Fodor's
Southeast
Asia

The complete guide, thoroughly up-to-date

Packed with details that will make your trip

The must-see sights, off and on the beaten path

What to see, what to skip

Mix-and-match vacation itineraries

City strolls, countryside adventures

Smart lodging and dining options

Essential local do's and taboos

Transportation tips, distances and directions

Key contacts, savvy travel tips

When to go, what to pack

Clear, accurate, easy-to-use maps

Books to read, videos to watch

Fodor's Travel Publications, Inc.
New York • Toronto • London • Sydney • Auckland
www.fodors.com

Fodor's Southeast Asia

EDITORS: Laura M. Kidder, Conrad Little Paulus

Editorial Contributors: Maya Besa, Bruce Bishop, David Brown, Andrew Chilvers, Mick Elmore, Doreen Fernandez, Nigel Fisher, Luis Francia, Wendy Hutton, Christina Knight, Natasha Lesser, Michael Mathes, Elizabeth V. Reyes, Helayne Schiff, M. T. Schwartzman (Gold Guide editor), Holly S. Smith

Editorial Production: Nicole Revere

Maps: David Lindroth, *cartographer*; Steven Amsterdam and Bob Blake, *map editors*

Design: Fabrizio La Rocca, *creative director*; Guido Caroti, *associate art director*; Jolie Novak, *photo editor*

Production/Manufacturing: Bob Shields

Cover Photograph: National Geographic Traveler/Paul Chesley/Photographers/Aspen

Copyright

Twenty-Second Edition

ISBN 0–679–00098–4

Special Sales

Contents

WHEN I PLAN A VACATION, the first thing I do is cast around among my friends and colleagues to find someone who's just been where I'm going. That's because there's no substitute for a recommendation from a good friend who knows your tastes, your budget, and your circumstances, someone who's just been there. Unfortunately, such friends are few and far between. So it's nice to know that there's *Fodor's Southeast Asia*.

In the first place, this book won't stay home when you hit the road. It will accompany you every step of the way, steering you away from wrong turns and wrong choices and never expecting a thing in return. Most important of all, it's written and assiduously updated by the kind of people you *would* hit up for travel tips if you knew them. They're as choosy as your pickiest friend, except they've probably seen a lot more of Southeast Asia. In these pages, they don't send you chasing down every town and sight but have instead selected the best ones, the ones that are worthy of your time and money. To make it easy for you to put it all together in the time you have, they've created itineraries and, in cities, neighborhood walks that you can mix and match in a snap. Will this be the vacation of your dreams? We hope so.

About Our Writers

The information in these pages is a collaboration of a number of extraordinary writers.

Born and raised in Nova Scotia, Canada, and a resident of Toronto, **Bruce Bishop** is a freelance writer/photographer and events coordinator. He has written for Canada's *The Globe and Mail*, Delta Air Lines' *Sky* magazine, Mexicana Airlines' *Vuelo* magazine, Montréal's *Doctor's Review,* and other publications in Canada, the United States, and Australia. Bruce spent two months in Singapore researching and updating the Singapore chapter.

Vietnam contributor **Andrew Chilvers,** who spent much of his life in London and Hong Kong, is a freelance journalist based in Ho Chi Minh City. He has written for newspapers and magazines in England, New Zealand, Vietnam, Thailand, and Japan, and hopes to extend his global reach.

Mick Elmore drove a beat-up old Chrysler across seven Indonesian islands in 1991 and has returned many times since. His most recent visits include a trip to Central Java in 1996 to walk for a week with Tom Stone, who's on a seven-year stroll around the world, and trips to both Sumatra and Java in 1998 for Fodor's. Mick has been a journalist since 1984—first in Texas, then in Australia and Cambodia. He is now based in Bangkok, where he writes for wire services and magazines.

Doreen G. Fernandez is a professor of literature and communication at the Ateneo de Manila University. When she's not busy teaching, she writes books and newspaper columns on food. In her update of the Manila dining section for this guide, she was assisted by **Maya Besa,** a freelancer who writes about food on the Internet.

Nigel Fisher—who updated Thailand, Cambodia, Laos, and Burma—is editor of the monthly travel publication *Voyager International.* He has traveled extensively throughout Asia and the world, and uses Bangkok as his Eastern base.

Born and raised in Manila and now a New York resident, Philippines chapter author **Luis H. Francia** is a published poet and has edited two anthologies of Philippine literature, including *Brown River, White Ocean*. He's the New York correspondent for Hong Kong's *Asiaweek,* and he writes for the New York weekly *The Village Voice*. He also teaches literature at Sarah Lawrence College.

Malaysia updater **Wendy Hutton** is a New Zealander by birth who has worked in Southeast Asia as a writer since 1967 and is currently based in Sabah on Borneo. A passionate explorer who's interested in places, peoples, and cuisines, Wendy has written many guidebooks and several cookbooks.

Michael Mathes is a freelance writer based in Hanoi. Vietnam has been his home since 1994, minus a brief hiatus in San Francisco. He's brave (or crazy) enough to travel around Hanoi by motorbike—wearing a helmet, of course—in search of the city's best *pho*, Vietnam's delicious noodle soup.

Elizabeth V. Reyes, who assisted with the Philippines chapter updating, is a Manila-based travel writer and magazine editor who has won awards for her travel writing on Manila and Bali. She's the coauthor of *The Philippines: A Journey around the Archipelago,* and *Filipino Style.*

Indonesia (Bali, Nusa Tenggara, and Sulawesi) updater **Holly S. Smith** is a freelance writer whose articles on travel and Southeast Asian history and culture have appeared in various international magazines. She has also written several books including *Aceh: Art and Culture,* and *Java: Garden of the East.* Holly's current projects include a book on heroines in Aceh (a province in northern Sumatra) and a collection of short stories inspired by her backpacking adventures in Southeast Asia and South America.

We'd also like to thank Amanresorts; Avis International; Gregory Bishop; Chia Boon Hee of BnF Travel Consultants, Singapore; Holiday Inn hotels; Hotel Tugu; Hyatt hotels; Garuda Indonesia Airlines; Northwest Airlines; the Oberoi hotel; Lara Constantino; Mariflor Lopez-Vito; Emiliano Yu, Rolando Estabillo, Joy Pasiliao, and Gigi Ezequiel of Philippine Airlines; the Philippine Department of Tourism in New York, Iloilo, Cebu, and Baguio; Sheraton ITT; Singapore Airlines; Tania Goh of the Singapore Tourism Board (STB) and Gerald Lee of the STB's office in Toronto.

Connections

We're pleased that the American Society of Travel Agents continues to endorse Fodor's as its guidebook of choice. ASTA is the world's largest and most influential travel trade association, operating in more than 170 countries, with 27,000 members pledged to adhere to a strict code of ethics reflecting the Society's motto, "Integrity in Travel." ASTA shares Fodor's devotion to providing smart, honest travel information and advice to travelers, and we've long recommended that our readers—even those who have guidebooks and traveling friends—consult ASTA member agents for the experience and professionalism they bring to your vacation planning.

On Fodor's Web site (www.fodors.com), check out the new Resource Center, an online companion to the Gold Guide section of this book, complete with useful hot links to related sites. In our forums, you can also get lively advice from other travelers and more great tips from Fodor's experts worldwide.

How to Use This Book

Organization

Up front is the **Gold Guide,** an easy-to-use section arranged alphabetically by topic. Under each listing you'll find tips and information that will help you accomplish what you need to in Southeast Asia. You'll also find addresses and telephone numbers of organizations and companies that offer destination-related services and detailed information and publications.

The first chapter in the guide, Destination: Southeast Asia helps get you in the mood for your trip. What's Where gets you oriented, Pleasures and Pastimes describes the activities and sights that make Southeast Asia unique, New and Noteworthy cues you in on trends and happenings, Fodor's Choice showcases our top picks, and Great Itineraries lays out a selection of complete trips.

The individual country chapters are arranged alphabetically. Each chapter covers exploring, dining, lodging, arts and nightlife, sports, and shopping in the country's best destinations; the chapter ends with an A to Z section that tells you how to get there, how to get around, and how to plan and enjoy your trip. The final country chapter, Other Destinations, covers three less-visited Southeast Asian nations; information on each country is arranged as in the individual country chapters. At the end of the book you'll find Portraits, including a time line of historical events in the region, an essay on religion, and suggestions for pretrip reading, both fiction and nonfiction, as well as videos to rent. A vocabulary chart and an index follow.

Icons and Symbols

★ Our special recommendations
✕ Restaurant
🏠 Lodging establishment
✕🏠 Lodging establishment whose restaurant warrants a detour
🐤 Good for kids (rubber duckie)
☞ Sends you to another section of the guide for more information
✉ Address
☎ Telephone number
🕐 Opening and closing times
💲 Admission cost (Those fees we give apply only to adults; substantially reduced fees are often available for children, students, and senior citizens. In those countries where favorable rates of exchange make most admission fees negligible, we note only if admission is charged or free.)

Numbers in white and black circles (e.g., ③ or ❸) that appear on the maps, in the margins, and within the tours correspond to one another.

Addresses

Not all listings in this guide include street addresses. In the older and less-industrialized cities and towns of Southeast Asia, systems of street naming and numbering often are not as rationalized as those in North America and Europe. Often a given attraction—a temple or monument or market—is a large-enough landmark that a street number is superfluous (much like Grand Central Station or the Eiffel Tower), or the town is sufficiently small that the establishment is easy to find; when in doubt, ask a local or take a taxi. Similarly, you may not find postal codes for all hotels; in some cases postal codes don't exist or, if they do exist, aren't used. For more details on addresses, see Contacts and Resources in the A to Z section at the end of each chapter.

Hotel Facilities

We always list the facilities that are available—but we don't specify whether you'll be charged extra to use them: when pricing accommodations, always ask what's included. In addition, assume that all rooms have private baths unless noted otherwise. When you book a room, be sure to mention if you have a disability or are traveling with children, if you prefer a private bath or a certain type of bed, or if you have specific dietary needs or other concerns.

Assume that hotels operate on the **European Plan** (EP, with no meals) unless we note that they use the **Continental Plan** (CP, with a Continental breakfast daily), **Breakfast Plan** (BP, with a full breakfast daily), or **Modified American Plan** (MAP, with breakfast and dinner daily), or are **all-inclusive** (including all meals and most activities).

Restaurant Reservations and Dress Codes

Reservations are always a good idea; we mention them only when they're essential or are not accepted. Book as far ahead as you can, and reconfirm as soon as you arrive. Unless otherwise noted, the restaurants listed are open daily for lunch and dinner. We mention dress only when men are required to wear a jacket or a jacket and tie. Look for an overview of local dining-out habits in the Pleasures and Pastimes section that follows each chapter introduction.

Credit Cards

The following abbreviations are used: **AE,** American Express; **DC,** Diners Club; **MC,** MasterCard; and **V,** Visa.

Don't Forget to Write

You can use this book in the confidence that all prices and opening times are based on information supplied to us at press time; Fodor's cannot accept responsibility for any errors. Time inevitably brings changes, so always confirm information when it matters—especially if you're making a detour to visit a specific place.

Were the restaurants we recommended as described? Did our hotel picks exceed your expectations? Did you find a museum we recommended a waste of time? Keeping a travel guide fresh and up-to-date is a big job, and we welcome your feedback, positive *and* negative. If you have complaints, we'll look into them and revise our entries when the facts warrant it. If you've discovered a special place that we haven't included, we'll pass the information along to our correspondents and have them check it out. So send us your thoughts via e-mail at editors@fodors.com (specifying the name of the book on the subject line) or on paper in care of the Southeast Asia editor at Fodor's, 201 East 50th Street, New York, New York 10022. In the meantime, have a wonderful trip!

Karen Cure
Editorial Director

Southeast Asia

CHINA

Guangzhou

Macao HONG KONG

Mandalay

Hanoi

Luang Prabang

Haiphong

UNION OF MYANMAR (BURMA)

HAINAN

LAOS

Pegu

Vientiane

Chiang Mai

Yangon (Rangoon)

THAILAND

Hue

Danang

Bangkok

VIETNAM

Angkor Wat

Andaman Sea

CAMBODIA

Phnom Penh

Ho Chi Minh City (Saigon)

Isthmus of Kra

Gulf of Thailand

Songkhla

South China Sea

Georgetown

PENINSULAR MALAYSIA

MALAYSIA

Bandar Seri Begawan

BRUNEI

SABA

Strait of Melaka (Malacca)

Medan

Kuala Lumpur

SARAWAK

Johor Bahru

SINGAPORE

Kuching

BORNEO

INDIAN OCEAN

SUMATRA

KALIMANTAN

Jambi

Karimata Strait

INDONESIA

Banjarmasin

KEPULAUAN

Palembang

GREATER SUNDA ISLANDS

Jakarta

Java Sea

0   500 miles

Bandung

Surabaya

0   750 km

Yogyakarta

JAVA

Malang

LE

BALI

LOMBO

N

Taipei

TAIWAN

PACIFIC OCEAN

LUZON

Quezon City

Manila

PHILIPPINES

MINDORO

PANAY
Ililo

Bacaloa

Cebu

NEGROS

Sulu Sea

SAMAR

PALAU

MINDANAO

Davao

Celebes Sea

HALMAHERA

THE MOLUCCAS

**PAPUA-
NEW GUINEA**

*SULUWESI
(The Celebes)*

BURU

SFRAM

IRIAN JAYA

Makassar Strait

Banda Sea

*KEPULAUAN
ARU*

Ujung
Pandang

Flores Sea

SSER SUNDA   ISLANDS

*KEPULAUAN
TANIMBAR*

FLORES

TIMOR

SUMBA

Timor Sea

AUSTRALIA

World Time Zones

Numbers below vertical bands relate each zone to Greenwich Mean Time (0 hrs.).
Local times frequently differ from these general indications,
as indicated by light-face numbers on map.

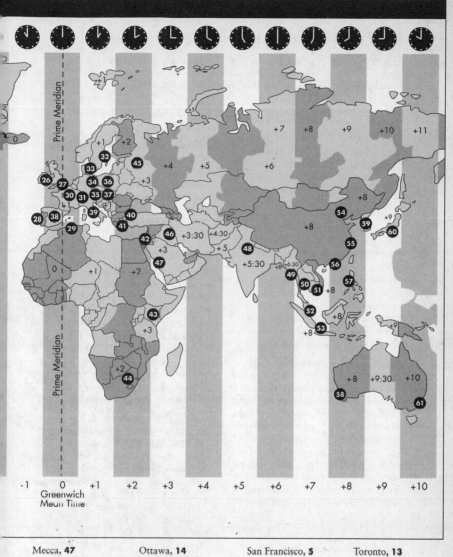

SMART TRAVEL TIPS A TO Z

Basic Information on Traveling in Southeast Asia, Savvy Tips to Make Your Trip a Breeze, and Companies and Organizations to Contact

AIR TRAVEL

BOOKING YOUR FLIGHT

Price is just one factor to consider when booking a flight: frequency of service and even a carrier's safety record are often just as important. Major airlines offer the greatest number of departures. Smaller airlines—including regional and no-frills airlines—usually have a limited number of flights daily. On the other hand, so-called low-cost airlines usually are cheaper, and their fares impose fewer restrictions, such as advance-purchase requirements. Safety-wise, low-cost carriers as a group have a good history—about equal to that of major carriers.

Nonstop flights from the United States to points in Southeast Asia are rare. A direct flight, which requires at least one stop, or a connecting flight, which requires a change of airplanes, will often be your only choice. Some flights, especially nonstops, may be scheduled only on certain days of the week. Depending upon your destination, you may need to make more than one connection. This is especially true for less popular cities.

Flights to Southeast Asia may be transpacific or transatlantic. Westbound, the major gateway cities are Los Angeles, San Francisco, Seattle, and Portland (Oregon). Eastbound, the major gateways are New York, Detroit, Chicago, and Dallas. Stopover points may include Bangkok, Hong Kong, Kuala Lumpur, Seoul, Singapore, Taipei, or Tokyo. Your best bet is to **use Hong Kong, Singapore, or Tokyo for your stopover, as many airlines fly nonstop here from the West Coast and these cities have the greatest number of connecting flights.** If time is not an issue and you're leaving from the Midwest or the East Coast of the United States you can often **add a stopover in Europe or the Middle East to your transatlantic flight** for a small charge.

Ask your airline if it offers electronic ticketing, which eliminates all paperwork. There's no ticket to pick up or misplace. You go directly to the gate and give the agent your confirmation number. There's no worry about waiting in line at the airport while precious minutes tick by.

CARRIERS

When flying internationally, you must usually choose between a domestic carrier, the national flag carrier of the country you are visiting, and a foreign carrier from a third country. National flag carriers have the greatest number of nonstops. Domestic carriers may have better connections to your home town and serve a greater number of gateway cities. Third-party carriers may have a price advantage.

➤ MAJOR AIRLINES: **Northwest** (☎ 800/225–2525) is the major U.S. airline that flies to Asia, with stops in Tokyo, Hong Kong, and Singapore, among other cities. **Continental** (☎ 800/525–0280), **Delta** (☎ 800/221–1212), and **United** (☎ 800/241–6522) also fly to Hong Kong, Singapore, and Tokyo; United also flies to Seoul and Continental flies to Denpasar. From North America, **China Airlines** (☎ 800/227–5118), **Japan Airlines** (☎ 800/525–3663), **Malaysia Airlines** (☎ 800/552–9264), **Philippine Airlines** (☎ 800/435–9725), and **Thai International Airways** (☎ 800/426–5204) all fly to Asia from the West Coast. Connections from points east are usually made via U.S. air partners, but **All Nippon Airways** (☎ 800/235–9262), **Korean Air** (☎ 800/438–5000), and **Singapore Airlines** (☎ 800/742–3333), also fly out of New York.

➤ FROM CANADA: Northwest and United also serve Asia from Canada;

Cathay Pacific (☎ 800/233–2742), Japan Airlines, Korean Air, Malaysia Airlines, and Singapore Airlines are the major Asian carriers serving the region. **Vietnam Airlines** (514/281–1333) has an office in Montreal.

➤ FROM THE U.K.: **British Airways** (☎ 800/247–9297, 0345/222–1111 in the U.K.), **Olympic Airways** (☎ 171/409–3440), and **Scandinavian Airways/SAS** (☎ 171/734–4020) fly to Asia from London.

➤ FROM AUSTRALIA AND NEW ZEALAND: **Air New Zealand** (☎ 800/663–5494 in the U.S. and Canada, 9/357–3000 in New Zealand, 132476 in Australia), **Ansett** (☎ 9/3022146 in New Zealand, 131767 in Australia), and **Qantas** (☎ 800/227–4500 in the U.S. and Canada, 9/3557–8900 in New Zealand, 131313 in Australia) reach Asia from most cities in Australia, New Zealand, and the South Pacific, but most Asian airlines also connect with these countries.

➤ SMALLER AIRLINES: In addition to the major air carriers, there are a number of smaller airlines that connect the countries of Southeast Asia (☞ *also* chapter A to Z sections), many with levels of comfort that equal or surpass those of Western carriers. Often, these airlines are less expensive, have more varied schedules, and will usually allow you to book last-minute and one-way tickets—without penalty, since they generally do not offer advance booking discounts.

CONSOLIDATORS

Consolidators buy tickets for scheduled international flights at reduced rates from the airlines, then sell them at prices that beat the best fare available directly from the airlines, usually without restrictions. Sometimes you can even get your money back if you need to return the ticket. Carefully read the fine print detailing penalties for changes and cancellations, and **confirm your consolidator reservation with the airline.**

➤ CONSOLIDATORS: **Cheap Tickets** (☎ 800/377–1000). **Discount Travel Network** (☎ 800/576–1600). **Unitravel** (☎ 800/325–2222). **Up & Away Travel** (☎ 212/889–2345).

World Travel Network (☎ 800/409–6753).

COURIERS

When you fly as a courier, you trade your checked-luggage space for a ticket deeply subsidized by a courier service. It's all perfectly legitimate, but there are restrictions: you can usually book your flight only a week or two in advance, your length of stay may be set for a certain number of days, and you probably won't be able to book a companion on the same flight.

CUTTING COSTS

The least-expensive airfares to Southeast Asia are priced for round-trip travel and usually must be purchased in advance. It's smart to **call a number of airlines, and when you are quoted a good price, book it on the spot**—the same fare may not be available the next day. Airlines generally allow you to change your return date for a fee. If you don't use your ticket, you can apply the cost toward the purchase of a new ticket, again for a small charge. However, most low-fare tickets are nonrefundable. To get the lowest airfare, **check different routings.** Compare prices of flights to and from different airports if your destination or home city has more than one gateway. Also price off-peak flights, which may be significantly less expensive.

Travel agents, especially those who specialize in finding the lowest fares (☞ Discounts & Deals, *below*), can be especially helpful when booking a plane ticket. When you're quoted a price, **ask your agent if the price is likely to get any lower** and **check both the routes and fares on more than one airline.** Good agents know the seasonal fluctuations of airfares and can usually anticipate a sale or fare war. They can also help you choose airlines that offer the least number of connections and amount of airport layover time. However, waiting can be risky: fares can go *up* as seats become scarce, and you may wait so long that your preferred flights sell out. A wait-and-see strategy works best if your plans are flexible, but if you must arrive and depart on certain dates, don't delay.

SPECIAL FARES

If you plan to visit multiple countries in Southeast Asia, **check into "Circle Pacific" fares or around-the-world "Globetrotter Fares."** These are flat-rate fares that are subject to advance-purchase restrictions, usually of 7–14 days, and other rules. "Circle Pacific" fares allow four stopovers, although travel may not be allowed to such countries as Vietnam, Burma, Laos, and Cambodia. Additional stopovers can be purchased for $50–$100. Around-the-world fares also have routing restrictions and require one transatlantic and one transpacific crossing. These tickets are based on either direction or mileage, and both have their advantages: direction-based fares can be less expensive, but mileage-based fares allow backtracking and multiple visits to a single city.

CHECK-IN & BOARDING

Airlines routinely overbook planes, assuming that not everyone with a ticket will show up, but sometimes everyone does. When that happens, airlines ask for volunteers to give up their seats. In return these volunteers usually get a certificate for a free flight and are rebooked on the next flight out. If there are not enough volunteers, the airline must choose who will be denied boarding. The first to get bumped are passengers who checked in late and those flying on discounted tickets, so **get to the gate and check in as early as possible,** especially during peak periods.

Although the trend on international flights is to drop reconfirmation requirements, many airlines still ask you to reconfirm each leg of your international itinerary. Failure to do so may result in your reservation being canceled.

Always **bring a government-issued photo ID to the airport.** You may be asked to show it before you are allowed to check in.

ENJOYING THE FLIGHT

For better service, **fly smaller or regional carriers,** which often have higher passenger-satisfaction ratings. Sometimes you'll find leather seats, more legroom, and better food.

For more legroom, **request an emergency-aisle seat.** Don't sit in the row in front of the emergency aisle or in front of a bulkhead, where seats may not recline.

If you don't like airline food, **ask for special meals when booking.** These can be vegetarian, low-cholesterol, or kosher, for example.

When flying internationally, try to maintain a normal routine, to help fight jet-lag. At night, **get some sleep.** By day, **eat light meals, drink water (not alcohol), and move around the cabin** to stretch your legs.

Some carriers have prohibited smoking throughout their systems; others allow smoking only on certain routes or even certain departures from that route. For flights within Asia, many airlines still have smoking sections, so **contact your carrier regarding its smoking policy.**

FLYING TIMES

See individual chapter A to Z sections for flying times to specific destinations.

HOW TO COMPLAIN

If your baggage goes astray or your flight goes awry, complain right away. Most carriers require that you **file a claim immediately.**

➤ AIRLINE COMPLAINTS: U.S. Department of Transportation **Aviation Consumer Protection Division** (✉ C-75, Room 4107, Washington, DC 20590, ☎ 202/366–2220). **Federal Aviation Administration Consumer Hotline** (☎ 800/322–7873).

AIRPORTS & TRANSFERS

AIRPORTS

The major airports of Southeast Asia are in Bangkok, Denpasar, Jakarta, Kuala Lumpur, Manila, and Singapore. Other busy international hubs include Chiang Mai in northern Thailand; Hanoi and Ho Chi Minh City, Vietnam; Medan, Indonesia; Penang, Malaysia; Phnom Penh, Cambodia; Vientiane, Laos; and Yangon, Myanmar (☞ individual chapter Essentials *and* A to Z sections for specific airport details).

TRANSFERS

Getting from the airport to downtown in Asia is rarely a problem, as a variety of transport is available at all hours. In addition to the taxis that serve these airports, there are many less expensive and equally comfortable options. For example, Singapore has a one-way shuttle that serves the major hotels, which will also drop off those staying at points in between, as well as a direct public bus. Kuala Lumpur and Jakarta also have non-stop airport shuttles that serve the train stations as well as the hotels. Shared hotel vans are the popular mode of transport in Hanoi, Vietnam; Denpasar; and Phnom Penh. However, for some airports, taxis still are the best choice, such as in Bangkok, where they're cheap, plentiful, and mercifully air-conditioned to keep out the noise and heat of the city; in Medan, where the airport is only 3 km (2 mi) outside of town; or in Vientiane, where there are few other options. Most drivers understand English, but it helps to have a hotel brochure or an address written out for you in the local language just in case.

BIKE TRAVEL

BIKES IN FLIGHT

Most airlines will accommodate bikes as luggage, provided they are dismantled and put into a box. Call to see if your airline sells bike boxes (about $5; bike bags are at least $100) although you can often pick them up free at bike shops. International travelers can sometimes substitute a bike for a piece of checked luggage for free; otherwise, it will cost about $100. Domestic and Canadian airlines charge a $25–$50 fee.

BUS TRAVEL

Most Asians don't own cars, so public transport is actually far more developed in Asia than in America, but it is, of course, crowded. Still, many countries offer luxury "super buses" that allow you to view the countryside in comfort. For example, Indonesia, Thailand, Singapore, and Malaysia all have first-class buses with extra-wide, reclining seats, air-conditioning, video, scheduled box or buffet meals, and rest rooms. Most booking agents speak some English, and the fares are inexpensive compared to flying; if you have the time you might consider this option to see more of a country.

For local bus travel, the main problem is language; in many countries signs are not in Roman letters. Even when numerals are the same and you know your route, city buses can still be very confusing, so get written instructions from your hotel clerk to show the driver. In your free time, buses can give you very cheap sightseeing tours. (*See also* individual chapter Essentials *and* A to Z sections.)

BUSINESS HOURS

See Opening and Closing Times *in* individual chapter A to Z sections.

CAMERAS & COMPUTERS

EQUIPMENT PRECAUTIONS

Always **keep your film, tape, or computer disks out of the sun.** Carry an extra supply of batteries, and **be prepared to turn on your camera, camcorder, or laptop** to prove to security personnel that the device is real. Always **ask for hand inspection of film,** which becomes clouded after successive exposure to airport X-ray machines, and **keep videotapes and computer disks away from metal detectors.**

TRAVEL PHOTOGRAPHY

➤ PHOTO HELP: **Kodak Information Center** (☎ 800/242–2424). *Kodak Guide to Shooting Great Travel Pictures,* available in bookstores or from Fodor's Travel Publications (☎ 800/533–6478; $16.50 plus $4 shipping).

CAR RENTAL

Given the traffic situations within the city limits of major Southeast Asian destinations, it's probably best to **leave the driving to the cabbies and chauffeurs** who rule the roads here. **If you must rent a car, use common sense about when to do so.** In certain locations such as Bali (Indonesia), the east coast of Malaysia, or Phuket (Thailand), renting cars is common practice, but in other locales traffic conditions and poor roads can make driving hazardous. Although hiring a car and driver (through your hotel or a travel agent) generally costs slightly more than simply renting a car, it's still relatively inexpensive.

Self-drive cars are available through large rental agencies, hotels, or travel agencies in major cities and tourist hubs. Although there are many inexpensive local agencies that waive the rules, if you want to be certain of the reliability of your vehicle it's best to **rent from a larger, well-known agency that can assist you if any problems occur.** Western agencies usually offer either sedans or four-wheel-drive vehicles, all with standard transmission, cassette decks, and air-conditioning; vehicles from local agencies can range from mini-Jeeps to full-size vans, but they may not have air-conditioning or extra comforts. Although there are no car seat requirements in Asia, those with traveling with small children can also **book infant and child seats in advance from Western agencies.**

➤ MAJOR AGENCIES: **Avis** (☎ 800/331–1084, 800/879–2847 in Canada, 008/225533 in Australia). **Budget** (☎ 800/527–0700, 0800/181181 in the U.K.). **Hertz** (☎ 800/654–3001, 800/263–0600 in Canada, 0345/555888 in the U.K., 03/9222–2523 in Australia, 03/358–6777 in New Zealand). **National InterRent** (☎ 800/227–3876; 0345/222525 in the U.K., where it is known as Europcar InterRent).

CUTTING COSTS

To get the best deal, **book through a travel agent who is willing to shop around.**

Also **ask your travel agent about a company's customer-service record.** How has the company responded to late plane arrivals and vehicle mishaps? Are there often lines at the rental counter? If you're traveling during a holiday period, does a confirmed reservation guarantee you a car? Finally, **look into special deals through airlines,** which may offer free days or coupons for 10%–25% discounts, or add miles to your frequent-flier account when you rent with a particular company.

INSURANCE

Insurance isn't required in Asia but it's definitely recommended.

When driving a rented car you are generally responsible for any damage to or loss of the vehicle. You also are liable for any property damage or personal injury that you may cause while driving. Before you rent, **see what coverage you already have** under the terms of your personal auto-insurance policy and credit cards.

REQUIREMENTS

Most car rental companies require (or would like you to have) your license from home *and* an International Driver's License. You can get one through the American or Canadian automobile associations, or, in the United Kingdom, through the Automobile Association or Royal Automobile Club. Most Western companies also have age requirements. For example, Avis requires that you be at least 25 years old, Hertz 21 years old, and National 18 years old.

SURCHARGES

Before you pick up a car in one city and leave it in another, **ask about drop-off charges or one-way service fees,** which can be substantial. Note, too, that some rental agencies charge extra if you return the car before the time specified in your contract. To avoid a hefty refueling fee, **fill the tank just before you turn in the car,** but be aware that gas stations near the rental outlet may overcharge.

CHILDREN & TRAVEL

CHILDREN IN SOUTHEAST ASIA

Youngsters are not only welcomed in Southeast Asia—they're embraced with delight in most areas. Only the strictest business establishments and stiffest upscale hotels and restaurants (ask before you book) frown upon children; otherwise, they're seen as a natural complement to life. You will be amazed at how many people will want to hold and play with your kids, and at how their presence will actually open conversations and cut through cultural boundaries. Because they'll be the center of attention, if your youngsters are very young or particularly shy, plan outings for off-peak hours. Many large hotels have playgrounds and special menus and activities for children; smaller places often have more personalized services. **Check to see what types of kid-friendly amenities a hotel offers.**

Be sure to plan ahead and **involve your youngsters** as you outline your trip. When packing, include things to keep them busy en route. On sightseeing days try to schedule activities of special interest to your children. If you are renting a car don't forget to **arrange for a car seat** when you reserve. Most hotels in Southeast Asia allow children under a certain age to stay in their parents' room at no extra charge, but others charge them as extra adults; be sure to **ask about the cutoff age for children's discounts.**

➤ BABY-SITTING: There are few formal sitting agencies in Asia. Large hotels and resorts have their own activity programs and baby-sitting services; smaller establishments will usually recruit a trusted family member or neighbor to provide any assistance you need. Some families hire a nanny from an au pair service before they depart.

FLYING

If your children are two or older, **ask about children's airfares.** As a general rule, infants under two not occupying a seat fly at greatly reduced fares or even for free.

In general the adult baggage allowance applies to children paying half or more of the adult fare. When booking, **ask about carry-on allowances for those traveling with infants.** In general, for babies charged a percentage of the adult fare you are allowed one carry-on bag and a collapsible stroller, which may have to be checked; you may be limited to less if the flight is full.

Experts agree that it's a good idea to use safety seats aloft for children weighing less than 40 pounds. Airlines, however, can set their own policies: U.S. carriers allow FAA-approved models but usually require

that you buy a ticket, even if your child would otherwise ride free, since the seats must be strapped into regular seats. Airline rules vary, so it's important to **check your airline's policy about using safety seats during takeoff and landing.** Safety seats cannot obstruct the movement of other passengers in the row, so get an appropriate seat assignment as early as possible.

When making your reservation, **request children's meals or a free-standing bassinet** if you need them; the latter are available only to those seated at the bulkhead, where there's enough legroom. Remember, however, that bulkhead seats may not have their own overhead bins, and there's no storage space in front of you—a major inconvenience.

CONSUMER PROTECTION

Whenever possible, **pay with a major credit card** so you can cancel payment or get reimbursed if there's a problem, provided that you can provide documentation. This is the best way to pay, whether you're buying travel arrangements before your trip or shopping at your destination.

If you're doing business with a particular company for the first time, **contact your local Better Business Bureau and the attorney general's offices** in your state and the company's home state, as well. Have any complaints been filed?

Finally, if you're buying a package or tour, always **consider travel insurance** that includes default coverage (☞ Insurance, *below*).

➤ LOCAL BBBs: **Council of Better Business Bureaus** (✉ 4200 Wilson Blvd., Suite 800, Arlington, VA 22203, ☎ 703/276–0100, ᴀ̳ᴁ 703/525–8277).

CRUISE TRAVEL

If you're interested in visiting a variety of Southeast Asian cities, **consider a cruise to the region.** Southeast Asia is one of the hottest destinations in cruising, and you can sail in many different styles. Choices range from a traditional ocean liner to a clipper-type tall ship to a luxury yacht. Ports of call include Bangkok, Singapore,

THE GOLD GUIDE / SMART TRAVEL TIPS

Bali, Komodo Island, and Ho Chi Minh City. To get the best deal, **book with a cruise-only travel agency.**

➤ CRUISE LINES: **Crystal Cruises** (✉ 2121 Ave. of the Stars, Los Angeles, CA 90067, ☎ 800/446–6620). **Cunard Line Limited** (✉ 555 5th Ave., New York, NY 10017, ☎ 800/528–6273). **Orient Lines** (✉ 1510 S.E. 17th St., Suite 400, Fort Lauderdale, FL 33316, ☎ 305/527–6660 or 800/333–7300). **Princess Cruises** (✉ 10100 Santa Monica Blvd., Los Angeles, CA 90067, ☎ 310/553–1770). **Radisson Seven Seas Cruises** (✉ 600 Corporate Dr., Suite 410, Fort Lauderdale, FL 33334, ☎ 800/333–3333). **Renaissance Cruises** (✉ 1800 Eller Dr., Suite 300, Box 350307, Fort Lauderdale, FL 33335-0307, ☎ 800/525–2450). **Royal Caribbean Cruise Line** (✉ 1050 Caribbean Way, Miami, FL 33132, ☎ 305/539–6000). **Seabourn Cruise Line** (✉ 55 Francisco St., San Francisco, CA 94133, ☎ 415/391–7444 or 800/929–9595). **Silversea Cruises** (✉ 110 E. Broward Blvd., Fort Lauderdale, FL 33301, ☎ 305/522–4477 or 800/722–9955). **Star Clippers** (✉ 4101 Salzedo Ave., Coral Gables, FL 33146, ☎ 800/442–0551).

CUSTOMS & DUTIES

When shopping, **keep receipts** for all of your purchases. Upon reentering the country, **be ready to show customs officials what you've bought.** If you feel a duty is incorrect, appeal the assessment. If you object to the way your clearance was handled, get the inspector's badge number. In either case, first ask to see a supervisor, then write to the appropriate authorities, beginning with the port director at your point of entry.

IN SOUTHEAST ASIA

See Customs *in* individual chapter A to Z sections.

IN AUSTRALIA

Australia residents who are 18 or older may bring back $A400 worth of souvenirs and gifts (including jewelry), 250 cigarettes or 250 grams of tobacco, and 1,125 milliliters of alcohol (including wine, beer, and spirits). Residents under 18 may bring back $A200 worth of goods.

➤ INFORMATION: **Australian Customs Service** (Regional Director, ✉ Box 8, Sydney, NSW 2001, ☎ 02/9213–2000, FAX 02/9213–4000).

IN CANADA

Canadian residents who have been out of Canada for at least seven days may bring in C$500 worth of goods duty-free. If you've been away less than seven days but more than 48 hours, the duty-free allowance drops to C$200; if your trip lasts 24–48 hours, the allowance is C$50. You may not pool allowances with family members. Goods claimed under the C$500 exemption may follow you by mail; those claimed under the lesser exemptions must accompany you. Alcohol and tobacco products may be included in the seven-day and 48-hour exemptions but not in the 24-hour exemption. If you meet the age requirements of the province or territory through which you reenter Canada, you may bring in, duty-free, 1.14 liters (40 imperial ounces) of wine or liquor *or* 24 12-ounce cans or bottles of beer or ale. If you are 16 or older you may bring in, duty-free, 200 cigarettes and 50 cigars.

You may send an unlimited number of gifts worth up to C$60 each duty-free to Canada. Label the package UNSOLICITED GIFT—VALUE UNDER $60. Alcohol and tobacco are excluded.

➤ INFORMATION: **Revenue Canada** (✉ 2265 St. Laurent Blvd. S, Ottawa, Ontario K1G 4K3, ☎ 613/993–0534, 800/461–9999 in Canada).

IN NEW ZEALAND

Although greeted with a *Haere Mai* (Welcome to New Zealand), homeward-bound residents with goods to declare must present themselves for inspection. If you're 17 or older, you may bring back $700 worth of souvenirs and gifts. Your duty-free allowance also includes 4.5 liters of wine or beer; one 1,125-milliliter bottle of spirits; and either 200 cigarettes, 250 grams of tobacco, 50 cigars, or a combo of all three up to 250 grams.

➤ INFORMATION: **New Zealand Customs** (✉ Custom House, 50 Anzac Ave., Box 29, Auckland, New Zealand, ☎ 09/359–6655 or 09/309–2978).

IN THE U.K.

From countries outside the EU, including those covered in this book, you may import, duty-free, 200 cigarettes or 50 cigars; 1 liter of spirits or 2 liters of fortified or sparkling wine or liqueurs; 2 liters of still table wine; 60 milliliters of perfume; 250 milliliters of toilet water; plus £136 worth of other goods, including gifts and souvenirs.

➤ INFORMATION: **HM Customs and Excise** (✉ Dorset House, Stamford St., London SE1 9NG, ☎ 0171/202–4227).

IN THE U.S.

U.S. residents may bring home $400 worth of foreign goods duty-free if they've been out of the country for at least 48 hours (and if they haven't used the $400 allowance or any part of it in the past 30 days).

U.S. residents 21 and older may bring back 1 liter of alcohol duty-free. In addition, regardless of your age, you are allowed 200 cigarettes and 100 non-Cuban cigars. Antiques, which the U.S. Customs Service defines as objects more than 100 years old, enter duty-free, as do original works of art done entirely by hand, including paintings, drawings, and sculptures.

You may also send packages home duty-free: up to $200 worth of goods for personal use, with a limit of one parcel per addressee per day (and no alcohol or tobacco products or perfume worth more than $5); label the package PERSONAL USE, and attach a list of its contents and their retail value. Do not label the package UNSOLICITED GIFT, or your duty-free exemption will drop to $100. Mailed items do not affect your duty-free allowance on your return.

➤ INFORMATION: **U.S. Customs Service** (✉ Inquiries, Box 7407, Washington, DC 20044, ☎ 202/927–6724; ✉ complaints, Office of Regulations and Rulings, 1301 Constitution Ave. NW, Washington, DC 20229; ✉ registration of equipment, Resource Management, 1301 Constitution Ave. NW, Washington DC 20229, ☎ 202/927–0540).

DISABILITIES & ACCESSIBILITY

ACCESS IN SOUTHEAST ASIA

Those with disabilities who are planning a trip to Southeast Asia will find the amenities woefully nonexistent. However, the situation is quickly changing at many hotels and tourist sites as the need for access is universally recognized. Singapore, with its wide sidewalks and modern facilities throughout the main city area, is the best option for those who have disabilities, but the newer hotels in other countries are also incorporating wheelchair ramps, wide doors, and appropriate rooms into their plans. Although international airlines are also becoming well versed in making proper accommodations for those with disabilities, the smaller regional airlines may not be able to offer the same access or comfort, so check before you book.

MAKING RESERVATIONS

When discussing accessibility with an operator or reservations agent, **ask hard questions.** Are there any stairs, inside *or* out? Are there grab bars next to the toilet *and* in the shower/tub? How wide is the doorway to the room? To the bathroom? For the most extensive facilities meeting the latest legal specifications, **opt for newer accommodations,** which are more likely to have been designed with access in mind. Older buildings or ships may have more limited facilities. Be sure to **discuss your needs before booking.**

TRANSPORTATION

➤ COMPLAINTS: **Disability Rights Section** (U.S. Department of Justice, Civil Rights Division, ✉ Box 66738, Washington, DC 20035–6738, ☎ 202/514–0301 or 800/514–0301, TTY 202/514–0383 or 800/514–0383, FAX 202/307–1198) for general complaints. **Aviation Consumer Protection Division** (☞ Air Travel, *above*) for airline-related problems. **Civil Rights Office** (U.S. Department of Transportation, Departmental Office of Civil Rights, S-30, ✉ 400 7th St. SW, Room 10215, Washington, DC 20590, ☎ 202/366–4648, FAX 202/366–9371) for problems with surface transportation.

TRAVEL AGENCIES & TOUR OPERATORS

As a whole, the travel industry has become more aware of the needs of travelers with disabilities. In the U.S., the Americans with Disabilities Act requires that travel firms serve the needs of all travelers. Note, though, that some agencies and operators specialize in making travel arrangements for individuals and groups with disabilities.

➤ TRAVELERS WITH MOBILITY PROBLEMS: **Access Adventures** (✉ 206 Chestnut Ridge Rd., Rochester, NY 14624, ☎ 716/889–9096), run by a former physical-rehabilitation counselor, offers tours throughout Asia, including Indonesia. **Accessible Journeys** (✉ 35 W. Sellers Ave., Ridley Park, PA 19078, ☎ 610/521–0339 or 800/846–4537, FAX 610/521–6959), for escorted tours exclusively for travelers with mobility impairments. **Flying Wheels Travel** (✉ 143 W. Bridge St., Box 382, Owatonna, MN 55060, ☎ 507/451–5005 or 800/535–6790, FAX 507/451–1685), a travel agency specializing in customized tours and itineraries worldwide. **Hinsdale Travel Service** (✉ 201 E. Ogden Ave., Suite 100, Hinsdale, IL 60521, ☎ 630/325–1335), a travel agency that benefits from the advice of wheelchair traveler Janice Perkins.

DISCOUNTS & DEALS

Be a smart shopper and **compare all your options** before making any choice. A plane ticket bought with a promotional coupon may not be cheaper than the least expensive fare from a discount ticket agency. For high-price travel purchases, such as packages or tours, keep in mind that what you get is just as important as what you save. Just because something is cheap doesn't mean it's a bargain.

CLUBS & COUPONS

Many companies sell discounts in the form of travel clubs and coupon books, but these cost money. You must use participating advertisers to get a deal, and only after you recoup the initial membership cost or book price do you begin to save. If you

plan to use the club or coupons frequently, you may save considerably. Before signing up, find out what discounts you get for free.

➤ DISCOUNT CLUBS: **Entertainment Travel Editions** (✉ 2125 Butterfield Rd., Troy, MI 48084, ☎ 800/445–4137; $20–$51, depending on destination). **Great American Traveler** (✉ Box 27965, Salt Lake City, UT 84127, ☎ 801/974–3033 or 800/548–2812; $49.95 per year). **Moment's Notice Discount Travel Club** (✉ 7301 New Utrecht Ave., Brooklyn, NY 11204, ☎ 718/234–6295; $25 per year, single or family). **Privilege Card International** (✉ 237 E. Front St., Youngstown, OH 44503, ☎ 330/746–5211 or 800/236–9732; $74.95 per year). **Sears's Mature Outlook** (✉ Box 9390, Des Moines, IA 50306, ☎ 800/336–6330; $19.95 per year). **Travelers Advantage** (✉ CUC Travel Service, 3033 S. Parker Rd., Suite 1000, Aurora, CO 80014, ☎ 800/548–1116 or 800/648–4037; $59.95 per year, single or family). **Worldwide Discount Travel Club** (✉ 1674 Meridian Ave., Miami Beach, FL 33139, ☎ 305/534–2082; $50 per year family, $40 single).

CREDIT-CARD BENEFITS

When you use your credit card to make travel purchases you may get free travel-accident insurance, collision-damage insurance, and medical or legal assistance, depending on the card and the bank that issued it. American Express, MasterCard, and Visa provide one or more of these services, so **get a copy of your credit card's travel-benefits policy.** If you are a member of an auto club, always **ask hotel and car-rental reservations agents about auto-club discounts.** Some clubs offer additional discounts on tours, cruises, and admission to attractions.

DISCOUNT RESERVATIONS

To save money, **look into discount-reservations services** with toll-free numbers, which use their buying power to get a better price on hotels, airline tickets, even car rentals. When booking a room, always **call the hotel's local toll-free number** (if one is available) rather than the central reservations number—you'll often get a better price. Always ask about special packages or corporate rates.

When shopping for the best deal on hotels and car rentals, **look for guaranteed exchange rates,** which protect you against a falling dollar. With your rate locked in, you won't pay more, even if the price goes up in the local currency.

➤ AIRLINE TICKETS: ☎ **800/FLY–4–LESS.**

➤ HOTEL ROOMS: **Steigenberger Reservation Service** (☎ 800/223–5652). **Travel Interlink** (☎ 800/888–5898). **VacationLand** (☎ 800/245–0050).

PACKAGE DEALS

Packages and guided tours can save you money, but don't confuse the two. When you buy a package, your travel remains independent, just as though you had planned and booked the trip yourself. Fly/drive packages, which combine airfare and car rental, are often a good deal.

ELECTRICITY

To use your U.S.-purchased electric-powered equipment, **bring a converter and adapter.** The electrical current in the countries covered in this book is 220 volts, 50 cycles alternating current (AC), except the Philippines, which, like the United States, runs on 110-volt, 60-cycle AC current.

If your appliances are dual-voltage, you'll need only an adapter. Don't use 110-volt outlets, marked FOR SHAVERS ONLY, for high-wattage appliances such as blow-dryers. Most laptops operate equally well on 110 and 220 volts and so require only an adapter.

GAY & LESBIAN TRAVEL

Many tourist areas—for example in Thailand, on Bali (Indonesia), and in the Philippines—offer an open environment for gay and lesbian travelers. Other areas, however—such as the strict Muslim regions of Malaysia and Indonesia—are not as tolerant. In more rural countries, such as Cambodia, Laos, and Vietnam, overt behavior is not encouraged, either. Outside of major tourist spots, discretion is advised.

➤ GAY- AND LESBIAN-FRIENDLY TOUR OPERATORS: **Hanns Ebensten Travel** (✉ 513 Fleming St., Key West, FL 33040, ☎ 305/294–8174, FAX 305/292–9665), one of the oldest operators in the gay market, offers packages such as the "Thai Experience" tour and "The Islands of Indonesia," which covers Java, Bali, and Kalimantan. **Toto Tours** (✉ 1326 W. Albion Ave., Suite 3W, Chicago, IL 60626, ☎ 773/274–8686 or 800/565–1241, FAX 773/274–8695) is currently coordinating trips to the region that may include the beaches of Thailand and a cruise around Bali.

➤ GAY- AND LESBIAN-FRIENDLY TRAVEL AGENCIES: **Corniche Travel** (✉ 8721 Sunset Blvd., Suite 200, West Hollywood, CA 90069, ☎ 310/854–6000 or 800/429–8747, FAX 310/659–7441). **Islanders Kennedy Travel** (✉ 183 W. 10th St., New York, NY 10014, ☎ 212/242–3222 or 800/988–1181, FAX 212/929–8530). **Now Voyager** (✉ 4406 18th St., San Francisco, CA 94114, ☎ 415/626–1169 or 800/255–6951, FAX 415/626–8626). **Yellowbrick Road** (✉ 1500 W. Balmoral Ave., Chicago, IL 60640, ☎ 773/561–1800 or 800/642–2488, FAX 773/561–4497). **Skylink Travel and Tour** (✉ 3577 Moorland Ave., Santa Rosa, CA 95407, ☎ 707/585–8355 or 800/225–5759, FAX 707/584–5637), serving lesbian travelers.

HEALTH

DIVERS' ALERT

Do not fly within 24 hours after scuba diving.

FOOD & DRINK

In Southeast Asia the major health risk is traveler's diarrhea, caused by eating contaminated fruit or vegetables or drinking contaminated water. So **watch what you eat.** Stay away from ice, uncooked food, and unpasteurized milk and milk products, and **drink only bottled water** or water that has been boiled for at least 20 minutes. Mild cases may respond to Imodium (known generically as loperamide) or Pepto-Bismol (not as strong), both of which can be purchased over the counter. Drink plenty of purified water or tea—chamomile is a good folk remedy. In severe cases,

THE GOLD GUIDE / SMART TRAVEL TIPS

rehydrate yourself with a salt-sugar solution (½ teaspoon salt and 4 table-spoons sugar per quart of water).

MEDICAL PLANS

No one plans to get sick while traveling, but it happens, so **consider signing up with a medical-assistance company.** Members get doctor referrals, emergency evacuation or repatriation, 24-hour telephone hot lines for medical consultation, cash for emergencies, and other personal and legal assistance. Coverage varies by plan, so **review the benefits of each carefully.**

➤ MEDICAL-ASSISTANCE COMPANIES: **International SOS Assistance** (✉ 8 Neshaminy Interplex, Suite 207, Trevose, PA 19053, ☎ 215/245–4707 or 800/523–6586, FAX 215/244–9617; ✉ 12 Chemin Riant-bosson, 1217 Meyrin 1, Geneva, Switzerland, ☎ 4122/785–6464, FAX 4122/785–6424; ✉ 10 Anson Rd., 14-07/08 International Plaza, Singapore 079903, ☎ 65/226–3936, FAX 65/226–3937).

SHOTS & MEDICATIONS

Although the countries in Southeast Asia don't require or suggest vaccinations before traveling, the United States Centers for Disease Control offer the following recommendations:

Tetanus-diphtheria and polio vaccinations should be up-to-date—if you haven't been immunized since childhood, **consider bolstering your tetanus vaccination.** You should also be immunized against (or immune to) measles, mumps, and rubella. If you plan to visit rural areas, where there's questionable sanitation, you'll need to **get an immune-serum globulin vaccination as protection against hepatitis A.** If you are staying for longer than three weeks and traveling into rural areas, antimalarial pills and a typhoid vaccination are recommended. If staying for a month or more, you should be vaccinated against rabies and Japanese encephalitis; for six months or more, against hepatitis B as well. For news on current outbreaks of infectious diseases, ask your physician and check with your state or local department of health.

According to the National Centers for Disease Control (CDC) there's a limited risk of malaria and dengue in certain areas of Southeast Asia. In most urban or easily accessible areas you need not worry. However, if you plan to visit remote regions or stay for more than six weeks, **check with the CDC's International Travelers Hotline.** In areas where malaria and dengue, both of which are carried by mosquitoes, are prevalent, use mosquito nets, wear clothing that covers the body, apply repellent containing DEET, and use spray for flying insects in living and sleeping areas. Also **consider taking antimalarial pills.** There is no vaccine that combats dengue.

➤ HEALTH WARNINGS: **National Centers for Disease Control** (✉ CDC, National Center for Infectious Diseases, Division of Quarantine, Traveler's Health Section, 1600 Clifton Rd. NE, M/S E-03, Atlanta, GA 30333, ☎ 404/332–4559, FAX 404/332–4565).

INSURANCE

Travel insurance is the best way to **protect yourself against financial loss.** The most useful plan is a comprehensive policy that includes coverage for trip cancellation and interruption, default, trip delay, and medical expenses (with a waiver for preexisting conditions).

Without insurance, you will lose all or most of your money if you cancel your trip, regardless of the reason. Default insurance covers you if your tour operator, airline, or cruise line goes out of business. Trip-delay covers unforeseen expenses that you may incur due to bad weather or mechanical delays. It's important to compare the fine print regarding trip-delay coverage when comparing policies.

For overseas travel, one of the most important components of travel insurance is its medical coverage. Supplemental health insurance will pick up the cost of your medical bills should you get sick or injured while traveling. United States residents should note that Medicare generally does not cover health-care costs outside the United States, nor do many privately issued policies. Residents of the United Kingdom can buy an annual travel-insurance policy valid for most vacations taken during the year in which the coverage is purchased. If you are pregnant or have a preexisting condition, make sure you're covered. British citizens should buy extra medical coverage when traveling overseas, according to the Association of British Insurers. Australian travelers should buy travel insurance, including extra medical coverage, whenever they go abroad, according to the Insurance Council of Australia.

Always **buy travel insurance directly from the insurance company**; if you buy it from a cruise line, airline, or tour operator that goes out of business you probably will not be covered for the agency or operator's default, a major risk. Before you make any purchase, **review your existing health and home-owner's policies** to find out whether they cover expenses incurred while traveling.

➤ TRAVEL INSURERS: In the U.S., Access America (✉ 6600 W. Broad St., Richmond, VA 23230, ☎ 804/285–3300 or 800/284–8300). Travel Guard International (✉ 1145 Clark St., Stevens Point, WI 54481, ☎ 715/345–0505 or 800/826–1300). In Canada, Mutual of Omaha (✉ Travel Division, 500 University Ave., Toronto, Ontario M5G 1V8, ☎ 416/598–4083, 800/268–8825 in Canada).

➤ INSURANCE INFORMATION: In the U.K., Association of British Insurers (✉ 51 Gresham St., London EC2V 7HQ, ☎ 0171/600–3333). In Australia, the Insurance Council of Australia (☎ 613/9614–1077, ℻ 613/9614–7924).

LODGING

Accommodations in Southeast Asia range from shoebox-size rooms with community or "squat" toilets to five-star luxury. Every major city and important resort has at least one— and probably several—opulent, international-style hotels (many are part of such international chains as Sheraton, Shangri-La, Regent, Hyatt, Hilton, Holiday Inn, and Inter-

Continental) that are famous for their service and amenities. If you can afford to splurge, this is the place to do it, for the prices of even the very top hotels are often still far lower than comparable digs elsewhere.

A good rule for medium and large hotels in popular areas is to **reserve your rooms at least two months prior to arrival.** This is especially true in December and January, during Chinese New Year, at the end of Ramadan, and during the Western summer holidays and local school breaks. The international chains have U.S. reservations offices. If you do arrive in an Asian capital without a hotel reservation, you will generally find a reservations desk at the airport that may be able to provide an immediate booking. This service is usually efficient and free, and often special discounts are available.

Most bottom-end accommodations are clustered in particular areas of cities or tourist hubs—and they're usually a little off the beaten path. Always **ask to see the room before committing to a stay in a budget hotel** and **comparison-shop for the best deal.** In Bangkok, try the Banglamphu section of town, especially along Khao San Road. In Kuala Lumpur, try the Jalan Tuanku Abdul Rahman. In Manila, look in the Ermita and Quiapo sections. In Singapore, try Bencoolen Street and Beach Road. In Jakarta, Jalan Jaksa is the budget hub, as are the gangs (alleys) around the train station in Yogyakarta, the back streets of Kuta beach on Bali and the outskirts of Rantepao in the Toraja area of south central Sulawesi.

You can find budget dormitory and hotel accommodations at the YMCAs in Bangkok, Kuala Lumpur, Manila, and Singapore, or at hostels and homestays in Thailand, the Philippines, Indonesia, and Malaysia. They vary greatly in quality but are generally inexpensive and clean. You will also find some interesting, uniquely Asian lodging alternatives. In Sarawak, Malaysia, for example, you can stay in tribal longhouses and observe the native lifestyle, joining in meal preparation and evening entertainments. In northern Thailand,

THE GOLD GUIDE / SMART TRAVEL TIPS

stays in village huts are part of many overnight treks to the hill tribes.

APARTMENT & VILLA RENTALS

If you want a home base that's roomy enough for a family and comes with cooking facilities, **consider a furnished rental.** These can save you money, especially if you're traveling with a large group of people. Home-exchange directories list rentals (often second homes owned by prospective house swappers), and some services search for a house or apartment for you (even a castle if that's your fancy) and handle the paperwork. Some send an illustrated catalog; others send photographs only of specific properties, sometimes at a charge. Up-front registration fees may apply.

➤ RENTAL AGENTS: **Hometours International** (✉ Box 11503, Knoxville, TN 37939, ☎ 423/690–8484 or 800/367–4668). **Property Rentals International** (✉ 1008 Mansfield Crossing Rd., Richmond, VA 23236, ☎ 804/378–6054 or 800/220–3332, ℻ 804/379–2073).

HOSTELS

No matter what your age, you can **save on lodging costs by staying at hostels.** In some 5,000 locations in more than 70 countries around the world, Hostelling International (HI), the umbrella group for a number of national youth hostel associations, offers single-sex, dorm-style beds and, at many hostels, "couples" rooms and family accommodations. Membership in any HI national hostel association, open to travelers of all ages, allows you to stay in HI-affiliated hostels at member rates (one-year membership is about $25 for adults; hostels run about $10–$25 per night). Members also have priority if the hostel is full; they're eligible for discounts around the world, even on rail and bus travel in some countries.

➤ HOSTEL ORGANIZATIONS: **Hostelling International—American Youth Hostels** (✉ 733 15th St. NW, Suite 840, Washington, DC 20005, ☎ 202/783–6161, ℻ 202/783–6171). **Hostelling International—Canada** (✉ 400-205 Catherine St., Ottawa, Ontario K2P 1C3, ☎ 613/237–7884, ℻ 613/237–7868). **Youth Hostel Association of**

England and Wales (✉ Trevelyan House, 8 St. Stephen's Hill, St. Albans, Hertfordshire AL1 2DY, ☎ 01727/855215 or 01727/845047, ℻ 01727/844126); membership in the U.S. $25, in Canada C$26.75, in the U.K. £9.30.

MONEY

For details on currency, costs, taxes, and tipping, *see* individual chapter A to Z sections.

CREDIT & DEBIT CARDS

Should you use a credit card or a debit card when traveling? Both have benefits. A credit card allows you to delay payment and gives you certain rights as a consumer (☞ Consumer Protection, *above*). A debit card, also known as a check card, deducts funds directly from your checking account and helps you stay within your budget. When you want to rent a car, though, you may still need an old-fashioned credit card. Although you can always *pay* for your car with a debit card, some agencies will not allow you to *reserve* a car with a debit card.

Otherwise, the two types of plastic are virtually the same. Both will get you cash advances at ATMs worldwide if your card is properly programmed with your personal identification number (PIN). Both offer excellent, wholesale exchange rates. And both protect you against unauthorized use if the card is lost or stolen. Your liability is limited to $50, as long as you report the card missing.

➤ ATM LOCATIONS: **Cirrus** (☎ 800/424–7787). **Plus** (☎ 800/843–7587) for locations in the U.S. and Canada, or visit your local bank.

➤ REPORTING LOST CARDS: To report lost or stolen credit cards, call the following toll-free numbers: **American Express** (☎ 800/327–2177); **Discover Card** (☎ 800/347–2683); **Diners Club** (☎ 800/234–6377); **MasterCard** (☎ 800/307–7309); and **Visa** (☎ 800/847–2911).

EXCHANGING MONEY

For the most favorable rates, **change money through banks.** Although fees charged for ATM transactions may be higher abroad than at home, Cirrus and Plus exchange rates are excellent, because they are based on wholesale rates offered only by major banks. You won't do as well at exchange booths in airports or rail and bus stations, in hotels, in restaurants, or in stores, although you may find their hours more convenient. To avoid lines at airport exchange booths, **get a bit of local currency before you leave home.**

➤ EXCHANGE SERVICES: **Chase Currency To Go** (☎ 800/935–9935; 935–9935 in NY, NJ, and CT). **International Currency Express** (☎ 888/842–0880 on the East Coast, 888/278–6628 on the West Coast). **Thomas Cook Currency Services** (☎ 800/287–7362 for telephone orders and retail locations).

TRAVELER'S CHECKS

Do you need traveler's checks? It depends on where you're headed. If you're going to rural areas and small towns, go with cash; traveler's checks are best used in cities. Lost or stolen checks can usually be replaced within 24 hours. To ensure a speedy refund, buy your own traveler's checks—don't let someone else pay for them: irregularities like this can cause delays. The person who bought the checks should make the call to request a refund.

PACKING

LUGGAGE

How many carry-on bags you can bring with you is up to the airline. Most allow two, but the limit is often reduced to one on certain flights. Gate agents will take excess baggage—including bags they deem oversize—from you as you board and add it to checked luggage. To avoid this situation, make sure that everything you carry aboard will fit under your seat. Also, get to the gate early, and request a seat at the back of the plane; you'll probably board first, while the overhead bins are still empty. Since big, bulky baggage attracts the attention of gate agents and flight attendants on a busy flight, make sure your carry-on is really a carry-on. Finally, a carry-on that's long and narrow is more likely to

remain unnoticed than one that's wide and squarish.

If you are flying internationally, note that baggage allowances may be determined not by piece but by weight—generally 88 pounds (40 kilograms) in first class, 66 pounds (30 kilograms) in business class, and 44 pounds (20 kilograms) in economy.

Airline liability for baggage is limited to $1,250 per person on flights within the United States. On international flights it amounts to $9.07 per pound or $20 per kilogram for checked baggage (roughly $640 per 70-pound bag) and $400 per passenger for unchecked baggage. You can buy additional coverage at check-in for about $10 per $1,000 of coverage, but it excludes a rather extensive list of items, shown on your airline ticket.

Before departure, **itemize your bags' contents** and their worth, and label the bags with your name, address, and phone number. (If you use your home address, cover it so that potential thieves can't see it readily.) Inside each bag, **pack a copy of your itinerary.** At check-in, **make sure that each bag is correctly tagged** with the destination airport's three-letter code. If your bags arrive damaged or fail to arrive at all, file a written report with the airline before leaving the airport.

PACKING LIST

Pack lightly, because porters can be hard to find and baggage restrictions are tight on international flights—be sure to **check on your airline's policies before you pack.** And either **leave room in your suitcase or bring expandable totes for all your bargain purchases.**

If you'll be traveling through several different types of climate, your wardrobe will have to reflect this. Light cotton or other natural-fiber clothing is appropriate for any Southeast Asian destination; drip-dry is an especially good idea, because the tropical sun and high humidity encourage frequent changes of clothing. **Avoid exotic fabrics, because you may have difficulty getting them laundered.**

Southeast Asia is generally informal: a sweater, shawl, or lightweight linen jacket will be sufficient for dining and evening wear, except for top international restaurants, where men will still be most comfortable in (and may in fact be required to wear) a jacket and tie. A sweater is also a good idea for cool evenings or overly air-conditioned restaurants. An umbrella can be helpful for shielding against both rain and sun.

The paths leading to temples can be rough; in any case, a pair of sturdy and comfortable walking shoes is always appropriate when traveling. Slip-ons are preferable to lace-ups, as shoes must be removed before you enter most shrines and temples.

It might be wise to **bring your favorite toilet articles** (in plastic containers, to avoid breakage and reduce the weight of luggage). Make sure that bottles containing liquids are tightly capped to prevent leakage. Allow for the tropical sun by bringing along a hat and sunscreen. Mosquito repellent is a good idea, and toilet paper is not always supplied in public places. Moist towelettes are great for cleaning off tropical grime and sweat, as well as for quick wash-ups before meals in more remote establishments where soap and water aren't always available. Small tissue packets are handy for spills and easier to tote than toilet paper, which is uncommon outside of resort areas.

In your carry-on luggage **bring an extra pair of eyeglasses or contact lenses** and **enough of any medication you take** to last the entire trip. You may also want your doctor to write a spare prescription using the drug's generic name, since brand names may vary from country to country. **Never put prescription drugs or valuables in luggage to be checked.** To avoid customs delays, carry medications in their original packaging. And don't forget to copy down and carry addresses of offices that handle refunds of lost traveler's checks.

PASSPORTS & VISAS

When traveling internationally, **carry a passport even if you don't need one** (it's always the best form of I.D.), and make **two photocopies of the data page** (one for someone at home and

another for you, carried separately from your passport). If you lose your passport, promptly call the nearest embassy or consulate and the local police.

ENTERING SOUTHEAST ASIA

See individual chapter A to Z sections for specific passport and visa requirements.

PASSPORT OFFICES

The best time to apply for a passport or to renew is during the fall and winter. Before any trip, be sure to check your passport's expiration date and, if necessary, renew it as soon as possible. (Some countries won't allow you to enter on a passport that's due to expire in six months or less.)

➤ AUSTRALIAN CITIZENS: **Australian Passport Office** (☎ 131–232).

➤ CANADIAN CITIZENS: **Passport Office** (☎ 819/994–3500 or 800/567–6868).

➤ NEW ZEALAND CITIZENS: **New Zealand Passport Office** (☎ 04/494–0700 for information on how to apply, 0800/727–776 for information on applications already submitted).

➤ U.K. CITIZENS: **London Passport Office** (☎ 0990/21010), for fees and documentation requirements and to request an emergency passport.

➤ U.S. CITIZENS: **National Passport Information Center** (☎ 900/225–5674; calls are charged at 35¢ per minute for automated service, $1.05 per minute for operator service).

SAFETY

Southeast Asia is generally a safe region for travelers of all ages and walks of life. Still, whether you're traveling as a couple, a family, a package tourist, a senior, or a solo backpacker, the general precautions of the road still preside. Except for when in resort areas, **dress modestly and don't flash your money around.** Carry travelers checks, keep large amounts of cash in a hidden money pouch, and use a credit card when possible, especially if they include insurance. Crime against travelers mainly occurs in large cities and tourist areas, where small-time thieves prey on unseasoned vacationers, so a little caution in how you act can go a long way. Pickpockets haunt crowded transport hubs and scam artists love to draw in naive travelers, so **keep your valuables hidden or back in the hotel safe** and **check out what you buy before you lay down the money**—fake jewels, fake name-brand items (handbags, shoes, perfume), bait-and-switch gifts "prewrapped" for Customs, and bogus shipping promises are the typical tricks of this region. Thankfully, most of this is limited to major tourist crossroads, and in the more remote areas, where neighbors are on a first-name basis and doors remain unlocked at night, crime of any sort is rarely a problem.

There are, however, several countries where the social climate has the potential for affecting your safety, including Cambodia, Indonesia, and Myanmar. With the death of Pol Pot and the decline of the Khmer Rouge, tourism to Cambodia is slowly on the rise again, but you should proceed with caution by staying within the geographic boundaries set by guides—particularly in the Siem Riap and Angkor temple areas, where stray land mines and unexpected guerrilla attacks still pose a threat. Indonesia, with its plummeting economy and tense political scene, is also a country to watch; although most antigovernment demonstrations have been on Java and Sumatra, particularly in the major cities, you should still **check with the state department for updates before departing.** Antigovernment friction is more serious in Myanmar, where, depending on the latest political activity and the whims of the officials, you may be prohibited from venturing too far outside the capital.

SENIOR-CITIZEN TRAVEL

There is no reason that active, well-traveled senior citizens shouldn't visit Southeast Asia, whether on an independent (but prebooked) vacation, an escorted tour, or an adventure trip. Before you leave home, however, determine what medical services your health insurance provider will cover outside the United States; note that Medicare does not provide for payment of hospital and medical services

outside the United States. If you need additional travel insurance, buy it (☞ Insurance, *above*).

To qualify for age-related discounts, **mention your senior-citizen status up front** when booking hotel reservations (not when checking out) and before you're seated in restaurants (not when paying the bill). Note that discounts may be limited to certain menus, days, or hours. When renting a car, **ask about promotional car-rental discounts,** which can be cheaper than senior-citizen rates.

➤ ADVENTURES: **Overseas Adventure Travel** (✉ Grand Circle Corporation, 625 Mt. Auburn St., Cambridge, MA 02138, ☎ 617/876–0533 or 800/221–0814, FAX 617/876–0455) offers tours to Java, Bali, Sumatra, Sulawesi, Nusa Tenggara, and Komodo Island in Indonesia, as well as to Malaysia, Singapore, Thailand, and Vietnam.

➤ EDUCATIONAL PROGRAMS: **Elderhostel** (✉ 75 Federal St., 3rd floor, Boston, MA 02110, ☎ 617/426–8056) coordinates trips to Indonesia, Malaysia, the Philippines, Thailand, and Vietnam. **Interhostel** (✉ University of New Hampshire, 6 Garrison Ave., Durham, NH 03824, ☎ 603/862–1147 or 800/733–9753, FAX 603/862–1113). **Folkways Institute** (✉ 14600 Southeast Aldridge Rd., Portland, OR 97236-6518, ☎ 503/658–6600 or 800/225–4666, FAX 503/658–8672).

STUDENT TRAVEL

TRAVEL AGENCIES

To save money, **look into deals available through student-oriented travel agencies.** To qualify you'll need a bona fide student I.D. card. Members of international student groups are also eligible.

➤ STUDENT IDs & SERVICES: **Council on International Educational Exchange** (✉ CIEE, 205 E. 42nd St., 14th floor, New York, NY 10017, ☎ 212/822–2600 or 888/268–6245, FAX 212/822–2699), for mail orders only, in the United States. **Travel Cuts** (✉ 187 College St., Toronto, Ontario M5T 1P7, ☎ 416/979–2406 or 800/667–2887) in Canada.

TELEPHONES

For details on making calls to, within, and from each country, *see* individual chapter A to Z sections.

INTERNATIONAL CALLS

AT&T, MCI, and Sprint international access codes make calling the United States relatively convenient, but you may find the local access number blocked in many hotel rooms. First ask the hotel operator to connect you. If the hotel operator balks, ask for an international operator, or dial the international operator yourself. One way to improve your odds of getting connected to your long-distance carrier is to travel with more than one company's calling card (a hotel may block Sprint, for example, but not MCI). If all else fails, call from a pay phone in the hotel lobby.

➤ To Obtain Access Codes: **AT&T Direct** (☎ 800/435–0812). **MCI WorldPhone** (☎ 800/444–4141). **Sprint International Access** (☎ 800/ 877–4646).

TOUR OPERATORS

Buying a prepackaged tour or independent vacation can make your trip to Southeast Asia less expensive and more hassle-free. Because everything is prearranged, you'll spend less time planning.

Operators that handle several hundred thousand travelers per year can use their purchasing power to give you a good price. Their high volume may also indicate financial stability. But some small companies provide more personalized service; because they tend to specialize, they may also be more knowledgeable about a given area.

BOOKING WITH AN AGENT

Travel agents are excellent resources. In fact, large operators accept bookings made only through travel agents. But it's a good idea to **collect brochures from several agencies**, because some agents' suggestions may be influenced by relationships with tour and package firms that reward them for volume sales. If you have a special interest, **find an agent with expertise in that area**; ASTA (☞ Travel Agencies,

below) has a database of specialists worldwide.

Make sure your travel agent knows the accommodations and other services. Ask about the hotel's location, room size, beds, and whether it has a pool, room service, or programs for children, if you care about these. Has your agent been there in person or sent others you can contact?

Do some homework on your own, too: local tourism boards can provide information about lesser-known and small-niche operators, some of which may sell only direct.

BUYER BEWARE

Each year consumers are stranded or lose their money when tour operators—even very large ones with excellent reputations—go out of business. So **check out the operator.** Find out how long the company has been in business, and ask several travel agents about its reputation. If the package or tour you are considering is priced lower than in your wildest dreams, **be skeptical.** Try to **book with a company that has a consumer-protection program.** If the operator has such a program, you'll find information about it in the company's brochure. If the operator you are considering does not offer some kind of consumer protection, then ask for references from satisfied customers.

In the U.S., members of the National Tour Association and United States Tour Operators Association are required to set aside funds to cover your payments and travel arrangements in case the company defaults. It's also a good idea to choose a company that participates in the American Society of Travel Agent's Tour Operator Program (TOP). This gives you a forum if there are any disputes between you and your tour operator; ASTA will act as mediator.

➤ Tour-Operator Recommendations: **American Society of Travel Agents** (☞ Travel Agencies, *below*). **National Tour Association** (✉ NTA, 546 E. Main St., Lexington, KY 40508, ☎ 606/226–4444 or 800/ 755–8687). **United States Tour**

Operators Association (✉ USTOA, 342 Madison Ave., Suite 1522, New York, NY 10173, ☎ 212/599–6599 or 800/468–7862, FAX 212/599–6744).

COSTS

The more your package or tour includes, the better you can predict the ultimate cost of your vacation. Make sure you know exactly what is covered, and **beware of hidden costs.** Are taxes, tips, and service charges included? Transfers and baggage handling? Entertainment and excursions? These can add up.

Prices for packages and tours are usually quoted per person, based on two sharing a room. If traveling solo, you may be required to pay the full double-occupancy rate. Some operators eliminate this surcharge if you agree to be matched with a roommate of the same sex, even if one is not found by departure time.

GROUP TOURS

Among companies that sell tours to Southeast Asia, the following are nationally known, have a proven reputation, and offer plenty of options. The classifications used below represent different price categories, and you'll probably encounter these terms when talking to a travel agent or tour operator. The key difference is usually in accommodations, which run from budget to better, and better-yet to best.

➤ SUPER-DELUXE: **Abercrombie & Kent** (✉ 1520 Kensington Rd., Oak Brook, IL 60521-2141, ☎ 630/954–2944 or 800/323–7308, FAX 630/954–3324). **Absolute Asia** (✉ 180 Varick St., New York, NY 10014, ☎ 212/627–1950 or 800/736–8187). **Travcoa** (✉ Box 2630, 2350 S.E. Bristol St., Newport Beach, CA 92660, ☎ 714/476–2800 or 800/992–2003, FAX 714/476–2538).

➤ DELUXE: **Globus** (✉ 5301 S. Federal Circle, Littleton, CO 80123-2980, ☎ 303/797–2800 or 800/221–0090, FAX 303/347–2080). **Maupintour** (✉ 1515 St. Andrews Dr., Lawrence, KS 66047, ☎ 785/843–1211 or 800/255–4266, FAX 785/843–8351). **Tauck Tours** (✉ Box 5027, 276 Post Rd. W, Westport, CT 06881-5027, ☎ 203/226–6911 or 800/468–2825, FAX 203/221–6866).

➤ FIRST-CLASS: **Brendan Tours** (✉ 15137 Califa St., Van Nuys, CA 91411, ☎ 818/785–9696 or 800/421–8446, FAX 818/902–9876). **DER Travel Services** (✉ 9501 W. Devon St., Rosemont, IL 60018, ☎ 800/937–1235, FAX 800/282–7474, 800/860–9944, for brochures). **General Tours** (✉ 53 Summer St., Keene, NH 03431, ☎ 603/357–5033 or 800/221–2216, FAX 603/357–4548). **Orient Flexi-Pax Tours** (✉ 630 Third Ave., New York, NY 10017, ☎ 212/692–9550 or 800/545–5540, FAX 212/661–1618). **Pacific Bestour** (✉ 228 Rivervale Rd., River Vale, NJ 07675, ☎ 201/664–8778 or 800/688–3288, FAX 201/722–0829). **Pacific Delight Tours** (✉ 132 Madison Ave., New York, NY 10016, ☎ 212/684–7707 or 800/221–7179, FAX 212/532–3406).

➤ BUDGET: **Cosmos** (☞ Globus, *above*).

PACKAGES

Like group tours, independent vacation packages are available from major tour operators and airlines. The companies listed below offer vacation packages in a broad price range.

➤ AIR/HOTEL: **Absolute Asia** (☞ Group Tours, *above*). **DER Travel Services** (☞ Group Tours, *above*). **Orient Flexi-Pax Tours** (☞ Group Tours, *above*). **Pacific Bestour** (☞ Group Tours, *above*). **Pacific Delight Tours** (☞ Group Tours, *above*). **United Vacations** (☎ 800/328–6877).

➤ IN THE U.K.: **Bales Tours** (✉ Bales House, Junction Rd., Dorking, Surrey RH4 3HB, ☎ 01306/876881 or 01306/885991). **British Airways Holidays** (✉ Astral Towers, Betts Way, London Rd., Crawley, West Sussex RH10 2XA, ☎ 01293/723171). **Hayes and Jarvis** (✉ Hayes House, 152 King St., London W6 0QU, ☎ 0181/748–5050). **Kuoni Travel** (✉ Kuoni House, Dorking, Surrey RH5 4AZ, ☎ 01306/740500).

THEME TRIPS

➤ CUSTOMIZED PACKAGES: **Pacific Experience** (✉ 63 Mill St., Newport,

RI 02840, ☎ 401/849–6258 or 800/279–3639, FAX 401/849–6158).

➤ ADVENTURE: **Asia Pacific Adventures** (✉ 826 S. Sierra Bonita Ave., Los Angeles, CA 90036, ☎ 323/935–3156 or 800/825–1680). **Geographical Expeditions** (✉ 2627 Lombard St., San Francisco, CA 94123, ☎ 415/922–0448 or 800/777–8183). **Himalayan Travel** (✉ 110 Prospect St., Stamford, CT 06901, ☎ 203/359–3711 or 800/225–2380, FAX 203/359–3669). **Mountain Travel-Sobek** (✉ 6420 Fairmount Ave., El Cerrito, CA 94530, ☎ 510/527–8100 or 800/227–2384, FAX 510/525–7710). **Naturequest** (✉ 934 Acapulco St., Laguna Beach, CA 92651, ☎ 714/499–9561 or 800/369–3033, FAX 714/499–0812). **Wilderness Travel** (✉ 1102 Ninth St., Berkeley, CA 94710, ☎ 510/558–2488 or 800/368–2794).

➤ ARCHAEOLOGY: **Archeological Tours** (✉ 271 Madison Ave., New York, NY 10016, ☎ 212/986–3054, FAX 212/370–1561).

➤ BICYCLING: **Backroads** (✉ 801 Cedar St., Berkeley, CA 94710-1800, ☎ 510/527–1555 or 800/462–2848, FAX 510/527–1444).

➤ CULINARY: **Geographical Expeditions** (☞ Adventure, *above*).

➤ LEARNING: **Earthwatch** (✉ Box 9104, 680 Mount Auburn St., Watertown, MA 02272, ☎ 617/926–8200 or 800/776–0188, FAX 617/926–8532) organizes research expeditions. **Smithsonian Study Tours and Seminars** (✉ 1100 Jefferson Dr. SW, Room 3045, MRC 702, Washington, DC 20560, ☎ 202/357–4700, FAX 202/633–9250).

➤ NATURAL HISTORY: **Questers** (✉ 381 Park Ave. S, New York, NY 10016, ☎ 212/251–0444 or 800/468–8668, FAX 212/251–0890). **Victor Emanuel Nature Tours** (✉ Box 33008, Austin, TX 78764, ☎ 512/328–5221 or 800/328–8368, FAX 512/328–2919).

➤ SCUBA DIVING: **Rothschild Dive Safaris** (✉ 900 West End Ave., #1B, New York, NY 10025-3525, ☎ 800/359–0747, FAX 212/749–6172). **Tropical Adventures** (✉ 111 2nd Ave. N, Seattle, WA 98109, ☎ 206/441–3483 or 800/247–3483, FAX 206/441–5431).

➤ YACHT CHARTERS: **Lynn Jachney Charters** (✉ Box 302, Marblehead, MA 01945, ☎ 617/639–0787 or 800/223–2050, FAX 617/639–0216). **Ocean Voyages** (✉ 1709 Bridgeway, Sausalito, CA 94965, ☎ 415/332–4681 or 800/299–4444, FAX 415/332–7460).

TRAIN TRAVEL

Trains are an option—and a recommended one—in many Southeast Asian countries, although cars with true first-class comfort are limited to journeys from Bangkok to Singapore. For more details, *see* individual chapter Essentials *and* A to Z sections.

TRAVEL AGENCIES

A good travel agent puts your needs first. Look for an agency that has been in business at least five years, emphasizes customer service, and has someone on staff who specializes in your destination. In addition, **make sure the agency belongs to a professional trade organization,** such as ASTA in the United States. If your travel agency is also acting as your tour operator, *see* Buyer Beware in Tour Operators, *above*).

➤ LOCAL AGENT REFERRALS: **American Society of Travel Agents** (ASTA, ☎ 800/965–2782 24-hr hot line, FAX 703/684–8319). **Association of British Travel Agents** (✉ 55–57 Newman St., London W1P 4AH, ☎ 0171/637–2444, FAX 0171/637–0713). **Association of Canadian Travel Agents** (✉ Suite 201, 1729 Bank St., Ottawa, Ontario K1V 7Z5, ☎ 613/521–0474, FAX 613/521–0805). **Australian Federation of Travel Agents** (☎ 02/9264–3299). **Travel Agents' Association of New Zealand** (☎ 04/499–0104).

TRAVEL GEAR

Travel catalogs specialize in useful items, such as compact alarm clocks and travel irons, that can **save space when packing.** They also offer dual-voltage appliances, currency converters, and foreign-language phrase books.

➤ CATALOGS: **Magellan's** (☎ 800/ 962–4943, FAX 805/568–5406). **Orvis Travel** (☎ 800/541–3541, FAX 540/ 343–7053). **TravelSmith** (☎ 800/ 950–1600, FAX 800/950–1656).

U.S. GOVERNMENT

Government agencies can be an excellent source of inexpensive travel information. When planning your trip, **find out what government materials are available.**

➤ ADVISORIES: **U.S. Department of State** (Overseas Citizens Services Office, ✉ Room 4811 N.S., Washington, DC 20520; ☎ 202/647– 5225 or FAX 202/647–3000 for interactive hot line; ☎ 301/946– 4400 for computer bulletin board); enclose a self-addressed, stamped, business-size envelope.

➤ PAMPHLETS: **Consumer Information Center** (✉ Consumer Information Catalogue, Pueblo, CO 81009, ☎ 719/948–3334 or 888/878–3256) for a free catalog that includes travel titles.

VISITOR INFORMATION

TOURIST INFORMATION

For details on regional and national tourist offices *see* individual chapter Essentials *and* A to Z sections.

WHEN TO GO

You can depend on the coastal areas of Southeast Asia to be warm and the interior highlands to be cool most of the time, but from here on, the climate slightly differs from country to country. Thailand has three seasons: hot (March to June), rainy (June to October), and cool (November to February). Monsoon winds whip the rain into peninsular Malaysia from September to December but take another month or so to reach Sabah

and Sarawak. November to January is Singapore's rainy season, although showers can still come regularly in June mornings and evenings. December to May is the dry season in the Philippines, with storms blowing in from June to November. Indonesia, while generally divided into the November–April rainy season and the May–October hot season, is also divided between east and west: Sumatra, Kalimantan, and Java have markedly wet winter monsoons, while Bali and points east are far more arid and have much hotter dry seasons. The best time to visit northern Vietnam is from October to December, when the weather is cool and the least rainy. Chilly, wet weather starts in December and continues through March; sweltering heat is common from May to early October. The country's central highlands are cool year round and dry from December to March. In the south, the best weather is from December to April when it's dry; May to November generally brings the wet season. The rainy southwest monsoon sweeps through Cambodia and Laos, leaving them cool and dry from December to February and hot and parched by March and April. But remember— especially with the lingering effects of El Nino—these are only generalizations. Winter mountain days can still be scorching, a brisk wind can bring a chill to the most dazzling dry-season beaches, and it can rain anywhere, at any time, so be prepared.

CLIMATE

For temperature charts, *see* individual chapter A to Z sections.

➤ FORECASTS: **Weather Channel Connection** (☎ 900/932–8437), 95¢ per minute from a Touch-Tone phone.

1 Destination: Southeast Asia

ASIA REVEALED

ANY ATTEMPT TO generalize about Southeast Asia is doomed to failure. This vast, varied region encompasses every level of civilization, from booming, bustling Singapore—with its ultraluxury hotels, sophisticated restaurants, and world-class shopping—to the tribal villages of Borneo, where headhunting was a way of life discarded only within recent memory.

A large part of Southeast Asia's fascination lies in the quiet beauty found in its rice-paddy landscapes—the glimpse into a simpler time that the West has left behind. But no matter where you go, do not expect to leave modern life entirely behind. As tourism among these societies grows, it subtly or grossly succeeds in changing them irrevocably.

WHAT'S WHERE

Indonesia

Indonesia is made up of five large and more than 17,000 small islands totaling more than 1,919,440 square km (741,052 square mi), with a population of 210 million. Its principal tourist destinations are Bali and Java. Java has the capital city of Jakarta (population close to 14 million), which is bursting at its seams with an influx of people swamping its Dutch-influenced past: local markets are crammed with regional produce and crafts; museums display the heritage of former kingdoms; the cuisine is a mixture of Indonesian, Chinese, and Dutch; and the architecture includes both pompous projects by recent governments and those of nobler days, some of the world's great Buddhist and Hindu monuments, and the palaces of sultans in Yogyakarta and Solo.

Bali is only about 145 km (90 mi) long but has more than 3 million people and probably more than 10,000 temples. Since the destruction of Tibet, this is one of the very last completely traditional societies in which all facets of life—agriculture, economics, politics, technology, social customs, and the arts—are welded together by religion. The beaches of Bali's southern coast are highly developed to accommodate tourists, but it is in the interior that you can fully appreciate Bali's passionate and beautiful way of life. To the east of Bali are the islands of the Nusa Tenggarra. Included in this chain are: Lombok, a tropical haven that's drawing those who find Bali too commercialized; Sumbawa, an island of both mountains and plains; Komodo, home of the famous dragons; Flores, a dive paradise; Timor, site of an ongoing struggle for independence; and Sumba, an island of bold ikat patterns and the site of ancient battles. Between these islands are Rinca, Roti, and many other islets.

North of the Nusa Tenggarra is Sulawesi (formerly known as the Celebes). This unique landmass has even more unique flora and fauna as well as a varied topography of rice fields, rain forests, mountains, and beaches and ancient tribes that inhabit its Toraja highlands. To the north and west of Java, Sumatra has lately become a tourist stop, with its indigenous tribes, hill stations around Brastagi, and a cool resort at Lake Toba.

Malaysia and Brunei

Malaysia

The country's more than 329,748 square km (127,316 square mi) are divided into two parts: the peninsula and the states of Sabah and Sarawak on Borneo. Malaysia's population of 21.1 million is made up of about 49% Malays, 29% Chinese, 10% Indians, 1% other indigenous groups (mostly in Sabah and Sarawak) and others. Peninsular Malaysia, with 81% of the population, contains the chief cities, sights, and resorts. The scenery is spectacular, with jungles and rugged hills in the interior, plantations and superb beaches in some of the coastal areas.

The capital, Kuala Lumpur (population 2 million), is clean and comfortable—if rather dull—with striking Victorian-Moorish architecture. The city is a 50-minute flight from Penang (the other main tourist center) and is near the Genting and Cameron highlands. The island of Langkawi, between Penang and the Thai border, is becoming a popular resort with the opening of deluxe hotels. Melaka, on the southwest coast, is the oldest city in Malaysia and has its share of historic charm. Off the southeast coast, Tioman Island is gaining renown for its scuba-diving facilities. Across the South China Sea on Borneo, Sarawak and Sabah are often considered frontier country. They have limited facilities (other than a few new luxury resorts) but offer virgin jungle and mountain scenery and fascinating close-up glimpses of tribal life.

Brunei

Primarily a stopover between Sabah and Sarawak on Borneo, Brunei covers less than 5,760 square km (2,226 square mi). The tiny sultanate is rich in oil revenues but still limited as to tourist facilities. Its population of 200,000 is found mostly in the sleepy tropical capital, Bandar Seri Begawan, and in *kampongs* (villages) on stilts at the waters' edge nearby.

The Philippines

The Philippines has a population of 70 million and an area of nearly 300,000 square km (115,831 square mi), including seven major and 7,100 minor islands. The economic, political, and cultural center is Manila (population 10 million). Tourism is concentrated in Cebu and the Metro Manila area, where there are modern hotels, restaurants, and shops. Elsewhere on the main island of Luzon, hill resorts, beaches, subtropical scenery, and friendly people are also draws. The nation contains about 55 ethnic groups, each with its distinctive language, customs, and traditions. The five major groups are the Ilocanos, Tagalogs, Visayans, Bicolanos, and Muslims.

Singapore

Singapore is something of an anomaly: an independent city-state, an efficient economy, a tightly run welfare system, and a remarkable multiracial social environment. With a population of 2.6 million and about 582 square km (225 square mi), Singapore's central shopping and business districts may have lost the mystery and romance of the "exotic Orient," but what

you will find instead is a bright, clean, modern tropical city—one that has neither the glamour of Hong Kong nor, mercifully, its brutal contrasts of wealth and squalor. Tucked into this tiny country's fringes are pockets of Chinese, Indian, Malay, and Arabic culture tucked into temples, gardens, and markets.

Thailand

Thailand, with a population of 54 million and an area of almost 513,998 square km (198,455 square mi), has become one of the world's top tourist destinations. Most of the traffic flows through the capital city of Bangkok (population 8 million), which is also the gateway for much of Southeast Asia. Bangkok has wonderful hotels, restaurants, nightclubs, shops, banks, and other big-city facilities. The level of development makes it very convenient, but the headlong rush into the 21st century has taxed its infrastructure to its limit.

Outside the capital, chief excursions are to important temples and ruins, mostly in smaller towns in the Bangkok basin—a hot, flat, wet, rice-growing plain that epitomizes subtropical Asia. The eastern and northeastern parts of the country are arid and poor; the areas' riches lie in their fantastic ruins, their spicy food, and a traditional Thai lifestyle. In the north, Chiang Mai, the rapidly developing second city, is a pleasant provincial town on a cool mountain plateau, with several good hotels, a tranquil atmosphere, and numerous temples in the Lanna style (12th–13th centuries). A number of beach resorts have established themselves on the world map. Pattaya, south of Bangkok, was the first: it's Asia's largest—and possibly tackiest—resort. Phuket, an island in the Andaman Sea, is now the most popular resort, though quieter Ko Samui in the gulf is preferred by many. Toward the Malaysian border are miles of sand beaches, fishing villages, and jungle regions.

Vietnam

Although it's rarely more than 150 km (90 mi) from the shores of the South China Sea at its western border, Vietnam snakes along the edge of the Indochinese peninsula for nearly 1,700 km (1,050 mi). The far northwest, bordered by China and Laos, is a remote mountainous region still inhabited by culturally unique hill tribes. Toward the coast lies Hanoi, the capital, surrounded by the fertile Red River Delta. The road north leads to the port of Haiphong on the Gulf of Tonkin, where the misty outcrops of Ha Long Bay were once the hideout of pirates but today are a renowned tourist attraction. South of Hanoi, Vietnam narrows; verdant fields hug hundreds of miles of largely unspoiled coastline, and low mountains and hills 50 km–200 km (30 mi–125 mi) inland form the western border with Laos and Cambodia. The former imperial city of Hue, Danang, and the sight-rich town of Hoi An are found midway down the coast of this central region; the beach town of Nha Trang and the mountain resort of Dalat are toward the southern end, surrounded by a wider swath of low mountains known as the Central Highlands. South of the mountains, Vietnam flattens into a broad floodplain that is home to Ho Chi Minh City (formerly Saigon) and the lush Mekong Delta.

Other Destinations

Burma (Myanmar)

Isolated for so long and still under a repressive government, Burma is just now opening up to tourism. Only a few destinations have facilities for the Western traveler who requires some comfort, but these are enough to hold anybody's interest for more than a fortnight. Rangoon (now called Yangon) is a capital city reawakening; it's also home to one of the most glorious pagodas in the Buddhist world, Shwedagon Pagoda. Mandalay is the old capital of Myanmar kings. Pagan (Bagan), another ancient capital, still has thousands of pagodas remaining from the 11th century. Inle Lake, often said to be the most beautiful in Southeast Asia, is a tranquil haven of floating islands.

Cambodia

Cambodia is recovering from years of civil war and still requires some fortitude from its visitors. It is worth much inconvenience however, to set eyes on one of the wonders of the world, Angkor, the long-lost, magnificent temple complex built in the 10th–13th centuries. To reach Angkor, you can fly direct from Bangkok or go by way of Phnom Penh, the country's capital, a city that's trying to overcome memories of the horrific "killing fields" of the late Pol Pot.

Laos

Laos sways to a slow rhythm of life, and the smiles of its people and charm of its small towns reward the visitor. You can see Vientiane, the capital city, in less than a day before proceeding north to Luang Prabang, with its enchanting palaces and temples. Southern Laos offers fascinating river journeys to thundering waterfalls and small villages settled along the banks of the Mekong Delta.

PLEASURES & PASTIMES

Beaches

Southeast Asia has some of the world's most exotic beaches, ranging from remote volcanic stretches in the Philippines to resort-strewn sites on Bali. The following is a brief rundown of the best beaches in each country.

Indonesia

The island of Lombok has a warm, dry climate and lovely unspoiled beaches. Surfers head for the waves at Kuta Beach in Bali, where an annual festival is held with local and Australian participants.

Malaysia

The peninsula's finest beaches are along its east coast and on islands just off the eastern shore. Several of these areas offer idyllic scenery and water sports facilities. The beaches of Langkawi, Penang and Pangkor, all islands off the west coast, are similarly developed, although hideaways with glorious private sands can be found on Langkawi and Pangkor Laut. In Sabah, there are fine sandy stretches and resorts along the west coast, not far from the capital, Kota Kinabalu.

Philippines

This tropical archipelago of more than 7,000 islands has an abundance of beaches, from pebble-strewn coastlines and black volcanic stretches to shady white expanses. Some of the most picturesque spots are on the smaller islands, particularly on Boracay, Iloilo, Palawan, and Cebu. Puerto Galera on Mindoro Island has several good beaches and is four hours from Manila by bus and ferry.

Thailand

With its long coastlines and warm waters, Thailand offers beach lovers lots of choices. Ko Samet, a popular Thai vacation spot, has many fine-sand beaches dotted with bungalows and cottages. On Phuket and nearby islands there are long, sandy beaches, cliff-sheltered coves, waterfalls, mountains, and excellent scuba diving. There are also Ko Samui, Ko Tao, and Ko Pha Ngan in the gulf and countless strands along the western coast.

Vietnam

Vietnam's unspoiled beaches, clear waters, and coral reefs beckon travelers. The south-central coast, with Nha Trang as the resort hub, boasts some of Vietnam's most beautiful beaches, as does the much less crowded Dai Lanh, 83 km (51 mi) north of Nha Trang. Equally beautiful are the beaches of Danang. Vung Tau, the popular seaside resort, is not as beautiful but is convenient from Ho Chi Minh City.

Dining

Hotels usually have several restaurants, from coffee shops serving both Western and Oriental cuisine to posh places staffed by famous European chefs. At the other end of the scale are outdoor stalls and markets where you can eat happily for a song.

Note: Though wine is available in Southeast Asia, it is relatively expensive. Furthermore, wine is not always the best accompaniment to local cuisines—whiskey or beer is often preferred. Mekong from Thailand is an excellent rice whiskey, and Thailand's Singha and Singapore's Tiger beers win international awards. If you are dining on European fare, consider Australian wines—they appear to survive the tropics better than do the French. If you want wine with Cantonese fare, check the wine list for Chinese wine (be sure that it's made from grapes and not rice)—Dynasty, for example, is a reasonable white Chablis-type wine.

Chinese

CANTONESE➤ Many Southeast Asian countries have significant ethnic Chinese populations, and Chinese restaurants are everywhere. The best-known regional Chinese cuisine is Cantonese, with its fresh, delicate flavors. Characteristic dishes are stir-fried beef in oyster sauce, steamed fish with slivers of ginger, and deep-fried duckling with mashed taro.

TEOCHEW➤ Though the cooking of the Teochew (or Chao Zhou), mainly fisherfolk from Swatow in the eastern part of Guangdong Province, has been greatly influenced by the Cantonese, it's quite distinctive. Teochew chefs cook with clarity and freshness, often steaming or braising, with an emphasis on fish and vegetables. Oyster sauce and sesame oil—staples of Cantonese cooking—don't feature much in Teochew cooking.

Characteristic Teochew dishes are *lo arp* and *lo goh* (braised duck and goose), served with a vinegary chili-and-garlic sauce; crispy liver or prawn rolls; stewed, preserved vegetables; black mushrooms with fish roe; and a unique porridge called *congee*, which is eaten with small dishes of salted vegetables, fried whitebait, black olives, and preserved-carrot omelets.

SZECHUAN➤ The Szechuan style of cooking is distinguished by the use of bean paste, chilies, and garlic, as well as a wide, complex use of nuts and poultry. The result is dishes with pungent flavors of all sorts, harmoniously blended and spicy hot. Simmering and smoking are common forms of preparation, and noodles and steamed bread are preferred accompaniments. Characteristic dishes are hot-and-sour soup, sautéed chicken or prawns with dried chilies, tea-smoked duck, and spicy string beans.

PEKINGESE➤ This style of cooking originated in the Imperial courts. It makes liberal use of strong-flavored roots and vegetables, such as peppers, garlic, ginger, leeks, and coriander. Dishes are usually served with noodles or dumplings and baked, steamed, or fried bread. The most famous Pekingese dish is Peking duck: the skin is lacquered with aromatic honey and baked until it looks like dark mahogany and is crackly crisp.

HAINAN➤ The greatest contribution made by the many arrivals from China's Hainan island, off the north coast of Vietnam, is "chicken rice": whole chickens are poached with ginger and spring onions; then rice is boiled in the liquid to fluffy perfection and eaten with chopped-up pieces of chicken, which are dipped into a sour-and-hot chili sauce and dark soy sauce.

FUKIEN➤ This cuisine emphasizes soups and stews with rich, meaty stocks. Wine-sediment paste and dark soy sauce are used, and seafood is prominent. Dishes to order are braised pork belly served with buns, fried oysters, and turtle soup.

HUNANESE➤ The Hunanese cooking style is dominated by sugar and spices and tends to be more rustic. One of the most famous dishes is beggar's chicken: a whole bird is wrapped in lotus leaves and baked in a sealed covering of clay; when it's done, a mallet is used to break away the hardened clay.

HAKKA➤ This food is very provincial in character and uses ingredients not normally found in other Chinese cuisines. Red-wine lees are used to great effect in dishes of fried prawns or steamed chicken, producing delicious gravies.

Indian

SOUTHERN INDIAN➤ This cuisine is generally chili-hot, relies on strong spices like mustard seed, and uses coconut milk liberally. Meals are very cheap, and eating is informal: just survey the cooked food displayed, point to whatever you fancy, then take a seat at a table. A piece of banana leaf will be placed before you, plain rice will be spooned out, and the rest of your food will be arranged around the rice and covered generously with curry sauce. The really adventurous should sample fish-head curry, with its hot, rich, sour gravy.

NORTHERN INDIAN➤ Generally found in the more posh restaurants, Northern Indian food is less hot and more subtly spiced than southern, and cow's milk is used as a base instead of coconut milk. Northern Indian cuisine also uses yogurt to tame the pungency of the spices and depends more on pureed tomatoes and nuts to thicken gravies. The signature Northern Indian dish is tandoori chicken (marinated in yogurt and spices and cooked in a clay urn) and fresh mint chutney, eaten with *naan*, *chapati*, and *paratha* (Indian breads).

Malay and Indonesian

MALAY➤ This cuisine is hot and rich. Turmeric root, lemongrass, coriander, *blachan* (prawn paste), chilies, and shallots are the ingredients used most often; coconut milk is used to create fragrant, spicy gravies. A basic method of cooking is to gently fry the *rempah* (spices, herbs, roots, chilies, and shallots ground to a paste) in oil and then, when the rempah is fragrant, add meat and either a tamarind liquid, to make a tart spicy-hot sauce, or

coconut milk, to make a rich spicy-hot curry sauce. Dishes to look for are *gulai ikan* (a smooth, sweetish fish curry), *telor sambal* (eggs in hot sauce), *empalan* (beef boiled in coconut milk and then deep-fried), *tahu goreng* (fried bean curd in peanut sauce), and *ikan bilis* (fried, crispy anchovies). The best-known Malay dish is *satay*—slivers of marinated beef, chicken, or mutton threaded onto thin coconut sticks, barbecued, and served with a spicy peanut sauce.

INDONESIAN➤ Indonesian food is very close to Malay; both are based on rice and do not use pork (except for dishes prepared by the non-Muslim Indonesians). Menus on Bali, a Hindu island, often do not include beef; however, pork is a popular main dish here. A meal called *nasi padang*—consisting of a number of mostly hot dishes, such as curried meat and vegetables with rice, that offer a range of tastes from sweet to salty to sour to spicy—originally comes from Indonesia.

Nonya (Nyonya or Peranakan)

When Hokkien immigrants settled on the Malay Peninsula, they acquired the taste for Malay spices and soon adapted Malay foods. Nonya (the cuisine was given this title, which is the Malay for word "woman" or "wife," because cooking was considered a feminine art), or Nyonya or Peranakan, food is one manifestation of the marriage of the two cultures, which is also seen in language, music, literature, and clothing. Nonya cooking combines the finesse and blandness of Chinese cuisine with the spiciness of Malay cooking. Many Chinese ingredients are used—especially dried ingredients like Chinese mushrooms, anchovies, lily flowers, soybean sticks, and salted fish—along with the spices and aromatics used in Malay cooking.

The Nonya cook uses preserved soybeans, garlic, and shallots to form the rempah needed to make *chap chay* (a mixed-vegetable stew with soy sauce). Other typical dishes are *husit goreng* (an omelet fried with shark's fin and crabmeat) and *otak otak* (a sort of fish quenelle with fried spices and coconut milk). Nonya cooking also features sourish-hot dishes like *garam assam,* a fish or prawn soup made with pounded turmeric, shallots, *galangal* (a hard ginger), lemongrass, shrimp paste, and preserved tamarind, a very sour fruit.

Philippine

Philippine cuisine starts with the same ingredients used in much of Southeast Asia—coconut and other native produce, meat, and fish. Added to these indigenous basics are layers of influences from several foreign cultures: Chinese (noodles, dumplings), Spanish–Mexican (rich stews, desserts), American (fast foods). The result is a cuisine that reflects the country's history and society.

Thai

Although influenced by the cooking of China, India, Indonesia, Malaysia, and even Portugal, Thai cuisine is distinctly different in taste. Thai food's characteristic flavors come from fresh mint, basil, coriander, and citrus leaves; extensive use of lemongrass, lime, vinegar, and tamarind keeps a sour-hot taste prevalent. On first tasting a dish, you may find it stingingly hot (tiny chilies provide the fire), but the taste of fresh herbs will soon surface. Not to say that all Thai food is hot; a meal is designed to have contrasting dishes—some spicy, others mild. The Thais don't use salt in their cooking. Instead, *nam pla* (fish sauce) is served on the side, which you add to suit your taste.

Popular Thai dishes include *mee krob,* crispy fried noodles with shrimp; *tom yam kung,* hot and spicy shrimp soup, *tom kha gai,* small pieces of chicken in a coconut based soup (both are popular with foreigners); *gai hor bai toey,* fried chicken wrapped in pandanus leaves; and *pu cha,* steamed crab with fresh coriander root and a little coconut milk. Thai curries may contain coconut milk and are often served with dozens of garnishes and side dishes. Most meals are accompanied by rice and soup. For drinks try Singha beer or *o-liang,* the national drink—a very strong, black, ice coffee sweetened with palm-sugar syrup.

Shopping

Some people travel to Southeast Asia exclusively to shop. Finely tailored clothing and unique handicrafts can be found at rock-bottom prices here. Indeed, with the devaluation of the currencies in the region that began in July 1997, prices for people with dollars have fallen to nearly criminally low levels. Further, although prices in department stores are generally fixed, you can bargain in small shops and markets. The final price will depend on your bargaining skill and the shopkeeper's mood, but generally will range from 10% to 40% off the original price.

If you can, carry your purchases with you instead of trusting shopkeepers and postal services to ship them safely home. If you're shopping for larger items, such as ceramic vases or furniture, the upscale shops are generally reliable. Some credit card companies, such as American Express, guarantee that items purchased with their card will arrive home safely. With any purchase, make sure you get a receipt for the amount paid, both for potential returns and for customs. Also, check on customs and shipping fees to make sure your bargain doesn't turn into a costly white elephant.

The following is a quick rundown of some of the most popular buys in individual Southeast Asian countries.

INDONESIA➤ Batik, shadow puppets, and silver jewelry from Yogyakarta and Bali; stone carvings and wooden masks, carvings, and furniture from Bali; gold and silver filigree from northern Sumatra.

MALAYSIA➤ Batik, pewterware, gold jewelry, silver, woven fabrics, and baskets.

PHILIPPINES➤ Traditional clothing, bamboo furniture, cigars, rum, rattan baskets, silver jewelry, and brassware.

SINGAPORE➤ Contemporary fashions, electronic equipment, and silk.

THAILAND➤ Silk, gems, jewelry, silverwork, ready-to-wear clothing, lacquerware, and pottery.

VIETNAM➤ Custom-made clothing, lacquerware, wood carvings, contemporary paintings, and pottery.

Sports

Bicycling is a popular diversion in Singapore, and mountain biking is fast catching on in parts of Malaysia. Fine **deep-sea fishing** is available around Pattaya (in the Thai Gulf) and Ranong and Phuket (in the Andaman Sea off Thailand's west coast). **Golf** aficionados will find quality courses in Thailand, Indonesia, Singapore, Malaysia, and the Philippines. If you plan to visit Thailand in March and April, look for **kite-fighting.** Many of Indonesia's wild rivers provide exciting **river rafting** opportunities. Southeast Asia's wealth of beaches and reef means that excellent spots for **scuba div-**

ing and snorkeling abound. Particularly recommended are Phuket and several marine national parks in Thailand; the Indonesian reefs around Manedo and Maluku; a number of islands of the Philippines (Batangas, Bohol, Cebu, and Palawan); the islands of Perhentian, Redang, Kapas, Tenggol off peninsular Malaysia; and Sipadan and Layang Layang off Sabah in Malaysian Borneo. **Surf's up** on Catanduanes island, off Southern Luzon in the Philippines. **Tennis** facilities are available in Singapore and the Philippines, as well as at many resort hotels around the region. Thailand and the Philippines offer opportunities for **windsurfing.**

NEW & NOTEWORTHY

Indonesia

There are many **new hotels and resorts** throughout the country, including Jakarta's Regent and Shangri-La hotels and Borobudur's Amanjiwo resort on Java; the Oberoi resort on Lombok; Jimbaran Bay's Ritz-Carlton, Bukit Peninsula's Bali Cliff, and Ubud's Four Seasons on Bali; and Ujung Padang's Radisson on Sulawesi. Many tour and adventure companies now offer **trips farther afield,** including those to central Sulawesi, the secluded homeland of the Toraja culture; northern Sumatra, where rain forests and volcanoes provide a stunning backdrop to serene Lake Toba and Gunung Leuser National Park; and eastern Kalimantan with its Dayak river cultures. Although luxury amenities are out of the question in these far reaches, simple yet comfortable accommodations are being built. Indonesia is the keeper of the world's third-largest rain forest area—filled with unique and rare species. The country's numerous **national parks** are receiving more attention than ever before, and much is being done to provide educational and ecosensitive facilities.

Malaysia and Brunei

MALAYSIA➤ **New hotels** from such well-known management companies as Mandarin Oriental, Hyatt, Regent, and Ritz-Carlton have all opened in the Golden Triangle. A number of lavish resorts have also opened on Langkawi, Malaysia's answer to Phuket. Strict adherence to Islam has curtailed licensing laws of Kelantan in the far northeast of the peninsula, although the east coast state of Terengganu is promoting its coastal and inland resorts. On Borneo, there has been a spate of hotel and resort construction in Sabah, most of it around Kota Kinabalu. In Sarawak, a number of new hotels have added additional rooms in both Kuching and Miri. Both Sabah and Sarawak are actively promoting tourism—especially **adventure and nature tourism.** Indeed, new lodges have made ecotourism on Sabah's east coast an attractive proposition.

Malaysia's **roads** have been improved. The North–South Highway (a toll road) runs all the way up the west side of the peninsula from Johor Bahru in the south to the Thai border. The East–West Highway across the top of the Malay Peninsula just south of the Thai border is finished, making the drive between Penang and Kota Bahru possible in six instead of 10 hours.

BRUNEI➤ Brunei recently entered the field of tourism, and it is actively cooperating with neighboring Sabah and Sarawak to encourage visitors to northern Borneo. Brunei's first **national park** established recently at Ulu Temburong offers a glimpse of virgin rain forest and its inhabitants. Bandar Seri Begawan's high-tech amusement park continues to charge no admission, making it a real draw for families.

Philippines

The **continuing volcanic activity** at Mt. Pinatubo, northwest of Manila, should not inconvenience most travelers, but it continues to wreak havoc in the lives of residents. There are ongoing efforts to control the flow of lava from the mountain, notably the construction of a permanent dike to channel the mud away from settled areas.

A number of new **transportation projects** should make it easier to get around Manila and Luzon. Manila's Light Elevated Transit line is being expanded; construction of additional track and stations began in 1997 and is due for completion in late 1999. The expressway to the north, toward Central Luzon, has been improved and widened.

Singapore

Singapore is always adding **new and sparkling hotels** to its huge inventory of rooms—in excess of 30,000. Three of the new ones, the Ritz-Carlton, the Inter-Continental, and the Four Seasons, are in the luxury category. The Raffles group has opened the Merchant Court Hotel, which is designed for those who want convenience, comfort, and efficiency, but not the high tariff. The **new convention center** at Suntec City has increased the number and size of conventions held in Singapore.

The **Singapore Art Museum,** which opened in 1996 on Bras Basah Road, was a decade in the making. Its permanent collection encompasses some 3,000 works from throughout Southeast Asia. The entire collection is accessible through the museum's Electronic Gallery, called E-mage, where you can call up digital images of artwork on computer monitors. Other new museums include the **Asian Civilisations Museum** and the **Philatelic Museum**; both offer impressive exhibits in their respective areas.

Despite the economic crisis, **Singapore Airlines** is offering more and better creature comforts. In economy look for personal video monitors (with games or movies), adjustable head and foot rests, gourmet meals (say, terrine of smoked salmon and asparagus), and free champagne. Business class offers wide, plush seats—more like those in first class on other craft—with reading lights, laptop power supplies, sleek video screens, and headphones that eliminate background noise. If the cheese-board hors d'oeuvres and elegant meals don't satisfy you, perhaps the biscotti with your espresso will. First-class minisuites have leather and wood touches, seats that recline all the way (yes, bedding and bedclothes are provided), a retractable working/dining surface, and a 14-inch fold-away video monitor. You choose when you'd like to eat: menus are by seven of the world's most renowned chefs; place settings are by Givenchy.

Thailand

Although the troubled economy has temporarily slowed the rush to build **hotels,** 1998–99 still saw two new establishments open in Bangkok—the Meridien Towers and the Peninsula. In Phuket, there's likely to be a shortage of hotel rooms since some tour operators have moved their packages from Bali to Phuket until Indonesia's stability returns. Demand for hotels is likely to be high in other resorts too, because more Thais are vacationing at home rather than abroad. Book your hotel well in advance, especially for peak periods.

Don't expect to find great bargains just because the Thai currency has dropped in value from 25 to 40 baht to the U.S. dollar. In response to the currency crisis the four and five-star hotels in tourist centers changed their rates from baht to dollars. Moderately priced hotels still quote in baht but have adjusted their rates upward. Other costs in tourist areas are climbing, so although a vacation in Thailand should cost less than before the devaluation, not everything is cheaper in dollar terms. The real bargains are in **shopping.** Thai-made goods still have irresistible prices.

Bangkok Airways has built an airport outside Sukhothai, which was once slightly off the beaten track. Now a daily flight arrives from Chiang Mai and Bangkok. The airline has also initiated direct flights between Bangkok and Siem Reap and between Singapore and Ko Samui. (Because Bangkok Airways is the only carrier with rights on Samui, flights there are already very expensive and likely to become truly exorbitant.) There's also a **new airport** at Krabi with flights to and from Bangkok. Bangkok is going ahead with plans for a second airport at Nang-Ngu Kao, 32 km (20 mi) east of town, to relieve congestion at Don Muang, and is finally addressing its auto traffic congestion. The **skytrain,** which should be operational by the end of 2000, will cross the city from north to south and east to west, and **new expressways** will also speed travel across town.

New tourist destinations are opening up. Vacationing Thais have moved down the coast from Pattaya to Ban Phe, near Rayong, and hardier travelers go even farther, to yet-to-be-developed islands of the Ko Chang group, near the Cambodian border. Thailand's last tourist frontier is still its northeast (I-san), the country's poorest region.

Vietnam

The government in Hanoi has loosened travel restrictions, beefed up travel facilities, and agreed to a number of joint ventures with foreign companies and investors. Unfortunately, the **new high-rise luxury hotels**—the Omnis, Sofitels, and Hyatts—that go up seemingly overnight tend to homogenize the cityscapes. Still, the Vietnamese are so keen on tourism that most lodging establishments—from mom-and-pop minihotels to five-star palaces—offer a wide range of **travel services.** Tours, in particular, are widely available: everyone from the central government worker to the corner café owner runs excursions, so nearly every attraction in every corner of the country is accessible.

Although the country is undergoing a **major road-improvement program,** precarious road conditions and suicidal driving habits persist, making car travel nerve-racking. The government has put a lot of money into **reliable air service,** and state-run Vietnam Airlines has seen considerable improvements. Planes generally run efficiently and frequently. American carriers are negotiating with the Vietnamese government for regular air service from the United States to Vietnam.

Other Destinations

Burma (Myanmar)
In desperation to bring foreign exchange into the country and prop up its dictatorship, SPDC, the ruling party, has opened the nation's doors to tourism, eased its visa restrictions, and begun to permit entry by land from Mae Sai in northern Thailand to Kengtung. You no longer need to purchase local currency at the official exchange rate (nine kyats to the dollar instead of 265 on the not-so-black market). Foreign investment is also welcomed. The result has been a rapid increase in hotel construction, development of a rudimentary tourist infrastructure, and an opportunity to visit a country that has been off-limits a long time. Only your conscience can tell you whether by visiting you are supporting one of the most inhumane governments in the world or helping the Burmese get an economic foothold and combat political repression.

Cambodia
Siem Reap, the base from which to visit the Khmer ruins of Angkor, is still, as of press time, open to tourists; you can now fly in direct from Bangkok, and the hotels there have been refurbished to meet the needs of the international traveler. Phnom Penh has quieted down since most of the United Nations personnel have moved out and reduced the inflationary pressure. An express bus now runs between Phnom Penh and Ho Chi Min City, Vietnam. Other parts of the country tend to be a little risky, with remnants of the Khmer Rouge roaming the forests. Once Cambodia neutralizes the Khmer Rouge and cleans up long-buried land mines, Angkor Wat at Siem Reap will be accessible across the Thai border.

Laos
Laos is opening up to foreign tourists in gentle steps, beginning with the Friendship Bridge crossing the Mekong river to Nong Khai. Visas are now obtainable there and at the Vientiane airport (be sure you can show your outbound ticket and preferably a hotel reservation). New hotels are opening in Vientiane and the former capital, Luang Prabang. Outside these two cities, accommodation is pretty rudimentary and scheduled travel uncertain, but if you're an intrepid traveler you'll be able to find your way around and you will be welcomed.

FODOR'S CHOICE

No two people will agree on what makes a perfect vacation, but it's fun and helpful to know what others think. We hope you'll have a chance to experience some of Fodor's Choices yourself in Southeast Asia. For detailed information about each entry, refer to the appropriate chapter.

Beaches

Indonesia
★ **Lombok Island.** Magnificent waves roll in on the deserted south-coast beaches.

Malaysia
★ **Langkawi.** With so many coves and beaches, you'll walk untrodden sands.

★ **Pangkor Laut.** A palm-grove beach on a private island with a charming hotel—what more could you want?

★ **Pantai Dalit, Sabah.** Golden sands stretch on either side of a resort, from a limpid estuary to a jungle headland.

Philippines

★ **Boracay Island, Panay.** One of the country's most beautiful beaches is here, with sands as fine as sugar.

★ **Mactan Island, Cebu.** Spend a few days lazing around at one of the resorts here.

★ **Samal Island, Davao.** Some of the Davao City area's nicest beaches are on Samal Island.

★ **Santa Cruz Island, Zamboanga.** This small island has a wonderful pink-coral beach and a lagoon in the middle.

Thailand

★ **Ao Nang Bay, Krabi.** Limestone pinnacles that rise curiously out of the blue sea will rivet your attention while you laze on the sands.

★ **Haad Tong Nai Pan Noi, Ko Pha Ngan.** Words can hardly describe such a perfect horseshoe bay.

★ **Ko Chang.** Only your footsteps will be printed in the sands of these islands.

★ **Nai Harn, Phuket.** As the sun sets dodging the tiny offshore islands, your tan will be golden.

★ **Pansea Beach, Phuket.** With a different beach for every day of your fortnight's Phuket island vacation, little Pansea Beach should be kept for the romantic interlude.

Vietnam

★ **Dai Lanh Beach, north of Nha Trang.** Sand dunes meet the sea at this semicircular beach, still virtually untouched by tourism.

★ **Doc Let, north of Nha Trang.** Doc Let is accessible only by hiring a private car, but beach-going doesn't get much better than these white sands and clear waters.

★ **Nha Trang.** Catch this beautiful resort beach before it becomes another Pattaya.

Dining

Indonesia

★ **Xin Hwa, Jakarta, Java.** Here spicy Szechuan dishes are served in refined surroundings. $$$$

★ **Sari Kuring, Jakarta, Java.** Very good Indonesian seafood is typified by the grilled prawns, which practically melt in your mouth. $$

★ **Ny Suharti, Yogyakarta, Java.** Forget charm and atmosphere and all the other items on the menu: you're here for the best fried chicken on the island, perhaps in all of Indonesia. $

Malaysia

★ **Mahsuri, Kuala Lumpur.** Treat yourself to a colonial curry tiffin, a sumptuous spread of delicately spiced dishes, available every Sunday at this historic mansion in KL's Lake Gardens. $$$$

★ **Lai Ching Yuen, Kuala Lumpur.** The city's best Cantonese fare is served in a room resembling two Chinese pavilions. $$$$

★ **Restoran Makanan Laut Selayang, Kuala Lumpur.** Delicious seafood is the specialty here, but if you're adventurous try the steamed river frogs and soups of squirrel, pigeon, or turtle. $$

Philippines

★ **Lantaw Gardens, Cebu City.** Feast on a splendid, well-priced buffet in an open-air, garden setting while enjoying a folk-dance show and scenic views of the city. $$$

★ **Bistro Remedios, Manila.** Pampanga regional cooking is served here in a setting of traditional furniture and paintings of Philippine landscapes. $$–$$$

★ **Alavar's, Zamboanga City.** This restaurant, a rambling house facing the sea, is justifiably famous for wonderful seafood. $$

★ **Ka Lui's, Puerto Prinsesa City.** Nothing is as fresh as the seafood here. $$

Singapore

★ **Club Chinois.** Superior surroundings set the tone for "nouvelle Chinoise," the best of creative Cantonese and French cuisine. $$–$$$

★ **Dragon City.** Many Singaporeans claim that this is the best place to enjoy the emphatic cuisine of Szechuan. $$–$$$

★ **Banana Leaf Apollo.** Come for robust South Indian curries, including the famous Singaporean fish head curry. $

Thailand

★ **Le Normandie, Bangkok.** For French food and an elegant evening out, this is the choice. $$$$

★ **Sala Rim Naam, Bangkok.** For dinner on royal Thai cuisine and a show of classical dancing, the Oriental's Sala Rim Naam is the best. *$$$*

★ **Huen Phen, Chiang Mai.** Northern Thai fare, well prepared and authentic, in an old teak house full of handicrafts and antiques. *$$*

★ **Spice Market, Bangkok.** Newcomers to Thai food should come here to try one of the world's finest cuisines. *$$*

★ **Prachak, Bangkok.** The best roast duck in town is served for less than a dollar. *$*

★ **White Orchid, Phuket.** Try this tiny outdoor café for fresh fish and a welcome smile. *$*

Vietnam

★ **Camargue, Ho Chi Minh City.** Unique Eurasian cuisine is accented by an elegant open-air villa setting. *$$$$*

★ **Lemongrass, Ho Chi Minh City.** Masterful Vietnamese standards and tasteful Franco-Viet decor make this an expat standby. *$$$*

★ **Ngoc Suong, Nha Trang.** Try some of the world's freshest and finest seafood while dining in a delightful garden. *$$*

★ **Ong Tao, Hue.** Imperial cuisine at its finest is served within the ruins of the ancient Imperial Enclosure. *$$*

★ **Hue Restaurant, Hanoi.** Wonderful pork-wrapped sugarcane and other delicious standards are served at this casual sidewalk café. *$*

★ **Ngoc Suong, Ho Chi Minh City.** Seafood perfection is served in a tree-house-like setting. *$*

Lodging

Indonesia

★ **Amandari, near Ubud, Bali.** The peaceful gardens and luxurious cottages here are in a private village setting overlooking the lush Ayung River valley. *$$$$*

★ **Amanjiwo, Borobudur, Java.** The 35 suites all have views of Borobudur temple from their private patios, 14 of which have swimming pools. *$$$$*

★ **Four Seasons, Sayan, Bali.** Given the captivating view of the Ayung River, you may never want to leave your private villa and pool to explore the rest of the island. *$$$$*

★ **Hotel Tugu, near Denpasar, Bali.** Art and artifacts abound here—in the public areas, the guest quarters, and the on-site museum. You can contemplate these works in your private cottage surrounded by quiet gardens. *$$$$*

★ **Mandarin Oriental, Jakarta, Java.** Expect refined, personal service in an atmosphere of understated elegance. *$$$$*

★ **Oberoi, Medan Beach, Lombok.** The ultimate secluded retreat has private thatched cottages at the shores of Medana Beach and within sight of Gili Air. *$$$$*

★ **Kusuma Sahid Prince Hotel, Solo, Java.** A former prince's residence becomes your home away from home. *$$$*

★ **Majapahit Mandarin Oriental, Surabaya, Java.** Built in 1910 and refurbished in 1996, the large grounds and personal service make you feel as if you're in a bygone era. *$$$*

Malaysia

★ **Datai, Langkawi.** Nature dictated the layout and structure of this luxury hideaway on the Andaman Sea. *$$$$*

★ **The Regent, Kuala Lumpur.** Luxurious guest rooms and grand public spaces make this the capital's smartest hotel. *$$$$*

★ **Shangri-La's Tanjung Aru Resort, Kota Kinabalu.** Set in 25 acres of landscaped gardens with its own small beach, Sabah's finest resort offers what is arguably the friendliest service in Borneo. *$$$$*

★ **Pangkor Laut Resort, Pangkor Laut.** Stay in a stilted house perched above the sea or in a bungalow in the forested hills on this private island. *$$$–$$$$*

Philippines

★ **Manila Peninsula, Manila.** The "Pen" exudes an informal elegance, and the well-kept rooms are spacious enough to seem more like suites. *$$$$*

★ **Fort Ilokandia, Vigan, northern Luzon.** Tiled walkways nestled among sand dunes connect several two-story buildings, whose style and room decor suggest the Old Quarter residences of Vigan. *$$$*

★ **Insular Century Hotel, Davao City.** The airy rooms at this hotel—on 20 lush acres with coconut groves, gardens, and a beachfront—come with verandas. *$$$*

★ **Westin Philippine Plaza, Manila.** Luxurious and grand—a veritable resort sans beachfront—the Plaza has an enormous lobby and a fabulous swimming pool. *$$$*

★ **Casa Amapola, Baguio City.** This quiet pension—once a family residence—retains a pleasing family-style informality. *$-$$*

Singapore

★ **Raffles Hotel.** Cliché though it may be, this world-famous hotel still oozes tradition and gentility in the midst of its modern, high-rise neighbors. *$$$$*

★ **Ritz-Carlton.** Wallow in your bathtub and watch the ships lying at anchor in Singapore harbor. *$$$$*

★ **Duxton Hotel.** In a city of skyscrapers, this boutique hotel in Chinatown is a wonderful alternative. *$$$*

★ **Regalis Court.** Housed in what was once a ballet academy, this Peranakan-style hotel is welcoming and economical. *$*

★ **RELC International House.** For the best value in inexpensive lodgings, this is the spot. *$*

Thailand

★ **Dusit Rayavadee, Krabi.** The only way to the duplex thatched cottages on this magical headland is by long-tailed boat. *$$$$*

★ **Oriental Hotel, Bangkok.** Nostalgia for the old days and views of the river bring people back here time and time again. *$$$$*

★ **The Regent, Bangkok.** For refined classical elegance including the best service, the Regent wins top honors. *$$$$*

★ **The Regent, Chiang Mai.** With Lanna Thai architecture built around rice fields and surrounded by the hills, the superb luxury is taken for granted. *$$$$*

★ **Santiburi, Ko Samui.** Steps away from your teak-floor bungalow are white sands shaded by swaying palms. *$$$$*

★ **River View Lodge, Chiang Mai.** One of the few small, charming, and personable hotels in the north. *$$*

★ **Tara Mae Hong Son, Mae Hong Son.** This hotel blends into a valley and seems at one with nature. *$$*

★ **Panviman Resort, Ko Pha Ngan.** Staggered up the cliff side, the bungalows look over the bay. *$-$$*

★ **The Atlanta, Bangkok.** Music played at teatime and old movies shown after dinner are part of what makes this small hotel a throwback to better times. *¢*

Vietnam

★ **Hotel Continental, Ho Chi Minh City.** The setting for Graham Greene's *The Quiet American,* the Continental is the most elegant accommodation in town. *$$$$*

★ **Omni Saigon, Ho Chi Minh City.** This super-slick new pleasure dome offers every conceivable service. *$$$$*

★ **Sofitel Hanoi/Metropole Hanoi.** Besides the beautifully renovated French-colonial architecture, there's impeccable food and service, to boot. *$$$$*

★ **Dalat Sofitel/Dalat Palace.** Set on the cool slopes of rolling green hills, this perfectly restored Old World resort is an ideal retreat, especially for golfers. *$$$-$$$$*

★ **Hotel Majestic.** New restorations have uncovered a slice of colonial Saigon in its heyday. *$$$*

Other Destinations

★ **Strand Hotel, Rangoon, Burma.** Not only is this the best hotel in Rangoon (Yangon), it is also one of the best in Asia—all the conveniences of the late 20th century with impeccable Edwardian style. *$$$$*

Museums

Indonesia

★ **Puppet Museum, Jakarta, Java.** Watch a shadow-puppet play or view an extensive collection of traditional Indonesian puppets, as well as examples from Thailand, China, Malaysia, India, Cambodia, and elsewhere.

★ **Puri Lukisan Museum, Ubud, Bali.** Bali's "palace of paintings" incorporates an overview of the island's famed artisan immigrants and native talents in a setting of tropical gardens and Balinese folklore.

Malaysia

★ **Sarawak Museum, Kuching.** Over a century old, this museum offers a superb collection illuminating Borneo's diverse cultures and their lifestyles.

Philippines

★ **Metropolitan Museum of Art, Manila.** An impressive display of contemporary fine arts, galleries of pre-Columbian pottery, and exquisite pre-Hispanic gold jewelry distinguishes this museum.

★ **University of San Carlos Museum, Cebu City.** This extensive collection includes seashells, fauna, and anthropological relics, as well as traditional clothing and ornaments of various tribal minorities.

Singapore

★ **Asian Civilisations Museum.** This cultural exhibition center has top-notch displays, many of which contain antiquities from mainland China.

★ **Pioneers of Singapore/Surrender Chambers.** Wax figures and tableaux provide fascinating, three-dimensional recounting of Singapore's early days.

Thailand

★ **National Museum, Bangkok.** The history of Thai art and culture is all here.

The Natural World

Indonesia

★ **Donau Toba, Sumatra.** The largest lake in Southeast Asia and one of the highest in the world, Lake Toba sits nearly 3,000 ft above sea level, surrounded by green mountains that plunge into its 1,500-ft deep waters.

★ **Gunung Bromo, Java.** You can stand on the rim of this active volcano just before dawn and watch it spew steam from a bubbling cauldron of water, ash, and sulphur.

★ **Keli Mutu, Flores.** Inside an extinct volcano cone, a triad of lakes mysteriously change colors.

Malaysia

★ **Cameron Highlands.** Cool forested trails are a welcome relief from the steamy concrete towns of the lowlands.

★ **Mt. Kinabalu from anywhere in Sabah.** Nature in its glory.

Philippines

★ **Banaue Rice Terraces, northern Luzon.** These spectacular rice paddies, terraced into the mountainsides more than 2,000 years ago, look like giant steps to the sky.

★ **Chocolate Hills, Bohol.** More than 50 of these 120-ft-high limestone oddities dot a plain on this southern island.

★ **Mt. Mayon, southern Luzon.** What may be the world's most symmetrical (and still active) volcano towers 8,189 ft over the Bicol countryside.

★ **St. Paul Subterranean National Park, Palawan.** The world's longest known underground river courses beneath this rain forest park and through caverns full of stalactites and stalagmites.

Singapore

★ **Botanic Gardens.** Escape from brick and mortar to appreciate tropical flora.

★ **Zoological Gardens and Night Safari.** The open plan of Singapore's zoo frees you from seeing nature's creations behind bars.

Thailand

★ **Golden Triangle, northern Thailand.** Misty mountains lure hikers with great trekking and unique hill-tribe villages.

★ **Phang Nga Bay, off Phuket.** These limestone rocks mysteriously rise out of the sea.

Vietnam

★ **Hoa Lu, south of Hanoi.** A quiet ride in a bamboo boat on the winding river through this incomparable landscape is unforgettable.

★ **Halong Bay, off Halong City.** Jutting dramatically from the South China Sea, Halong Bay's limestone archipelago is a water-bound sculpture garden.

★ **Sapa, northern Vietnam.** Hill-tribe cultures thrive in the verdant highlands, undisturbed by the modern age.

Palaces and Unique Structures

Indonesia

★ **The Kraton Sultans' Palace of Yogyakarta, Java.** The original palace of Javanese sultans, built in 1757, is an extensive open complex of gardens and pavilions where there are performances of traditional Javanese dance and gamelan music daily.

★ **Traditional Clan Houses of the Toraja, Sulawesi.** The carved and painted *tongkonans* are built on piles and topped by massive roofs shaped like a ship or buffalo horns.

Philippines

★ **Intramuros, Manila.** This ancient walled city, built by the Spaniards in the 16th century, is still formidable, with cannon emplacements atop the 30-ft-thick walls and a strategic location facing the bay.

★ **Malacañang Palace, Manila.** Notable colonial Spanish architecture and interior decor here demand a look, especially the three chandeliers in the reception hall; beautiful hardwoods used for the grand staircase; portraits and memorabilia of former presidents; and the exquisite music room.

Thailand

★ **Suan Pakkard Palace, Bangkok.** Here you'll find the harmony of Thai architecture at home.

Sacred Places

Brunei

★ **Masjid Sultan Omar Ali Saifuddin, Bandar Seri Begawan.** This superb example of modern Islamic architecture was built in 1959 of imported white marble, gold mosaic, and stained glass.

Indonesia

★ **Borobudur Temple, Central Java.** It took perhaps 10,000 men 100 years to build this giant stupa, which illustrates the earthly and spiritual life of the Buddha with thousands of relief carvings and statues.

★ **Prambanan Temple Complex, Central Java.** These remarkable 9th-century temples celebrate the Hindu pantheon.

Philippines

★ **Quiapo Church, Manila.** This 16th-century church is home to the famed Black Nazarene, a dark-hardwood statue of Jesus of Nazareth said to perform miracles.

★ **San Agustin Church, Manila.** The second-oldest stone church in the country has 14 side chapels, a trompe l'oeil ceiling, and seats of hand-carved *molave*—a beautiful tropical hardwood.

Singapore

★ **Sri Mariamman Temple.** The oldest Hindu temple in the city is also one of the most colorful and ornate.

★ **Sultan Mosque.** The focus of the Malay community is all golden domes and minarets.

Thailand

★ **Wat Benjamabophit, Bangkok.** In this temple, classical lines of perfection harmonize the spirit.

★ **Wat Chaimongkol, Chiang Mai.** This is a personal temple by the river.

★ **Wat Phanan Choeng, Ayutthaya.** Memories and fate are embedded in this monument.

★ **Wat Phra Keo, Bangkok.** Ornate and dramatic, this is a spiritual magnet.

★ **Wat Traimitr, Bangkok.** Buddha's image shines with the love of gold here.

Vietnam

★ **Jade Emperor's Pagoda, Ho Chi Minh City.** A Vietnamese "It's a Small World," this pagoda is lined with carnival-like sculptures and reliefs of gods and mythical figures.

★ **Marble Mountain, Quang Nam-Danang.** Remarkable cave temples house dozens of statues of the Buddha, some said to have magical powers.

Other Destinations

★ **Ankgor Temple Complex, Cambodia.** More than 300 structures, including the monumental Angkor Wat, make up one of the world's greatest architectural marvels.

★ **Pagan Archeological Zone, Burma.** More than 2,000 ruined stupas, shrines, and monasteries remain from the 6,000 built during the Pagan Dynasty.

★ **Shwedagon Pagoda, Rangoon, Burma.** The 320-ft spire of this gaudy 2,500-year-old pagoda complex is covered with 70 tons of gold and encrusted with thousands of precious stones.

Shopping

Indonesia

★ **Antique wayang kulit on Bali or in Yogyakarta on Java.** These puppets conjure up the shadows of Hindu epics.

★ **Batiks and leather in Yogyakarta, Java.** Fabulous designs on batik and crafted bags in leather are real temptations.

★ **Silver filigree on Bali and in Yogyakarta on Java.** Delicate spiderwebs of creations in dainty, intricate shapes.

★ **Stone and wood carving on Bali.** Guardians sculpted in stone and masks in wood are essential to keep evil spirits at bay.

Malaysia

★ **Batik Malaysia Berhad, Kuala Lumpur.** The best quality and patterns of Malay fabric are found here.

★ **Kompleks Budaya Kraf, Kuala Lumpur and Langkawi.** All the regional crafts are here.

★ **Main Bazaar, Kuching.** The best of Borneo, with old (and new) antiques, basketware, mats and tribal artifacts.

★ **Selangor pewter, throughout Malaysia.** Malaysia is famous for its tin and has been producing pewter for centuries.

Myanmar

★ **Precious stones and lacquerware** are the specialities here.

Philippines

★ **Baguio Public Market, Baguio City.** Handicrafts, antiques, and fresh produce are available in abundance.

★ **Madrazo Fruit District, Davao City.** Most fruit vendors will let you sample the more exotic produce before you buy.

★ **Yakan Village, Zamboanga.** The hand-woven tribal cloth from this village is remarkable.

Singapore

★ **Arab Street.** Stores and shops spill out onto the sidewalk with an array of Malay and Indonesian wares.

★ **China Silk House.** This boutique has a deservedly high reputation for Chinese silks.

★ **P. Govindasamy Pillai.** Come here for the best-quality Indian silks.

Thailand

★ **Night Bazaar in Chiang Mai.** So much for so little, be it fake or authentic, is for sale here.

★ **Sapphires and rubies in Bangkok.** The center for gems is here.

★ **Thai silk in Chiang Mai, Bangkok, and I-san.** In all patterns, Thai silk is irresistible.

Vietnam

★ **Hoi An.** This perfectly preserved ancient port is almost entirely dedicated to seamstress boutiques and to souvenir shops that sell pottery and paintings by local artists.

★ **Linh Phuong Maison de Couture, Ho Chi Minh City.** This shop specializes in custom clothing made from Japanese and Vietnamese silks and cottons.

★ **Sapa Weekend Market.** Hill tribes from around the Sapa area convene at this colorful outdoor market to sell and exchange their chartreuse-embroidered, indigo-dyed clothing, as well as other handicrafts and food staples.

★ **Tien Dat, Hanoi.** The best tailor in town for casual custom clothing, Tien Dat has the finest silks and cottons.

GREAT ITINERARIES

The itineraries that follow suggest ways you can combine destinations for a trip that suits your interests, and give an idea of reasonable (minimum) amounts of time needed in various places. Don't try to see every one, but use this material for ideas on how to mix and match your destinations.

The Whirlwind Grand Tour

Southeast Asia is more diverse than Europe, yet there's a temptation on a first visit to cover the entire area on one European-style Grand Tour. Such a trip is physically and mentally taxing and cannot begin to do justice to the complexities of Asian cultures. Even with three weeks to see the capitals and a few highlights, it's best to skip a couple of places to spend more time in each.

Begin in exciting, exotic Bangkok, for a leisurely round of sightseeing interspersed with shopping. Go up to Chiang Mai in northern Thailand before flying into Burma to visit Mandalay, Pagan, and Yangon. From there, fly to Kuala Lumpur in Malaysia, before a stop in Singapore. Then it's on to Jakarta, Bali, and Manila.

Duration: 3 weeks

Transportation

Stopping in all the major regions of Southeast Asia requires the use of different airlines. Coming from the United States, you may want to use Thai Airways International or Northwest, a U.S. airline that best covers the capital cities, as your major carrier. From Great Britain, British Airways serves many of Asia's capitals. From Australia, check out Qantas' fares and routes.

Itinerary

BANGKOK: FOUR NIGHTS➤ Arrive in Thailand's capital and catch some zzz's before taking in some of its 300 temples, old teak houses, markets, and restaurants. Go on a morning tour to Damnoen Saduak's floating market and a full-day tour to Ayutthaya, the ancient capital.

CHIANG MAI: TWO NIGHTS➤ Fly to Chiang Mai (or take the night train the evening before from Ayutthaya). Visit the major temples in and around town, including Doi Suthep. Spend a morning at the elephant training camp at Mae Sa and an afternoon browsing the craft showrooms and workshops along the Golden Mile.

MANDALAY AND PAGAN: THREE NIGHTS➤ Fly on Air Mandalay to upper Burma's unofficial capital for one night, before continuing to Pagan for two nights.

RANGOON (YANGON): ONE NIGHT➤ Fly to Rangoon for one night, and try to visit both the Shwedagon Pagoda and Bogyoke Aung San Market.

KUALA LUMPUR: ONE NIGHT➤ Take the Myanmar/Malaysian Airways flight to the capital. Much of the city is modern with shining skyscrapers, but enough grand buildings remain from colonial days to excite your interest for 24 hours.

SINGAPORE: TWO NIGHTS➤ In Singapore, explore Chinatown, Little India, and the Arab district; take a stroll along the Padang, the heart of colonial Singapore, check out the shops on Orchard Road, and dine sumptuously on Singapore's multiethnic cuisines. Make a day trip to the historic city of Melaka. (You could go by land from Kuala Lumpur to Singapore, stopping off at Melaka.)

JAKARTA: ONE NIGHT➤ It's an hour's flight from Singapore to the Indonesian capital, a congested city of modern high-rises, an old town with Dutch colonial buildings, and slums. You can see the major sights in a day.

BALI: FOUR NIGHTS➤ Fly into Denpasar on Bali. Exploring the temples, craft shops,

and villages of this exotic island will take at least three days, especially if you want to spend some time on the beach.

MANILA: THREE NIGHTS➤ Fly to the Philippine capital (via Hong Kong) to explore the Spanish colonial sights, especially Intramuros, the walled city. The next day, visit Pagsanjan's waterfalls and rapids, or visit the Villa Escudero and its museum and gardens.

The Indochina Tour

Take a circular tour of former French Indochina using Bangkok as a starting and ending point.

Duration: 3 weeks

Transportation

Northwest Airlines has the best flights from the United States to Thailand. British Airways flies to Bangkok from London, Qantas from Australia. Use Bangkok Airways from Bangkok to Siem Reap, and either Air Cambodge or Vietnam Airlines for the hop to Phnom Penh.

Itinerary

THAILAND: THREE NIGHTS➤ Start in Bangkok with a leisurely round of sightseeing, shopping, and dining while you get over your jet lag. Make a couple of side trips, to Ayutthaya, and to Damnoen Saduak and the Bridge over the River Kwai.

CAMBODIA: THREE NIGHTS➤ Fly directly to Siem Reap for two nights to visit the fantastic Khmer ruins at Angkor, then fly or take a boat down to Phnom Penh for a day.

VIETNAM: SIX NIGHTS➤ Fly to Ho Chi Minh City (formerly Saigon) to explore for a day, then fly to Da Nang and take a taxi to Hoi An for two nights. A tourist bus will take you, via Marble Mountain and Da Nang's Cham Museum, to Hue. Spend the night there, and fly to fascinating Hanoi for the rest of your stay.

LAOS: THREE NIGHTS➤ From Hanoi take a plane to Luang Prabang, the former capital and still the country's artistic center. After two nights, fly to Vientiane for one night.

THAILAND: TWO OR MORE NIGHTS➤ Cross over the Mekong on the new Friendship Bridge to Nong Khai for the day. Take the night train to Bangkok to spend another day, and fly out that night or the following morning.

2 Indonesia

In this land of contrasts and diversity, cultural attractions compete for your time with the pursuit of the pleasure principle. From the temples and beaches of Bali to the great architectural wonders around Yogyakarta, from fascinating animist rites on Sulawesi to the rush into the 21st century in Jakarta, Indonesia will enthrall you.

By Nigel Fisher
and Lois
Anderson

Updated by
Holly S. Smith
and Mick
Elmore

THE SHEER SIZE OF INDONESIA is mind-boggling. This nation is the world's fourth most populous and covers more than 17,000 islands (over one-third of them uninhabited) that stretch for more than 5,161 km (3,200 mi) from the Pacific to the Indian Ocean. From north to south, the islands form a 1,774-km-long (1,100-mi-long) bridge between Asia and Australia.

From Jakarta's tall steel-and-glass office buildings to Irian Jaya's thatched huts, Indonesia embraces an astonishing array of cultures. Today Indonesia's 210 million people—Asmat, Balinese, Batak, Dayak, and on down through the alphabet—speak more than 300 languages, though a national language, Bahasa Indonesia, is officially recognized as a means of binding the population together.

It's this size and diversity that make Indonesia so fascinating. You can relax in one of Bali's luxury resorts or take a river trip through the jungles of Borneo. If you do venture off the beaten path—really the way to fall in love with the country's charms—remember that patience is a key to enjoying your trip. Since tourism is a new priority for Indonesia, the infrastructure is often rudimentary. Only in areas slated for tourist development can you expect to find services approaching international standards. Elsewhere, expect only modest accommodations and casually scheduled transport.

Don't mistake this lack of development for a lack of history, however. The nation has seen a succession of conquerors and revolutions, even receiving its name from one of its earliest colonizers: "Indonesia" comes from two Greek words—"indos," meaning Indian, and "nesos," meaning islands—a testament to the Indian traders who roamed the islands in the 1st century AD. By the 7th century, powerful Buddhist and Hindu kingdoms had emerged, and by the 1300s the Majapahit Hindu empire had united much of what is now Indonesia. During the next two centuries, however, Arab traders began setting up communities and spreading the teachings of Islam, the religion now followed by about 90% of the population, making Indonesia the world's largest Muslim country.

Contact with the west came in 1509, when Portuguese traders arrived. A century later they were displaced by the Dutch, and by the 18th century, Dutch rule encompassed most of Indonesia, known to the West as the Dutch East Indies. Except for a brief interlude of British rule during the Napoleonic Wars of 1811–16, the Dutch remained in power until the outbreak of World War II. After the surrender of the occupying Japanese in 1945, a bloody fight for Indonesian independence ensued. In 1949 Indonesia won its sovereignty, and the name Dutch East Indies became one more piece of colonial history.

The man behind the independence movement was Sukarno (many Indonesians have only one formal name), who became president of the new republic and implemented a leftist nationalist policy. He forcibly prevented ethnic groups from forming their own republics and extended Indonesia's borders by annexing part of New Guinea, now the province of Irian Jaya. Despite imprisoning his opposition, he lost control of the movement, the economy suffered under an annual inflation rate of 650%, and Indonesia dissolved into chaos.

On the night of September 30, 1965, Communists (or so it was said) abducted and murdered six top generals and their aides and, it is alleged, were about to seize power. Major-General Suharto intervened, and blood flowed by the gallon. Anyone accused of being a Commu-

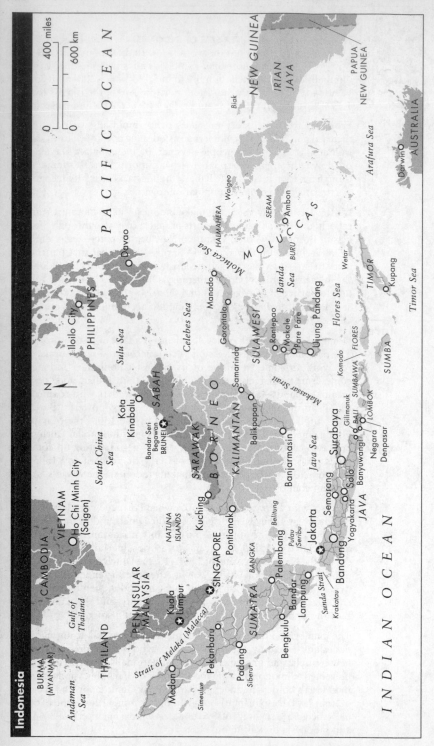

Indonesia

nist was slaughtered. Rampaging mobs massacred thousands—some estimates place the number of dead at 500,000.

Suharto became president in 1967 and ruled for seven consecutive terms until the growing economic and social turmoil that began with the 1997 Asian financial crisis—and the consequent devaluation of the rupiah by more than 75%—had the country riding waves of anxiety and expectation. Repressive policies toward the independence-minded people of Timor, the one island that remained more Portuguese than Dutch, didn't help either, particularly since Timor freedom fighters Bishop Carlos Ximenes Belo and José Ramos-Horta attracted the international spotlight when they shared the 1996 Nobel Peace Prize. In May 1998, after weeks of student demonstrations against Suharto's government, which culminated in riots that ricocheted throughout the islands, Suharto allowed Vice President B. J. Habibie to assume rule of the country. However, for the students and general public, Habibie—a known Suharto supporter—is only an interim solution at best, and at press time, the country was in the process of drawing up new electoral parties and candidates. As for Indonesia's political and economic future, everything will depend on how Habibie handles his power and how strongly his opponents are supported by the masses. At worst, the country could fall into a far more fragmented archipelago of isolated, individualist islands; at best, it could pull together as a stronger, more experienced, and more enthusiastic nation.

Pleasures and Pastimes

Dance

Dance is everywhere on the islands: at celebrations, purification ceremonies, temple rituals, weddings, birthdays, processions to the sea. On Java, court dances are still performed at the sultan's palace in Yogyakarta and, in the summer, dance troupes of several hundred performers act out the Hindu legend of the Ramayana by full-moon light at the Prambanan Temple. For the Javanese, the slow, smooth movements are almost like a ballet in which each subtle turn of the head or lift of the finger has meaning. Sumatra's dance traits have the added elements of liveliness and simultaneous movements that include claps, snaps, kneeling dances, and chanting as music is played in the background for performances like the *saudati*. Other dances symbolize offerings of peace, such as northern Sumatra's *meusekat*; or, like the *tob daboh,* they can mimic battlelike action using dancers who are armed with real daggers.

On Bali, perhaps the island best known for its colorful and elegant performing arts, dancers move low to the ground, with bent knees, arched backs, and controlled steps, arms at right angles with elbows pointing up and fingers spread wide. The female dancers flutter their long-nailed fingers. They move slowly across the stage, then turn quickly but precisely with a staccato movement. Head movements are staccato, too, without facial expression except for their darting and flashing eyes. They wear petaled or gold headdresses. The men have to do battle and get killed, and their movements are more varied.

Most dances are accompanied by the traditional gamelan orchestra of gongs, drums (mostly hand-beaten), a type of xylophone with bronze bars, violinlike instruments, and a flute. Balinese dancing is far more exuberant than Javanese, and the Balinese gamelan is sharper and louder, with more crescendo. Behind every dance is a legend with a moral theme.

BARONG

The Barong is a dance of Good versus Evil. The Good is Barong, a dragon with a huge, bushy, lionlike head and a long flower-bedecked beard. Bells ring as he snaps his head. The two dancers inside the costume use complicated motions to make Barong humorous and good natured, but fe-rocious when he meets Evil, in the form of the witch Rangda. Rangda's horrifying mask is white, with bulging eyes and tusks extending from her mouth. Her long braided hair sweeps down to the floor amid men-acing, red, mirrored streamers. She rushes threateningly back and forth across the stage. There are also beautiful female dancers with petaled headdresses, tasseled girdles, and gold-and-green sarongs, and male war-riors whose prince is crowned with gold and flowers. Rangda forces the warriors to turn their kris (dagger) blades on themselves, but Barong's powers keep the blades from harming them. A bird dancer enters and is killed—the required sacrifice to the gods—and Rangda is banished.

LEGONG

The Legong is a glittering classical dance. The story involves a young princess kidnapped by an enemy of her father. Three young girls in tight gold brocade and frangipani headdresses perform several roles. Their movements are rapid and pulsating; they punctuate the music with quick, precise movements and flashing eyes. It's an exacting dance—girls start training for the roles at five and retire before they're 15.

KECAK

The dramatic Kecak, the Monkey Dance, depicts the monkey armies of Hanuman, who rescued Rama and his love, Sita, from the forests of Ceylon in the *Ramayana,* the great Hindu epic. No gamelan is used; all sound comes from the chorus, who, in unison, simulate both the game-lan and the chattering, moaning, bellowing, and shrieking of monkeys. This dance is often performed at night under torchlight. The dark fig-ures, again in unison, make wild arm gestures and shake their fingers. (The Kecak isn't a classical dance but a product of this century.)

Dining

The choice of foods in Indonesia is wide ranging: Indonesian, Chinese, and Western cooking are available in every major town and resort. To meet the needs of an increasing number of Japanese tourists, you'll also find Japanese restaurants in Jakarta and on Bali.

Warungs are Indonesian street-food stalls, sometimes with benches and tables in the open, under canvas, or sheltered by a sheet of galvanized tin. The food here varies from drab to tasty, but it's always cheap: you can eat well for Rp 1,000. Warungs are often clustered together at a *pasar malam,* or night bazaar.

Rumah makan are just like warungs, only with fixed walls and roofs. Another step up is the *restoran,* a very broad category of small dining establishments. Most are Chinese-owned and serve both Indonesian and Chinese cuisine. Hotel dining rooms generally offer Chinese, In-donesian, and Western fare; the native specialties are usually toned down. If you enjoy spicy food, you'll be happier at more authentic eateries.

Nasi (rice) is the staple of the Indonesian diet. It's eaten with break-fast, lunch, and dinner, and as a snack, but it mainly serves as a back-drop to an exciting range of flavors. Indonesian food can be very hot, particularly in Sumatra. Your first sample might be *sambal,* a spicy rel-ish made with chilies that's placed on every restaurant table. Indone-sians cook with garlic, shallots, turmeric, cumin, ginger, fermented shrimp paste, soy sauce, lime or lemon juice, lemongrass, coconut, other nuts, and hot peppers. Peanut sauce is common; two dishes frequently en-countered are *gado gado,* a cold vegetable salad dressed with spiced peanut sauce, and *saté* (or *satay*), slices of skewered meat charcoal-broiled and dipped in a flavored peanut sauce. *Mie* (noodles) are also used in a variety of popular fare, such as *mie goreng,* an entrée of stir-fried noodles with meat and vegetables.

You'll find dishes with such meats as *ayam* (chicken), *babi* (pork), *daging* (beef), and *kambing* (lamb), though, naturally, fresh fish and shellfish abound. *Ikan* (fish) is often baked in a banana leaf with spices, grilled with a spicy topping, or baked with coconut. *Udang* (shrimp) come cooked in coconut sauce, grilled with hot chilies, made into prawn-and-bean-sprout fritters, or, in Sulawesi, with butter or Chinese sweet-and-sour sauce. *Cumi-cumi* (squid) and *kepiting* (crab) are also featured.

For dessert, Indonesians eat fresh fruit: papaya, pineapple, rambutan, salak, and mangosteen. Because this is a mostly Muslim country, wine and alcohol—when available—are expensive additions to a meal; beer is your best bet. Hard liquor is generally only available in popular bars and Western restaurants in the major cities, although local whiskey brews, called *arak,* are found throughout the islands.

Most food comes cut into small pieces, and finger bowls are provided. Even in Jakarta, you'll see well-dressed Indonesians eating with their fingers. Visitors normally receive forks, although the combination of a spoon (held in the right hand to eat with) and a fork (held in the left hand to help push food into the spoon) is commonly used as well. In more remote areas, the right hand is the main eating implement. (The left hand, traditionally used in Asian lavatory hygiene, is considered unclean and is never used for dining, touching, or pointing.) Note that water in Indonesia is not potable, so stick with the bottled variety. Ice used in restaurants and hotels is supposed to be the kind made under government supervision with the claim that it's safe; as you have no way to check whether or not the proper ice is used, you may want to forego it.

Here are a few more food terms that appear frequently on Indonesian menus:

bakmi goreng—fried noodles with bits of beef, pork, or shrimp; tomatoes; carrots; bean sprouts; cabbage; soy sauce; and spices
dendeng ragi (or rendang)—thin squares of beef cooked with grated coconut and spices
gudeg—chicken with jackfruit
kelian ayam—Sumatran chicken curry
nasi campur—steamed rice with bits of chicken, shrimp, or vegetables with sambal; often topped with a fried egg and accompanied by *krupok,* delicious puffy prawn crisps
nasi goreng—fried rice with shallots, chilies, soy sauce, and ketchup; it may include pork (in Bali), shrimp, onions, cabbage, mushrooms, or carrots; it's often studded with tiny fiery green peppers in Sumatra
nasi rames—a miniature rijsttafel
rijsttafel—literally, "rice table"; steamed rice with side dishes such as sayur lodeh, gudeg, or kelian ayam
sayur lodeh—a spicy vegetable stew
soto ayam—chicken soup, varying from region to region but usually including shrimp, bean sprouts, spices, chilies, and fried onions or potatoes; mie soto ayam is chicken noodle soup.

Price categories throughout the chapter are based on the following ranges:

CATEGORY	COST*
$$$$	over $30 (over Rp 324,000)
$$$	$20–$30 (Rp 216,000–Rp 324,000)
$$	$10–$20 (Rp 108,000–Rp 216,000)
$	under $10 (under Rp 108,000)

per person for a three-course dinner, excluding tax, service, and drinks.

Lodging

You'll find superb resorts—such as the Four Seasons on Bali and the Mandarin Oriental in Jakarta—that cost half what you might pay in the Caribbean. All such establishments generally include room service and air-conditioning as part of their long lists of amenities. New hotels open all the time in Bali's popular areas; Ubud doesn't yet have any mammoth hotels, which has helped it maintain a small-town feel, but the number of small hotels (20–50 rooms) multiplies every year.

The government classifies hotels with star ratings, five stars being the most luxurious. Its criteria are somewhat random, however. (No hotel without a garage gets four stars, for example, despite the fact that many visitors don't need a garage.) Besides hotels, most Indonesian towns offer three types of rooming houses: *penginapan, losmen,* and *wisma*. Theoretically, the penginapan is cheapest, with thin partitions between rooms, and the wisma most expensive, with thicker walls. The term "losmen" is often used generically to mean any small rooming house. Facilities vary widely throughout the islands: some Bali losmen are comfortable and social, with shared living areas and rest rooms; others are quieter and more private, with separate sitting areas and individual baths. At the bottom range in the less touristed areas you'll usually get a clean room with a shower and an Asian toilet—either an in-ground porcelain "squatter" or a seatless Western "throne"—for less than $5 a night. Losmen on Bali often include a light breakfast, and free tea, coffee, and snacks are part of the hospitality in many areas. Note that although there a few luxury exceptions, as a rule the standards in accommodations on Lombok and islands farther east as well as in some parts of Sumatra and Sulawesi often fall below those in, say, Jakarta or Bali—be prepared to rough it.

Price categories throughout the chapter are based on the following ranges:

CATEGORY	COST*
$$$$	over $150 (over Rp 1,620,000)
$$$	$100–$150 (Rp 1,080,000–Rp 1,620,000)
$$	$75–$100 (Rp 810,000–Rp 1,080,000)
$	$40–$75 (Rp 432,000–Rp 810,000)
¢	under $40 (under Rp 432,000)

for a standard double room in high season, excluding 10% service charge and 11% tax.

Scuba Diving and Snorkeling

Scuba diving is becoming popular, and licensed diving clubs have sprung up around the major resort areas. Bali (off Sanur and the north coast), Lombok's Gili Islands, Flores, and North Sulawesi have some of the world's best diving. The best times for diving in Indonesia are March–June and October–November.

Shopping

Arts and crafts in Indonesia are bargains by U.S. standards. If you have the time, custom-made items can be commissioned. Consider bringing pictures or samples of items that you'd like built or reproduced—anything from clothing and jewelry to furniture and board games.

From Java the best buys are batik cloth and garments, traditional jewelry, musical instruments, leather *wayang* puppets, and leather accessories. In Bali, look for batiks, stone and wood carvings, bamboo furniture, ceramics, silver work, traditional masks, and wayang puppets. Sumatra is best for thick, handwoven, cotton cloth; carved-wood panels and statues, often in primitive, traditional designs; and silver and gold jewelry. Sulawesi is known for its silver-filigree jewelry, hand-woven silks and cottons, hand-carved wood panels, and bamboo

goods. Be aware that machine-produced goods are sometimes sold to
visitors as handcrafted.

Exploring Indonesia

Indonesia is an archipelago of more than 17,000 islands that stretch 5,200
km (3,224 mi) along the Equator from the Indian Ocean to the Pacific.
It's the largest archipelago in the world, resting just above Australia and
below peninsular Southeast Asia. Three of the planet's six largest islands
are found here, and some 210 million people who speak more than 500
languages are spread throughout 6,000 or so bits of land within this fast-
growing country. More than 90% of the population are followers of Islam,
making Indonesia the largest Muslim nation in the world.

Java is the archipelago's economic and political core, and it's also the
most crowded island; 14 million people live in the capital area of
Jakarta alone. Yet this is still a land of great natural power, with more
than two dozen active volcanoes—including the infamous Krakatau—
and 15 peaks that rise above 1,860 ft. The Great Britain–size isle is
also a natural haven, with nearly two dozen national parks and reserves.
Between these are found clusters of five main cultural groups: the Islamic Sundanese and the reclusive Badui of West Java, the traditional
Javanese of the central areas, the Tenggerese of the east, and the
Madurese of Madura Island.

Bali is the country's most popular getaway for foreigners, just a pint-
size nub of land 140 by 80 km (87 by 50 mi) in size. Its distinction is
that it is the only Hindu island in an overwhelmingly Islamic country,
yet the religions peacefully coexist. The dominant natural force in Bali
is Gunung Agung, the "mother mountain," which the Balinese worship as the abode of the gods. Temples are built facing the volcano,
and rituals are regularly performed in its honor.

Sumatra is the world's sixth-largest island, comprising more than 100
volcanoes that stretch 2,000 km (1,240 mi) north to south. More than
15 are currently active, including Gunung Leuser near Medan and Gunung Marapi near Jambi. This island also has some very large tracts
of pristine rain forest, and much of its southern swamps have yet to
be explored. The westernmost point in the archipelago is here, at
Pulau Weh at the tip of the northern province of Aceh, also the region
where Arabic traders originally landed in the 13th century before
spreading the religion of Islam throughout the islands. Sumatra also
encompasses Nias Island and the Mentawais in the Indian Ocean,
where primitive cultures still exist, and the Riau Archipelago in the
Melaka Strait, home to seafaring peoples. Near Medan is 1,797-square-
km (1,114-square-mi) Lake Toba, the largest lake in Southeast Asia,
where the Christian Batak culture thrives. The Bukittinggi area just to
the west is the home of the matriarchal Minangkabau tribe.

To the southeast of Sumatra, the island of Borneo is the word's third-
largest, and the lower three-fourths, called Kalimantan, belongs to Indonesia. Its name means "river of diamonds," and it is, indeed, an island
of powerful waterways—from the 720-km (446-mi) Mahakam to the
880-km (546-mi) Barito to the 1,140-km (707-mi) Kapuas, the
archipelago's longest river. Naturally, then, life here is based on the rivers,
where many of the approximately 300 Dayak cultures live in raised
longhouses over the water. Kalimantan is also the site of several of the
region's major natural havens, such as Tanjung Puting National Park
and Tanjung Harapan orangutan reserve in the south.

Sulawesi is one of the world's most uniquely shaped islands; its four
arms are bits of Australia, Antarctica, Borneo, and New Guinea that

smashed together over the eons. As these islands slowly came together, they created a haven for some of the world's most unusual species, such as the anoa "dwarf buffalo," the babirusa "pig deer," and the black Celebes macaque. The island is also a shelter for unusual cultures, from the Bajau and Bugis sea gypsies in the south to the Christian Minihasans in the north. Perhaps the best-known and most intriguing culture here, though, is that of the Tanatoraja, where highland villages in the southwest peninsula are still the site of elaborate funeral celebrations, cliff-side graves, and life-size effigies of the dead.

Once known as the "Spice Islands," the miniarchipelago of Maluku lies just east of Sulawesi. A region comprising 851 square km (527 square mi) of island volcanoes and coral atolls—more than 90% of it underwater—Maluku has for centuries drawn international trade to the region and is one of the world's best dive areas. South of Maluku and just 500 km (310 mi) above Australia, the "southeast islands" of Nusa Tenggara include Lombok, Sumbawa, Komodo, Flores, Sumba, and Timor, once known for their abundant sandalwood and wild horses. At the archipelago's far eastern edge is New Guinea, the second-largest island in the world, the western half of which is Indonesia's Irian Jaya. Even today, relatively few visitors make the journey to view the Stone Age Dani cultures of the interior Baliem Valley; even fewer have attempted the rugged slopes of 3,131-ft Puncak Jaya, the highest point in the archipelago, or explored the thick, mountainous rain forest and coastal swamps at the island's edges.

Great Itineraries

It could easily take an active traveler years to explore all of Indonesia, and even to see the limited number of destinations covered in this book would still require a whirlwind month or two. This guide discusses only those areas that have a range of amenities for all travelers and have sights or attractions that are of particular interest. If you haven't been to Bali, then that island should be on your itinerary. It would be very easy to spend an entire vacation at one of Bali's resorts—**Kuta, Nusa Dua,** and **Sanur** are the best known—but assuming that you have the itch to see more, then Java's **Yogyakarta** and the famed temple of **Borobudur** should be your second destinations. Or consider visiting **Lombok** and the western islands of Nusa Tenggara as an extension of a holiday in Bali. North Sumatra, including the peaceful Lake Toba area and the rain forest of Gunung Leuser National Park, and south-central Sulawesi, including the beaches and waterfalls around Ujung Pandang and the mountainous Toraja highlands, are also recommended options. **Jakarta,** while enmeshed in the typical trappings of big-city traffic and smog, is actually worth a look for its cultural and historical sites, including a variety of museums, a cobblestone neighborhood known as Old Batavia, and a waterfront that has for centuries been a crux of Southeast Asian trade.

IF YOU HAVE 7 DAYS

Fly into Bali and spend the first two days exploring the temples and villages, using **Ubud** as your base; be sure to see at least one dance performance. Then take an hour's flight to **Yogyakarta** and spend two nights there, making sure to visit **Borobudur, Prambanan,** and the sultans' palaces in Yogyakarta and **Solo.** Return to Bali for a couple of days at a beach resort before flying out.

IF YOU HAVE 10 DAYS

Enter Indonesia by way of **Medan,** taking three days to visit **Brastagi** and **Lake Toba.** Depart from Sumatra and spend one night in **Jakarta.** On the fifth day take the early morning flight into **Yogyakarta** and visit **Prambanan** in the afternoon. The next morning drive out to **Borobudur** and then take the late afternoon flight to Bali. Split your final days between the beach and sightseeing around the island. Be sure to visit Ubud and other craft and cultural villages clustered southeast of the island's center.

IF YOU HAVE 14 DAYS

With two weeks in Indonesia, you could follow the 10-day itinerary and add a side trip from Bali to Sulawesi. Fly into **Ujung Pandang** for a night, taking the afternoon to explore the natural beauty of Bantimurung park, then proceed to **Rantepao** for a three-day exploration of Toraja. If time permits, head north and take a two-day dive trip on the coral reefs of Bunaken Marine Park near Manado before heading home.

IF YOU HAVE 15-21 DAYS

Temples and Ancient Cultures: Fly into Jakarta and spend the night; hire a car and driver the next morning, and take in the Botanic Gardens and Presidential Palace in Bogor. From the capital, fly to Yogyakarta that evening and spend two full days visiting the Sultan's Palace, the ruins of Taman Sari, and the Prambanan and Borobudur temples. From Yogyakarta, fly to Bali for two days and hire a car to visit Besakih, Tanah Lot, Ulu Watu, and some of the island's smaller temples. Next, fly to Ujung Pandang, where you can spend the afternoon at the massive Ft. Rotterdam before flying up to Tanatoraja the next morning. After two days in Toraja, head back to Ujung Pandang and catch a connecting flight to Balikpapan, where you can spend three days learning about the Dayak river cultures and seeing the longhouses. From Balikpapan, head back to your international gateway.

National Parks and Wildlife Overview: Fly into Medan, hire a car, and head south for Gunung Leuser National Park, where you can spend three days viewing orangutans and rain-forest life. Next, fly to Jakarta and spend the night; the next morning catch a boat to Ujung Kulon National Park, for three days of snorkeling, hiking, and spotting wildlife on Pulau Peucang and the mainland. Using Jakarta as your base, fly to Labuanbajo, Flores, and catch a boat for a three-day Komodo adventure. Back in Jakarta, fly to Ujung Pandang and then Poso, where you can spend three days exploring Lore Lindu National Park; then head north to Manado, for three days of diving or snorkeling around the beautiful reefs or Pulau Bunaken Marine Park before flying home.

The Grand Dive Tour: Fly into Jakarta and head down to Ujung Kulon National Park by boat, where you can spend three days diving the many reefs around Pulau Peucang. Head back to Jakarta and fly or travel overnight by road to Bali, where you can take four days to explore the numerous reefs and wrecks along the eastern coast. Cross over to Lombok by ferry and spend three days diving the reefs around northwest Senggigi and the Gili islands. Cross back to Denpasar and then fly to Manado for five days of diving the excellent reefs of Pulau Bunaken Marine Park. Finally, fly to Ambon, hire a boat, and spend three days diving the Maluku reefs before flying back to Jakarta. (Caution: If you follow this itinerary be sure to rest or just snorkel rather than dive within 24 hours of flying.)

When to Tour Indonesia

In June and July, popular areas (especially Torajaland) are crammed with visitors. Bali hotels also tend to be fully booked around Christmas and New Year's. Be sure to keep track of Muslim holidays, such as Ramadan, the fasting month when many establishments are closed during the day. During Idul Fitri, the Islamic New Year, and the weeks around Chinese New Year, vacationing Indonesians crowd the transport systems and hotels, so book early if you must visit during these times. Be aware that many national museums are closed on Mondays.

Also, in observance of the Muslim holy day, museums and offices usually close by 11 AM on Friday. The best months for traveling are April–May and September–October, when you're most likely to miss both the seasonal rains and the crowds. (*Also see* When to Go *in* Indonesia A to Z, *below.*)

Numbers in the text correspond to numbers in the margin and on the maps.

JAVA

Java could be a big country all by itself. It's the heart, soul, and financial center of Indonesia. And with more than 100 million people squeezed into an area about the size of Louisiana, it's the world's most populous island. Strangely enough, however, you can still find places of great solitude. This thin isle—about 1,100 km (684 mi) from east to west and between 100 km (62 mi) and 200 km (124 mi) wide—is full of volcanoes (many of them active), pounded by big surf from the Indian Ocean, and buffeted by the much calmer Java Sea. Divided into three provinces—West, Central, and East Java—and two special territories—Jakarta the capital and Yogyajakarta the cultural center—it's easy to see in bite-size sections. The road and rail systems are extensive (although in places they're pushed to their limits), the people are friendly, and English isn't as foreign a tongue as you might expect.

It seems that every bit of land—from the fertile valleys to the steep mountain slopes—is cultivated, taking advantage of the rich volcanic soil. But such landscaping is one of the few constants here. Java's long and varied history is evident in Borobudur, the world's largest Buddhist monument; Cirebon, a city on the north coast that dates back more than 500 years; ancient Hindu sites; and remnants of old Javanese empires. Islam, which arrived in the 13th century and remains the most prominent religion, has its share of monuments, too. The Dutch made Java one of their colonies in the early 1800s, and their influence is still reflected in such cities as Bandung and Bogor in West Java. The capital, Jakarta—with its tall modern buildings casting shadows on shacks and shanties—seems a tribute to a contemporary age in which the collision of old ideas and new ones has caused confusion and upheaval.

Indonesia, with Java leading the way, is entering an exciting yet worrying time. Exciting because of the promise of new freedoms and opportunities and worrying because of the uncertainty of economic crisis. As you travel, you'll notice a huge gulf between rich and poor—particularly in Jakarta—and it may take some getting used to. Further, the floating rupiah and inflation are playing havoc with prices. With this come great bargains, but also considerable commercial instability. Companies—including travel agents, airlines, and other tourism-related businesses—open and close seemingly overnight. Some tolerance will be needed. Your patience and compassion, however, will be amply rewarded by the rich sights and experiences that Java, and the rest of Indonesia, offer.

Jakarta

Indonesia's capital is a place of extremes. Modern multistory buildings look down on shacks with corrugated-iron roofs. Wide boulevards intersect with unpaved streets. Elegant hotels and high-tech business centers stand just a few blocks from overcrowded kampongs. BMWs accelerate down the avenues while pedicabs (which are officially banned from the city) plod along backstreets.

Although the government has tried to prepare for the 21st century, Jakarta has had trouble accommodating the thousands who have flocked to it each year from the countryside. Because of the number of migrant workers who arrive each day, it's difficult to accurately estimate the city's population. The census reports 8.5 million, but the true number is closer to 14 million. The crowds push the city's infrastructure to the limit. Traffic often grinds to a standstill, and a system of canals, built by the Dutch to prevent flooding in below-sea-level Jakarta, can't accommodate the heavy monsoon rains, so the city is sometimes under water for days. The heat and humidity take getting used to, though air-conditioning in the major hotels, restaurants, and shopping centers provides an escape. Early morning and late afternoon are the best times for sightseeing.

Exploring Jakarta

At Jakarta's center is the vast, parklike Merdeka Square, where Sukarno's 433-ft National Monument is topped with a gold-plated flame symbolizing national independence. Wide boulevards border the square, and the Presidential Palace (the president doesn't live here), the army headquarters, City Hall, Gambir Railway Station, the National Museum, and other government buildings are here.

Immediately south of the square along Jalan M. H. Thamrin (*jalan* means "street") is the Menteng district with many international hotels and embassies. Farther south, Jalan Thamrin changes its name to Jalan Jentral Sudirman, is the downtown of New Jakarta, home to most banks, large corporations, and more international hotels. This area is also known as the Golden Triangle.

North and west of Merdeka Square, around the port of Sunda Kelapa at the mouth of the Ciliwung River, is the Kota area, known as Old Batavia. This is where the Portuguese first arrived in 1522. A century later, in 1619, the Dutch secured the city, renamed it Batavia, and established an administrative center for their expanding Indonesian empire.

Dutch rule came to an abrupt end when, in World War II, the Japanese occupied Batavia and changed its name back to Jayakarta. The Dutch returned after Japan's surrender, but by 1949 Indonesia had won independence and, abbreviating the city's old name, established Jakarta as the nation's capital.

Old Batavia

Old Batavia, or Kota, is down by the port, where the Dutch administration was centered. As Jakarta expanded after World War II, Old Batavia was neglected. Its stately colonial buildings fell into decay, its streets and sidewalks caved in, and its shophouses became warehouses and repair shops. Prior to the economic crisis, an appreciation for Jakarta's heritage was awakened, and a revitalization of Old Batavia began. Many of the old buildings were restored and the area experienced an economic rejuvenation and beautification. (Note that despite gentrification, it's best to visit Old Batavia by day; some of the streets are scary to walk along at night.)

A GOOD TOUR

To cover a lot of ground before the midday heat, a combination of walking and taking cabs is prudent for this tour. Start by taking a taxi to the **fish market** ①, which is best seen early in the day. If you walk through the back of the market, you can save on the entrance fee to **Sunda Kelapa Harbor,** where vessels dock with goods from Indonesia's outer islands. Head south and stop at the **Maritime Museum** ②, then veer left, over to Jalan Tongkol, which becomes Jalan Cengkeh. Turn right onto

Jalan Kunir, and follow it a short distance to Jalan Pintu Besar Utara. Turn left and head down to the heart of Old Batavia, **Fatahillah Square** ③. On the west side of the square, which was the city's central plaza in the days of the Dutch, is the **Puppet Museum** ④ (often called the Wayang Museum); on the east side is the **Jakarta Fine Art Gallery** ⑤, in the former Palace of Justice. The old Town Hall, on the square's south side, is now the **Museum of Old Batavia** ⑥. Behind the Town Hall, on Jalan Pangeran Jayakarta and opposite the Kota Railway Station, is the **Portuguese Church** ⑦, the oldest in Jakarta. From the square head south to explore **Glodok,** Old Batavia's Chinatown; wander around and marvel at all the activity in its narrow streets.

TIMING

To experience the frenetic activity of the fish market, start your tour early, at around 7 AM. If you're visiting on a Sunday, there's an abbreviated wayang *kulit,* or shadow-puppet play, performed at 10 AM at the Puppet Museum. Since the heat builds as the day progresses, try to finish your walk soon after midday.

SIGHTS TO SEE

③ **Fatahillah Square.** At the heart of the old city is Fatahillah Square, cobbled with ballast stones from old Dutch trading ships. In its center is a fountain, a reproduction of one originally built here in 1728. Near the fountain, criminals were beheaded while their judges watched from the balconies of Town Hall (☞ Museum of Old Batavia, *below*). Just to the north is an old Portuguese cannon whose muzzle tapers into a clenched fist, a Javanese fertility symbol; childless women have been known to straddle the cannon for help in conceiving.

① **Fish Market.** The Pasar Ikan is as remarkable an introduction to the denizens of Indonesia's seas as a visit to an aquarium—and more chaotic and exciting. It's colorful, noisy, smelly, and slimy, and there are great photo opportunities. Be sure to come early, when it's in full swing. ⊠ *Sunda Kelapa Harbor.*

Glodok. Much of Chinatown has been demolished, but there are still sights and smells that evoke the days when Chinese were brought in as laborers and worked like slaves to become merchants. Many now run successful businesses, and this has caused resentment in other ethnic groups. During the riots that rocked the capital in May 1998, ethnic Chinese were targeted by furious mobs who felt that the Chinese received unfair government protection. Though businesses were looted and burned throughout the city, Glodok was, obviously, hit hard. More than 1,000 people died in the rioting (mostly looters who were trapped in torched shopping malls), and many Chinese fled to neighboring countries. Some came back, but many of those who lost homes and/or loved ones vowed never to return. Today, there's little evidence of the riots, but for locals, they're a powerful part of the area's history. Wander around Glodok Plaza (a landmark shopping center and office building), and you can still find small streets crowded with Chinese restaurants and shops that sell herbal medicines. Glodok is also an entertainment district at night, but unless you know your way around, it's better left to the locals.

⑤ **Jakarta Fine Art Gallery.** The Belai Seni Rupa Jakarta is in the former Palace of Justice, built between 1866 and 1870, on the east side of Fatahillah Square. The gallery's permanent collection includes paintings by Indonesia's greatest artists; contemporary works, such as wood sculptures; and the Chinese ceramic collection of Adam Malik, a former Indonesian vice-president. A museum in the southeast of the Menteng district, the **Adam Malik Museum** (⊠ Jl. Diponegoro 29, ☎ 021/

337400 or 021/337388), displays even more of his works. ⊠ *Jl. Taman Fatahillah 2,* ☎ *021/676090.* ▧ *Admission.* ☉ *Tues.–Sun. 9–2.*

Café Batavia (⊠ Jl. Taman Fatahillah 2, ☎ 021/691–5531), on the north side of Fatahillah Square, is a friendly place in which to enjoy Indonesian hors d'oeuvres, an Indonesian or European entrée, or a bit of ice cream. Its collection of nostalgic bric-a-brac, including a sketch of Winston Churchill, makes it quite cheerful. Choose a table by the window and watch the goings-on in the square below.

2 **Maritime Museum.** Two former Dutch East Indies warehouses have been restored to house the Museum Bahari. One warehouse is devoted to models of Indonesian sailing vessels; the other contains ancient maps and documents that tell the history of the spice trade. Neither exhibit is very thorough. ⊠ *Jl. Pasar Ikan 1,* ☎ *021/669–0518.* ▧ *Admission.* ☉ *Tues.–Sun. 9–2.*

6 **Museum of Old Batavia.** On the south side of Fatahillah Square is the old Town Hall, built by the Dutch in 1707. Preserved as an historic building, it now houses the Museum Sejarah Jakart, commonly known as the Jakarta Museum. The history of Batavia is chronicled with antique maps, portraits, models of ancient inscribed Hindu stones, antique Dutch furniture, weapons, and coins. Unfortunately, the exhibits have few explanations in English, and the museum is rather gloomy. Beneath the halls are the dungeons where criminals once awaited trial. Prince Diponegoro, the Indonesian patriot who nearly evicted the Dutch from Java in 1830, was imprisoned here on his way to exile in Manado. All you see of the dungeons are the double-barred basement windows along Jalan Pintu Besar. ⊠ *Jl. Taman Fatahillah 1,* ☎ *021/679101.* ▧ *Admission.* ☉ *Tues.–Thurs. 9–2:30, Fri. 9–noon, Sat. 9–1, Sun. 9–3.*

7 **Portuguese Church.** Opposite the Kota Railway Station, behind the Museum of Old Batavia, is the oldest church in Jakarta. It was built by the Portuguese—among the first Europeans to arrive in Indonesia—in the 17th century. Its exterior is plain, but inside you'll see carved pillars, copper chandeliers, solid ebony pews, and plaques commemorating prominent Dutch administrators. ⊠ *Jl. Pangeran Jayakarta.*

★ ✋ **4** **Puppet Museum.** On the west side of Fatahillah Square, in a former Protestant church, is the Museum Wayang. Here you'll find an extensive collection of traditional Indonesian wayang kulit figures, the intricately cut leather shadow puppets used to perform stories from the Hindu epics *Ramayana* and the *Mahabarata*. The museum also has wayang *golek* figures (wooden puppets used in performing Arabic folk tales or stories of Prince Panji, a legendary Javanese prince associated with the conversion of Java to Islam), as well as puppets from Thailand, China, Malaysia, India, Cambodia, and elsewhere. An abbreviated wayang kulit is performed on Sunday morning at 10. Also on display are puppets that are employed in social education projects, including those used by the Yogyakarta family-planning program. ⊠ *Jl. Pintu Besar Utara 27,* ☎ *021/679560.* ▧ *Admission.* ☉ *Tues.–Thurs. and weekends 9–2, Fri. 9–1.*

Sunda Kelapa Harbor. At the back of the fish market is the wharf, where Makassar and Bugis *prahus* (sailing ships) are docked at oblique angles to the piers. They look like beached whales, but they still sail the Indonesian waters as they have for centuries, trading between the islands. You can negotiate a small punt (about Rp 2,500–3,000) to take you on a 30-minute tour of the harbor. Government plans to develop a tourist marina here are on hold owing to Indonesia's fiscal crisis, so the evocative setting is safe for a while yet. ▧ *Admission.* ☉ *Daily 8–6.*

New Jakarta

In many developing countries, the capital becomes a symbol of national pride in shaking off the yoke of economic, and often colonial, servitude. In pre–economic crisis Jakarta, this attitude led to the construction of wide avenues, tall skyscrapers (many of which are bank offices), palatial government buildings, and extravagant monuments. Modern Jakarta has little aesthetic appeal, but it's an interesting example of how an evolving nation attempts to thrust itself into the modern age.

A GOOD TOUR

New Jakarta is almost impossible to cover on foot. The distances between sights are long, the streets aren't pedestrian-friendly, and the equatorial heat will melt you. Taxis are very cheap. Use them to get from one sight to another.

Start your tour in vast Merdeka Square, at the towering **National Monument** ⑧, taking its interior elevator up to the top for a bird's-eye view of the city. Then head for the monument's basement to visit the Museum of National History. Next head west to the **National Museum** ⑨ and its outstanding collection of Indonesian antiquities and ethnic artwork. From the museum, you may want to ride around the square in a taxi. On the northwest corner is the Presidential Palace; on the northeast corner is the **Istiqlal Mosque** ⑩, Indonesia's largest (guided tours are available); and a bit farther down the east side is **Emmanuel Church** ⑪. Keep the taxi and continue south down Jalan Cikini Raya to the **Jakarta Cultural Center** ⑫, known by the acronym TIM, where you're bound to find a cultural performance of some kind in progress. (If you walk, it's about 15 minutes from the south side of the square.) Directly west from TIM and about 10 minutes by taxi is the **Textile Museum** ⑬, with a collection of more than 300 kinds of Indonesian textiles and a small workshop where batik making is demonstrated.

TIMING

It shouldn't take much more than a half a day to cover these sights. Do plan to spend at least a couple of hours in the National Museum. If possible, time your visit to coincide with one of the free tours given in English—Tuesday, Wednesday, and Thursday at 9:30 AM—and you'll appreciate the museum a thousand times more; on Sunday morning there's Javanese or Sundanese gamelan music from 9:30 to 10:30.

SIGHTS TO SEE

⑪ **Emmanuel Church.** This classical Dutch Protestant church, off Merdeka square in the shadow of the ☞ **National Monument,** was built in 1835. Today its modest simplicity seems wonderfully incongruous in contrast to the grandeur of the surrounding monuments. ⊠ *Jl. Merdeka Timur 10.*

⑩ **Istiqlal Mosque.** On the northwest corner of Merdeka Square is Indonesia's largest mosque. If you haven't come to pray, you probably won't be encouraged to enter on your own. To appreciate the mosque's size and open layout, however, you can arrange to join a guided tour through your hotel or a travel agent. ⊠ *Jl. Veteren.*

⊙ ⑫ **Jakarta Cultural Center.** There's something happening at the Taman Ismail Marzuki (TIM) from morning to midnight. Most evenings, either the open-air theater or the enclosed auditorium stages some kind of performance, from Balinese dance to imported jazz, from gamelan concerts to poetry readings. Your hotel will have a copy of the monthly program. Two art galleries display paintings, sculpture, and ceramics. Also within the complex are an art school, an art workshop, a cinema, a planetarium, and outdoor cafés. ⊠ *Jl. Cikini Raya 73,* ☎ *021/*

342605. ⊠ Admission. ⊙ Daily 8–8. Planetarium shows: Tues.–Sun. at 7:30; Sun. at 10, 11, and 1.

⑧ National Monument. Merdeka Square is dominated by the towering Monument Nasional (MONAS). Local wags have taken to calling the Russian-built tower commemorating Indonesia's independence "Sukarno's last erection." Some of this bitterness may stem from the fact that the World Bank supplied funds for 77 pounds of pure gold to coat the "flame of freedom" atop the column while many Indonesians starved. Regardless of how you feel about it, the monument serves as a useful landmark. Take its interior elevator up to just below the flame for a panoramic view of the city.

In the basement is the **Museum of National History,** with a gallery of 48 dioramas that illustrate Indonesia's history and struggle for independence. The Hall of Independence contains four national treasures: the flag raised during the independence ceremony in 1945; the original text of the declaration of independence; a gilded map of the Indonesian Republic; and the Indonesian coat of arms, which symbolizes the five principles of the Indonesian Republic (belief in one supreme god; a just and civilized humanity; unity of Indonesia; consensus arising from discussion and self-help; and social justice). ⊠ *Jl. Silang Monas, Merdeka Square,* ☎ *021/681512 museum.* ⊠ *Admission (one price for both monument and museum).* ⊙ *Monument: Sat.–Thurs. 9–4, Fri. 9–11. Museum: Tues.–Thurs. and Sat. 9–2:30, Fri. 9–11:30 AM.*

★ ⑨ National Museum. On the west side of Merdeka Square stands the Museum Nasional, recognizable by the bronze elephant in front—a gift from the King of Siam (Thailand) in 1871. The museum has the most complete collection of Indonesian antiquities and ethnic artwork in the country. There are five sections: Hindu and Buddhist stone carvings from the 7th to 15th centuries; an exhibit of prehistoric skulls, weapons, and cooking utensils dating back 4,000 years; Indonesian ethnic crafts; a treasure room with gold trinkets, jeweled weapons, and Buddhist statues; and one of the largest collections of Chinese ceramics outside China. Free tours are given in English on Tuesday, Wednesday, and Thursday at 9:30 AM, and on Sunday morning you can hear gamelan music from 9:30 to 10:30. To the right, as you face the museum, is the **museum shop,** which sells such items as shadow puppets and books on Indonesia. ⊠ *Jl. Merdeka Barat 12,* ☎ *021/381–2346.* ⊠ *Admission.* ⊙ *Tues.–Thurs. and weekends 8:30–1, Fri. 8:30–11.*

⑬ Textile Museum. With its rich collection of Indonesian fabrics and small workshop where batik-making is demonstrated, the Museum Tekstil will give you an idea of what to expect by way of design and quality in the textiles you'll come across as you travel about the country. ⊠ *Jl. K. Sasuit Tubun 4,* ☎ *021/365367.* ⊠ *Admission.* ⊙ *Tues.–Thurs. and Sun. 9–2, Fri. 9–11, Sat. 9–1.*

Jakarta's Green Spaces

Jakarta has made an attempt to attract visitors and to give local residents recreational opportunities. At the same time, the government has wanted to make Jakarta an example of the diversity that is Indonesia. Thus, many of the city's parks are celebrations of the nation's different ethnic and cultural groups.

A GOOD ROUTE

You may not want to visit both of these recreational attractions—choose the one that best satisfies your interests. North of Kota and stretching east along the bay is **Dunia Fantasi at Ancol;** billed as Southeast Asia's largest recreation area, it provides entertainment around the clock. About 12 km (7 mi) southeast of Merdeka Square and 30 minutes by taxi is the **Beautiful Indonesia in Miniature Park.** Its 250 acres hold 27 full-size traditional houses, as well as various museums.

TIMING

You may want to spend the afternoon at Dunia Fantasi at Ancol after touring Old Batavia, since it's north of Kota. However, avoid it on the weekends, when it's thronged with Jakarta families. You'll want to allow a good half a day at Beautiful Indonesia in Miniature Park, perhaps arriving in time for lunch.

SIGHTS TO SEE

☙ **Beautiful Indonesia in Miniature Park.** The Batak house of North Sumatra, the Redong longhouse of the Kalimantan Dayaks, the cone-shape hut of Irian Jaya, and the Toraja house of South Sulawesi are just a few of the 27 full-size traditional houses—one from each Indonesian province—on display at the Taman Mini Indonesia Indah. There are even miniature Borobudur and Prambanan temples. Other attractions at the 250-acre park include a 30-minute movie, *Beautiful Indonesia*, shown daily from 11 to 5; the Museum Indonesia, with traditional costumes and handicrafts; a stamp museum; the Soldier's Museum, honoring the Indonesian struggle for independence; the Transportation Museum; and Museum Asmat, highlighting the art of the master carvers of the Asmat people of Irian Jaya. The park also has an orchid garden, an aviary, a touring train, cable cars, horse-drawn carts, paddleboats, and places for refreshment. English-speaking guides are available, if you call in advance. The park is about 12 km (7 mi) southeast of Merdeka Square and 30 minutes by taxi. ⊠ *12 km (7 mi) south of central Jakarta, off Jagorawi Toll Rd.,* ☎ *021/849525.* ⊡ *Admission.* ☉ *Museums, daily 9–3; outdoor attractions, daily 9–4.*

☙ **Dunia Fantasi at Ancol.** A village unto itself, this 24-hour park has hotels, nightclubs, shops, and amusement centers, including an oceanarium with dolphin and sea lion shows, a golf course, a race-car track, a four-pool complex with a wave pool, and water slides. Africa is represented by a comedy of mechanized monkeys, America by a Wild West town, Europe by a mock Tudor house, and Asia by buildings from Thailand, Japan, India, and Korea. Rides, shooting galleries, and food stalls surround these attractions, all set on 1,360 acres of land reclaimed from the bay in 1962. ⊠ *Taman Impian Jaya Ancol,* ☎ *021/681512.* ⊡ *Admission.* ☉ *Daily.*

Dining

All the major hotels have Western and Indonesian restaurants, and many of the latter also offer Chinese food. Outside the hotels, dining options range from restaurants with a formal atmosphere and fine cuisine to Western fast-food outlets, including the more upscale ones such as TGI Friday's and Planet Hollywood, to inexpensive street stalls.

Chinese

$$$$ ★ ✕ **Xin Hwa.** The Malay chef at this elegant 100-seat restaurant in the Mandarin Oriental hotel (☞ Lodging, *below*) prepares spicy Szechuan specialties, including sliced, braised chicken with hot-pepper oil and abalone soup with fermented black beans. Try the excellent bird's nest soup and the stir-fried lobster in a hot black-bean sauce. Dinner reservations are highly recommended. ⊠ *Jl. M. H. Thamrin,* ☎ *021/391–6438. AE, DC, MC, V. No lunch weekends.*

Contemporary

$$$ ✕ **Asiatique.** The concept of marrying Asian spices with Western culinary concepts isn't new in California, but it is in Jakarta. At this restaurant in the Regent hotel (☞ Lodging, *below*), chefs Kenji Salz

Dining ●
Asiatique, **21**
Brasserie, **29**
Le Bistro, **9**
Gandy, **15**
Green Pub, **8,23**
Handayani, **6**
Manari, **24**
Mira Sari, **27**
Nadaman, **19**
Natrabu, **7**
Oasis, **10**
Omar Khayyam, **3**
Paregu, **25**
Pondok Laguna, **2**
Sari Kuring/Sari
Nusantara, **5**
Tamnak Thai, **14**
Xin Hwa, **17**

Lodging ○
Grand Hyatt, **12**
Hotel Borobudur Inter-
Continental, **4**
Hotel Wisata
International, **16**
Interhouse, **26**
Jayakarta Tower, **1**
Kebayoran Inn, **28**
Mandarin
Oriental, **18**
Marcopolo, **13**
President Hotel, **11**
Regent, **22**
Shangri-La, **20**

Jakarta Dining and Lodging

(formerly of the Four Seasons Bali) and Derek Watanabe (a graduate of New York's Culinary Institute of America) are the innovators. They blend elements from different Asian cuisines to produce tempting combinations. You can order most dishes as an appetizer or a main course; a broad selection of appetizers is a good way to satisfy your curiosity. Especially tasty are the lemongrass-spiked tandoori salmon and the fried chili and lobster with peppers and lotus root. ⊠ *Jl. H. R. Rasuna Said,* ☎ *021/252–3456. AE, DC, MC, V. No lunch.*

Eclectic

$$$ ✕ **Oasis.** Fine international cuisine, as well as a traditional rijsttafel, ensure that, even after decades, the Oasis remains popular with Western visitors. A specialty is medallions of veal Oscar—served in a cream sauce with mushrooms, crabmeat, and asparagus. The atmosphere lives up to the cuisine in this lovely old house decorated with tribal art and textiles. A combo alternates with Batak singers to provide music nightly. ⊠ *Jl. Raden Saleh 47,* ☎ *021/326397. Reservations essential. AE, DC, V. Closed Sun.*

French

$$$ ✕ **Brasserie.** French-born Gil D'Harcour opened this cozy restaurant in 1997 in Kemang, a trendy neighborhood in the south of the city where many expats live. The atmosphere in the dining room and on the patio is casual, and the food—traditional French dishes made with fresh, local ingredients—is good. The wine list has an extensive selection of French varieties. ⊠ *Plaza Bisnis, Jl. Kemang Raya 2,* ☎ *021/718–3422. AE, MC, V.*

$$$ ✕ **Le Bistro.** Candlelighted and intimate, with checked tablecloths and copper pots, the ambience here puts you in the mood for the classic Provençal menu—simple food, prepared with herbs, from the south of France. Try the roast chicken with rosemary and thyme. The circular piano bar at the back of the dining room is the perfect spot for an after-dinner liqueur. ⊠ *Jl. K. H. Wahid Hasyim 75,* ☎ *021/364272. AE, DC, V.*

Indian

$ ✕ **Omar Khayyam.** In addition to an Indian buffet lunch, this restaurant offers such specialties as curries and tandoori dishes. The decor pays homage to the eponymous Persian poet: some of his poetry is inscribed on the walls. Try the chicken *tikka makhanwalla*—boneless tandoori chicken with tomato, butter, and cream sauce—or the marinated fish that's wrapped in a banana leaf and deep-fried. ⊠ *Jl. Antara 5–7,* ☎ *021/356719. Reservations not accepted. No credit cards.*

Indonesian

$$ ✕ **Handayani.** This true neighborhood restaurant has friendly service and some English-speaking staffers. Decor isn't its strong point—lines of tables and chairs fill a bare room—but Handayani draws locals for its food rather than its sparse interior. You may have to be a bit bold to sample some of the dishes, such as chicken bowels steamed in banana leaves, beef intestine satay, and goldfish fried or grilled. If you're timid try the lobster-size king prawns cooked in a mild chili sauce or the nasi goreng Handayani, a special version of the Indonesian staple. ⊠ *Jl. Abdul Muis 35E,* ☎ *021/373614. DC, V.*

$$ ✕ **Manari.** Locals often bring their foreign guests here. The menu is primarily Indonesian, though there are dishes from China (Canton) and Thailand, too. The food is really secondary, however, to the varied dinnertime cultural performances—dances and songs that demonstrate Indonesia's multiethnic heritage. ⊠ *Jl. Jendral Gatot Subroto 14,* ☎ *021/ 516102. Reservations essential. AE, MC, V.*

$$ ✕ **Mira Sari.** Comfortable rattan chairs with soft pillows, fresh flowers, and friendly service make this a congenial spot. Regional Indonesian specialties are served in the air-conditioned dining room, in the garden, or on the terrace. The menu includes a very good version of Indonesian chicken soup; excellent spiced, grilled fish; prawns grilled with spices and chilies; and roast or fried spiced chicken. ⊠ *Jl. Kemang Utara 1, 33 Patiunus 15,* ☎ *021/799–7997. Reservations essential. No credit cards.*

$$ ✕ **Natrabu.** Decor at this popular Padang (the spicy cuisine of the Minangkabau people in the Padang area of West Sumatra) restaurant is minimal: bare tabletops and side booths, red Sumatran banners hanging from the ceiling, and a model of a Minangkabau house set in a corner. Padang waiters wearing head scarves from the region deliver bowls of food from the moment you sit down. You can order, or you can select from the dishes they bring—you pay for the ones you try. ⊠ *Jl. H. A. Salim (often called Jl. Sabang) 29A,* ☎ *021/335668. Reservations not accepted. MC, V.*

$$ ✕ **Pondok Laguna.** Here, the large dining room, divided by water
★ pools and falls, is always crowded with families and young couples. The noise level is fairly high and the service casual. Some of the staff speaks English; all are anxious to help foreign guests. Fish is the specialty—either fried or grilled and accompanied by different sauces ranging from hot to mild. Whatever you choose, expect it to be fresh and cooked to perfection. ⊠ *Jl. Batu Tulis Raya 45,* ☎ *021/359994. Reservations not accepted. AE, DC, MC, V.*

$$ ✕ **Sari Kuring.** This restaurant near Merdeka Square serves very good
★ Indonesian seafood, especially the grilled prawns and the Thai fish à la Sari Kuring, marinated in spices then quickly fried. The restaurant is large, but connected on many levels by stone steps, so there's some feeling of intimacy. If you can't get a table here, try next door at **Sari Nusantara,** where the fare is similar except for a slight Chinese influence in the cooking and fewer spices in the sauces. ⊠ *Jl. Silang Monas Timur 88,* ☎ *021/352972. AE, V.*

Japanese

$$$ ✕ **Nadaman.** This restaurant in the Shangri-La hotel (☞ Lodging, *below*) offers a varied selection of traditional and newer Japanese dishes. The 56-seat main dining room is decorated with rice-paper lanterns and black lacquer tables; there are also private rooms, some with tatami mats and one with tables and a sushi bar. ⊠ *Jl. Jendral Sudirman Kav 1,* ☎ *021/570–7440. AE, DC, MC, V.*

Mexican

$$ ✕ **Green Pub.** The two branches of the Green Pub are recommended not only for their Mexican food but for their live country-and-western music (6:30–9) and jazz (9:30–1). The decor is somewhere between a Western saloon and a Mexican ranch, with tapestries adorning the walls. The burritos and enchiladas are quite authentic, and the menu also includes such Tex-Mex dishes as barbecued spareribs. ⊠ *Jakarta Theater Building, Jl. M. H. Thamrin 9,* ☎ *021/359332. Reservations not accepted. AE, V.* ⊠ *Jl. H. R. Rasuna Said, Setia Budi Building 1,* ☎ *021/517983. Reservations not accepted. AE, V.*

Steak House

$$ ✕ **Gandy.** There are several Gandys in Jakarta, but this one is the most interesting. Stepping into this popular place is like stepping back into the 1960s: the staff wears uniforms that seem outdated by about 30 years but fit in well with the wooden decor and steak-house setting. Some of the beef and imported lamb dishes—the specialities here—arrive on a hot plate and keep cooking at your table. Things become lively

after 7 PM or 8 PM, when a jazz band with a singer starts to perform. ⊠ *Jl. Hos. Cokroaminoto 90,* ☎ *021/629–0539. AE, DC, MC, V.*

Thai

$$ ✕ **Tamnak Thai.** The friendly staff here serves good, standard Thai food in the comfortable, 30-odd-table dining room or the separate VIP room. The menu includes pictures—for the uninitiated—and the chef will prepare dishes for you as if you were in Thailand or tone down the spices if you like. Seafood dishes are standouts. ⊠ *Jl. Hos Cokroaminoto 78,* ☎ *021/315–0833. MC, V.*

Vietnamese

$$ ✕ **Paregu.** This place serves the best Vietnamese food in town. The decor is simple, with Asian embellishments, and the service is top-notch. Try the Vietnamese version of spring rolls; the fried rice with scrambled eggs, chicken, shrimp, and a blend of herbs and spices; or the herbed seafood. ⊠ *Jl. Sudan Cholagogue 64,* ☎ *021/774892. No credit cards.*

Lodging

Jakarta has many world-class hotels with all the modern amenities and countless budget establishments with few frills. Most accommodations are just south of Merdeka Square.

$$$$ ▦ **Grand Hyatt.** Glitter and shining-marble modernity characterize this 1992 hotel. You enter the four-story atrium lobby and climb a palatial staircase (or take the escalator) to the reception area. One more short flight up brings you to the expansive Fountain Lounge, where you can watch the stalled traffic on Jalan M. H. Thamrin. On the fifth floor is the pool garden, an extensive area of greenery with a seafood terrace restaurant. Rooms are spacious, and each has two bay windows; bathrooms have separate shower stalls and toilets. Furnishings are in the ubiquitous pastels, but pleasant nonetheless. Beneath the Hyatt is the Plaza Indonesia (☞ *also* Shopping, *below*), with restaurants, nightclubs, and more than 250 shops. In a city that sprawls, this proximity to a "social center" is an advantage. ⊠ *Jl. M. H. Thamrin (Box 4546), 10045,* ☎ *021/390–1234 or 800/233–1234 in the U.S.,* ☒ *021/310–7300. 413 rooms, 47 suites. 6 restaurants, bar, pool, massage, 6 tennis courts, health club, jogging, squash, business services. AE, DC, MC, V.*

$$$$ ▦ **Hotel Borobudur Inter Continental.** Billed as "your country club in Jakarta," this large, modern complex sits on 23 acres of landscaped gardens and has excellent facilities. Floor-to-ceiling windows at the back of the Pendopo Lounge look out onto the greenery, making it a delightful place for afternoon tea, cocktails, or snacks. Most of the compact guest rooms have a modern Javanese design; the Garden Wing has suites with kitchens. Request a room that overlooks the gardens and the pool or risk staying in one that faces the parking lot. ⊠ *Jl. Lapangan Banteng Selatan (Box 329), 10710,* ☎ *021/380–5555 or 800/327–0200 in the U.S.,* ☒ *021/380–9595. 712 rooms, 140 suites. 5 restaurants, 2 bars, room service, pool, miniature golf, 8 tennis courts, badminton, health club, jogging, racquetball, squash, dance club, playground, business services, meeting rooms. AE, DC, MC, V.*

$$$$ ▦ **Mandarin Oriental.** Jakarta's most sophisticated hotel was completely
★ renovated in mid-1997. The elegant circular lobby has three tall, beautifully carved Batak roofs, each housing a Sumatran statue. An open mezzanine above the lobby provides comfortable seating for tea or cocktails and some fine shops, including a gallery for Ida Bagus Tilem, Bali's master wood-carver. Guest rooms are spacious and have top-quality furnishings: thick russet carpeting, floral bedspreads, off-white draperies on picture windows, and dark wood furniture. Complimentary afternoon tea and hors d'oeuvres are delivered to your room. Most rooms

are "executive," with butler service; for a nominal extra fee you can have complimentary breakfast and cocktails as well as use of the executive lounge and concierge services. The hotel's location is central, and with the Plaza Indonesia shopping complex and the Grand Hyatt across the square, there are shops, restaurants, and bars within a two-minute walk. On-site restaurants include the Xin Hwa (☞ *Dining, above*). ✉ *Jl. M. H. Thamrin (Box 3392), 10310,* ☎ *021/314–1307 or 800/526–6566 in the U.S.,* FAX *021/314–8679. 438 rooms. 4 restaurants, bar, pool, sauna, health club, business services, meeting rooms. AE, DC, MC, V.*

$$$$ 🏨 **Regent.** The architects made the most of space and natural light at
★ this property, which sits on 6 acres in the Golden Triangle, the city's booming business district. In the lobby, 10 shades of granite and marble are set off by honey-color teak paneling and Indonesian art. Guest rooms are large—a minimum of 500 square ft—and double layers of masonry between them keep things soundproof. Double-glazed, sliding glass doors lead out onto small balconies; framed Indonesian tapestries adorn the walls; and marble baths have deep tubs and separate shower stalls. Phones have two lines, modems, and voice mail. The Regent Club, on the 17th floor, has a commodious lounge where complimentary breakfast and evening cocktails are served amid a backdrop of great city views. Service throughout the hotel is friendly and enthusiastic. ✉ *Jl. H. R. Rasuna Said, 12920,* ☎ *021/252–3456 or 800/545–4000 in the U.S.,* FAX *021/252–4480. 378 rooms. 3 restaurants, bar, pool, sauna, 2 tennis courts, health club, business services, meeting rooms. AE, DC, MC, V.*

$$$$ 🏨 **Shangri-La.** At this opulent hotel, chandeliers adorn the huge lobby, where a string quartet plays classical music during much of the day. Rooms are spacious and comfortable; baths have tubs as well as separate shower stalls. A stay here includes free use of the well-equipped Horizon Health Club, which is like a resort in and of itself and has one of the city's best pools. The hotel's location in the Golden Triangle area makes it a convenient place for business travelers. ✉ *Jl. Jendral Sudirman Kav 1, 10220,* ☎ *021/570–7440 or 800/942–5050 in the U.S.,* FAX *021/570–3530. 628 rooms, 40 suites. 6 restaurants, 2 bars, pool, massage, putting green, 3 tennis courts, health club, jogging, business services, meeting rooms. AE, DC, MC, V.*

$$$ 🏨 **Hotel Wisata International.** Ranked as a three-star hotel by the government, the ungainly Wisata is off Jakarta's main thoroughfare. Corridors are long and narrow, guest rooms compact but clean. Each has a king-size bed; a TV and a safe take up most of the remaining space. Rooms on the executive floor are only marginally larger. Still, the price, the convenient coffee shop off the lobby, and the central location make the Wisata a reasonable choice. ✉ *Jl. M. H. Thamrin, 10230,* ☎ *021/230–0406,* FAX *021/324597. 165 rooms. Bar, coffee shop, meeting rooms. AE, DC, MC, V.*

$$$ 🏨 **President Hotel.** Like many hotels in the Japanese Nikko Hotel group, the President has a spare, utilitarian atmosphere but is equipped with all the modern amenities. Guest rooms are simple, with blue-and-navy striped fabrics, plain wood furniture, and small bathrooms. The on-site Ginza Benkay restaurant serves Japanese food, the Kahyangan serves Japanese and Indonesian, and the Golden Pavilion serves Chinese. ✉ *Jl. M. H. Thamrin 59, Jakarta 10350,* ☎ *021/230–1122,* FAX *021/314–3631. 354 rooms. 3 restaurants, bar, coffee shop, meeting rooms. AE, DC, MC, V.*

$$ 🏨 **Jayakarta Tower.** This moderately priced hotel is within walking
★ distance of Old Batavia. The marble lobby is accented with hand-blown-glass chandeliers and carved-wood panels. Each spacious room has a double or two twin beds, with Javanese-pattern spreads, plus a table

and two chairs and a vanity/desk. Executive rooms have minibars. For on-site meals your choices are the Dragon (a Chinese restaurant), as well as a coffee shop that serves Western and Indonesian specialties; ask to see the Thai menu at both. The hotel is affiliated with KLM's Golden Tulip properties, so you can make reservations through the airline. ✉ *Jl. Hayam Wuruk 126 (Box 803), 11001, ☎ 021/629–4408, FAX 021/626–5000. 435 rooms. 2 restaurants, coffee shop, room service, pool, health club, meeting rooms. AE, DC, MC, V.*

$ 🖫 **Interhouse.** This hotel is in the Kebayoran expatriate neighborhood and shopping district. Rooms are comfortable, though not large, and have air-conditioning; pleasant, homey furnishings; and pastel color schemes. ✉ *Jl. Melawai Raya 18–20 (Box 128/KBYB), 10305, ☎ 021/270–0408, FAX 021/720–6988. 130 rooms. Restaurant. AE, V.*

$ 🖫 **Kebayoran Inn.** Just south of the center of Jakarta is this quiet, residential-type lodging. The clean, air-conditioned rooms are simply decorated, with an Indonesian batik or ikat here and there. ✉ *Jl. Senayan 87, Jakarta 12180, ☎ 021/716208, FAX 021/560–3672. 61 rooms. Restaurant. AE, V.*

$ 🖫 **Marcopolo.** The staff at this basic, economical hotel is helpful, and
★ although the carpeted rooms are plain, they're clean, adequate, and air-conditioned. The restaurant serves good Chinese and European food. ✉ *Jl. T. Cik Ditiro 19, 10350, ☎ 021/325409, FAX 021/310–7138. 181 rooms. Restaurant, pool, nightclub. AE, DC. MC, V.*

Nightlife and the Arts

Nightlife

Owing to the economic crisis, Jakarta's night scene is surely in for some volatile times; nightspots will, no doubt, quickly come and go. When you arrive, you'll have to check out what's happening. Hotel staffers are terrific resources, and concierges can make reservations for you if necessary. Another good resource is *Jakarta Week,* which lists upcoming events and is found at most hotels. The places detailed below seemed, at press time, the ones most likely to survive the test of both time and economics.

Fashion Cafe. Opened in late 1996, the two-floor Fashion Cafe (the largest of the chain, which includes places in New York and London) has become *the* place to see and be seen. Its high-energy, futuristic, techno design makes for a terrific night out; wear black, and you'll fit right in. You can order such dishes as Naomi's Fish and Chips (named after fashion model Naomi Campbell) and Claudia's (as in Claudia Schiffer) New York Strip or just stick to drinks at the bar. Sometimes there's a show. ✉ *Jl. Jendral Sudirman Kav 1, ☎ 021/574–5111. ☉ Daily 11 AM–1 AM.*

Green Pub. After dinner at this pub-restaurant (☞ *also Dining, above*) consider hanging out with the expats and listening to music performed by local bands. ✉ *Jakarta Theater Building, Jl. M. H. Thamrin 9, ☎ 021/359332.*

Hard Rock Cafe. You'll find the same American fare and rock-and-roll paraphernalia here as at its brethren in cities around the world. The live music starts at about 9 PM. The stage has a huge, stained-glass-window backdrop that depicts Elvis Presley. ✉ *Sarinah Building, 2nd floor, Jl. M. H. Thamrin 11, ☎ 021/390–3565. ☉ Daily 11 AM–1 AM.*

Harry's Captain's Bar. This comfortable spot in the Mandarin Oriental hotel (☞ *Lodging, above*) is good for a relaxed evening of music by a small international or local group. ✉ *Jl. M. H. Thamrin, ☎ 021/ 321307. ☉ Nightly 8 PM–1 AM.*

Jaya Pub. This long-established piano bar is across from the Sarinah department store. It's popular with older expats and Indonesians alike, in part because the owners are two former Indonesian movie stars, Rimi Melati and Frans Tumbuan. ⊠ *Jl. M. H. Thamrin 12,* ☎ *021/327508.* ◷ *Daily noon–2 AM.*

O'Reiley's Pub and Bar. Built to resemble an Irish pub, this spot in the Grand Hyatt hotel (☞ Lodging, *above*) offers beer on tap. Stop by for a few drinks and some conversation early in the evening or a few pints and some live music later at night. ⊠ *Jl. M. H. Thamrin,* ☎ *021/390–1234.* ◷ *Daily 11 AM–1 AM.*

Planet Hollywood. You can't, it seems, have the Fashion and Hard Rock cafés without also having a Planet Hollywood. You can dine amid the movie memorabilia or just sip drinks and chat about your favorite films. There's live entertainment on Thursday, Friday, and Saturday after 10 PM. As it's in the east section of sprawling Jakarta, it's best to take a taxi. ⊠ *Jl. Gatot Subroto Kav 16,* ☎ *021/526–6727.*

Tanamur. Here's a place that just about every hotel staff member will suggest when asked for tips on nightspots. (Many staffers smile about Tanamur, and some say they don't go because their boyfriend or girlfriend would frown on it—though most have been at least once.) This Jakarta institution has good jazz and soft rock and is usually the most crowded disco in town. What goes on as couples huddle against the dimly lit walls is better left unsaid; a bevy of hostesses is ready to dance and drink with guests who don't have a date. ⊠ *Jl. Tanah Abang Timur 14,* ☎ *021/353947.* ◷ *Nightly 9 PM–2 AM.*

The Arts

For information on Jakarta's art events, check the daily *Indonesian Observer* newspaper or the monthly *What's On* magazine (available in many hotels) or contact the City Visitor Information Center (☞ Visitor Information *in* Jakarta Essentials, *below*).

DANCE AND THEATER

Beautiful Indonesia in Miniature Park. This park offers various regional dances on Sunday and holidays from 10 to 2 (☞ *also* Jakarta's Green Spaces *in* Exploring Jakarta, *above*). ⊠ *Off Jagorawi Toll Rd.,* ☎ *021/849525.*

Bharata Theater. Every night but Monday and Thursday, from 8:15 to midnight, this theater stages performances of traditional wayang *orang* (dance-dramas), depicting stories from the *Ramayana* or the *Mahabharata.* Sometimes the folk play *Ketoprak,* based on Javanese history, is also performed. ⊠ *Jl. Kalilio,* ☎ *no phone.*

Jakarta Hilton Cultural Program. Each week, the Hilton offers regional dance programs. Every afternoon from 4 to 6, the famous and very old Cakra Dalem Raya gamelan orchestral set is played. ⊠ *Indonesia Bazaar, Jakarta Hilton, Jl. Jendral Sudirman and Jl. Jendral Gatot Subroto,* ☎ *021/583051.*

Taman Ismail Marzuki. This arts center hosts plays, music and dance performances, art shows, and films. Monthly schedules of events are distributed to hotels. ⊠ *Jl. Cikini Raya 73,* ☎ *021/342605.*

PUPPET SHOWS

National Museum. Here there are biweekly performances using leather shadow puppets to depict stories from the *Ramayana* or the *Mahabharata,* or wood puppets to depict Islamic legends. ⊠ *Jl. Merdeka Barat 12,* ☎ *021/360976.*

Puppet Museum. This museum frequently offers performances; check with the staff for dates and times. ⊠ *Jl. Pintu Besar Utara 27,* ☎ *021/679560.*

Outdoor Activities and Sports

Diving
Dive Indonesia (⊠ Hotel Borobudur Inter-Continental, Jl. Lapangan Banteng Selatan, ☎ 021/370108) specializes in underwater photography and arranges trips to Flores and Sulawesi. **Jakarta Dive School and Pro Shop** (⊠ Indonesia Bazaar, Shop 32, Jakarta Hilton, Jl. Jendral Sudiman and Jl. Jendral Gatot Subroto, ☎ 021/583051, ext. 9008) offers open-water lessons and equipment rental.

Golf
At last count greater Jakarta had 20 golf courses. The Indonesia Golf Course Association, together with the Indonesia Tourism Promotion Board, publishes *The Official Golf Map of Indonesia,* available free at travel agencies and tourist offices. There are two well-maintained, 18-hole courses open to the public, though both are extremely crowded on weekends. Greens fees are generally Rp 150,000 on weekdays and Rp 250,000 on weekends; caddy fees run Rp 25,000 (tips are appreciated). The **Ancol Golf Course** (⊠ Dunia Fantasi at Ancol, Taman Impian Jaya Ancol, ☎ 021/681511) has pleasant sea views. **Kebayoran Golf Club** (⊠ Jl. Asia-Afrika, Pintu 9, ☎ 021/654–1156) is popular with expats.

Health and Fitness Centers
The **Clark Hatch Physical Fitness Center** has two facilities (⊠ Hotel Borobudur Inter-Continental, Jl. Lapangan Banteng Selatan, ☎ 021/370108; ⊠ Jakarta Hilton, Jl. Jendral Sudirman and Jl. Jendral Gatot Subroto, ☎ 021/583051) with up-to-date equipment, as well as massage, heat treatments, a sauna, and a whirlpool.

Other gyms are: **Club Olympus Fitness Center** (⊠ Fifth floor, Grand Hyatt, Jl. M. H. Thamrin, ☎ 021/390–1234), **Executive Fitness Center** (⊠ Ground floor, South Tower, Kuningan Plaza, Jl. H. R. Rasuna Said, ☎ 021/578–1706), **Medical Scheme** (⊠ Setia Budi Bldg. L, Jl. H. R. Rasuna Said, Kuningan, ☎ 021/515367), and **Pondok Indah Health and Fitness Center** (⊠ Jl. Metro Pondok Indah, ☎ 021/764906).

Running
The **Hash House Harriers/Harriettes,** a world-wide club known for mixing outrageous antics into its runs, has a chapter in Jakarta (⊠ HHH Box 46/KBY, Jakarta, ☎ 021/799–4758). Men run Monday at 5 PM, women Wednesday at 5 PM, and there's socializing in between. Write or call for meeting places and routes.

Tennis and Squash
Many of Jakarta's hotels have tennis and/or squash courts where non-guests can play. Call first to reserve a court. The **Grand Hyatt** (⊠ Jl. M. H. Thamrin, ☎ 021/390–1234), the **Hotel Borobudur Inter-Continental** (⊠ Jl. Lapangan Banteng Selatan, ☎ 021/370108), and the **Jakarta Hilton** (⊠ Jl. Jendral Sudirman and Jl. Jendral Gatot Subroto, ☎ 021/583051) have both tennis and squash facilities.

Shopping

Indonesia became a shoppers' paradise when the rupiah's value went from about 2,500 to the U.S. dollar in mid-1997 to 17,000 in the first half of 1998. (At press time, it was hard to tell where the rupiah's value would go and what inflation would do to prices.) All this has been bad news for Indonesians; indeed, when import prices increased, it put a lot of items out of reach for many citizens. But for visitors with dollars, such locally produced items as batik fabric, wood carvings, and clothing were, at press time, nearly criminally cheap.

Department Stores

Pasaraya (⊠ Jl. Iskandarsyah 1½, in Blok M, ☎ 021/739–0170).
Jakarta's largest department store tempts you to visit its multistory complex to see Indonesia's latest in women's fashions and handicrafts by
paying your taxi fare if you're staying at a five-star hotel. Check with
your hotel's concierge for a coupon.

Plaza Indonesia (⊠ Jl. M. H. Thamrin, ☎ 021/310–7272). Under the
Grand Hyatt and across the square from the Mandarin Oriental, this
is a central and convenient shopping center. Among its 250 stores are
upscale boutiques, art and antiques galleries, bookshops, travel agents,
Sogo's food store, and restaurants.

Plaza Senayan (⊠ Jl. Asia-Africa 8, ☎ 021/572–5555). One of the
city's newest shopping complexes has upscale boutiques with designer-
label fashions.

Sarinah Mataram (⊠ Jl. M. H. Thamrin 11, Menteng, ☎ 021/327425).
This four-story department store not only sells a variety of goods from
its convenient location, but is also connected to the Hard Rock Cafe—
a great place to rest your feet after all that shopping.

Markets

Jalan Surabaya Antiques Stalls (⊠ Pasar Barang Antik Jalan Surabaya,
in Menteng residential area). The city's daily (9–6) "flea market," sells
mundane goods at either end, but in the middle you might find delft-
ware, Chinese porcelain, old coins, old and not-so-old bronzes, and
more. You *must* bargain.

Pasar Melawai (⊠ Jl. Melawai, in Blok M). This series of buildings
and stalls offers everything from clothing to toys, cosmetics, and fresh
foods. English is spoken; hours are daily 9–6.

Specialty Stores

ANTIQUES

For serious antiques shopping, try the stores along Jalan Paletehan I
(Kebayoran Baru); Jalan Maja Pahit and Jalan Gajah Mada (Gam-
bir/Kota); Jalan Kebon Sirih Timur and Jalan H. A. Salim (Mentang);
and Jalan Ciputat Raya (Old Bogor Road).

Cony Art Antiques (⊠ Jl. Malawai Raya 180E, ☎ 021/716554). This
shop in the Kebayoran district is worth a visit for antique Chinese
porcelain.

Madjapahit Art and Curio (⊠ Jl. Melawai III/4, ☎ 021/715878). This
reputable store is behind the Sarinah Jaya, near Block M.

Nasrun (⊠ Jl. Kebon Sirih Rimur Dalam) has a large collection of
Chinese porcelain, antique batik, and Javanese and Sumatran wood
carvings.

NV Garuda Arts, Antiques (⊠ Jl. Maja Pahit 12, Kota, ☎ 021/342712).
NV Garuda is another reliable shop.

HANDICRAFTS

Sarinah Mataram (⊠ Jl. M. H. Thamrin 11, Menteng, ☎ 021/327425).
The third floor of this department store is devoted entirely to handi-
crafts, which you can also find in abundance at its larger sister store,
Pasaraya (☞ *above*).

TEXTILES

Batik Berdikari (⊠ Jl. Masjid in Palmerah, southwest of Merdeka Sq.,
☎ 021/548–2814). This shop (and factory) sells various types of Indonesian batik and has demonstrations of the ways in which batik is
made (either hand-drawn or printed).

Batik Danar Hadi (⊠ Jl. Raden Saleh 1A, ☎ 021/342748). The batik
selection here is quite large.

Batik Mira (✉ Jl. Mar. Raya 22, ☎ 021/761138). This is the place for expensive but excellent-quality batik. Its tailors will do custom work, and you can also ask to see the factory at the rear of the store.
Batik Semar (✉ Jl. Tornang Raya 54, ☎ 021/567–3514). Here you'll find top-quality batik with many unusual designs.
Bin House (✉ Jl. Panarukan 33, ☎ 021/335941). This shop carries Indonesian handwoven silks and cottons, including ikat, as well as antique textiles and objects d'art.
Plaza Indonesia (✉ Jl. M. H. Thamrin, ☎ 021/310–7272). This is a good place for chic, fashionable batiks, especially on the first floor.
PT Ramacraft (✉ Jl. Panarukan 25, ☎ 021/333122). PT Rarnacraft is the name of both the label and company run by Iwan Tirta, a famous designer of batik fabrics and clothing for men and women.

Jakarta Essentials

Arriving and Departing

BY AIRPLANE

Jakarta's airport, **Soekarno Hatta** (☎ 021/550–5307), is a modern showpiece, with glass-walled walkways and landscaped gardens. Although most of it isn't air-conditioned, it's breezy and clean. There's a small duty-free shopping area. Terminal One handles international flights, and Terminal Two serves all Garuda Indonesia Airways flights (both international and domestic) and all other domestic airlines. (For information on carriers and flights, ☞ Indonesia A to Z, *below*.) Between the two terminals, a **Visitor Information Center** (☎ 021/550–7088) is usually open Monday through Saturday 8 AM–10 PM, though sometimes it's closed seemingly because the staff feels like it. In both terminals there are **Indotel desks** (☎ 021/550–7179) where you can make hotel reservations, often at discounted rates.

From the Airport to Downtown: The airport is 35 km (20 mi) northwest of Jakarta. A toll expressway takes you three-quarters of the way to the city quickly, but the rest is slow going. To be safe, allow a good hour for the trip on weekdays.

Taxis *from* the airport add a surcharge of Rp 2,300 and the road toll (Rp 4,000) to the fare on the meter. The surcharge doesn't apply going *to* the airport. Blue Bird Taxi (☞ By Taxi under Getting Around, *below*) offers a 25% discount on the toll charge either way. The average fare to a downtown hotel is Rp 20,000. However, if it's raining and there are likely to be traffic jams, you'll need to negotiate a fare—Rp 40,000 should do it. On request, some hotels, such as the Mandarin Oriental, will arrange to have a chauffeur-driven car waiting for you. The cost is Rp 55,000.

Air-conditioned buses, with DAMRI in big letters on the side, operate every 20 minutes between the airport and six points in the city, including the Gambir Railway Station, Rawamangun Bus Terminal, Blok M, and Pasar Minggu Bus Terminal. The cost is Rp 3,000.

BY BUS

Bus terminals are off Merdeka Square and Blok M; buy tickets at the terminals or at travel agencies. **Pulo Gadang** (✉ Jl. Perintis Kemerdekaan, ☎ 021/489–3742) serves Semarang, Yogyakarta, Solo, Surabaya, Malang, and Denpensar. Use **Cililitan** (✉ Jl. Raya Bogor, ☎ 021/809–3554) for Bogor, Sukabumi, Bandung, and Banjar. **Kalideres** (✉ Jl. Daan Mogot) is the depot for Merak, Labuhan, and major cities in Sumatra (which include a ferry ride as part of a bus journey).

BY TRAIN

Use the **Tanah Abang Railway Station** (✉ Jl. KH Wahid Hasyim, southwest of Merdeka Sq., ☎ 021/340048) for trains to Sumatra. (You get off the train for the ferry across the Sunda Straight to Sumatra, and then catch another train in Bandarlampang.) Trains for destinations other than Sumatra—to Bogor and Bandung or to the east Java cities of Semarang, Yogyakarta, Solo, Surabaya, Madiun, and Malang—start from one of two other stations: the **Kota Railway Station** (✉ Jl. Stasiun Kota, south of Fatahillah Sq., ☎ 021/678515 or 021/679194) or the **Gambir Railway Station** (✉ Jl. Merdeka Timur, east side of Merdeka Sq., ☎ 021/342777 or 021/348612). You can buy tickets from travel agencies (☞ Tour Operators and Travel Agents, *below*) or at the station at least an hour before departure.

Getting Around

BY BUS

Non-air-conditioned public buses charge a flat Rp 350; the (green) air-conditioned buses charge Rp 600. All are packed during rush hours, and pickpockets abound. The routes can be labyrinthine, but you can always give one a try and get off when the bus veers from your desired direction. For information, contact these companies: **Hiba Utama** (☎ 021/413626 or 021/410381), **P. P. D.** (☎ 021/881131 or 021/411357), or **Mayasari Bhakti** (☎ 021/809–0378 or 021/489–2785).

BY CAR

Though rental cars are available, they're not advised. Traffic is horrendous, and parking is very difficult. If you do decide to rent a car, be aware that traffic police supplement their income by stopping you, even for infractions that you never knew you made. The police will suggest Rp 70,000 to forget the matter; you're expected to negotiate, and Rp 30,000 should make you both happy.

You can rent cars from: **Avis** (✉ Jl. Doponegoro 25, ☎ 021/331974), **Hertz** (✉ Jl. Tenku, C. K. Ditoro 11E, ☎ 021/332610), or **National** (✉ Hotel Kartika Plaza, Jl. M. H. Thamrin 10, ☎ 021/333423).

You can hire air-conditioned, chauffeur-driven cars for a minimum of two hours, at hourly rates of Rp 11,375 for a small Corona or Rp 21,000 for a Mercedes. Daily charters cost Rp 105,000 and Rp 210,000, respectively. Try Blue Bird Taxi (☞ *below*) or Hertz (☞ *above*).

BY MOTOR BECAK

These dirty, little, orange put-puts are, believe it or not, very good for short, one-way trips. Flag them down on the street. Most rides are Rp 2,000 to 5,000. You sit in the back, though it's a bit of a squeeze for anyone bigger than average.

BY TAXI

A cheap and efficient way of getting around, Jakarta's metered taxis charge Rp 900 for the first kilometer (½ mi) and Rp 450 for each subsequent 100 meters. You can flag taxis on the streets, and most hotels have cab stands. Be sure that the meter is down when you set off, and avoid taxis with broken meters or none at all, or you will be seriously overcharged. For a radio-dispatched taxi, call **Blue Bird Taxi** (☎ 021/798–9000 or 021/798–9111).

Contacts and Resources

EMERGENCIES

Ambulance: ☎ 118. **City Health Service:** ☎ 119.

Doctors and Dentists. A group-practice clinic, **Bina Medica** (✉ Jl. Maluku 8–10, ☎ 021/344893) provides 24-hour service and English-speaking doctors. **Doctors-on-Call** (☎ 021/683444, 021/681405, or 021/514444) has English-speaking doctors who make house calls. Payment in cash is required. Dental services are provided at the **Metropolitan Medical Center** (✉ Wisata Office Tower, 1st floor, Jl. M. H. Thamrin, ☎ 021/320408). English-speaking staff (including dentists) are available at the 24-hour clinic and pharmacy **SOS Medika Vayasan** (✉ Jl. Prapanca Raya 32–34, Kebayoran Baru, ☎ 021/771575 or 021/733094).

Pharmacies. Melawai Apotheek (✉ Jl. Melawai Raya 191, ☎ 021/716109) has a well-stocked supply of American medicines. SOS Medika Vayasan (☞ *above*) also has a pharmacy.**Police:** ☎ 110. **Traffic accidents:** ☎ 118.

ENGLISH-LANGUAGE BOOKSTORES

Major hotel shops carry magazines, newspapers, paperbacks, and travel guides in English. For a wide book selection, try **PT Indira** (✉ Jl. Melawi V/16, Blok M, ☎ 021/770584). The **Family Book Shop** (✉ Kemang Club Villas, Jl. Kelurahan Bangka, ☎ 021/799–5525) has quite a few titles. The largest selection is at the **Times Bookshop** (✉ Jl. M. H. Thamrin 28–30, ☎ 021/570–6581), on the lower floor of Plaza Indonesia.

TOUR OPERATORS AND TRAVEL AGENTS

Hotel tour desks will book the following tours or customize outings with a chauffeured car: "City Tour" (6 hrs) covers the National Monument, Pancasila Monument, Beautiful Indonesia in Miniature Park, and Museum Indonesia; "Indocultural Tour" (5 hrs) visits the Central Museum, Old Batavia, the Jakarta Museum, and a batik factory; "Beautiful Indonesia Tour" (3–4 hrs) takes you by air-conditioned bus through the Beautiful Indonesia in Miniature Park; and "Jakarta by Night" (5 hrs) includes dinner, a dance performance, and a visit to a nightclub. Tours beyond Jakarta include the following: a nine-hour trip to Pelabuhanratu, a former fishing village that's now a resort; an eight-hour tour to the safari park at Bogor and the Botanical Gardens, 48 km (30 mi) south of Jakarta at a cool 600 ft above sea level, and to the Puncak Mountain Resort; and a two-day tour into the highlands to visit Bandung and its volcano, with stops at Bogor and Puncak.

Gray Line (✉ Jl. Hayam Wunuk 3–P, ☎ 021/639–0008) covers most of Jakarta and its surrounding attractions. If you show up at **Jakarta City Tourist Center** (✉ Lapangan Binteng, Bantung Square, ☎ no phone), which opens at 8 AM, you can join any of the tours operating that day, usually at a discounted rate.

Travel agencies arrange transportation, conduct guided tours, and can often secure hotel reservations more cheaply than you could yourself. **Natourin** (✉ 18 Buncit Raya, Jakarta 12790, ☎ 021/799–7886) has extensive facilities and contacts throughout Indonesia. Although the following agents specialize in train travel, they can also help you with other travel needs: **Carnation** (✉ Jl. Menteng Raya 24, ☎ 021/384–4027 or 021/386–5728), **P. T. Bhayangkara** (✉ Jl. Kebon Sirih 23, ☎ 021/327387), and **Iwata Nusantara** (✉ Jl. Riau 19, ☎ 021/314–8957).

Large government-owned travel agencies with branch offices at most Indonesian tourist destinations include the following: **Nitour** (✉ Duta Merlin, Jl. Gajah Mada 3–5, ☎ 021/346346); **Satriavi** (✉ Jl. Prapatan 32, ☎ 021/380–3944); and **Pacto Ltd. Tours and Travel** (✉ Jl. Surabaya 8, ☎ 021/332634), the Indonesian representative of American Express.

VISITOR INFORMATION

The comprehensive *Falk City Map of Jakarta* is available at bookstores for Rp 9,200. The *Jakarta Program,* available at most hotel newsstands for Rp 4,000, is a monthly magazine listing attractions and events.

The **City Visitor Information Center** (✉ Jakarta Theatre Building, Jl. M.
H. Thamrin 9, ☎ 021/354094) has brochures, maps, and information
on bus and train schedules to other Java destinations. The center is open
Monday–Thursday 8–3, Friday 8–11:30 AM, and Saturday 8–2.

The **Indonesian tourist office** (✉ Jl. K. H. Abdurrohim 1, at Dimas Pari-
wisata, Kuningan Barat, ☎ 021/525–1316) is charged with dispens-
ing information on destinations across the archipelago, but it's difficult
to find and the assistance given is minimal.

West Java

Java's western province has coastline, mountains, and fertile valleys
that are intensively farmed. The province also has the impressive Ujung
Kulon National Park, which is set on a peninsula in the island's southwestern corner. Just north of the park is Pulau Krakatau, an active island volcano. There are wild areas in the southeast corner, too, around
the resort town of Pangandaran. Cosmopolitan Bandung, Indonesia's
third-largest city, has a few reminders of the days when the Dutch flocked
here to escape Jakarta's sweltering heat.

Most of the people in West Java are Sundanese and have their own language and cuisine (for a long time, the region was known as Sunda).
The people are friendly and inquisitive; all also speak Bahasa Indonesia, Indonesia's national language, and many speak some English.

The Thousand Islands

🔟 *16 km–32 km (10 mi–20 mi) northwest of Jakarta; an hour or two
by boat.*

In the Java Sea, northwest of Jakarta, are the little Thousand Islands—
really a misnomer, because there are only 113 of them. Their white-sand
beaches, lined with coconut palms, offer a retreat from the heat and
bustle of the capital. If the concrete and noise of Jakarta are getting to
you, consider a day trip to **Pulau Seribu** (*pulau* means island) to walk
on the sands in a sea breeze. You can hire a motorboat from the **Marina Jaya Ancol** (✉ Jakarta, ☎ 021/681512), or take a **hovercraft** (✉
the port is at Jl. Donggala 26A, Tanjun Priok, Jakarta, ☎ 021/325608).

Lodging

Several islands have rustic getaways; accommodations are available on
Pulau Putri (021/828–1093), **Pulau Matahari** (021/380–0521), **Pulau
Bidadari** (021/680048), and **Pulau Laki** (021/314–4885). Contact each
island's Jakarta office (listed above) to make reservations and to arrange transport to the island. Room rates are usually quoted as all-inclusive packages that include food and transport.

$$$ 🏨 **Kotok Island Resort.** Set on 42 unspoiled acres of coconut groves and
tropical foliage, this resort owns all but the island's very eastern tip, which
belongs to a private Japanese club. In this back-to-nature environment,
the accommodations are rustic, the plumbing primitive. The 22 bun-
galows have bamboo walls, basic bamboo furniture, and tiled baths with
showers. Eight units are air-conditioned, but thanks to the sea breezes,
the rest are comfortable with just overhead fans. The dining room—an
open-air pavilion over the water—serves well-prepared Indonesian spe-
cialties. Licensed instructors give scuba-diving courses, and there's good
snorkeling. The resort provides a launch service from Jakarta; the run
takes 90 minutes. ✉ *Reservation office: Duta Merlin Shopping Arcade,
3rd floor, Jl. Gajah Mada 3–5, Jakarta, ☎ 021/634–2948, FAX 021/633–
6120. 22 rooms. Restaurant, bar, beach, dive shop, snorkeling. No credit
cards, unless you book through a travel agent.*

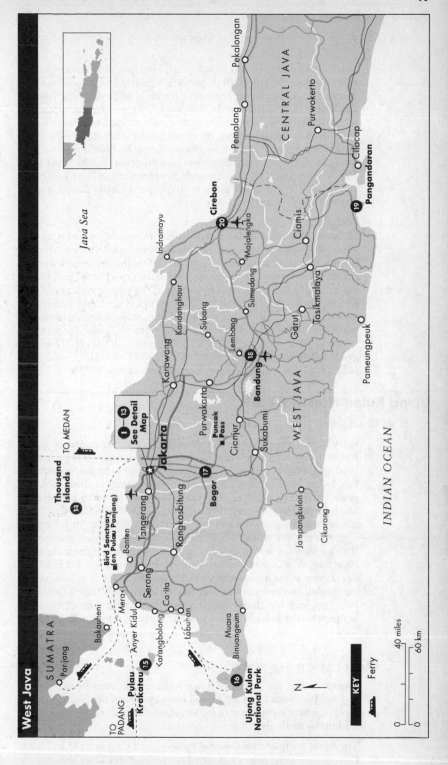

West Java

SUMATRA

TO MEDAN

TO PADANG

Java Sea

INDIAN OCEAN

CENTRAL JAVA

WEST JAVA

Parjang

Bakauheni

Merak

Anyer Kidul

Karangbolong

Carita

Labuhan

Serang

Banten

Tangerang

Rangkasbitung

Pulau Krakatau

Ujong Kulon National Park

Muara Binuangeum

Bird Sanctuary (on Pulau Panjang)

Thousand Islands

Jakarta

See Detail Map

Bogor

Puncak Pass

Cianjur

Sukabumi

Purwakarta

Karawang

Kandanghaur

Subang

Lembang

Sumedang

Majalengka

Indramayu

Cirebon

Bandung

Garut

Tasikmalaya

Ciamis

Pameungpeuk

Jampangkulon

Cikarang

Pemalang

Pekalongan

Purwokerto

Cilacap

Pangandaran

① — ⑬

⑭

⑮

⑯

⑰

⑱

⑲

⑳

KEY

⚓ Ferry

N

40 miles

60 km

Pulau Krakatau

⑮ *2 to 4 hours by boat from Carita Beach, which is 150 km (95 mi) south-west of Jakarta.*

You'll need to make an overnight trip to see the famous Krakatau (Krakatoa) Island, in the Sunda Strait between Sumatra and Java. The active volcano, Anak Krakatau, is actually the child of Krakatau, a volcano that erupted in 1883, killing 36,000 people and creating marvelous sunsets around the world for the next two years. Anak Krakatau emerged from the sea between three other islands by early 1928—45 years after its predecessor's eruption. (Note: Access by boat is an on-again, off-again venture as the volcano has been erupting intermittently since 1993. If you do go, take care; people have been injured by flying rocks and debris.) The popular place to overnight is **Carita Beach,** a quiet resort that's pleasant in its own right.

Lodging

$$ 🏨 **Carita Krakatau Beach Hotel.** There are two advantages to this hotel: air-conditioned buses leave daily from its reservation office in Jakarta, and the hotel arranges trips (including the two-hour sea crossing) to the volcano. The rooms are modest, but most of the time you're out on the beach or taking refreshment at the terrace restaurant. The historic Krakatau photos and news clippings in the lobby breezeway, as well as the seaside vistas of the volcano, make a visit here worthwhile even if you don't plan to spend the night. ⊠ *Carita Beach; reservations office at Hotel Wisata International, Jl. M. H. Thamrin, ground-floor arcade, Jakarta,* ☎ *0254/21043 or 021/314–0252 in Jakarta. 45 rooms. Restaurant, beach, waterskiing. MC, V.*

Ujung Kulon National Park

★ ⑯ *200 km (124 mi) southwest of Jakarta.*

Forty or so endangered Javan rhinos still hide in the jungles of Ujung Kulon National Park, a World Heritage Site with nearly 800 square km (340 square mi) of peninsular and island wilderness that few people venture to see. It's a great place to trek (the snorkeling is good, too), but getting here is tough; the easiest way is by boat. If you're adventurous and have the time (at least two or three days, though four days or more is best) and the gear, you can arrange a tour with guide in Jakarta or Carita or go on your own. Note that you'll need to buy supplies before setting out; there are no facilities in the park, although there are basic guest bungalows, a few small stores, and a new World Wildlife Fund visitors center at the main entrance in Taman Jaya. Hotels in Jakarta can recommend tour operators (☞ *also* Tour Operators *in* West Java Essentials, *below*); a four-day, three-night trek usually costs between $200–$300 per person. You can also hire a guide at the park office in Taman Jaya.

Bogor

⑰ *60 km (36 mi) south of Jakarta.*

The sprawling, smoky city of Bogor hides several attractions. Drop in at Jalan Pancasan 17 to see a **gong foundry,** one of the few remaining on Java, where instruments of the gamelan orchestra are still made using traditional methods.

The white-porticoed **Presidential Palace**—first built in 1745 by Dutch Governor General Gustav Willen Baron Van Imhoft and then rebuilt in 1856 after being destroyed by an earthquake—has a fine collection of paintings and sculptures. The palace is on the west side of Bogor's main attraction, the **Kebun Raya Bogor** (Botanical Gardens) founded in 1817 by the first English governor-general of Indonesia, maintained by the Dutch, and adopted by Sukarno. The 275-acre garden has 15,000 species of plants, hundreds of trees, an herbarium, cactus gardens, and ponds with enormous water lilies. The monument in the park is of Olivia Raffles, first wife of Sir Stanford Raffles, who died here at the Bogor Palace. Guides are available at Rp 6,000 an hour. ☒ *Admission.* ⊘ *Daily 9–5.*

Lodging

$$$ ⊞ **Novotel Bogor.** Bogor's best hotel looks like an alpine resort, albeit one that's surrounded by banana trees. The grounds are so lush that you can't help but think that the city's beautiful botanical garden provided inspiration. Rooms are spacious, and you can lounge by the pool or play golf or tennis. The hotel's only drawback is its location 4 km (3 mi) from town. ☒ *Golf Estat Gogor Raya, 16710,* ☎ *251/271555 or 800/2214542 in the U.S.,* ☒ *251/271333. 180 rooms. Restaurant, pool, 18-hole golf course, 2 tennis courts, health club, jogging, business services. AE, DC, MC, V.*

En Route The road from Bogor to Bandung winds through tea plantations and rain forests, past waterfalls and lakes. This is the Puncak region, where on clear days you'll get views of the Gede, Pangrango, and Salak mountains. Just over the summit of Puncak Pass is the **Puncak Pass Hotel,** a famous stop for travelers that serves excellent afternoon teas and vistas.

Bandung

⓲ *187 km (120 mi) southeast of Jakarta, 127 km (84 mi) southeast of Bogor.*

Situated on a plateau at 2,500 ft and shadowed by majestic volcanoes, Bandung was transformed into a Dutch oasis at the turn of the last century. European architects put up Art Deco buildings, café society copied fashions from Paris and Amsterdam, and Bandung became Indonesia's cultural and intellectual heart. There was even speculation that the capital might be transferred from steamy Jakarta to this mountain-fresh hill town.

The city's status waned after World War II. With independence, the political focus shifted to the tightly centralized government in Jakarta, and the Sundanese reasserted their own complex language and customs. Today, Bandung is an appealing mix of European and Asian cultures. With overcrowding burdening Jakarta's infrastructure, Bandung has, in recent years, attracted high-tech businesses with its intellectual environment and its 13 universities, including the prestigious Institute Teknologi Bandung. Although brochures exaggerate the city's attractions, it does have a pleasant climate—warm days and cold nights—and it's small and pedestrian-friendly enough to cover on foot.

In the days when Bandung called itself the "Parijs van Java," **Jalan Braga** was the "Rue St. Honoré." In the last few years the city made a successful attempt to rejuvenate the area, and it's once again a nice place to walk. There aren't many remnants of Bandung's glory days, but the classic, Art Deco **Savoy Homann Hotel** (☞ *also* Lodging, *below*) has been restored at great pains by its current owners. Near the Savoy hotel on Jalan Asia-Africa is the **Freedom Building** (Gedung Merdeka), where in 1955 Chou En-lai, Ho Chi Minh, Nehru, Nasser, and U Nu attended the famous Asia-Africa Conference of nonaligned nations.

Walking north back past the Savoy Homann, you'll reach the *alun-alun* (town square), the heart of Bandung. Just off the square is **Market Street,** which is worth a stroll at night, when book and magazine sellers take over one side and food stalls popular with locals take over the other. If you continue north along Jalan Braga you'll pass several cafés that offer great cakes and coffee for a break. If you're looking for evening entertainment, karaoke bars have taken over some of the side streets in this area.

At the **Geological Museum** (✉ Jl. Diponegoro), which is open daily 9– 5 and is free, you'll find replicas of the fossils of Java Man (*Homo erectus*; a predecessor of Homo sapiens). North of the Geological Museum is the **Institut Teknologi Bandung,** designed by Maclaine Pont, a proponent of the Indo-European integrated style, exemplified here by the upturned, Minangkabau-style roofs; beyond the institute are the Dago Tea House and a waterfall with a splendid panorama of the city.

The hills surrounding Bandung are known as Parahyangan (Abode of the Gods) and are sacred to the Sundanese. The first stop on a tour of this area is usually the pleasant hill town of Lembang, just less than 10 km (6 mi) north of Bandung. The **Tangkuban Perahu Nature Reserve,** 10 km (6 mi) north of Lembang, contains Indonesia's only active volcano whose rim is accessible by car. From the preserve's entrance, the narrow road winds 4 km (2½ mi) to the crater's edge. The souvenir stands and hawkers are a nuisance, but the crater, boiling and seething with sulfurous steam, is dramatic. Several kilometers southeast of the crater are the **Crater Hot Springs,** with public baths where you can soothe your soul.

Dining and Lodging

$$$ ✕ **Braga Permai.** You can sit at tables on a streetside patio and order from the large selection of Indonesian and Western dishes that make this restaurant popular with both locals and tourists. It's a good place for lunch, dinner, or a break from a walk along Jalan Braga (the cakes are great). At night a piano player adds to the ambiance. ✉ *Jl. Braga 58,* ☎ *022/420–1831. AE, DC, MC, V.*

$$ ✕ **Sari Sunda.** This Sundanese restaurant first opened in the early 1990s and proved so successful with locals that now there are three branches. This branch is in a wooden building with bamboo furniture and lots of plants—very relaxing. The Sundanese dishes are spicy but not spicy enough to stun your taste buds. You can't go wrong with the fried fish covered in sweet-spicy topping or the chicken steamed in bamboo. The fruit drinks are also highly recommended. ✉ *Jl. Lengkong Sesar 77,* ☎ *022/438125. AE, DC, MC, V.*

$ ✕ **Naripan Steak.** A 10-minute walk off Jalan Braga will bring you to this open-to-the-street, meat-lovers grill. The dining room, with its basic tables and hard-back chairs, is sparse, but the food is tops. The satay beef and chicken are real treats. ✉ *Jl. Naripan 30,* ☎ *022/426–4453. No credit cards.*

$$ 🏨 **Savoy Homann.** It's neither the priciest nor the most up-to-date hotel ★   in town, but the Savoy Homann is loaded with character. Built in the 1880s, it acquired its Art Deco details in 1930. In the evening, guests gather at the bar in the central courtyard to listen to a band. Superior rooms are the size of small suites; most have sitting areas and look onto either the street (windows are double-glazed) or the courtyard. The English-speaking staff is very friendly. ✉ *Jl. Asia-Afrika 112, 40261,* ☎ *022/250–0303,* 🇫🇦🇽 *022/250–0301. 153 rooms. Restaurant, bar, coffee shop. AE, DC, MC, V.*

$$ 🏨 **Sheraton Inn.** Though this hotel is in a residential neighborhood 15 minutes by taxi from downtown, many travelers are drawn by its modern facilities, its well-trained staff, and its tranquility. The best rooms overlook the circular courtyard and its pool. Dining is a relaxed affair, either on the terrace by the pool or inside with air-conditioning.

The Sheraton-style architecture and ambience are more American than Indonesian. ✉ *Jl. Ir. H. Juanda 390 (Box 6530), 40065,* ☎ *022/210303, 800/325–3535 in the U.S.,* ᖴᐱᕽ *022/210301. 111 rooms. Restaurant, pool, 2 tennis courts, business services. AE, DC, MC, V.*

$ 🏨 **Lembang Grand Hotel.** Built in 1926 and used by the Dutch as a hill resort, the Grand still stands and offers simple accommodation just north of Bandung. ✉ *Jl. Raya Lembang 228, Lembang,* ☎ *022/82393. 26 rooms. Pool, 2 tennis courts. MC, V.*

Outdoor Activities and Sports

In many villages near Bandung, Sunday morning is the time for the weekly *adu domba* (ram fights). Facing off two at a time, prize rams bang, crash, and lock horns until one contestant decides that enough is enough and scampers off. It's as much a social event as a serious sport (though the wagerers take it seriously); don't miss it if you're around on a weekend.

Pangandaran

★ ⑲ *210 km (130 mi) southeast of Bandung, 370 km (230 mi) southeast of Jakarta.*

Pangandaran, a beach resort on a peninsula about halfway between Bandung and Yogyakarta, is popular with Bandung residents on weekends. If possible, visit during the week when you share it only with the local fisherfolk. The surf from the Indian Ocean pounds the black sandy beaches and can be dangerous. Still, there are sections protected by the bulb at the end of the peninsula—great places to splash about in calmer waters.

Though the peninsula is small enough to see on foot, there are plenty of becaks if you get tired. You might take one to the entrance of the small national park, passing rows of booths that sell mostly clothing along the way. The staff at your hotel can recommend a guide who's familiar with the park's jungled terrain; they can also arrange longer trips to Green Canyon, a larger and more spectacular wilderness area a couple hours away (☞ *also* Tour Operators *in* West Java Essentials, *below*).

Dining and Lodging

$$ ✕ **Bunga Laut Restaurant.** Though this small restaurant in a bunga-low doesn't look like much, it has great Sundanese food—a bit spicy but yummy. ✉ *Jl. Bulak Laut 2,* ☎ *no phone. No credit cards.*

$ ✕ **Fish Market.** If you hanker for seafood, check out the collection of
★ open-air restaurants here. Good choices include **Ditha**, in a bamboo building next to the road, and **Risma**, a concrete structure (its walls stop at waist level) next to the gravel parking area. At both you get to choose your fish and then have it cooked however you want. ✉ *Jl. Pantai Timur, about halfway up the peninsula,* ☎ *no phone. No credit cards.*

$$$ 🏨 **Pantai Indah Timur.** This resort and its sister property, **Pantai Indah Barat** (on the peninsula's west side), are the most upscale in the region. The grounds at both are very well kept, with lots of trees and brick footpaths. The wooden one- and two-story buildings fit in well with the environment. Rooms are spacious and comfortable though not lux-urious. ✉ *Jl. Kidang Pananjung 139,* ☎ *265/379004,* ᖴᐱᕽ *265/379327. 21 rooms, 2 suites, 7 bungalows. 2 restaurants, pool, 2 tennis courts. AE, DC, MC, V.*

$$ 🏨 **Adam's Home Stay.** The air-conditioned bungalows here are grouped near the pool and just a two-minute walk from the beach. There are also fan-cooled rooms in the old Dutch-era main house, which faces the ocean. The view and sound of the ocean from these rooms can't be beat, and the library-bookshop—which has English-language titles—

is just down the stairs next to the restaurant. You can have a cappuccino and stock up on reading material. ✉ *Jl. Pamugaran Bulak Laut, 46396,* ☎ *265/639164,* FAX *265/639164. 9 rooms, 3 bungalows. Restaurant, bar, pool, bicycles, library. MC (sometimes).*

Cirebon

Ⓩ *130 km (81 mi) northeast of Bandung, 250 km (155 mi) southeast of Jakarta.*

Cirebon is situated on a mangrove coast where, unfortunately, there are no beaches and few remaining mangroves. Over the centuries this port town has been influenced by many cultures; today it's something of a commercial crossroads and, as such, is a little wealthier than most Indonesian cities. The people here are friendly, and the distances between sights are manageable on foot. There are also plenty of fancy, painted becaks; you can catch a ride to almost anywhere in town for less than a dollar. City Hall, near the train station, is an Art Deco building right out of old Los Angeles or Miami. Cirebon also has a couple of cinemas that show slightly dated Hollywood movies, so, if you missed something in the past year or two, this could be your chance to catch up.

Start your tour in the south of the city at the **Kraton Kesepuhan,** a walled palace built in 1529 and set on 30 acres of peaceful grounds. The 13th generation of sultans still lives in a section that's closed to the public. You can still get a look inside by visiting the museum. The ornate carriage (circa 1549) on display is alone worth the visit. Just north of here is **Mesjid Agung,** one of Java's oldest and most interesting mosques—note its tiered roof. From the mosque, it's a few minutes' walk north along Jalan Lemah Wungkuk to the **Kraton Kanoman,** a palace with tranquil grounds and a huge banyan tree in its courtyard. A few minutes up the road from here is the **Vihara Dewi Welasasih,** a colorful temple that's a testament to the Chinese influence in the city. On the coast near the temple there's an odd little **amusement park** with a few rides and a rickety old boardwalk out over the water.

Dining and Lodging

$$ ✕ **Helena.** Seafood tops the menu at this big, air-conditioned, dining hall; if you want it spicy the chef will cook it Thai style. You'll also find a wide selection of Indonesian rice and chicken dishes. ✉ *Jl. Ade Irma Suryani Nasution,* ☎ *231/201882. No credit cards.*

$$ ✕ **Jumbo Restaurant and Sea Food.** This restaurant in the heart of Cirebon has an extensive seafood menu as well as other chicken and meat dishes. The dark-wood dining room is quite comfortable. ✉ *Jl. Siliwangi 191,* ☎ *231/203606. MC, V.*

$$$ ▣ **Bentani.** Here you'll find all the amenities of a world-class hotel, but with more homegrown, personal service. Guest rooms are comfortable and spacious, and there are several on-site nightlife options, including karaoke. ✉ *Jl. Siliwangi 69, 45121,* ☎ *231/207526,* FAX *231/207527. 64 rooms, 20 suites. 2 restaurants, 2 bars, pool, sauna, health club, dance club. AE, MC, V.*

$$–$$$ ▣ **Hotel Prima.** This hotel opened in 1991 across from the city hall. The rooms are comfortable, and the staff is friendly. ✉ *Jl. Siliwangi 107, 45124,* ☎ *231/205411,* FAX *231/205407. 88 rooms, 8 suites. Restaurant, bar, pool, 2 tennis courts. AE, MC, V.*

$$ ▣ **Hotel Sidodadi.** Air-conditioning, clean rooms, and complimentary breakfast are all part of the package at this moderately priced establishment in in Cirebon's hotel row. ✉ *Jl. Siliwangi 72,* ☎ *231/202305,* FAX *231/204821. 50 rooms. Restaurant. MC, V.*

West Java Essentials

Arriving and Departing

BY AIRPLANE

Jakarta is the hub for flights to points in West Java (☞ By Airplane under Arriving and Departing *in* Jakarta Essentials, *above*). There has been talk of making Bandung more of a gateway, but with the economic turmoil of the late 1990s, it may be a while till anything gets off the ground (so to speak).

BY BOAT

Boat travel between Jakarta and Sumatra is an option, albeit a slow one. The KM *Lawit,* and KM *Kerinci* make a 40-hour trip between Jakarta and Padang about every two weeks. There are also ferries every hour between Merak (110 km/68 mi west of Jakarta) to Bakauheni on the southern tip of Sumatra.

BY TRAIN

The trip to Bandung from Yogyakarta is eight hours, and there are three or more trains a day. The night train has *ekeskutif* (first-class) compartments with reclining seats, air-conditioning, and blankets. The day train lacks these amenities but offers *biznis* (business) class, with padded seats and windows that you can open.

Getting Around

BY AIRPLANE

There are flights to Bandung's Husein Sastranegara airport from Jakarta with **Merpati** and **Garuda** (⊠ Jl. Asia Afrika 73, ☎ 022/441226), which share an office across from the Savoy Homann in Bandung.

BY BOAT

Each of the Thousands Islands resorts has its own boat transport; contact them directly to make arrangements. Boats for Pulau Krakatau leave Carita Beach at around 8 AM; the trip takes 2½ hours by speedboat (Rp 100,000), four hours on a slower boat (about Rp 40,000). It's best to visit with a reputable tour operator, and you can make arrangements for this in Jakarta or Carita. Don't venture out if the waters are rough, even though there are plenty of boatmen in Carita who will offer to take you despite high seas (these are the people to avoid). Note also that sometimes you won't be able to visit Pulau Krakatau owing to volcanic activity.

Boats to Ujung Kulon National Park leave from Labuan, just south of Carita. You can take the *Wanawisata,* which costs about Rp 324,000 one way and takes about six hours. (You'll have to ask about its schedule, which is ever-changing). Alternatively, you can charter a boat (about Rp 400,000) that can carry as many as 20 people. Another option, and probably the best one, is to organize a three- or four-day tour with a travel agent in Carita (ask your hotel staff for recommendations).

BY BUS

The road from Jakarta to Bandung offers spectacular views, and many minibuses make the trip each day—though fretful passengers may spend more time watching the next curve than the scenery. The larger air-conditioned buses are a better bet. You can travel from Jakarta to Carita Beach by public bus in about three hours, but the minivans of **P. J. Krakatau** (⊠ Ujung Kulon Tours, Hotel Wisata International, Jakarta, ☎ 021/314–0252) are a lot more comfortable.

BY CAR

You can rent a car and drive yourself, but unless you know the language and the country it's not recommended. Its best to hire a car with a driver to take you from major hubs to surrounding sights. Such arrangements don't cost very much, and they leave you free to watch the scenery.

There are numerous trains between Jakarta's Gambir Station and Bogor each day (it's almost like a commuter service as many people live along the hour-long route). Four express trains make the four- to six-hour trip from Gambir to Cirebon daily. Trains between Surabaya and Jakarta also pass through Cirebon. The trip from Jakarta to Bandung—approximately three hours from Gambir Station, with nine departures daily—is quite scenic: the train travels through flat rice lands before climbing mountains along a curving track and over trestle bridges built by the Dutch. Rates are Rp 20,000 for executive class with air-conditioning and reclining seats, RP 7,000 for business class with open windows and padded seats, and *really* cheap for third class, in which case you get what you pay for.

Contacts and Resources

EMERGENCIES
Hospital: Adventist Hospital (✉ Jl. Cihampelas 161, Bandung, ☎ 022/234-386).

ENGLISH-LANGUAGE BOOKSTORES
In central Bandung there are several book shops along Jalan Braga.

TOUR OPERATORS
The **Bandung City Tour** (☎ 022/520–4650) is a half-day bus trip to Bandung's major sites. Contact the **Indonesian Guide Association** (✉ Jl. Kidang Pananjung 21, Pangandaran, ☎ 265/639296) to arrange for treks to wilderness areas around Pangandaran. Sudrajad Pujo Adi at **Kirana Wisata** (✉ Wisata International Hotel, Jl. M. H. Thamrin 48, ☎ 021/390–8008) has been taking visitors to Ujung Kulon National Park since 1990.

VISITOR INFORMATION
Bandung Tourist Information Office (✉ Alun-alun, Jl. Asia Afrika, ☎ n phone). **Bogor Tourist Information Office** (✉ Jl. Merak 1, ☎ 251/ 325701)). **West Java Provincial Tourist Office** (✉ Jl. Soekarno-Hatta, Km 11, Bandung, ☎ 022/780–5739).

Central and East Java

Central Java—and the special province of Yogyajakarta within its borders—is the cultural heart of Indonesia. The region nurtured some of the country's great Indian kingdoms in the 8th and 9th centuries, including the Buddhist Sailendras, who built the Borobudur temple, and the Hindu Sanjayans, who made Prambanan their religious center. Today visitors generally use Yogyakarta as a base for seeing these temples. However, if you prefer less commercialism and tourist hustling, the ancient city of Solo, 64 km (40 mi) to the east, is a good bet. From this quiet city you can easily drive out to Sukuh Temple and to Sangiran, the site where Java Man was discovered.

Five hours northeast of Yogyakarta is Surabaya, a good base from which to explore East Java, a free-spirited province ideally suited to adventurous, unorthodox travelers. It has three regions; the north coast, including Madura Island; the Brantas River basin; and the volcanoes that dominate the south. Mt. Bromo, an active volcano from whose rim you can peer down into nature's cauldron, is a provincial highlight.

Central and East Java

BALI
Gilimanuk
Ketapang
Banyuwangi
Bondowoso
Jember
Situbondo
Lumajang
Probolinggo
Pasuruan
Mt. Bromo (Gunung Bromo) 32
Surabaya 31
Gresik
Bangkalan
MADURA ISLAND
Sumenep
Java Sea
Lamongan
Tuban
Mojokerto
Jombang
Malang
Kertosono
Kediri
Solo
Bojonegoro
Lasem
Cepu
Madiun
Tulungagung
EAST JAVA
Ponorogo
Trenggalek
Rembang
Kudus
Sangiran 29
28 Suku Temple
30
Semarang
Salatiga
Solo (Surakarta)
Klaten
Prambanan Temple Complex
27
Jepara
Temanggung
Parangtritis
Kalasan
Kota Gede
Ambarawa
Yogyakarta 26
Wonosobo
Wates
CENTRAL JAVA
Dieng Plateau Reserve
Borobudur Temple
Kendal

INDIAN OCEAN

See Detail Map 21 — 25

KEY
Ferry

0 — 40 miles
0 — 60 km

N

Yogyakarta

㉑–㉕ *618 km (371 mi) southeast of Jakarta, 431 km (251 mi) southeast of Bandung.*

Every Indonesian has a soft spot for Yogyakarta, or Yogya (pronounced *joeg-jakarta* or *joeg-ja*), a city of some 300,000 on a fertile plain in the shadow of three volcanoes. Students from Yogya's Gajah Mada University account for some 20% of the city's population, and dance and choreography schools, wayang troupes, and poetry workshops make it an artist's mecca. Every evening, classical drama and dance performances are staged somewhere in the city. Leading Indonesian painters and sculptors display their work in numerous galleries, and crafts shopping is a major activity. The batik here and in Solo (☞ *below*) is said to be superior even to that found on Bali.

Exploring Yogyakarta

Yogya sprawls. Unless you stay at the Garuda (☞ Lodging, *below*) or one of the less expensive city hotels, chances are you'll be a few miles from Jalan Malioboro, the main thoroughfare.

SIGHTS TO SEE

㉕ **Affandi Museum.** Out toward the airport, about 8 km (5 mi) southeast of Yogya, is the home and studio of Indonesia's best-known painter, Affandi (1907–90). A permanent collection of his works, along with paintings by young artists, is exhibited in an oval, domed extension to the traditional paddy-field house. ⊠ *Jl. Laksda, Adisucipto 67,* ☎ *no phone.* ⊠ *Free.* ☉ *Daily 9–3.*

㉔ **Diponegoro Monument.** This is the reconstructed residence of Prince Diponegoro, who rebelled against the Dutch and led a bloody guerrilla battle in the Java War (1825–30). The house is now a museum, displaying the prince's krises, lances, and other revered possessions. ⊠ *Tegalrejo (4 km/2½ mi west of Yogyakarta),* ☎ *0274/563068.* ⊠ *Donation appreciated.* ☉ *Open by appointment only.*

Jalan Malioboro. This is where the action is, day and night. It's the main shopping street, not only for established stores but also for sidewalk vendors. They set up cardboard stands that sell handicrafts until about 9 PM, then convert to food stalls serving Yogya's specialties: nasi gudeg (rice with jackfruit in coconut milk) and ayam goreng (marinated fried chicken). Malioboro is a fascinating street; arrive by 8 PM, and you can catch both the shops and the food. Haggle for prices over items on the street or look for good deals at the indoor market, **Pasar Beringharjo,** at the top of the street; it's worth visiting just to see the stacked merchandise—everything from jeans to poultry.

★ ㉑ **Kraton.** At the southern end of Malioboro stands the Kraton, or Sultan's Palace. The large, grassy square in front of it—a walled city within the city—is the **alun-alun,** where the townspeople formerly gathered to trade, gossip, and hear the latest palace news. The Yogya Kraton has special significance to Indonesians as the bastion against Dutch colonialism. During the War of Independence (1945–49), Yogya's Sultan Hamengku Buwono allowed the Indonesian freedom fighters—including guerrilla commander Suharto—to use the Kraton as a base. Built in 1756, it's a vast complex of pavilions and buildings, part of which—strictly off-limits to the public—is home to the present sultan. The complex is protected by 400 guards (in blue shirts) and maintained by 1,000 servants (in red shirts).

At the center of the white, green-trimmed palace is the **Bengsal Kengono** (Golden Pavilion), an open hall with carved teak columns and a black-and-gold interior, where weddings, cremations, and coronations

Yogyakarta

KEY

AE American Express Office
— Rail Lines
i Tourist Office

Winongo River
Jl. Magalang
Buntung River
Jl. A.M. Sangaji
Jl. C. Simanjuntak
Jl. Colombo
Jl. Kyai Mojo
Jl. Diponegoro
Hotel Phoenix
Jl. Jend. Sudirman
Jl. Solo
25
TO AIRPORT AND AMBARRUKMO PALACE HOTEL
JETIS
Garuda Airlines
Jl. Mangkubumi
Jl. Dr. Wahidin
Jl. Pengok
24
Railway Station
AE
Jl. Atmo
Sukarto
Jl. Lempuyangan
Jl. Kom. Pol Bambang Suprato
Jl. H.O.S. Cokroaminoto
Jl. Let. Jend. Suprapto
Garuda Hotel
Jl. Pringgokusuman
Jl. Kemetiran anlor
Sosrowijayan
Jl. Kemetiran Kidul
Jl. Dagan
Jl. Mataram
DANU REJAN
Jl. Mas Suharto
Jl. Macanan
Jl. Dr. Sutomo
GEDONG TENGEN
Jl. A.I.P.K.S. Tubun
Jl. Malioboro
Mutiara Hotel
i
PAKUALAMAN
Jl. Bausaran
Jl. Cayam
NGAMPILAN
Jl. Jend. A. Yami
Melia Hotel
Jl. Laksamana R.E. Martadinata
Jl. K.H. Ahmad Dahlan
Jl. P. Senopati
Jl. Sultan Agung
Jl. Kusumanegara
Jl. Batikan
Winongo River
Jl. K.H. Wakhidhasyim
Jl. H. Agus Salim
Jl. Kauman
22
North Palace Sq.
Jl. Dwikora
GONDOMANAN
Jl. Taman Siswa
21
Jl. Palawijan
Jl. Palawijan
Jl. Let. Jend. S. Parman
23
KRATON
South Palace Sq.
Jl. Brig. Jend. Katamso
Cade River
MERGANGSAN
Jl. Sugeng Jeroni
Jl. Let. Jend. Haryono M.T.
Jl. May. Jend. Sutoyo
Jl. Kol. Sugiyono
Jl. Menteri Supeno
N
Agastya Art Institute
Jl. Bantul
MANTRIJERON
Jl. Suryodiningratan
Jl. May. Jend. Panjaitan
Jl. Tirtodipuran
Jl. Parangtritis
Jl. Prawirotaman
Jl. Sisingamangaraja
Batik Plentong

0   500 yards
0   500 meters

Affandi Muscum **25**
Diponegoro Monument, **24**
Kraton, **21**
Sono Budoyo Museum, **22**
Taman Sari, **23**

are held. The complex includes a gallery that displays a collection of gamelan instruments. Try to time your visit to catch the Sunday classical dance rehearsal (10:30 and noon, except during Ramadan). In another pavilion is a collection of sedan chairs. The last one was used in 1877; now a Rolls-Royce transports the sultan on ceremonial occasions. ☎ *No phone.* ⊠ *Admission.* ⊙ *Sun.–Thurs. 8:30 AM–1 PM, Fri.–Sat. 8:30 –11:30 AM.*

㉒ **Sono Budoyo Museum.** Of Yogya's several museums, the most interesting and well-maintained is the Sono Budoyo Museum, on the square in front of the Kraton. Inside this traditional Javanese-style building is a collection of crafts and batiks from Java and Bali. Its archaeological treasures include a small gold Buddha, and the display of wayang golek, the wood puppets used in Muslim theater, is charming. ☎ *0274/ 562775.* ⊠ *Admission.* ⊙ *Tues.–Thurs. 8 AM–1 PM, Fri. and Sun. 8– 11 AM, Sat. 8–noon.*

㉓ **Taman Sari.** Behind the Kraton is the recreational Water Palace constructed by the same sultan who built the main palace. A large artificial lake, sunken bathing pools, underground passageways, and towers where gamelan orchestras serenaded the royal party were all part of this noble retreat. It was abandoned in the 18th century and fell into ruin; the restored sections give a sense of what the privileged enjoyed. Visit the ornate bathing pools used by the princesses, the underground mosque, and the tower from which the sultan watched his concubines lounge by the water. ☎ *No phone.* ⊠ *Admission.* ⊙ *Sun.–Thurs. 8 AM–1 PM, Fri. 8–11 AM.*

Dining

For Western food, you can dine at the major hotels. Many also offer a performance of segments from the *Ramayana,* charging an extra fee to see the show. The Indonesian fare at local restaurants is inexpensive and good.

$$ ✕ **Pesta Perak.** Smartly decorated with wrought-iron furniture and
★ a sultan-costumed maître d', Pesta Perak has excellent Javanese cuisine. Its rijsttafel includes satays, gudeg, and fish wrapped in banana leaves. An à la carte menu is also offered, but customers rarely choose this. A gamelan trio plays traditional music. Use a becak to get there, and have it wait for you; the fare from Jalan Malioboro, including waiting time, is less than Rp 4,000. ⊠ *Jl. Tentura Rakyat Mataran 8,* ☎ *0274/586255. MC, V.*

$$ ✕ **Pringsewu Garden Restaurant.** For relaxed alfresco dining at tables tucked between shrubs and trees, this restaurant is a delight. It offers some of the best fare in the region, served by a friendly staff attired in colorful batiks. The cooking is from West Sumatra. Try the ayam goreng *mantega* (with a butter sauce) or the ikan *mas baket* (grilled and served in ginger sauce). ⊠ *Jl. Magelang, Km 6,* ☎ *0274/564993. AE, DC, MC, V.*

$$ ✕ **Sintawang.** Though the tables are Formica, the restaurant is clean and offers a wide range of outstanding seafood, either cooked Javanese-style or grilled for Western palates. Try the udang *bakar* (marinated and grilled), udang *pais* (spiced and grilled in a banana leaf), or ikan *asam manis* (in a sweet-and-sour sauce). ⊠ *Jl. Magelang 9,* ☎ *0274/512901. Reservations not accepted. AE, DC.*

$ ✕ **Legian Garden Restaurant.** Choose a table next to the open windows at the edge of its terrace and watch fellow tourists *jalan jalan* (amble around) on the street below. Since the food is pretty average (primarily Western, with a few Indonesian alternatives), you may just want to stop by for a beer. ⊠ *Jl. Perwakilan 9 (off Jl. Malioboro), 1st floor,* ☎ *0274/564644. Reservations not accepted. No credit cards.*

$ ✕ **Ny Suharti.** It's worth the Rp 3,500 cab ride here from Malioboro
★ for the best fried chicken in Java. Forget charm and atmosphere and
the other items on the menu: you're here for a bird—boiled, marinated
in spices, then cooked up crisp. Order one for two people, with rice
on the side, and enjoy it out on the veranda. If you pay by credit card,
a 3% surcharge will be added to your bill. ✉ *Jl. Laksda Adisucipto,
Km 7,* ☎ *0274/515522. Reservations not accepted. MC, V.*

$ ✕ **Via Via.** This little restaurant sets the standard for backpacker fare
★ of cheap, simple cuisine. The small Indonesian and Western menu is
very good, as are the fruit shakes. This is also a good place to pick up
travel information. ✉ *Jl. Prawirotaman 24,* ☎ *no phone. No credit
cards.*

Lodging

In the 1990s, the number of hotels in Yogyakarta grew in leaps and
bounds, and the quality of existing establishments improved greatly.
Now there are accommodations to meet every pocketbook. The world-
class Amanjiwo, which opened in 1997 near the Borobudur Temple,
is one of the best hotels in Southeast Asia (with prices to match its reputation). In Yogya itself there are countless new medium-range hotels
as well as two blocks of guest houses in the southern part of town. Just
off Jalan Malioboro (across from the Garuda and two blocks from the
railway station), there's a good selection of small, budget hotels. With
so many lodging options, prices are competitive. There are discounts
of as much as 50% on offer—just be sure to ask about them.

$$$$ 🏨 **Amanjiwo.** Superlatives don't do this hotel justice. Designed by
★ American Ed Tuttle, who also created Bali's Amankila and the Amanpuri in Phuket, Thailand, it has 35 suites, each in its own building; 14
of them have private pools of a reasonable size, though there's also a
40-meter communal pool. Rooms are spacious and airy with king-size
beds; big, sliding-glass doors; outdoor sunken tubs; indoor showers;
and two dressing areas with closets. The grounds are at the base of
steep mountains, and there are views of Borobudur Temple from each
suite. You can continue to pay homage to the temple while swimming
laps in the pool, dining in the open-air restaurant, or relaxing in the
bar. To top it off, the hotel offers a sunrise tour of Borobudur (reservations are recommended). ✉ *About 6 km (4 mi) south of Borobudur
Temple and up a slight incline (Box 333, Magelang 56553),* ☎ *0293/
88333,* 𝖥𝖠𝖷 *0293/88355. 35 suites. Restaurant, bar, café, pool, massage,
bicycles, travel services. AE, DC, MC, V.*

$$$$ 🏨 **Ambarrukmo Palace.** Yogyakarta's premier in-town hotel is built
on the grounds of a former royal country retreat. Guest rooms are large,
decorated with light Indonesian-pattern fabrics and mahogany furniture, and full of amenities. The best rooms have balconies that overlook the gardens. This hotel is very popular with American tour groups,
and some rooms are little worn; if yours isn't up to standard, don't be
shy about asking for another. Every evening sees some type of entertainment, usually dances from the *Ramayana.* ✉ *Jl. Laksda Adisucipto,
55281,* ☎ *0274/566488,* 𝖥𝖠𝖷 *0274/563283. 266 rooms. 2 restaurants,
bar, minibars, pool, travel services. AE, DC, MC, V.*

$$$–$$$$ 🏨 **Melia.** Part of the Spanish-owned Sol Melia chain, this hotel is con-
veniently close to Jalan Malioboro. Some of its spacious, comfortable
rooms have doors that connect them with other rooms—perfect op-
tions for families or other groups. The hotel is built around a big pool
and garden area, where you can get a foot massage and take it really
easy. ✉ *Jl. Suryotomo 31, 55122,* ☎ *0274/589521,* 𝖥𝖠𝖷 *0274/588070.
295 rooms. Restaurant, coffee shop, pool, massage, health club, meet-
ing rooms, shops, travel services. AE, DC, MC, V.*

$$-$$$ ⊞ **Garuda.** The draws at this imposing old hotel are its central loca-
tion and its moderate prices. Standard guest rooms are plainly furnished
but do have all the latest conveniences, including a TV with a VCR
and a minibar. Ask for one of the newer rooms as the older ones have
a faint musty odor; note, however, that all rooms have suffered from
the steady stream of tour groups (there are black scrape marks on walls
and stains on carpets). The restaurants offer Indonesian and Western
food. ⊠ *Jl. Malioboro 60, 55271,* ☎ *0274/566353,* FAX *0274/563074.
235 rooms. 2 restaurants, coffee shop, minibars, pool, tennis court,
exercise room, business services, travel services. AE, DC, MC, V.*

$$ ⊞ **Radisson Yogya Plaza.** New in 1996, there is a pleasing fresh-
ness to this hotel, which calls itself a resort within a city. Guest rooms, most
with king-size beds, are modern and functional; the best for light and
peace are those overlooking the courtyard, where you'll find the pool
and a café and terrace off to the side. In the evenings, a local band plays—
sometimes a string quartet, sometimes a gamelan orchestra—and later
a performance of the *Ramayana* is given. Off the large atrium lobby,
which contains a comfortable sitting area, the dining room serves
Western and Indonesian fare and excellent buffet breakfasts. The
downside to this property is that it's more than a 30-minute walk to
downtown Yogyakarta; a shuttle bus does run back and forth, but dis-
tance precludes a spontaneous walk. ⊠ *Jl. Gejayan, Complex Columbo,
55821,* ☎ *0274/584222,* FAX *0274/584200. 120 rooms. 2 restaurants,
bar, pool, massage, 2 tennis courts, health club, business services,
meeting rooms. AE, DC, MC, V.*

$ ⊞ **Batik Palace Hotel.** For modest accommodations in the center of
Yogya, this hotel offers worn but clean rooms, each with twin beds,
table, and chair. The lobby, decorated with batiks and crafts, is a com-
fortable place to relax. ⊠ *Jl. Mangkubumi 46 (Box 115), 55153,* ☎
0274/562229, FAX *0274/562149. 38 rooms. Restaurant, pool. V.*

$ ⊞ **Data Guest House.** Along Jalan Prawirotaman to the south of the
Kraton are a score of inexpensive guest houses. Data is one of the best,
with clean rooms and reasonable prices, and its position down a nar-
row street makes it one of the quietest. The very basic double rooms
(around $15) have two narrow beds, cold-water showers, and fans—
there are, however, no windows. Twice as much will get you a "gar-
den view" (the guest house's fancy term for the courtyard),
air-conditioning, and a hot-water shower. Since there are only eight of
these deluxe rooms, reserve ahead. The owners speak excellent English
and are only too happy to assist in travel planning. Prices include a
modest American buffet breakfast. (Be sure you find Data Guest
House—many other hotels in the neighborhood have "Data" in their
names.) ⊠ *Jl. Prawirotaman 26/1, 55153,* ☎ *0274/372064. 32 rooms.
Breakfast room. AE, DC, MC, V.*

$ ⊞ **Mutiara.** Two buildings on Jalan Malioboro make up this hotel. The
newer south wing has fresher rooms that, despite their pale-green-and-
orange-flecked decor, are worth the extra $5. Cracked plaster and
stained carpets notwithstanding, all the rooms are swept clean, fresh
towels are supplied though the day, and the cheerful staff is always ready
to give advice. The restaurant serves meals all day long, but stick to
the breakfast. A small combo plays every evening on the ground floor.
⊠ *Jl. Malioboro 18, 55153,* ☎ *0274/563814,* FAX *0274/561201. 109
rooms. Restaurant, coffee shop, pool. AE, DC, MC, V.*

$ ⊞ **Rose Guest House.** The rooms here are very modest, but they do
have private baths and either air-conditioning or overhead fans. The
rates include breakfast and airport transfers, so this hotel is an extremely
good value. ⊠ *Jl. Prawirotaman 22, 55153,* ☎ *0274/727991. 29
rooms. Restaurant, pool. No credit cards.*

Nightlife and the Arts

If you hanker for a beer and maybe some local music, try the restaurants along Jalan Prawirotaman or Jalan Malioboro. Indeed, after dark Jalan Malioboro is transformed from a crowded market street into one long, open restaurant—the hub of social life in the city. Magicians perform tricks and singers wander between tables strumming guitars, and conversations and coffee continue long after the last dish has been cleared from the table.

Most often there will be a gamelan orchestra playing in your hotel, but a performance in the sultan's palace is not to be missed. Portions of the *Ramayana* are performed at different venues throughout the city, but the most dramatic setting is at Prambanan (☞ *below*). Wayang kulit shows, usually based on stories from the *Ramayana*, are also given.

DANCE, MUSIC, AND THEATER

The **Kraton,** the sultan's palace, hosts traditional gamelan music on Monday and Wednesday from 10:30 to noon. In addition, every Sunday from 10:30 AM to 12:30 PM, the **Kraton Classic Dance School** rehearses here. Actors perform stories from the *Ramayana* nightly at 7 in **Taman Hiburan Rakyat** (People's Park; ⊠ Jl. Brig. Jen. Katamso). Shows last about two hours.

PUPPET SHOWS

Wayang kulit shows take place Sunday through Friday from 3 to 5 PM at the **Agastya Art Institute** (⊠ Jl. Gedongkiwo MDIII/237, ☎ no phone).

Eight-hour wayang kulit performances of the full *Ramayana* or *Mahabharata* are usually held every second Saturday of the month at **Sasono Hinggil,** a theater just south of Yogya's Kraton, on the opposite side of the alun-alun. These plays begin at 9 PM and last until dawn. Shorter versions lasting two to three hours are given at other times. Your hotel should have the schedule, or check at the information booth outside the theater.

At the **Ambar Budaya** (Yogyakarta Crafts Center; ⊠ Jl. Laksda Adisucipto, opposite the Ambarrukmo Palace Hotel), hour-long wayang kulit performances take place every Monday, Wednesday, and Saturday at 9:30 PM.

Shopping

Shopping for batiks is a delight, and you should make the time to watch batik being made at one of the many small factories. Yogyakarta is also a center for painters, and their works are displayed in scores of galleries. Leather goods here are usually well made and inexpensive. Yogyakarta may be a shopper's dream, but be selective—there's a lot of tacky merchandise alongside the treasures—and bargain gracefully. After you've offered your next-to-last price, walk away; you'll probably be called back. There are any number of scams to lure you into shops—for instance, the claim that a student art exposition is being held and the works are being sold without commercial profit. Don't believe it!

Jalan Malioboro is lined with shops; the handicraft stalls turn into food stalls around 9 PM. Most of the merchandise is junk, but it's worth picking through. This is a convenient area to buy T-shirts or shorts, but prices are on the high side.

You'll find good prices—prices that locals may pay—at the modern indoor market, **Pasar Beringharjo,** at the top end of Jalan Malioboro, across from the Kraton. This fascinating market offers countless spices and foodstuffs, as well as pots and pans, clothes, and electronics.

HANDICRAFTS

In addition to batik, Yogya handicrafts include small hand-tooled leather goods, pottery (items decorated with brightly colored elephants, roosters, and animals from mythology are made in Kasongan, just south of Yogya), and wayang kulit and wayang golek. All the shops and stalls on Jalan Malioboro and around the Kraton sell puppets and other handicrafts. The **Yogyakarta Handicrafts Center** (✉ Jl. Adisucipto, ☎ no phone), not far from the Ambarrukmo Palace Hotel, sells handicrafts by artisans with disabilities.

The patterned Indonesian textiles called batik—made by drawing on fabric with wax, then dyeing the unwaxed areas—can be found in all the stalls in Yogyakarta. Many prints with batik design are machine-made, however, so beware. Before you buy, try to visit a batik factory where you can watch the process and browse the showrooms.

One place to see batik being created is **Batik Plentong** (✉ Jl. Tirtodipurun 28, ☎ 0274/562777), which has everything from yard goods to pot holders and batik clothing—all hand-stamped and hand-drawn. Visit **Iman Batik Workshop** (✉ Jl. Dagen 76B, just off Jl. Malioboro, ☎ no phone), where Iman Nuryanto, the owner, holds changing exhibitions of local artisans. Don't pay more than 50% of the asking price. The **Koperasi (Cooperative) Fine Arts School** (✉ Jl. Kemetiran Kidul, ☎ no phone), south of the railway station, has batik designed by talented artisans—just be sure to bargain.

You'll find high-quality leather goods **Kusuma** (✉ Jl. Kauman 50, parallel to Malioboro, ☎ 0274/565453). There's room for modest bargaining, but no credit cards are accepted.

If you're interested in ceramics and pottery, head for **Kansongan,** 8 km (5 mi) southwest of Yogya. There are more than 30 pottery workshops in the little town, which is slowly being engulfed by Yogya but still far enough away to keep its identity. Pottery isn't the easiest merchandise to transport, but there are many pots and sculptures that are truly worth buying. Taxis all know where Kansongan is, or you can take a bus heading toward Bantul, get out at the town entrance, and walk the last kilometer.

Many silversmiths have workshops and salesrooms in **Kota Gede,** 6 km (3½ mi) southeast of Yogya. The largest in Kota Gede, **Tom's Silver** (✉ Jl. Ngaksi Gondo, Kota Gede 3-1 A, ☎ 0274/525416) also offers the best workmanship. Also try **MD Silver** (✉ Jl. Keboan, Kota Gede, ☎ 0274/375063).

Borobudur Temple

★ **26** *42 km (26 mi) northwest of Yogyakarta.*

That the temple of Borobudur took perhaps 10,000 men 100 years to build becomes credible the moment you set eyes on its cosmic structure, in the shadow of the powerful volcanoes that the Javanese believe are the abode of God. Try to go early in the morning—plan to end your two-to three-hour visit before noon, while the temperature is still relatively cool. Guided coach tours run from Yogya hotels, or you can hire a minibus and guide (usually more informed) through a Yogya travel agency. If you'd like to visit on your own, take the public bus that heads toward Samarung, then change at Muntilan for the Ramayana bus to Borobudur.

Borobudur was abandoned (the reasons are still debated) soon after completion in AD 850, and the forest moved in. The man who founded modern Singapore, Thomas Stamford Raffles (then the English lieutenant-governor of Java), and his military engineer, H. C. C. Cornelius, rediscovered the temple in 1814. A thousand years of neglect had left much of it in ruins, and the temple has undergone two mammoth restorations, first from 1907 to 1911, and then again from the 1960s to the 1980s with the help of UNESCO and $25 million.

The temple is a giant stupa (dome-shape structure): five lower levels contain 1,500 relief carvings depicting the earthly life of Siddhartha in his passage to enlightenment. Start at the eastern staircase on the first level and walk clockwise around each gallery to follow the sequence of Lord Buddha's life.

Above the reliefs are 432 stone Buddhas. Even higher, above the square galleries, are three circular terraces with 72 latticed stupas that hide statues depicting the Buddha's departure from the material world and existence on a higher plane. The top stupa symbolizes the highest level of enlightenment. Looking out at the surrounding mountains from the upper level of Borobudur, you feel some of the inspiration that created this grand monument. If you go around each of the nine galleries, you will have walked roughly 5 km (3 mi) closer to heaven. On weekends the complex is fairly crowded—another reason to come early. In 1990, a museum opened on the grounds, charging an additional admission that its contents do not justify. ☎ *No phone.* 🎟 *Admission.* ⊙ *Daily 6:15–5.*

OFF THE BEATEN PATH	**CANDI PAWON AND MENDUT** – About 1.5 km (1 mi) east of Borobudur, on the way back to the main road, is a small temple, **Candi Pawon,** built around the same time as Borobudur. It's thought that worshipers purified themselves here on their way to Borobudur. Another kilometer or so farther east is the small temple **Mendut,** also from the 9th century. The exterior of this friendly temple is superbly carved with some 30 large relief panels depicting scenes from the Buddha's previous incarnations. Inside stands a magnificent 10-ft statue of Buddha, flanked by the bodhisattvas Avalokitesvara and Vajrapani.

Prambanan Temple Complex

★ ㉗ *16 km (10 mi) northeast of Yogyakarta, a 30-min drive via the Solo road.*

When the Sanjayan kingdom evicted the Buddhist Sailendras, the Sanjayans wanted to memorialize the return of a Hindu dynasty and, supposedly, undermine Borobudur. To this end they built Prambanan. When the 9th-century complex was rediscovered in 1880, it had fallen into ruin from centuries of neglect and enveloping vegetation. In 1937 reconstruction began, and the work continues to this day.

The temple was built with an outer stage for commoners, a middle stage for high-ranking nobility, and a main temple area for royalty. Of the original 244 temples, eight major and eight minor temples are still standing, in the highest central courtyard of the Prambanan plain.

The center temple, dedicated to Shiva the Destroyer, is the highest (155 ft) and the best-restored; Vishnu's is to the north; and Brahma's to the south. Originally the temples were painted—Shiva's red, Brahma's white, Vishnu's a dark gray—but only traces of the paint remain. To the east of these temples are three smaller ones, which contained the "vehicles" of each god: Shiva's bull, Vishnu's elephant, and Brahma's goose. Only the bull survives.

In part because the complex was dedicated to Shiva, and in part because Shiva's temple is the best restored, this is where you'll want to spend most of your time. Over the entrance is the head of Kali, a protection against evil from land. On the balustrade, the *naga* (serpent) guards against evil from the sea. The base has medallions with lions (an imported figure) as well as half-bird, half-human figures flanked by trees of good hope. Above these, on the outer balustrade, are carvings of classical Indian dancers and celestial beings.

The inner wall of the balustrade is carved with lively, sometimes frivolous, reliefs that tell the story of the *Ramayana*. From the east gate, walk around the temple clockwise to follow the story in sequence. The reliefs show free-flowing movement, much humor, and a love of nature. In contrast to Borobudur's reliefs, these carvings combine a celebration of the pleasures and pains of earthly life with scenes from Hindu mythology. They're more fun to look at (monkeys stealing fruit and bird-women floating in air), but the drama they portray—the establishment of order in the cosmos—is just as serious.

In the main chamber, at the top of the east stairway, a four-armed statue of Shiva the creator and destroyer stands on a lotus base. In the south chamber, Shiva appears as divine teacher, with a big beard and big stomach. The statue in the western chamber is Ganesha, Shiva's elephant-headed son. And in the northern chamber, Shiva's consort, Durga, kills the demon buffalo. An **archaeological museum** was opened in 1990, but its exhibits won't add much to your appreciation of the imposing architecture of the temples. However, you may want to stop at the information desk at the entrance to clarify any questions you have about the complex. Note that if you book through a tour operator, you can combine Prambanan with a visit to Borobudur or to Solo, 46 km (29 mi) northeast of Yogya. Minibuses go out to Prambanan from the Jalan Solo terminus in Yogya. If you hire a taxi, the round-trip will cost Rp 35,000. ☎ *No phone.* ▣ *Admission.* ◎ *Daily 6–5.*

OFF THE BEATEN PATH

CANDI SAMBISARI – The numerous other Buddhist and Hindu temples between Yogyakarta and Prambanan are in various states of ruin but merit at least a day of exploring. A great way to see them is to rent a bike and pack a lunch. Signs on the Yogya–Solo road point the way to the temples. Most are off the road, down small paths, and charge a small admission. Candi Sambisari, a small temple off the highway and 3 km (2 mi) back toward Yogya, is set in a sunken garden and is usually deserted—ideal for a quiet rest.

The Arts

Within walking distance of the temple is the **Prambanan theater complex,** where performances of the *Ramayana* are given in the evening, either at the Ramayana Theatre (open-air) or the Trimurti Theatre (indoor). The Ramayana ballet—an elaborate presentation with scores of dancers, a full-blown orchestra, and armies of people in monkey costumes strutting around the stage—is performed at various times throughout the year. From January through March, shows are usually once a week on Thursday. April through June and October through December, there are at least three performances (Tuesday, Wednesday, and Thursday). July through September features up to five performances a week—always on Tuesday, Wednesday, and Thursday, and usually on Saturday and Sunday. Hotel tour desks can arrange tickets and transportation, or you can share a taxi from the Tourist Information Center in Yogyakarta (☞ Visitor Information *in* Central and East Java Essentials, *below*) at 6:30. Public buses pass the theater's entrance, but they can be unreliable, and the drivers tend to gouge foreigners. ⊠ *Jl. Raya Yogya-Solo, Km 16,* ☎ *0274/63918.* ▣ *Admission.*

Solo

② *60 km (38 mi) northeast of Yogyakarta, 40 km (25 mi) northeast of Prambanan.*

Solo (also known as Surakarta or Sala) is less Westernized than Yogya, with fewer tourists and much less hustling. The city has its own traditional batik designs and its own style of dance. And although its people are devoutly Muslim, their daily life is less religious. During the unrest that led to Suharto's resignation, Solo was the scene of widespread looting, and many banks and businesses were torched. As was the case in Jakarta, the ethnic Chinese were singled out, partly because of an economic imbalance and partly because of cultural tensions that go way back. Conflict with the Chinese-Indonesians started in Solo in the 18th century when Chinese merchants supported a rebellion against Keraton Kartosuro. Then, in 1965, the "year of living dangerously," there were conflicts between political factions dominated by the Chinese and other groups. A riot on November 19, 1983, again targeted Chinese, and much of their property was damaged or destroyed.

On the west side of town is the **Kraton Mangkunegaran,** a palace complex of carved, gilded, teak pavilions. The outer center pavilion, or *pendopo,* serves as the audience hall and is typical of a Javanese royal building. The Italian marble floor laid in 1925, the guardian lions from Berlin, and the 50-ft roof supported by teak pillars make the pendopo very grand. Its ceiling is painted with a flame motif bordered by symbols from the Javanese zodiac, designed with the eight mystical colors (yellow to ward off sleep, green to subdue desire, purple to keep away bad thoughts, etc.). The effect is gaudy but dramatic.

The museum, in the ceremonial pavilion just behind the main pendopo, displays dance ornaments, masks, jewelry, chastity belts for men and women, and wayang kulit and wayang golek. At center stage is the enclosed bridal bed (originally a room reserved for offerings to the rice goddess). To the left of the museum are the official reception rooms: a formal dining room, with a Javanese-style stained-glass window (made in Holland) and an ivory tusk with carvings that depict the wedding of Arjuna, one of the heroes of the *Mahabharata*; a mirrored parlor area; and a "bathing" room for royal brides. ✉ *Jl. Sugiyopranoto,* ☎ *no phone.* ✉ *Admission.* ☉ *Mon.–Thurs. and Sat. 9–noon, Fri. 9–11 AM.*

Solo's second palace, **Kraton Kasuhunan** (sometimes called Kraton Solo), is being rebuilt because it suffered terrible damage (its elaborate ceremonial pavilion was gutted) during a fire in 1985. Luckily, the museum—one of Central Java's best—was unharmed by the blaze. It contains a priceless collection of silver and bronze Hindu figures and Chinese porcelain, but the real treat is three royal carriages given to the sultanate by the Dutch in the 18th century. The English-speaking guide will help you appreciate the collection. ✉ *Jl. Coyudan,* ☎ *0271/ 44046.* ✉ *Admission.* ☉ *Sat.–Thurs. 9–noon.*

Dining and Lodging

$$ ✕ **Kusuma Sari.** This spotless restaurant is excellent for Indonesian fare, be it ayam goreng or a snack such as *resoles ragout* (chicken wrapped in a soft pancake)—and you can dine until 11 PM nightly. The tile floors, glass-topped wood tables, and plate-glass windows don't offer a lot of atmosphere, but choose a table by the window and watch the flow of pedestrians and becaks on the town's main street. ✉ *Jl. Slamet Riyadi 111,* ☎ *0271/37603. Reservations not accepted. No credit cards.*

$ ✕ **Ramayana.** For good, inexpensive local cuisine try this plain dining room a two-minute walk from the Kusuma Sahid Prince Hotel (☞ *below*). Dishes include such Indonesian staples as nasi goreng and satays. ✉ *Jl. Imam Bonjol 49,* ☎ *0271/46643. No credit cards.*

$$$ ✕🏨 **Kusuma Sahid Prince Hotel.** Here three two-story buildings and
★ outlying bungalows are set back from the street on 5 acres of landscaped gardens. The lobby veranda—the original *pendopo agung* (prince's courtyard)—is a wonderful place for tea or a cool drink. The quiet guest rooms are well maintained, and all the accoutrements—from the linens to the orchids—are quite fresh. Some rooms have a view of the enormous pool; those in the newer wing have up-to-date furnishings and always-welcome climate control. The formal Kasuma Sahid restaurant is light and airy, with white linen and polished silver. The menu includes such Indonesian specialities as chicken with jackfruit and fish wrapped in banana leaves—with the restaurant's own special blend of spices. Western dishes with nouvelle French influences and Indonesian accents are featured as well. ✉ *Jl. Sugiyopranoto 22,* ☎ *0271/46356,* ☎ *0271/44788. 103 rooms. Restaurant, bar, pool, shops, meeting rooms, travel services. AE, DC, MC, V.*

$ 🏨 **Wisata Indah.** Though the plastered walls have hand smudges and the bathrooms are *mandi* style (a tub of water with a small bucket used to throw water over yourself; it doesn't sound like much, but it works quite well), the hot water is hot, the sheets are freshly laundered, and the staff is friendly and helpful. Outside each room are tables and chairs for breakfast (included in the price) and other meals that you can order from the bellboys. Negotiate the room rate before you sign in. ✉ *Jl. Slamet Riyadi 173,* ☎ *0271/46770. 27 rooms. MC, V.*

The Arts

At Solo's **Mangkunegaran Palace,** a gamelan orchestra performs each Saturday from 9 to 10:30 AM. Dance rehearsals are held on Wednesday from 10 to noon and on Monday and Friday afternoon.

Shopping

Solo's main shopping street is **Jalan Secoyudan.** In addition to a score of goldsmiths, you'll find antiques stores selling curios from the Dutch colonial days, as well as krises and other Javanese artifacts. Between Jalan Slamet Riyadi—which has many antiques shops—and Mangkunegaraan Palace, and just off Diponegoro is **Pasar Triwindu,** Solo's daily flea market, where hundreds of stalls sell everything from junk to old coins to batik. Bargain like crazy.

Solo has its own batik style, often using indigo, brown, and cream, as opposed to the brighter colors of Yogya's batiks. Prices are better in Solo, and you have some 300 batik factories to choose from. Aside from the shops along Jalan Secoyudan, visit **Pasar Klewer,** a huge batik market just outside the Kraton Solo with a fine selection of goods on the second floor. An established shop that sells batik and has batik-making demonstrations is **Dinar Hadi Batik Shop** on Jalan Dr. Rajiman (there's no phone).

Sangiran

㉙ *15 km (9 mi) north of Solo.*

In the late 19th century, Sangiran was the center for excavations in search of evidence to support Charles Darwin's theory of evolution. In 1891 Dutch physician Eugene Dubois discovered what he called "Java Man" (*Homo erectus*) in East Java not far from Sangiran, and the paper he published on his find rocked the scientific community. Afterward, older and more important Java Man finds were made, mostly around

Sangiran. (Note that Sangiran is not to be confused with Sanggarahan, a village just outside Yogya known for its pleasure houses.) The museum here contains good exhibits about these discoveries, including a replica of a Java Man cranium (the originals are in musuems around the world); models of these ancestors of the Homo sapiens who lived some 250,000 years ago; and fossils of other forms of life, such as now-extinct elephants. To get here you can take a bus to Kaliso, then walk 30 minutes to the site; or take a taxi (Rp 15,000 round-trip from Solo). ☎ *No phone.* ☷ *Admission.* ☉ *Mon.–Sat. 9–4.*

Sukuh Temple

30 *35 km (21 mi) east of Solo.*

Sukuh Temple stands mysteriously and exotically alone and contains elements of Hinduism, Buddhism, and animism. Looking like an abbreviated pyramid, the delightful temple is full of cult symbols and objects with erotic suggestions. The structure dates from the 15th century, but no one knows who built it or what traditions were practiced in it. The place has a mystical atmosphere, enhanced by the lush surrounding rice terraces. A hired car (Rp 20,000) is the most convenient way to get here; the journey takes a good hour along winding, hilly roads. You can also come by bus, but it requires three changes: at Tertomoyo catch the bus to Tawangmangu, then get off at Karangpandan for a minibus to Sukuh. ☷ *Admission.* ☉ *Daily 9–4.*

Surabaya

31 *260 km (150 mi) northeast of Solo, 320 km northeast of Yogyakarta.*

Surabaya isn't on the traditional tourist route, but with a rapidly expanding business and industrial base—it's Indonesia's second-largest city and for centuries its most important eastern seaport—it's looking for visitors. Hope springs eternal in the human breast.

The city's rich history includes its capture by Kublai Khan in the 13th century and by the Japanese during World War II. On November 10, 1945, the Dutch and their allies virtually flattened the community while trying to reclaim it after the Japanese surrender. The Surabayans resisted and raised the red-and-white Indonesian flag above the Hotel Majapahit. (November 10 is now celebrated throughout Indonesia as Revolutionary Heroes' Day, symbolizing the country's determination to throw off the colonial yoke.) Despite all the history here, the Hotel Majapahit and a 1950s Soviet submarine on display by the river are the only real sights.

Surabaya is the maritime jumping-off point for the little-visited island of Madura (famous for its bullfights) and for Sulawesi (☞ *below*); a transfer point for flights to Singapore, Hong Kong, and cities in Japan; and a good base from which to visit Mt. Bromo.

Dining and Lodging

$$$ ✕ **Indigo Restaurant and Bar.** Connected to the Hotel Majapahit (☞ *below*) and done in the same art-deco style, this 130-seat restaurant—with its long, dark-wood bar and its booths—feels like a posh café. The good "Euro-Asian" food includes such dishes as pizza cooked in a wood-burning oven. The baked goods are delicious, and the coffee is strong. ✉ *Jl. Tunjungan 65,* ☎ *031/545–4333. AE, DC, MC, V*

$$$ ✕ **Kuningan.** Fish is the specialty here, particularly shellfish. The traditional Chinese-style dining room is a comfortable place to peruse the extensive menu. ✉ *Jl. Kalimantan,* ☎ *031/534–5103. MC, V.*

$$–$$$ ✕ **Cafe Venezia.** Set in a charming old villa that has a garden, this eatery is a great place to take a break from the hectic streets. The intriguing mix of tasty food includes steaks and hamburgers as well as Japanese and Korean cuisine. ⊠ *Jl. Ambengan 16,* ☎ *031/534–3335. MC, V.*

$$$ 🏨 **Hotel Majapahit.** Built in the center of town in 1910 by the Sarkies
★ brothers (of Singapore's Raffles fame), this is one of Indonesia's few heritage hotels. Its expansive courts and green lawns became derelict after World War II, but in 1994 the Mandarin Oriental Hotel Group took over; a $27 million restoration was completed in 1996. Although modern luxuries were added, many of the original details were retained, including stained-glass windows, terrazzo floors, and colonial-style balconies and verandas. Rooms on the ground floor are large, but those upstairs are slightly quieter. The Presidential Suite, the largest of its kind in Indonesia, is more than 8,600 square ft. Furnishings are Javanese, and some are antiques. Batiks from Yogyakarta add splashes of color. There's a pool bar as well as three restaurants: Sarkies for Oriental seafood, Indigo for Eurasian, and Shima for Japanese. ⊠ *Jl. Tunjungan 65, 60011,* ☎ *031/545–4333,* 𝔽𝔸𝕏 *031/545–4111. 135 rooms, 15 suites. 3 restaurants, bar, pool, tennis court, health club, business services, meeting rooms. AE, DC, MC, V.*

$$$ 🏨 **Hyatt Regency Surabaya.** This large, modern hotel has an 11-story wing and the 27-story Regency Tower with Regency Club rooms, meeting rooms, two business centers, and offices. An added convenience is an airline ticketing office. Rooms are typical Hyatt—comfortable; beige; fairly large; and furnished with wooden cabinets, king-size beds, and ferns in huge clay pots. The main lobby is popular with locals who come to drink and listen to a trio that plays sentimental favorites. Expats gather in the Tavern for drinks and light meals. ⊠ *Jl. Jendral Basuki Rakhmat 106-128, 60275,* ☎ *031/531–1234 or 800/233–1234 in the U.S.,* 𝔽𝔸𝕏 *031/532–1508. 500 rooms. 2 restaurants, lobby lounge, coffee shop, pool, exercise room, shops, business services, meeting rooms, travel services. AE, DC, MC, V.*

Mt. Bromo

★ ㉛ *Tosari, a village on the mountain, is 90 km (55 mi) southeast of Surabaya.*

It's truly a thrill to approach the circular crater of this active volcano, one of a triad of precipitous peaks, and then look down into what seems like the depths of hell—a bubbling cauldron of water, ash, and sulphur that spews clouds of hot steam. The elemental eeriness of this sight is compounded by having to get up very early in the morning, hike to the top through the chilly air, and worship the sun as it comes up.

Part of the pleasure of visiting Mt. Bromo (Gunung Bromo) is that you're allowed much closer to the rim than at other volcanoes (those in Hawaii, for example), but be surefooted: in 1994 one American peering down the 350 ft to the crater's bottom fell in and never came out. Additionally, before you make any Bromo-related travel plans, verify that the mountain is open: sometimes the volcano is so active that the government prohibits people from visiting. However, the Tengger and Semaru peaks, which also surround the dusty valley here, are popular alternatives for trekking.

One way to visit Mt. Bromo is on an organized tour (☞ Guided Tours *in* Central and Eastern Java Essentials, *below*) that gets you to the rim of the caldera just before dawn. You can either leave Surabaya in the afternoon and stay overnight in a small bungalow hotel, or leave in the wee hours of the morning and return by lunchtime. Either way, the predawn walk will be chilly, so bring a sweater.

Central and Eastern Java Essentials

Arriving and Departing

BY AIRPLANE

Adisucipto Airport (☎ 274/566–666) is 10 km (6 mi) east of Yogyakarta. From Jakarta's Soekarno-Hatta Airport, **Garuda** (☎ 0274/563706 in Yogyakarta, 031/545–7747 in Surabaya, or 021/334425 in Jakarta) offers several daily flights; flying time is about 45 minutes. Seats fill up quickly, so reservations are essential. There are also flights into Yogya from Denpasar (Bali) and Surabaya on **Merpati** (☎ 0274/514272 in Yogyakarta, 031/568–8111 in Surabaya, or 021/424-3608 in Jakarta). There are flights to Surabaya's **Juanda Airport,** about 20 km (12 mi) from downtown, on Garuda and Merpati from most Javanese cities, as well as from Bali and Lombok.

Between the Airport and Yogyakarta. A minibus runs until 6 PM from airport to the terminal on Jalan Senopati for Rp 250; from here you can catch a three-wheel becak to your hotel. Taxis to or from downtown charge Rp 5,500. The major hotels send their own minibuses to the airport.

Between the Airport and Surabaya. A taxi to town is your best bet. Cabs cost about Rp 15,000 and work on a coupon system so you need not bargain with the driver.

BY BUS

Night buses from Jakarta to Yogyakarta take about 14 hours and cost about Rp 12,250. Buses also run from Denpasar on Bali (12 hours), Bandung (7 hours), and Surabaya (8 hours) For information in Jakarta, contact: **Antar Lintas Sumatra** (✉ Jl. Jati Baru 87A, ☎ 021/320970) or **PT. ANS** (✉ Jl. Senen Raya 50, ☎ 021/340494).

BY CAR

Although the scenery may be beautiful, the long drive from Jakarta is slow going, and service areas are few and far between. It is advisable to hire a driver when traveling through Indonesia.

BY TRAIN

Trains from the Gambir Railway Station in Jakarta leave several times daily for Yogya's **Tugu Railway Station** (✉ Jl. Pasar Kembang, ☎ 274/514270 or 274/513785). The trip takes 7–12 hours and costs Rp 6,700–Rp 21,500, depending on whether the train is an express or a local and on the class of the ticket. The most comfortable trip is via the *Senja Utama Express,* which has sleeping cars and leaves Gambir at 7:20 PM and arrives in Yogya at 4:50 AM. The fares are Rp 18,000 for B class, Rp 21,000 for A class, and Rp 44,000 for executive class. There are also day and night trains from Bandung (an eight-hour trip) and from Surabaya (seven hours) as well as service to Surabaya from Jakarta, Yogyakarta, and Solo. (Note: Trains to and from Jakarta and points east and west use Surabaya's Pasar Turi terminal on Jalan Gresik in the north of the city; the Gubeng Train Station, on Jalan Gubeng Sumatra in the central part of Surabaya is used by trains going to and from Solo, Yogya, and Bandung.)

Another line links Surabaya (from the Pasar Turi terminal) to Banyuwangi, on the eastern tip of Java; from here ferries depart every 30 minutes for the 20-minute crossing to Bali. This is a slow train, though, and most non–air travelers prefer the night express buses. The train between Jakarta and Surabaya takes 14 hours overnight but, oddly, sleepers aren't available. The executive class (Rp 21,000), however—with air-conditioning, reclining seats, and dinner service—is quite comfortable. Business and Economy cost less, but you'll feel worse for wear after an overnight trip. Another option is to break the trip in Cirebon, a charming coastal town four hours east of Jakarta on the fast train, and about 10 hours west of Surabaya.

Getting Around

BY BECAK

Becaks (three-wheel pedicabs) are the main form of public transportation in most Javanese towns and cities (except Surabaya and Jakarta, where they're banned). Yogya alone has about 25,000 of them, most with paintings of mountains on their fenders. Solo has quite a few, as well. In nice weather, they're a relaxing way to travel. The proper fare is about Rp 1000 per km (½ mi); be sure to negotiate with your driver before starting out.

BY BICYCLE

In Yogya, you can rent bicycles for Rp 4,000 a day from the **Hotel Indonesia** (⊠ Sosromenduran IV, ☎ 0274/587659). The **Restaurant Malioboro** (⊠ Jl. Malioboro 67, ☎ no phone) also has bikes for rent.

BY BUS

As a rule, you can simply go to the bus station in any Javanese city and catch a bus for most anywhere on the island. The shorter bus trips are tolerable; for longer hauls it's best to stick with trains. For day trips between cities minibuses are a favored way to go. They leave for Solo throughout the day (7–5) from Yogyakarta's **Terminal Terban** (⊠ Jl. Diponegoro near Jl. P.Mangkubumi) or from Jalan Sudirman or Jalan Solo. From Solo's **Gilligan minibus station,** which is next to the main Tirtonadi Bus Terminal on Jalan Dr. Setiabudi in the northwest of town, take a *bemo,* or minivan (Rp 300), or a becak (Rp 750) the 3 km (1.8 mi) into town. To reach Mt. Bromo, you can take a bus from Surabaya's **Bungurasih Bus Station** to Probolinggo and change for a bemo up to Pasuruan; from there take a minibus up to Tosari. To get from Tosari to the crater's rim, another 7½ km (4½ mi), you can rent a four-wheel-drive vehicle or, if you're fit, make the two-hour uphill trudge.

BY TAXI

In Yogya you can catch taxis in front of the larger hotels; in general, they don't cruise the streets. Taxis are metered; the flag-fall charge is Rp 800 and covers the first kilometer. A shared taxi from Yogya to Solo costs Rp 2,500 per person.

BY TRAIN

The train from Yogya to Solo takes about one hour; from Solo to Surabaya takes about four. The train is a great way to watch Java pass by. Executive class is air-conditioned and has comfortable reclining seats, business has padded seats but no air-conditioning, and third class can be like chaos on the rails.

Contacts and Resources

EMERGENCIES

Ambulance: ☎ 118. **Hospitals:** Bethesda Hospital (⊠ Yogyakarta, ☎ 0274/588876), **Dr. Sardjito Hospital** (⊠ Yogyakarta, ☎ 0274/587333), **RS Budi Mulia** (⊠ Surabaya, ☎ 031/534–1821), **RS Darmo** (⊠ Surabaya, ☎ 031/561–8824), and **RSUD Dr. Soetomo** (⊠ Surabaya, ☎ 031/550–1111). **Fire:** ☎ 113. **Police:** ☎ 110.

ENGLISH-LANGUAGE BOOKSTORES

There are several stores with used books along Jalan Prawirotaman in the south of Yogyakarta. In Surabaya the best bookshops are in the three main malls: **Surabaya Mall** (⊠ Jl. Kusuma Bangsa 116, ☎ 031/534-3002), **Surabaya Plaza** (⊠ Jl. Pemuda 31-37, ☎ 031/531–5088), and **Tunjungan Plaza** (⊠ Jl. Basuki Rachmat 8-12, ☎ 031/531–1507).

Hotels and travel agencies in Yogya can arrange the following tours, either in a private chauffeured car or as a group tour by bus:

Art and Handicrafts. A five-hour tour of the local craft centers for leather puppets, wood carving, silver work, batik, and pottery.
Borobudur. An eight-hour tour of Yogyakarta; the countryside; and the Borobudur, Mendut, and Pawon temples.
Prambanan. A three-hour tour of the temple complex.
Yogya City. A three-hour tour including the sultan's palace, Sono Budoyo Museum, Kota Gede silver works, and batik and wayang workshops.
Yogya Dieng Plateau. A 10-hour tour of the Dieng Plateau, with its spectacular scenery, sulfur springs, and geysers, plus a visit to Borobudur.

In Surabaya, the largest tour agency is **Orient Express** (⊠ Jl. Jendral Basuki Rakhamat 78, ☎ 031/515253), which will meet you at the airport or anywhere else in Surabaya. Day tours (Rp 436,000 per person) depart Surabaya at 1 AM. Overnight tours (Rp 927,000 per person) depart at 3 PM for the Bromo Cottages in Tosari, where the accommodation is simple, modern, and clean. You rise at 3:30 AM and travel by Jeep up Mt. Penanjakan (9,088 ft) for spectacular sunrise views. Afterward the Jeep takes you to the sea of sand—an area of fine volcanic ash bleached by the sun—and then to the stairway to the rim of the Bromo crater; finally it's back to the cottages for breakfast before returning to Surabaya.

You can also rent a chauffeured car and do the trip independently for about Rp 100,000, plus the fee for a Jeep on the last leg of the journey. Try **P. T. Zebra Nusantart** (⊠ Jl. Tegalsari 107, Surabaya, ☎ 031/511777); the firm also has a representative at the Surabaya Hyatt.

Yogya's main companies include **Nitour** (⊠ Jl. K. H. A. Dahlan 71, ☎ 0274/375165) and **Satriavi** (⊠ Hotel Ambarrukmo Palace, ☎ 0274/566488, ext. 7135). American Express cardholders can contact **Pacto Ltd. Tours and Travel** (⊠ Garuda Hotel, Jl. Malioboro 60, ☎ 0274/565345). The locally operated **Intan Pelangi** (⊠ Mutiara Hotel, Jl. Malioboro 18, ☎ 0274/562895) is also helpful.

In Surabaya: American Express cardholders can contact **Pacto Ltd. Tours and Travel** (⊠ Jl. Jendral Basuki Rachmad 106, ☎ 031/532–6385) and **Nitour Incorporation** (⊠ Jl. Urip Sumoharjo 63, ☎ 031/534–1247).

Yogyakarta's **Tourist Information Office** (⊠ Jl. Malioboro 16, ☎ 0274/562811) has maps, schedules of events, bus and train information, and a helpful staff. It's open Monday through Saturday from 8 to 8. There's also a tourist booth at the railway station. The **Solo Tourist Information Office** (⊠ Jl. Slamet Riyadi 275, ☎ 0271/46501) is open Monday–Saturday 8–5.

In Surabaya you can try the **Surabaya Tourist Office** (⊠ Jl. Darmakali 35, ☎ 031/575448) or the **East Java Tourist Office** (⊠ Jl. Pemuda 118, ☎ 031/532–4499). Both are open weekdays 8:30 to 5.

BALI

The "magic" of Bali has its roots in the fact that the island is religiously distinct from the rest of Indonesia: unlike their Muslim neighbors, the Balinese are Hindus. Their faith also contains elements of Buddhism and of ancient animist beliefs indigenous to the archipelago. Hindu culture came to Bali as early as the 9th century; by the 14th century, the island was part of the Hindu Majapahit empire of East Java. When that empire fell to Muslim invaders, Majapahit aristocrats, scholars, artists, and dancers fled to Bali, consolidating Hindu culture and religion here.

To the Balinese, every living thing contains a spirit; when they pick a flower as an offering to the gods, they first say a prayer to the flower. All over the island, from the capital city of Denpasar to the tiniest village, plaited baskets filled with flowers and herbs lie on the sidewalks, on the prows of fishing boats, and in markets. These offerings are made from dawn till dusk, to placate evil spirits and honor helpful ones. *Garudas* (stone figures) guard entries to temples, hotels, and homes. The black-and-white-checked cloths around the statues' waists symbolize the balance between good and evil. Maintaining that harmony is the life work of every Balinese.

The island's geography also contributes to Bali's religion and rituals: the focus of offerings to the spirits is on Gunung Agung, the 9,866-ft "Mother Mountain," which is considered the holiest site on the island. Agung is also known for its deadly eruption in 1963, but other active volcanoes rise 6,560–9,840 ft along Bali's mountainous interior. It's the ash fallout from these high summits, and the dependable rainfall from storms caught between them, that provides fertile valleys for the famed emerald rice terraces. At its edges, Bali is framed by thick mangrove swamps, sweeping white beaches, and lively coral reefs, offering a variety of ecosystems for wildlife such as mousedeer, monkeys, dolphins, giant turtles, and more than 300 bird species, including the rare Bali starling.

Although the island is only 140 km (84 mi) long by 80 km (48 mi) wide, a week wouldn't be enough to fully appreciate Bali's beaches, temples, volcanoes, and towns. With Indonesia's most developed tourist infrastructure, Bali has several beach areas on its southern coast, where 90% of its visitors stay. Each has its own appeal, and all are within easy reach of one another.

Jimbaran Bay

★ ❶ *1,100 km (682 mi) southeast of Jakarta, 3 km (2 mi) south of Ngurah Rai Airport, 20 km (12 mi) southwest of Denpasar.*

Once a sleepy fishing village, Jimbaran Bay is now a playground for guests of several luxury resorts. On the western side of the Bukit Peninsula to the south of Kuta, the area's white-sand beaches, glowing sunsets, and sapphire waves with colorful fishing boats create a captivating scene. An offshore reef offers makes the waters gentle enough for swimming.

OFF THE BEATEN PATH   **PURA LUHUR ULU WATU** – About 15 km (9 mi) south of Jimbaran—at the end of the Bukit Peninsula—is this cliff-side temple overlooking the ocean. Originally constructed in the 11th century as one of Bali's six main territorial places of worship, Ulu Watu was rebuilt 500 years later and has been renovated several times since, giving the current structure a mix of old and new styles. The split-gate entrance imitates a curving set of garuda wings and leads to the outer courtyard, where a second gate is framed by statues of Ganesha (the elephant-headed god and son of Shiva) and topped by a fearsome guardian. The inner court houses a smaller, three-tier temple. The sunsets from here are spectacular (visitors arrive in droves to view them), and the nearby beaches offer fine surfing.

Dining and Lodging

$ ✕ **Kakul Cafe.** This upbeat, open-air café brings the cuisine of the southwestern United States to one of Bali's poshest corners. Its bright, mango-color exterior makes it hard to miss; its mango-color tablecloths, moss-green chairs, and funky geometric wall art make it hard to forget. The hearty fare includes a tasty shrimp-and-pepper salad; baked-potato soup; pepper steak; and the familiar pizza, pasta, and quesadillas. ⊠ *Jl. Bukit Permai 5c,* ☎ *0361/702815. AE, MC, V.*

$$$$ ✕⌂ **The Ritz-Carlton, Bali.** The breathtaking opulence here is appar-
★ ent as soon as you step into the entryway: a series of pools descend in falls toward a stunning view of the Indian Ocean. Unpolished marble surrounds the fountains and koi ponds; carved antique wooden benches adorn the hallways; and a replica of Klungkung's Kertagosa Palace mural graces the lobby ceiling. The pool area not only has a two-tiered pool but also a walk-through grotto with an 11,000-gallon saltwater aquarium. Most rooms in the four-story main building have ocean views; all have a Western-style decor with a slightly Balinese flair. The thatched-roof villas have striking Balinese accents, *bale bungong* (cushioned lounging areas), and private plunge pools. At the 130-seat Langit Theatre and open-air restaurant, you can watch Balinese dancing while dining. The intimate Padi's restaurant overlooks the bay and is next to a pond lined with yellow and red heliconias. Try the sweet-and-sour shrimp with turmeric or the yellow chicken curry in a clay pot. There's also a rijsttafel buffet that offers a taste of Indonesia's most famous dishes. ⊠ *Jl. Karang Mas Sejahtera, 80364,* ☎ *0361/702222,* FAX *0361/702555. 277 rooms, 16 suites, 36 villas. 6 restaurants, 6 bars, pool, massage, spa, putting green, tennis court, beach, snorkeling, windsurfing, boating, children's programs, meeting rooms. AE, DC, MC, V.*

$$$ ✕⌂ **Bali Cliff Resort and Hotel.** The grounds here are a little run down, but you can't beat the locale along rough-hewn cliffs, 10 km (6 mi) southeast of Jimbaran and at the very tip of the island. Rooms are done up tastefully in pastels; suites and villas offer more space and elegance, with marble floors; hand-carved furnishings; sitting areas; spa baths; and balconies. You can stroll through mazes of gardens and fountains to an on-site temple. Dances are performed on the lower beach as you dine by candlelight in a nearby cave—an unusual and memorable experience. A ride down a sloping, glass-enclosed tram takes you to the multilevel Ocean restaurant, whose tables are in thatched-roof pavilions overlooking the surf. Although portions aren't huge, the food is tasty—spring rolls are crispy and hot, and the grilled fish is very fresh. Just beware of the mean local macaque troop, which will rush the tables for tidbits if not shooed away from afar. ⊠ *Jl. Purah Batu Pageh, Ungasan,* ☎ *0361/771992,* FAX *0361/771993. 180 rooms. 3 restaurants, 3 bars, coffee shop, in-room safes, pool, spa, health club, shops, theater, laundry service, meeting rooms. AE, MC, V.*

$$$$ ⌂ **Four Seasons Resort.** Set on 35 acres, this veritable village of lux-
★ ury bungalows rises from the shore some 150 ft up a hill. The most elevated bungalows have terrific bay views, and you needn't worry about hiking down to the public areas from them—an electric taxi will shuttle you to and fro. Once you enter your villa courtyard (through a pair of carved, painted Balinese doors), you're in your own personal oasis. Stepping stones, surrounded by luminous green pebbles, lead to a private pool beside which water splashes gently in a fountain. The living-dining pavilions look onto the pool and bay beyond. Bedrooms have peaked bamboo-and-thatch roofs; bathrooms have huge, deep tubs and separate showers—one inside and one out in a small courtyard garden. Down by the beach, the pool spills over a 20-ft waterfall into a free-form soaking area below. A new 10,000-square-ft spa features nine spacious treatment rooms, a fitness facility, a refreshment center, and

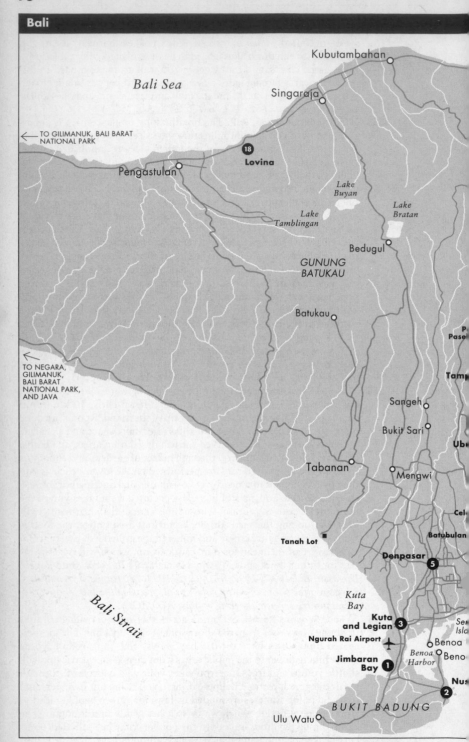

Bali Sea

Kubutambahan

Singaraja

← TO GILIMANUK, BALI BARAT
NATIONAL PARK

18 **Lovina**

Pengastulan

*Lake
Buyan*

*Lake
Bratan*

*Lake
Tamblingan*

Bedugul

*GUNUNG
BATUKAU*

Batukau

P.
Pase

← TO NEGARA,
GILIMANUK,
BALI BARAT
NATIONAL PARK,
AND JAVA

Tamp

Sangeh

Bukit Sari

Ub

Tabanan

Mengwi

Cel

Batubulan

Tanah Lot

Denpasar
5

Bali Strait

*Kuta
Bay*

**Kuta
and Legian** **3**

*Se
Isla*

Ngurah Rai Airport ✈

Benoa

**Jimbaran
Bay** **1**

Benoa Beno
Harbor

Nus

2

BUKIT BADUNG

Ulu Watu

Bali Sea

Penulisan

Kintamani

Gunung
(Mount)
Batur

9

Lake
Batur

Penelokan

Tulamben
17

GUNUNG
AGUNG

Pura Besakih

Mt. Seraya

Pura Panti
ek Gel Gel

Tirta Empul

Pura Gunung Kawi

paksiring **8**

10 Pura Kehen

Karangasem

Tegalalang

Bangli

16 Tenganan

Pejeng

Balina
Beach and
Manggis **14**

15 Candidasa

7

6 Bedulu

Amuk
Bay

ud

Goa Gajah

Mas

Gianyar

11 Klungkung

13 Padangbai

Kemenuh

12

Batuan

Goa Lawah

TO LOMBOK

lok

Sukawati

n

4 Sanur

Badung Strait

Lembongan
Island

rangan
and
Port

Ceningan
Island

Sakti

Karengsari

oa

NUSA PENIDA

sa Dua

N

Strait of Lombok

| 0 | | | | 4 miles |
| 0 | | | | 6 km |

complete beauty services. The Four Seasons is very much a self-contained resort; there are no villages within a couple of miles, and the nearest building is the Ritz-Carlton, a mile or so down the beach. ⊠ *Jl. Bukit Permai, 80361,* ☎ *0361/701010,* 𝖥𝖠𝖷 *0361/701020. 147 bungalows. 5 restaurants, pool, massage, spa, 2 tennis courts, beach, snorkeling, windsurfing, boating, shops, laundry service, meeting rooms, travel services. AE, DC, MC, V.*

$$$ – $$$$ 🏨 **Hotel Inter-Continental Bali.** Five stone garudas wrapped in black-and-white checked cloths greet you from their posts in a large lotus pond at the entrance. Their brooding presence conveys a deeper sense of Indonesian formality here than is found at other large resorts nearby. Opulence readily mixes with tradition in the ornate building's design, from the intricately detailed pavilions to the carefully chosen interior decorations that highlight every room. Hardwood floors, light-wood furniture with cream and rose cushions, and carefully hewn stone and metal ornaments adorn the guest quarters. A blue-tile pool rests just over the bay; next to it, a large thatch-roof pavilion with oversize decorative fish dangling from its eaves is an ideal place for sunsets. ⊠ *Jl. Uluwatu 45, 80361,* ☎ *0361/701888,* 𝖥𝖠𝖷 *0361/701777. 214 rooms. 2 restaurants, 2 bars, pool, massage, beach, snorkeling, windsurfing, boating, dance club, laundry service, meeting rooms, travel services. AE, MC, V.*

$$$ 🏨 **Pansea Puri Bali.** Luxury is reasonably priced at this resort down
★ a narrow, one-lane road and at the edge of Jimbaran's beach. A black-tile entryway dripping with ivy leads to a bridge between two ponds where large koi play follow-the-leader in packs. To the left of the bridge and facing the beach is the dining pavilion. Scattered throughout the gardens are villas whose roofs are thatched with rice straw. Inside, marble floors and wood paneling complement the Balinese textiles, paintings, and carvings. Special treats that are standard here include wraparound terraces, spacious bathrooms with sunken tubs, and private gardens with open-air showers. A free-form pool that edges up to the beach and lagoon makes the best of the bay. ⊠ *Jl. Uluwatu, 80361,* ☎ *0361/701605,* 𝖥𝖠𝖷 *0361/701320. 41 villas. Restaurant, bar, pool, beach, snorkeling, windsurfing, boating, library, laundry service, travel services. AE, MC, V.*

$$ – $$$ 🏨 **Keraton Bali Cottages.** The ornate stone bas-reliefs and sparkling marble floors of its pagoda-like entrance belie this hotel's reasonable prices. The "cottages" are actually rooms angled out to face the beach so that they offer more privacy than typical rows of hotel rooms—and the concept works. Thick gardens tumble around a narrow central walkway lined by the dwellings' small raised porches. All rooms have garden views—but no tubs (only showers); suites also have balconies, sitting rooms, and whirlpool tubs. The decor is simple and neat, and the large grounds, numerous facilities, and reasonable rates attract many European and Indonesian guests. ⊠ *Jl. Mrajapati (Box 2023), 80361,* ☎ *0361/701961,* 𝖥𝖠𝖷 *0361/701991. 89 rooms, 10 suites. 2 restaurants, 3 bars, coffee shop, pool, snorkeling, windsurfing, boating, billiards, theater, laundry service, travel services. AE, MC, V.*

$ 🏨 **Puri Bamboo Bungalows.** This small hotel offers comfortable accommodations and a convenient location without the added expenses for opulent facilities. Each neat, two-story cottage has four rooms—two upstairs and two down—all with small, simply furnished bedrooms. Bathrooms have tubs and stone gardens; sinks are in the main room. Superior suites have porches, and deluxe suites include a sitting area. In the middle of the cottages, a pool with a swim-up bar is the center of activity, even though the beach is just steps away. ⊠ *Jl. Pangeracikan, 80361,* ☎ *0361/701377,* 𝖥𝖠𝖷 *0361/701440. 20 rooms, 18 suites. Restaurant, bar, pool, beach, gift shop, laundry service, travel services. AE, MC, V.*

Nightlife

Nightlife here is centered on resort bars. If you tire of the bars at your hotel, barhopping from resort to resort is an option. The **Kakul Kafe** (✉ Jl. Bukit Permai 5c, ☎ 0361/702815) attracts a crowd on weekends. The **Monkey Forest Fun Pub and Disco** (☎ 0361/701888) at the Hotel Inter-Continental Bali is a popular hangout. The **Tarian Open Stage** (☎ 0361/701961) at the Keraton Bali hotel offers cultural dances on Saturday nights, including an Indonesian buffet dinner.

Nusa Dua

➋ *10 km (6 mi) southeast of Jimbaran Bay, 8 km (5 mi) southeast of Ngurah Rai Airport, 30 km (18 mi) southeast of Denpasar.*

Nusa Dua, a former burial ground, consists of two tiny islands linked to the mainland by a reinforced sand spit. Unlike Kuta and Sanur, this is an entirely planned resort, with no indigenous community. Although you have to travel inland from here to see the real Bali, Nusa Dua's beaches are wide and peaceful, and its self-contained hotels are luxurious.

Dining and Lodging

$ ✗ **Cafe Gong Bali.** At a bend in the road leading into Benoa (3 km/2 mi north of Nusa Dua), you'll come to a wooden temple–style structure with a fish-shape sailboat out front. Although the busy roadside locale and loud reggae music add little to the ambience, this watering hole is still popular with Westerners. The reasonably priced Indonesian fare includes snacks of spring rolls and gado gado, a rijsttafel buffet, and à la carte entrées such as crispy Balinese duck or fresh lobster. ✉ *Jl. Pratama 88, Tanjung Benoa,* ☎ *0361/773738. AE, MC, V.*

$ ✗ **Ulam.** Right on Nusa Dua's prime shopping street, Ulam is favored by travelers for its Indonesian dishes and seafood. Upon being seated in the dark, cozy dining room, women diners receive flowers to put in their hair—and after dinner a free glass of local whiskey is served. Set meals are a specialty: the "seafood parade" consists of juice or soda; avocado-and-shrimp cocktail or crab-and-corn soup; a selection of grilled fish, shrimp, crab, and squid; and fresh fruit or a Balinese pancake. The busy bar caters to the Western crowd, and there's free transportation to and from Nusa Dua hotels. ✉ *Jl. Pantai Mengiat 14,* ☎ *0361/771590. AE, MC, V.*

$$$$ ✗🏨 **Amanusa.** The rough, winding road through the Bali Golf & ★ Country Club and to the Amanusa disguises the resort's opulence. Shining marble floors and thick columns welcome you into the stone main building, which towers above a reflection pond and a wide, sapphiretile swimming pool. From here, the views of the forested peninsula stretch to the Indian Ocean, and most of the enormous villas— built into the land's gentle folds—share this vista at least partially. Each also has checkered-marble floors; rich teak furniture; a canopy bed; a garden; a sunken marble tub; and an outdoor shower. Individual bale bungong are outside on the terraces; eight villas also have plunge pools. Chauffeurs will drive you to the resort's beach club—on a pristine strip of sand five minutes' away—where there are sun chairs, cushioned *bales* (raised, open resting pavilions), and a restaurant. You can toast the sunset—seated beneath a canopy of bougainvillea beside the pool—while gamelan music is played. Afterward, the Terrace restaurant's candlelighted tables provide a romantic dinner setting above the peninsula's twinkling lights. Indonesian and Thai food are the highlights. Try the prawn salad with coconut, chili, lemon, and basil and the rich, red curry with chicken, peanuts, and coconut. Sumptuous desserts include chocolate-caramel-mousse cake and date pudding with butterscotch sauce. ✉ *Jl. Nusa Dua Selatan (Box 33), 80363,* ☎ *0361/772333,* 🅵🅰🆇 *0361/*

772335. 35 villas. 2 restaurants, pool, golf privileges, 2 tennis courts, spa, windsurfing, boating, mountain bikes, library, laundry service, meeting rooms. AE, DC, MC, V.

$$$–$$$$ ✕🖼 **Sheraton Laguna.** The garden setting here attracts an international
★ crowd intent on relaxation and seclusion. (Those here on business stay next door at the Sheraton Nusa Indah convention center complex.) The central courtyard has free-form swimming pools, lagoons, and waterfalls that are connected by stone steps and curving wooden bridges. Ground-level rooms have balconies or patios; upper suites have large balconies that drip with bougainvillea; and suites have large sitting areas and marble baths with oversize tubs. One staff member is assigned to take care of all your needs. If that's not enough pampering, visit the spa, where you'll find indoor and outdoor whirlpool baths; a long bathing pool with several waterfalls; and a massage and treatment villa with marble floors and a cushioned bale. La Trattoria restaurant has a familiar Italian look, and its bright decor and garden views make it a popular gathering place. The breakfast buffet includes meats, fresh baked goods, and local fruits. Indonesian, Italian, and other Western specialities are offered throughout the day, and theme buffets and live entertainment are scheduled nightly. ✉ Jl. Raya Nusa Dua (Box 2077), 80363, ☎ 0361/771327 or 800/325–3535 in the U.S., 🆋 0361/771326. 211 rooms, 65 suites. 4 restaurants, in-room safes, pool, wading pool, 2 tennis courts, spa, exercise room, business services, travel services. AE, DC, MC, V.

$$$ ✕🖼 **Hotel Melia Benoa.** The furnishings at this hotel just north of Nusa Dua are more Pier One than local Bali, but the decor goes well with the casual, international atmosphere. (Owing to the optional all-inclusive rates, this hotel is popular with tour groups.) Open lounges and terraces, tall white buildings, and pools create a sense of space. Rooms are large and have marble floors, wood trim, and balconies with garden or sea views. The gardens are full of cattails and lotus ponds, and there are bread boxes for feeding the koi. The open-air Dwarawati Coffee House offers reasonable prices and a comfortable family atmosphere. The decor is no-frills—basic round tables, dark wood chairs, and a stone floor—but the breakfast buffet is well-rounded, the mix of Indonesian and Western dishes fresh and creative. Entrées include *puscilli al tono* (pasta salad with tuna, olives, tomato, and parsley) and paprika chicken with roasted potatoes and seasoned vegetables. ✉ Jl. Pratama, Tanjung Benoa (Box 52, Nusa Dua 80363), ☎ 0361/771714, 🆋 0361/771713. 156 rooms. 2 restaurants, 2 bars, coffee shop, in-room safes, pool, massage, spa, health club, laundry service, meeting rooms, travel services, car rental. AE, MC, V.

$$$–$$$$ 🖼 **Bali Hilton International.** At this resort, set on 30 acres of landscaped gardens along 984 ft of beach, a spectacular floodlighted waterfall sets the scene. Five-story buildings on either side of the vast, open reception area create a "U" around Balinese-theme courtyards and an enormous lagoon. All rooms in the enormous, pagoda-style, red-tile-roof main buildings have balconies that look onto the lagoon or the sea. Interior corridors connect the structures, which also feature central gardens, pools, and fountains that are open to the sky. Ayodya Club rooms are slightly larger and have a separate check-in area. The Hilton also caters to Japanese visitors with such special amenities as a Japanese-speaking staff, Japanese newspapers, green tea, and slippers. Travelers with disabilities will also be pleased by the hotel's facilities. ✉ Jl. Raya Nusa Dua (Box 46), 80363, ☎ 0361/771102 or 800/ HILTONS in the U.S., 🆋 0361/771616. 538 rooms. 7 restaurants, in-room safes, 3 pools, spa, 4 tennis courts, exercise room, squash, theater, meeting rooms. AE, DC, MC, V.

$$$–$$$$ ⛵ **Grand Hyatt Bali.** Forty acres of gardens and cascading waterfalls are the setting for the Hyatt's four "ethnic village" compounds, each with its own small lagoon or swimming pool. Rooms are large and have a traditional Balinese decor, king-size beds, and small sitting enclaves with banquette seats. Bathrooms have separate shower stalls and wooden shutters that open to the bedrooms. Regency Club rooms feature balconies, marble bathrooms, private pools, butler service, and the Club Lounge, where complimentary breakfast and cocktails are served. The hotel's Balinese character is heightened by the Pasar Senggol open-air night market of 11 food stalls and an amphitheater where traditional dances are performed. ⌧ *Jl. Raya Nusa Dua (Box 53),* ☎ *0361/771234 or 800/233–1234 in the U.S.,* FAX *0361/772038. 750 rooms. 5 restaurants, 4 bars, in-room safes, 6 pools, putting green, 3 tennis courts, health club, squash, shops, theater, children's programs, playground, meeting rooms. AE, DC, MC, V.*

Nightlife and the Arts

Some of the livelier resort locales include: **Club Taboh** (⌧ Nusa Dua Beach Hotel, Jl. Raya Nusa Dua next to the Sheraton Nusa Indah, ☎ 0361/977120), which features karaoke and an all-night disco Tuesday through Sunday; the Grand Hyatt's **Lila Cita** (☎ 0361/771234), which has weekly fashion shows and live bands; and the Sheraton Laguna's **Quinn's** (☎ 0361/7711237), which offers live entertainment nightly.

Along Jalan Pantai Mengiat, the jazz bar at **Poco Loco** (☎ 0361/773923) rocks on weekends in peak season, **Ulam** (☎ 0361/771590) is always crowded, and **Koki Bali** (☎ 0361/772406) has Balinese dancing at 8 PM every Tuesday and Thursday. There are several bars in the Nusa Dua Galeria shopping plaza (all offer free transport to and from area resorts), including: **Arak Bali** (☎ 0361/774612), **Uno** (☎ 0361/773654), and **Harry's** (☎ 0361/772655).

Balinese cultural performances are scheduled regularly at the **Galeria stage** (⌧ Galeria Nusa Dua Shopping Centre, Jl. Raya Nusa Dua, ☎ 0361/771662). In summer live bands also perform here on Saturday night.

Outdoor Activities and Sports

The 18-hole, 6,839-yard course of the **Bali Golf & Country Club** (☎ 0361/771791), on the Bukit Peninsula in Nusa Dua, has $125 greens fees (including caddy) and $27 club rental. Most of the hotels have mountain bikes and maps for the area's numerous cycling paths.

Shopping

Each Nusa Dua resort has at least one shop where you can pick up postcards and souvenirs, but you'll find the best prices and selection outside the hotels. Along Jalan Pantai Mengiat, in the center of town, clothing shops and trinket stalls filled with carvings and textiles are tucked between small, open-air restaurants. If you're shy about bargaining, head for the **Galeria Nusa Dua Shopping Centre** (⌧ Jl. Raya Nusa Dua, in the center of town) where you'll find clothing at **Bali Lotus** (☎ 0361/772539), pretty lace creations at **Uluwatu** (☎ 0361/771309), textiles at **Batik Shanti** (☎ 0361/771308) and **Tenun Ikat Bali** (☎ 0361/772081), art at **Batik Keris** (☎ 0361/771303), and jewelry at **Unique Gold & Silver** (☎ 0361/771038) and **Surya Silver** (☎ 0361/773856). Be sure to get a discount book from the Galeria Information desk before you shop or eat.

Shops and bargains abound in the village of **Benoa** (not to be confused with the Tanjung Benoa ship port on the opposite side of Benoa Harbor), a five-minute drive north of Nusa Dua along the eastern peninsula's beach strip. The busy, two-lane road to the northeast end of the beach buzzes with traffic and tour buses from dawn to long past dusk.

The village markets, including the **Pasar Seni art market** at the bend in the road into town, offer a refreshing change of scenery if you've been cooped up too long in your resort.

Kuta and Legian

❸ *8 km (5 mi) km northwest of Nusa Dua, 4 km (3 mi) northeast of Ngurah Rai Airport, 12 km (7 mi) southwest of Denpasar.*

In recent years, Bali's first resort area, Kuta, has become extremely commercial and somewhat tawdry. Its once-splendid golden swatch of sand is now smothered by people and scattered with litter, and its main street, just two blocks from the beach, is crammed with boutiques, Western fast-food chains, bars, discos, and—after hours—ladies of the night. Still, the sunsets are stunning, the energy of the youthful vacationers (including many backpackers) give the town a festive atmosphere, and there are enclaves of the real Bali down many a narrow, quiet street.

Legian Beach to the north is quieter and less congested than Kuta; it's for those who like to be close to the action but not right in it. Just to the south of Kuta is Tuban, another area of hotels designed to attract families and those looking for quieter vacations.

Dining and Lodging

$$ ✕ **Glory Bar & Restaurant.** The Glory stands out for the freshness of its fish, mud crabs, and lobster. The ambience is convivial, and the prices are fair. The Wednesday Indonesian buffet includes corn soup, fried chicken, sweet-and-sour pork, batter-fried fish, satay, and noodles. ⊠ *Jl. Legian 445, Legian,* ☎ *0361/751091. AE, DC, MC, V.*

$$ ✕ **Indah Sari.** This seafood-and-barbecue restaurant on the main drag serves well-prepared dishes—from prawns to grouper—that you can order either spicy or bland. The freshness of the food makes up for the impersonal service and lack of intimacy. ⊠ *Jl. Legian, Kuta,* ☎ *0361/751834. AE, MC, V.*

$$ ✕ **Poppies.** Surrounded by high-volume, high-energy shops and dives, Poppies is a garden haven enclosed by tall, thin walls. Vines and blossoms tumble through trellises above the well-spaced tables, and the staff is quick to please. The relaxed alfresco atmosphere makes the creative variety of fresh, tasty Indonesian and Western dishes all the more enjoyable. Items range from Greek salads and *tom yam* (spicy Thai prawn soup) to grilled fish and succulent spareribs. ⊠ *Poppies La. (off Jl. Legian), Kuta,* ☎ *0361/751059. MC, V.*

$$ ✕ **Un's.** With its pebbled entryway, small trees strung with white lights, and U-shape pavilion lined with Balinese paintings, the feel here is that of a secret temple tucked away in the center of a bustling town. Margaritas are the happy-hour special, and entrées include both Indonesian and Western specialties—mushroom ravioli, Venetian chicken breast, cordon bleu, and grilled snapper and prawns. At day's end, the bar in the center of the garden is a great place to unwind, and strolling Batak musicians occasionally perform. ⊠ *Jl. Pantai, Poppies La. (off Jl. Legian), Kuta,* ☎ *0361/752607. AE, MC, V.*

$$ ✕ **Warung Kopi.** Five marble-top tables facing the street and another 10 in the rear garden provide an oasis from the surrounding honkytonk scene. The menu is eclectic: Indonesian fish, vegetable, and rice dishes; Indian curries; Western beef and lamb. This is also a fine place to stop for just a beer and an appetizer or coffee and dessert. ⊠ *Jl. Legian Tengah 427, Legian,* ☎ *0361/753602. MC, V.*

$ ✕ **Bakung Mas Garden.** This peaceful, romantic restaurant belongs to the Segara Village Hotel. There are only six tables under its thatched roof, though there's a tiny bar in case you have to wait. The food has a Chinese influence: try the stir-fried vegetables with pork or the *semur* *daging* (thinly sliced beef with a rich sauce of mushrooms and onions). ✉ *Jl. Bakung Sari, Kuta,* ☎ *0361/788407. No credit cards.*

$$$$ ✕▥ **The Oberoi.** At the far western end of Legian Beach, the Oberoi's
★ 15 acres offer tranquility, privacy, and friendly service. Guest quarters dot the gardens of bougainvillea, hibiscus, and frangipani. The thatched cottages have verandas, and the villas have balconies and garden courtyards; some of the luxury villas have private pools and all have traditional Balinese inner courtyards. Hand-carved teak furnishings and locally made silk-screen prints and draperies are used throughout. Balinese dance is performed in the resort's amphitheater two or three evenings a week. Before the show, consider dining beneath the bamboo ceiling of the Kura Kura restaurant, perhaps near the lotus pond and its fountain. A Swiss chef and a Balinese sous-chef turn out both an Indonesian buffet and à la carte items with a Continental flair. The *bebek betutu*—a Balinese favorite of whole duck stuffed with mild spices, wrapped in banana leaves, and slowly steamed—is a standout dish. ✉ *Jl. Kayu Aya, Basangkasa, Legian Beach (Box 3351, Denpasar 80033),* ☎ *0361/ 730361 or 800/5–OBEROI in the U.S.,* ℻ *0361/730391. 60 cottages, 13 villas. Restaurant, bar, café, pool, spa, tennis court, health club, beach, windsurfing, theater, laundry service, meeting rooms, car rental. AE, DC, MC, V.*

$$$–$$$$ ✕▥ **Kul Kul Beach Resort.** This is one of the most interesting and attractive structures on Kuta Beach. The sundeck is built over rocks on one side of the pool, and you clamber down boulders to have a dip or get a drink. The modern bungalows contain deluxe bathrooms as well as sitting rooms and bedrooms furnished in rattan and bamboo. The attentive service adds to the sense of harmony you feel amid the Balinese architecture. The restaurant serves everything from Italian pastas to New Zealand lamb to Indonesian rice dishes. In the evening, a wayang kulit performance is given in English, an Indonesian singer entertains in the bar, and a video is shown on a wide screen. ✉ *Jl. Raya Pantai Kuta, Legian 80361,* ☎ *0361/752520,* ℻ *0361/752519. 55 bungalows. Restaurant, bar, pool, dance club. AE, MC, V.*

$$–$$$ ✕▥ **Bali Dynasty.** At the Dynasty, two wings branching out from the main building house the guest rooms, which have a standard rectangular layout with a double bed or two twins against one wall, a writing table along the other, and a couple of easy chairs; an extra $10 gets you a garden view. The pool is close to the beach. You can take meals in the Western-style restaurant or in the noteworthy Golden Lotus Chinese restaurant, whose Singaporean chef has a sure hand with spices. ✉ *Jl. Dewi Kartika, Tuban 80361,* ☎ *0361/752403, 800/942–5050 in the U.S., or 0181/747–8485 in the U.K.;* ℻ *0361/752402. 225 rooms, 12 suites. 2 restaurants, 2 bars, pool, tennis court, beach, dance club, travel services. AE, DC, MC, V.*

$$$–$$$$ ▥ **Bali Imperial.** Here you'll find peace and quiet, yet all the action on the Kuta/Legian strip is just a 10-minute walk away. The relaxed, expansive lobby is glass and marble. Guest rooms have high ceilings, lightwood furniture, shining wood floors, two twin beds or one king-size bed, balconies that face the sea or the garden, and marble baths with separate showers. The resort is under the same management as the Imperial Hotel in Tokyo, and there's an emphasis on service (the staff-to-guest ratio is three to one). If you ring your butler for coffee or tea (complimentary), he'll no doubt bring it to you immediately. ✉ *Jl. Dhyana Pura, Seminyak (Box 3384, Denpasar 80001),* ☎ *0361/ 754545, 212/692–9001 in the U.S., or 0171/355–1775 in the U.K.;* ℻ *0361/751545. 121 rooms, 17 bungalows. 2 restaurants, 2 pools, 2 tennis courts, beach, travel services. AE, DC, MC, V.*

$$ ▥ **Kuta Palace Hotel.** Set on 11 acres, this hotel consists of two-story buildings that surround a courtyard with gardens and pools. Rooms

are simply but pleasantly decorated with Balinese-patterned fabrics and a cream-and-rust color scheme. All have ocean or garden views. ✉ *Jl. Pura Bagus Taruna, Legian (Box 3244, Denpasar 80001),* ☎ *0361/751433,* FAX *0361/752074. 422 rooms. Restaurant, refrigerators, pool, 4 tennis courts, beach, laundry service. AE, DC, MC, V.*

$$ 🖼 **Poppies Cottages.** At this, one of Kuta's top small hotels, you can stay in a traditional thatched cottage for a fraction of what it would cost at a larger resort. Set amid fragrant gardens—highlighted by arching bridges, hidden pools, and flowing waterfalls—each cottage has one double bed or two single beds and a large, secluded balcony. Bathrooms have sunken tubs and are in screened, private gardens. A set of pools is nestled among rocks with landscaped sunbathing terraces and waterfalls, and the pavilion houses a small library and game area. Convenience is another advantage here: Kuta's shops and beaches are a five-minute walk down the road. ✉ *Poppies La., Kuta (Box 3378, Denpasar 80033),* ☎ *0361/751059,* FAX *0361/752364. 20 cottages. Restaurant, bar, 2 pools, library, travel services, car rental. AE, DC, MC, V.*

Nightlife and the Arts

Tourist life on Bali focuses on sightseeing and beach activities; by late evening, most areas quiet down, with one exception: Kuta Beach. Here the activity begins with drinks at cafés—one of the most consistently popular is **Poppies** restaurant (☞ Dining and Lodging, *above*)—in the early evening, followed by more drinks in cafés or dancing and drinks in discos, most of which charge a modest cover.

A stroll down Jalan Pantai along the beach leads past many small, open-air bars right on the sand. **Cactus Biru** (☎ no phone) and **Geria Cafe** (☎ no phone), next to the Dunkin' Donuts stand on the northern end of the beach, are usually packed. **Kacang Bali** (☎ 0361/754412), otherwise known as "Peanuts," sponsors a weekly pub crawl that hits many watering holes on the strip.

The new **Hard Rock Cafe Beach Club** (✉ Jl. Legian 204, Kuta, ☎ 0361/755661) is one of the most consistently popular places in town. There's no cover unless a live band is playing; generally, the action starts rolling at 9 PM and grinds down at 2 AM.

Some of the old standbys include: **Gado-Gado** (✉ Jl. Dhyana Pura, ☎ 0361/775225), open Wednesday–Sunday, an open-air disco near the ocean; **Kayu Api** (✉ Jl. Legian and Jl. Melasti, ☎ no phone), which has live music, often of international caliber; and **Koala Blu** (✉ Jl. Kuta, ☎ no phone), which attracts mostly Australians. For informality, drop in at the **Kuta Jaya Jazz Corner** (✉ Jl. Raya. Pantai Kuta, ☎ 0361/752308).

Shopping

Kuta's shopping scene of small stores crammed onto both sides of the main street has moved decidedly upscale and now includes a range of boutiques and specialty shops. However, if you take your time, you'll still find many bargains. Try to buy crafts directly from village workshops; items to look for include silver objects and jewelry, Indonesian crafts, batik clothing and art, paintings, and wood carvings. Skip the fake watches and bogus tapes sold by roving vendors and go for the Indonesian gamelan music CDs, guaranteed to bring back memories when played at home.

Animale (✉ Jl. Pantai Kuta, ☎ 0361/485450) has unique prints for men and women. The **Cleopatra Boutique** (✉ Jl. Pantai Kuta 21, ☎ 0361/755456)—which caters to the Japanese market as well as Westerners—is a good place for textiles, clothes, and accessories. For men, **Handy's** (✉ Jl. Pantai Kuta 20C, ☎ 0361/751247) has an extensive selection of batik shirts and shorts. **Indigo Kids** (✉ Jl. Pantai Kuta, Jl. Legian Kuta, and Jl. Arjuna 23, ☎ 0361/730447 general factory) is the place to buy batik clothing for babies through teens. **Inspirations** (✉ Jl. Pantai Kuta, ☎ 0361/483616) has a terrific variety of knick-knacks, carvings, and woven goods.

For customized jewelry, check out **Mayang Bali** (✉ Kuta Square, Blok A-12, ☎ 0361/752902). **Natural Field** (✉ Jl. Tegal Wangi, Kuta, ☎ 0361/752124) sells lovely textiles, sarongs, dresses, and accessories. For a wonderful selection of high-quality batik, ikat, dresses, accessories, and gifts, step into **Pusaka** (✉ Jl. Pantai Kuta 20D, ☎ 0361/761810; ✉ Jl. Legian 338, ☎ 0361/758110). **Sarayu Silver** (✉ Jl. Pantai Kuta, ☎ no phone) sells jewelry.

Sanur

④ *12 km (7 mi) northeast of Kuta, 15 km (9 mi) northeast of Ngurah Rai Airport, 9 km (5 mi) southeast of Denpasar.*

Sanur was Bali's second beach resort, and today it's a good mix of Kuta and Nusa Dua: the energy of the former without the frenzy, and the class of the latter without the high prices. Hotels, restaurants, and shops are spread out, and this helps to keep the pace slow. The wide beach, which is framed by a shallow coral reef, is calm—perfect for snorkeling, boating, and windsurfing.

Dining and Lodging

$$$ ★ ✕ **Telaga Naga.** The name means "dragon's pond," though the lily ponds in the tropical garden set a peaceful—rather than fearsome—tone. The Cantonese and Szechuan cuisine is exquisite. Try the sautéed chicken with dried red chili or the fried prawns with Szechuan sauce, both house specialties. ✉ *Jl. Danau Tamblingan, across from Bali Hyatt,* ☎ *0361/288-1234. Reservations essential. AE, DC, MC, V.*

$$ ✕ **Le Gong.** The gong hangs in a central garden, and although the restaurant is on Sanur's main street, its woven bamboo walls and set-back tables give it a relaxing atmosphere. To make the most of the traditional Balinese menu, order a few dishes and share them. Some suggestions: soto ayam, prawns in butter sauce, fish grilled with spices, and nasi goreng. Fresh papaya or pineapple are refreshing desserts, but the coup de grâce is the Balinese equivalent of a banana split, swathed in a honey treacle. ✉ *Jl. Legong,* ☎ *0361/588066. No credit cards.*

$$ ✕ **Lotus Pond.** This thatched-roof restaurant is large and open, with square dining tables along one side, a cushioned lounge area along the other, and an extensive Indonesian buffet in the middle. Gardens with lotus ponds surround the pavilion. The atmosphere is breezy and casual, the service amicable. Western offerings, such as club sandwiches and salads, are popular as are the spiced-down Indonesian dishes; the rijsttafel buffet is outstanding. ✉ *Jl. Danau Tamblingan,* ☎ *0361/289398. AE, MC, V.*

$$ ✕ **Penjor Restaurant.** Set back from the main street, this bamboo-walled restaurant surrounds an open courtyard where tables are set up in fine weather. Each night a different Balinese dance-drama is presented, and the set menu rotates between Balinese, Indonesian, Chinese, and Indian dinners. Owner Ida Bagus Ketut Oka speaks English fluently and loves to chat with his guests. ✉ *Jl. Batu Jumbar,* ☎ *0361/88226. AE, DC, MC, V.*

$$$$ ✕🏨 **Tandjung Sari.** This renowned hotel, whose unique design has been featured in books on architecture, is a peaceful "village" of Balinese-style bungalows on tropical grounds with small stone temples and statues. The open-pavilion lobby is decorated with carvings, and the gardens overflow with blossoms year-round. Bungalows have split-bamboo walls and such touches as minibars, handwoven fabrics, and an antique or two. Most bathrooms have skylights. Prawns, curries, fritters, and a dozen other items are served in a romantic setting just back from the beach; Wednesday night sees a superb rijsttafel. ⊠ *Jl. Danau Tamblingan (Box 25, Denpasar 80001),* ☎ *0361/288441,* ℻ *0361/ 287930. 24 bungalows. Restaurant, bar, minibars, beach, pool, windsurfing, snorkeling. No credit cards.*

$$$–$$$$ ✕⊡ **Bali Hyatt.** For a hotel that's part of a large international chain, this has a surprisingly Balinese feel. The green-tile pool has a waterfall replica of the entrance to the Goa Gajah (Elephant Cave); at the nearby pavilion, an Indonesian buffet is served during a Balinese dance performance on Saturday night. In the open-air spa, specialists perform a range of therapeutic treatments native to the archipelago. Tropical gardens cover the expansive grounds to the 6-km-long (4-mi-long) beach esplanade, where colorful *jukung* fishing boats depart each morning. Rooms are in four-story buildings, and though they're slightly worn, each has an island-style decor and a balcony. The Wantilan Cafe is a great place to try Balinese cuisine. An extensive breakfast buffet is served on the terrace overlooking the lily pond and fountain. For dinner, a rijsttafel buffet of 30-plus dishes—all labeled with their ingredients—is laid out on a lotus altar in the center of the room. The hotel is within walking distance of local markets, shops, and restaurants. ⊠ *Jl. Danau Tamblingan (Box 392, Denpasar 80001),* ☎ *0361/281234,* ℻ *0361/287693. 390 rooms. 5 restaurants, 4 bars, in-room safes, minibars, 2 pools, spa, 3-hole golf course, 2 tennis courts, jogging, beach, snorkeling, windsurfing, boating, children's programs, meeting rooms, car rental. AE, DC, MC, V.*

$$$ ⊡ **Hotel Sanur Beach.** Most of the action here takes place around the pools, the beach, and the patio bars. All rooms have balconies, and most have huge double beds (a few in the older wing have twins); the best rooms face the pool. Twenty-six self-contained bungalows offer more privacy. Classical Balinese dance performances and buffet dinners are offered most nights. ⊠ *Jl. Kalianget (Box 3279, Denpasar 80001),* ☎ *0361/288011,* ℻ *0361/287566. 298 rooms, 26 bungalows. 3 restaurants, coffee shop, 2 pools, 4 tennis courts, badminton, beach, windsurfing, recreation room, meeting rooms. AE, DC, MC, V.*

$$ ⊡ **Segara Village.** At the north end of Sanur Beach, this small, family-owned hotel consists of Balinese-style thatch-roof cottages. The open lobby houses both of the hotel's restaurants, so it can be busy. Rooms have balconies or verandas and private baths. The decor is very simple, but the hospitality is genuine. ⊠ *Jl. Segara Ayu (Box 91, Denpasar 80001),* ☎ *0361/288407,* ℻ *0361/287242. 40 rooms. 2 restaurants, 4 bars, 2 pools, 2 tennis courts, bicycles, children's programs, playground. AE, DC, MC, V.*

Nightlife and the Arts

Most hotels here have some form of entertainment, often a live band. The **Lotus Pond** (⊠ Jl. Danau Tamblingan, ☎ 0361/289398) is a tranquil haven where a casual, upscale crowd gathers for evening cocktails. Across the street, Bali socialites and twentysomething tourists meet for drinks at the **Janger** bar (⊠ Jl. Danau Tamblingan 21, ☎ 0361/ 288888) and late-night dancing at the cavernous, techno-modern **Subek** disco (⊠ Jl. Danau Tamblingan 21, ☎ 0361/288888).

Outdoor Activities and Sports

BOATING

For yacht charters, contact **Jet Boat Tours** (⊠ Jl. Pantai Karang 5, ☎ 0361/28839). Sanur's **Bali Hyatt** (☞ Dining and Lodging, *above*) has two deep-sea fishing boats available for charter. You can hire the *Bali Hai* (☎ 0361/720331) for a luxurious excursion around the island as well as for dive and surf trips. The vessel departs from Tanjung Benoa, about 9 km (6 mi) south.

SCUBA DIVING AND SURFING

You can rent scuba equipment and a ride out to the reef at Sanur from **Bali Marine Sport** (✉ Jl. Bypass Ngurah Rai, ☎ 0361/87872). **Ocean Dive Center** (✉ Jl. Bypass Ngurah Rai, ☎ 0361/88652) organizes dives out to reefs.

Nusa Lembongan, the island opposite Sanur Beach and next to Nusa Penida, has surfing and diving opportunities. For the best surfing, however, you really should head to Pura Luhur Ulu Watu, on the western side of the Bukit Peninsula. Both dive shops listed above rent boards and arrange transportation; you can also rent boards at the beaches, but they tend to be of lesser quality, and you'll be responsible for any damage done to them.

Shopping

There are interesting shops along Jalan Bypass and Jalan Danau Tamblingan. Look for handwoven fabrics, jewelry, ceramics, baskets, and kites. The **Sanur Beach Market** is worth a browse for handcrafted souvenirs. **Bagus Drugstore,** on Jalan Duyung next to the Bali Hyatt, sells groceries and has a large bookshop (with English-language titles) and souvenir area.

Denpasar

⑤ *9 km (5 mi) northwest of Sanur, 16 km (10 mi) northeast of Ngurah Rai Airport.*

Most people don't stay overnight in this busy market town of about 400,000 people, but Denpasar is worth a day trip to visit its museums, markets, and monuments. You can book city tours through your resort, or you can see Denpasar on your own, by taxi or bemo.

Where Jalan Gajahmada intersects with Jalan Veteran is a large **statue of Brahma.** Its four faces look in the cardinal directions. To the left is the **Natour Bali Hotel** (✉ Jl. Veteran 3, ☎ 0361/225681), in a building dating from the Dutch colonial period.

Continue through this intersection past Puputan Square—a park on the right-hand side, with its Sukarno-inspired heroic statue of the common man—to reach **Pura Agung Jagatnatha,** Bali's state temple. (Go right at the end of the park onto Jalan Letkol, and the entrance is on your left.) The temple's center stupa is surrounded by a moat and rises eight levels; at the top is a statue of Shiva with flames coming from his shoulders. The stupa is supported by the cosmic turtle (on whose back the real world symbolically sits, according to Balinese legend) and protected by a huge carved face with a red cloth tongue. Nagas entwine the base; around the bottom are relief carvings.

Farther down Jalan Letkol is the **Bali Museum,** with Balinese art dating from prehistoric to present times. The buildings are excellent examples of Balinese temple and palace architecture. ✉ *Jl. Letkol,* ☎ *0361/ 222680.* 🎫 *Admission.* ⊙ *Tues.–Thurs. and weekends 8–5, Fri. 8– 3:30.*

Another Denpasar attraction is **Taman Wedhi Budaya Arts Center,** where year-round dance performances are held (don't miss the island's annual summer arts festival, held here from mid-June to mid-July). Changing exhibits of modern paintings, batik designs, and wood carvings are also on display. ✉ *Jl. Nusa Indah,* ☎ *0361/222776.* 🎫 *Admission.* ⊙ *Daily 10–4.*

OFF THE   **TANAH LOT** – This famous temple stands on a small rocky islet 15 km (9
BEATEN PATH   mi) west of Denpasar (it's accessible via a small causeway except at
high tide, when it turns into an island). Though people flock here for the
postcardlike setting, the Balinese revere this pagoda-style temple as
deeply as they do the mountain shrines. It has the added mystery of
snakes that secret themselves in the rock holes and are said to guard the
spirits residing at Tanah Lot. Ideally, you should arrive an hour before
sunset; this will give you enough time to see the snakes. Cross the causeway to the temple, then return to the shore to watch it become silhouetted against the burning sky as the sun goes down. Not even the
hawkers and the lines of snapping cameras can spoil the vision.

Dining and Lodging

$$$$ ✗⌧ **Hotel Tugu Bali.** The island's most memorable hotel is 11 km (8
★   mi) west of the city in a bucolic landscape of rolling hills and rice paddies along the edge of the Bali Sea. Nearly every element here is a piece
of Balinese and Indonesian history—from the ornately carved teak doors
and window frames and the ancient Chinese temple reconstructed on
the grounds to the 39—the number needed to show respect to and ask
protection from the wrath of the gods—*boma* (faces) looking down
from teak columns. You enter the lower level of each two-story guest
villa by a boardwalk over a lotus pond; access to the upper floors is
via an outdoor spiral staircase. Each villa also has a back terrace with
a plunge pool. Inside, you'll find marble floors, huge canopy beds, and
exquisite antiques. Bath and toilet areas are small but have such winning touches as stained-glass windows. You can also stay in (or just
tour) the Puri Le Meyeur, a bungalow and monument to Belgian artist
A. J. Le Meyeur De Merpres, and the Pavilion, which commemorates
artist Walter Spies and is modeled after his home at the palace in Yogyakarta, Java. Other on-site amenities include an art gallery, the
Puputan Museum brimming with artifacts and old photos, and a traditional medicine and spice stall. Even if you don't stay here, pop in
for tea at the small Tugu Restaurant. The selection is varied and delightful: crispy rice cakes, fried tempeh, spring rolls, fresh fruit tarts,
and chocolate cake squares. Don't miss the ginger tea—truly refreshing on a hot afternoon. A dinner of such Thai dishes as stir-fried
chicken with cashews, grilled red snapper, or crab soup is also an option. Just save room for dessert. ⌧ *Jl. Batu Bolong, Canggu,* ☎ *0361/*
731701, ℻ *0361/731704. 25 villas. 2 restaurants, bar, pool, spa, li-*
brary, business services, meeting rooms. AE, MC, V.

Shopping

Along the Badung River (near the bridge off Jalan Gajahmada) is the
large, two-story **Pasar Badung,** the liveliest market in town. Packed
with spice vendors and farmers selling vegetables, meats, and flowers,
it's busiest in the early morning, though commerce continues until early
afternoon. The little girls who volunteer to guide you around get com-
missions from any vendor you patronize; of course, the price of anything you buy is raised accordingly. If you're in Denpasar in the evening,
head for the **night market** in the riverside parking lot of the multilevel
shopping center at Kumbasari. It's a gathering place for locals, who
come to chat, shop, and feast on Balinese food. The **Mega Art Gallery**
(⌧ Jl. Gajahmada, ☎ 0361/224592) sells new and antique puppets,
wood carvings, and paintings.

Crafts Villages

From Denpasar north, a strand of crafts villages is laced together by slim,
twisting roads that slip between mountain folds and fertile rice fields. In
just a day, you can cover the main sights; with a little more time, you

can explore off-the-beaten-path shops that often double as the artisans' homes. In any case, these crafts villages are among the highlights of any trip to Bali, and the quality, variety, and affordability of the items sold in them will make a venture to these towns truly memorable.

Batubulan

The first crafts village is 19 km (12 mi) northeast of Denpasar on the main road to Ubud. Batubulan is famous for the stone carvers whose workshops and displays line the road. You'll see small, open factories where boys chip at the soft sandstone and sculptures are for sale out front. Wares range from the classic guardian figures that stand before Balinese temples and houses to smaller statues. Most workshops make small carvings that are easier to transport home. **I. Made Sura** (☎ no phone) is one of the better shops; it also carries some wood carvings, old wooden ornaments, and carved doors.

At 9:30 each morning, **dance-dramas** are performed at each of the village's three theaters, along the main road (the same show is done at all three). Travel agencies in Ubud and many hotels can arrange for you to see the show as part of a cultural tour. Admission is around Rp 20,000.

Tohpati

Balinese batik tends to be more colorful than that of Java, and the designs are often floral rather than geometric. A good source of hand-drawn batiks is **Popiler** (☎ 0361/36498) in the village of Tohpati, on the northern outskirts of Batubulan. If you pay cash instead of using a credit card, you increase your bargaining power by around 20% for the yard goods, paintings, garments, and household items here. Behind the shop, you can watch girls outlining the designs with wax.

En Route   German businessman and Balinese resident Ed Swoboda chose Singapadu (just north of Batubulan; take the smaller road that runs straight rather than following the main road around the right curve) as the site of the **Taman Burung** (Bali Bird Park). Designed with Balinese thatched roofs, the aviaries of the 4-acre park house birds from around the world, including such rare species native to Indonesia as the Bali starling and birds of paradise from Irian Jaya. A 160-seat restaurant makes a good stop for breakfast in a lush setting. ⊠ *Jl. Serma Lok Ngurah Gambir, Singapadu,* ☎ *0361/299352.* 🎫 *Admission.* ⊙ *Daily 9–6.*

Celuk

Celuk, 2 km (1 mi) northeast of Batubulan, is a village of silversmiths, and the main road through town is jammed with small shops announcing their specialties. In workshops behind the stores, you can watch boys working the silver and setting semiprecious stones. As a rule, the jewelry you find here is 90%–92% silver, the tableware 60%–70%. Filigree pieces with detailed, imaginative designs—ships, flowers, butterflies—are among the best items to buy, but don't visit in the morning, when all the tour buses stop here; come in the afternoon when prices return to reasonable levels. If you have time, you can custom-order pieces. Remember that with quiet patience and a smile you might drive the cost of a $125 bracelet down to $80. (Bargaining is the rule, especially where price tags are in dollars.)

At least 30 shops line the main road and surrounding streets, although a severe shortage of sidewalks can make browsing on foot potentially life-threatening. The goods vary little from store to store—rings, earrings, pins, and hair clips are perennial favorites—but some establishments display more merchandise. One shop with a large selection is **Dewi Sitha** (☎ no phone), on the left side of the road going north. Other places include: **Antara** (☎ 0361/298091) and **Celuk Ministore** (☎ 0361/298350). Along the same road, stop in **Bali Ayu Batik** (☎ 0361/

298193) and the nearby **Bali Pottery Center** (☎ no phone) for an assortment of crafts.

Sukawati

Four kilometers (2 miles) northeast of Celuk, Sukawati is known for its specialized crafts, including kites, mobiles, wind chimes, temple umbrellas, woven baskets, and shadow puppets. Stalls lining the road also sell baskets, hats, and furniture. **Pasar Seni,** the crafts market on the east side of the main road, sells a range of works by some of the island's most talented artisans, but lines of tour buses stop here mid-morning, so arrive early to beat the crowds. If you bargain determinedly, you may find some of the best prices in Bali. A kilometer (½ mi) west, the village of Puaya is one of the best places to shop for wayang kulit puppets and wayang topeng wooden masks.

Batuan

Batuan, 2 km (1 mi) north of Sukawati, is a weaving village and a painting center, where the famous black-and-white style of Balinese painting originated. Small galleries line the main road, and the backstreets have signs pointing to artists' homes. Impromptu visits are welcome in both.

The hand-cut, painted, shadow puppets sold on Bali are usually new, but you can buy antique ones at the **Jati Art Gallery** (✉ Along the main road, ☎ no phone), which also sells paintings, old masks and temple ornaments, handwoven ikat, batiks, wood carvings, and new puppets. **Mario Antique** (☎ 0361/298541) is a huge, open factory on the left side of the same road, where you can watch dozens of workers honing various pieces of furniture. You can't miss the giant elephants outside the **Antique Furniture Warehouse** (☎ 0361/298269) on the right; this is a fine place to search for both antiques and reproductions.

Find time in this village to visit the 10th-century **Pura Puseh Pura Desa** (Temple of Brahma), where the seldom-seen *gambuh*—the oldest known form of dance drama on Bali—takes place at every full moon. Once performed only for royal celebrations or temple festivals, these dances are the ultimate in classical Balinese style and have influenced numerous other dramas, including the wayang *wong,* in which humans perform the roles of the wayang kulit shadow puppets, and the *legong,* a famous court dance performed by young girls. The gambuh dance dramas are accompanied by a gamelan orchestra that features the long, resonant flutes that are unique to the area.

The brick-and-sandstone temple has three parts. You enter the outer courtyard through a classic Balinese split gate. The bell tower, in the second courtyard, is hung with the ubiquitous black-and-white-checked cloth. In the main courtyard, a stone screen protects the temple from bad spirits (because such spirits can't turn a corner, they can't go around the screen). In one corner of this courtyard is a shrine to Brahma, where a hermaphroditic figure is guarded by two nagas. This is the main shrine and, as in every Balinese temple complex, it faces Gunung Agung, the home of the gods. Nearby, another shrine has three roofs representing Brahma, Shiva, and Vishnu. Over the gate entrances, the face of the god Boma guards against evil from the earth, and the nagas provide protection against evil from the sea. ✉ *Jl. Raya, Batuan.* 🎫 *Rp 15,000.* ☉ *Daily sunrise to sunset except during ceremonies. Dance performances at 8 PM.*

Kemenuh

On the main road in Kemenuh, 3 km (2 mi) northeast of Batuan, the house of **Ida B. Marka** (☎ no phone), a famous wood-carver, is open to the public, providing a rare look inside a Balinese home. The showroom is in front, but there's no pressure to buy. Behind are a court-yard and a cluster of buildings that serve as the family complex. The centerpiece is the building used for weddings and other rites of passage; this is where the oldest family member sleeps. Other structures include the family temple, a granary, and a cooperative workshop where other villagers help to carve and polish.

Mas

There are some 4,000 wood-carvers on Bali, and most of them live in Mas, 5 km (3 mi) northwest of Kemenuh. Unique crafts found here include framed wooden carvings of Balinese rural scenes, intricately detailed wooden statues of Hindu goddesses, wooden chessboards, and carvings of creatures and characters. The village is also known for its mask making, samples of which can be found in shops down the back lanes. The brightly painted masks, most of which represent characters in Balinese folklore, make great wall hangings.

The famous wood-carver **Ida Bagus Tilem** (✉ Ubud Rd., ☎ 0361/6414) lives in Mas; his work, which has been exhibited internationally, is sold in his small shop. In Mas you'll also find **Taman Harum Cottages** (✉ Mailing address: Box 216, Denpasar, ☎ 0361/35242), which consist of 17 compact adjoining duplexes. Here you can take wood-carving classes or just shop for finished products in the **Tantra Gallery**, which also has displays of work by master carver Nyana. The **Tinem Gallery** (☎ 0361/35136) contains works by Nyana's brother, Ida Bagus Nyana. A variety of quality carvings are found at **Ary Puja Gallery and Workshop** (✉ Jl. Raya, Mas, ☎ 0361/975195), whose collection includes rooms full of polished wood statues, rural scenes, masks, and ornate framed pictures. **Nyoman Nurga** (☎ 0361/975200) carves made-to-order items.

Bedulu

6 *5 km (3 mi) northeast of Mas, 26 km (16 mi) northeast of Denpasar.*

This was once the capital of the last Balinese kingdom to stand against the conquering forces of Java in the 14th century. Today Bedulu's main claim to fame is the **Goa Gajah** (Elephant Cave), 2 km (1 mi) to the right of the intersection of Jalan Mas and Jalan Pengosekan (the entrance is on the right through a parking lot lined with souvenir vendors). Discovered in 1923 by a farmer cultivating his field, this cave temple is thought to have been built in the 11th century. In the court-yard, water spouts from the hands of six stone nymphs into two pools. It's believed that worshipers purified themselves here before passing through the mouth of the giant face of Boma carved on the entrance. (The Balinese consider the face protective even though it contains the same symbolic features as the face of Kali, the goddess of destruction, found at other Hindu temples.) To enter the cave, worshipers must pass through the mouth.

The cave is pitch dark—hope that your guide has a flashlight. To the left is a niche with a statue of Ganesha, the elephant-headed god and son of Shiva. In the center, to the right of a crumbled statue, are three *linga* (upright carved stones symbolizing male fertility), each with three smaller *yoni* (female forms).

NEED A BREAK?	Atop the hill above the cave, is **Puri Suling** (☎ no phone), a pleasant restaurant with a terrace that looks out over the rice fields and down to the cave area. The Western food is dull, but the Indonesian dishes are excellent.

Also of interest in Bedulu is the **Pura Saman Tiga** temple, on the left side of the road several yards beyond the Bedulu junction. Legend has it that this 11th-century temple was the site where a group of holy men once met to establish laws of religious tolerance and unity on Bali. A little farther on is the **Bedulu Archaeological Museum** (☎ no phone), which houses numerous early Balinese artifacts, including pottery and sarcophagi. The museum is open Monday–Thursday 8–2 and Friday–Saturday 8–1.

Ubud

❼ *5 km (3 mi) northwest of Bedulu, 25 km (15 mi) northeast of Denpasar.*

Ubud gained fame as an art colony in the 1930s and has since grown into the island's main cultural center of galleries, crafts shops, and traditional Balinese dance troupes (there are performances nearly every day). It has also grown more commercial. Many artists still have workshops in the region, but hotels, restaurants, ice-cream parlors, and souvenir stalls are taking over more and more ground. Ubud may no longer be a quiet place in which to immerse yourself in Balinese culture, but it still offers many more opportunities to experience authentic Balinese life than do the coastal resort areas. It's also an excellent base from which to explore Bali's interior. Step out of town and walk the many trails that lead through the countryside to small villages, and you'll find the "real Bali."

Ubud was placed on the world map when artists Walter Spies from Germany and Rudolf Bonnet from Holland introduced the Balinese to the three-dimensional form and convinced them that using real people, not courtly officials, in a free-flowing background was legitimate art. From that point on, a naturalism was seen in Balinese art. Exhibits at the
★ **Puri Lukisan Museum,** set in gardens at the west end of the main street, show the evolution of this art style from the 1930s to the present. Works are arranged chronologically, so you can see the transition from formal religious art to more natural, realistic depictions of dances, festiv.¹s, and rice harvesting. ⊠ *Jl. Raya (west of intersection with Monkey Forest Rd.),* ☎ *0361/975136.* 💷 *Admission.* ⊙ *Daily 8–4.*

For an overview of Balinese and Indonesian art styles, visit Ubud's finest collection of paintings at the **Neka Gallery,** at the east end of the main street. The works are organized by style in seven buildings, one of which has paintings by foreign artists, including Spies and Bonnet. Be sure to visit Building 6, devoted to works by Affandi, an Indonesian artist of international renown. Building 4 houses works by I Gusti Nyoman Lempadi, who is recognized as one of the first true Bali artists. ⊠ *Jl. Raya.* ☎ *0361/975074.* 💷 *Admission.* ⊙ *Daily 9–4.*

The **Agung Rai Museum of Art (ARMA)** in Pengosekan, a small community just southeast of Ubud, is a cultural complex whose emphasis is on the Balinese arts. Here you'll find several galleries with permanent displays by Indonesian and European artists; a library; a bookshop; workshops; and the elegant Kokokan Hotel (☞ *also* Dining and Lodging, *below*). The museum offers dance, art, and music classes, and arts performances take place throughout the week; call or stop by the museum for a current schedule. ⊠ *Jl. Pengosekan,* ☎ *0361/976659.* 💷 *Free.* ⊙ *Daily 9–6.*

In the center of town is the beautiful **Hotel Puri Saren Agung,** which was once part of the palace of Ubud's royal family. The structure was rebuilt after it was decimated by a 1917 earthquake; the current prince's living quarters are at the end of the courtyard. There are slightly run-down guest pavilions on the grounds; better to just stop

Ubud and Vicinity

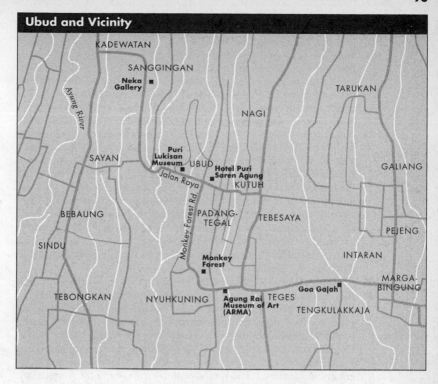

by for a look at the fine antiquities or for a listen to the gamelan music that's played here nightly.

Across from Puri Saren is Monkey Forest Road, which has many souvenir and T-shirt shops and inexpensive restaurants. Farther along are small hotels and losmen, where you can find simple and very affordable accommodations. Keep walking and you'll reach the **Monkey Forest,** where a small donation gets you a close-up view of monkeys so accustomed to people that the little monsters will steal your camera from your hands or tear jewelry from your neck and scamper off with their loot into the trees.

OFF THE BEATEN PATH

TEGALALUNG – The roads north out of Ubud pass through lovely countryside with patchwork rice fields in different stages of cultivation. Men ankle-deep in mud plant and weed while ducks paddle and dip for their lunch. Out in the fields stand shrines to Dewi, the goddess of rice, and raised wooden platforms where farmers rest or eat. In the village of Tegalalung, artisans carve intricate flower designs into wood. It's delicate work, where a slip of the chisel can ruin the whole piece. You don't have to buy anything—though to do so would make the artisans happy. Just watch and marvel at the incredible craftsmanship.

Dining and Lodging

$$
✕ **Ary's Warung.** This Ubud classic is right on the main street. The open, multilevel layout is welcoming, but in peak season the small tables are placed so closely together that you'll probably bump elbows with the person sitting next to you. Still, the delicious Indonesian and Western fare—including salads, sandwiches, and snacks—is worth putting up with the close quarters. On quieter days, Ary's is a great place to browse through your guidebook or people-watch while sipping tea or coffee. The desserts are fabulous (one taste of the white-

chocolate cheesecake, and you'll be hooked). ✉ *Jl. Raya,* ☎ *0361/975053. AE, MC, V.*

$$ ✕ **Café Lotus.** Owned and managed by a Balinese man and his Australian wife, this peaceful, charming restaurant in the center of Ubud has tables in the courtyard gardens of a royal temple. You can't beat the setting: cool stone floors, intimate tables, small waterfalls hither and yon, and a magnificent lotus pond in back. From the creative menu consider ordering the avocado with diced peanuts, the roast chicken, or a homemade pasta dish. ✉ *Jl. Raya,* ☎ *0361/975660. AE, MC, V. Closed Mon.*

$$ ✕ **Kokokan Club.** Bali's best Thai restaurant is hidden in a corner lot
★   next to the ARMA (☞ *above*). Tucked into the folds of a forest beside a river that flows through rice terraces, the two-story, thatched-roof pavilion is just a quick step across a stone bridge. Both the views and the food are memorable. The steamed spring rolls are fresh, soft, and hot; the onion, tomato, and cucumber salad with lettuce, peanuts, and chilies is crisp and zesty; the fish entrées are fresh and sumptuous. Even the standard *phad thai* (fried noodles) are top-notch and beautifully arranged. Round tables, candlelight, and river breezes make this a popular dinner place, but the views are best in the late afternoon. ✉ *Jl. Pengosekan,* ☎ *0361/96495. AE, MC, V.*

$$ ✕ **Murni's Warung.** Beside a small ravine just outside Ubud, this mul-
★   tilevel restaurant is spacious yet intimate. The street-level dining room bustles with activity; one steep flight of stairs below, a second dining room is often empty and has terrific views (particularly of a nearby waterfall), as does the downstairs bar. Throughout, the shadowy wood interior is complemented by simple bamboo furniture and Indonesian art, creating a rustic and very Balinese feel. Both Indonesian and Western dishes are served, and special buffets are available on Western holidays. The Balinese duck—stuffed with spices and baked so thoroughly that the meat falls off the bones—is tried and true. The friendly, cheerful staff is ready to offer advice on local activities or simply rock babies while parents eat. A shop on the upper floor is a veritable gallery of Balinese items. Murni's also has some on-site accommodations, including two rooms, a bungalow, and a house—all moderately priced. ✉ *Jl. Raya,* ☎ *0361/975233. AE, MC, V.*

$ ✕ **Kafe Batan Waru.** Expats favor this café for its great service, decent food, and laid-back Ubud ambiance. Two dozen or so tables edge right up to the sidewalk, and the wait staff is quick to deliver drinks and plates of food even at the busiest times. A combination of Indonesian and Western fare graces the menu, including a tasty assortment of gado gado, mie goreng, nasi campur, and grilled seafood. ✉ *Jl. Dewi Sita,* ☎ *0361/977528. AE, MC, V.*

$ ✕ **Tutmak.** A stone's toss from Kafe Batan Waru is this small, neat coffee shop and espresso counter, where the beans are roasted fresh daily. Duck in for simple meals or pastries and a real cup of "java." ✉ *Jl. Dewi Sita,* ☎ *0361/975754. No credit cards.*

$$$$ ✕🏨 **Kupu Kupu Barong.** This luxurious complex is on the precipice of a deep valley, with glorious views of rice terraces and the Ayung River. Guest quarters vary in size and cost; all require stout legs, since they're built into the hillside (note because of the many levels, steps, and balconies, this hotel isn't recommended for families with young children). The older bungalows blend with the landscape and have woven rattan or stone-face walls and unique crafted furnishings. Duplexes have wood paneling and indulgently large bathrooms. The path to the restaurant is trellised with banana leaves, hibiscus, and clove. Seated on a rattan chair at a marble-top table, you can make your selection from such dishes as chicken casserole with coconut, chili, and lemongrass; prawn curry with yellow jasmine rice and green mango pickles; or smoked chicken and avocados with tropical fruit and black-current dressing. ⊠ *Desa Kedewatan, 80571,* ☎ *0361/975478, 800/561–3071 in the U.S., or 0171/742–7780 in the U.K.,* FAX *0361/975079. 19 suites. Restaurant, 2 bars, 2 pools, massage, bicycles, travel services. AE, DC, MC, V.*

$ ✕▥ **Ananda Cottages.** In the rice paddies of Campuan, just up the hill from Ubud, is this friendly, relaxed hotel. The open-air lounge-lobby surrounds a central garden. The thatched-roof brick bungalows have two units above and two below. Room decor is simple, with rattan furniture and ikat bedcovers; upper rooms have not only better views but also better baths. The open-air restaurant serves such specialities as satay and bebek betutu. ⊠ *Jl. Raya (Box 205, Denpasar 80364),* ☎ *0361/975376,* FAX *0361/975375. 30 rooms. Restaurant, bar, pool. No credit cards.*

$$$$ ▥ **Amandari.** The modern architecture here elegantly reflects local cul-
★ ture and customs. As you walk along stone paths and past lotus ponds, the only thing that might break the serenity is an occasional, distant rooster's crow. The spacious public areas include an open-air lobby, a book and CD library, and a restaurant overlooking a dramatic pool that appears to drop off into infinity. Tall stone walls enclose thatched-roof villas, most of which overlook rice terraces. The light-filled suites have dark wood, marble floors, heavy cream upholstery, spacious showers, dressing areas, and sunken outdoor tubs; six suites have private plunge pools. In duplexes, a spiral staircase leads to an upstairs bedroom. After a workout in the gym—with all its modern equipment—you might head for the spa for a traditional Balinese treatment. If you'd like do some shopping afterward, drivers are available to take you to and from downtown Ubud. ⊠ *Desa Kedewatan (Box 33), 80571,* ☎ *0361/975333, 800/ 447–7462 or 212/223–2848 in the U.S., 0800/282684 in the U.K.,* FAX *0361/975335. 30 suites. Restaurant, bar, pool, spa, tennis court, health club, hiking, bicycles, library, travel services. AE, DC, MC, V.*

$$$$ ▥ **Four Seasons Resort at Sayan.** The journey to this 17-acre prop-
★ erty begins with a walk along a wooden bridge above rice terraced mountain slopes and the Ayung River. The path ends at a large elliptical lotus pond on the roof of the central three-story structure. A polished wood staircase descends to the reception area and a lounge and bar with a spectacular 180-degree vista. Two-story suites are in the main building; villas are set into the hillside all the way down to the riverbank. Rooms are accented with rich teak and stone and have custom-made furnishings and tapestries from Bali and Java. The very modern spa offers Balinese massage and natural treatments. There's also a health club and, on a curving terrace, two sunken whirlpools that seem to hang out over the valley. Golf carts transport you along cement paths to the main building, the villas, and the free-form pool beside the river. Garden plots along the way contain ginger, corn, chilies, and other spices and vegetables used in the kitchen; rice grown on site is given away to local villages. ⊠ *Desa Sayan, 80571,* ☎ *0361/977577,* FAX *0361/ 977588. 18 suites, 28 villas. 2 restaurants, bar, pool, hot tubs, spa, health club, shops, library, meeting rooms. AE, DC, MC, V.*

$$$$ ▥ **Ibah Luxury Villas.** Tucked into the hills above a bend in Ubud's main road, Ibah is an unexpected pleasure. To reach the thatched-roof villas you stroll through stone archways, follow stepping stones across lily ponds, and hike trails that wind up the slopes. Villas have large windows with heavenly views, wood floors, ornate antique wood doors, and bathrooms with marble tubs and garden vistas. The picturesque pools across the parking lot are surrounded by cushioned seating areas carved into a stone wall built into the hill. The cozy spa above the restaurant is secluded and intimate, with treatment rooms right beneath its eaves. ⊠ *Jl. Raya (Box 193), 80571,* ☎ *0361/974466,* FAX *0361/974467. 11 villas. Restaurant, bar, 2 pools, hot tub, spa, health club, laundry service, travel services. AE, MC, V.*

$$$$ 🏨 **Pita Maha.** A member of Ubud's royal family modeled the Pita Maha after a Balinese village and built it on the edge of the Oos River valley. The architecture of the villas is traditional, the interior touches tastefully luxurious: marble floors, ornate window panels, wicker furniture with cream-color cushions, woven mats. Tall, sliding glass panels open to private terraces; most villas also have plunge pools. Bathrooms have curving sunken tubs, decorative stone walls, and open gardens. The restaurant and large, "infinity-edge" pool look onto the river valley. A stay at this hotel also gives you privileged access to local museums, temples, tours, and activities—compliments of your royal host. ✉ *Jl. Sanggingan (Box 198),* ☎ *0361/974330,* FAX *0361/974329. 29 villas. Restaurant, 2 bars, in-room safes, pool, spa, shop, library, laundry service, travel services. AE, MC, V.*

$$–$$$ 🏨 **Kokokan Hotel.** Scattered in the hills above the sacred Tirta Tawar River like small, forgotten temples, the stone-and-brick buildings of this charming hotel reflect the aura of their magical setting. Rooms have marble floors; terraces; huge bathrooms (no tubs, though, only showers); and ornate, hand-carved wooden doors and window panels. Balinese textiles and paintings accent the warm wood. Deluxe rooms have carved sandstone walls and sliding door panels that separate the large bedroom area from the bath. Room rates include a full breakfast; you can also dine in the poolside café or at the nearby Kokokan Club (☞ *above*). The on-site museum offers workshops that teach Balinese art forms such as gamelan playing, puppet and mask making, weaving, and dance—an excellent opportunity for parents to learn about Bali with their children. ✉ *Jl. Pengosekan, 80571,* ☎ *0361/975742,* FAX *0361/ 975332. 15 rooms. Restaurant, pool, laundry service, children's programs. AE, MC, V.*

$$ 🏨 **Puri Bunga Village Hotel.** This quiet oasis offers the same views as the Amandari and the Kupu Kupu for a fraction of the price. Although the furnishings aren't spectacular, rooms are spacious, and all but two face the Ayung River valley. Two junior suites have whirlpools; the Honeymoon Suite is the most luxurious and private. A small pool in the garden is beside an open-air restaurant. You're better off having your own wheels here; otherwise it's a 10-minute taxi ride into Ubud's center. ✉ *Desa Kedewatan (Box 141), 80000,* ☎ *0361/975448,* FAX *0361/ 975073. 14 rooms. Restaurant, pool. MC, V.*

$$ 🏨 **Tjampuhan.** On the main road just out of Ubud—atop a ravine overlooking a holy river—Tjampuhan was once an artists' colony, and the grounds still contain the former house of German painter Walter Spies. The lobby is no more than an open terrace off the road; paths lead to the bungalows, which are set in lovely gardens and have carved and gilded wood doors, woven bamboo walls, bamboo furniture, and handwoven fabrics and batiks. During the rainy season, rooms tend to be a little damp. You can ring for breakfast with bamboo bells. A new spa down the lane from the restaurant offers a variety of traditional treatments in a tropical setting. ✉ *Jl. Campuan (Box 15, Denpasar 80364),* ☎ *0361/975368,* FAX *0361/975137. 63 bungalows. Restaurant, bar, pool, spa, 2 tennis courts, bicycles, car rental. MC, V.*

$–$$ 🏨 **Puri Gong.** The front is an art gallery, but beyond a slim stone doorway, a path leads back to three large villas overlooking rice terraces. Rooms are bright, spacious, and breezy (there are four in each building, two on the upper level and two on the lower); each has tile floors, large teak canopy beds, and private bathrooms. Lower rooms have verandas, but upper ones have wonderful views through large windows that pull in the afternoon light. Breakfast is included in the price. ✉ *Jl. Hanoman, Raya Pengosekan, Ubud,* ☎ *0361/975343,* FAX *0361/ 298269. 12 rooms. Restaurant, bar, pool, laundry service, travel services. MC, V.*

$ 🏠 **Agung Raka.** Four rooms at this lodging in a developing area off
Monkey Forest Road are duplexes: downstairs are a covered patio and
a small lounge area; up steep wooden steps is the main bedroom with
a canopy bed and a small balcony overlooking the rice fields. The bathroom and shower are outside, enclosed but open to the sky. The remaining rooms, which cost about a quarter less, are in small two-story
houses; those on the ground-floor have patios, those upstairs, balconies.
Rates include breakfast. ✉ *Jl. Pengosekan, 80571,* ☎ *0361/975757,*
FAX *0361/975546. 12 rooms. Restaurant, pool. MC, V.*

Nightlife and the Arts

Ubud shuts down early—by the time most dance performances let out,
around 9 or 9:30, many cafés and restaurants are closing. One or two
spots along Jalan Raya stay open later, including **Ary's Warung** (☎ 0361/
975053) and **Café Lotus** (☎ 0361/975660), which often have live jazz
or Indonesian music. **Rai Bar** (☎ no phone) on Monkey Forest Road
attracts a crowd after everything else has shut down. The **Kokokan Club**
(✉ Jl. Pengosekan, ☎ 0361/96495) in Pengosekan has live music on
Saturday.

Ubud is the dance center of Bali, and you should see more than one of
the varied performances during your visit—not a problem, as at least
three troupes perform nightly. Dance shows at hotels are often commercially adapted and shortened; those held elsewhere around Ubud
are more genuine. (☞ Pleasures and Pastimes, *above,* for a discussion
of the most popular dances.) Try to attend at least one performance
in the village of Peliatan (it's just east of Ubud), whose troupes enjoy
some renown. The Puri Saren, Ubud's palace, is a pleasant, atmospheric
venue. Avoid the Kecak dance in the village of Bona, 3 km (2 mi) east
of Blahbatuh, as traffic noise distracts from the chant.

Consult your hotel or the *Bali Tourist Guide* and the *Bali Guide to
Events,* available free at most hotels and travel agencies, for current
schedules. **Ubud Tourist Information** (☞ Visitor Information *in* Bali Essentials, *below*) has a weekly dance-performance schedule and sells tickets (Rp 5,000–Rp 7,000) that include transportation to shows not held
in Ubud proper.

Outdoor Activities and Sports

GOLF

Forty-five minutes north of Ubud, the 18-hole, 6,432-yard **Bali Han-
dera Country Club** (✉ Bedugul, ☎ 0361/788994) is in a volcanic
crater and has beautifully landscaped gardens along its fairways.
Greens fees are $87 on weekends and $72 during the week. Caddies
cost $7 a round.

RAFTING

It takes 2½ hours to drift and bump through gorges and rapids down
the Ayung River, ending in the gentle valley near Ubud. Several companies organize rubber-raft trips for around $55, including the reliable
Australian outfit **Bali Adventure Rafting** (✉ Jl. Tunjung Mekar, Legian,
☎ 0361/751292). For agencies that specialize in adventure and rafting tours, *see also* Travel Agencies *in* Bali Essentials *below.*

Shopping

Ubud's main street is lined with shops that sell art, textiles, clothing, and
other handicrafts. On most days you'll also find a street market, but the
big "market day" takes place every third day from dawn until noon. The
clusters of shops along Jalan Monkey Forest and the surrounding streets
are also filled with bargains on jewelry, batik clothing and textiles, and
handcrafted bags. **Ary's Book Shop** (☎ 0361/96351) is the best place to
find English-language publications on regional culture and nature. For

clothing and books, try **Mutiara** (☎ 0361/975145). **Kunang-Kunang I and II** (☎ 0361/975714 and 0361/975716, respectively) have wonderful collections of textiles, carvings, art pieces, and antiques for sale.

The **Puri Gong Art Gallery** (✉ Jl. Raya, Pengosekan, ☎ 0361/974697) purveys antique sculptures, furniture, ceramics, and masks. The gallery next to the **Rudana Museum** (✉ Jl. Cokgederai, ☎ 0361/26564) sells collectors' pieces of hand-painted batik and paintings at reasonable prices. The **Seniwati Gallery of Art by Women** (✉ Jl. Sri Wedari, ☎ 0361/975285) displays and sells the works of many local female artists.

Ubud has its own style of wood carving; it's somewhat more ethereal than the work done in Mas. The slightly dusty shops of **Kamasan** (✉ Jl. Raya, Peliatan, ☎ 0361/974697) have an array of hand-carved items in endless themes, sizes, and styles. Look for handcrafted furniture at **Mario Antiques** (✉ Peninjauan Sukawati, Gianyar, ☎ 0361/98541), just outside Ubud. A good place to see both old and new work is the **Nyana Tilem Gallery** (✉ Jl. Raya, Mas, ☎ no phone). **Siadja** (✉ Jl. Raya, Mas, ☎ 0361/975710) is a small shop with numerous colorfully painted items.

En Route   Pejeng fell to the Javanese in the mid-1300s, but its temples still stand as testament to a great kingdom. Take time to walk through the **Pura Penataran Sasih,** Pejeng's former state temple, with its centuries-old Moon of Pejeng bronze drum. Also interesting is the **Pura Pusering Jagat,** possibly the crux of an ancient Balinese kingdom in which carvings and a large urn depict tales of the Mahabharata. Don't miss the **Pura Kebo Edan,** the "crazy buffalo" temple, with its famous 10-ft statue of its namesake.

Tampaksiring

❽ *19 km (12 mi) northeast of Ubud.*

This town is an excellent base for visiting three sacred Balinese sites. Since there are few accommodations or restaurants in the area, it's best to make Tampaksiring a day trip from Ubud.

Outside of town follow signs to **Pura Gunung Kawi,** a monument to an 11th-century ruler and one of the oldest temples in Bali. From the access road, a stone stairway leads down to a lush valley. You pass beneath a stone arch to the canyon floor where there are two rows of memorial temples, carved in niches in the face of two cliffs. According to legend, the giant Kebo Iwa carved these in one night with his fingernails.

Beyond the outskirts of Tampaksiring, the road forks. To the right is the famous temple at **Tirta Empul,** where people from all over Bali come to bathe in the holy spring. According to legend, the spring was created when the god Indra pierced a stone to produce magical waters that revived his army, whose soldiers had been poisoned by the demon king Mayadanava.

At the **Pura Panti Pasek Gel Gel** holy spring, a few miles north of Tirtal Empul, the hawkers are less demanding, and fewer visitors interrupt the sanctity of the temple than at Tirtu Empul. The temple is dedicated to Vishnu, whose many responsibilities include water and irrigation. The main shrine stands in the center of a pool filled with holy water and fat goldfish. Bathing pools are segregated by sex and age.

Gunung Batur

❾ *11 km (7 mi) north of Tampaksiring, 62 km (37 mi) north of Ubud.*

West toward the villages of Penaka and Sebatu and north of Tampaksiring, the vanilla- and clove-bordered road climbs quickly. Roadside stalls sell fruits and vegetables rather than souvenirs and handicrafts. And then there's the majestic bulk of 5,632-ft Gunung Batur (Mt. Batur). Dark lava flows are visible within the volcano's vast crater—nearly 29 km (18 mi) in diameter and 600 ft deep—where a new volcano has arisen and cool Lake Batur has formed. Penelokan, a village at the edge of the old crater, affords a great view of the lake and caldera.

An alternative route to Gunung Batur that captures Bali's enchanting rural scenes can be done in an afternoon, leaving around 3 PM to catch the best light of the day. The narrow, two-lane Sayan–Kedewatan road along the eastern border of Ubud passes a gathering of resorts through Payangan. Women carrying baskets of vegetables on their heads walk along the forest-lined route. As the lane heads north, you'll glimpse the Ayung River valley to the left; banana and palm trees crowd the right. The terrain then evens out into steeply stacked rice terraces that shine in the late afternoon light. Flocks of cranes cruise through the blue sky above them. About 12 km (8 mi) from the town of Kintamani (☞ *below*), the forest occasionally opens to offer views of the river valley to the left and mountains to the right. The truly breathtaking scenes, however, begin 3 km (2 mi) outside Kintimani, when the triumvirate peaks of Gunung Agung, Gunung Batur, and Gunung Abang appear east to west. A thin pine forest surrounds the road as it climbs into the mountains and comes to the junction with the main northern road. Here, you can't help but stop to gape at the shadowy slopes surrounding Lake Batur far below.

Quiet **Kintamani** is used as a rest stop by hikers who climb Gunung Batur. Guided hikes cost of about Rp 10,000 per person with a minimum of four in the group. To find a guide, inquire at the Yayasa Bintang Danu tourist office (☎ 0366/23370) opposite the turnoff to Lake Batur from Penelokan.

In the village of Penulisan, an old stairway leads up a hill to the ancient temple of **Pura Sukawana.** Most of the decaying sculptures are from the 11th century, but look closely and you will find older, pagan phallic symbols. The view, which stretches across Bali to the Java Sea, is breathtaking, especially at sunrise.

Dining and Lodging

$ ×🔢 **Lakeview Restaurant and Homestay.** Of the cluster of small, inexpensive hotels and restaurants beside the volcano's rim in Penelokan, this very simple hotel is one of the most popular. Rooms are very basic but clean, and the proximity to local activities makes up for the lack of amenities. Budget quarters are without bath; superior rooms are the largest and have private baths. The indoor-outdoor restaurant has decent Indonesian fare and memorable views—tour buses often stop here for a buffet lunch en route through the mountains. ⊠ *Jl. Raya, Penelokan,* ☎ *0366/51464. 20 rooms. Restaurant, bar, laundry service. No credit cards.*

$ ×🔢 **Segara Bungalows.** Six kilometers (4 miles) down the caldera road past Penelokan, this pleasant hotel is almost at the edge of Lake Batur. The no-frills rooms are clean; all have private baths but not all have hot water, so make sure to specify your preference. An open-air restaurant offers tasty Indonesian and Western dishes in a quiet mountain setting. Tours of the area are available, and the management is very helpful. The hotel is often used as a base for hiring trekking guides. ⊠ *Jl. Danau Batur, Penelokan,* ☎ *0361/958001. 38 rooms. Restaurant, travel services. AE, MC, V.*

Pura Kehen

 35 km (21 mi) south of Gunung Batur. The drive south from Penelokan to Bangli is a quick run downhill. On the outskirts of Bangli is an S-curve; here take a left, and at the foot of the hill is Pura Kehen.

Pura Kehen, a 12th-century temple dedicated to Shiva, is considered one of Bali's most beautiful: it rises up the mountainside and culminates in an 11-tier shrine. You step through an ornate entrance and into a courtyard with a giant holy banyan tree and a bell tower used to summon the villagers for ceremonies. The entrance to the inner courtyard is up steep steps. At the top center are the "closed gate" and a boma, which blocks evil spirits. Within the inner courtyard, the main shrine sits on a cosmic turtle, symbolizing the spiritual world, entwined by nagas, symbolizing the material. Material binds the spiritual—another example of Balinese harmony.

OFF THE
BEATEN PATH

PURA BESAKIH – Known as the Mother Temple of Bali, Pura Besakih is the most sacred of all. Situated on the slopes of Gunung Agung, the complex has 30 temples—one for every Balinese district—on seven terraces. It's thought to have been built before Hinduism reached Bali and subsequently modified. The structure consists of three main parts, the north painted black for Vishnu, the center white for Shiva, and the south red for Brahma. You enter through a split gate.

Much of the temple area was destroyed in 1963 when Gunung Agung erupted, killing 1,800 of the faithful, but diligent restoration has repaired most of the damage. You aren't allowed into the inner courtyard, but there's enough to see to justify the steep 2-km (1-mi) walk from the parking lot past souvenir stands and vendors. Besakih is 40 km (25 mi) northeast of Bangli, 45 km (28 mi) north of Klungkung, and 60 km (35 mi) north of Denpasar. The temple can be reached from Bangli (if you're coming from Gunung Batur), Klungkung (the best route if you're coming from Ubud, Denpasar, or points south), or Candidasa—take the road inland to Amlapura, where the road splits; keep going to Rendang, then turn right to climb the 11 km (7 mi) to the temple.

Klungkung

 28 km (18 mi) southeast of Ubud, 46 km (29 mi) east of Denpasar.

Klungkung is a former dynastic capital. In the center of town stands the **Kerta Gosa** (Hall of Justice), part of the 18th-century Royal Palace destroyed by the Dutch in the early 20th century and restored again by the remorseful Dutch two decades later. The raised platform in the hall supports three thrones—one with a lion carving for the king, one with a dragon for the minister, and one with a bull for the priest. The accused brought before this tribunal could look up at the painted ceiling and contemplate the horrors in store for convicted criminals: torches between the legs, pots of boiling oil, decapitation by saw, and dozens of other punishments to fit specific crimes. To the right of the Hall of Justice is the **Bale Kambang** (Floating Pavilion), a moat-encircled palace that was also decimated and rebuilt by the Dutch. Part of the motif of its painted ceiling relates stories of the hero Sang Sutasoma, whose supernatural powers could turn arrows and spears into flowers. The **Museum Semarajaya,** across the courtyard, is also worth a look for its collection of island relics as well as black-and-white photos and newspaper clippings that depict palace life and relate historic events.

Goa Lawah

⑫ *10 km (6 mi) southeast of Klungkung.*

East of Klungkung, the road drops south to run along the coast and through the area of Kusamba, speckled with the thatched roofs of salt-panning huts. Just beyond is Goa Lawah, the bat cave. Unless you really long to see thousands of bats hanging from the ceiling, you may not want to subject yourself to the aggressive hawkers, postcard sellers, and young girls who throw you a flower, then angrily demand payment when you leave. The cave is said to lead all the way to Gunung Agung.

Padangbai

⑬ *5 km (3 mi) northeast of Goa Lawah.*

Continuing east from Goa Lawah along the coast will bring you to Padangbai, a quiet village next to one of the island's main ports. Because most people simply pass through it en route to other sights, Padangbai has remained a charmingly offbeat center for water sports and romantic getaways. The only time the town seems at all frenzied is right after the four-hour ferry from Lombok arrives or when the occasional cruise ship docks—hawkers set up stands and set to work as passengers disembark. There's a tourist office at the docks, and there are plenty of boats for hire. There are also plenty of small losmen where you can while away the afternoons walking along the thin brown crescent of beach filled with colorfully painted fishing pontoons.

Balina Beach and Manggis

★ **⑭** *5 km (3 mi) north of Padangbai.*

The curving stretch of Balina Beach, at the other end of Amuk Bay, is just as serene as Padangbai—but with the feel of an upscale resort. Several luxury hotels are set back into the forested slopes along the road between the village of Manggis, 11 km (7 mi) north of Padangbai, and Candidasa.

Dining and Lodging

$$$$ ✕▥ **Amankila.** This hillside resort has views of the Bandung Straits.
★ Luxurious thatched-roof pavilions are connected by long, raised, cement walkways. Each guest villa has a terrace, a bedroom with a king-size canopy bed, and a spacious bath with a sunken tub and separate shower; some villas have private pools. You'll feel like royalty basking in the sun beside the tri-level communal pool, whose waters rush down in wide falls from one level to the next. The beach is a stiff downhill climb, or you can ride to it in a chauffeured Jeep. The large, warm library has an extensive collection of books on Indonesian and regional travel and history; in its cushioned sitting area, experts often present slide shows or give talks on topics related to local culture. At the Terrace restaurant, you choose from three menus—Indonesian, Nonya (Malay), and Western. The chef comes to your table to make recommendations tailored to your tastes, and the rest of the staff maintains this high level of service throughout your meal. Savory appetizers include the Thai-style crab and coconut salad and the *bosonboh,* a light, crispy, stir-fried salad with squid, tofu, bean sprouts, and vegetables. Succulent pork satay, juicy beef rendang, and curry *kapitan* (a wild-chicken curry flavored with lemongrass) are standout entrées. Each night a gamelan trio plays as the sun sets. ✉ *Pantai Buitan (3 km/2 mi northeast of Padangbai turnoff), Manggis 80871,* ☎ *0366/ 21993, 800/447–7462 or 212/223–2848 in the U.S., 0800/282684 in the U.K.;* 🖷 *0366/21995. 35 villas. 2 restaurants, bar, pool, mas-*

sage, hiking, beach, snorkeling, windsurfing, library, travel services. AE, DC, MC, V.

$$$–$$$$ ✕▥ **The Serai.** When sunlight washes the pale golden walls and marble floors, you get a true sense of this resort's warmth. Rooms are in the two-story buildings with gold walls, wood furnishings, and cream-color upholstery. Superior rooms don't have tubs (only showers), but they do have outer sitting areas that face the pool and beach; in deluxe rooms the baths are fully equipped and the balconies have built-in sofas overlooking the pool and gardens. A range of outdoor activities and tours to local sights are available so you can readily experience the local flora, fauna, and culture. In the restaurant, small square tables and butterscotch wicker chairs are arranged in a raised, sheltered pavilion surrounded by a lotus pond. Must-try Asian dishes include steamed duck breast, spicy prawn mango curry with yellow rice, and Thai green chicken curry. If you crave a Western dish, try the wild-rice mushroom risotto or the grilled peppered tuna. Round woven mats, deep-blue cups and plates with lemon-color starfish, and yellow spice and sugar bowls accentuate the food's artistic presentation. The on-site cooking school gives you a chance to learn more about Indonesian cuisine. ⊠ *Pantai Buitan (6 km/4 mi northeast of Padangbai turnoff), Manggis 80871,* ☎ *0363/41011,* ﬀ *0363/41015. 58 rooms. Restaurant, bar, beach, dive shop, travel services. AE, DC, MC, V.*

$ ▥ **Balina Beach Bungalows.** Popular with scuba and snorkel enthusiasts for its diving club, this hotel has one- and two-story thatched cottages near a sandy beach 3 km (1.8 mi) west of Candidasa. All rooms have private baths and ceiling fans. The best rooms, upstairs in the two-story bungalows, have sitting areas and terraces; the one-story garden-view rooms have open-air bathrooms and large corner tubs as well as large cushioned bales overlooking the rice fields. ⊠ *Pantai Buitan (8 km/5 mi northeast of Padangbai turnoff), Manggis 80870,* ☎ *0363/ 41002,* ﬀ *0363/41001. 42 rooms. Restaurant, bar, pool, beach, dive shop, travel services. AE, DC, MC, V.*

Outdoor Activities and Sports

The **Balina Diving Association** (⊠ Balina Beach, ☎ 0361/80871) arranges dives out to Nusa Penida.

Candidasa

⑮ *3 km (2 mi) east of Balina Beach, 6 km (4 mi) east of Manggis, 14 km (9 mi) northeast of Padangbai.*

Candidasa, once a budget traveler's escape from the 24-hour partying of the southwestern beaches, now encompasses a throng of small hotels, restaurants, tourist shops, and travel agencies. Still, the area is more peaceful than Kuta or Legian, and less expensive than Nusa Dua or Jimbaran. A lively coral reef 300 yards offshore calms the waves and makes the water ideal for snorkeling. If you prefer scuba diving, you can easily hire one of the many fishing boats that park close to the beach.

Dining and Lodging

$ ✕ **TJ's.** Don't let the dressed-down setting of chipped blue chairs, a mishmash of tables, and scuffed brick floors put you off—the food is terrific. There is Asian and Western fare, and a bar along the side wall serves up every drink you can imagine (it's a popular evening hangout). Among the best dishes are the Thai green chicken curry, the spicy Thai red prawn curry, and the nasi campur. ⊠ *Jl. Raya,* ☎ *no phone. AE, MC, V.*

$ ✕ **Warung Candi Agung.** Fresh, tasty food and very affordable prices have made this eatery on the main road popular with travelers. With a very basic decor and motorcycles and trucks flying by, there isn't much ambiance. But the list of Western, Indonesian, and seafood dishes is long; the service is prompt; and the staff is eager to please. A stage is the site of free weekly Legong performances, and the restaurant operates a free shuttle to and from town. ⊠ *Jl. Raya,* ☎ *0363/41157. No credit cards.*

$$ ⊞ **The Watergarden.** This resort's name couldn't be more appropriate. ★ Cool, thatched-roof cottages with high ceilings, marble floors, warm brick walls, and simple island furnishings are complemented by wide wooden terraces overlooking lily ponds. Each dwelling is nestled into tropical gardens, with rushing waterfalls and koi ponds around every corner. From the white-sand beach across the road, the views of Gunung Agung are superb. Friendly staffers might offer to take you to their villages so that you can see Balinese culture and ceremonies up close. ⊠ *Jl. Raya,* ☎ *0363/41540,* FAX *0363/41164. 13 rooms. Restaurant, bar, pool, beach, snorkeling, library, laundry service, travel services. V.*

$ ⊞ **Fajar Candidasa Beach Bungalows.** Whistling songbirds and chuckling mynahs welcome you to this small hotel; indeed, dozens of birdcages decorate the back of the reception area. Tall, redbrick, templelike bungalows and neat gardens line the walkway. All rooms have small terraces and oversize sunken tubs; only deluxe rooms have air-conditioning, however. The small swimming pool and terrace are right next to the ocean breakwater. The facilities are clean and the grounds are quiet. ⊠ *Jl. Raya,* ☎ *0363/41539,* FAX *0366/41538. 33 rooms. Restaurant, bar, pool, beach, boating, laundry service, travel services. AE, MC, V.*

$ ⊞ **Pandan Bungalows.** Here cozy bungalows with bamboo doors and walls are connected by red-tile terraces beneath a thatched roof. The garden setting stretches to the sea. Bathrooms are open and feature a shower and small stone garden. There's no air-conditioning, but fans are available, as is hot water. You can dine in the restaurant that's next to a small pool and the ocean or in the dining area out front. Continental breakfast is included in the price. ⊠ *Jl. Raya (Box 126, Amlapura 80801),* ☎ *0363/41541,* FAX *0363/41541. 24 rooms. 2 restaurants, bar, pool, laundry service. MC, V.*

Tenganan

⑯ *8 km (5 mi) northwest of Candidasa.*

On the western side of Candidasa, the road turns inland to Tenganan, an ancient walled village of the Bali Aga—the people who lived on the island well before the conquerors of Java's Majapahit kingdom arrived. The village consists of two parallel streets lined on either side with identical walled compounds. Inside the compounds, houses face each other across a grassy central strip, where the public buildings stand (no cars are allowed). Tenganan people seldom marry outside the village, and they adhere to their traditions—it is, for example, one of the few places in Indonesia where double ikat is still woven and traditional Balinese script is transcribed onto palm leaves. Several unique and sacred types of music and dance are still performed here: the gamelan *selendeng,* the orchestra of the ancient Balinese; the gamelan *gambing,* composed of a pair of seven-key bronze xylophones and four wooden-key xylophones; and the *rejang* dance, which features ornate headdresses and costumes made of the fine *geringsing* cloth woven only in Tenganan.

Tulamben

⑰ *40 km (24 mi) northeast of Candidasa.*

The main road from Candidasa cuts west around the foothills of 3,854-ft Gunung Serai and continues up and around the north coast. Although Tulamben isn't a large town, it's visited by many people who have one goal in mind: to dive the wreck of the *Liberty,* a World War

II ship that sank just offshore. The reefs here add to the attraction, and the beaches are more serene than others nearby.

Dining and Lodging

$–$$ ✕🏨 **Mimpi Resort.** The accommodations are basic and pleasant at this dive resort set between the sea and the foothills of Gunung Agung. Rooms have a traditional Balinese design with understated island decor; all have air-conditioning and private outdoor showers. The on-site restaurant has Indonesian and Western fare that's hearty enough to please the appetites of underwater adventurers. In addition to dive tours and snorkeling, the hotel also offers sea kayaking. ⊠ *Desa Kubu, Karangasem,* ☎ *0363/21642,* 𝖥𝖠𝖷 *0363/21939. 40 rooms. Restaurant, bar, pool, spa, beach, snorkeling, dive shop, travel services. AE, MC, V.*

Lovina

★ ⑱   *70 km (42 mi) northwest of Tulamben.*

Calm seas, black-sand beaches, and lovely sunrises and sunsets are what you'll find at these peaceful northern settlements. The cluster of villages here—including Anturan, Bunut Panggang, Kalibukbuk, Temukus, and Tukad Mungga—is known as "Lovina," a pleasant name bestowed on this stretch of coastline in the 1950s by Prince Anak Agung Panji Tisna simply in honor of love. Although a number of hotels and restaurants line the main road, the landscape to the south is all mountains and farmland, and that to the north is all ocean. Travelers have long headed to Lovina for respite, but the large resorts have only laid down roots in the last decade. Diving, dolphin-watching, trekking, and cultural explorations are the prime activities.

Dining and Lodging

$ ✕ **Lian.** Savory scents from this restaurant's satay grill waft into the large dining pavilion, tantalizing you as you wait for your Indonesian, Western, or Chinese fare. If you arrive when it's busy, the wait can be long. Have a beer and relax amid the cheerful chatter and loud Western music. Prices are inexpensive, but portions are small. Note that some of the best dishes—such as the Balinese duck—have to be ordered in advance. ⊠ *Jl. Raya,* ☎ *0362/41480. MC, V.*

$ ✕ **Puri Ratus Restaurant.** Guarded by two large chickens in woven cages and a pair of carved wooden lions, this red-tile-roof pavilion has decent, reasonably priced Indonesian and Western fare. Menu items are basic—mie goreng, seafood, curries, and fruits. Breakfast and lunch buffets are offered daily. ⊠ *Jl. Raya Lovina,* ☎ *0362/41059. MC, V.*

$$–$$$ 🏨 **Hotel Aneka Lovina.** It's worth visiting this resort just to see the variety of ornately carved wooden doors. Each room has a traditional Balinese entry, honed with different images and painted in different colors. A winding brick walkway runs through the gardens between the rows of thatched-roof, two-story buildings; fuchsia and orange bougainvillea trickle over their balconies. Rooms are clean and simple with peach curtains, white-tile floors, and Balinese paintings. The seafood restaurant and the large pool are at the end of the resort grounds, next to the ocean. ⊠ *Jl. Raya Seririt,* ☎ *0362/41121,* 𝖥𝖠𝖷 *0362/41827. 59 rooms. Restaurant, 2 bars, pool, beach, dive shop, windsurfing, boating, playground, laundry service, travel services. AE, MC, V.*

$$–$$$ 🏨 **Sol Lovina.** Set in slightly overgrown grounds, this large resort is all-inclusive, so you never need leave. Rooms are decorated in gold and pale green, with pale peach floors and wood furniture. All have triangular terraces with garden views. Secluded behind high stone walls and ornate green wood doors with gold trim, villas are also decorated in gold and have ample dressing areas, large bathrooms, and outdoor gardens; some have private plunge pools. The communal pool, seafood

grill, and garden restaurant are down by the sea. ✉ *Jl. Raya Seririt,* ☎ *0362/41775,* FAX *0362/41659. 118 rooms, 10 villas. 2 restaurants, bar, pool, health club, beach, dive shop, meeting rooms, travel services. AE, MC, V. All-inclusive.*

$–$$ 🏨 **Hotel Mas Lovina.** Also known as Las Brisas Cottages, these two-story, bullet-shape, traditional Balinese villas are made of dark wood. Bedrooms, which are upstairs, have long windows and views of the pool and the bay. Downstairs, some accommodations have a living area, others have a kitchen—be sure to specify your preference when booking. Each cottage has a redbrick terrace, bamboo furniture, and a large shared backyard with fruit trees. A restaurant serving Indonesian, Western, Chinese, and Japanese food catches the breeze off the water. Breakfast is included in the price, and discounts are available in low season. The Spice Islands Dive Center office is in the reception building. ✉ *Jl. Raya Seririt,* ☎ *0362/41237,* FAX *0362/41236. 20 rooms. Restaurant, bar, pool, beach, dive shop, travel services. AE, MC, V.*

$ 🏨 **Aditya Bungalows.** The ornate reception building right on the main road in central Lovina has an Indian flair but is actually an old Balinese structure. Guest quarters are down long paths through well-maintained gardens, and many have yards just steps from the sand. Rooms are large and open, with back entrances, raised front porches, tile floors, and very basic furnishings. Note: check the toilet, tub, and refrigerator to make sure they're working, and keep food wrapped up, as ants can be a problem in this area. The staff is very helpful and friendly, and a breakfast buffet is included in the price. ✉ *Jl. Raya Lovina (Box 134, Singaraja 81101),* ☎ *0362/41059,* FAX *0362/41342. 80 rooms. Restaurant, bar, refrigerators, pool, spa, laundry service, car rental, travel services. AE, MC, V.*

$ 🏨 **Baruna Beach Cottages.** Off the main road at the edge of the beach, this hotel's dark-stone, two-story, thatched-roof bungalows face the ocean. Agung Rooms have red-tile floors; carved, dark-teak furniture; woven rattan walls and ceilings; terraces overlooking the bay; and bathrooms with a half-tub and a shower hose. The cottage-style rooms are in the back garden and have redbrick terraces with small, temple-style doors; large baths with stone gardens; and batik sarong towels. The pavilion restaurant has a stage for dance performances. (Note: If you mention that you read about this hotel in Fodor's, you may just get a discount of 30%–50%). ✉ *Desa Pemaron (Box 149),* ☎ *0362/41745,* FAX *0362/41252. 18 rooms. Restaurant, bar, pool, spa, beach, dive shop, travel services. AE, MC, V.*

Bali Barat National Park

90 km (54 mi) southwest of Lovina, 140 km (87 mi) northwest of Denpasar.

With 188,491 acres of arid forests and mangrove swamps, Bali Barat (West Bali) National Park is a valuable natural treasure. It's one of the few areas left unsculpted by rice terraces, tourist complexes, and other human endeavors. In addition, it's home to several very rare species; foremost is the Bali starling—the island's mascot. Also known as Rothschild's mynah, this soft, white bird has a band of blue around its eyes; the world's last 100 or so of these winged creatures are here, and an on-site breeding program is trying to save the species. Bali Barat also protects approximately three dozen rare Javan *banteng* (buffalo).

There are several unspoiled coral reefs off Menjangan Island, which is just north of the park's mainland. Local dive shops organize scuba and snorkeling trips. If you prefer to stay on land, there's a network of fairly flat trails around the park's edges. You can arrange guided treks at the park office in Cekik, 6 km (4 mi) west of the park entrance at Labuan Lalang (at the crossroads of the main Denpasar and Singaraja roads and on the left side just before Gilimanuk). Permits are required for travel within the park—dive shops usually take care of this formality, but for hiking trips, you'll need to stop at the park office yourself. Another option is a boat trip. You can hire craft at Labuan Lalang, along the Singaraja road, where there are also simple guest houses.

Bali Essentials

Arriving and Departing

BY AIRPLANE

About 13 km (8 mi) southwest of Denpasar, Bali's airport, **Ngurah Rai,** handles international and domestic flights. **Garuda** (☎ 0361/227825) is the main domestic carrier, with flights from Jakarta, Surabaya, Yogyakarta, Medan, Mataram, Ujung Pandang, and Banjarmasin, among other cities. Although the most of its flights were suspended at press time, you could also check with **Merpati** (☎ 0361/221188) to see whether its service between Bali and other Indonesian cities has resumed. For details on international carriers, *see* Indonesia A to Z, *below.*

Between the Airport and Hotels. Most hotels will have a car or minivan waiting to meet you if you let them know in advance. Otherwise, order a taxi at the counter outside customs; the fixed fare varies depending on the location of your hotel. You can also catch a bemo ghoutside the airport, but make sure that you're going in the right direction and that if you enter an empty van you're not hiring it for yourself—unless that's your intention.

BY BOAT

Ferries make the 35-minute crossing every hour between Ketapang in eastern Java and Gilimanuk in western Bali for about Rp 1,000 for passengers and Rp 11,000 for vehicles. *See* Nusa Tenggara Essentials, *below,* for information on ferry service between Bali and Lombok.

BY BUS

Buses from Yogyakarta to Denpasar (16 hours) use the ferry; an air-conditioned bus costs around Rp 17,000. Bus service is available also from Jakarta and Surabaya. You can buy tickets in advance through any travel agent, or you can simply show up at the bus terminal a few hours before you'd like to depart and ask an agent of one of the many bus companies.

Getting Around

BY BEMO

Bemos (minibuses) ply the main routes from Denpasar to Sanur and Kuta and from Kuta to Ubud. You can catch them at the main bemo terminals, where fares and schedules are posted, or simply flag one down along the road. Bemos can be crowded with people and goods, but they are quite inexpensive and give you a glimpse of everyday Balinese life.

BY CAR

Renting cars or Jeeps in Bali is convenient. Daily rates vary from Rp 540,000 at Avis to Rp 454,000 at a small operator, including insurance and unlimited mileage. If you rent from an upscale hotel, the cost of the car will be considerably higher than if you rent off the hotel property. Legally you have to have an international driver's license, though some agencies will not ask for it. Note: if you plan to travel farther than Bali—to Lombok or Java, say—you need a special permit from your rental agent, so be sure to mention your itinerary before you sign the contract. Although prices vary, depending on the places you wish to visit (and the distance covered), a car with a driver will run about Rp 702,000 for 12 hours. Most hotels and agencies can provide drivers.

Try **Andika** (⊠ Jl. Batur 12 A, Denpasar, ☎ 0361/240032), **Bagus Rent Car** (⊠ Jl. Duyung, Sanur, ☎ 0361/287794), or **Lina Biro Jasa** (⊠ Jl. Bakungsari, Kuta, ☎ 0361/51820). **P. T. Multi Sri Bali** (⊠ Jl. Raya Uluwatu 8A, Jimbaran, ☎ 0361/701770) represents Avis, which also has branches in several hotels.

Though there is a highway along the island's perimeter, most roads run north to south owing to the mountainous interior. One of the two main north–south thoroughfares heads from Denpasar out toward Sanur and Gianyar, traveling up through Ubud to Gunung Batur; the other cuts off the southwestern highway to head north through Bedugul to Singaraja. On the Bukit Peninsula, the main highway splits just beyond the Ngurah Rai Airport; the east road goes to Nusa Dua, the west to Pura Uluwatu, and a smaller road links points in between.

BY TAXI

Taxis are available in the main tourist areas; you can flag one down on the street or book one from any hotel or restaurant. Kuta, Sanur, Nusa Dua, and Denpasar have metered taxis. Make sure that the meter is used. The charge is Rp 450 per km (½ mi). The 15-minute ride from Kuta to Nusa Dua, for example, is Rp 9,000; from Sanur to Nusa Dua, Rp 15,000. For longer journeys, set rates are negotiable—count on about Rp 15,000 per hour in the southern tourist towns, Denpasar, and Ubud. To order a cab, call the **dispatcher** (☎ 0361/701000 or 0361/289090). You can also try the **airport taxis** (☎ 0361/751011) for rides to and from Ngurah Rai Airport, and **Praja Taxi** (☎ 0361/289090) or **Bali Taxi** (☎ 0361/701111) to travel elsewhere.

Contacts and Resources

EMERGENCIES

Ambulance: ☎ 118. **Fire:** ☎ 113.

Doctors and Dentists: Denpasar: Sangleh Public Hospital (⊠ Jl. Sangleh, ☎ 0361/227911) and Kasih Ibu (⊠ Jl. Teuku Umar 120, ☎ 0361/223036). **Kuta:** Kuta Clinic (⊠ Jl. Raya Kuta, ☎ 0361/753268), or Dr. N. Sugita (⊠ Jl. Tuban, ☎ 0361/751301) for pediatric emergencies. **Nusa Dua:** Nusa Dua 24-hour Clinic (⊠ Jl. Pratama 81A, ☎ 0361/771324) and Nusa Dua Dental Clinic (⊠ Jl. Pratama 81A, ☎ 0361/771324). **Sanur:** Clinic Bali Hyatt Sanur (⊠ Bali Hyatt Hotel, Jl. Danau Tamblingan, ☎ 0361/288271). **Ubud:** Ubud Clinic (⊠ Jl. Ubud, Campuhan, ☎ 0361/974911).

Scuba-Diving Emergencies: Baruna (⊠ Jl. Raya Seririt, Lovina, ☎ 0362/41084) has a decompression chamber. **Pharmacies:** Bali Farma Apotik (⊠ Jl. Melatig, Denpasar, ☎ 0361/22878) provides reliable service and advice. **Indonesia Farma Apotik** (⊠ Jl. Diponegoro, Denpasar, ☎ 0361/27812) is another recommended pharmacy. **Police:** ☎ 110.

ENGLISH-LANGUAGE BOOKSTORES

Most large resorts sell some cultural and mass market fiction books, and in major budget tourist areas, such as Kuta, used-book shops thrive on the main strip. Sanur's **Bagus Drugstore** (☎ 0361/287794) has a good selection of culture and nature books. The **Nusa Dua Galeria** supermarket has an entire section of books on regional travel and culture, as well as paperback best-sellers and magazines. **Ary's Bookstore** (☎ 0361/96351) in Ubud is one of the best for regional culture and history.

TOUR OPERATORS

The best way to explore Bali is with a private car *and* a knowledgeable guide. Should you visit the crafts villages north of Denpasar, note that most guides get a commission on your purchases. If your guide stops at every shop along the road, speak up—there's too much to see in Bali to spend all your time in such a way. A car, driver, and guide can be hired through local or international car rental agencies, as well as most travel agencies or hotels. For a personal guide, contact **I Made Ramia Santana** (✉ Jl. Planet 9, Denpasar, ☎ 0361/725909).

Many group tours by bus or van are conducted daily. They range from full-day trips into the countryside—stopping at temples, volcanos, and caves—to short in-town Denpasar tours or those that take you to Ubud's arts sights and nearby handicrafts villages. Companies with a great variety of tours include: **Kunang–Kunang** (✉ Jl. Pengosekan, Ubud, ☎ 0361/977388), **Kuta Emas** (✉ Jl. Pantai Kuta 23D, Kuta, ☎ 0361/751925), **Mesti Oriental** (✉ Jl. Nangka Paksimas, Denpasar, ☎ 0361/722283), and **P. T. Putri Mandalika Tours & Travel** (✉ Jl. Hang Tuah Raya II, Sanur, ☎ 0361/297450).

Cruises around the island and to Nusa Lembongan are specialties of: **Bali Hai Cruises** (✉ Benoa Harbor, ☎ 0361/720331), **P. T. Island Explorer** (✉ Jl. Sekar Waru 14D, Sanur, ☎ 0361/289856), **Quicksilver** (✉ Jl. Segara Kedul 3, Benoa Harbor, ☎ 0361/771997), and **Waka Louka** (✉ Jl. Pratama, Tanjung Benoa, ☎ 0361/723629).

Agencies that specialize in dive trips are: **Bali Club Diver** (✉ Jl. Tamblingan 110, Sanur, ☎ 0361/287263), **Bali Diving Perdana** (✉ Jl. Danau Poso, Gang Tanjung, Sanur, ☎ 0361/286493), **Baruna** (✉ Jl. Raya Seririt, Lovina, ☎ 0362/41084), **Geko Dive** (✉ Jl. Silayukti, Padangbai, ☎ 0363/41516), **Nusa Dua Dive Center** (✉ Jl. Pratama 93A, Tanjung Benoa, Nusa Dua, ☎ 0361/774711), and **Sea Star Dive Center** (✉ Jl. Bypass Ngurah Rai 45, Sanur, ☎ 0361/286492).

For adventure tours—including white-water rafting, kayaking, trekking, and cycling—try: **Ayung River Rafting** (✉ Jl. Diponegoro 150B, Denpasar, ☎ 0361/283789), **Baleraf** (✉ Jl. Tamblingan 82, Sanur, ☎ 0361/287256), **Bali Adventure Tours** (✉ Jl. Bypass Ngurah Rai, Kuta, ☎ 0361/721480), **Bali International Rafting** (✉ Jl. Tirta Ening 7, Bypass Ngurah Rai, Sanur, ☎ 0361/281408), and **Sobek** (✉ Jl. Tirta Ening 9, Bypass Ngurah Rai, Sanur, ☎ 0361/287059).

TRAVEL AGENCIES

Nitour (✉ Jl. Veteran 5, Denpasar, ☎ 0361/736096) is a reliable travel agency and tour operator. **Pacto Ltd. Tours and Travel** (✉ Bali Beach Hotel, Jl. Tanjung Sari, Sanur, ☎ 0361/788449) provides tour and travel services and also represents American Express. **Satriavi Tours & Travel** (✉ Jl. Cemara 27, Semawang, Sanur, ☎ 0361/287494) offers a comprehensive selection of tours and also arranges custom tours. Since Satriavi is a subsidiary of Garuda Indonesia Airlines, it's well equipped to handle onward flight reservations.

Additional travel agencies with a range of services include: **Bali Griyasari Tours & Travel** (✉ Jl. Gatot Subroto 49, Denpasar, ☎ 0361/461910), **Bintang Balindo Tours & Travel** (✉ Jl. Legian, Gang Meubel, Blk 14, Kuta, ☎ 0361/758402), and **P. T. Lis Bali** (✉ Jl. Tamblingan 32, Sanur, ☎ 0361/286014).

VISITOR INFORMATION

Denpasar: Dipardi Bali (✉ Jl. Raya Puputan Renon, ☎ 0361/238184). **Kuta:** Bali Tourist Information Center (✉ Central Tourist Plaza, ground floor, Jl. Benasati 7, Legian, ☎ 0361/754090). **Ubud:** Ubud Tourist Information (✉ Jl. Raya, west of Monkey Forest Rd., ☎ 0361/973285).

NUSA TENGGARA

Dozens of islands that spill out eastward from Bali are part of the Nusa Tenggara, the southeastern (*tenggara*) islands (*nusa*). They were formed eons ago when shards of land broke from Sulawesi 300 km (180 mi) to the north and Australia, just 500 km (310 mi) south. Best known are the stepping stones immediately east of Bali: Lombok, a serene tropical haven whose tourism industry is slowly growing; Sumbawa, a golden arc of mountains and plains; Komodo, home of the dragons; Flores, a dive paradise ringed by coral reefs; Timor, site of an ongoing struggle for independence; and Sumba, island of bold ikat patterns and site of ancient battles between warriors on horseback. Between these islands are a smattering of islets: Rinca, Roti, and the Solor and Alor archipelagos, to name a few.

Despite their relatively diminutive size, these arid islands are home to many superlative natural sights. More than 40 volcanoes jut upward from the sea in this province. The explosion of Sumbawa's Gunung Tambora in 1814 was one of the largest in world history, and the 12,221-ft summit of Lombok's Gunung Rinjani still rumbles threateningly from time to time. Tiny Komodo is a mass of parched, dormant slopes smothered in long, green-gold grasses. Flores has 14 active volcanoes of its own. The islands' main wildlife includes birds—cockatoos, parrots, lories, and other Australian types—insects, and reptiles, such as the famous Komodo dragon.

Most Nusa Tenggara inhabitants, like the people throughout much of Indonesia, adhere to Islam. Still, there are subtle differences. The Sasaks of Lombok resisted the influx of Hindu Balinese from the west and have maintained unique brands of Islam: Wektu Telu (Three Prayers) and Wektu Lima (Five Prayers). Farther east, the Sumbawanese have upheld the more traditional Muslim rites brought by the Bugis and Makassarese of Sulawesi—although many people incorporate a healthy dose of animism into their practices. Animism is also evident in the beliefs of the 1,000 or so villagers who live on Komodo. On Flores, 85% of the people are Catholic, thanks to missionaries who have been coming to this island since the 16th century.

The earliest outsiders were the intrepid 12th- and 13th-century traders who discovered the islands' treasures of cinnamon, tortoiseshell, and sandalwood during voyages around the Spice Islands of Maluku to the north. To this day, Nusa Tenggara remains well off the beaten travelers' path. Life has continued here in much the same way for five centuries. Even the modes of travel haven't changed much: aside from a few air routes (whose schedules are undependable), access is by daily ferries or weekly ships. Although there are long-distance buses that journey—on dusty mountain roads—between towns, in-town transport is primarily by horse-drawn cart or by bicycle. Development will no doubt work its way east from Bali. But these sunny islands are likely to remain untainted for a little while longer.

Lombok

The island of Lombok is just 45 km (27 mi) east of Bali, but it seems to exist several decades back in time. The beaches are superior to those of Bali and the level of commercialism is substantially lower. Further, Lombok's drier climate is a distinct advantage during the rainy season (December–May).

Lombok, named for the island's well-known *lombok* (chili pepper), is home to two cultures: the Balinese Hindu and the Sasak Muslim. Most of the Balinese, who ruled the island until 1894, live on the western

Nusa Tenggara

Bali Sea

Flores Sea

PULAU
SANGEANG

Mt.
Tambora ▲

Pulau Moyo

7

6 Sumbawa
Besar

Utan

Dompu

S U M B A W A

8

Bima
and Raba

9 Sape

Waworada

10 Pulau
Komodo

PULAU
RINCA

11 Labuanbajo

Sumba Strait

S U M B A

Parado

Taliwang

Labuhan
Lombok

Bayan

Lombok 1–5
See Detail
Map

Kuta

Mataram

INDIAN OCEAN

B A L I

Denpasar

Padangbai

Kuta and
Legian

N

EAST
TIMOR

ALOR

Kalabahi

PANTAR

Lewoleba

LOMBLEN

ADONARA

SOLOR

Larantuka

Maumere

Savu Sea

KEY

⛴ Ferry

N

60 miles

80 km

0

0

13 Keli Mutu

12 Ende

Flores Sea

Pota

Reo

Ruteng

Bajawa

F L O R E S

11 Labuanbajo

Sumba Strait

S U M B A

side of the island around Ampenan, Mataram (the provincial capital), and Cakranegara (known for its handwoven textiles). Here you will find Balinese temples of interest, though none are as fully developed as in Bali. The Sasaks, who centuries ago came to Indonesia from northern India, live mainly in Lombok's central and eastern regions and comprise the majority of the island's 2.4 million population. Although they're included in the country's census of Islamic peoples, their religious practices are more animist and Hindu than Muslim. They're divided into two sects: the Wektu Telu (Three Prayers), whose rituals display more of a mix of doctrines, and the Wektu Lima (Five Prayers), who more stringently follow the guidelines of Islam.

Enjoy Lombok while you can, as the unspoiled atmosphere is changing fast: Senggigi Beach is now crowded with hotels, the beaches on the Gili coral atolls are already lined with low-priced bungalows, and at press time there were plans in the works for an international megaresort at beaches to the south.

Ampenan, Cakranegara, and Mataram

❶ *24 km (14 mi) north of Lembar (the port for Bali ferries), 1,200 km (744 mi) southeast of Jakarta.*

Most visitors are introduced to Lombok by way of Ampenan, Cakranegara, and Mataram—the string of towns that make up the most populated area on this serene island. Each settlement has a separate function: Western Ampenan is the port where travelers arrive by ship, ferry, and hydrofoil; Cakranegara, the former capital of Lombok, today is a trading center; and Mataram is the island's administrative core and the site of the airport.

On the central town border between Mataram and Cakranegara is **Pura Meru,** the largest Balinese temple on Lombok. Constructed in 1720, Puru Meru is arranged around three courtyards full of small Meru shrines. The three most important—those to Shiva, Vishnu, and Brahma—are in the central courtyard.

Across from Pura Meru is **Taman Mayura,** once a Balinese royal palace, now a large artificial pool filled with lotus. In the center of the pool is Bale Kembang, a floating pavilion that's similar to, but smaller and less ornate, than the one in Klungkung, Bali.

The **Museum Negeri Nusa Tenggara Barat** (Museum of West Nusa Tenggara) has intriguing displays of island weaponry, decorative arts, and artifacts. ✉ *Jl. Panji Tilar Negara,* ☎ *no phone.* ☞ *Rp 200.* ☺ *Tues.–Sun. 8–4.*

OFF THE BEATEN PATH

NARMADA TAMAN – Lombok's most famous temple-palace complex is Narmada Taman (10 km/6 mi east of Cakranegara), built in 1727. The architecture is an interesting mix of Hindu, Islamic, and Sasak, but the temple is notable for its man-made lagoon, which symbolizes the lake of the holy mountain, Gunung Rinjani, in north Lombok. The faithful explain that the replica's purpose was to permit an aging king to fulfill his religious obligations of throwing offerings into the mountaintop lake when he became too old to make the climb. However, more likely it was built so that the monarch could spy on the maidens washing in the pools.

Five kilometers (3 miles) north of Narmada is **Lingsar Temple,** built in 1714 by the first migrating Balinese and reconstructed in conjunction with Sasak Muslims as a symbol of their unity. Nearby is **Suranadi,** a cool hill town with a Hindu temple, especially venerated for its spring water and eels. Both promise good fortune to the pilgrim.

Lombok

Shopping

The public market in Cakranegara has many silver and gold items and straw baskets. In Sweta, just outside Cakranegara, you can shop for spices and beautifully made cane baskets that entrepreneurs buy and take back to Bali to sell at inflated prices. (Note that Sweta is also a hub for buses to other points east.)

Artha Studio and Gallery (⊠ Jl. Arjuna 12, Mataram, ☎ 0370/36715), owned by a local painter, has a collection of wonderful pastels of Lombok life, some of which grace the walls of the island's finest resorts. For a glimpse of the region's handwoven textiles, head to **Pertenunan Rinjani** (⊠ Jl. Pejanggik 46, Mataram, ☎ 0364/23169). **Sasak Pottery** (⊠ Jl. Koperaso 102, Ampenan, ☎ 0370/31687) has traditional handmade pottery.

En Route As you approach Senggigi from Mataram, you can spot the **Batu Bolong** (Rock with a Hole) temple from alongside the road just a short way south. Perched above the ocean upon a huge outcrop that does, indeed, have a natural hole, the temple faces west toward Gunung Agung and the sunset. Beautiful maidens were supposedly tossed into the sea (as divine sacrifices) here in ancient days, reason enough why residents claim that sharks haunt these waters.

Senggigi

★ ❷ *12 km (7 mi) northwest of Mataram.*

The narrow, curving strip of sand that comprises Senggigi was once a backpackers' escape from the crowded beaches of Bali. Inexpensive accommodations are still available, but expensive resort hotels have begun to dominate the beach. Senggigi is still a pleasant place to relax, but it's no longer a quiet hideaway.

Dining and Lodging

$-$$ ✕ **Graha Restaurant.** The red-tile floors and red-check tablecloths add cheer to this thatched-roof restaurant. An outdoor terrace looks right out over the sea, and soft jazz plays in the background. Specialties include grilled shrimp, *graha lumpia* (deep-fried spring rolls with sweet-and-sour sauce), and *ikan bumbu kuning* (fried and with a yellow sauce). Entrées come with garlic sauce and a choice of four kinds of sambal. ✉ *Jl. Raya Senggigi,* ☎ *0370/93101. MC, V.*

$-$$ ✕ **Restaurant Naga.** The Chinese lanterns and eye-popping, vivid-yellow sign—CHINESE FOOD THAI FOOD SEAFOOD—out front compel you to stop for a bite. Specialties include cashew chicken, Hong Kong duck, and Szechuan crab; specials might include Japanese seafood stew or baked spareribs. Free transport is available to and from area hotels. ✉ *Jl. Raya Senggigi,* ☎ *0370/93207. MC, V.*

$ ✕ **Cafe Alberto.** For a quick meal of pizza, barbecued items, sushi, or sashimi, try this basic, open-air restaurant in a pavilion behind the Dynasty (☞ *below*). Business booms at lunchtime. ✉ *Jl. Raya Senggigi,* ☎ *0370/93758. MC, V.*

$ ✕ **Dynasty.** Two locally carved and painted wooden horses at the entrance beckon you to climb the steps into the casual dining room. Westerners come for the familiar fare of pasta—spaghetti, tagliatelli, ravioli—all of which is homemade. Seafood is also a specialty. Red couches and candlelight make this a popular evening spot. There's karaoke nightly and traditional dancing lessons and performances of Joget Gandrung and Putri Mandalika Thursday at 7. ✉ *Jl. Raya Senggigi,* ☎ *0370/93313. MC, V.*

$ ✕ **Lombok Coconut.** Over a meal of seafood, pizza, or pasta, you can chat about the dozens of stone carvings that decorate this restaurant's facade, about the birds that twitter in their cages, or about the eclectic collection of tables in assorted sizes and shapes. Eavesdropping on the oft-interesting conversations of other travelers is also an option. ✉ *Jl. Raya Senggigi,* ☎ *0370/93195. No credit cards.*

$ ✕🏨 **Hotel Panorama.** Although it's not on the beach, this hotel does have captivating views of the bay from the hills on the eastern side of Senggigi's main road. The brown and white cottages with red-tile roofs are clean and simply furnished. All have tile floors, wood furniture, and garden bathrooms; lower rooms have terraces and upper ones have balconies. Six deluxe bungalows offer more space and privacy. Rich food and reasonable prices make a meal—or afternoon tea—in the restaurant memorable. Consider ordering the steamed fish in a clay pot with hot garlic sauce or the chicken topped with chopped prawns and butter sauce. For dessert you'll find mocha cake, apple pie, lemon pie, and raisin and banana breads. ✉ *Jl. Raya Senggigi, Km 8 (Box 1063, Mataram 83015),* ☎ *0370/939000,* FAX *0370/93603. 30 cottages. Restaurant, bar, pool, laundry service, travel services. MC, V.*

$$-$$$ 🏨 **Lombok Intan Laguna.** Beside the ocean it may be, but the Itan's focal point is really its curving pool with an arched stone bridge and round, thatched-roof bar. The two-story cottages have a mix of traditional and modern architecture. Their rooms are spacious, with tile floors, wood furniture, and indoor-outdoor bathrooms. Less-expensive rooms are in a more modern, white, three-story building. At the open-air restaurant, the smell of flowers from the gardens is carried along on cooling sea breezes. A stay here also puts you within walking distance of Senggigi's main shopping area. ✉ *Jl. Raya Senggigi (Box 1049, Mataram 831235),* ☎ *0370/93090,* FAX *0370/93185. 146 rooms. 2 restaurants, bar, pool, 2 tennis courts, exercise room, beach, shops. AE, DC, MC, V.*

$$-$$$ 🏨 **Senggigi Beach Hotel.** Sunsets from here are splendid. On a peninsula that juts into the Lombok Straits, this resort has thatched-roof cottages—each with several guest rooms—on 25 acres of grass, coconut

trees, and white-sand beach. Modest rooms have twin beds, tables, chairs, and TVs; bathrooms have shower stalls rather than tubs. The open-sided dining room, overlooking the pool, serves mostly buffet-style breakfasts and dinners. ⊠ *Jl. Raya Senggigi (Box 1001, Mataram 83125),* ☎ *0364/93210,* ℻ *0364/93200. 182 rooms. Dining room, pool, 2 tennis courts, badminton, beach, snorkeling, windsurfing, boating, travel services. AE, DC, MC, V.*

$$–$$$ ⊞ **Sheraton Senggigi Beach Resort.** The lobby, with its polished an-
   ★   tiques and bay views, immediately conveys the subtle elegance found throughout. Landscaped grounds, thick with blossoms, embrace the three-story terraced buildings. Rooms have sumptuous wood and wicker furniture and Lombok craftwork; all look onto the gardens and free-form pool, and many offer a glimpse of the beach beyond. The main restaurant offers indoor and outdoor dining, and the on-site stage is used for dance performances. ⊠ *Jl. Raya Senggigi (Box 1154, Mataram 83015),* ☎ *0370/93333 or 800/325–3535 in the U.S.,* ℻ *0370/93140. 156 rooms. 3 restaurants, 2 bars, 2 pools, 2 tennis courts, health club, beach, snorkeling, windsurfing, boating, travel services. AE, DC, MC, V.*

$$ ⊞ **Holiday Inn Resort Lombok.** This familiar Western establishment does a good job of mixing local traditions with foreign comforts. It has an exotic location on a lovely sweep of sand with rolling blue waves. Stone walkways lead through gardens to connected chalets and the larger, separate bungalows (each with several guest rooms); both types of accommodations have porches and large garden bathrooms. A layered pool surrounds a swim-up bar and a hot tub. Beside the pool is a dining terrace where local musicians stroll nightly. Upstairs in reception, the adept travel staff can help you arrange tours anywhere on the island. ⊠ *Senggigi Beach (Box 1090, Mataram 83015),* ☎ *0370/93444,* ℻ *0370/93092. 145 rooms, 14 bungalows. 2 restaurants, 3 bars, pool, massage, spa, health club, beach, snorkeling, windsurfing, boating, shops, laundry service, meeting rooms, travel services, car rental. AE, DC, MC, V.*

$ ⊞ **Graha Beach.** Set on the beach, the Graha is one of the best of several inexpensive hotels and losmen in Senggigi. Clean, air-conditioned rooms have twin beds, tile floors, TVs, and private showers and toilets. There's a restaurant, small souvenir shop, and money exchange counter. Tours of the island can be arranged—prices are negotiable. ⊠ *Senggigi Beach,* ☎ *0364/93401,* ℻ *0364/93400. 29 rooms. Restaurant, beach, travel services, car rental. No credit cards.*

Nightlife and the Arts

Senggigi's main strip, Jalan Raya Senggigi, has a number of small bars and dance places that are busy on weekends. The **Dynasty** (☎ 0370/93313) is a popular hangout with a curving wood bar, cozy red couches, candlelight, and karaoke nightly. On Thursdays at 7, you receive free traditional dance lessons before the Joget Gandrung and Putri Mandalika dance performance. The **Tropical Bar and Restaurant** (☎ 0370/93712) is particularly crowded on Saturday, especially the **C. V. Discotheque** on the first floor. The **Sheraton Senggigi** (☎ 037093333) features various cultural performances weekly.

To explore local art, check out the shops at the **Pasar Seni** art market at the center of town, right on Jalan Raya Senggigi. Across from the art market, the **Pamour Art Gallery** (☎ 0370/93104) has exhibitions of Lombok and regional art, craft-making demonstrations, and an extensive collection of crafts and furnishings.

Outdoor Activities and Sports

For scuba and snorkeling trips to the Gilis, many travelers begin from Senggigi. Try **Baruna** (⊠ Jl. Raya Senggigi, in the Holiday Inn, ☎ 0370/

93314), an extension of one of Bali's best-known operations. Also on Jl. Raya Senggigi are **Albatross** (☎ 0370/93399), **Blue Coral** (☎ 0370/93251), and **Batu Surya Utama** (☎ 0370/93345).

Gili Islands

❸ *5–8 km (3–5 mi) off the coast from Bangsal-Pameneng, which is 31 km (19 mi) northeast of Senggigi.*

A 30-minute drive north of Senggigi brings you to the Bangsal ferry dock, near Pameneng, where a small boat will zip you across to one of three coral atolls known collectively as the Gili Islands. All three islands have cottage bungalows that are popular with backpackers. Most of these lodgings are simple bamboo huts (Rp 108,000–Rp 216,000) with a cold-water *mandi* (dip-bucket bath) and squat toilets; a few of the more upscale places have electricity. Most losmen rent snorkeling equipment, and dive trips can be arranged. Bring cash as, outside of a few hotels, credit cards are rarely accepted and travelers checks can be difficult to exchange.

Gili Air

Gili Air is closest to shore and requires only a quick 10-minute sea crossing in a motorized prahu. Here dazzling white sand meets crystal-clear water, and the coral reef is home to brightly colored tropical fish. The atmosphere is calm and uncluttered, the scenery simple and rural—a great place to clear your head.

DINING AND LODGING

$ ✕🅷 **Hotel Gili Air and Restaurant.** Gili Air's largest hotel has bungalows encircled by tropical gardens. The modest, clean rooms have basic furnishings accented with touches of island decor. Private bathrooms with flush toilets and running water are standard and most rooms have beach and sea views; only 14 have air-conditioning and hot water, however. Continental breakfast is included in the price, and the onsite restaurant is open all day; pizzas are a specialty and beachfront barbecues take place weekly. There's good snorkeling right off the beach, and the friendly staff can help with tours around the islands. ✉ *Desa Gili Indah, Pameneng,* ☎ *0370/34435. 26 rooms. Restaurant, beach, snorkeling, travel services. MC, V.*

$$$$ 🅷 **The Oberoi, Lombok.** Hidden away on Lombok's northwest coast
★ and within sight of the palm-fringed beach of Gili Air just across the strait, this resort offers the ultimate in upscale seclusion. Spacious terrace pavilions with lovely views are set on well-groomed grounds. High stone walls surround the private villas, each with a garden, fountain, and raised dining pavilion; some have plunge pools. Interiors have high, thatched-roof ceilings; marble floors; dark teak furniture; oversize canopy beds; wicker seating areas; and sliding glass panels that open to garden or ocean views. Bathrooms are of a good size and have separate toilet and shower compartments enclosed by glass doors, double marble sinks, large walk-through closets, and sunken tubs near a lotus pond in the garden. Service is discreet and unobtrusive. The spa and fitness center offer deluxe traditional treatments in open-air bales or air-conditioned rooms. Two large pools face the ocean, and a boat is available to take you snorkeling at nearby reefs or to the Gilis. ✉ *Pantai Medana, Tanjung (Box 1096, Mataram 83001),* ☎ *0370/38444,* 🅵🅰🆇 *0370/32496. 20 villas, 30 terrace pavilions. 5 restaurants, bar, in-room safes, 2 pools, beauty salon, spa, health club, beach, snorkeling, windsurfing, library, laundry service, car rental. AE, DC, MC, V.*

OUTDOOR ACTIVITIES AND SPORTS

Blue Marlin (☎ no phone) has an office in south Gili Air and can co-ordinate trips out to the reefs. On the east side of the island you'll find **Reefseekers Pro Dive** (☎ 0370/34387).

Gili Meno

For even more pristine waters, the next atoll, Gili Meno, has a greater abundance of sea life—red-lined triggerfish, starfish, five-line damsel, and the occasional shark—and, for scuba divers, there's unique blue coral 50–80 ft below the surface. This is the quietest island, and it has earned its place as a divers' haven. Its accommodations and restaurants are basic, but that's part of its charm.

Gili Trawangan

Although it's the farthest island from Lombok, Gili Trawangan is the party island of the three Gilis, where most visitors come to get away from Bali crowds. The beaches are excellent here, and the diving is memorable. Despite the rapid rise in tourism, there are plenty of inexpensive accommodations and restaurants.

OUTDOOR ACTIVITIES AND SPORTS

Located nearly on top of one another on the east side of Gili Trawangan are **Albatross** (☎ 0370/30134), **Blue Coral** (☎ 0370/34497), and **Blue Marlin Dive Center** (☎ 0370/32424), which make regular dive excursions around the islands. A two-dive day trip is about Rp 540,000 and introductory through full-certification courses are available.

En Route   Back on the mainland, on the way to Gunung Rinjani, consider a stop in **Bayan.** Its mosque stands on a stone platform and is said to be more than three centuries old—Lombok's oldest religious structure. This village is also rumored to be where the island's indigenous Wektu Telu (the less stringently Muslim of the island's two Hindu-Muslim-animist Sasak sects) religion was born. Among the highlights of Bayan and its environs are the tall, spade-shape, traditional houses and rice barns that loom above the arid landscape. The settlements here are small, quiet clusters of life where men till the wide fields and women create beautiful original textiles. This is also a burgeoning tourist area where you're welcome to learn about and interact with the Sasak way of life.

Gunung Rinjani

❹ *77 km (50 mi) southeast of Bangsal, 82 km (51 mi) northeast of Mataram.*

The second-highest mountain in Indonesia, after Puncak Jaya (16,564 ft) in Irian Jaya, 12,221-ft Gunung Rinjani is one of the most revered and feared summits in the country. Revered because, like Gunung Agung on Bali, it's considered a sacred summit, a place of the gods; feared because the mountain still shudders and spews fiery lava from time to time. Its beauty is stark and magnificent, a smoldering peak against blue sky and ocean, with the green crescent of Lake Segera Anak shimmering 6 km (4 mi) across outside the crater. The trek up the slope is breathtaking, both for the natural views and village scenes as well as the physical effort. (The hike to the rim and down to the lake can be dangerous and should only be attempted by those who are in good shape and who are blessed with good balance.)

From Bayan, the trail around the rim has several approaches through the village settlements of Batu Koq and Senaru, 5 km (3 mi) and 8 km (5 mi) farther on. A 2-km (1-mi) side trip between them is to the Sendang Gila (Sindanggile) waterfall, where monkeys peer down from the trees alongside the path. Simple losmen abound here, as well as in the eastern villages of Sembulan Lawang and Sembulan Bintang. Most trekkers plan on a three-day journey from Senaru or Batu Koq, taking time to explore nearby hot springs and falls one day and hiking up to the crater the next.

Take comfortable hiking boots, warm layers, a sleeping bag, a tent, a stove, cooking utensils, and a flashlight—most of which you can rent from losmen in Batu Koq and Senaru. Stock up on foodstuffs and water in Mataram, where there's more variety and where prices are lower. Several outfitters arrange organized treks (☞ Tour Operators *in* Nusa Tenggara Essentials, *below*).

Kuta and Environs

★ ⑤ *143 km (89 mi) southwest of Bayan, 30 km (18 mi) southeast of Mataram.*

Once a tiny village on the shores of the Indian Ocean, **Kuta** is still quiet, but development plans by large hotels are on the horizon. The curving sandy beach, known as Putri Nyale Beach, is now cluttered with the activity of budget travelers who made this area famous, most of whom stay at one of the many losmen on the other side of the road.

Five kilometers (3 miles) southeast along the coast is the horseshoe-shape **Tanjung Aan,** one of the island's most beautiful beaches. Its fine, soft, white sands are usually deserted, except for a few hopeful vendors selling watermelons and brave hearts windsurfing. All this may change—at press time the beach was slated for development, with wealthy Jakarta businessmen putting up the money for several luxury hotels.

There are several small Sasak settlements just north of Kuta on the road to Mataram, including the village of **Rambitan.** Here, the long, sloping thatched roofs of traditional Sasak houses and *lumbing* (a type of rice barn) are clustered together, and a few of the villagers sell batik sarongs at surprisingly low prices. Try to get a glimpse inside the houses, each of which has two main areas: the outer area where the men sleep and the inner one reserved for the women.

Farther north along the main road is **Penujak,** where lovely terracotta *gerabah* pottery is created, you'll also spot *gantong* (vessels), *jangkih* (traditional stoves), and wooden masks here. Cruise the main street to get a sense of design, selection, and quality. Although **Sukarara**'s fame as a traditional textile center has made it something of a tourist attraction (the costumed weavers at the looms in front of shops are just for show; the real weaving is done in the villages), it's definitely *the* place to see the creative, colorful works of Lombok artisans.

Dining and Lodging

$ ×▥ **Matahari Lombok Hotel and Restaurant.** Owned by a Lombok man, his Swiss wife, and their three boys, this friendly establishment caters mainly to budget travelers, although its lovely setting and cleanliness make it seem more upscale. Three houses are available, one with 12 double rooms, one with four, and one with three—all with basic but pleasant local decor, but not all with private baths. A bungalow with two double rooms is also available. Two on-site restaurants offer a mix of Indonesian and basic Western dishes; one has a dance floor that hops in high season. The hotel is in the village but is within walking distance of the beach; a pool is in the hotel's future plans. ✉ *On Kuta's main thoroughfare,* ☎ *0370/54832,* ☏ *0370/54909. 19 rooms, 1 bungalow. 2 restaurants. MC, V.*

Sumbawa, Komodo, and Flores

Sumbawa

Sumbawa is an island of strict Islamic beliefs and stunning scenery, where boys race wild horses through golden plains, men practice bare-fisted *berempah* boxing in the high mountain villages, water buffalo are still used to pull plows through rice fields, and the lavender shadow of Gunung Tambora towers over the bright central shoreline.

Sumbawa Besar

⑥ *100 km (62 mi) east of Labuhan Lombok, 1,360 km (843 mi) southeast of Jakarta.*

Once the center of the Sumbawa sultanate that dominated the western half of the island, Sumbawa Besar, or Big Sumbawa, is, despite its name, a rather small settlement. Located on the northwest coast, a two-hour drive from the ferry terminal at Poto Tano and less than an hour's flight from Mataram, it's usually just a pass-through point for those heading to the wildlife reserve at Pulau Moyo (☞ *below*). Still this clean, quiet, welcoming town has a few noteworthy sights.

On Jalan Batu Pasak, the **Dalam Loka,** or old sultan's palace, is an assembly of raised, gray, wooden, structures with tiered roofs built in 1885 and restored in the early 1980s. The original structure has 99 pillars to honor the 99 names given to Allah. You can stroll around the outer grounds for a look at Sumbawan architecture, or ask around for the manager, who can give you a tour of the various rooms and explain the significance of the few vestiges of palace days—mostly drawings and decorations—on display inside. Sumbawan dances are performed here most Sunday mornings; at press time plans were afoot to refurbish the buildings and create a museum.

Today, the sultans' descendants reside at the **Bale Kuning** on Jalan Wahidin, where many of the royal families' possessions are still kept; the tourist office (☞ Visitor Information *in* Nusa Tenggara Essentials, *below*) can arrange a visit with advance notification. A black-sand beach at **Kencana** 11 km (7 mi) west of town has decent reefs for snorkeling and views of northern Pulau Moyo.

LODGING

$–$$ 🏨 **Tambora Hotel.** This midsize hotel, just five minutes from the airport, is your best option for a stay right in town. Rooms are simple and clean, and service is attentive. The hotel is a good base for day trips around the area, and it also has a minimart, an art shop, and a copy center on site. Rooms rates include breakfast. ✉ *Jl. Kebayan,* ☎ *0371/21585. 49 rooms. Restaurant, travel services. AE, MC, V.*

$ 🏨 **Kencana Beach Cottages.** Just 15 minutes from the airport, this pleasant hotel is set in gardens surrounded by bamboo and palm trees. A gathering of colorful and very spacious traditional bungalows face a black-sand beach where the clear water offers hints of the coral below. Wooden floors, white walls, high ceilings, and traditional woven art and paintings complete the elegantly simple decor. The location is quiet, but if you need more activity than just sipping drinks from coconut shells by the pool all day, there's plenty to keep you busy. The amicable staff at the on-site travel office can arrange trips to buffalo races, traditional villages, waterfalls, and Pulau Moyo. Before you set out, you can have a good breakfast, which is included in the price of your room. ✉ *Jl. Raya Tano, Km 11, Badas,* ☎ *0371/22555,* 𝐅𝐀𝐗 *0371/ 22439. 25 bungalows. Restaurant, bar, pool, massage, beach, dive shop, snorkeling, laundry service, travel services. No credit cards.*

Pulau Moyo

★ ⑦ *20 km (12 mi) northeast of Sumbawa Besar.*

The focal point of the nature reserve on Moyo Island, just off Sumbawa's northeastern coast, is 402-ft Gunung Moyo. Although wildlife spotting is a draw, the main attraction is diving and snorkeling, and the island's remote location, extensive reefs, and upscale resort have made it the the darling of expensive package tours. Some of the best reefs are around Tanjung Pasir and Aik Manis. For maps and permits, contact the **Dinas Perlindungan dan Pengawetan Alam (PHPA)**—otherwise known as the Forest Authority—office in Sumbawa Besar office in Sumbawa Besar (☞ Visitor Information *in* Nusa Tenggara Essentials, *below*). For package tours, try the **Hotel Tambora** or the **Kencana Beach Cottages** (☞ *above*), the latter of which can charter a speedboat for two dozen people at a daily rate of about Rp 350,000. If you'd like to visit the island independently, you can take a half-hour ride in a local fishing vessel (around Rp 10,000 each way) from Aik Bari on the coast.

DINING AND LODGING

$$$$ ✕▣ **Amanwana.** Its name, which means "peaceful forest," couldn't ★ be more appropriate. Nestled into a wooded setting facing a secluded beach, the large, luxurious tents mimic a mix of camping and island-bungalow features: simple yet spacious individual bale pavilions are surrounded by smooth terraces and protected by graceful, sloping canvas roofs held up by strong ropes and wooden poles. Despite their simple appearance, rooms are opulent and comfortable, with collectors' pieces of traditional art; polished wood floors; soft, sumptuous couches; king-size beds; writing desks; and large bathrooms. Although the pavilions are enclosed, only one wall is solid; the rest are panels that slide back to reveal huge glass windows, which afford a spectacular 270-degree view of the surrounding forest and bay. A library in the main building has spotless wood floors and glowing golden walls, as well as an intriguing selection of books and works of art. The open-air bar-lounge has a thatched roof and overlooks the bay—an intimate setting amid the wilds. ✉ *Pulau Moyo,* ☎ *0371/22233 or 0361/ 771267 (for reservations),* ℻ *0371/22288. 20 luxury tents. Restaurant, bar, dining room, lobby lounge, hiking, beach, snorkeling, windsurfing, boating, library, laundry service, travel services, airport shuttle. AE, DC, MC, V.*

Bima and Raba

⑧ *230 km (143 mi) east of Sumbawa Besar.*

Seven hours' drive from Sumbawa Besar, the neighboring towns of Bima and Raba are Sumbawa's main eastern settlements. Bima is the island's major port and the former sultanate that shared power over the island with the royal family of western Sumbawa; Raba is the main bus transit point 5 km (3 mi) east.

Things to see in these towns include the old **Sultan's Palace** in Bima on Jalan Sultan Ibrahim, which doubles as a museum of artifacts from the royal family and the region. Included in the collection here are books, furniture, and weaponry. The palace is open 7–5 daily except Islamic holidays. There's a suggested donation of Rp 1,000; guides will be grateful for another Rp 1,000. For a contrast, explore the new **Royal Palace** on Jalan Sumbawa, where the sultans' descendents have a collection of formal attire, decorative jewelry, and royal valuables on display. Book an appointment to visit through the tourist office (☞ Visitor Information *in* Nusa Tenggara Essentials, *below*).

Sape

❾ *50 km (31 mi) southeast of Bima and Raba.*

The muted clip-clop of horses' hooves on soft dirt roads echoes through the hills of Sape (*sah*-pay), the easternmost town of Sumbawa. This sublime port—teeming with lively markets selling produce and colorful woven crafts—is the road traveler's stopping point en route to Komodo. Low, one-story homes line narrow streets traversed by horse-drawn carts (known here as Ben Hurs because they resemble the chariots used in the movie); occasionally, soulful Islamic music can be heard. The nearby rough, grassy mountains make for a good day's hike to supreme views over the town and the bay. Ferries to Komodo and Flores leave at 8 AM daily except Friday, and the morning crowd at the docks can be quite festive. For those stuck in town when the ferry breaks down—not an uncommon occurrence—things to do include visiting local weaving workshops, hiking in the hills, and practicing Indonesian with local tour guides who want to polish their English.

DINING AND LODGING
Most losmen will dish up a home-cooked meal for their guests. Fried rice, fried noodles, fried vegetables, or grilled fish with white rice are what you'll find across the board. There are a number of small losmen along the main road, each offering a half dozen clean, quiet rooms with private Indonesian cold-water baths. Try **Losmen Friendship,** near the port, or **Losmen Mutiara,** a two-story, shared-bath hotel next to the docks.

Pulau Komodo

★ ❿ *320 km (198 mi) east of Sumbawa Besar, 90 km (56 mi) east of Bima, 40 km (25 mi) east of Sape.*

On the approach to Komodo, a tiny island just 36 km (22 mi) long and 16 km (9 mi) across at its widest point, it's hard to imagine that it's home to the fearsome dragons described by explorers of the late 1800s. Komodo's soft curves and parched golden grasses slide up over the topaz bay of lively coral reefs, glass-clear waters, and white-sand beach. But then you remember that this innocent looking island is, indeed, inhabited by 13-ft, 220-pound adult *ora,* as the dragons are known locally. Don't be frightened, though: although stories of European tourists and village children disappearing run rampant, a trip here is quite safe. The park office is right at the docks, and from it a mild 2-km (1-mi) walk along a sandy path brings you to the dragons' lairs. You'll see them sunning themselves in forest ravines or snuggling up in shallow caves inside cliff walls.

Local legends say that the dragons are descendents of a lost child who once took refuge in one of their burrows. Modern science reports that the dragons evolved from dinosaurs that lived in Asia some 130 million years ago. They're the largest lizards on earth, with a population of around 2,000, and they live only on Komodo, the nearby island of Rinca, and parts of Flores. Their soft, white eggs hatch in April or May, with a three-to-one ratio of males to females. The dragons have sharp hearing and a keen sense of smell (they can pick up the scent of carrion, their favorite treat, 7 mi away). They're fast, too, running at speeds of up to 18 mph and eating at a rate of six pounds of meat a minute. (At one time goats were slaughtered twice a week to attract the dragons, but these slaughters now take place much less frequently so that the dragons can be observed in the wild.) The dragons are also excellent swimmers—to the chagrin of those who are tempted to snorkel in the calm bay at the park's eastern edge. But the dragons aren't the only danger here: this is also an island of giant spiders, vipers, and scorpions. Thus, a guide must accompany everyone outside the main park compound, and you're encouraged to walk carefully and be aware of your surroundings at all times.

Travel to Komodo doesn't have to be the arduous journey of days past, thanks to luxury tour packages via speedboats from Bali, Lombok, and Flores. However, these are only short ventures; to stay longer and explore this fascinating island, you must prepare for a much simpler lifestyle. Komodo does have its amenities, namely an open-air restaurant that serves up simple fare, sells supplies, and rents a half dozen raised wooden cabins. A 2-km (1-mi) low-tide beach walk from the park office, Kampung Komodo is a local settlement of a few dozen raised huts and colorful fishing boats. Here you can meet the islanders and hear their stories. English-speaking guides can be hired at the park office to translate.

Dining and Lodging

$ X🏠 **Pulau Komodo Bungalows.** A half dozen simple, raised wooden cabins grace the edge of a wide lawn and overlook grazing deer and scampering pigs by dusk and dawn. Each structure has four small bedrooms, a shared cold-water mandi, a common living area, and a wide balcony; the double rooms in front are the largest and coolest. The afternoon breeze eliminates the need for fans, as does the shortage of electricity, which only runs from 6 PM to 10 PM. A restaurant across the yard serves basic Indonesian fare, but you may want to bring your own food supplements if you're staying more than one night. Note: keep all luggage sealed and all food out of the rooms, as animals have been known to raid the cabins in search of cracker crumbs and banana peels, among other things. This is the only place to stay on the island; otherwise, it's necessary to stay aboard a tour boat in the bay. ⊠ *Loh Liang, 100 yards northwest of PHPA office,* ☎ *no phone. 12 rooms. Restaurant, beach, snorkeling. No credit cards.*

Outdoor Activities and Sports

Komodo may be small, but there's plenty to do if you're the intrepid sort and you have a few days. You can hire guides (Rp 20,000 for up to five people) to hike to the 1,731-ft **Gunung Ara** and other peaks. Overnight camping trips can also be arranged. You can spot still more wildlife on a side trip to **Pulau Rinca.** The snorkeling around this island's reefs is also spectacular. Divers can organize trips from Labuanbajo, Flores (☞ Outdoor Activities and Sports *in* Labuanbajo, *below*). Since there's no regular boat transport to Rinca, you must sign up for an organized tour or hire your own boat from Labuanbajo.

Flores

Originally named Cabo de Flores, or Cape of Flowers—owing to its blossoming coastlines—by 16th-century Portuguese traders, Flores is a rugged, arid island of smoldering volcanic peaks and teal bays ripe for exploring. Although they were once under the control of Sulawesi's Bugis and Makassarese peoples, the inhabitants of Flores are actually closer in culture to Melanesia the early Melanesian civilizations that migrated west to the Indonesian archipelago; this heritage is reflected in their physical features. In addition, Flores's population is 85% Catholic, a significant statistic in an archipelago that's 90% Muslim. However, the island's draw is not really its culture, but rather its diving. The reefs here are some of Indonesia's best.

Labuanbajo

⑪ *100 km (62 mi) northeast of Sape on Sumbawa.*

A tiny settlement of one-story shops, homes, and losmen now does brisk business as a tourist jumping-off point for travelers heading by boat or plane west to Komodo, east to the gem-color lakes of Keli Mutu, or around the island on lengthy dive trips. Don't miss the Pasar Malam night market at the south end of town, where you can pick up a cheap bite to eat while finding numerous inexpensive souvenirs. There are many simple, comfortable places to stay and numerous beaches and reefs to explore.

If you have an afternoon, check out **Batu Cormin,** a cave 4 km (2 mi) outside of town. Several nearby islands have beaches that are worth a visit, including **Batugosok, Kanawa, Bididari, Sabolo Besar,** and **Sabolo Kecil**; the latter three also have excellent reefs for diving and snorkeling.

DINING AND LODGING

Most losmen have their own small restaurants, and on a scenic stroll along the main road you peruse the diverse menus. There are more than a dozen small losmen along Jalan Yos Sudarso as well. Touts will try to strike bargains with you as you step off the ferry. Always insist on seeing the accommodations first before making a deal, though; most places are simple and clean, but you never know if it's what you want until you see it. Walking along the main road is also a good way to check out the many travel booths and find out about the trips that they offer, as well as learn about additional accommodations and activities on the islands within an hour's boat ride of town.

$ ✕⛫ **Gardena Bungalows.** Just a few yards from the ferry dock, this hotel offers traditional wooden bungalows with verandas above the bay in a setting of tropical gardens. There's no air-conditioning, but fans are provided; all rooms also have beds with mosquito nets and private bathrooms with showers. This is a popular place, and the friendly staff can assist you with tours to Komodo and Rinca, snorkeling trips to Bididari and Sabolon islands, and bus and ferry tickets. A small restaurant serves Indonesian, Chinese, and Western fare; breakfast is included in the price. ✉ *Jl. Yos Sudarso, 86554,* ☏ *0385/41258,* ℻ *0385/41200. 19 bungalows. Restaurant, laundry service, travel services. No credit cards.*

$ **New Bajo Beach Hotel & Cottages.** This hotel is on the secluded, white-sand Phe'de Beach, with its thriving coral reefs, about about 2 km (1 mi) from Labuanbajo. Rooms are simple, clean, and decorated with Nusa Tenggara carvings and textiles; cottages have air-conditioning, private baths with hot water, and TVs. You can make tour arrangements—by car, speedboat, and fishing boat—at the travel desk. The restaurant offers a mix of Asian and Western dishes. ✉ *Pantai Pede 86554,* ☏ *0385/41047,* ℻ *0385/41069. 16 rooms, 10 bungalows. Restaurant, beach, snorkeling, travel services, airport shuttle, car rental. No credit cards.*

$ ⛫ **Puri Komodo Resort.** On a peninsula at the northwest tip of Flores,
★ this back-to-nature retreat is a relaxing hideaway. The 50-acre resort sits on a long stretch of sugar-white sand at the edge of a huge coral reef, making it a prime spot for dive trips. The 12 basic, clean bungalows (at press time, 12 more were being built) are surrounded on three sides by breezy balconies and are equipped with American-style spring mattresses. Bathrooms are outside of the rooms and include traditional bamboo showers; the toilet facilities are Western, however. The spacious two-story chalet has six rooms, two on each level and each with a private indoor bathroom. The serene gardens are a lovely place to walk in the cool evenings before dining in the seaside restaurant. The resort is 20 minutes by boat from Labuanbajo, but transfers and trips into town are free. Tours to Komodo, Rinca, and other area attrac-

tions can be arranged on site. ✉ *Batu Gosok, 86554,* ☎ *0385/41319,* ℻ *0385/41030. 12 bungalows, 1 chalet. Restaurant, beach, snorkeling, travel services. No credit cards.*

OUTDOOR ACTIVITIES AND SPORTS

Puri Komodo Resort (☞ Dining and Lodging, *above*) offers trips to Komodo and Rinca, as well as dive tours around Flores. The **Sea Transportation Cooperative** (☎ no phone) organizes boat trips to Komodo, Rinca, and other points around Flores, as do **Kencana, Perama,** and **Suamarnik.** All of these are on Jalan Yos Sudarso, the town's 2-km (1-mi) main strip. Not all tours offer the same amenities, so it pays to check out what you'll get for your money; accommodations, food, equipment, supplies, entrance fees, and souvenirs may or may not be included.

Ende

⑫ *250 km (155 mi) southeast of Labuanbajo.*

At the base of a mountain slope and the edge of the sea, Ende is a waiting point for many travelers catching ships to other parts of Nusa Tenggara and those heading east to Keli Mutu (☞ *below*). You can wander the lively **daily market** on Jalan Pasar at the waterfront for a taste of local culture and walk through the town to see its amazing variety of tailor shops with ancient Singer sewing machines. The **Ende Museum** on Jalan Perwira is actually a house where former President Sukarno was exiled by the Dutch in 1933. Knock on the door, and the manager will let you in to view the old photographs that are on display. For those interested in architecture, the neighboring village of **Wolotopo** is a good place to have a look at traditional woven textiles and the local style of raised wooden houses.

SHOPPING

To find quality ikat textiles from both Flores and Sumba, try the **market** on the corner of Jalan Pasar and Jalan Pabean. Eight kilometers (5 miles) east of Ende, the village of **Ndona** is the home of many traditional weavers. The blankets sold here are good buys.

Keli Mutu

★ ⑬ *66 km (41 mi) northeast of Ende.*

A volcanic crater filled with a triad of gem-color lakes, Keli Mutu has attracted visitors worldwide for more than a century. The magic of the site is that these three lakes change color—and no one knows why. (Scientists have theorized that the variations are caused by minerals in the soil or water.) In the 1960s, they were rust, navy, and cream; now they are teal, olive, and ebony. The view of the sunrise over the crater is one of the archipelago's most memorable.

The mountain is reached from Ende via the town of Moni, which is 14 km (9 mi) from the mountaintop. Trucks and minibuses make the journey up the 14-km (9-mi) road before dawn and return between 7 and 8 AM, but many visitors prefer to ride up and then make the 2½-hour walk back down to Moni. There are also a number of hot springs and waterfalls just outside of Moni. You can stay in a losmen in Moni or make this a day trip from Ende.

Nusa Tenggara Essentials

Arriving and Departing

By Airplane

Garuda (☎ 0364/22226) and its subsidiary, **Merpati** (☎ 0364/22226), run shuttle service, with flights every hour beginning at 7 AM, from Denpasar to Lombok's **Selaparang Airport** in Mataram. The last flight is at 3 PM. You can buy tickets at the airport an hour before departure. For trips from Lombok to Denpasar, Bali, you can only reserve a seat if you have a connecting flight. Note that flights tend to be late and are frequently canceled.

Elsewhere in the Nusa Tenggara, the main airports are at Sumbawa Besar, Bima, Labuanbajo, and Ende. Flights to Mataram on Lombok, Denpasar on Bali, Ujung Pandang on Sulawesi, and Jakarta on Java depart several times weekly, but schedules are unpredictable and flights are often canceled. For details on air transport, contact **Merpati** (☏ 0371/21416 in Sumbawa Besar or 0374/42697 in Bima). The airport in Sumbawa Besar is just yards from the Hotel Tambora, but bemos make the journey from other points in town for around Rp 250. Bima's airport is 16 km (10 mi) from town, Rp 10,000 by taxi. The Labuan-bajo airport is 3 km (2 mi) from town, a Rp 5,000 taxi ride. Ende's airport just outside town at the junction of Jalan Ahmad Yani, Jalan Keli Mutu, Jalan El Tari, and Jalan Gatot Subroto; backpackers walk it, but you can also take a bemo for about Rp 400.

By Boat

Ferries make the four-hour crossing from Padangbai, east of Denpasar on Bali, to Lembar, south of Ampenan on Lombok, every two hours around the clock; the fare is Rp 5,000. Since the ferry docks some distance from the tourist centers on both Bali and Lombok (it takes three bemos to travel from Lembar Harbor to Senggigi), a bus/ferry package—between Ubud, Kuta, or Sanur on Bali and Mataram or Senggigi on Lombok—is a good idea. Fares are reasonable (e.g., Rp 13,000 from Kuta to Senggigi), and most travel agents can make the bookings. Try **Dewi Sri Murni Tours** (☏ 0361/730272) in Kuta on Bali. On Lombok, contact **Perama Travel** (☞ Tour Operators, *below*).

The *Mabua Express* (☏ 0370/81195 in Lembar) luxury hydrofoil takes just 2½ hours to cross from Tanjung Benoa in southern Bali to Lembar. It leaves at 8 AM and 2:30 PM from Tanjung Benoa and at 10:30 A ʿ and 5 PM from Lembar. The fare is Rp 119,000 in economy, Rp 216,000 in Emerald Class, and Rp 302,000 in Diamond Class; the latter includes transport from to Kuta, Nusa Dua, or Sanur on Bali and to Bangsal, Mataram, or Senggigi on Lombok.

Ferries depart hourly between dawn and dusk for the 1½-hour journey to Poto Tano on the west coast of Sumbawa; fares are around Rp 3,600 for air-conditioned (and smoke-filled) quarters and Rp 2,300 for deck class; vehicles transport costs Rp 6,000–20,00. On the west end of Sumbawa, it costs Rp 10,000 to make the seven-hour ferry crossing to Komodo and Rp 11,500 for the 10-hour continuing journey to Labuanbajo, Flores. In theory, the ferry departs at 8 AM every day but Friday, but check on the schedule and the condition of the ferry with locals before you show up at the docks (crossings have been canceled for weeks at a time for boat repairs).

The national fleet of Pelni ships (large, cruise ship–type vessels) stop at Sumbawa Besar's satellite port of Badas, 7 km (4 mi) to the west, every two weeks. Pelni also pauses at Sumbawa Besar weekly, alternating journeys between Lembar on Lombok and a route that encompasses Waingapu, Sumba, Ende, Flores, Kupang, and Timor. Costs range from about Rp 15,000 per segment for economy class (bunk beds in shared rooms of 100 or more, shared baths, and three simple meals a day) to about Rp 70,000 or more per segment for first-class (a two-bed cabin and more elaborate meals).

From Labuanbajo, regular ferries depart daily at 8 AM (except Friday) for the three-hour journey (Rp 4,000) west to Komodo; they then continue on seven more hours to Sape on Sumbawa (Rp 11,500). In Ende, the Pelabuhan Ipi dock is 3 km (2 mi) from town; the Pelni office at Jalan Kemakmuran and Jalan Pabean has schedule details. A regular ferry also cruises south to the island of Sumba on Tuesday and east to Kupang on Timor on Saturday.

By Bus

Buses/ferries are an important form of transportation between islands in Nusa Tenggara. Sumbawa Besar has a new terminal 6 km (4 mi) northwest of town; vehicles leave for Lombok at 6, 8, and 9 AM and again at 9 PM and depart for Bima between 7 and 9 AM and at 8 PM. Bima's terminal for points west is just outside of the town center; buses to Lombok leave in the evening and smaller buses to towns on Sumbawa run between 6 AM and 5 PM. Express buses to Lombok and Bali meet the ferries from Labuanbajo in Sape, Sumbawa's eastern port. Buses from Sape transfer in Bima for towns west. Those from Labuanbajo head east for Ende around 7 AM and then again around 4 PM when the ferry from Sape arrives.

Getting Around

By Bemo and Horse-Drawn Cart

Public transport on Lombok consists primarily of crowded bemos and the *cidomo,* a horse-drawn cart that seats four or five and costs approximately Rp 500 per km (½ mi). Elsewhere in the Nusa Tenggara, bemos are the way to get around towns and to nearby sites; most cost around Rp 250 for short distances; you can bargain with drivers for longer jaunts. Many areas still have horse-drawn carriages called *dokars,* also known as Ben Hurs in Sape.

By Bus and Taxi

The central terminal on Lombok is in Sweta, just outside Cakranegara. Government-set fares are posted, although they may be out of date, so don't balk if you're charged slightly more. Do bargain, however, if the price seems outrageous. Metered taxis are available from the airport and at hotels (though you can also hire them for a flat fee to take tours); a taxi from the airport to Senggigi should cost less than Rp 7,000 (though you'll be asked for at least Rp 10,000 initially). There's a taxi stand in Senggigi, right on the main road next to the art market.

Unless you've hired your own vehicle to drive east through the other islands, buses are the only way to reach the small towns. Taxis are available in the larger settlements, but usually only for short-distance trips.

By Car

On Lombok, rental cars cost about Rp 45,000 a day or Rp 75,000 with driver. Try **Rinjani Rent Car** (☎ 0370/32259), on Jalan Bung Karno in Mataram across from the Hotel Granada, or **Metro Rent Car** (☎ 0370/32146) on Jalan Yos Sudarso in Ampenan, which rents Suzuki Jimmys for Rp 45,000–Rp 60,000 including insurance. You can also rent a car or hire a car and driver through major hotels.

Contacts and Resources

Emergencies

Scuba-Diving Emergencies: The closest decompression chamber is operated by **Baruna** (✉ Jl. Raya Seririt, Lovina, ☎ 0362/41084) in northwest Bali.

Ambulance: ☎ 118. **Medical:** Klinik Senggigi Medical Services (☎ 0370/93210). **Fire:** ☎ 113. **Police:** ☎ 110.

Medical and Police. Bima: Bima Police Station ☎ 0374/21110. **Labuan-bajo:** Public Hospital of Labuanbajo (✉ heading away from docks on the main road, take first left after BRI Bank). **Sumbawa Besar:** Public Hospital of Sumbawa (☎ 0371/21087); Sumbawa Besar Police Station (☎ 0371/21142).

English-Language Bookstores

Most major Lombok resorts have at least a few books, news magazines, and international papers available. Used bookstores come and go in the tourist areas of Senggigi and Kuta; ask at your hotel. The **Senggigi Supermarket and Department Store** on Jalan Raya Senggigi (☎ 0370/93738) sells books and maps. Aside from this, however, you will find few bookshops selling English-language material on the island.

If you're desperate for reading material on the other islands, local hotels usually have a few books to trade, or you can trade with fellow travelers. Unfortunately, outside of the more touristed areas, the bookstore concept hasn't caught in Indonesia.

Tour Operators

Baruna (✉ Holiday Inn Lombok, Jl. Raya Senggigi, Senggigi, ☎ 0370/93093) arranges dive trips. **Bidy Tour and Travel** (✉ Jl. Ragigenep 17, Ampenan, ☎ 0370/32127) offers treks, island cruises, dive packages, visits to cultural villages, and fishing trips. **Dream Divers** (✉ Jl. Raya Senggigi, Senggigi, ☎ 0370/93738; ✉ Gili Air, ☎ 0370/3454) has dive trips around the island. **Satriavi Tours & Travel** (✉ Senggigi Beach Hotel, ☎ 0364/23430, ext. 8602) organizes different tours of the island, including treks to Gunung Rinjani. **Perama** (✉ Jl. Pejanggik Mataram, ☎ 0370/35936; ✉ Jl. Raya Senggigi, Senggigi, ☎ 0370/93007) coordinates treks to Gunung Rinjani, day tours of Lombok, and land/sea adventure tours to Komodo. Golf tours are available through **Rinjani Country Club** (✉ Jl. Sriwijaya 396, Mataram, ☎ 0370/37316).

Grand Komodo Adventures and Diving (✉ Jl. Sukarno-Hatta 45, Bima, ☎ 0374/42018; ✉ Jl. P. W. Papu, Labuanbajo, ☎ 0385/41277) organizes dive trips throughout Nusa Tenggara on live-aboard boats. **Puri Komodo Resort** (✉ Batu Bosok, Labuanbajo, ☎ 0385/41319) coordinates a variety of tours and treks.

Travel Agencies

The following Lombok companies can make travel arrangements and organize guided tours: **Bidy Tour and Travel** (☞ Tour Operators, *above*), **Discover Lombok** (✉ Pasar Seni market, Jl. Raya Senggigi, Senggigi, ☎ 0370/36781), **Lombok Indah Tour and Travel** (✉ Jl. Raya Senggigi, Senggigi, ☎ 0370/93838), **Lombok Wisata Indah** (✉ Pasar Seni market, Jl. Raya Senggigi, Senggigi, ☎ 0370/32815), **Nazareth Tours and Travel** (✉ Jl. Raya Senggigi, Senggigi, ☎ 0370/93033). **Perama** (☞ Tour Operators, *above*) also has an office on Jalan Yos Sudarso in Labuanbajo on Flores.

Visitor Information

The **Regional Office of Tourism** (✉ Jl. Singosari 2, Mataram, ☎ 0364/21730) is open Monday–Thursday 8–3 and Friday–Saturday 8–12.

The **Labuanbajo Tourist Office** (⊠ Off Jl. Yos Sudarso, ☎ 0385/41170) keeps odd hours, though they're supposed to be open daily 10–6; if you want information, it's best to stop by as soon as you get off the ferry from Sape.

The **Bima Tourist Office** (⊠ Jl. Soekarno Hatta, ☎ 0374/44331) is open 7–3 Monday through Friday. The **PHPA Office Information Booth** (⊠ Jl. Yos Sudarso, Bima, ☎ no phone) provides general information on Komodo and Rinca. It's open Monday–Thursday 8–4 and Friday–Saturday 8–11. The **Sumbawa Besar Tourist Office** (⊠ Jl. Garuda, near Hotel Tambora, ☎ 0371/21632) has hours Monday–Thursday 8–4 and Friday–Saturday 8–11. For information on the national parks, try the **PHPA Office** (⊠ Jl. Garuda 12, Sumbawa Besar, ☎ 0371/21358), which is open 8–2 weekdays.

SULAWESI

To the north and east of Bali and Java is the island of Sulawesi, formerly called the Celebes. Four long peninsulas radiate from a central mountainous area, giving the island an orchid shape. Its topography is dramatic—from rice fields, rain forests, and mountains to bays where crescents of sugar-white sand gently slip into sapphire water and dazzling coral reefs. Sulawesi is actually a puzzle of land masses that were pieced together over millions of years, its arms once connected to Borneo, New Guinea, and even Antarctica. The island also inherited plenty of natural power from the "ring of fire" into which it was born, for Sulawesi has 11 active volcanoes. The crushing tectonic forces that pushed the island's arms into place resulted in a chain of mountains that stretch 1,300 km (806 mi) from north to south. Still, no point on the island is more than 100 km (62 mi) from the sea.

With its pieces sliding together from all over the earth, Sulawesi is the home of many unique species; in fact, two-thirds of its mammals and one-third of its birds are found nowhere else in the world. Included in its rare cast of wildlife are the *babirusa,* (deer pig) and two types of *anoa* (pygmy buffalo). Several national parks, including Morowali, Lore Lindu, Tangkoko Batuangus Dua Saudara, and Pulau Manado Bunaken Tua, are prime spots for trekking and wildlife watching—if you're the adventurous sort. At present, Sulawesi is virtually unspoiled, its tourist infrastructure confined mostly to the southwestern port of Ujung Pandang, central Tanatoraja, and northeastern Manado.

The earliest human inhabitants were seafaring tribes who sailed through the straits from other parts of Asia and from Australia. The first major settlement was southern Soppeng, which was soon overshadowed by Mankasara—now Ujung Pandang—and northern Manado, both busy trading hubs on the way to and from the Spice Islands of Maluku. Mankasara in particular rose to prominence in the 16th century as the aggressive Bajau "sea gypsies" and Bugis tribes took over the waters. In fact, the Bugis were so feared by Asian and Western traders venturing into the region that they became the basis for the modern-day term "Boogey (Bugi) Man." However, it took just a century or so for the Dutch to dominate trade in the region and later take over much of the island, changing the capital's name to Makassar in the process. As Islam spread through the lower peninsula in the early 1600s, the Dutch began working their way north and inland to a region the Bugis called Tanatoraja, the fabled "Land of the Kings"—a secluded, mountainous area where head-hunting, witchcraft, human sacrifice, and elaborate funeral rites were practiced. It was well into the 1900s before missionaries arrived bringing Christianity with them, and well into the 1940s before the Dutch relinquished power, allowing the island to become part of the Republic of Indonesia.

Today, more than 12 million people live on Sulawesi; around four-fifths follow Islam, and the rest—mostly in Tanatoraja and northern Manado—are Christian. The people's physical attributes and their traditions have Arabic, Austronesian, Chinese, and Indian roots; indeed, the island's culture is its primary attraction. There are the southern Bugis, who once sent bands of pirates to prowl the waters and raid ships and whose glorious 200-ton, dual-masted *pinisis* can still be seen in the water at Ujung Pandang and at the shipyards of Maru Masa, 7 km (4 mi) from Bira at the peninsula's opposite end. The Bajau, too, are expert sailors who still spend nearly all their time on the water; their village homes are clustered together over the bays of the south coast. Perhaps the most famous culture here, though, is that of Tanatoraja, where traditional clan houses—the carved and painted *tongkonan*—are built on stilts and topped by massive, curving roofs like a graceful pair of buffalo horns soaring skyward. To the north, the Minihasans around Manado follow Christian beliefs (20% of them are Catholic, 80% are Protestant) introduced by 15th-century Spanish and Portuguese missionaries.

Travel on Sulawesi is challenging at best. Most of the numerous flights between the southwest peninsula and Tanatoraja and northeastern Manado were, at press time, suspended owing to the economic crisis. With the Ujung Pandang–Manado highway recently completed, buses are a viable alternative until the airlines reestablish service; however, the central terrain is mountainous, vehicles are rarely in good condition, and trips are often arduous. Sea travel is the third, and perhaps most pleasant option if you have the time—ships only call weekly or biweekly at various island ports. Renting a car and driving yourself isn't advised and, unfortunately, if you're planning to venture far from Ujung Pandang, long-distance drivers aren't always available. On this island, perhaps more than any other, you must keep your traveler's sense of humor, making every effort to consider the journey as much a part of the fun as the destination.

Ujung Pandang

➊ *1,630 km (1,011 mi) northeast of Jakarta, 770 km (477 mi) northeast of Denpasar, 322 km (200 mi) north of Labuanbajo.*

Most visitors fly into Ujung Pandang and use it as their base for travel throughout Sulawesi. The city has several old forts and palaces that can easily be seen on short trips along the coast just outside of town. Ujung Pandang's port is busy and colorful, with everything from small, slim prahu outriggers to sleek pinisi to huge modern Pelni (a state-owned company) ships. Natural wonders are also plentiful, including vast, empty beaches, waterfalls, and tropical gardens less than a two-hour drive away.

Benteng Ujung Pandang, better known as Ft. Rotterdam, is by the harbor in the center of the Old City. Once a fortified trading post for the Sulawesi Gowan dynasty, the fort was captured and rebuilt by the Portuguese in 1545, then captured by the Dutch in 1608 and reinforced again. Several municipal offices are housed in the complex, including the Conservatory of Dance and Music. You can occasionally see unofficial dance performances (the children practice on the stage in the fort's center) as well as the official ones frequently held on Saturday night at 8; the staff at your hotel should have a schedule. The fort also includes the **Galigo Museum,** the state's museum, which is divided into ethnology and history sections. The ethnographic museum is the more interesting, with a large collection of artifacts from different areas of Sulawesi. ✉ *Free to fort; admission fee for museums.* ◷ *Fort: Daily 8–5. Museums: Tues.– Thurs. 8 AM–1 PM, Fri. 8 AM–10 AM, weekends 8–4.*

The lovely blossoms at the **Clara Bundt Orchid Garden,** just south of the fort off Jalan Hasanuddin, include those from varieties from all over the world. Some of the plants here grow to more than 13 ft high. There's also an extensive seashell collection that includes several giant clams. ✉ *Jl. Mochtar Lufti 15,* ☎ *0411/22572.* ✉ *Free.* ◷ *Daily 10–4.*

Across the harbor from Ujung Pandang is **Samalona Island,** which has been developed into a recreational center, mostly appealing to locals. It can be reached in 45 minutes. The sports you can participate in here include snorkeling and waterskiing.

For a look at southern Sulawesi's culture and crafts, head for **Taman Mini Sulsel,** southeast of the ports and Benteng Ujung Pandang and about 5 km (3 mi) east of the Orchid Garden (☞ *above*). This combination amusement park and cultural complex includes examples of architecture, textiles, and costumes from all over the archipelago, but it makes a decent introduction to the area's history and sights, including the curved-roof tongkonan of Toraja. ⊠ *Jl. Dangko.* ⊡ *Admission.* ⊙ *Daily 10–10.*

For an overview of exquisite silk textiles, visit the **Tenunan Sutera Alam** silk factory in the city's southern Chinese quarter. Here, women still practice their craft each step of the way, from gathering and dyeing the strands to spinning and weaving the garments. ⊠ *Jl. Ontah 408,* ☎ *no phone.* ⊡ *Free.* ⊙ *Daily 10–3.*

For those interested in religion and architecture, there are also a number of Chinese temples in the southern part of the city, particularly around Jalan Sulawesi. You can wander through them at anytime during daylight hours, as long as there are no religious ceremonies taking place; the friendly caretakers will most likely be pleased to provide a quick tour. **Ibu Agung Bahari** (⊠ Jl. Sulawesi 41), is a 350-year-old structure filled with carvings and colorful paintings. The brilliant colors and ornate detailing of the 18th-century **Tian Hou Gong Temple** (⊠ Corner of Jl. Sulawesi and Jl. Serui) make it hard to miss. The large, wooden building is dedicated to Tian Hou, the "Heavenly Queen," who is both a goddess of fertility and a patron of the sailors who still worship here. Her figure, which graces the central altar, is surrounded by three lower levels, where the faithful also worship venerated deities of medicine and motherhood as well as of fertility. Just down the street is **Long Xian Gong Temple** (Corner of Jl. Sulawesi and Jl. Bali), or "Dragon Ghost" temple, built in 1868. This temple has classic Chinese architectural lines and houses three altars: the left one is dedicated to Tu Di Gong, the god of the earth and wealth; the right one to Mi Lo Fo, the protector of jewelers; and the central one to Xian Mu, a mother of the gods.

About 4 km (2 mi) southeast of town is the **Diponegoro Tomb,** the grave of and monument to a great Javanese hero. Prince Diponegoro of Yogyakarta led the fight against the Dutch successfully for five years during the Java War (1825–30). The Dutch finally put a stop to his leadership by summoning him to their headquarters on the pretense of negotiating peace and then taking him prisoner. His sentence was exile to Sulawesi and imprisonment at Ft. Rotterdam, which was where he spent his final 26 years. ⊠ *Jl. Diponegoro.* ⊡ *Free.* ⊙ *Daily sunrise–sunset.*

Four centuries ago, the kingdom of Gowa—which merged with the kingdom of Tallo to form the island's first true center of power—was the site of the palace of the Makassar rulers and a key port. The ruins of "Old Gowa" begin 7 km (4 mi) south of Ujung Pandang at **Sombaopu,** the fort that protected the sultanate with massive brick walls (10 ft thick and 23 ft high) and a clever locale overlooking the sea. The Dutch—in cohorts with Makassar rival Bugis troops—decimated the fort in 1669 and the elements pounded the ruins for the next three centuries. Indonesian archaeologists restored them in the late 1980s. Besides strolling around the fort area, you can also visit the historical museum, which displays artifacts and ammunition uncovered in the excavation, as well as four "living cultural villages" that represent four of the region's ethnic groups' crafts and rituals. ⊠ *Off Jl. Tallo along the Ujung Pandang–Sunguminasa Hwy.,* ☎ *no phone.* ⊡ *Admission.* ⊙ *Daily 8–5.*

The **Tomb of Sultan Hasanuddin** and other kings of Gowa are in a cemetery between the fort and the Sungguminasa Palace (☞ *below*). Besides the grave of Hasanuddin, the most famous of the Gowan kings and a national hero for his ferocious battle against the Dutch, you'll also find the **Pelantikan stone,** or *tomanurunga,* the coronation stone of the Kingdom of Gowa. Legends of the kingdom tell of the goddess Tomanurunga, who started the line of Gowan kings when she married a mortal named Karaeng Bayo at this site. Afterward the stone became the place where the sultans were crowned. Fifteen minutes' walk from the tomb is the 1603 **Mesjid Katangka,** Ujung Pandang's oldest mosque (now rebuilt) and the site of more graves.

The traditional, raised, wooden palace of **Sungguminasa** (4 km/3 mi south of Sombaopu) was built in 1936. The **Ballalompoa Museum** here is a must-see, full of ornate royal jewelry and ceremonial costumes. ✉ *Jl. Cenderawasih, off Jl. Tallo and the Ujung Pandang–Sungguminasa Hwy.,* ☎ *no phone.* 🎫 *Admission.* ⊙ *Mon.–Thurs. 8–1, Fri. 8– 10:30, Sat. 8–12.*

North of the city are several noteworthy sights. The remains of **Tallo,** Gowa's 16th-century satellite kingdom and ally are 3 km (2 mi) north of Ujung Pandang in the rice paddies off Jalan Tallo Umar. Just 4 km (2 mi) north of town is **Paotare,** the harbor where the Bugis bring their pinisi to unload cargo, mend sails, and prepare for the next voyage. Watching these elegant wooden schooners set off along the warm, bright water is a timeless sight. Sunsets from here are singular, but the pier has missing planks and gaping holes, so watch your step. **The ports of Sukarno and Hatta** along Jalan Martadina southwest of Paotare are a good place to watch large modern ships and two-masted prahu glide in from all parts of Indonesia.

Dining and Lodging

$$ ✕ **Shogun.** On the waterfront road, Sulawesi's original Japanese restaurant is clean and busy. Menu items include such traditional fare as sushi and sashimi. Try anything served with the fresh local seafood—especially the fish. Sake is a nice complement to an evening meal. ✉ *Jl. Penghibur 2,* ☎ *0411/324102. AE, MC, V.*

$$ ✕ **Surya Supercrab.** This restaurant serves some of the best seafood in Ujung Pandang—count on crowds and a wait for a table. The large, bright room has no notable decor or atmosphere, but the crab-and-asparagus soup is delicious, as are the gigantic prawns. ✉ *Jl. Nusakambangan 16,* ☎ *0411/317066. No credit cards.*

$$–$$$ ✕🖃 **Radisson Ujung Pandang.** What this hotel lacks in charm it makes up in efficiency and a grand waterfront location on the waterfront. Rooms are boxlike but comfortable and well equipped, with such amenities as hair dryers and in-room safes. The coffee shop looks out onto the water and offers a combined taste of the West and of Asia—tiger prawns with a hint of lemongrass and barbecued duck in a light curry sauce. There's also a Chinese restaurant that serves both Szechuan and Cantonese fare. ✉ *Jl. Somba Opu 235, 90111,* ☎ *0411/3333111,* FAX *0411/333222. 90 rooms. Restaurant, coffee shop, health club, meeting rooms. AE, DC, MC, V.*

$$–$$$ 🖃 **Hotel Sedona.** This comfortable, deluxe, 10-story hotel has a scenic location on the southern Losari Beach. The spacious lobby has beige polished-marble floors and floor-to-ceiling windows that offer sweeping sea views. Rooms and suites are awash in pastels and decorated with contemporary furnishings tailored for modern travelers, including queen-size beds, desks, minibars, and sizable baths; six rooms have terraces. A large ballroom and meeting rooms with many facilities make this hotel popular with business travelers. ✉ *Jl. Somba Opu 297, 90111,* ☎ *0411/870555,* FAX *0411/870222. 218 rooms, 12 suites. 3 restaurants, 2 bars, pool, health club, beach, shops, laundry service, business services, meeting rooms. AE, MC, V.*

$$–$$$ ⊡ **Makassar Golden Hotel.** Right on Losari Beach, this hotel has Toraja-style roofs on its main building. Most of the comfortable rooms and cottages face the sea and have wall-to-wall carpeting, with beige decor and woven bedcovers in a Toraja design. All rooms have private baths, minibars, and TVs. ⊠ *Jl. Pasar Ikan 50, 90111,* ☎ *0411/ 314408,* 🖷 *0411/320951. 50 rooms, 10 cottages. Restaurant, coffee shop, minibars, pool, beach, dance club, laundry service, meeting rooms. AE, DC, MC, V.*

$$ ⊡ **Makassar City Hotel.** Toraja-style carved-wood panels are the focus here. The hotel is affordable and centrally located, but its facilities and furnishings have seen better days: rooms are spacious, with sitting areas, king-size beds, TVs, and minibars, but stains on the carpets and scuff marks on the walls attest to their age. The lounge has tired crushed-velvet sofas and lumpy leather chairs. ⊠ *Jl. Khairil Anwar 28, 90111,* ☎ *0411/317055,* 🖷 *0411/311818. 89 rooms. Restaurant, bar, pool, meeting rooms. AE, DC, MC, V.*

$ ⊡ **Hotel Ramayana.** Between the airport and Ujung Pandang, this place is clean but purely utilitarian. It's conveniently located across from the Liman Express office, which runs buses to Tanatoraja. ⊠ *Jl. G. Bawakaraeng 121, 90111,* ☎ *0411/442479,* 🖷 *0411/322165. 35 rooms. Restaurant, travel services. No credit cards.*

Nightlife and the Arts

Sunset viewing and snack munching are the prime activities on the patios of the expat hangouts **Kios Semarang** and **Eva Ria** along Jalan Penghibur. Local bands often play at the **Makassar Golden Hotel** (⊠ Jl. Pasar Ikan 50–52, ☎ 0411/314408). Dancers can try the disco at the **Marannu City Hotel** (⊠ Jl. Sultan Hasanuddin 3-5, ☎ 0411/315087).

Shopping

Ujung Pandang's position at the crossroads of trade routes between east and west Indonesia, as well as those north and south between Asia and the South Pacific, makes it one of the most diverse shopping spots in the country. Start east of the waterfront and south of Benteng Ujung Pandang at **Jalan Somba Opu,** which is lined with crafts shops filled with shells, spices, carvings, silks, gold, fine Gowan brasswork, and musical instruments. **Asia Art and Curio** (⊠ Jl. Somba Opu, ☎ no phone) has a variety of antiques. **Asia Baru** (⊠ Jl. Somba Opu, ☎ no phone) is a good place for porcelain. **Kanegbo Art Shop** (⊠ Corner of Jl. Somba Opu and Jl. Pattimura, ☎ no phone) sells silk textiles, baskets, and pieces of fine jewelry made in the region. The **Maryam Art Shop** (⊠ Jl. Pattimura 6, 2nd floor, ☎ no phone) also has old pieces.

Leang Leang Caves and Bantimurung Falls

② *38 km (24 mi) northeast of Ujung Pandang.*

The extensive underground chambers of the **Leang Leang Caves** (also known as the Maros Caves) make up an archaeological park that protects some of the archipelago's most valuable prehistoric artwork. In the midst of breezy, forested hills, the park's rugged limestone cliffs hide Mesolithic paintings of wildlife and human images from 5,000–10,000 years ago. Visit Leang Pettae and Leang Peta Kere to see eerie sets of human handprints in all different sizes, or Ulu Leang and Leang Burung I and II to see fossils. More than 60 caves have been found in the region, including Salukan Kalang, which at 11 km (7 mi) is the island's longest.

Three kilometers (2 miles) northeast of Leang Leang is a serene forest haven with tropical scenery, cool streams, quiet caves, and the thundering **Bantimurung Falls,** made famous by 1800s naturalist Alfred Russel Wallace, who came here to collect butterflies. Although the park is overrun with locals on weekends and holidays and it now takes patience to find the spectacular giant birdwings so common in Wallace's day, the area is nevertheless a good place to observe Sulawesi's natural beauty.

Bone

❸ *79 km (49 mi) northeast of Bantimurung, 110 km (68 mi) northeast of Ujung Pandang.*

In the 17th century, this town (formally known as Watampone) was a regional core of power and a semiautonomous state ruled by the rebel king, Aru Palakka. The Dutch eventually conquered the city—three times—and remnants of their presence include colonial houses along some of the streets. The Dutch weren't the only outsiders to live in Bone, though; the seafaring Bugis also maintained a presence, and an 1881 Bugis house, the **Bola Soba,** can be seen behind the Hotel Watampone on Jalan Sudirman. The former palace is now the **Museum Lapawawoi,** with an extensive collection of photos, charts of royal successions, and an array of court artifacts. The museum is open daily 8–5; there is an admission fee.Bone is also a base for visiting one of the peninsula's largest cave systems, the **Mampu Caves,** 40 km (25 mi) south of town.

Dining and Lodging

$ ✕ **Pondok Selera.** This small, friendly place is consistently recommended by both visitors and expats as the best restaurant in town. The back garden is a pleasant spot in which to enjoy savory Indonesian and Chinese dishes. Any of the seafood entrées with hot rice and mixed vegetables are guaranteed to satisfy. ⊠ *Jl. Biru 28,* ☎ *no phone. No credit cards.*

$ 🏨 **Wisma Bola Ridie.** Owned by a descendent of the last prince of Bone, this hotel is in a charming 1930s Dutch building. Its name means "The Yellow House," and its yellow exterior is a symbol of South Sulawesi nobility. Large, comfortable rooms, tile floors, and congenial hospitality all add to the delightful setting five minutes' walk from the main town. Breakfast and tea are included in the price. ⊠ *Jl. Merdeka 6,* ☎ *0419/21412. 6 rooms. No credit cards.*

$ 🏨 **Wisma Watampone.** This modern-style building with touches of Sulawesi decor offers more Western comforts than expected outside of Ujung Pandang, including air-conditioning and private baths in all rooms. Quarters are simple, spacious, and clean, and the English-speaking staff members are happy to assist with travel plans. ⊠ *Jl. Biru 14,* ☎ *0419/ 21362. 20 rooms. Restaurant, coffee shop, pool, laundry service. AE, MC, V.*

En Route Forty kilometers (25 miles) northwest of Bone (via Uloe) are the **Mampu Caves,** a network of underground limestone passages that comprises Sulawesi's largest cave system. You can hire guides in the village next to the site, and they will point out an imaginative variety of characters found in the unusual stalactite and stalagmite shapes. Local lore has it that these images are the former court of a lazy local princess, turned to stone when she dropped her spool and promised to marry whoever picked it up for her but then broke her vow when it was returned by a dog.

Sengkang

❹ *65 km (40 mi) northwest of Bone, 175 km (109 mi) northeast of Ujung Pandang.*

Sengkang (Singkang) is an unexpectedly pleasant lakeside resort town in the center of the southwestern peninsula. A large, shallow lake—

Danau Tempe—gives the town a relaxed, mountain-hideaway feel, and the, scenic gardens, lush hills, and "floating" houses (Bugis houses that are raised on stilts) have made it quite a draw. There are also numerous weaving cooperatives in the area where you can observe the creation of silk textiles from the worm to the loom to the market shelves. Check out **Toko Sumber Sutera** (⊠ Jl. Magga Amirulla 140, ☎ no phone) for an idea of selection and price.

Soppeng

5 *25 km (15 mi) southwest of Sengkang, 75 km (46 mi) northwest of Bone.*

Soppeng, or Watansoppeng, is another silk-production hub. Along the northern road from here to Pangkajene are groves of mulberry trees where silkworms are cultivated; many of the worms that hatch here are sent to Sengkang. Among the town's other attractions are its gardens, some of the most prized in the region, and the hundreds of fruit bats that live in the trees near the central mosque. Soppeng's true richness, however, lies in its cultural treasures, such as the **Taman Purbakala Kompleks Makam Kuno** (Sultans' Graves), a gathering of unique stone structures just outside town on the road to Ompo.

Pare Pare

6 *70 km (43 mi) northwest of Soppeng, 180 km (108 mi) north of Ujung Pandang.*

From Ujung Pandang the four-hour drive north to Pare Pare—halfway between Ujung Pandang and Rantepao in the Tanatoraja region—takes you through rice fields and past the Makassar Strait. Bugis houses, which are built on stilts and have crossed roof beams, line the road. At some you'll see fish hanging from the rafters, curing in the sun. With 90,000 people, Pare Pare is Sulawesi's second-largest town. The Bugis *bago* ships—smaller and more agile than the 100-ton pinisi cargo ships—and other craft sail from its port, perhaps on their way to Kalimantan on Borneo. At the **Museum Bangenge,** 2 km (1 mi) south of town at Cappa Galung, you'll find a collection of traditional weapons, costumes, and ornaments overseen by curator Haji Hamzah, a descendent of the last ruler of the region's Bacu Kiki kingdom. ⊠ *Desa Cappa Galung,* ☎ *no phone.* 🖾 *Admission.* ⊙ *Daily 10–4.*

Dining

$ ✕ **Bukit Indah.** Perched on a hill, this smart, pristinely clean restaurant has a view of the bay and catches a nice breeze. The crab-and-corn soup is delicious; if you're feeling daring, try the fried frogs' legs. To reach Bukit Indah, take a right turn up the hill from the main street just before entering downtown Pare Pare. (Note that six clean, simple rooms are available if you wish to stay the night.) ⊠ *Jl. Sudirman 65,* ☎ *0421/21886. No credit cards.*

$ ✕ **Sempurna.** On Pare Pare's main street is a clean, Formica-furnished, air-conditioned restaurant that serves tasty Indonesian and Chinese fare. Seafood dishes dominate the menu; try the sweet-and-sour shrimp. ⊠ *202 Jl. Bau Massepe,* ☎ *0421/21573. No credit cards.*

En Route   The route from Pare Pare north to Tanatoraja wasn't paved until 1980; before then, the rutted, stony track took hours to cover. Even today, travel on this thin, two-lane road can be arduous, if not terrifying, as it winds along steep, jagged cliffs before it twists and turns inland, climbing into limestone hills forested with tropical pines and palms. Shimmering in the distance are the steely blue mountains that locked out intruders for centuries. Farther north are the smooth tucks and folds of soft, green, mountain slopes. The sky is enormously wide and, in the dry season, the air is clear and warm, allowing a glimpse of what regional legends maintain is the realm of gods.

NEED A
BREAK?

About 54 km (32 mi) before Makale is a roadside restaurant, **Puntak Lakawan,** with a terrace that affords spectacular views of Tanatoraja. Stop for the vistas, the strong coffee, and the "tourist only" Western toilet facilities—not for the food.

Tanatoraja (Torajaland)

★ **7** *Makale is 328 km (205 mi) northeast of Ujung Pandang, 110 km (68 mi) northeast of Pare Pare; Rantepao is 17 km (11 mi) northeast of Makale.*

The so-called Land of the Kings, which dominates south-central Sulawesi, was put in the international limelight in the early 1900s, when word of its animist cultures and their traditions first reached the West. Then, as now, people were captivated by tales of Tanatoraja's graceful tongkonans, whose curving roofs point east and west to the heavens out respect for ancestors; of its life-size *tau tau* (wooden effigies) that mark graves in limestone cliffs; of its wedding ceremonies and their elaborate costumes of gold and silk brocade; of its exciting *sisemba* kick-boxing contests and buffalo fights; and of its funerals involving hundreds of people and dozens of animal sacrifices.

The more popular sights are between Makale, the administrative center, and Rantepao, the commercial and tourist hub to the north. From Rantepao a network of roads peels off into the countryside to Toraja villages. To see the highlights, you'll need at least three full days; plan on a week to visit the more remote villages. If you drive to the area, add a day each way for the trip to and from Ujung Pandang. Although the dry season runs from April to October, many of the celebrations take place in July and August when the crops are harvested. This is when most people visit the area—particularly the towns around Rantepao. To avoid crowds, schedule a trip around these months or venture into the northwestern or eastern regions, which are the least infiltrated by Western visitors.

A good way to experience Tanatoraja is by hiking from one village to the next through hills and rice paddies along small, rugged paths. (Be sure to wear strong, ankle-supporting shoes and a hat—for sun protection—and bring binoculars so that you can clearly see the tau tau.) A trip that combines bus travel and short hikes is another option, though the going will be slow. You can also hire a minivan or a Jeep. Regardless of how you travel, a good, professionally trained guide is essential. Such a guide will not only serve as your translator, but also your ambassador and teacher—explaining the culture's beliefs and ceremonies, relating local legends, and introducing you to the lesser-known settlements.

Of all the rituals, the funeral ceremony is probably the most important to the peoples of the Tanatoraja, and you should attend one if you get the chance. Funerals here are celebrations of life after death rather than a lament for the departed soul. They can take months to arrange, with relatives arriving from all over the archipelago, and can last for days. Palm wine is drunk, feasts are shared, and animals are slaughtered. Wealth is measured in buffalo (it's believed that the dead arrive in the hereafter riding a large white buffalo): the more buffalo sacrificed at the funeral, the more honor to the dead, the family, and the clan. Even those who have converted to Christianity continue the funeral ritual to demonstrate their prestige, keep tradition, and make sure the dead have plenty of influence with the gods.

Another large ritual takes place when a clan erects a new tongkonan. At these housewarming ceremonies the whole clan—often hundreds of people—is present. Buffalo, chickens, and pigs are sacrificed, both as dishes for the huge feast and as a show of prestige. All tongkonan face north—toward the land of the gods, according to one legend. Another legend contends that they face the direction from which the first settlers sailed (they are then purported to have used their upturned boats as shelters, hence the buffalo-horn shape of the roofs today). Houses are raised and have high gables with geometric designs and, perhaps, a few buffalo skulls; they also usually face a row of large rice barns.

Makale

Set amid the mountains and around a man-made lake, Makale is the entrance to Tanatoraja. Although it gleams with whitewashed Dutch churches and has an interesting market, this cool highland town attracts few visitors. Indeed, if you're in the area during peak season, you might consider making this your hub rather than crowded Rantepao. Although Makale isn't within walking distance of the main sights, you can easily hire a vehicle and a guide here. The **town market,** held every six days off Jalan Pasar Baru, is a riot of color and activity. Several trails on the outskirts of town lead to small villages—perfect for day hikes and picnics. A path from Jalan Ihwan Rambe runs west toward **Tondon,** where there are several secluded tau tau.

Rantepao and Environs

Rantepao is a small, easygoing town of dirt roads, cool mountain breezes, and a quietly booming tourist business year-round. Its big event occurs every sixth day, when the "weekly" market at the town crossroads attracts shoppers from miles around. Even on off days, the market shops sell wood carvings, cloth, and other Toraja-crafted goods. Rantepao's inexpensive restaurants and hotels are clean, comfortable, and friendly, and its semi-backwoods location and Christian-animist character give it an honest, genteel aura.

Some of the best-known Tanatoraja villages and sights are a short walk or drive from Rantepao. (Note: When you visit a village, plan to give a small donation of at least Rp 1,500, as tourism helps with these communities' upkeep. Also bring gifts of cigarettes or food to show your respect.) In **Karasik,** a traditional village on the southern outskirts of town, a group of elegant tongkonan surround several megaliths. Four kilometers (2 miles) south of Rantepao is **Kete Kesu,** a wood-carving village with hanging graves beneath the cliffsides; you'll also spot coffins and piles of bones along the thin forest paths. Ten minutes' walk from Kete Kesu is **Sulukeng,** where megaliths mark several graves.

In **Londa,** 8 km (5 mi) south of Rantepao, long, twisted passageways run deep into the cliffs and are lined with piles of skulls and bones. Coffins are tucked into some of the cave shelves as well, many with more than one body inside (it's customary to bury family members together). You don't need a guide for the caves, but you will need a bright flashlight; if you don't have one, there are plenty of guides—many of whom speak English and are excellent storytellers—with gas lamps for hire near the snack stands outside. Within walking distance of the Londa caves is **Pabalsenam,** a tree of hanging graves for babies who died before teething. Five kilometers (3 miles) south of Londa is **Lemo,** one of the best places for viewing tau tau in the cliff faces; try to arrive here early in the morning, because the figures face east and are bathed in shadows by midday.

At **Marante,** 5 km (3 mi) northeast of Rantepao, you'll find burial caves in a limestone cliff as well as the remnants of poles used to support

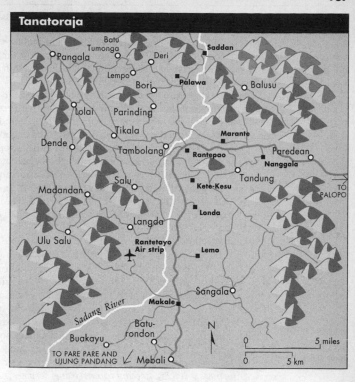

Tanatoraja

hanging coffins, some old carved coffins, and a funeral bier shaped like a traditional house—a ship to carry the deceased to the next life. At one end of the village is a modern home with a prow projecting from the roof and a wooden buffalo head attached to its front post—a fabulous anachronism.

Ten kilometers (6 miles) east of Rantepao is quiet **Nanggala.** Here the tongkonan are built on poles with soaring prow-shape roofs and are lined up facing north; *lumbung* (granaries, smaller than the houses but similar in shape) stand opposite. The tongkonan is cared for by the clan leader. A noble clan may decorate all the walls with carved and painted designs symbolizing the buffalo, the sun, and important crops. A middle-ranking clan is permitted to decorate only the front gable. When you see a wooden buffalo head or the horns of sacrificed buffalo affixed to the front pole of the house, you're looking at the house of a noble clan.

In the very old village of **Palawa,** 7 km (4 mi) north of Rantepao, hundreds of horns of sacrificed buffalo hang on the houses. Eight of the traditional homes contain shops that sell Toraja carvings, textiles, old coins, and, well, junk. In **Saddan** (3 km/2 mi northeast of Pulawa), Toraja women weave and sell their colorful textiles, which have mainly primary colors in geometric patterns.

DINING AND LODGING

$ ✕ **Pondok Torsina.** A few miles south of Rantepao, this small hotel and ★ restaurant serves good Indonesian food on a veranda overlooking the rice paddies. Try the asparagus soup, shrimp in spicy butter sauce, or grilled fish. If possible, make arrangements a day in advance to have the *piong,* a traditional Toraja meal cooked in bamboo. The Toraja owner is very helpful in filling in any information gaps left by your guide. ⊠ *Tikunna Malenong,* ☎ *0423/21293. No credit cards.*

$ ✕ **Restaurant Rachmat.** Right across from the traffic circle in the center of town, this Chinese-operated restaurant has design elements based on a traditional Toraja house. The menu includes standard Indonesian, Toraja, and Chinese dishes and caters to tour groups, so it can be busy and noisy. Local specialties include fried buffalo steak and black rice. ⊠ *Jl. Abdul Sari 8. No credit cards.*

$$$ ✕⊡ **Marante Highland Resort.** At this hotel just outside Marante, request a room in one of the traditional structures with roofs that look like upside-down boats. These have Indonesian fabrics and terraces that overlook the landscaped grounds, and all rooms have good, long bathtubs. The pool has an adjoining terrace café, the coffee shop serves Western food and a few Indonesian dishes, and the barbecue restaurant offers an array of Southeast Asian dishes. The hotel staff can arrange excursions to the surrounding villages and cliffside graves. ⊠ *Jl. Jurusan Palapo (Box 52, Rantepao 91831),* ☎ *0423/216169,* ℻ *0423/21122. 111 rooms. 3 restaurants, pool, shops, travel services, meeting room. AE, DC, MC, V.*

$$ ✕⊡ **Hotel Misiliana.** The lovely setting for this massive collection of traditional bungalows is a hilly, landscaped area 4 km (2 mi) northeast of town. The courtyard garden has a row of tongkonan with rice barns opposite; guest rooms surround the courtyard and are in two- or four-unit bungalows designed to complement the houses. The rooms themselves are spotless and have twin beds with colorful native spreads as well as modern tile baths. Set-menu breakfasts and dinners are included in the room price. A cultural show takes place some evenings. ⊠ *Jl. Pongtiku 27 (Box 01), 91831,* ☎ *0423/21212,* ℻ *0423/21512. 96 rooms. 2 restaurants, bar, coffee shop, pool, tennis court, laundry service, business services, meeting rooms, travel services, car rental. AE, DC, MC, V.*

$$ ✕⊡ **Toraja Prince Hotel.** This large complex in the hills 4 km (2 mi) northeast of town is as upscale as you'll get in the region. The buildings have flourishes of traditional architecture. Rooms are spacious, comfortable, and clean; bright Torajan textiles complement the dark woods. The Japanese restaurant is a refreshing alternative to the abundance of Indonesian fare in town; a second restaurant serves Torajan, Chinese, and Western dishes. The friendly, professional management team operates a very thorough travel service; they take great pride in being helpful. ⊠ *Jl. Pakubalasalu, 91831,* ☎ *0423/21430,* ℻ *0423/21304. 95 rooms. 2 restaurants, bar, pool, shop, laundry service, travel services. AE, MC, V.*

$ ✕⊡ **Pia and Poppies Hotel and Restaurant.** Mr. Paul worked for years
★ as a chef at different Bali resorts before returning to Rantepao and opening this inn. His wonderful property is sleepy and serene, with panoramic valley views from the terrace, and skylighted, rock-inlaid showers. Mr. Paul and his family also preside over one of the most sophisticated Torajan dining rooms around; save room for the pumpkin soup. ⊠ *Jl. Pongtiku 27A (a few blocks south of Rantepao on the road to Makale), 91831,* ☎ *0423/21121,* ℻ *0423/25059. 10 rooms. Restaurant, bar. No credit cards.*

$$ ⊡ **Toraja Cottages.** Just 3 km (2 mi) east of Rantepao, and set among tropical gardens, this hotel consists of rows of attached cottages around the main building. The small, clean rooms have twin beds. Westernized Indonesian food is served in a veranda restaurant with rattan furniture, and, amusingly, a model of the Statue of Liberty on a corner table. People like to gather in the small bar off the lobby. ⊠ *Kampung Bolu (reservations: Jl. Somba Opu 281, Ujung Pandang 91831),* ☎ *0423/21089 or 0411/84146 in Ujung Pandang,* ℻ *0423/21304 or 0411/ 873083 in Ujung Pandang. 58 rooms. 2 restaurants, bar, pool, shops, travel services. AE, DC, V.*

Manado

❽ *2,500 km (1,550 mi) northeast of Jakarta, 1,900 km (1,178 mi) northeast of Ujung Pandang, 1,600 km (992 mi) northeast of Rantepao.*

As the hub for ships sailing between the Philippines, Borneo, and the Spice Islands and as the capital of a collection of northern states united in the province of Minihasa, Manado is a cosmopolitan city. Yet despite its international flavor and port town status, it's a surprisingly clean, open, congenial place.

★ For most people, *the* reason to come here is scuba diving. The waters and reefs of the nearby Bunaken Manado Tua National Marine Reserve offer some of the world's most spectacular dive sites. Live coral gardens and diverse marine life make for some fascinating and colorful exploration. Most trips begin from Manado or Malayang village, where powerboats zip you out to **Pulau Bunaken,** the main island of this archipelago (10 km/6 mi off shore) in just over an hour. Dive operations know this territory well and offer a variety of trips to the reefs around Pulau Bunaken. Area dive sites include the **Manado Wreck,** the 196-ft skeleton of a Dutch ship that sunk during World War II; the reefs off **Pulau Manado Tua,** a dormant volcano now covered with forest; and the coral gardens around **Pulau Siladen, Pulau Montehage,** and **Pulau Nain.**

When you come up for air, Manado has an abundance of markets, little shops, museums, and memorials. The **Sam Ratulangi Monument,** on Jalan Sam Ratulangi, honors the "father" of the Minihasan people, who was the first governor of east Indonesia. The **Ibu Walanda Maramis Monument** memorializes a pioneer of the Indonesian women's movement. The **Toar Lumimuut Monument** on Jalan Sudarso commemorates the legendary goddess Lumimuut and her son—who, as the stories go, mistakenly married each other. **The Provincial Museum of Northern Sulawesi** on Jalan Supratman provides a good overview of the region's culture. There is an admission fee to the museum, which is open Monday–Thursday 8–5, Friday 8–11, and Saturday 8–2.

Lodging

$$–$$$ 🏨 **Novotel Manado.** Right on the waterfront esplanade near the Matahari Department store, this large hotel is one of the town's newest and most luxurious. Standard rooms are comfortable and have touches of local decor amid the mainly Western furnishings. Suites have spacious sitting areas; for a fine bay view, request one of the two suites that have balconies. A sixth-floor pool also commands a stunning view of the water; the bar here is an early-evening hot spot. Blue Banter Marina, Tour, and Diving Center, in front of the hotel, offers dive tours to area reefs as well as dive classes and provincial tours. ✉ *Jl. Piere Tendean, 95111,* ☎ *0431/855555,* 𝖥𝖠𝖷 *0431/868888. 190 rooms, 14 suites. Restaurant, 2 bars, coffee shop, pool, health club, dive shop, children's programs, laundry service, business services, meeting rooms, travel services. AE, DC, MC, V.*

$$ 🏨 **Hotel New Queen.** Just 10 minutes from the airport, this newly renovated establishment offers clean, convenient accommodations at reasonable prices. Rooms are basic in decor but have such amenities as refrigerators. The price includes airport transfers, breakfast, dinner, or laundry service. ✉ *Jl. Wakeke 12-14, 95111,* ☎ *0431/855551,* 𝖥𝖠𝖷 *0431/ 864440. 35 rooms. Restaurant, bar, coffee shop, refrigerators, laundry service, meeting room. AE, DC, MC, V.*

$$ 🏨 **Nusantara Diving Center (NDC).** Manado's best-known dive orga-
★ nization also runs a hotel and restaurant right on Molas Beach, 5 km (3 mi) north of town. You can check in, make your scuba plans, and be out on the Bunaken reefs the next day. Rooms are basic and small

and not all of them have air-conditioning. But the place is friendly, and most guests don't mind the limited indoor space as they're here solely for the underwater action. The on-site dive shop has all the equipment necessary for dive and snorkel tours and classes, and the travel desk can organize trips to the countryside, including visits to area volcanoes. All-inclusive dive, boat, and hotel packages are available. ⊠ *Molas Beach, 95001,* ☎ *0431/863988,* FAX *0431/860638. 43 rooms. Restaurant, 2 bars, beach, dive shop, dance club, travel services. AE, MC, V.*

Outdoor Activities and Sports

Package rates for the three top dive operators in the area run Rp 648,000–Rp 972,000, including equipment, boat, and meals. **Barracuda** (⊠ Jl. Sam Ratulangi 61, Manado, ☎ 0431/62033) has a fleet of dive boats as well as several chalets on Molas Beach so that you can put together hotel and boat dive packages. **Murex** (⊠ Jl. Sudirman 28, Manado, ☎ 0431/66280) also has a dive resort and a number of boats that run to the Sangihe and Talaud islands north of Manado, among other places. The **NDC** (☞ Lodging, *above*), considered one of the friendliest and most professional outfits in the region, offers all-inclusive hotel, dive tour or class, and boat packages.

Sulawesi A to Z

Arriving and Departing

By Airplane

Garuda (☎ 0411/322543) flies to Ujung Pandang's **Hasanuddin Airport** (☎ 0423/62411) from Jakarta and Surabaya on Java and from Denpasar on Bali, among other places.

Merpati (☎ 0411/24114 in Ujung Pandang or 0423/21485 in Rantepao) once flew each morning between Ujung Pandang and the **Rantetayo Airport** (☎ 0423/62423) near Rantepao; this is the only air route to Tanatoraja, and at press time flights were suspended. However, due to the popularity of this region, service was expected to resume; contact your travel agent or Merpati for updates. In any case, even when flights are scheduled, the runway can become unserviceable in the rainy season, causing frequent cancellations.

All flights to Manado's **Sam Ratulangi Airport** (☎ 0431/51060) from the south are via Ujung Pandang on **Garuda** (☎ 0431/51544). **Merpati** (☎ 0431/64027) may also have flights to different points on the island. **Bouraq** (☎ 0431/62757) serves the city from Gorontalo on the northeast peninsula, Palu in the central area, and the northeast island of Ternate. Internationally, you can enter Manado nonstop from Davao in the Philippines or from Singapore (☞ *also* Arriving and Departing *in* Indonesia A to Z, *below*).

Between the Airport and Downtown. The Hasanuddin Airport is 22 km (14 mi) east of Ujung Pandang; a taxi to town costs about Rp 15,000. You can buy a coupon inside the terminal, next to the baggage claim. You can also hire a minivan—perfect for groups or those with lots of dive gear—outside the arrivals area for around Rp 10,000. Rantetayo Airport is 24 km (15 mi) southwest of Rantepao. You can catch a bus into town or book one for a ride to the airport from your hotel for about Rp 5,000. From Sam Ratulangi Airport, 13 km (8 mi) east of Manado, metered taxis run roughly Rp 7,000.

By Boat

Pelni (⊠ Jl. Angkasa 18, Jakarta, ☎ 021/421–1921) ships from **Surabaya** (☎ 031/21041) pass through **Ujung Pandang** (☎ 0411/331393) every seven days and moor at Pelabuhan Hatta Harbor, a short becak ride from the center of town. Because Ujung Pandang is the gateway to eastern Indonesia, many other shipping companies take passengers from here aboard freighters to Maluku and other eastern islands and to Kalimantan, on Borneo. **Manado**'s port is Bitung, 30 km (19 mi) from town, where **Pelni** (✉ Jl. Sam Ratulangi 7, Manado, ☎ 0423/62844) ships pass through en route to Ambon, Jayapura, Ujung Pandang, and other points along the Sulawesi coast.

Getting Around

Because the country between Ujung Pandang and Rantepao is breathtaking both from alongside and above, the ideal way to visit Tanatoraja is to make the outbound journey by road and return by air (that is, of course, if there's air service).

BY BECAK

For short journeys bicycle rickshaws are popular. Bargain hard—a trip in a town should cost about Rp 1,000, even if the driver begins by asking Rp 5,000.

BY BEMO

In Ujung Pandang, bemo minivans run along Jalan Jendral Sudirman/Ratulangi; Jalan Hasanuddin/Cenderawasih; and Jalan Bulusaraung/Mesjid Raya to Leang Leang (sometimes detouring to the airport). Public minibuses to towns outside Ujung Pandang leave from Jalan Sarappo whenever they're full.

BY BUS

The best bus service north from Ujung Pandang to Tanatoraja and points in between is **Liman Express** (☎ 0411/315851). Buses run from Manado to Gorontalo and all the way south to the Ujung Pandang; however, as the "highways" are often unpaved, in a state of disrepair, or washed out altogether, for road trips in the Minihasa province it's far more convenient to hire a car and driver from one of the many travel agencies; for longer distances it's far more convenient to fly.

The bus to Tanatoraja from Ujung Pandang takes nine to 12 hours, depending on weather and road conditions, plus an hour lunch break. There are morning and evening departures in both directions. At Rp 15,000, it's an economical way to go. Since the countryside is not to be missed, make sure to make at least one trip during daylight.

BY CAR

You can hire a car and a driver through most hotels and travel agencies in Ujung Pandang, Rantepao, Makale, and Manado. For in-town and short regional excursions from Ujung Pandang, taxis are the most widely used form of transport; ask at your hotel for recommendations and count on Rp 324,000–Rp 540,000 per day. In Tanatoraja, travelers often hire minibuses to shuttle them between sights, with prices around Rp 54,000 and hour or Rp 432,000 a day. Taxis may be hired for around Rp 32,500 an hour in Manado.

BY TAXI

You can hail cabs on the street in Ujung Pandang or pick one up outside a hotel. Taxis are metered; the fare is roughly Rp 1,000 per km (½ mi). Two large companies are: **Amal Taxi** (☎ 0411/313131) and **Omega** (☎ 0411/22679). Taxis are available in Tanatoraja and Manado, but the more popular public transport modes are bemos and *mikrolets* (a Manado-style bemo), respectively. In Manado, you can also try **Dian Taksi** (☎ 0421/862421).

Contacts and Resources

EMERGENCIES

Ambulance: ☎ 118. **Hospitals:** Elm Hospital (✉ Jl. A Yani, Rantepao); Pancaran Kasih (✉ Jl. Sam Ratulangi, Manado); **Rumah Sakit Umum**

(✉ Jl. Yos. Sudarso, Manado); **Rumah Sakit Umum** (✉ Jl. Gunung Bawakaraeng, next to Hasanuddin University, Ujung Pandang); **Stella Maris Hospital** (✉ Jl. Panghibur, Ujung Pandang).

Pharmacy: Kimia Firma (✉ Jl. A Yani, Ujung Pandang). **Police:** ☎ 110 or 7777. **Scuba Diving Emergencies:** The only public decompression chamber is operated by **Baruna Watersports** (✉ Jl. Bypass Ngurah Rai 300B, Kuta, ☎ 0361/753820) on Bali.

ENGLISH-LANGUAGE BOOKSTORES

All the major hotels in Ujung Pandang and Manado have shops or kiosks with English-language newspapers, magazines, and the occasional guidebook or novel.

TOUR OPERATORS

In Ujung Pandang, **Toraja Highland Tours and Travel** (✉ Jl. Rambutan 3, ☎ 0411/852495) offers a full range of tours throughout the southern province and specializes in trips to Toraja. **Intravi** (✉ Jl. Urip Sumoharjo 225, ☎ 0411/319747) is also a reputable agency. Besides arranging tours, **Pacto Ltd. Tours and Travel** (✉ Jl. Jendral Sudirman 56, ☎ 0411/873208) represents American Express. **Ramayana Tours** (✉ Jl. Bulukunyi 9A, ☎ 0411/871791) is particularly good for tours into Tanatoraja because many of its guides come from there. It also offers excursions to the southeast peninsula, famous for boatbuilding and a reclusive Muslim village, and arranges customized trips such as Jeep treks across the island or canoe visits to the weavers of Galumpang in central Sulawesi. In Manado, try **Helista Tour and Travel** (✉ Jl. Bethesda 75, ☎ 0423/628880), which also offers dive tours, or **Manado Land and Sea** (✉ Jl. Diponegoro 5, ☎ 0431/64476).

TRAVEL AGENCIES

Ceria Nugraha (✉ Jl. Usmar Jafar 9, 90111, ☎ 0411/311846) and **Limbunan** (✉ Jl. Gunung Bawakaraeng 40–42 [Box 97], 90111, ☎ 0411/323333) are reliable agencies in Ujung Pandang. In Tanatoraja, try **Ramayana Satrya** (✉ Jl. Pong Tiku, Rantepeo, ☎ 0423/21615). In Manado, **Natrabu** (☎ 0431/853716), **Pandu Express** (✉ Jl. Sam Ratulangi 91, ☎ 0431/851188)), and **Pola Pelita Express** (✉ Jl. Sam Ratulangi 113, ☎ 0431/852231) offer a range of travel services.

VISITOR INFORMATION

In Ujung Pandang, the **South Sulawesi Tourist Office** (✉ Jl. Sultan Alauddin 105 B, ☎ 0411/83897) is open Monday–Thursday and Saturday 7–2, Friday 7–11. The **North Sulawesi Provincial Tourism Office** (✉ Jl. 17 Augustus, ☎ 0431/64911) can help with maps and dive details; it's open Monday–Thursday 7–2, Friday 7–11, and Saturday 7–12:30. The **Manado Tourist Office** (✉ Jl. 17 Augustus, ☎ 0431/64299) has general information on the area and is open Monday–Thursday 7–2, Friday 7–11, and Saturday 7–12:30. If you're headed to one of the region's national parks, contact the **National Parks Office** (PHPA; ✉ Jl. Babe Palar 67, ☎ 0431/62688). It's open Monday–Thursday 9–4, Friday 9–11, and Saturday 9–12:30. The **Tourist Information and Booking Center** (✉ Bunaken Souvenir Shop, Jl. Sam Ratulangi 178, Manado) also has maps and regional information available. It's hours are Monday–Thursday 9–4, Friday 9–11, and Saturday 9–4.

SUMATRA

Although Sumatra's amenities have improved in recent years, this is still an island for the adventurous and the tolerant—not for those who need exact schedules, fixed prices, and luxury. The world's fifth-largest island (about the size of Japan or Spain), and Indonesia's most northern one, lies off the west coast of the Malaysian peninsula. Its rubber and palm-oil plantations and oil and gas fields make it a gold mine for the country. Medan, the capital of North Sumatra province, is an important commercial center. The capital of West Sumatra province, Padang, is a large port. But not all of Sumatra's resources have been exploited, not all of its lands developed: it has rain forests that teem with wildlife as well as beautiful lakes, mountains, and beaches.

Before Jakarta exploded into the violence that led to the end of President Suharto's 32-year-rule, riots in Medan (in early May) caused large business areas of the city to close. Medan is a commercial center and has one of Indonesia's largest ethnic-Chinese populations (the Chinese, who many believe receive unfair government protection and assistance, are often the target of disenfranchised Indonesian workers). The city is also home to several universities whose student bodies often agitate for more political freedom. And then there is Aceh—the province on the northern tip of Sumatra—whose zealous Muslim inhabitants have always wanted more independance from Jakarta. (The Dutch never fully controlled this region, and the Indonesian government only did so with strong-arm tactics.) All the turmoil aside, the Sumatrans are an intriguing and diverse people—from the former headhunter Bataks in the north to the matrilineal Miningkabau tribes in the west. Many islanders are also freewheeling entrepreneurs who understand the value of tourism; some speak a little English, and most are friendly and quick to offer help and information.

To do Sumatra right, you'll need at least a week. It's best to enter at Medan in the north and travel overland to Padang on the west coast (or vice versa). Taxis and a comprehensive bus system link small towns, and domestic airlines connect provincial capitals. (Note that, at press time, the airports in Medan and Padang had not been greatly affected by the economic crisis, though air service elsewhere was less comprehensive than in better financial times.)

North Sumatra

Outside of Medan, the provincial capital and a bustling commercial center, much of North Sumatra remains wilderness. Among its highlights are the 100-km-long (62-mi-long) Danau Toba and its island, Samosir, which are in the caldera of a massive volcano; the rain forests of Gunung Leuser National Park; and the Bukit Lawang Orangutan Rehabilitation Center. Although many sights are along the Trans-Sumatran Highway (also called the Asian Highway), which runs the length of Sumatra from north to south, others take a lot more effort to reach. Luckily North Sumatra's people are friendly and helpful, making much of the island a joy to see—regardless of problems with the infrastructure.

Medan

❶ *1,350 km (840 mi) northwest of Jakarta, 625 km (390 mi) northwest of Singapore, 575 km (360 mi) northeast of Padang.*

Medan, the capital of North Sumatra and the fourth-largest city in Indonesia, developed into a bustling plantation town early this century and is now only second (after Jakarta) in terms of business importance. The general population of more than 2 million people jostles about in a city designed for 500,000. Cars, taxis, bemos, motor scooters, bicycles, and pedestrians compete for positions on streets that are in various states of repair.

Banda Aceh

Andaman
Sea

ACEH

Takengon

Langsa

Blangkejeren

Pulau
Simeulue

Medan ①

Tebingtinggi

Brastagi ②
Lingga ■

Pematangsiantar

Ambarita
Tuk Tuk
Tomok

③ **Prapat**
■ **Binanga**

Tanjungbalai

**Danau Toba and
Pulau Samosir** ④

Sibolga

Rantauprapat

Langgapayung

Pulau
Rupat

Pulau
Nias

Padangsidempuan

NORTH
SUMATRA

MALAYSIA

Kuala Lumpur

Strait of Melaka (Malacca)

RIAU

Mentawai Strait

Bonjol ⑤
**Danau
Maninjau** ⑥ **Bukittinggi**
⑦ ⑧ **Batusangkar**

Padangpanjang

Pulau
Siberut

⑨ **Padang**

WEST
SUMATRA

Rengat

Pulau
Pagai

Sungaipenuh

Muarabungo

JAMBI

Bangko

Jambi

INDIAN
OCEAN

SOUTH
SUMATRA

Bengkulu

Palembang

N

0 _____ 100 miles
0 _____ 150 km

Kotabumi

The two major in-town sights are the large, multidome **Mesjid Raya Mosque** (✉ near the intersection of Jl. Mesjid Raya and Jl. Sisinga Mangaraja in the southeast of town) built in 1906 and one of Indonesia's largest, and the Sultan's Palace, the **Istana Sultan Deli** (✉ Jl. Katamso just west of the mosque) built in 1880. Special permission from the tourist office (☞ Visitor Information *in* North Sumatra Essentials, *below*) is required to visit the inside of the palace.

The **Orangutan Rehabilitation Station** in Gunung Leuser National Park is just a 2½-hour drive outside of town. You can hire a taxi and a guide for about Rp 810,000. It's best to leave Medan by about 11 AM to reach the park by 2 PM. You will then have a 30-minute walk in tropical heat up to the ranger's hut. A further 15-minute hike up the mountain takes you to the feeding platform where rangers, at 3:30 PM, spend 35 minutes feeding and inspecting the orangutans, preparing them for life in the wild. You need to be relatively fit to make the 45-minute hike, which involves rugged terrain and crossing a creek by raft, but the experience is well worth the effort.

Dining and Lodging

Western fast food has arrived in Medan. There's a McDonald's near the Mesjid Raya Mosque, a Pizza Hut in Deli Plaza, and, it seems, Kentucky Fried Chicken is everywhere else. For more upscale Western fare, try the restaurants in the larger hotels. On the Asian side, many eateries—including the food stalls in the park across from the mosque—serve good Padang cuisine. Padang food originated, of course, in Padang on Sumatra's west coast, but it is known throughout the archipelago. Dishes are similar to curries, and most are quite spicy.

$$–$$$ ✗ **Miramar.** Near several antiques shops in central Medan, this restaurant serves Chinese and Padang dishes (seafood is a specialty) in an air-conditioned dining room with big padded chairs around large tables. The menu has pictures so you get a good idea of what you're ordering, and the service is good. ✉ *Jl. Pemua 11,* ☏ *061/325491. AE, MC, V.*

$$ ✗ **RM Famili.** A short walk down Jalan Sisingamangaraja from the Mesjid Raya Mosque, this is a great place to sample Padang food. There are many selections in a glass display case as you walk into the large, open-air dining room. Smiling waiters will bring small plates and bowls of food to your table and serve you rice. You eat what you want and pay accordingly. It's best to get a seat close to the waterfall fountain to drown out the traffic noise outside. ✉ *Jl. Sisingamangaraja 33,* ☏ *061/ 718787. No credit cards.*

$–$$ ✗ **Tip Top.** Opened in 1935, Tip Top is a Medan institution. It offers a selection of Indonesian, Chinese and Padang food (all of it good) and some Western food (not as good). The front dining room opens onto a very busy street, but there are quieter, air-conditioned dining rooms in the back. The cake and coffee are tops. ✉ *Jl. Jendral A. Jani 92,* ☏ *061/24442. No credit cards.*

$$$ 🏨 **Hotel Danau Toba.** The city's first major hotel (circa 1972) is more like an urban resort with its lagoonlike pool (complete with landscaped islands), its many restaurants, and its karaoke bar and disco. Despite their age, public areas and guest rooms are well maintained. ✉ *Jl. Imam Bonjol 17, 20235,* ☏ *061/557000,* 🏠 *061/530053. 268 rooms, 4 suites. 4 restaurants, 4 bars, pool, massage, health club, dance club, meeting rooms. AE, DC, MC, V.*

$$$ 🏨 **Novotel Soechi.** This central Medan establishment has the city's only cybercafé (with eight terminals), making it a good choice for those who can't bear to be disconnected from the rest of the world. Rooms are of a good size and some have doors that connect them to other rooms—

perfect for families or other groups traveling together. There's a 24-hour restaurant on site, and you have a good selection of both dining and shopping options in the adjoining Hong Kong Plaza. ⊠ *Jl. Cirebon 76-A, 20235,* ☎ *061/561234,* FAX *061/57222. 232 rooms, 15 suites. Restaurant, 4 bars, café, pool, tennis court, health club, business services, meeting rooms. AE, DC, MC, V.*

$$$ ⊞ **Tiara Medan Hotel.** Although Medan's many new hotels have given it a run for the money, the clean, smart Tiara has remained Medan's best. Guest rooms are spacious and well maintained, and the staff is friendly and quick to help. The lobby restaurant offers standard Chinese, European, and Indonesian fare for lunch, and the more formal Amberita Restaurant serves dinner. ⊠ *Jl. Cut Mutia, 20152,* ☎ *061/516000,* FAX *061/51076. 316 rooms, 16 suites. 2 restaurants, bar, pool, 2 tennis courts, health club, squash, business services, meeting rooms, travel services. AE, DC, V.*

$$ ⊞ **Natour Dharma Deli Medan.** Although this hotel, part of Indonesia's Natour chain, is right in central Medan, it has a lovely pool with bar service and shaded areas—the perfect escape from urban buzz and equatorial sun. Though rooms are on the boxy side, each is comfortably furnished with two queen-size beds, two chairs, a coffee table, a desk, and satellite TV. The coffee shop serves Indonesian, Chinese, and Western food. ⊠ *Jl. Balai Kota 67, 20111,* ☎ *061/327011,* FAX *061/327153. 180 rooms. Coffee shop, pool, massage, exercise room. AE, DC, MC, V.*

$ ⊞ **Hotel Sri Deli.** This wooden, brightly painted, four-story hotel is near the mosque. Rooms are clean and each has its own bath (with hot water)—a real plus in a budget hotel; some rooms have air-conditioning as well. A few members of the friendly staff speak a little English, and many tour guides hang out downstairs. ⊠ *Jl. S. M. Raja 30, 20214,* ☎ *061/713571. 53 rooms. Café. No credit cards.*

Shopping

For a variety of contemporary goods, try **Deli Plaza** (⊠ Jl. Guru Patimus) in the north of town. In central Medan, the many shops in the **Hong Kong Plaza** (⊠ Jl. Cirebon) are your best bets.

Jalan Jendral A. Yani has several good curio and antiques shops. Among them they offer goods from all corners of Indonesia. Note that only good, old-fashioned, hard currency is accepted, and haggling is de rigueur: **Toko Bali** (⊠ Jl. Jendral A. Yani 68, ☎ 061/512556), **Dagang Sepalat** (⊠ Jl. Jendral A. Yani 61, ☎ no phone), **Rufino** (⊠ Jl. Jendral A. Yani 56, ☎ 061/567165), and **Selatan** (⊠ Jl. Jendral A. Yani 44, ☎ 061/518149). If the heat and the bargaining tire you, take a break at the nearby Tip Top or Miramar restaurants (☞ Dining and Lodging, *above*).

Brastagi

② *68 km (41 mi) southwest of Medan.*

Brastagi, two hours from sweltering Medan on one of two routes to Danau Toba, is a refreshing hill station 4,600 ft above sea level and set between two volcanoes. It retains an Old World air from the days when Dutch planters came here to escape the heat.

Several groups of the Karo Bataks have their villages in the highlands, and one worth a visit is **Lingga,** 15 km (9 mi) southwest of Brastagi and just a little off the road to Danau Toba. Here you can see 250- to 300-year-old multifamily tribal houses that are still used today. Karo Bataks, as well as the Toba Bataks, are descendants from proto-Malay tribes who originally inhabited the border areas of what is now Myanmar (Burma) and Thailand. They chose this mountainous region for its isolation, and their patrilineal society remains virtually intact—despite the increasing numbers of sightseers.

Dining and Lodging

$$–$$$ ✕🏨 **Bukit Kubu Hotel.** This wonderful, old, colonial-style hotel is the
★ area's best. Ask for a double suite with a view of the mountains (the price is only Rp 54,000 more than that for a standard room). Lunch is served on a breezy terrace; dinner, inside, is in the formal dining room. Starched linen and billowing lace curtains are reminiscent of the 1930s, when Dutch planters came here to relax. Today, the hotel is popular with wealthy folk from Medan who come for weekends in the cool mountain air. ⊠ *Jl. Sempurna 2, 22151; booking office: Jl. Jendral Sudirman 36, Medan 20100);* ☎ *0628/20832 or 061/519636 in Medan. 40 rooms. Restaurant, laundry service. AE, V.*

Prapat

❸ *120 km southeast of Brastagi, 176 km (110 mi) south of Medan.*

From Brastagi it's an easy two-hour bus or taxi ride south to Prapat, the resort town near Danau Toba where ferries leave for Pulau Samosir. The last 30 minutes of the journey are the most dramatic. The road winds through tropical vegetation to a pass, where the lake suddenly appears below. (Note that if you're coming directly from Medan—a four-hour drive—you can take the Trans-Sumatran Highway. The views aren't quite as fantastic and you'll miss charming Brastagi, but the route is fast.) If you arrive in Prapat late and miss the last boat (about 4:30 PM) there are a few good places to eat and to rest your travel-weary bones.

Dining and Lodging

$$–$$$ ✕ **Singgalang.** The first version of this family restaurant opened 40 years ago. This new edition, an air-conditioned dining room just off the highway, carries on the tradition of offering good Chinese and international fare. (There are also a couple of fan-cooled guest rooms if you're stuck for a place to stay.) ⊠ *Trans-Sumatran Hwy. 52,* ☎ *0664/ 41260. AE, DC, MC, V.*

$$ ✕ **Trogadero.** For good Indonesian cuisine—satays, nasi goreng, and the like—try this one-room restaurant near the water. You'll find it easy to relax in the easygoing atmosphere. ⊠ *Jl. Haranggaol 110,* ☎ *0664/ 41148. No credit cards.*

$$$–$$$$ 🏨 **Niagara.** One of Prapat's best hotels—as many a tour group has discovered—is on a hill behind town with spectacular views of the lake and a big pool. Guest rooms are spacious and comfortable, and the huge dining room has an international menu. There's a free shuttle bus into town. ⊠ *Jl. Pembangunan 1, 21174,* ☎ *0664/41028,* FAX *0664/ 41233. 178 rooms, 4 suites. Dining room, bar, pool, 4 tennis courts, bicycles, dance club. DC, MC, V.*

$$ 🏨 **Natour Hotel Prapat.** The best quarters here are in the bungalows on landscaped slopes that face the lake. Rooms, though worn, are comfortably large and well furnished and have patios. Like all Natour hotels, this one is not spectacular but it is a bargain. ⊠ *Jl. Marihat 1, 21174,* ☎ *0664/41012,* FAX *0664/41019. 85 rooms. Dining room, bar, beach. AE, V.*

$$ 🏨 **Risis Hotel.** This clean, whitewashed hotel on the street that leads to the market square is a good bet if you're on a tight budget. Some rooms have private baths; all have bare walls and floors and minimal furniture. Although there's no on-site restaurant, Trogadero (☞ *above*) and all its Indonesian fare is nearby. ⊠ *Jl. Haranggaol 39, 21174,* ☎ *0664/41392. 20 rooms. No credit cards.*

Danau Toba and Pulau Samosir

★ ❹ *Samosir Island is 45 minutes by boat from Prapat.*

Danau Toba, the largest lake in Southeast Asia and one of the highest in the world, sits 2,950 ft above sea level, surrounded by steep slopes that plunge headlong into the water to depths of 1,475 ft. Prapat may be the major resort town *on* the lake, but most visitors prefer to stay *in* the lake—on Samosir, a hilly 777-square-km (300-square-mi) island that's home to the Toba Bataks. The island remains agriculturally based. Even the people who run guest houses in touristed Tuk Tuk (☞ *below*) continue to plant their rice fields.

In **Tomok,** you'll find the tombs of King Sidabutar, who ruled in the 1800s; his son; his grandson; and several warriors of rank. Nearby are several Batak houses with curving roofs and intricately carved beams and panels. To reach these attractions, walk ½ km (¼ mi) up from the ferry dock past stalls selling souvenirs, artifacts, and batik cloth. Keep in mind that the actual purchase price is 30%–40% of the initial asking price.

Tuk Tuk, on a peninsula that juts into the lake, has been greatly developed as a tourist hub during the last 10 years (indeed, some areas are virtual guest-house ghettos, with one lodging after another). Still, quiet retreats remain and a stay in one can be pleasant. There are few vehicles; many visitors get around by bicycle, just as the easygoing locals do. (Note that the locals are fond of chess and are usually eager to play. If you're good you might give them a game; if you're *very* good you might even win.) To reach Tuk Tuk, it's best to take the passenger ferry (a 45-minute ride), which stops at several hotels on the peninsula. **Ambarita** is a village where, in the past, miscreants had their heads lopped off. You can still see the courtyard where the king held council. Ancient, weathered stone chairs and tables form a ring in front of the chief's traditional house. The village is a nice two-hour bicycle outing from Tuk Tuk.

At the northern tip of Samosir is **Simanindo,** site of a fine old traditional house, once the home of a Batak king. The village has been declared an open-air museum, and the one house not to miss is the Long House (Rumak Bolon), with its fine carvings and the sculpted depiction of the god Gajah Dompak. His job was to frighten off evil spirits, and by the look of him, he must have been good at it.

In nice weather, consider making the pleasant ride (by motorcycle) to the small **Danau Sidihoni** toward the center of Pulau Samosir island. On the way, you can contemplate the fact that you'll soon be visiting what has to be the world's only lake on an island in a lake on an island.

Passenger boats cost Rp 1,500 one-way to Tuk Tuk, slightly more for Ambarita and Simanindo. They leave from Prapat's lakeshore market. A little ways down the coast there's a car ferry to Tomok. The passenger boats are more frequent and enjoyable. For a more extensive look at the island you can charter a powerboat for a three-hour trip to Tomok, Tuk Tuk, Ambarita, and Simanindo, which will cost about Rp 40,000. It could be your only opportunity to get seasick at 3,000 ft. For travel around Samosir, minibus taxis make irregular trips, and there are motorbikes for rent (about Rp 20,000 a day).

Dining and Lodging

Accommodations here are pleasant, albeit a bit rustic. All the hotels have restaurants, but you should trying eating at a few places because the best lodging doesn't necessarily have the best food.

$–$$ ✕ **Bagus Bay.** For a good selection of Indonesian food, very edible pizza and sandwiches, and terrific fruit shakes, check out this big open-air eatery. You'll also find an extensive used bookshop with some English-language titles. Once a week (the days vary) there's an evening performance of traditional dance and music put on by local Bataks. ✉ *Jl. Slamet Riyadi, Tuk Tuk,* ☎ FAX *0625/41481. No credit cards.*

$–$$ ✕⊞ **Toba Vegetarian Restaurant.** Toba has seven guest rooms, four of them in a Batak house that was moved here and refurbished. It has hot water and a balcony facing the lake. Room 7, on the second floor, is the best room. The food here is good, especially the freshly baked cakes and the dark German bread. ✉ *Jl. Slamet Riyadi 111, Tuk Tuk 22395,* ☎ *0271/37603. 7 rooms. Restaurant. No credit cards.*

$$$ ⊞ **Toledo.** This is one of the bigger resorts, but the owners have done a reasonable job fitting it into the environment. Though the hotel caters to tour groups, you can stay here without feeling overwhelmed. Ask for a room with a patio facing the lake; make your second choice a room next to the pool. Activities here include boat rides on the lake and outings to island sights. ✉ *On both sides of the road along the northeast side of the Tuk Tuk peninsula, Tuk Tuk 22395,* ☎ *0271/46356,* FAX *0271/44788. 140 rooms. Restaurant, bar, pool, massage, beach, boating, shops, meeting rooms, travel services. AE, DC, MC, V.*

$$ ⊞ **Carolina Cottage.** Tuk Tuk's first accommodation remains its best.
★ Rooms—in Batak houses at the edge of the lake—all have spectacular views and baths; most also have hot running water. The service is friendly and helpful. For convenience and a great view, request a room down by the beach and the swimming area. Continental breakfasts, snacks, and dinners are served. ✉ *On a small lane off Jl. Slamet Riyadi, Tuk Tuk 22395,* ☎ *0625/41520,* FAX *0625/41521. 50 rooms. Restaurant, bar, beach. No credit cards.*

En Route On the Trans-Sumatran Highway from Prapat to Bukittinggi is Binanga (sometimes known as Lumban Binanga) and 15 km (9 mi) southwest of Prapat are five traditional houses. Park at the side of the highway (you'll see a sign), and walk down the hill past some new houses and terraced paddy fields to these 100- to 200-year-old Batak houses. Few tourists come here, so Binanga has much less bustle than the villages on Samosir.

North Sumatra Essentials

Arriving and Departing

BY AIRPLANE

Air service in Indonesia went into a tailspin with the financial crisis in 1997. Several airlines folded, others cut routes, and all adjusted their schedules. Flights are sure to continue to Medan, but you should double-check schedules. **Garuda Indonesian Airways** (☎ 061/516066) and **Silk Air** (☎ 061/537744) have daily hour-long flights from Singapore to Medan's **Polonia Airport** (☎ 061/538444) right on the south edge of town. **Malaysia Airlines** (☎ 061/519333) flies from Penang, Malaysia. There are also flights to Jakarta on Java and Padang in West Sumatra. **Merpati** (☎ 061/514102) also serves Medan. The only way into Medan from the airport is by taxi. A fixed rate of Rp 4,800 applies.

BY BOAT

The least expensive and more adventurous way to reach Medan is on one of the daily five-hour "fast boats" from Penang, Malaysia. At 96 Malaysian ringgit it's a bargain, but the Melaka Straights often get rough. Contact **Kuala Perlis-Langkawi Ferry Service** (☎ 04/262–5630) in Penang or **Perdana Express** (☎ 061/545803) in Medan.

Getting Around

BY AIR

If you only have enough time for a few of Sumatra's highlights, the best strategy is to use Medan as a sightseeing hub and then fly to Padang to see its area sights—or vice versa. For details on airports and carriers in Medan, *see* By Airplane *in* Arriving and Departing, *above*.

BY BUS

Buses range from the air-conditioned express variety to crowded local vehicles. Long-distance bus travel—such as the 14- to 16-hour journey from Medan's Amplas bus station to Padang—can be an adventure. (Motion sickness is a concern, as is all the smoke from the clove Kretek cigarettes that are popular with so many passengers.) Short day trips by bus are quite tolerable, however. Bus stations are never far from town centers, and you'll generally find a bus leaving for nearby destinations within 30 minutes of your arrival at the station. A travel agent can arrange the bus trip, too. In Medan, contact **Trophy Tours** (☞ Tour Operator and Travel Agent, *below*).

BY CAR

Although many sights are along the Trans-Sumatran Highway—a well-sealed two-lane (for the most part) highway—renting a car and driving yourself is a risky business on Sumatra. It's best to hire a car and a driver—leaving the work to someone who knows the terrain and the language. A travel agent (☞ Tour Operator and Travel Agent, *below*) and the staff at major hotels can make arrangements for you.

BY TAXI

In Medan, you'll find car and motorcycle taxis at hotels, the bus station, the airport, and the dock. Some taxis have meters; with others, you must negotiate the fare before you get in. The original asking price will usually be about 20% to 40% higher—if you look gullible, it will be higher still—than what you should pay. For a shared taxi, try **Indah Taxi** (✉ Brig-jen Katamso 60, ☎ 061/510036).

Contacts and Resources

EMERGENCIES

Ambulance: ☎ 118. **Fire:** ☎ 113. **Hospital:** Dr. M. Jamil (✉ Jl. Perintis Kemerdekaan, ☎ 061/22355 for English speakers). **Police:** ☎ 110.

ENGLISH-LANGUAGE BOOKSTORES

Try the bookshop in the **Tiara Medan Hotel** (✉ Jl. Cut Mutia, Medan, ☎ 061/574000). The **Toko Buku Bookshop** (✉ Jl. Ahmad Yani 48, Medan, ☎ no phone) is another good bet.

TOUR OPERATOR AND TRAVEL AGENT

Trophy Tours (✉ Jl. Brig-jen Katamso 33, Medan, ☎ 061/555666) can help you with tours and trips on Sumatra as well as with other travel arrangement.

VISITOR INFORMATION

The **tourist office** at Polonia Airport—between the domestic and international terminals—has lists of accommodations in the region. The staff will happily make reservations and arrange ground transportation.

Some information can be obtained from **North Sumatra Regional Office of Tourism** (✉ Jl. Alfalah 22, Kampung Baru, Medan, ☎ 061/762220). More helpful is the **Provincial Tourist Service** (✉ Jl. Jendral A. Yani 107, Medan 20151, ☎ 061/511101).

West Sumatra

Much of mountainous West Sumatra remains covered in virgin jungle with volcanoes, rivers, elephants, endangered tigers, and rhinos—a nature-lover's delight. It has three regions: the volcanic highlands, a coastal plain, and islands covered in jungle. The long plain is heavily inhabited, the highlands and islands less so. Nearly 90% of the population are members of the matrilineal Minangkabau tribe (here women inherit the family property). Extended families live in *rumah gadang* (big houses) with roofs that have a series of curving spikes—similar to buffalo horns—that point skyward.

Bonjol

5 *600 km (372 mi) south of Medan, 220 km (136 mi) north of Padang.*

There's really not much here—just a funky concrete globe of the world, a park, some coffee stalls, and a souvenir shop—but it *is* the site of the equator and hence merits at least a little respect. You can get a certificate that you visited at the souvenir shop, which might make Bonjol worth a stop if you're driving south from Medan to Padang on the Trans-Sumatran Highway. If you're a geography junkie, you can also make Bonjol a day trip from Bukittinggi. (☞ *below*).

Bukittinggi

6 *120 km (75 mi) southeast of Bonjol, 550 km (341 mi) southwest of Prapat, 94 km (58 mi) north of Padang.*

Nestled in the highlands north of Padang, picturesque Bukittinggi is the area's cultural and tourist hub. At 3,051 ft above sea level on the Agam Plateau it offers cool relief from the heat. The Dutch called it Ft. de Kock; although some foundations and a few rusty cannon are all that remain of the actual fort, their hilly site offers good views.

The **Jam Gadang** clock tower is the landmark of Bukittinggi's center. The nearby town market is a lively place to shop for local items or sample local food at one of the numerous stalls. The **Rumah Gadang Museum,** a refurbished, 19th-century, Minangkabau home that's also near the clock tower, offers free dance performances on Sunday and public holidays.

On the south end of town are the extensive **Japanese Tunnels,** dug with forced labor during World War II as a defense against an attack by the Allies. They're worth the small admission charge, and it's easy enough to tour them by yourself because there are lights along the main tunnel. If you want a more extensive look you can hire a guide who knows the history, and perhaps more importantly carries a flashlight so you can see all the nooks and crannies. Nearby the Japanese Tunnels is **Sianok Canyon,** which winds south of the city. A one-hour walk through the canyon from Bukittinggi brings you to the village of **Kota Gadang,** whose inhabitants are known for their silver work—particularly silver filigree. Even if you're not in the market the walk here makes a nice half-day outing.

Pandai Sikat (12 km/8 mi south of Bukittinggi) is known for its furniture and woodworking factories, but it's also a weaving center, with several hundred looms turning out cloth. The furniture is beautiful to some, a bit overdone for others, and too big for most travelers to transport home. However, there are some smaller wood carvings for sale here, too.

Dining and Lodging

$ ✕ **Lapan Nasi Sederhana.** It doesn't look like much—just a room that's open to the street and food displayed in a glass case—but the Padang dishes are spicy and good. Point to what you want, and it will be brought to your table with a bowl of rice. This place is popular with locals and can be packed. ⊠ *Jl. Minangkabau 61,* ☎ *no phone. No credit cards.*

$ ✕ **Simpang Raya.** Like its Padang cousin, this branch serves a good selection of such Indonesian staples as nasi goreng and satays in a simple dining room. Expect crowds at lunchtime. ⊠ *Jl. Sudiman 8,* ☎ *0751/ 22163. No credit cards.*

$$$ ▦ **Melia Comfort Pusako.** The Melia's location 4 km (2 mi) from the center of town gives it the feel of a resort. Rooms here are spacious and have views of the surrounding mountains. You can bike into town or ask the hotel staff to arrange for transportation—making the location seem less remote. They can also coordinate golf outings at a local course. ⊠ *Jl. Soekarno-Hatta 7, 26129,* ☎ *0752/32111,* ℻ *0752/32667. 184 rooms, 7 suites. 2 restaurants, bar, pool, massage, 2 tennis courts, health club, bicycles, business services. AE, DC, MC, V.*

$$$ ▦ **Novotel.** In a building that looks like a cross between a medieval fort and a Middle Eastern palace, this hotel is a commanding presence above the center of town. It also has many of the amenities you would expect of an international chain establishment, including a pleasant pool and gardens. You can walk or bike around town from here, and the on-site Shaan Holidays office will arrange guided tours of the area or trips to the local golf course. ⊠ *Jl. Laras Datuk Bandaro, 26113,* ☎ *0752/35000,* ℻ *0752/23800. 93 rooms, 6 junior suites, 1 suite. Restaurant, bar, pool, bicycles, travel services. AE, DC, MC, V.*

$–$$ ▦ **Benteng Hotel.** This budget hotel—a simple concrete structure—offers rich views from its location right next to what remains of Ft. de Kock on the highest hill in town. The basic rooms have TVs, well-kept old furniture, hot water in private baths, and air-conditioning—though you hardly need it with the cool highland breezes. The staff is friendly. ⊠ *Jl. Benteng 1, 26113,* ☎ *0752/21115,* ℻ *0752/22596. 15 rooms. Restaurant, bar. MC, V.*

Danau Maninjau

➐ *40 km (25 mi) west of Bukittinggi.*

Smaller than Danau Toba and, perhaps, not as spectacular, this lake is still quite beautiful. The steep crater walls are mostly forested, though there are terraced rice fields in places. The drive here from Bukittinggi is something of a thrill; the final descent from the rim of the crater to the lake involves 44 hairpin turns. You can calm your nerves and soothe your soul with a swim in the lake's deep blue waters.

Batusangkar

➑ *50 km (31 mi) southwest of Bukittinggi.*

According to legend, Batusangkar is the cradle of Minangkabau culture, and it has many unique traditional houses as well as a countryside full of terraced rice fields. It's best to visit with a driver and guide from Bukittinggi or Padang. Be sure to stop in Balimbang village, which has many traditional Minangkabau houses, including one reputed to be 350 years old.

Padang

➒ *575 km (360 mi) southwest of Medan, 900 km (560 mi) northwest of Jakarta, and 490 km (304 mi) southwest of Singapore.*

The capital of West Sumatra is also the largest port in the west of the island. Sitting on a coastal plain, it's hot and has the laid-back atmosphere and attitude that often accompanies such a climate. Many of the city's structures have Minangkabu roofs with their hornlike spikes. The clip-clop of horse-drawn carts is a more common sound than the ear-splitting whine of motorcycle taxis so often heard in Medan. The city's old quarter, next to the river, is worth a stroll. The century-old shops look a bit worn (somehow, this adds to their appeal), and the boats in the river are colorfully painted. But the highlight here is the food. Don't miss the chance to sample spicy Padang food *in Padang*.

In a traditional Minangkabu house on the corner of Jalan Diponegoro and Jalan H. O. S. Cokroaminoto, the **Adiyawarman Museum** has a collection of regional antiques. The museum is open daily 9 to 5.

Although Padang is on the coast, most of its beaches aren't that great. The exception is **Bungus Bay**, 20 km (12 mi) south of town. The sand is soft and white, and the surf is calm. Further, this crescent-shape bay is surrounded by rice fields and hills. Several islands just off the coast from Padang also have beautiful beaches.

Dining and Lodging

$$–$$$ ✕ **Sari.** One of Padang's fancier restaurants is near a quaint little mosque with loudspeakers that blast the call to prayer early in the evening. Seated in the air-conditioned dining room or on the patio (which is nicer if it's not too hot) you can order local and imported steaks or Indonesian and Padang dishes. ⊠ *Jl. Thamrin 71B,* ☎ *0751/31838. MC, V.*

$$ ✕ **Simpang Enam.** This restaurant tops the competition that surrounds ★ it. Although the menu has a selection of Chinese dishes, anything made with the fish, fresh from the waters nearby, will be delicious (the pepper crab is a good choice). You order in the simple air-conditioned dining room, and then watch the chefs cook your meal through a window. ⊠ *Jl. H. O. S. Cokroaminoto 44,* ☎ *0751/25044. AE, V.*

$–$$ ✕ **Simpang Raya.** In an old house off a busy road Simpang Raya offers a good selection of Indonesian staples, including a noteworthy chicken satay. There are tables in an air-conditioned room, in a fan-cooled room, and on a patio. ⊠ *Jl. Aziz Chan 24,* ☎ *0751/24894. No credit cards.*

$$$ 🏨 **Bumi Minang.** Opened in 1995 as a Sedona chain hotel, this impressive seven-story property was bought by local owners in 1997—although people still often refer to it as the Sedona. It's centrally located and offers all the amenities you'd expect from a hotel with international roots. A band plays local music in the lobby, the rooms are comfortable, and the staff is professional. ⊠ *Jl. Bundo Kandung (Box 135), 25118,* ☎ *0751/37555,* FAX *0751/37567. 138 rooms, 26 suites. 5 restaurants, pool, 2 tennis courts, business services. AE, DC, MC, V.*

$$$ 🏨 **Sol Inn Pusako, Sikuai Island Resort.** A 20-minute boat ride from Padang, this resort has 99-acre Sikuai Island all to itself. Each of its 54 timber cottages has a balcony view of white sandy beach and gentle surf. Though the decor is nothing fancy, rooms are spacious and comfortable with air-conditioning, hot water, and TVs. The restaurant serves Indonesian, Japanese, Chinese, and Western cuisine. You can work off all that food by participating in one of the resort's many water sports activities. ⊠ *Jl. Muara 38, Padang 25118,* ☎ *0751/35311 or 800/336–3542 in the U.S.,* FAX *0751/22895. 54 cottages. Restaurant, 3 bars, 2 pools, jogging, beach, dive shop, snorkeling, boating, jet skiing, fishing. AE, DC, MC, V.*

$$-$$$ ⊡ **Batang Arau Hotel.** In Padang's old quarter and next to the river,
★   this former bank—yes, bank (circa 1808)—was converted into a hotel
       in 1995. It's run by a German, Norma Dulfer, and a stay here is a mem-
       orable experience. Though each room is unique, all are outfitted with
       solid wooden furniture and iron beds (with mattresses, of course) and
       decorated in local Minangkabau style. Two rooms have balconies.
       Breakfast is included in the rate. ⊠ *Jl. Batang Arau 33, 25118,* ☎ *0751/
       27400,* 𝖥𝖠𝖷 *0751/31404. 6 rooms. Bar, billiards. AE, V.*

$$ ⊡ **Paradiso Village, Cudadak Island.** For a very basic island escape—
       one where your days are filled only with sunbathing and reading—try
       Paradiso Village, a 90-minute boat ride or a 90-minute drive and a 10-
       minute boat ride from Padang. Built by an Italian scuba diver who fell
       in love with the area in the early 1990s, the resort offers two-story bun-
       galows with mosquito nets and fans, although sea breezes usually keep
       things cool enough. The reasonable room rates include all your meals—
       very reasonable, indeed. ⊠ *Rimbun Sumatra Tours, Jl. Batang Arau
       33, Padang 25118,* ☎ *0751/31403,* 𝖥𝖠𝖷 *0751/31404. 10 bungalows.
       Restaurant, beach. AE, MC, V.*

$-$$ ⊡ **Wisma Mayang Sari.** On a busy Padang street, this small establishment
       in an old Dutch-era house still feels like someone's home—right down
       to its front yard and its living room. Rooms are basic, though each has
       air-conditioning or a fan, a private bath with hot water, and a refrig-
       erator. Breakfast is included in the price of a room. ⊠ *Jl. Jendral Sudi-
       man 19, 25118,* ☎ *0751/22647. 15 rooms. V.*

West Sumatra Essentials

Arriving and Departing

BY AIRPLANE

Though service to Padang will no doubt continue despite the economic crisis, service to other destinations may be cut back or even dis-
continued; always double-check schedules. Padang's **Tabing Airport,**
north of town, is served by **Garuda** (☎ 0751/58487), **Merpati** (☎ 0751/
32010), and **Silk Air** (☎ 0751/38122), a Singapore airline.

BY BOAT

If you're a patient traveler and have a lot of time, arriving and departing by boat travel is another option. Check with **Pelni** (☎ 0751/33624)
about its service. The line travels weekly to many of the nearby islands
and also has service to Jakarta and coastal cities on mainland Sumatra.

BY BUS

If you're a glutton for punishment there are overnight buses on the Trans-
Sumatran Highway from Jakarta to Padang. The Padang bus station
is on Jalan Pemuda near the intersection with Jalan M. Yamin.

Getting Around

BY AIRPLANE

There are regular flights between Padang and Medan. For more information, *see* Arriving and Departing *in* North Sumatra Essentials,
above.

BY BUS

There are 14- to 16-hour bus trips between Padang and Medan—not
the most comfortable way to go. For hops between nearby towns, however, bus travel is fine, though some local buses don't have air-conditioning and can be crowded. You can buy your ticket at the bus
station—usually near the town center—right before you depart or you
can have a travel agent make arrangements for you in advance. In Padang
contact **Lintas Andalas Terminal** (⊠ Jl. Pemuda, ☎ 0751/23216).

BY CAR

Despite the relatively good condition of the Trans-Sumatran Highway, driving a rental car yourself can be dangerous unless you already know the country and you speak the language. It's best to make arrangements to hire a car and a driver through a travel agent (☞ Tour Operators and Travel Agencies, *below*) or the staff of a major hotel.

You can pick up cabs or becaks at hotels, bus stations, airports, and docks. If your cab isn't metered, be sure to negotiate the price before you get into the car; don't hesitate to bargain hard. In both Padang and Bukittinggi, horse-drawn carts are another public transport option. You can also share a cab with four or five strangers and split the cost. For a shared taxi in Padang, contact **Safa Marwa** (✉ Jl. Pemua 33, ☎ 0751/25244). **Patax** (✉ Jl. Pintu Kebun, ☎ 0752/21163) is a good company in Bukittinggi.

Contacts and Resources

EMERGENCIES

Ambulance: ☎ 118. **Fire:** ☎ 113. **Hospitals:** RSUP Dr. M. Djamil (✉ Jl. Perintis Kemerdekaan, Padang, ☎ 0751/26585), or **General Hospital** (✉ Jl. A. Rivai, Bukittinggi, ☎ 0752/21013). **Pharmacy:** Yani (✉ Jl. A Yani 42, Padang, ☎ 751/27948). **Police:** ☎ 110.

ENGLISH-LANGUAGE BOOKSTORES

In Padang try **Gramedia** (✉ Jl. Damar 63, ☎ 0751/37003) a few blocks north of the museum and bus station. It has a few English-language pulp-fiction titles. In Bukittinggi there are several used bookshops with some English-language novels on Jalan Ahmad Yani.

TOUR OPERATORS AND TRAVEL AGENCIES

In Padang, **Pacto** (✉ Jl. Tan Malaka, ☎ 0751/33335) can help you with a variety of travel arrangements. **Rimbun Sumatra Tours** (✉ Jl. Batang Arau 33, ☎ 0751/31403) is, as its name suggests, good for tours.

In Bukittinggi try: **Pt. Maju Indosari** (✉ Jl. Muka Jam Gadang 17, ☎ 0752/21671), or **Shaan Holidays** (✉ Jl. Pemuda 9, ☎ 0752/32530).

VISITOR INFORMATION

In Padang, contact the **Indonesian Tourist Promotion Office** (✉ Jl. Khatib Sulaeman, ☎ 0751/55711). In Bukittinggi, contact the **Bukittinggi Tourism Information Office** (✉ Jl. Syech Bantam 1, ☎ 0752/22403).

INDONESIA A TO Z

Arriving and Departing

By Airplane

AIRPORTS

International flights to Jakarta's **Soekarno Hatta Airport** (☎ 021/550–5307) land at Terminal One, with the exception of Garuda Indonesia Airways flights, which are processed through Terminal Two. Medan's **Polonia Airport** (☎ 021/550–1562) and **Bali's Ngurah Rai International Airport** (☎ 0361/751026) are also major international gateways.

Many travelers use one airline into an Asian capital such as Bangkok, Seoul, Singapore, Taipei, or Tokyo, then transfer to one of the numerous Asian airlines that fly to Indonesia. Others take advantage of international routes that utilize less common entry points such as Davao, the Philippines, to Manado, Sulawesi; Darwin, Australia to Kupang, Timor; and Kuching, Malaysia, to Pontianak, Kalimantan.

CARRIERS

Prior to the economic crisis, **Garuda Indonesian Airways** (☎ 021/2572241 in Jakarta, 0361/227825 in Denpasar, or 061/515277 in Medan), the national carrier, offered a direct, two-stop flight from Los Angeles to Jakarta or Bali; at press time, however, this service was suspended. Check with the airline or your travel agent for an update.

Northwest Airlines (☎ 800/225–2525), the best-known U.S. carrier that flies to Asia—and the first to fly there as well—has numerous routes from its hubs throughout North America to 19 major transit points in Asia, from which you can fly on a regional airline to Bali, Medan, Jakarta, or elsewhere in the archipelago.

Other airlines with service from North America include: **Cathay Pacific** (☎ 021/515–1741 in Jakarta or 0361/286001 in Denpasar), **Continental** (☎ 0361/288511 in Denpasar), **Japan Airlines** (☎ 021/672–3211 in Jakarta or 0361/287576 in Denpasar), **Malaysia Airlines** (☎ 021/522–9682 in Jakarta, 0361/285071 in Denpasar, or 061/519333 in Medan), **Singapore Airlines** (☎ 021/520–6881 in Jakarta, 0361/287940 in Denpasar, or 061/537744 in Medan), and **Thai Airways International** (☎ 021/320607 in Jakarta, 0361/288141 in Denpasar, or 061/510541 in Medan).

From London, **Garuda** (☞ *above*) flies to Jakarta and Bali. **Cathay Pacific** (☞ *above*) also flies to Bali.

Qantas (☎ 021/230–0277 in Jakarta or 0361/288331 in Denpasar) has nonstop flights from Sydney. **Air New Zealand** (☎ 021/391–5501 in Jakarta or 0361/756170 in Denpasar) and **Ansett Australia** (☎ 021/315–4462 in Jakarta or 0361/289636 in Denpasar) offer nonstop service from both Australia and New Zealand.

FLYING TIMES

Transpacific flying times to Bali are approximately 19 hours from Los Angeles, 23 hours from Chicago, 25 hours from New York, and 22 hours from Vancouver. Flying the eastbound route, the flight time from New York is 23 hours to Jakarta and hours 25 to Bali. Allowing for stops, it's 26 hours from Toronto and Montréal to Jakarta and 28 to Bali. From London it's 16 and 18 hours to Jakarta and Bali, respectively. From Sydney and Melbourne, it's 7 and 4 hours to Bali and 9 and 6 hours to Jakarta. From Auckland, it takes 9 hours to reach Bali and 11 hours to Jakarta. (For details on flying times within Indonesia, *see* By Airplane *in* Getting Around, *below.*)

By Boat

High-speed ferries depart from Penang, Malaysia, every day but Sunday to Belawan (the port of Medan), Sumatra, five hours later. Return trips depart around noon from Belawan every day except Monday. Contact **Perdana Express** (☎ 061/545803 in Medan) or **Kuala Perlis-Langkawi Ferry Service** (☎ 04/262–5630 in Penang).

Another popular ferry route is that from Singapore to the Riau Archipelago's Batam—there are departures every hour during the day—where you can pick up a domestic flight to anywhere in Indonesia. Another ferry route from Singapore is to Tanjung Pinang, also in the Riau Archipelago and just a 90-minute ferry ride, and from there you can take a Merpati flight to another Indonesian destinations.

Getting Around

By Airplane

Reservations are strongly advised on popular routes—between Jakarta and Yogyakarta, for example. Expect delays, especially during the monsoon rains, which can make air travel impossible. Besides the major air hubs in Medan, Jakarta, and Bali (☞ Arriving and Departing, *above*), official air entry points include: Ambon, Maluku; Balikpapan, Kalimantan; Bandung, Java; Batam, Riau; Biak, Irian Jaya; Manado, Sulawesi; Mataram, Lombok; Padang, Sumatra; Pekanbaru, Sumatra; Pontianak, Kalimantan; and Surabaya, Java.

CARRIERS

Garuda Indonesian Airways (☞ Arriving and Departing, *above*), **Merpati** (☎ 021/424–7404 in Jakarta), and **Sempati** (☎ 021/835–1612 in Jakarta) cover all 27 provinces. **Bouraq** (☎ 021/628–8827 in Jakarta) flies into small towns with limited landing facilities, such as destinations in Kalimantan on Indonesian Borneo. Note: always check with the airlines the day before your flight, because flights are often canceled and schedules changed owing to the country's financial crisis.

FLYING TIMES

Flying within Indonesia requires patience and flexibility, as schedules run on the infamous *jam karet*, or "rubber time," and long hauls may incorporate unscheduled stops. From Jakarta it's 40 minutes to Bandung, 1¼ hours to Yogyakarta, and 1½ hours to Surabaya on Java; 1½ hours to Denpasar on Bali; 2 hours to Ujung Pandang on Sulawesi; 2¼ hours to Medan on Sumatra; and 2¼ hours to Mataram on Lombok. From Denpasar, it's 40 minutes to Mataram and almost 1½ hours to Ujung Pandang.

PASSES

Garuda Indonesia offers a **Visit Indonesia Pass** for $300 good for three flights within Indonesia, and additional flight coupons for $100 each. It's best to buy the pass before your arrival (allow at least a week for processing), but if you don't have time to purchase one before your trip, you can buy one in Indonesia if you show a local airline office a copy of your international tickets. One hitch to the deal, though, is that you must fly in and out of the country on Garuda Indonesia; otherwise, a surcharge of $60 is added.

By Bajaj

Although scooting through traffic in these three-wheel orange contraptions can be faster, more exciting, and less expensive than taxis, keep in mind that they are also hot (no air-conditioning) and loud (no glass in the windows). A few blocks will cost Rp 500–Rp 1,000; 1 km (½ mi) will run Rp 2,000–Rp 5,000, depending on your negotiating skills. Drivers are notorious for overcharging, so bargain hard—and finalize the price *before* you get in.

By Becak

These three-wheeled pedicabs are useful for short distances. In Jakarta they're permitted only in the outlying neighborhoods, but elsewhere in Indonesia they're plentiful. A few blocks will cost Rp 200–Rp 500; 1 km (½ mi) can run Rp 1,000–Rp 3,000. Becak drivers are tough bargainers, but if one doesn't meet your price, another may. Just be sure to sort out the fare with the driver beforehand.

By Bemo

A bemo is a converted pickup truck or minivan—a standard form of transport for short trips. Most bemos follow regular routes and will stop anywhere along the way to pick up or discharge passengers. You pay when you get out. Try to learn the fare (they vary according to distance) from another passenger; otherwise you'll be overcharged. An empty bemo will often try to pick up Western travelers, but beware: unless you clarify that it's on its regular route, you will be chartering it as a taxi.

By Boat

Ferries run between many of the islands. Hotel travel desks and travel agencies have schedules; you buy your tickets at the terminals. For longer trips, **Pelni** (⊠ Jl. Angkasa 18, Jakarta, ☎ 021/421–1921; ⊠ Jl. Martadinata 38, Ujung Pandang, ☎ 0411/331393), the state-owned shipping company, serves all the major ports with ships accommodating 1,000 to 2,000 passengers in four classes. First-class cabins are air-conditioned and have private bathrooms—but don't expect comfort or opulence; this is not a luxury cruise. Schedules and tickets are available from Pelni's head office or at travel agencies. Official entry and exit points by sea are: Ambon, Maluku; Batam, Riau; Belawan, Sumatra; Benoa, Bali; Dumai, Riau; Jakarta, and Surabaya, Java; Padangbai, Bali; Semarang, Java; and Tanjung Pinang, Riau.

By Bus

Buses are an important form of surface transportation in Indonesia, though they offer varying degrees of comfort. Long-distance expresses have air-conditioning, reclining seats, rest rooms, meals, videos—even karaoke. Local buses, however, can be crowded and steaming hot. It's an inexpensive means of transport—the 14-hour trip between Jakarta and Yogyakarta, for instance, costs Rp 17,500 on an air-conditioned express. Tickets and schedules are available from terminals, travel desks, or travel agencies. Tourist offices also provide schedules. The only international land crossing from Indonesia is between Kuching, Malaysia, and Pontianak, Kalimantan.

For Java and Sumatra, contact **Antar Lintas Sumatra** (⊠ Jl. Jati Baru 87A, Jakarta, ☎ 021/320970) or **Bintang Kejora** (⊠ Jl. K. H. Mas Mansyur 59, Jakarta, ☎ 021/336677). For Java, Bali, and Sumatra, try **P. T. ANS** (⊠ Jl. Senen Raya 50, Jakarta, ☎ 021/340494), **Java Indah Express** (⊠ Jl. Diponegoro 14, Denpasar, ☎ 361/227329), or **Lorena** (⊠ Jl. Hasannudin 3, Denpasar, ☎ 361/234941). To book a seat on one of the smaller vehicles that run east through Nusa Tenggara, try the numerous Denpasar transport agencies on Jalan Diponegoro and Jalan Hasannudin; otherwise, you can ask the drivers at any ferry terminal if seats are available. **Liman Express** (⊠ Jl. Timor, Ujung Pandang, ☎ 0411/315851) makes daily runs to Tanatoraja on Sulawesi.

By Car

Given the traffic situations within the city limits of major Indonesian destinations, it's probably best to leave the driving to the cabbies and chauffeurs who rule the roads here. If you must rent a car, use common sense about when to do so. On Bali, renting cars is common practice and relatively safe, but in other locales traffic conditions and poor roads can make driving hazardous. Although hiring a car and driver (through your hotel or a travel agent) generally costs 25%–50% percent more than simply renting a car (about Rp 324,000–Rp 540,000), it's still relatively inexpensive.

EMERGENCY ASSISTANCE

Prompt assistance is part of the service at major international car rental agencies as well as at the more popular local companies. Otherwise, you're pretty much on your own. However, if you break down or run into trouble, Indonesians are in general very helpful and will be able to direct you to the nearest auto service facility—if not actually stay with you and help you fix your vehicle.

GASOLINE

Gas prices are higher than in the States, the equivalent of around $1.65 for a U.S. gallon. Stations are few and far between, so don't set out with less than a quarter tank, and check your fuel gauge frequently

to make sure that it works. Pertamina is the major gas station operator, but there are numerous small vendors alongside the roads; be sure,
however, that you know how to ask for the right type of fuel.

PARKING

Except at the larger resort hotels, where guests usually park free in designated lots or garages, parking in Indonesia is for the most part "take
what you find"; curbside is your only option.

RENTALS

Self-drive cars are available through large rental agencies, hotels, or
travel agencies in major cities and tourist hubs, including Jakarta, Yogyakarta, and Bali. Most Indonesian car rental companies require (or
would like you to have) your license from home *and* an International
Driver's License. You can get one through the American or Canadian
automobile associations, or, in the United Kingdom, through the Automobile Association or Royal Automobile Club. Most Western companies
also have age requirements. For example, Avis requires that you be at
least 25 years old, Hertz 21 years old, and National 18 years old.

Always discuss your itinerary with the agent before signing the contract. Some rental contracts may limit the areas to which you can
drive. For example, you need a special permit—really just a letter from
the rental agency—to cross from Bali to Lombok.

Western agencies usually offer either sedans or four-wheel-drive vehicles, all with standard transmission, cassette decks, and air-conditioning; vehicles from local agencies can range from mini-Jeeps to
full-size vans, but they may not have air-conditioning or extra comforts. The rental charge for a four-wheel-drive vehicle from an international firm starts at about $45 a day. For details on agencies, *see* the
Essentials sections *in* specific regions.

ROAD CONDITIONS

Indonesia's main roads are paved and in good condition, but side and
back roads can be poor. Tourist areas are often very congested, with
small trucks, bemos, scooters, bicycles, and pedestrians adding to car
traffic. Off the main highways, expect village animals—cows, goats,
dogs, chickens—to appear in the road without warning.

RULES OF THE ROAD

The most important rule to remember here is that there are no rules:
drivers routinely ignore red lights and policemen, yet stop mid-road
for a chat with a passing vehicle or to buy cigarettes from a wandering vendor. Keep your eyes open and your reflexes sharp at all times.
Driving is on the left, and passing is on the right. Road signs reading
HATI HATI mean "warning" and exclamation points mean "Caution!"
for a variety of reasons: sharp curves, steep embankments, construction, or bad roads in general. Hint: Tap your horn as a warning before passing on two-lane roads and as you round blind curves on
less-used thoroughfares.

There are no formal seat belt laws, but make sure yours works and
that you wear it. Although they aren't required in Indonesia, it's wise
to use car seats if you're traveling with young children. To get such a
seat, you'll need to rent your car in advance through a Western agency
and request it when booking.

By Horse Cart

Horse-drawn carts are disappearing fast, but they remain popular in
Lombok, Sumbawa, and other tourist areas. The typical fare for distances up to a km (½ mi) is Rp 200–Rp 500.

By Taxi

Registered taxis and hired cars may be hailed on city streets—look for the yellow number plates. Except in Jakarta, Surabaya, parts of Bali, and at most airports, you negotiate the fare with the driver before setting out. Most hotels have taxi stands.

By Train

Java is the only island with reliable train service. The line runs from Jakarta through Yogyakarta to Surabaya and Banyuwangi, and it's a worthwhile mode of transport if you have time. Executive and business classes include air-conditioning, comfortable swivel seats, TV, and meals. Economy offers fan-cooled cars and open windows that let you view the lush countryside as it slides by. Early morning departures are best for avoiding the midday heat. Night trains are also a viable alternative though sleeper cars are rarely offered. Schedules and tickets are available through hotel travel desks, travel agencies, or at the train stations; be sure to get tickets well in advance. Between Jakarta and Yogyakarta, it's around Rp 55,000 in executive class, Rp 23,000 in business, and Rp 14,000 in economy; to Surabaya, it's around Rp 57,000 in executive, Rp 38,000 in business, and Rp 10,000 in economy. For more information, contact the **Regional Operational Office** (KADAOPS; ✉ Jl. Taman Stasiun 1, Jakarta Kota, Jakarta, ☎ 021/6929083).

Contacts and Resources

Customs and Duties

ON ARRIVAL

Two liters of liquor and 200 cigarettes may be brought into Indonesia duty-free. Restrictions apply on the import of radios and television sets. Of course, no drugs, weapons, or pornography are allowed; neither are cassette players or printed matter in Indonesian or Chinese. Note: carry all prescription medicines in their original containers and keep a copy of the doctor's slip with you.

ON DEPARTURE

You may not export more than 50,000 rupiah per person. Other forbidden exports include valuable antiques (generally more than 100 years old and worth $100 or more), artifacts, cultural treasures, and products made from endangered plants and animals, such as furs, feathers, and the tortoiseshell items sold in Bali.

Electricity

The electrical current in Indonesia is 220 volts, 50 cycles alternating. If you're coming from North America you'll need an adapter and a converter unless you have dual-voltage appliances, in which case you'll need only an adapter. Electricity may flicker out at any time, even in Jakarta and Bali. Carry a small flashlight with extra batteries and keep computers charged at all times just in case.

Embassies and Consulates

AUSTRALIAN

Consulate: (✉ Jl. Prof. Mochtar Yamin Kav 51, Renon, Denpasar, ☎ 0361/235092). **Embassy:** (✉ Jl. H. R. Rasuna Said Kav. C15–16, Jakarta, ☎ 021/522–7111).

CANADIAN

Embassy: (✉ Jl. Jendral Sudirman Kav. 29, 5th floor, Wisma Metropolitan 1, Jakarta, ☎ 021/510709).

NEW ZEALAND

Embassy: (✉ Jl. Diponegoro 41, Jakarta, ☎ 021/330680).

UNITED KINGDOM

Consulate: Medan (✉ Jl. Ahmad Yani 2, ☎ 061/518699). **Embassy:** Jakarta (✉ Jl. M. H. Thamrin 75, ☎ 021/330904).

UNITED STATES

Consulates: Denpasar (✉ Jl. Hayam Wuruk 188, ☎ 0361/233605); Medan (✉ Jl. Imam Bonjol 13, ☎ 061/322200); **Sanur** (✉ Jl. Segara Ayu 5, ☎ 0361/288478); and Surabaya (✉ Jl. Raya Dr. Sutomo 33, ☎ 031/568–2287). **Embassy:** Jakarta (✉ Jl. Medan Merdeka Selatan 5, ☎ 021/3442211).

Health and Safety

Drink only bottled water, and avoid ice in any beverage (although ice at luxury hotels, such as those on Bali, is often made from distilled water and may be safe). It's best to steer clear of raw, unpeeled fruits and vegetables, raw seafood, and undercooked meat. Although malaria is rare in the tourist areas, it has not been eradicated from the outer regions, so it's best to take precautions before you leave. Inoculations for hepatitis and tetanus should also be up to date. If you're a hiker or diver, be aware that these islands are home to a number of dangerous and poisonous creatures—know what to watch out for before you head into the wild.

Owing to the downward spiral of the Indonesian economy and general political dissatisfaction, large public demonstrations have occurred in major cities throughout the islands, including riots in Jakarta and Bandung. Tourists should be safe in any case, but be wary of the social climate before you travel, pay attention to travelers' advisories, and steer clear of areas embroiled in political upheaval, especially during elections.

Crime against travelers mainly occurs in large cities and tourist areas, where small-time thieves prey on unseasoned visitors, so a little caution in how you act can go a long way. Dress modestly and don't flash your money around. Carry travelers' checks and keep large amounts of cash in a hidden money pouch or locked in hotel safes. Pickpockets haunt crowded transport hubs, and scam artists love to draw in naive travelers. Check out what you buy before you lay down the money—fake jewels, fake name-brand items (handbags, shoes, perfume), bait-and-switch gifts "prewrapped" for customs, and bogus shipping promises are the typical tricks of this region.

Although it's common practice for Indonesian men and women to walk hand-in-hand with friends of the same sex, gay and lesbian travelers should practice discretion, even in Bali, since homosexuality is not readily accepted in this overwhelmingly Muslim country. For advice and information on gay and lesbian activities, contact the organization **Gaya Nusantara** (✉ Jl. Mulyosari Timur 46, Surabaya, ☎ 031/593–4924).

Language, Culture, and Etiquette

Although some 300 languages are spoken in Indonesia, Bahasa Indonesia has been the national language since independence. English is widely spoken in tourist areas.

Indonesians are extremely polite. Begin encounters with locals by saying "*Selemat pagi*" ("Good morning"), "*Selamat siang*" ("Good day"), "*Selamat sore*" ("Good afternoon"), or "*Selamat malam*" ("Good evening"), depending on the time of day. Two phrases you'll use often are "*Terima kasih*" ("Thank you") and "*Ma'af*" ("Excuse me" or "I'm sorry"). Shaking hands has become a common practice, and Indonesians are very tactile, so expect to be touched often in conversation. Smiling is the national pastime, so do it frequently and you'll have a much easier time traversing language barriers. Some etiquette no-nos are pointing with your index finger (gesture with your whole hand instead), crossing your arms, and placing your hands on your hips (signs of anger). Most important, avoid touching food or people with your left hand, which is considered unclean.

The more formal or sacred an occasion, the more formally dressed you should be. When visiting mosques, women should wear something on the head and shouldn't enter during menstruation. Men should wear long trousers and have at least their upper arms covered. Don't walk in front of those who are praying. At Balinese temples, you must wear a sash to enter; these are usually rented on-site for a few rupiah. Shorts (and other above-the-knee clothing) are considered improper temple attire, so avoid them or borrow a sarong when visiting any holy place.

Mail

POSTAL RATES

Two kinds of airmail are available: *pos udara* (regular) and *kilat* (express). Kilat rates to the United States or the United Kingdom are Rp 1,200 and Rp 1,300 respectively for postcards and Rp 1,600 and Rp 1,700 for 1 gram (.035 oz.) letters. Postcards are Rp 600 to all foreign countries. Pos udara letters less than 21 grams are Rp 1,600 to North America and Europe and Rp 1,200 to Australia and New Zealand.

RECEIVING MAIL

For letters or packages to reach you in any major town in the islands, have them sent to the main post office—usually open Monday through Thursday 8–4, Friday 8 AM–11 AM, and Saturday 8 AM–12:30 PM. You can have mail sent to you "poste restante" care of local post offices. Just be sure that letters addressed to you have your surname (underlined and in capital letters), followed by your name, to avoid filing confusion. A small fee may be charged to pick up a letter. Most hotels will also accept mail and hold it. Do not have anyone send cash.

WRITING TO INDONESIA

Indonesian addresses are straightforward. All you need for a proper address are the name, street address (Jl. or Jln. stand for "Jalan," or road), number (though many addresses in small towns won't have this), town, island, and postal code. Finally, be sure to follow all this information with "Republik Indonesia."

Money and Expenses

COSTS

Prices in Indonesia depend on what you're buying. The basic cost of living is low and domestic labor is cheap, but you'll pay a premium for anything imported. Thus, camera film is expensive, food is not. Regionally, costs rise in direct relation to tourism and business development. Prices in Bali and Jakarta are relatively high, particularly at deluxe hotels and restaurants. Sumatra and Sulawesi, by contrast, are bargains.

Major cities have shopping complexes and department stores where prices are fixed, but at small shops and street stalls bargaining is not only expected but part of the whole shopping experience. Bargaining is, in fact, having a dialogue with the vendor, and a certain respect is established between you and the seller. It's also an art, so try to develop your own technique. Start by offering half the asking price, even a third in the tourist areas. You'll finish somewhere in between. Shops with higher-quality merchandise are likely to take credit cards, but payment in cash puts you in a better bargaining position. The keys to good negotiation in Asia are a positive attitude and flexibility.

Sample Prices: Cup of coffee: 25¢–$2.00; small bottle of beer, $1–$4; small bottled water, 25¢–$2; can of soda: 50¢–$3; bottle of house wine:

$7–$15; sandwich: $2–$7; 2-km (1-mi) taxi ride, 75¢–$3 (depending on traffic); city bus ride: 10¢–$2; museum: 25¢–$3.

CURRENCY

Indonesia's unit of currency is the rupiah. Bills come in denominations of 100, 500, 1,000, 5,000, 10,000, 20,000, 50,000, and 100,000 Rp, coins in 25, 50, 100, 500, and 1,000 Rp. The exchange rate at press time was Rp 10,800 to the U.S. dollar, Rp 6,940 to the Canadian dollar, 18,000 to the U.K. sterling, Rp 6,300 to the Australian dollar, and Rp 5,300 to the New Zealand dollar.

SERVICE CHARGES, TAXES, AND TIPPING

High-end hotels charge 21% tax, of which only 10% is the regular government tax also seen on the bill at moderate hotels; the rest comprises various service charges. Departing passengers on international flights pay an airport departure tax of around Rp 25,000. Domestic airport taxes are from Rp 6,500 to Rp 11,000, depending on the point of departure.

The more expensive tourist restaurants include a service charge; if not, tip 10%. Above the hotel service charge, plan to tip bellboys Rp 10,800 per bag; you may also want to tip room-service personnel if you request a special service. Porters at the airport should receive about Rp 5,400 per bag. Taxi drivers aren't tipped except in Jakarta and Surabaya, where Rp 500, or small change, is the minimum. For a driver of a hired car, Rp 21,600 for half a day would be the minimum tip. Private guides expect a gratuity, perhaps Rp 32,400–Rp 54,000 per day.

Opening and Closing Times

Banks are open from around 9 AM to 3 PM or 4 PM, but they may close during the lunch hour. Bank branches in hotels may stay open later. **Government offices** are open Monday–Thursday from approximately 8 to 3 and Friday 8–11:30 AM. Some are also open on Saturday 8–2. **Offices** have varied hours, usually around 9–5 weekdays and a half day on Saturday. Most **museums** are open Tuesday–Thursday and weekends 9–2 (although some larger museums stay open until 4 or 5), Friday 9–noon. **Shops** are generally open Monday–Saturday 9–5. Offices and stores in Muslim areas are only open until 11 AM on Friday.

NATIONAL HOLIDAYS

Start of Ramadan, the Islamic month of fasting (Dec. 9, 1999; Nov. 27, 2000); New Year's Day; Idul Fitri, the end of Ramadan (Jan. 19, 1999; Jan. 8, 2000; Dec. 27, 2000); Isra Miraj Nabi Mohammed, Mohammed's Ascension (Feb./Mar.); Good Friday (Apr. 2, 1999; Apr. 21, 2000); Ascension Day (May 13, 1999; June 1, 2000); Waicak, Birth of Buddha (May/June); Haji, commemorating Mecca pilgrimages (July); Independence Day (Aug. 17); Birth of Mohammed (Oct.); Christmas Day.

Outdoor Activities and Sports

Swimming pools, health clubs, tennis, badminton, and sometimes squash and racquetball are available at the major hotels. There are golf courses near the larger cities and in resort areas. Special adventure tours can be arranged through tour operators. Traditional sports include bull races in Madura, Java; bullfights (bull against bull) at Kota Baru, near Bukittinggi, Sumatra; and cockfighting (though it is illegal) in Java, Bali, and Sulawesi.

For scuba-diving information, contact the Indonesian diving organization, **Possi** (✉ Jl. Prapatan 38, Jakarta, ☎ 021/348685), or try **Pulau Seribu Paradise** (☎ 021/380–8426) in Jakarta, **Baruna Water Sports** (☎ 361/753820) at Kuta Beach in Bali, or **Nusantara Diving Center** (☎ 437/3988) in Manado. A helpful guide for divers interested in Indonesian reefs is *Underwater Indonesia* (by Kal Muller, Periplus Editions, Singapore, 1995).

Passports and Visas

The Indonesian government stipulates that passports must be valid for at least six months from arrival date, and all travelers must have proof of onward or return passage. For stays up to 60 days, visas are not required for citizens of Australia, Canada, New Zealand, the United Kingdom, and the United States as long as you enter the country through one of the major gateways. These include the airports at Ambon, Bali, Balikpapan, Bandung, Batam, Biak, Jakarta, Kupang, Manado, Mataram, Medan, Padang, Pekanbaru, Pontianak, and Surabaya, as well as the seaports of Ambon, Balikpapan, Batam, Belawan, Benoa, Jakarta, Kupang, Manado, Padangbai (Bali), Pontianak, Semarang, Surabaya, and Tanjung Pinang. The only international land crossing allowed is between Kuching, Malaysia and Pontianak, Kalimantan. Other ports of entry may require a visa.

Telephones

CALLS TO INDONESIA

To call Indonesia from overseas, dial the country code, 62, and then the area code, omitting the first 0.

LOCAL CALLS

Prior to the economic crisis, efforts were being made to upgrade and standardize Jakarta's phone system, but there has been little progress since (hence, some phone numbers in Jakarta have five or six digits and others have seven). Further, upgrades have not even been started in some parts of Indonesia—phone numbers vary in length and service varies in quality. You're better off using hotel phones despite the small surcharges; that way you don't need to amass quantities of coins, and an operator can help with translation and information. Your best chance of finding a phone is in hotel lobbies and Telekom offices. Some travel agencies have phones you can use for local calls, and the staff will let you send and receive faxes for a small fee.

For local calls, three minutes costs Rp 100. Older public phones take Rp 100 coins, but the newer ones accept only phone cards—a recent introduction restricted to the larger cities and tourist areas. For long distance, dial the area code before the number. For operator and directory assistance, dial 108 for local calls, 106 for the provinces.

INTERNATIONAL CALLS

Major Indonesian cities are now hooked into the International Direct Dialing (IDD) system via satellite. Dial 001 plus the respective country code. For towns without the IDD hookup, go through the operator (in tourist destinations many speak English). If you want to avoid using hotel phones, the most economical way to place an IDD call is from the nearest Kantor Telephone & Telegraph office. For international directory assistance, dial 102.

You can make collect calls to Australia, Europe, and North America; for other countries, you need a telephone credit card. Reduced rates on international phone calls are in effect 9 PM–6 AM daily. For most Western countries, Indonesia also has special "home country" phones in its Telekom offices and many hotels. With these you can contact an operator in your home country just by pushing a button. Like a collect call, the bill is charged to whomever you're calling, or you can use one of the calling cards that are sold everywhere.

AT&T, MCI, and Sprint long-distance services make calling home relatively convenient, but you may find the local access number blocked in many hotel rooms. First ask the hotel operator to connect you. If the hotel operator balks, ask for an international operator, or dial the international operator yourself. One way to improve your odds of getting connected to your long-distance carrier is to travel with more than one company's calling card (a hotel may block Sprint, for example, but not MCI). If all else fails, call your phone company collect in the United States or call from a pay phone in the hotel lobby. Here are some long-distance access codes in Indonesia: **AT&T** (☎ 001–801–10), **MCI** (☎ 001–801–11), and **Sprint** (☎ 001–801–15).

Visitor Information

OUTSIDE INDONESIA

Australia has an **Indonesian Embassy** (⊠ 8 Darwin Ave., Yarralumla ACT 2600, ☎ 06/2733222) and an **Indonesian Tourist Office** (⊠ Level 10, S. Elizabeth St., Sydney NSA 2000, ☎ 02/92333630). At press time, there was no Indonesian tourism office in Canada. Contact the **Embassy of Indonesia** (⊠ 287 MacLaren St., Ottawa, Ontario, Canada K2P 0L9, ☎ 613/236–7403). New Zealand also has an **Indonesian Embassy** (⊠ 70 Glen Rd., Kelburn, Wellington, ☎ 04/475–8697). In the United Kingdom, contact the **Indonesian Tourist Office** (⊠ 3 Hanover St., London W1R 9HH, ☎ 0171/493–0030). In the United States, contact the **Indonesia Tourist Board** (⊠ 3457 Wilshire Blvd., Los Angeles, CA 90010, ☎ 213/387–2078).

WITHIN INDONESIA

The Directorate General of Tourism in Indonesia (⊠ Jl. Merdeka Barat 16–19, Jakarta 10110, ☎ 021/386–7588). For details on specific tourist offices throughout the country, *see* the Essentials section *in* each region.

When to Go

Indonesia's low-lying regions are uniformly hot and humid year-round. Temperatures can reach 90°F (32°C) soon after midday, and they drop no lower than 70°F (21°C) at night. The weather at higher altitudes is up to 20°F (11°C) cooler.

The best months to visit Indonesia are April–May and September–October, when crowds are lighter and you're not so likely to get drenched: the west monsoon, from November through March, brings heavy rains. It can drizzle for several days in a row or pour half the day, with only occasional dry spells. Since most of Indonesia's attractions are under the open sky—temples and other architecture, beaches, and outdoor festivals—the monsoon can very literally dampen your enjoyment. Like many locals, you may want to keep an umbrella on hand at all times for protection from both rain and sun.

In the peak tourist months, June and July, popular areas (especially Tanatoraja) are crammed with visitors. Bali hotels also tend to be fully booked around Christmas and New Year's; transport and accommodations in the rest of the country are full around Muslim holidays. Unless you plan to stay only on Bali, consider carefully before visiting during Ramadan, the Islamic month of fasting, when many restaurants, offices, and tourist attractions are closed until sundown.

CLIMATE

The following are average temperatures in Jakarta:

Jan.	84F	29C	**May**	88F	31C	**Sept.**	88F	31C
	74	23		74	23		74	23
Feb.	84F	29C	**June**	88F	31C	**Oct.**	88F	31C
	74	23		74	23		74	23
Mar.	85F	30C	**July**	88F	31C	**Nov.**	85F	30C
	74	23		74	23		74	23
Apr.	86F	30C	**Aug.**	88F	31C	**Dec.**	85F	30C
	74	23		74	23		74	23

Festival dates depend on the type of calendar prevalent in the region where they take place. Most of Indonesia uses the Islamic calendar; the Balinese use a lunar calendar. The **Indonesia Calendar of Events**, with listings for the entire archipelago, is available at Garuda airline offices, or contact tourist information offices.

Dec.–Jan.: Idul Fitri, two days marking the end of Ramadan (a month of fasting during daylight), is the most important Muslim holiday. Festivals take place in all the villages and towns of Muslim Indonesia. **Kesodo** ceremonies are held by the Hindu Tenggerese at the crater of Mt. Bromo on Java.

Mar.: Nyepi, the Balinese New Year, falls on the vernal equinox, usually around March 21. New Year's Eve is spent exorcising evil spirits, which are first attracted with offerings of chicken blood, flowers, and aromatic leaves, then driven away with noise as masked youths bang gongs and tin pans. The island falls silent: no fires or lamps may be lit, and traffic is prohibited.

May: Waicak Day, a public holiday throughout Indonesia, celebrates the Buddha's birth, death, and enlightenment. The **Ramayana Ballet Festival** is held at the Prambanan temple near Yogyakarta during the full-moon week each month, beginning in May and continuing through October. A cast of 500 performs a four-episode dance-drama of the *Ramayana* epic.

July: Galungan, Bali's most important festival, celebrates the creation of the world, marks a visit by ancestral spirits, and honors the victory of good over evil. Celebrants make offerings in family shrines and decorate their villages. On the 10th and last day they bid farewell to the visiting spirits with gifts of *kuningan,* a saffron-yellow rice.

Aug.: Independence Day is celebrated on the 17th throughout Indonesia with flag-raising ceremonies, sports events, and cultural performances.

Oct.: The town of Pamekasan on Java holds **bull-racing finals** in mid–October. A jockey stands on skids slung between two yoked bulls. The animals are decorated, and there's mass dancing before they run. The winner is the bull whose feet cross the finish line first. **Sekaten** commemorates the birth of Mohammed. In Yogyakarta the sultan's antique gamelan—a unique Indonesian musical instrument—is played only on this day. The concert is performed in the gamelan pavilion of the kraton, the sultan's palace complex. Then the celebrants form a parade, carrying enormous amounts of food from the kraton to the mosque, where they distribute it to the people.

3 Malaysia and Brunei

Malaysia offers a haunting olfactory experience. In city streets the acrid aroma of diesel fumes blends with that of chilies frying in vendor stalls, sweet incense from Indian shops, pungent curry powders from spice merchants, and hints of frangipani and other flowers abloom. The jungle has a damp, fermenting scent. In neighboring Brunei, the smell of money permeates. This tiny country is one of the richest in the world, and with Malaysia it shares not only a tropical climate and jungle terrain but also a mix of Malay and Muslim traditions.

THE EARLIEST INHABITANTS of the Malay Peninsula were Neolithic Negrito peoples whose descendants— the Orang Asli—still live simply in jungle uplands. Several waves of progressively more Mongoloid groups brought Iron and Bronze Age cultures to the peninsula and spread out over the entire archipelago. Later, with the emergence of the Java-based Majapahit, the Malay Peninsula came under the influence of a Hindu-Javanese empire that exerted little political control but strong cultural influence. This was once seen in the *wayang kulit* (shadow puppet plays)—a form of storytelling performed in villages in Kelantan until banned by the extremist Islamic state government in 1992—as well as in traditional ceremonies and customs (such as batik making and folktales) that are still practiced today.

By Nigel Fisher

Updated by
Wendy Hutton

In the 15th century, Islam entered Malaya (as the peninsula was once was once called) from northern Sumatra and became the official religion of the powerful state of Melaka (Malacca) during the reign of Sultan Iskandar Shah. Islam solidified the system of sultanates, in which one person and his family provided both political and religious leadership. (Today Malaysia still has nine sultans; every five years one is elected to serve a term as constitutional monarch. The head of government in this parliamentary democracy is the prime minister.)

For the next 200 years the peninsula was a hornets' nest of warring sultanates, marauding pirates, and European adventurers who, while searching for spices and gold, introduced guns and cannons. The Portuguese conquered Melaka, and were followed by the Dutch, who established a stronghold in Java and outposts in Sumatra and Melaka. An 1824 treaty gave the British Dutch-held Melaka, which became part of the British Straits Settlements along with Singapore and Pinang (Penang). With the British dominating Malaya and the Dutch in Sumatra, the two regions—which shared similar histories, cultures, and religious customs—began to split and follow the lead of the Europeans.

In the mid-19th century, war and famine forced millions of Chinese to flee their homelands and seek employment in Malaya's rapidly expanding tin industry. Soon after their arrival, the rubber industry began to flourish. Rubber requires intensive labor, and still more workers were brought in from India. Other groups came from India to trade, open shops, or lend money. While in India the British trained many civil servants and professionals who also came to Malaya. This Indian community maintained strong ties with home. (To this day Indians sometimes request brides or grooms from an ancestral village—many marriages are still arranged—and often retire in their native land.)

These patterns of life in Malaya continued until World War II. Malays continued their traditions in *kampungs* (communal villages), where time flowed slowly. Sultans prospered under British protection, combining the pleasures of East and West. The Chinese became the peninsula's economic backbone, and the Indians performed various middleman roles. The British maintained a benevolent rule. Each community flourished separately, with little cultural exchange.

The war had little impact on life in Malaya until the Japanese attack on Pearl Harbor and subsequent invasion of Malaya. Japanese forces landed in the northeastern state of Terengganu and moved rapidly down through the jungle, taking Singapore in March 1942. Life on the Malay Peninsula changed overnight. The British had farthest to fall. Many women and children were evacuated to Australia, but the men remained. Former planters, bankers, executives, and soldiers were thrust from a

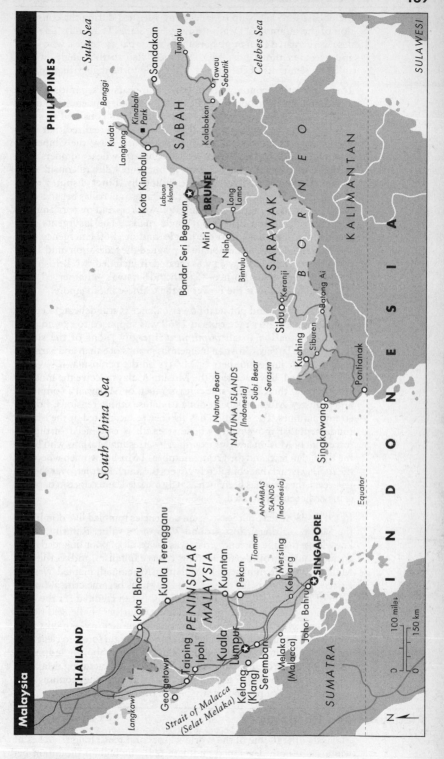

Malaysia

life of ease into hardship or jail. Many perished during the construction of the infamous "Death Railway" in Siam (Thailand). The Chinese were treated even more harshly by the Japanese forces, who jailed and executed thousands. Many Chinese fled to the jungle, where, aided by remnants of the British army, they formed guerrilla bands.

The war left the economy floundering, and years of separatism made unification and development difficult. Prior to independence and under a federation of Malaysian states in 1957, politics consisted of struggles between two racial groups. The Malays, who realized that independence would remove British protection and leave the Chinese in control, became politically active. The Chinese, whose numbers were greatly diminished by the occupation but who still had considerable economic clout, failed to organize politically. Bitter disputes raged among the local leadership. In 1948 the Chinese guerrillas began a campaign of terrorism, harassing plantation workers and owners and ambushing Malays and British on jungle roads. (The insurgents were gradually pushed back into the jungle, and in 1960 emergency policies were lifted.) Ethnic factionalism plagued the federation until 1963, when the nation of Malaysia was created. It included two British protectorates in northern Borneo—Sabah and Sarawak—that served as an ethnic balance against the power of the Chinese in Singapore.

Malaysia's racial and political power balance is still delicate. Legislation introduced after race riots in 1969 was supposed to extend positive discrimination to all *bumiputra* (literally "sons of the soil"), including the largely Christian indigenous groups of Sabah and Sarawak as well as the large numbers of Malays on the peninsula. It's widely acknowledged, however, that the Muslim Malays receive the most assistance, and the Chinese still control much of Malaysia's commerce and industry. Much has been done to defuse ethnic tensions, but the strain continues. The situation has also been exacerbated by the Islamic fundamentalist movement, whose strength is evidenced in the enforcement of Muslim law (for example, by arresting Muslims who break the Ramadan fast) and the greater number of Muslim women who wear the *tudung* (scarf that completely covers the hair). Further, over the last few years, the press has been increasingly muzzled, and criticism of politicians has been suppressed.

In 1997–98, when Southeast Asian currencies tumbled like dominoes, the Malaysian ringgit lost around 70% of its value. Refusing to acknowledge that the currency crisis was the result of poor financial management, uncontrolled bank lending, crony capitalism, and corruption, Malaysia's prime minister, Dr. Mahathir Mohamad, blamed Western currency speculators for the crash. Malaysians became critical (in private) of Dr. Mahathir, who had previously been credited for the double-digit annual growth rate. Malaysia was further challenged by the severe haze created by the worst drought of the century—thanks to El Niño—and by the indiscriminate burning of the rain forest to clear land for plantations in Sumatra and Kalimantan, in neighboring Indonesia. Still, with its petroleum, palm oil, timber, and manufacturing, Malaysia seems certain to weather the current crisis, although the economy isn't expected to pick up significantly before the new century.

Pleasures and Pastimes

Malaysia offers some of the world's best coral reefs; long stretches of white sand (both developed and deserted); the highest mountain between the Himalayas and New Guinea; hill resorts that provide recreation and escape from the tropical sun; spectacular limestone outcroppings and impressive caves in Sarawak's Gunung Mulu National

Park; vast areas of primary jungle; and networks of rivers perfect for white-water rafting. Though there are increasingly more amenities and facilities throughout the country, the major destinations remain Melaka, Kuala Lumpur, Pinang, and Langkawi on the west coast; Kuantan and Tioman Island on the east coast; the Cameron and Genting highlands in the center; Kota Kinabalu in Sabah; and Kuching in Sarawak.

Beaches

Despite its countless beautiful beaches, resorts are a relatively new concept in Malaysia. Still you'll find some terrific establishments on Langkawi Island (a pet project of the prime minister), even though its beaches are only so-so. Although Pinang was the first region to promote beaches, its Batu Ferringhi Beach pales in comparison with those on the Pangkor Islands (off the west coast) and along the eastern coast from Terengganu to Johor. The lovely islands of Perhentian and Redang embody the idea of tropical paradise, complete with scuba diving and other resort facilities. Farther south, around Cherating, you'll find miles of tranquil sandy stretches and traditional Malay fishing villages. Several islands off Mersing, notably Tioman, offer resorts that range from super-luxurious to the simple feet-in-the-sand variety.

On Borneo, Sarawak's rivers tend to carry silt to the ocean, making for muddy waters. Damai Beach, just outside Kuching, has a resort complex, but Sarawak's best beach is in the somewhat remote Similajau National Park. In Sabah, there are countless beaches along the west coast, with resorts in Tanjung Aru and Tuaran, near Kota Kinabalu, which also offers five lovely islands in a marine national park just minutes from downtown.

Dining

Ordering a meal from street vendors (paying each for the individual dish he or she makes) and sharing a table with locals is a great way to immerse yourself in Malaysian cuisine and culture. Just look at what others are eating, and if it appeals to you, point and order. You're likely to find a mix of food—Chinese, Malay, and Indian—in one cluster of stalls. One Chinese favorite is the *popiah,* a soft spring roll filled with vegetables. The *meehon* and *kweh teow* (fried noodles) are also tasty and cheap. Perhaps the best-known Malay dish is *satay*—slivers of marinated beef, chicken, or mutton threaded onto thin sticks, barbecued, and served with a spicy peanut sauce. Be cautious with the local *nasi kandar*—the chilies rule the spicy prawns and fish-head curry. Malaysia's breakfast dish, *nasi lemak* (a bundle of rice with salt fish, curry chicken, peanuts, cucumber, and boiled egg), is worth a taste.

Because fruit is so plentiful and delicious, Malaysians consume lots of it, either fresh from the ubiquitous roadside vendors or fresh-squeezed— try star fruit, watermelon, and orange juice. Mangoes, papayas, rambutans, mangosteens, and finger-size bananas are widely available. The "king" of fruits is the durian, but be prepared: the smell isn't sweet, even though the taste is (it's sort of like vanilla pudding). Hotels have strict policies forbidding durians in guest rooms, so you'll have to select a fruit, have the seller cut it open, and then eat the yellow flesh on the spot.

Authentic Malay food isn't as widely available in sit-down restaurants as Chinese or even American fast-food fare. Thai and Japanese restaurants are plentiful, and the food of the Nonyas or Straits-born Chinese (a fusion of Malay and Chinese cuisines) is perennially popular. In Kuala Lumpur, you'll find establishments that serve a variety of Indian cuisines—southern, northern, and Muslim. Eating rice and curry from a banana leaf with your hand (right hand only, please), as is done in the southern Indian restaurants, is an experience you'll no doubt savor. The following terms are likely to appear on the menus in Malaysia:

asam—sour; a reference to the sourness provided by the tamarind fruit used in some dishes.

dim sum—Chinese snacks, eaten at breakfast or lunch, made with meat, prawns, or fish, and usually steamed or deep-fried

garoupa—a local fish with tender flesh and a sweet flavor

green curry—a Thai curry made with green chilies, lots of fresh herbs, small green *brinjals* (eggplants), and chicken or red meat

ice kacang—shaved ice heaped over red beans, jelly, sweet corn, and strips of green mung-pea flour, sweetened with syrup and drenched with coconut milk or evaporated milk.

kacang—(pronounced ka-chang); signals the presence of beans or nuts

kaya—a jam made from steaming a mixture of eggs, sugar, and coconut cream

kerabu—a hot-and-sour Nonya salad of chicken, jellyfish, unripe mango, squid, beef, or almost anything else, dressed with onions, lemongrass, lime juice, and small chilies

rendang—meat simmered for hours in spices, chilies, and coconut milk until nearly dry

roti—bread

sambal—a thick, hot condiment of chilies, local roots, and herbs; if it has plenty of shrimp paste, it's known as *sambal belacan*

tandoori—meat or seafood roasted in a clay oven, northern Indian style

tom yam—a very sour, hot, and lemony Thai soup usually made with seafood

Price categories are based on the ranges below.

MALAYSIA

CATEGORY	COST*
$$$$	over $30 (over RM108)
$$$	$20–$30 (RM72–RM108)
$$	$8–$20 (RM29–RM72)
$	under $8 (under RM29)

per person, based on three dishes shared between two people, excluding tax, service, and drinks

BRUNEI

CATEGORY	COST*
$$$$	over US$30 (over B$45)
$$$	US$20–US$30 (B$30–B$45)
$$	US$8–US$20 (B$12–B$30)
$	under US$10 (under B$12)

per person for a three-course dinner, excluding tax, service, and drinks.

Golf

Golf is part of the British legacy in Malaysia, and you'll find around 200 courses—many of them excellent—throughout the country. Among the best are the Royal Selangor Golf Club and the Saujana Golf and Country Club (the country's most prestigious golf resort) in Kuala Lumpur, the Bukit Jambul Golf and Country Club in Pinang, the Datai Bay Golf Club in Langkawi, the Borneo Golf and Country Club in Sabah, and the Damai Beach Golf Course near Kuching.

Hiking

The Malaysian Tourism Promotion Board, or MTPB (☞ Visitor Information *in* Malaysia and Brunei A to Z, *below*), has a useful brochure that describes the country's 19 national parks and their trails and lodging options. (In some places, particularly Sarawak, the accommodations are surprisingly upscale.) Hiking opportunities range from full-scale backpacking through dense jungle to short treks combined with road and river transport. The best climb in Southeast Asia is Sabah's Mt. Kinabalu. Paths around the park headquarters there offer rewarding but less arduous walking. Trekking in Sarawak's Gunung Mulu National Park ranges from a grueling hike to the razor-sharp Pinnacles to three to four days following the Headhunter's Trail. The trekking in the remote Kelabit Highlands, also in Sarawak, is excellent. On peninsular Malaysia you can arrange jungle hikes in Taman Negara, a national park north of Kuala Lumpur. For leisurely hikes in cooler temperatures, try the hills of the Cameron Highlands.

Jungle Treks and River Trips

Rain forest threaded by rivers and rapids still covers much of Borneo. Intrepid travelers can trek through the jungle interior on foot or by Jeep, ride a longboat upriver (transportation in the interior is often by river, where boats take the place of buses), and stay overnight in a tribal longhouse. The tourist industry is only now being developed in these regions, so you won't trip over other visitors. And though you'll find signs of modernity even in the most remote longhouses, native lifestyles and hospitality are largely unaltered. Insects hum, invisible creatures croak and grunt, water gurgles and sighs. Equally mysterious are the groaning and screeching of trees that, burdened by age and debris, finally crash through the jungle growth. Sabah's scenic white-water rivers also guarantee exciting outdoor adventures.

Lodging

You'll find many new luxury hotels—shining marble-and-glass towers that provide smiling service and every comfort—particularly in Kuala Lumpur. Hotels in smaller provincial capitals aren't quite as grand, though they certainly provide quality and comfort. In bare-bones establishments the furnishings may be worn and the plaster walls may have cracks, but the bed linen will be fresh and the bathrooms clean. Resorts run the gamut from modern, self-contained complexes with many amenities to cramped, down-at-the-heel Chinese hotels where the shared bath is down the hall.

Only three exceptional hotels of character and charm come to mind: Pangkor Laut, on a private island, brings back the exotic feeling of a Malay village; Datai, on Langkawi, is architecturally innovative and marvelously designed to blend into the environment; Carcosa Seri Negara, in Kuala Lumpur, the former governor's mansion, has been restored resplendently. Your more exotic options include stays in a Dayak (an indigenous group in Sarawak) longhouse or a small thatched beach bungalow (albeit one with primitive plumbing) on a small island off the peninsula's east coast.

Bathrooms in the city generally have Western-style commodes; Asian-style squat facilities are common in rural areas. Better hotels have in-house movies available on color TVs. The government censors the media, including the channels offered by Astro and Mega satellite broadcasting, although all major hotels offer CNN. All hotels are air-conditioned unless otherwise stated, and room service is available in all the $$$ and $$$$ hotels.

Rest houses—government bungalows normally rented to officials—are available to tourists at low rates when government officers aren't using them, but they are difficult to book in advance and they're always fully booked during school holidays. For more information, contact the MTPB (☞ Visitor Information *in* Malaysia and Brunei A to Z, *below*) or **Utell**

International (☎ 800/44–UTELL in the U.S.), which represents more than 30 Malaysian hotels.

Price categories are based on the ranges below.

MALAYSIA

CATEGORY	COST*
$$$$	over $115 (over RM415)
$$$	$90–$115 (RM343–RM415)
$$	$60–$90 (RM217–RM343)
$	under $60 (under RM217)

*for a standard double room in high season, excluding 10% service charge and 5% tax.

BRUNEI

CATEGORY	COST*
$$$$	over US$120 (over B$180)
$$$	US$90–US$115 (B$135–B$180)
$$	US$60–US$90 (B$90–B$135)
$	under US$60 (B$90)

*for a standard double room in high season, excluding service charge and tax.

Scuba Diving

Sipadan Island, off Sabah's east coast in the Celebes Sea, is one of the best dive spots in the world. Here you can explore a spectacular 2,000-ft wall of vertical coral and swim with sea turtles. Islands off Semporna, and the atoll of Layang Layang off Sabah's west coast also offer spectacular diving. Sarawak has the Luconia Shoals, which are accessible via Miri or Brunei. Off the peninsula, you should head for Tioman Island; the small islands around Mersing; or the islands of Perhentian, Redang, Kapas, and Tenggol—all off Terengganu on the east coast.

Shopping

Malaysia's hand-printed batiks, with layers of rich colors and elaborate traditional designs, have become high fashion worldwide. You can buy shirts and simple skirts and dresses or lengths of fabric. Pewter is another specialty, since it's made from one of the country's abundant raw material, tin. The best-known manufacturer is Selangor Pewter, which markets its goods through its own showrooms as well as in department stores, gift shops, and handicraft centers.

Handicrafts, especially those from Sarawak, are well made and appealing. Typical items are rattan baskets, handwoven straw goods, and handmade silver jewelry from Kelantan. The Iban people create weavings called *pua kumbu,* which have primitive patterns and a faded look like that of an antique carpet. Tribal sculptures also have an allure. Perhaps the most unusual handcrafted material is *kain songket,* an extraordinary tapestrylike fabric with real gold threads woven into patterns.

Exploring Malaysia and Brunei

Malaysia is composed of two parts: Peninsular Malaysia (known as Malaya before the formation of Malaysia in 1963) and the two Borneo states of Sabah and Sarawak. (Borneo, the world's third-largest island, also includes the Sultanate of Brunei and the Indonesian provinces of Kalimantan.) Peninsular Malaysia has 11 states. Those covered in this guide include Kedah, Perak, Pinang, Negeri Sembilan, Melaka, Johor, Pahang, Terengganu, Selangor, and the federal territory of Kuala Lumpur.

Although Sabah and Sarawak have a much larger area than the peninsula, the land is largely covered by rain forest or plantations; 80% of the people live on the peninsula. Malaysia's population of some 21.1 million is about 49% Malay; 29% Chinese; 21% Indian and various minorities; and 1% non-Malay indigenous groups including the Kadazan, Iban, and other tribes of Borneo. Although Malaysia is officially a Muslim country, freedom of worship is permitted. The Chinese are mostly Buddhist or Christian, the Indians Hindu or Muslim. Sabah and Sarawak are primarily Christian, as a result of 20th-century missionaries who converted most of the non-Muslim natives.

This mix of cultures is one of Malaysia's main fascinations. It's especially noticeable in the cities, where, interspersed with businessmen in Western garb and teenagers in T-shirts and jeans, you'll see Malay women in floral-print sarongs, conservative Muslim women with traditional head coverings, Chinese in the pajama-type outfits called *samfoo,* and Indian men in *dhotis* (saronglike garments). It manifests itself in a lively and varied food scene, with a proliferation of vendors who sell everything from exotic fruits and juices to Hokkien noodles and Malay satay. And it proclaims itself joyously in the street festivals and religious ceremonies that different cultures celebrate throughout the year.

On the west coast of the peninsula is Kuala Lumpur, Malaysia's capital and the gateway through which most people enter the country. It's a sprawling, clamorous, modern city that nevertheless retains many reminders of the past. The beach resort island of Pinang is a wonderful place to tool about in a trishaw or pedicab through streets lined with lively shops and graceful colonial architecture. North of Pinang is the duty-free island of Langkawi, whose idyllic setting has attracted the attention of resort developers. For a sense of Malaysia's colonial history, a visit to Melaka, with ruins and restored buildings from successive European colonizers, is a must.

The peninsula's east coast is less developed, allowing a glimpse of a quieter Malaysia. Terengannu's islands of Perhentian, Redang, Kapas, and Tenggol, as well as a couple coastal spots, offer superb beaches and a range of resorts. Farther south, around Kuantan and Cherating you'll find outstanding beaches and first-rate resorts; Mersing, south of Kuantan, is the jumping-off point for several islands, including Tioman, where the film *South Pacific* was shot. The scenery of this island is as idyllic today as it was then; several resort hotels offer a perfect base for a water-sports or jungle-hiking vacation. Much of the rest of the peninsula is covered with rubber estates, oil palm plantations, and cool hill stations. Sabah and Sarawak deliver all the adventure that the word *Borneo* promises, including trips through dense jungle on foot or by longboat to visit the descendants of headhunters at their longhouses—a rare opportunity to learn about a culture so very different from what you've left at home.

Great Itineraries

If you seek only sun, sea, and relaxation, Pangkor Laut, Pinang, Langkawi, Kuantan, the east coast, or around Kota Kinabalu in Sabah are ideal. Alternatively, the diversity of Malaysia is such that a trip could be specifically geared to special-interest travel, such as river trips in Borneo or hiking through the national parks. The itineraries below are as diverse as possible within limited time frames.

IF YOU HAVE 3 DAYS

With this time limit, you'll probably want to focus on seeing **Kuala Lumpur,** though you really should try to get out into the country; **Melaka,** with its colonial past, is only a two-hour drive away. You could also limit Kuala Lumpur to only one day and spend two in **Pinang** or at the beach on the island of **Pangkor Laut.**

Start your visit with two full days in **Kuala Lumpur** before going north to the **Cameron Highlands** to stay at Ye Olde Smokehouse for a night. Then continue north up to **Pinang** to spend a couple of nights in **Georgetown,** renting a car one day to tour the island. Then take a plane to **Langkawi** for two days of sun and a beach vacation.

Although 10 days won't permit you to cover all of Malaysia's highlights, it does offer some flexibility. Give yourself a full day in **Kuala Lumpur** and then pick up a car to drive to the **Cameron Highlands** for a night. The next day, continue on to Pinang and spend the night in **Georgetown.** On the following day, drive over the mountains to the east coast and **Kuantan.** You'll want to rest up and spend a couple of nights there or slightly up the coast at **Cherating.** On the sixth day drive down to **Johor Bahru** to drop off the car and pick up a flight to **Kota Kinabalu** in Sabah. Give yourself at least a couple of days here. From Kota Kinabalu you may want to fly into **Bandar Seri Begawan** in Brunei for the night before continuing on to **Kuching** in Sarawak. Spend two nights in Sarawak, making sure that you go into the interior for a river trip and a visit to a Dayak village. From Kuching, you can take a direct flight back to peninsular Malaysia or Singapore.

When to Tour Malaysia and Brunei

The wet season runs from late October through February on peninsular Malaysia's east coast (where flooding is common), in Sarawak, and on Sabah's east coast. Sabah's west coast is more likely to receive heavy rain from May through July. Islam is the state religion of Malaysia, and Islamic law is strictly enforced. Friday is the holy day, and government offices close between 11:45 AM and 2 PM to allow Muslims to visit the mosque. During the month of Ramadan, Muslims aren't allowed to eat or drink from sunup to sundown (if caught, offenders are punished). Muslim restaurants are therefore usually closed during the day. Incidentally, the stress of fasting during Ramadan makes believers a little grumpy and not their normal hospitable selves. (☞ *also* When to Go *in* Malaysia and Brunei A to Z, *below.*)

Numbers in the text correspond to numbers in the margin and on the maps.

KUALA LUMPUR

Kuala Lumpur (or KL as it's commonly called), the capital city of Malaysia, is in a special region—called a federal capital territory—surrounded by the state of Selangor. Gleaming skyscrapers sit next to century-old, two-story shophouses, and on six-lane superhighways, rush hour traffic often appears to be an elongated parking lot. Somewhat surprisingly, there are still remnants of the old kampungs, traditional Malay villages, within parts of KL.

KL was founded by miners who discovered tin in this spot where the Klang (Kelang) and Gombak rivers formed a broad delta. Those pioneers were a rough, hardy lot, and the city retains some of that early boomtown character. Despite its bustling, cosmopolitan style, KL is at heart an earthy place, where people sit around the *kedai kopi* (coffeehouse) and talk about food, religion, and business. It's also the center of the federal government, and since government is dominated by the easygoing Malays and business by the hyperactive Chinese, the city's tone is schizophrenic at best. Although it's not one of the world's great destination cities, KL does have first-rate hotels, excellent and varied cuisines, a lively blend of cultures, architectural styles that range from Moorish to Tudor to modern, a generally efficient infrastructure, and some of the lowest prices of any major Asian city.

Exploring Kuala Lumpur

394 km (246 mi) northwest of Singapore, 481 km (300 mi) south of Alor Setar (near the Thai border).

In the last 20 years, KL has mushroomed outward and upward in a most confusing manner. Most visitors spend their time in a section known as the Golden Triangle, which has the city's best hotels and shopping areas, as well as a number of sights. Here you'll find symbols of Malaysia's boom time, with the towering Petronas Twin Towers and the KL Tower as the most recent additions. The city's colonial center is marked by the Sultan Abdul Samad Building, which faces the open green (Merdeka Square) and the quaint Tudor-style Royal Selangor Club. Nearby Chinatown is still a busy center for trading and commerce.

Downtown Kuala Lumpur

A GOOD TOUR

Begin on the edge of Chinatown at the **Central Market** ①, a renovated art deco building with a lively bazaar and tempting food stalls. Exit onto Jalan Hang Kasturi, and turn left onto Jalan Hang Lekir in the heart of old Chinatown, where the shops sell traditional medicine, incense, and intriguing dried produce. Just past the temple, **See Yeoh** ②, take the alleyway known as Penajaja Gallery Jalan Tun H. S. Lee, where produce and dry goods are sold at a morning market. Follow it through to busy Jalan Petaling, which is lined with stalls purveying such items as wallets, umbrellas, cheap clothing, and music cassettes. (At night the street is closed to auto traffic and becomes a full-scale market.) Wander down Jalan Petaling and turn right onto Jalan Sultan to return to Jalan Tun H. S. Lee. Turn right to reach the city's major Hindu temple, **Sri Mahamariamman** ③. When you leave the temple, pass the garland sellers and turn right back onto Jalan Tun H. S. Lee. At Jalan Balai Polis turn left, passing the small temple for the Sikhs in the police force. If you're thirsty or feel like a snack, you can stop at the **Old China Cafe** before visiting **Chan See Shu Yuen** ④, the most atmospheric temple in Chinatown.

From the temple you have a couple of touring choices: you can take a cab west to see the classic architecture of the **Railway Station** ⑤, the contemporary architecture of the **Masjid Negara** ⑥, and the exhibits at the **Galeri Seni Lukis Negara** ⑦ or **Muzium Negara** ⑧—all followed by a stroll through the greenery of the **Taman Tasik Perdana** ⑨. Alternatively, you could take a cab east to see the exhibits and the huge mural at **Pudu Prison,** and then return to Chan See Shu Yuen to continue sightseeing (and shopping) on foot. To continue the walking tour, leave the temple and take Jalan Sultan to Jalan Silang. If you veer right off Silang you'll come to the **Menara Maybank** ⑩, which houses the Numismatic Museum. If you veer left, Silang leads to Leboh Pasar Besar and out onto Jalan Sultan Hishamuddin and **Merdeka Square** ⑪. Across from the square is the magnificent Moorish **Sultan Abdul Samad Building** ⑫. Just beyond here, at the confluence of the Klang and Gombak rivers, is **Masjid Jamek Bandaraya** ⑬, the city's oldest mosque (enter via Jalan Tun Perak). Pass by **Masjid India** ⑭, a modern Indian mosque on Jalan Masjid India, where vendors sell herbal medicine and cosmetics.

Head north up **Jalan Tuanku Abdul Rahman,** past a few turn-of-the-century shophouses (note the decorative flourishes along the roofline) and several colorful sari shops, bookstores, stationers, Indian Muslim restaurants, and stores of an indeterminate nature. Notice the land-

Kuala Lumpur

To Batu Caves
and National Zoo

Jln. Tunku

Jln. Tun Ismail

Jln. Mahameru

Jln. Tun Ismail

Jln. Dato' Onn

Jln. Mahameru

Jln. Tamingsari

Jln. Parlimen

Jln. Bukit Aman

Lake
Gardens

Jln. Kebun Bunga

Jln. Tembusu

Jln. Perdana

Deer
Park

Jln. Lembah Perdana

Jln. Tugu

Jln. Cenderasari

Jln. Perdana

Jln. Persekutuan

Jln. Damansara

Jln. Travers

Sungai Gombak

Jln. Kuching

Jln. Raja Laut

Jln. Medan
Tuanku

Jln. Dang Wangi

Jln. Tuanku Abdul Rahman

Lbg. Tuanku Abdul Rahman

Jln. Masjid India

Jln. Munshi Abdullah

Sungai Banus

Dorai

Jln. A

Jln. Melayu

Bukit Nanas

Leboh Ampang

Jln. Sultan Hishamuddin

Leboh Pasar Besar

Gereja

Jln. Tun H.S. Lee

Jln. Hang Lekiu

Jln. Tun Perak

Jln. Silang

Jln. Hang Kasturi

Jln. Hang Lekir

Jln. Cheng Lock

Jln. Sultan

Jln. Wesley

Jln. Sultan

Jln. Petaling

Jln. Tun
H.S. Lee

Old
China
Cafe

Jln. Kinabalu

Jln. Sulaiman

Jln. KG. Atap

Jln. Maharajalela

9

17

15 AE

16

14

13

11 12

1

3 2

10

6

5

7

8

4

KEY

AE American Express Office

Jln. Mayang

Jln. Ampang

19

0   400 yards

0   400 meters

Jln. Raja Abdullah

Sungai Kelang

Jln. Raja Ali

Jln. Yap Kwan Seng

oraisam

Jln. Ramlee

Jln. P.

Jln. Pinang

Jln. Sultan Ismail

Jln. Perak

Jln. Kia Peng

Ct. Kia Peng

n Ampang

20

Jln. Stonor

Jln. Tengah

AE

Jln. Conlay

18

Jln. Raja Chulan

Bukit Ceylon

Jln. Ct. Bukit Bintang

Lrg. Ceylon

Jln. Nagasari

Jln. Bukit Bintang

Jln. Ceylon

Jln. Sahabat

Jln. Berangan

Jln. Pudu Lama

Jln. Alor

Jln. Bukit Bintang

Jln. Walter

Jln. Jati

Jln. Inai

Jln. Kampong

Jln. Kemining

Jln. Tong Shin

Jln. Utara

Jln. Pudu

Jln. Melati

Jln. Wesley

Jln. Imbi

Jln. Meror

Jln. Selatan

Jln. Barat

Jln. Ckt. Stadium

Jln. Hang Jebat

■ **Pudu Prison**

Jln. Stadium

Ckt. Tambi Dollah

Jln. Davis

Jln. Hang Tuah

Jln. Pudu

Jln. Pelandok

elela

Jln. Berunai

mark **Coliseum Theatre** ⑮, one of the capital's first movie houses. Across from it on Jalan Bunus, lots of little shops and vendors congregate in the shadow of the Mun Loong department store. Around the theater's parking lot, near the traffic signal, are *tandas* (public toilets) and a number of American fast-food outlets. Or stop in at the **Coliseum Cafe,** which serves superb sizzling steaks and British pints.

Continue north on Jalan Tuanku Abdul Rahman to the **Selangor Pewter Showroom** ⑯. At the meeting of Jalan Dang Wangi and Jalan Tuanku Abdul Rahman, the Odeon Theatre occupies one corner, and the huge shopping center of **Kompleks Pertama** ⑰ takes up another. After browsing in the shops, you might want to continue on to other sights by cab at this point. If, however, you have some energy left, you can certainly continue on foot: first turn right onto Jalan Dang Wangi and then turn left onto Jalan Ampang. At the next corner turn right onto Jalan Sultan Ismail. At Jalan Raja Chulan, turn left and then take the second road to your left, Jalan Conlay. Here you'll find the new **Kompleks Budaya Kraf** ⑱, where a wide range of handicrafts from all over Malaysia are on display. From here, you can walk up Jalan Stonor and left onto Jalan Kia Peng, which leads—via Jalan Penang—to **Kuala Lumpur City Centre** ⑲ and the gleaming skyscrapers of the Petronas Twin Towers and the state-of-the-art Suria KLCC shopping complex. A perfect ending for the day is an elevator ride to the top of the **Menara Kuala Lumpur** ⑳ for a view of the city.

TIMING

The walk can be done in about four to six hours, depending on how long you linger along the way. Don't hesitate to talk to locals—they are, by and large, open and friendly.

SIGHTS TO SEE

❶ **Central Market.** This lively bazaar, housed in an art deco building in the heart of KL, was once the city's produce market. Today it's the commercial, cultural, and recreational hub of downtown daily from 10 to 10. You can wander through its many shops and stalls that sell herbs (for cooking or for medicine), kites, batik clothing, jewelry, antiques, rattan baskets, and wood and bamboo crafts. In addition, food vendors offer Malaysian dishes at reasonable prices.

❹ **Chan See Shu Yuen.** Built in 1906, this temple has an impressive roof decorated with figures depicting Chinese mythology. Just off the southern end of Jalan Sultan, the temple is somewhat isolated from the rest of Chinatown.

⑮ **Coliseum Theatre and Cafe.** The landmark Coliseum, one of KL's first movie houses, shows Malaysian and Indonesian films with Chinese subtitles, so it's not really the place to stop for a movie unless you're a linguist. Consider, however, taking a break at the **Coliseum Cafe** (☞ *also* Dining, *below*), a favorite local watering hole that may well serve the best steak in town. ⊠ *98–100 Jln. Tuanku Abdul Rahman,* ☎ *03/292–6270.*

★ ❼ **Galeri Seni Lukis Negara.** This four-story building was the old Majestic Hotel until its conversion into the National Art Gallery in 1984. The permanent collection reflects native artists' visions and concerns. They tend to work in contemporary modes—conceptual pieces, pop images, bold sculptures, humorous graphics, and realistic landscapes. The gallery is a bit funky, with its ceiling fans, linoleum floors, and some dimly lit rooms, but the museum is slated for a complete renovation. The on-site shop sells witty posters, prints, cards, and artsy T-shirts at reasonable prices. ⊠ *1 Jln. Sultan Hishamuddin,* ☎ *03/230–0157.* ⊠ *RM1.* ☉ *Sat.–Thurs. 10–6, Fri. 10–12:15 and 2:15–6.*

Jalan Tuanku Abdul Rahman. Locals still often refer to this street by its old name, Batu Road, as it was once the main road to the Batu Caves. Regardless of what you call it, the street is home to a number of colorful sari shops, bookstores, stationery shops, Indian Muslim restaurants, and stores of an indeterminate nature. By day you can shop and stop for some people-watching and a bowl of steaming noodle soup at one of the open-air coffee shops with marble-top tables and bentwood chairs. A troupe of blind musicians with bongo drums and electric piano often entertains passersby. Note, however, that after midnight the atmosphere changes dramatically as *pondans* (transvestites) take to the street.

Across the road from the theater on Jalan Bunus, lots of little shops and vendors press on in the shadow of the bustling **Mun Loong** department store. Farther along, at Number 223, the **Peiping Lace Shop** sells Chinese linens, lace, jewelry, and ceramics. Neighboring **China Arts**, a branch of Peiping Lace, is full of decorative coromandel screens, carved writing desks, teak and camphor chests, and antique vases.

★ ⑱ **Kompleks Budaya Kraf** The two-story Handicraft Complex, once called the Karyaneka Handicraft Centre, is the ideal place to learn about Malaysia's handicrafts and do some serious souvenir shopping. At the entrance there are several shops; at the back is a museum with exhibits on batik, wood carving, ceramics, silver, pewter, and brass. ⊠ *53 Jln. Conlay.* 🎫 *Free.* ⊙ *Daily 10–10.*

⑰ **Kompleks Pertama.** Pertama (which means "first") is typical of most KL shopping centers: it has clothing, shoe, appliance, and record shops. It also has such recreational facilities as a video-game room, a pool hall, and a nightclub. ⊠ *Jln. Dang Wangi and Jln. Tukanu Abdul Rahman.*

⑲ **Kuala Lumpur City Centre.** On the site of the old racecourse, the massive KLCC development project symbolizes Malaysia's aspirations of attaining developed-nation status by the year 2020. It includes the 88-story **Petronas Twin Towers Complex,** completed in 1996 and currently the world's tallest structure. It's ostentatious, to say the least, but the Malaysians are proud of it. The twin towers are linked by a 175-ft-long skybridge at the 41st and 42nd floors.

The complex also includes the **Suria KLCC,** a shopping and entertainment center that has two department stores, more than 300 specialty shops, two food courts, and a cinema complex. Work on the whole KLCC project will continue for the next 10–12 years; also planned are a *surau* (Islamic prayer hall), a 645-room Mandarin Oriental hotel, and a 50-acre park that will preserve some of the trees from the grounds of the Selangor Turf Club, a private club that once occupied the site.

⑭ **Masjid India.** Outside the modern Indian Muslim mosque, in the center of Little India, street vendors sell local *ubat* (medicine) or *jamu* (cosmetics) with all the theatricality of carnival barkers and snake-oil salesmen. They lure potential customers with elaborate stories and "magic" acts in which audience members participate.

⑬ **Masjid Jamek Bandaraya.** At the confluence of the Klang and Gombak rivers is the city's oldest (and most charming) mosque, its two minarets only slightly taller than the coconut palms on the grounds. It was designed by a British architect and was completed in 1909. A vendor beside the main gate sells tape recordings of those hypnotic prayer chants.

⑥ **Masjid Negara.** The contemporary architecture of the National Mosque features a towering 240-ft minaret spire, a purple roof, and geometric-pattern grillwork. Though not the largest mosque in Asia, it can accommodate 10,000 worshipers. The entrance is on Jalan Lembah Perdana. Signs remind you to dress modestly, to remove your shoes when entering, and to be aware that certain areas are off-limits, especially during prayer times. The mosque complex also houses a library and a mausoleum. ⊠ *Jln. Sultan Hishamuddin.* ⊙ *Sat.–Thurs. 9–6, Fri. 2:45–6.*

㉚ Menara Kuala Lumpur. For a dramatic overview of KL and the surrounding area, take an elevator ride up the 1,380-ft Kuala Lumpur Tower or, simply, KL Tower. In addition to an observation platform you'll find food outlets, a revolving restaurant, and gift and souvenir shops. On the rare clear day, you can even see the Straits of Melaka from here. ⊠ *Jln. Puncak (off Jln. P. Ramlee).* ▨ *RM8.* ⊙ *Daily 10–10.*

⑩ Menara Maybank. On the imposing hill at the corner of Jalan Tun Perak and Jalan Raja Chulan stands the Maybank Building, designed to resemble the handle of a kris (dagger with a wavy blade), the national emblem. At the top of the escalators, you can walk around the soaring (five-story) bank lobby during business hours. The **Numismatic Museum,** which exhibits Malaysian bills and coins from the past, can supply information on the nation's major commodities and adjoins a gallery of contemporary art. ☎ *03/280–8833, ext. 2023.* ▨ *Free.* ⊙ *Mon.– Sat. 10–6.*

⑪ Merdeka Square. Once known as the Padang, this open green square has been the site of everything from rugby and cricket matches to Merdeka (Independence) Day celebrations. With its mania for trying to get into the *Guinness Book of World Records,* the Malaysian government erected the world's tallest flagpole at one end. At the back of the square is the black-and-white, pseudo-Tudor **Royal Selangor Club,** once called the "Spotted Dog," and for years the haunt of British colonials.

⑧ Muzium Negara. The distinctive architecture of the National Museum makes it easily identifiable; the building is modeled after an old-style Malay village house, enlarged to institutional size. Burial totem poles from Sarawak line the path to it. On its facade two large mosaic murals depict important moments in history and elements of Malay culture.

The **Cultural Gallery,** to the left as you enter, emphasizes Malay folk traditions and Chinese culture in Malaysia. A model Nonya (Peranakan or Straits-born Chinese) home exhibits classical Chinese furniture and such exquisite antiques as carved canopy beds and a table-and-chair set with mother-of-pearl inlay. The **Historical Gallery** has models of homes from different regions, traditional costumes, a collection of ceramic pottery, gold and silver items, and other artifacts. Displays trace the stages of British colonization from the late 18th century to the British withdrawal in the mid-20th century. Photos and text outline the Japanese occupation during World War II and Malaysia's move toward independence. The **Natural History Exhibit** upstairs is devoted to indigenous wildlife, with stuffed flying lemurs, birds, insects, and poisonous snakes.

Behind the museum, the **Transportation Shed** has displays of every form of transport used in the country, from a Melaka bullock cart—with its distinctive upturned roof—to the pedal trishaws that are still used in Pinang. Don't miss the Malay-style house, called **Istana Satu** (First Palace). Built on stilts, the simple little wooden structure is open and airy—perfectly suited to the tropics—and has decorative wood carvings. ⊠ *Jln. Damansara,* ☎ *03/238–0255.* ▨ *Free.* ⊙ *Sat.–Thurs. 9– 6, Fri. 9–12:15 and 2:45–6.*

OFF THE
BEATEN PATH   **PUDU PRISON** – The walls of what was once KL's main prison are covered with a beautifully painted tropical landscape, done by inmates. It's the longest mural in the world, according to the *Guinness Book of World Records*. The building, no longer used as a jail, has exhibits of photographs, artifacts, and videos that show everyday prison life. You can even see the old execution chamber—definitely high on the list of macabre attractions. ⊠ *Jln. Imbi and Jln. Hang Tuah.* ☉ *Daily 9–5.* ☞ *RM12.*

⑤ Railway Station. The imposing Moorish structures that make up the city's main railway station and the administrative offices of **Kereta-api Tanah Melayu (KTM)**, the national rail system, have become a common postcard shot of KL. Built in the early 20th century and renovated since, the station was designed by a British architect to reflect the Ottoman and Mogul glory of the 13th and 14th centuries. The KTM building itself blends Gothic and Greek designs and has wide, distinctive verandas.

② See Yeoh. Chinatown's oldest temple was founded by Yap Ah Loy, the first head of KL's Chinese community, in 1885. It's somewhat disappointing inside, however, especially compared with the Chan See Yeun temple nearby.

⑯ Selangor Pewter Showroom. Tin was a major Malaysian export, so it was only natural that the country would develop a pewter industry. The most famous name is Selangor, and this showroom has a full range of the sorts of wares made in Malaysia for more than 100 years. Most designs are simple and of superior quality. A few items, such as a photo frame encrusted with Garfield the Cat, are pure kitsch. In its Heritage Collection, Selangor has replicas of *caping*, fig-leaf-shape "modesty discs" that nude children once wore to cover their genitals; now teenagers wear them on chains as pendants. In the back of the shop you can see a pewter-making demonstration. ⊠ *231 Jln. Tuanku Abdul Rahman.*

③ Sri Mahamariamman. A temple was built on this site by the Tamil community from southeast India back in 1873. The exuberantly colored figures that adorn the five-tier *gopuram* (gateway) were created only in 1960 and refurbished in mid-1998. During the annual Thaipusam festival, the chariot from this temple is taken through the streets on its way to Batu Caves.

NEED A
BREAK?   The **Old China Cafe** (☞ *also* Dining, *below*), a charming antiques-filled café-restaurant, is a great place to stop for a snack after visiting Sri Mahamariamman. Try the *pie-tee* (crunchy savories) or *bubur cha-cha*, an intriguing dessert of sweetened coconut milk with diced yam and sweet potato. Even if you're not hungry, it's worth popping in to have a drink and soak up the atmosphere. ⊠ *11 Jln. Balai Polis,* ☎ *03/232-5915.* ☉ *11–11.*

⑫ Sultan Abdul Samad Building. This massive structure—erected in 1897 and bedecked with Moorish arches, copper domes, and a clock tower—is considered the center of the old city. (Preservationists fought to have it restored in the early 1980s.) Originally occupied by the state secretariat (Dewan Bandaraya), it now houses the judicial department and high courts, along with a handicrafts museum and salesroom called **Infokraf Malaysia.** ⊠ *Jln. Sultan Hishamuddin,* ☎ *03/293–4929 (Infokraf).* ☞ *Free.* ☉ *Sat.–Thurs. 9–6.*

⑨ Taman Tasik Perdana. Behind the National Museum are the scenic Lake Gardens, more than 200 acres where you can enjoy a leisurely stroll and join city dwellers relaxing, picnicking, and boating on the lake.

Also in the park are the **National Monument,** a bronze sculpture dedicated to the nation's war dead, and an **orchid garden** with more than 800 species (the garden is open daily from 10 to 6; admission is free).

Around Kuala Lumpur

In the past couple of decades, KL has grown so much that sights once considered part of the countryside are now thought of as part of the suburbs. Satellite towns such as Petaling Jaya and the congested Klang Valley are best avoided. However, two outlying sights worth seeing are the Batu Caves and the Zoo Negara (National Zoo); you can readily reach both by cab or bus. To get a glimpse of KL's outskirts as well as several in-town attractions, consider taking the tourist board's "Country Tour" (☞ Tour Operators *in* Kuala Lumpur Essentials, *below*).

SIGHTS TO SEE

Batu Caves. About 11 km (7 mi) north of KL, these vast, beautiful caverns are in a limestone outcrop that was discovered in 1878 by American naturalist William Hornaday, who was searching for new species of moth larvae. To reach the caves you must climb a flight of 272 steps; a wide path with an iron railing leads you through the recesses, and colored lights illuminate stalagmites and other formations. The caves are the site of the spectacular but gory Thaipusam festival (held around February). The main cave houses a Hindu temple dedicated to Lord Subramaniam; behind the immense Dark Cave (it's 1,200 ft long and 400 ft at its highest point) is a third cave—the Art Gallery—with elaborate sculptures of figures from Hindu mythology. The caves are open daily 7 AM–9 PM. To get to them, take a taxi (about RM30–RM40 round-trip) or Bus 68 or 70 from Lebuh Ampang in Chinatown.

Zoo Negara. The National Zoo is 14 km (9 mi) north of KL center, and you can reach it by taxi (about RM20 round-trip) or by Bus 17 or 174 from Lebuh Ampang in Chinatown. The zoo sprawls over a large area of gardens; a shuttle bus (RM1) takes you around and stops at major attractions. Be sure to check out the indigenous species, which include tigers, bearded pigs, rhinoceros, civet cats, and orangutans. Vividly colored coral-reef fish do much to dispel the gloom of the aquarium that's at the back of the zoo. ⊠ *Jln. Ulu Klang,* ☎ *03/406–9887.* ⊠ *RM6.* ☉ *Daily 9–6.*

Dining

Though KL isn't a coastal city, seafood is the rage among locals, who wash it down with ice-cold beer (outdoor restaurants that serve both have sprung up all over). Indian, Chinese, Japanese, Thai, and Nonya cuisine are also all available, as is a wide range of Western cuisine. The lack of purely Malay restaurants seems somewhat surprising, but as the locals know, the best Malay food—which still has that home-cooked flavor—is available at street stalls and at food complexes in shopping centers. In addition, major hotels serve Malay buffets and à la carte dishes. Food festivals that feature regional specialties from different Malaysian states are also common.

There are many establishments in the Golden Triangle, in the area around Jalan Bukit Bintang and Jalan Sultan Ismail, and in Chinatown and central KL. Still, don't hesitate to try places that are farther afield, perhaps in the trendy suburb of Bangsar (about 3 km/2 mi south of the city center and about RM3–RM4 by taxi) or to the north of KL. Eating out almost everywhere is informal. Jackets and ties are seldom worn except at the swankiest hotels. Expensive restaurants add a 10% service charge—in which case you don't need to tip. In addition, some expensive restaurants are classified as "tourist class" and charge 5%

sales tax. Lunch is normally served from 11:30 AM to 2:30 PM, dinner from 6:30 to 11 (last orders for food are taken between 9:30 PM and 10 PM). Seafood restaurants are usually open from 5 PM to 3 AM.

Golden Triangle

CHINESE

$$$$
★ ✕ **Lai Ching Yuen.** The extensive menu at this widely acclaimed Cantonese restaurant in the Regent Hotel (☞ Lodging, *below*) features shark's fin, bird's nest, abalone, pigeon, chicken, duck, and barbecue specialties. The dining room is designed as two Chinese pavilions; illuminated glass etchings, modern Chinese art, silver panels, a Burmese teak ceiling, and silver-and-jade table settings create an elegant ambience. Traditional music on Malay instruments accompanies dinner. ⊠ *126 Jln. Bukit Bintang,* ☎ *03/241–8000. Reservations essential. Jacket and tie. AE, DC, MC, V.*

$$ ✕ **Teochew Restaurant.** Soothingly decorated in cream and brown, this spacious eatery has well-spaced tables and screened-off private dining rooms. It's popular on weekends and holidays, when 100 varieties of dim sum are served for breakfast and lunch. Typical Teochew Chinese dishes include noodles made entirely of fish; sea cucumber stuffed with scallops, crab, mushrooms, and water chestnuts; and sizzling prawns. Try also the *oh wee,* a sweet yam dessert with ginkgo nuts that's served with tiny cups of bitter Teochew tea. ⊠ *270–272 Jln. Changkat Thamby Dollah, off Jln. Pudu,* ☎ *03/241–5851. Reservations essential. AE, DC, MC, V.*

CONTEMPORARY

$$$$ ✕ **Regent Grill.** Choosing between Shangri-La's Lafite and the Regent Hotel's (☞ Lodging, *below*) Regent Grill is a gourmet's dilemma. The Grill aims to impress, and it is a little more expensive than Lafite (☞ *below*). Wood paneling, leather upholstery, and stark earth-tone walls make the white German Schoenwald china and Schoff Zweisel crystal stand out. The menu varies, but frequent items are panfried goose liver and honey-braised endive, or dill-marinated salmon rolls in Turkish dough. As might be expected from the name, charcoal-grilled prawns, salmon, and beef are always featured. A set menu (RM75) offers appetizers and desserts from a buffet and your choice of a red or white meat, fish, or pasta main course. The wine list is comprehensive— there are some 300 selections, and many are surprisingly affordable. ⊠ *160 Jln. Bukit Bintang,* ☎ *03/241–8000. Reservations essential. Jacket and tie. AE, DC, MC, V. No lunch.*

$$$–$$$$ ✕ **FIC's.** The food at this at this restaurant in the Kuala Lumpur Hilton (☞ Lodging, *below*) is excellent, and the decor is striking. A spiral staircase winds down into two spacious dining areas that are separated by a man-made stream. Huge windows look out onto an enclosed garden, and granite slabs on the floor and walls are inset with metal letters that spell out recipes or wine descriptions. The European cuisine, which often features Mediterranean or Asian accents, avoids heavy sauces and uses plenty of fresh herbs. You can order from the à la carte menu or the set lunch (RM49) and dinner (RM72) menus. Dishes vary from month to month, but one constant is lamb shank braised in wine and served with potato puree, shiitake mushrooms, deep-fried onions, and fresh herbs. The crème brûlée is to die for. ⊠ *Jln. Sultan Ismail,* ☎ *03/ 242–2122. Reservations essential. AE, DC, MC, V.*

ECLECTIC

$$$ ✕ **Citrus Cafe.** Situated beside its sister restaurant, Scalini (☞ *below*), Citrus wears several hats at once. You'll find a counter where you can enjoy fine Japanese sushi and sashimi; a glass-enclosed restaurant; and a large, partially open section with a dining area, a long bar, and a dance

Kuala Lumpur Dining and Lodging

Dining ●

Annalakshmi, **10**
Bangsar Seafood, **11**
Chikuyo-tei, **23**
Cili Padi Thai
Restaurant, **2**
Citrus Cafe, **12**
Coliseum Cafe, **4**
FIC's, **21**
Happy Hour Seafood
Restaurant, **33**
Kedai Makanan Yut
Kee, **3**
Lafite Restaurant, **14**

Lai Ching Yuen, **25**
Mahsuri, **5**
Old China Cafe, **9**
Rasa Utara, **28**
Regent Grill, **26**
Restoran Makanan
Laut Selayang, **1**
Scalini, **13**
Seri Melayu, **24**
The Taj, **30**
Terrace Garden, **18**
Teochew
Restaurant, **34**

Lodging ○

Carcosa Seri
Negara, **6**
Cardogan Hotel, **29**
Concorde Hotel, **16**
Equatorial Hotel, **19**
Federal Hotel, **31**
Holiday Inn on the
Park, **17**
Hotel Malaya, **7**
Kuala Lumpur
Hilton, **22**
Lodge Hotel, **20**

Park Avenue
Hotel, **32**
Regent Hotel, **27**
Shangri-La Hotel, **15**
Swiss Inn, **8**

KEY

AE American Express Office

Jln. Mayang

Jln. Ampang

Jln. Raja Abdullah

Sungai Kelang

Jln. Raja Ali

Jln. Yap Kwan Seng

raisam

12 13

16

Jln. Sultan Ismail

Ramlee

Jln. P.

Jln. Pinang

17

Jln. Perak

Ampang

14 15

Jln. Tengah

20

19

Jln. Kia Peng

Ck. Kia Peng

Jln. Stonor

AE

Jln. Raja Chulan

Bukit Ceylon

Jln. Cr. Bukit Bintang

Lrg. Ceylon

Jln. Nagasari

21 22

Jln. Conlay

23 24

25 26 27

Jln. Ceylon

Jln. Berangan

Jln. Bukit Bintang

Jln. Sahabat

Jln. Pudu Lama

Jln. Tong Shin

Jln. Alor

Jln. Bukit Bintang

28

Jln. Walter

Jln. Jati

Jln. Kampong

Jln. Inai

Kemining

Jln. Pudu

29

Jln. Utara

Jln. Melati

Jln. Wesley

Jln. Hang Jebat

30 31

32

Jln. Imbi

33

Jln. Melar

Jln. Barat

Jln. Selatan

Ckt Stadium

Jln. Stadium

Jln. Hang Tuah

Jln. Pudu

Ckt. Tambi Dollah

34

Jln. Davis

10 11

ela

Jln. Berunai

Jln. Pelandok

18

N

0   400 yards

0   400 meters

floor (there's music and a DJ). The cuisine is East–West fusion with dishes such as seared pepper tuna with wasabi-and-soy dressing or tempura fish-and-chips with wasabi mayonnaise. The service is very friendly. ⊠ *19 Jln. Sultan Ismail,* ☎ *03/248–5188. AE, MC, V.*

FRENCH

$$$$ ✕ **Lafite Restaurant.** The Shangri-La Hotel's (☞ Lodging, *below*) Lafite Restaurant—named for France's finest vineyard—serves classic French and innovative cuisine in a romantically lit setting with fine crystal, oil paintings, and pastel wallpaper and upholstery. An impressive wine cellar is the dining room's centerpiece. In addition to the à la carte menu, which is modified periodically, you can partake of a buffet lunch (weekdays only) or dinner. The buffet selections are extensive: at least six main courses and a daily roast are offered, as are many salads and desserts. ⊠ *11 Jln. Sultan Ismail,* ☎ *03/232–2388. Reservations essential. Jacket and tie. AE, DC, MC, V.*

INDIAN

$$ ✕ **The Taj.** Northern Indian cuisine, with its mildly spiced creamy curries and tandoor-baked dishes, is the specialty at this restaurant in the Federal Hotel (☞ Lodging, *below*). Although there's an extensive menu, it's hard to bypass the tandoori chicken, unless you opt for the sinfully rich butter chicken: tandoori chicken smothered in a buttery tomato sauce. The *naan* (bread) is also delicious; consider washing it down with a glass of *lassi* (salted yogurt drink). ⊠ *35 Jln. Bukit Bintang,* ☎ *03/248–9166. AE, MC, V.*

ITALIAN

$$$–$$$$ ✕ **Scalini.** The ever-popular Scalini has three dining areas—four if you count the garden, which is sometimes opened to accommodate patrons. The mood is minimalist and modern; the menu mainly Italian. You'll find pizza (baked in a wood-fired oven), beef carpaccio, clam and mussel soup, and squid-ink pasta with prawns as well as broad beans and shiitake mushrooms or honey-glazed duck breast. The wine list has varieties from around the world; if you don't want a bottle, you can order b. the glass (around RM16). ⊠ *19 Jln. Sultan Ismail,* ☎ *03/245–3211. AE, MC, V.*

JAPANESE

$$$ ✕ **Chikuyo-tei.** Despite its rather dismal entrance (into the basement of an office complex) the oldest Japanese restaurant in the city has a warmly lit, woody interior with tatami rooms and other sectioned-off dining areas. It serves excellent *unagi kabayaki* (grilled eel) and *nigirisushi,* a variety of sushi made with tuna, herring, salmon eggs, and squid. The *teppanyaki*—meat, seafood, and vegetables sliced, seasoned, and cooked on a hot plate in front of you—is popular. ⊠ *See Hoy Chan Plaza, Jln. Raja Chulan,* ☎ *03/230–0729. Reservations essential. AE, DC, MC, V. No lunch Sun.*

MALAYSIAN

$$ ✕ **Seri Melayu.** Here you can opt to eat Malay style—seated on a *tikar* (woven mat)—while taking in a show of Malaysian music and dance. There's an à la carte menu as well as a buffet with an excellent selection of spicy and mild curries, vegetable dishes, and *kuih* (cake). Dishes not to be missed include the rich, meaty rendang; *ulam* (vitamin-rich herbs that you dip into a spicy sauce); and, for dessert, *pengat* durian, made with that oh-so controversial fruit. ⊠ *1 Jln. Conlay,* ☎ *03/245– 1833. AE, D, MC, V.*

$ ✕ **Rasa Utara.** The decor here may be somewhat impersonal, but the Malay dishes—including many Kedah specialties from the north—are outstanding. There are reasonably priced set menus (written in English and Malay) for two, four, or six or more diners, as well as à la carte choices. The meal for two comes with rice, chicken curry, mixed vegetables, an omelet, fruit, and a soft drink for only RM15 per person. The *roti jala* (pancakes with chicken or beef curry) are lovely. Consider refreshing yourself with a glass of coconut water. ✉ *B5003, Basement 1, Bukit Bintang Plaza, Jln. Bukit Bintang,* ☎ *03/241–9246. AE, DC, MC, V.*

SEAFOOD

$$ ✗ **Happy Hour Seafood Restaurant.** Strings of lights decorate the front of this restaurant, and tables spill out onto the walkway (for a little more atmosphere, request a seat outdoors rather than in the brightly lit, functional interior). Steamed, baked, or fried crabs filled with rich red roe are specialties. Other good choices are the prawns steamed with wine and ginger or the deep-fried garoupa. ✉ *53 Jln. Barat (off Jln. Imbi),* ☎ *03/248–5107. AE, DC, V. No lunch.*

Chinatown and Central Kuala Lumpur

CHINESE

$ ✗ **Kedai Makanan Yut Kee.** This 65-year-old family-run Hainanese
★ restaurant is one of the few that hasn't been torn down in the name of progress. Big and airy but rather noisy from the city traffic, the casual dining area is filled with marble-top tables and regular customers who insist on their favorite seats. Recommended is *roti babi,* a sandwich with pork filling dipped in egg and deep-fried (douse it liberally with Worcestershire sauce). The black coffee is the best around, and the Swiss roll filled with kaya makes a fine dessert. As befits the coffee-shop feel, meals are served starting at 7 AM; service stops at 6 PM. ✉ *35 Jln. Dang Wangi,* ☎ *03/298–8108. Reservations not accepted. No credit cards. Closed Mon.*

CONTINENTAL

$$ ✗ **Coliseum Cafe.** The aroma of sizzling steak—the house specialty—fills the air in this café. It was established before World War II, and a nostalgic, slightly seedy colonial ambience prevails: the waiters' starched white jackets are a bit frayed, and the walls are cracked and brown with age. Steaks are served with brussels sprouts, steak fries, and salad. Another favorite here is crab baked with cheese. The Sunday lunch, or *tiffin,* of light curry dishes, is not to be missed. ✉ *98–100 Jln. Tuanku Abdul Rahman,* ☎ *03/292–6270. Reservations not accepted. No credit cards.*

NONYA

$$ ✗ **Old China Cafe.** This charming café-restaurant, tucked away at the bottom end of Chinatown, is an absolute treasure. Set in a Chinese guildhall that was built at the turn of the century, it has large mirrors, calligraphy, photographs, and other memorabilia from that period. All the tables, chairs, porcelain pieces, and other fixtures are antiques. The Pinang-born chef offers a delectable range of Nonya dishes, including curry *kapitan* (chicken in spiced coconut milk) and *udang asam pedas* (prawns in sour hot gravy). ✉ *11 Jln Balai Polis,* ☎ *03/232–5915. AE, MC, V.*

Farther Afield

CHINESE

$$ ✗ **Restoran Makanan Laut Selayang.** Food, not decor, is this restau-
★ rant's raison d'être. You can eat outside, under a zinc roof, or in a simple air-conditioned room that seats 30 at three large, round tables. Adventurous diners can try steamed river frogs and soups of squirrel, pigeon, or turtle. Also good are the deep-fried soft-shell crabs and the prawns fried with butter, milk, and chilies. The house specialty is *fatt*

thieu cheong ("monk jumps over a wall"), a soup of shark's fin, sea cucumber, dried scallops, mushrooms, and herbs, which must be ordered in advance. If you aren't in the mood for seafood, try the black chicken—a small bird with black skin and white feathers—steamed in a coconut. ⊠ *Lot 11, 7½ mi, Selayang,* ☎ *03/627–7015. AE, V.*

CONTINENTAL

$$$ ✕ Terrace Garden. Soothing shades of green and gray, white walls, black-framed windows, and pale green trellis dividers blend well in this restaurant converted from a house. Dolly Lim runs the place sweetly and efficiently, the service is very friendly, and there's live music every night but Sunday. The chef recommends either the char-broiled spareribs or the sea bass with martini sauce and black pepper. ⊠ *308 Jln. Ampang,* ☎ *03/457–2378. Weekend reservations essential. AE, DC, MC, V.*

ECLECTIC

$$$$ ✕ Mahsuri. In the dining room of the Carcosa Seri Negara hotel (☞ Lodging, *below*)—which is made up of a pair of colonial mansions—a new French chef offers excellent French country cooking and fine Malaysian cuisine. The afternoon tea here is famous (partake of it, and you won't want dinner); the curry tiffin is a must if you happen to be in KL on a Sunday. You can enjoy this sumptuous spread of Anglo-Indian and Malay dishes on a wide veranda or in an air-conditioned restaurant. To work off the excess weight you may have gained after your thoroughly British Pimms cocktail and a meal, you can indulge in a game of croquet on the lawn. ⊠ *Taman Tasik Perdana,* ☎ *03/282–1888. Reservations essential. AE, DC, MC, V.*

INDIAN

$$ ✕ Annalakshmi. This Bangsar restaurant, decorated with Indian artifacts and antiques, is the most elegant place in KL in which to sample Indian vegetarian food. It's staffed by volunteers of the Temple of Fine Arts (a group devoted to the propagation of Indian arts and culture), and the food is so beautifully spiced that it's a real treat even for confirmed carnivores. Although there's an à la carte menu, you'll be able to sample a much wider range of dishes at the buffet full of savories, spiced vegetable dishes, curries, side dishes, breads, and desserts. ⊠ *46 Jln. Maarof,* ☎ *03/282–3799. AE, D, MC, V.*

SEAFOOD

$$$ ✕ Bangsar Seafood. In the trendy suburb of Bangsar, which has some of KL's hottest restaurants and pubs, this restaurant offers 30 tables in the open air and another 30 inside. Feast on market-fresh seafood (some of it still swimming in tanks) cooked just about any way you want. ⊠ *Jln. Telawi Empat,* ☎ *03/284–7297. AE, MC, V.*

THAI

$$ ✕ Cili Padi Thai Restaurant. Named after the Malay word for the fiery hot little bird's-eye chili, this restaurant offers Thai cuisine at moderate prices. There's a wide range of typical Bangkok food with perennial favorites such as spicy lemon prawn soup, crispy catfish on green mango salad, and steamed fish mousse in banana leaf. The restaurant is spacious and unassuming; it's the sort of place where families come. Still, couples are made to feel welcome with set menus for two people that cost RM40 to RM47. ⊠ *Shop 31, Second level, The Mall, 100 Jln. Putra,* ☎ *03/442–9543, AE, D, MC, V.*

Lodging

Many hotels are north of the train station, with some of the best near the intersection of Jalan Sultan Ismail and Jalan Bukit Bintang, the heart of the commercial district and one corner of the Golden Triangle. The range is broad. Establishments at the top level can compete with the world's best in terms of luxury and service; at the lower level, you can find nearly unbeatable prices. There are particularly good deals in hotels on Jalan Tuanku Abdul Rahman and in Little India.

$$$$ ⊞ **Carcosa Seri Negara.** These two colonial mansions in the Lake Gardens, just 10 minutes from downtown, once housed the governor of the Straits Settlement. There are seven suites in Carcosa, the main house, and six more an eight-minute walk away in Seri Negara, the guest house. Both properties were completely renovated in 1997–98 and are once more impeccable. A stay here isn't ideal for families or scene makers; come if you want luxurious Victorian accommodation—including your own butler—with all the modern conveniences. The Mahsuri dining room (☞ *also* Dining, *above*) is one of KL's best. If you don't stay or dine here, at least stop by for the lavish afternoon tea or the Sunday curry tiffin. ⊠ *Taman Tasik Perdana, 50480,* ☎ *03/ 282–1888; 212/223–2848 or 800/447–7462 in the U.S.;* ℻ *03/282– 7888. 13 suites. Restaurant, pool, 2 tennis courts, massage, sauna, exercise room, business services, meeting rooms. AE, DC, MC, V.*

$$$$ ⊞ **Kuala Lumpur Hilton.** Though dated, KL's first high-rise luxury hotel still maintains its world-class standards for service and quality. The mood of crisp elegance is set in the lobby, with fresh flowers and glowing chandeliers. The pastel-decorated rooms have bay windows, sitting areas, and desks. Rooms with the best views look down onto the hotel's pool and the burgeoning KLCC and the Petronas Twin Towers. FIC's (☞ also Dining, *above*) restaurant serves outstanding contemporary Western fare. ⊠ *Jln. Sultan Ismail, 50250,* ☎ *03/248–2322 or 800/HILTONS in the U.S.,* ℻ *03/244–2157. 581 rooms. 4 restaurants, bar, coffee shop, pool, 2 tennis courts, health club, squash, business services, meeting rooms. AE, DC, MC, V.*

$$$$ ⊞ **Regent Hotel.** This hotel, across from the Star Hill Shopping Cen-
★ tre, opened in 1990 and has maintained its crisp newness. Spacious guest rooms have plenty of light, a decor of natural woods and pastel fabrics, and opulent marble bathrooms with huge tubs and separate glass-enclosed showers. The large atrium lobby is tiered, with each level separated by flower boxes. The fifth-floor pool overlooks the city and a crowded public pool across the avenue. The Regent Grill and the Lai Ching Yuen (☞ Dining, *above*) restaurants vie for top culinary honors with the Hilton's and Shangri-La's European and Chinese restaurants. ⊠ *126 Jln. Bukit Bintang, 55100,* ☎ *03/241–8000 or 800/ 545–4000 in the U.S.,* ℻ *03/242–1441. 454 rooms. 3 restaurants, coffee shop, tea shop, pool, sauna, health club, squash, business services, meeting rooms. AE, DC, MC, V.*

$$$$ ⊞ **Shangri-La Hotel.** Since opening in 1985, this central hotel has attracted a glamorous set that parades through its spacious, opulent lobby. Businesspeople favor it for its business services, meeting rooms, and proximity to the city's financial institutions. All guest rooms are large and furnished with dark wood furniture to give them a traditional feel. The higher floors are quieter, and guests paying a premium to stay on the Horizon Floor receive more personalized service. In addition to the gourmet Japanese, French, and Chinese dining rooms, there's a poolside café for daytime relaxation and a pub for congenial evening socializing. The basement Gourmet Corner offers delicatessen treats that are ideal for lunch or afternoon tea. ⊠ *11 Jln. Sultan Ismail, 50250,* ☎ *03/232–2388 or 800/44–UTELL in the U.S.,* ℻ *03/230–1502. 722 rooms. 4 restaurants, pub, pool, 2 tennis courts, health club, squash, dance club, business services, meeting rooms. AE, DC, MC, V.*

$$$ ⊞ **Equatorial Hotel.** This 16-story hotel near the Hilton doesn't have a warm or appealing layout, but it serves well the businessperson on

a budget. Deluxe rooms are spacious and equipped with such amenities as hair dryers and phones in the bathrooms. Rooms in the rear are quieter. The basement café serves a "hawker" buffet of authentic local dishes, and the reasonably priced lunches at the Kampachi Japanese restaurant have become deservedly well known. ⊠ *Jln. Sultan Ismail, 50250,* ☎ *03/261−7777 or 800/44−UTELL in the U.S.,* ℻ *03/261−9020. 300 rooms. 4 restaurants, bar, pool, business services, meeting rooms. AE, DC, MC, V.*

$$$ 🏨 **Federal Hotel.** In the heart of the shopping district, this old-style hotel is distinguished by a revolving restaurant on its roof and an 18-lane bowling alley downstairs. The front of the hotel, with its street-level coffee shop, is decidedly urban, but the landscaped pool area has a tropical atmosphere. The guest rooms have large windows and the usual amenities. ⊠ *35 Jln. Bukit Bintang, 55100,* ☎ *03/248−9166 or 800/44−UTELL in the U.S.,* ℻ *03/248−2877. 450 rooms. Restaurant, coffee shop, pool, dance club, meeting rooms. AE, DC, MC, V.*

$$$ 🏨 **Holiday Inn on the Park.** Just off the main drag, this 14-story hotel is surrounded by trees and is the smarter of the city's two Holiday Inns. Many guest rooms are decorated in ghastly corporate green and white, but they do have complimentary extras such as in-room movies and coffee- and tea-making facilities. The continuous passage of tour groups has taken its toll on the furnishings, however. ⊠ *Jln. Penang, 50732,* ☎ *03/248−1066 or 800/HOLIDAY in the U.S.,* ℻ *03/248−1930. 200 rooms. 4 restaurants, pool, sauna, tennis court, exercise room. AE, DC, MC, V.*

$$$ 🏨 **Park Avenue Hotel.** Formerly the Prince, this high-rise is near the major shopping district. Its rooms were renovated when the hotel changed hands in 1989. An 18th-floor restaurant serves Western fare. ⊠ *Jln. Imbi, 55100,* ☎ *03/242−8333,* ℻ *03/242−6623. 300 rooms. 2 restaurants, coffee shop, pool, dance club, business services. AE, MC, V.*

$$−$$$ 🏨 **Concorde Hotel.** This large, centrally located property has been completely—if somewhat impersonally—refurbished. But the rooms are bright and fresh, and the price is right. Pay more for the concierge floor if you want more personalized service, including complimentary breakfast. The large lobby is often filled with tour groups. ⊠ *2 Jln. Sultan Ismail, 50250,* ☎ *03/244−2200,* ℻ *03/244−1628. 600 rooms. 3 restaurants, coffee shop, pool, health club, 3 concierge floors. AE, DC, MC, V.*

$$ 🏨 **Cardogan Hotel.** This is mainly a business hotel with few frills, but the clean, smart rooms—most of which have king-size beds—have air-conditioning, TVs, and minibars. The staff is cheerful, and the coffee shop is good for a quick meal. Best of all is the Golden Triangle location, close to many restaurants and hawker stands. ⊠ *64 Jln. Bukit Bintang, 55100,* ☎ *03/244−4856,* ℻ *03/244−4865. 61 rooms. Coffee shop, minibars, exercise room, business services. MC, V.*

$$ 🏨 **Hotel Malaya.** Right in the heart of Chinatown, this 10-story hotel has a bright modern lobby with marble floors and a cheerful restaurant that serves local and Western cuisine. All rooms are spotless and have minibars, international-direct-dial (IDD) telephones, TVs, and tea- and coffee-making facilities. Standard rooms are small and lack windows; it's better to choose a superior or deluxe room. ⊠ *Jln. Hang Lekir, 50000,* ☎ *03/232−7722,* ℻ *03/230−0980. 238 rooms. Restaurant, bar, minibars, meeting rooms, free parking. AE, DC, MC, V*

$−$$ 🏨 **Swiss Inn.** This hotel fills two buildings that are between Jalan Sultan and Jalan Petaling, in the heart of Chinatown. The main entrance is on Jalan Sultan, but the terrace restaurant—a great place to watch the world go by—is right on Jalan Petaling. The pleasantly furnished rooms have a faintly Old World feeling, with dark wooden dressing tables and wardrobes. To be sure that your quarters will have a window, request a superior or deluxe room. ✉ *62 Jln. Sultan, 50000,* ☎ *03/232–3333,* ⟨FAX⟩ *03/201–6699. 110 rooms. Restaurant, bar, café. AE, DC, MC, V.*

$ ⌨ **Lodge Hotel.** Across from the Hilton in the Golden Triangle, the Lodge offers basic air-conditioned accommodations. Everything is a little shabby—carpets have stains and bathrooms need some plaster repair—but the rooms are clean, and the service is friendly. The pool is tiny, but the coffee shop stays open, albeit sleepily, 24 hours a day. ✉ *Jln. Sultan Ismail, 50250,* ☎ *03/242–0122,* ⟨FAX⟩ *03/241–6819. 50 rooms. 2 restaurants, bar, coffee shop, pool. AE, DC, V.*

Nightlife and the Arts

The free monthly *Malaysia Now* guide is available at hotels and MTPB offices (☞ Contacts and Resources *in* Kuala Lumpur Essentials, *below*). The "Time Out" pages in Thursday's *Sun* include an excellent calendar of all that's going on in town as well as restaurant reviews. The "Metro Diary" column of the daily *Star* also lists such happenings.

Most government-sponsored events are of the folk rather than the fine-arts variety. Free, traditional cultural programs are regularly presented on Friday evening from 8 to 9 on Level 2 of the **Putra World Trade Center** (✉ Jln. Tun Ismail). The **Central Market**'s outdoor stage (☎ 03/274–6542) is the site of free performances Saturday and Sunday at 7:45 (with the occasional weeknight show as well). Offerings include fashion shows and jazz concerts. The Central Market puts a schedule of events in its monthly leaflet, which is distributed at hotels and MTPB offices.

Dance Clubs
Pubs close at around 11 PM, which is about when the action at the discos cranks up (it continues until 1 AM or 2 AM on Saturday and public holidays). Sometimes you'll find live bands as well as DJs, and many establishments have restaurants. Be prepared for cover charges at some places and a drink minimum at others.

Baze-2 (✉ Lower ground floor, Plaza Ampang, ☎ 03/264–3404) is the place for soul, reggae, and dance music. The **Boom Boom Room** (✉ 11 Lebuh Ampang, ☎ 03/232–6906) has an outrageously funny and thoroughly professional drag show every night, as well as pulsating music. Popular and easy to find is the **Shark Club** (✉ Jln. Sultan Ismail, ☎ 03/241–7878), where you can enjoy live music or shake your thing in the disco; outside is a casual restaurant where you can refuel. **The Jump** (✉ 241 Jln. Tun Razak, ☎ 03/245–0046) is currently regarded as the best dance club in town. On Wednesday evening, ladies are admitted free and given a free drink.

Hotel Lounges
At the lounges and clubs of the major hotels, the atmosphere is international and the tabs are pricey. Most have entertainment every night but Sunday. The **Aviary Lounge** (✉ Kuala Lumpur Hilton, Jln. Sultan Ismail, ☎ 03/242–2222) becomes darkly romantic when its jazz combo plays Monday through Saturday. A live combo often plays at the **Blue Moon Lounge** (✉ Equatorial Hotel, Jln. Sultan Ismail, ☎ 03/261–7777); sometimes P. Ramlee—Malaysia's favorite singer of the '50s and '60s—performs golden-oldies. The **Casablanca Club** at the (✉ Holiday Inn City Centre, Jln. Raja Laut, ☎ 03/293–9233) has pop singers. You'll find a piano bar and a singer in the **Lobby Lounge** (✉ Pan Pacific Hotel, Jln. Putra, ☎ 03/442–5555). For nostalgic tunes, check out the **Sky Room Supper Club** (✉ Federal Hotel, 35 Jln. Bukit Bintang, ☎ 03/248–9166).

Pubs and Bars

Once upon a time, pubs were modeled after their British counterparts. Nowadays you'll find American-style bars with country-western, blues, jazz, or pop bands; Irish pubs; karaoke bars; and wine bars and other cosmopolitan places. Bangsar, just south of the city center, is the hottest area for pubs and bars, which come and go with amazing speed. It's best to just take a cab here and cruise between Jalan Telawi and Jalan Maarof to see where it's all happening.

Expats flock to **Branigans** (⊠ 1 Lorong Perak, off Jln. P. Ramlee), where there's a bi-level bar and dance area. **Coliseum Bar** (⊠ 98 Jln. Tuanku Abdul Rahman), in the famous old Coliseum Hotel, is totally unpretentious; it's easy to chat with locals over a beer here. The **Hard Rock Cafe** (⊠ Wisma Concorde, 2 Jln. Sultan Ismail, ☎ 03/244–4062) is adjacent to the Concorde Hotel; by 10 PM a line forms outside. Lively **Modesto's** (⊠ 10 Lorong Perak, off Jln. P. Ramlee, ☎ 03/248–9924)— which is jam-packed on weekends—has darts, pool, and other amusements. The **Pub** (⊠ Shangri-La Hotel, 11 Jln. Sultan Ismail, ☎ 03/232–2388) has a cozy wood-paneled ambience in which to relax, have a pint and a snack, and play backgammon. At **Riverbank** (☎ 03/274–6651), a small spot in a corner of Central Market, you can sit on the terrace above the river while a DJ inside plays music. Why not watch your stocks go up as your drink slips down at **Wall Street** (⊠ Ground floor, Menara TA 1, 22 Jln. P. Ramlee, ☎ 03/466–6666)?

Outdoor Activities and Sports

Beaches

Although the Mines Resort, built around what was once the world's biggest and deepest tin mine just south of KL, claims to have a beach (some sand dumped at the edge of the man-made lake), the beach nearest KL is really at Port Dickson, about 1½ hours away. Intercity buses from Pudu Raya station take you to the Port Dickson terminal; from there local buses will drop you off anywhere you want along the coast road. Alternatively, you can charter a taxi for around RM150 round-trip. The beach stretches for 16 km (10 mi) from Port Dickson (a good place to begin a walk is the fifth milestone from town) to Cape Rachado, with its 16th-century Portuguese lighthouse. On the coast road, stalls sell the fruits of the season. Be aware that the sea isn't suitable for swimming; the water is shallow, hot, and often polluted.

Golf

Hotels can make arrangements for you to use local courses, including the **Royal Selangor Golf Club** (☎ 03/984–8433), whose two 18-hole championship courses have an outstanding reputation. Greens fees range from RM120 to RM200; the caddy fee is RM20.

Horse Racing

Malaysians have a passion for horse racing, and a regional circuit includes race days in KL, Pinang, Ipoh, and Singapore. Races are held on weekends year-round. Off-course betting is permitted at all the courses, regardless of where the actual race is being run; punters get to watch the action on huge TV screens. For information call the relevant **Turf Club** (☎ 03/985–3888 in Sungei Besi, near KL, 04/229–9284 in Pinang, or 05/254–8084 in Ipoh).

Shopping

Malaysia's shopping scene has been transformed in the last five years. There's a wider range of better-quality goods than ever before. Prices have dropped considerably (many items are duty free), and—since the recession first hit in 1997—the sales have been almost endless. Watches and electronics are now cheaper in KL than in Singapore. Prescription eyeglasses (ready in a day or two) and high-fashion items are also surprisingly inexpensive, and you can pick up locally made jeans and shirts for much less than in North America and Europe. Add to this to the depreciation of the ringgit, and you have the ideal conditions for amazing bargains. If you can't find a particular product or service, call **Infoline** (☎ 03/230–0300), a telemarketing company whose staff members will try to steer you in the right direction.

Centers and Markets
CENTERS
Billed as "Malaysia's premier shopping center," **Suria KLCC** is part of the new development on the grounds of what was once the Selangor Turf Club. The center is in a six-story, crescent-shape complex in front of the Petronas Twin Towers. Pass beneath the striking skylight of its main entrance and on to any of the 273 shops (including department stores) and restaurants. There's also a cineplex.

The upscale **Star Hill,** opposite the Regent Hotel, may be the most beautiful complex in the Golden Triangle. It has a branch of a well-known Singapore department store as well as high-fashion outlets and food centers with inexpensive local and international fare. Almost next door, on Jalan Bukit Bintang and Jalan Sultan Ismail, are KL's most popular shopping centers: **Lot 10, Bukit Bintang Plaza,** and **Sungai Wang Plaza** (Bukit Bintang Plaza somewhat confusingly adjoins Sungai Wang Plaza, and you may not realize that you have passed from one to the other). All have major department stores (Isetan, Metrojaya, Parkson), bookstores, boutiques, pharmacies, gadget shops, and food centers.

For arts and crafts try **Yow Chuan Plaza** on Jalan Tun Razak. **The Mall** on Jalan Putra has a department store and numerous specialty shops, including an excellent bookstore. **The Weld** on Jalan Raja Chulan is decidedly upscale, with a marble interior and such shops as Crabtree & Evelyn, Benetton, Bruno Magli, and Etienne Aigner. Those interested in computer hardware and software should head for **Imbi Plaza** on Jalan Imbi.

MARKETS
At KL's street markets, stalls sell everyday goods, from leather handbags to pocketknives to pop music cassettes. Bargaining is the rule, and only cash is accepted. The large market on Chinatown's **Jalan Petaling** starts late in the morning and runs well into the night. The nightly market, **Chow Kit,** is on upper Jalan Tuanku Abdul Rahman. On Saturday between 6 PM and 11 PM **lower Jalan Tuanku Abdul Rahman,** near the Coliseum Theatre is closed for a market. In the **Kampung Baru** area on Sunday, a *pasar minggu* (open-air bazaar) offers Malay handicrafts and food.

Specialty Items
ANTIQUES
China Arts (✉ 235 Jln. Tuanku Abdul Rahman, ☎ 03/292–9250), next to the Peiping Lace Co., has Chinese arts and crafts. For Nonya antiques, try **Le Connoisseur** (☎ 03/241–9206) in Yow Chuan Plaza. The shop is normally open only in the afternoon, but call Mrs. Cheng to visit at other times. For Chinese arts and crafts, look in at **Peiping Lace Co.** (✉ 223 Jln. Tuanku Abdul Rahman, ☎ 03/298–3184). The **Treasure Chest** (✉ Jaya Supermarket, Petaling Jaya, ☎ 03/755–3942) has Nonya and colonial antiques.

ART

Art Folio (⊠ 2nd floor, City Square, 182 Jln. Tun Razak) offers expensive oil paintings, water colors, and ceramics. There's a selection of Chinese brush paintings and ceramics at **Art House** (⊠ 2nd floor, Wisma Cosway, Jln. Raja Chulan). Watercolors and portraits finished or in progress can be found at the **Central Market** (⊠ Jln. Cheng Lock, ☎ 03/274–6542). **Collectors' Focus** (⊠ 3rd floor, Lot T, City Square, 182 Jln. Tun Razak) has art at affordable prices. Top-quality artwork from Malaysia and other Southeast Asian countries is on sale at **Valentine Willie Fine Art** (⊠ 1st floor, 17 Jln. Telawi 3, Bangsar Baru, ☎ 03/284–2348).

HANDICRAFTS

Batik Malaysia Berhad (⊠ Jln. Tun Perak, ☎ 03/291–8606) has a wide selection of batik fabrics, shirts, dresses, and handicrafts. The stalls of the **Central Market** (☞ *above*) offer handicrafts as well as a wide range of other souvenirs, including portraits, painted tiles, jewelry, and antiques. For the widest range of Malaysian handicrafts—including rattan baskets, straw handbags, wood carvings, Kelantan silver jewelry, and batik fashions—try the new **Kompleks Budaya Kraf** (⊠ Jln. Conlay, ☎ 03/262–7533).

The best selection of modern pewter designs is available at the **Selangor Pewter Showroom** (⊠ 231 Jln. Tuanku Abdul Rahman, ☎ 03/298–6244). At the **Selangor Pewter Factory** (⊠ 4 Jln. Usahawan 6, ☎ 03/422–3000), a few miles north of the city in the suburb of Setapak, you can see how pewter is made (from refined tin, antimony, and copper) and then formed into pitchers, candelabra, and the like. You can buy duty-free souvenirs here, too. The factory is open Monday–Saturday 8:30–4:45 and Sunday 9–4.

JEWELRY

Try **Jade House** (☎ 03/241–9640), on the ground floor of KL Plaza. **Jewellery by Selberan,** with showrooms in KL Plaza (☎ 03/241–7106) and Yow Chuan Plaza (☎ 03/243–6386) does fine work with precious gems.

Kuala Lumpur Essentials

Arriving and Departing

BY AIRPLANE

Kuala Lumpur International Airport (KLIA; ☎ 03/843–1002) in Sepang around 60 km (37 mi) south of KL, opened in mid-1998, replacing the old Subang Airport, which is now used only for charter flights and for domestic flights, except those to Pinang, Kota Kinabalu, and Kuching, which depart from KLIA. (☞ Malaysia and Brunei A to Z, *below,* for information on international arrivals and departures and on domestic carriers and flights.)

From the Airport to Downtown. A normal limousine to the city costs RM70; a more luxurious limo, RM90. Regular taxis aren't available. KL City Bus offers service to downtown (the trip takes about 1½ hours) aboard air-conditioned coaches; the fare is about RM25. By the year 2000 the travel time by public transportation will take only 30 minutes on an Express Rail Link (ERL) between the airport and the city (your bags will be checked in before you board).

BY BUS

Regional buses bring you to the main **Puduraya Terminal** on Jalan Pudu, across from the Maybank Building, where you can get a taxi or local bus to your city destination. KL–Singapore express buses cost RM22; KL–Butterworth, RM17. For Kota Bharu and other destinations on the east coast, buses and shared taxis use the Putra Bus Station opposite the Putra World Trade Center on Jalan Tun Ismail.

BY CAR

Roads into and out of KL are clearly marked, but traffic jams are legendary. It's best to avoid the morning and late-afternoon rush hours if possible. Tropical downpours also cause delay. It's strongly recommended that you hire a taxi or chauffeur-driven car to get around the city and its immediate environs rather than driving yourself; if you want to rent a car to travel farther afield, pick it up just as you are leaving the city. Luxury hotels in KL generally have parking lots, and guests are usually given a 50% discount on regular rates.

BY TRAIN

All trains from Butterworth and Singapore deposit passengers at the **railway station** (☎ 03/274–7435) on Jalan Sultan Hishamuddin, a short distance from the city center. (There are always cabs at the taxi stand here.) The second-class train fare (in an air-conditioned car) to KL from either Singapore or Butterworth is approximately RM34; first class is about RM68.

Getting Around

Conditions in KL aren't ideal for walking—distances between sights seem a long way in the heat and humidity, sidewalks have potholes, and many streets are partially dug up for a monorail project (construction was stopped at press time, and it's unlikely that work will resume until the economy picks up again). Crossing streets requires a reckless disregard for danger; best to wait until a few locals form a group and then cross with them en masse. Travel by taxi may seem preferable—until you're caught in your first KL traffic jam. On the other hand, buses are overcrowded and confusing, and neither they nor the LRT system seem worth the bother when taxis are so reasonably priced. The best plan is a combination of foot and cab travel: arm yourself with a map, choose the sights that you wish to see, and dress in comfortable walking shoes and loose, light clothing (cotton fabrics will keep you cooler than synthetics). When it's a long way to your next destination (or you simply tire out), take a taxi.

BY BUS

Buses cover most of the metropolitan area, and stops are usually marked. Note, however, that bus route maps simply don't exist, so before you get on a bus, ask the driver whether his route serves your destination. Fares are based on distance, starting at 50 sen up to RM2. Just tell the conductor where you want to go, and have small change ready, because ticket sellers don't like to break large bills. Minibuses, which used to hurtle recklessly about town, are now banned from the city center. The two major bus terminals are Pudu Raya on Jalan Pudu and the Klang terminal on Jalan Sultan Mohamed.

BY CAR

Major car rental agencies in KL are: **Avis** (✉ 40 Jln. Sultan Ismail, ☎ 03/241–7144), **Budget** (✉ 29 Jln. Yap Kwan Seng, ☎ 03/242–5166), **Hertz** (✉ International Complex, Jln. Sultan Ismail, ☎ 03/243–3433), and **National** (✉ Wisma HLA, Jln. Raja Chulan, ☎ 03/242–5166). In view of the distance to the KL International Airport, it might be sensible to check with the rental agency about whether or not you can drop off the car there just before your departure.

BY TAXI

Taxis—which are metered and air-conditioned—are plentiful, except during rainstorms or rush hour. You can catch them at stands, hail them on the street, or request them by phone (pickup costs extra). Most taxi drivers speak passable English, but make sure they understand where you want to go and know how to get there before you set off. Also make sure that the driver turns on the meter—cabbies are notorious for not using their meters and charging visitors more than twice the correct fare. The flag fare is RM2 for the first 2 km (1 mi), and 10 sen for each additional 200 meters. A 50% surcharge applies between midnight and 6 AM, and extra passengers (more than two) pay an additional 20 sen each per ride. Luggage, if placed in the trunk, is an additional RM1. You can also hire a cab by the hour for around RM40 for the first hour and RM30 per hour afterward.

There's an RM1 surcharge for booking a cab by phone. Radio-dispatch taxi companies include: **Comfort Radio Taxi** (☎ 03/733–0507), **Federal Territory & Selangor Taxi Assn.** (☎ 03/293–6213), **Koteksi** (☎ 03/781–5352), **Mesra Radio Taxi Service** (☎ 03/442–1019), and **Teletaxi** (☎ 03/221–1011).

BY TRAIN

The first phase of the new light-rail system, the LRT, is now running. It connects Sultan Ismail, Dang Wangi, Masjid Jamek, Plaza Rakyat, Hang Tuah, and Pudu stations before going on to finish at Ampang. For information and a route map, stop by any of the stations (these are clearly visible as the rail runs on raised ramps above the road, or contact the LRT Customer Service Hotline, ☎ 03/298–4977).

Contacts and Resources

EMERGENCIES

Ambulance, Police, and Fire: ☎ 999. **Doctors and Dentists:** The telephone directory lists several government clinics (look under the heading "Kementerian Kesihatan") that treat walk-in patients for a cash fee; these are open during normal business hours. Alternatively, ask your hotel to make a recommendation. There's a pharmacy in every major shopping center, though it will be open only during business hours.

ENGLISH-LANGUAGE BOOKSTORES

Because English is widely used in Malaysia, reading material is easy to find, especially on Jalan Tuanku Abdul Rahman; **Minerva Book Store** at Number 114 is recommended. You'll also find bookshops in major shopping centers, including **Berita Book Centre** (⊠ 002-003, 1st floor, Bukit Bintang Plaza), **MPH** (⊠ 002, Ground floor, Bukit Bintang Plaza), and **Times Books** (⊠ D3, 3rd floor, Star Hill Plaza).

TOUR OPERATORS

The **MTPB** (☞ Visitor Information, *below*) maintains a list of all licensed tour operators; you can also get brochures in most hotel lobbies and information from local travel agents. The **Malaysian Tourist Information Center** (MATIC; ☞ Visitor Information, *below*) offers a daily, three-hour, "Country Tour" that leaves from the MATIC office at 9:30 AM and takes in Kompleks Budaya Kraf; Ambassadors' Row; the remains of a rubber plantation; pewter and batik factories; a butterfly and insect farm; the oldest Malay house in the KL area; and the Batu Caves. The cost is RM25. **Mayflower Acme Tours** (⊠ 18 Jln. Segambut Pusat, ☎ 03/626–7011; ⊠ Ming Court Hotel lobby, ☎ 03/261–1120) is one of the biggest operators. Another major operator is **Reliance** (⊠ 3rd floor, Sungei Wang Plaza, Jln. Sultan Ismail, ☎ 03/248–0111).

TRAVEL AGENCIES

American Express (⊠ MAS Bldg., 5th floor, Jln. Sultan Ismail, ☎ 03/261–0000). **Thomas Cook** (⊠ Wisma Bouftead, Jln. Raja Chulan, ☎ 03/241–7022). *See also* Tour Operators, *above*.

VISITOR INFORMATION

The staff at the **KL Visitors Center** (✉ 3 Jln. Hishamuddin, ☎ 03/230–1369) supplies city maps, directions, and assistance in finding hotels weekdays 8–4:15 and Saturday 8–12:45 PM. The **MATIC** (✉ 109 Jln. Ampang, ☎ 03/264–3929) is in a restored colonial mansion that's open daily from 9 to 6. You can pick up information on KL and the rest of Malaysia, and the staff is very helpful. In addition you can make arrangements to visit the National Park (Taman Negara) at a private agency here. City and country tours depart from MATIC at 9:30 AM (☞ Tour Operators, *above*), and there are cultural shows given on the first floor every Tuesday, Thursday, Saturday, and Sunday at 3:30 PM; admission is RM2. There are also information counters at the airport and the railway station. The **MTPB** (✉ 26th floor, Menara Dato Onn, Putra World Trade Center, Jln. Tun Ismail, ☎ 03/293–5188) has information on all of Malaysia. It's open Monday to Thursday from 8 to 12:45 and from 2 to 4:15, Friday from 8 to noon and from 2:30 to 4:15, and Saturday from 8 to 12:45 PM.

NORTHWEST COAST AND CENTRAL HIGHLANDS

North of KL and inland you'll find cool, lovely highlands. Off the coast of Perak state are the delightful resort islands of Pulau Pangkor and Pangkor Laut. Farther north, the state of Kedah is known mainly for the resort island of Langkawi. The recently completed North–South Highway makes travel along the west coast rapid and easy.

Perak

Perak means "silver" in Malay, although it's a far less glamorous metal that made the state rich. It once had the richest tin field in the world, and this attracted thousands of migrant Chinese to the region during the 1880s and '90s. Rubber plantations took over when the tin boom ended, and although there are still plenty of tin deposits, the low price for this commodity has caused the mines to cease operation. The most striking geographic feature of Perak is the strange limestone peaks found around Ipoh, the capital. Although the royal town of Kuala Kangsar, where the Sultan of Perak resides, has romantic royal palaces and mosques, most visitors to the state head for the Pangkor islands or inland (and just over the border into Pahang state) to the Cameron Highlands.

Cameron Highlands

★ ❶ *190 km (118 mi) north of KL.*

A colonial atmosphere still lingers at this hill station, which was built for British plantation owners and civil servants. The genteel, civilized tone is epitomized by Ye Olde Smokehouse hotel (☞ Dining and Lodging, *below*), where you can sip a pink gin by the fireplace and imagine yourself in dear old England. Though you'll see tea plantations, terraced vegetable gardens, and jungle, much of the landscape makes you feel as if you're hallucinating—it's Great Britain in the middle of Malaysia (and only 322 km/200 mi from the equator). This is particularly true once you pass through the town of Tanah Rata. The tropical air gives way to a Scottish crispness; Tudor and Edwardian bungalows and English row houses (built for laborers) begin to appear.

En route to the small village of Brinchang, 5 km (3 mi) north of Tanah Rata, you'll pass the large, lavish **Sam Poh** Chinese temple, which was

Peninsular Malaysia

built in 1965. Another 5 km (3 mi) north of Brinchang, the **Butterfly Farm** has many beautiful—often flashy—local species fluttering among the flowers. The farm is open daily 8–6, and admission is RM3. Even more interesting is the **Robertson Rose Garden**, 2 km (1 mi) northwest of Brinchang, where you can wander for free (daily from 10 to 4) among the roses, buy local honey and dried flowers, and enjoy marvelous views of the tea plantations in the surrounding hills. If want to actually visit a tea plantation, you can take a free tour of the **Sungai Palas Tea Estate,** which is just beyond the rose garden and is open everyday but Monday from 8:30 to 3. You'll learn how the tea is picked, processed, and packaged, and then enjoy a cup of it in the on-site café.

Dining and Lodging

Most Cameron Highlands eateries are very informal places that don't take reservations; many are in Tanah Rata. The Malay food stalls opposite the post office on the main road are open in the evening and sell good, inexpensive food. You're unlikely to pay more than RM5–RM8 per person for a satisfying meal here. In Tapah, the small town you pass through heading up to Cameron Highlands, try the local *roti canai* (rice and curry) at any of the Indian Muslim coffee shops along the main street.

$–$$ ✕ **Jasmine Restaurant.** This restaurant is best known for its rijsttafel, a set meal of rice with lots of curries and condiments. Another reasonably priced set meal consists of four Chinese dishes. ⊠ *45 Main Rd., Tanah Rata,* ☎ *05/527–8205. No credit cards.*

$–$$ ✕ **Restoran Orient.** For a warming "steamboat," where pieces of meat, fish and vegetable are dipped into boiling stock in a sort of fondue set in the center of the table, try to this popular spot. There's also a standard Chinese menu. Like all the restaurants on the Main Road, this one is fairly basic but comfortable. ⊠ *38 Main Rd., Tanah Rata,* ☎ *05/491–1633. No credit cards.*

$$$ ✕⊡ **Ye Olde Smokehouse.** To really breathe the true spirit of this hill
★ station, consider a stay at this a-little-down-at-the-heel but ever-so-charming hotel. Stuffed with delightful British clutter, the suites have superb mountain views and plenty of odd corners in which to sit and think. You can dine in style (jacket and tie are required) on typically English dishes, such as a roast beef dinner (around RM75). Just as in colonial India, British "rules of deportment" are followed here: you order from the bar and wait until the maître d' invites you to your table; later you can return to the bar and linger over brandy or port. Late-afternoon tea—with scones, strawberry jam, and cream—on the terrace is another delightful option. ⊠ *Golf Course Rd., Tanah Rata 39100,* ☎ *05/491–1215,* ℻ *05/491–1214. 20 suites. Restaurant, bar. AE, MC, V.*

Outdoor Activities and Sports

Time at the Cameron Highlands is best spent breathing in the glorious mountain air and walking. Although the highly touted jungle walks are exciting, the trails aren't well marked, and trail maps are merely suggestive. It's best to hire a guide so that you can relax and admire the scenery rather than worrying about whether the search party will find you. The Tanah Rata Tourist Office (on the right on the main road as you enter town) can recommend a guide, or you can inquire about one at Ye Olde Smokehouse (☞ *above*). The official trails vary in length and difficulty. You can walk the relatively easy Trail 4 in about an hour, passing a waterfall and a lookout tower with views over Brinchang.

Ipoh

❷ *121 km (95 mi) north of Brinchang in the Cameron Highlands, 205 km (127 mi) northwest of KL.*

The third-largest town on peninsular Malaysia has a number of magnificent colonial buildings around its *padang*, or open green. The railway station, city hall, and Hongkong Bank are particularly noteworthy. The main attractions, however, are the Chinese temples built inside caves just outside Ipoh. Also of interest is an abandoned mansion on a rubber estate.

The remains of **Kellie's Castle**—a mansion with Moorish arches, apricot-color bricks, and a four-story tower—stand in the Kinta Kelas Rubber estate 12 km (7½ mi) south of Ipoh. Named after the Scottish rubber planter who built it, the grandiose mansion was never completed because Kellie died while on a trip to Portugal. You can see a painting of Kellie himself, wearing *solar topee* (pith helmut) and a planter's jacket, on the facade of the nearby Sri Maha Mariamman Temple, which he reputedly built after a number of Tamil laborers working on his mansion died of a mysterious illness.

Some 6 km (4 mi) south of Ipoh is the oldest and largest cave temple, **Sam Po Kong,** founded in the 1890s by a Buddhist monk. Landscaped gardens lead to a huge chamber, which is filled with statues of the Buddha and has a pool of tortoises that are considered sacred. ⊠ *Free.* ◎ *Daily 8–4:30.*

The **Perak Tong** cave temple, 6 km (4 mi) north of town, has a 49-ft statue of Buddha and impressive wall paintings of various Chinese deities. The temple, built in 1925, can be very atmospheric when worshipers ring the huge, century-old bell during their devotions. At the back, if you climb 385 steps up from the cave, you'll be rewarded with a view of the surrounding countryside. ⊠ *Free.* ◎ *Daily 8–6.*

Dining and Lodging

Ipoh is renowned for its Cantonese cuisine, particularly the noodles. There are a number of simple coffee shops along Jalan Bandar Timah (Kedai Kopi Kong Meng, at Number 65, is famous for its *kway teow,* meltingly soft fresh rice-flour noodles with chicken and seasonings).

$ ✕ **FMS.** You can enjoy a simple Western meal at what is probably Malaysia's oldest restaurant. Named after the Federated Malay States, of which Perak was a member in 1906 when the restaurant opened, it was redecorated in an indeterminate style in the 1950s. However, the beer is cold, the fish-and-chips are fine, and the "uncle" behind the bar has been running the place for 50 years and is happy to chat about the past. ⊠ *2 Jln. Sultan Yussof and Jln. Sultan Idris Shah (opposite the Padang),* ☏ *05/254–0591. No credit cards.*

$$$ ✕🏨 **Casuarina Parkroyal Hotel.** Although slightly outside of Ipoh, this hotel has the most amenities of any in area. There's a swimming pool in the nicely landscaped gardens and a tourism information office on the ground floor. If you hanker for expensive Western cuisine, the upscale restaurant serves up a good steak. ⊠ *18 Jln. Gopeng, 30250,* ☏ *05/255–5555,* 𝔽𝔸𝕏 *05/255–8177. 200 rooms. Restaurant, bar, pool, shops, dance club, car rental. AE, DC, MC, V.*

$ 🏨 **Majestic Station Hotel.** If you're a nostalgia freak who wants to know what it was like to stay in a hotel during the colonial era, consider a room at the Majestic Station. On the top level of the magnificent Moorish Ipoh railway station, which is all colonnades and cupolas, the hotel was recently renovated with an eye toward retaining a charming, old-fashioned ambience. Request one of the rooms that opens onto the veranda, where ceiling fans whir lazily above. Although these rooms aren't luxurious, they do have wooden parquet flooring; dark wooden furniture; refrigerators; TVs; IDD phones; air-conditioning; and spotless, thoroughly modern bathrooms. ⊠ *Ipoh Station, 3rd* *floor, 30000,* ☎ *05/255–5605,* FAX *05/255–3393. 86 rooms. Restaurant, café, meeting rooms. AE, DC, MC, V.*

Pulau Pangkor and Pulau Pangkor Laut

❸ *84 km (52 mi) southwest of Ipoh, 175 km (109 mi) northwest of KL.*

Just off the coast and part of Perak state, Pulau Pangkor is an island known for its fishing and its western shore beaches. Aside from the major stretches of sand at Teluk Nipah, Teluk Belanga, and Pasir Bogok, there are quieter coves at Tortoise Bay and Teluk Chempedak. The jumping-off point for the island is the small coastal town of Lumut, a one-hour taxi ride from Ipoh (it costs about RM40 one-way for an air-conditioned cab). An express ferry runs to and fro about every 20 minutes. What really makes a journey here worthwhile is a stay in the exclusive resort on Pulau Pangkor Laut—a private islet just south of Pulau Pangkor. Private ferries transport resort guests from the larger island to the smaller one. If you like to travel in style all the way, you can arrange limo service from KL or Pinang through the resort; the cost is about RM300.

Dining and Lodging

$$$$
★
✕⊞ **Pangkor Laut Resort.** As you approach Pulau Pangkor Laut, you will see what looks like a traditional Malay fishing village but what is really a collection of smart resort villas. Set on stilts that are connected by walkways 15 ft above the ocean, the water villas have private balconies and peaked roofs that keep the air circulating (helped, of course, by air-conditioning). The two villas that contain suites have private decks, huge bathrooms with baths that are suspended over the water, and raised platforms with glass-paned trapdoors that reflect light from the sea below. Those who prefer terra firma should opt for a villa on the palm-studded beach or in the forested hills. These villas also have oversize baths (those for beach villas are outside) as well as cream-color cotton spreads and polished wood floors. The resort has everything you need for the perfect beach vacation, including a spa, many land and water activities, and a variety of restaurants. The Fisherman's Cove offers a dinner menu of seafood specialities. When it comes to dining in style, the romantic Samudra, poised on stilts over the bay, is the place to be. ✉ *Pulau Pangkor Laut, 32200,* ☎ *05/699–1100,* FAX *05/699–1200. 186 villas. 6 restaurants, 2 pools, massage, spa, 3 tennis courts, health club, hiking, squash, dive shop, snorkeling, windsurfing, boating, library. AE, DC, MC, V.*

Kuala Kangsar

❹ *50 km (31 mi) northwest of Ipoh, 255 km (158 mi) northwest of KL.*

The royal capital of Perak state for the past 250 years is set on a bend of the Perak River. The charm of Kuala Kangsar is such that one Victorian writer admitted liking it "better than any place that I have been at in Asia." This very Malay town's most famous landmark is the exuberant **Ubudiah Mosque,** an Arabian Nights' fantasy completed in 1919 and built of black-and-white Italian marble topped by gilded domes. (Ask permission before entering the mosque, and avoid visiting it during Friday's midday prayers.) ✉ *Jln. Istana.*

The Sultan of Perak lives in the modern, white-marble Istana Iskandariah, which is closed to the public. However, you can visit another royal residence, the **Istana Kenangan,** which now houses the **Royal Museum.** A fine example of traditional Malay woodworking skills, this building was constructed entirely without nails. Notice the carved friezes and split bamboo wall panels. The museum has an interesting collection of old photographs of sultans and various British gentlemen. ⊠ *Jln. Istana,* ☏ *no phone.* ▣ *Free.* ⊙ *Sat.–Wed. 9:30–5, Thurs. 9:30–12:45.*

Taiping

❺ *36 km (22 mi) north of Kuala Kangsar; 291 km (180 mi) northwest of KL.*

Taiping's main claim to fame is that it's the wettest town on the peninsula. Despite the fact that the town's Chinese name means "everlasting peace," Taiping (then known as Larut) was the scene of fierce fighting between rival Chinese tin miners in the 1870s. This predominantly Chinese town has a scenic garden, **Taman Tasik** (Lake Gardens), built around a couple of disused tin mining pools. The main area attraction, however, is Malaysia's smallest and oldest hill station—**Bukit Larut** (☏ 05/807–7241 for superintendent/reservations), formerly known as Maxwell Hill. The 3,395-ft ascent to the resort was once made by sedan chair; today, you can travel by government Land Rover or walk for two to three hours along the 9-km (6-mi) road. You'll find the same wooden bungalows, lawns, flower beds, pine trees, and misty morning views that enchanted and soothed the colonials. You can stay either in one of five well-equipped bungalows—requesting that the caretaker arrange meals for you—or in the three-bedroom Rest House, which serves Western and Malaysian dishes. There's not much to do apart from relaxing, strolling, or playing tennis. But inactivity is part of Bukit Larut's charm.

Pinang

Tucked between the states of Perak and Kedah, Pinang (Penang) state is most famous for its eponymous island—a major vacation destination and home to the state capital of Georgetown. Known as the Pearl of the Orient for its natural beauty, Pulau Pinang respects tradition but is neither stodgy nor sleepy. The island offers gracious colonial architecture, vibrant Chinese communities, Indian temples and mosques, beach resorts, and some of Malaysia's most exciting food.

Thanks to its safe anchorage and strategic position in the Straits of Melaka, the island caught the eye of an English trader in the late 1700s. He persuaded the Sultan of Kedah to grant him the island in exchange for British protection, and Pinang quickly grew into a thriving and cosmopolitan entrepôt. Today the island's population is primarily Hokkien Chinese, though a sizable Indian community thrives, particularly in Georgetown, and many Malays reside in the countryside.

Butterworth

❻ *94 km (58 mi) northwest of Taiping, 164 km (102 mi) northwest of Ipoh.*

Butterworth is Pinang state's major industrial area. Its only truly noteworthy characteristic is that it's the main jumping-off point for Pulau Pinang. If you're driving, you'll probably cross the 13-km-long (8-mi-long) bridge that joins the southeast corner of island with the mainland, not far from Penang International Airport. There's also a 24-hour car-and-passenger ferry service (☞ Arriving and Departing By Boat *and* By Car *in* Northwest Coast and Central Highlands Essentials, *below*).

Georgetown

❼–㉕ *7 km (4 mi) west off the shore of Butterworth, 370 km (229 mi) northwest of KL.*

Georgetown is a great place to tour on foot, by bicycle, or by trishaw; of course, you'll have to stop frequently to browse in the city's many intriguing shops and to sample its world-famous cuisine. In recent years, many streets have been renamed, but locals prefer to use the older—often simpler—colonial names (understandably, you're more likely to hear "Pitt Street" than "Jalan Masjid Kapitan Kling").

The best place to begin a tour is near the Swettenham Pier, where there are offices of the Penang Tourist Association and the MTPB (☞ *also* Visitor Information *in* Northwest Coast and Central Highlands Essentials, *below*). Opposite the tourism offices is a **Victorian clock tower,** donated to the city by a Pinang millionaire to commemorate Queen Victoria's diamond jubilee. The tower is 60 ft tall, one foot for every year of her reign up to 1897.

Head from the Victorian clock tower up Jalan Tun Syed Barakbah past **Ft. Cornwallis,** the harborside site where city founder Captain Sir Francis Light of the British East India Company first landed on the island in 1786. On the outside, the 1810 compound's moss-encrusted ramparts and cannons give the impression of a mighty fortress, but it never saw any real action. On the inside are an open-air amphitheater, shade trees, and public toilets.

The **Esplanade**—an open, grassy field next to Ft. Cornwallis—is a pleasant site for a stroll, especially in the evening, when the sea breezes roll in and the hawkers set up their stands. The Esplanade is often used for festivals and recreational sports. A monument surrounded by palms honors soldiers who died in World War I.

Pinang's hub used to be Lebuh Pantai (Beach Street), near the ferry terminal in the heart of the banking district. But the city center has gravitated toward the huge new KOMTAR (☞ *below*) shopping and office complex. Even the city government has moved to this complex, and its former home—the stately, early 20th-century **Municipal Council Building** is now used for special exhibitions.

The **Dewan Sri Pinang,** next to the Municipal Council Building, is the city's major auditorium, seating some 1,300 for concerts, plays, and other events. Coming cultural activities are posted on a billboard in front. The **Pinang Library** is on the first floor.

The colonial structure across from Dewan Sri Pinang houses the **High Court.** Malaysia's legal system is based on that of Britain, and although lawyers are now supposed to speak Bahasa Malaysia, the courts still conduct much of their business in English. Cases are open to the public, so you can wander in and immerse yourself in a local legal drama. Inside the compound is a marble statue dedicated to James Richardson Logan, a lawyer and newspaper editor who devoted his life to public service and who advocated law, order, and free speech.

Behind the High Court is the **Penang Museum and Art Gallery.** The statue outside the 1897 building, which was used as the Penang Free School for more than a century, is of Sir Francis Light. The museum reopened in late 1997 after a three-year renovation; it's currently considered one of Malaysia's top museums and contains fascinating exhibits that emphasize Pinang's multiculturalism. Right beside the museum building is an old railcar that was once used on the Pinang Hill funicular and now houses a shop run by the Pinang Heritage Trust. Here you can buy postcards (including old ones), books, prints, coins, antique porcelain, and *kebaya* (Nonya blouses). ✉ *Lebuh Farquhar,* ☎ *04/657–7888.* ☎ *Free.* ☺ *Sat.–Thurs. 9–5.*

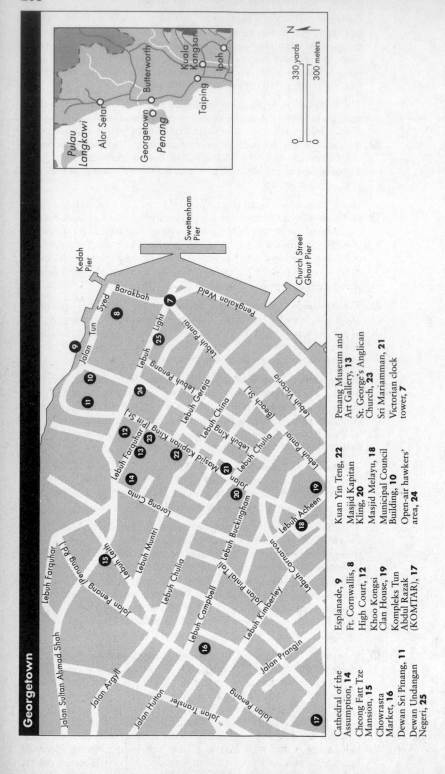

Georgetown

330 yards

300 meters

Swettenham Pier

Kedah Pier

Church Street Ghaut Pier

Barakbah

Pulau Langkawi

Alor Setar

Georgetown Penang

Taiping

Butterworth

Kuala Kangsar

Ipoh

N

Jalan Sultan Ahmad Shah

Lebuh Farquhar

Jalan Penang (Penang Rd.)

Jalan Argyll

Jalan Hutton

Jalan Transfer

Jalan Penang

Lebuh Campbell

Lebuh Chulia

Lebuh Muntri

Lebuh Leith

Jalan Pintal Tali

Lebuh Carnavon

Lebuh Kimberley

Lebuh Buckingham

Lebuh Acheen

Jalan Prangin

Lorong Cinta

Lebuh Farquhar

Lebuh Light

Lebuh Penang

Lebuh Gereja

Lebuh King

Lebuh China

Lebuh Chulia

Masjid Kapitan Kling (Pitt St.)

Jalan Pintal

Lebuh Pantai

Lebuh Victoria

Beech St.

Pengkalan Weld

Jalan Tun Syed

Cathedral of the Assumption, **14**
Cheong Fatt Tze Mansion, **15**
Chowrasta Market, **16**
Dewan Sri Pinang, **11**
Dewan Undangan Negeri, **25**

Esplanade, **9**
Ft. Cornwallis, **8**
High Court, **12**
Khoo Kongsi Clan House, **19**
Kompleks Tun Abdul Razak (KOMTAR), **17**

Kuan Yin Teng, **22**
Masjid Kapitan Kling, **20**
Masjid Melayu, **18**
Municipal Council Building, **10**
Open-air hawkers' area, **24**

Penang Museum and Art Gallery, **13**
St. George's Anglican Church, **23**
Sri Mariamman, **21**
Victorian clock tower, **7**

⑭ Next door to the museum and art gallery is the **Cathedral of the Assumption,** one of the oldest Roman Catholic churches in Malaysia.

⑮ Beyond the cathedral, at the top of Lebuh Leith, is one of the most stunning traditional houses in all Malaysia, the **Cheong Fatt Tze Mansion.** Built in the early part of this century by a Chinese immigrant who amassed a fortune in Malaya and Indonesia, the house has exquisite gilded carved screens, cast-iron columns, intricate mosaic panels made from pieces of broken pottery, art nouveau stained-glass windows, and ornate spiral staircases. Its 38 rooms and five courtyards were used as a setting for the film *Indochine.* Rescued from dereliction in 1990, the bright-blue mansion and five shophouses (once housing for the staff and lesser wives of Cheong Fatt Tze, and now Pinang's trendiest bar-restaurant complex, 20 Leith Street) across from it are being restored. A one-hour mansion tour is given at 11 AM every Monday, Wednesday, and Saturday; admission is free and tours cost RM10.

Lebuh Leith runs into **Jalan Penang,** the city's main shopping strip. In the labyrinth of stalls along it and in its alleyways, you'll find such basics as underwear, belts, handbags, and luggage. In the first block a series of handicrafts and antiques shops carry gift items including Asian jewelry and Thai and Indonesian wood carvings. All along the road, trishaw drivers—mostly older men—will solicit you. If you take one of them up on an offer to sightsee, consider heading up Lebuh Muntri past some of the city's best examples of traditional architecture, turn left onto Lorong Cinta (Love Lane), turn right, and pass the museum. From here you can head back down Jalan Masjid Kapitan Kling, passing the famous temple of Kuan Yin and Masjid Kapitan Kling (☞ *below*) before turning right into Lebuh Buckingham. This becomes Lebuh Campbell (great for coffee-shop breakfasts) and runs into to Jalan Penang.

⑯ South of Lebuh Campbell, off Jalan Penang, is the indoor **Chowrasta Market,** where local produce is sold. Shops in front of the entrance sell produce including pickled and dried nutmeg (grown on Pinang); candies made from ginger root, coconut, and durian; and *dodol,* durian cake that's sold in little triangular pieces or foot-long rolls. In the morning, the market spills out onto three of the surrounding streets, where you'll find everything from freshly netted prawns to wooden Chinese clogs to barbecued wafers of sweet pork and bowls of noodles.

⑰ At the bottom of Jalan Penang is the **Kompleks Tun Abdul Razak (KOMTAR),** named to honor Malaysia's second prime minister (it was also called the Tower of the East when it was still the tallest building in Southeast Asia). The complex is totally out of scale with the neighboring buildings and can be confusing owing to its size and many entrances. Still, you can conduct business (all the government offices are here), shop, eat, and even sleep here. The **Shangri-La Penang** hotel (☞ Lodging, *below*) is connected to the complex via a small department store on level two; there are a number of fast-food outlets that serve hamburgers, fried chicken, and pizza in the center of the mall; one of the city's best Chinese restaurants, **Supertanker** (☞ Dining, *below*), is on the upper level; the third-floor **Tourism Information Centre** has helpful staffers who dispense maps, brochures, and advice; and **Chin's Art Gallery,** next to the Malaysia Airline System (MAS) office on the third level, will engrave your initials in a stone *chop* (seal) for RM60–RM150, depending on the size and quality of the stone. Among the tower's busiest tenants are hip young tailors with trendy haircuts and smart outfits who scurry about fitting customers with garments cut from the bolts of fabric they stack in every corner of their tiny shops.

⑱ At the junction of Lebuh Acheen and Jalan Masjid Kapitan Kling is the oldest mosque in Pinang. The **Masjid Melayu,** also known as the Acheen Street Mosque, was restored and repainted in 1998. The walk along quiet back lanes to reach it is as interesting as the mosque itself, which has Chinese architectural touches in its design.

⑲ On the north side of Lebuh Acheen, look for a small sign posted above an entrance to an alley announcing the **Khoo Kongsi Clan House,** a complex of structures that may be the most elaborately decorated in Malaysia. Restored in the early 1990s, the **Leong San Tong** (Dragon Hall) temple is a showcase of Chinese architecture and art, constructed by 19th-century master craftsmen. Virtually no surface is unadorned. Notice the relief sculptures depicting Chinese legends and the heavily gilt dragons. Visitors are welcome weekdays 9–5, and Saturday 9–1. Permission to enter must be obtained from the office. The open theater across the square is used for opera performances.

⑳ Not only is Jalan Masjid Kapitan Kling often referred to by its colonial name, Pitt Street, but it's also called the Street of Harmony because temples, mosques, and churches from four major religions are situated along and just off it. The **Masjid Kapitan Kling** is at the Lebuh Buckingham intersection. Built in the early 1800s, the mosque has been recently renovated and continues to serve the Indian Muslim community. (You need permission to enter.) Also along this section of Pitt Street is a row of small jewelry shops run by Indians who deal in gold and semiprecious stones. Many are also licensed money changers. These street bankers can handle almost any type of foreign currency and work much longer hours than regular banks. Some are also numismatists who sell to collectors.

㉑ Past the gates of the Teochew Association House, on the corner of Pitt and Lebuh Chulia, is the temple in the heart of the Indian district, **Sri Mariamman,** on Lebuh Queen. The entrance is topped by a gopuram covered with statues of Hindu deities. Inside, the ceiling features the symbols for the planets and signs of the zodiac. The most prized possession of the faithful is a statue of Lord Subramaniam, which is covered with gold, silver, diamonds, and emeralds. The statue is paraded about during the Thaipusam festival. You can enter the temple, with permission.

㉒ The nearby temple dedicated to the goddess of mercy, **Kuan Yin Teng,** is the busiest in the city—perhaps because it's associated with fertility. Built in 1800, it serves the Cantonese and Hokkien communities. A
㉓ block east of Kuan Yin Teng, on Lebuh Farquhar, is the stately **St. George's Anglican Church,** with its gracious flowering trees and gazebo. Built in 1818 by convicts, this symbol of the British role in Pinang's early history is now attended mostly by Indians.

㉔ On the corner of Lebuh Light and Lebuh King, at an **open-air hawkers' area,** old Chinese men often bring their caged pet birds when they come for a cup of coffee and a breath of morning air. In this area, you may also see elderly men writing letters on old portable typewriters. These public scribes serve clients who need help dealing with the bureaucracy or illiterates who simply want to write a friend.

㉕ Traveling east on Lebuh Light, before you reach the Victorian clock tower you'll see the **Dewan Undangan Negeri,** a majestic colonial building with massive columns. This is the state assembly, and the luxury cars parked out front belong to its illustrious members. You're now across from Ft. Cornwallis again—near the ferry if you're hopping back to the mainland and a waterfront cab ride away from the beach hotels.

Dining

Pinang has a superb array of cuisine: Chinese, southern Indian, Indian Muslim, Malay, and the local style of Nonya cuisine, which mixes Thai flavors in with those of China and Malaysia. Dishes are still prepared in old, time-consuming ways, giving the food an authenticity not always found in other Malaysian cities. Furthermore, hundreds of stalls all over the island offer dishes that the cooks seem to have been perfecting for a lifetime. For elegant dining with attentive service, the major hotels are your best bet, but it would be a shame to miss out on some of Malaysia's best stall food. You can find excellent Chinese food (including a renowned oyster omelet) every night at the stalls around the junction of Macalister Road and Lorong Bahru, near the Church of Seven Sorrows (near the junction of Macalister Road and Jalan Penang). Even nicer is the long line of stalls along Gurney Drive, about 10 minutes by taxi out of Georgetown on the road north to Batu Ferringhi. The stalls once followed the sea wall but are now concentrated in a sort of parking-lot area (there's also a big seafood restaurant here). However, the food—most of it Hokkien, though you'll find Malay and Indian cuisine, too—is as good as ever. There are other hawker centers at Lebuh Campbell and the Esplanade.

Local stall-food specialties include: *char* kway teow (flat rice noodles fried smooth and soft with bean sprouts, prawns, and eggs), Hokkien *mee* (noodles, pork, and bean sprouts in a spicy shrimp soup topped with fried onions), the famous Pinang *rojak* (savory fruit and vegetable salad with a pungent dressing), and Pinang *laksa* (rice-flour noodles in a sour, fishy gravy topped with herbs, shredded cucumber and pineapple). For dessert consider trying *cendol* (green mung-bean noodles and red beans in fresh coconut milk and ice) or the Nonya *bubur cha cha* (sweet potatoes, yams, and red beans in coconut milk sweetened with palm sugar).

CHINESE

$$ ✕ **Supertanker.** The noise and crowds at this restaurant are its testimonials: locals love the food and the prices. Favorites on its Teochew menu are the crisp roast suckling pig and the rice porridges that come with a range of salty accompaniments. ✉ *KOMTAR,* ☎ *04/261–6393. AE, MC.*

$ ✕ **E. T. Steamboat.** At this restaurant named after the do-it-yourself Chinese stew, waiters bring vegetables, seafood, tofu, and a fondue pot full of rich broth to your table; you custom-cook your own dinner. For variety, try *lowbak* (pork rolls) or the spicy tom yam soup. ✉ *4 Jln. Rangoon,* ☎ *04/226–6025. AE, MC.*

CONTINENTAL

$$$ ✕ **Brasserie.** Recorded fusion jazz music sets the mood at this restau-
★   rant in the Shangri-La Penang hotel (☞ Lodging, *below*). You select a main course from the menu—which has a wide range of Western options—and then help yourself from the buffet for soups, salads, and dessert. Dishes have Mediterranean influences with some interesting cross-cultural touches—herb-crusted sole with Szechuan pepper aioli, for example, or grilled citrus salmon with mango. ✉ *Jln. Magazine,* ☎ *04/262–2622. Reservations essential. AE, DC, MC, V.*

$$ ✕ **Eden.** A downtown restaurant with a funky decor, Eden makes
★   fresh oxtail soup every day and is famed for its shredded lamb in black pepper sauce. The lunch menu caters to Westerners, with sandwiches, salads, and ice-cream sundaes. ✉ *15 Jln. Hutton,* ☎ *04/263–9262. AE, DC, MC, V.*

INDIAN

$ ✕ **Hameediyah.** This simple downtown restaurant excels with its nasi kandar rice—served with spicy mutton, fish, and chicken curries—or *murtabak,* an Indian-style pizza filled with spicy mutton and onions. ✉ *164 Lebuh Campbell,* ☎ *04/261–1095. No credit cards. Closed Fri.*

MALAY

$$ ✕ **Eliza: The Malay Restaurant.** This elegant (but not formal) restau-
★ rant has award-winning Malay cuisine and fantastic views of Pinang and the Strait of Melaka from the 13th floor of the City Bayview hotel (☞ Lodging, *below*). At lunch you can opt for the buffet (very popular) or order from the menu. Evenings are rather quiet; instead of a buffet there's a very reasonably priced set dinner. Signature dishes include a coconut-rich and lightly spiced beef rendang, delightful clear prawn soup, and stuffed chicken wings. Traditional Malay music adds to the ambience; if you want to go totally local, you can sit on mats on a raised platform at one side of the restaurant. ✉ *25A Lebuh Far-quhar,* ☎ *04/263–3161. AE, D, MC, V.*

NONYA

$$ ✕ **Dragon King.** People come here for the food—a blend of Malay and Chinese cuisines—not the atmosphere or modest decor. Try the spicy curried chicken and the kerabu salad. Come early; the place closes at 9 PM. ✉ *99 Lebuh Bishop,* ☎ *04/261–8035. AE, MC, V.*

$$ ✕ **Hot Wok.** Considered one of Pinang's best Nonya restaurants, this attractively decorated place is on the ground floor of a block of modern shophouses next to Island Plaza (RM8 by taxi from Georgetown or around RM15 from Batu Ferringhi). The atmosphere is relaxed and friendly and the furniture mostly ornate antique Peranakan pieces, with plenty of British colonial clutter (cigarette posters, portraits of Queen Elizabeth) in one of the two dining rooms. The menu includes all the Pinang Nonya classics. Try the *inche kabin,* spiced deep-fried chicken with a dip based on English Worcestershire sauce, and the pork *cincalok,* intriguingly flavored with preserved tiny shrimps. The mango kerabu is uncompromisingly spicy but excellent; request that the chef tone down the chili a little if you can't take it hot. ✉ *125 Desa Tanjung, Jln. Tan-jung Tokong,* ☎ *04/899–0858. AE, D, MC, V.*

Lodging

$$$$ ▥ **Equatorial Hotel.** Although not in Georgetown proper and far from the beaches, this hotel is close to the airport and the golf course and is geared toward business travelers. Note the unique 10-story atrium garden with bubble elevators. One restaurant, The View, offers a range of Western dishes with a smattering of Asian ones; the view, by the way, is of the ships moving through the straits. At press time, the hotel was being expanded. ✉ *1 Jln. Bukit Jambul, Bayan Lepas 11900,* ☎ *04/ 643–8000 or 800/44–UTELL in the U.S.,* ℻ *04/644–8000. 415 rooms. 3 restaurants, coffee shop, 2 tennis courts, golf privileges, health club, squash, business services, meeting rooms. AE, DC, MC, V.*

$$$$ ▥ **Shangri-La Penang.** The glitziest hotel in Georgetown is linked with the KOMTAR shopping and office complex downtown. Its efficient rooms are comfortably decorated and offer great views of the city. The Shang Palace, a Cantonese restaurant, serves dim sum daily and the Brasserie (☞ Dining, *above*) prepares Continental cuisine. Guests are a mix of tourists and business travelers seeking modernity and efficiency. ✉ *Magazine Rd., 10300,* ☎ *04/262–2622, 800/942–5050 in the U.S., or 081/747–8485 in the U.K.;* ℻ *04/262–6526. 426 rooms, 16 suites. 3 restaurants, coffee shop, lobby lounge, pool, health club, dance club, business services, meeting rooms. AE, DC, MC, V.*

$–$$ 🏨 **City Bayview.** This well-equipped, modern high-rise offers you a great deal for your money, including a convenient downtown location, great views, and a pool. It began life as the Merlin, the first of Pinang's modern hotels, and underwent extensive renovation in 1998. There's a Japanese restaurant, a revolving restaurant on the 14th floor, and Eliza (☞ Dining, *above*), which serves good Malay food on the 13th floor. ✉ *25A Lebuh Farquhar, 10200,* ☎ *04/263–3161,* 🅕🅐🅧 *04/263–4124. 159 rooms. 3 restaurants, bar, coffee shop, pool, dance club, meeting rooms. AE, DC, MC, V.*

$ 🏨 **Malaysia.** All the rooms in this hotel, conveniently located on upper Jalan Penang, have baths, TVs, and refrigerators. ✉ *7 Jln. Penang Rd., 10000,* ☎ *04/263–3311,* 🅕🅐🅧 *04/263–1621. 126 rooms. Restaurant, bar, refrigerators, exercise room, dance club. AE, MC, V.*

Nightlife and the Arts

Arts events are advertised on posters and in the newspapers. Festivals include street events, such as Chinese opera.

BARS

Downtown Georgetown still has seedy bars, with dim lights and ladies of indeterminate age and profession. However, there's a number of more tasteful options. The **Babylon Boom Boom** (✉ Lebuh China Ghaut, ☎ 04/262–2601)—a huge establishment with a café-restaurant to one side—has a hilarious and thoroughly professional drag show every evening, though most guests are decidedly straight and enjoy dancing on the disco floor before and after the show. Ken and Pat run the **Cheers Beer Garden** (✉ 22 Jln. Argyll, ☎ 04/263–7971) with an eye to assisting travelers. At the bright-blue **20 Leith Street** (☎ 04/261–8573)— a row of five converted houses that were once part of the Cheong Fatt Tze mansion—there's a small beer garden, a North Indian restaurant, and a Japanese restaurant with a bar, pool tables, a dartboard, and music videos. If you want a look at a tacky bar that was popular with the Australian armed forces who were once based in Butterworth, try the **Hong Kong Bar** (✉ 371 Lebuh Chulia, ☎ 04/261–9796).

DANCE CLUBS

Sol Fun (✉ Pengkalan Weld, ☎ no phone) is a converted warehouse housing a gay disco. Straights will also enjoy dancing in this imitation of the Babylon Boom Boom (☞ *above*).

LOUNGES

For a drink and a panoramic city view, head for the revolving restaurant atop the **City Bayview** hotel (✉ Farquhar St., ☎ 04/263–3161). In the **Shangri-La Penang's** (✉ Jln. Magazine, ☎ 04/262–2622) lobby lounge, a string quartet—playing everything from classical pieces to waltzes to pop—alternates evenings with a Latin combo.

Outdoor Activities and Sports

GOLF

Pinang has two 18-hole golf courses that are open to the public—Batu Gantung and Bukit Jambul. For information, fees, and tee times, call the golf section of the **Penang Turf Club** (☎ 04/229–9284) or the **Bukit Jambul Country Club** (☎ 04/884–2255).

HIKING

For hiking, your best bet is the tropical **Rima Rekreasi** (Recreational Forest), 1½ km (1 mi) past the village of Teluk Bahang. The forest also has a museum, a playground, and picnic tables. A Malayan Nature Society brochure with six other treks around the hills of Pinang is available at tourist information centers (☞ Visitor Information *in* Northwest Coast and Central Highlands Essentials, *below*).

In Air Itam (Ayer Itam), about 9 km (6 mi) southwest of Georgetown, runners or walkers can explore the track around the reservoir that provides Pinang with drinking water. The path cuts through a tropical forest and across a dam. There's no bus service up to the area, so getting here is a workout in itself. It's best as an early morning outing.

Shopping

Jalan Penang is the main shopping street, with Lebuh Campbell and Jalan Burmah as offshoots. For a wide selection of goods—including some that are duty-free—sold in air-conditioned surroundings, a trip to the KOMTAR complex is a must. Most shops are open 10–9.

The **Chowrasta Market** (☞ Exploring, *above*) on Jalan Penang is primarily a fresh produce market with additional shops and stalls outside. Upstairs, clothing and miscellaneous goods are available. On Sunday morning, a **flea market** with a mixture of junk and antiques is held on Jalan Pintal Tali.

ANTIQUES

Many of the curio and junk shops that used to crowd Pinang have disappeared. You could try **Saw Joo Ann** (☎ 04/261–9851), on the corner of Lebuh Hong Kong, for high-quality Malaysian artifacts. (If it's not open during normal business hours, ask at the coffee shop next door and someone will let you in to browse). The **Eccentric Gift Shop** (✉ Jln. Burma, ☎ 04/227–4181), in the Midlands Park Centre, has antiques and bric-a-brac as well as handicrafts from Vietnam, Indonesia, and other Asian countries.

HANDICRAFTS

On Upper Jalan Penang, shops sell crafts from Malaysia, Thailand, Indonesia, China, and India. The best selection of batik prints is at **BMB** (☎ 04/262–1607) in KOMTAR. **Penang Butterfly Farm** (✉ 803 Mk. 2, Jln. Taluk Bahang, ☎ 04/881–1253) sells items from all over Southeast Asia.

Batu Ferringhi

14 km (8 mi) northwest of Georgetown.

Most of Pulau Pinang's northern coast is broken up into small rocky coves—except, that is, for the shore at Batu Ferringhi. In the 1960s, this beach—its fine, golden sands shaded by casuarina and coconut trees—made Pinang one of the best-known vacation islands in Southeast Asia. Since then the north coast has been greatly developed, and today a strip of resorts starts from about 12 km (7 mi) northwest of Georgetown and extends all the way to Teluk Bahang.

Though not Miami Beach, Batu Ferringhi does have a similar ambience—a strip of fancy hotels that primarily provide blocks of rooms to package tours. (You'd never want to pay the published room rate here unless you don't mind your fellow guests paying half that amount.) Batu Ferringhi may be a popular choice for a week's stay, but it has fewer charms for day-trippers (public facilities, such as showers and changing rooms, are nonexistent). Don't go to a great effort to drive out unless you're really desperate for a day at the beach.

Dining and Lodging

$$$ ✕ **Eden Seafood Village.** This huge, open-air, beachfront restaurant caters to tourists with a nightly cultural show. Its Chinese-style specialties include crab cooked in a spicy chili-tomato sauce, steamed prawns in ginger sauce, lobster, and fried squid. ✉ *Batu Ferringhi,* ☎ *04/881–1852. Reservations essential. AE, DC, MC, V.*

$$ ✕ **End of the World Restaurant.** By the jetty in Teluk Bahang, 5 km (3 mi) beyond Batu Ferringhi, this simple wooden place specializes in seafood. It's so highly regarded that people drive out all the way from Georgetown just for dinner. Everything is good, though the black-pepper crab is especially recommended. ✉ *Jln. Teluk Bahang, Teluk Bahang,* ☎ *04/881–1189. No credit cards. No lunch.*

$$$$ ✕▦ **Penang Mutiara Beach Resort.** The luxury starts in the white-marble lobby, with its fountains and floor-to-ceiling windows. It continues
★ to the rooms, all of which have ocean views, rattan furniture, batik wall prints, and Malay-pattern rugs; ceiling fans, shutters, and balconies that drip with bougainvillea add to the overall tropical elegance. Restaurant choices include a seafood spot that's aptly named The Catch, and the outstanding Farfalla, whose chic, retro-style decor and impeccable service are matched by sublime northern Italian cuisine. (The chef has a way of combining ingredients in inventive ways, as evidenced by the spiced duck breast with glazed pear and the fillet of lamb in olive crust accompanied by sautéed clams.) ✉ *Jln. Teluk Bahang, Teluk Bahang 11050,* ☎ *04/881–2828 or 800/44–UTELL in the U.S.,* ℻ *04/881–2829. 443 rooms. 5 restaurants, 2 bars, 2 pools, 4 tennis courts, health club, windsurfing, boating, dance club. AE, DC, MC, V.*

$$$ ✕▦ **Shangri-La Golden Sands Resort.** The beachfront Golden Sands has lush tropical landscaping around two pools and an open-air lounge and café with a spectacular indoor-outdoor garden effect. Each room is decorated in soft pastels accented with cane; ask for a room that has a private balcony with a view of the sea or hills. Such activities as jungle walks and sand castle–building competitions are arranged, and special poolside events, such as Chinese buffet dinners or barbecues, are held most nights. The hotel's most popular restaurant, Peppino, serves a wide variety of antipasti, pizzas, and pasta. ✉ *Batu Ferringhi Beach, 11100,* ☎ *04/881–1911, 800/942–5050 in the U.S., or 081/747–8485 in the U.K.;* ℻ *04/881–1880. 395 rooms. 2 restaurants, bar, coffee shop, 2 pools, wading pool, snorkeling, windsurfing, boating. AE, DC, MC, V.*

$$$ ✕▦ **Shangri-La's Rasa Sayang Resort.** There's enough activity—programmed and otherwise—here to keep you busy day and night. If you need a break, have a seat by the large pool (the one between the main building and the beach) and wait for it to be transformed—as it is each evening—into a colorfully floodlighted fountain. The resort has a Japanese restaurant (which pleases the many Japanese who stay here) as well as a Chinese restaurant and one that serves European fare. ✉ *Batu Ferringhi Beach, 11100,* ☎ *04/881–1811, 800/942–5050 in the U.S., or 081/747–8485 in the U.K.;* ℻ *04/881–1984. 514 rooms. 3 restaurants, bar, coffee shop, 2 pools, putting green, 4 tennis courts, health club, squash, volleyball, snorkeling, windsurfing, boating, dance club, meeting rooms. AE, DC, MC, V.*

$$ ✕▦ **Casuarina Beach Hotel.** Large (yet cozy) rooms, a low-key pace, and attentive service make this established resort a favorite. Named for the willowy trees that mingle with the palms along the beach, the hotel has a pleasant pool area and offers champagne brunches and country-and-western music nights. Il Ritrovo, an Italian bistro that's decorated with travel posters and candles in wine bottles, is a standout among the hotel's three restaurants. Its excellent three-course meal is good value: you can start with a perfect *antipasti tutti mare* (seafood antipasto), followed by an impressive range of pasta, veal, lamb, and chicken dishes and classic Italian *dolci* (sweets). A Filipino band plays diners' requests. ✉ *Batu Ferringhi Beach, 11100,* ☎ *04/881–1711,* ℻ *04/881–2155. 175 rooms. 3 restaurants, bar, pool, snorkeling, windsurfing, boating. AE, DC, MC, V.*

$$ ▦ **Holiday Inn Penang.** This seven-story hotel surrounds a large pool right on the beach. It's popular with Australians, and it offers such ac-

tivities as bike rides and jungle walks, snooker and Ping-Pong tournaments, and tennis and windsurfing lessons. Rooms face either the hill or the sea. Nonguests can use the hotel's facilities during the day for a fee. ⊠ *Batu Ferringhi Beach, 11100,* ☎ *04/881–1601 or 800/ HOLIDAY in the U.S.,* 🖷 *04/881–1389. 350 rooms. 3 restaurants, 3 bars, 2 tennis courts, pool, hiking, Ping-Pong, windsurfing. AE, DC, MC, V.*

$ 🏨 **Lone Pine.** The best bargain on the beach is somewhat faded, with no pool and few amenities, but its huge beachfront lawn is shady and pleasant. The air-conditioned rooms are spacious if spartan; all have baths, TVs, and refrigerators. Rates include breakfast and morning tea. ⊠ *97 Batu Ferringhi Beach, 11100,* ☎ *04/881–1511. 54 rooms. Restaurant, bar, refrigerators. AE, DC, MC, V. BP.*

Nightlife and the Arts

CULTURAL EVENTS

Eden Seafood Village (☎ 04/881–1852) in Batu Ferringhi holds a cultural show for diners every evening. The show features Malay dancers, Indians laden with bells, and noisy Chinese lion dancers.

The **Pinang Cultural Center** (⊠ Jln. Teluk Bahang, Teluk Bahang, ☎ 04/881–1175), which re-creates a kampung with a *balai* (community center), an Orang Ulu longhouse, a padang for outdoor activities, and an exhibition hall. Three 2½-hour tours, which are conducted every day, introduce you to all aspects of Malaysian culture. A 45-minute performance (held at 10:15, noon, and 3:15) of dance and traditional music is part of the tour. 🎫 *RM35.* ⊘ *Sat.–Thurs. 9:30–5.*

LOUNGES AND CLUBS

The Penang Mutiara Beach Resort's serene **Palmetto Lounge** (⊠ Teluk Bahang, ☎ 04/881–2828) has a resident pianist. The dance floor at **Cinta** (⊠ Batu Ferringhi, ☎ 04/811–1811, ext. 1151), in the Shangri-La Rasa Sayang Resort, draws an international crowd nightly.

Kedah

The state of Kedah, the nation's "rice bowl," surrounds Pinang state to the east and the north, and it includes the vacation islands of Langkawi. Kedah may well be one of Malaysia's most historic states. Here you'll find 7th-century Hindu/Buddhist ruins and a sultanate that dates from pre-Islamic times. The Thais ruled the state from 1821 until 1846, and though it still shares a border with Thailand, this border was greatly reduced when the state of Perlis was created out of Kedah's northwest corner in 1842.

Alor Setar

🕸 *269 km (167 mi) north of Butterworth, 462 km (287 mi) northwest of KL.*

Alor Setar (pronounced, and sometimes spelled, without the "e"), the capital of Kedah, has a number of attractive mosques and royal residences, most of which are in the center of town. A good place to begin is on Jalan Raja at the **Balai Besar,** the Thai-influenced Great Audience Hall, once used for royal receptions. The current open-sided structure with columns and wood carvings was built in 1904 to replace an 18th-century building. Near the hall is the three-tier, octagonal **Balai Nobat,** built to house the sacred musical instruments of the royal orchestra. Unfortunately, you can only go inside if you make prior arrangements in the government office across from it.

The **Muzium di Raja** (Royal Museum) near the Balai Besar was built in 1763. Used as a royal residence until 1983, today it houses a collection of memorabilia and photographs of previous sultans. Some of the rooms remain as they were when the last sultan lived here. ⊠ *Jln. Raja,* ☎ *no phone.* 🎟 *Free.* 🕐 *Sat.–Thurs. 10–6, Fri. 10–12 and 2:30–6.*

On the corner of Jalan Pekan Melayu and Jalan Kampung Perak, the **Masjid Zahir,** an imposing Moorish-style mosque with the usual onion domes and minarets, was built in 1921. On Jalan Tengku Ibrahim you'll find the building that houses the **Bali Seni Negeri** (State Art Gallery). The gallery's collections aren't really worth your time, but you should make a point of pausing to look at the lovely colonial architecture (1912) of the former courthouse.

If you're interested in seeing some stone artifacts recovered during the archaeological excavations at Lembah Bujang (literally "Bachelor Valley"), as well as antique Chinese ceramics, head for the **Muzium Negeri** (National Museum) about 2 km (1 mi) north of Alor Setar. ⊠ *Jln. Lebuhraya Darulaman,* ☎ *no phone.* 🎟 *Free.* 🕐 *Sat.–Thurs. 10–6, Fri. 10–12 and 2:30–6.*

Before you leave town, soak up some local atmosphere at the "Wednesday Centre" or **Pekan Rabu,** a market somewhat confusingly opened every day of the week from early morning until late in the evening. A large modern building on Jalan Tuanku Ibrahim, right in the middle of town, houses a range of stalls where you can find everything from handicrafts to local Malay delicacies.

Langkawi

🟢 *30 km (19 mi) off the coast from Kuala Lipis, which is 171 km (106 mi) northwest of KL.*

Langkawi is an archipelago of 101 islands (there are only 99 at high tide) north of Pinang and just south of Thailand. A couple of decades ago, it was a Robinson Crusoe hideaway; today it's one of Malaysia's hottest destinations, and the government hopes to see it become even more popular. (Prime Minister Mahathir is from Kedah state, and he has thrown his not inconsiderable weight behind its development.) Virtually all the development—including the building of an international airport—has taken place on the major island, Pulau Langkawi, after which the whole group is named. To further encourage tourism, the whole region is a duty-free zone. (Though beer, wine, and spirits are much cheaper here than elsewhere in the country, you may have a hard time finding alcohol outside your hotel owing to the region's devout Muslim population. Indeed, most activity is focused around the hotels and resorts.)

The main town of Kuah—which is 4 km (2 mi) from the ferry terminal in the southeast of Pulau Langkawi—has a few hotels and shopping blocks. Most resorts are along the island's southwest coast, particularly around Pantai Cenang, Pantai Tengah, Pantai Kok, and Teluk Burau; there are a few more resorts along the northwestern and northeastern coasts. In the northwestern corner, there are also pristine rain forests. Though Langkawi is still largely rural—and many of its residents live simple, traditional lifestyles—it has a good system of well-maintained and well-signposted roads, making driving around easy. Try to get out and explore the beaches not only on the main island but also on the other 100 islands. There are boats for hire as well as organized trips (☞ Tour Operators *and* Visitor Information *in* Northwest Coast and Central Highlands Essentials, *below*). Take a boat, find your island, snorkel, dive, and laze away the day on your own beach.

Pulau Langkawi has a number of theme parks, most of them of limited appeal to non-Malaysian visitors. You could, however, spend half a day or so exploring these parks and learning about the archipelago's legends (Langkawi is often billed as the "Isles of Legends"). Some of these tales are rendered in stone at **Lagenda Langkawi,** between the ferry terminal and a large square dominated by a vast, ugly statue of an eagle. Visit late in the afternoon or risk sweltering in the heat (there's no shade anywhere, and no refreshment stands). ⊠ *RM5.* ⊙ *Daily 9–9.*

★ In the north of Pulau Langkawi, far from the resorts, is the huge **Kompleks Budaya Kraf Langkawi.** Here handicrafts from all over Malaysia are a sold in a lavish mosquelike series of white-stone galleries. The complex has a sister operation in KL (☞ Exploring *in* Kuala Lumpur, *above*). ⊠ *Teluk Yu,* ☎ *04/959–1913.* ⊠ *Free.* ⊙ *Daily 9–6.*

Also in the north is the **Galleri Perdana,** which houses more than 10,000 state gifts presented to the Malaysian prime minister. Some are amazingly tacky and others are quite impressive. Don't miss the collection of automobiles. ⊠ *Kilim,* ☎ *04/959–1498.* ⊠ *RM2.* ⊙ *Tues.– Thurs. and weekends 10–5, Fri 10–12:15 and 3–5.*

You certainly won't be the only one around if you take a trip to the popular **Pulau Paya Marine Park,** about three hours south of Pulau Langkawi, for a look at a coral reef. The excursion offered by Sriwani Tours & Travel (☞ Tour Operators *in* Northwest Coast and Central Highlands Essentials, *below*) is recommended. The trip includes hotel transfers, a high-speed catamaran ride to the park, lunch, and a stop at a glass-bottom reef-viewing platform from which you can snorkel.

Dining and Lodging

Although the best places to eat in Langkawi are generally inside the resorts, there are a few independent restaurants that merit a visit. Around Kuah you'll find some simple, locally owned stalls that offer good food. (Note, however, that alcohol isn't served, and English is rarely spoken.) Your lodging choices range from luxurious, expensive resorts to local hotels with ultracheap, fan-cooled rooms.

$$ ✕ **Bon Ton at the Beach.** Housed in an open-sided, Balinese-style pavilion, Bon Ton is just south of the airport and north of Pantai Cenang. The very good East–West cuisine, delightful ambience for both lunch and dinner, and rich cakes (they're legendary) have made this restaurant popular with Pulau Langkawi's "in crowd." You'll also find a gift shop at the entrance to the restaurant pavilion and right on the main road, as well as an informal food stall with inexpensive local food, the Warung Kopi, run by the same team that operates the main establishment. ⊠ *Mukim Kedawang, Pantai Cenang,* ☎ *04/955–3643. AE, D, MC, V.*

$$ ✕ **Charlie's Place.** This restaurant, which is part of the Langkawi Yacht Club, just east of Kuah, offers sea breezes, sea views, and good Western and local food. Try the grilled lamb chops. ⊠ *Jln. Datuk Syed Omar, Kuah,* ☎ *04/966–7193. AE, DC, MC, V.*

$$$$ 🛏 **Datai.** Tucked away on Pulau Langkawi's northwestern tip (a 40-
★ minute drive from most attractions), this hideaway resort faces the turquoise Andaman Sea and is backed by a rain forest. The large, open-air main building—which serves as a reception area and lounge—overlooks a small valley that carves its way steeply down to the beach, a 10-minute walk away. Open-air corridors link the lobby to the guest quarters, many of which also look down into the valley. The large rooms are decorated in silk and red *merbau,* a warm Malaysian hardwood that shines from the floors to the walls. Each room has a bedroom with a king-size bed; a living room with a bar and two daybeds; and a grand bathroom with two vanities, a shower, a bath, and luggage space. Vil-

las and suites are almost twice as big and have decks with sun lounges and elevated verandas. Though the food here isn't innovative, it's of a high quality and is well orchestrated (note that only hotel guests are permitted to eat in the restaurants). Fine Thai cuisine is available every evening in the gorgeous open-sided Pavilion restaurant. As a guest at Datai, you also have the option of having dinner at the adjacent Andaman resort, which is managed by the same hotel group. The Andaman's Kamogawa restaurant offers refined Japanese cuisine. ⊠ *Jln. Teluk Datai, 07000,* ☎ *604/950–2500, 603/245–3515 in KL, 800/ 447–7462 in the U.S, or 0800/181535 in the U.K.;* ℻ *604/959–2600 or 603/245–3540 in KL. 54 rooms, 40 villas, 14 suites. 2 restaurants, bar, minibars, 2 pools, 18-hole golf course, 2 tennis courts, health club, hiking, beach, windsurfing, boating, mountain bikes, meeting rooms. AE, DC, MC, V.*

$$$ ⊞ **Berjaya Langkawi Beach & Spa Resort.** Set below the forest-covered hills in the far northwest of Pulau Langkawai, the Berjaya reflects its Malay heritage in the architecture. All rooms have a balcony or terrace that overlooks the bay. Perhaps the main attraction here is the outstanding spa (open to guests and nonguests alike) with its wide range of health and beauty treatments—everything from Oriental reflexology to flotation-tank treatments to aromatherapy facials. ⊠ *Teluk Burau 07000,* ☎ *04/959–1888,* ℻ *04/959–1886. 150 suites. Restaurant, bar, pool, beauty salon, massage, sauna, spa, steam room, 2 tennis courts, beach, dance club. AE, DC, MC, V.*

$$$ ⊞ **Pelangi Beach Resort.** Management intended to recreate the atmosphere of a kampung here, but with such facilities as a pool with a swim-up bar, the atmosphere is really that of a large (25 beachfront acres) resort—albeit one where the service, amenities, and architecture are tops. In the center of the large lobby is a relaxing lounge where you can take tea or sip cocktails. Guest rooms are small, and the extensive use of (compressed) wood and heavy carpeting makes them seem even smaller; fortunately, they come with balconies as well as air-conditioning and fans. About a third face the sea, another third a man-made lake, and the remainder the back lot (as usual, room rates reflect these views). The beach isn't spectacular, but at low tide you can wade across to a nearby island for privacy. ⊠ *Pantai Cenang 07000,* ☎ *04/ 955–1001 or 03/261–0393 in KL,* ℻ *04/955–1122. 302 rooms, 55 suites. 2 restaurants, pool, sauna, 3 tennis courts, exercise room, squash, travel services. AE, DC, MC, V.*

Northwest Coast and Central Highlands Essentials

Arriving and Departing

By Airplane

Penang International Airport (☎ 04/643–0811) in Bayan Lepas (about 18 km/11 mi south of Georgetown) is served by Malaysia Airline System (MAS), Singapore Airlines, Cathay Pacific, and Thai Airways International. Pinang is about a 40-minute flight from KL. Airport taxis use a coupon system with fixed fares. A one-way ride into the city costs RM19; to Batu Ferringhi it's RM30. A public bus (Yellow No. 83) just outside the airport entrance will take you to the KOMTAR terminal in the city center for RM1.40. Buses run hourly 6 AM–midnight.

Langkawi International Airport (☎ 04/955–1311) is at Padang Matsirat, in the southwest of Pulau Langkawi and about 20 km (12 mi) from Kuah. There are several daily MAS flights from Pinang, Johor Bahru, and KL as well as flights from Singapore (SilkAir as well as MAS),

Japan, and Taiwan. MAS flights are often fully booked, so make reservations far in advance and reconfirm them. Unless your resort can arrange for pickup, you'll need to take a taxi from the airport. Cabs are plentiful and fares are fixed; pick up a coupon at the taxi counter. You shouldn't have to pay more than RM10–RM15 to any destination.

Ipoh's **Sultan Azlan Shar Airport** (☎ 05/312–2460) is served by daily flights from KL. It's 5 km (3 mi) west of the city, and taxis charge RM10 for the trip.

By Boat

Ferries to Pinang from Butterworth operate 24 hours a day, running about every 20 minutes 6 AM–midnight and hourly midnight–6 AM. The fare is RM1 per vehicle *and* 60 sen per person. Daily express ferries ply between Pinang and Sumatra, Indonesia, departing from Georgetown at 9 AM and arriving at Medan's port of Belawan five hours later (no visa required for American and British citizens). The return trip departs from Belawan at 9 AM. The one-way fare is RM96. The terminal office is next to the tourist information office on Lebuh Pantai, near Ft. Cornwallis.

An air-conditioned express ferry departs from Pinang to Langkawi at 8 AM daily and makes the return journey at 6 PM. The hour-long trip costs RM35 one way. You can also reach Langkawi aboard a ferry from Kuala Kedah (near Alor Setar). Ferries depart frequently between 8 AM and 7:30 PM daily; the trip takes a little over an hour and costs RM15 one way. There's also ferry service from Kuala Perlis, near the Thai border; the trip takes 45 minutes and costs RM13. Ferries to Langkawi from Thailand depart three times daily from Satun, on the Thai border; the journey takes 1½ hours and costs RM15 one way.

By Bus

The **main bus station** (☎ 04/634–4928) serving Pinang is on the Butterworth side near the ferry terminal. Coach service to Singapore can be booked through **Hosni Express** (☎ 04/261–7746). The fare from KL to Pinang is around RM17.

By Car

To reach Pulau Pinang, you can either drive across the Penang Bridge from Butterworth (RM7 toll) or take your car across on the ferry (☞ By Boat, *above*). There's no bridge connecting the mainland to Langkawi; neither is there vehicular ferry service.

By Train

The train station serving Pinang is next to the bus and ferry terminals in Butterworth. You can buy a ticket at the **Butterworth Station** (☎ 04/331–2796) or at a booking station at the Pinang **ferry terminal** (✉ Pengkalan Weld, Georgetown, ☎ 04/261–0290). It's not a long walk from Butterworth station to the ferry, but you'll have to carry your own luggage. On the Pinang side, porters and taxi drivers will help.

The Ekspres Langkawi rail service runs from KL to Alor Setar, where you can take a bus or taxi to Kuala Kedah for the ferry service across to Langkawi.

Getting Around

By Bus

Five bus companies operate on Pulau Pinang. Blue buses, which run to the north of the island (including Batu Ferringhi), and green buses, which run through Georgetown toward Ayer Itam, leave from the station near the Pengkalan Weld ferry terminal. Red-stripe buses serve Georgetown and depart from a station on Leubh Vistoria. All buses eventually pass through the station at KOMTAR. You buy tickets from conductors on the bus and pay according to the distance you travel. For information on routes and schedules, call 04/262–9357.

It's scarcely worth bothering with the limited public transport in Langkawi, where the three bus routes leaving from the town of Kuah depart once every hour or two. You're better off taking a taxi, or hiring a car or motorbike.

By Car
Avis (☎ 04/643–9633 and 04/811–1522), **Hertz** (☎ 04/263–5914), and **National** (☎ 04/643–4205) have counters at Pinang airport and in Georgetown. In Langkawi, rental cars are available at the airport through **Angkaland Tours & Travel** (☎ 04/955–5797) and **Bayou Tours & T Travel** (☎ 04/955–7007).

Instead of renting a vehicle and driving to the Cameron Highlands yourself, consider hiring a chauffeured, air-conditioned car. From the KL International Airport the five- to six-hour drive will cost about RM350 (the six-hour drive south from Pinang costs about the same). A few words of caution if your destination is Ye Olde Smokehouse: despite assurances that drivers will go all the way up the mountain to the hotel, they may try to leave you at the taxi station in Tanah Rata. Your best recourse is to refuse to pay the fare until the driver has arranged for a second taxi to go the rest of the way up the hill.

By Taxi
You can pick up what's known as an "outstation taxi" from cab stands next to the bus stations in all major Malaysian towns. On Pulau Pinang, you'll find stands near many hotels. The minimum charge is RM3, more for air-conditioned cars. Though taxis have meters, the drivers prefer not to use them. Establish the price before you get in. Two companies are **Syarikat Georgetown Taxi** (☎ 04/261–3853) and **Island Taxi** (☎ 04/262–5127). There are always taxis available at Langkawi airport and ferry terminal, as well as in Kuah. Your resort will probably need to phone a cab if you wish to hire one.

By Trishaw
Pulau Pinang's Georgetown is one of the few places in Malaysia where trishaws—large tricycles with a carriage for passengers and freight—are not only available, but also provide a safe, pleasant, and inexpensive way to sightsee. (Not only tourists but some residents—mainly elderly Chinese women and children heading for school—rely on them.) Don't be alarmed if your trishaw heads the wrong way up a one-way street; Pinang motorists are used to making allowances for these vehicles. Negotiate the route and fare before you get in. A short trip is likely to cost only RM5. If you want to hire a trishaw for longer, the usual hourly rate for one passenger is from RM15–RM20. The driver will, of course, ask for more, but negotiate.

Contacts and Resources

Emergencies
Pulau Pinang. Ambulance and police: ☎ 999; the Penang Adventist Hospital (☎ 04/637–3344) also sends ambulances. **Fire:** ☎ 994. **Hospitals and clinics:** Hospital Besar (✉ Jln. Residency, Georgetown, ☎ 04/637–3333) or the Specialists Centre (✉ 19 Jln. Logan, Georgetown, ☎ 04/636–8501). All hospitals and clinics are able to dispense medication.

Pulau Langkawi. Ambulance and police: ☎ 999. **Fire:** ☎ 994. **Hospitals and clinics:** Daerah Langkawi (✉ Jln. Bukit Teguh, ☎ 04/966–3333),

Perdana Polyclinics (⌧ Lot 110, Pusat Daganan Kelana Mas, Kuah, ☎ 04/966–8526). All hospitals and clinics can provide medication.

English-Language Bookstores

Once you're outside the major tourist areas, English is a rare commodity. It's best to stock up on reading material at major resorts or in shops in KL, Pinang, or Langkawi. On Pulau Pinang, the **Times Bookstore** is on the first floor of the Penang Plaza shopping complex (⌧ 126 Jln. Burmah, Georgetown, ☎ 04/262–3443). Other Georgetown bookstores include: **City Book Centre** (⌧ 11 Lebuh Bishop, ☎ 04/265–1593) and **Academic** (⌧ 23 Lebuh Bishop, ☎ 04/261–5780).

On Langkawi, major resorts have their own souvenir and gift shops that sell books and magazines. You can also try **Pustaka Langkawi** (⌧ 55 Persiaran Mutiara, Pusat Dagangan Kelana Mas, Kuah, ☎ 04/966–3323).

Tour Operators

Several companies offer general tours of Pulau Pinang. The most popular is a 73-km (45-mi), 3½-hour drive around the island. From Batu Ferringhi it goes through Malay kampungs, rubber estates, and nutmeg orchards; stops at the Snake Temple; cruises past the Universiti Sains Malaysia campus and through Georgetown; and then returns via the beach road. The principal tour companies also offer such excursions as "Pinang Hill and Temples," "City and Heritage," and "Pinang by Night," in addition to trips to the world's largest butterfly farm (at Teluk Bahang) and the Botanical Gardens. Operators can also arrange such harbor cruises as a sunset dinner voyage, a waterfront and Pinang Bridge trip, and a Monkey Beach excursion.

Pinang's major companies include: **Mayflower Acme Tours** (⌧ Shangri-La Inn, Jln. Magazine, Georgetown, ☎ 04/262–3724; ⌧ Tan Chong Building, 23 Pengkalan Weld, Georgetown, ☎ 04/262–8196) and **Tour North East** (⌧ Golden Sands Hotel, Batu Ferringhi, ☎ 04/881–1662; ⌧ Penang Plaza, 4th floor, Georgetown, ☎ 04/261–9563). Also, the **Penang Tourist Guides Association** (☞ Visitor Information, *below*) offers tours of Georgetown for RM29.

There are at least 10 tour companies in Langkawi that can arrange coach tours to such main-island sights as Mahsuri's Tomb, as well as to nearby islands. Try **Mayflower Acme Tours** (⌧ Pelangi Beach Resort, ☎ 04/966–1871) or **Reliance Sightseeing** (⌧ Delima Resort, Kuala Muda, ☎ 04/955–2016). For cruises by high-speed catamaran down to Pulau Payar Marine Park, about an hour from Langkawi, contact **Sriwani Tours & Travel** (⌧ Jetty Point Complex, near Kuah, ☎ 04/966–7318).

Travel Agencies

On Pulau Pinang try: **American Express** (⌧ Pan Chang Building, 274 Lebuh Victoria, Georgetown, ☎ 04/262–3724) or **Thomas Cook** (⌧ 1 Pengkalan Weld, Georgetown, ☎ 04/261–0511). On the third floor of Georgetown's KOMTAR complex on Jalan Penang you'll find a branch of **MAS** (☎ 04/262–0011) as well as **Ace Tours and Travel** (☎ 04/261–1205), which often sells airline tickets for less than MAS.

Langkawi also has an office of the **MAS** (⌧ Lot 1598 Bangunan Tabung Haji, Pokok Asam, ☎ 04/966–6622).

Visitor Information

In Georgetown, the **MTPB** (☎ 04/643–0501 airport or 04/262–0066 KOMTAR) has a counter at the airport, an office opposite the clock tower near Ft. Cornwallis, and an office in KOMTAR; hours are weekdays 8:30–4:45 and Saturday 8:30–1. The **Penang Tourist Guides Association** (☎ 04/261–4461 KOMTAR or 04/261–6663 Ft. Cornwallis) distributes information from centers on Level 3 of the KOMTAR building and downtown near Ft. Cornwallis at the intersection of Lebuh Pantai and Lebuh Light. Both booths are open weekdays 8–noon and 2–4 and Saturday 8–12:30.

In Langkawi, there's a tourism information counter at the airport where you can pick up free brochures. For more detailed information, try the **Langkawi Tourist Information Centre** (✉ Jln. Persiaran Putra, Kuah, ☎ 04/966–7789). It's open daily 9–5.

THE SOUTHERN PENINSULA AND THE EAST COAST

Although the peninsula's southern tip and eastern coast are becoming more developed, they're still very much places for visitors with a sense of adventure. Along coastal roads—from Desaru all the way up to the Thai border—towns and resorts are few; beaches, though tempting, have few facilities; and public transportation is sporadic.

Increased tourism has brought some development to the coastal towns of Pahang state. In Terengganu state, changes have been wrought both by tourism and the discovery of petroleum a couple decades ago. Still, along the state's coast you're as likely to find a hotel consisting of simple thatch chalets as you are a luxury resort with all the trimmings. The tourist infrastructure of the offshore islands, the best known of which is Pulau Tioman, has been developed, and many now have scuba facilities. Outside these areas, however, the east coast still putters along with an economy based largely on fishing and agriculture. But that's really what makes it a delight.

Negri Sembilan

Between KL and Melaka is an area called Negri Sembilan (Nine States). Although it's not a major tourist destination it does offer you the chance to see a different side of Malaysia. Negri Sembilan is unique in that its Malay peoples are originally from the matriarchal Minangkabau tribe of western Sumatra, and their traditional law, or *adat*, differs from that of other Malays.

Seremban

28 *64 km (37 mi) southwest of KL, 320 km (200 mi) northwest of Singapore.*

Negri Sembilan's capital is a busy city with attractive botanical gardens and a cultural center where there are several examples of early Minangkabau architecture. In both Negeri Sembilan and West Sumatra, roofs have a buffalo-horn shape, commemorating the victory of a Sumatran buffalo over a buffalo representing the invading Javanese. (The tribal name of "minangkabau" means "victory of the buffalo.")

The main reason for leaving the North–South Highway, which bypasses Seremban, is to visit the **Taman Seni Budaya Negeri.** Just 3 km (2 mi) outside Seremban itself and close to the highway, this center showcases local culture. Exhibits in the main museum aren't remarkable, but on the grounds are three superb original wooden houses that were reconstructed here almost 50 years ago. The most elaborate of these, the **Istana Ampang Tinggi,** is a fine example of the wood-carver's art. ✉ Jln. Labu. 🎫 *Free.* 🕐 *Tues., Wed., and weekends 10–6; Thurs. 8:15–1; Fri. 10–12:15 and 2:45–6.*

OFF THE
BEATEN PATH

SRI MENANTI — Thirty kilometers (19 miles) east of Seremban is what was once the royal capital, Sri Menanti. Here you can visit an ancient royal burial ground; the "new" *istana* (palace), which was built in the 1930s; and the old istana—constructed in 1902 in the Minangkabau style (built entirely without nails) and used by the sultan until 1931. The drive to Sri Menanti takes you through hilly country, where bougainvillea and hibiscus abound. ▣ *Free.* ⊙ *Tues., Wed., and weekends 10–6; Thurs. 8:15–1; Fri. 10–12:15 and 2:45–6.*

Melaka

The state of Melaka (Malacca), once an important Muslim sultanate, has been reduced to a tiny wedge of land along the strait named after it, with Negri Sembilan to the north and Johor to the south and east. However, the state's eponymous capital—Malaysia's oldest city—is full of interesting sights. On its northern outskirts, the region of Air Keroh (Ayer Keroh) has been developed as a recreational area with a number of attractions.

Air Keroh

㉙ *70 km (44 mi) southeast of Seremban, 134 km (83 mi) southeast of KL.*

You could spend a pleasant half day in Air Keroh, either on your way south from KL to Melaka City or as a side trip from Melaka City (a taxi from town should cost around RM7). Start at the **Hutan Rekreasi** (Recreational Forest), where you can stroll along paths through undisturbed vegetation and learn about the various plants from the helpful labels. ☎ *06/232–8401.* ▣ *Free.* ⊙ *Daily 7–6.*

If you haven't yet seen a Malaysian zoo, you could have a look at the small **Melaka Zoo** near the Recreational Forest. It has around 50 species of wildlife from Southeast Asia and Africa. ☎ *06/232–4053.* ▣ *RM3.* ⊙ *Weekdays 10–6, weekends 9:30–6:30.*

The **Taman Rama Rama** resolves any question you may have had about whether or not Malaysia is a lepidopterist's paradise. At this attractive Butterfly Farm, some 200 local species fly freely. ☎ *06/232–0033.* ▣ *RM4.* ⊙ *Daily 8:30–5:30.*

If you only have time for one attraction, head straight for **Taman Mini Malaysia,** attractive gardens where traditional houses typical of all 13 Malaysian states are showcased. The grounds also contain the **Mini ASEAN Village,** where you can view structures from Malaysia's neighbors in the Association of Southeast Asian Nations (ASEAN). ☎ *06/231–6089.* ▣ *RM3.* ⊙ *Weekdays 10–6, weekends 9:30–6:30.*

Melaka City

㉚ *10 km (6 mi) south of Air Keroh, 155 km (97 mi) southeast of KL.*

Established as the capital of a Malay sultanate in the 14th century, Melaka City was captured in 1511 by the Portuguese, who built fortifications; in 1641 the Dutch invaded and took possession. The city thrived owing to its port—once the most important in Southeast Asia—which saw many a ship from China, India, and Arabia. Eventually, however, it became a sleepy backwater as the Dutch and British established more important trading centers elsewhere, including the entrepôt of Singapore. (The tomb of the Sultan of Johor—the man who signed over the rights of the island of Singapura to Raffles in 1819—is in Melaka City's Tranquerah Mosque, a 150-year-old building of Sumatran design.)

The British took over Melaka in 1824 and remained in control until Malaysian independence in 1957. After a long period of languishing in the doldrums, Melaka is now enjoying a rebirth. Construction has spread out along the coast, an oil refinery has been built to the north, factories have sprung up in the vicinity, and a vast land-reclamation project has been completed at the mouth of the Melaka River estuary. Despite all the industrial development, Melaka is still Malaysia's most historic town, with impressive buildings and ruins that date from all its periods of colonial rule.

The center of historic Melaka is the small square in front of the Stadhuys and Christ Church. This is backed by St. Paul's Hill and its various historic sights. There are several museums within walking distance of both the square and the hill. Across the river from the Stadhuys is the old Chinatown, with its temples, antique shops, and fine examples of 19th-century Melaka architecture.

Start at one of the city's oldest Portuguese ruins, dating from 1521, **St. Paul's Church,** atop St. Paul's Hill. The statue at the summit commemorates St. Francis Xavier, who was buried here before being moved to his permanent resting spot in Goa, India, where he began his missionary career.

Come down the hill and explore the **Porta de Santiago,** an entrance gate that is all that remains of A Famosa, a Portuguese fortress. This gate has become the symbol of the state of Melaka.

Near the Porta de Santiago is the **Muzium Budaya,** whose exhibits on Muslim culture and royalty are housed in a re-creation of a traditional wooden palace known as the Sultanate Palace. ✉ *Jln. Kota,* ☎ *06/ 282–7464.* 🎫 *RM2.* ⊙ *Mon.–Thurs. and Sat.–Sun. 9–6, Fri. 9–12:15 and 2:45–6.*

Firmly aground on the riverbank—on your left as you head toward the square surrounding the Stadthuys (☞ *below*)—is a re-creation of a Portuguese ship that sank off the coast of Melaka. It houses the **Maritime Museum,** which offers a glimpse of the sailing vessels and trade at the height of the Melaka sultanate in the 14th century. ✉ *Off Jln. Merdeka,* ☎ *no phone.* 🎫 *RM2.* ⊙ *Mon.–Thurs. and Sat.–Sun. 9– 6, Fri. 9–12:15 and 2:45–6.*

The **Stadthuys** complex is good and solid, in true Dutch style. Note the thick masonry walls, the heavy hardwood doors, and the windows with wrought-iron hinges. The complex was erected between 1641 and 1660 and used until recently for government offices. It has now been restored and converted into a museum with artifacts from both the Dutch and Portuguese eras. Across from the Stadthuys is another fine example of Dutch architecture. **Christ Church** was built in 1753 of salmon-pink bricks brought from Zeeland (Netherlands) and faced in red laterite.

Cross the Melaka River to the west bank and the **Chinese quarter** of narrow streets that are lined with traditional shophouses, ancient temples, and clan houses (note the interesting carved doors). The **Cheng Hoon Teng Temple** is one of the country's oldest Chinese temples. You'll recognize it by its ceremonial masts, which tower over the surrounding houses, and by the porcelain and glass animals and flowers that decorate its eaves. Built in the Nanking style, the temple embraces three doctrines: Buddhist, Taoist, and Confucian. You can tell the monks apart by their robes; the Taoists, for example, expose their right shoulder. On your way out, you can buy sandalwood (the scent that permeates the temple) as well as papier-mâché houses and cars and symbolic money ("hell money"), used to burn as offerings during funerals.

Close by on **Temple Street** are the papier-mâché craftspeople, who fashion legendary figures of Chinese mythology. Wander on, turning right onto Jalan Hang Lekiu and right again onto Jalan Hang Jebat, and you'll find good pork satay at No. 83, and several coffee shops that sell wonderful noodles.

From Jalan Hang Jebat take a left onto Jalan Kubu, then another left onto Jalan Tun Tan Cheng Lock. This street was once called Millionaires' Row because of its glorious mansions, built by wealthy Babas (Peranakan men) in the 19th century. The **Baba and Nyonya Heritage Museum** is set in a superb town house that's furnished with many items that belonged to the original owners. The museum offers a good deal of insight into the lifestyle and architecture of the Peranakans (Straits Chinese), whose culture and cuisine assimilated many Malay elements. ⊠ *48-50 Jln. Tun Tan Cheng Lock,* ☎ *06/283–1273.* ⊡ *RM7.* ⊙ *Daily 10–12:30 and 2–4:30.*

From the Baba and Nyonya museum, take a taxi to **Bukit China** (Chinese Hill), about 10 minutes northeast of the city center, for a glimpse of more Chinese history. Six centuries ago, a Ming emperor's envoy set up the first trade arrangements in this ancient Malay capital; a daughter of the emperor was sent to Melaka as wife to Sultan Mansor Shah. She and her 500 ladies-in-waiting set up housekeeping on Bukit China. The early Chinese traders and notables who lived and died in Melaka were buried on this hill, and their 17,000 graves remain, making this the largest Chinese cemetery outside China. Stop off at the **Sultan's Well,** at the foot of Bukit China. Tossing a coin into the well—a custom that dates from the founding of Melaka by Raja Iskandar Shah in the 14th century—is said to ensure your return to the city.

Dining and Lodging

For a delicious, inexpensive dinner, head for the row of stalls known as Glutton's Corner. It used to be on the seafront, but reclamation has pushed it far inland, close to the big Mahkota Square shopping center.

$$ ✕ **Bunga Raya Restaurant.** Also known as Madam Fatso's (after its not-so-slender proprietor), Bunga Raya is perfect for a seafood feast. The place is basic—bright neon lights over a semi-open-air cluster of tables—but the food is good. There are huge Sri Lankan crabs (live for steaming or for transformation into chili crab) as well as good steamed fish and prawns. Ask Madam or her daughter for recommendations on what's best the night you visit. ⊠ *Jln. Merdeka,* ☎ *no phone. No credit cards. No lunch.*

$–$$ ✕ **Jonkers.** Melaka's prettiest place to eat also has some of the most delicious food, but unfortunately it's only open from 11 AM to 5 PM. In the historic heart of the town, it's housed in a lovingly resorted Peranakan town house that's amid several antiques shops. You pass through a tastefully stocked gift shop before entering an open internal courtyard with a well surrounded by colorful tiles. The light, tasty offerings include several imaginative East–West dishes, a Nonya set lunch, and excellent cakes. ⊠ *17 Jln. Hang Jebat,* ☎ *06/283–5578. AE, DC, MC, V.*

$$$ ✕⊡ **Century Mahkota Hotel.** The newest luxury hotel in town sits on reclaimed land behind the Mahkota Parade shopping complex. The hotel is glossy and spacious and has a good number of recreational facilities. Rooms are tastefully furnished and well equipped. You can enjoy freshly made pizza at the Pizza Terrace, international fare at the Cafe Mahkota, or a variety of Asian cuisines at the aptly named Spices restaurant. Though the hotel is a short walk from several sights, there's free shuttle service to the center of town. ⊠ *Jln. Merdeka, 75000,* ☎ *06/ 281–2828,* ℻ *06/281–2323. 295 rooms. 3 restaurants, 2 bars, piano* *bar, 2 pools, beauty salon, golf privileges, 2 tennis courts, squash, business services, meeting rooms. AE, DC, MC, V.*

$$$ ⊞ **Renaissance Melaka Hotel.** Operations at this 24-story hotel run
★ smoothly, making it a good choice whether you're visiting on business or for pleasure. Guest rooms are bright (be sure to ask for one that overlooks the gardens), decorated in pastel colors, and equipped with IDD phones, color TVs and VCRs, and refrigerators; rooms on the Renaissance floor have private concierge services. In the evening there's usually live entertainment in the Famosa Lounge. Special package rates may be 60% lower than the listed room rates; ask about discounts when making reservations. ⊠ *Jln. Bendahara, 75100,* ☎ *06/284–8888,* FAX *06/284–9269. 295 rooms. 2 restaurants, bar, no-smoking floors, refrigerators, pool, exercise room, squash, business services, meeting rooms, travel services. AE, DC, MC, V.*

$$ ⊞ **City Bayview.** This modern 14-story high-rise stands in contrast to the older buildings of Melaka. The look of the hotel is strictly functional (read: no personality), but the rooms, with motel-like furniture and IDD phones, are clean and satisfactory. ⊠ *Jln. Bendahara, 75100,* ☎ *06/239–7888,* FAX *06/236–7699. 181 rooms. 2 restaurants, coffee shop, pool, exercise room, dance club, laundry service, business services, meeting rooms. AE, DC, MC, V.*

Nightlife

Melaka's sights are brought to life nightly in a **sound-and-light show,** in which the city's history is told to the accompaniment of Malay music, sound effects, and illuminated monuments. The first show is at 8:30 PM; the second, narrated in English, is at 9:30 PM. They're held in the stadium between Jalan Merdeka and Jalan Parameswara.

Johor

The state of Johor, which covers the southern tip of the peninsula, has huge oil palm and pineapple plantations, old rubber estates, canning factories, and a considerable amount of industry. The state was founded by the sultan of Melaka in 1511, when he was ousted by the Portuguese, and it has been ruled with an iron hand by subsequent sultans ever since. The capital, Johor Bahru, is at the very tip of the peninsula and is connected to Singapore by a causeway—built in the '20s, bombed by the British, and rebuilt by the Japanese during World War II—and, farther east by a bridge that opened in 1998. Eastern Johor state is less developed, and its attractive beaches and lovely islands are attracting more and more visitors, especially from Singapore.

Johor Bahru

③ *368 km (221 mi) southeast of KL, 206 km (128 mi) southeast of Melaka, 1 km (½ mi) north of Singapore.*

At the southern tip of peninsular Malaysia and connected to Singapore, the royal and administrative capital of Johor state, Johor Bahru (JB), suffers from a lack of town planning that stands in sharp contrast to Singapore's orderliness. There's no center and streets follow no grid or other logical plan but rather run into one another higgledy-piggledy. The pace used to be noticeably different, too, but JB's days as a laid-back escape from the planned sterility of its neighbor are over. Because labor costs are lower than in Singapore, the last few years have seen rapid commercial and industrial development. The pace is picking up, taxis are smarter, and there are new first-class hotels; congestion and pollution are also on the rise. Although JB makes an excellent hub for exploring the east and west coasts of the peninsula, spending more than a couple hours here may prove tiresome.

The town's major sight is the **Istana Besar** (⊠ Jln. Tun Dato Ismail), the old palace of the sultans of Johor. This neoclassical, rather institutional-looking building, erected in 1866, has been converted into a museum; it holds hunting trophies as well as ceremonial regalia and ancient weapons. You can see the displays daily 9–5 for RM18. The new sultan's palace, the **Istana Bukit Serene** (⊠ Jln. Straits View), was built in 1933 and is noted for its gardens, which are popular with joggers.

Masjid Sultan Abu Bakar (⊠ Jln. Gerstak Merah, off Jln. Tun Dato Ismail), built in 1900 in European Victorian style, is one of Malaysia's most beautiful mosques, with sparkling white towers and domes surrounding the main prayer hall. It can accommodate more than 2,000 worshipers. At the cemetery on Jalan Muhamadiah, the **Sultan Abu Bakar Mausoleum** has been the final resting place for the Johor royal family since it left Singapore. You can't enter the mausoleum, but a number of impressive Muslim tombs surround it.

Dining and Lodging

Although there are smart restaurants at Johor's top hotels, the local favorite dining option is outdoors at one of the Tepian Tebrau food stalls along the seafront on Jalan Skudai. Seafood steamboat is the speciality, but Malay curries and Chinese dishes are also offered.

$$–$$$ ✕ **Straits Garden Seafood.** This popular spot is a short distance (RM5 by taxi) from the center of town. The Filipino band that plays here can be a little exuberant, but you can always ask for a quieter spot near the fishponds. The tiger prawns, either grilled or fried, are expensive but are a must. ⊠ *Jln. Skudai,* ☎ *07/237–5788. AE, DC, MC, V. No lunch.*

$$$$ ✕⊞ **Hyatt Regency Johor Bahru.** The grand, modern Hyatt is built on a slight rise facing the Straits of Johor. The mammoth building forms an arc around landscaped gardens through which a two-tier pool meanders. Guest rooms are large (more than 350 square ft) with all the latest technological gadgetry in bedside controls. You can increase the feeling of space by opening the wooden shutter between the bedroom and the spacious bathroom. Four restaurants offer you the choice of Western, Japanese, Szechuan, and Italian cuisine. ⊠ *Jln. Sungai Chat (Box 222), 80720,* ☎ *07/223–1234,* ℻ *07/223–2718. 406 rooms. 4 restaurants, bar, pool, 2 tennis courts, health club, business services, meeting rooms. AE, DC, MC, V.*

$$$ ⊞ **Puteri Pan Pacific.** This hotel opened in 1991 adjacent to the Kotaraya Complex—the city's newest and most prestigious office and shopping mall. The design makes use of round, timber-clad columns and colorful batiks in an open-court lobby. Guest rooms, decorated in pastels, are fully equipped with modern amenities. ⊠ *Jln. Salim (Box 293), Johor Bahru 80000,* ☎ *07/223–3333,* ℻ *07/233–6622. 500 rooms. 5 restaurants, in-room safes, pool, business services. AE, DC, MC, V.*

Desaru

㉜ *94 km (58 mi) east of JB, 436 km (282 mi) southeast of KL.*

Since the west coast of Johor and nearby Singapore have few decent beach resort areas, Desaru was developed to fill the bill. The beach here is, indeed, beautiful (just beware of the dangerous currents), and there's also a seaside golf course. Still, Desaru is something of a desultory playground. Development plans for a theme park, two more golf courses, and more water-sports facilities and vacation homes along the 17-km (10-mi) stretch of jungle-fringed beach have not yet come to fruition.

Dining and Lodging

$$$–$$$$ ✕⊞ **Desaru Golden Beach Resort.** At this full-service luxury resort set in seaside gardens, all the rooms have color TVs, VCRs, minibars, and

balconies with views of the South China Sea. A wide variety of facilities—including the nation's longest swimming pool—is available, and pickup in Singapore can be arranged. As there's nowhere to eat in Desaru outside the hotels, you can try one of the three establishments here (the Chinese seafood restaurant is noteworthy), or you can walk along the beach to the restaurants at the Desaru Perdana Beach Resort (☞ below). ✉ *Tanjung Penawar (Box 50), Kota Tinggi 81900,* ☎ *07/822–1101,* FAX *07/822–1480. 204 rooms, 16 villas. 3 restaurants, bar, minibars, pool, 4 tennis courts, golf privileges, miniature golf, hiking, beach, dive shop, bicycles, dance club, recreation room, playground, meeting rooms. AE, MC, V.*

$$–$$$ ✗🏨 **Desaru Perdana Beach Resort.** The newest hotel along Desaru's beach, this luxurious resort consists of a series of five-story buildings grouped around a huge pool. Rooms are equipped with all the modern amenities. One on-site restaurant serves international and Malaysian food, another Chinese fare; the third is Desaru's only Japanese restaurant. ✉ *Tanjung Penawar (Box 29), Kota Tinggi 81900,* ☎ *07/822–2222,* FAX *07/822–2223. 188 rooms, 22 suites. 3 restaurants, coffee shop, pool, hot tub, sauna, 2 tennis courts, golf privileges, beach, hiking, volleyball, baby-sitting, meeting rooms. AE, MC, V.*

Outdoor Activities and Sports
GOLF

The **Desaru Resort Golf Club** (✉ Kota Tinggi, ☎ 07/822–2333) is open to guests at all Desaru hotels. It has an undulating 18-hole course designed by Robert Trent Jones, Jr. and made more difficult by strong sea breezes. Greens fees are RM150 on weekends, RM 90 weekdays; caddies cost RM 20.

Pahang

Until relatively recently, Pahang—the largest and arguably the most beautiful state on the peninsula—was isolated from the rest of the country by jungle-covered mountains. Access was by sea and then by plane until the construction of the road (now a highway for most of the distance) across from KL and a coastal road linking it with JB. Most of a huge national park, the Taman Negara, falls within Pahang's boundaries, and there are also miles of glorious beaches and many quaint Malay fishing villages. The lush island of Tioman is part of Pahang (though it's reached via the low-key market town of Mersing in neighboring Johor state), and there are beaches north of Kuantan, the state capital, up through Cherating.

Pulau Tioman

③③ *Two hours by ferry from Mersing, which is 146 km (91 km) north of Desaru, 161 km (100 mi) northeast of JB, and 353 km (212 mi) southeast of KL.*

The largest of the islands off the shore of Mersing (in Johor state) was used as the setting for Bali Hai in the movie *South Pacific*. The mountainous, tropical Pulau Tioman hasn't changed much since then, but virtually every beach now has tourist accommodations. You can sunbathe in sandy coves, swim in clear waters, try the nine-hole golf course, or walk through jungle-clad hills (the highest is Gunung Kajang at 3,400 ft). In addition, there are plenty of water-sports options (brightly colored fish and coral make for especially enjoyable snorkeling), and you can hire boats and rent bicycles to get around.

Express ferries to Tioman stop at several of its bays; they generally depart in the morning and are dependent on the tide. The trip takes about two hours and costs around RM25–RM30 one-way. Timetables are posted inside the R&R Plaza near the Mersing jetty. Though there are many tour operators around the jetty, **Zaid Mohammed Lazim** (✉ 17 Jln. Abu Bakar, R&R Plaza, ☎ 07/799–4280) can not only book your ferry ride, but also make reservations at the island lodging of your choice. (Note that you can also fly from KL or Singapore to Tioman; for details ☞ Arriving and Departing *in* The Southern Peninsula and the East Coast Essentials, *below*).

Tioman, although peaceful and quiet by most standards, does get a little busy. For a really quiet haven, check out the other nearby islands. Three of them have resorts with simple bungalow accommodations, including: **Sea Gypsy Village Resort, Pulau Sibu** (☎ 07/222–8642), **Rawa Safarai's Island Resort, Pulau Rawa** (☎ 07/799–1204), and **Radin Resort & Safaris, Pulau Besar** (☎ 07/799–4152).

For boats to other islands, inquire at the tour operator offices on the Mersing jetty or stop by the Mersing Tourist Information Centre (☞ Visitor Information *in* The Southern Peninsula and the East Coast Essentials, *below*) about 400 yards from the wharf. The helpful staffers can provide maps and information and recommend reliable hotels in Mersing and on the islands.

Dining and Lodging

If the room rates at the Berjaya Tioman Beach Resort (☞ *below*) seem too steep, you can drop by to use its facilities but stay at one of the inexpensive chalets around Kampung Tekek and Kampung Air Batang. The best places to eat are inside the various resorts; the only independent restaurant worth mentioning is Liza in the main bay of Tekek just north of the Berjaya resort. Here you'll pay around RM20 for a meal of Western food (slightly more if you order seafood).

$$$$ ✕▨ **Berjaya Tioman Beach Resort.** A full renovation in 1993 transformed this property into a full-service hotel and resort complex. Rooms are decorated in soft colors and equipped with TVs and minibars. If the attractive nine-hole golf course and the large pool aren't enough to keep you occupied, the activities desk can arrange pony rides, diving and snorkeling excursions, and boat trips around the island. ✉ *Pulau Tioman, 86807,* ☎ *09/414–5445,* 🅵🅰🆇 *09/414–5718. 375 rooms. 2 restaurants, bar, coffee shop, pool, 9-hole golf course, 2 tennis courts, dive shop, jet skiing, windsurfing, boating, meeting rooms. AE, MC, V.*

En Route   Although there are numerous traditional kampungs and colorful fishing villages along the east coast between Mersing and Kuantan, the only main town is **Pekan** (107 km/66 mi north of Mersing). It's the home of the sultan, and you can see his modern palace—with its manicured lawns and, of course, its polo field—but only from outside the gates. Don't bypass this town, as the signposts suggest; drive through the center instead. Built on the western shore of a river, it's a delightfully old-fashioned community with two-story shophouses along its main street.

Kuantan

㉞   *177 km (110 mi) northwest of Mersing, 259 km (156 mi) northeast of KL.*

The east coast's major beach and resort area is just north of the state capital, Kuantan (to get here from the capital, take Jalan Teluk Sisek just past the Hotel Suraya). At the sandy, crescent-shape bay of Teluk Chempedak you'll find several hotels, four or five restaurants and bars, discos, and a small but attractive beach. Sunbathers come for the company of other vacationers rather than for solitude. If you prefer privacy, continue a few miles north, where smaller hotels dot a long stretch of virtually untrodden sand.

Dining and Lodging

$$$ ✕ꔮ **Hyatt Regency Kuantan.** Here, breezes from the South China Sea
★ blow through lush, cultivated gardens and ripple across two swimming pools just steps from the golden beach. Rooms are in three courts that are also near the shore. It's worth paying the premium rate for a room that faces the sea (rather than one that faces the hills at the back) so that you can sleep with your balcony doors open to the sounds of the surf. Guest rooms are carpeted and have either king-size or twin beds as well as bathrooms with separate shower stalls. A six-story business wing at the rear of the main hotel has conference rooms and 52 business suites. The Kampung Café is set on stilts facing the sea and is made all the more romantic by candlelight that's reflected off sparkling crystal and silver. The food is a mix of Malay and European; the seafood dishes are the best. ✉ *Teluk Chempedak, Pahang Darul Makmur 25730,* ☎ *09/513–1234,* FAX *09/567–7577. 275 rooms, 52 suites. Restaurant, café, 2 pools, sauna, golf privileges, 3 tennis courts, exercise room, squash, beach, dance club, business services, meeting rooms. AE, MC, V.*

$–$$ ꔮ **Coral Beach Resort.** Set on endless sands along the South China Sea, this modern resort hotel has a wide-open lobby and a clientele of both business-seminar participants in shirts and ties and bathing-suit-clad sun worshipers. At night, both types of guests relax in the bars or the disco. Guest rooms have utilitarian furnishings, king-size or twin beds, and adequate bathrooms. A light-filled coffee shop serves Malay and European fare, and there are Japanese and Chinese restaurants for more elaborate meals. ✉ *152 Sungai Karang, Beserah 26100,* ☎ *09/544–7544,* FAX *09/544–7543. 162 rooms. 2 restaurants, 2 bars, coffee shop, pool, 2 tennis courts, health club, squash, beach, dance club, meeting rooms. AE, DC, MC, V.*

$ ꔮ **Tanjung Gelang Motel.** This small, Chinese-owned establishment has simple chalets that face the beach and are packed rather tightly together. The motel's main advantage is its price (RM80–RM100 a night); there are no frills, just the basics and a small restaurant that serves Chinese and European food. Still, the Coral Bay Resort and all its facilities are right next door. ✉ *Jln. Kemaman (Km 15), Pahang Darul Makmur 26100,* ☎ *09/544–7254,* FAX *09/544–7388. 40 rooms. Restaurant. AE, MC, V.*

OFF THE **GUA CHARAH** – Some 25 km (15 mi) into the jungled hills west of Kuan-
BEATEN PATH tan are the Gua Charah (Pancing Caves). Traveling from Kuantan, you first pass rubber and oil-palm plantations before arriving at the bottom of a small hill. Now comes the hard part: to reach the caves, you must climb 220 steps. Buddhists still live here, and there are many altars. Don't miss the cave with the reclining, 30-ft-long Buddha, carved by a Thai monk who devoted his life to the task.

Cherating

③⑤ *30 km (19 mi) northeast of Kuantan, 289 km (175 mi) northeast of KL.*

Half an hour's drive north of Kuantan is the peaceful village of Cherating, a rustic haven for beachcombing along miles of white, clean beaches that are fanned by gentle breezes rustling through the coconut trees. Club Med was one of the first to stake its claim on a fine stretch of sand here, responding to the spirit of the place with its Malay-style bungalows built on stilts. Since then, numerous resorts have sprung up along the main highway, but they always seem to have more than enough empty rooms to offer good discounts.

Opportunities for **turtle-watching**—one of the east coast's most popular attractions—begin at Cherating and continue north. The best viewing place is said to be Chendor Beach, an hour north of Kuantan or 20 minutes up from Cherating. Most nights between May and September (the peak month is August), enormous leatherback turtles slowly make their way ashore to lay around 100 eggs each. Signs at the hotels will tell when and where to go, and the crowds do gather to watch as the 1,000-pound turtles laboriously dig their "nests" before settling down to their real work.

Dining and Lodging

$$$$ ✕🍽 **Club Med Cherating.** This Malaysian-style Club Med village is on its own bay, surrounded by 200 acres of parkland. Accommodation is in twin-bedded bungalows with air-conditioning and showers. As with all Club Meds, use of all sports facilities and participation in such activities as arts-and-crafts workshops are included in the price, as are buffet-style meals. The resort was refurbished in 1994 and is quieter and more low-key than the Club Meds found in the Caribbean. ⊠ *Jln. Kuantan–Kemaman (Km 29), 26080,* ☎ *09/581–9131 or 03/261– 4599 in KL,* 🕿 *09/581–9524. 600 rooms. 2 restaurants, pool, 6 tennis courts, aerobics, archery, exercise room, squash, beach, windsurfing, children's programs. AE, MC, V. All-inclusive.*

$$$$ ✕🍽 **Impiana Resort Cherating.** This low-rise sprawl of modern luxury on 32 acres at the edge of Cherating's beach offers you more independence than Club Med. The vast lobby, flooded by natural light and cooled by sea breezes, is the focal point. Beyond is the two-tier pool, and beyond that the sea. You can have Malay, Chinese, or Western food from the three restaurants or try a little of everything at the evening buffet. Standard rooms are in the main building; there are also two- and three-bedroom chalets. Most guest quarters face the sea, and all have four-poster wooden beds, ceiling fans, and air-conditioning. For recreation, there's a fully equipped water-sports center. ⊠ *Km 32, Jln. Kuantan–Kemaman, Cherating, Pahang 26080,* ☎ *09/581–9000,* 🕿 *09/581–9090. 119 rooms and chalets. 3 restaurants, bar, beach, jet skiing, meeting rooms. AE, DC, MC, V.*

$$ ✕🍽 **Cherating Holiday Villa Beach Resort.** From the central building that houses the reception and dining area, buildings fan out toward the beach, enclosing a pool and gardens. The structures vary, with each taking some architectural aspect, usually a roof style, from a different region of Malaysia. Rooms are equally diverse: from modern, Western-style accommodations to chalets designed in the Malay style with bare wooden floors and a minimum of furniture. Most are wood-paneled, with sliding-glass doors facing the pool (rooms on the second floor offer more privacy). The restaurant serves dinners that are a mix of Italian-inspired fare and Malay cooking; a beach barbecue is held twice a week. ⊠ *Lot 1303, Mukim Sungei Karang, 26080,* ☎ *09/581– 9500 or 03/262–2922 in KL,* 🕿 *09/581–9178 or 03/262–2937 in KL. 94 rooms. 2 restaurants, coffee shop, 2 pools, 3 tennis courts, badminton, exercise room, squash. AE, MC, V.*

$ 🍽 **Cherating Beach Mini-Hotel.** If your reason for staying in Cherating is beachcombing, then this budget hotel is perfect. The chalets are very small and sparsely furnished, but the beach is at the front door. The staff is wonderfully low-key and friendly, and the restaurant does its best to cook up European food (though it's better at Malaysian dishes). ⊠ *Batu 28 Kampung, Jln. Kemaman, 2608,* ☎ *09/581–9335. 20 chalets. Restaurant. No credit cards.*

Taman Negara

*176 km (109 mi) from Kuantan to Jerantut, 250 km (19 mi) north-
east of KL.*

Malaysia's oldest protected area, Taman Negara (National Park),
sprawls across the borders of Pahang, Terengganu, and Kelantan states,
roughly in the center of the Malay peninsula. Covering 4,343 square
km (1,677 square mi), the park is where a large percentage of the peninsula's plant and animal life is protected. Access is by road or rail to
Kuala Tembeling or Jerantut, and then a three-hour boat ride to the
headquarters area at Kuala Tahan. Within the park, you can trek, explore the rain forest by canoe, stay overnight to watch for mammals,
or go fishing.

The best accommodation in the park is the privately run **Taman Negara Resort** (☎ 09/266–3500, ℻ 09/2661500) where the luxurious
two-story, two-bedroom bungalows have their own kitchens and balconies and go for almost RM600 per night; less expensive are the twin-
bed chalets with attached bathrooms for RM201. You can make
reservations through the resort itself or through MATIC in KL (☞ Visitor Information *in* Kuala Lumpur Essentials, *above*).

Terengganu

The sultanate of Terengganu, like that of Kelantan to the north, paid
annual tribute to Siam (Thailand) until it came under British control
in 1909. Separated from the western part of the peninsula by jungle-
covered mountains, Terengganu state remained a peaceful backwater
with an overwhelming Malay population largely engaged in fishing and
small-scale agriculture until the discovery of petroleum a couple of
decades ago.

The recent establishment of several luxurious coastal and inland resorts, an increase in the number of accommodations and scuba facilities on the offshore islands, and the gradual development of Lake Kenyir
as an ecotourism destination all make a visit to Terengganu less of a
challenge than it used to be. Its endless beautiful beaches where giant
sea turtles come ashore to lay their eggs, its exquisite coral-girt islands,
its traditional villages and handicrafts, and its jungled interior are
more accessible than ever before.

Rantau Abang

🏖 *150 km (93 mi) northwest of Kuantan, 399 km (211 mi) northeast
of KL.*

Not so much a village as a scattering of guest houses along the coastal
road, the protected, 10-km (6-mi) stretch of beach of Rantau Abang
is one of the places where the giant leatherback turtle comes ashore
to lay its eggs (between May and September each year). These magnificent and endangered turtles lumber ashore after dark to dig a hole and
deposit around 100 eggs in the sand. They then cover the hole and head
back to sea, leaving the eggs to hatch around 50 to 60 days later. These
eggs are transferred to protected hatcheries, and when the baby turtles emerge, they're transferred to the beach to begin their watery existence. Amazingly, the hatchlings will return to exactly the same spot
some 20 years later to breed and repeat the cycle.

The **Turtle Information Centre** has a video and other displays relating
to the turtles. Admission to the center is free, and it's open May–August, Saturday–Thursday 9–1, 2–6, and 8–1 and Friday 9–12 and 3–
11; from September to April, the hours are daily 8–12:45 and 2–4.

Lodging

The finest place to stay in the area is the award-winning **Tanjung Jara Beach Hotel** (☎ 09/844–1801), a luxurious resort built in traditional Malay style just 9 km (5 mi) south of Rantau Abang. At press time, however, the hotel was closed for a complete renovation and wasn't slated to reopen till some time in 1999. You shouldn't hesitate to contact the hotel to see whether it will be operational when you plan to visit, as a stay here is highly recommended.

$$ 🏨 **Awana Kijal Beach & Golf Resort.** Roughly 60 km (37 mi) south of Rantau Abang, this huge beachfront resort has plenty of activities—from golf to arts-and-crafts workshops. (If you're seeking peace and quiet, try elsewhere—especially during school holidays). The lobby soars up to an impressive height, but despite allusions to classical Malay architecture, the decor and furnishings throughout are of questionable taste. Most rooms face the sea, although they don't have balconies. ⊠ *Jln. Kemaman-Dungun (Km 28), 24100,* ☎ *09/864–1188 or 03/200– 6288 in KL,* 🖷 *09/864–1688. 263 rooms. 4 restaurants, 2 bars, pool, wading pool, 18-hole golf course, tennis court, health club, Ping-Pong, beach, dive shop, snorkeling, fishing, playground, business services, meeting rooms. AE, DC, MC, V.*

Kuala Terengganu

㊲   *209 km (130 mi) north of Kuantan, 162 km (101 mi) north of Cherating, 455 km (282 mi) northeast of KL.*

Kuala Terengganu, the state capital, is basically a big village trying to get used to being a town. Giant mango trees shade old, wooden houses with terra-cotta roofs. Next to such houses sit modern office blocks constructed with the wealth provided by the petrochemical industry.

The true heart of the town is the **Central Market,** where a fascinating array of fresh and dried produce is sold on the ground floor. (This is where you'll find *keropok lekur,* a local speciality made of pureed fish and sago flour that's boiled or deep fried. Keropok is also dried into wafers that can later be fried to a crisp; buy a packet to take home.) Upstairs in the market there's a collection of tiny shops where you can bargain for batik, kitchen implements, and local handicrafts; there are also food stalls that serve tasty, inexpensive Malay cuisine.

Near the market is a jetty where boats leave for **Pulau Duyung,** a large island in the Terengganu estuary famous for its traditional boat building. Opposite the jetty, on Jalan Sultan Zainal Abidin, you'll find a complex of traditional buildings, including the **Terengganu Tourist Information Centre** (☞ Visitor Information *in* The Southern Peninsula and the East Coast Essentials, *below*), beside some souvenir shops. You can pick up a range of brochures and get helpful advice here.

One of the few old sights in town is **Bukit Puteri** (Princess Hill), where the remains of a fort and several cannons can be seen atop the small hill. You pay RM1 to climb the stone steps at the side of the tourism office; unfortunately, it closes daily at 5:45 PM, too early to see the sunset. Around the corner from Bukit Puteri, on Jalan Masjid Abidin, is the attractive **Istana Maziah,** the sultan's old palace, now used only for ceremonial functions (the new, architecturally uninteresting palace is on the main road south). Completed in 1903, Istana Maziah and its grounds are closed to the public, but you get a good view of it from the road.

The small **Chinatown** of this overwhelmingly Malay community (it's one of the very few in the country where Malays predominate) is basically one street, Jalan Bandar. Walk along this road, which runs to one side of the Central Market, and notice the beautiful old houses and shops, particularly Number 151. This attractive building with faded decorative tiles is the home of Teratai, a shop with a good range of arts and crafts.

If you have time for only one sight in Kuala Terengganu, then it must be to the **Terengganu State Museum,** 5 km (3 mi) southwest of the town center. A taxi trip (RM7) or bus ride (50 sen) takes you through the still-charming district of Kampung Losong to the museum complex. Set in landscaped gardens on the Terengganu River, the main part of the museum is housed in four large blocks that cleverly echo the traditional style of a Terengganu house. You might want to bypass several of the 10 galleries, but don't miss the Bangunan Utama (Main Building), where there are displays of textiles, traditional clothing, handicrafts, and royal regalia.

Located nearer the river is a **fisheries museum** (where you can see some lovely old carved and painted canoes); a **maritime museum** (check out the two huge wooden boats permanently beached on the lawn); and a group of magnificent old wooden houses reconstructed in the gardens. The finest of these is the **Istana Tengku Long,** built in 1888 and constructed entirely without nails. The curving roof gables have gilded wooden screens, carved with verses from the Koran. The istana and other houses are often closed, but if you ask, the security guard will open them so you can look around inside. ⊠ *Bukit Losong,* ☎ *09/ 622–1444.* ⊑ *RM5.* ◷ *Sat.–Thurs. 10–6, Fri. 10–12 and 3–6.*

Dining and Lodging

There are surprisingly few restaurants in Kuala Terengganu, apart from a few Indian Muslim places downtown. Your best bet is to eat in one of the two major hotels.

$$$ ✕▥ **Primula Parkroyal Hotel.** This premier hotel, which was completely refurbished in 1997, is right on the beach less than a mile from the town center. The spacious, carpeted rooms have all the modern conveniences as well as small verandas. The pool area and gardens are very attractive, and recreational activities are organized daily. The hotel also counts a medical clinic among its amenities. The Rhusila Coffee House offers buffets for breakfast, lunch, and dinner, as well as an interesting à la carte menu with local and Western dishes. Try a steamboat or a pizza at the casual poolside Pelangi restaurant. ⊠ *Jln. Persingahan (Box 43), 20904,* ☎ *09/622–2100,* ℻ *09/623–3360. 249 rooms. 3 restaurants, bar, pool, beach, bicycles, shops, children's programs, business services, meeting rooms. AE, DC, MC, V.*

$$ ✕▥ **Yen Tin Midtown Hotel.** As its name implies, this hotel offers comfortable, well-equipped rooms right in the center of town. The Midtown Cafe on the second level is famous for its roti jala and its ulam. Likewise, if you hanker for a steak or fish-and-chips—as well as a beer—this is the place. ⊠ *Jln. Tok Lam, 20100,* ☎ *09/623–5288,* ℻ *09/623–4399. 144 rooms. Restaurant, business services, meeting rooms. AE, DC, MC, V.*

$$$$ ▥ **Ariyani.** If you want a tiny patch of paradise where the most strenuous activity is taking in a dip in the pool to the sounds of a live gamelan orchestra, head 45 km (28 mi) north of Kuala Terengganu to the Ariyani, outside the village of Merang (not to be confused with Marang, south of Kuala Terengganu). Owned and designed by a member of the Terengganu royal family, this resort is a blissful combination of pavilions, gardens, lotus ponds, discreetly situated villas, and white-sand beach. It's all reminiscent of a small resort on Bali, and indeed, you'll find Indonesian as well as local handicrafts used in the decor. The hotel's spa is in a restored, century-old Malay house; a traditional Malay body massage here is a must. If you crave activity, you can rent a bike or ask the staff to arrange a diving or snorkeling expedition to nearby Pulau Redang or a trip to Lake Kenyir, the Sekayu Falls, or the museum in Kuala Terengganu. ⊠ *Jln. Rhu Tapai-Merang, 21010,* ☎ *09/624–1111 or 03/269–6410 in KL,* FAX *09/624–8007. 40 rooms. 3 restaurants, pool, massage, spa, beach, library. AE, DC, MC, V.*

Pulau Besar, Pulau Kecil, and Pulau Redang

Pulau Redang is 50 km (31 mi) off the coast from Merang; Pulau Besar and Pulau Kecil are 21 km (13 mi) off the coast from Kuala Besut.

Scattering the waters of the South China Sea—from Terengganu's border with Kelantan state down almost to Pahang—islands with white-sand beaches, limpid waters, and coral reefs beckon. Owing to the strong winds, rain, and rough seas during the year-end northeast monsoon, the season for visiting these islands is from March to October. Facilities for snorkeling and scuba diving are available at all the major hotels.

Accessible from the village of Merang, which is 40 km (25 mi) north of Kuala Terengganu, **Pulau Redang** is about two hours by boat from the coast. Redang (which is composed of Redang, Pulau Pinang and seven islets) is part of a marine park, but this hasn't protected its once-tranquil villages, forest, and bays. Trees were felled and hilltops were bulldozed to create a 9-hole golf course, and villagers have been relocated to to make room for new resorts. Although Redang still offers excellent scuba diving and snorkeling, it's no longer an untouched tropical paradise.

The **Perhentian Islands** are a 1½-hour boat ride from Kuala Besut, 123 km (76 mi) north of Kuala Terengganu. Part of a marine park, Perhentian is composed of two islands, Besar (Big) and Kecil (Little), each with a scattering of simple villages and range of accommodations.

Lodging

$$$$ 🏨 **Berjaya Redang Beach Resort.** Situated at Pulau Redang's northernmost bay, this resort has an exquisite beach of powdery-white sands lapped by turquoise waters. Unfortunately, the chalets are crowded too closely together for privacy. Still, the rooms are air-conditioned and have all the facilities you'd expect of a top hotel, including TVs with VCRs. The hotel also operates its own ferry service to and from Merang. ⊠ *Teluk Dalam Kecil (Box 126, Main Post Office), 20928,* ☎ *09/697–3988 or 03/242–9611 in KL,* FAX *09/697–3899 or 03/245–5408 in KL. 152 rooms. 2 restaurants, 3 bars, pool, tennis court, hiking, volleyball, beach, dive shop, snorkeling, meeting rooms. AE, DC, MC, V.*

$$ 🏨 **Perhentian Island Resort.** This Pulau Besar resort offers the least cramped and most tasteful accommodations of any hotel on Terengganu's islands. On a private beach backed by jungle you'll find comfortable chalets, each with four, twin-bed-equipped, rooms. The hotel has its own ferry service to the mainland. ⊠ *Teluk Pauh (Mailing address: Menara Promet, 22nd floor, Jln. Sultan Ismail, KL 50250),* ☎ *010/903–0100 or 03/244–8530 in KL,* FAX *03/243–4984 in KL. 106 rooms. Restaurant, pool, tennis court, volleyball, beach, dive shop, snorkeling, windsurfing. AE, DC, MC, V.*

The Southern Peninsula and the East Coast Essentials

Arriving and Departing

By Airplane

Senai Airport (☎ 07/334–1001) is 25 km (16 mi) north of JB (there are air-conditioned buses into the city). MAS offers direct flights to JB from KL, Pinang, Kota Kinabalu (Sabah), and Kuching (Sarawak). MAS flies into **Sultan Ahmad Shah Airport** (☎ 09/538–1291), 15 km (9 mi) west of Kuantan from KL and Kuala Terengganu; SilkAir flies in from Singapore. **Sultan Mahmud Airport** (☎ 07/414–6301) is 13 km (8 mi) northwest of Kuala Terengganu and has direct flight service from KL and Kuantan. **Kerteh Airport** (☎ 09/666–3062) serves the town of Kerteh and surrounding petrochemical industrial estates and is 12 km (7 mi) from the Awana Kijal Resort south of Rantau Abang. **Pulau Tioman** (☎ 07/414–6301) has a small airport at Kampung Tekek; MAS has service from KL and Kuantan; SilkAir flies from Singapore.

By Boat

The ferry between Dumai (on Sumatra in Indonesia) and Melaka takes four hours, costs RM80, and departs (usually) every day at 10 AM. Citizens of Canada, the United States, and the United Kingdom don't need a visa to enter Indonesia. Boats to Tioman and other islands off Mersing run from the Mersing jetty; you can find the latest timetables and make reservations at Mersing's R&R Plaza or at ticket offices belonging to the individual resorts—all are near the jetty. An express ferry from Pulau Tioman to Singapore is operated by **Tioman Island Resort Ferries** (☎ 65/271–4866 in Singapore).

By Bus

Johor Bahru, as the southern end of the line for peninsular Malaysia, has comprehensive, efficient, and inexpensive bus service. Departures are frequent from the main terminal, which is 3 km (2 mi) north of town, and both air-conditioned and non-air-conditioned buses are available. Bus 170 makes the run across the causeway between Johor Bahru and Singapore.

Melaka is served by frequent express buses from KL's Puduraya Terminal (☞ Arriving and Departing by Bus *in* Kuala Lumpur Essentials, *above*); the trip costs RM7. There are also frequent direct buses—so many that you don't need to book in advance—to Singapore. Express buses also link Kuantan with KL, JB, and Kuala Terengganu. Kuala Terengganu has express service to Ipoh, KL, JB, Kuantan, and Kota Bharu; these operate out of the Central Bus Station at Jalan Syed Hussain.

By Car

The North–South Expressway between KL and JB bypasses Seremban and Melaka, though exits for these towns are clearly indicated. An expressway from KL toward Kuantan goes as far as Karak, where it's replaced by a regular two-lane roadway. The coastal road north from Kuantan to Kuala Terengganu is well marked but sometimes slow-moving, owing to trucks and country buses.

By Taxi

Either privately chartered or shared taxis between major destinations are a good proposition (a private charter fare is four times as much as a shared fare). You can pick up what's known as an "outstation taxi" from cab stands next to the bus stations in all major Malaysian towns. A chartered taxi from KL to Melaka costs approximately RM80–RM90.

A round-trip will cost slightly less than twice the one-way fare, but a KL taxi driver is unlikely to know his way around Melaka. Cabs to Kuantan from KL cost around RM100, from JB, RM120. From Kuantan to Kuala Terengganu by shared taxi will cost RM60.

By Train

As train service to the south and the east coast is far less frequent, much slower, and more expensive than buses or long-distance taxis (especially since the completion of the North–South Highway), it's not worth using except for perhaps KL–JB trips. Melaka doesn't have a train station, but you can get off in Tampin, 38 km (24 mi) north of the city and take a taxi into town (about RM3). For information, call **Malayan Railways,** also known as KTM (☎ 06/223091 in Melaka), or the **Tampin train station** (☎ 06/411034).

Getting Around

By Trishaw

In Melaka, the best way to get around the historical area is on foot or by trishaw, which will cost you a minimum of RM5 and around RM20 per hour. You can also take a trishaw in Kuala Terengganu. In all other towns, a local taxi will be both inexpensive (RM5 for about 3 km/2 mi) and efficient.

By Car

You can rent cars at the following places throughout the region: **Kuantan:** Orix Car Rental (✉ Kuantan airport, ☎ 09/538–8394) and Mayflower Car Rental (✉ Kuantan airport, ☎ 09/538–3490). **Melaka:** Avis (✉ 124 Jln. Bendahara, ☎ 06/284–6710) and National (✉ 36 Jln. Laksamana, ☎ 06/284–8871). **Johor Bahru:** Avis (✉ Tropical Inn, Jln. Gerja, ☎ 07/2237971) and Hertz (✉ Johor Information Centre, ☎ 07/223–7520). **Kuala Terengganu:** Kapas Rent A Car (✉ Kuala Terengganu Airport, ☎ 018/896–6676 or 101/983–3103 [mobile-phone numbers]); ✉ Primula Parkroyal Hotel, ☎ 09/624–5915), **Wata Car Rental** (✉ 1762A Jln. Kamarudding, ☎ 09/624–7440), and **Kijal Travel & Tours** (✉ Awana Kijal Beach & Golf Resort, Km 28 Jln. Kemamam-Dungun, ☎ 09/864–1069).

Contacts and Resources

Emergencies

Ambulance and Police: ☎ 999. **Fire:** ☎ 994. **Hospitals and Clinics:** Johor Public Hospital (☎ 07/223–1666); Kuantan Public Hospital (☎ 09/222–3333); or Melaka Public Hospital (☎ 06/282–2344). **Scuba-Diving Accidents:** The only decompression chamber on the peninsula is at the Malaysian Navy Base in Lumut, on the coast near Ipoh. Dive masters should be able to fill you in on emergency procedures.

English-Language Bookstores

Books and magazines in English are very limited outside hotel sundry shops in this region. In Melaka, the long-established **Lim Brothers** (✉ Jln. Laksamana, ☎ no phone) has some pleasant surprises. You'll find the best selection at **MPH** (✉ Mahkota Parade shopping complex, ☎ 06/283–2960), also in Melaka. JB also has a branch of **MPH** (✉ Plangi Leisure Mall, Jln. Serampang, ☎ 07/335–2672).

Tour Operators and Travel Agencies

Most of the tour operators cited below can help you make general travel arrangements including airline reservations and hotel bookings. Several companies organize day trips to Melaka from KL in an air-conditioned limousine (RM250–RM300) or by bus (about RM70). These may be arranged through most hotels. The best-known tour guide in

Melaka is **Robert Tan Sin Nyen** (✉ 256-D Jln. Parameswara, ☎ 06/ 284–4857). You can take a 45- or 90-minute **river tour** (☎ 06/283– 6538) of the city from the dock on Jalan Quayside.

In Kuantan, tour operators include: **Eastern Skyline** (✉ Lot A126, Ground floor, MARA Building, ☎ 09/528811), **SMS Travel** (✉ 158 Bangunan LKNP, Jln. Besar, ☎ 09/514–3888), and **Jelai Holiday** (✉ 9 Bangunan LKNP, Jln. Besar, ☎ 09/552016).

Kijal Travel & Tours (✉ Awana Kijal Beach & Golf Resort, Km 28, Jln. Kemamam-Dungun, ☎ 09/864–1064) offers fishing and snorkeling trips, handicraft and shopping tours, treks to Sekayu Falls, and night-time turtle-watching forays to the Rantau Abang area. **Kapas Travel & Tours** (✉ Primula Parkroyal Hotel, ☎ 09/623–5915) offers a range of city tours in Kuala Terengganu; day trips to Sekayu Falls, Lake Kenyir, and Pulau Kapas; and turtle-watching, fishing, scuba diving, and boating excursions.

Visitor Information

MTPB (✉ Tun Abdul Razak Complex, ground floor, Jln. Wong Ah Fook, JB, ☎ 07/222–3591). **Melaka Tourist Information Center** (✉ Jln. Kota, ☎ 06/283–6538). **Mersing Tourist Information Centre** (✉ 1 Jln. Abu Bakar, ☎ 07/799–5212). **Pahang Tourist Information Centre** (✉ Jln. Mahkota, Kuantan, ☎ 09/517–1623). **Terengganu Tourist Information Centre** (✉ Jln. Sultan Zainal Abidin, Kuala Terengganu, ☎ 09/622– 1553).

NORTHERN BORNEO

Until the period of colonial expansion in the 18th and 19th centuries, the Sultan of Brunei held sway over all of northern Borneo. However, with the granting of Sarawak to James Brooke (the first "white rajah"), and the sale of the northern tip of Borneo (Sabah) to the British North Borneo Company, the lines on the map were redrawn. Today, Brunei consists of two tiny pieces of land surrounded by Sarawak, with Sabah adjoining Sarawak's northern border. The eastern and southern borders of Sarawak adjoin Kalimantan, the Indonesian portion of the island of Borneo. Although both Sarawak and Sabah became part of Malaysia, Brunei has remained an independent sultanate.

Sarawak

Sarawak's modern history began in 1841 after an English adventurer, James Brooke, was formally ceded land around the Sarawak River in exchange for settling a rebellion against the local rajah, an uncle of the Sultan of Brunei. Raja Brooke instituted a benevolent family regency that lasted until the Japanese occupation during World War II. Sarawak then became a British colony as the Brookes could not afford to restore it following the war. In 1963, the Federation of Malaysia was formed by the incorporation of Malaya with Sarawak and Sabah (Singapore was initially part of Malaysia, but left after two years). Sarawak, like neighboring Sabah, was permitted to retain a number of special rights, including control over immigration.

The native peoples of Sarawak are ethnically different from those of the peninsula, and the Chinese who have settled here are better integrated, often through intermarriage with non-Muslim natives. Although proud to be Malaysians, the peoples of Sarawak have a very strong sense of their unique history and identity. Despite the fact that modern trappings such as generators and satellite TV have reached far into the interior, many tribespeople still live in communal wooden longhouses, with as many as 60 or even 100 families—entire villages, really—under one roof.

Sarawak is Malaysia's largest state, with some 1.9 million people inhabiting its 124,450 square km (48,342 square mi). Almost 500,000 live around the capital city of Kuching, a pleasant, fairly modern town that still retains many of its Victorian buildings and Chinese shophouses. Some 30% of Sarawak's population is Iban, 27% is Chinese, and 20% is Malay; the rest is a mixture of indigenous ethnic groups. As in Sabah, Christians outnumber Muslims.

Sarawak's principal attractions are its magnificent national parks—particularly Gunung Mulu with its spectacular caves, and the archaeologically important Niah Caves National Park—as well as the native longhouses. Some tour operators have built comfortable lodges adjacent to upriver longhouses, so you can stay overnight and learn about the lifestyle and culture of the local people without sacrificing too many creature comforts.

Kuching

❶ *920 km (575 mi) southeast of KL, 832 km (520 mi) southwest of Kota Kinabalu.*

Kuching is one of the most charming cities in the region, and a walk around the Old Town near the river will give you some feeling for its history. You'll note the gentle, unhurried pace as you stroll along the landscaped **waterfront,** which runs along the Sarawak River and has benches, food stalls, gardens, and a small stage where performances are often held. The **lookout tower** at the upriver end of the waterfront affords a fine view of downtown Kuching and the surrounding countryside.

One of the finest Brooke-era buildings is the white **courthouse,** completed in 1874. Topped by ironwood shingles, the building has shady verandas and Romanesque columns; the clock tower was added in 1883. Behind the courthouse on Jalan Tun Haji Openg stands the **pavilion,** a pleasant architectural mishmash that's being transformed into a costume and textile museum. Opposite, the **post office** is an attractive building with Corinthian columns.

At the downriver end of the waterfront, next to the Kuching Hilton, is the town's oldest building. At the 1843 **Tua Pek Kong** Chinese temple, you can watch worshipers lighting incense and making paper offerings. This temple is on a site considered highly auspicious by the Chinese, where the Mata Kuching River, after which the city was named, once flowed into the Sarawak River (the Mata Kuching has long since disappeared into a drainage tunnel).

★ A stroll through the waterfront's **main bazaar** takes you past curio and antiques shops where you can find everything from a beaded Dayak baby carrier to a strand of old beads. Wonderful for basketwork, wood carvings, and souvenirs, the bazaar also has fascinating old coffee shops, stores that sell such items as processed birds' nests and Sarawak pepper, and old-style provision shops.

The small streets off the bazaar lead to **Jalan Carpenter,** the heart of Kuching's Chinatown. Here you'll find a couple of interesting temples, some restaurants and food stalls, and a number of goldsmiths and other artisans.

Across the river is **Ft. Margherita,** built in 1879 by Rajah Charles Brooke (James' Brooke's nephew). Take a quaint *tambang* (river taxi)

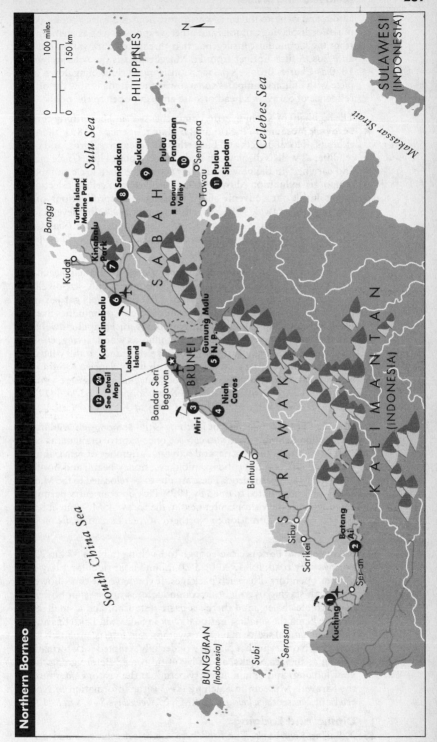

Northern Borneo

across and explore the fort, which now houses a rather funky police museum displaying cannons and other weapons as well as memorabilia from the Communist insurgency that threatened Sarawak in the '60s and '70s. A little upriver from Ft. Margherita sits the **Astana,** built in 1870 as Charles Brooke's palace. Consisting of three bungalows, complete with military ramparts and a tower, the Astana is now the official residence of Sarawak's head of state and isn't open to the public.

The highlight of Kuching is the comprehensive and beautifully curated
★ **Sarawak Museum.** In the original building, opened in 1891, there are exhibits of local insects and butterflies, sea creatures, birds, and other wildlife, as well as displays on body tattoos, burial items, face masks, and carvings. In the newer building across the road are a number of temporary exhibitions downstairs, as well as an excellent selection of books inside the souvenir shop. Upstairs are reproductions of the dwellings of Sarawak's different ethnic groups (including several longhouses) that are full of artifacts. There's also a model of the Niah Caves and a good collection of ceramics and beads. ⊠ *Jln. Tun Haji Openg,* ☎ *082/244232.* ☜ *Free.* ⊙ *Daily 9–6.*

The award-winning **Sarawak Cultural Village** at Damai Beach (☞ Outdoor Activities and Sports, *below*), contains the life-size dwellings of seven major Sarawak ethnic groups, all set in a lovely garden at the foot of Mt. Santubong. People from the different communities live and work in the various longhouses, farmhouses, or kampung dwellings, and they give demonstrations of such things as woodcarving, cooking local cakes, weaving, or using a blowpipe. Entrance to the village includes admittance to a cultural show with lively dances. A restaurant serves local dishes, and there's a good souvenir shop where you can even buy CDs of tribal music. ⊠ *Santubong,* ☎ *082/846411.* ☜ *RM45.* ⊙ *Daily 9–5; cultural shows daily at 11:30 and 4:30.*

About 22 km (14 mi) south of Kuching is the **Semonggoh Wildlife Rehabilitation Centre,** where you can see once-captive orangutans being trained to return to their natural habitat. A number of other animals such as macaque and proboscis monkeys, honey bears, and hornbills are held in a sort of minizoo. These are due to be relocated to the Matang Wildlife Centre, slated to open by 1999. Pick up your entry permit for Semonggoh at the visitor center next to the Sarawak Museum in Kuching (☞ Visitor Information *in* Northern Borneo Essentials, *below*). ☜ *Free.* ⊙ *Daily 8–4.*

Bako National Park is close enough to Kuching (a mere 37 km/23 mi northeast by road, followed by a 20-minute boat ride) for a day trip; all tour operators offer such packages. If you have the time, however, it's worth staying overnight; accommodations range from hostels to comfortable chalets, and there's a basic restaurant and a small store. Despite being the smallest national park in Sarawak, Bako has a wide variety of natural sights: mangrove swamps, rain forests, proboscis monkeys, carnivorous pitcher plants, wonderfully sculpted rock formations known as the Sea Stacks, and a beautiful beach. Before going, book your lodgings and obtain an entry permit at the visitor center next to the Sarawak Museum in Kuching (☞ Visitor Information *in* Northern Borneo Essentials, *below*). ☜ *RM3.* ⊙ *Weekdays 8–4, Sat. 8–12:45.*

Dining and Lodging

$$ ✕ **Beijing Riverbank.** The food here—light refreshments and drinks downstairs, a more elaborate Cantonese and Western menu upstairs—is acceptable. What really draws people to this modest building shaped like a Bidayuh tribal head house is its location overlooking the river. ⊠ *Kuching Waterfront,* ☎ *082/234126. MC, V.*

$$ ✕ **Lok Thian.** This large restaurant is renowned for its gourmet Chinese food, including Cantonese barbecue. The ground floor has a Thai restaurant; Chinese and Japanese food are served upstairs. ⊠ *319 Jln. Padungan,* ☎ *082/331310. AE, DC, V.*

$$ ✕ **Tsui Hua Lau.** Better for a Chinese banquet than a dinner for two, this brightly lighted, two-story restaurant has an extensive menu with Cantonese, Szechuan, and Shanghainese fare. The unusual entrées include braised turtle, sea cucumber, and bird's nest soup. The barbecued duck and Szechuan-style shredded beef meet high standards. ⊠ *22 Ban Hock Rd.,* ☎ *082/414560. AE, DC, V.*

$ ✕ **Topspot Food Court.** Don't miss the chance to eat as the locals do in the somewhat unlikely setting of the landscaped roof of a parking garage. Clean and brightly lighted during the evening, the food court has stalls that serve a wide range of cuisines, including several with excellent fresh seafood. Choose your own fish or prawns and specify how you want them cooked. There are also Chinese clay-pot specials (food slow-cooked in an earthenware pot) and Malay satay. ⊠ *Top floor of parking garage on Jln. Bukit Mata Kuching,* ☎ *no phone. No credit cards.*

$$–$$$ ✕🏨 **Holiday Inn Kuching.** The first international hotel in Kuching enjoys an unrivaled location right on the river. The rooms are compact, with standard amenities. The view of the road is rather dreary, so request a room with a river view. The Executive Floor has rooms with locally inspired furnishings and a shared lounge with a splendid river view of the river. The gaudily decorated Meisan Szechuan restaurant serves spicy Szechuan fare; you'll also find a variety of dim sum at its popular Sunday brunch (reservations essential). Note that if you'd like to trade an in-town lifestyle for one at the seashore, you can make arrangements to split your stay between this property and one of the two Holiday Inns on Damai Beach. ⊠ *Jln. Tuanku Abdul Rahman (Box 2362), 93100,* ☎ *082/423111, 800/HOLIDAY in the U.S., or 0171/ 722–7755 in the U.K.;* FAX *082/426169. 305 rooms. 2 restaurants, bar, pool, sauna, tennis court, exercise room, dance club, playground, business services. AE, DC, MC, V.*

$$$$ 🏨 **Kuching Hilton.** This 15-story luxury hotel on the Sarawak River, just
★ across from Ft. Margherita, has become a landmark for quality service and fine dining. Its spacious rooms have light-wood furniture, including a desk. The Penthouse Floor and the two Executive Floors have such extra amenities as separate check-in, personal butlers, and private lounges. The views—and all the restaurants have them—are far better than those at the newer Crowne Plaza Riverside Kuching next door. The serene, ground-floor Waterfront Cafe is a great place to watch the river traffic. Its menu has Malay, Chinese, and Indian favorites plus Western specialties. It's also the best place in town if you're longing for a fresh salad, good bread, and delicious noodle dishes. ⊠ *Jln. Tuanku Abdul Rahman (Box 2396), 93748,* ☎ *082/248200 or 800/HILTONS in the U.S.,* FAX *082/428984. 322 rooms. 4 restaurants, bar, pool, exercise room, business services, meeting rooms. AE, DC, MC, V.*

$$$ 🏨 **Holiday Inn Resort Damai Beach.** This is one of two Holiday Inn resorts set virtually side by side on a stretch of beach about 24 km (15 mi) from Kuching. (A shuttle bus serves the two resorts from the Holiday Inn Kuching.) The beach itself is only so-so, but the setting—backed by lush rain forest and cradled by Mt. Santubong—is glorious. The large, well-furnished rooms have an outdoorsy feeling, owing to their glass patio doors. For a little more seclusion, opt to stay in one of the 80 deluxe rooms or 20 suites; they're housed in buildings with various indigenous architectural styles on the breezy slopes overlooking the main hotel. The word *damai* means "harmony and peace," but to find it here you must walk away from the hotel's many activities. ⊠ *Damai Beach*

(Box 2870), 93756, ☎ 082/411777, 800/HOLIDAY in the U.S., or 0171/722–7755 in the U.K.; FAX 082/428911. 282 rooms, 20 suites. 3 restaurants, snack bar, pool, sauna, golf privileges, miniature golf, 2 tennis courts, exercise room, hiking, squash, snorkeling, windsurfing, boating, bicycles, dance club, recreation room, business services, meeting rooms. AE, DC, MC, V.

$$$ 🏨 **Holiday Inn Resort Damai Lagoon.** Newer than the adjacent Holiday Inn Resort Damai Beach (☞ *above*), this resort has an enormous lagoon-shape swimming pool. Some of its pleasant rooms are in an austere multistory block; others are in attractive Malay-style chalets near the pool and the beach. As with its sister hotel, Damai Lagoon offers many recreational options, including water sports and jungle treks. ⊠ *Damai Beach (Box 3159), 93756, ☎ 082/846900, 800/HOLIDAY in the U.S., or 0171/722–7755 in the U.K.; FAX 082/846901. 256 rooms. Restaurant, 2 snack bars, 2 bars, pool, hot tub, massage, sauna, golf privileges, 2 tennis courts, health club, hiking, squash, snorkeling, windsurfing, boating, bicycles, business services, meeting rooms. AE, DC, MC, V.*

$ 🏨 **Borneo Hotel.** This well-located, well-established hotel is a good deal. Its rooms are modestly furnished, but they're clean and have air-conditioning, TVs, phones, and private baths. The staff is friendly, and the small restaurant serves good local curries. ⊠ *30C-F Jalan Tabuan, ☎ 082/244122, FAX 082/254848. 65 rooms. Restaurant, deli, piano bar. AE, DC, MC, V.*

Nightlife and the Arts

Evening entertainment in Kuching tends to run along the lines of karaoke lounges and bars. The Holiday Inn Kuching has a popular world-music lounge known as **Tribes** (⊠ Jln. Tuanku Abdul Rahman, ☎ 082/423111); it's open Monday–Saturday 4 PM–1 AM. The town's favorite disco is **Peppers** (⊠ Jln. Tuanku Abdul Rahman, ☎ 082/248200) in the Kuching Hilton. For traditional dance performances, you can't beat the cultural show at **Sarawak Cultural Village** (☎ 082/846411) in Santubong.

Outdoor Activities and Sports

BEACHES

Damai Beach is about 24 km (15 mi) northwest of Kuching (35 minutes by taxi), at the foot of Mt. Santubong. The two Holiday Inn resorts here (☞ *Lodging, above*) allow nonguests to use their facilities for windsurfing, catamaran sailing, kayaking, and waterskiing. To be honest, the sea here doesn't really invite swimming (it's rough in monsoon season and shallow and murky at other times), but the forested hills backing the beach make it a very pleasant spot to relax.

GOLF

The **Sarawak Golf Club** (☎ 084/440966) at Petra Jaya, about 15 minutes from downtown Kuching, is open to guests of major hotels. Greens fees are RM84–RM126, caddies RM8–RM12. The **Damai Beach Golf Course** (⊠ Jln. Santubong, ☎ 082/846088), designed by Arnold Palmer, is close to the Damai resorts and is open to nonmembers. Greens fees are RM150–RM180, caddy fees are RM15–RM25, and you can rent carts for about RM30.

Shopping

The handicrafts in Sarawak are among the most fascinating in all of Malaysia. Especially distinctive are the handwoven Iban textiles or *pua kumbu*, whose intricate designs have ceremonial significance. Baskets, hats, and mats are made from a variety of materials including rattan, palm leaves, and reeds; their designs vary according to the ethnic group. Wood carvings often bear the motif of the hornbill, the national emblem. Pottery designs show a Chinese influence, as do brass and silver objects. Many tribal artifacts from Indonesian Kalimantan are also sold in Kuching.

The best place to browse for antiques, curios, handicrafts, and other souvenirs is the **main bazaar,** which runs parallel to the waterfront. There are close to 20 shops whose irresistible bric-a-brac literally spills out onto the pavement. Try the **Atelier Gallery** (No. 104); **Nelson's Gallery** (No. 84), which is run by the most knowledgable antiques dealer in town; and **Arts of Asia** (No. 68). Although prices are amazingly low to start out, bargaining is expected (just be sure to ask whether the item you're haggling over is a genuine antique or a skillful copy). Goods can be shipped anywhere, and major credit cards are accepted in most shops.

A **Sunday market** in the parking lot of Bank Bumiputra on Jalan Satok sells everything from fruit to heirlooms. The market actually starts on Saturday afternoon and is a good place to catch the local atmosphere.

Batang Ai

➋ *Approximately 100 km (60 mi) southeast of Kuching.*

Few people visit Sarawak without making a trip to a tribal longhouse. Some are as close as a 1½-hour drive from Kuching; others involve a longer drive followed by a boat trip. You can visit for a day or stay for a week. Either way, your hosts welcome you with a mixture of hospitality and polite indifference.

The Skrang River was the first area to be used by tour operators as a destination for longhouse excursions. However, with the construction of the huge Batang Ai hydroelectric dam and the opening of the four-star Hilton Batang Ai Longhouse Resort (☞ Lodging, *below*), there are more accommodation options now than before. Many operators use the resort (to reach it you must make a half-hour boat ride across the lake) as the hub for day trips to or overnight stays at longhouses along the rivers that feed the Batang Ai Reservoir. (☞ Tour Operators and Travel Agencies *in* Northern Borneo Essentials, *below.*) Popular longhouse destinations are the Engkari River and the Batang Ai (*batang* means "river" in Iban). At the huge Batang Ai National Park (where you have a good chance of spotting wild orangutans) your only lodging option is camping.

The route to Batang Ai takes you by car or bus through pepper plantations, run mostly by Chinese families, where you can pause and look at one of Sarawak's major exports being grown and dried. Most tours also stop at the interesting market in the little town of Serian and later make a break for a local meal. The entire trip from Kuching to the Batang Ai Lake takes around 4½ hours. Note that most visitors stay in separate accommodations near the longhouse, rather than actually sleeping in the longhouse itself. These purpose-built lodges are simple but adequate, with mosquito netting, flush toilets, and running water. The attraction is seeing, close at hand, a lifestyle that has changed little in centuries. Tour operators can advise you on dress and comportment.

Lodging

$$$$ 🏨 **Hilton Batang Ai Longhouse Resort.** This resort, which opened in 1994, is an alternative to the spartan accommodations available on longhouse tours. Designed on the lines of a traditional Iban timber longhouse, it stands on a small island in Batang Ai Lake, surrounded by hills and with a patch of rain forest behind. Rooms are comfortably furnished with native woods and have air-conditioning and ceiling fans.

Another longhouse contains a large dining room with a terrace that overlooks the lake. Treks and longboat excursions to Iban communities are the main options for daily activities. Hilton International will make travel arrangements through a local tour operator. ✉ *Reservations: Kuching Hilton, Jln. Tuanku Abdul Rahman (Box 2396), Kuching 93748,* ☎ *082/248200 or 800/HILTONS,* 🖷 *082/428984. 100 rooms. Restaurant, meeting rooms. AE, DC, MC, V.*

Miri

③ *544 km (340 mi) northeast of Kuching.*

This once sleepy fishing village is now the administrative capital of northeastern Sarawak, thanks primarily to Shell, which began exploiting its offshore oil in 1910. Several flights daily link this economic center with Kuching, Bandar Seri Begawan in Brunei, and Kota Kinabalu in Sabah. You'll find comfortable hotels; karaoke clubs and bars; and the exotic Tamu Muhibbah native market, which sells all sorts of weird produce—from edible stems harvested in the jungles to sago worms, a local delicacy eaten either blanched or barbecued.

Most visitors use Miri as a jumping-off point for the famous Gunung Mulu National Park (several flights daily) and the archaeologically important Niah Caves, a bus or taxi ride away. It's also possible to travel by bus from here to Kuala Belait, and then cross the border into Brunei. Miri was once a popular hub for trips up the Baram River to the longhouses of the Kayan and Kenyah tribes. However, increased logging activities in the region have made such trips less attractive. Enthusiastic scuba divers can visit the Luconia Shoals, northwest of Miri, on a live-aboard dive boat that operates between April and October.

Lodging

$$$ 🏨 **Holiday Inn Miri.** On the beach at the mouth of the Miri River, this international hotel is slightly closer to town than its neighbor, the Rihga Royal (☞ *below*). Popular with both leisure and business travelers, it has a swimming pool and a gym as well as the usual room amenities. The Western food served in the coffee shop is often surprisingly good, and there's also a popular Chinese restaurant. ✉ *Jln. Temenggong Oyang Lawai, 98998,* ☎ *085/418888,* 🖷 *085/419999. 168 rooms. Restaurant, bar, coffee shop, pub, pool, health club, dance club, business services, meeting rooms. AE, DC, MC, V.*

$$$ 🏨 **Rihga Royal Hotel.** On the edge of the beach and a five-minute taxi ride from the town center, this modern hotel sits on 20 acres of landscaped grounds. Three buildings surround a courtyard that fans out to the grounds, the pool, and the guest chalets. Rooms throughout are smart, efficient, and functional; each has air-conditioning that's individually controlled and coffee- and tea-making facilities. A cascading waterfall is the centerpiece of the atrium lobby, off which is a pub for a convivial chat and a game of darts. ✉ *Jln. Temenggong Oyang Lawai, 98998,* ☎ *085/421121,* 🖷 *085/421099. 170 rooms. 3 restaurants, pub, pool, health club, dance club, business services, meeting rooms. AE, DC, MC, V.*

Niah Caves

④ *109 km (68 mi) south of Miri.*

The Niah Caves in Niah National Park are the most important archaeological site on Borneo, yielding evidence of human habitation some 25,000 to 30,000 years ago. Artifacts uncovered include stone, bone, and iron tools; wall paintings; Chinese ceramics; and 1,000-year-old wooden coffins. Unfortunately, most of these items have been removed to Kuching's Sarawak Museum for safekeeping, and the Painted Cave, where the wall paintings and coffins remain, is closed to the public for reasons of preservation.

However, the caves are still worth visiting, especially when birds' nests are gathered twice a year. Edible nests formed from the hardened saliva of a couple of varieties of swiftlet are scraped off the walls and roofs of the cave in a death-defying operation by collectors, who scale flimsy poles and ropes to climb as much as 100 ft above the cave floor. The collectors are convinced that the risks are justified by the high price paid by the Chinese, who believe that the nests have medicinal properties and generally make them into a soup. Year-round, the local Ibans gather guano from the cave floors for fertilizer.

The park is about a 1½-hour bus or taxi ride (RM80) from Miri. If you're adventurous you can walk 45 minutes along a well-maintained boardwalk through the rain forest to explore the caves with or without a guide. The park offers a range of accommodations, including comfortable chalets, and there's a canteen that serves drinks and basic meals. You can make lodging reservations at the Miri visitor center (☞ Visitor Information *in* Northern Borneo Essentials, *below*).

Gunung Mulu National Park

⑤ *35-minute flight or eight-hour trip by both bus and boat from Miri.*

The most dramatic feature of Sarawak's vast Gunung Mulu National Park is the world's largest limestone cave system, set amid virgin rain forest. Although the complex ecosystem of the forest is impressive, it's the "show caves" (those open to the public) that are unforgettable. Strategic lighting and boardwalks make it possible to explore four caves: Deer Cave, which could hold London's St Paul's Cathedral five times over; Lang's Cave, with its beautiful stalactites and stalagmites; Clearwater Cave, which has a river running through it and is the longest cave in Southeast Asia; and Wind Cave, with lovely flowstones and other interesting formations. Those with a sense of adventure can arrange with a tour operator to travel underground from one cave passage to another. Hikers can visit the sharp limestone Pinnacles or trek out from the park along the Headhunters' Trail, finishing the trip by boat downriver to Limbang.

The park offers a variety of accommodations near its headquarters at Mulu, and there are private hotels just outside the park's boundaries. The hostels that are run by various tour operators are very basic, but fortunately, a surprising degree of comfort in the midst of the jungle is offered by the attractive Royal Mulu Resort. Access from here to the park headquarters is by longboat.

The best way to reach Mulu is by the Twin Otter planes run by MAS (generally there are four flights per day from Miri). The trip takes 35 minutes and offers a panoramic view of the rain forest, especially over Brunei, where logging has not encroached. An alternative way to reach Mulu is by bus from Miri to Kuala Baram, then by a series of express boats and longboats up the Baram River; this takes at least eight hours and because of deforestation and erosion along the river, it's a depressing rather than scenic ride.

Lodging

$$$ 🏨 **Royal Mulu Resort.** This charming resort consists of a series of timber chalets and larger buildings with rooms, all linked by boardwalks and set high on stilts at a river junction. The attractively furnished guest quarters have parquet floors, private baths, air-conditioning, and satellite TVs. The resort also has a pool, a walk-in aviary, and a library with interesting reference books. *Reservations through Royal Rhiga Hotel:* ✉ *Jln. Temenggong Oyang Lawai, Miri 98998,* ☎ *085/421121,* FAX *085/425057. 88 rooms. Restaurant, bar, pool, library, meeting room. AE, DC, MC, V.*

Sabah

Sabah—known as the "Land Below the Wind" because it lies below the typhoon belt—occupies the northern tip of Borneo. It shares its southwestern border with Sarawak and the rest of its southern border with the Indonesian province of Kalimantan. Its primary resource is timber, from which fortunes have been made. Although vast tracts of forest have been replaced by oil palm plantations, a sizable portion of land is protected in national parks or conservation areas. These majestic forests and freshwater swamps contain abundant wildlife—and relatively few people. Although the state's area is some 75,500 square km (29,388 square mi), it only has about 2 million people, of which the Kadazans are the largest ethnic group. Along the west coast, the Bajaus grow rice and raise ponies; on the east coast a group related to the Bajau, but who speak a different language, are mostly fishermen. The Chinese, who run much of Sabah's commerce, live mostly in the towns and make up about 10% of the population.

Borneo's forbidding interior made it far less attractive to early traders and explorers than neighboring areas, so Sabah remained unexploited by the British until the late 19th century. In 1963, it joined Sarawak, Malaya, and Singapore (which later seceded) in forming the Federation of Malaysia. Most Sabahans are Christians, although the official religion of Malaysia is Islam. Sabah's native arts, crafts, and social customs are still retained, and Bahasa Malaysia, the national language, is still a second tongue for most Sabahans.

The capital, Kota Kinabalu, is a relatively new town, rebuilt after it was destroyed by Allied bombing during World War II. It contains few sights but is an important transportation hub. Most travelers to Sabah visit Mt. Kinabalu, the legendary mountain in the less-developed interior. At 13,450 ft, this is the highest peak in Southeast Asia outside the Himalayas, and it's part of a huge national park. You can hike from the park headquarters to the summit and back in two days. For beachcombers, the seas around Sabah offer a kaleidoscope of marine life. You can scuba dive in some of the world's top dive spots or simply snorkel or putter about the reefs in a glass-bottom boat.

Kota Kinabalu

❻ *1,584 km (990 mi) east of KL.*

The capital, called Jesselton when Sabah was known as British North Borneo, was razed during World War II. It was renamed in 1967, four years after Sabah became part of the Federation of Malaysia. Little of historic interest remains—the oldest part of the city is vintage 1950s. The multistory shophouses sell hardware and other practical goods; the upper floors are dwellings. The central market on the waterfront sells produce and handicrafts. Next to the central market is a smaller collection of stalls that sell produce from the Philippines.

Kota Kinabalu's main draw is the **Sabah Museum,** on a hilltop off Jalan Penampang about 3 km (2 mi) south of the city center. The building resembles a traditional longhouse, and its exhibits are a good introduction to local history, archaeology, botany, and ethnography. Perhaps the most interesting feature is the group of life-size traditional houses in the garden setting of **Kampung Warisan** (Heritage Village), on the slopes behind the museum parking lot. Within the museum you'll find many antique *tajau* (Chinese ceramic jars)—heirlooms with a practical purpose that are common throughout Asia. ✉ *Jln. Kebajikan,* ☎ *088/253199.* ⛟ *Free.* ⊙ *Museum Sat.–Thurs. 10–6; Heritage Village Sat.–Thurs. 9–1 and 2–5.*

Three seas wash the shores of Sabah, and they're all accessible from Kota Kinabalu. Just offshore are five small, delightful islands that make up the **Tunku Adbul Rahman Marine Park** (☎ 088/211652 for the Sabah Parks Office in Kota Kinabalu). You can make a day trip to picnic and snorkel among the reefs at **Pulau Gaya** and walk the 20 km (12 mi) of trails through the mangrove swamps and tropical forests. **Pulau Sapi** is popular with sun worshipers and snorkelers (note that it can get very crowded). **Pulau Mamutik** is a quiet little island where a well-known dive operator has a base. **Pulau Manukan** is the most developed island, with chalets for rent, a restaurant, a small swimming pool, and a campground. **Pulau Sulug,** the island farthest offshore, is the least visited. However, a dive operator has plans to erect a number of chalets here.

OFF THE
BEATEN PATH

KAMPUNG BAVANGGAZO – This small, peaceful kampung is in the Kudat district, about three hours north of Kota Kinabalu. The people who live here are members of the Rungus tribe, a subgroup of the Kadazan tribe and the most traditional of Sabah's people. Here you'll learn about the lifestyle of the Rungus farmers, sample local food and rice wine, see a cultural show after dinner, and stay in a longhouse (beds have mosquito netting, and proper toilet and shower facilities are available). You'll also see handicrafts being made and can buy the finished products at remarkably low prices. You can either make arrangements with a tour operator (☞ Tour Operators and Travel Agencies *in* Northern Borneo Essentials, *below*) or rent a car and drive here yourself. The whole operation is run as a cooperative by the villagers; contact the Sabah Tourism Promotion Corporation (☞ Visitor Information *in* Northern Borneo Essentials, *below*) for information and reservations if you opt to visit independently.

Dining and Lodging

$$–$$$ ✕ **Port View Seafood Restaurant.** This place has grown from a simple, open-sided eatery to a brightly tiled and gaily decorated (even if pink is not to everyone's taste) restaurant that's very popular with Asian tour groups. The seafood is spanking fresh (even live, if you want); the steamed prawns and butter prawns are superb. ✉ *Jln. Haji Saman (opposite Marine Police base),* ☎ *088/221753. AE, MC, V. No lunch.*

$$ ✕ **Nam Xing.** The locals who patronize this Chinese restaurant order the dim sum for breakfast or lunch, but there are also tasty seafood dishes—chili crab, squid, and prawns. The noise and gusto of the clientele provide a lively distraction from the bland decor. ✉ *32 Jln. Haji Saman,* ☎ *088/212900. No credit cards.*

$ ✕ **Wishbone Cafe.** Located in the Jesselton, an attractive boutique hotel, this perennially popular restaurant is informal but comfortable and always busy at lunchtime. Local food (the Hainanese-style chicken rice is recommended) and simple Western fare are available. The service is very good. ✉ *69 Jln. Gaya,* ☎ *088/223333. AE, DC, V.*

$$$$ ✕🏨 **Hyatt Kinabalu.** Eager to keep its place as a leader among downtown hotels, the Hyatt underwent a top-to-toe renovation during 1997–98, and it now looks considerably more glamorous. Rooms are spacious and comfortable; many have views of the port and nearby islands. Rooms on the top two Regency Club floors have extra ameni-

ties. The hotel also has the best Japanese restaurant in town, the Nagisa, and a very popular pub, Shenanigan's. You can get good pizzas and cakes—perfect for picnics—in the delicatessen. ⊠ *Jln. Datuk Salleh Sulong, 88994,* ☎ *088/221234 or 800/223–1234 in the U.S.,* FAX *088/225972. 288 rooms, 14 suites. 3 restaurants, 2 bars, pool, business services. AE, DC, MC, V.*

$$$$ ✕▣ **Shangri-La's Tanjung Aru Resort.** This luxury establishment is
★   near the airport and 10 minutes from downtown (there's a shuttle into town and to Shangri-La's Rasa Ria Resort about an hour away). No longer a quiet getaway, it has become a major resort that bustles with activity when it's full. Wicker furniture gives the rooms an airy feel; each room also has a balcony that overlooks the hotel's 25 landscaped acres and the sea beyond. There's a marina that arranges windsurfing, scuba diving, waterskiing, and sailing excursions as well as trips to the nearby marine park islands. You can play tennis and pitch-and-putt golf or go biking; the small beach is a great place to relax, build sand castles, or play volleyball. Tour operators in the hotel's shopping arcade offer white-water rafting excursions and trips to Sepilok, Sukau, and Danum Valley. Of the four restaurants, Peppino is noteworthy for its Mediterranean food with Italian accents. ⊠ *Jln. Aru (Locked Bag 174), 88999,* ☎ *088/225800 or 800/942–5050 in the U.S.,* FAX *088/ 244871. 500 rooms. 4 restaurants, bar, 2 pools, 4 tennis courts, exercise room, volleyball, dock, dive shop, snorkeling, windsurfing, waterskiing, boating, bicycles, shops, dance club, business services, travel services. AE, DC, MC, V.*

$$$$ ▣ **Shangri-La's Rasa Ria Resort.** Set on 400 acres of tropical vegetation
★   along a long sandy beach, this resort is about an hour's drive from Kota Kinabalu International Airport. The split-level rooms are a touch on the small side, but you probably won't be spending much time in your room owing to all the recreational facilities. In addition to tennis and the usual water sports, you'll find horseback riding, crab catching, and golf at the nearby 18-hole Dalit Bay Golf and Country Club among the list of activities. At the adjacent nature reserve, the stars are a pair of orangutans. The only drawback to this resort is the lack of a nearby village or town with alternative places to eat. ⊠ *Pantai Dalit (Box 600), Tuaran 89208,* ☎ *088/792888 or 800/942–5050 in the U.S.,* FAX *088/792777. 330 rooms. 4 restaurants, bar, grocery, pub, pool, outdoor hot tub, golf privileges, 2 tennis courts, health club, hiking, horseback riding, beach, dive shop, snorkeling, windsurfing, boating, jet skiing, bicycles, video games, children's programs, business services. AE, DC, MC, V.*

$$$ ▣ **Promenade Hotel.** One of several hotels that have recently opened
★   in Kota Kinabalu, Promenade is near the waterfront overlooking Pulau Gaya and a five-minute drive from the city center. It caters more to Malaysian businessmen than to leisure travelers. Rooms are small though adequately furnished; only the lobby has fancy decor. The pub, Le Rendezvous, is a popular place at night. ⊠ *4 Lorong Api Api 3, Api Api Centre, 88000,* ☎ *088/265555,* FAX *088/246559. 451 rooms. 2 restaurants, pub, pool, fitness center, dance club, business services. AE, DC, MC, V.*

$ ▣ **Casuarina Hotel.** Two minutes' walk from Tanjung Aru Beach and less than 10 minutes from the airport, this attractive boutique hotel is nicely furnished. The staff is very friendly, and there's a free shuttle service to downtown. ⊠ *Lorong Ikan Lais, off Jln. Mat Salleh, 88100,* ☎ *088/243899,* FAX *088/223000. 44 rooms. Restaurant, bar. AE, MC, V.*

Nightlife and the Arts

CULTURAL SHOWS

The best place to see a cultural show with a variety of Sabahan dances is at the **Malam Kampung** (Village Night; ☎ 088/225800 for reservations) in the Pulau Bayu restaurant of Shangri-La's Tanjung Aru Resort (☞ Dining and Lodging, *above*). Held every Sunday at 8, the evening includes a buffet of Malaysian food or selections from the à la carte menu. Cultural shows are also given at the **Monsopiad Cultural Village** (☎ 088/761336) in a rural setting about 20 minutes from town. Although the House of Skulls—a minimuseum devoted to the trophies of the famous, long-dead headhunter, Monsopiad—is open daily, the cultural performance and buffet dinner are normally given only for groups. Check with any Kota Kinabalu tour operator (☞ Tour Operators and Travel Agencies *in* Northern Borneo Essentials, *below*) about trips to see the show.

DANCE CLUBS

The Hyatt hotel's **Shenanigan's** (⊠ Jln. Datuk Salleh Sulong, lower level, ☎ 088/221234) is the most popular place in town, with lively music and a friendly atmosphere. You may also want to try the Promenade Hotel's **Le Rendezvous** (⊠ 4 Lorong Api Api 3, Api Api Centre, 88000, ☎ 088/265555). For a relaxing evening where you can sip a drink, play pool or board games, and enjoy light meals and the occasional live show, try the spacious, two-level **Something Al's** (⊠ Jln. Aru, ☎ 088/266480) at Shangri-La's Tanjung Aru Resort.

Outdoor Activities and Sports

BEACHES

The closest beaches to Kota Kinabalu are on the islands of the **Tunku Abdul Rahman Marine Park** (☎ 088/211652 for the Sabah Parks Office in Kota Kinabalu) a 15-minute speedboat ride from the small jetties in front of the Hyatt hotel downtown. Except for Pulau Sapi, which tends to get crowded, peace and privacy prevail. Pretty coral formations and marine life attract snorkelers and divers (☞ Scuba Diving, *below*). Tour operators (☞ Tour Operators and Travel Agencies *in* Northern Borneo Essentials, *below*) will arrange trips complete with a picnic lunch or barbecue.

DIVING

Kota Kinabalu is a great place to arrange trips to some of the world's best dive spots. Sipadan, an oceanic island off Sabah's southeast coast, is renowned for its 2,000-ft wall dive, turtles, and pelagic fish. North of Sipadan, islands such as Mabul and Pandanan offer pristine corals and rich marine life. Far off Sabah's west coast is the atoll of Layang Layang, where a dive resort gives enthusiasts a chance to discover the underwater world and see the thousands of migratory birds that nest here.

Borneo Divers (⊠ 4th floor, Wisma Sabah, Locked Bag 194, Kota Kinabalu 88999, ☎ 088/222226), a 5-star PADI facility, arranges diver training and excursions to most of Sabah's dive sites. They were the first company to offer dive trips to Sipadan, where their chalets occupy a prime location. **Tanjung Aru Dive Centre** (⊠ The Marina, Shangri-La's Tanjung Aru Resort, WDT 14, Kota Kinabalu 89459, ☎ 088/256676) offers diver training and dives around Kota Kinabalu, and runs a small, exclusive dive resort on Pandanan island, off Sabah's east coast.

GOLF

There are three private golf courses within Kota Kinabalu and several others within a two-hour drive of the city; note that it's best to make arrangements to play in advance through your hotel. The 18-hole course of the **Sabah Golf and Country Club** (⊠ Jln. Kolom, ☎ 088/247533) at Bukit Padang is quite popular. Greens fees are RM70–RM150. Also popular is the 27-hole course of **Sutera Harbour Golf and Country Club** (⊠ Sutera Harbour Blvd., ☎ 088/252266), where greens fees are RM200–RM250; golf carts are compulsory and cost RM25. The 9-hole course of the **Kinabalu Golf Club** (☎ 088/234904) is near the beach at Tanjung Aru. Greens fees are RM105 and caddies cost RM27 (note that visitors aren't permitted to play on weekends). Other fine courses include those at Karambunai and Pantai Dalit, north of Kota Kinabalu, and the Borneo Golf and Country Club south of town at Bongawan. The Mt. Kinabalu Golf Course, at around 6,000 ft on the slopes of Mt. Kinabalu, offers some spectacular vistas and a cooler climate at its 18-hole course.

Shopping

To see how the locals shop, visit the Sunday morning **street fair** on Jalan Gaya. Stalls sell everything from fresh fruit to orchids, clothing to bric-a-brac, and basketwork to live puppies. For a wide assortment of goods, try the **Centrepoint** complex on the Coastal Highway, where stores sell clothing, shoes, photographic equipment, and souvenirs; you'll also find money changers and several restaurants, including those that serve Western fast food. Nearby, a little beyond the Promenade Hotel, the new **Wisma 2020** complex has a large department store and a wide range of shops; there are food stalls on the fourth floor.

Sabah handicrafts are less elaborate than those of Sarawak, but they do have character. In Kota Kinabalu, **Borneo Craft** (⊠ Ground floor, Wisma Merdeka, ☎ 088/237936) has a small but interesting collection of local handicrafts, as well as a good range of books on Borneo. Also in the same shopping complex, **Rafflesia Gift Centre** (☎ 088/239287) has a wide range of handicrafts and souvenirs. They also have a branch, **Classic Batik & Craft,** on the ground floor of Centrepoint complex. The gift shop inside the **Sabah Tourism Promotion Corporation** (⊠ 51 Jln. Gaya, ☎ 088/218620) is worth checking out. If you're driving to Mt. Kinabalu, stop at the handicraft stalls at **Nabalu Market,** where the locally made basketwork is interesting and cheap, and the vendors are as colorful as the products they sell.

Kinabalu Park

❼ *90 km (56 mi) east of Kota Kinabalu.*

Kinabalu Park, about 1½ hours from Kota Kinabalu, is regarded as having the richest assemblage of plants in the world within its 754 square km (291 square mi). Nature lovers can walk miles of well-marked trails through jungle dense with wild orchids, carnivorous pitcher plants, bamboo, mosses and vines, and unusual geologic formations. The wildlife is shy, but you're likely to see a variety of birds (some endemic), squirrels, and tree shrews. To reach the Kinabalu Park Headquarters on your own, take one of the frequent minibuses that depart from the Padang in Kota Kinabalu for Ranau (the one-way fare is RM8); they pass the park's entrance. The cost to enter the park is RM2. Many Kota Kinabalu tour operators (☞ Tour Operators and Travel Agencies *in* Northern Borneo Essentials, *below*) also offer organized trips. For general information, contact the **Sabah Parks Office** (☎ 088/211652) in Kota Kinabalu.

★ For some, the main event is scaling **Mt. Kinabalu,** at 13,450 ft the highest mountain in Southeast Asia outside the Himalayas; it's also a place of spiritual significance (souls of the departed are believed to reside here) for the Kadazan people. Hikers can trek from the park headquarters to the peak and back in two days. The view from the summit on a clear morning is worth every step, so most people catch their second wind at 11,000 ft in the rest house at Panar Laban (☞ *also* Lodging, *below*) before leaving at 2 AM to reach the summit by dawn.

Poring Hot Springs, on the southeastern side of Kinabalu Park about 40 km (25 mi) from the park headquarters, is popular for day trips. If you have the time, however, it's pleasant to stay overnight in the chalets. The hot sulphur springs are piped into attractive open-air baths; there's a pool of mountain-temperature water for a refreshing plunge afterwards. You can also make the steep 3,000-ft climb to Poring's canopy walkway, which is strung high above the ground and offers a bird's-eye view of the rain forest. If you like your entertainments to be less strenuous, you can visit the Butterfly Farm to see many live, native—often amazing—species. Good, inexpensive food is available in the restaurant overlooking a pool.

On the east side of Mt. Kinabalu, **Mesilau Plateau** is reached via the vegetable-growing district of Kundasang about 30 minutes from the park headquarters. Just beyond the scenic 18-hole Mt. Kinabalu Golf Course, a series of beautiful wooden hostels and chalets, together with a restaurant and an information center, opened in mid-1998. There are also plans to create a trail from here up to Panar Laban.

Lodging

Although there's a range of accommodations in Kundasang, about 5 km (3 mi) from the park, it's infinitely better to stay in the park's superb forested environment. Accommodations at Panar Laban, the park headquarters, Poring Hot Springs, and Mesilau Plateau were privatized in mid-1998, although everything else pertaining to the park is still managed by Sabah Parks. Beds in the heated rest house at Panar Laban cost RM25 per person; bunk beds in the nearby mountain hostel cost RM5. At the park headquarters, you'll find the Nepenthes Villas (two bedrooms with twin beds as well as a sitting room and a kitchen) for RM250 a night and the Twin Bed Cabins offer (you guessed it) twin beds as well as attached bathrooms for RM50. Two hostels offer dormitory-style accommodations for RM10 per person. Make advance reservations for any of the park lodgings through **Kinabalu Gold Resorts** (✉ 3rd floor, Block C, Kompleks Karamunsing, Kota Kinabalu, ☎ 088/243629, 🖷 088/242861).

$ 🏨 **Hotel Perkasa.** The Perkasa sits on a hilltop about 6 km (4 mi) from the park headquarters. It overlooks the vegetable farms of Kundasang, and it faces Mt. Kinabalu, to which excursions can be arranged. Rooms offer a mountain view as well as heaters—a rarity in the tropics—to warm the brisk mountain air, but that's the extent of the luxury. The hotel is a 2½-hour drive from the airport in Kota Kinabalu. ✉ *WDT 11, Ranau 89300, ☎ 088/889511, 🖷 088/889101. 74 rooms. Restaurant, bar, golf privileges, tennis court, exercise room, business services, travel services. AE, DC, MC, V.*

Sandakan

❽ *386 km (241 mi) east of Kota Kinabalu.*

The coastal town of Sandakan was the capital of British North Borneo until it was completely destroyed by the Allies toward the end of the Japanese occupation during World War II. The capital was transferred to Jesselton (now Kota Kinabalu), but Sandakan came back to life in the 1970s as the center for the logging industry. That natural resource has been largely exhausted and the land is now replanted with oil palm plantations. No longer a boomtown, Sandakan is nonetheless worth visiting as it's within a couple of hours of some of Borneo's most accessible wildlife sights.

No visit to Sabah is complete without a trip to the **Sepilok Orang-Utan Rehabilitation Center,** set in a rain forest reserve just 25 km (15 mi) from Sandakan. Here, illegally captured animals are prepared for a return to the wild. You can watch the twice-daily feeding of the semi-wild orangutans, who come in from the forest for a meal of bananas and milk until they're ready to go it alone. During the various fruiting seasons, when plenty of food is available in the wild, the number of animals visiting the feeding platform is likely to be greatly reduced. From Sandakan's Labuk Road station, buses depart for the center at 9:20, 11:30, 1:30, and 3 each day. To arrive in time for the first feeding, take a minibus for "Batu 14," or take a taxi and ask the driver to wait for you (around RM25). ☎ *089/531180. ▤ RM10. ☉ Daily 8–6; feeding times 10 AM and 2:30 PM.*

Three islands, Selingan, Bakungan, and Gulisan (almost one hour by speedboat north of Sandakan), and their surrounding waters make up the **Turtle Islands Marine Park.** Throughout the year, green and hawksbill turtles come to their shores to dig nests and lay their eggs in the warm sands. The eggs are then gathered by rangers and transferred to hatcheries in an effort to conserve these endangered marine animals. To visit the islands, tour operators in Kota Kinabalu or Sandakan (☞ Tour Operators and Travel Agencies *in* Northern Borneo Essentials, *below*) can arrange for a boat and an overnight stay at one of the three chalets on Selingan.

Sukau

❾ *134 km (83 mi) southeast of Sandakan.*

The Kinabatangan, Sabah's largest river, flows through a vast tract of freshwater swamp that's home to a rich variety of wildlife, including the orangutan; the big-nosed, pot-bellied proboscis monkey found only in Borneo; and a host of glorious birds. The village of Sukau, on the mid-reaches of the Kinabatangan and about two hours by road from Sandakan, is a focal point for wildlife-viewing trips along the river and its tributaries. Five tour operators maintain simple but comfortable tourist lodges along the Kinabatangan and take visitors by boat at dusk and at dawn to look for proboscis monkeys. Make arrangements in Kota Kinabalu with Wildlife Expeditions or Borneo Eco Tours (☞ Tour Operators and Travel Agencies *in* Northern Borneo Essentials, *below*).

OFF THE
BEATEN PATH

DANUM VALLEY – Anyone with a serious interest in discovering the complex beauty of the virgin rain forest should make a trip to the Danum Valley Conservation Area. To get here you must fly (40 minutes) from Kota Kinabalu to Lahad Datu on Sabah's east coast and then drive 85 km (53 mi). Apart from the field center, where scientists carrying out studies of the forest are based, there's accommodation at the **Borneo Rainforest Lodge** (☎ 088/244100), where fan-cooled wooden chalets on stilts are clustered near the Danum River. From here you can follow trails through the forest, watch for birds and other wildlife from the stunning canopy walkway, and go on night drives. Nature interpretation is provided by knowledgeable guides; you'll also gain a greater understanding of conservation by visiting some of the projects where experiments in reforestation are being conducted.

Pulau Pandanan

❿ *Reaching Pandanan involves a 45-minute to an hour flight from Kota Kinabalu to Tawau, followed by a 1½-hour minibus ride to Semporna, and then a 45-minute speedboat ride.*

Many beautiful coral-fringed islands are found to the east and northeast of Semporna; as yet, only one of these has been developed as a dive resort. Pasir, a private resort on the minute island of Pandanan, offers simple but comfortable accommodation and excellent macro diving. To make arrangements for a dive excursion here, contact the Tanjung Aru Dive Centre (☞ Scuba Diving *in* Outdoor Activities and Sports *under* Kota Kinabalu, *above*).

Pulau Sipadan

⑪ *45-minute flight from Kota Kinabalu to Tawau, followed by a 1½-hour minibus ride to Semporna, and then a 1-hour boat ride from Semporna.*

Until a decade ago, the tiny oceanic island of Sipadan, around 30 km (18 mi) south of Semporna, was visited only by nesting sea turtles. Jacques Cousteau's proclamation that the island was "an untouched piece of art" combined with the establishment (in 1989) of a small dive resort changed all that. Scuba divers began arriving in ever-increasing numbers to explore the pristine waters and coral reefs.

The island rises 2,000 ft directly from the floor of the Celebes Sea, offering a dive wall that goes on forever. Unchecked development has resulted in a total of five resorts now on the island, with even more divers coming in daily from a Japanese-owned resort on nearby Mabul Island. Federal legislation was introduced in early 1998 to restrict the number of divers to 80 per day, but at press time, this wasn't being enforced. Sipadan still offers a remarkable diving experience, even if it is being challenged by the presence of too many people. For trips and accommodations, contact Borneo Divers (☞ Scuba Diving *in* Outdoor Activities and Sports *under* Kota Kinabalu, *above*).

Brunei

Surrounded by both the Malaysian state of Sarawak and the South China Sea, Brunei is a tiny nation different from any other in Southeast Asia. Since 1929, when oil was discovered off its shores, the sultanate of Brunei Darussalam—no larger than the state of Delaware and with a population of only 280,000—has become one of the richest countries in the world. Although Brunei shares with its Malaysian neighbor a tropical climate and a jungle terrain, its people enjoy an unmatched standard of living.

In the 16th century, Brunei was nominally in control of an empire that stretched as far north as Manila. The nobility, however, was cruel and unpopular, and its power was gradually eroded by internal politics and revolts. In 1841, the first white rajah of Sarawak, James Brooke, obtained a grant for the land around the Sarawak River from the Sultan of Brunei. For the next 60 years, Brooke and his successor extended Sarawak's borders farther and farther, so that by the beginning of the 20th century, Brunei was a tiny, insignificant state. It became a British protectorate in 1888, and although oil was discovered in 1903, the wealth didn't start flowing until 1931. Britain helped quell a rebellion against the sultanate in 1962; political stability followed, and Brunei was granted full independence in 1984.

Brunei's 29th sultan, Hassanal Bolkiah, has ruled since 1967, when his father abdicated. Like his predecessors, he takes his role as a guardian of Islamic values seriously and has banned the sale of alcohol in Brunei. His fabulous personal fortune (he's estimated by *The Guinness Book of Records* to be the world's wealthiest man) also makes him a major player in global politics: his US$10 million contribution to the Nicaraguan rebels linked his name with the Iran-Contra arms scandal. Bragging about his extravagance—his passion for polo ponies, Italian sports cars, the Boeing jet he gave his daughter for her 18th birthday—is a national pastime. His 50th birthday celebrations included hiring Michael Jackson to perform; Whitney Houston did the singing honors at the wedding of his daughter. He's also famous for his beneficence. His government uses oil revenues to finance free public education, health care, and cultural programs. He has even donated an amusement park to the citizens of Brunei, making it the only one in the world where admission and rides are free. Brunei's business and real-estate investments abroad have ensured that the sultanate's prosperity will continue long after its oil and gas are exhausted.

You can get a quick overview of Brunei with a full day in Bandar Seri Begawan, its capital. The city is situated on a wide river, and many of its citizens dwell at the Kampung Ayer (Water Village) in houses built on stilts. If you're looking for adventure and undisturbed wilderness, consider a trip inland. More than 80% of Brunei is forest, mostly primary rain forest dominated by giant dipterocarp trees and populated by eagles, bears, wildcats, bats, and monkeys of all kinds—not to mention ants, snakes, and other of the less attractive jungle dwellers. You can take a day trip to Ulu Temburong National Park, although it's really better to plan an overnight stay.

Bandar Seri Begawan

⑫–㉔ *900 km (560 mi) northeast of Kuching, 300 km (186 mi) southwest of Kota Kinabalu.*

Unlike most Asian cities, where imposing modern office buildings and hotels dominate the skyline, Bandar Seri Begawan (BSB) has a traditional look. Its buildings are appealing—and the space around them is well landscaped—but few are more than six stories tall. This low profile makes the downtown mosque's stately minarets and huge golden dome—the first thing you see as you drive in—all the more impressive. Combining walking trips with short taxi or bus rides, you can easily visit all the main attractions in a day; indeed, many sights are near the mosque in the central district, with the sultan's palace and several fine museums a short distance away.

★ ⑫ Start near the Brunei River at one of the city's most famous landmarks, the beautiful **Masjid Sultan Omar Ali Saifuddin.** This superb example of modern Islamic architecture was built in 1959 of imported white marble, gold mosaic, and stained glass—all made possible by petrodollars. The exterior is constructed of granite from Hong Kong, the interior is covered with marble from Italy, the chandeliers come from England, and the prayer rugs were brought from Iran. Be sure to take the elevator up the 145-ft minaret for a terrific view of the city. The mosque's beauty is further enhanced by being partly surrounded by a lagoon, where a religious stone boat called the *Mahaligal* floats year-round, as elegant and ornate as the mosque itself. ⊠ *Jln. Elizabeth II and Jln. Stoney.* ☉ *Public viewing: Sat.–Wed. 8–noon, 1:30–3:30, and 4:30–5:30; Fri. 4:30–5:30.*

⑬ From the mosque, walk down Jalan Pretty toward the river, passing the attractive shopping and commercial **Yayasan Hassanal Bolkiah complex.** The architecture is inspired by traditional Malay houses, and the buildings are set around a large courtyard. This is BSB's most upscale shopping area, and it's a good spot to grab a coffee and croissant (perhaps at the Delifrance Cafe) or to discover local food at the sparkling clean stalls in the air-conditioned, third-floor food court.

⑭ In front of the Yayasan you'll see wide steps (beside the Port View Seafood restaurant; ☞ *also Dining and Lodging, below*) leading to the river. This is one of the main departure points for the small boats that zip at alarming speed across the river to stilt houses of **Kampung Ayer.** Almost one-third of the city's population lives in the solidly built wooden homes in this river community (actually, there are 28 separate kampungs that are linked by concrete-and-wood bridges and by systems for water, electricity, and sewage). Schools, clinics, and small mosques stand among the houses, all of which all bristle with TV antennae. Each kampung used to have its own speciality trade such as boatbuilding, weaving, or making brassware. Today, however, most of the residents commute by water taxi or private boat to work on terra firma, generally in some branch of government service. You can hire a boat (expect to pay around B$20 for half an hour), explore the waterways, and follow some of the boardwalks that link the homes. You may even be invited in for a drink by the friendly inhabitants.

Ask your boatman to return you to the city side of the river, and then retrace your steps to the mosque. Across from it on Jalan Elizabeth II, ❶ note the scenes of village life depicted in the mosaic mural on the facade of the **public library.**

Continue down Jalan Elizabeth II and turn left onto Jalan Sultan. Follow it (note that you'll pass the Brunei History Centre, which really ❶ doesn't merit a visit) until you reach the **Royal Regalia Building,** which opened in 1992 to celebrate the sultan's silver jubilee. The semicircular building, with its lavish marble floors and carpets, is basically a museum devoted to the life and times of the current sultan. There are a great many photos (women will enjoy studying the costumes and shoes of notable ladies), a wonderfully ornate crown, the coronation carriage, and even a golden hand and forearm that the sultan used to support his chin during the coronation ceremony. 🎫 *Free.* 🕐 *Sat.–Thurs. 8:30–5, Fri. 9–1:30 and 2:30–5.*

❶ The **Royal Ceremonial Hall,** across Jalan Sultan from the Royal Regalia Building, isn't officially open to the public. Still, you can get a glimpse of the impressive interior with its pillars leading up to the royal throne at the end.

Continue south along Jalan Sultan and turn left back onto Jalan Queen Elizabeth II; at Jalan Sungei Kianggeh turn right. This road runs along (18) the river and passes the town's main **Chinese temple,** where, if you happen to be visiting during an important festival, you may see Chinese opera performed on an outdoor stage. On the opposite side of the river, (19) accessible via a footbridge, is the **Tamu Kianggeh,** a native market where interesting produce is sold (most of the activity takes place fairly early in the day).

At the bottom of Jalan Sungei Kianggeh, turn left and cross the bridge onto Jalan Residency. About 1 km (½ mi) along this road and on your (20) right is the **Brunei Arts and Handicrafts Centre.** The eight-story building, shaped like the scabbard of a kris, contains workshops for silversmithing, brassmaking, weaving, and basketmaking. The silver goods—including such oddities as miniature cannons and boats—are exquisite. Crafts are for sale in the showroom, but prices are steep. ☎ *02/240676.* ⌨ *Free.* ⊙ *Mon.–Thurs. 7:45–12:15 and 1:30–4:30, weekends 8:30–2.*

In front of the center, you should be able to pick up a Central Line bus (21) (B$1) to take you the 4 km (2 mi) to the **Brunei Museum.** The obligatory gallery on oil and gas donated by Shell Petroleum is of limited interest. It's best to head right upstairs to the Islamic Art Gallery, where there are some outstanding ceramics, jewelry, prayer rugs, Korans, and other items from around the Islamic world. ☎ *02/244545.* ⌨ *Free.* ⊙ *Tues.–Thurs. and weekends 9–5, Fri. 9:30–11:30 and 2:30–5.*

(22) At the back of the Brunei Museum steps lead down to the **Malay Technology Museum** at the river's edge. Exhibits here focus on the traditional crafts of the Malays, including boatmaking, fishing, house-building, metalworking, and goldsmithing. In Gallery Three, there are interesting displays—including models of houses—relating to the Kedayan, Murut, Dusun, and Iban people. ☎ *02/242862.* ⌨ *Free.* ⊙ *Sat.–Mon. and Wed.–Thurs. 9–5, Fri. 9:30–11:30 and 2:30–5.*

From the Malay Technology Museum you can take a bus to the Jalan Cator bus station in the center of BSB. From here it's well worth tak-(23) ing a taxi or a Circle Line bus to the **Masjid Jame 'Asr Hassanil Bolkiah,** the largest mosque in Brunei. No expense was spared in the construction and furnishing of this superb mosque to mark the 25th anniversary of the sultan's accession to the throne. Generally referred to by the locals as the Kiarong Mosque (after a nearby village), it's set in immaculate gardens and is a symphony of golden domes, minarets, and blue tiles. ☎ *02/440676.* ⌨ *Free.* ⊙ *Sat.–Wed. 12–1:30 and 4:30–5:30.*

If you have time you can take a bus or taxi back to town and on to (24) the **Istana Nurul Iman** (Sultan's Palace), about 3 km (2 mi) west of the city along Jalan Tutong. It's officially closed to the public except for a three-day open house during the annual Hari Raya Puasa festival, when you can greet the sultan or his two official wives (gender segregation is the rule of the day; only women are permitted to meet the wives, and only men can meet the sultan). Built in the shape of a Borneo longhouse at a cost of US$500 million, it's the largest (1,788 rooms including a throne room that seats 2,000) and one of the most opulent homes in the world. The sultan, his first wife, and their children actually live here; in addition, the sultan's oldest son has his own palace, as does the sultan's second wife. If you can't visit the interior, drive by just to glimpse the massive arched roofs, gold domes, and expanses of imported marble. Near the palace wall is a sculpture garden, a permanent ASEAN exhibit that features modern works from neighboring countries, all based on the theme "Harmony in Diversity."

OFF THE
BEATEN PATH

JERUDONG PARK – Combining Moorish architecture with all the latest high-tech rides (maintained by a crew of Western technicians), this state-of-the-art amusement park is a cross between an Arabian Night's fantasy and Disneyland. It has been unkindly said that the park was created to give people something to do at night after the banning of the sale of alcohol in 1991. Be that as it may, entrance to the park and all the attractions within it are absolutely free. In addition to some adrenaline-pumping rides (especially the "Pusing Lagi"), there's a spectacular musical fountain with a laser light show. Just opposite the entrance is a collection of food stalls, where you can enjoy a meal before entering. The only hitch to Jerudong Park, which is near the sultan's private polo grounds about 20 km (12 mi) out of town, is getting here and back. There's no public bus service, and it's almost impossible to pick up a taxi when you wish to return. The best way is to arrange round-trip transportation (about B$60 per person) with your hotel. ☎ *No phone.* 🎟 *Free.* ⊙ *Sun.–Wed. and Fri. 5–midnight, Thurs. and Sat. 5 PM–2 AM.*

ULU TEMBURONG NATIONAL PARK – Brunei's only national park is on the small wedge of land separated from the rest of Brunei by the Limbang district of Sarawak, Malaysia. Getting here is half the fun. You take a 45-minute speedboat ride through the mangrove swamps from BSB to the small town of Batang. From here you take a vehicle along Temburong's only road to Batang Duri, where you then transfer to a longboat for a delightful ride through beautiful rain forest—where Iban boatmen skillfully negotiate the rapids—to the park headquarters. From here on, travel is on foot, and you need to be fit—the steep hillsides mean you're always either climbing or descending. A highlight of the park is its canopy walk, a somewhat intimidating structure of aluminium towers and walkways strung high above the forest floor. Provided you've got a good head for heights and the fitness for the demanding trek along the trail to the start of the walkway, you get a fantastic view from the top—not just of acre after acre of forested hills, but also of the plant and animal life. You may spot gibbons (especially if you go early in the morning), hornbills, and orchids. Sunshine Borneo Tours and Travel (☞ Tour Operators and Travel Agencies *in* Northern Borneo Essentials, *below*) offers day trips to Ulu Temburong—complete with a barbecue lunch—and can also arrange for longer stays.

Dining and Lodging

Although it has a few noteworthy restaurants, BSB isn't a great place for eating out. Hotel coffee shops are popular with locals as well as visitors, and if you enjoy low-cost hawker food, visit the open air stalls near the Edinburgh Bridge and along the river on Jalan Kianggeh, near Jalan Pemancha. There are also food stalls—albeit slightly more expensive ones—on the third level of the Yayasan Hassanal Bolkiah complex. Note that many restaurants close at 10:30 PM. Compared with its neighbors, Brunei is an expensive place, and it hasn't made any attempt to encourage tourists. Accommodations are limited, and advance reservations are advised. Apart from Jerudong Park House and the Sheraton, most hotels are plain, but clean and comfortable. All listed below have a private bath, air-conditioning, and a TV in each room. For price categories, *see* the charts *in* Pleasures and Pastimes, at the start of this chapter.

$$$ ✕ **Port View Seafood.** Right on the riverbank opposite the Yayasan Hassanal Bolkiah complex, this attractive new restaurant has plate-glass windows that overlook the water and Kampung Ayer on one side.

Although the emphasis is on seafood, *halal* Chinese dishes (prepared without pork) are also available. ⊠ *Jln. MacArthur,* ☎ *02/231465. AE, DC, MC, V. No lunch.*

$$ ✕ **Fratini.** This relatively new restaurant on the ground floor of the Yayasan Hassanal Bolkiah complex is a welcome addition to BSB's dining scene. The food is Italian—with lots of pasta dishes and pizza options—though you'll find other cuisines as well. ⊠ *G24, Block C, Yayasan Hassanal Bolkiah Complex,* ☎ *02/232892. AE, DC, MC, V.*

$$ ✕ **Rasa Sayang.** On the fifth floor of a central business district office/shopping complex, the Rasa Sayang has excellent dim sum at lunchtime. The Malaysian waitresses are happy to help you make your selections, which include everything from steamed buns to barbecue ribs. For something more substantial, the fish dishes (particularly pomfret with onions and a soy-based sauce) are better than the beef. ⊠ *Top floor, Bangunan Guru 2 Melayu,* ☎ *02/223600. AE, DC, V.*

$$$$ ✕🏨 **Sheraton Utama.** The smartest, most professionally managed hotel in BSB is in the central business district. Rooms are on the dark side owing to their small windows (the best view you'll get is one of the pool), but light fabrics and furnishings add some cheer. Superior rooms, with two queen-size or a king-size bed, are worth the extra B$20, and two- and three-room suites are also available. Bathrooms are functional rather than luxurious, though they're equipped with toiletries and bathrobes. The formal dining room, Deal's, offers the only respectable European fare beyond the coffee-shop variety. In a small, personable room with Regency-style decor, the German chef serves Dover sole, U.S. prime beef, and New Zealand lamb, as well as local seafood. Recipes are simple but professionally executed. The more casual Café Melati serves a buffet breakfast, lunch, and dinner from 7 AM to 10:30 PM. On most evenings, there are barbecue or fondue dinners served poolside. The bar is a friendly meeting place. ⊠ *Jln. Tasek (Box 2203), 1922,* ☎ *02/244272, 800/325–3535 in the U.S., or 0800/353535 in the U.K.;* 🖷 *02/221579. 156 rooms and suites. 2 restaurants, bar, pool, exercise room, business services. AE, DC, MC, V.*

$$ 🏨 **Brunei Hotel.** In the heart of the central business district, this hotel has neat, clean, minimally furnished but pleasant rooms with oak trim. The Coffee Garden restaurant serves local and Western food (seafood is the best thing to order); there's usually a theme buffet in the evening. The VIP Room serves classic Cantonese fare. ⊠ *95 Jln. Pemancha (Box 50), 1900,* ☎ *02/242372,* 🖷 *02/226196. 75 rooms. 2 restaurants. AE, DC, V.*

$$ 🏨 **Terrace Hotel.** This hotel offers clean rooms at modest prices. You'll also find a pool surrounded by well-landscaped grounds. ⊠ *Jln. Tasek Lama (Box 49), 1900,* ☎ *02/243554,* 🖷 *02/227302. 80 rooms. Bar, coffee shop, dining room, pool, beauty salon. AE, DC, MC, V.*

Shopping

The **open market** alongside the Kianggeh River is a fun place to browse for inexpensive goods. The best place to shop for a wide assortment of items is the attractive, new **Yayasan Sultan Hassanal Boliah** complex, generally referred to simply as the Yayasan. There's a large basement supermarket opposite a good drugstore and bookstore (where you can pick up secondhand books). On the ground floor of the same block are the **Delifrance Cafe**; the Italian restaurant, **Fratini** (☞ *also* Dining and Lodging, *above*); and a branch of the **Body Shop**. On the upper level, you'll find a reasonable book store—the **Times Bookshop**—as well as trendy boutiques; the third level has an air-conditioned food court. The department store in the other block is rather disappointing.

The showroom at the **Brunei Arts and Handicrafts Centre** (☞ *above*) has the best selection of local work, but its prices—especially for finely worked silver—are high. Popular items include kris (ornamental daggers) and *kain songket,* a cloth containing gold or silver thread.

Gold jewelry (24 karat) is popular among Brunei's citizens, so goldsmiths offer a wide selection. Check out **Chin Chin Goldsmith** (✉ 33 Jln. Sultan, ☎ 02/222893). At **Million Goldsmith and Jewelry** (✉ Teck Guan Plaza, Jln. Sultan, ☎ 02/429546), you'll find necklaces, brooches, and bracelets in interesting designs.

Northern Borneo Essentials

Arriving and Departing

By Airplane

SARAWAK

Malaysia Airlines is the primary carrier to Sarawak, although Royal Brunei also flies into **Kuching International Airport** (☎ 082/454242); this spacious airport is about 11 km (7 mi) south of town, and the unmetered taxis charge RM15 for the trip. Singapore Airlines has two flights a week from Singapore to Kuching, and Dragonair operates flights linking Hong Kong and Kuching. Royal Brunei also operates daily flights from BSB to Kuching and Miri.

SABAH

Malaysia Airlines is the primary carrier to Sabah; in addition, Royal Brunei, Singapore Airlines, TransAir, and Dragonair fly into **Kota Kinabalu International Airport** (☎ 088/238555). A taxi ride from the airport to the city center costs RM15; purchase the taxi voucher from the counter marked TEKSI.

BRUNEI

Brunei International Airport (☎ 02/331747)) near BSB, is sleek, modern, and efficient. The national carrier, Royal Brunei Airlines, has routes throughout Southeast Asia, as well as to Europe and Australia. Malaysia Airlines flies to Brunei from Kuching in Sarawak and Kota Kinabalu in Sabah. Singapore Airlines, and Thai Airways International also serve Brunei. The quickest way to get downtown from the airport is by taxi, although air-conditioned minibuses (B$2) leave from the covered bus depot about 100 yards from outside the arrival hall. Taxis are unmetered, but the fare is currently fixed at B$22.

By Boat

You can get to Brunei from Limbang in northern Sarawak via a riverboat that takes half an hour and costs about B$7; there's also service to Brunei from Lawas, Sarawak. Express boats run between Muara, which is about 30 minutes and B$2 by air-conditioned minibus from BSB, and the Malaysian island of Labuan (there are express boats to the island from Kota Kinabalu in Sabah); the trip takes about one hour, and the fare is B$20. It's much cheaper to do the trip in reverse, as the fare from Labuan to Muara is RM20.

Getting Around

By Airplane

Sarawak has an excellent system of internal air links, with frequent MAS flights between Kuching, Sibu, Bintulu, Miri, Limbang and Lawas. Smaller destinations such as Mulu, Mukah, Kapit, and Bario can be reached via the subsidized MAS Rural Air Service. Sabah has flights connecting Kota Kinabalu with Tawau, Lahad Datu, and Sandakan on the east coast, while the Rural Air Service operates from Kota Kinabalu to Kudat, and links Kudat with Sandakan. There are no internal flights in Brunei.

By Boat
SARAWAK

In a land where rivers are often still the major highways, boats are an essential means of transport. Fast, air-conditioned express boats link Kuching with Sibu, where you can get other express boats up the Rajang River to Kapit and on up the Baleh River. There are also express boats along another river system, the Baram, operating from Kuala Baram north of Miri up to Marudi and Long Lama. Canoes equipped with outboard engines, known locally as longboats, ply the smaller rivers.

BRUNEI

Water taxis—small, open boats—to the Kampung Ayer are available from several places, including near the market off Jalan Sungai Kianggeh and the steps near the Yayasan shopping complex. Bargain with drivers for fares; a complete tour should cost between B$20 and B$25. Trips to the Temburong District of Brunei involve travel by speedboat through a network of mangrove forest.

By Bus
SARAWAK

Long-distance buses—from Lundu, on the northwest coast, to Kuching and from Kuching right up through Sri Aman, Sibu, Bintulu and Miri—advertise their timetables in the daily English-language newspapers. In Kuching, the main terminal is the Jalan Penrissen Bus Station, south of town. A handy map showing the various local bus stations in Kuching and their routes is available at the Visitors' Information Centre near the Sarawak Museum (☞ Visitor Information, *below*).

SABAH

Private buses, both minibuses and large air-conditioned coaches, serve the towns and the countryside, and link Kota Kinabalu with Kudat in the north as well as Sandakan, Lahad Datu, and Tawau on the east coast. It's also possible to travel by bus south to Lawas in Sarawak. Kota Kinabalu's main terminal for long-distance buses is near the Padang; this is also the departure point for minibuses to Ranau, which pass in front of Kinabalu Park. Local buses leave for Tanjung Aru from opposite the post office; minibuses leave from an empty lot in front of Centrepoint shopping complex.

BRUNEI

A paved road links Kuala Belait, 112 km (70 mi) southwest of BSB, with the Malaysian town of Miri in Sarawak. It's slow going and involves a river crossing by ferry and two immigration-control stops. And if you want to go on to BSB, you have to take another bus. The best way to do the trip from Miri right to BSB is aboard one of the air-conditioned, private minibuses owned by **Mr. Nee Tien Poh** (☎ 02/222945 in BSB or 085/433898 in Miri). The extra comfort and speed makes the cost of B$60 seem well worth your while.

By Car
SARAWAK AND SABAH

Four-wheel-drive vehicles are recommended for driving in the interiors of both states. Car rental prices are high—starting at RM140–RM160 a day. In Kuching, try: **Mayflower Car Rental** (✉ Kuching airport, ☎ 082/236889) or **Pronto Car Rental** (✉ Kuching airport, ☎ 082/410110). In Kota Kinabalu, try: **E&C** (☎ 088/239996) or **Kinabalu Rent A Car** (☎ 088/232602), which has desks at the airport and at major hotels.

BRUNEI

Two rental agencies have counters at the airport: **Avis** (☎ 02/442284) and **National Car Rental** (☎ 02/224921). Rates are B$100–B$150 per day.

By Taxi

SARAWAK AND SABAH

Cabs are more expensive here than on the peninsula, and they're un-metered. Always agree on the price with your driver before setting out. To ensure that things go smoothly, ask at your hotel about nearby taxi stands, the usual fares to various destinations within cities, and how to arrange trips to rural areas. Hiring a car with driver for three hours in Kuching or Kota Kinabalu costs about RM80; it should be slightly cheaper outside the state capitals.

In Kuching, drivers gather in front of the Holiday Inn and opposite the Crowne Plaza. Shared taxis and minibuses congregate near the bus terminals, and river taxis leave from marked departure points (*pangkalan*) along the waterfront. In Kota Kinabalu you can always find a cab near the Hyatt downtown. Summoning cabs by telephone isn't very reliable, but you can try a **taxi company** (☎ 088/51863 or 088/25669) in Kota Kinabalu.

BRUNEI

You can hire a private taxi for sightseeing, but drivers often speak little English. Hotels will arrange such service for around B$50 an hour, often with a minimum of three hours.

By Train

SABAH

Sabah State Railways (☎ 088/254611) runs the only rail service on Borneo from Kota Kinabalu south to Tenom. The 49-km (31-mi) stretch between Beaufort and Tenom passes through the spectacular Crocker Range and Padas Gorge. The locomotive from Beaufort to Tenom (RM2.25) is very slow and uncomfortable; however, a quaint small railcar takes 1½–2 hours and costs RM8.85.

Contacts and Resources

Emergencies

SARAWAK AND SABAH

Major private hospitals maintain high standards and doctors speak English. Your hotel will be able to arrange for a doctor or dentist should the need arise. Pharmacies are well stocked and the pharmacists speak English (if not the counter staff). Scuba divers should note that the only decompression chamber in the region is in Labuan, off Brunei Bay.

Hospitals: Normah Medical Centre (✉ Jln. Tun Datuk Patinggi, Kuching, ☎ 082/440055); **Sabah Medical Centre** (✉ Kingfisher Park, Kota Kinabalu, ☎ 088/424333). **Police:** ☎ 082/241222 in Kuching; ☎ 088/242111 in Kota Kinabalu.

BRUNEI

Brunei's medical services are of a high standard and are staffed by English-speaking doctors and nurses. **Ambulance:** ☎ 99. **Fire:** ☎ 995. **Hospital:** Jerudong Park Medical Centre (✉ Jerudong Park, ☎ 02/671433).

English-Language Bookstores

SARAWAK AND SABAH

In Sarawak, Kuching is the best place to find English-language books and magazines. Recommended shops include: **The Curio Shoppe** (✉ Kuching Hilton, Jln. Tuanku Abdul Rahman, ☎ 082/248118), **The Curio Shoppe** (✉ Sarawak Museum, Jln. Tun Haji Openg, ☎ 082/253977), and **Mohamed Yahiah Sons** (✉ Holiday Inn Kuching, Jln. Tuanku Abdul Rahman, ☎ 082/254282).

In Sabah, Kota Kinabalu shops include: **Borneo Craft** (✉ Ground floor, Wisma Merdeka, ☎ 088/237936), or **Iwase** (✉ Ground floor, Wisma Merdeka, ☎ 088/233757).

In BSB, try: **Times Bookshop** (✉ 1st floor, Yayasan Sultan Haji Hassanal Bolkiah Complex, ☎ 02/220964) or **Far Eastern Books** (✉ G4 Guan Teck Plaza, Jln. Sultan, ☎ 02/242539).

Tour Operators and Travel Agencies

Note that many of the companies cited below can help you make general travel arrangements—airline reservations, hotel bookings, and so on—as well as organize tours.

SARAWAK

It takes about three hours to see Kuching's historic sites, including a drive past the central market and a Malay village and a stop at the Sarawak Museum. You can take guided nature walks within the orangutan sanctuary at Semenggoh; visit a crocodile farm; or take a trip to the Bako National Park or the Kubah National Park, where the Matang Wildlife Centre is due to open. Tour organizers also arrange backpacking and spelunking excursions into mountain regions and ancient caves.

In Kuching you'll find the itineraries and prices comparable at: **Asian Overland Services** (✉ 286A, 1st floor, Westwood Park, Jln. Tabuan, ☎ 082/251162), **Ibanika** (✉ Lot 435, Lorong 9, Jln. Ang Cheng Ho, ☎ 082/424022), and **Singai Travel Services** (✉ 2nd floor, Lot 168, Chan Chin Ann Rd., ☎ 082/412778). **Borneo Adventure** (✉ 55 Main Bazaar, ☎ 082/245175) has won awards for its longhouse tours and also offers a wide range of other tours in Sarawak, Sabah, and Brunei. In Miri **Tropical Adventure** (✉ Ground floor, Mega Hotel, Jln. Merbau, ☎ 085/419337) specializes in adventure tours to Gunung Mulu National Park and the Bario Highlands; they also offer dive trips on live-aboard boats to Luconia Shoals from April to October.

SABAH

A Kota Kinabalu city tour covers the highlights in just two hours. Country tours often stop at Mengkabong, a stilted village of Bajau fisherfolk 30 km (19 mi) out of Kota Kinabalu. On the way you'll pass rice fields; rural kampungs; and the town of Tamparuli, famed for a nearby suspension bridge. Other excursions include the Sunday market at Kota Belud, a day trip to Tenom, and the Sepilok Orang Utan Rehabilitation Center. Two- and three-day trips are offered to the wildlife haven of Sukau in the Kinabatangan region, to the Turtle Islands off Sandakan, and to Danum Valley. Tour operators also offer whitewater rafting as well as hiking safaris into the interior (including visits to native villages); some specialize in dive trips.

Tour operators in Kota Kinabalu include: **Borneo Eco Tours** (✉ 12A, 2nd floor, Lorong Bernam 3, off Jln. Kolam, ☎ 088/234009); **Borneo Adventure** (✉ 10th floor, Gaya Centre, Jln. Tun Razak, ☎ 088/238731); and **Borneo Divers** (✉ 4th floor, Wisma Sabah, Jln. Tun Razak, ☎ 088/222226), which offers diving courses and diving excursions to Sipadan and the reefs of Tunku Abdul Rahman National Park and has packages with Malaysia Airlines.

Several operators are based at Shangri-La's Tanjung Aru Resort (near the airport and 10 minutes from downtown), including: **Borneo Expeditions** (☎ 088/222948); **Tanjung Aru Tours & Travel** (☎ 088/256676), which offers resort diving and scuba training and has a private dive resort on Pandanan Island north of Sipadan; and **Wildlife Ex-**

peditions (☎ 088/246000), which specializes in trips to Sepilok, Sukau, Turtle Islands, and the Danum Valley.

Two tour companies specializing in tours of Brunei are based in BSB. The best-known operator is **Sunshine Borneo Tours and Travel** (✉ Block A, No. 4, first floor, Abdul Razak Complex, Km 3½, Jln. Gadong, ☎ 02/446812). They organize tours of the capital, river trips, and tours to Iban longhouses both in Brunei and across the border in Sarawak, and day trips to Ulu Temburong National Park. **Freme Travel Service** (✉ Unit 4038 Wisma Jaya, Jln. Pemancha, ☎ 02/335025) offers similar tours in both Brunei and neighboring Sabah and Sarawak.

Visitor Information

SARAWAK

Sarawak has an efficient network of tourist information offices, and staffers are unfailingly friendly and helpful; these centers also handle accommodation bookings and issue visit permits for the various national parks in the vicinity. They include: **Visitors Information Centre** (✉ 31 Jln. Masjid [next to Sarawak Museum], Kuching, ☎ 082/410944); **Visitors Information Centre** (✉ 32 Ground floor, Jln. Cross, Sibu, ☎ 084/340980); and **Visitors Information Centre** (✉ 452 Jln. Melayu [opposite Tamu Muhibbah], Miri, ☎ 085/434181).

In Kuching, the **MTPB** (✉ Rugayah Building, Jln. Song Thian Cheok, ☎ 082/246775) has information on all of Malaysia but not a great deal on Sarawak itself. The **Sarawak Tourist Association** maintains a small information center on the Kuching waterfront (☎ 082/240620) and at the Kuching airport (☎ 082/456266).

SABAH

The **Sabah Tourism Promotion Corporation** (✉ 51 Jln. Gaya, ☎ 088/219400) has an office that's conveniently located in downtown Kota Kinabalu and one on the first level of the Kota Kinabalu airport (☎ 088/223767). In Kota Kinabalu you'll also find an office of the **MTPB** (✉ Wing On Life Building, Jln. Segunting, ☎ 088/211732).

BRUNEI

Brunei only recently begun to actively encourage tourism and cannot match the tourism information services of its neighbors. There's a tourist information booth at the airport, where you can pick up the brochure, *Explore Brunei,* but there is no tourism office in downtown BSB.

MALAYSIA AND BRUNEI A TO Z

Arriving and Departing

By Airplane

AIRPORTS

The brand-new **Kuala Lumpur International Airport** opened in June 1998 and is the major gateway to Malaysia. This large, modern facility, 51 km (32 mi) from downtown, has updated check-in, baggage-handling, and security procedures; two hotels; and bus links into the capital. Given the congestion in and around KL, getting to the airport can take as long as two hours; when the direct rail link is operational (expected by 2000), it will be the fastest way to go. The old airport at Subang is now used only for charter flights. **Brunei International Airport** (☎ 02/331747) near BSB, is also a modern gateway.

CARRIERS

Malaysia Airlines (☎ 03/261–0555 in KL), the national carrier, offers six weekly flights from Los Angeles to KL with a stop in Tokyo or Taipei, three weekly flights from New York to KL with a stop in Dubai, and two weekly flights from Vancouver to KL with a stop in Taipei. MAS also has frequent flights to KL from six cities in Australia as well as from Auckland, New Zealand. Among the many airlines that serve Kuala Lumpur are **British Airways** (☎ 03/242–6177), **Air Canada** (☎ 03/242–4311), **Singapore Airlines** (☎ 03/292–3122), and **Thai Airways International** (☎ 03/293–7100). During the day both MAS and Singapore Airlines fly hourly between KL and Singapore; you can cut the fare in half by buying a standby air-shuttle ticket at the airport.

Brunei is served by its national carrier, **Royal Brunei Airlines** (☎ 02/242222 in BSB), which has direct daily flights to London, and three flights a week to Frankfurt. The airline also has services to Perth, Darwin, and Brisbane in Australia and to Bangkok. Daily flights connect Brunei with both Singapore and KL. Singapore Airlines and Thai Airways International also serve Brunei.

FLYING TIMES

The flying time to KL is 19 hours from Los Angeles, 17 hours from Vancouver, 15 hours from New York (eastward), 12½ hours from London, 8 hours from Sydney, and 10½ hours from Auckland. The flying time to Brunei is 16½ hours from London, 8 hours from Brisbane, 2½ hours from Bangkok, and 2 hours from KL and Singapore.

Getting Around

By Airplane

Malaysia Airlines flies to 35 towns and cities in the country (for air hub information, ☞ Arriving and Departing by Plane *in* individual region's Essentials sections). Domestic flights are relatively inexpensive and often fully booked, especially during school holidays and festivals. Still, there's no need to reconfirm reservations. There are no internal flights within Brunei.

AIR PASSES

Malaysia Airlines offers a Discover Malaysia Pass that enables international visitors to travel on domestic routes for about half the normal fare. You may make flight reservations and purchase tickets overseas or in Malaysia. There's a catch, though: you must show that your entry into Malaysia will be or is on Malaysian Airlines.

By Boat

There's no passenger service between peninsular Malaysia and Sabah and Sarawak, nor from Singapore to Brunei. In Malaysian port cities there's regular **ferry service** to the nearby islands. To get to Pangkor, catch the ferry in Lumut; for Langkawi, ferries leave from Kuala Perlis, Kuala Kedah, and Pinang. Ferries to Pulau Redang leave from Merang, and those to the Perhentian islands leave from Kuala Besut. Launches serve Tioman Island from Mersing and the islands of the Tunku Abdul Rahman Marine Park from Kota Kinabalu. Frequent passenger launches run from BSB to Limbang, and express boats to Labuan depart from Brunei's port of Muara.

By Bus

Bus service is extensive and cheap, but generally only coaches traveling between major cities are air-conditioned. Local buses are often crowded, noisy, and slow, but it's a great way to people-watch and sightsee at the same time. Brunei has an excellent public bus service in the BSB, using small, air-conditioned coaches. For information on schedules, contact the nearest tourism information service or ask at your hotel.

By Car

EMERGENCY ASSISTANCE

The **Automobile Association of Malaysia** (✉ Hotel Equatorial, Jln. Sultan Ismail, KL, ☎ 03/261–3713 or 03/261–2727) can offer advice in case of a roadside emergency. There's no such service in Brunei; in case of mechanical problems, contact your car-rental agency.

GASOLINE

Stations charge about RM1.08 per liter (RM4.86 per gallon) and generally offer full service; in KL however, government policy has forced many gas stations to operate self-service pumps. In the cities, most stations operate 24 hours; elsewhere, they're closed at night. Fuel costs B53 cents per liter (B$2.38 per gallon) in Brunei, and service stations generally close at night.

PARKING

Except for KL, Georgetown, and JB, on-street parking is generally adequate in Malaysia. In some towns, meters are installed (and closely monitored), though you're just as likely to have a parking attendant issue you a receipt. Major cities also have multistory parking garages. In Brunei, parking is generally on the street, though BSB has a parking garage.

RENTAL AGENCIES

In Malaysia, you don't need an international driving license to rent a car; a valid permit from home is adequate. Cars are available for hire only in major towns. Rates run from as little as RM70 a day in Langkawi to around RM170 in Kota Kinabalu, with unlimited mileage. Inquire about special three-day and weekend rates. These can offer significant rate reductions. One-way rentals are possible for additional drop-off fees. In Brunei, both self-drive and chauffeured cars are available in BSB. Major car-rental offices in Malaysia include Avis, Budget, Hertz, Mayflower, and Thrifty; in Brunei, you'll find Avis and National Car Rental systems. For details on these and smaller, local agencies, *see* Getting Around By Car *in* the individual region's Essentials sections.

ROAD CONDITIONS

The North–South Highway runs along the western side of the peninsula from the Thai border past Butterworth (near Pinang), Ipoh, KL, and Melaka, down to JB, where it's linked by a causeway and a new bridge to Singapore. The East–West Highway runs from Butterworth across to Kota Bharu. Other roads, especially near industrial centers, have heavy traffic day and night. Slow moving trucks, motorcycles, and bicycles make driving somewhat treacherous. Back roads are narrow but paved, and the pace is relaxed—you'll weave around dogs sleeping in the road. Mountain roads are often single-lane, and you must allow oncoming cars to pass. Brunei has one major road that links BSB with Kuala Belait in the southwest; note that you can't drive to the Temburong area of Brunei.

RULES OF THE ROAD

In both Malaysia and Brunei, seat belts are compulsory for drivers and front-seat passengers, and stiff fines are imposed on those caught without them. Driving is on the left side of the road. The police use radar traps frequently, and fines are heavy—about RM300 for driving 20 kph over the limit. Don't be tempted to bribe your way out of a fine; however, given the traditional courtesy of Malaysians and Bruneians, a smile from a helpless tourist sometimes saves the day. Some common traffic signs in both countries include: AWAS (caution), JALAN SEHALA (one way), KURANGKAN LAJU (slow down), and IKUT KIRI (keep left). Directions are *utara* (north), *selatan* (south), *timur* (east), and *barat* (west).

By Taxi

Both Malaysian and Bruneian taxi operators near bus terminals call out destinations for long-distance, shared-cost rides; drivers leave when they get four passengers. Single travelers who want to charter a taxi pay four times the flat rate and leave whenever they want. The quality of service depends on the condition of the vehicle and bravado of the driver.

City taxis are plentiful and relatively cheap. Taxis on peninsular Malaysia are metered. However, taxi drivers in KL will sometimes attempt not to use the meter and, instead, charge you a fixed price. Console yourself with the thought that the locals, too, are subjected to such treatment, especially during rush hour or when it's raining hard. Taxis in Sabah and Sarawak are not metered—set the fare with the driver in advance. Between midnight and 6 AM, rides cost 50% more than what's on the meter. In Brunei, taxis are metered in the capital; a 50% surcharge is added 9 PM–6 AM.

By Train

Malayan Railways (☎ 03/273–9118) known as KTM, offers relatively comfortable service on the peninsula. However, trains are slower and more expensive than the buses, or even long-distance taxis. Beginning at Singapore, one train line runs northwest to Butterworth (for Pinang) via KL; at Butterworth, you can make a connection with the International Express to Bangkok (which runs three times a week) or a local train to Hat Yai, Thailand. Another train line runs to Kota Bharu, at the peninsula's northeastern tip; at Pasir Mas, a trunk line connects KTM with the Thai railway, 23 km (14 mi) to the north. Both express and local service, and both air-conditioned and non-air-conditioned cars, are available. Passengers with tickets for distances of more than 200 km (124 mi) can stop off at any point on the route for one day per 200 km (124 mi) traveled: *the stationmaster must endorse the ticket immediately upon arrival at the stop-off station.* On long trips movies are shown, but the passing scenery is always more interesting. In some sections the route goes through jungle and you may see wild monkeys. Sleepers are available on overnight service for a supplemental charge. Dining-car food is simple, cheap, and tasty. For information on the rail line in Sabah, *see* Getting Around By Train *in* Northern Borneo Essentials, *above.*

A luxury (and superexpensive) train service, the *Eastern & Oriental Express,* which is modeled after the *Orient Express,* makes the 41-hour trip between Singapore and Bangkok with stops in Malaysia at KL and Butterworth. For information in the United States, call 800/524–2420.

RAIL PASSES

Foreign visitors can buy the KTM Railpass, which permits unlimited travel for 10 days (US$55) or 30 days (US$120), at main railway stations in Malaysia and in Singapore. Prices are reduced for children between 4 and 12 years old and for youths under the age of 30 and who hold the ISIC, YIEE Card, or Youth Hostel Card.

Contacts and Resources

Customs and Duties

MALAYSIA

Such items as cameras, watches, pens, lighters, cosmetics, perfume, portable radio cassette players, cigarettes (up to 200), and liquor (1 liter) may be brought into Malaysia duty-free. If you're bringing in dutiable goods, such as video equipment, you may have to pay a deposit (up to 50% of the item's value) for temporary importation, which is refundable when you leave. If you have to pay a tax or deposit, be sure to get an official receipt. The importation of illegal drugs into Malaysia carries the death penalty. Restrictions exist on the export of antiquities. If in doubt about any purchase, check with the director of the Muzium Negara in KL.

You're allowed to import 200 cigarettes and 60 milliliters of perfume. The import of alcohol is restricted to two bottles (about 2 quarts) of liquor and 12 cans of beer for non-Muslims over 17 years of age. A declaration must be completed on arrival.

Electricity
The electrical current in both Malaysia and Brunei is 220 volts, 50 cycles alternating current (AC). You should bring an adapter and converter, or, if your appliances are dual voltage, just an adapter. Wall outlets take a variety of plug styles, including plugs with two round oversize prongs and plugs with three prongs. It is a good idea to bring a surge protector for your laptop.

Embassies and Consulates
MALAYSIA
Australia (✉ 6 Jln. Yap Kwan Seng, KL, ☎ 03/242–3122). **Canada** (✉ Plaza MBF, 5th floor, Jln. Ampang, KL, ☎ 03/261–2000). **New Zealand** (✉ Menara IMC, Jln. Sultan Ismail, KL, ☎ 03/238–2533). **United Kingdom** (✉ 185 Jln. Ampang, KL, ☎ 03/248–2122). **United States** (✉ 376 Jln. Tun Razak, KL, ☎ 03/248–9011).

BRUNEI
Australia (✉ 4th floor, Teck Guan Plaza, Jln. Sultan, BSB, ☎ 02/229433). **United Kingdom** (✉ Hongkong Bank Chambers, Jln. Pemancha, BSB, ☎ 02/225547). **United States** (✉ 3rd floor, Teck Guan Plaza, Jln. Sultan, BSB, ☎ 02/229670).

Health and Safety
FOOD AND DRINK
As a rule, in both Malaysia and Brunei, food handlers are inspected by health-enforcement officers, but the best advice is to patronize popular places: consumers everywhere tend to boycott stalls with a reputation for poor hygiene. Avoid eating precooked food from outdoor food stalls, where lack of refrigeration increases the risk of contamination; places where food is cooked for you only when ordered are recommended. Bottled water is widely available and preferred by many locals; ice is, by law, made from boiled water.

OTHER PRECAUTIONS
As elsewhere in Southeast Asia, you should find out whether there are stinging jellyfish in the water before you wade in. Some trees in the rain forest can cause allergies; if you are trekking with a guide, you'll be warned of any possible dangers. Gay and lesbian travelers should be aware that both Malaysia and Brunei officially frown upon such relationships; to avoid embarrassment, discretion is recommended.

Language, Culture, and Etiquette
MALAYSIA
The official language is Bahasa Malaysia, though local variations can differ greatly from the official version. English is widely spoken in government, business, and tourism establishments, and it's the interracial lingua franca. The Chinese generally speak several dialects, including Cantonese, Teochew, Hakka, and Hokkien; the Indians are primarily Tamil speakers. In Sabah and Sarawak, as many as 50 tribal languages are spoken, though all schoolchildren throughout the country are educated in the national language.

Being neatly dressed is respected by Malaysians. As this is officially a Muslim country, conservative dress is recommended. Revealing clothes, shorts, and short skirts should be worn only at resorts. To enter mosques, women must wear something, a scarf for example, over their heads (in some mosques, women are requested to wear a coverall that's handed to them at the door by mosque officials). Everyone must remove their shoes before entering a mosque or any private home. Avoid using the left hand to give or receive anything, as this is considered offensive to Muslims.

BRUNEI

The official language is Malay, but English and the Hokkien Chinese dialect are widely spoken. Bruneians are even more conservative in dress than most Malaysians, so it's prudent to dress modestly. As in Malaysia, remove your shoes before entering a mosque or a private home, and avoid using the left hand to give or receive anything.

Mail

Addresses in Malaysia and Brunei do not always include street numbers; often the name of a large office building, a shopping complex, or a hotel is sufficient. Note that in addresses for a shop in a large complex, you might see a digit with a decimal in it, such as 3.26. The "3" indicates the floor or level within the complex, and the "26" indicates the shop number on that floor/level.

POSTAL RATES

In Malaysia, stamps and postal information are generally available at hotel front desks. Postcards cost 55 sen to the Americas, 50 sen to Europe, and 45 sen to Australia and New Zealand; airmail letters cost RM1.10 (½ oz) to the Americas, 90 sen to Europe, and 55 sen to Australia and New Zealand. Aerograms are the best value of all, at 50 sen— regardless of where they're being sent.

Brunei charges B30 cents for postcards, B45 cents for aerograms, and B90 cents for airmail letters to any overseas destination. Obtain stamps from your hotel or the post office.

RECEIVING MAIL

American Express (✉ Bangunan MAS, 5th floor, Jln. Sultan Ismail, KL, ☎ 03/213–0000; ✉ 4th floor, Shell Building, Jln. Sultan, BSB, ☎ 02/228225) will hold mail for 30 days at no charge, as long as you can produce identification and either an American Express card or American Express traveler's checks. In addition, you can have mail sent to you labeled "poste restante" care of the main post office in various cities or towns; check both your first name and surname as the locals sometimes file mail by the first name that appears on the envelope.

WRITING TO MALAYSIA AND BRUNEI

Although postal codes are officially in use in both countries, mail will still be delivered without them. Address envelopes in the normal fashion and you can expect them to reach their destination. The efficiency of the Malaysian mail system is such that many Malaysians prefer to use courier service for urgent mail, and register all important mail (another RM1).

Money Matters

COSTS

The Malaysian ringgit, like other Asian currencies, lost dramatically against the U.S. dollar and other currencies in mid-1998. This means that for many visitors, the country offers real value. As might be expected, prices in the cities are higher than elsewhere, though mostly rural Sabah is the most expensive state in the country. Prices in most shops and larger stores are fixed, but you can discreetly ask for a discount. In street markets, flea markets, and antiques stores, bargaining is expected. Taxes on alcohol mean that a glass of beer or bottle of wine is surprisingly expensive in Malaysia. Brunei is a rich country, and the Brunei dollar is strong. Things here cost almost twice as much as they do in Malaysia.

Sample Costs in Malaysia: Cup of coffee/tea in a hotel, RM5; cup of tea in open-air *kedai,* 80 sen; small bottle of water RM1.10; bottle of beer, RM8.50; bowl of noodles at a stall, RM3.50; 2-km (1-mi) taxi ride, RM4-5; city bus ride, 50 sen–80 sen.

Sample Costs in Brunei: Breakfast of toast, eggs, and coffee, B$10–B$15; coffee in a hotel B$5; bowl of noodles B$3–B$4; taxi ride, B$4 for first mile, B60 cents per mile thereafter; city bus ride B$1.

CURRENCY

Malaysian ringgit are issued in denominations of RM1, RM5, RM10, RM20, RM50, RM100, RM500, and RM1,000. The ringgit is divided into 100 sen, and there are coins worth 1, 5, 10, 20, and 50 sen and RM1. The exchange rate at press time was RM3.61 to the U.S. dollar, RM2.53 to the Canadian dollar, RM6.04 to the pound sterling, RM2.37 to the Australian dollar, and RM2.11 to the New Zealand dollar.

Brunei dollars are issued in notes of B$1, B$5, B$10, B$50, B$100, B$500, and B$1,000. Coins come in denominations of 1, 5, 10, 20, and 50 cents. The Brunei dollar is at par with the Singapore dollar, which also circulates in Brunei. At press time the exchange rate was B$1.50 to the U.S. dollar, B$2.25 to the pound sterling, B$1.11 to the Canadian dollar, B$1.03 to the Australian dollar, and B$0.88 to the New Zealand dollar.

SERVICE CHARGES, TAXES, AND TIPPING

In Malaysia, a 5% tax is added to bills of hotel and restaurants classified as tourist class, along with a 10% service charge in a system that the locals call "plus plus." (You'll see the "++" symbols where this applies.) In nontourist class restaurants and local coffee shops, tipping isn't expected. All departing passengers pay an airport tax of RM40 to international destinations, RM10 to Singapore and Brunei, and RM5 for domestic destinations. Tip porters RM1 per bag. It would be insulting to tip less than 50 sen. Malaysians usually tip taxi drivers with their coin change. Otherwise, when you want to acknowledge fine service, 10% is generous, though not expected.

In Brunei, there's a service charge of 10% in hotels and also in air-conditioned restaurants. Hotel porters should be given B$1 per bag. The driver of a hired car appreciates B$10 for a morning's work, but there's no need to tip taxi drivers. Departing passengers pay an airport tax of B$12 on international flights, B$5 to Singapore or Malaysia.

Opening and Closing Times

In Malaysia: Restaurants normally serve lunch from 11:30 AM to 2:30 PM and dinner from 6:30 PM to 11 PM, with last orders at 9:30 or 10 PM. **Shops** are generally open 9:30 AM–7 PM; department stores and supermarkets, 10–10. Many places are closed Sunday, except in the states of Johor, Kedah, Perlis, Kelantan, and Terengganu, where Friday is the day of rest. **Banks** are open weekdays 9:30–3 and Saturday 9:30–11:30. **Post offices** are open from Monday to Thursday 8–5 and Friday 8–12.30. **Government offices** have hours Monday–Thursday 8–12:45 and 2–4:15, Friday 8–12:45 and 2:45–4:15, and Saturday 8–12:45.

In Brunei: Government offices are open from 7:45 to 12:15 and 1:30–4.30, except on Friday and Sunday, when they are closed. Most **shopping centers** open daily from 10–10. Restaurants generally close early, between 9 and 10.

NATIONAL HOLIDAYS

Note that the dates of some religious holidays change from year to year.

In Malaysia: Chinese New Year (Jan./Feb.), Labor Day (May 1), Hari Raya Aidilfitri (Jan.), King's Birthday (June 4), Hari Raya Haji (Jan.), National Day (Aug. 31), Prophet Muhammad's Birthday (Aug.), Deepavali (Nov.), Christmas (Dec. 25).

In Brunei: Hari Raya Aidilfitri (Jan.), National Day (Feb. 23), Anniversary of the Royal Brunei Army (May 31), Sultan's Birthday (July 15), Prophet Muhammad's Birthday (Aug.), Hari Raya Aidiladha (Jan.)

Passports and Visas

IN MALAYSIA

Citizens of Australia, Canada, New Zealand, the United States, and the United Kingdom do not need visas for stays of less than 90 days. All visitors must be in possession of a passport that's valid for three months from the date of arrival on peninsular Malaysia, and for six months on the date of arrival in Sabah or Sarawak.

IN BRUNEI

All visitors must be in possession of a valid passport. For stays of up to 14 days, citizens of Canada, New Zealand, the United Kingdom, and the United States don't need visas. Australians must obtain visas in advance (note that you can't get them in Sabah or Sarawak). To apply for visas, Australians should contact any Royal Brunei Airlines office or the **Brunei High Commission** (⌧ 16 Bulwarra Close, O'Malley, Canberra ACT 2606, Australia, ☎ 06/290–1801).

Student and Youth Travel

Youth Hostels Association (⌧ 9 Jln. Vethavanam, off Jln. Ipoh, KL, ☎ 03/971–7373) operates hostels throughout Malaysia. However, these are generally out of the way and no cheaper than other budget accommodations. (The same is true of YMCA and YWCA lodgings.) Many national parks, especially in Sarawak and Sabah, offer either camping sites or inexpensive hostels.

Telephones

CALLS TO MALAYSIA AND BRUNEI

To call Malaysia from overseas, dial the country code, 60, and then the area code, omitting the first 0. The area code for KL is 3; for Pinang and Langkawi, 4; for Melaka, 6; for Tioman and JB, 7; for Cherating and Kuala Terengganu, 9; for Kuching, 82; and for Kota Kinabalu, 88. To call Brunei from overseas, dial the country code, 673, and then the area code, omitting the first 0. The area code for BSB is 2.

LOCAL CALLS

Malaysia: Public pay phones take 10 sen, 20 sen, 50 sen, and RM1 coins (time unlimited on local calls). Remember to press the release button, which allows your coins to drop down, when the person you call picks up the receiver. Phone cards are becoming increasing popular for use at public pay phones. There are three types of cards: Kadfon, Unicard, and Cityfon, which can only be used in the appropriate phone booth, where instructions for using them are displayed. The cards come in denominations from RM5 to RM50 and can be purchased at airports, Shell and Petronas gas stations, and most 7-Eleven and Hop-In stores. A limited number of pay phones accept major international credit cards. For assisted local calls, dial 102. Dial 103 for directory information.

Brunei: Pay phones use phone cards in values of B$10, B$20, B$50, and B$100, on sale at Telekom offices and post offices.

LONG-DISTANCE AND INTERNATIONAL CALLS

In Malaysia: You can make direct-dial calls overseas from many hotel-room phones. If you want to avoid the hotel charges, local phone books give pages of information in English on international calling, rates, and locations of phone offices. Pay phones where international calls can be made have an orange IDD sign over them, and can generally be found outside post offices. For assisted international calls, dial 108.

When calling the States, you can dial the following **access numbers** to reach a U.S. long-distance operator: AT&T (☎ 800–0011); MCI (☎ 800–0012); Sprint (☎ 800–0016). To use AT&T's UKDirect to Britain, dial 800–0044.

In Brunei: You can make direct-dial international calls from the major hotels or from the Central Telegraph Office on Jalan Sultan. To call the operator for assistance on overseas calls, dial 01; for directory information, 113.

Visitor Information

MALAYSIA

For information and brochures, contact the **Malaysia Tourism Promotion Board** (MTPB; ✉ 595 Madison Ave., Suite 1800, New York, NY 10022, ☎ 212/754–1113, www.tourism.gov.my; ✉ 57 Trafalgar Sq., London WC2 5DU, ☎ 0171/930–7932).

BRUNEI

Brunei does not have any tourism information office either at home or abroad. Before coming, inquire at the local office of Brunei's national airline, Royal Brunei Airlines. They may be able to give you a copy of their in-flight magazine, *Muhibbah*.

When to Go

Malaysia's equatorial climate is fairly uniform throughout the year: temperatures range from the low 90s during the day to low 70s at night. The mountains may be 10° cooler than the lowlands. Relative humidity is usually about 90%. Rain is common all year, but showers don't last long and shouldn't slow you down much. A rainy season brought on by monsoons lasts from November through February on the east coast of the peninsula, from October through April in Sarawak, and from October through February in Sabah. The heavy rains can cause delays. During school holidays, locals tend to fill hotels, so book in advance if you plan to visit in early April, early August, or from mid-November to early January.

Brunei lies between 4° and 6° north of the equator, and temperatures don't vary much from one season to the next: it's hot and humid year-round, and the equatorial sun is fierce. (The annual mean temperature is 80°F.) Though sudden, brief rainstorms are prevalent throughout the year (particularly November–May), the wettest months are December and January. Even during the monsoon season, be prepared for blasts of heat between downpours. There's no peak tourist season.

CLIMATE
The following are average temperatures in KL:

Jan.	89F	32C	May	91F	33C	Sept.	89F	32C
	72	22		74	23		74	23
Feb.	91F	33C	June	91F	33C	Oct.	89F	32C
	72	22		74	23		74	23
Mar.	91F	33C	July	89F	32C	Nov.	89F	32C
	74	23		72	22		74	23
Apr.	91F	33C	Aug.	89F	32C	Dec.	89F	32C
	74	23		74	23		72	22

FESTIVALS AND SEASONAL EVENTS IN MALAYSIA

Malaysia's multiracial society celebrates numerous festivals, since each ethnic community retains its own customs and traditions. The dates of some holidays are fixed, but most change according to the various religious calendars.

Jan.–Feb.: During **Chinese New Year,** Chinese families visit Buddhist temples, exchange gifts, and hold open house for relatives and friends. The Hindu festival **Thaipusam** turns out big crowds for a street parade in Pinang and a religious spectacle at the Batu Caves near KL. Indian devotees of the god Subramaniam pierce their bodies, cheeks, and tongues with steel hooks and rods. **Hari Raya Puasa or Aidilfitri** marks the end of Ramadan, the fasting month. It's a time of feasting and rejoicing and often includes a visit to the cemetery followed by mosque services. Tourists are welcome at the prime minister's residence in Kuala Lumpur during open-house hours. (Because the Islamic calendar follows the lunar cycle, each Gregorian year Ramadan begins roughly 10 days earlier.)

May–June: The **Kadazan Harvest Festival** is celebrated May 30 and 31 in Kota Kinabalu, Sabah, with feasting, buffalo races, games, and colorful dances in native costumes. The Sabah Fest, which runs in the capital for two weeks from mid-May, features cultural performances, sales of handicrafts, and special food in major shopping complexes and hotels. **Gawai Dayak,** a weeklong harvest festival, is celebrated in Sarawak with dances, games, and feasting in the longhouses. The official celebration is held in Kuching on June 1. The **Dragon Boat Festival** features boat races off Gurney Drive in Pinang early in the month. On June 5 every state marks the **King's Birthday** (Yang Di-Pertuan Agong) with parades. In KL's Merdeka Stadium, a trooping of the colors is held.

Aug.–Sept.: Merdeka Day, on August 31, is Malaysia's Independence Day. Arches are erected across city thoroughfares, buildings are illuminated, parades are arranged, and in KL there's a variety show in Lake Gardens. On **All Souls' Day,** or the Feast of the Hungry Ghosts, Chinese honor their ancestors by burning paper objects (for the ancestors' use in the afterlife) on the street. Chinese opera is performed in various locations in Pinang and other cities.

Oct.–Nov.: During **Deepavali,** the Hindu festival of lights that celebrates the triumph of good over evil, houses and shops are brightly decorated.

Dec.: During the **Chingay Procession** in late December, Malaysian Chinese parade through the streets of Pinang and JB doing stunts with enormous clan flags on bamboo poles, accompanied by cymbals, drums, and gongs. It's a noisy, colorful, folksy pageant. **Christmas** is widely celebrated, with decorations, food promotions, music, and appearances of Father Krismas.

Brunei's Muslim festivals are generally low-key affairs involving visits to the mosque and to relatives. **Royal Brunei Armed Forces Day** on May 31 consists of military parades and displays at the Taman Haji Sir Omar Ali Saifuddien in BSB. On the **Sultan's Birthday,** celebrated July 15, parades and festivities take place throughout the country, with fireworks and night markets in the evening.

4 Philippines

A feast of islands awaits you in the Philippines. Luzon has historic Metro Manila, with its vibrant nightlife, the breathtaking Cordillera and Sierra Madre mountain ranges to the north, and Spanish-era architecture and churches. The Visaya Islands have some of the country's best sandy stretches and music-loving inhabitants, and Mindanao has towering Mt. Apo and rare flora and fauna. All three regions enjoy translucent seas, tropical beaches, and highlands to trek.

By Luis H.
Francia

Updated by
Luis H.
Francia,
Doreen
Fernandez,
Elizabeth V.
Reyes, and
Maya Besa

THIS ARCHIPELAGO OF 7,107 ISLANDS, extending between Taiwan to the north and Borneo to the south, seems like a misplaced Latin American country. Indeed, Filipinos are often referred to as the "Latins of the East." While the dominant racial stock is Malay—akin to the indigenous populations of Indonesia, Borneo, and Malaysia—most people's names are Hispanic and their faith Roman Catholic (the Philippines is the only predominantly Catholic nation in Asia). To add to this cultural mix, the government is headed by a democratically elected president and English is widely spoken here, making the Philippines the fourth-largest English-speaking nation in the world, after the United States, the United Kingdom, and India. These features reflect four centuries of Spanish and American colonization. As celebrated Philippine writer Carmen Guerrero Nakpil put it, the Philippines spent more than 300 years in a convent and 50 in Hollywood.

The cultural potpourri began around the 10th century, when the native Malays intermarried with Arab, Indian, and Chinese traders. By the 14th century, Islam had established itself in southern Mindanao with the conversion of tribal royalty. Muslim tenets started to spread north to the Visayas and Luzon, but in 1521, Ferdinand Magellan—a Portuguese navigator in the service of the Spanish throne, heading the first expedition to circumnavigate the world—landed on the island of Homonhon, off the coast of Samar, and claimed the country for Spain. The intrepid Magellan moved on to Cebu (which was then known as Zubu and which was, as now, an important trading port) and was killed shortly thereafter by Lapu-Lapu, a native chieftain. Spanish rule was uneasy, periodically interrupted by regional revolts that culminated in the 1896 nationwide revolution, the first of its kind in Asia. Nationalist aspirations were aborted, however, when the United States, after defeating Spain in the Spanish-American War, took over in 1898—but not without the ensuing bitter, five-year Philippine-American War, a conflict characterized by guerrilla tactics on the part of the poorly armed Philippine soldiers.

American rule, interrupted by Japanese occupation during World War II, came to an end on July 4, 1946, when Manuel Roxas took over as the first postcolonial president. Except during the dictatorial rule of Ferdinand Marcos from 1972 until 1986 (when he was ousted by the bloodless four-day People Power revolution), the government has since been a democratically elected one. The new constitution adopted in 1987 under President Corazon Aquino limits presidential tenure to one term of six years. Elections in 1992 to determine her successor resulted in former general Fidel V. Ramos's winning the presidency. The current president is Joseph Estrada, Ramos's vice president and a former screen actor, elected in 1998.

After more than two decades of unrest, a nationwide Communist insurgency—with its roots in agrarian and social injustice—has been on the decline, with ongoing peace talks between rebel leaders and the government. A Muslim secessionist movement in southern Mindanao has come to terms with Manila, though a radical splinter group has engaged the Philippine military sporadically. The military, after several coup attempts in the late '80s, has adjusted to civilian leadership.

Because of its colonial history and its people's innate warmth, the Philippines today is a country open to visitors and tolerant of cultural idiosyncrasies. Filipinos are a gregarious, fun-loving people whose hospitality is legendary. ("No" is a word frowned upon; a Filipino will find countless ways to decline a request without sounding negative, smoothing over a potentially disruptive moment. Westerners should be aware that insistent straightforwardness can be counterproductive.) Filipinos love to joke and tease and have a natural sense of the absurd. These qualities come in handy in a society full of paradoxes and contradictions, where medieval Catholic values coexist with tropical hedonism; a freedom-loving people still contends with such feudal practices as private armies; and poverty persists amid sunshine and rich natural resources.

Pleasures and Pastimes

The Philippines may not have world-class museums or a monumental ruin at every turn, but the nation's three island groupings—Luzon (the largest), the Visayas, and Mindanao—have twice the coastline of the continental United States and offer diverse attractions. The indigenous tribes—from the Ifugao in northern Luzon to the T'boli in Mindanao—offer glimpses of ancient traditions. The outstanding beauty of the land, the many picturesque towns and villages, the abundance of uncrowded islands and beaches, the excellent dining, and the hospitality and gaiety of the people offer rewards all their own.

Beaches

The Philippines has an abundance of beaches, from pebble-strewn coastlines and black volcanic stretches to brilliant white expanses of sand. The advantage of being on a tropical archipelago (remember, more than 7,000 islands!) is that you're never far from the sea. Some of the loveliest beaches—Boracay, Panay, Bohol, and Cebu—are in the Visayas region. Palawan is possibly the least developed island and the wildest in terms of flora and fauna.

Churches

The heart of the typical Philippine town is its Catholic church—along with the adjacent plaza and the town hall—where communal rites are observed and in front of which you can witness the languorous rhythms of daily life. Churches from the Spanish colonial era are evident in most of the country, except of course in the Muslim south and in the higher reaches of northern Luzon. These churches have been dubbed "earthquake baroque" for the massive walls and buttresses built (not always successfully) to withstand earthquakes; their ornate facades combine classical Western influences with folk art motifs. Some of the more distinctive churches are in the Ilocos region (along the coast of northern Luzon), in the metropolitan Manila area, and in the Visayas, particularly on such islands as Cebu, Bohol, Leyte, and Panay.

Dining

Including as it does both patently Asian and Western dishes, Philippine food may puzzle you. History is responsible: on a matrix of native (Austronesian or Malay) dishes akin to those in the rest of Southeast Asia, Chinese traders input their culinary culture, Spanish colonizers added touches of Spain and Mexico (through which the islands were governed), Indian and Arab interaction influenced the food of Mindanao, and U.S. colonization brought in American cooking.

The indigenous cuisine consists of seafood or meat broiled or stewed in vinegar (for preserving without refrigeration) or sour-stewed in broth with tamarind or tomato (which are cooling in hot weather), or in other liquids such as coconut water (*pinais*) or coconut milk (*laing*). Coconut is prominent—as a vegetable (the bud, the heart of palm), as a drink (called *tuba* when its taken from the sap, *lambanog* when it's distilled), as coco milk or cream in which to cook fruits and vegetables (*ginataan*), and as flesh grated into desserts and sweets.

Rice is a staple: when steamed to go with meals, it's a shaper of other tastes; when ground into flour, it's transformed into myriad cakes for snacks and feasts. One such cake is *bibingka,* baked on and beneath hot coals and topped with freshly grated coconut, salted duck's eggs, and slices of *carabao* (water buffalo) milk cheese; another is leaf-wrapped *suman,* sticky rice cooked with coconut milk and eaten with ripe mangoes.

The Chinese connection is apparent in such foods as vegetable- or pork-filled *lumpia* (spring rolls), and especially in *pansit* noodles (rice, mung bean, wheat; fresh or dried; fat or thin) sautéed with vegetables, pork, or seafood—the ingredients differ from region to region and from cook to cook.

Spanish dishes have become fiesta food: *lechon,* spit-roasted suckling pig; chicken *relleno* stuffed with pork, sausage, and spices; paella rich with crabs, prawns, sausages, ham, and clams; *pochero,* a beef stew given local character with a vegetable relish; *callos* (tripe) with chickpeas and pimientos; *caldereta,* goat or beef stew with olive oil, bell peppers, and olives.

The American regime, which began in 1898, brought in convenience (sandwiches and salads), quick cooking (fried chicken, hamburgers), and a new food culture. The East–West range is therefore wide, but it has been made more Philippine through time by local ingredients, dipping sauces (such as *patis,* a fish sauce, or *bagoong,* a salted shrimp or fish paste), cooking styles, and general fine-tuning.

In a nation with some 90 ethno-linguistic groups, there are, of course, regional variations. The Bicol people (from southeast Luzon) like chili-hot food; so do the Maranaws, who live around Lake Lanao in Mindanao. Dare to try the Bicol *pinangat* (shrimp or pork wrapped in taro leaves, cooked with coco cream, ginger, and chilies) or the Maranaw catfish (cooked with turmeric, coco milk, and chilies). The Ilocano north favors *pinakbet,* a vegetable stew made with bagoong, and often with the bittersweetness of *ampalaya* (bitter melon). It is now the pan-Philippine vegetable dish—everyone cooks it with regional variations (steamed or sautéed, for example, with shrimp or with pork). Leyte and Samar (eastern Visayan provinces) folk have many dishes cooked in coconut milk (such as prawns or chicken with ginger). Tagalog dishes lean toward a controlled sourness, as in beef, pork, or chicken *sinigang.* The food of the Pampanga province (60 km/37 mi north of Manila) is one of the richest regional cuisines; it includes a plethora of sweets and such exotica as stuffed frogs (*betute*).

You can sample many of these regional cooking styles—and most international cuisines—in Metro Manila restaurants, as well as in food malls, street stalls, and market *turo-turo* (point-point) counters that offer an array of cooked foods. But venturing into the provinces is the best way to get a real taste of the Philippines. Price categories throughout the chapter are based on the following ranges:

CATEGORY	COST*
$$$$	over P880 (over US$20)
$$$	P440–P880 (US$10–US$20)
$$	P264–P440 (US$6–US$10)
$	under P264 (under US$6)

per person for a three-course dinner, excluding tax, service, and drinks.

Lodging

Major urban areas, such as Manila, Cebu, Baguio, and Davao, have lodgings for every type of traveler, from the hedonist with deep pock-

The Philippines

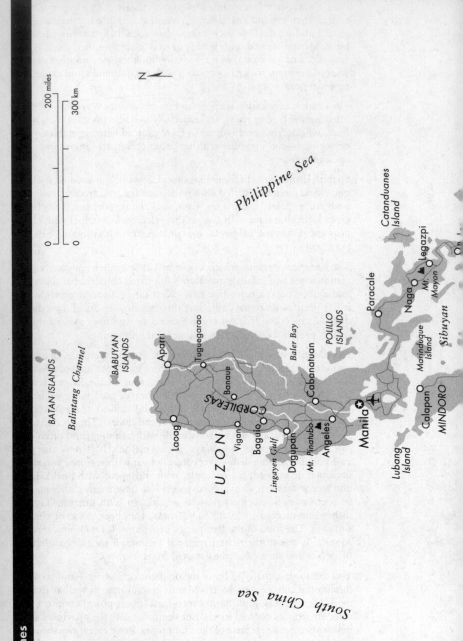

The Philippines

Philippine Sea

South China Sea

200 miles
300 km

BATAN ISLANDS

Balintang Channel

BABUYAN ISLANDS

Aparti
Tuguegarao
Banaue
CORDILLERAS
Laoag
Vigan
Baguio
Lingayen Gulf
Dagupan
Mt. Pinatubo
Angeles
Manila

LUZON

Baler Bay
Cabanatuan

POLILLO ISLANDS

Paracale

Catanduanes Island

Naga
Mayon
Mt. Legazpi

Sibuyan

Morinduque Island

Lubang Island

Calapan

MINDORO

Bislig

Butuan City

Surigao

Dinagat
Island

Tagum

Davao City

Tacloban

SAMAR

Digos

General Santos
City

MINDANAO

Mt.
Apo

LEYTE

Bulan

Macton
Island

Ormoc City

CEBU

BOHOL

Cagayan
de Oro

Iligan

Polomolok

Masbate

MASBATE

VISAYAS

Cebu
City

Ozamiz

Cotabato

Midsayap

Sea

Roxas

PANAY

NEGROS

Bacolod City

Celebes Sea

Iloilo City

Basilan
Island

Zamboanga City

Isabela

SULU

Sulu Sea

Jolo

SULU ARCHIPELAGO

CALAMIAN
GROUP

Puerto Princesa

PALAWAN

Sandakan

MALAYSIA

BORNEO

BRUNEI

ets to the backpacker who must count pennies. Large towns usually feature a couple of reasonably priced, comfortable hotels and lower-scale inns and pensions. In the more rustic areas, accommodations tend, not surprisingly, toward the basic. Popular beach areas have resorts made up of anything from pricey air-conditioned cabanas to inexpensive cottages. Small cities and towns offer mostly family-run hotels, sometimes short on amenities but generally well maintained and clean and with a courteous and helpful staff. For the more expensive hotels and beach resorts, it's best to make reservations during the peak season (November to February). Price categories throughout the chapter are based on the following ranges:

CATEGORY	COST*
$$$$	over P9,680 (over US$220)
$$$	P4,400–P10,000 (US$100–US$220)
$$	P2,640–P4,400 (US$60–US$100)
$	under P2,640 (under US$60)

*for a standard double room in high season, excluding 10% service charge and 13.7% tax.

Mountain Climbing
Mt. Pulog in the Cordilleras, Mt. Mayon in southern Luzon, Mt. Kanlaon on Negros Island, Mt. Hibok-Hibok on Camiguin Island, and Mt. Apo in Mindanao—all have known trails and local guides for hire.

Shopping
The Philippines can yield great bargains if you know what to look for and where. There are handicraft stores all over the country, usually near the public market in small- to medium-size cities and towns and in shopping centers in such large urban areas as Manila, Cebu, and Baguio. In Manila, the country's commercial capital, you'll find regional goods, though prices are higher than elsewhere. Focus on handicrafts special to the region you're visiting. Look for handwoven rattan baskets, blankets, and backpacks from northern Luzon; handwoven cloth from northern Luzon, Iloilo City, and southern Mindanao; items crafted of si..ll from Cebu City and Zamboanga City; handwoven *pandan* (a type of palm tree) mats with geometric designs from Zamboanga City and Davao City; brassware from southern Mindanao; bamboo furniture from central Luzon; gold and silver jewelry from Baguio City and Bulacan province; and cigars from the Ilocos region. Bargaining is acceptable in public markets, flea markets, and small, owner-run stores. Department stores and big shopping areas have fixed prices.

Water Sports
The tropical waters are ideal for a variety of water sports, from scuba diving to waterskiing. Many resorts in different regions offer equipment and facilities. The country has some of the best dive sites in the world, with more than 40 known spots, most around Palawan, the Visayas, and Batangas Province (on Luzon). Many more wait to be discovered. Most resorts rent out snorkeling equipment; the tonier ones have scuba gear as well. Surfers have discovered the Philippines, though there are still only a handful of surf centers. Most are on the island of Catanduanes off southern Luzon, on the Pacific coast.

Exploring the Philippines

Great Itineraries
To truly appreciate what the country has to offer, you need at least two weeks, given the variety of attractions and their diverse locations. If you have less time, however, here are some suggested itineraries.

IF YOU HAVE 3 DAYS

With such little time, your best bet is to concentrate on **Metro Manila,** with an all-day trip to Pagsanjan Falls, a two-hour drive from the city, and a stop at Tagaytay Ridge to view Taal Volcano (a volcano within a lake within a volcano). In the city, two days should be sufficient to visit such sights as Intramuros, Malacañang, the Coconut Palace, Rizal Park, and such colorful neighborhoods as Binondo, Quiapo, and the tourist districts of Ermita and Malate.

IF YOU HAVE 7 DAYS

Spend two days exploring Metro Manila, then either join a tour or proceed on your own to the Cordilleras in northern Luzon. Plan on an overnight stay in **Banaue** to visit the magnificent rice terraces, built more than two millennia ago. Nearby is **Sagada,** a picturesque town with unique limestone formations and burial caves. From Sagada, proceed to **Baguio** and spend two days there.

IF YOU HAVE 10 DAYS

Spend two days in **Metro Manila,** then head north to the rice terraces in **Banaue** and to **Baguio.** On the sixth day, fly back to Manila and take a connecting flight to **Cebu.** Two days in the Queen City of the South should suffice to see its sights and to spend a lazy day at a beach on nearby Mactan Island. The last two days could be spent either in **Zamboanga City,** on the western coast of Mindanao, or **Davao City,** on the eastern coast. Both have local culture and beach resorts. Zamboanga is an older city, the southernmost bastion of Spanish rule in the archipelago; Davao City is a boomtown, near the country's tallest peak, Mt. Apo, and the site of huge agribusiness and trading concerns.

When to Tour the Philippines

The ideal time to visit is from mid-October to February (the peak tourist season being from late November to February), right after the monsoon rains and before the start of the scorchingly hot period from March to May. Besides having perfect beach weather, the hot months coincide with the Lenten season, when reenactments of Christ's Passion take place in towns and cities, and flagellants, whipping themselves into a bloodied frenzy, stagger through the streets, particularly in Central Luzon. There are fiestas every month, but during May every town in the country seems to have some kind of celebration. If you happen to be in the Philippines in the rainy season, from June to mid-October, be sure to pack a raincoat and waterproof shoes. (☞ When to Go *in* Philippines A to Z, *below.*)

Numbers in the text correspond to numbers in the margin and on the maps.

METRO MANILA

The urban sprawl that is metropolitan Manila (it's made up of the cities of Manila, Makati, Pasay, Quezon, Caloocan, and Pasig, plus 12 towns) is a fascinating, even surreal, combination of modernity and tradition. In Manila's streets you'll see horse-drawn *calesas* (carriages) alongside sleek Mercedes-Benzes, Japanese sedans, passenger buses, and the ubiquitous passenger jeepneys—once converted World War II Jeeps but now manufactured locally.

Built by the Spanish conquistadors in 1571 as Intramuros, a fortified settlement on the ashes of a Malay town, Manila spread outward over the centuries, so that the oldest districts are those closest to Intramuros. Yet very few buildings attest to the city's antiquity, since it suffered extensive damage during World War II, the most except for Warsaw, Hiroshima, and Nagasaki. Among Manila's older districts are the centrally located, bay-front Ermita and Malate, which make up the Tourist Belt (so-called because of its many hotels, clubs, restaurants, boutiques, and coffee shops). At the upper end of the scale is Makati City, the country's financial center, with its wide, well-kept boulevards; high-rise apartment and office buildings; ultramodern shopping centers, and well-guarded walled enclaves of the fabulously rich.

Because Metro Manila is a conglomeration of cities and towns, it lacks a defined center, and you certainly won't find an easy-to-navigate grid layout. Adding to the confusion is a lack of consistent urban planning. Like many cities in developing nations, Metro Manila has its share of congestion, pollution, haphazard planning, and poverty. The large slum of Tondo is dominated by a huge pile of garbage known as Smoky Mountain for the endless burning of trash fires. Here the poor live in cardboard shanties and scavenge for a living. But the 10 million inhabitants of the "noble and ever loyal city"—as Manila was described by its Spanish overlords—have a joie de vivre that transcends their struggles. Manilans bear their burdens with humor and a casual grace, and the fortuitous blend of Latin and Southeast Asian temperaments makes for an easygoing atmosphere, where play is as important as work. The nightlife here may well be Southeast Asia's liveliest—comparable to that in Bangkok—with myriad restaurants, discos, coffeehouses, nightclubs, massage parlors, topless bars, music lounges, and beer gardens. Certainly the bands—rock, Latin, or jazz—have a reputation for being the finest in Southeast Asia. Enjoy the city's mix of the terrible and marvelous, for it's a microcosm of Philippine society.

Exploring Metro Manila

Metropolitan Manila has a roughly crescent shape, with Manila Bay and the scenic Roxas Boulevard that runs along it forming the western boundary. The Epifanio de los Santos Highway (EDSA) forms the eastern border. The Pasig River divides the city into northern and southern sections, with the oldest districts, including the ancient walled city of Intramuros, near where the river empties into Manila Bay.

Intramuros

Manila's ancient walled city, built by the Spaniards in the 16th century, is a compact 7.5 sq km (3 sq mi). Within this small area, churches, schools, convents, offices, and residences were constructed—the latter reserved for the Spanish and Spanish mestizos only. In its heyday Intramuros—with its seven drawbridges and its encircling moat—must have presented a magnificent sight to visiting galleons. The moat, filled in by the Americans to prevent the spread of disease, is now used as a golf course, but the 30-ft-thick walls are still formidable, with cannon emplacements and a strategic location facing the bay.

A GOOD WALK

Ft. Santiago ① is where the Spanish established their first settlement and where you should begin your explorations. Across from the fort is **Manila Cathedral** ②. Walking along General Luna Street, which borders the cathedral, you will come to **San Agustin Church** ③. Across the street is the Barrio San Luis Complex, which includes **Casa Manila** ④. General Luna Street ends near one of Intramuros's fortified gates, Puerta Real, which has a display of antique church silver. Bearing left onto Muralla Road, note the famed (if largely reconstructed) walls—gray, stately, and seemingly invincible. You will pass lookout towers and other fortifications. Muralla Road winds around in a semicircle, bringing you to Puerta Isabel. This gate houses a fascinating display of baroque floats bearing statues of saints.

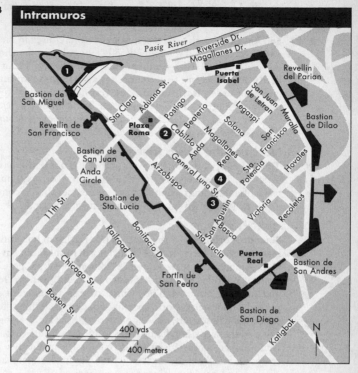

Intramuros

TIMING

It's best to explore the Walled City early in the morning to beat the heat. Exploring Intramuros on foot should take about half a day, or rent a *caretela* (a horse-drawn cart that can carry several persons) on the grounds for about P300.

SIGHTS TO SEE

4 **Casa Manila.** The main attraction of the **Barrio San Luis Complex** is not the shops but this splendid re-creation of a 19th-century Spanish patrician's three-story domicile. It's complete with a carriage entrance, an inner courtyard, and a grand stairway. Upstairs is a display of period furniture and accessories. ⊠ *General Luna St.,* ☎ *2/527–4084.* ⛶ *Admission.* ☾ *Daily 9–6.*

1 **Ft. Santiago.** This stone fort overlooking the mouth of the Pasig River is on the site where the original Malay Muslim settlement stood. Previously used by the Spanish, Americans, and Japanese, it's now a pleasant park with an open-air theater where plays in Pilipino (the national tongue) are staged among the ruins. The fort has a grim history: Philippine revolutionaries (including the national hero José Rizal) were imprisoned here by the Spanish; they often drowned in the dungeons, which were below the high-tide level. ⛶ *Admission.* ☾ *Daily 8 AM–9 PM.*

2 **Manila Cathedral.** Dedicated to the Immaculate Conception of the Virgin Mary, this Romanesque edifice (a reconstruction of the original 1600 structure) has three arched doorways that form an imposing facade. The middle door is made of bronze, with eight panels that portray the cathedral's history. Inside, the clerestory's stained-glass windows depict the history of Christianity in the Philippines. Underneath the main altar is a crypt where the remains of the former archbishops are entombed. Fronting the church is **Plaza Roma,** where bullfights were once staged. Its centerpiece is a monument to three Philippine priests executed in 1872 for their nationalism. ⊠ *General Luna and Postigo Sts.,* ☎ *2/733–4945.* ☉ *Mon.–Sat. 6–5, Sun. 6–6.*

★ ❸ **San Agustin Church.** The second-oldest stone church in the country has 14 side chapels and a trompe l'oeil ceiling. Up in the choir loft, note the hand-carved 17th-century seats of *molave,* a beautiful tropical hardwood. Adjacent to the church is a small **museum** run by the Augustinian order, featuring antique vestments, colonial furniture, and religious paintings and icons. ⊠ *Gen. Luna and Real Sts.,* ☎ *2/734–7421 or 2/733–3721.* ☜ *Admission to museum.* ☉ *Church daily 7–7:30 AM and 5–6 PM; museum daily 9–noon and 1–5.*

North of the Pasig River

This is a poor and crowded part of the city, but it also has an old, historic feel. The streets are narrow, with a mix of small businesses and residential buildings. Manilans say a foreigner should come here to get a true feel for down-home Philippine neighborhoods.

SIGHTS TO SEE

Binondo. Forbidden by the Spanish from living in Intramuros, Chinese merchants and their families settled north of the Pasig River, and a sizable community—now known as Binondo—grew here in the 18th century. Bounded by the river, Claro M. Recto Avenue, Del Pan Street, and Avenida Rizal, Manila's Chinatown is a jumble of small streets packed with jewelry shops, sporting-goods and clothing stores, apothecaries, kung fu schools, movie houses that show Hong Kong flicks, magazine stalls, seedy hotels, brothels, and restaurants that usually offer Amoy and Fukienese cuisine (which emphasize minimally seasoned, fresh seafood). Stroll about, especially on Ongpin, the main street, or stop a calesa and have the driver take you around.

❺ **Binondo Church.** This 16th-century church still has its original stone walls. Note the replica of St. Peter's dome at the main altar and the Madonna encased in glass. The first Philippine saint, Lorenzo Ruiz, started here as an altar boy. ⊠ *Paredes St. at Plaza Calderon de la Barca,* ☎ *2/242–4850.* ☉ *Daily 6 AM–7 PM.*

★ ❽ **Malacañang Palace.** Once the seat of the colonial Spanish and American governor-generals, this palace is the official residence of Philippine presidents and is sometimes referred to as the Philippine White House. During her term, Corazon Aquino preferred to live in the guest house, a symbolic gesture meant to disassociate her from the dictatorial Ferdinand Marcos. Now open to the public, Malacañang's colonial Spanish architecture and interior decor are worth a look, especially the three chandeliers in the reception hall, the beautiful hardwoods used for the grand staircase, the portraits of former presidents, and the exquisite music room. The Marcoses' personal effects are gone (those shoes and that bulletproof bra!), and the rooms converted to the Malacañang Heritage Museum, featuring memorabilia of past presidents. ⊠ *J. P. Laurel St.,* ☎ *2/742–2451.* ☜ *Admission.* ☉ *Tues.–Wed. 9–noon; Thurs. mornings for guided tours only; Fri.–Sat. 9–3.*

★ ❼ **Quiapo Church.** East of Binondo, not far from the foot of Quezon Bridge and facing Plaza Miranda—where orators of varying skills and persuasions harangue passersby—is this 16th-century church, later enlarged. Its crowded environs are as close to an authentic Philippine neighborhood as you can get in Manila. On side streets vendors sell amulets and herbal cures for a wide variety of ailments. The church is home to the famed **Black Nazarene,** a dark hardwood statue of Jesus of Nazareth made by a Mexican craftsman and brought via galleon from Mexico in the 18th century. Many believe that praying to the statue can produce miracles. It isn't unusual to see supplicants crawling on their knees from

Binondo Church, **5**
Coconut Palace, **17**
Malacañang Palace, **8**
Malate Church, **14**
Manila Hotel, **9**
Manila Zoo, **15**
Metropolitan
Museum of Art, **16**
National Museum, **11**
Paco Park, **13**
Quiapo Church, **7**
Quinta Public
Market, **6**
Rizal Park, **10**
Tabacalera Factory, **12**

the entrance to the altar. As part of the Quiapo Fiesta, each January 9 the Nazarene is paraded through the district's narrow streets by bare-chested male devotees who compete for the honor of pulling the float that carries the statue. ⊠ *Plaza Miranda and Quezon Blvd.,* ☏ 2/733–4945. ☼ *Daily 6 AM–7 PM.*

❻ Quinta Public Market. Bargain-price handicrafts, from handwoven mats to rattan baskets and straw brooms, are the specialty of this market near Quiapo Church. You'll find more handicrafts in the small arcade right beneath the nearby bridge. You can also get a snack or light meal of native dishes. Be mindful of your wallet or bag, and be especially wary of people offering to buy your dollars. ⊠ *Below Quezon Bridge.* ☼ *Daily 5 AM–8 PM.*

South of the Pasig River: The Tourist Belt and Around

The Ermita and Malate districts that form the so-called Tourist Belt are bordered by Roxas Boulevard to the west, Taft Avenue to the east, Intramuros to the north, and Pablo Ocampo Senior Street to the south. On Roxas are nightclubs, the Cultural Center of the Philippines complex, hotels, restaurants, apartment buildings, Rizal Park, and Intramuros. On Taft Avenue are the Light Rail Transit line, universities, shops, stores, and several hospitals. In between are bars and cocktail lounges, the infamous go-go joints (especially on M. H. del Pilar and A. Mabini streets), massage parlors, coffeehouses, more restaurants and hotels, office buildings, boutiques, and shopping malls.

SIGHTS TO SEE

★ ⑰ Coconut Palace. South of Malate on Roxas Boulevard is this $10 million project of former first lady Imelda Marcos, so named because more than 70% of the construction materials were derived from the coconut tree. The grandiose structure, within the Cultural Center complex, faces Manila Bay and was constructed for Pope John Paul's visit in 1981 (he refused to stay here). Each of the seven (the Marcoses' lucky number) palatial suites is named and styled after a different region of the country. The Pangasinan Room, for example, features *piña* (pineapple fiber) bed covers and a fabulous mother-of-pearl table set. Several of Imelda's jet-set friends stayed here at one time or another, among them Van Cliburn and Brooke Shields. ⊠ *Roxas Blvd. in Cultural Center complex,* ☏ 2/832–0223 or 2/831–1756. ☐ *Admission.* ☼ *By appointment only; 5-person minimum.*

⑭ Malate Church. Photographers love to shoot the picturesque, well-kept facade of this gray-stone church, an intriguing mixture of Romanesque and baroque styles. Its interior, however, is unremarkable. Between the church and Roxas Boulevard is Rajah Sulayman Park, the centerpiece of which is a statue of Rajah Sulayman, a pre-Spanish (16th-century) ruler of Manila. ⊠ *Corner of Remedios and M. H. del Pilar Sts.* ☼ *Mon.–Sat. 5:30–noon and 3–7; Sun. 5:30 AM–8 PM.*

NEED A BREAK?   Around Malate Church are innumerable places for lunch or a snack. You can walk eastward (away from the bay) on Remedios Street and choose from several cafés around Remedios Circle. Besides the cafés listed in Nightlife and the Arts (☞ *below*) try the 24-hour **Aristocrat** (⊠ Roxas Blvd. at San Andres St., ☏ 2/524–7671), a favorite with everyone from gangsters to businesspeople; prices are reasonable, and the food is decent.

❾ Manila Hotel. On the edge of Rizal Park and a short stroll from the Rizal Monument is the doyen of Philippine hotels, built in 1912 (☞ *also* Lodging, *below*). This is where General Douglas MacArthur lived during much of his time in the Philippines; Ernest Hemingway also stayed here once. The spacious lobby is gracious in an Old World way; note the ceiling and woodwork, made entirely of precious Philippine hardwoods, the floors of Philippine marble, and the *capiz* (translucent-shell) and brass chandeliers. ⊠ *Rizal Park at Bonifacio Dr.,* ☎ *2/527–0011.*

NEED A
BREAK?

Manila Hotel has an airy, pleasant poolside coffee shop, **Café Ylang-Ylang** (☎ 2/527–0011). The menu offers solid local and Continental fare; in the afternoon you'll find a mouthwatering dessert buffet that's ever so hard to resist.

⑮ Manila Zoo. This small zoo in the Tourist Belt has the usual assortment of wild animals, including such local species as the *tamaraw* (a peculiar water buffalo), the rare mouse deer (the smallest deer in the world), and the Palawan pheasant. ⊠ *Quirino Ave. at Adriatico St.,* ☎ *2/575–7061 or 2/525–4602.* ⊠ *Admission.* ⊙ *Daily 7–6.*

★ **⑯ Metropolitan Museum of Art.** This impressively designed museum has exhibits of classical and contemporary fine arts. Each year there are four major exhibitions by renowned Filipino and foreign artists. In the basement galleries you'll find displays of pre-Colombian pottery and an exquisite collection of pre-Hispanic gold jewelry from the central bank collection. ⊠ *Roxas Blvd., central bank complex, across from Cultural Center,* ☎ *2/523–7855 or 2/521–1517.* ⊠ *Admission.* ⊙ *Mon.–Sat. 10–6.*

⑪ National Museum. Once the site of Congress, this building now houses displays that range from archaeological treasures to paintings, including an impressive array of the 19th-century artist Juan Luna's works. Three nearby government buildings have been incorporated into the museum, alleviating the crowded displays. Two permanent exhibitions have been installed: "The Story of the Filipino People" and "The Treasures of San Diego," which features a sunken 17th-century galleon's treasures. ⊠ *Rizal Park at Padre Burgos St.,* ☎ *2/527–1207.* ⊠ *Admission.* ⊙ *Mon.–Sat. 9–noon and 1–5.*

⑬ Paco Park. On the south side of the Pasig River, this petite but beautiful circular park of moss-covered stone—with a picturesque chapel in the middle that's a favorite site for weddings—was a cemetery until it was declared a national park in 1966. Its two concentric walls served as burial niches for the Spanish elite and, for a while, the national hero José Rizal. No burials have been performed here since 1912. Free concerts are offered on Friday at 6 PM. ⊠ *San Marcelino and General Luna Sts.,* ☎ *2/524–2011.* ⊠ *Admission.* ⊙ *Daily 8–5.*

⑩ Rizal Park. Stretching from Taft Avenue toward the bay is a 128-acre oasis where Manilans can jog, do Tai Chi, stroll through the **Chinese Garden**, a pleasant arboretum, or just lie on the grass. The park is named after José Rizal, a national hero who was, among other things, a doctor, linguist, botanist, novelist, poet, educator, and fencer. Executed in 1896 by the Spanish because of his reformist views, he was originally buried at Paco Park but now lies under the **Rizal Monument**, designed by Swiss artist Richard Kissling and erected in 1912. Nearby, towering above the statue, is a stately 50-ft obelisk marking the spot where three local 19th-century priests were garroted by the Spanish for their nationalist views. The 24-hour guards, like honor guards everywhere, try to be as impassive as possible. Rizal's poem *Mi Ultimo Adios* (My Last Farewell), composed just before his death, is inscribed on a bronze slab set into a nearby octagonal wall; in addition to the original Spanish, it appears in English and several other languages. ☎ *2/523–8058 (park administration).* ⊠ *Admission to Chinese Garden.* ⊙ *Park daily dawn–dusk; Chinese Gardens daily 8–6.*

⑫ **Tabacalera Factory.** The full, rather grandiloquent name of this company is La Flor de Isabela, Compañía General de Tabacos de Filipinas (Flower of Isabela, General Company of Philippine Tobacco). Founded during the Spanish colonial era, it has a well-deserved reputation for fine cigars. The factory offers free tours (call in advance) that enable you to view the time-honored process of cigar making. Cigars and humidors are for sale. ✉ *900 Romualdez St. at United Nations Ave.,* ☎ *2/524–8026.* ⊙ *Mon.–Sat. 9–5.*

OFF THE
BEATEN PATH

A RIDE ON THE LRT – The Light Rail Transit (LRT) is an excellent way to travel beyond the usual tourist sights. For only a few pesos, you can ride from one end of the 15-stop line and back (a 1¼-hour trip), taking in the heart of Manila. Baclaran, the southernmost terminal, is not far from Baclaran Church, which on Wednesday is packed with devotees for special services to the Virgin Mary. Moving north, you pass through congested neighborhoods and can often peer into offices, apartments, and backyards. It's worth getting off at the R. Papa station, taking a pedicab, and visiting the remarkable Chinese Cemetery (there's a small entrance fee). The mausoleums are virtual mansions with architectural styles that range from Chinese classical to baroque, a reminder that wealth makes a difference even in death. At the last stop, Monumento, walk a short distance to the monument marking the spot where Philippine revolutionaries began their struggle against Spain.

Dining

Reservations are a good idea on holidays and weekends. Most places close only on Christmas, New Year's Day, All Souls' Day, Maundy Thursday, and Good Friday. Hours are normally noon to 2:30 for lunch and 7 to 11 for dinner; some restaurants are also open for breakfast (7–10) and *merienda* (afternoon snack; 4–6). Few require formal dress; jackets or the long-sleeve *barong tagalog* for men suffice at even the most upscale establishments, and most others draw the line only at athletic shorts and tank tops. Restaurants build a 10% VAT into their charges. Ask whether or not a service charge is included; if it isn't, a 10%–15% tip is expected.

Chinese

$$–$$$ ✕ **The Good Earth Tea Room.** Inside a spare, gracious art gallery is this
★   gem, where Chinese culinary tradition is distilled with intelligence and creativity. Start with such appetizers as duck *siopao* (steamed buns); slivered jellyfish and century eggs; minced chicken and fried wood-ear-mushroom pouches. Move on to chow mein; blue marlin with black beans; chili-spiced shrimp with buttery cashews; or deep bowls of noodles in a perfect clear broth with meat-filled wontons, prawns, and scallion ribbons. Sweet endings might be hot banana fritters, pandan-flavored gelatin, or dark coffee jelly topped with ice cream. Chef-owner Henry Cheung's devotees were only too pleased when he opened a branch across town called **The Good Earth Chinese Cuisine.** ✉ *101 Building, Magallanes Commercial Center, Makati City,* ☎ *0915/702–7786 (cellular). AE, DC, MC, V. Closed Sun.* ✉ *Silhouette Tower, 5 Eisenhower St. at Annapolis St., Greenhills, San Juan,* ☎ *2/723–8982. AE, DC, MC, V. Closed Mon.*

$$ ✕ **North Park Noodle House.** It was a tragedy when the original San Juan restaurant burned down, but now this establishment is back with not one but two locations. Both do a very brisk business owing to the long opening hours, reasonable prices, and good, simple food. Pot stickers and steamed buns are on the menu along with crisp prawn dumplings, roast Long Island duck, King Dao spareribs, and rice fried with salted

fish and chicken bits. And, of course, you'll find noodles—*canton*, flat Shanghai, herb, or whole wheat—in steaming broth with a rainbow of savory topping choices (Nanking beef, mushrooms, pork ribs, ox tripe). The thick, creamy *congee* (rice porridge) brims with such treasures as Pacific clams, snapper, sea abalone, beef, century eggs, shiitake mushrooms, and curly scallion strips. On Saturday night, the Makati City location is open around the clock, and the crowd never seems to subside. ⊠ *1200 Makati Ave., Makati City,* ☎ *2/895–3471, 2/896–3482, or 2/896–3490. No credit cards.* ⊠ *869 Banawe Ave., Quezon City,* ☎ *2/412–9505 or 2/413–7063. No credit cards.*

Contemporary

$$$ ✕ **Grassl's.** Here you can have fresh lobster served three ways: as crisp
★ cool sashimi (not cooked or passed through fire) flavored with ginger; as a freshly made bisque; or grilled with *calamansi* (Philippine lime) butter or baked with tarragon, mascarpone, and whipped spinach. Other fine options include tamarind-glazed king salmon; five-spice pork roast with walnut-apple glaze, wild rice, and a balsamic sauce; or soft-shell crab tempura on sweet-sour mango salad. For dessert consider the white-chocolate and cognac crème brûlée. Chef Markus Gfeller calls his food "innovative market cuisine," because his creations depend on what's fresh in the market. Excellent service in elegant surroundings complete the experience. ⊠ *5F Benpres Building, Meralco Ave. and Exchange Rd., Pasig City,* ☎ *2/632–1203 or 2/632–1204. AE, DC, MC, V. Closed Sun.*

Eclectic

$$$ ✕ **Le Soufflé Restaurant and Wine Bar.** Three chefs own and operate
★ this restaurant, where large picture windows overlook a public garden. Theirs is a light, fresh cuisine, generally Mediterranean but with salutes to Asia and eclecticism. When ingredients are available, the chefs can accommodate requests not on the menu. Specialties range from pan-fried goose liver in raspberry sauce to shiitake mushroom salad, wild rice risotto, baked salmon in phyllo pastry, and desserts such as chocolate soufflé with berry sauce and *halo-halo* parfait (the innovative pastry chef's take on a traditional Philippine snack, which translates as "mix-mix"; mixed, sweetened fruits and beans topped with crushed ice). ⊠ *2F Josephine Building, Greenbelt Dr. at Makati Ave., Makati City,* ☎ *2/812–3287, 2/894–1269, or 2/894–3253. AE, DC, MC, V.*

$ ✕ **SM Megamall Food Court.** In the air-conditioned basement of a huge shopping mall, some 40 food stores ring the tables. The offerings include Philippine food: bibingka at **Ferino's;** lechon at **Lydia's;** pansit and regional dishes at **Aristocrat** and **Kamay Kainan;** Chinese vegetarian food at **Bodhi;** Cantonese cuisine at **Golden Cantonese;** Japanese food at **Moshi-Moshi;** Korean dishes at **Kimchi;** French fare at **Le Coeur de France;** and American-style pizzas, hamburgers, fried chicken, pies, cookies, and salads. The food court opens at 10 and closes at 9. ⊠ *SM Megamall, Building A, EDSA and Julia Vargas St., Pasig City,* ☎ *2/633–5012. Reservations not accepted. No credit cards.*

French

$$$$ ✕ **Prince Albert Rotisserie.** This elegant room in the Inter-Continental Manila hotel (☞ Lodging, *below*) has served excellent French food for 29 years. A set lunch menu includes a Mediterranean appetizer buffet. The regular menu has such items as grilled lobster *feuillantine* (between thin, leaflike layers of pastry), veal mignon with sage butter, chicken breast with truffles, and Black Angus beef. Sweet tooths will savor desserts like hot mango soufflé with strawberry sorbet or chocolate tart with a Grand Marnier sauce. The wine list is reasonable in selection, scope, and price. ⊠ *1 Ayala Ave., Makati City,* ☎ *2/815–9711. AE, DC, MC, V. Closed Sun. No lunch Sat.*

290

Dining ●

Aristocrat
Restaurant, **4**

Bistro Remedios, **5**

Carpaccio Ristorante
Italiano, **10**

Flavours and
Spices, **14, 29**

The Good
Earth, **12, 30**

Grassi's, **28**

North Park Noodle
House, **25, 26**

Prince Albert
Rotisserie, **19**

Restoran Barasoain, **11**

SM Megamall
Food Court, **31**

Le Soufflé Restaurant
and Wine Bar, **16**

Sugi, **18, 27**

La Tasca, **15**

Via Mare Seafood
Specialty
Restaurant, **13, 32**

Lodging ○

Adriatico Arms, **3**

Century Park
Hotel, **6**

Dusit Hotel Nikko, **17**

Heritage Hotel, **9**

Hyatt Regency, **8**

Inter-Continental
Manila, **20**

Mandarin Oriental, **24**

Manila Diamond
Hotel, **2**

Manila Hotel, **1**

Manila Peninsula, **23**

New World
Renaissance, **21**

Shangri-La Makati, **22**

Westin Philippine
Plaza, **7**

Manila Dining and Lodging

Italian

$$$ ✕ **Carpaccio Ristorante Italiano.** Here, the interior is cool and dimly lit, and the tables are all arranged around a central bar. You can start your meal with beef, lamb, salmon, and tuna carpaccio or a spicy Sicilian seafood salad. Pastas here are enhanced by traditional or innovative sauces. Entrées include cod or salmon fillet, saltimbocca, Black Angus rib eye, and lamb tenderloin. Weekly specials (crepes, risottos) and a constellation of pizzas add to your options. Desserts include such classics as homemade gelato and tiramisu. ✉ *7431 Yakal St., San Antonio Village, Makati City,* ☎ *2/843–7286. AE, DC, MC, V. Closed Sun.*

Japanese

$$$ ✕ **Sugi.** The Japanese and Philippine chefs here have developed a wide-ranging menu: sushi, tempura, *teppanyaki* (cooked on a grill built into the table) steak, sukiyaki, grilled *gindara* (silver cod), *shabu-shabu* (thinly sliced, blanched beef with a dipping sauce), and *soba* (buckwheat) and *udon* (wheat) noodles served hot or cold. Specials may include *kana koura age* (creamed crab with mushrooms), inventive seafood dishes, and emperor's soup (slivers of squid, prawn, mushrooms, and radish sprouts served in a tiny pot with a spout). The decor is Japanese, the service is exemplary, and the menu is regularly updated. ✉ *Greenbelt Mall, Ayala Centre, Makati City,* ☎ *2/816–3885 or 2/816–3886. AE, DC, MC, V.* ✉ *Greenhills Commercial Center, Ortigas and Connecticut Aves., San Juan,* ☎ *2/725–0208 or 2/723–9496. AE, DC, MC, V.*

Philippine

$$–$$$ ✕ **Bistro Remedios.** Traditional flavor and country cooking, especially
★ that of the Pampanga province, are featured here in an urban setting. Taste the local culture through *adobong palos* (freshwater eel in coconut milk, *kamias*—a small acidic fruit commonly used for souring—and chili), *gising-gising* (chopped chili with minced pork in coconut cream), crisp-fried beef ribs, prawns in crab-fat sauce, pinais *na itlog ng isda* (fish roe with lemongrass, leeks, and ginger broiled in banana leaf); *guinumis* (gelatin, tapioca, coco milk, and shaved ice) is a cooling favorite. Breakfast is a popular option here—perhaps one of garlic rice, eggs, sausages, and a cup of thick hot chocolate. The Bistro keeps long daily hours: 6 AM–10 AM for breakfast, 11 AM–2 PM for lunch, 5 PM–2 AM for dinner. ✉ *1911 Adriatico St., Malate,* ☎ *2/523–9153 or 2/524–3795. AE, DC, MC, V.*

$$ ✕ **Restoran Barasoain.** In this restaurant—named after the site of the first Philippine Constitutional Congress—you can get a taste of hometown cooking, particularly that of Bulacan and Pampanga, two of the provinces nearest Manila. The *sawsawan*—dipping sauces or accompanying relishes with which Filipinos fine-tune food to their individual tastes—are particularly noteworthy here. Vinegar, fish sauce, tamarind, garlic, ginger, tomatoes, and other ingredients can be mixed and matched to complement such dishes as boneless milkfish with black beans, ginger, and tomatoes; blue marlin in lemongrass-coconut sauce; and chicken simmered in tamarind broth. Desserts include sherbet of young coconut and halo-halo. ✉ *Mezzanine floor, Mile Long Building, Amorsolo St. at Herrera St., Makati City,* ☎ *2/812–4719 or 2/843–9596, AE, DC, MC, V.*

$–$$ ✕ **Aristocrat Restaurant.** Since opening in 1936, the Aristocrat has been run by four generations of the Reyes family, and although there are other branches, the one by the bay is the signature outlet. Drop by any time—it's open 24 hours—for the moderate prices and basic dishes: barbecued chicken or pork with Javanese rice, *satay* (sweet-spicy Indonesian peanut sauce), and papaya pickles; pansit *luglog* (with a shrimp and duck-egg sauce); honey chicken. Consider a Philippine breakfast of rice, dried beef or marinated milkfish, and coffee or hot choco-

late. ⊠ *432 San Andres St. at Roxas Blvd., Malate,* ☎ *2/524–7671.
No credit cards.*

Seafood

$$$ ✕ **Via Mare Seafood Specialty Restaurant.** This place is an institution—
★ a gracious setting for seafood in many guises. Fat live oysters are flown
in daily from the Visayas, and prime seafood—salmon and trout,
Alaskan cod and blue marlin, scallops and lobster—is transformed into
international and Asian delights such as Thai chili crab, country-style
Philippine milkfish, and *bacalao a la Vizcaina* (salt cod in the Spanish
manner, with olive oil, potatoes, and pimientos). ⊠ *Greenbelt Com-
mercial Complex, Paseo de Roxas, Makati City,* ☎ *2/893–2306 or 2/
893–2746. AE, DC, MC, V. No lunch Sun.* ⊠ *Penthouse, Tektite East
Tower, Exchange Rd., Ortigas Center, Pasig City,* ☎ *2/631–7980 or
2/631–7981. AE, DC, MC, V. No lunch Sun.*

Spanish

$$$ ✕ **La Tasca.** Manila's well-deserved fame for the best Spanish cuisine
★ in Asia owes much to restaurants like this one. The basic menu offers
such favorites as *sopa de ajo* (garlic soup); paella Valenciana, *marinera*
(all seafood), or *negra* (with squid); *fabada Asturiana* (bean stew with
bacon); and bacalao a la Vizcaina. For dessert you might try *canon-
igo* (meringue, mangoes, and syrup). There are also changing specials.
⊠ *Legaspi St., Greenbelt Commercial Center, Makati City,* ☎ *2/893–
8586 or 2/893–8556. AE, DC, MC, V. Closed Sun. No lunch Sat.*

Thai

$$$ ✕ **Flavours and Spices.** The grandest of the city's many Thai restau-
rants, this is also a store for spices and condiments. Popular dishes in-
clude *tom yam* soups (soured and spiced with lime leaves, lemongrass,
and cilantro); chicken in pandan leaf; red, green, and yellow curries;
catfish salad with green mango; *phad thai* (a dish done differently by
each Thai cook from the same basic ingredients: noodles and bean
sprouts, prawns, bits of scrambled egg, and scallions), little *takho*
cakes (steamed rice cakes in banana-leaf cups with coconut cream and
sweet corn in the bottom), and crushed-ice desserts like *tub tim grob*
(mixed fruit and gelatin bits with crushed ice) or *ruam-mit* (water chest-
nuts, sweet potatoes, jackfruit strips, and coconut milk with crushed
ice). But try as well the coconut milk soup, Thai congee, or the hot pot
in which meat, seafood, and vegetables are cooked then dipped in a
sesame-seed hot sauce. ⊠ *Garden Sq., Greenbelt Commercial Center,
Makati City,* ☎ *2/815–3029, 2/819–1375, 2/894–5624, or 2/894–
5625.* ⊠ *Ortigas Center, Ruby Rd. at Julia Vargas Ave., Pasig City,* ☎
2/632–7153, 2/632–7154, or 2/632–7155. AE, DC, MC, V.

Lodging

As the largest urban area in the country, metropolitan Manila has lodg-
ings that run the gamut from small, intimate establishments to five-
star hotels whose lobbies accentuate the grand and the grandiose.
Most hotels are in two areas: the Tourist Belt (Malate and Ermita dis-
tricts) in downtown Manila or in Makati City, Manila's Wall Street
and fashionable residential enclave. Unless otherwise noted, rooms have
private baths.

Ermita/Malate

The advantages of staying in the Tourist Belt are Manila Bay, with its
fabled sunsets, and the area's assortment of restaurants, bars, clubs,
coffeehouses, shops, and such museums as the National Museum and
the Metropolitan Museum of Art. The Cultural Center of the Philip-

pines (☞ Nightlife and the Arts, *below*) is right on Roxas Boulevard, the scenic main road that flanks the bay.

$$$$ ⊞ **Century Park Hotel.** The sunny, six-story atrium—with a two-level lobby—has been redone and given expansive marble floors and a giant chandelier. A string quartet serenades lobby loungers every evening from 4 to 8. The rooms, done in muted but cheery tones, are spacious. Ask for one with a full bay view; some rooms overlook the adjacent parking lot and shopping complex. ⊠ *Pablo Ocampo Senior St. (formerly Vito Cruz),* ☎ *2/528–8888,* FAX *2/528–1811. 500 rooms, 28 suites. 8 restaurants, bar, coffee shop, deli, pool, exercise room, nightclub, business services. AE, DC, MC, V.*

$$$$ ⊞ **Manila Hotel.** This is where General MacArthur had his unofficial
★ headquarters before World War II. Other luminaries who have stayed here include Ernest Hemingway and Douglas Fairbanks. The lobby exudes an Old World feeling, with floors of Philippine marble, *narra* wood and mahogany ceilings, and mother-of-pearl and brass chandeliers. The MacArthur Club, which is reached by a private elevator, serves complimentary breakfast. Room decor re-creates the colonial era with nostalgic artwork and intricate wood paneling that recalls traditional motifs. The best rooms face the bay and the pool. ⊠ *Rizal Park, adjacent to Quirino Grandstand,* ☎ *2/527–0011,* FAX *2/527–0022. 440 rooms, 70 suites. 7 restaurants, bar, pool, 2 tennis courts, exercise room, dock, business services. AE, DC, MC, V.*

$$$ ⊞ **Hyatt Regency.** Right on the main boulevard, this medium-size establishment has a spare but elegant lobby—graced by capiz chandeliers—that never seems crowded. The rooms all have bay views as well as wood-and-straw headboards and cane chairs. ⊠ *2702 Roxas Blvd.,* ☎ *2/833–1234,* FAX *2/833–5913. 132 rooms, 28 suites. 3 restaurants, bar, pool, exercise room, nightclub, business services, meeting rooms. AE, DC, MC, V.*

$$$ ⊞ **Manila Diamond Hotel.** The style of the lobby (or, as the staff calls it, the "tea lounge") is a mix of art deco and postmodern. The hotel fronts Manila Bay, and all the rooms have a view of the ocean. Room decor combines dark-wood paneling with art-deco touches; the eclectic motifs, with both ethnic and modernist designs, verge on the pleasantly gaudy. ⊠ *Roxas Blvd. at J. Quintos St.,* ☎ *2/526–2211,* FAX *2/ 526–2255. 472 rooms, 28 suites. 8 restaurants, bar, pool, sauna, health club, business services, meeting rooms. AE, DC, MC, V.*

$$$ ⊞ **Westin Philippine Plaza.** Luxurious and grand—a veritable resort
★ *sans* beachfront—the newly renovated Plaza has an enormous lobby with two levels. Not only is the swimming pool huge, but it also has a snack bar smack in the middle of it as well as slides for the kids. All rooms have terraces with views either of Manila Bay or of reclaimed land. The decor features rattan furnishings and a beige-and-white color scheme. ⊠ *Cultural Center complex, Roxas Blvd.,* ☎ *2/551– 5555,* FAX *2/551–5610. 552 rooms, 48 suites. 3 restaurants, bar, 3 snack bars, pool, spa, driving range, putting green, 4 tennis courts, health club, nightclub, business services, meeting rooms. AE, DC, MC, V.*

$$ ⊞ **Adriatico Arms.** This small, cozy hotel, with armchairs in the lobby and a combination coffee shop–deli, is in the heart of the Tourist Belt. The rooms are tastefully—if simply—furnished in basic black and white. The small staff treats guests like family. ⊠ *560 J. Nakpil St. at Adriatico St.,* ☎ *2/521–0736,* FAX *2/525–6214. 28 rooms. Coffee shop. AE, DC, MC, V.*

$$ ⊞ **Heritage Hotel.** Barely four years old, the spanking-white Heritage fronts the bay and isn't far from the airport. The smart-looking lobby is done in marble, brass, and colored stone inlays. The decor in the guest rooms repeats the motif of stone and brass, with deep-blue upholstery. ⊠ *Roxas Blvd. at EDSA,* ☎ *2/891–8888,* FAX *2/891–8833. 425 rooms, 28 suites. Restaurant, bar, coffee shop, pool, health club, casino. AE, DC, MC, V.*

Makati City

This district, the business capital of the country and neighbor to the airport, is not as congested as the Tourist Belt. The streets and sidewalks are wide, making it easier than elsewhere to walk around, and the hotels are near the gigantic Makati Commercial Center, which has everything from movie houses to money changers.

$$$$ 🏨 **Inter-Continental Manila.** Conservative in beige and brown motifs, this hotel reeks of sobriety—and no-nonsense security checks at the entrance. The rooms are spacious, if a bit stolid, and have access to the Internet via the TV. Businesspeople can avail themselves of rooms with work stations, fax-scanners, swivel chairs, and office supplies. ⊠ *1 Ayala Ave.,* ☎ *2/815–9711,* FAX *2/812–4389. 266 rooms, 70 suites. 6 restaurants, bar, pool, health club, disco, business facilities, meeting rooms. AE, DC, MC, V.*

$$$$ 🏨 **Mandarin Oriental.** The ambience here is discreet and elegant, with
★ a small but stately lobby done in black marble and illuminated by a cut-crystal chandelier. The rooms are scrupulously maintained and similarly elegant, with muted but rich colors. The staff is unfailingly professional and courteous, another reason (along with management's sensitivity to noise and security) that it's a favorite with many travelers. ⊠ *Makati Ave. and Paseo de Roxas St.,* ☎ *2/750–8888,* FAX *2/817–2472. 430 rooms, 29 suites. 7 restaurants, bar, pool, exercise room, nightclub, business services, meeting rooms. AE, DC, MC, V.*

$$$$ 🏨 **Manila Peninsula.** The Pen, as Manilans call it, exudes an informal
★ elegance, expressed in the wide lobby—under a giant sun-sculpted ceiling—and the understated furnishings and decor of the well-kept rooms, which are spacious enough to seem more like suites. The lobby is known as a "power spot," where politicians and others in Manila society gather for breakfast or a late-night drink. ⊠ *Makati and Ayala Aves.,* ☎ *2/810–3456,* FAX *2/815–4825. 453 rooms, 47 suites. 4 restaurants, bar, deli, pool, nightclub, business services. AE, DC, MC, V.*

$$$$ 🏨 **New World Renaissance.** A modern 25-story edifice built in 1995, this property has what's termed "internationalist" style, from its lobby to its rooms: ultramodern decor and furnishings meant to make businesspeople feel that they're really not too far from home. All the rooms have centralized bedside controls for everything—TV, lights, air-conditioning. The staff is quiet, fast, and efficient. ⊠ *Esperanza St. at Makati Ave.,* ☎ *2/811–6888,* FAX *2/811–6777. 583 rooms, 28 suites. 3 restaurants, bar, coffee shop, lobby lounge, pool, barbershop, beauty salon, health club, business services. AE, DC, MC, V.*

$$$$ 🏨 **Shangri-La Makati.** After the luxurious, soaring, light-filled lobby, the rooms here are something of a disappointment: although they're spacious and sparking clean, they have a bland, modern decor. The hotel does, however, have the metropolitan area's hottest disco, Zu. ⊠ *Ayala Ave. at Makati Ave.,* ☎ *2/813–8888,* FAX *2/813–5499. 608 rooms, 95 suites. 4 restaurants, bar, deli, pool, exercise room, dance club, business services. AE, DC, MC, V.*

$$$ 🏨 **Dusit Hotel Nikko.** Formerly the Nikko Manila Garden, this new incarnation opened in 1997. It has an elegant Spanish-Mediterranean style, including a light-filled lobby with black-marble floors and wrought-iron and wood trim. The staff is very gracious, and the location in Makati Commercial Center—with restaurants, cinemas, boutiques, and department stores—is most convenient. ⊠ *Ayala Center at EDSA,* ☎ *2/867–3333,* FAX *2/867–3888. 490 rooms, 59 suites. 7* *restaurants, bar, coffee shop, pool, health club, business services, meeting rooms. AE, DC, MC, V.*

Nightlife and the Arts

The Arts

Good guides to the city's cultural life are the *Expat Weekly* and *What's on in Manila,* distributed free by major hotels, restaurants, and tourist information centers. Check the entertainment pages of the dailies, particularly the Sunday editions.

The **Cultural Center of the Philippines** (✉ Roxas Blvd. facing Pablo Ocampo Senior St., ☎ 2/832–1125) is the country's premier institution for music, theater, dance, and the visual arts. It has a resident dance company and a theater group. The government-run center also hosts internationally known artists and musicians, sometimes in cooperation with the various cultural arms of the foreign embassies. The center's two art galleries display contemporary and traditional art.

ART GALLERIES

Ateneo de Manila Gallery (✉ Ateneo de Manila University, Katipunan Rd., Loyola Heights, Quezon City, ☎ 2/924–4432) owns a stellar collection of Philippine modern art. **Ayala Museum Galleries** (✉ Makati Ave. at Ayala Ave., ☎ 2/821–1191, 2/821–1192, or 2/821–1193) has works by well-established modern artists. **Crucible Gallery** (✉ SM Megamall, EDSA and Julia Vargas St., Building A, Artwalk, 4th floor, ☎ 2/635–6061) exhibits contemporary Philippine artists. **Galleria Duemila** (✉ SM Megamall, EDSA and Julia Vargas St., Building A, Artwalk, 4th floor, ☎ 2/633–6687) focuses on young, contemporary artists. An hour and a half's drive southwest of Manila is the **Geronimo Berenguer de los Reyes, Jr. Museum** (✉ Gateway Park, General Trias, Cavite, ☎ 2/892–2916) which has an extensive collection of 19th-century photographs, rare books, maps, and prints. Two pavilions house Chinese antiques, from the neolithic period to the Qing Dynasty.

Hiraya Art Gallery (✉ 530 United Nations Ave., Ermita, ☎ 2/523–3331) favors up-and-coming artists whose work incorporates social-consciousness themes. **Luz Gallery** (✉ Makati Ave. at Ayala Ave., ☎ 2/815–6906) is a well-known venue for established modern artists. The new, government-run **Museo ng Sining** (✉ Cultural Center complex, GSIS Building, Roxas Blvd., ☎ 2/891–6161, ext. 4940) offers a surprising range of Filipino art—from traditional to wildly modern.

CONCERTS

Free concerts are given at Rizal Park on Sunday beginning at 5 PM, usually featuring a program of popular Western and Philippine music. Well-known singers and musicians are featured. Paco Park and Puerta Real in Intramuros offer similar programs, at 6 PM on Friday and Saturday respectively, during the dry season.

DANCE

The **Cultural Center of the Philippines** (✉ Roxas Blvd.) has an acclaimed resident dance company, Ballet Philippines (☎ 2/831–7082). Two other ballet companies are **Philippine Ballet Theater**(☎ 2/631–7436) and **Ballet Manila** (☎ 2/525–1584), which performs with Russian flair. The country's premier folk-dance company is **Bayanihan Philippines** (☎ 2/521–7829), with an extensive, stylish repertoire.

FILM

Metro Manila has many cinema houses, but many of the English-language films are either the substandard B type or the Hollywood blockbuster type, though good films do turn up. During the two-week **Metro**

Manila Film Festival in June and December, only Philippine films are shown in the cinemas.

The **Alliance Française de Manille** (✉ 220 Gil Puyat Ave., Makati City, ☎ 2/813–2681), **Goethe Institute** (✉ 687 Aurora Blvd., Quezon City, ☎ 2/722–4671), **Thomas Jefferson Library** (✉ 395 Buendia Ave. Ext., Makati City, ☎ 2/818–5484), and the **University of the Philippines Film Center** (✉ Diliman campus, Quezon City, ☎ 2/963–640) offer free film screenings, ranging from silent classics to contemporary movies. The **Mowelfund Film Institute** (✉ 66 Rosario Dr., Cubao, Quezon City, ☎ 2/721–7702) holds a yearly film festival, **Pelikula at Lipunan** (Film and Society), with a selection of the best of commercial and independent Philippine films.

THEATER

The **CCP Little Theater** (✉ Cultural Center complex, Roxas Blvd., ☎ 2/832–1125, ext. 270) performs original works or plays translated into Pilipino. The **PCIB Theater** (✉ PCI Bank Tower, Paseo de Roxas, ☎ 2/840–7000, ext. 2360), presents classical chamber music and intimate dramas. **Repertory Philippines** (✉ Shangri-La Plaza Mall, Ortigas Ave., ☎ 2/633–4821 or 2/633–4825) usually does Broadway musicals.

Nightlife

Metropolitan Manila is a pleasure-seeker's paradise, with an array of nighttime activities, from the soothing to the sinful. You can listen to jazz or rock, have a drink at a bar while ogling scantily clad performers of either sex, dance madly at a disco, or have a snack and cappuccino in a lively coffeehouse.

BARS

There are really two types of bars in Manila: "girlie" bars with skimpily attired dancers and disco music, and music bar-lounges with varied musical fare. Most of the girlie bars are in Pasay City, along Roxas Boulevard. You'll also find some in Quezon City, around the Tomas Morato–Quezon Avenue intersection. They range from basic pub-cum-strip-joints to upscale places offering high-priced drinks and high-priced hostesses who will drink with gentlemen patrons and listen sympathetically as they unburden their troubles.

Music bar-lounges are scattered throughout Makati, the Tourist Belt, and beyond. **Calesa Bar** (✉ Hyatt Regency hotel, 2702 Roxas Blvd., ☎ 2/833–1234) has a reputation for launching new and noteworthy singers. **Captain's Bar** (✉ Mandarin Oriental hotel, Makati Ave. and Paseo de Roxas St., Makati, ☎ 2/750–8888), is favored by businessmen for its soothing tunes. **Guernica's** (✉ 1856 Bocobo St., Malate, ☎ 2/521–4415) features Spanish music, ballads, and folk songs. **Harry's Bar and Grill** (✉ Ayala Town Center, Alabang, ☎ no phone) is known for Harry's jazz sounds and his wife's fine bar chow. At the **Jazz Box** (✉ 1903 M Adriatico St., Malate, ☎ 02/524–5526), they place the latest jazz fusion recordings and serve finger food starting at about 5 PM. The **Prince of Wales** (✉ New Plaza Building, Greenbelt, Makati, ☎ 02/815–4274) pub packs in the expats. **San Mig Pub** (✉ Garden Mall, Greenbelt Park, Makati Ave., Makati, ☎ 2/893–8556) attracts yuppies because of its friendly buzz and its techno and disco sounds. The **Tap Room** (✉ Manila Hotel, 1 Rizal Park, ☎ 2/527–0011) has small jazz and pop ensembles.

CAFÉS

The largest concentration of cafés is in the Malate district, in and around Remedios Circle. During the dry season the café owners sometimes sponsor a street fair, with live music. **Cafe Adriatico** (✉ 1790 Adriatico St., ☎ 2/525–2509) features Philippine food, classical music, and a low-key atmosphere. **Cafe Caribana** (⊠ J. Nakpil St., ☎ 2/524–8421) has jam sessions and Caribbean-inspired food. The folks at the jungle-theme **Endangered Species Cafe** (⊠ Adriatico St., ☎ 2/524–0167) serve good international fare. **Penguin Cafe** (⊠ 604 Remedios St. at Bocobo St., ☎ 2/631–2088), which doubles as an art gallery, has a great outdoor patio, an artistic crowd, and good homemade pasta. **Windows Cafe** (⊠ 513 Remedios St., ☎ 2/526–2066) serves tasty soups and pastas and has a good view of street life.

CASINOS

Manila has three government-sanctioned casinos, each in a major hotel. **Grand Boulevard Sofitel** (⊠ 1990 Roxas Blvd., ☎ 2/507–818) occupies the hotel's entire mezzanine, with a room reserved for high rollers. **Holiday Inn-Manila Pavilion Hotel** (⊠ Maria Orosa St. at United Nations Ave., ☎ 2/522–2911). **Heritage Hotel** (⊠ Roxas Blvd. at EDSA, Pasay City, ☎ 2/891–7856). All three casinos are open 24 hours a day; games include baccarat, blackjack, roulette, and poker. You must be 18 to enter (bring your passport), and dress is smart casual (though at the Heritage you might want to err on the "smart" side).

DISCOS

Manila discos tend to be cavernous. The beat is generic and follows Western fashions. The trendiest places combine the disco fever with a few karaoke rooms and, on some nights, ballroom dancing. In Quezon City, a popular gay disco is **Club 690** (⊠ 690 Amoranto St. at Biak-na-Bato St., ☎ 2/712–3662), with shows featuring dancers and impersonators. **Euphoria** (⊠ Hotel Inter-Continental, Makati Commercial Center, Ayala Ave., ☎ 2/815–9711) is a trendy yuppie hangout. **Cats** (⊠ New World Renaissance hotel, Esperanza St. at Makati Ave., ☎ 2/811–6888) is one of the liveliest scenes for disco and ballroom dancing. **Studebaker's** (⊠ Quad III, Ayala Center, in front of Shangri-La Makati hotel, Makati, ☎ 2/892–0959) has three floors: one with a café, the second with a karaoke lounge, and the third with an often crowded disco. **Zu** (⊠ Shangri-La Makati hotel, Makati Ave. at Ayala Ave., Makati, ☎ 2/813–8888) is the current hot spot, where everyone from yuppies to entertainment celebrities to fast-rising politicos comes to see and be seen.

FOLK AND ROCK HOUSES

Chatterbox (⊠ 41 West Ave., Quezon City, ☎ 2/928–7539) caters to the college-age grunge set. **Club Dredd** (⊠ 570 EDSA at Tuason St., ☎ 2/912–8464) favors hard-core rock. **Hobbit House** (⊠ 1801 A. Mabini St., ☎ 2/521–7604) is memorable for its wait staff of little people and regular roster of folk singers; Freddie Aguilar, who's famous throughout Southeast Asia, performs twice a week. **Mayric's** (⊠ 1320 Espana St., in front of the University of Santo Tomas, ☎ 2/732–3021) has bands that alternate between punk and grunge. In Quezon City, the **'70's Bistro** (⊠ 46 Anonas St., ☎ 2/922–0492) has a mix of students and professionals listening to folk-rock bands.

NIGHTCLUBS AND CABARETS

Manila nightclubs offer floor shows that vary from performances of well-known bands and cultural presentations to highly choreographed "model" shows, in which a lot of skin is bared. **Siete Pecados** (⊠ Westin Philippine Plaza, Cultural Center complex, Roxas Blvd., ☎ 2/551–5555) favors showy bands and Latin music. **Top of the Century** (⊠ Century Park Hotel, Pablo Ocampo Senior and Harrison Sts., ☎ 2/522–1011) has well-known jazz and pop singers who have reached the top of the music scene. **Zamboanga** (⊠ 1619 Adriatico St., ☎ 2/521–9836) serves Philippine cuisine and presents regional folk dances.

Outdoor Activities and Sports

Basketball

Basketball is the Philippines' premier sport, an enduring legacy of the American colonial era. Tournaments are held by the professional **Philippine Basketball Association** (☎ 2/833–4103), as well as by the **University Athletic Association of the Philippines** (UAAP) and the **Philippine Amateur Basketball League** (PABL). The major courts are the Rizal Coliseum (☎ 2/525–2171) in Malate, and the Cuneta Astrodome (☎ 2/832–7000) in Pasay City.

Golf

Visitors are welcome at **Club Intramuros** (☎ 2/527–6613), which has 18 holes right beside the historic walls of Intramuros. Greens fees are P1,200 by day, P2,000 at night (last tee off at 8:30 PM); you can rent clubs for P500. You can play at **Puerto Azul Beach and Country Club** (⊠ Ternate, Cavite, ☎ 2/525–9248), a championship 18-hole course in a tropical resort by the sea (a 90-minute drive from Manila), for P1,800; cart rentals cost P885 and clubs rent for P600–P900. The **Westin Philippine Plaza** (⊠ Cultural Center complex, Roxas Blvd., ☎ 2/551–5555) has a putting green (P175 an hour) and a driving range (P450 for an hour and 160 balls).

Horse Racing

The **Santa Ana Race Track** (⊠ J. Rizal St., Santa Ana, ☎ 2/843–0971) and the **San Lazaro Hippodrome** (⊠ Manila Jockey Club, Felix Huertas St., ☎ no phone) feature races on Tuesday and Wednesday evenings and Saturday and Sunday afternoons.

Tennis

The **Westin Philippine Plaza Hotel** (⊠ Cultural Center complex, Roxas Blvd., ☎ 2/551–5555) has four (grass or Multiflex) lighted courts. Court fees are P270 during the day, P370 at night; lessons cost P170 an hour. The **Velayo Sports Center** (⊠ Domestic Airport Rd., ☎ 2/832–2316) has five sheltered, lighted courts on which you can play weekdays for P220–P295 an hour and on weekends for P230–P300 an hour. An hour's lesson costs P150. The **Rizal Memorial Stadium** (⊠ Pablo Ocampo Senior St., Malate, ☎ 2/525–6434) also has courts; call for details.

Shopping

As the nerve center of the country, Manila has all the shopping options, from sidewalk vendors and small retail stores to market districts and shopping centers. Nothing beats shopping in the market districts for color, bustle, and bargains—in a word, for atmosphere. Here haggling is raised to a fine art. Located in the older areas of the city, each encompasses several blocks and is a neighborhood unto itself. Crowds can be intense, and, as in any urban area, they include pickpockets. Don't be paranoid; just be alert. Shopping malls are found in relatively newer areas, such as Makati's commercial center, and in Quezon City. The malls make up in convenience what they lack in charm; prices are fixed, however, so bargaining is pointless.

Districts and Markets

Baclaran. The many stalls on Roxas Boulevard specialize in ready-to-wear clothing. Prices are supposedly lowest on Wednesday, when the weekly devotions to Our Lady of Perpetual Help are held at the nearby Baclaran Church. The disadvantages of Wednesday shopping are the crowds and worse-than-usual traffic jams.

Divisoria. North of Binondo, this is the largest old-fashioned market district, with everything from fresh produce to cooking utensils and hardware to leather goods and handicrafts. Savvy Manilans come to browse among the assorted stalls, emporia, and department stores until they see what they want at the right price. Be especially careful of pickpockets.

A. Mabini Street. This street and those just off it have several small antiques and handicraft shops. Some reputable stores are: **Likha Antiques** (✉ 1415 A. Mabini St., ☎ 2/525–1620), **Padua Gallery** (✉ 1171 A. Mabini St., ☎ 2/562–7772), **Riba Artifacts** (✉ 1337 M. H del Pilar, ☎ 2/523–0084), **Terry Baylosis** (✉ 1185 San Marcelino, ☎ 2/523–7878 for an appointment), **Tesoro's** (✉ 1325 A. Mabini St., ☎ 2/524–3936), and **Via Antica** (✉ 1411 A. Mabini St., ☎ 2/522–0869), and **VM Antiques** (✉ 1153 M. H. del Pilar, ☎ 2/524–8243).

San Andres Market. This 24-hour Tourist Belt market is noted for its tropical and imported fruits. Bright and neatly arranged, the piles of mangoes, watermelons, custard apples, and jackfruit are above average. It's pricey, but you can bargain.

Malls and Centers

EDSA Malls. On EDSA, between Shaw Boulevard and Ortigas Avenue, loom three gigantic air-conditioned shopping malls—**Robinson's**, **Shangri-La Plaza**, and **SM Megamall**. All three have shops selling clothing, electronics, record and books, as well as fast-food areas, fine restaurants, art galleries, cinemas, and several department stores (Robinson's, Shoemart, and Rustan's). There's even an ice-skating rink. Being relatively near one another, the three malls make one monstrous bazaar, where sophisticated urbanites, foreigners, and visitors from the provinces all mingle in air-conditioned comfort. Shops and fast-food restaurants close at 9 PM; fine-dining establishments close at 10. The malls themselves shut at midnight, or whenever the last film screening lets out.

Harrison Plaza. This huge Tourist Belt center adjacent to the Century Park Hotel, on Adriatico and Pablo Ocampo Senior Streets, has department stores, supermarkets, jewelers, drugstores, boutiques, record and electronics shops, video rentals, restaurants and snack bars, and four movie houses. Opening hours vary, but all shops close at 7:30 PM, except the fast-food restaurants, which are open until 8:30.

Lao Center. Some of the better antiques shops—Katutubo, Tawalisi, Osmundo's, and JoLiza's—have recently moved to this center. It's on Arnaiz Avenue in Makati and is open Monday through Saturday 10 AM–7 PM.

Makati Commercial Center. Bounded by Makati Avenue on the west, Ayala Avenue on the north, EDSA on the east, and Pasay Road on the south, this is the biggest shopping center in the country, including several malls, a couple of gigantic department stores, two hotels, and a multitude of smaller shops. There are plazas where you can rest your feet and watch humanity stream by. Opening hours vary; shops and fast-food restaurants close at 9 PM, fine-dining establishments close at 10, and the malls themselves close at midnight or so.

Metro Manila Essentials

Arriving and Departing

BY AIRPLANE

Ninoy Aquino International Airport (NAIA; ☎ 2/832–3011 or 2/832–1901), the international air hub of the Philippines, is in Paranaque on the southern edge of Metro Manila. Domestic flights land at **Manila Domestic Airport** (☎ 2/832–0991 or 2/832–0932). For specific information on international arrivals and departures and on domestic carriers and flights, *see* Philippines A to Z, *below*.

From the Airports: The major Manila hotels have shuttles; look around for one before using another means of transport. Cabbies generally charge a fixed fee of P300 or higher for trips to the Tourist Belt. Avis (☎ 2/ 833–7897) has a taxi-coupon service, with rates averaging P450. (You buy a coupon at the booth outside customs for a fixed price of, say P350 or P400, for travel from the airport to a designated area in the city.) There are no taxi stands in the arrivals area, so you must go to the departure area on the third level. Limousine service is available for P1,600–P1,700; check at the arrivals hall. For rental cars, Hertz, Avis, and National have booths in the arrival area. To the right of the airport building at the end of the driveway are stops for public buses that pass by the Tourist Belt via Makati. They leave every 15 minutes.

In light traffic, it's a 30-minute ride from the domestic airport to Makati's hotels; getting to the Tourist Belt takes close to an hour. Manila Domestic Airport is a two-building affair with a parking area and a designated taxi line. Here airport police make sure cabbies use their meters. A ride to Makati should cost no more than P100, P150 to the Tourist Belt.

BY BUS

There are about 20 major bus companies in the Philippines and almost as many terminals in Manila. Those closest to downtown Manila and Makati are at Plaza Lawton (now called Liwasang Bonifacio, but bus signboards still say LAWTON) and along a portion of EDSA in Pasay City, not far from Taft Avenue. Another important terminal is farther north on EDSA, at the corner of New York Street, in the district of Cubao, Quezon City.

Bus companies include: **BLTB** (✉ EDSA at Aurora St., Pasay City, ☎ 2/833–5501), **Dangwa** (✉ 1600 Dimasalang, Sampaloc, ☎ 2/731– 2859), **Pantranco** (✉ 325 Quezon Blvd. Ext., near Roosevelt Ave., Quezon City, ☎ 2/833–5061), **Philtranco** (✉ EDSA and Apelo Cruz St., Pasay City, ☎ 2/833–1369), **Saulog Transit** (✉ 1377 Quirino Ave., Paranaque, ☎ 2/827–2926, 2/827–2927, 2/827–2928, 2/827–2929, or 2/827–2930), and **Victory Liner** (✉ EDSA at Aurora St., Pasay City, ☎ 2/833–0293, 2/833–5020, or 2/832–2456).

BY CAR

The best routes for leaving or entering the city are the Epifanio de los Santos Avenue (known as EDSA), the South Superhighway, the C-5 Highway, and the EDSA–North Diversion link. EDSA is the main artery connecting Pasay, Makati, Mandaluyong, Quezon, and Caloocan. The North Diversion begins in Caloocan, at a junction of EDSA, and leads to points north. The South Superhighway originates in Manila, passes through Makati with EDSA as a junction, and leads to points south. C-5 is a circumferential road that connects Pasig (a district adjacent to the EDSA malls) to the South Superhighway and destinations farther south, allowing you to bypass the often congested stretch of EDSA through Makati and Mandaluyong.

Parking has become a problem, with Manila becoming more congested. In Makati, there are parking lots and meter maids collecting P10 to P15 per hour. Be on the lookout for designated tow-away zones in Makati.

BY TRAIN

The main rail terminal, Tutuban Station in the Tondo district, has recently been completely transformed into a shopping mall. The two operational train stations are in the Paco and Makati districts. A commuter train, Metro-Tren, operates on a north–south axis during rush hours, from Paco, in Manila, to Alabang, a southern suburb.

Getting Around

Manila isn't a city for walking, though you can do so within certain areas, particularly in the Tourist Belt, on Roxas Boulevard, and in some parts of Makati. Sidewalks are generally narrow, uneven, and sometimes nonexistent. Instead, choose from a vast array of transportation, public and private, from horse-drawn carriages to elevated trains.

BY BUS AND JEEPNEY

Public buses and jeepneys (a cross between a van and a Jeep) crisscross Metropolitan Manila and are the cheapest form of travel for areas not served by the LRT, the light-rail system. Buses make sense for longer trips, and jeepneys are best for short ones. For example, a bus is recommended to reach Quezon City from Ermita, but within Ermita, or between districts, take a jeepney. The latter can accommodate 12 to 15 passengers and is perhaps the city's most colorful form of public transport, gaudily decorated and with the driver's favorite English slogan emblazoned in front. Fares average P5 to P10.

BY CAR

Between the frustration and the smoke emissions, traffic jams in Manila can reduce drivers to tears. If you don't have to drive within the city, don't. Public transportation is plentiful and cheap. If you do drive, improvisation—such as sudden lane changing—is the rule rather than the exception. Many of the nonarterial roads are narrow and become clogged during morning (7:30–10) and afternoon (3:30–7:30) rush hours. On the other hand, a car gives you flexibility (though parking has become somewhat of a problem), and you don't have to deal with cabs, some of whose meters may run faster than a speeding bullet.

Some car-rental agencies include: **Ace** (☎ 2/810–5147 or 2/812–4892), **Avis** (☎ 2/525–2206 or 2/844–8498), **Budget** (☎ 2/818–7363 or 2/816–6682), **Dollar** (☎ 2/896–9251), **Executive** (☎ 2/832–5368), **Hertz** (☎ 2/832–0520), and **National** (☎ 2/897–9023). Hiring a chauffeur-driven sedan from an agency for 10 hours will cost you, on the average, P3,000.

BY CARETELA OR CALESA

Good for short hops within a neighborhood are the horse-drawn carriages called calesas and caretelas (larger versions of calesas). They're available mostly in the older neighborhoods, such as Binondo (Chinatown), and they are inexpensive (about P30 a ride).

BY LIGHT RAIL

The **Light Rail Transit** (☎ 2/832–0423) is an elevated, modern railway, with 16 stops on a north–south axis; additional stations are under construction. It's the fastest, cleanest, and safest mode of transport in the city. The southern terminal is at Baclaran in Pasay City, the northern at Monumento in Caloocan City. A new line is being added, along EDSA; when it's completed (in early 2000 or so), it will essentially render the LRT an elliptical route. Currently, most stops are in Manila. Hours of operation are from 4 AM to 9 PM. The fare between any two stations is P5. Each station displays a guide to the routes.

BY PEDICAB OR TRICYCLE

Pedicabs (bicycles) and motorcycles with attached sidecars (tricycles) are found everywhere and provide amazingly inexpensive (P2–P5) short hops.

BY TAXI AND LIMOUSINE

Taxis aren't as inexpensive as other means of public transport, but they're still fairly cheap: a metered 3 km (2-mi) cab ride should cost about P100 (assuming you don't get caught in a traffic jam, a commonplace occurrence), plus tip. However, although rates are theoretically standard, a number of cab companies tolerate their drivers' tampering with the meters. If you feel the fare registered is exorbitant, say so politely. Often the driver will allow you to pay less than what's shown. Try to take a taxi from the better hotels, where cabs are always waiting and hotel doormen note the taxi number, which is useful in case of problems. **Avis Taxi** (☎ 2/532–5758 or 2/532–0605) is a reputable radio-cab company that adds P35 to the meter rate as a pick-up fee.

Major hotels have limo service and use mostly Mercedes-Benzes or luxury Toyota sedans. Costs are P7,000 to P8,500 for 10 hours.

Contacts and Resources

EMERGENCIES
Doctors: Call the **Philippine Medical Association** (☎ 2/928–2132) for referrals. **Dentists:** The **Philippine Dental Association** (☎ 2/899–6332 or 2/890–4609) can suggest a dentist. Finer hotels also usually have a doctor and/or dentist either on premises or on call.

Hospitals: There are emergency rooms at **Makati Medical Center** (⊠ Corner of Amorsolo and de la Rosa Sts., ☎ 2/815–9911 to –9944) and at **Manila Doctors' Hospital** (⊠ 667 United Nations Ave., near UN station on LRT, Ermita, ☎ 2/524–3011). **Pharmacies:** Mercury Drug Store, a citywide chain, has 24-hour branches in Quiapo, Plaza Miranda (☎ 2/733–2112) and Guadalupe Commercial Center, Makati, (☎ 2/843–4327). **Police:** The **Metropolitan Police Command** now has one line for all emergencies (☎ 166). The **Tourist Assistance Police** (☎ 2/524–1660 or 2/524–1724, 24 hours) can assist in cases of theft, missing luggage, or other untoward incidents.

ENGLISH-LANGUAGE BOOKSTORES
National Book Store is the biggest chain. In the Tourist Belt, try the **Harrison Plaza** branch (⊠ Adriatico and Pablo Ocampo Senior Sts., ☎ 2/525–8205). In Makati, try the **Quad Arcade** branch (☎ 2/892–5767) at the Makati Commercial Center, or the newest outlet, **Powerbooks** (☎ 2/844–3237), a cybercafé on the second floor. **Filipinas Heritage Bookshop** (⊠ Old Nielson Tower across from Manila Peninsula hotel, ☎ 2/892–1801) specializes in Philippine-published books. **Solidaridad** (⊠ 531 Padre Faura St., ☎ 2/525–5038), owned by well-known novelist F. Sionil José, is frequented by Manila's literati. The store offers political, literary, and popular titles.

TOUR OPERATORS
The average city tour takes five hours and can be arranged by the staff of most hotels or by any of the following travel agencies, which also handle out-of-town tours: **American Express** (⊠ Ground floor, Philam Life Building, in front of Holiday Inn–Manila Pavilion Hotel, United Nations Ave., ☎ 2/521–9492), **Baron Travel Corp.** (⊠ Pacific Bank Building, H. V. de la Costa St. and Ayala Ave., Makati, ☎ 2/817–4926), **Clique Traveler** (⊠ 24 Platinum St., Camella Homes, Phase 14, Las Piñas, ☎ 2/805–5714 or 2/806–6274), and **Rajah Tours** (⊠ 3/f Physicians' Tower, 533 United Nations Ave., ☎ 2/522–0541).

The Department of Tourism (☞ Visitor Information, *below*) can provide a list of English-, Spanish-, Japanese-, French-, Italian-, German-, Indonesian-, and even Hebrew-speaking guides. Guided standard day tours around Manila or to nearby Tagaytay or Pagsanjan cost P650 and up, per person, with lunch included.

Bay Cruise (☎ 2/716–0204 or 2/713–1463) offers a nightly dinner cruise of Manila Bay on a tanker-turned-luxury-cruiser, the *Tennessee Walker*. The boat leaves at 7:30 from the Manila Hotel's dock.

TRAVEL AGENCIES

The agencies that offer guided tours (☞ *above*) are travel agencies as well. There's also the venerable **Thomas Cook** (⊠ G/F Skyland Plaza, Gil Puyat Ave., Makati City, ☎ 2/816–3701 or 2/812–2446).

VISITOR INFORMATION

The **Department of Tourism** has an information center on the ground floor of its main offices (⊠ Tourism Building, Agrifina Circle, Rizal Park, T. M. Kalaw Ave., Manila, ☎ 2/522–7082, 2/524–2384, or 2/524–1703), at the mezzanine and arrival mall of the Ninoy Aquino International Airport (☎ 2/832–2964 or 2/877–1000), and at Manila Domestic Airport (☎ 2/832–3566). For information on the old walled city, contact the **Intramuros Administration** (☎ 2/527–3155).

SIDE TRIPS FROM METRO MANILA

Las Piñas

12 km (8 mi) south of Manila. Drive south from Rizal Park on Roxas Blvd., turn left on Airport Rd., turn right on Quirino Ave. and continue for 10 km (6 mi) to Las Piñas.

The world's only bamboo organ is housed in Las Piñas's 18th-century **San José Church.** The organ, built in 1795, has 121 metal pipes, 832 bamboo pipes, 22 registers, and a five-octave manual. Every February the church holds its Bamboo Organ Festival, which features well-known local and international organists. Not far from San José church is the **Sarao Motor Works,** largest manufacturer of the ubiquitous and gaudy jeepney, its original prototype a converted U.S. Army Jeep. The works are open to the public for free tours weekdays 9–5.

Tagaytay Ridge

60 km (37 mi) south of Manila. Take South Expressway to the Carmona or the Santa Rosa exit; join up with the Aguinaldo Highway, which leads to the town of Silang and right into Tagaytay.

Trees and rice fields run alongside the South Expressway, which heads south from downtown Manila to Tagaytay Ridge, 2,500 ft above sea level. Here you can view what may be the world's smallest volcano, **Taal Volcano.** It's actually a volcano within a volcano: the ridge on which you stand is the rim of a giant caldera that exploded centuries ago, forming the lake below, which encloses Taal, an active volcano. With cool temperatures and scenic vistas, Tagaytay provides welcome relief from Manila's heat and congestion.

Laguna Resorts

★ *Hidden Valley is 75 km (34 mi) southeast of Manila; Villa Escudero is 11 km (7 mi) beyond Hidden Valley. Take South Expressway to its end and turn right toward Lucena City; bear left at the Santo Tomas intersection onto the road to San Pablo City and follow it to Alaminos.*

Tucked in the foothills of two Laguna mountains is the popular **Hidden Valley** resort. Daytrippers and overnight visitors alike come here for the six natural, spring-fed pools with their pristine, bubbly (like soda!) waters whose temperatures range from lukewarm to cool. You can also hike through a rain forest dotted with giant *amlang* trees. If you opt for an overnight stay, there are 22 exquisite and peaceful cottages. The resort also offers fine dining with ever-changing menus. ⊠ *Alaminos, Laguna,* ☎ 2/818–4034 or 2/840–4112, ℻ 2/812–1609.

Villa Escudero offers the chance to experience a 1,600-acre rice and coconut plantation. Just 90 minutes from Manila, the resort makes a perfect day trip; if you like, you can stay overnight in one of the all-bamboo cottages. Upon arrival you may be greeted by children dressed in traditional outfits and playing native instruments. After being serenaded, consider a visit to the on-site museum, with its eclectic and colorful collections of war memorabilia, religious artifacts and altars, paintings, stuffed animals, and celadon pottery. For lunch, you can dine on dishes made with fresh local produce; afterward, you can go rafting on a sleepy river and dip your feet in the cool waters of a man-made waterfall. ⊠ *San Pablo, Laguna*, ☎ *2/521–0830 or 2/523–0392.* 🖂 *P670 for a day visit (includes food, entertainment, and museum entry).*

Pagsanjan

★ *130 km (80 mi) south of Manila. Take South Expressway to its end, then turn left toward Calamba (there are signs). Turn right at the first major intersection and follow signs to Pagsanjan.*

About an hour and a half southeast of Manila, the town of Pagsanjan was used by Hollywood director Francis Ford Coppola for his epic film *Apocalypse Now* (older residents complain the town hasn't been the same since). Pagsanjan is known for its rapids and the numerous waterfalls that empty into the Magdapio River. The last set, the **Magdapio Falls,** cascade from about 100 ft. You can take to the river in small boats guided through the rapids by skillful oarsmen. A raft trip under the Magdapio Falls into a cave caps off the ride. This exhilarating trip offers a glimpse of rural life: villagers bathing and laundering in the river as well as an occasional carabao cooling off. Be sure to dress appropriately, and wrap your camera or other nonwaterproof gear in plastic. Life preservers aren't provided, so think twice about taking children along. The round-trip takes 2½–3 hours, and the fee is P600 per head, two per boat (oarsman appreciate a tip of P100 or so).

Corregidor Island

57 km (26 mi) due west of Manila, one-hour boat ride

In 1942, just months after the bombing of Pearl Harbor, Corregidor—a small island in Manila Bay—became a World War II battleground. It was the last bastion of Filipino and American forces fighting the Japanese. Known as "The Rock," Corregidor still has eerie battle-scarred ruins: cement roads linking the old military installations, bombed-out barracks, and giant mortars. The highlight of a tour of the island—now a national shrine—is the sound-and-light show inside the historical Malinta Tunnel. Day trips, available through Sun Cruises (☎ 2/831–8140 or 2/831–5736), cost P1,720 per person, including lunch. You can also stay overnight at the Corregidor Inn.

Legaspi City

545 km (338 mi) southeast of Manila (an hour by plane; about 11 hours by car).

Legaspi City—near the tip of southern Luzon, an hour's flight from Manila—has what may be the world's most symmetrical (and still active) volcano, towering 8,189 ft over the Bicol countryside. Aside from
★ the lure of the two- to three-day climb, **Mt. Mayon** has a volcanology/seismography station at about 2,500 ft, with a rest house that offers panoramic views of the volcano and the surrounding terrain. The station has geological displays relating to volcanoes, earthquakes, and tidal waves. You can also see a seismograph in operation.

Just 5 km (3 mi) northwest of Legaspi City are the **Cagsawa Bell Tower and Ruins,** what remains of a church buried in an 1814 eruption; more than 1,000 people who sought refuge inside perished.

NORTHERN LUZON

In northern Luzon you'll find the rugged Cordillera and the Sierra Madre ranges—with breathtaking views at elevations of 3,000 to 9,500 ft—and the narrow, beautiful, coastal plains of the Ilocos region. This area is home to hard-working, highland peoples, the Cordillerans, who are less Westernized than their lowland counterparts and whose origins can be traced to migratory groups older than the Malays. Over the centuries highland and lowland cultures have mingled through commerce, religion, education, and conflict. Nowhere is this more evident than in Baguio: many of its inhabitants are lowlanders (businesspeople, retirees, artists, students), so you're as likely to hear Pilipino as Ilocano, the regional tongue. At 5,000 ft above sea level among pine-covered slopes, Baguio is a lovely respite from the lowland heat and is a good base from which to explore the rice terraces of Banaue or the towns and Spanish-era churches of the Ilocos region. (Note that the region can be chilly at night, especially from November through February, and torrential rains mid-June through October can cause rock slides that make roads impassable.)

Baguio

❶ *246 km (153 mi) north of Manila, 196 km (121 mi) south of Vigan.*

At 5,000 ft above sea level, the air in Baguio is crisp, invigorating, and laden with the fragrance of pine trees. Billed as the "summer capital of the Philippines," this resort city was developed as a hill station during the American colonial era and is now the commercial, educational, and recreational hub of the Cordilleras. Avoid the city during the Christmas holidays and Easter week, when both the population of 280,000 and the prices of everything practically triple.

The **Mansion House** was built in 1908 as the summer residence of the American governor-generals and now serves as a site for local and international conferences. You enter through gates that replicate those of Buckingham Palace in London, and you can wander through the pleasant gardens (including one with roses). On your walk, you'll no doubt sense the leisurely pace and elegance of a vanished era. ✉ *Leonard Wood Rd.,* ☎ *74/442–2703.* 🎟 *Admission.* ⊘ *Daily 8–5.*

Across the road from the Mansion House is the 300-ft-long, pine-tree-bordered **Pool of Pines** From the vine-covered stone trellis at the far end of the pool, a long, grand staircase leads down to **Wright Park,** the most popular horseback-riding park in town (☞ *also* Outdoor Activities and Sports, *below*).

At **Baguio Botanical Garden** (✉ Leonard Wood Rd.), a pleasant arboretum a short drive or jeepney ride toward downtown Baguio from Mansion House, you'll find floral displays, ornamental plants, and sculptures of *anitos* (native gods). For a small fee, natives dressed in traditional tribal finery will pose for photos.

On a slope off the Leonard Wood Road is the **Teachers' Camp** educational/recreational compound. It's dotted with chalet-style school buildings built by the Thomasites, as the first American schoolteachers to arrive in the early days of the American colonial era were called. (They came across the Pacific on the USS *Thomas*.)

Northern Luzon

From Leonard Wood Road head to **Session Road,** downtown Bagio's steep 1-km-long main street, so named because it was the route to the government session hall during the American colonial era. Today, it's crowded with bazaars, restaurants, movie houses, offices, and cafés. This is where Baguio residents promenade.

From Session Road, a long flight of steps leads up to what may be the Philippines' only cathedral painted a light, cheery pink. With its hints of Norman architecture, **Baguio Cathedral** won't inspire raves, but it is a good perch from which to get a panoramic view of the town. The cathedral was one of the few buildings to survive World War II bombs, and it served for a while as a refugee center and trading place. ⊠ *Post Office Loop,* ☎ *74/442–4256.* ⊙ *Mon.–Sat. 6 AM–8 AM and 5 PM– 6 PM, Sun. 5 AM–10 AM and 4 PM–6 PM.*

NEED A BREAK?	**Mario's** has a first-rate Caesar salad, good steaks, seafood, and daily specials. Its success has spawned two branches in Metro Manila. ⊠ *176 Session Rd.,* ☎ *74/442-5445. AE, DC, MC, V.*

Beside the cathedral is the old **Post Office,** a tiny stone structure that harks back to colonial days. Down a steep, winding road below the cathedral is the **General Aguinaldo Museum,** named after the leader of the revolution against Spain and the subsequent war against America. Displays include historical photos, memorabilia, and a replica of the first flag of the Philippine Republic. ⊠ *Happy Glen Loop Rd.,* ☎ *74/ 444–8334.* ☜ *Admission.* ⊙ *Weekdays 1:30–5.*

★ You haven't fully experienced Baguio until you've visited its **public market,** which is between a hill and Magsaysay Avenue at the bottom of Session Road. A series of alleys with stalls on either side, the market has sections devoted to fish and meat; rice, vegetables, and strawberries, for which Baguio is famous; antiques; dry goods that range from traditional loincloths to army surplus items; and regional handicrafts such as rattan backpacks, silver jewelry, and tribal ornaments. The money changers here offer better rates than hotels or banks.

South of Session Road lies the pleasant oasis of **Burnham Park.** Named for American landscape architect Daniel Burnham, who helped plan the city, the park has spacious grounds that are perfect for an idyllic stroll or a picnic. It's popular with families and crowded on weekends. You can boat on the artificial lake or rent bicycles and go for a ride. Along the park's western edge you'll find the **Baguio Orchidarium,** where—as the name implies—vendors sell orchids, as well as the new **Pine Tree Park,** where international varieties of coniferous pine are being cultivated for research and display.

The **Club John Hay** (a former U.S. military base) is a placid, green, recreation center. Enjoy these green environs while you can; there are nascent plans to transform the grounds into an upscale resort. ⊠ *Loakan Rd. and South Dr.,* ☎ *74/442–7902 or 74/442–2101.* ☞ *Admission.* ☉ *Daily 8–5.*

Dining and Lodging

$$ ✕ **Barrio Fiesta/Pinoy Hotpot.** You can dine on Philippine dishes, including food served in a hot pot, while admiring or critiquing the 10 giant Igorot wooden statues and other carvings that decorate the interior. ⊠ *North Dr. and Session Rd.,* ☎ *74/442–6049. AE, DC, MC, V.*

$$ ✕ **Bonuan.** In a quiet neighborhood below the cathedral, this establishment specializes in seafood and Philippine cuisine. ⊠ *10-B Happy Glen Loop,* ☎ *74/442–5175. AE, V.*

$$ ✕ **O Mai Kan.** Featuring an all-you-can-eat menu, this establishment offers a style of cooking they call "Mongolian": you fill a large bowl with various meats and vegetables and select the spices you like; the staff cooks it for you. ⊠ *12 Otek St.,* ☎ *74/442–5885. AE, DC, V.*

$ ✕ **Biscotti et Cioccolate.** A variety of coffees, pastries, and home-cooked dishes are served at this tiny, charming café. The paintings hung on the wall here reveal the calling of the owners, two artists. ⊠ *Unit 5, Nevada Sq., near Club John Hay,* ☎ *74/442–7420. No credit cards.*

$ ✕ **Ionic Cafe.** Midway along Session Road, this hip place, favored by students and local bohemians, has good coffee, a full bar, salads, pastas, and sandwiches. Its second-floor windows are excellent for people-watching. ⊠ *Session Rd.,* ☎ *74/442–3867. No credit cards.*

$ ✕ **Solana's Manna.** This bakery sells mountain coffee and products made from *camote* (yam) flour as well as serving breakfast and lunch. ⊠ *Club John Hay,* ☎ *74/442–7902. No credit cards. No dinner.*

$ ✕ **Star Cafe.** The menu at this bright, busy Chinese restaurant is extensive. All the dishes are tasty and most of them are reasonably priced. ⊠ *Session Rd.,* ☎ *74/442–3148. AE, DC, MC, V.*

$$ 🛏 **Benguet Prime Hotel.** Right in the heart of busy downtown, this architecturally challenged hotel has no lobby to speak of and little in the way of decor. But what it lacks in charm it makes up for in convenience, and its rooms are spacious and clean. ⊠ *Session Rd. at Calderon Rd.,* ☎ *74/442–7066,* FAX *74/442–8132. 51 rooms. Restaurant, room service. AE, DC, V.*

$$ 🛏 **Burnham Hotel.** Rooms at this small hotel near Session Road are clean and wood-paneled. Avoid those on the ground floor, which can be noisy. ⊠ *21 Calderon Rd.,* ☎ *74/442–2331 or 74/442–5117,* FAX *74/442–8415. 18 rooms. Restaurant, room service. AE, DC, V.*

$$ 🛏 **Mountain Lodge.** In a quiet area, this cozy establishment is decorated with local artifacts and has a dining area with a terrace and a lobby with a fireplace. Guest rooms are clean and simply furnished.

✉ *27 Leonard Wood Rd.,* ☎ *74/442–4544,* ꜰᴀx *74/442–6175. 21 rooms. Restaurant, bar. DC, MC, V.*

$$ 🏨 **Munsayac Inn.** Small but well maintained, this family-run hotel has a pleasant ambience. Long patronized by missionaries, the inn will appeal to those who like their lodgings on the quiet side. The rooms are neat, with locally woven blankets, TVs, and refrigerators. ✉ *125 Leonard Wood Rd.,* ☎ *74/442–2451. 20 rooms. Restaurant, lobby lounge, refrigerators. AE, DC, MC, V.*

$–$$ 🏨 **Casa Amapola.** Once a family residence, this pension retains a fam-
★ ily-style informality. What was once the living room is now a lounge where guests meet informally, and there's a terrace where you can breakfast while watching the fog lift from the surrounding hills. If you want more privacy, ask to stay in one of the three-story chalets with verandas and kitchens. ✉ *46 First Rd., Quezon Hill,* ☎ *74/442–3406,* ꜰᴀx *74/443–7911. 13 rooms, 3 chalets. Dining room. AE, V.*

$ 🏨 **Tepeyac Hotel.** Placed high among the pine trees and removed from city bustle, Tepeyac has clean, comfy, motel-style rooms and nice pine furnishings in the airy hallways. It's quiet and informal. ✉ *177 Leonard Wood Rd.,* ☎ ꜰᴀx *74/442–3956. 19 rooms. Café, lobby lounge. AE, DC, MC, V.*

Nightlife and the Arts

THE ARTS

Baguio has a lively arts scene, inspired by the tribes and indigenous Cordillera cultures. Poetry readings, art exhibits, dance, music, and performance art constitute a cornucopia of creative activity. Every February the city holds the Flower Festival, centered on Session Road. On alternate years, usually around October, the Fiber Web event showcases hand-loom weavers. The **Baguio Arts Guild** (☎ 74/442–8489) and other civic groups organize the biannual Baguio Arts Festival in late November or early December. **Christine's Art Gallery** (✉ 23 Chuntug St., ☎ 74/443–9659), is a showcase for contemporary local artists.

NIGHTLIFE

Perk Cafe and Pub (✉ Top of Session Rd. YWCA, ☎ 74/442–3568) hosts folk and rock bands on weekends. **Rumors** (✉ 55 Session Rd., ☎ no phone) is a low-key bar-lounge with tasty appetizers; you can also hear live music here from time to time. **Spirits** (✉ 22 Otek St. at Burnham Park, ☎ 74/442–3097) is a lively disco in a rambling, wooden, colonial-era house, which, with its gingerbread details, is itself worth a close look.

Outdoor Activities and Sports

HORSEBACK RIDING

There are ponies and larger horses for both children and adults at **Wright Park**; the fee is P100 an hour. You can ride among the casuarina groves in the park or along a trail around the mountain toward Mansion House. The Baguio "pony-boys" act as guides and/or riding instructors; their hourly fee is about P120.

Shopping

Easter Weaving School (✉ Easter School Rd., ☎ 74/442–4972) sells highland blankets and clothing woven on the premises. For silvercraft, try **Ibay's** (✉ Lion Center, Governor Pack Rd., ☎ 74/442–7082). At **Munsayac's Handicraft** (✉ 21 Leonard Wood Rd., ☎ 74/442–2451) you'll find good wood carvings, brass, and silverware For items made of ikat, try **Narda's** (✉ 151 Upper Session Rd., ☎ 74/442–2992). **PNKY Woodworks** (✉ Nevada Sq., in front of John Hay, ☎ 74/444–5418) has tasteful wood furnishings—antique and brand-new. The **St. Louis Silver Shop** (✉ St. Louis High School, Assumption Rd., ☎ 74/442–2139) sells conventional, well-crafted silver items. **Tu-**

cucan (⊠ Upper Level, Maharlika Building, Baguio Public Market, ☎ 74/442–4169) has unusual artifacts, from baskets to beads.

BALATOC MINES – Experience the life of a gold miner on a tour of these nonoperational mines, a 40-minute ride via Loakan to the town of Itogon, 17 km (10 mi) southeast of Baguio. First you'll view a small museum with displays of rock samples and mining equipment. Afterward, outfitted in miner's gear, you'll take a train ride into the mine with a guide who explains the milling of gold ore and the production of gold bullion. ⊠ *Benguet Lab, 141 Abanao St. Ext., Baguio,* ☎ *74/447–2610.* ☜ *Admission.* ⊘ *Daily 7–4.*

TAM-AWAN VILLAGE – At the area's newest cultural attraction, a 15-minute ride from Baguio's city hall, you can see nine reconstructions of traditional grass-roof houses. You can also learn about the tribal life of the Ifugao—one of the Cordilleras's indigenous peoples—take a traditional-art workshop, and have a great cup of coffee. ⊠ *Pinsao Rd., Pinsao,* ☎ *73/446-2949.* ☜ *Admission.* ⊘ *Daily 8-5.*

Banaue

★ ❷ *196 km (122 mi) northeast of Baguio on mountain roads with dizzying switchbacks and long unpaved stretches.*

Looking like giant steps to the sky, the Banaue rice terraces are spectacular, man-made paddies terraced into the mountainsides of Mayaoyao and Carballo by the Ifugao, a highland tribe, more than 2,000 years ago. If placed end to end, these terraces would extend for 22,500 km (14,000 mi) or halfway around the world. Some of the terraces can be seen from Banaue itself, but the best views are in the countryside. A 1½-hour hike (ask for directions) or a 20-minute drive from Banaue proper will take you to a scenic viewpoint on a promontory. Wizened Ifugao women in native dress will pose for a little money.

Dining and Lodging

$ ✕ **Cool Winds.** Simple, inexpensive fare is the speciality of this spot near the town market. It's a favorite of locals and backpackers. ⊠ *Town Market,* ☎ *73/386–4023. No credit cards.*

$$ ✕🏨 **Banaue Hotel.** Each room here has a terrace and a good view of the town and valley. The decor throughout is reminiscent of that in a country lodge. The informal restaurant serves American-style breakfasts, Continental food, and such Philippine regional dishes as pinakbet. The dining room is large and airy—with bright red decor, native wall hangings, and a garden view—and the service is superb. The hotel also puts on a cultural show of Ifugao dances (free for guests) nightly at 8. Afterward the dancers try to get you to join in for an impromptu session. ⊠ *Banaue,* ☎ FAX *73/386–4087;* ☎ *2/812–1984 in Manila. 90 rooms. Restaurant, lobby lounge, pool. AE, DC, MC, V.*

$ 🏨 **Banaue View Inn.** In this pleasant inn high above the town, the rooms are comfortable and clean. What distinguishes this place is its family museum, which contains a well-known anthropologist's documents and memorabilia—probably the best cultural attraction in Banaue. ⊠ *Off the rd. to Bontoc,* ☎ *73/486–4078. No credit cards.*

$ 🏨 **Sanafe Lodge.** Near the city market, Sanafe is a combination dormitory and hotel, with a small lobby overlooking rice terraces. Private rooms are small but clean; eight of them have private baths. There are two less-expensive dorm rooms that sleep eight and are spartan but also clean. The resident manager is a gold mine of information on the area. ⊠ *Banaue,* ☎ *73/386–4085; 2/721–1075 in Manila. 16 rooms. Restaurant. No credit cards.*

Outdoor Activities and Sports

HIKING

The main outdoor activity in the Banaue area is hiking, and you can hire a guide for about P300 and up, per person. Several well-marked trails go to and through the rice terraces, for hikes that range from a couple of hours to a whole day. Check with the local visitor information center for more information (☎ 73/386–4085) or contact the **Banaue Hotel** (☞ Dining and Lodging, *above*), which has a list of treks and guides and even has walking sticks available, free of charge.

Shopping

Near the town market, which has handicrafts stalls, is the small **trade center,** where you'll find such souvenirs as baskets, handwoven backpacks, and wood carvings.

Batad and Banga-An

❸–❹ *9 km–16 km (6 mi–10 mi) northeast of Banaue on rough roads.*

Even more spectacular than Banaue are the Ifugao villages of Batad and Banga-An, both set among the rice terraces. To reach them from Banaue you can take a 60-minute jeepney ride along the main and only road to the Bangaan Inn, and then hike the easy trail down to Banga-An (another 30 minutes). Alternatively, you could ask the jeepney driver to drop you at "the junction" from which you can then make the 90-minute hike up to Batad. (Note that for about P40, you can spend the night in an Ifugao rest house in Batad). En route you'll pass pine-covered slopes; green valleys dwarfed by clouded peaks; far-off, pyramid-shape Ifugao huts improbably perched on crags; and mountain streams irrigating the terraces. Village life goes on pretty much as it has for centuries: rice is planted in age-old rituals and plowed with the help of the ubiquitous water buffalo. Dogs, pigs, and ducks wander about native huts, which are elevated on wooden posts. Handicrafts—rattan backpacks, baskets, and ornaments—are sold for low prices.

Sagada

❺ *50 km (31 mi) northwest of Banaue, 150 km (93 mi) northeast of Baguio.*

Deep in the central Cordilleras, among the rice terraces, is a small, tightly knit Igorot community. A favorite with adventurous backpackers, Sagada has several burial caves with hanging coffins, an underground river, waterfalls, limestone formations, and hiking trails. At the edge of the village are fruit orchards, smaller rice terraces, and the occasional *dap-ay*—the circular stone meeting place where village elders once gathered to discuss communal matters. It's worth spending at least two days here to savor the unspoiled charm, the laid back atmosphere, and the striking scenery—no phones, no malls, no pollution. Just be respectful of local customs: don't take photographs of townspeople without asking permission. Never point at individuals (it's considered intolerably rude), and, of course, don't disturb the hanging coffins.

You can begin a walk through town from **Masferre's Studio,** 15 minutes south of the town center. A Spanish mestizo who settled in Sagada and married a local, the late Eduardo Masferre chronicled the lives of the Cordilleran peoples for decades, starting in the 1930s. A collection of his photos, which have been exhibited in several countries, is on display here, and prints and postcards are for sale. ⊠ *Bontoc-Banga-An Rd.,* ☎ *no phone.* ☜ *Free.* ⊙ *Irregular hrs.*

Sagada Weaving, closer to town than Masferre's studio, is a well-known purveyor of such quality hand-loomed products as sturdy backpacks,

shoulder bags, and blankets. You can watch the Igorot women skill-
fully plying their trade, incorporating traditional designs into their weaving. ✉ *Main rd.,* ☎ *no phone.* ☉ *Daily 9–4.*

Across from Sagada Weaving, a trail winds down to a small valley where
it's easy to spot the mouth of **Matangkib Cave** and the burial coffins
stored in niches within. Respect for these remains is a must. Enter the
cave (you'll need flashlights) and you can hear the roar of an **underground river.** At press time, the cave was closed temporarily.

Not far from Sagada Weaving—proceeding south and on the same side
of the main road—is a trail that cuts across a narrow river. The trail
leads to the small **Bokong Waterfall,** set amid rice terraces, with a deep
pool that's perfect for cooling off in after a day of hiking.

Dining and Lodging

In this small village, most of the restaurants are close to the center of
town, near the town hall and the market. Prices are truly a bargain,
but credit cards are useless. The lodgings are equally a bargain—the
average cost per night is $3–$4.

$ ✕ **Country Cafe.** Come to enjoy the big fireplace and strong native cof-
fee. Short-order meals, ice cream, and homemade cakes are available.
✉ *North of town hall, on rd. to Besao,* ☎ *no phone. No credit cards.*

$ ✕ **Log Cabin Cafe.** This quiet, friendly spot serves very good dishes that
reflect some European influence. ✉ *North of town hall, on rd. to Besao,*
☎ *no phone. No credit cards.*

$ ✕ **Shamrock Cafe.** Overlooking the market, this café is one of the old-
est in town and offers breakfast, lunch, dinner, snacks, and drinks. ✉
South of town hall, on rd. to Demang, ☎ *no phone. No credit cards.*

$ 🏠 **Mapiya-aw Pension.** This pleasant guest house is surrounded by strik-
ing limestone formations and pine groves. The staff is friendly and helpful and will serve meals on request. ✉ *East of town hall, on rd. to Bontoc,*
☎ *no phone. 12 rooms. Laundry service. No credit cards.*

$ 🏠 **Masferre Cafe & Inn.** The rooms here are large, and the restaurant
has a view of rice terraces. You'll also find a gift shop that sells postcards and T-shirts. ✉ *South of town hall, on rd. to Demang,* ☎ *no
phone. 10 rooms. Laundry service. No credit cards.*

$ 🏠 **St. Joseph's Rest House.** The largest accommodation in the area is
slightly elevated, with a good view of the town and the Episcopalian
church. Rooms are spartan but clean. ✉ *East of town hall, opposite
church,* ☎ *no phone. 15 rooms. Laundry service. No credit cards.*

Outdoor Activities and Sports

The Sagada area is perforated with caves and underground rivers,
making spelunking the most exciting activity in town. For information
about which caves are open or to hire a guide, visit the **Sagada Environmental Guides Association** in the town hall. Rates for a guide depend on the size of the party but are eminently affordable. Hiking is
the area's other main outdoor activity; you can hire a guide for this as
well, or you can head into the fields and pine groves by yourself.

A pleasant trek would be a leisurely 30-minute walk to **Banga-An.** Take
in the fresh air, groves of pine trees, and scenic rice terraces. If you have
the stamina, ask the guide to take you through rice terraces to Fedil-
isan Waterfalls.

Vigan

❻ *196 km (122 mi) north of Baguio, 78 km (48 mi) south of Laoag.*

The capital of the Ilocos Sur province, a scenic four-hour drive from
Baguio, is Vigan, a small coastal city that dates from the early years

of Spanish colonization. It has some of the best-preserved Spanish-influenced architecture in the country, suggesting how Manila's Intramuros would have looked had it not been heavily damaged during World War II. The Viva Vigan Festival is celebrated during the first week of May, the best time to see Ilocano culture proudly unfurl. There's a crafts fair, and several colonial-era homes are opened to the public.

Set in a colonial-era residence that used to be occupied by a revolutionary priest, the **Burgos Museum** has a collection of dioramas, artifacts, and paintings (including a series that depicts a local revolt) relating to the area's history, as well as period furniture. ⊠ *Burgos St.,* ☎ *no phone.* 🖭 *Admission.* ⊘ *Tues.–Sun. 9–noon and 1–5.*

It's about a 10-minute walk from the Burgos Ayala Museum to the town's main landmark, the 16th-century **Vigan Cathedral** (also known as the Cathedral of St. Paul), a massive, whitewashed, brick-and-wood structure with a tile roof. Chinese lions guard the portals and the gleaming silver altar within. It's a short stroll northwest of the cathedral to the **Old Quarter,** which you can explore in about half a day. The buildings have whitewashed brick walls, tile roofs, sliding capiz windows, and lofty interiors. General Luna, Crisologo, De los Reyes, and Bonifacio streets have row upon row of these edifices—perfect backdrops for Westerns or Gothic films, for which, in fact, they have been used.

Dining and Lodging

Seafood dishes and vegetables are the specialty on the Ilocos coast. Try fried squid, shrimp marinated in vinegar and peppers, or the grilled catch of the day. In Vigan's plaza, you can taste the local delicacy, an empanada stuffed with vegetables. Also worth trying are *ipon,* delicious small fish caught seasonally, and pinakbet flavored with bagoong.

$ ✕ **Cool Spot.** Choose one of the tasty regional dishes on display behind a glass counter in this wide, airy, thatch-and-bamboo hut. ⊠ *Burgos St.,* ☎ *77/722–2588. No credit cards.*

$$ 🖭 **Cordillera Inn.** The rooms at this inn, a colonial-era building with broad stairways and good views of the Old Quarter, are on the bare side but clean. Climb up to the roof for an excellent panorama. ⊠ *General Luna and Crisologo Sts.,* ☎ *77/722–2526. 23 rooms. Restaurant, laundry service. No credit cards.*

$ 🖭 **Villa Angela.** This lovely turn-of-the-century home with period furniture and a pleasant garden has been converted into a pension. The living room has family memorabilia on display. In keeping with the spirit of the place, the rooms have high ceilings, four-poster beds, mosquito nets, and capiz windows. ⊠ *Quirino Blvd. at Liberation St.,* ☎ *77/722–2914. 6 rooms. Laundry service. No credit cards.*

Shopping

In the bustling **central market** you'll find the usual assortment of produce and handicrafts. You should also check out the *burnay,* or **potters' district,** about a 15-minute walk from the cathedral. Here you can buy terra-cotta jars and urns from the potters themselves.

Check out **Ciudad Fernandina** (⊠ 888 Plaza Burgos, ☎ 77/722–2888), a shop that sells antiques in the Old Quarter. **Lucy's Antique Shop** (⊠ 14 Crisologo St., ☎ 77/722–2099) is also in the Old Quarter. You'll find woven items at **Rowilda's Handloom Weaving** (☎ 77/722–2732) right across from the Cordillera Inn. In the town of Santiago, just south of Vigan, there's **Cora's Ethnic Handwoven,** where prized local weaving is for sale.

En Route North of Vigan are a number of good beaches (most without resorts) near the towns of Cabugao, Sinait, Currimao, and Pangil. Fishermen store their boats and nets on Sinait's white-sand beach, Pug-os.

Paoay

★ ❼ *258 km (160 mi) north of Baguio, 50 km (31 mi) north of Vigan, 20 km (12 mi) south of Laoag.*

Between Vigan and Laoag are towns whose churches are fine examples of what a local writer once termed Filipino baroque—unique, even rococo, combinations of Western and Asian styles. Among the most impressive are Santa Maria, with its 85 stately broad steps, and Magsingal, with a small but intriguing museum nearby. But the majestic **Paoay Church** is a must-see. The crenellations and turrets, massive curlicued buttresses, exterior stairways, and niches are reminiscent of a Javanese temple. Beside this splendid fusion of styles is a belfry made of limestone, used as an outpost during the Revolution of 1896 against Spain and by guerrillas during the Japanese occupation in World War II.

Laoag

❽ *78 km (48 mi) northeast of Vigan, 278 km (172 mi) north of Baguio.*

Laoag, another coastal Spanish colonial town, doesn't have the wealth of architecture and sights of Vigan. Still, the 17th-century **Laoag Cathedral** and its **Sinking Bell Tower** are worth visiting. The church is heavily buttressed (a protection against earthquakes) and has two exterior stone stairways, urn ornamentation, and foliate capitals. North of the church is a bell tower that has sunk a little more than a yard, so that its portal is barely visible.

Dining and Lodging

$$$ ✕▢ **Fort Ilokandia.** This sprawling hotel is made up of several two-story
★   buildings, whose style and room decor suggest the Old Quarter residences of Vigan. Tiled walkways connect the buildings, which are nestled among sand dunes (the hotel has a good, black-sand beach). The spacious, wood-paneled Pamulinawen restaurant serves very solid Philippine dishes—including pinakbet and beef *tapa* (cured, dried strips of meat served with a vinegar-and-garlic sauce)—as well as some Continental fare. ✉ *Barangay 37, Calayab,* ☎ *77/772−1166,* ☏ *77/772−1411. 264 rooms. Restaurant, bar, pool, beach, dance club. AE, DC, MC, V.*

OFF THE   **THE BATANES −** The country's northernmost islands, the Batanes are
BEATEN PATH   closer to Taiwan than to Luzon. The rugged cliffs, rolling grassy fields akin to the Scottish moors, scenic coastline, and idyllic towns with unique stone-walled homes make for great treks. It's best to visit between November and May, the relatively dry season before the onslaught of monsoon storms (these isles are in the middle of the typhoon belt). Allow yourself extra time here; a sudden wind even in the dry season may lead to a flight's cancellation. PAL (☞ Northern Luzon Essentials, *below*) flies from Manila to Basco, the capital, thrice weekly, with a stopover in Laoag. Be sure to book your flight well in advance, as these islands are popular with locals.

Northern Luzon Essentials

Arriving and Departing

BY AIRPLANE
Philippine Air Lines (PAL; ☎ 74/442−2695 or 74/442−6627) flies from Manila Domestic Airport to Loakan Airport in Baguio; a cab ride

from the airport into town should cost approximately P100. PAL also has flights to Laoag Airport; there are public jeepneys available at Laoag Airport that ply the Vigan–Laoag route. (Note that, at press time, PAL was working through financial difficulties and labor disputes that may have affected schedules; contact the airline for details on service.)

BY BUS

A number of bus companies run daily trips from Manila to northern Luzon—particularly to Baguio, Vigan, and Laoag—on an hourly basis. For information, contact the Manila offices of Pantranco or Victory Liner (☞ Metro Manila Essentials, *above*). There are no nonstop bus routes to Sagada from Manila; you have to change in Baguio, at the terminal in front of the market, or catch a jeepney from Banaue.

BY CAR

From Manila it's a relatively smooth six-hour drive to Baguio via the North Diversion Highway, which begins at EDSA, links up to the MacArthur Highway, and leads to the zigzagging Kennon Road. If Kennon is closed for repairs, you can take Naguilian Road or the Marcos Highway (which has a Mt. Rushmore–like bust of the late dictator), farther north along the coast. Add an extra hour for these routes to Baguio. Because of rough road conditions, it isn't advisable to drive to Banaue—take a bus or join a tour group originating in Manila.

Getting Around
BY BUS

Buses between towns are numerous and cheap, and most terminals are near the public markets. Buses to and from Manila and Vizan arrive at and depart from Baguio's terminal on Governor Pack Road, at the top of Session Road. You can catch buses to Sagada Baguio's second terminal on Magsaysay Avenue. For tickets contact Lizardo Bus Company (☎ 74/442–2741 or 74/443–8719).

BY CAR

On the coastal plains and around the cities of Baguio, Vigan, and Laoag, the roads range from good to excellent. Northeast of Baguio, however, deeper into the Cordilleras, they can be very bad, and public transportation is a better bet.

BY JEEPNEY

Plentiful and good for short routes, jeepneys begin and end their routes at or near the public market. They can also be hired for out-of-town trips. The average cost of a ride, for about a kilometer (½ mi), is a mere P2.

BY TAXI

Baguio has the region's only cabs—small Japanese models. Rides within the central part of town average P80.

Contacts and Resources
BOOKSTORES

In Baguio city, paperbacks are available at **The Bookmark** (✉ EDT Building, Session Rd., ☎ 74/442–4912).

EMERGENCIES

Fire: ☎ 74/160 or 74/442–2222. **Hospital:** General Hospital (✉ Governor Pack Rd., Baguio, ☎ 74/169 or 74/442–4216). **St. Louis University Hospital** (✉ Assumption Rd., Baguio, ☎ 74/442–5701). **Pharmacy:** Mercury Drug Store (✉ Session Rd. near Magsaysay Rd., Baguio, ☎ 74/442–4310) is open until 9 PM. **Police:** ☎ 74/166.

TOUR OPERATORS

It's best to arrange tours to and throughout northern Luzon with tour operators and travel agencies in Manila.

VISITOR INFORMATION
Baguio: ⊠ Governor Pack Rd., ☎ 74/442–7014.

THE VISAYAS, MINDANAO, AND PALAWAN

While northerners are known for their industry and frugality, southerners are easygoing, gregarious, and musical. The land and seas are especially fertile, yet some of the worst pockets of poverty are also found here, arising out of centuries-old feudalism, an overdependence on cash crops, and the often tragic effects of militarization in areas where the New People's Army (NPA) is active. (The Communist/Maoist NPA, around since 1969, has a socialist vision that's violently at odds with the Philippine government.) You need not worry about being caught up in the conflict: armed clashes almost always occur in remote rural areas, and left-wing insurgency is on the decline.

Geographically, the Visayas are the center of the Philippines—bound on the north by Luzon and on the south by Mindanao. This group of islands has some of the best beaches and resorts in the country, unusual natural attractions, and non-Hispanicized minority cultures. The populations of Mindanao (the nation's second-largest island) and Palawan (the westernmost isle) are intriguing mixes of Christians, Muslims, and indigenous cultures. Large areas of both islands have been settled by mostly Christian migrants from Luzon and the Visayas. In Mindanao, this has led to an ongoing radical Muslim secessionist movement, though peace talks are being conducted between the government and leaders of the movement. To really enjoy the region, take the time to appreciate the affectionate, fun-loving ways of its people, explore the beaches and beautiful scenery, and take in the charm of small, often historic towns and cities. Note that the places discussed below are all easily accessible by plane from Manila or from Cebu.

Cebu City

❶ *1 hour by plane from Manila.*

This small but strategically important port has the advantages of a big city—restaurants, shops, lodgings, and businesses—but few of the drawbacks. The "Queen City of the South" and capital of Cebu Island, it's not far from Homonhon, where Ferdinand Magellan claimed the country for Spain in 1521. Founded by the conquistador Miguel Lopez de Legaspi in 1571, Cebu was the first Spanish settlement in the Philippines. Though little is left of the original town, you can still spend a fascinating and rewarding day of sightseeing here. Most of the historical sights are within walking distance of one another in the downtown area near the port.

Fort San Pedro, the country's oldest and smallest fort, was built in 1565. The three bastions with turrets for cannons give it a triangular shape. The parapets afford a good view of the sea—a necessity in the days when the settlement was a target for pirate raids. ⊠ *Port area,* ☎ *32/96518.* 🎫 *Admission.* ⊙ *Daily 8–noon and 1–5.*

From Fort San Pedro it's a 10-minute walk to Plaza Rizal, where **Magellan's Cross,** the original cross brought over by the famed Portuguese navigator, is housed. You won't actually *see* the original: residents believe the cross has miraculous powers and used to take slivers from it, so it has been encased within the hollow wooden cross that's suspended from the ceiling of a pavilion on Magallanes Street.

The Visayas, Mindanao, and Palawan

Romblon
Odiongan
Tablas Island
Sibuyan Island
Masbate
Uson
MASBATE
Balud
Cotarman
Laoang
Palapag
3
SAMAR
Calbayog City
Catbalogan
4 Boracay Island
Kalibo
THE VISAYAS
Roxas City
Visayan Sea
Biliran Island
Culasi
PANAY
Passi
1
Cadiz City
Bantayan Island
Escalante
Silay City
Talisay
2
Iloilo City
San Carlos City
CEBU
Miagao
3
Bacolod City
Guimaras Strait
Guimaras Island
Cebu City **Matcan Island**
1
Panay Gulf
Naga
Carcar
Kabankalan
Tañon Strait
Badian Island
Bohol Strait
Cauayan
Bais City
Sipalay
NEGROS
Tanjay
Hinob-an
Bayawan
Santa Catalina
Dumaguete City
1
Siquijor Island
LEYTE
Burauen
Ormoc City
Leyte Gulf
2
Baybay
Hilongos
Maasin
Panaon Island
Dinagat Island
BOHOL
Tagbilaran City
Chocolate Hills
Mindanao Sea
Camiguin Island
Surigao City
Cabadbaran
1
Butuan City
Gingoog City
Cagayan de Oro City
1
Puerto Princesa
Palawan
9
Dapitan City
Dipolog City
Oroquieta City
7
Iligan City
Marawi City
MINDANAO
Valencia
Lake Lanao
Quezon
Sulu Sea
N
Pagadian City
Tagum
3
Parang
Mt. Apo National Park
Davao City
7
5
Zamboanga Peninsula
Cotabato City
Sultan Kudarat
Dinaig
Magpet
Samal Island
6
8 Zamboanga City
Moro Gulf
Pikit
Kidapawan
Santa Cruz Island
Lamitan
5
Davao Gulf
Isabela
Basilan Island
N
Malita
Celebes Sea
Polomolok
General Santos City
Glan
N

0 ___ 100 miles
0 ___ 150 km

Opposite Magellan's Cross is the 18th-century **Basilica Minore** (closed daily noon–2 PM), built in typical Spanish baroque style. It houses the nation's oldest Catholic image—that of **Santo Niño**, the Holy Infant— brought over by Magellan and presented to Queen Juana of Zebu. En- shrined in glass and ornamented with gold and precious stones, the icon stands atop a side altar, venerated by a constant stream of devotees. The candle-bearing, middle-age women outside the church will, for a small fee, pray to and dance for the Santo Niño on your behalf.

A short stroll from Basilica Minore is the oldest street in the country, named after Cristóbal Colón, otherwise known as Christopher Colum- bus. Formerly the heart of the Parian District (or Chinatown), **Colón Street** is now downtown Cebu's main drag. Here modernity crowds in on you in the form of movie houses, restaurants, department stores, and other commercial establishments.

NEED A BREAK?   At the **Lighthouse Restaurant,** a classic Cebu place, you'll find Filipino seafood dishes and a native ambience. ⊠ *Gen. Maxilom Ave.,* ☎ *32/ 78126. AE, DC, MC, V.*

From the eastern end of Colón Street, it's a short walk to **Casa Gorordo,** the former residence of Cebu's first bishop, Juan Gorordo. Now re- stored, the century-old wood house has a tile roof, capiz windows, a wide veranda, and a fine collection of furnishings from the last cen- tury. The ground-floor art gallery displays contemporary works by Philip- pine artists. ⊠ *35 Lopez Jaena St.,* ☎ *32/255–5630.* 🖼 *Admission.* ⊙ *Daily 9–noon and 2–5:30.*

★   The **University of San Carlos Museum,** a 20-minute walk from Casa Gorordo, has an extensive collection of seashells, fauna, and relics: local prehistoric stone and iron tools, burial jars, and pottery. Another sec- tion focuses on traditional clothing and ornaments of various tribes. ⊠ *Rosario and Junquera Sts.,* ☎ *32/72419.* 🖼 *Admission.* ⊙ *Week- days 9–noon and 1:30–5:30; weekends and holidays by appointment.*

Incongruously set in an expensive suburb known as Beverly Hills is a **Taoist Temple,** dedicated to the teachings of the 6th-century BC Chi- nese philosopher Lao-tzu. You can get here from downtown Cebu by taxi (referred to as a PU, for "public utility") for about P80. A flight of 99 steps leads up to the temple from the road. Come for the panoramic views of the city, the colorful and ornate Chinese architec- ture, and to have your fortune read. ⊠ *Beverly Hills,* ☎ *32/93652.* 🖼 *Free.* ⊙ *Daily until dark.*

Dining and Lodging

Sinugba is a Cebuano method of grilling fish and shellfish over coals. Western- and Asian-style dishes are also available. As the second- largest city in the Philippines, Cebu City has a full range of accom- modations, from the inexpensive to the costly. A number of nearby islands, namely Badian and Mactan, have attractive beach resorts.

$$$ ✕ **Lantaw Gardens.** Here you can feast on a splendid, well-priced
★   buffet in an open-air garden setting while enjoying a folk-dance show and scenic views of the city. ⊠ *Cebu Plaza, Nivel Hills, Lahug,* ☎ *32/ 231–1231. AE, DC, MC, V.*

$ ✕ **Golden Cowrie.** This informal, screen-enclosed, outdoor establish- ment serves inexpensive grilled seafood as well as typical Philippine cuisine. ⊠ *Salina at La Guardia St.,* ☎ *32/92633. No credit cards.*

$ ✕ **Grand Majestic.** Dim sum and other Chinese fare are served here at
★   reasonable prices. ⊠ *Archbishop Reyes Ave.,* ☎ *32/232–1103. AE, DC, MC, V.*

$ ✕ **Vienna Kaffeehaus.** The Austrian proprietor of this establishment
★ has re-created the ambience of a Viennese coffeehouse, complete with
Viennese food, newspapers, and magazines. ⊠ *Ground floor, Wayne's
Inn, Banilad, Mandaue,* ☎ *32/253–1430. No credit cards.*

$$$$ 🏨 **Badian Beach Club.** On Badian Island, just off the southwest coast
of Cebu and about a three-hour drive from the city, this resort has a
lovely beachfront, scenic bay views, sailboats, and a variety of water
sports. The staff schedules a cultural show during the buffet dinners.
⊠ *Badian Island,* ☎ *32/253–6452 or 32/253–6364,* FAX *32/253–
3385. 34 cottages, 16 suites. 3 restaurants, 3-hole golf course, beach,
dive shop, dock, snorkeling, boating. AE, DC, MC, V.*

$$$$ 🏨 **Cebu Plaza.** A luxurious hotel, the Cebu Plaza has panoramic views,
★ sprawling grounds, and a clientele consisting mainly of Japanese and
Chinese tourists. The best rooms are those with a view of the city. ⊠
Nivel Hills, Lahug, ☎ *32/231–1231,* FAX *32/231–2071. 417 rooms.
2 restaurants, 3 bars, pool, 2 tennis courts, shops, dance club, meeting rooms. AE, DC, MC, V.*

$$$$ 🏨 **Maribago Bluewater Beach Resort.** About 30 minutes from the city,
this upscale resort has all the comforts and water sports you'd want.
The brightly decorated guest rooms are furnished with locally made
rattan furniture. ⊠ *Buyong St., Maribago, Mactan Island,* ☎ *32/253–
1620,* FAX *32/492–0218. 76 rooms. 3 restaurants, coffee shop, pool,
barbershop, driving range, tennis court, exercise room, beach, dive shop,
dock, snorkeling, windsurfing, boating, fishing. AE, DC, MC, V.*

$$$$ 🏨 **Shangri-La's Mactan Island Resort.** On a stunningly landscaped site
near the airport, this palatial luxury resort has its own beach cove, two
lagoon-style swimming pools, and lush tropical gardens. The comfortable, well-maintained rooms are done in tropical motifs and have
such amenities as satellite TV. ⊠ *Punta Engano Rd., Mactan Island,*
☎ *32/813–8888,* FAX *32/813–5499. 490 rooms, 56 suites. 8 restaurants, bar, coffee shop, 2 pools, massage, 2 tennis courts, exercise
room, beach, boating, dive shop, fishing, nursery. AE, DC, MC, V.*

$$ 🏨 **Marriott Hotel.** A smart business address, this 12-story building is
smack in the heart of the Cebu Business Park, by the doorstep of the
Ayala Shopping Center. Rooms are cheery and modern. ⊠ *Cardinal
Rosales Ave.,* ☎ *32/232–6100,* FAX *32/232–6101. 303 rooms, 22
suites. 2 restaurants, coffee shop, pool, health club, business services,
meeting rooms. AE, DC, MC, V.*

$$ 🏨 **Montebello Villa.** This hotel has nice gardens, cheerfully decorated
rooms, and a cultivated colonial-era ambience. It's in a quiet neigh-
borhood. ⊠ *Banilad,* ☎ *32/231–3681,* FAX *32/231–4455. 142 rooms.
2 restaurants, coffee shop, pool, 2 tennis courts, casino, meeting rooms,
travel services. AE, DC, MC, V.*

$$ 🏨 **Park Place Hotel.** In the heart of downtown, this neat, cozy estab-
lishment is patronized mostly by businessmen on moderate budgets.
⊠ *Fuente Osmena Ave.,* ☎ *32/253–1131,* FAX *32/634–7509. 114
rooms. Restaurant, bar, café, shops, meeting rooms. AE, DC, MC, V.*

Outdoor Activities and Sports

BEACHES

In and around Cebu are a number of beaches and beach resorts (☞
Dining and Lodging, *above*). Day visitors can use the beaches for a fee.

TENNIS

Both the Cebu Plaza and Montebello Villa (☞ Dining and Lodging,
above) hotels have tennis courts that nonguests can use for a fee.

Nightlife

BARS

Philippine Dream (⊠ Cebu Yacht Club, Lapu-Lapu City, ☎ 32/340–3888, ℻ 32/340–3083) is a huge cruise ship anchored at a deep-water dock close to the airport. This floating entertainment complex has restaurants, bars, and discos. Europeans like the informal **St. Moritz Bar** (⊠ Gorordo Ave., Lahug, ☎ 32/231–0914), part of a hotel of the same name. **Thunderdome** (⊠ 175 F. Ramos St., ☎ 32/54534) is a midtown bar favored by yuppies; it has a first-rate sound system.

CASINO

The **Waterfront Cebu City Hotel and Casino** (⊠ Salinas Dr. Ext., Lahug, ☎ 32/231–1404 or 32/231–5652) has a decor that mimics a picturesque turn-of-the-century plaza. The action at the gaming tables runs from 5 PM to 5 AM. You must be 18 years old to enter (bring your passport), and dress is smart casual (no sleeveless T-shirts or shorts allowed). **Montebello Villa** hotel (⊠ Banilad, ☎ 32/231–3681) has a small, unremarkable casino with similar age and dress requirements.

DANCE CLUBS

The fashionable set dances at the strobe-lit **Bai Disco** (⊠ Cebu Plaza Hotel, Nivel Hills, Lahug, ☎ 32/231–1131). **Balls Disco** (⊠ Gen. Maxilom Ave., ☎ 32/79305) has live bands from 7 to 10 PM. From 10 on, the dance floor fills up with a mixed, mostly young crowd.

Shopping

One of the best handicraft stores in the city is the **Cebu Display Center** (⊠ 11–13 Magallanes and Lapu-Lapu Sts., ☎ 32/52223 or 32/52224), which has an excellent collection of regional crafts, particularly items made using shells. Prices aren't inflated for tourists. You may want to visit **Carbon Public Market,** a 20-minute walk from Magellan's Cross and a good place for handicrafts. You can find Cebu's unique crafts at **Regalos de Cebu** (⊠ 51 Gorordo Ave., ☎ 32/232–0147).

OFF THE
BEATEN PATH   **CHOCOLATE HILLS, BOHOL ISLAND** – These are about 50 striking limestone hills, with an average height of 120 ft, that look like overturned teacups without handles. About a two-hour bus ride from the market in Tagbilaran City—a half-hour flight from Cebu City, or a 1½-hour ride on Aboitiz's Supercat Ferry—the hills turn chocolate-brown during the dry months (February through May). In July they become green again, their grasses nourished by rain.

Iloilo City

❷ *½-hour flight from Cebu City.*

A small and gracious aggregate of six districts, Iloilo (pronounced "*ee*- lo-*ee*- lo"), the capital of Iloilo Province on Panay Island, has a genteel air and loads of charm. The city and its surrounding area have several noteworthy churches—all accessible by public transportation—where you can get a feel for Iloilo's civic and social pulse.

Near the city center and across from the provincial capitol building is the **Museo Iloilo** (Iloilo Museum), which has an excellent collection of pre-Hispanic artifacts dug up mainly on Panay Island. These include fossils, Stone Age flake tools, and gold death masks. Other exhibits, some supplemented by video presentations, focus on liturgical art and the treasures of a British frigate shipwrecked nearby in the 19th century. ⊠ *Bonifacio Dr. at General Luna St., ☎ 33/72986.* ▣ *Admission.* ⊙ *Daily 8–noon and 1–5.*

Molo Church, in a pleasant park in the downtown Molo district, is a twin-spired Gothic structure erected in the late 19th century. It has an intricate facade, with a kind of domed pergola that's complete with Greek columns. Note the row of female saints that line the nave.

Jaro Cathedral, 3 km (2 mi) north of downtown, is larger than Molo Church but also shows Gothic influences. In front is a balcony with a statue of the Virgin that locals consider miraculous. Across the street is the church's reconstructed belfry. Nearby is a statue of **Graciano Lopez Jaena,** a journalist who wrote against the Spanish regime and died in Barcelona in 1896, at the outset of the revolution against Spain. Take some time to walk around the district and look at the grand, colonial-style residences, with their intricate grillwork and capiz windows.

The 200-year-old **Miagao Fortress Church,** 40 km (25 mi) south of the city, has two bell towers—of different design, as they were erected by two different friars—that also served as watchtowers against invasions by Muslim pirates. If you promise to be careful, the bell ringer will let you climb one of them. The sandstone facade depicts, amid floral designs, St. Christopher planting a coconut tree.

Dining and Lodging
Iloilo is well known for its *pancit molo* (chicken, pork, and shrimp dumplings in noodle soup), *la paz batchoy* (a tripe stew), *binakol* (chicken-and-coconut soup cooked in a bamboo tube), and pastries.

$ ✕ **Breakthrough sa Baybay.** The tasty dishes at this popular seafood place are served in the open air. ✉ *Santo Nino Norte Rd., Arevalo District,* ☎ *33/73027. No credit cards.*

$$ ✕▥ **Hotel del Rio.** Although modest, this well-run 30-year-old prop-
★ erty is quiet and appealing. The clean, spacious rooms get lovely breezes off the Iloilo River. In the Owari restaurant, the city's best place for Japanese cuisine, local fish is used to good advantage. The more formal Igmaan restaurant serves native cuisine on a breezy terrace with a river view; if you time your meal right, you can also enjoy a beautiful sunset. Afterward, take in the nightlife at the hotel bar. ✉ *M. H. del Pilar St., Molo District,* ☎ *33/335–1171,* 🖷 *33/70736. 57 rooms. 3 restaurants, bar, pool, dance club. AE, DC, MC, V.*

$$ ▥ **Sarabia Manor.** This hotel has a cosmopolitan feel and a friendly, well-informed staff. Ceilings are low, but the rooms are otherwise spacious and well kept. The hotel's bar is a good place for a night out. ✉ *General Luna and Ybiernas Sts.,* ☎ *33/335–1021,* 🖷 *33/79127. 100 rooms. 3 restaurants, bar, pool, dance club. AE, DC, MC, V.*

$ ▥ **La Fiesta Hotel.** Florid wrought-iron banisters spiral all the way up this pleasant three-story inn, and cream-color terrazzo tiles are used throughout. Rooms are spacious and colorfully decorated. ✉ *M. H. del Pilar St., Molo District,* ☎ *33/338–0044,* 🖷 *33/79508. 29 rooms, 2 suites. Restaurant, coffee shop. AE, DC, MC, V.*

Shopping
At **Asilo de Molo Molo** (✉ Avancena St., Molo District, ☎ 33/74717), an orphanage for girls, the skills of fine embroidery, especially for church vestments, are taught by nuns. Exquisitely embroidered cloth for dresses and intricate barong tagalogs are sold at nonnegotiable prices. **Ilonggo Producers Association Showroom** (✉ Basa St., ☎ 33/76893) gathers native crafts and souvenirs (made of wood, paper, roots, and cloth) in one convenient place. **Sinamay Dealer** (✉ Osmeña St., Arevalo District, ☎ 33/74221) is an outlet for fine hand-loomed textiles and runners made from *jusi* (silk), cotton, and pineapple fiber.

Guimaras Island

❸ *45-minute boat ride southeast of Iloilo City.*

This lush island, just off the coast of the city, is justly famous for its luscious mangoes. It has a number of fishing villages, rice paddies and cornfields, and a Trappist Monastery that doesn't encourage visitors. It's home to two of the more rustic, if moderately expensive, resorts in the area.

Lodging

$$$ ⌂ **Costa Aguada.** A satellite isle of Guimaras, this 2,200-acre eco-resort has white-sand beaches, a forest, a minizoo, and a turtle nursery. You can participate in water sports, go horseback riding, or play tennis. ⊠ *Guimaras Island,* ☎ *2/895–8624 (reservations in Manila),* FAX *2/833–0357. 68 rooms. Restaurant, bar, coffee shop, pool, 2 tennis courts, health club, horseback riding, beaches, dive shop, snorkeling, boating. AE, DC, MC, V.*

$$$ ⌂ **Isla Naburot.** Guest quarters here are in native-style cottages without electricity. The owner's daughter prepares exceptional dishes using mostly homegrown produce or freshly caught fish; she'll urge you to eat till you're near to bursting. Go ahead and indulge; you can work off all that food by participating in one of several water sports. ⊠ *Guimaras Island,* ☎ *33/76616. 18 cottages. Dining room, beach, dive shop, snorkeling, fishing. No credit cards.*

Boracay Island

★ ❹ *2 hours by plane and boat from Manila.*

Famous among Europeans, this small, bow-tie-shape island off the coast of Panay has one of the Philippines' most beautiful beaches, with sands as fine and smooth as refined sugar. This is the only attraction, and lazing on the beach or engaging in the water sports available at the various resorts—which range from basic to luxurious—are the main activities.

Lodging

$$$ ⌂ **Friday's Beach Resort.** The island's oldest upscale resort is well maintained. Rooms are in cottages that have a bamboo-and-thatch decor and a terrace. ⊠ *Boracay Island,* ☎ *2/521–2283,* FAX *2/521–1072. 22 rooms. Restaurant, bar, snorkeling, fishing. AE, DC, MC, V.*

$$$ ⌂ **Lorenzo Grand Villa.** This hotel's cliff-top location guarantees two things: a grand view and privacy. The decor throughout is a blend of native and Mediterranean. ⊠ *Boracay Island,* ☎ *2/926–4152. 32 rooms. Restaurant, bar, pool, beach, snorkeling, boating, fishing. AE, MC, V.*

$$ ⌂ **Pink Patio.** Air-conditioned rooms at this motel-like resort, five minutes from the beach, face a pleasant garden. ☎ *2/812–9551,* FAX *2/810–8282. 57 rooms. Restaurant, snack bar. AE, DC, MC, V.*

Nightlife

The central section of the beach has several distinctly different establishments: **Bazura Bar** is a disco, sometimes with all-night partying. **Beachcomber** is a mellow spot, often with a folk singer entertaining. **Moondog's Shooter Bar** offers an array of imaginative tropical drinks.

Davao City

❺ *1½ hours by plane from Manila.*

One of the largest cities in the world in terms of area (1,937 square km/748 square mi), Davao City is busy and booming. It's also probably the most ethnically diverse urban area in the country, with Muslim, Christian, Chinese, and indigenous tribal communities. It's surrounded by banana plantations and fruit and flower farms and bounded on the west by Mt. Apo and on the east by Davao Gulf.

★ Davao is justly famous for its tropical fruits, especially the durian, said to "smell like hell and taste like heaven." (The fruit has an oval shape with a thick yellow-green rind and a creamy white pulp; it smells worse than old gym socks, but it has a caramel taste.) The **Madrazo fruit district,** near downtown, is an excellent place to get to know these unusual fruits; most vendors will let you have a sample before you buy.

The large, intricate **Lon Wa Buddhist Temple** has three altars made of Italian marble, gold, and bronze respectively. Photos of deceased faithful are enshrined here. A resident Buddhist monk will tell your fortune if you ask. ⊠ *Rd. to airport,* ☎ *no phone.* 🎟 *Donation requested.*

The **Davao Museum,** not far from the airport and the Insular Century Hotel Davao (☞ Dining and Lodging, *below*), has fascinating displays of tribal artifacts and costumes. ⊠ *Insular Village, Lanag St.,* ☎ *82/235–1876.* 🎟 *Admission.* ☉ *Mon.–Sat. 8–5.*

Philippine Eagle Nature Center, a not-for-profit organization in Calinan, about 36 km (22 mi) from the city center, attempts to preserve the Philippine eagle, an endangered species, through breeding in captivity. These majestic birds have 6-ft wingspans, and their diet includes monkeys. The fierce-looking warriors-of-the-air are truly an awesome sight. The center also has captive crocodiles. At the visitors center (at the entrance), you can watch a short documentary on the eagles. ⊠ *Malagos, Calinan,* ☎ *82/298–2663.* 🎟 *Admission.* ☉ *Daily 8–5.*

Dining and Lodging

$$ ✕ **Luz Kinilaw.** Fishermen bring their catches directly to this shore-area restaurant, where the specialties are coal-grilled tuna tail and jaw and sashimi. ⊠ *Salmonan, Quezon Blvd.,* ☎ *82/226–4612. DC, V.*

$ ✕ **Kanaway Restaurant.** The walls of this eatery are adorned with artwork depicting different types of fish—a dead giveaway as to the kinds of delights you'll find on the menu. ⊠ *Magsaysay Park Complex,* ☎ *82/221–8594. DC, MC, V.*

$ ✕ **Molave.** This friendly eatery is well known for its truly greaseless fried chicken. ⊠ *Matina District,* ☎ *82/225–3184. No credit cards.*

$ ✕ **Tai Huat Clay Pot.** The inexpensive and delicious Chinese food here is popular with Davao's Chinese community. ⊠ *141 Magsaysay Ave.,* ☎ *82/226–4576. No credit cards.*

$$$ 🏨 **Insular Century Hotel Davao.** Close to the airport and about 3 km
★ (2 mi) from town, this hotel sits on 20 lush acres with coconut groves, gardens, and a beach. Nearby is a small settlement of an indigenous tribe, the T'boli. Twice a day tuba gatherers climb the tall trees to collect the sap. The airy rooms, done in native-style decor, have verandas. ⊠ *Lanang,* ☎ *82/234–3050,* 🖷 *82/235–0902. 153 rooms. 3 restaurants, bar, coffee shop, pool, 2 tennis courts, squash, beach, dock, shops, meeting rooms. AE, DC, MC, V.*

$$ 🏨 **Apo View.** This downtown hotel—with its pleasant, busy lobby and its comfortably furnished rooms—is popular with businesspeople. It has many repeat guests. ⊠ *J. Camus and Bonifacio Sts.,* ☎ *82/221–6430 or 2/893–1288 (in Manila),* 🖷 *82/221–0748 or 2/894–1223 (in Manila). 205 rooms. 2 restaurants, bar, coffee shop, pool, dance club. AE, DC, MC, V.*

$$ 🏨 **Casa Leticia.** This small but friendly establishment has a cozy, casual lobby and clean, well-maintained rooms. The top-floor Toto's Bar and Café—with its photos of rock stars, album covers, and other rock

memorabilia—hops almost every night; the owner himself often serves as the DJ. ⊠ *J. Camus and Palma Gil Sts.,* ☎ *82/224–0501. 41 rooms. Restaurant, bar, coffee shop. AE, DC, MC, V.*

Shopping

The downtown **Aldevinco Shopping Center** is a complex of neat rows of small stores that sell Mindanao tribal crafts, woven mats, brassware, antiques, batik cloth, and wood carvings. A 10-minute walk away is the **Madrazo fruit district** (☞ *above*), where vendors sell tropical fruits.

Samal Island

⑥ *15 minutes by motorized launch from the Insular Century Hotel Davao.*

Some of the Davao City area's nicest beaches are on nearby Samal Island. The island has several resorts where you can spend the day or stay overnight. For a schedule of trips to the island, ask at the Insular Century Hotel Davao (☞ Dining and Lodging, *above*) front desk.

Lodging

$$$$ ⊡ **Pearl Farm Beach Resort.** Formerly an aquaculture enterprise, this pricey resort has beautifully designed bungalows on a hillside overlooking Davao Gulf. On the grounds is a weaving center of the Mandayas, an indigenous tribe. ☎ *82/231–9976, 82/231–9977, 82/231–9978, 82/231–9979, or 2/832–0893 (in Manila), ℻ 82/221–9979 or 2/526–4484 (in Manila). 73 rooms. Restaurant, bar, pool. AE, DC, MC, V.*

$$$–$$$$ ⊡ **Paradise Park and Beach Resort.** This pleasant beach resort, complete with a small zoo, is good for a day trip or an overnight stay. ☎ *82/234–1229, ℻ 82/234–2926. 22 rooms. Restaurant, beach. AE, DC, MC, V.*

Mt. Apo National Park

⑦ *40 km (25 mi) west of Davao City.*

Davao City is a good base from which to explore Mt. Apo, at 9,689 ft the tallest peak in the country. The mountain, considered sacred by the indigenous people that live on and around it, is part of the Mt. Apo National Park. Trails pass through rain forests, sulfur springs, and, toward the summit, sparse vegetation. The average time for getting to the summit and back is five days; you can climb at any time of year, but it is best to do so during the dry season between March and May. For essential information and to hire a guide, contact the Davao City tourist office (☞ Visitor Information *in* Visayas, Mindanao, and Palawan Essentials, *below*).

OFF THE BEATEN PATH **CAMIGUIN ISLAND–** A three-hour trip from Cagayan de Oro City on the northwest coast of Mindanao, this lovely unspoiled isle is still heavily forested and has seven volcanoes. Hibok-Hibok, the largest of them, can be climbed with a hired guide. The best place to secure guides is Ardent Hot Springs, not far from Mambajao, which is also a good place to begin—and end—the climb. Accommodations are basic but cheap and clean, and the local people are friendly. There are hot springs, trekking opportunities, beaches, and waterfalls.

Zamboanga City

⑧ *45-minute flight from Cebu City or Davao City.*

Zamboanga City is famous for its bright flowers (its early name, Jambangan, meant "land of flowers"), which grow profusely in every garden. The roadsides are lined with bougainvillea and bright-red-flowered *gumamela* bushes. It's also a city with a sizable Muslim population, made up mainly of the Yakan, Badjao, Samal, and Tausug tribes; the Christian and Muslim populations live, for the most part, peaceably but in separate enclaves.

Begin exploring the city at **Plaza Pershing,** the town square named after "Blackjack" Pershing, the first American governor of the region, which was formerly known as Moroland and was said to have spurred the development of the .45 pistol. (Legend has it that fanatic Muslim warriors couldn't be stopped by a .38, hence the need for a more powerful gun.) Two blocks southeast of Plaza Pershing, on Valderrosa Street, is the **city hall**; built by the Americans in 1907, it's a curious combination of Arab and baroque styles.

East from city hall on Valderrosa Street is **Fort Pilar,** an old Spanish fortress. **Rio Hondo,** beyond Fort Pilar, is a small riverine Muslim village with its own mosque. Many of the houses are on stilts. Men wear white skullcaps, and women wear the distinctive *malong,* a brightly decorated wraparound dress.

North of downtown is **Climaco Freedom Park** (named after a beloved mayor slain many years ago) with its **Ecumenical Holy Hill**—Stations of the Cross on a roadside cliff leading to a giant white cross at the top, where there's a good view of the city. In **Pasonanca Park,** also north of downtown, you'll find the **Pasonanca Treehouse.** If you contact city hall (☎ 62/991–2295) in advance you can stay here for a night or two (albeit without a bathroom)—a fun Tarzan-and-Jane experience for young couples or couples who are young at heart.

About 16 km (10 mi) north of Zamboanga City is the Muslim village of **Taluksangay.** At the back of the town's distinctive red-and-white mosque is a prominent Muslim family's burial plot with headstones shaped like boats and with the ever-present crescent. The community is made up of seaweed gatherers; everywhere piles of seaweed dry in the sun. Stroll along the many catwalks and watch as women weave and sell straw mats. Remember to bargain; prices quoted at first will be high.

Dining and Lodging

Zamboangueños like steamed crabs, barbecued meats, and raw fish marinated in vinegar and hot green peppers.

$$ ✕ **Alavar's.** Run by a husband-and-wife team (he cooks, she manages),
★ this restaurant is justly famous for wonderful seafood. Prawns, clams, and blue marlin are served in this rambling house, but the specialty is *curacha,* crabs in a creamy, sweet-spicy sauce that is the chef's secret. Down your food with refreshing *buko* (young coconut) juice. ✉ *Don Alfaro St., Tetuan District,* ☎ 62/991–2483. DC, MC, V.

$ ✕ **Lotus.** Here tasty Filipino and Chinese dishes are served in a pleasant, informal setting. ✉ *Mayor Jaldon St.,* ☎ 62/991–2510. AE, DC, MC, V.

$ ✕ **Palmeras.** Feast on barbecued meats—the house specialty—on a pleasant, shady, garden terrace. The wait staff here is friendly. ✉ *Santa Maria Rd.,* ☎ 62/991–3284. AE, V.

$$ 🏨 **Grand Astoria Hotel.** Near the airport and 15 minutes from downtown by jeepney, this hotel has sunny, tiled rooms with tropical decor. The staff is friendly and efficient. ✉ *Mayor Jaldon St.,* ☎ 62/991–2510, FAX 62/991–2510. 52 rooms. 2 restaurants, bar, coffee shop, room service. AE, DC, MC, V.

$$ 🏨 **Lantaka.** Right by the waterfront, this establishment has well-appointed rooms and gracious service. The terrace abuts the sea, where Badjaos, a gypsylike tribe, sell mats and seashells from their outrigger

boats. Watch the sunset and the sea from the lovely, open-air Talisay Bar. Unfortunately, the hotel cuisine is mediocre. ⊠ *Valderrosa St.,* ☎ *62/991–2033,* FAX *62/991–1626. 112 rooms. Restaurant, bar, coffee shop, pool, meeting room, travel services. AE, DC, MC, V.*

$ ⊞ **Zamboanga Hermosa Inn.** This hotel in a quiet area of the city has a small, informal lobby with a restaurant. Guest rooms are small but comfortably furnished and clean. ⊠ *Mayor Jaldon St.,* ☎ *62/991–2042. 33 rooms. Restaurant, laundry service. DC.*

Shopping

In Zamboanga's colorful **city market** (⊠ Alano St.) you'll find the woven mats (Row C in the handicrafts section has a good selection) for which the city is famous. You'll also find brassware, antiques, items crafted from shells (for which Zamboanga is also noted), and batik from Indonesia. The market is open from dawn to dusk.

San Luis Shell Industries (⊠ San José Rd., ☎ 62/991–1044) has a wide selection of shells. For the tribal weavings prized by Philippine designers, visit the **Yakan Weaving Village,** 7 km (3 mi) from the city on the west coast. The weave is so fine it takes at least a week to finish a yard of cloth. You'll find a good selection of shells at **Zamboanga Home Products** (⊠ San José St. at Jaldon, ☎ 62/991–1717).

OFF THE   **SANTA CRUZ ISLAND –** This small island has a wonderful pink-coral
BEATEN PATH   beach, which is open daily 7–4, and a lagoon. At the beach's eastern end is a Muslim burial ground, ornamented with stars, crescents, and tiny boats—to provide passage to the next life. In this life, your passage to the island is best accomplished by renting a *banca,* a native canoe fitted with outriggers, at the Lantaka hotel (☞ Dining and Lodging, *above*). The trip takes 25 minutes; rates are officially set at P400 roundtrip. Be sure to pack water and refreshments, as there are no food or beverage stands.

Palawan

❾ *90-minute flight from Cebu City or Manila to Puerto Princesa.*

Shaped like a long dagger, Palawan is the archipelago's westernmost island and one of its most isolated and least developed. Here you'll find beautiful beaches, with excellent snorkeling and diving spots, as well as unique flora and fauna including giant turtles, peacocks, mouse deer, scaly anteaters, purple herons, and seven-color doves. If you really want to get away from it all, you'll find some of the Philippines' most secluded (and often most luxurious) resorts on smaller islands off Palawan's northwestern coast.

The lack of development means that you'll need a little patience on a visit to the island. Outside the island's only city, Puerto Princesa, roads are unpaved and tend to be almost impassable after a heavy rain. (The points of interest listed here are those accessible by public transportation.) And as the island has malaria-bearing mosquitoes, you should take preventive medication at least two weeks before arriving and bring plenty of insect repellent.

The usual port of entry is the capital, **Puerto Princesa.** Although the city is pleasant (it regularly wins honors as the country's cleanest city) and makes a logical hub from which to explore the rest of the island, there isn't a great deal to see in it. The **Palawan Museum** (⊠ Old City Hall Building, J. Valencia St., ☎ no phone) does have good ethnographic and crafts displays. Admission is charged.

★ North of the capital is **St. Paul Subterranean National Park,** a national rain forest park with the world's longest known underground river, **St. Paul's River,** most of which runs through St. Paul's Peak, the mountain that comprises almost all of the park. There's a small beach hamlet, **Sabang,** about a three-hour jeepney ride from Puerto Princesa. At Sabang, you can hire a banca to take you to the river and the gigantic caverns—with their stalactite and stalagmite formations—through which it courses. You have to obtain a permit to tour the river and the caves at a ranger station at the mouth of the river. There's no charge for the permit, but be sure to tip the boatmen.

You can also hike from Sabang to the river, about 2 km (1¼ mi) away. A well-marked trail starts from the beach, goes up through rain forest, and emerges at the main ranger station, where you can obtain a visitor's pass. From the station the hike continues by the beach and onto the **Monkey Trail,** a bamboo stairway that winds among limestone rocks and through forest inhabited by monitor lizards, parrots, and—of course—monkeys. ⊠ *St. Paul Subterranean River National Park office, 150 Manalo St., Puerto Princesa,* ☎ *48/433–2409.*

A five-hour bus ride south of Puerto Princesa, near the coastal town of Quezon, are the **Tabon Caves,** discovered in 1962. These caves—numbering about 200 but with only a small number explored—were among the earliest inhabited sites in the country. Although you won't see any artifacts in the caves (most are in the National Museum in Manila), just being here and imagining life millennia ago is a worthwhile experience.

At the Quezon branch of the **National Museum** you can arrange banca trips to the Tabon Caves (prices are reasonable) and view the regional artifacts and marine specimens on display. ⌨ *Admission.* ☉ *Mon.–Sat. 9–noon and 1–5.*

Dining and Lodging

PUERTO PRINCESA

$$$ ✗ **Cafe Puerto.** This upscale restaurant serves Continental cuisine, including seafood and chops, in one of the city's more formal settings. ⊠ *Rizal Ave.,* ☎ *48/433–2266. AE, DC, M, V.*

$$ ✗ **Ka Lui's.** Puerto's free spirits hang out here to dine on fresh seafood
★ and delicious fruit shakes served on an airy bamboo veranda. The owner-chef has a small lending library on the premises, with a variety of English-language titles. ⊠ *Rizal Ave.,* ☎ *48/433–2580. No credit cards.*

$$$ 🏨 **Asia World.** Although this concrete structure is incongruous in a city where preserving the environment is an issue, it meets the demands of travelers who prefer urban comforts. Rooms are spacious, air-conditioned, and well maintained. ⊠ *San Miguel National Highway,* ☎ *48/433–2022 or 2/242–6546 (reservations in Manila),* FAX *48/433–2515. 109 rooms, 14 suites. 2 restaurants, bar, coffee shop, pool, tennis court, health club, travel services. AE, DC, MC, V.*

$$ 🏨 **Badjao Inn.** A pleasant low-key atmosphere and a veranda recommend this inn, although many of the rooms are cheerless. ⊠ *350 Rizal Ave.,* ☎ *48/433–2761. 26 rooms. Restaurant, laundry service. AE.*

$$ 🏨 **Casa Linda.** Constructed of bamboo, wood, and thatch, this inn has a veranda, as well as a courtyard garden and parrots. The staff is cheerful and helpful. ⊠ *Trinidad Rd.,* ☎ *48/433–2606. 13 rooms. Restaurant, laundry service. AE.*

$$ 🏨 **Hotel Fleuris.** This new hotel in a three-story, neoclassic-style building has a smoked-glass atrium and lobby. Located downtown, it provides well-furnished, comfortable rooms; good dining; and reliable service. ⊠ *Lacao St.,* ☎ *48/233–3380. 48 rooms. Restaurant, bar, coffee shop, business services. AE, DC, MC, V.*

$$$$ ⌂ **Amanpulo.** A private island in the Cuyo Archipelago, roughly halfway between northern Palawan and the Visayas' Panay Island, has been turned into a luxurious getaway with gourmet dining and lush surroundings. Here, spacious, secluded casitas—with tropical decor, verandas, cable TV, and VCRs—line white-sand beaches. You have access to golf carts to get around the manicured grounds. ✉ *Pamalican Island,* ☎ *2/532–4041, 2/532–4042, 2/532–4043, 2/532–4044 (reservations in Manila); 212/223–2848 or 800/447–7462 (reservations in the U.S.);* 🖷 *2/532–4040 in Manila. 50 casitas. Restaurant, bar, room service, pool, massage, 2 tennis courts, beach, dive shop, snorkeling, boating, fishing, library, meeting rooms. AE, DC, MC, V.*

$$$$ ⌂ **El Nido.** This resort, spread over two islands off northern Palawan, is in a beautiful marine park and has its own ecological and environmental protection programs, such as a fish nursery. Packages include meals, charter-air transportation, lodging, and the use of water-sports facilities. Guest cottages are patterned after native huts—bamboo, thatching, shell, and wood abound. ✉ *Miniloc and Lagen islands, near the town of El Nido,* ☎ *2/810–7291 or 2/894–5644 in Manila. 82 rooms. Restaurant, beach, dive shop, dock, snorkeling, windsurfing, boating, fishing. AE, DC, MC, V.*

$$$ ⌂ **Club Paradise.** This resort, on a small isle near the larger Busuanga Island off the coast of northern Palawan, has native-style thatch cottages and rustic surroundings. It's popular with resident expatriates on weekends. ✉ *Dimakya Island,* ☎ *2/816–6871 (reservations in Manila). 50 rooms. Restaurant, pool, beach, dive shop, dock, snorkeling, boating, fishing. AE, DC, MC, V.*

$$ ⌂ **Marina del Nido.** One of the most unusual resorts off the coast of
★   northern Palawan was built in 1994. Sailboats and yachts moor here, and their crews stock up on necessary supplies or just enjoy the resort's cuisine. For landlubbers, there are bungalows (not air-conditioned) built in the native style. The cuisine here is simple but superb. The staff, drawn from the local community, can arrange diving and snorkeling tours and camping trips in the rain forest. ✉ *Malapacao Island,* ☎ *2/831–1487 (reservations in Manila). 4 cottages. Restaurant, snorkeling, boating, fishing. AE, DC, MC, V.*

Nightlife and the Arts

Nightlife in Puerto Princesa is limited to hotels, where people gather in lounges for a drink and conversation. **Bistro Valencia** (✉ E. Valencia St., ☎ no phone) has local folksingers. Patrons are encouraged to try their vocal cords with the featured singers at **Erick's Sing-Along Bar** (✉ Rizal Ave. Ext., ☎ no phone). **Kamayan Folkhouse and Restaurant** (✉ Rizal Ave., ☎ 48/433–2019) serves native dishes as folk bands strut their stuff. If you're in the mood to dance, check out the discotheque **Prism** (✉ Asia World hotel, San Miguel National Highway, ☎ 48/433–2111).

Shopping

Along Puerto Princesa's Rizal Avenue, handicrafts, antiques, and baskets can be purchased at Mencoco, Culture Shack, or Karla's. The public market is a good source as well: try Macawili Handicraft for baskets and brassware.

The Visayas, Mindanao, and Palawan Essentials

Arriving and Departing

BY AIRPLANE

Philippine Air Lines (PAL; ☎ 32/254–3870 in Cebu City; 82/234–0073 in Davao City) has flights from Manila to major cities in the region. Check with the airline for details about service. **Singapore Airlines/Silkair** (☎ 32/253–1343 in Cebu City) has direct flights from Singapore to Cebu.

BY BOAT

Cebu City is a busy port and a primary stop for interisland ships. All the major lines have trips between Cebu and ports all over the archipelago. The Cebu–Manila voyage takes 21 hours, Cebu–Davao, 12 hours. Some companies are: **Aboitiz Shipping** (☎ 32/95661 or 32/253–3143), **Escaño Lines** (☎ 32/77253 or 32/62122), **Negros Navigation** (⊠ Port Area, ☎ 32/253–3831 in Cebu City; 2/816–3481 or 2/818–3804 in Manila).

High-speed ferry services have transformed interisland traffic, with trips to most central Visayan ports averaging a little less than three hours. **WG&A** (☎ 2/894–3211 or 2/893–2211 in Manila) operates what it calls its SuperFerry service between the cities of Cebu, Iloilo, Davao, and Puerto Princesa; their cruise ships have suites, on-board entertainment, and dining. Other companies include: **Delta Cat** (☎ 32/232–1356 in Cebu City), **Negros Navigation** (☎ 32/253–3831 in Cebu City), **Supercats** (☎ 32/95661 in Cebu City), and **Waterjet** (☎ 32/232–1356 in Cebu City).

BY BUS

If you can't get enough of bus travel, bridges and ferry service make it possible to travel overland from Manila to Davao City in Mindanao; the **Philtranco** (☎ 2/833–5061 in Manila) bus lines make the trip in approximately 44 hours.

Getting Around

BY AIRPLANE

Cebu City's **Mactan International Airport** (☎ 32/340–5522) is the regional hub, providing a crucial link between Manila and Mindanao, other parts of the Visayas, and Palawan. From Cebu, the flight to Iloilo City is 30 minutes; the flight to Zamboanga City is 45 minutes; and flights to Davao City and Puerto Princesa on Palawan Island last an hour. You can arrange flights to the northern Palawan resorts by contacting the resorts directly.

BY BUS

Buses, a main form of public transportation on the islands, usually begin and end their routes in the vicinity of the public market, whether in Cebu or Puerto Princesa. Get to the market early in the morning to secure a good seat. Air-conditioned buses, not as common on islands other than Luzon, are of course more expensive.

BY CAR

Roads in the urban areas, especially those in and around Iloilo City, are in good shape. The exception is Palawan, where roads are largely unpaved and often impassable during the rainy season. Although having a car gives you freedom and privacy, taxi and jeepney fares are low, and local drivers know the area better than you do. Your best bet—particularly on Palawan—is to travel by "hire-car" in local parlance—by the hour or the day. Ask about going rates at local tourist offices (☞ Visitor Information, *below*).

Car-rental agencies in Cebu City include: **Avis** (☎ 32/340–2486 or 32/340–8527), **Cattleya** (☎ 32/73074), and **Guani** (☎ 32/253–5465). In Iloilo City contact: **Avis** (☎ 33/271171). Agencies in Davao include **Avis** (☎ 82/221279 or 82/221–6430) and **Guani** (☎ 82/221–5000).

BY JEEPNEY

Jeepneys generally begin and end their trips at public markets. Fares are very low: a 2-km (1¼-mi) ride within Cebu City costs only P2.

BY TAXI

Taxis in Cebu are metered, while in Iloilo, Zamboanga, and Davao prices are agreed upon beforehand. The average taxi ride in Cebu costs P80, while trips to Mactan Airport and to out-of-town destinations start at P250. In Davao, a ride to the airport averages P80.

BY TRICYCLE

The tricycle, the ubiquitous motorized pedicab, is good for within-a-neighborhood trips. In Puerto Princesa, however, it's the main form of public transport for trips inside the city or to outside destinations. Prices are negotiable but are routinely a bargain.

Contacts and Resources

BOOKSTORES

Bookstores in Cebu City include: **National Bookstore** (⊠ Ayala Center, Cebu Business Park, ☎ 32/231–4006) and **Bookmark** (⊠ 260 Osmena Blvd., ☎ 32/253–8246). In Puerto Princesa, the **Palawan Museum** (⊠ Old City Hall Building, J. Valencia St., ☎ no phone) has a small library with books on Palawan, anthropology, and ethnography. **Ka Lui's Restaurant** (⊠ Rizal Ave., ☎ 48/433–2580) has a collection of paperbacks (left by various travelers) that are lent out on an honor system.

EMERGENCIES

Cebu: ☎ 32/95676 or 32/74642. **Davao:** ☎ 82/119. **Iloilo:** ☎ 33/75511.

TOUR OPERATORS

Trips can be arranged through tour operators and travel agencies in Manila. You can also consult local tourism offices (☞ *below*) for suggestions and a list of guides. In addition, many of the larger hotels have tour operators' desks.

VISITOR INFORMATION

Cebu City (⊠ Ground floor, LDM Building, Lapu-Lapu St., ☎ 32/254–2811 or 32/254–6077). **Davao City** (⊠ 7 Magsaysay Ave. at Magsaysay Park, ☎ 82/221–6798 or 82/221–6955). **Iloilo City** (⊠ Capitol Grounds, Bonifacio Dr., ☎ FAX 33/335–0245). **Puerto Princesa** (⊠ City Hall, ☎ 48/433–2154; ⊠ Provincial Capitol, ☎ 48/433–2983). **Zamboanga City** (⊠ Lantaka Hotel, Valderrosa St., ☎ 62/991–0217 or 62/991–0218).

PHILIPPINES A TO Z

Arriving and Departing

By Airplane

AIRPORTS

Manila's **Ninoy Aquino International Airport** (☎ 2/877–1109) is the major international and domestic air hub for the Philippines. Although it's used mainly by domestic flights (which make it the country's second-busiest airport), some international flights also use Cebu City's **Mactan International Airport** (☎ 32/340–5522), particularly those from Japan, Singapore, and Australia. The **Laoag International Airport** (☎ no phone) is now an alternative port of entry into the country for travelers coming from Taipei.

CARRIERS

At press time **PAL** (☎ 2/816–6691 or 2/832–3011), the national carrier, was working to overcome financial difficulties and labor disputes, and this may have affected schedules. Check with the airline directly for details about domestic and international service (☞ *also* Air Travel *in* the Gold Guide at the front of this book). **Northwest** (☎ 2/819–

7341) has flights to Manila from Chicago and Los Angeles with one stop in either Tokyo or Osaka.

Other carriers with service to Manila include: **China Airlines** (☎ 2/523–8021), **Cathay Pacific** (☎ 2/848–2747), **Japan Airlines** (☎ 2/810–9781), **Korean Air** (☎ 2/815–8911), **Malaysian Airlines** (☎ 2/525–9404), **Singapore Airlines** (☎ 2/810–4951), and **Thai Airways** (☎ 2/815–8421).

FLYING TIMES

Manila is 16 hours from San Francisco; 15 from Los Angeles; 20 hours from Chicago; and 22 hours from New York, Toronto, and Montréal. From London, Manila is 16 hours away; flights from Sydney are about 8½ hours.

Getting Around

By Airplane
It's always wise to confirm your domestic flight at least two days in advance. **PAL** (☞ *also above*) has traditionally covered most of the archipelago, serving 43 cities and towns. Owing to the company's recent economic and labor woes, however, there may have been cuts in service. Smaller, privately owned companies have regular flights to some cities and resorts. These include: **Aerolift** (☎ 2/817–2369 or 2/818–4223), **Air Philippines** (☎ 2/832–1961), **Asian Spirit** (☎ 2/817–1176), **Cebu Pacific Air** (☎ 2/893–9607), **Grand Air** (☎ 2/833–8090), and **Pacific Air** (☎ 2/832–2731, 2/832–2732, or 2/833–2390).

By Boat
Much of the local populace travels by boat, the cheapest way to get from island to island. One-way rates from Manila to Cebu City (a 24 hour trip) range from P2,200 for luxury on **W G&A SuperFerry** (☎ 2/894–3211) to P722 for economy. Were you to fly, the same one-way trip on PAL would cost P2,600 but take only 70 minutes.

Speed, reliability, and safety vary from line to line. **Aboitiz** (☎ 2/525–9303), **Negros Navigation** (☎ 2/816–3481 or 2/816–3481), and **Sweet Lines** (☎ 2/912–2332) generally have well-kept ships and good records. **Sulpicio** (☎ 2/241–9701) and **Gothong** (☎ 2/214121) lines have lesser reputations.

By Bus
The Philippines has an excellent bus system, with 20 major lines covering the entire archipelago. Service between major destinations is frequent, often on an hourly basis. This is a cheap, generally safe way to travel. You can also go island-hopping by bus and ferry. Such routes are usually limited to islands close together, though these days you can get from Manila to Davao City on the Philtranco line in 44 hours.

In Manila there are several bus terminals. Outside Manila, most terminals are next to public markets. Companies that serve the major routes have coaches with or without air-conditioning. Some bus lines are: **BLTB** (☎ 2/833–5501), **Dagupan Bus Co.** (☎ 2/929–6123), **Pantranco** (☎ 2/833–5061), **Philtranco** (☎ 2/833–1369), and **Victory Liner** (☎ 2/833–0293, 2/833–5019, or 2/833–5020).

By Car
EMERGENCY ASSISTANCE

There are no road-service organizations, but if your car breaks down, passing motorists and townsfolk will gladly lend a hand.

GASOLINE

A gallon costs approximately P50. Gas stations are readily found in and around cities and major towns, with a majority of those in urban areas open 24 hours.

PARKING

Parking can be difficult in Manila. In Makati, there are parking lots (the average cost is P15–P20 for three hours); on some streets meter maids approach you to collect P15 per hour. In other areas of Metro Manila where street parking is available, young men or kids offer to "watch your car" for a few pesos. It's worth it. Major hotels used to provide free parking for guests but now charge major fees. Newer malls have parking levels; fees are nominal.

RENTAL AGENCIES

The larger car-rental agencies represented in the Philippines are: **Avis** (☎ 2/741–0394 or 2/734–5872), **Budget** (☎ 2/818–7363), **Carlines** (☎ 2/810–5421), **Dollar** (☎ 2/811–6849), and **National** (☎ 2/890–3252 or 2/897–9101). On the average, a self-driven car costs about P2,000 per day. Rates vary for chauffeur-driven cars, depending on the agency and the destination.

ROAD CONDITIONS

Road conditions vary from excellent, with smooth cement or asphalt highways (generally around such metropolitan areas as Manila, Cebu City, and Baguio), to bad, where "road" is a euphemism for a dirt track that's dusty and badly rutted in summer and muddy during the rainy season. Although there are official speed limits—95 kph (60 mph) maximum and 55 kph (35 mph) minimum—they are not displayed on highways and are rarely enforced, so you can go as fast as you dare on the open road. Use prudence in populated areas and where children or farm animals are nearby.

RULES OF THE ROAD

Driving is on the right, and you must have a valid foreign or international driver's license to rent a car. Drive defensively—this is not a car culture, so driving rules tend to be honored in the breach.

By Train

Only Luzon has a railway system, the **Philippine National Railways** (PNR; ☎ 2/361–1125), a single-rail system that has deteriorated. Trains no longer run north of Manila, traveling only south to Guinobatan in Luzon's Bicol region. (Plans have long been drawn to extend rail service north, to La Union, and farther south, to Legaspi City, but they're continuously shelved.) Fares are slightly lower than those for bus travel, but trips take longer.

Contacts and Resources

Customs and Duties

ON ARRIVAL

Personal effects (a reasonable amount of clothing and a small quantity of perfume), 400 cigarettes or two tins of smoking tobacco, and 2 liters of liquor may be brought into the Philippines duty-free.

ON DEPARTURE

There are restrictions on the export of antiques, religious and historical artifacts, coral, orchids, monkeys, and birds (including endangered species such as the Philippine eagle).

Electricity

The electrical current in the Philippines, runs on 220-volt, 60-cycle AC current, though major hotels in Manila provide 110 outlets. Wall outlets take a variety of plug styles, including Continental-type plugs, with two round prongs, and plugs with two flat prongs.

Embassies and Consulates

Australia (✉ Dona Salustiana S. Ty Tower, ground floor, 104 Paseo de Roxas, Makati, ☎ 2/817–7911). **Canada** (✉ Allied Bank Center, 9th floor, 6754 Ayala Ave., Makati, ☎ 2/810–8861). **New Zealand** (✉ Far East Bank Center, 23rd floor, Sen. Gil Puyat Ave., Makati, ☎ 2/891–5358). **United Kingdom** (✉ LV Locsin Building, 15th–17th floors, 6752 Ayala Ave., Makati, ☎ 2/816–7116 or 2/816–4849; ✉ Maria Luisa Park, Banilad, Cebu City, ☎ 32/346–0525). **United States** (✉ 1201 Roxas Blvd., Manila, ☎ 2/521–7116; ✉ Fourth floor, PCI Building, Gorordo Ave., Cebu City, ☎ 32/231–1261).

Health and Safety

FOOD AND DRINK

Water is usually potable, though in cities such as Manila it's heavily chlorinated. If your stomach is sensitive, you might want to stick to bottled water. On the road be sure to bring water for the trip. The food, whether Western-style or Filipino, shouldn't cause any problems, though it would be better to avoid street offerings, tempting as they may seem. Peeling fresh produce is is a good idea.

OTHER PRECAUTIONS

The most common scam is when someone offers you much higher rates of exchange for your currency. In crowded areas, a money belt under your clothing is a good idea, and you should avoid wearing expensive jewelry. Unaccompanied women generally won't be bothered, except, perhaps, by flirts. Still, it's best to dress modestly. Although there are no largely gay areas, gay and lesbian travelers will find that Filipinos aren't really concerned about sexual orientation.

Language, Culture, and Etiquette

The Philippines is an English-speaking country, a legacy of its years as a U.S. colony. Communicating is rarely a problem, either in the cities or in the countryside. A second lingua franca is Pilipino, which is based on the regional language of Tagalog. Spanish is still spoken by many members of the country's elite; in Zamboanga City a form of Creole Spanish known as Chavacano is spoken.

Two simple rules of etiquette will smooth your way: don't point and don't raise your voice. The main principle to bear in mind when in public and in the company of locals is a very Eastern one: never cause anyone to lose face. Filipinos place a premium on what they call Smooth Interpersonal Relations, or SIR. In terms of dress, this being a tropical country, informal attire is fine, but neatness and a well-groomed appearance are musts. Only a few restaurants have a dress code, but shorts, sandals, and tank tops are frowned upon by many establishments. Dress conservatively when visiting churches or mosques.

You'll have no problem taking pictures of most lowland Filipinos—they may even jump in front of your camera. Tribal highlanders, on the other hand, often shy away from being photographed; they may even become angry if you try to photograph them without receiving permission or offering payment for the privilege. In Baguio and Banaue, the costumed tribespeople expect a few pesos for posing.

Mail

POSTAL RATES

For letters to foreign countries, stamps cost P13; the cost is P8 for a postcard or an aerogram.

RECEIVING MAIL

Letters sent care of "poste restante" to the **Manila General Post Office** (⊠ Plaza Lawton, Manila, ☎ 2/527–8327 or 2/527–0069) will be held for you. Otherwise, have your mail addressed to you care of **American Express** (⊠ Philam Life Building, ground floor, United Nations Ave., Ermita, Manila, ☎ 2/521–9492).

WRITING TO THE PHILIPPINES

In urban areas addresses follow the standard Western format, except that postal codes are infrequently used, and the name of the building is often given in lieu of the street number. For example: XYZ Co., Insular Life Building, Ayala Avenue, Makati, Metro Manila. In rural areas, addresses may seem less than complete to Western eyes (indeed, they may not include a street name, let alone a street number).

Money and Expenses

COSTS

The Philippines remain a bargain, thanks to low inflation and the weakening of the peso against the dollar due to the economic crisis throughout Asia. Predictably, Metro Manila is the most expensive destination. Other urban areas, such as Baguio and Cebu City, are less expensive, and the surrounding provincial areas are cheapest of all.

Sample Costs: Cup of instant coffee, 25¢; fresh-brewed native coffee, 50¢–$1; bottle of beer, 50¢–$1; Coca-Cola, 60¢; hamburger, $1.50; 2-km (1-mi) cab ride, $2; 2-km (1-mi) bus ride, 50¢; museum admission, 75¢–$3.

CURRENCY

The unit of currency is the peso, made up of 100 centavos. Bills come in denominations of 2, 10, 20, 50, 100, 500, and 1,000 pesos. Coins range from 25 centavos to P5.

The exchange rate at press time was P28 to the Canadian dollar, P44 to the U.S. dollar, P75 to the pound sterling, P26 to the Australian dollar, and P22 to the New Zealand dollar. Licensed money changers in Manila's Tourist Belt, especially those on M. H. del Pilar and A. Mabini streets, often offer better exchange rates than banks. Unless otherwise indicated, prices quoted throughout this chapter are in pesos.

SERVICE CHARGES, TAXES, AND TIPPING

The international airport departure tax is P500, while domestic airports charge, on the average, P50. Hotels add a 10% service charge (as do most restaurants) and a government tax of 13.7%. In addition to a 4% sales tax, a value added tax (VAT) of 10% is charged by all businesses.

Tipping is now an accepted practice, and 10% is considered standard for waiters, bellboys, and other hotel and restaurant personnel. In restaurants and hotels that tack the 10% service charge onto the bill, tipping is optional (though it is customary to leave loose change). At Ninoy Aquino International Airport, you pay P30 per cart, and porters expect P10 for each piece of luggage (in addition to P10 per piece paid to the porter office). Hotel doormen and bellboys should get about the same. For taxi drivers, P15 is fine for the average 2-km (1-mi) ride.

Opening and Closing Times

Most businesses follow the 9 to 5 routine, though a few begin the day at 8. **Banks** are open 9–3. **Museums** have varying hours, though they generally close for an hour or two at midday and are rarely open on Sunday and holidays. Large **post office** branches are open weekdays 8–5 and Saturday 8–noon; hours at smaller branches may differ. **Store** hours vary depending on the type of establishment: shops and supermarkets are usually open 9:30–7:30, with mall stores remaining open till 8; public markets' hours are dawn to dusk. Except during Holy Week, most stores remain open on holidays.

NATIONAL HOLIDAYS
New Year's Day (Jan. 1), Holy Week—from Maundy Thurs. through Easter Sunday (Apr. 1–4, 1999; Apr. 21–23, 2000, Apr. 13–15, 2001); Labor Day (May 1); Day of Valor (May 6); Independence Day (June 12); All Saints' Day (Nov. 1); Andres Bonifacio Day (Nov. 30); Christmas (Dec. 25); José Rizal Day (Dec. 30).

Passports and Visas

Visas are not required of Australians, New Zealanders, Canadians, or U.K. or U.S. citizens for stays of up to 21 days, provided that travelers have a ticket for a return or onward journey.

Telephones

CALLS TO THE PHILIPPINES
To call the Philippines from overseas, dial the country code, 63, and then the area code. Area codes for some key destinations are: Baguio, 74; Cebu City, 32; Davao City, 82; Iloilo City, 33; Manila, 2; Puerto Princesa, 48; Vigan and Laoag, 77; Zamboanga City, 62.

LOCAL CALLS
Local calls are untimed, except for those made on a pay phone, which cost P2 for the first three minutes. For directory assistance, dial 114. All operators speak English. Outside of Manila, phone numbers vary in length from five to seven digits—you may even find phone numbers of varying lengths within one town. The Philippines is in the process of updating its phone system, but the conversion is taking place in fits and starts; hence there are still variations.

LONG-DISTANCE AND INTERNATIONAL CALLS
For domestic long-distance calls, you need to go through an operator by dialing 109, unless your phone has direct dialing, now being introduced in stages. The big hotels have direct overseas dialing. Otherwise, dial 108 to reach the operator. Whether or not the party is at the other end, a connection fee of about $1 is charged. International access codes for the Philippines are as follows: **AT&T** (☎ 10512), **MCI** (☎ 10515), and **Sprint** (☎ 10517).

Visitor Information

Before leaving home, Americans and Canadians should contact the **Philippine Center** (✉ 556 5th Ave., New York, NY 10036, ☎ 212/575–7915; ✉ 3660 Wilshire Blvd., Suite 825, Los Angeles, CA 90010, ☎ 213/487–4527; ✉ 447 Sutter St., Suite 507, San Francisco, CA 94108, ☎ 415/956–4060). Visitors from the United Kingdom can contact the **tourism office** in London (✉ 17 Albermarle St., W1X 7HA, ☎ 0171/449–5443). In Australia, there's a **tourism office** in Sydney (✉ 301 George St., 2000, ☎ 612/299–6815).

When to Go

The Philippines has two seasons: dry and wet. The dry season generally runs from late October through May, with temperatures ranging from cool and breezy—even chilly—in the northern highlands to scorching hot in the lowland cities. Within this seven-month span, the coolest stretch is from November through February and, since it coincides with winter months in the West, it's also the peak tourist season. Popular spots are crowded, major hotels have high occupancy rates, and airfares are higher. Still, there are plenty of beaches and unspoiled places where crowds are either sparse or nonexistent.

If you enjoy crackling summer heat, then March through May are the best months to visit. The Catholic penitential rites of Lent are observed in late March or early April, climaxing in nationwide rituals during Holy Week, when business and government offices shut down. May is harvest—and fiesta—time. If you find yourself in the Philippines during the rainy season—June through September—note that most of Mindanao lies outside the typhoon belt, which cuts across Luzon and most of the Visayas. Mindanao gets rain, but not much more than during the rest of the year. Manila, on the other hand, is subject to frequent floods, and the highlands of northern Luzon become waterlogged; mud and rock slides frequently make the roads impassable. Be sure to pack a good raincoat and waterproof boots. The following are maximum and minimum temperatures for Manila.

CLIMATE

Jan.	86F	30C	May	93F	34C	Sept.	88F	31C
	70	21		75	24		75	24
Feb.	88F	31C	June	92F	33C	Oct.	88F	31C
	70	21		75	24		74	23
Mar.	91F	33C	July	88F	31C	Nov.	88F	31C
	72	22		75	24		72	22
Apr.	93F	34C	Aug.	88F	31C	Dec.	86F	30C
	74	23		75	24		70	21

FESTIVALS AND SEASONAL EVENTS

The most spectacular festivals are in honor of Jesus Christ, as the Holy Infant (Santo Niño) or Son of God, and the Virgin Mary.

Jan.: Three orgiastic, dancing-in-the-streets carnivals take place this month: the **Ati-Atihan** (third weekend of the month in Kalibo, Aklan), the **Sinulog** (third weekend of the month in Cebu City), and the **Dinagyang** (last weekend of the month in Iloilo City). In all three, the Holy Infant is the object of veneration. Kalibo's Ati-Atihan, the oldest and most popular, is also the noisiest, as competing town bands thump enthusiastically night and day. All three cities get crammed to the gills, and plane, ship, and room reservations must be made two or three months in advance. In contrast, on January 9, the **Black Nazarene** procession of the Quiapo district in Manila is a more somber but equally intense show of devotion, as the faithful compete to pull the carriage holding a statue of Christ that's believed to be miraculous.

Jan.–Mar.: With the **Hari Raya Puasa,** Muslims celebrate the completion of Ramadan, a holy month of fasting and abstention that commemorates the revelation of the Koran to the Prophet Mohammed by the Angel Gabriel. (The Islamic calender follows the lunar cycle; Ramadan begins and ends on different dates each year.)

Late Mar.–early Apr.: Christ's final sufferings are remembered during the last week of Lent, Holy Week. In the central Luzon towns of Bulacan and Pampanga, masked and bleeding flagellants atoning for their sins are a common sight. Groups of old women and children gather at makeshift altars and chant verses describing Christ's passion. The **Turumba** in Pakil, Laguna (held the second Tuesday and Wednesday after Holy Week), honors Our Lady of Sorrows. Devotees dance through the streets trying to make her smile.

May: All over the country, the **Santacruz de Mayo** commemorates St. Helen's discovery of the Holy Cross in 324. The celebrations include colorful processions, complete with floats of each town's patron saint, beautifully gowned young women acting as May queens, and local swains dressed in their Sunday best. One of the more unusual feasts is in Lucban, Quezon Province, where multicolored rice wafers, called *kiping,* are shaped into window ornaments, usually in the form of fruits and vegetables.

Sept.: The **Peñafrancia** (3rd weekend of the month) is the biggest festival in the Bicol region, drawing as many as 10,000 spectators to Naga City in southern Luzon. A procession of floats on the river honors the Virgin of Peñafrancia.

Dec.: 'Tis the season for carolers, midnight masses, and such feasts as the **Maytinis** in the town of Kawit, Cavite—a 90-minute drive from Manila. Christmas Eve is celebrated with 13 colorful gigantic floats. Be there by 6 PM to get a good view.

5　Singapore

Don't let first impressions lead you
to write Singapore off as just another
modern international capital. Although
it may no longer be the exotic, romantic
city so vividly documented by Conrad
and Kipling, Singapore is yet a unique
metropolis, where the flavor, spirituality,
and gentle manners of the East
peacefully coexist with the comforts,
conveniences, and efficiency of the West.

By Nigel Fisher

Updated by
Bruce Bishop

TO ARRIVE IN SINGAPORE is to step into a world where the muezzin call to prayer competes with the bustle of capitalism; where old men play mah-jongg in the streets and white-clad bowlers send the ball flying down well-tended cricket pitches; where Chinese fortune-tellers and high-priced management consultants advise the same entrepreneur. This great diversity of lifestyles, cultures, and religions thrives within the framework of a well-ordered society. Singapore is a spotlessly clean—some say sterile—modern metropolis, surrounded by green, groomed parks and populated by 2.7 million extremely well-mannered people.

Although the Malays, Chinese, and Indians account for 97% of Singapore's population, other ethnic groups—from Eurasians to Filipinos, from Armenians to Thais—contribute significantly to the nation's cultural mix. Understandably, the heritage of the British colonial stay is profoundly felt even though Singapore became an independent nation in 1965.

In a part of the world where histories tend to be ancient and rich, Singapore is unique in having almost no history at all. Modern Singapore tends to date its history from the early morning of January 29, 1819, when a representative of the British East India Company, Thomas Stamford Raffles, stepped ashore at Singa Pura (Sanskrit for "Lion City"), as the island was then called, hoping to establish a British trading settlement on the southern part of the Malay Peninsula. The two sons of the previous sultan, who had died six years earlier, were in dispute over who would inherit the throne. Raffles backed the claim of the elder brother, Tunku Hussein Mohamed Shah, and proclaimed him sultan. Offering to support the new sultanate with British military strength, Raffles persuaded him to grant the British a lease allowing them to establish a trading post on the island in return for an annual rent; within a week the negotiations were concluded. (A later treaty ceded the island outright to the British.) Within three years, the small fishing village, surrounded by swamps and jungle and populated by only tigers and 200 or so Malays, had become a boomtown of 10,000 immigrants, administered by 74 British employees of the East India Company.

As Singapore grew, the British erected splendid public buildings, churches, and hotels, often using Indian convicts for labor. The Muslim, Hindu, Taoist, and Buddhist communities—swelling rapidly from the influx of fortune-seeking settlers from Malaya, India, and South China—built mosques, temples, and shrines. Magnificent houses for wealthy merchants sprang up, and the harbor became lined with *godowns* (warehouses) to hold all the goods passing through the port.

By the turn of the century, Singapore had become the entrepôt of the East, a mixture of adventurers and "respectable middle classes." World War I hardly touched the island, although its defenses were strengthened to support the needs of the British navy, for which Singapore was an important base. When World War II broke out, the British were complacent, expecting that any attack would come from the sea and that they would be well prepared to meet it. But the Japanese landed to the north, in Malaya. The two British battleships that had been posted to Singapore were sunk, and the Japanese land forces raced down the peninsula on bicycles.

In February 1942 the Japanese captured Singapore. Huge numbers of Allied civilians and military were sent to Changi Prison; others were marched off to prison camps in Malaysia or to work on the notorious "Death Railway" in Thailand. The 3½ years of occupation was a time of privation and fear; an estimated 100,000 people died. The Japanese surrendered on August 21, 1945, and the Allied forces returned to Singapore. However, the security of the British Empire was never again to be felt, and independence for British Southeast Asia was only a matter of time.

In 1957 the British agreed to the establishment of an elected 51-member legislative assembly in Singapore. General elections in 1959 gave an overwhelming majority—43 of 51 seats—to the People's Action Party (PAP), and a young Chinese lawyer named Lee Kuan Yew became Singapore's first prime minister. In 1963 Singapore became part of the Federation of Malaysia, along with the newly independent state of Malaysia.

Mainly due to Malays' anxiety over a possible takeover by the ethnic Chinese, the federation broke up two years later and Singapore became an independent sovereign state. The electorate remained faithful to Lee Kuan Yew and the PAP. In 1990, Lee resigned after 31 years as prime minister, though as a senior minister he maintains his strong grip. His firm leadership of the party, his social and economic legislation, and his suppression of criticism led to his reputation as a (usually) benevolent dictator; yet Singaporeans recognize that his firm control had much to do with the republic's economic success and high standard of living. Lee is rumored to be grooming his son for the reins of the PAP—though the fact that the party is receiving fewer votes than in the past suggests a disaffection with the (virtually) one-party system. In the meantime, Lee's hand-picked successor, Goh Chok Tong, has established a power base of his own during his years as prime minister.

Pleasures and Pastimes

Dining

Eating is an all-consuming passion among Singaporeans, and you'll soon discover why. There's a stunning array of cuisine from around the world, particularly from the three major cultures that make up the island nation: Chinese, Malay, and Indian. It also won't take you long to discover that Singaporeans love spices. But spicy doesn't necessarily mean hot. It can also mean tastes that are mellow, as in thick, rich coconut gravies; pungent, as in Indian curries; tart, as in the sour and hot tamarind-, vinegar-, and lime-based gravies of Thailand, Malaysia, Indonesia, and Singapore; or sweet and fragrant, as in Indian desserts and beverages. Price categories throughout the chapter are based on the following ranges:

CATEGORY	COST*
$$$$	over S$60 (over US$36)
$$$	S$35–S$60 (US$21–US$36)
$$	S$15–S$35 (US$9–US$21)
$	under S$15 (under US$9)

All prices are per person for a three-course meal excluding tax, service charge, and drinks.

Gardens and Parks

You can escape from the concrete and glass that is modern downtown Singapore to visit orchid farms or the wonderfully kept Botanic Gardens. If you have a lot of energy, you can hike the trails of Bukit Timah Nature Reserve—the tigers have long gone, but the sounds and smells of the jungle are still here. If you want to see a tiger or two, as well as animals from as far away as the North Pole, Singapore has a pleasant zoo, designed on the open-moat concept. And because many animals are nocturnal, there's another zoo, the Night Safari, where tigers and rhinoceros wake up at dusk to feed.

Lodging

Although Singapore isn't the same indulgent retreat it once was, it's hard to match the standard of comfort, efficiency of staff, and level of services that Singapore hotels offer. The luxury establishments cater to every whim—and so they should at more than S$300 a night—but you can find good service, freshly decorated rooms, cleanliness, and modern facilities for around S$200. For less money, there are simple, clean hotels (often more personal than the larger ones), with rooms for about S$90. If you're on a tight budget, the youth hostels are spotless, cosmopolitan, and cheap. Price categories throughout the chapter are based on the following ranges:

CATEGORY	COST*
$$$$	over S$375 (over US$223)
$$$	S$275–S$375 (US$164–US$223)
$$	S$175–S$275 (US$104–US$164)
$	under S$175 (under US$104)

All prices are for a standard double room, excluding 4% tax and 10% service charge.

Shopping

Once upon a time Singapore, a duty-free republic, was a haven for shoppers. And though shopping is still the major pastime, nowadays the shoppers tend to be rich and sassy. Except for a lucky find in an antiques store, bargains are hard to come by. Still, nowhere else will you find so many shops that carry the latest fashions and electronic equipment. Browsing here is as much a pleasure as shopping.

Theme Parks

No other country of Singapore's size has put so much effort into creating attractions for both its citizens and its visitors. Singapore may have spent millions destroying its heritage buildings, but private enterprise has also spent a fortune re-creating the old at theme parks, usually designed to educate and entertain. Haw Par Villa emphasizes Chinese mythology, and the Tang Dynasty Village displays life in ancient China.

EXPLORING SINGAPORE

The main island of Singapore is shaped like a flattened diamond, 42 km (26 mi) east to west and 23 km (14 mi) north to south. Near the peak is the causeway leading to peninsular Malaysia—Kuala Lumpur is less than four hours away by car. At the foot is Singapore city, with its gleaming office towers and working docks. Offshore are Sentosa and some 59 smaller islands—most of them uninhabited—that serve as bases for oil refining or as playgrounds or beach escapes from the city. To the east is Changi International Airport, connected to the city by a parkway lined for miles with amusement centers of one sort or another. Of the island's total land area, less than half is built up, with the balance made up of farmland, plantations, swamp areas, and forest. Well-paved roads connect all parts of the island, and Singapore city has an excellent public transportation system.

Colonial Singapore

You'll find the heart of Singapore's history and its modern wealth in Colonial Singapore. The area stretches from the skyscrapers in Singapore's financial district to the Raffles Hotel, and from the super-modern convention centers of Marina Square to the National Museum and 19th-century Fort Canning. Although most of old Singapore has been knocked down to make way for the modern city, in Colonial Singapore most of the major landmarks have been preserved, including early 19th-century buildings designed by the Irish architect George Coleman.

Numbers in the text correspond to numbers in the margin and on the Colonial Singapore map.

A Good Walk

A convenient place to start is at **Collyer Quay** ① ("quay" is pronounced "key") and Clifford Pier, where most European colonizers first set foot on the island. Leaving Clifford Pier, walk up the quay—toward the Singapore River—until you come to the **former General Post Office** ②, a proud Victorian building of gray stone that, rumor has it, is slated to become a hotel complex. Walk down the short, narrow, tree-lined street alongside the post office to cross the gracious old iron-link **Cavenagh Bridge** ③. If you walk along the river's south bank before crossing the bridge, you'll find what was once a wide towpath and is now a paved pedestrian street of restaurants and bars—**Boat Quay** ④. The second building on your left houses Harry's Bar, which gained international attention in 1995 as a haunt of derivatives trader Nick Leeson, the young whippersnapper who brought down the venerable Barings Bank.

Once over the Cavenagh Bridge, take a left onto North Boat Quay. Slightly back from the river is **Empress Place** ⑤, a huge white building. A bit farther along the quay is the **statue of Sir Thomas Stamford Raffles** ⑥, who is believed to have landed on this spot in 1819. Turn right onto St. Andrew's Road until you come to **Parliament House** ⑦ on your left, the oldest government building in Singapore, and on your right, **Victoria Memorial Hall** ⑧, built in 1905 as a tribute to Queen Victoria. Across the road is the old **Singapore Cricket Club** ⑨. Just past it, on your right as you continue up St. Andrew's Road, is the **Padang** ⑩, or playing field. To your left are the **Supreme Court** ⑪ and **City Hall** ⑫, two splendidly pretentious, imperial-looking buildings. Continuing northeast on St. Andrew's Road, which runs along the Padang, cross Coleman Street toward the green lawns that surround the Anglican **St. Andrew's Cathedral** ⑬.

Northeast of the cathedral is the huge **Raffles City** ⑭ complex, easily recognized by the towers of the two Westin hotels. Take the MRT underpass north across Stamford Road, and walk through Raffles City to Bras Basah Road. Across the street is the venerable **Raffles Hotel** ⑮. After touring the hotel, continue up Bras Basah Road to Queen Street and make a right to the **Singapore Art Museum** ⑯. After touring the exhibits, cross Bras Basah Road and walk down to Victoria Street, where you'll no doubt find a place to rest and people-watch at the **Chijmes** ⑰ complex. Continue southwest on Victoria Street (it becomes Hill Street after Stamford Road); the **Armenian Church** ⑱ will be on your right just before Coleman Street. From here, stamp collectors should turn left onto Coleman and visit the **Singapore Philatelic Museum** ⑲; culture vultures should go right on Coleman and than right again onto Armenian Street to visit the **Asian Civilisations Museum** ⑳. To see the **National Museum and Art Gallery** ㉑ instead, return to Stamford Road and make a left. You may wish to conclude your tour with a stroll through **Fort Canning Park** ㉒, pausing at the European Cemetery and the Tomb of Iskander Shah, and/or a visit to **Clarke Quay** ㉓, south of the park, with its restaurants and shops.

TIMING

This walking tour, with time factored in to wander through the Raffles Hotel and view the exhibits at one or more of the area's four museums, should take a full day. Allow an hour for the Raffles, including time out for a Singapore sling in the Long Bar. Allow at least an hour to view the exhibits at each museum.

Sights to See

⑱ Armenian Church. More correctly, the **Church of St. Gregory the Illuminator** is one of the most endearing buildings in Singapore. It was built in 1835, which makes it the republic's oldest surviving church, and it's still used for regular Armenian Orthodox services. The Armenians were but one of many minority groups that came to Singapore in search of fortune. A dozen wealthy Armenian families supplied the funds for the ubiquitous architect George Coleman to design this church. The main internal circular structure is imposed on a square plan with four projecting porticoes. In the churchyard is the weathered tombstone of Agnes Joaquim, who bred the parent plants of Singapore's national flower. The orchid, with a purplish pink center, was discovered in her garden in the 1890s and still carries her name.

★ ⑳ Asian Civilisations Museum. Formerly the Tao Nan School, this grand colonial building re-opened in 1997 as the first phase of the Asian Civilisations Museum. (Phase II is slated to open in 2000 at ☞ **Empress Place**.) With a mandate to provide an Asia-wide insight into the legacies of the past and the cultural traditions of the peoples who live in the region, the museum is a fascinating blend of permanent and changing exhibitions. Chinese furniture, ceramics, jade, and a faithfully recreated Chinese scholar's study are on permanent display. ⊠ *39 Armenian St.,* ☎ *338–0000.* ☞ *S$3.* ☉ *Tues.–Sun. 9:30–5:30.*

④ Boat Quay. Right next to the financial district, along the Singapore River, is this popular new restaurant area with both indoor and outdoor dining. Local entrepreneurs have created a mélange of eateries and nightclubs to satisfy diverse tastes. Between 7 PM and midnight, the area swells with people, who stroll along the pleasant quay, stopping to take a meal or refreshment. At the end of Boat Quay and named after Lord Elgin, a governor general of India, **Elgin Bridge** was built to link Chinatown to the colonial quarter. The original rickety wooden structure was replaced in 1863 with an iron bridge imported from Calcutta; the current ferroconcrete bridge was installed in 1926.

③ Cavenagh Bridge. This gracious old iron-link bridge is named after Major General Orfeur Cavenagh, governor of the Straits Settlements from 1859–67. The bridge, built in 1868 from iron girders imported from Scotland, was once the main route across the river; now Anderson Bridge bears the brunt of the traffic.

⑰ Chijmes. Built in 1840 as Caldwell House, the original structure became the Convent of the Holy Infant Jesus—where Catholic nuns housed and schooled abandoned children—in 1852. The church was added between 1901 and 1903. After World War II, both the convent and the church fell into disrepair. The buildings received a S$100 million renovation and were reopened in 1996 as this shopping and entertainment complex. Today the lovingly restored church is rented out for private functions. The new name "Chijmes" (pronounced "chimes") is an acronym of the convent's name, a nod at the complex's noble past.

⑫ City Hall. Completed in 1929, this building now houses a number of government ministries, including the Ministry of Foreign Affairs. It was here that the British surrender took place in 1942, followed by the surrender of the Japanese in 1945. Each year on August 9, the building's steps serve as a reviewing stand for the National Day Parade, celebrating Singapore's independence from Great Britain and the birth of the republic.

Singapore City

NEWTON

Kampong
Park

Stevens Rd.

Bukit Timah Rd.

Orchard Road

Cairnhill Rd.

Clemenceau Ave.

Nassim Rd.

Claymore Hill

Scotts Rd.

ORCHARD

Orchard Rd.

Bideford Rd.

Cavenagh Rd.

Wilkie Rd.

Tanglin Rd.

Edinburgh Rd.

Orchard Blvd.

Paterson Rd.

One Tree
Hill

SOMERSET

Colonial Singap

Grange Rd.

Exeter Rd.

Oxley

DHOBY
GHAUT

Grange Rd.

Rise

Fort Canning Rd.

Fort
Canning
Park

River Valley Rd.

Clemenceau

River Valley Rd

Singapore River

River Valley Rd

Zion Rd.

Kim Seng Rd.

River Valley Rd.

Coleman
Bridge

Alexandra Rd.

Havelock Rd.

Havelock Rd.

Havelock Rd.

Pickering St.

**TIONG
BAHRU**

New Bridge Rd.

South Bridge Rd.

Henderson Rd.

Tiong Bahru Rd.

Outram
Park

Jalan Bukit Merah

Outram Rd.

**OUTRAM
PARK**

Craig Rd.

Pagar Rd.

Maxwell Rd.

Cecil St.

0   1000 meters

0   1000 yards

N

Neil Rd.

Cantonment Rd.

**TANJONG
PAGAR**

Bahru Rd.

Spottiswoode
Park

Chinatown

Keppel Rd.

Subway & Rail Lines

Keppel Rd.

South Quay

North-South MRT line
East-West MRT line
Railroad lines
Subway stop

Empire Dock

Little India

Farrer Park
Farrer Park Rd.
Verdun Rd.
Race Course Rd.
Syed Alwi Rd.
Serangoon Rd.
Jalan Besar
Kichener Rd.
Jalan Besar
Lavender St.
Jalan Besar
Canal Rd.

KALLANG

Kallang Rd.
Victoria St.
Crawford St.
Kallang River
Gay World Amusement Park
Nicoll Hwy.
Merdeka Bridge

Rochor Canal
Selegie Rd.
St.
St.
Jalan Sultan
Arab St.
Ophir Rd.
Beach Rd.
Nicoll Hwy.

Arab District

BUGIS

apore
Bencoolen St.
Middle St.
Waterloo St.
Victoria St.
North Bridge Rd.
Rochor Rd.
Beach Rd.
Nicoll Hwy.
Merlion Ave.
Geylang River
Tanjong Rhu

Bras Basah Rd.
Rd.
Stamford Rd.

CITY HALL

East Coast Parkway

Hill St.
Coleman St.
Stamford Rd.
Temasek Blvd.
Raffles Blvd.
Rochor Rd.
Merlion Blvd.
High St.

Queen Elizabeth Walk

MARINA SQUARE
Raffles Blvd.
Raffles Ave.

Land Under Reclamation

Anderson Bridge
Benjamin Sheares Bridge

St.
Church St.
Market St.
Cross St.
Shenton Way

Marina Bay

Clifford Pier

RAFFLES PLACE

East Coast Parkway

Land Under Reclamation

MARINA BAY

Singapore Strait

Clarke Quay. Named in remembrance of Sir Andrew Clarke, the second governor of Singapore, this quay functions as a festival village that offers entertainment, food, and shopping. Here you can observe a tinsmith demonstrating his skill, see a band perform in the central square's small gazebo, and watch stilt-walkers wobble down pedestrian-only streets. Be aware that prices in the shops and restaurants are inflated. The river here is close to being the sleepy waterway it was when Raffles first arrived; cargo vessels are banned from entering. You can board one of the bumboats (small launches) that offer daily 30-minute cruises along the river and into Marina Bay; it's a pleasant ride, and a respite for tired feet.

Collyer Quay. Land reclamation in 1933 pushed the seafront back, and Collyer Quay, which now fronts Telok Ayer Street, is three blocks from its original site. In the 19th century, the view from the quay would have included a virtual wall of anchored ships. Today, you look out upon a graceful bridge that carries the East Coast Parkway from one landfill headland to another, enclosing what's now called Marina Bay. **Clifford Pier,** a covered jetty with high, vaulted ceilings, still reveals some of the excitement of the days when European traders arrived by steamship and Chinese immigrants by wind-dependent junks. Now Indonesian sailors sit around smoking clove-scented cigarettes, and seamen from every seafaring nation come ashore to stock up on liquor and duty-free electronics. The atmosphere here is seedy (this is one of the few places in Singapore where women might feel uncomfortable by themselves). Passengers from the ocean liners no longer come ashore here (they now arrive at the World Trade Centre cruise terminal), but it's still possible to set sail from here on a day cruise around Singapore's harbor and to the outlying islands. Bumboats wallow in the bay, waiting to take sailors back to their ships or carry other visitors wherever they want to go for about S$30 an hour. In **Merlion Park,** at the end of the quay near Anderson Bridge, stands a statue of Singapore's tourism symbol, the Merlion—half lion, half fish. In the evening, the statue—on a point of land looking out over the harbor—is floodlit, its e, ·s are lighted, and its mouth spews water. You can see an even bigger one on Sentosa Island. This creature is based upon the country's national symbol, the lion (from which the name Singapore was derived). The Merlion symbolizes courage, strength, and excellence.

Empress Place. This huge, white, neoclassical building was meticulously restored as an exhibition hall but is now closed until the year 2000, when it will reopen as Phase II of the ☞ **Asian Civilisations Museum.** Constructed in the 1860s as the courthouse, the building has since had four major additions and has housed nearly every government body, including the Registry of Births and Deaths and the Immigration Department. Virtually every adult Singaporean has been inside this building at one time or another.

Former General Post Office. The post office recently moved to the suburbs from this proud, anachronistic, Victorian building—all gray stone and huge pillars. The government has promised not to knock the structure down to make way for yet another glass-and-steel high-rise. But rumor has it that the building will become yet another hotel and shopping complex. To the left as you face the old post office is **Fullerton Square,** a rest stop for cycle-rickshaw drivers.

Fort Canning Park. Until recently Fort Canning was hallowed ground, a green sanctuary from the city's mass of concrete commercialism. Alas, like so much in Singapore, the park is undergoing extensive renovations. The government recently added a 19th-century walk, with guideposts

Colonial Singapore

Armenian Church, **18**

Asian Civilisations
Museum, **20**

Boat Quay, **4**

Cavenagh Bridge, **3**

Chijmes, **17**

City Hall, **12**

Clarke Quay, **23**

Collyer Quay, **1**

Empress Place, **5**

Former General Post
Office, **2**

Fort Canning
Park, **22**

National Museum
and Art Gallery, **21**

Padang, **10**

Parliament House, **7**

Raffles City, **14**

Raffles Hotel, **15**

St. Andrew's
Cathedral, **13**

Singapore Art
Museum, **16**

Singapore Cricket
Club, **9**

Singapore Philatelic
Museum, **19**

Statue of Sir Thomas
Stamford Raffles, **6**

Supreme Court, **11**

Victoria Memorial
Hall, **8**

pointing you to all the park's 19th-century sites. There are designated picnic areas, and a country club is being built at the park's edge.

What still remains, though, are the tombstones of the **European ceme-tery.** Once divided into areas for Protestants and for Catholics, the tomb-stones have been moved to form a wall around an open field. It's hard to read the inscriptions on the weathered plaques, but their brevity sug-gests the loneliness of the expatriates who had sought fortune far from home.

Seven centuries ago **Fort Canning Rise,** as the park was once called, was home to the royal palaces of the Majapahit rulers, who no doubt chose it for the cool breezes and commanding view of the river. The last five kings of Singa Pura, including the legendary Iskandar Shah, are said to be buried on the hill. Some dispute this, claiming that Iskandar Shah escaped from Singa Pura before its destruction in 1391.

For several hundred years the site was abandoned to the jungle. It was referred to by the Malays as Bukit Larangan, the Forbidden Hill, a place where the spirits of bygone kings roamed on sacred ground. Then Raf-fles came and, defying the legends, established a government house (head-quarters for the colonial governor) on the rise. Later, in 1859, a fort was constructed; its guns were fired to mark dawn, noon, and night.

OFF THE
BEATEN PATH

MARINA SQUARE – A minicity all its own, Marina Square has three malls and five smart atrium hotels—the Pan Pacific, the Marina Man-darin, the Oriental, the Ritz-Carlton, and the Conrad International Cen-tennial (☞ *also* Lodging, *below*). The mammoth convention center and shopping mall, Suntec City, had its opening in 1995, only to be fol-lowed by the opening of an even bigger mall, the Millennia Walk, with its three-story duty-free shop, in late 1996. The Marina Square Shop-ping Mall provides an eclectic mix of boutique bargain shopping. An arts center, The Esplanade, is slated to open in 2001 across the road from this mall and along the Queen Elizabeth Walk, which opened in 1953 to mark her coronation. The entire Marina Square complex sym-b lizes much of what Singapore has become: a modern convention city built on landfills and dotted with theme parks and festival malls de-signed to entertain delegates and their spouses.

㉑ **National Museum and Art Gallery.** Housed in a grand colonial build-ing topped by a silver dome, this museum is also referred to as the Sin-gapore History Museum and was originally opened as the Raffles Museum in 1887. Included in its collection are 20 dioramas that de-pict the republic's past; the Revere Bell, donated to the original St. An-drew's Church in 1843 by the daughter of American patriot Paul Revere; the 380-piece Haw Par Jade Collection, one of the largest of its kind; ethnographic collections from Southeast Asia; and many his-torical documents. ⊠ *Stamford Rd.,* ☎ *332–3659.* ▨ *S$3; free guided tour 11 AM Tues.* ☉ *Tues.–Sun. 9–5:30.*

❿ **Padang.** Today the Padang, which seemingly constitutes the backyard of the ☞ **Singapore Cricket Club,** is used primarily as a playing field (an appropriate usage, as *padang* is Malay for "field" or "plain"). It has traditionally been a social and political hub. Once called the Es-planade, it was only half its current size until an 1890s land reclama-tion expanded it, giving colonial gentry still more room to stroll and exchange pleasantries and gossip. Its other uses have not been as po-lite: during World War II, 2,000 British civilians were gathered here by the Japanese before being marched off to Changi Prison and, in many cases, to their deaths.

Beyond the northeastern edge of the Padang, across Stamford Road and the Stamford Canal, are the four 230-ft, tapering, white columns of the **War Memorial,** known locally as "The Four Chopsticks." The monument honors the thousands of civilians from the four main ethnic groups (Chinese, Malay, Indian, and European) who lost their lives during the Japanese occupation. The highest column represents the Chinese, who were the most persecuted—some 25,000 were immediately executed for being too Western; others were sent to help build the bridge over the River Kwai.

Along the Padang's eastern edge, just across Connaught Drive, are several other monuments. The **Major General Lim Bo Seng Memorial** honors a well-loved freedom fighter of World War II who was tortured and died in a Japanese prison camp in 1944. The imposing **Cenotaph War Memorial** honors the dead of the two world wars.

❼ Parliament House. George Coleman designed the Parliament House in 1827 for a wealthy merchant, but it went unoccupied until the government bought it for S$15,600 in 1841 to use as a courthouse. It's considered the oldest government building in Singapore. Additions were built, and in the 1870s it became the meeting place for parliament. The bronze elephant in front of the building was a gift from King Chulalongkorn of Siam during his state visit in 1871. ✉ *Corner of High St. and St. Andrew's Rd.,* ☎ *335–8811.* ☜ *Free.* ☽ *Daily by appointment.*

⓮ Raffles City. The Raffles City complex of offices and shops contains Asia's tallest hotel, the Westin Stamford, not to be confused with the Westin Plaza, which is in the same building and operates as a semi-separate hotel (☞ *Lodging, below*). There's a beautiful view of downtown and the harbor from the Compass Rose restaurant atop the Stamford.

⓯ Raffles Hotel. Once a "tiffin house," or tearoom, the Raffles Hotel started life as the home of a British sea captain. In 1887 the Armenian Sarkies brothers took over the building and transformed it into one of Asia's grandest hotels. The Raffles has had many ups and downs, especially during World War II, when it was first a center for British refugees, then quarters for Japanese officers, and then a center for released Allied prisoners of war. There's a delicious irony to the Raffles: viewed as a bastion of colonialism, it was not only the creation of Armenians, but in its 130 years of hosting expatriates, it only once had a British manager. Even so, service has been unfailingly loyal to the colonial heritage. Right before the Japanese arrived, the Chinese waiters took the silverware from the dining rooms and buried it in the Palm Court garden, where it remained safely hidden until the occupiers departed.

After the war the hotel deteriorated, surviving by trading on its heritage rather than its facilities. However, in late 1991, after two years of renovation and expansion, the Raffles reopened as the republic's most expensive hotel. You can no longer just roam around. Instead you're channeled through new colonial-style buildings to take in a free museum of Raffles memorabilia and then, perhaps, to take refreshment in a reproduction of the **Long Bar,** where the famous Singapore Sling was created in 1903 by the bartender Ngiam Tong Boon. The sling here is still regarded as the best in Singapore; note that your S$17.15 tab includes service and tax, but not the glass—that's another S$8. Also note that some consider the new Long Bar a travesty, with manually operated *punkahs* (fans) replaced by those that are electrically powered. Although casual visitors are discouraged from entering the original part of the hotel, if you crave authenticity (and you have few qualms about being persistent) the **Tiffin Room** and the **Bar and Billiard Room** are much better bets than the Long Bar. If you aren't feeling brazen, you can simply browse in the arcade's 65 shops, stop by **Doc Cheng's** restaurant for a taste of its "transethnic" cuisine, or head to the tiny **Writers Bar** for a drink.

⑬ St. Andrew's Cathedral. This Anglican (Episcopal) church, surrounded by a green lawn, is the second one built on this site. The first was constructed in 1834, but after being struck twice by lightning, it was demolished in 1852. (Locals took the bolts from the heavens as a sign that the site was bedeviled. It was suggested that before another place of worship was built, the spirits should be appeased with the blood from 30 heads; fortunately, the suggestion was ignored.) Indian convicts were brought in to construct a new cathedral in the English Gothic style. The structure, completed in 1862, has bells cast by the firm that made Big Ben's, and it resembles Netley Abbey in Hampshire, England. The British overlords were so impressed by the cathedral that the Indian convict who supplied the working drawings was granted his freedom. The church was expanded once in 1952 and again in 1983. Its lofty interior is white and simple, with stained-glass windows coloring the sunlight as it enters. Around the walls are marble and brass memorial plaques, including one remembering the British who died in a 1915 mutiny of native light infantry and another in memory of 41 Australian army nurses killed in the Japanese invasion. Services are held every Sunday.

⑯ Singapore Art Museum. When this 1852 building—once the all-boys Catholic St. Joseph's Institution—closed in 1987 it did not reopen as a museum until 1996. (Names of school donors still adorn the porch at the entrance.) When Prime Minister Goh Chok Tung opened it, he described a vision of Singapore "reliving, through its museums, its historic role as an entrepôt for art, culture, civilization, and ideas." Collections here include modern art from Singapore and traditional art from other parts of Southeast Asia. The **E-Image Gallery** has interactive programs that feature 20th-century Southeast Asian art presented on large, high-definition monitors. ⊠ *71 Bras Basah Rd.,* ☎ *332–3222.* ☞ *S$3.* ☼ *Tues.–Sun. 9–5:30; free guided tours Tues., Fri., and Sat.– Sun. 11 AM.*

NEED A BREAK? At the back of the Singapore Art Museum you'll find the **Olio Dome** (☎ 339-0792), a casual breakfast and lunch spot. The Dome, one of several in Singapore, serves a Western menu of soups, salads, and sandwiches—but it really specializes in coffee. A latte goes for S$4.20. You can eat outside on the curving neoclassical porch or inside in a 1920s-style bistro.

---

⑨ Singapore Cricket Club. Founded during the 1850s, this club became the main center for the social and sporting life of the British community. It now has a multiracial membership of more than 4,000 and offers facilities for various sports, in addition to bars and restaurants. If you're going to be in Singapore for more than a couple weeks, you can apply, with the support of a member, for a visiting membership. The club isn't open to the general public, but from the Padang you can sneak a quick look at the deep, shaded verandas, from which members still watch cricket, rugby, and tennis matches.

⑲ Singapore Philatelic Museum. Housed in a 92-year-old building, once part of the Anglo Chinese School, is Southeast Asia's first stamp museum. It has a fine collection of local and international stamps as well as an audiovisual theater, a resource center, interactive games, and a souvenir shop. ⊠ *23B Coleman St.,* ☎ *337–3888.* ☞ *S$2.* ☼ *Tues.– Sun. 9–4:30.*

In case you want to be welcomed there.

We're here to see that you're always welcomed at establishments everywhere. That's why millions of people carry the American Express® Card – for peace of mind, confidence, and security, around the world or just around the corner.

do more

Cards

And just in case.

We're here with American Express® Travelers Cheques and Cheques *for Two*.® They're the safest way to carry money on your vacation and the surest way to get a refund, practically anywhere, anytime.

Another way we help you...

do more ®

Travelers Cheques

6 **Statue of Sir Thomas Stamford Raffles.** This statue near Empress Place on North Boat Quay is on the spot where Raffles purportedly landed in Singapore early on the morning of January 29, 1819. Pause here a moment to observe the contrast between the old and the new. Once this river was the organ of bustling commercial life, packed with barges and lighters that ferried goods from cargo ship to dock. There were no cranes—the unloading was done by teams of coolies. Swarms of them tottered under their heavy loads, back and forth between lighter and riverside godowns, amid yells from *compradores* (factotums).

11 **Supreme Court.** In the neoclassical style so beloved by Victorian colonials, the Supreme Court has Corinthian pillars and the look of arrogant certainty. However, it's not as old as it seems. The building was completed in 1939, replacing the famous Hôtel de l'Europe, where Conrad once propped up the bar eavesdropping on sailors' tales that he later used in novels. The pedimental sculptures of the Greek-temple-like facade portray Justice and other allegorical figures. Inside, the echoing hall and staircase are grand and, high above, the vast paneled ceiling is an exercise in showmanship. All of this was completed just in time for the Japanese to use the building as their headquarters.

8 **Victoria Memorial Hall.** The Memorial Hall was built in 1905 as a tribute to Queen Victoria. Along with the adjacent **Victoria Theatre,** built in 1862 as the town hall, it's currently the city's main cultural center, offering regular exhibitions, concerts, and theatrical performances of all types (☞ Nightlife and the Arts, *below*).

Chinatown

In a country where 76% of the people are Chinese, it may seem strange to name a small urban area Chinatown. But Chinatown was born some 170 years ago, when the Chinese were a minority (if only for half a century) in the newly formed British settlement. In an attempt to minimize racial tension, Raffles allotted sections of the settlement to different immigrant groups. The Chinese were given the area south of the Singapore River. Today, the river is still the northern boundary of old Chinatown; Maxwell Road marks its southern perimeter and New Bridge Road its western one. Before the 1933 land reclamation, the western perimeter was the sea. The reclaimed area between Telok Ayer Street and Collyer Quay–Shenton Way has become the business district whose expansion has caused Chinese shophouses to be knocked down all the way to Cross Street.

Inside a relatively small rectangle, immigrants—many of them penniless and half-starved—from mainland China were crammed. Within three years of the formation of the Straits Settlement, 3,000 Chinese had arrived; this number increased tenfold over the next decade. The Hokkien people, traders from Fukien Province, made up about a quarter of the community. Other leading groups were the Teochews, from the Swatow region of Guangdong Province, and their mainland neighbors, the Cantonese. In smaller groups, the Hainanese, the nomadic Hakkas, and peoples from Guangxi arrived in tightly packed junks, riding on the northeast monsoon winds.

Most immigrants came with the sole intention of exchanging their rags for riches, then returning to China. They had no allegiance to Singapore or to Chinatown, which was no melting pot but, rather, separate pockets of ethnically diverse groups, each with a different dialect; a different cuisine; and different cultural, social, and religious attitudes. In the shophouses—two-story buildings with shops or small factories on the ground floor and living quarters upstairs—as many as 30 lodgers

would share a single room. Life was a fight for space and survival. Crime
was rampant. What order existed was maintained by Chinese guilds,
clan associations, and secret societies, all of which fought—sometimes
savagely—for control of lucrative aspects of community life.

Until recently, all of Chinatown was slated for the bulldozer, to be wiped
clean of its past and replaced by uniform concrete structures. The traditional ways of the Chinese groups were to melt away into the modern Singaporean lifestyle. In the name of "progressive social engineering,"
much of the original community was disassembled and entire blocks
were cleared of shophouses. However, the government finally recognized not only the people's desire to maintain Chinese customs and family ties, but also the important role these play in modern society.
Chinatown received a stay of execution, and an ambitious plan to restore a large area of shophouses is almost complete. Fortunately,
enough of the old remains to permit the imaginative visitor to experience a traditional Chinese community.

*Numbers in the text correspond to numbers in the margin and on the
Chinatown map.*

A Good Walk

Begin at the Elgin Bridge, built to link Chinatown with the colonial
administration center. At the south end of the bridge, logically enough,
South Bridge Road begins. Off to the right is Upper Circular Road, on
the left-hand side of which is **Yeo Swee Huat** ① at No. 13, which sells
paper replicas of houses, cars, and other worldly goods intended to be
burned at Chinese funerals. (You'll encounter other such shops during your walk.) Circular Road, once home to cloth wholesalers, now
has bars and restaurants. Walk down **Lopong Telok Street** ②, with its
architecturally interesting shops and clan houses, and take a right onto
North Canal Road. Here are stores that sell Chinese delicacies—dried
foods, turtles for soup, sea cucumbers, sharks' fins, and birds' nests.
Trace your steps back along North Canal to Chulia Street. Follow it
to Phillip Street and turn right to reach the recently restored **Wak Hai
Cheng Bio Temple** ③.

Return to North Canal Road. Continue to New Bridge Road, turn left,
and walk past the Furama Singapore Hotel and the People's Park Centre, now home to the Singapore Handicrafts Centre. Cross Upper
Cross Street and take a left onto **Mosque Street.** The old shophouses
here—now being redeveloped into offices—were originally built as stables. Turn right onto South Bridge Road. The **Jamae Mosque** ④ will
be on your right. On the next block is the **Sri Mariamman Temple** ⑤,
the oldest Hindu temple in Singapore.

If you take the next right, onto **Temple Street,** you may be fortunate
enough to see one of the few remaining scribes in Singapore. At the
junction of Trengganu Street, notice the old building on the corner. Reliable sources say this was once a famous **brothel** ⑥. You are now in
the core of Chinatown, an area known as **Kreta Ayer.** Trengganu Street
leads to the new **Chinatown Centre** ⑦. Leaving the market, walk along
Sago Street to see more family factories that make paper models to be
burned for good fortune at funerals. Parallel to Sago Street is Sago Lane.
There's nothing to see here now, but the street was once known for its
death houses, where Chinese waited out their last days.

If you turn right onto South Bridge Road, you'll come to the intersection of **Tanjong Pagar Road** and Neil Road. The **Jinriksha Station** ⑧
was once a rickshaw depot, but it is now a food court. After strolling
down Tanjong Pagar Road to see the restored shophouses and trendy
restaurants, head back to South Bridge Road. **Smith Street,** on the left,

has stores that sell everything from chilies to ground rhinoceros horn. Ann Siang Road, on the other side of South Bridge Road, is full of old shops and is the site of the **Guild for Amahs** ⑨. From Ann Siang Road, turn left onto Club Street, and then right at Gemmill Lane. When you get to Telok Ayer Street, turn right, and you'll find the **Nagore Durghe Shrine** ⑩—an odd mix of minarets and Greek columns decorated with Christmas lights—built by South Indian Muslims in the early 19th century. Continue down the road to the interesting **Thian Hock Keng Temple** ⑪, which, at press time, was undergoing renovation as part of a new housing-shopping complex on Telok Ayer Street. Across from the temple is the China Square Food Centre, home of the unusual House of Mao (☞ Dining, *below*) restaurant. A little farther down the street is the **Al Abrar Mosque** ⑫, built in 1827. Walk east along McCallum Street toward the bay and take a left onto Shenton Way. At Boon Tat Street, you'll see the **Telok Ayer Market** ⑬, the largest Victorian cast-iron structure in Southeast Asia. Here you can refresh yourself at the food court, then take the subway back to Raffles Place on Collyer Quay.

TIMING

Allow two to three hours for this walk, and factor in a half an hour each for the Wak Hai Cheng Bio, Thian Hock Keng, and Sri Mariamman temples. Owing to all the construction and restoration projects in this area, you may need a little more patience than usual to get around.

Sights to See

⑫ **Al Abrar Mosque.** Also known as Kuchu Palli (the Tamil word for "small mosque"), this structure dates from 1850. The original mosque, built in 1827, was one of the first for Singapore's Indian Muslims.

OFF THE BEATEN PATH

BIRD-SINGING CAFÉS – A special Sunday-morning treat is to take breakfast with the birds. Bird fanciers bring their prize specimens, in intricate bamboo cages, to coffee shops and hang the cages outside for training sessions: by listening to their feathered friends, the birds learn how to warble. Bird-singing enthusiasts take their hobby seriously and, incidentally, pay handsomely for it. For you, it costs only the price of a cup of coffee to sit at a table and listen. One place to try is the Seng Poh Coffee Shop on the corner of Tiong Bahru and Seng Poh roads, west of Tanjong Pagar; arrive at around 9 AM.

⑥ **Brothel.** Reliable sources say this was a famous brothel. Opium dens and brothels played important roles in the lives of Chinese immigrants, who usually arrived alone and worked long days, with little time for relaxation or pleasure. Many immigrants took to soothing their aching minds and bodies at opium dens; as only 12% of the community were women, men often sought female companionship from professionals. Gambling was another popular pastime. (Except for the state lottery and the official horse-race-betting system, gambling is now outlawed by the government. But you can be sure that when you hear the slap of mah-jongg in a coffeehouse, a wager or two has been made.) Raffles tried to ban gambling, but to no avail—the habit was too firmly entrenched. One legendary figure, Tan Che Seng, who had amassed a fortune subsidizing junks bringing immigrants to work in the warehouses, resolved to give up gambling. As a reminder of his resolution, he cut off half of his little finger. Still, he continued to gamble!

⑦ **Chinatown Centre.** This market is mobbed inside and out with jostling shoppers. At the open-air vegetable and fruit stands, women—toothless and wrinkled with age—sell their wares. Inside, on the first floor, hawker stalls sell a variety of cooked foods, but it's the basement floor that fascinates: here you'll find a wet market—so called because water

Chinatown

is continually sloshed over the floors—where an amazing array of meats, fowl, and fish are bought and sold. Some of the sights may spoil your appetite; at the far left corner, for example, live pigeons, furry white rabbits, and sleepy turtles are crammed into cages, awaiting hungry buyers.

9 Guild for Amahs. Club Street is full of old buildings that continue to house clan associations, including the professional guild for *amahs*. Though their numbers are few today, these female servants were once an integral part of European households in Singapore. Like the *samsui* (women who vowed never to marry)—a few of whom can still be observed in their traditional red headdresses passing bricks or carrying buckets at construction sites—the amahs choose to earn an independent living, however hard the work, rather than submit to the servitude of marriage. (In traditional Chinese society, a daughter-in-law is the lowest-ranking member of the family.) In the past, when a woman decided to become an amah or samsui, she went through a ritual—a sort of substitute for marriage. Family and friends gathered and even brought gifts. The woman then tied up her hair—to indicate she wasn't available for marriage—and moved to a *gongxi,* or communal house, where she shared expenses and household duties and cared for her sisters.

4 Jamae Mosque. Popularly called Masjid Chulia, the simple, almost austere mosque was built in the 1830s by Chulia Muslims from India's Coromandel Coast. So long as it isn't prayer time and the doors are open, you're welcome to step inside for a look (you must be dressed conservatively and take your shoes off before entering; women may need shawls or scarves to cover their heads).

8 Jinriksha Station. This station was once the bustling central depot for Singapore's rickshaws, which numbered more than 9,000 in 1919. Now there's nary a one, and the station has been converted into a food market on one side and an office block on the other. This is a good place to sit down with a cool drink.

Kreta Ayer. Named after the bullock carts that carried water for cleaning the streets, this is the core of Chinatown.

7 Lopong Telok Street. Nos. 27, 28, and 29 on this architecturally interesting street have intricately carved panels above the shop doorways. Across the street are old clan houses whose stonework facades appear to have a Portuguese influence—possibly by way of Malacca, a Portuguese trading post in the 17th century until the Dutch, and then the British, took possession of it.

Mosque Street. The old shophouses here—mercifully spared demolition—were originally built as stables. Now they house Hakka families selling second- or, more likely, thirdhand wares, from clothes to old medicine bottles.

10 Nagore Durghe Shrine. This odd mix of minarets and Greek columns was built by South Indian Muslims between 1828 and 1830. Inside it's now decorated with Christmas tree lights.

Sago Street. At No. 20, Fong Moon Kee, the best tikar mats—used by the older Chinese instead of soft mattresses—are sold. They're easy to carry and excellent for picnics, although prices begin at S$60. A cake shop at No. 34 is extremely popular for fresh baked goods, especially during the Mooncake Festival. Nearby, at No. 26, is Ban Yoo Foh Medical Hall, a store that sells dried snakes and lizards, for increasing fertility, and powdered antelope horn, for curing headaches and cooling the body.

Smith Street. Stores here sell chilies, teas, and soybeans. A medicine hall offers ground rhinoceros horn (a controversial product owing to wildlife protection issues) to help overcome impotency and pearl dust to help ladies' complexions.

★ ⑤ **Sri Mariamman Temple.** The oldest Hindu temple in Singapore, the building has a pagodalike entrance topped by one of the most ornate *gopurams* (pyramidal gateway towers) you are ever likely to see. Hundreds of brightly colored statues of deities and mythical animals line the tiers of this towering porch; glazed cement cows sit, seemingly in great contentment, atop the surrounding walls. The story of this Hindu temple smack in the heart of Chinatown begins with Naraina Pillay, who came to Singapore on the same ship as Raffles in 1819 and started work as a clerk. Within a short time, he had set up his own construction business, often using convicts sent over to Singapore from India, and quickly made a fortune. He obtained this site to build a temple on, so that devotees could pray on the way to and from work at the harbor. This first temple, built in 1827 of wood and *atap* (wattle and daub), was replaced in 1843 by the current brick structure. The gopuram was added in 1936. Inside are some spectacular paintings that have been recently restored by Tamil craftsmen brought over from South India.

Tanjong Pagar Road. The center of an area of redevelopment in Chinatown, the area has 220 shophouses restored to their 19th-century appearance—or rather a sanitized, dollhouselike version of it. They now contain teahouses, calligraphers, mah-jongg makers, and other shops. More shophouses are presently being restored and, at current rents, will probably be occupied by upscale boutiques and restaurants.

⑬ **Telok Ayer Market.** This market, which looks a lot like a chicken coop, is the largest Victorian cast-iron structure left in Southeast Asia. Already a thriving fish market in 1822, it was redesigned as an octagon by George Coleman in 1894. It has been transformed into a planned food court, with hawker stalls offering all types of Asian fare. By day it's busy with office workers. After 7 PM Boon Tat Street is closed to traffic and the mood turns festive: hawkers wheel out their carts, and street musicians perform.

Temple Street. Here you may be fortunate enough to see one of the few remaining practitioners of a dying profession. Sometimes found sitting on a stool here is a scribe, an old man to whom other elderly Chinese who have not perfected the art of writing come to have their letters written. The street is slated to become a pedestrian street in the near future.

⑪ **Thian Hock Keng Temple.** Though at press time this—the Temple of Heavenly Happiness—was closed for renovations and it was unclear when the work would be finished, you should at least pass by to see the exterior. The temple was completed in 1841 to replace a simple shrine built 20 years earlier. It's one of Singapore's oldest and largest Chinese temples, built on the spot where, prior to land reclamation, immigrants stepped ashore after a hazardous journey across the China Sea. In gratitude for their safe passage, the Hokkien people dedicated the temple to Ma Chu P'oh, the goddess of the sea. Thian Hock Keng is richly decorated with gilded carvings, sculptures, tiled roofs topped with dragons, and fine carved stone pillars. The pillars and sculptures were brought over from China, the exterior cast-iron railings were made in Glasgow, and the blue porcelain tiles on an outer building came from Holland. On either side of the entrance are two stone lions. The one on the left is female and holds a cup, symbolizing fertility; the other, a male, holds a ball, a symbol of wealth. If the temple is open, note that as you enter you must step over a high threshold board. This serves a dual function. First, it forces devotees to look downward, as they should, when entering the temple. Second, it keeps out wandering ghosts—ghosts tend to shuffle their feet, so if they try to enter, the threshold board will trip them.

Inside, a statue of a maternal Ma Chu P'oh, surrounded by masses of burning incense and candles, dominates the room. On either side of her are the deities of health (on the left if your back is to the entrance) and of wealth. The two tall figures you'll notice are her sentinels: one can see for 1,000 miles, the other can hear for 1,000 miles. The gluey black substance on their lips—placed there by devotees in days past—is opium, to heighten their senses. While the main temple is Taoist, the temple at the back is Buddhist and dedicated to Kuan Yin, the goddess of mercy. Her many arms represent how she reaches out to all those who suffer on earth. This is a good place to learn your fortune. Choose a number out of the box, then pick up two small, stenciled pieces of wood at the back of the altar and let them fall to the ground. If they land showing opposite faces, then the number you have picked is valid. If they land same-side up, try again. From a valid number, the person in the nearby booth will tell you your fate, and whether you like it or not, you pay for the information. Leave the grounds by the alley that runs alongside the main temple. The two statues to the left are the gambling brothers. They will help you choose a lucky number for your next betting session; if you win, you must return and place lighted cigarettes in their hands.

❸ Wak Hai Cheng Bio Temple. Built between 1852 and 1855 by Teochew Chinese from Guangdong Province and dedicated to the goddess of the sea, restoration of this temple was completed in 1998. Its wonderfully ornate roof is covered with decorations—including miniature pagodas and human figures—depicting ancient Chinese villages and scenes from opera. Chinese temples, incidentally, are invariably dusty, thick with incense, and packed with offerings and statuary—evidence of devotees asking for favors and offering thanks for favors granted. To a Chinese, a sparkling clean, spartan temple would suggest unsympathetic deities with few followers. Where burning joss sticks have left a layer of dust and continue to fill the air with scent, the gods are willing to hear requests and grant wishes. If word spreads that many wishes have been realized by people visiting a particular temple, it can, virtually overnight, become the most popular temple in town.

❶ Yeo Swee Huat. At No. 13 Upper Circular Road, you'll see a cottage industry designed to help Chinese take care of one obligation to their ancestors: making sure they have everything they need in the afterlife. Here, paper models of the paraphernalia of life—horses, cars, boats, planes, even fake money—are made, to be purchased by relatives of the deceased (you can buy them, too) and ritually burned so that their essence passes through to the spirit world in flames and smoke. Note that although the items may elicit chuckles, this custom is a very serious part of Chinese beliefs; try not to offend the proprietors.

Little India

Indians have been part of Singapore's development from the beginning. While Singapore was administered by the East India Company, headquartered in Calcutta, Indian convicts were sent here to serve their time. These convicts left an indelible mark on Singapore, reclaiming land from swampy marshes and constructing a great deal of the city's infrastructure, including public buildings, St. Andrew's Cathedral, and many Hindu temples. The enlightened penal program permitted convicts to study a trade of their choice in the evenings. Many, on gaining their freedom, chose to stay in Singapore.

Other Indians came freely to seek their fortunes as clerks, traders, teachers, and moneylenders. The vast majority came from the south of India—both Hindu Tamils and Muslims from the Coromandel and Malabar coasts—but there were also Gujaratis, Sindhis, Sikhs, Parsis, and Bengalis. Each group brought its own language, cuisine, religion, and customs, and these divisions remain evident today. The Indians also brought their love of colorful festivals, which they now celebrate more frequently and more spectacularly than is done in India itself. The gory Thaipusam is among the most fascinating (☞ Festivals and Seasonal Events *in* Singapore A to Z *below*).

The area Raffles allotted to the Indian immigrants was north of the British colonial district. The heart of this area—known today as Little India—is Serangoon Road and the streets east and west of it between Bukit Timah and Sungei roads to the south and Perumal Road to the north. Although new buildings have replaced many of the old, the sights, sounds, and smells will make you believe you're in an Indian town.

Numbers in the text correspond to numbers in the margin and on the Little India map.

A Good Walk

Try to plan your walk for a weekday morning when crowds are at their thinnest and temperatures are at their lowest. Avoid Sunday afternoons, when the neighborhood teems with people. A good starting point is the junction of Serangoon and Sungei roads. As you walk along Serangoon, your senses will be sharpened by the fragrances of curry powders and perfumes, by tapes of high-pitched Indian music, by jewelry shops selling gold and stands selling garlands of flowers. (Indian women delight in wearing flowers and glittering arm bangles, but once their husbands die, they never do so again.) Other shops supply the colorful dyes used to mark the *tilak*—the dot seen on the forehead of Indian women. Traditionally, a Tamil woman wears a red dot to signify that she's married; a North Indian woman conveys the same message with a red streak down the part of her hair. However, the modern trend is for an Indian girl or woman to choose a dye color to match her sari or Western dress. Occasionally you'll see an unmarried woman with a black dot on her forehead: this is intended to counter the effects of the evil eye.

The first block on the left is **Zhujiao Centre** ①, one of the largest wet markets in the city. The streets to the right off Serangoon Road—Campbell Lane (home of **P. Govindasamy Pillai** ②, famous for its beautiful silk saris) and Dunlop Street—as well as **Clive Street,** which runs parallel to Serangoon, are filled with shops that sell such utilitarian items as pots and pans as well as rice, spices, brown cakes of palm sugar, and every other type of Indian grocery imaginable. You'll also see open-air barbershops and tailors working old-fashioned treadle sewing machines, and everywhere you go you'll hear sugar-sweet love songs from Indian movies. Along **Buffalo Road,** to the left off Serangoon, are shops specializing in saris, flower garlands, and electronic equipment. Above the doorways are strings of dried mango leaves, a customary Indian sign of blessing and good fortune. (If you detour down Dunlop Street, to the right off Serangoon Road, you'll come to the **Abdul Gaffoor Mosque** ③, with its detailed facade of green and gold.)

A little farther down Serangoon Road on the left (opposite Veerasamy Road), you'll notice the elaborate gopuram of the **Sri Veeramakaliamman**

Temple ④, built in 1881 by indentured Bengali laborers working the lime pits nearby. Take Kinta Road to the **Burmese Buddhist Temple** ⑤ with its 11-ft-tall white marble Buddha. Turn right on Race Course Road to **Farrer Park** ⑥, site of Singapore's original racecourse. Farther along Race Course Road is the charming **Long San Chee Temple** ⑦, dedicated to Kuan Yin. Across the road is Sakya Muni Buddha Gaya Temple, more commonly referred to as the **Temple of 1,000 Lights** ⑧. Backtrack on Race Course Road to Perumal Road; to the left is the **Sri Srinivasa Perumal Temple** ⑨. Dedicated to Vishnu the Preserver, the temple is easy to recognize by the 59-ft-high monumental gopuram, depicting Vishnu in nine forms. If you continue along Race Course Road, you'll come to the Banana Leaf Apollo, an excellent place for a drink and a curry (☞ Dining, *below*).

TIMING

This whole Race Course Road area has been under construction for a new MRT (subway) line and may require a couple of detours while walking. Even so, you should be able to do this tour in three to four hours. Factor in a half an hour extra for the temples.

Sights to See

❸ **Abdul Gaffoor Mosque.** This small, personable temple at No. 41 Dunlop Street has none of the exotic, multicolor statuary of the Hindu temples. But it still woos you with an intricately detailed facade in the Muslim colors of green and gold. When entering, make sure your legs are covered to the ankles, and remember to take off your shoes. Note that only worshippers are allowed into the prayer hall. Out of respect you shouldn't enter during evening prayer sessions or at any time on Friday.

Buffalo Road. Shops here specialize in saris, flower garlands, and electronic equipment. Also along this short street are a number of moneylenders from the Chettiar caste—the only caste that continues to pursue in Singapore the role prescribed to them in India. You'll find them seated on the floor before decrepit desks, but don't let the simplicity of their style fool you: some of them are very, very rich.

❺ **Burmese Buddhist Temple.** Built in 1878, this temple houses an 11-ft Buddha carved from a 10-ton block of white marble from Mandalay. The other, smaller Buddhas were placed here by Rama V, the king of Siam, and high priests from Rangoon, Burma (now called Yangon, Myanmar).

Clive Street. On this byway off Sungei Road, you'll find shops that purvey sugar, prawn crackers, rice, and dried beans. The older Indian women you'll notice with red lips and stained teeth are betel-nut chewers. If you want to try the stuff, you can buy a mouthful from street vendors.

❻ **Farrer Park.** This is the site of Singapore's original racetrack. It's also where the first aircraft to land in Singapore came to rest en route from England to Australia in 1919.

❼ **Long San Chee Temple.** Its main altar is dedicated to Kuan Yin—also known as Bodhisattva Avalokitesvara—and framed by beautiful, ornate carvings of flowers, a phoenix, and other birds.

❷ **P. Govindasamy Pillai.** This shop is famous for Indian textiles, especially saris. It sits on Campbell Lane amid other shops that sell spices, nuts, flower garlands, plastic flowers, and plastic statues.

❾ **Sri Srinivasa Perumal Temple.** Dedicated to Vishnu the Preserver, the temple is easy to recognize by the 60-ft-high monumental gopuram, with tiers of intricate sculptures depicting Vishnu in the nine forms in which he has appeared on earth. Especially vivid are the depictions of

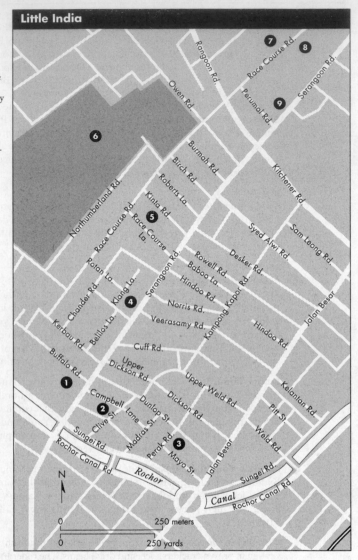

Little India

Vishnu's manifestations as Rama, on his seventh visit, and as Krishna, on his eighth. Rama is thought to be the personification of the ideal man; Krishna was brought up with peasants and, therefore, was a manifestation popular with laborers in the early days of Singapore. Sri Srinivasa Perumal is very much a people's temple. Inside you'll find devotees making offerings of fruit to one of the manifestations of Vishnu. This is done either by handing the coconuts or bananas, along with a slip of paper with one's name on it, to a temple official, who will chant the appropriate prayers to the deity and place holy ash on your head, or by walking and praying, coconut in hand, around one of the shrines a certain number of times, then breaking the coconut (a successful break symbolizes that Vishnu has been receptive to the incantation). The Temple is open from 6:30 AM to noon and 6 PM to 9 pm. Dress conservatively, and don't wear shoes inside.

❹ **Sri Veeramakaliamman Temple.** Built in 1881 by indentured Bengali laborers working the lime pits nearby, this temple is dedicated to Kali the Courageous, a ferocious incarnation of Shiva's wife, Parvati the Beautiful. Inside is a jet-black statue of Kali, the fiercest of the Hindu deities, who demands sacrifices and is often depicted with a garland of skulls. More cheerful is the shrine to Ganesh, the elephant-headed god of wisdom and prosperity. Perhaps the most popular Hindu deity, Ganesh is the child of Shiva and Parvati. (He was not born with an elephant head but received it in the following way: Shiva came back from a long absence to find his wife in a room with a young man. In a blind rage, he lopped off the man's head, not realizing that it was his now-grown-up son. The only way to bring Ganesh back to life was with the head of the first living thing Shiva saw; he saw an elephant.) Unlike some of Singapore's temples, which are open all day, this one is only open 8 AM−noon and 5:30−8:30 PM. During these times, you will see Hindus going in to receive blessings: the priest streaks devotees' foreheads with *vibhuti,* the white ash from burned cow dung.

⑧ Temple of 1,000 Lights. The Sakya Muni Buddha Gaya is better known by its popular name because, for a small donation, you can pull a switch that lights countless bulbs around a 50-ft Buddha. The entire temple, as well as the Buddha statue, was built by the Thai monk Vutthisasala, who, until he died at the age of 94, was always in the temple, ready to explain Buddhist philosophy to anyone who wanted to listen. The monk also managed to procure relics for the temple: a mother-of-pearl-inlaid cast of the Buddha's footprint and a piece of bark from the bodhi tree under which the Buddha received Enlightenment. Around the pedestal supporting the great Buddha statue is a series of scenes depicting the story of his search for Enlightenment; inside a hollow chamber at the back is a re-creation of the scene of the Buddha's last sermon.

⑨ Zhujiao Centre. One of the largest wet markets in the city, it has a staggering array of fruits, vegetables, fish, herbs, and spices. On the Sungei Road side of the ground floor are food stalls that offer Chinese, Indian, Malay, and Western foods. Upstairs are shops selling brass goods, "antiques," porcelains, and textiles.

The Arab District

Long before the Europeans arrived, Arab traders plied the coastlines of the Malay Peninsula and Indonesia, bringing with them the teachings of Islam. By the time Raffles came to Singapore in 1819, to be a Malay was also to be a Muslim. Traditionally, Malays' lives have centered on their religion and their villages, known as kampongs. These consisted of a number of wood houses, with steep roofs of corrugated iron or thatch, gathered around a communal center, where chickens fed and children played under the watchful eye of mothers and the village elders while the younger men tended the fields or took to the sea in fishing boats. The houses were usually built on stilts above marshes and reached by narrow planks serving as bridges. If the kampong was on dry land, flowers and fruit trees would surround the houses.

Except for a Malay community on Pulau Sakeng (reachable only by private boat), all traditional kampongs have fallen to the might of the bulldozer in the name of urban renewal. Though all ethnic groups have had their social fabrics undermined by the demolition of their old communities, the Malays have suffered the most, since social life centered on the kampong.

The area known as the Arab District, or Little Araby, while not a true kampong, remains a Malay enclave, held firmly together by strict observance of the tenets of Islam. At the heart of the community is the Sultan Mosque, or Masjid Sultan, originally built with a grant from the East India Company to the Sultan of Jahore. Around it are streets whose very names—Bussorah, Baghdad, Kandahar—evoke the fragrances of the Muslim world. The pace of life is slower here: there are few cars, people gossip in doorways, and closet-size shops are crammed with such wares as *songkok* hats (the white skullcaps presented to hajji, those who have made the hajj, as the pilgrimage to Mecca is called) as well as Indonesian batiks, leather bags, and herbs whose packages promise youth and beauty, or many children.

The Arab District is a small area, bounded by Beach and North Bridge roads to the south and north and spreading a couple of blocks to either side of Arab Street. It's a place to meander, taking time to browse through shops or enjoy Muslim food at a simple café. Much of this neighborhood has undergone extensive renovation since 1996, but this only seems to be adding to the area's quiet charm.

Numbers in the text correspond to numbers in the margin and on the Arab District map.

A Good Walk

This walk begins at the foot of **Arab Street,** a street of specialty shops just off **North Bridge Road.** Wander past the shops and take a right onto Baghdad Street; watch for the dramatic view of the **Sultan Mosque** ① where **Bussorah Street** opens to your left. Leaving the mosque, return to Arab Street and take the first left onto Muscat Street, turn right onto Kandahar Street, and then left onto Baghdad Street. At Sultan Gate, you'll find **Istana Kampong Glam** ②, the sultan's Malay-style palace, built in the 1840s. Baghdad Street becomes Pahang Street at Sultan Gate, where traditional Chinese stonemasons create statues curbside. At the junction of Pahang Street and Jalan Sultan, turn right and, at Beach Road, left, to visit the endearing **Hajjah Fatimah Mosque** ③, built in 1845. It leans at a 6° angle. Return to Jalan Sultan and take a right. Past Minto Road is the **Sultan Plaza** ④, which houses fabric stores. Continue along Jalan Sultan, crossing **North Bridge Road,** to the junction of Victoria Street and the **Malabar Jama-Ath Mosque** ⑤.

Follow Victoria Street down to **Bugis Street** ⑥. Three blocks beyond where Bugis Street becomes Albert Street—between the Fu Lu Shou shopping complex (whose shops mostly sell clothes) and the food-oriented Albert Complex—is Waterloo Street. Near the corner is the **Kuan Yin Temple** ⑦, one of the most popular Chinese temples in Singapore.

TIMING

This walking tour shouldn't take more than two hours, including stops to look around the temples and mosques. But take your time. This is one of the friendliest places in Singapore.

Sights to See

Arab Street. On this street of specialty shops, you'll find baskets of every description—stacked on the floor or suspended from the ceiling. Farther along shops that sell fabrics—batiks, embroidered table linens, rich silks and velvets—dominate.

⑥ **Bugis Street.** Until recently Bugis Street was the epitome of Singapore's seedy but colorful nightlife; locals and visitors delighted in its red lights and bars. The government wasn't delighted, though, and the area was razed to make way for a new MRT station. So strong was the outcry that Bugis Street has been re-created, just steps from its original site, between Victoria and Queen streets, Rochor Road, and Cheng Yan Place. The shophouses have been resurrected; hawker food stands compete with open-fronted restaurants (Kentucky Fried Chicken has

363

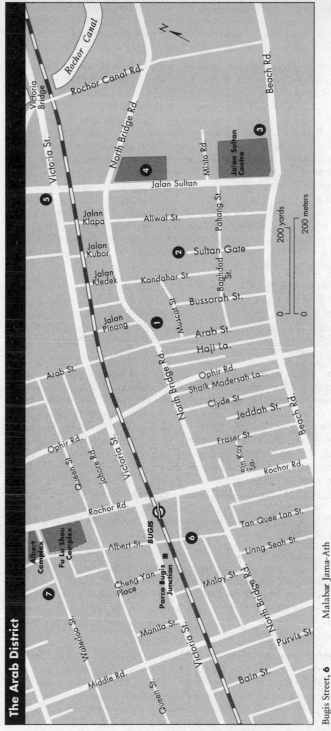

The Arab District

Bugis Street, **6**
Hajjah Fatimah
Mosque, **3**
Istana Kampong
Glam, **2**
Kuan Yin Temple, **7**

Malabar Jama-Ath
Mosque, **5**
Sultan Mosque, **1**
Sultan Plaza, **4**

a prominent spot on a corner). Closed to traffic, the streets in the center of the block are the places to find bargain watches and CDs; you'll also find the Parco Bugis Junction, an upscale shopping center that's quite a contrast to all the area's dollar stores and souvenir shops.

③ Hajjah Fatimah Mosque. In 1845 Hajjah Fatimah, a wealthy Muslim woman married to a Bugis trader, commissioned a British architect to build this mosque. (Hajjah is the title given to a woman who has made the pilgrimage to Mecca.) The minaret is reputedly modeled on the spire of the original St. Andrew's Church in colonial Singapore, but it leans at a 6° angle. No one knows whether this was intentional or accidental, and engineers brought in to see if the minaret could be straightened have walked away shaking their heads. Islam forbids carved images of Allah. The only decorative element usually employed is the beautiful flowing Arabic script in which quotations from the Qur'an (Koran) are written across the walls. This relatively small mosque is an intimate oasis amid all the bustle. It's extremely relaxing to enter the prayer hall (remember to take your shoes off) and sit in the shade of its dome. French contractors and Malay artisans rebuilt the mosque in the 1930s. Hajjah Fatimah, her daughter, and her son-in-law are buried in an enclosure behind the mosque.

② Istana Kampong Glam. The sultan's Malay-style palace, rebuilt in the 1840s on a design by George Coleman, has been refurbished, and next door is another grand royal bungalow: the home of the sultan's first minister. Notice its gateposts surmounted by green eagles. Neither building is open to the public, but through the gates you can get a glimpse of the past.

⑦ Kuan Yin Temple. The dusty, incense-filled interior of this popular temple, its altars heaped with hundreds of small statues of gods from the Chinese pantheon, transports you into the world of Chinese mythology. Of the hundreds of Chinese deities, Kuan Yin is perhaps most dear to the hearts of Singaporeans. Legend has it that just as she was about to enter Nirvana, she heard a plaintive cry from Earth. Filled with compassion, she gave up her place in Paradise to devote herself to alleviating the pain of those on Earth; thereupon, she took the name Kuan Yin, meaning "to see and hear all." People in search of advice on anything from an auspicious date for a marriage to possible solutions for domestic or work crises come to her temple, shake *cham si* (bamboo fortune sticks), and wait for an answer. The gods are the most receptive on days of a new or full moon.

For more immediate advice, you can speak to any of the fortune-tellers who sit under umbrellas outside the temple. They'll pore over ancient scrolls of the Chinese almanac and, for a few dollars, tell you your future. If the news isn't good, you may want to buy some of the flowers sold nearby and add them to your bathwater. They're said to help wash away bad luck. A small vegetarian restaurant next to the temple serves Chinese pastries.

⑤ Malabar Jama-Ath Mosque. The land on which this mosque sits was originally granted to the Muslim Kling community (Muslims from either Malaysia or the Philippines) in 1848 by Sultan Ally Iskander Shah as a burial ground. The mosque they erected here was abandoned and later taken over by the Malabar Muslims (those with ancestors from India or Ceylon, now Sri Lanka), who rebuilt it in 1963.

North Bridge Road. North Bridge Road is full of fascinating stores that sell costumes and headdresses for Muslim weddings, clothes for traditional Malay dances, prayer beads, scarves, perfumes, and much more. Interspersed among the shops are small, simple restaurants that serve

Muslim food. Toward the Sultan Mosque, the shops tend to concentrate on Muslim religious items, including *bareng haji*, the clothing and other requisites for a pilgrimage to Mecca.

★ ❶ **Sultan Mosque.** The first mosque on this site was built early in the 1820s with a S$3,000 grant from the East India Company. The current structure, built in 1928 by Denis Santry—the architect who designed the Victoria Memorial Hall—is a dramatic building with golden domes and minarets that glisten in the sun. The walls of the vast prayer hall are adorned with green and gold mosaic tiles on which passages from the Qur'an are written in decorative Arab script. The main dome has an odd architectural feature: hundreds of brown bottles, stacked five or more rows deep, are seemingly jammed in neck first between the dome and base. No one seems to know why. Five times a day—at dawn, 12:30 PM, 4 PM, sunset, and 8:15 PM—the sound of the muezzin, or crier, calls the faithful to prayer. At midday on Friday, the Islamic sabbath, seemingly every Malay in Singapore enters through one of the Sultan Mosque's 14 portals to recite the Qur'an. During Ramadan, the month of fasting, the nearby streets, especially Bussorah, and the square before the mosque are lined with hundreds of stalls selling curries, cakes, and candy; at dusk, Muslims break their day's fast in this square. Non-Muslims, too, come to enjoy the rich array of Muslim foods and the party atmosphere.

❹ **Sultan Plaza.** Inside, dozens of traders offer batiks and other fabrics in traditional Indonesian and Malay designs.

Orchard Road

If "downtown" is defined as where the action is, then Singapore's downtown is Orchard Road. Here are some of the city's most fashionable shops, hotels (which often, like the Hilton, for example, have expensive, upscale malls all their own), restaurants, and nightclubs. The street has been dubbed the Fifth Avenue or Bond Street of Singapore but, air of luxury aside, it has little in common with either of those older, relatively understated marketplaces for the wealthy. Orchard Road is an ultra-high-rent district that's very modern and very, very flashy—especially at night, when millions of lightbulbs, flashing from seemingly every building, assault the senses. In addition to all those glittering lights and windows, Orchard Road offers a number of sights with which to break up a shopping trip. Still, if the urge to splurge has overtaken the need to sightsee, you'll find additional information on the malls and stores mentioned in this tour *in* Shopping, *below.*

Numbers in the text correspond to numbers in the margin and on the Orchard Road map.

A Good Walk

Start at the bottom of Orchard Road and head toward the junction with Scotts Road, the hub of downtown. You'll see the enormous **Is-tana** ①, once the official residence of the colonial governor and now that of the president of the republic. Senior Minister Lee Kuan Yew also keeps his office here. On the other side of Orchard Road, and a few steps down Cleamenceau Avenue, is the lovely old **Tan Yeok Nee House** ②. Built in 1815 for a wealthy Chinese merchant, the house used to be a museum, but now it's being redeveloped. Turn on Tank Road and continue to the **Chettiar Temple** ③, which houses the image of Lord Subramaniam. Return to Orchard Road and turn left. On the right is Cuppage Road, with a market (open every morning) known for imported and unusual fruit and a row of antiques shops.

Returning once more to Orchard Road, you'll pass the block-long **Centrepoint**; immediately after it is **Peranakan Place** ④, a celebration of Peranakan culture. A bit farther along and on the other side of Orchard Road is the **Mandarin Singapore** ⑤ hotel, which has an interesting art collection. Cross back to the other side of Orchard Road and follow it to the intersection of Scotts Road, where you'll find **Shaw House** ⑥, which has Isetan as its major anchor. A detour up Scotts Road leads to the landmark **Goodwood Park Hotel,** which offers one of the most civilized high teas in town. Farther up Scotts Road is the **Newton Circus** ⑦ food hawker center.

Retrace your steps to the intersection of Scotts and Orchard roads. Walk up the left side of Orchard Road, past the Lane Crawford building. Taxi drivers call it "the rocket", and you'll see why. **Planet Hollywood** opened at the Liat Towers on Orchard Road in early 1997 and still gets its share of visiting celebrities. As you continue up Orchard Road, the **Palais Renaissance** will be on your right. Where Orchard turns into Tanglin, you'll find the **Tanglin Shopping Centre.** The second floor has some of the best antiques shops in town.

TIMING

Orchard Road has so many shopping diversions that you should allow three to four hours for the walk. Allow half an hour for the Chettiar Temple and, if you are an antiques fan, at least an hour for the Tanglin Shopping Centre.

Sights to See

Centrepoint. One of the liveliest shopping complexes, spacious and impressive Centrepoint has the **Robinsons** department store as its largest tenant. It also has **Marks & Spencer**; leading watch retailer **The Hour Glass**; jewelry, silverware, and fashion clothing shops; furniture stores that sell Philippine bamboo and Korean chests; and a large basement supermarket. For those craving a Big Mac, a popular **McDonald's** is also here.

❸ **Chettiar Temple.** This southern Indian temple, home to numerous shrines, is a recent (1984) replacement of the original, which was built in the 19th century. The 70-ft-high gopuram, with its many colorful sculptures of godly manifestations, is astounding. The chandelier-lit interior is lavishly decorated; 48 painted-glass panels are inset in the ceiling and angled to reflect the sunrise and sunset. The temple's daily hours are more limited than those at most Singapore temples; it's open from 8 AM to noon and then again from 5:30 to 8:30.

Goodwood Park Hotel. Though not as well known as the Raffles and 30 years younger, this hotel (☞ also Lodging, below) is just as much a landmark. Partaking of an elegant afternoon tea here—accompanied by live piano music—is the perfect way to take a break from all that shopping. Tea is served from 2:30 to 6 and costs about S$21.

❶ **Istana.** Once the official residence of the colonial governor and now that of the president of the republic, the building is open to the public only on National Day. On the first Sunday of each month, there's a changing-of-the-guard ceremony: the new guards leave Bideford Road at 5:30 PM and march along Orchard Road to the Istana, reaching the entrance gate punctually at 6. Former prime minister and senior minister Lee Kuan Yew has his office here.

❺ **Mandarin Singapore.** In the main lobby of this hotel is an exquisite mural delineated by real gold etched into white marble. The 70-ft-long work, by Yuy Tang, is called *87 Taoist Immortals* and is based on an 8th-century Tang scroll. It depicts 87 mythical figures paying homage

Orchard Road

Chettiar Temple, **3**
Istana, **1**
Mandarin
Singapore, **5**
Newton Circus, **7**

Peranakan Place, **4**
Shaw House, **6**
Tan Yeok Nee
House, **2**

to Xi Wangmu, Mother of God, on her birthday. While in the Mandarin, you may want to wander around to see the other works of art displayed. In the Mezzanine Lounge is Gerard Henderson's floor-to-ceiling mural *Gift to Singapore*. Henderson, half Chinese and half Irish, also created a powerful series of eight canvases titled *Riders of the World*. Five of these vibrant paintings dominate the wall adjoining the lobby. They depict the untamed and unconquered, including a 13th-century Japanese samurai, a Mandarin of the Ming Dynasty, a 9th-century Moor, and a 20th-century cossack. Don't miss the huge abstract batik mural by Seah Kim Joo, one of Singapore's best-known contemporary artists, that adorns three walls of the Mandarin's upstairs gallery.

7 **Newton Circus.** This is one of the best-known hawker centers in town. (The "circus" refers to the rotary, as in Piccadilly Circus.) Some of the stalls are open all day, but the best times to go are either around 9 AM, when a few stalls serve Chinese breakfasts, or after 7 PM, when all the stores are open and the Circus is humming with the hungry.

Palais Renaissance. The Palais Renaissance complex is chic, opulent, and overpriced but a delight to wander through. Boutiques such as **Ralph Lauren, Dunhill, Chanel,** and **Gucci** are for the shopper seeking status labels at high prices.

4 **Peranakan Place.** A celebration of Peranakan (also called straits-born Chinese, Baba, or Nonya) culture, an innovative blending of Chinese and Malay cultures that emerged in the 19th century as Chinese born in the straits settlements adopted (and often adapted) Malay fashions, cuisine, and architecture. At Peranakan Place, six old wooden shophouses, with fretted woodwork and painted in pastel colors, have been beautifully restored. Notice the typical Peranakan touches, such as the use of decorative tiles and the unusual fence doors.

☜ **Planet Hollywood.** The Liat Towers, formerly home to Galleries Lafayette, the French department store, was transformed into a branch of the now ubiquitous Planet Hollywood. With leopard-print sofas, California cuisine, and film memorabilia adorning the walls, Planet Hollywood remains popular. Teenagers sit across from the entrance waiting for a glimpse of their favorite North American celebrities, who often sign autographs here when in town.

6 **Shaw House.** Japan's large **Isetan** department store is the major anchor in this shopping complex at the corner of Scotts and Orchard roads. **Kinokuniya** bookstore, in the older Shaw Centre, is especially good for publications about Japan, but also carries English-language books.

Tanglin Shopping Centre. At the corner of Napier and Tanglin roads, this suburban mall was built to cater to the surrounding wealthy neighborhood. It has an excellent food court in its basement.

2 **Tan Yeok Nee House.** The house was built around 1885 for Tan Yeok Nee (1827–1902), a merchant from China who started out here as a cloth peddler and became a very wealthy man through trade in opium, gambier, and pepper. Whereas most homes built in Singapore at that time followed European styles, this town house was designed in a style popular in South China—notice the keyhole gables, terra-cotta tiles, and massive granite pillars. After the railway was laid along Tank Road in 1901, the house became the stationmaster's. In 1912, St. Mary's Home and School for Girls took it over. Since 1940 the Salvation Army has made the place its local headquarters. The house is now being redeveloped.

Side Trips Around Singapore and Beyond

Although there's a great deal to see and do in Singapore, you may want to escape to areas just outside the city or to small islands just off the coast. A jaunt to the nearby Indonesian island of Bintan—with its pristine shores, mangrove swamps, and hideaway resorts—will no doubt add still more dimension to your Southeast Asia journey.

The East Coast

Two decades ago, Singapore's eastern coastal area contained only coconut plantations, rural Malay villages, and a few undeveloped beaches. Today, however, it is totally different. At the extreme northeastern tip of the island is Changi International Airport, one of the finest in the world. Between the airport and the city, numerous satellite residential developments have sprung up, and vast land-reclamation projects along the seashore have created a park 8 km (5 mi) long, with plenty of recreational facilities.

Numbers in the text correspond to numbers in the margin and on the East and West Coasts and the Green Interior map.

A GOOD TOUR

A trip to the east coast is a relaxing way to spend a morning or afternoon. This two- to three-hour tour is best done by taxi, which will cost you roughly S$8–S$15 each way. Catch a cab at the junction of Nicoll Highway and Bras Basah Road, near the Raffles Hotel and Marina Square.

Nicoll Highway leads onto East Coast Road, and heading east along it, you come to the Kallang area. Cross the Rochar and Kallang rivers by the Merdeka (Independent) Bridge and you'll see, to the left and right, an estuary that was once the haunt of pirates and smugglers. A few shipyards are visible to the left, where the old Bugis trading schooners once anchored. (The Bugis, a seafaring people from the Celebes—now Sulawesi—Indonesia, have a long history as great traders; their schooners, called *prahus,* still ply Indonesian waters.) To the right is the huge National Stadium, where international sporting events are held. Just past the stadium, Mountbatten Road crosses Old Airport Road, once the runway of Singapore's first airfield. One of the old British colonial residential districts, this area is still home to the wealthy, as attested by the splendid houses in both traditional and modern architectural styles.

Ask the driver to take you up East Coast Parkway, so that you can visit the **Crocodilarium** ① (for still more reptile fun you can head up to the **Singapore Crocodile Farm**) or the **East Coast Park** ②. Stop to eat at the **East Coast Park Food Centre** or the **UDMC Seafood Centre.** Catch another taxi to take you farther east to the infamous **Changi Prison** ③.

SIGHTS TO SEE

❸ **Changi Prison.** This home to Nick Leeson, the young Englishman who broke the Barings Bank, is well worth a visit. The sprawling, squat, sinister-looking place, built in 1927 by the British, was used by the Japanese in World War II to intern some 70,000 prisoners of war, who endured terrible hardships here. Today it houses some 2,000 convicts, many of whom are here owing to Singapore's strict drug laws. This is where serious offenders are hanged at dawn on Friday.

If you're not part of an organized tour (☞ Tour Operators *in* Singapore A to Z, *below*), you can really only visit the **Changi Prison Chapel and Museum,** whose walls hold poignant memorial plaques to those interned here during the war. It's a replica of one of 14 chapels where

Johore Bahru

Causeway

Johore Straits

Admiralty Rd. W.

WOODLANDS

YISHUN

Yishun Ave. 2

Sarimbun Reservoir

Lim Chu Kang Rd.

Kranji Reservoir

Kranji War Memorial

Mandai Rd.

Seletar Reservoir

Singapore Zoological Gardens **11**

12 **13**

Night Safari

Sembawang Rd.

Murai Reservoir

Jalan Behar

Mandai Orchid Garden

BUKIT PANJANG

Poyan Reservoir

Choa Chu Kang Rd.

Upper Bukit Timah Rd.

Bukit Timah Expwy.

Upper Peirce Reservoir

Lower Peirce Reservoir

Upper Thomson Rd.

Kong M San Ph Kark S Temple

Bukit Timah

Pan Island Expwy.

JURONG WEST

Upper Jurong Rd.

Chinese Garden **7**

Japanese Garden **8**

9 Singapore Science Centre

Tang Dynasty City **10**

Jalan Ahmad Ibrahim

5 **6** Jurong Crocodile Paradise

Jalan Buroh

Singapore Mint Coin Gallery

14 Bukit Timah Nature Reserve

MacRitchie Reservoir **15**

Bukit Timah Rd.

Upper Ayah Rajah Rd.

Holland Rd.

Queensway

Farrer Rd.

Botanic Gardens **16**

Tanglin Rd.

Orchard Rd.

Jurong Bird Park

Pandan Reservoir

West Coast Hwy.

New Ming Village

Ayah Rajah Rd.

P. Pesek

P. Merlimau

Terumbu Retan Laut

Mt. Faber

Haw Par Villa **4**

Telok Blangah Rd.

World Trade Centre Ferry Terminal

P. Ayer Chawan

P. Seraya

P. Sakra

P. Ayer Merbau

P. Bakau

Sentosa Island

P. Br

P. Te

P. Busing

P. Bukum

P. Ular

P. Hantu

↓ TO P. SAKENG, P. SENANG

Sister's Islands

0 ——————— 4 miles
0 ——————— 6 km

WEST
MALAYSIA

P. Seletar

TO DESARU,
MALAYSIA

Johore Straits

P. Seletar

P. Ubin

P. Serangoon

TO P.
TEKONG

Yio Chu Kang Rd.

PUNGGOL

P. Ketam

Serangoon
Harbour

CHANGI

SERANGOON

S. Serangoon

Punggol Rd.

ng Meng
an Phor
ark See
mple

Central Expwy.

Upper Serangoon Rd.

Tampines Rd.

Loyang Ave.

U. Changi Rd.

Changi
Airport

Singapore
Crocodile Farm

Changi
Prison

Airport Blvd.

Chang. Coast Rd.

Siong Lim
Temple and
Gardens

Paya Lebar Rd.

BEDOK

New Upper Changi

③

Serangoon Rd.

Pan Island Expressway

Upper Changi Rd.

Kallang Rd.

Sims Ave.

Geylang Rd.

East Coast Rd.

N

KATONG

Mountbatten Rd.

East Coast Parkway

②

East Coast
Park Food Centre

d Rd.

Nicoll Hwy.

National
Stadium

UDMC
Seafood
Centre

East Coast
Park

Crocodilarium

①

Recreational
Centre

Strait of Singapore

P. Brani

Buran
Darat

P. Tekukor

P. Renggit

Kusu Island

Lazarus Island

St. John's Island

85,000 Allied POWs and civilians gained the faith and courage to overcome the degradation and deprivation inflicted upon them by the Japanese. The museum contains drawings, sketches, and photographs by POWs depicting their wartime experiences. ☎ *545–1441.* 🖾 *Donations accepted.* ☉ *Chapel and museum: Mon.–Sat. 9:30–4:30; visitors welcome at 5:30 PM Sun. service.*

Organized guided tours may take you through the old British barracks areas to the former RAF camp. Here, in **Block 151**—a prisoners' hospital during the war—you'll see the simple but striking murals painted by a British POW, bombardier Stanley Warren. (Fax the prison's public affairs department at 764–6119 for approval to view the murals if you're visiting on your own.) The scale of military spending in the 1930s by the British—who put up these well-designed barracks to accommodate tens of thousands of men—is amazing. You can clearly see why the British believed Singapore was impregnable! This is still a military area; most of the barracks are used by Singapore's servicemen during their 2½-year compulsory duty.

① **Crocodilarium.** More than 1,000 of the jaw-snapping crocodiles here are bred to be skinned. You can watch crocodile wrestling Tuesday through Sunday at 1:15 and 4:15 PM; a definite feeding time is Tuesday at 11 AM. Naturally, there's a place to buy crocodile-skin bags and belts—at inflated prices. ☎ *447–3722.* 🖾 *S$2.* ☉ *Daily 9–5.*

② **East Coast Park.** Between the highway and the sea, this park has a wide variety of water sports and other recreational facilities. A cool sea breeze makes it the best place in town for running. (☞ *also* Outdoor Activities and Sports, *below.*)

East Coast Park Food Centre. Next to the Europa Sailing Club, this alfresco center offers dining from many stalls and a great view of the harbor.

OFF THE
BEATEN PATH
SINGAPORE CROCODILE FARM – Yet more of these popular creatures—plus alligators, snakes, and lizards—are on view at a 1-acre breeding farm 6½ km (4 mi) northwest of the Crocodilarium. Feeding time is 11 AM Tuesday through Sunday. At the factory, observe the process of turning hides into accessories that—along with imported eel-skin products—are sold at the farm shop. ⊠ *790 Upper Serangoon Rd.,* ☎ *288–9385.* 🖾 *Free.* ☉ *Daily 8:30–5:30.*

UDMC Seafood Centre. This gathering of eight outdoor restaurants is a popular evening destination (☞ *also* Dining, *below.*)

The West Coast

The satellite city of Jurong is Singapore's main industrial area. It's estimated that more than 70% of the nation's manufacturing workforce is employed here by more than 3,000 companies. Though this may seem an unlikely vacation destination, there are actually several interesting attractions in or around Jurong. A garden environment exists here, demonstrating that an industrial area doesn't have to be ugly.

A GOOD TOUR

West Coast attractions are far from the center of town and far from one another. Allow a half day for each sight (except the Crocodile Paradise, which deserves an hour at most). You can arrange a tour through your hotel or take taxis alone or in combination with the MRT. A cab ride from the center of town to Jurong will cost about S$15. **Haw Par Villa** ④ amusement park is much closer to town than the other sights. The nearest MRT station is Buona Vista Station, from which you must transfer to Bus 200 (though air-conditioned express coach service is available from hotels along Orchard Road). Haw Par Villa is also near one of the main jumping-off points to Sentosa Island, a short ride away, so consider pairing a visit to the villa with one to the island (☞ *also* Sentosa Island, *below*).

On another day, you might start with a visit to **Jurong Bird Park** ⑤. An MRT ride to Clementi will cost about S$1.50, depending on where you start your journey, and a taxi from here to the park itself will cost another S$5 or so. If take a taxi the whole way, plan to spend S$30 round-trip. Exploring the park is tiring, so take a break (or two) in one of the on-site restaurants. If you haven't tired of all the fauna, check out the **Jurong Crocodile Paradise** ⑥, directly across the parking lot from the bird park. If, however, you're ready to view some flora, spend your afternoon at the **Chinese Garden** ⑦ and the **Japanese Garden** ⑧ (take the MRT to the Chinese Garden Station to get here).

Alternatively, you could spend your afternoon at the **Singapore Science Centre** ⑨ or the **Tang Dynasty City** ⑩. If you don't want to spring for a taxi from Orchard Road (about a 20-minute ride), you can take the west-bound MRT to the Jurong East Station, and then transfer to Bus 335 or make the 10-minute walk to the Science Centre's Omni-Theatre. To reach Tang Dynasty City, simply take the MRT to the Lakeside Station. Other area sights include the **Singapore Mint Coin Gallery,** where coins are made and displayed, and pottery demonstrations at **New Ming Village.**

SIGHTS TO SEE

🖐 ❼ **Chinese Garden.** This 34.6-acre reconstruction of a Chinese imperial garden (one inspiration for it was the garden of the Beijing Summer Palace) has pagodas, temples, courtyards, and bridges. Lotus-filled lakes and placid streams are overhung by groves of willows. Rental rowboats allow a swan's-eye view of the grounds, and there are re-freshment facilities. Within the main garden you'll find the **Ixora Garden,** with several varieties of the showy flowering ixora shrub; the **Herb Garden,** showcasing plants used in herbal medicines; and the **Garden of Fragrance,** where many newlyweds have their photographs taken against stone plaques with auspicious Chinese engravings. If you're com-ing directly from Singapore, take the MRT to the Chinese Garden stop; it's only a short walk to the garden itself. ⊠ *Off Yuan Ching Rd.,* ☎ *264–3455.* 🎟 *S$4.50 (includes admission to Japanese Garden).* ☉ *Mon.–Sat., 9–7, Sun. 8:30–7. Last admission at 6 PM daily.*

🖐 ❹ **Haw Par Villa.** Also known as the Tiger Balm Gardens, the villa pre-sents Chinese folklore in theme-park fashion. Part of an estate owned by two eccentric brothers in the 1930s, after World War II the gardens were opened to the public. They fell into disarray and were sold to a soft-drink-bottling company that spent S$85 million on their trans-formation. Haw Par Villa was reopened in late 1990 and today it has both traditional amusements and multimedia presentations. The most popular attractions are a boat ride ("Tales of China") through the in-side of a dragon whose entrails have scenes from the 10 courts of hell; a slide presentation ("Legends and Heroes") of Chinese mythology that explains why we have only one sun; a 3-D movie ("Creation of the World"); and a water roller coaster ("Wrath of the Water Gods"). These and seven other attractions will keep your child's interest, though you will be either bored or amused by the corniness of the sanitized pro-duction sets. The best time to start your visit is at 9:30 AM, before the crowds and long lines. ⊠ *262 Pasir Panjang Rd.,* ☎ *774–0300.* 🎟 *S$16.50 (includes all attractions).* ☉ *Daily 9–6.*

🖐 ❽ **Japanese Garden.** Adjacent to the Chinese Garden, this delightful for-mal garden is one of the largest of its kind outside Japan. Its classic simplicity, serenity, and harmonious arrangement of plants, stones, bridges, and trees induce tranquility. (Indeed, the garden's Japanese name, Seiwaen, means "Garden of Tranquility.") A miniature waterfall spills into a pond full of water lilies and lotus. ⊠ *Off Yuan Ching Rd., Jurong,* ☎ *264–3455.* ⊠ *S$4.50 (includes admission to Chinese Garden).* ⊙ *Mon.–Sat. 9–7, Sun. 8:30–7; last admission at 6.*

⑤ Jurong Bird Park. Built on 50 landscaped acres, the world's largest walk-in aviary includes a 100-ft man-made waterfall that cascades into a stream. More than 3,600 birds from 365 species are here, including the colorful, the rare, and the noisy. It's a shock to stand atop Jurong Hill, amid the twittering birds and lush vegetation, and look down on factories that crank out Singapore's economic success. For an overview of the park with sweeping vistas, consider taking the 10-minute ride on the Panorail, an air-conditioned monorail train.

If you arrive here early, try the breakfast buffet from 9 to 11 at the **Song Bird Terrace,** where birds in bamboo cages tunefully trill as you help yourself to sausages, eggs, and toast. From here you can walk over to the **Penguin Feeding** (held at 10:30). In the afternoon (at 3), you might catch the JBP All Star BirdShow, at the **Pools Amphitheatre.** The nocturnal-bird house allows a glimpse of owls, night herons, frogsmouth, kiwi, and others usually cloaked in darkness. The bee-eaters and starlings are fed at 10:30 AM, 11:30 AM and 4:30 PM; you can be fed throughout the day at the **Waterfront Cafe** or **Burger King.** ⊠ *2 Jurong Hill, Jalan Ahmad Ibrahim,* ☎ *265–0022.* ⊠ *S$10.30, Panorail S$2.* ⊙ *Daily 9–6.*

⑥ Jurong Crocodile Paradise. Singaporeans seem to be fascinated with crocs, and at this 5-acre park you'll find 2,500 of them in landscaped streams, at a feeding platform, or in a breeding lake. You can feed the crocodiles, watch muscle-bound showmen (and a showlady) wrestle with them, or buy crocodile-skin products at the shop. You can also watch the beasts through glass, in an underwater viewing gallery. A seafood restaurant and fast-food outlets provide refreshments, and there are rides for children. ⊠ *241 Jalan Ahmad Ibrahim,* ☎ *261–8866.* ⊠ *S$7.* ⊙ *Daily 9–6; wrestling at 11:45, 2, and 4.*

New Ming Village. At this small complex of buildings not far from the Jurong Bird Park, demonstrations of the art of Chinese pottery making are given, and copies of Ming Dynasty blue and white porcelain are produced and sold. ⊠ *32 Pandam Rd.,* ☎ *265–7711.* ⊠ *Free.* ⊙ *Daily 9–5:30.*

Singapore Mint Coin Gallery. Close to the ☞ Singapore Science Centre and just east of the Boon Lay MRT station, you can watch minting operations. There are also displays of coins, medals, and medallions from Singapore and around the world. ⊠ *20 Teban Garden Crescent,* ☎ *566–2626.* ⊠ *Free.* ⊙ *Weekdays 9:30–4:30.*

⑨ Singapore Science Centre. Here, subjects such as aviation, nuclear science, robotics, astronomy, and space technology are entertainingly explored through audiovisual and interactive exhibits. You can walk into a "human body" for a closer look at vital organs or test yourself on computer quiz games. You'll also find a flight simulator of a Boeing 747 and the Omni Theatre, which presents two programs: "Oasis in Space" travels to the beginning of the universe and "To Fly" simulates the feel of space travel. Children of any age are sure to get a thrill from the brave new world of science presented here. ⊠ *Science Centre Rd., off Jurong Town Hall Rd.,* ☎ *560–3316.* ⊠ *S$3; Omni Theatre S$9.* ⊙ *Tues.–Sun. 10–6.*

Tang Dynasty City. This theme park re-creates the 7th-century Chinese village of Chang'an (present-day Xian) with pagodas, gilded imperial courts, and an underground palace of the royal dead guarded by 1,000 terra-cotta warriors. The Imperial Palace is really a cluster of six palaces built to scale. Restaurants and entertainment facilities are modern intrusions, but artisans make and sell traditional wares, and acrobats, rickshaws, and oxcarts add to the authenticity. A tram takes you around. ✉ *2 Yuan Ching Rd.,* ☎ *251–1116.* ✍ *S$15.45 (including tram ride).* ⊙ *Daily 10–6:30.*

Into the Garden Isle

Singapore is called the Garden Isle, and with good reason. Although the government seems obsessed with reinforced concrete, it has also established nature reserves, gardens, and a zoo. This excursion from downtown takes you into the center of the island to enjoy some of its greenery. If you have only a little time to spare, at least visit the zoo— it's truly exceptional. If you want to learn more about Singapore's natural habitats and plant life, contact the nature society (☎ 253–2179).

A GOOD TOUR

Much of Singapore's natural world is miles from the center of the city. Because of the heat, walking through nature here is tiring, so you probably won't be able to see all the sights in one day. Taxis or hotel tours are the favored ways of getting to the orchid garden, the zoo, and the Night Safari—all of which you can tour in the space of an afternoon and an evening. The **Mandai Orchid Garden** ⑪ is a must for flower-lovers; a taxi here from the center of town will cost about S$16, or you can take SBS Bus 138 from the Ang Mo Kio MRT station. Spend about an hour here, then visit the **Singapore Zoological Gardens** ⑫. The taxi ride here from the orchid garden will cost about S$6 (though you can also take Bus 138). If you arrive by 3 PM sharp, you'll be in time for tea with an orangutan. You can then get a good look at the zoo before it closes at 6 and head over to **Night Safari** ⑬ for dinner in the restaurant at its entrance (the grounds don't open till 7:30).

To reach the **Bukit Timah Nature Reserve** ⑭ take Bus 171, which departs from the Newton MRT station. From the Orchard MRT station to **MacRitchie Reservoir** ⑮ it's about a S$6.50 taxi ride. Plan to spend about S$4 on a cab to reach the **Botanic Gardens** ⑯ from the city center or you can catch Bus 7, 105, 106, 123, or 174 from the Orchard MRT station. Allow two hours for the Botanic Gardens and another two for the reservoir. Allow about three hours for the nature reserve.

On a trip to this area, culture vultures can work in visits to the **Kong Meng San Phor Kark See Temple** and the **Siong Lim Temple and Gardens**; nature lovers can check out the **Selatar Reservoir**; and history buffs can stop by the **Kranji War Memorial.**

SIGHTS TO SEE

★ **Botanic Gardens.** The gardens were begun in the days of Queen Victoria as a collection of tropical trees and plants (indeed, the 19th-century bandstand perpetuates the image of carefully conceived British gardens). Later, botanist Henry Ridley experimented here with rubber-tree seeds from South America; his work led to the development of the region's huge rubber industry and to the decline of the Amazon basin's importance as a source of the commodity.

Spread over some 74 acres, the grounds contain a large lake, masses of shrubs and flowers, and magnificent examples of many tree species, including fan palms more than 90 ft high. Locals come here to stroll along nature walks, jog, practice tai chi, feed geese, or just enjoy the serenity. The combined fragrance of frangipani, hibiscus, and aromatic herbs that pervades is delightful. ⊠ *Corner of Napier and Cluny Rds.,* ☎ *800/467–1540.* ⊡ *Free.* ⊙ *Daily 5* AM–*midnight.*

Inside the Botanic Gardens, the 7.4-acre **Singapore Orchid Garden** was opened in 1995 by Senior Minister Lee Kuan Yew, the former prime minister. Here you can see more than 3,000 orchids in all their glory. ⊡ *S$2.* ⊙ *Daily 8:30–6.*

⑭ **Bukit Timah Nature Reserve.** If you like your nature a little wilder than what's found in manicured urban parks, then this is the place for you. In these 148 acres around Singapore's highest hill (574 ft), the tropical forest runs riot, giving you a feel for how things might have been when tigers roamed the island. Wandering along structured, well-marked paths, you may be startled by flying lemurs, civet cats, or—if you're really lucky—a troupe of long-tailed macaques. The view from the hilltop is superb. Wear good walking shoes—the trails are rocky, sometimes muddy, paths. You can buy trail maps from the visitor center. ⊠ *177 Hindhede Dr.,* ☎ *800/468–5736.* ⊡ *Free.* ⊙ *Daily 8:30–6:30.*

Kong Meng San Phor Kark See Temple. The Bright Hill Temple, as it's commonly known, is a relatively modern complex of Buddhist temples typical of the ornate Chinese style, with much gilded carving. ⊠ *88 Bright Hill Dr., 1½ km (1 mi) west of Bishan MRT station.*

Kranji War Memorial. This cemetery, a tribute to the forces who fought to defend Singapore in World War II, is in the north of the island, near the causeway off Woodlands Road. Rows of Allied dead are grouped with their countrymen in plots on a peaceful, well-manicured hill. This is a touching experience, a reminder of the greatness of the loss in this and all wars.

ⓒ ⑮ **MacRitchie Reservoir.** This 30-acre park has a jogging track with exercise areas, a playground, and a tea kiosk. The path around the reservoir is peaceful, with only the warbling of birds and chatter of monkeys to break your reverie. Crocodile spotting became a favorite pastime after baby crocs were found in the reservoir in early 1996. Don't go in the water. ⊠ *Lornie Rd., near Thomson Rd.,* ☎ *no phone.* ⊡ *Free.* ⊙ *Daily dawn–dusk.*

⑪ **Mandai Orchid Garden.** Less than a kilometer down the road from the zoo (TIBS Bus 171 links the two) is a commercial orchid farm. The hillside is covered with the exotic blooms, cultivated for domestic sale and export. There are many varieties to admire, some quite spectacular. However, unless you are an orchid enthusiast, and since it is a good 30-minute taxi ride from downtown, a visit here is worth it only when combined with a visit to the zoo. The ☞ **Botanic Gardens** are closer to downtown and also have orchids. ⊠ *Mandai Lake Rd.,* ☎ *269–0136.* ⊡ *S$2 (refunded if you make a purchase).* ⊙ *Weekdays 8:30–5:30.*

ⓒ ⑬ **Night Safari.** Right next to the ☞ **Singapore Zoological gardens,** the safari claims to be the world's first nighttime wildlife park. Here 80 acres of secondary jungle provide a home to 100 species of wildlife that are more active at night than during the day. Some 90% of tropical animals are, in fact, nocturnal, and to see them active—instead of snoozing—gives their behavior a new dimension. Night Safari, like the zoo, uses a moat concept to create open, natural habitats; areas are floodlit with enough light to see the animals' colors, but not enough to limit their normal activity. You're taken on a 45-minute tram ride along 3 km (2 mi) of road, stopping frequently to admire the beasts and their antics. On another kilometer or so of walking trails you can observe some of the small cat families, primates (such as the slow loris and tarsier), and the *pangolin* (scaly anteater). Larger animals include the

Nepalese rhino (the largest of rhinos, with a single, mammoth horn) and the beautifully marked royal Bengal tigers—which are somewhat intimidating to the nearby mouse deer, *babirusa* (pig deer with curled tusks that protrude through the upper lip), *gorals* (wild mountain goats), and *bharals* (mountain sheep). ✉ *80 Mandai Lake Rd.,* ☎ *269–3411.* ☞ *S$15.45.* ⊘ *Daily 7:30 PM–midnight.*

Seletar Reservoir. Larger and wilder than the MacRitchie Reservoir, the Seletar is the largest and least developed natural area on the island. ✉ *Mandai Rd., near the zoo, no phone.* ☞ *Free.* ⊘ *Daily dawn–dusk.*

★ ✋ ⑫ **Singapore Zoological Gardens.** You get the impression that animals come here for a vacation and not, as is often the case elsewhere, to serve a prison sentence. The Singapore zoo has an open-moat concept, wherein a wet or dry moat separates the animals from the people. (Interestingly, a mere 3-ft-deep moat will keep humans and giraffes apart, for a giraffe's gait makes even a shallow trench impossible to negotiate. A narrow water-filled moat prevents spider monkeys from leaving their home turf for a closer inspection of visitors.) Few zoos have have been able to afford the huge cost of employing this system, which was developed by Carl Hagenbeck, who created the Hamburg, Germany, zoo at the turn of the century. The Singapore zoo has managed by starting small and expanding gradually. It now sprawls over 69 acres of a 220-acre forested area.

Try to arrive at the zoo in time for the buffet breakfast. The food itself isn't special, but the company is. At 9:30 AM, Ah Meng, a 24-year-old orangutan, comes by for her repast. She weighs about 250 pounds, so she starts by taking a table by herself, but you're welcome to join her for a snack. (Ah Meng also takes tea promptly at 3.) Afterward, from glass windows that look into a watery grotto, you can watch polar bears dive for their own fishy breakfast. At the reptile house, be sure to check out the Komodo dragon lizards, which can grow to 10 ft in length. Then it will be time for the primate-and-reptile show, in which monkeys, gibbons, and chimpanzees have humans perform tricks, and snakes embrace volunteers from the audience.

There are performances by fur seals, elephants, free-flying storks, and other zoo inhabitants at various times throughout the day. In numerous miniparks that re-create different environments, giraffes, Celebese apes, bearded pigs, tigers, lions, and other of the zoo's 1,700 animals from among 160 species take life easy. ✉ *80 Mandai Lake Rd.,* ☎ *269–3411.* ☞ *S$10.30; breakfast or tea with Ah Meng S$15.* ⊘ *Daily 8:30–6; breakfast with Ah Meng Tues.–Sat. 9–10 AM; high tea at 3.*

Siong Lim Temple and Gardens. The largest Buddhist temple complex in Singapore was built by two wealthy Hokkien merchants between 1868 and 1908. Set among groves of bamboo, the temple is guarded by the giant Four Kings of Heaven, in full armor. There are a number of shrines and halls, with many ornate features and statues of the Lord Buddha. The goddess of mercy, Kuan Yin, has her shrine behind the main hall; another hall houses a number of fine Thai Buddha images. The oldest building in the complex is a small wood shrine containing antique murals of the favorite Chinese legend "Pilgrimage to the West." ✉ *184 E. Jalan Toa Payoh, about 1 km (½ mi) east of the Toa Payoh MRT station.*

Sentosa Island

In 1968 the government decided that Sentosa, the Isle of Tranquillity, would be transformed from the military area it was into a resort playground, with museums, parks, golf courses, restaurants, and hotels (☞ Lodging, *below*). A lot of money has been spent on development, and some find Sentosa an enjoyable getaway. However, this "pleasure park" is likely to hold little interest for travelers who have come 10,000 miles to visit Asia, a fact lost on the Singapore government. That said, there are two good reasons to visit the island: the visual drama of reaching it—particularly via cable car—and its wax museum.

In addition to all its historical and scientific exhibitions, Sentosa has a secondary jungle; a *pasar malam* (night market) with 40 stalls, open Friday–Sunday 10–6 PM; campsites by the lagoon; and a wide range of recreational activities. You can swim in the lagoon and at a small ocean beach, though owing to all the cargo ships—you'll see hundreds of them anchored off the coast—the waters leave a lot to be desired. If golf is your game, consider a few rounds at the Sentosa Golf Club (☞ Outdoor Activities and Sports, *below*) or putt away on one of Won-derGolf's 45 uniquely landscaped greens.

The best way to make the 2-km (1-mi) trip to Sentosa is by cable car (small gondolas that hold four passengers each). Other options include a shuttle bus or taxi via the causeway or a ferry ride (☞ *also* Getting Around *in* Singapore A to Z, *below*). The island's S$5 admission price will get you into many attractions, though some have separate entrance fees. Sentosa has a monorail, which operates daily from 9 AM to 10 PM. It has stations close to the major attractions (a recording discusses each sight as you pass it), and unlimited rides are included in the price of the island admission. A free bus can also take you to most of the sights; it runs daily from 9–7:30 with night service from 7:30 to 10:30 at 10-minute intervals. A small train runs along the south coast for about 3 km (2 mi); bicycles are available for rent at kiosks throughout the island; and, of course, you always have your own two feet. For more information about Sentosa and its facilities, call the **Sentosa Development Corporation**'s Sales Department (☎ 275–0388).

Numbers in the text correspond to numbers in the margin and on the S⌐tosa Island map.

A GOOD TOUR

This tour will take three to five hours. Start at the World Trade Centre, where you'll take a ferry or cable car (from the nearby station) to Sentosa. Between the ferry terminal and the cable car station on the Sentosa side is **WonderGolf** and **Asian Village & Adventure Asia** ①, a mini-theme park (the **Fountain Gardens** and **Sentosa Orchid Garden** are also nearby). From Asian Village you can follow the signs to the **Pioneers of Singapore/Surrender Chambers** ②, a wax museum that gives you an idea of what Singapore was like 100 years ago. Close by is the **Butterfly Park and World Insectarium** ③. After seeing all the bugs, board the monorail for a trip to **Underwater World** ④, a popular aquarium. Next to that, you will find **Ft. Siloso** ⑤, an old British fort whose cannons were pointed the wrong way during World War II. From here, take the monorail again to the swimming lagoon.

After a drink at the **Sunset Bar,** where you can sit on the wooden deck, gaze out at the view, and watch the nonstop volleyball, head up the hill behind the bar to the **Merlion** ⑥, Singapore's 10-story mascot. The view from the top is good—the city and the container port on one side, the harbor, the refineries, and the Indonesian islands of Bintan and Bataam on the other. Such watery scenery gets you in the mood for the **Maritime Museum** ⑦, which is due east from the Merlion. On the way there, you can stop at **VolcanoLand** or **Fantasy Island.**

SIGHTS TO SEE

① Asian Village & Adventure Asia. Adjacent to the ferry terminal, this village contains three independent "communes" representing East Asia, South Asia, and Southeast Asia. In each village, street performances, demonstrations, merchandise, and food stalls do what they can to add life to an eclectic mix that, for example, combines Thai and north Sumatran architecture in one village and a Japanese torii gate and a Chinese teahouse in another. At Adventure Asia you can go on as many amusement rides as you like for one price. *Asian Village: free. Adventure Asia: S$10. ⊘ Daily 10–9.*

③ Butterfly Park and World Insectarium. This park has a collection of 2,500 live butterflies from 50 species, 4,000 mounted butterflies and insects, plus lots of other insects—like tree-horn rhino beetles, scorpions, and tarantulas—that still creep, crawl, or fly. The park has an Asian landscape with a moon gate, streams, and bridges. *S$5. ⊘ Daily 9–6:30.*

Fantasy Island. This is a great place to escape Singapore's heat. Among other attractions, you'll find a water slide and an action river with whitewater rapids. *S$20. ⊘ Fri.–Tues. 10–7.*

NEED A BREAK?	You may want to enjoy high tea or an early dinner at the **Rasa Sentosa Food Centre,** open daily 10 AM–10:30 PM, next to the ferry terminal. More than 40 stalls offer a variety of foods for alfresco dining in groomed tropical surroundings.

⑤ Ft. Siloso. The fort covers 10 acres of gun emplacements and tunnels created by the British to fend off invasions by the Japanese. Unfortunately, the Japanese arrived by land (through Malaysia) instead of by sea, so the huge guns were pointed in the wrong direction. (The guns could have been redirected, but they were designed to fire shells that pierced ships' armor, not to deal with land forces.) Gun buffs will enjoy the range of artillery pieces. Photographs document the war in the Pacific, and dioramas depict the life of POWs during the Japanese occupation. *S$3. ⊘ Daily 9–6.*

Fountain Gardens. Several times each evening, visitors to the gardens, conveniently close to the ferry terminal, are invited to dance along with the illuminated sprays from the fountains to classical or pop music. This activity is not for introverts. Performances by traditional dance groups are sometimes held.

⑦ Maritime Museum. A small but interesting collection of ship models, pictures, and other items show Singapore's involvement with the sea in business and in war. A fishing gallery displays nets, traps, and spears used in the area throughout the centuries; a collection of full-size native watercraft traces the development of local boatbuilding from dugout canoes to Indonesian prahus. *S$2. ⊘ Daily 10–7.*

⑥ Merlion. This monument, which some find to be in questionable taste, is Singapore's tourism mascot—a 10-story, off-white "lion fish" creature that emits laser beams from its eyes and smoke from its nostrils. It even glows in the dark. To get to the observation tower, you walk through a pirate cave exhibition. The walls are covered with TV screens, some showing "The Legend of the Merlion," others showing advertisements for the rest of Sentosa. The ride up to the 10th story is by elevator, then you climb two stories to the top where there's a view of Singapore and the Indonesian islands of Bataam and Bintan. *S$3. ⊘ Daily 9–10.*

★ **②** **Pioneers of Singapore/Surrender Chambers.** This wax museum stands out from all the rest of Sentosa's attractions. Galleries trace the de-

Sentosa Island

Keppel Harbour

Brani Shoals

Pulau Brani

Selat Sengkir

Duran Darat

Berhala Reping

Serapong Hill Rd.

Woolwich Loop

Golf Course

Allanbrooke Rd.

Beaufort Hotel

Bukit Manis Rd.

Maritime Museum ⑦

Fantasy Island

Jetty Rd.

Fountain Gardens

Sentosa Orchid Garden ①

Artillery Ave.

Asian Village & Adventure Asia

TO SINGAPORE

School Rd.

Carlton Hill Rd.

Volcanoland

Merlion ⑥

Swimming Lagoon

Tanjong Beach

Wonder-Golf

Cable Car Station ③

②

Sunset Bar

Butterfly Park and World Insectarium

Sentosa Beach Resort

Siloso Rd.

Pioneers of Singapore/ Surrender Chambers

MONORAIL

Siloso Beach

Rasa Sentosa Hotel

Underwater World ④

Ft. Siloso ⑤

Singapore Strait

N

KEY

—— Rail lines

⛴ Ferry

•••• Cable Car

0   1000 meters

0   1000 yards

velopment of Singapore and depict the characters who profoundly influenced its history. Though the wax figures aren't the most lifelike, the scenes and the running narrative offer a vivid picture of 19th-century life in Singapore and a rare opportunity, in the modern Singapore, to ponder the diversity of cultures that were thrust together in the pursuit of trade and fortune. In the Surrender Chambers, wax tableaux show the surrender of the Allies to the Japanese in 1942 and the surrender of the Japanese to the Allies in 1945. (Originally, there was only the scene representing the Japanese surrender; as the numbers of Japanese visitors to Singapore increased, however, museum officials decided to show both.) Photographs, documents, and audiovisuals highlight events in the Japanese occupation and the various battles that led to their defeat. ⌨ *S$5.* ⊙ *Daily 9–9.*

☺ **Sentosa Orchid Garden.** This exotic garden is filled with orchids from around the world. You'll also find a flower clock, a carp pond, and a Japanese teahouse. ⌨ *S$2.50.* ⊙ *Daily 9–7.*

Sunset Bar. Expatriates hang out here to play volleyball and other beach games to the beat of rap music.

☺ ❹ **Underwater World.** Completed in 1991, Underwater World reverses the traditional aquarium experience by placing you right in the water. Two gigantic tanks house thousands of Asian Pacific fish and other marine life; you walk through a 100-yard acrylic tunnel that curves along the bottom. In total, there are 6,000 marine creatures from 350 species. The latest inhabitants (acquired in 1998) are a giant octopus, wolf eels, and giant spider crabs. ⌨ *S$13.* ⊙ *Daily 9–9.*

☺ **VolcanoLand.** This multisensory theme attraction creates a simulated journey to the center of the earth. There are also exhibits on the Maya civilization. ⌨ *S$10.* ⊙ *Daily 10–8.*

☺ **WonderGolf.** A first for southeast Asia, this course features 45 holes for putting in picturesque surroundings, including caves, ravines, streams, and ponds. Three greens deliver different experiences and challenges. ⌨ *S$8.* ⊙ *Daily 9–9.*

The Outer Islands

Singapore consists of one large island and some 60 smaller ones. Though many of the outer islands are still off the beaten track—with few facilities—some are being developed as beach destinations. Island hopping by ferry, bumboat, or water taxi is relatively easy to arrange. (☞ Getting Around *in* Singapore A to Z, *below*).

KUSU

Kusu, also known as Turtle Island and sacred to both Muslims and Taoists, is an ideal weekday retreat (it gets crowded on weekends) from the traffic and concrete of Singapore. There's a small coffee shop on the island, but you may want to bring a picnic lunch to enjoy in peace on the beach. A number of stories attempt to explain the association with turtles; all the tales in some way relate to a turtle that saved two shipwrecked sailors—one Chinese and one Malay—who washed up on the shore. Turtles now are given sanctuary here, and an artificial pond honors them with stone sculptures.

The hilltop **kramat kusu** (shrine) is dedicated to a Malay saint—a pious man named Haji Syed Abdul Rahman, who, with his mother and sister, is said to have disappeared supernaturally from the island in the 19th century. To reach the shrine, you climb the 122 steps that snake up through a forest. Plastic bags containing stones have been hung on the trees by devotees who have come to the shrine to pray for forgiveness of sins and the correction of wayward children. If their wishes are granted, believers must return the following year to remove their bags and give thanks.

Tua Pekong, a small, open-fronted Chinese temple, was built by Hoe Beng Watt in gratitude for the birth of his child. The temple is dedicated to Da Bo Gong, the god of prosperity, and the ever-popular Kuan Yin, goddess of mercy. Here she's also known by her Chinese surname, Sung Tzu Niang ("Giver of Sons"), and is associated with longevity, love of virtue, and fulfillment of destiny. Sung Tzu had a difficult childhood. She was determined to become a nun, but her father forbade it. When she ran away to join an order, he tried to have her killed. In the nick of time she was saved by a tiger and fulfilled her destiny. In gratitude, she cut off her arm as a sacrifice. This so impressed the gods that she was then blessed with many arms. Hence, when you see her statue in many of the Chinese temples in Singapore, she is depicted with six or eight arms. This temple has become the site of an annual pilgrimage. From late October to early November (or in the ninth lunar month), some 100,000 Taoists bring exotic foods, flowers, joss sticks, and candles, and pray for prosperity and healthy children.

PULAU UBIN
Here amid the *kelongs* (fishing huts) and duck and prawn farms the lifestyle hasn't changed much in 30 years. The island is a natural haven for plants, birds and insects found in its mangrove and forest areas. There are colorful Thai *Ma Chor* temples along the seashore.

ST. JOHN'S
St. John's was first a leper colony, then a prison camp. Later it became a place to intern political enemies of the republic, and now it has become an island for picnicking and overnight camping. Without any temples or particular sights, it is quieter than Kusu. There are plans to develop camping facilities, which will surely take away some of the peaceful solitude one can experience here now.

SISTER'S ISLAND
One of the most beautiful of the southern islands is also one of the best for snorkeling and diving. To get there, you'll have to hire a water taxi (S$50 per hour) at the Jardine Steps or Clifford Pier or take an organized day cruise (check with your hotel). Some of the boatmen know where to find the best coral reefs. If you plan to dive, be advised that the currents can be very strong.

Bintan Island, Indonesia
From the tallest building in Singapore you can see the nearby islands of Indonesia's Riau Archipelago. In 45 minutes, you can cross the straits on a ferry south (☞ *also* Getting Around *in* Singapore A to Z, *below*) to the Bataam Islands. Bataam itself is undergoing a vast development project that includes a duty-free industrial zone and a tourist complex. However, Bataam and its resorts have been overshadowed by the more interesting island of Bintan.

Today the *orang laut* (sea people; island inhabitants who are descendants of pirates and traders) still live in houses on stilts over the sea—an interesting contrast to the six modern beach resorts here. Overnight trips to Bintan, more than twice the size of Singapore, can include a stay at a five-star hotel with your own private pool or a more adventurous jaunt in a sampan to the 16th-century palace of a Malaysian sultan. Make hotel reservations as far in advance as possible (☞ Lodging, *below*). You may also want to consider booking a guided tour of the island (☞ Contacts and Resources *in* Singapore A to Z, *below*). Note that citizens of Canada, the United Kingdom, and the United States need only passports for stays in Indonesia of less than one month.

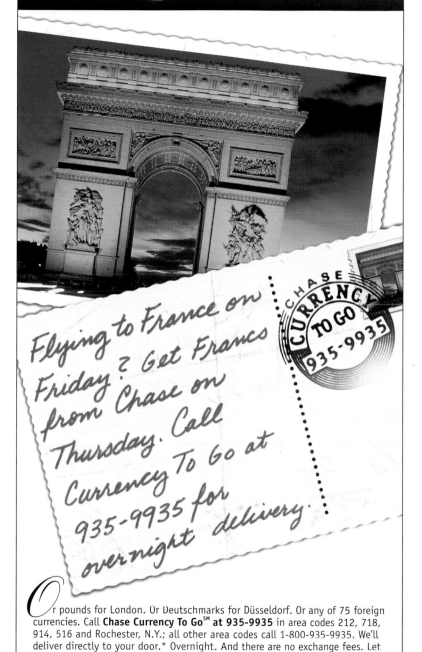

Flying to France on Friday? Get Francs from Chase on Thursday. Call Currency To Go at 935-9935 for overnight delivery.

CHASE CURRENCY TO GO 935-9935

*O*r pounds for London. Or Deutschmarks for Düsseldorf. Or any of 75 foreign currencies. Call **Chase Currency To Go**ᔆᴹ **at 935-9935** in area codes 212, 718, 914, 516 and Rochester, N.Y.; all other area codes call 1-800-935-9935. We'll deliver directly to your door.* Overnight. And there are no exchange fees. Let Chase make your trip an easier one.

CHASE. The right relationship is everything.ᔆᴹ

BONUS MILES MAKE GREAT SOUVENIRS.

Earn Miles With Your MCI Card.

Take the MCI Card along on this trip and start earning miles for the next one. You'll earn frequent flyer miles on all your calls and save with the low rates you've come to expect from MCI. Before you know it, you'll be on your way to some other international destination.

Sign up for MCI by calling 1-800-FLY-FREE

Earn Frequent Flyer Miles.

Is this a great time, or what? :-)

Easy To Call Home.

1. To use your MCI Card, just dial the WorldPhone access number of the country you're calling from.
2. Dial or give the operator your MCI Card number.
3. Dial or give the number you're calling.

#Bahrain	800-002
#Brunei	800-011
#China ❖	108-12
For a Mandarin-speaking operator	108-17
#Cyprus ♦	080-90000
#Egypt(CC)♦ (Outside of Cairo, dial 02 first)	355-5770
#Federated States of Micronesia	624
#Fiji	004-890-1002
#Guam(CC)	1-800-888-8000
#Hong Kong(CC)	800-96-1121
#India (CC) ❖	000-127
#Indonesia(CC)♦	001-801-11
Iran ÷	(Special Phones Only)
#Israel(CC)	1-800-940-2727
#Japan(CC)♦	
To call using KDD ■	00539-121▶
To call using IDC ■	0066-55-121
To call using ITJ ■	0044-11-121
#Jordan	18-800-001
#Korea(CC)	
To call using KT ■	009-14
To call using DACOM ■	00309-12
Phone Booths ÷ Red Button 03, then press ★	
Military Bases	550-2255
#Kuwait	800-MCI (800-624)
Lebanon ÷ Collect Access	600-MCI (600-624)
#Macao	0800-131
#Malaysia(CC)♦	1-800-80-0012
#Philippines(CC)♦	
To call using PLDT ■	105-14
Collect access via PLDT in Filipino ■	105-15
Collect access via ICC in Filipino ■	1237-77
#Qatar ★	0800-012-77
#Saipan (CC)÷	950-1022
#Saudi Arabia (CC)÷	1-800-11
#Singapore	8000-112-112
#Sri Lanka (Outside of Colombo, dial 01 first)	440-100
#Syria	0800
#Taiwan(CC)♦	0080-13-4567
#Thailand ★	001-999-1-2001
#United Arab Emirates ♦	800-111
Vietnam ●	1201-1022
Yemen	008-00-102

Bintan's main town is **Tanjung Pinang,** where the primary activity is shopping at **Pasar Pelantar Dua.** Tanjung Pinang is a jumping-off point for some interesting nearby sites.

You can take a tour from Tanjung Pinang's Pelentar Pier up the **Snake River** through the mangrove swamps to the oldest **Chinese temple** in Riau. As the boatman poles his way up the small tributary choked with mangroves, the sudden view of the isolated 300-year-old temple with its murals of hell will send chills down your spine. Have the boatman take you back down the river to **Tanjung Berakit,** where tiny huts perch on stilts. Friendly villagers live in spartan homes without electricity or water—this only an hour and a half from Singapore.

Another good stop by motorboat is **Pulau Penyengat** (Wasp Island), once the heart of the Riau sultanate and the cultural hub of the Malay empire. In the 16th century, the Malay sultanate fled here after being defeated by the Portuguese in Malacca. The island is just 15 minutes by motorboat from Tanjung Pinang's Pelentar Pier. Sites include royal graves, the banyan-shrouded ruins of the palace, and the **Mesjid Raya** (Sultan's Mosque)—a bright yellow building that was plastered together with egg yolks.

DINING

Singapore offers the best feast in the East. You'll find restaurants that serve home-grown Nonya (or Peranakan) fare; others that specialize in cuisine from all parts of Asia; and still others that offer European and American dishes. Some cultures consider atmosphere, decor, and service more important than food. In Singapore, however, the food's the thing: you're as likely to find gourmet cooking (and high standards of cleanliness) in unpretentious food stalls as you are in elegant eateries.

Many of the poshest restaurants are in hotels. Such establishments offer fine dining, complete with the freshest ingredients, displays of roses and orchids, polished silver and gleaming crystal, waiters dressed in tuxedos, and impeccable service. Several hotels also offer high tea (generally served 3 PM–6 PM at a cost of about S$20 per person without tax or service charge). The Singapore version of this British tradition is usually served buffet style and includes dim sum (called *dian xin* here) and fried noodles as well as finger sandwiches and scones. Standout teas include those at the Oriental, Goodwood Park, the Raffles, the Four Seasons, and the Ritz-Carlton.

If you prefer coffee and a casual setting to tea in formal surroundings, you'll be pleased to note that alfresco coffeehouses have taken Singapore by storm. Starbucks, Spinellis, and Delifrance have locations everywhere and are very popular despite the humidity. In addition, widespread building restoration has given rise to several chic dining addresses. Boat Quay—a riverside strip of cafés, restaurants, and bars—may well be the busiest place in town at night. Restaurants to look for here include Kinara (North Indian) and Warung Wayan (Indonesian). At Clarke Quay, another massive restoration project, you can dine on a moored *tongkang,* a type of boat that once plied the river; sample the horrible-to-smell, good-to-eat durian fruit at Durian House; or try seafood at Key Largo, Thai cuisine at Thanying Restaurant, or Mediterranean fare at Bastiani's. Other dining areas include Chinatown's Tanjong Pagar—with such trendy restaurants as Da Paolo (Italian) and L'Aigle d'Or (French)—and Robertson Quay.

Food is a route to cultural empathy, especially if it's consumed at a stir-fry stall (fondly called "wok-and-roll" stalls) or at a vendor's stall in an open-air hawker center. You'll find many stir-fry stalls—most are half restaurant and half parking lot—on East Coast Road. They open at about 5 PM and serve such simple, freshly cooked dishes as deep-fried baby squid and steamed prawns—accompanied, of course, by fried noodles.

The hawker centers have quite a history. At one time, food vendors moved through the streets, each one serving a single dish (often made using a secret family recipe). A hawker advertised by sounding a horn, knocking bamboo sticks together, or simply shouting. Hearing the sound, people dashed from their houses to place orders. After everyone had eaten, the hawker collected and washed the crockery and utensils and continued up the road. Many hawkers might have passed a house in a day. Several years ago, the government gathered the hawkers into large centers for reasons of hygiene (and rest assured that everything is *very* clean; health authorities are strict). Today, these centers enable you to see the raw materials and watch the cooking methods in stall after stall. Then you simply find a seat at a table, note the table number, relate your order and this number to the vendor, and sit down to wait for your food. (Someone will come to your table to take a drink order.) Though you sometimes pay at the end of the meal, paying when you place your order is more the norm. Most dishes cost S$4 or slightly more; for S$12, you can get a meal that includes a drink and fresh fruit for dessert.

The sheltered hawker center at Marina South has hundreds of stalls. The most touristy open-air center is the raucous, festive Newton Circus. Come here for the experience, but avoid the seafood stalls, which are known to fleece tourists. Feast instead at stalls that offer traditional one-dish meals and that have prices displayed prominently. (When you place an order, specify whether you want a S$2, S$3, or S$4 portion.) Other open-air centers include the historic Lau Pa Sat Festival Market in the downtown financial district, Telok Ayer Transit Food Centre on Shenton Way, and Bugis Square at Eminent Plaza. Indoor, air-conditioned food centers are a great way to beat the midday heat. Those in the Orchard Road area include Picnic in the basement of Scotts Centre and the Food Chain in the basement of Orchard Emerald (opposite and just down from the Mandarin Singapore hotel). The following are dishes and food names that you'll often encounter at hawker centers:

char kway teow—flat rice noodles mixed with soy sauce, chili paste, fish cakes, and bean sprouts and fried in lard.
Hokkien prawn mee—fresh wheat noodles in a prawn-and-pork broth served with freshly boiled prawns.
laksa—a one-dish meal of round rice noodles in coconut gravy spiced with lemongrass, chilies, turmeric, shrimp paste, and shallots. It's served with a garnish of steamed prawns, rice cakes, and bean sprouts.
mee rebus—a Malay version of Chinese wheat noodles with a spicy gravy. The dish is garnished with sliced eggs, pieces of fried bean curd, and bean sprouts.
rojak—a Malay word for "salad." Chinese rojak consists of cucumber, lettuce, pineapple, *bangkwang* (jicama), and deep-fried bean curd—tossed with a dressing made from salty shrimp paste, ground toasted peanuts, sugar, and rice vinegar. Indian rojak consists of deep-fried lentil and prawn patties, boiled potatoes, and deep-fried bean curd, all served with a spicy dip sweetened with mashed sweet potatoes.
roti prata—an Indian pancake made by tossing a piece of wheat-flour dough into the air until it's paper-thin and then folding it to form many

layers. The dough is fried until crisp on a cast-iron griddle, then served with curry powder or sugar. An ideal breakfast dish.

satay—small strips of meat marinated in fresh spices and threaded onto short skewers. A Malay dish, satay is barbecued over charcoal and eaten with a spiced peanut sauce, sliced cucumbers, raw onions, and pressed rice cakes.

thosai—an Indian rice-flour pancake that's a popular breakfast dish, eaten with either curry powder or brown sugar.

In sit-down restaurants, plan on small servings of four to five dishes for four people or three dishes for two people. Food is either served family-style—placed all at once at the center of the table so everyone can dig in—or, for more formal meals, served a course at a time, again with diners sharing from a single dish at the center of the table. Each diner is given a plate or bowl of rice. Most Chinese restaurants automatically add a charge of about S$2 per person for tea, peanuts, pickles, and rice.

Most restaurants are open from noon to 2:30 or 3 for lunch and from 7 to 10:30 PM (last order) for dinner. Some hotel coffee shops (and the Indian coffee shops along Changi Road) are open 24 hours a day; others close between 2 and 6 AM. At hawker centers, some stalls are open for breakfast and lunch while others are open for lunch and dinner. Late-night food centers such as Eminent Plaza in Jalan Besar are in full swing until 3 AM.

Competition among Singapore's restaurants has kept the overall meal prices low, but liquor has remained expensive. A cocktail or a glass of wine costs S$8–S$12; a bottle of wine is a minimum of S$50. Seafood is inexpensive (though expensive delicacies such as shark's fin, dried abalone, and lobster are served in some Chinese restaurants). Dishes marked "market price" on the menu are premium items. Before ordering, find out exactly how much each dish will cost, and don't be surprised if you're charged for the napkins and cashew nuts that arrive at the start of your meal. Note that smoking is banned in air-conditioned restaurants and banquet/meeting rooms, though many establishments now offer outdoor patios with a seating area for smokers.

What to Wear

Except at the fancier hotel dining rooms, Singaporeans don't dress up to eat out. The weather calls for lighter wear than a jacket and tie. (Some restaurants tried to enforce a dress code for men but found that their customers went elsewhere to eat. Now an open-neck shirt and a jacket represent the upper limit of formality.) Generally, though, shorts, sleeveless cotton T-shirts, and track suits aren't appropriate. If you're sensitive to cold, bring a sweater—many restaurants are air-conditioned to subarctic temperatures.

Chinese

$$$$ ✕ **Chang Jiang.** Meals in this Goodwood Park hotel (☞ Lodging, *below*)
★ Shanghainese restaurant are served Western-style (portions are presented on dinner plates, and you don't serve yourself from a central platter). The kitchen staff was trained by the chef of Shanghai's leading restaurant, Yang Zhou. Recommended dishes are the chicken and goose surprise, fresh crabmeat in a yam basket, baby kale with scallops, and sliced beef stir-fried and served with leeks. Presentation is an art here. Even the chopsticks are gold-plated. The service and surroundings are very formal. ⊠ *22 Scotts Rd.,* ☎ *737–7188. AE, DC, MC, V.*

$$$$ ✕ **Hai Tien Lo.** Sit in the right place at this 37th-floor restaurant and you'll get a view of the sea, the Padang, and City Hall. The Cantonese cuisine,

the decor, and the service are all extremely elegant: plates are changed with every course, waitresses wear *cheongsams* (Chinese dresses with high collars and side slits) with black with gold trim, and the delicate white china is hand-painted with cherry blossoms. For lunch, opt for the dim sum, priced at a premium because of the top-quality ingredients. Other specialties include roast chicken with crispy golden-brown skin and tender, juicy flesh; beef cubes fried with black pepper and oyster sauce; and deep-fried fresh scallops stuffed with minced prawns and tossed in a salty black-bean sauce. The pièce de résistance is Monk Jumps over the Wall—dried abalone, whole chicken, ham, fish stomach lining, dried scallops, and shark's fin steamed together for hours. At S$100 per serving (or S$1,000 for 10 people), it's one of the most expensive dishes in town, but the broth is the best in the world—the really rich simply drink it and leave the rest. ⊠ *Pan Pacific Hotel Singapore, Marina Square, 6 Raffles Blvd.,* ☎ *336–8111. AE, DC, MC, V.*

$$$$ ✕ **Jiang Nan-Chun.** On the second floor of the Four Seasons hotel (☞ ★ Lodging, *below*), this dining room is home to the innovative creations of one of the youngest master chefs in Singapore, Sam Leong. His delicious Cantonese food has Thai and Japanese influences. Although a set menu is offered, the restaurant's regular customers often request the chef's favorites, which may include deep-fried scallops with pear sauce, baked oysters with bok choy, or fried prawns with sesame and lime mayonnaise. The presentation is unusual and artistic (the double-boiled seafood soup, for example, is served in a hollowed coconut), the service is attentive, and the ambience is understated and relaxed. ⊠ *190 Orchard Blvd.,* ☎ *734–1110. Reservations essential. AE, DC, MC, V.*

$$$$ ✕ **Shang Palace.** Locals and expats alike frequent this elegant Cantonese dining room in the Shangri-La hotel (☞ Lodging, *below*). Large and decorated in brilliant red and gold, the room can be noisy during a full house, but the delicious food more than compensates. The staff is very knowledgeable about the menu, prepared by Hong Kong–born chef Lo Ka Cheung. Try the prawns deep fried with minced shrimp and sesame seeds, or the steamed asparagus served with a poached egg and caviar. For connoisseurs, there are more than 11 Chinese teas from which to choose. ⊠ *22 Orange Grove Rd.,* ☎ *737–3644. Reservations essential. AE, DC, MC, V.*

$$$–$$$$ ✕ **Li Bai.** The dining room in the Sheraton Towers hotel (☞ Lodging, ★ *below*) evokes richness without overindulgence—deep maroon wall panels edged with black and backlighted, elaborate floral displays, jade table settings, ivory chopsticks. The service is very fine, as is the cooking, which is modern and innovative, yet deeply rooted in the Cantonese tradition. The chef's unusual creations include deep-fried diamonds of egg noodles in a rich stock with crabmeat and mustard greens; fried lobster in black-bean paste; and double-boiled shark's fin with Chinese wine and *jinhua* ham. The restaurant is small, seating fewer than 100 people. ⊠ *39 Scotts Rd.,* ☎ *737–6888. AE, DC, MC, V.*

$$$ ✕ **Cherry Garden.** At the Oriental hotel (☞ Lodging, *below*), a wooden- ★ roof pavilion with walls of antique Chinese brick encloses a landscaped courtyard that makes a fine setting for a meal. The artwork is tastefully chosen and displayed, the service is impeccable, and the Hunanese food is a welcome change from the usual Cantonese fare. Try the minced-pigeon broth with dried scallops steamed in a bamboo tube or, in season, served in a fragrant baby melon; the superior Yunnan honey-glazed ham served between thin slices of steamed bread; or the camphor-smoked duck in a savory bean-curd crust. ⊠ *Marina Square, 6 Raffles Blvd.,* ☎ *331–0538. AE, DC, MC, V.*

$$$ ✕ **Golden Peony.** "Refined" is the word that best describes everything—from the service and the table settings to the decor and ambience—in the Cantonese dining room at the Conrad International

Centennial hotel (☞ Lodging, *below*). All dishes are exquisitely pre-pared and ultrafresh. Specialties include deboned crispy chicken with bean curd skin and Yunnan ham (eaten like a sandwich); steamed crab claw in Hua Tiao wine and ginger juice; and steamed Canadian bass and salmon with mushrooms. ⊠ *2 Temasek Blvd.,* ☎ *334–8888, ext. 7482. AE, DC, MC, V.*

$$$ ✕ **Min Jiang.** Housed in a Chinese pavilion on the grounds of the Good-wood Park hotel (☞ Lodging, *below*), Min Jiang is always packed, thanks to its delicious Szechuan food, fast service, and longtime man-ageress, the friendly Shirley Neow. The decor is attractive—a restrained and elegant interpretation of Chinese style. The camphor-smoked duck and the long beans fried with minced pork are favorites. ⊠ *22 Scotts Rd.,* ☎ *737–7411. AE, DC, MC, V.*

$$$ ✕ **Pine Court.** Baked tench, marinated lamb, and fried dry scallops are just a few of the dishes that distinguish the Pekingese cooking at this restaurant in the Mandarin Singapore hotel (☞ Lodging, *below*). The restaurant's Peking duck is famed for its crisp, melt-in-your-mouth skin and delicate pancake wrapping. Dinner here is the best meal; the more economical lunch (frequently a buffet) is less inspired. The carved-wood wall panels will make you feel as if you're in a Chinese mansion; the award-winning service is fine and caring. ⊠ *333 Orchard Rd.,* ☎ *737–4411. AE, DC, MC, V.*

$$–$$$ ✕ **Dragon City.** Many Singaporeans consider Dragon City the best place
★ for Szechuan food. Set in a courtyard and entered through a flamboyant, red, moon-gate door, the large dining room looks Chinese but is not particularly appealing. All artistry is reserved for the food. Choose from such delicious staples as kung po chicken, minced-pork soup in a whole melon, steamed red fish with soybean crumbs, or smoked duck. The service is fast. If you don't quite know how to order your meal, ask for Wang Ban Say, the restaurant's manager and one of the own-ers. ⊠ *Novotel Orchid Inn, Plymouth Wing, 214 Dunearn Rd.,* ☎ *250–3322. AE, DC, MC, V.*

$$–$$$ ✕ **Imperial Herbal Restaurant.** The Chinese believe that "you are what you eat" and that food can be used to maintain or restore health. In the Metropole Hotel's (☞ Lodging, *below*) unique restaurant, an herbalist—rather than a chef—runs the kitchen, and there's a tradi-tional pharmacy near the entrance where herbs are stored (and sold). The menu includes dishes that are decidedly exotic as well as those that are deceptively simple. A must is the delicate quick-fried egg white with scallops and herbs served in a crunchy nest of potato threads. The eel fried with garlic and fresh coriander and the eggplant with pine nuts are equally delicious; the crispy fried ants on prawn toast are not only a conversation piece but totally inoffensive. It's nice to know that that the food that's satisfying your taste buds is also doing you good. Beer and wine are available, as are restorative tonics and teas. ⊠ *41 Seah St., 3rd floor,* ☎ *337–0491. AE, MC, V.*

$$–$$$ ✕ **Lei Garden.** This aesthetically pleasing restaurant has built up a de-voted following with branches in Hong Kong and Kowloon. The food represents the nouvelle Cantonese style with its pristine tastes and del-icate textures. One old-fashioned item is the soup of the day, cooked just the way mother did—assuming that mother had the time to stew a soup lovingly for many hours over low heat. The menu also offers a long list of double-boiled tonic soups (highly prized by the Chinese), barbecued meats, and seafood (including a variety of shark's fin dishes). Dim sum is available and extremely popular at lunch; recommenda-tions include Peking duck, grilled rib-eye beef, and fresh scallops with bean curd in black-bean sauce. ⊠ *Chijmes, No. 01-24, 30 Victoria St.,* ☎ *339–3822. AE, DC, MC, V.*

Singapore Dining

L'Aigle d'Or, **29**
Alkaff Mansion, **28**
Annalakshmi, **36**
Aziza's, **20**
Banana Leaf
Apollo, **24**
Bastiani's, **26**
Beng Hiang, **34**
Blue Ginger, **19, 32**
Café Modestos, **7**
Chang Jiang, **11**
Cherry Garden, **43**

Club Chinois, **8**
Compass Rose
Restaurant, **38**
Dragon City, **5**
Golden Peony, **51**
Gordon Grill, **13**
Hai Tien Lo, **48**
House of Mao, **35**
House of Sudanese
Food, **44, 50**
Imperial Herbal
Restaurant, **40**
Ivin's Restaurant, **16**

Jiang Nan-Chun, **9**
Keyaki, **49**
Latour, **2**
Lee Kui (Ah Hoi)
Restaurant, **31**
Lei Garden, **37**
Li Bai, **15**
Long Jiang, **18**
Madras New
Woodlands
Restaurant, **25**
Min Jiang, **12**
Moi Kong, **33**

Muthu's Curry
Restaurant, **23**
Nadaman, **4**
Our Village, **46**
Palm Beach
Seafood, **53**
Paolo & Ping's, **10**
Pine Court, **17**
Rajah Inn, **22**
Ristorante
Bologna, **42**
Samy's Curry
Restaurant, **1**

Shang Palace, **3**
Shima, **14**
Suntory, **6**
Tandoor, **21**
Thanying, **27, 30**
Tiffin Room, **39**
Tsui Hang Village, **47**
UDMC Seafood
Centre, **52**
Warung Wayan, **45**
Yhingthai Palace, **41**

$$–$$$ ✕ **Long Jiang.** Perhaps the greatest draw of this Szechuan restaurant in the Crown Prince Hotel (☞ Lodging, *below*) is the "all-you-can-eat" offer. For a set price (around S$24), you can sample nearly 40 items on the menu, including hot-and-sour soup, shark's fin soup, smoked duck, and kung po chicken. It's not unlike most other Chinese restaurants in appearance, but the service is above average. ⌧ *270 Orchard Rd.,* ☎ *732–1111. AE, DC, MC, V.*

$$–$$$ ✕ **Tsui Hang Village.** The decor of this well-regarded Cantonese restaurant includes green tiles, brick walls, and rooflike overhangs that give it a courtyard ambience. The seafood is fresh and flown in from Hong Kong (the superior braised shark's fin is among the best in town). At lunch, try the inexpensive dim sum or one of the set menus. The deep-fried roast chicken pleases most palates. ⌧ *Marina Square, No. 02–142, 6 Raffles Blvd.,* ☎ *338–6668. AE, DC, MC, V.*

$$ ✕ **Beng Hiang.** At this restaurant in a restored shophouse just outside the financial district, you'll find peasant-style Hokkien cooking: hearty, rough, and delicious. *Kwa huay* (liver rolls) and *ngo hiang* (pork-and-prawn rolls) are very popular and are eaten dipped in sweet plum sauce. *Hay cho* (deep-fried prawn dumplings) are another Hokkien staple. Beng Hiang also serves *khong bak* (braised pig's feet) and what is reputedly the best roast suckling pig in Singapore. ⌧ *112–116 Amoy St.,* ☎ *221–6695. Reservations not accepted. No credit cards.*

$$ ✕ **House of Mao.** Opened in the spring of 1998 to great fanfare, this kitschy, pop-art homage to the late dictator is an amalgamation of Warhol meets Julia Child's favorite Chinese (specifically, Hunanese) dishes. The memorabilia and the staff's Red Army uniforms are only two of the reasons to come; the tasty, contemporary Hunanese food is the third. The service can be uneven due to the crowds that have been flocking here since its opening. ⌧ *No. 03-02 China Square Food Centre, 51 Telok Ayer St.,* ☎ *533–0660. Reservations not accepted. AE, DC, MC, V.*

$$ ✕ **Lee Kui (Ah Hoi) Restaurant.** This unassuming storefront restaurant in the heart of Chinatown serves you at large tables (if your party is small, you may have to share a table with others); it's busy, noisy, and often crowded. The distinctive flavors of Teochew cuisine are evident: try the cold crab as a starter, followed by winter melon soup, prawns with young chives and *ngohiang* (minced pork rolls). Your glass of tea will be constantly replenished. It may be helpful to go with a Mandarin-speaking person, as the staff speaks little English. ⌧ *46 Mosque St.,* ☎ *222–3654. Reservations not accepted. No credit cards.*

$$ ✕ **Moi Kong.** At this unpretentious Chinese (Hakka) eatery, try the prawns fried with red-wine lees, the steamed chicken with wine, or the *khong bak mui choy* (braised pork in dark soy sauce with a preserved salted green vegetable), delicious with rice. ⌧ *22 Murray St.,* ☎ *221–7758. Reservations not accepted. AE, DC, V.*

Continental

$$$$ ✕ **Gordon Grill.** The Scottish country/hunting lodge look here is light-
★   ened with celadon and apple greens, light-wood chairs, and glass panels etched with delicate drawings of Scottish lairds. Tradition is served up here—not surprising for a Goodwood Park hotel (☞ Lodging, *below*) restaurant—so you won't find any trendy "fusion" cooking, only Continental dining at its best. Specialties include excellent roast beef, perfect steaks, and the best sherry trifle in town. The service is very good. ⌧ *22 Scotts Rd.,* ☎ *737–7411. AE, DC, MC, V.*

$$$$ ✕ **Latour.** At press time, the very highly regarded Latour was—owing
★   to renovations—being moved from one part of the Shangri-La hotel

(☞ Lodging, *below*) to another. It was slated to reopen on the 24th floor, with a "less stuffy" atmosphere, according to the mâitre d'. When it does open, the wine list will no doubt still be one of the best in town, and diners will still be able to order such popular dishes as the panfried duck liver and the seasonal salad flavored with a truffle sauce. ✉ *22 Orange Grove Rd.*, ☎ *737–3644. Reservations essential. AE, DC, MC, V.*

Eclectic

$$$ × **Bastiani's.** Mediterranean food with New World accents stars at this
★ restaurant in a restored riverside warehouse. Downstairs there's a comfortable bar and a patio; upstairs the spacious dining room has a terrace (where renegade smokers can indulge in their habit). With its Asian rugs on polished wood floors, eclectic furniture, and open kitchen—hung with garlic, salamis, and the like—Bastiani's has a casual elegance. The menu changes every two months, but it always emphasizes fresh vegetables and herbs; grains such as couscous and polenta; and grilled or baked poultry, red meat, and fish. Pizza is cooked in a wood-fired oven. The more than 4,000 bottles in the wine cellar should satisfy the most fastidious wine buff. ✉ *Clarke Quay*, ☎ *433–0156. AE, DC, MC, V.*

$$$ × **Compass Rose Restaurant.** This elegant restaurant is spread out over three floors of the Westin Stamford hotel (☞ Lodging, below); on a clear day, the view from the 70th floor includes Malaysia and some Indonesian islands. Indulge in the luxurious lounge (where high tea and drinks are served) or in the more formal dining room, where artistically presented meals preside. "East meets West" is the theme in such dishes as sautéed veal tenderloin and grilled goose liver, lobster bisque, and broiled king prawns topped with coriander and macadamia pesto. Lunches are considerably less expensive than dinners, and the noontime seafood buffet (S$42) has an amazing variety of dishes. There's always a line at night for seats in the lounge. ✉ *2 Stamford Rd.*, ☎ *338–8585. AE, DC, MC, V.*

$$–$$$ × **Club Chinois.** When Tan Zhuan Qing opened the prestigious Club
★ Chinois in Shanghai in 1925, he couldn't have imagined that a Singaporean restaurateur, Andrew Tjioe, would model another restaurant on it more than 70 years later. Here, in the Orchard Parade Hotel (☞ Lodging, *below*) you'll find a delectable fusion of Cantonese and French cuisine, aptly directed by famed Canadian chef Susar Lee. The decor is swank and breezy: cream-color tablecloths are accented by turquoise monogrammed napkins and Wedgwood china. Mandarin cha-cha music from the '20s and '30s fills the room as the Armani-clad staff serves delightful dishes. Try the olive-oil-blanched tuna and lobster salad; the soybean bisque with morels; and a chili-marinated rack of lamb with tamarind, orange, and onion marmalade and soft pumpkin cake. ✉ *No. 02-18, 1 Tanglin Rd.*, ☎ *834–0660. AE, DC, MC, V.*

$$ × **Paolo & Ping's.** Though the mix of Chinese and Italian dishes may seem odd, this place has been very popular since its opening in the Royal Crowne Plaza Singapore hotel (☞ Lodging, *below*) in mid-1997. Though the turquoise and yellow-ocher interior is a bit noisy (owing to an open-kitchen layout) for intimate dinners, you can request a seat in the quieter Ping's Tea Room and Paolo's Tables section or on the outdoor terrace. Try the spaghetti *con aragosta* (with lobster, tomato, and fresh herbs) or the wok-fried beef with garlic on potato dumplings. For dessert, the deep-fried bittersweet chocolate "wontons" are a decadent treat. The restaurant has live entertainment most evenings until 1 AM. ✉ *25 Scotts Rd.*, ☎ *731–7985. AE, DC, MC, V.*

French

$$$ ✕ **L'Aigle d'Or.** Glittering crystal contrasts with gaily decorated floral plates at this small, cheerful restaurant in the Duxton Hotel (☞ Lodging, *below*). A five-course *menu dégustation* (sampling menu) for about S$100 may include lobster consommé, sautéed fresh foie gras, baked John Dory fillets, and roast rack of lamb. Desserts come in pairs; you'll rave about the hot lemon soufflé in a chocolate shell. A set lunch menu changes daily and costs about S$36 per person. ⊠ *83 Duxton Rd.,* ☎ *227–7678. AE, DC, MC, V.*

Indian

$$$ ✕ **Tandoor.** The food has a distinctly Kashmiri flavor at this luxuri-
★ ous restaurant, where Indian paintings, rust and terra-cotta colors, and Indian musicians (at night) create the ambience of the Moghul court. The tandoor oven, which you can see through glass across a lotus pond, dominates the room. After you order tandoori chicken, lobster, fish, or shrimp—marinated in yogurt and spices, then roasted in the oven—sit back and watch the chef work. Also cooked in the oven is the northern Indian leavened bread called *naan*; the garlic naan is justifiably famous. The tender, spice-marinated roast leg of lamb is a favorite with regulars. Spiced *masala* tea is a perfect ending to the meal. Service is exceptionally attentive. ⊠ *Holiday Inn Park View, 11 Cavenagh Rd.,* ☎ *733–8333. AE, DC, MC, V.*

$$–$$$ ✕ **Annalakshmi.** Run by a Hindu cultural organization, this restaurant in the Excelsior Hotel (☞ Lodging, *below*) is considerably more elegant and more expensive than the average vegetarian eatery. The lunch buffet is very popular with Indian businessmen. At night, the paper-thin *dosai* pancakes are delicious in the special Sampoorna dinner. The selection often includes cabbage curry, *channa dhal* (chickpea stew), *kurma* (a mild vegetable curry cooked with yogurt or cream), *poori* (puffy, deep-fried bread), *samosa* (deep-fried, vegetable-stuffed patties), and *jangri* (a cold dessert). The flavors are delicate; spices are judiciously employed to enhance—rather than mask—the taste. ⊠ *5 Coleman St.,* ☎ *339–9993. AE, DC, MC, V. Closed Sun.*

$$ ✕ **Our Village.** There are considerably more attractive—and expensive—
★ Indian restaurants along Boat Quay, but aficionados swear that the food here is superior. Look for the narrow corridor that leads to the restaurant's elevator, which will take you to the fifth floor and a rooftop terrace that's delightfully cool and has excellent views. The menu contains all the usual North Indian favorites, yet the food, cooked home-style rather than prepared hours in advance, has a particular freshness and intensity of flavor. The *sag paneer* (spinach with homemade cheese) and *bhindi bhartha* (okra) are very good; so are the naan and any of the dishes cooked in the tandoor. ⊠ *46 Boat Quay, 4th and 5th floors,* ☎ *538–3058. AE, MC, V.*

$ ✕ **Banana Leaf Apollo.** Along Race Course Road are a host of South
★ Indian restaurants that serve meals on fresh rectangles of banana leaf. This down-home cafeteria-style spot was recently transformed into a stylish restaurant that specializes in fish-head curry (S$18–S$25, depending on the size). The food is fabulous, though it's often so hot that you may wind up with tears streaming down your face. Each person is given a large piece of banana leaf; steaming-hot rice is spooned into the center; then two *papadam* (deep-fried lentil crackers) and two vegetables, with delicious spiced sauces, are arranged neatly around the rice. Optional extras such as the fish-head curry or spicy mutton may be added. ⊠ *54–58 Race Course Rd.,* ☎ *293–8682. AE, MC, V.*

$ ✕ **Madras New Woodlands Restaurant.** Many locals have quite an al-
★ legiance to this simple restaurant in the heart of Little India. The zesty

food is vegetarian, combining northern and southern styles. For a full meal, order a *thali:* a large platter of dosai pancakes served with three spiced vegetables, curd, dhal, *rasam* (hot and sour soup), *sambar* (spicy sauce), sweet *raita* (chopped vegetables with yogurt), and papadam. Ask for the paper dosai, which is particularly crisp and comes in an enormous roll; it's served with two spiced coconut sauces and a rasam and is wonderful enough to make a meal on its own. The milk-based sweetmeats are irresistible. ⊠ *14 Upper Dickson Rd.,* ☎ *297–1594. Reservations not accepted. No credit cards.*

$ ✕ **Muthu's Curry Restaurant.** Curry aficionados argue endlessly over which sibling serves the better food, Muthu or his brother, who owns the Banana Leaf Apollo (☞ *above*) down the street. The decor is similar, and Muthu's also has air-conditioning. ⊠ *78 Race Course Rd.,* ☎ *293–7029. Reservations not accepted. AE, MC, V.*

$ ✕ **Samy's Curry Restaurant.** It's *très* chic to lunch at this restaurant on the grounds that used to be home to the Ministry of Defense, not least because there's no way you can stumble upon it by chance—you have to be in the know. The old, no-fuss, civil-service clubhouse is a legacy of the British rule. The decor and service are equally no-fuss. The food—spicy-hot South Indian curries that are served on banana leaves—is excellent. There's no air-conditioning, which means that you sweat it out in true colonial fashion. It's cooler in the evening, but arrive no later than 7 PM for the best dishes. ⊠ *Singapore Civil Service Club House, Block 25, Dempsey Rd.,* ☎ *472–2080 or 296–9391. Reservations not accepted. AE, DC, V. No dinner Thurs.*

Italian

$$$ ✕ **Ristorante Bologna.** The Bologna, in the Marina Mandarin hotel (☞ Lodging, *below*) insists on making pastas fresh and on using fresh herbs in such dishes as *agnello al dragoncello* (roast rack of lamb stuffed with snow peas and tarragon). Ingredients are flown in from Italy to ensure authenticity. Waiters in vests provide impeccable service. The decor is light, airy, and luxurious; Renaissance-inspired murals adorn the walls, Carrera marble tiles the floor, and a cascading waterfall tops off the view. ⊠ *Marina Square, 6 Raffles Blvd.,* ☎ *338–3388. Reservations not accepted. AE, DC, MC, V.*

$$–$$$ ✕ **Café Modestos.** Blessed with an unbeatable location on the ground
★ floor of the Orchard Parade Hotel (☞ Lodging, *below*), at the corner of Orchard and Tanglin roads, Café Modestos does more than just wait for folks to wander in. It *draws* them in with its reasonably priced menu of Italian favorites and live entertainment. You can feast on chef Frederico's creative pizza and pasta on the outdoor patio, in the semi-outdoor area (which smokers appreciate), or in the air-conditioned main dining room. There's also a cigar lounge and a wine cellar. Try the carpaccio *di manzo ai funghi misti* (with mushrooms and Parmesan), the linguine *alla modesto* (with assorted seafood), or the *branzino patate e capperi* (sea bass with roasted potatoes in a caper and white-wine sauce). The best pizza has to be the *nera ai frutti di mare* (a squid-ink crust topped with tomatoes and seafood). ⊠ *1 Tanglin Rd.,* ☎ *235–7808. AE, DC, MC, V.*

Japanese

$$$–$$$$ ✕ **Suntory.** Owned by a Japanese beer company, this is reputedly the most expensive Japanese restaurant in town. You'll find a *teppanyaki* room (you're seated at large tables around a large griddle where fish, meat, vegetables, and rice are lightly seared), a sushi counter, tables for *shabu-shabu* (a kind of fondue meal where seafood and meats are lightly swished in boiling stock, then dipped in a variety of sauces),

tatami rooms, and a very attractive lounge. The decor is exquisite, the staff well trained, and the food excellent. ⊠ *Delfi Orchard, No. 06–01/02, 402 Orchard Rd.,* ☏ *732–5111. AE, DC, MC, V.*

$$$ ✕ **Keyaki.** A Japanese farmhouse has been re-created in a formal Japanese garden with a golden-carp pond on the rooftop of the Pan Pacific Hotel (☞ Lodging, *below*). The waitresses in kimonos, the waiters in *happi* coats, and the Japanese lacquerware and porcelain make you feel as if you're in Japan (despite the European-looking wood chairs). The teppanyaki may be the best in Singapore, with a distinctive garlic fried rice and excellent beef, scallops, salmon, and shrimp. ⊠ *Marina Square, 7 Raffles Blvd.,* ☏ *336–8111. AE, DC, V.*

$$$ ✕ **Nadaman.** There's nothing quite so exciting as watching a teppa-
★ nyaki chef perform his culinary calisthenics. The Nadaman, in the Shangri-La hotel (☞ Lodging, *below*) offers sushi, sashimi (the fresh lobster sashimi is excellent), teppanyaki, tempura, and *kaiseki* (a formal Japanese banquet). Try one of the *bento* lunches—fixed-price meals (around S$35) beautifully decorated in the Japanese manner and served in lacquer trays and boxes. The decor is distinctly Japanese, and the service is discreetly attentive. ⊠ *22 Orange Grove Rd.,* ☏ *737–3644. AE, DC, MC, V.*

$$–$$$ ✕ **Shima.** Strangely, "German baronial" is perhaps the best way to describe the look of this Japanese restaurant in the Goodwood Park hotel (☞ Lodging, *below*). Teppanyaki, shabu-shabu, and *yakiniku* (grill-it-yourself slices of beef, chicken, or fish) are the only items on the menu. You sit around a teppanyaki grill, watching the chef at work, or at the shabu-shabu and yakiniku tables cooking for yourself. Copper chimneys remove the smoke and smell. ⊠ *22 Scotts Rd.,* ☏ *734–6281/2. AE, DC, MC, V.*

Malay and Indonesian

$$$ ✕ **Alkaff Mansion.** Once the estate of wealthy merchants, this 19th-century house on Mt. Faber Ridge, a short distance southwest of the city center, opened as a restaurant in 1991. You can sit inside under twirling fans inside or out on a veranda decorated to reflect the diverse tastes of the old Arab traders. Downstairs there's a huge Malay-Indonesian dinner buffet; on the balconies upstairs, 10 sarong-clad waitresses serve a multicourse rijsttafel. Western food—from steaks to seafood bordelaise—is also offered on a three-course luncheon menu and a more elaborate à la carte dinner menu. Overall, the delightful turn-of-the-century ambience and the presentation are more rewarding than the food. ⊠ *10 Telok Blangah Green,* ☏ *278–6979. AE, DC, MC, V.*

$$$ ✕ **Tiffin Room.** For a taste of nostalgia and of a typical British "curry tiffin," part of the Malay colonial tradition, a visit to the Tiffin Room in the landmark Raffles Hotel (☞ Lodging, *below*) is a must. Despite its popularity with tour groups, the light, airy restaurant with its marble floors is still gracious; the service is courteous if a fraction slow during busy lunches. The lunch and dinner buffets are tempting spreads of largely Indian dishes. Forget that concession to modern tastes, the salad bar, and head straight for the mulligatawny, a spicy curry soup. There's a large array of spicy (but not necessarily chili-hot) vegetable, meat, poultry, and seafood dishes, and far more pickles, chutneys, and other condiments than a genuine Indian meal would provide. If you've still got room, you can choose from one or two local desserts as well as Indian and international favorites. ⊠ *1 Beach Rd.,* ☏ *331–1612. AE, DC, MC, V.*

$$ ✕ **Aziza's.** It's the spicy cooking of the Malay Peninsula you get here—lots of lemongrass, shallots, pepper, coriander, cloves, and cinnamon. Try the *rendang* (beef simmered for hours in a mixture of spices and coconut milk), *gado gado* (a light salad with a spiced peanut sauce), or *bergedel* (Dutch-influenced potato cutlets). The oxtail soup is especially delicious. Ask for *nasi ambang,* and you'll get festive rice with a sampling of dishes from the menu. The friendly setting makes this an easy place to experiment with Malay food. ⊠ *180 Albert St.,* ☎ *235–1130. AE, DC, MC, V.*

$$ ✕ **Rajah Inn.** In the lobby of the charming Regalis Court boutique hotel (☞ Lodging, *below*), this surprisingly large Indonesian restaurant is decorated in warm yellow and white tones and has ceiling fans as well as the ubiquitous air-conditioning. Try the *sambal goreng udang* (fried shrimp with chili) for a spicy sensation, *sayur lodeh* (local vegetables cooked in coconut milk), or *kambing gan lembu* (mutton or beef in a mild curry sauce). Prices are very reasonable, but call ahead to make sure the restaurant won't be feeding a tour group at the time you'd like to dine here. ⊠ *64 Lloyd Rd.,* ☎ *734–7117. AE, MC, V.*

$$ ✕ **Warung Wayan.** Indonesian cuisine reigns at this riverside restaurant. The charcoal-grilled items are particularly good. If you want to sample Balinese as opposed to Javanese or Indonesian-Chinese food, order the Balinese *satay* (pieces of beef, pork, and chicken on a wooden skewer and that are barbecued or roasted; but don't eat them with peanut sauce; they don't go together in Balinese cooking) and *ayam panggang Wayan* (barbecued chicken) with its wonderful tangy sauce. A Javanese speciality— *tahu telor* (meltingly soft bean curd deep-fried with a crunchy egg coating)—is a must. Prices for wine and beer are very reasonable by Singapore standards. ⊠ *50A Boat Quay,* ☎ *538–3889. AE, DC, MC, V.*

$–$$ ✕ **House of Sudanese Food.** Sudanese food, born of an isolated province
★ in western Java, is a cuisine unique from the rest of Indonesia. It combines raw, fresh vegetables with meat and fish in a piquant sweet-spicy mix. Order several small dishes and one seafood entrée and share them with your travel companions. You might start with *keredok,* a vegetable salad in a spicy peanut dressing; continue with *taupok goreng isi,* bean-curd-skin rolls stuffed with scallops, prawns, water chestnuts, and mushrooms; and *sedap ikan snapper bakar,* broiled red snapper basted in a sweet sauce. The prices at all three locations are very reasonable, making them hits with the lunchtime business crowd. ⊠ *55 Boat Quay,* ☎ *534–3775. AE, DC, MC, V.* ⊠ *Suntec City Mall, No. B1-063, Fountain Terrace, 3 Temasek Blvd.,* ☎ *334–1012. AE, DC, MC, V.* ⊠ *218 East Coast Rd.,* ☎ *345–5020. AE, DC, MC, V.*

Nonya

$$ ✕ **Blue Ginger.** Singapore's most popular Peranakan restaurant has two convenient locations—one in Chinatown, the other on Orchard Road. Furnishings are stylish and elegant, and colorful paintings by local artist Martin Loh abound. You might try such dishes as *udang goreng tauyu lada* (sautéed prawns with pepper in a sweet soya sauce), *ayam panggang Blue Ginger* (boneless chicken grilled and flavored with spiced coconut milk), and the mouthwatering *ngo heong* (homemade rolls of minced pork and prawns seasoned with five spices). If you're brave, sample the dessert made from the local infamous durian fruit (a large, thorny bit of produce that smells like old gym socks but has a caramel flavor). At the Tanjong Pagar location, request a second-floor table for an entertaining view of the street below. ⊠ *97 Tanjong Pagar Rd.,* ☎ *222–3928. AE, DC, MC, V.* ⊠ *The Heeren, No. 05-02C, 260 Orchard Rd.,* ☎ *835–3928. AE, DC, MC, V.*

$$ ✕ **Ivin's Restaurant.** Housed in the upscale suburb of Bukit Timah, just north of the city center (you'll need a cab to get here), this casual restaurant serves traditional Nonya food à la carte. Specialties include *ayam buah keluak* (chicken in a spicy-sour gravy with a black Indonesian nut that has a creamy texture and the smokiness of French truffles),

babi pongteh (pork stewed in soy sauce and onions), *udang masak nanas* (prawns cooked with pineapple), and *pong tauhu* (a soup with bamboo shoots and minced chicken, prawn, and bean-curd dumplings). ⊠ *19/21 Binjai Park,* ☎ *468–3060. AE, DC, MC, V.*

Seafood

$$–$$$ ✕ **Palm Beach Seafood.** Forty years ago, this restaurant was on a beach, with tables set under coconut trees—hence the name. It's now in a shopping and leisure complex next to the National Stadium and covers three floors, with its downstairs restaurant seating around 550. What the place lacks in ambience, it more than makes up for in food quality, and the prices may well be the best in town for seafood. The most popular dishes include chili crabs served with French bread to mop up the sauce; prawns fried in black soy sauce or in butter and milk with curry leaves; and deep-fried crisp squid. Don't miss the *yu char kway,* deep-fried crullers stuffed with a mousse of squid and served with a tangy black sauce. ⊠ *Leisure Park, 5 Stadium Walk, Kallang Park,* ☎ *344–3088. Reservations not accepted. AE, MC, V.*

$$–$$$ ✕ **UDMC Seafood Centre.** You *must* visit this place at the East Coast Parkway, near the entrance to the lagoon, to get a true picture of the way Singaporeans eat out, as well as real value (prices here are cheaper than in most other seafood restaurants). Walk around the eight open-fronted restaurants before you decide where to eat. Chili crabs, steamed prawns, steamed fish, pepper crabs, fried noodles, and deep-fried squid are the specialties.. Restaurants include **Chin Wah Heng** (☎ 444–7967), **Gold Coast Seafood** (☎ 448–2020), **Golden Lagoon Seafood** (☎ 448–1894), **Jumbo Seafood** (☎ 442–3435), **Lucky View Seafood Restaurant** (☎ 241–1022), and **Red House Seafood Restaurant** (☎ 442–3112). ⊠ *East Coast Pkwy. Reservations not accepted. AE, DC, MC, V. No lunch.*

Thai

$$–$$$ ✕ **Thanying.** The owners and chefs at this restaurant in the Amara Hotel
   ★   (☞ Lodging, *below*) are Thai, so it's no wonder that it has such exquisite, aristocratic, Thai decor and that the food (redolent of kaffir-lime leaves, basil, mint, ginger, and coriander) is cooked in the best palace tradition. Indeed, this restaurant has been so successful that the owners have opened a second one on Clarke Quay. Try the *gai kor bai toey* (marinated chicken in pandanus leaves and char-grilled to perfection), an exquisite Thai salad like *yam sam oh* (shredded pomelo tossed with chicken and prawns in a spicy lime sauce), *pla khao sam rod* (grouper, deep-fried until it's so crispy you can practically eat the bones), or one of the Thai curries. And of course, you won't want to miss the sour and hot *tom yam* soup. ⊠ *Amara Hotel, Level 2, 165 Tanjong Pagar Rd.,* ☎ *222–4688. AE, DC, MC, V.* ⊠ *Clarke Quay, Block D,* ☎ *336–1821. AE, DC, MC, V.*

$$ ✕ **Yhingthai Palace.** The no-nonsense decor of this small, simple restaurant—just around the corner from the famous Raffles Hotel—makes it clear that food is the prime concern. Although the service can be slow, the well-prepared and moderately priced food is worth waiting for. The *yam ma muang* (sour mango salad) is an excellent and refreshing dish, while *hor mok talay,* seafood mousse served in charming terra-cotta molds, is light and flavorful. If you enjoy spicy dishes with plenty of herbs, try the *phad kra kai* (stir-fried minced chicken). The *kuay teow phad Thai* (fresh rice noodles fried with seafood) is delicious, and one of the lemony tom yam soups is almost obligatory. ⊠ *13 Purvis St.,* ☎ *337–9429. AE, MC, V.*

LODGING

Over the years Singapore has been transformed from a popular tourist destination to a conventioneers' mecca teeming with tour groups and delegates. Singapore's lodging has visibly changed to accommodate this clientele: extensive refurbishment and growth with more automated service has been the trend. With that said, though, luxury still abounds, and there are places where exceptional personal service hasn't completely fallen by the wayside.

Singapore's hotels were once considered inexpensive compared to those in other world-class cities. Today, however, costs rival those in New York or London—a superior double room in a deluxe hotel can run more than S$400 a night; one with a private bath in a modest hotel, about S$150 a night. Further, during conventions and the peak months of August and December, hotel rooms can be scarce and prices can rise. Still, there are enough discounts and deals that no thrifty visitor should ever have to pay the published price (if you use a travel agent, make sure that he or she asks for a discount). There are also budget hotels (with shared bathroom facilities) with rates less than S$85 a night. And if all you're looking for is a bunk, walk along Bencoolen Street, where there are dormitory-style guest houses that charge no more than S$25 a night. (For more information on affordable lodgings, contact the Singapore Tourism Board or STB—*see* Visitor Information *in* Singapore A to Z, *below*— for its annually updated brochure, "Budget Hotels.")

Booking ahead—particularly for stays in August and December—will probably save you money and will definitely save you headaches. If, however, you gamble and arrive without reservations, the Singapore Hotel Association has two counters at Changi Airport that are staffed by people who can set you up with a room—often at a discount—with no booking fee.

Establishments in the $$$–$$$$ range offer such amenities as International Direct Dial (IDD) phones with bathroom extensions, TVs with international cable stations, room service, minibars, data ports for modems, no-smoking rooms or floors, in-room safes, and business and fitness centers loaded with the latest equipment. On the flip side, some smaller hotels—particularly those in converted shophouses—have a few rooms that lack windows, so be sure to ask for one that has them. For of all Singapore's high-tech advances—including traffic signals that chirp at you when it's safe to cross the street—there are some establishments that don't offer rooms equipped for people with mobility problems; those that do are indicated below. Unless otherwise noted, all rooms have air-conditioning and private baths.

Singapore

Singapore's hotels have developed in clusters. The best-known grouping is at the intersection of Orchard and Scotts roads. The luxurious Four Seasons is tucked behind the Hilton off Orchard Road, and the recently refurbished Grand Hyatt is on Scotts Road. Close by is the new Traders Hotel, which cuts out the frills and frippery found at luxury hotels, providing all the basic comforts at low rates.

In Raffles City, the megalithic Westins—the Plaza and the Stamford—stare down at the Raffles, the grande dame of Singapore's hotels, and the Inter-Continental's black-and-white marble gleams alongside turn-of-the-century shophouses. At the south end of the Shenton Way commercial district are a number of business-oriented hotels; to the south of the Singapore River, still another cluster has sprung up, one with boutique hotels as well as the Raffles-owned Merchant Court. Marina Square—a minicity created by a reclamation project that pushed back the seafront to make way for the Suntec City convention complex, more than 200 shops, and many restaurants—has a half dozen hotels, including the Pan Pacific and the Conrad International Centennial.

If you can't get enough of Sentosa Island's attractions, you'll find a couple of hotels there. If you like shopping and nightlife, then the Orchard and Scotts roads area is for you. If you're attending a convention or simply want an urban landscape with open spaces and river views, Marina Square is the logical choice. If you're doing business in the financial district, a hotel close to Shenton Way is ideal; if your business plans include a trip to the industrial city of Jurong, then a hotel on the Singapore River is best. Regardless of where you stay, it's easy to get around this compact city. Taxis and public transportation, especially the subway, make it possible to travel between areas swiftly, and no hotel is more than a 30-minute cab ride from Changi Airport.

$$$$ ★ 🏨 **Four Seasons.** Opened in 1995 by the owner of the adjacent Hilton, the Four Seasons is quieter and—dare we say it?—more refined, with luxuries intended to make it outshine the city's older hotels. (Drawn by the modern elegance, Britain's Spice Girls taped a music video here in 1998.) Guest rooms are spacious and gracious, with soft fabrics, peaceful Asian art, large bathrooms, two-line speakerphones with modem hookups, laser video, and CD players. Of the three restaurants, the Cantonese Jiang-Nam Chun (☞ Dining, *above*) is the most memorable for its stunning art deco and art nouveau decor and its exotic fare. Some of the tennis courts are air-conditioned, and there's even a golf simulator. The hotel is linked to Orchard Road via an elevated passageway to the Hilton. ⊠ *190 Orchard Blvd., 248646,* ☎ *734–1110,* 🖷 *733–0682. 237 rooms, 20 suites. 3 restaurants, bar, 2 pools, 4 tennis courts, health club, shops, business services, meeting rooms. AE, DC, MC, V.*

$$$$ 🏨 **Goodwood Park.** This venerable institution began in 1900 as a club for German expatriates and has since hosted the likes of the Duke of Windsor, Edward Heath, Noël Coward, and the great Anna Pavlova, who performed here. It has recently been renovated to bring its facilities up to world-class standing, though it still lacks many plush extras found in other luxury hotels. The Parklane Suites, each with a bedroom and a living-dining room, can be rented (for short- or long-term stays) for less than a double room in the main hotel; the drawback is the five-minute walk to all the hotel's facilities. Restaurants—which are popular with local diners—include the Gordon Grill, Min Jiang, and Chang Jiang (☞ Dining, *above*). ⊠ *22 Scotts Rd., 228221,* ☎ *737–7411 or 800/772–3890 (reservations in the U.S.),* 🖷 *732–8558. 171 rooms, 64 suites. 3 restaurants, coffee shop, 3 pools, beauty salon, exercise room, baby-sitting, business services, meeting rooms. AE, DC, MC, V.*

$$$$ 🏨 **Grand Hyatt Singapore.** Formerly the Hyatt Regency, this centrally located luxury hotel was extensively refurbished in 1998. Room rates here are among the highest in town, but promotional packages are frequently offered. The Grand Wing consists of one-, two-, and three-room apartments with two-line phones, extra bathrooms, work areas, and private mailboxes. Standard rooms are adequate but small. Dine at Pete's Place, for excellent pasta dishes; mezza9 for authentic Asian; and Scotts Lounge, for afternoon tea. Travelers with disabilities will find the amenities here to their liking. ⊠ *10–12 Scotts Rd., 228211,* ☎ *738–1234,* 🖷 *732–1696. 266 rooms, 427 apartments. 3 restaurants, coffee shop, pool, beauty salon, massage, sauna, 2 tennis courts, badminton, exercise room, squash, business services. AE, DC, MC, V.*

$$$$ 🏨 **Hotel Inter-Continental Singapore.** This Bugis Junction hotel, built in 1995, appears to be just another modern, marbleized, posh hotel with all the latest amenities (including facilities for people with disabilities and "cyber-relations" officers, or computer consultants, on call). But in its 83 Shophouse Rooms—each one different from the next—the Peranakan style (the distinctive Malay-Chinese-European mix of design influences) reminds you of Singapore's multicultural heritage. There's a S$10 surcharge a night for a stay in these rooms, but a complimentary American breakfast is included. The remaining guest rooms have classical, clean, European lines. For a surcharge of S$50 a night you'll get more attentive service, a Continental breakfast, and evening cocktails. ✉ *80 Middle Rd., 188966,* ☎ *338–7600,* ℻ *338–7366. 406 rooms. 3 restaurants, pool, health club, business services, meeting rooms. AE, DC, MC, V.*

$$$$ 🏨 **The Oriental.** Inside this pyramid-shape Marina Square hotel, the
★ level of service on everyone's part—from student trainees to seasoned doormen—is second to none. Subdued, modern elegance and personal attention are the hallmarks here. Rooms are understated, with soft hues of peach and green, handwoven carpets, and paintings of old Singapore. Of special note are the Italian-marble-tiled bathrooms with phones and radio and TV speakers. One-bedroom suites have lovely sitting rooms and separate washrooms. The Cherry Garden (☞ Dining, *above*) prepares outstanding Hunanese food. Morton's, the Chicago-based steak house, has opened its first Asian branch here. More casual dining is available at Café des Artistes. Note that the hotel has facilities for people with disabilities. ✉ *5 Raffles Blvd., 039797,* ☎ *338–0066,* ℻ *339–9537. 422 rooms, 100 suites. 5 restaurants, pool, massage, sauna, golf privileges, 2 tennis courts, health club, jogging, business services, meeting rooms, travel services. AE, DC, MC, V.*

$$$$ 🏨 **Raffles Hotel.** Opened by the Sarkies brothers in 1887 and visited
★ by such writers as Joseph Conrad, Rudyard Kipling, and Somerset Maugham, Raffles was the belle of the East during its heyday in the '20s and '30s but fell on hard times after World War II. True to form in this planned republic, millions of dollars have been spent to replace Singapore's noble old charm with a sanitized version of colonial ambience. The new Raffles is a glistening showpiece, especially from the outside; inside, antique furniture blends well with modern amenities (including facilities for people with disabilities). There are two lobbies: one for guests and the other for the constant flow of diners and curious tourists. Guest suites have teak floors, 14-ft ceilings, overhead fans, and '20s-style furnishings that tend to be stiff. Some suites are named after famous literary figures who once stayed here. ✉ *1 Beach Rd., 189673,* ☎ *337–1886,* ℻ *339–7650. 104 suites. 2 restaurants, 2 bars, pool, exercise room, shops, business services. AE, DC, MC, V.*

$$$$ 🏨 **Ritz-Carlton.** The most dramatic of the luxury hotels in Marina Bay
★ is the Ritz-Carlton. It opened in 1996 with 32 floors of unobstructed water views as well as sculptures by Frank Stella and limited-edition prints by David Hockney and Henry Moore. All rooms are unusually large (travelers with disabilities will appreciate the facilities in some) and have bathrooms that seem better stocked than your local drugstore. Floors 30 to 32 are Club Floors where, for S$60 more a night, you can enjoy complimentary breakfast, noon snacks, afternoon tea, evening cocktails, after-dinner cordials, and personalized concierge services. For dining, there's Snappers for seafood, the Summer Pavilion for Cantonese cuisine, and the Asian- and European-accented Greenhouse. Check out the exclusive health club (local memberships cost S$25,000) and the live jazz in the lobby lounge every evening. ✉ *7 Raffles Ave., 039799,* ☎ *337–8888,* ℻ *338–0001. 541 rooms, 59*

Singapore Lodging

suites. *3 restaurants, pool, spa, tennis court, health club, business services, meeting rooms. AE, DC, MC, V.*

$$$$ 🏨 **Shangri-La.** This hotel has consistently been among Singapore's
★   top three since opening in 1971. To give the other two a run for their
        money, approximately S$57 million has been earmarked for extensive
        renovations of this hotel's Tower Wing, pool, lobby areas, and food
        and beverage outlets in 1998–99. While refurbishments continue, the
        Valley Wing (built at the start of the '90s) and its 137 rooms will be
        the site of business-as-usual hotel activity. Prime Ministers and presidents have stayed here, but all travelers are treated to the same excellent service. The Coffee Garden, designed after an English conservatory,
        has light meals and a lunch buffet; you'll find haute Cantonese cuisine
        in Shang Palace (☞ Dining, *above*); and the Nadaman (☞ Dining, *above*)
        serves Japanese fare. (Travelers with disabilities take note: this hotel
        has amenities for you.) ⊠ *22 Orange Grove Rd., 258350,* ☎ *737–
        3644, 0181/747–8485 (reservations in the U.K.), or 800/942–5050
        (reservations in Canada or the U.S.);* 𝖥𝖠𝖷 *737–3257. 823 rooms. 4 restaurants, bar, putting green, 4 tennis courts, health club, squash, business
        services, meeting rooms. AE, DC, MC, V.*

$$$$ 🏨 **Sheraton Towers.** The pastel-decorated guest rooms here have all
        the deluxe amenities, including small sitting areas with a sofa and easy
        chairs. The Tower Rooms, at about S$60 more, include complimentary butler service and breakfast. The best vantage point for the dramatic cascading waterfall (the rocks are fiberglass) is from the Terrazza
        restaurant, which has a superb high tea. Other restaurants are Domus
        for Italian food and Li Bai (☞ Dining, *above*) for refined Cantonese.
        The hawker stalls at Newton Circus are close by. A large, comfortable
        lounge has live music in the evening. ⊠ *39 Scotts Rd., 228230,* ☎ *737–
        6888,* 𝖥𝖠𝖷 *733–4366. 606 rooms. 2 restaurants, café, coffee shop,
        pool, massage, sauna, dance club, business services, meeting rooms.
        AE, DC, MC, V.*

$$$ 🏨 **ANA Singapore.** Don't be deceived by the antique tapestries and
        wood-paneled walls in the lobby of this glistening 14-story hotel near
        the Botanic Gardens and the embassies. It has a full range of modern
        facilities. Rooms are decorated in light colors and have writing desks,
        bedside remote controls, and coffee- and tea makers. The Hubertus Grill
        serves seafood, prime rib, and Continental cuisine; the Unkai specializes in Japanese food. ⊠ *16 Nassim Hill, 238467,* ☎ *732–1222,* 𝖥𝖠𝖷
        *732–2222. 445 rooms, 17 suites. 2 restaurants, café, coffee shop,
        pool, exercise room, dance club, business services. AE, DC, MC, V.*

$$$ 🏨 **The Beaufort.** This resort on Sentosa Island caters to leisure visitors,
        but its remote location makes it seem more suited to business seminars. Its best feature is the swimming pool, which overlooks the
        Malacca Straits and is flanked by a romantic, open-air, seafood restaurant. The rooms—down concrete corridors, past pond-filled courtyards,
        and in two symmetrical low-rise wings—don't share these fine views;
        instead they look onto tropical parkland. Standard rooms (called
        deluxe) aren't very large (though bathrooms are of a good size) and
        have undistinctive pastel furniture. The Garden Rooms have larger bedrooms and work areas with better-quality furniture such as handmade
        tortoiseshell desks, mosaic tables, and French banquette sofas. There
        are also four luxurious two-bedroom villas, each with its own pool.
        (This hotel has facilities for travelers with disabilities.) ⊠ *2 Bukit
        Manis Rd., Sentosa Island, 099891,* ☎ *275–0331 or 800/637–7200
        (reservations in the U.S.),* 𝖥𝖠𝖷 *275–0228. 175 rooms, 34 suites, 4 villas. 3 restaurants, pool, 2 tennis courts, exercise room, squash, business services, meeting rooms. AE, DC, MC, V.*

$$$ 🏨 **Boulevard Hotel.** A floor-to-ceiling sculpture dominates the airy
        atrium lobby of this hotel, which caters to traveling executives. Guest

rooms have large desks and coffee- and tea makers. Rooms come in three sizes: standard; deluxe, with a corner pantry; and executive, with a work desk area. The hotel is at the top end of Orchard Road, away from the main thoroughfare. ⊠ *200 Orchard Blvd., 248647,* ☎ *737–2911,* FAX *737–8449. 521 rooms. 3 restaurants, coffee shop, 2 pools, beauty salon, exercise room, dance club, business services, travel services. AE, DC, MC, V.*

$$$ 🏨 **Carlton Hotel.** This stark, pristine hotel near Raffles City has achieved a more relaxed ambience than when it first opened in 1988. Your footsteps will still echo through the lobby, but you'll find that the lounges to the side are quiet enclaves for sipping afternoon tea. All the hotel's amenities (including those for travelers with disabilities) are up-to-date. The upper five stories contain concierge floors, with express check-in, complimentary breakfast, and evening cocktails. Published prices have climbed recently; unless you can get a decent discount, they're steep for what the hotel offers. ⊠ *76 Bras Basah Rd., 189558,* ☎ *338–8333,* FAX *339–6866. 463 rooms, 14 suites. 2 restaurants, bar, café, coffee shop, lobby lounge, pool, exercise room, business services, meeting rooms. AE, DC, MC, V.*

$$$ 🏨 **Conrad International Centennial Singapore.** Though this impressive hotel is a high-rise—new in 1997—it's almost lost among the other towers of Marina Square. It's adjacent to the Singapore International Convention and Exhibition Centre (SUNTEC or Suntec City), so many of its rooms are often booked. The lobby is dominated by a grand marble staircase and a gold-leaf ceiling. The Asian art on permanent display was commissioned from the island's top artists and complements the Far Eastern decor and ambience. Rooms are similarly decorated, and have large bathrooms with the usual amenities. Travelers with disabilities will appreciate that the hotel has taken their needs into consideration; businesspeople will be grateful for the 24-hour business center and the well-equipped function rooms. The Golden Peony (☞ Dining, *above*) serves one of the best dim sum lunches in the city. ⊠ *2 Temasek Blvd., 038982,* ☎ *338–8830,* FAX *338–8164. 484 rooms, 25 suites. 3 restaurants, 3 bars, pool, exercise room, business services, meeting rooms, travel services. AE, DC, MC, V.*

$$$ 🏨 **Crown Prince Hotel.** The large, sparse lobby greets you with Italian marble and glass chandeliers. For more drama, glass elevators run along the outside of the building so you can check out the traffic on Orchard Road. Though the pastel rooms are neat and trim, efficiency outweighs warmth here. The Cafe de Prince serves local and Western food, the Long Jiang (☞ Dining, *above*) offers Szechuan food from a set menu, and the Sushi Nogawa is Japanese-owned. ⊠ *270 Orchard Rd., 238857,* ☎ *732–1111,* FAX *732–7018. 297 rooms, 6 suites. 3 restaurants, pool, business services, meeting rooms. AE, DC, MC, V.*

$$$ 🏨 **The Duxton.** Singapore's first boutique hotel consists of eight smartly
★ converted shophouses in Chinatown's Tanjong Pagar district. It remains a breath of fresh air: intimate and tasteful, with a whiff of Singapore's character before it sold out to steel girders and glass. The standard rooms, at the back of the building, are small and have colonial reproduction furniture. You may want to spend the extra S$120 a night for a small duplex suite. Breakfast is included, and afternoon tea is served in the lounge. The excellent French restaurant, L'Aigle d'Or (☞ Dining, *above*), is off the lobby. ⊠ *83 Duxton Rd., 089540,* ☎ *227–7678 or 800/272–8188 (reservations in the U.S.),* FAX *227–1232. 38 rooms, 11 suites. Restaurant, business services. AE, DC, MC, V.*

$$$ 🏨 **Grand Plaza Parkroyal.** The builders of this two-year-old property integrated the century-old shophouses of the neighborhood with modern architecture, making an appealing statement at the junction of Coleman and Hill streets. The superb location has meant compromise,

however, as the pool, fitness facilities, and regular rooms are smaller than those at similarly priced properties. The hotel has one large and prestigious tenant, though: the St. Gregory Marine Spa covers 7,000 square ft and has separate floors for men and women. There's also a medical clinic within the complex. ✉ *10 Coleman St., 179809,* ☎ *336–3456,* FAX *339–9311. 338 rooms. 2 restaurants, bar, coffee shop, spa, exercise room, business services, meeting rooms. AE, DC, MC, V.*

$$$ 🏨 **Hilton International.** It may be short on glitter and dazzle, but the Hilton's rooms have all the amenities (including those for people with disabilities) of a modern deluxe property and at highly competitive rates. It's near shopping arcades that house some of Singapore's most exclusive boutiques. The rooms on the street side still have views, but those at the back have been blocked by the adjacent Four Seasons. The former Givenchy suites are now Executive Club floors with 72 rooms and suites and a clubroom all decked out in contemporary furniture with warm tones and black steel trim. Executive rooms, many with balconies, have two phone lines and a modem connection. Within the hotel are Checkers Brasserie; Tradewinds, a spot for rooftop and poolside dining; and the Harbour Grill, which has seafood and French cuisine. ✉ *581 Orchard Rd., 238883,* ☎ *737–2233,* FAX *732–2917. 351 rooms, 72 suites. 3 restaurants, 2 bars, pool, health club, business services, meeting rooms. AE, DC, MC, V.*

$$$ 🏨 **Hotel New Otani.** Off by itself on the north bank of the Singapore River, this orange-brick-fronted hotel is striking against the greenery of Fort Canning Park. It attracts many Japanese travelers as part of the Liang Court complex, which houses more than 40 specialty shops, and the large Japanese department store Daimaru. Rooms come with coffee-, tea-, and soup makers. The hotel's location is best suited to business travelers who want to be close to Shenton Way. ✉ *177A River Valley Rd., 179031,* ☎ *338–3333,* FAX *339–2854. 408 rooms. 2 restaurants, bar, pool, exercise room, business services, meeting rooms. AE, DC, MC, V.*

$$$ 🏨 **Hotel Phoenix.** During recent renovations, the Phoenix installed PCs with Internet access and exercise equipment in all its rooms, as well as a computerized massage chair in each of its executive rooms and suites. In the warmly decorated rooms, beds are dressed in down quilts and have electronic control panels beside them; the Business Executive Rooms can be converted into offices during the day. There's no on-site health club, so if the in-room gear isn't enough, take advantage of the free passes to the California Fitness Center two blocks away. The Phoenix Garden Café serves very good local and Western fare, but it can be noisy during dinner, perhaps owing to its basement location. The hotel is in the heart of the Orchard Road district and a five-minute drive to the convention center. ✉ *277 Orchard Rd., 238858,* ☎ *737–8666,* FAX *732–2024. 290 rooms, 22 suites. Restaurant, bar, patisserie, nightclub, business services. AE, DC, MC, V.*

$$$ 🏨 **Mandarin Singapore.** The grand main lobby has translucent white-and-black Italian marble and a huge mural, *87 Taoist Immortals,* based on an 8th-century Chinese scroll. Guest rooms on the upper floors command fabulous views of the harbor, the city, and Malaysia beyond. The best rooms have VCRs and bedside remote controls; some have amenities for travelers with disabilities. Rooms in the South Tower have black-lacquer furniture with colorful silk cushions. Overall, however, the Mandarin is a little disappointing; tour groups are its mainstay. Dining options include the Pine Court (☞ Dining, *above*); the Top of the M, a revolving restaurant; Chikuyotei, with Japanese fare; the 24-hour Chatterbox coffeehouse; and hawker-stand Chinese food. ✉ *333 Orchard Rd., 238867,* ☎ *737–4411,* FAX *732–2361. 1,200 rooms. 3 restaurants, coffee shop, pub, pool, beauty salon, massage, sauna, ten-*

nis court, exercise room, squash, dance club, business services, meeting rooms. AE, DC, MC, V.

$$$ ⊞ **Marina Mandarin.** Here, the John Portman–designed atrium narrows as it ascends 21 floors to a tinted skylight, and the lobby is relatively peaceful. Pastel guest rooms are modern and smart and have coffee- and tea makers; for the best view, ask for a room overlooking the harbor. Rooms on the concierge floor—the Marina Club—cost about 25% more and have such extras as terry-cloth robes, butler service, and free breakfast and cocktails. Also available are accommodations for businesspeople who don't need all the extras of the concierge floor but who do need efficient hotel services. The on-site Peach Blossoms restaurant serves Chinese cuisine for lunch and dinner and the Ristorante Bologna (☞ Dining, *above*) has northern Italian fare; the Cricketeer pub is a pleasant place for an evening drink. ⊠ *6 Raffles Blvd., 039594,* ☎ *338–3388,* FAX *339–4977. 575 rooms. 3 restaurants, pub, pool, massage, sauna, 2 tennis courts, exercise room, squash, dance club, business services. AE, DC, MC, V.*

$$$ ⊞ **Merchant Court Hotel.** The trend toward developing "no frills" hotels for business travelers led the Raffles Group to open Merchant Court in 1997. It's across from Clarke Quay and is a free shuttle ride away from the Raffles City Shopping Centre. Standard rooms, albeit small, are comfortable; larger executive rooms have a few more amenities. A stay in a Merchant Club room gets you free use of laptop computers and fax machines as well as complimentary breakfast and cocktails. All rooms have refrigerators for you to stock, and there's a coin-op laundry with video games on the second floor. In addition, the hotel can comfortably accommodate travelers with disabilities. The Ellenborough Market Café offers a nightly Asian/Western buffet. The fitness facilities are top-notch, though the locker rooms are cramped and ill-equipped. ⊠ *20 Merchant Rd., 058281,* ☎ *337–2288,* FAX *334–0606. 470 rooms, 6 suites. Restaurant, 2 bars, refrigerators, pool, exercise room, business services, meeting rooms. AE, DC, MC, V.*

$$$ ⊞ **Meridien Singapore Orchard.** Slightly away from much of the hustle and bustle on Orchard Road, this hotel—its large atrium lobby reminiscent of a train station—is part of what seems to be an abandoned shopping complex. Rooms are done in pastels and have such Asian touches as silk-screen murals; some rooms have balconies loaded with potted plants. Quarters on Le Club Président concierge level have extra amenities. In addition to the hotel's dining room, you'll find rotisserie buffets, local specialties, and Western fare in the relaxed Café Georges. ⊠ *100 Orchard Rd., 238840,* ☎ *733–8855,* FAX *732–7886. 407 rooms. 2 restaurants, bar, pool, exercise room, business services. AE, DC, MC, V.*

$$$ ⊞ **Orchard Hotel.** Its location close to the activity on Orchard Road, several embassies, and the Botanic Gardens has no doubt contributed to this hotel's popularity. The pastel guest rooms are comfortable and functional, and there are facilities for people with disabilities. Rooms in the 17-story Orchard Wing are larger and more expensive than standard rooms. Rooms on the top four floors are part of the Premier and Harvesters' clubs; amenities here include separate check-in, in-room fax services, and complimentary breakfast and evening cocktails. The formal Hua Ting restaurant offers Cantonese and Shanghainese dishes, and the Orchard and Sidewalk cafés serve light fare till 1 AM. ⊠ *442 Orchard Rd., 238879,* ☎ *734–7766,* FAX *733–5482. 680 rooms. Restaurant, 2 cafés, bar, tea shop, pool, exercise room, business services, meeting rooms, travel services. AE, DC, MC, V.*

$$$ ⊞ **Orchard Parade Hotel.** Previously known as the Ming Court Hotel, this 30-year-old property at the corner of Tanglin and Orchard Roads

underwent a S$40-million transformation that was completed in mid-1998. Mediterranean in style (there's a Spanish feel throughout the place), the rooms are spacious, especially the Junior Suites. Several of these are set aside for families with young children and have one or two extra single beds and a dining area. The hotel's location makes it a favorite with leisure travelers, and all the on-site restaurants are leased to well-known eateries. Club Chinois (☞ Dining, *above*) adds a touch of elegance to this "new" kid on the block. ✉ *1 Tanglin Rd., 247905,* ☎ *737–1133,* FAX *733-0242. 368 rooms, 19 suites. 4 restaurants, bar, coffee shop, dance club, nightclub, meeting rooms, travel services. AE, DC, MC, V.*

$$$ 📺 **Pan Pacific.** Of the five Marina Square hotels, this one is the largest (which can make it seem impersonal) and the least expensive (which may enable you to overlook its impersonal air). It caters to tour groups and conventioneers, with amenities (such as PCs in all the rooms) to please the budgets and needs of business travelers—from junior executives to senior management. Upper-floor guest rooms have better views and more amenities; those on the Pacific Floor have butler service and complimentary breakfast and cocktails. Your eatery options include the rooftop Chinese restaurant and the Japanese and Italian dining rooms. ✉ *7 Raffles Blvd., 039595,* ☎ *336–8111,* FAX *339–1861. 747 rooms, 37 suites. 4 restaurants, café, coffee shop, pool, 2 tennis courts, exercise room, playground, business services, meeting rooms. AE, DC, MC, V.*

$$$ 📺 **The Regent.** A good 10-minute walk from Orchard and Scotts roads, the Regent appeals to those who want a quiet haven. Relaxed, comfortable public rooms are done in soft tones and decked out with Asian carpets and wood paneling. The clubby second-floor cocktail lounge, The Bar, is a peaceful refuge within this refuge. Rooms have pastel color schemes, big beds, writing desks, and marble bathrooms; some have balconies. The Tea Lounge serves, of course, high tea daily. Capers offers an alfresco setting for its international cuisine, the Summer Palace serves Cantonese cuisine prepared by Hong Kong chefs; and Maxim's de Paris has a belle epoque decor and French cuisine. (Travelers with disabilities take note: this hotel has amenities for you.) ✉ *1 Cuscaden Rd., 249715,* ☎ *733–8888,* FAX *732–8838. 393 rooms, 48 suites. 4 restaurants, bar, lobby lounge, pool, spa, business services. AE, DC, MC, V.*

$$$ 📺 **Royal Crowne Plaza Singapore.** The lobby here makes a statement with Italian marble floors, two grand staircases, Burmese teak paneling, stained-glass skylights, and handwoven tapestries. Rooms were recently upgraded to the tune of S$20 million, and there are facilities for travelers with disabilities. The Executive Club floor has a private lounge for complimentary breakfast and evening cocktails. Paolo & Ping's (☞ Dining, *above*) is a fun, informal restaurant off the lobby. ✉ *25 Scotts Rd., 228220,* ☎ *737–7966,* FAX *737–6646. 495 rooms. 2 restaurants, bar, pool, exercise room, business services, travel services. AE, DC, MC, V.*

$$$ 📺 **Singapore Marriott.** Formerly the Dynasty, this striking 33-story, pagoda-inspired property dominates Singapore's "million-dollar corner"—the Orchard and Scotts roads intersection. Before Marriott took over, the three-story lobby was done in rich, deep red—the Chinese color for good fortune—with 24 remarkable carved-teak wall panels. Such decoration has been replaced by light-color walls and fake palm trees. Rooms are Western in style, with light-gray carpets, pink vinyl wallpaper, pink-gray upholstery, and ample wood; there are amenities for people with disabilities. The hotel's location—rather than its character—is now its selling point, though it may be the only lodging in the country with an outdoor basketball court. The Crossroads Café is a

great spot for people-watching. ✉ *320 Orchard Rd., 238865,* ☎ *735–5800,* ℻ *735–9800. 364 rooms, 19 suites. 2 restaurants, café, coffee shop, pool, basketball, exercise room, nightclub, business services, meeting rooms. AE, DC, MC, V.*

$$$ ▦ **Westin Plaza and Westin Stamford.** Catering to business executives, the Plaza is the smaller and higher-priced of these Raffles City twins; the 70-story Stamford, one of the tallest hotels in the world, attracts tours and conventions. These hotels are a hub of their own, with a dozen restaurants—of which the Compass Rose (☞ Dining, *above*) is the highlight—more than 100 shops, and convention facilities (including the largest column-free meeting rooms in the world). All rooms have balconies, and the hotel can fulfill the needs of those with disabilities. The 29 Stamford Crest Suites are extremely well appointed with such amenities as a complimentary breakfast and minibar and a separate exercise room. ✉ *2 Stamford Rd., 178882,* ☎ *339–6633,* ℻ *336–5117. Stamford 1,263 rooms; Plaza 764 rooms, 29 suites. 12 restaurants, 2 pools, 6 tennis courts, health club, squash, dance club, business services, convention center, meeting rooms, travel services. AE, DC, MC, V.*

$$ ▦ **Albert Court Hotel.** Rare in Singapore are small hotels that have gone
★   to the expense and effort of restoring existing structures (and installing facilities for people with disabilities). The Albert Court, which is only a few minutes' walk to Little India, is one. Furnishings are simple, but wood paneling creates a warm, comfortable atmosphere. The staff is enthusiastic, and this attitude infects the mostly European guests. You can relax and grab a bite at the small coffee shop, open from 7 AM to 11 PM. ✉ *180 Albert St., 189971,* ☎ *339–3939,* ℻ *339–3253. 135 rooms, 1 suite. Bar, coffee shop. AE, MC, V.*

$$ ▦ **Allson.** This hotel's published rates are lower than those at similar hotels, such as the nearby Carlton. All rooms have rosewood furniture and little extras such as coffee- and tea makers and IDD phones. Rooms on the Excellence Floor are more expensive but more spacious. This hotel has a great location: it's near Raffles City Tower, Marina Square, the historic colonial district, Little India, Bugis Street, and the Arab District, and it's only a 10-minute subway or bus ride to Orchard Road. ✉ *101 Victoria St., 188018,* ☎ *336–0811,* ℻ *339–7019. 450 rooms. 3 restaurants, café, coffee shop, pool, business services. AE, DC, MC, V.*

$$ ▦ **Amara Hotel.** At the south end of the business district, this 18-story hotel is convenient to the train station and the commercial and port facilities and is one of Singapore's better deals if you get a discount (usually available). Although the hotel itself lacks character, it's part of a vibrant shopping and entertainment complex and close to Chinatown's Tanjong Pagar. Rooms are warm, with pastel colors, large sofas, one king-size or two queen-size beds, and bedside remote-control panels. The Royal Club concierge floor has butler service. Don't miss the nightly S$22 poolside steamboat and barbecue buffet with more than 40 items. (Travelers with disabilities should consider a stay at this hotel.) ✉ *165 Tanjong Pagar Rd., 088539,* ☎ *224–4488,* ℻ *224–3910. 337 rooms. 2 restaurants, coffee shop, pool, 2 tennis courts, jogging, squash, nightclub, business services. AE, DC, MC, V.*

$$ ▦ **Apollo Singapore.** Another business-traveler haven, this semicircular, 19-story hotel has relatively inexpensive, clean, and bright rooms. There are on-site Chinese, Indonesian, and Japanese restaurants; a coffee shop; and evening entertainment. The hotel is south of the Singapore River and west of Chinatown and the business district. A daytime shuttle bus runs hourly to Orchard Road. ✉ *405 Havelock Rd., 169633,* ☎ *733–2081,* ℻ *733–1588. 345 rooms. 3 restaurants, coffee shop, exercise room, dance club. AE, DC, MC, V.*

$$ ▦ **The Concorde.** Once appropriately called the Glass Hotel, the Concorde has a glass canopy that curves down from the ninth story over

the entrance, which faces southeast for good fortune. Decorated in autumn hues, rooms are modern and have standard amenities. A stay in one on the three executive floors gets you complimentary breakfast and cocktails. For dining and entertainment, head for the fourth floor, where there are French, Japanese, and Chinese restaurants; the Chinese restaurant frequently has floor shows. The hotel lies just south of the Singapore River and west of the business district. ⊠ *317 Outram Rd., 169075,* ☎ *733–0188,* ₣ₐₓ *733–0989. 515 rooms. 3 restaurants, pool, massage, sauna, steam room, exercise room, tennis court, business services, meeting rooms. AE, DC, MC, V.*

$$ 🏨 **Elizabeth Hotel.** Once the truly budget Queen's Hotel, this establishment in a quiet area off Orchard Road was expanded in 1997 and was given a new name and higher rates. Standard rooms are modest; those in the four-story deluxe wing have refrigerators. Travelers with disabilities will be comfortable here. ⊠ *24 Mt. Elizabeth, 228518,* ☎ *738–1188,* ₣ₐₓ *732–3866. 247 rooms. Restaurant, bar, coffee shop, pool, exercise room, business services, meeting rooms. AE, DC, MC, V.*

$$ 🏨 **Excelsior Hotel.** This central-city hotel is across the street from nearly 1,000 shops; close to its older sister, the Peninsula hotel; and a block from Raffles City. Guest rooms are reasonably large and well maintained and have IDD phones. Its popular Annalakshmi restaurant (☞ Dining, *above*) serves vegetarian Indian fare, and there's a 24-hour café. ⊠ *5 Coleman St., 179805,* ☎ *338–7733,* ₣ₐₓ *339–3847. 266 rooms, 5 suites. 3 restaurants, bar, pool, travel services. AE, DC, MC, V.*

$$ 🏨 **Furama Hotel.** This modern curvilinear building, on the doorstep of Chinatown and a 10-minute walk from the commercial district, stands out amid the surrounding shophouses. Tour groups and Japanese businessmen call this place home. The helpful staff will direct you to interesting sights, and there are daily guided walking tours through Chinatown. After hoofing it around, you can rest in the popular poolside café. ⊠ *10 Eu Tong Sen St., 059804,* ☎ *533–3888,* ₣ₐₓ *534–1489. 356 rooms. 2 restaurants, bar, café, pool, beauty salon, sauna, steam room, business services, meeting rooms. AE, DC, MC, V.*

$$ 🏨 **Harbour View Dai Ichi.** If you want to be away from all the hurly-burly but still still near the business district, this 29-story hotel will be perfect for you. Rooms are small, neat, and functional; two are in Japanese tatami style (most of the clientele is from Japan), and the hotel's main restaurant is the Kuramaya. There's also a Continental restaurant. ⊠ *81 Anson Rd., 079908,* ☎ *224–1133,* ₣ₐₓ *222–0749. 416 rooms. 2 restaurants, coffee shop, pool, massage, sauna, exercise room, business services. AE, DC, MC, V.*

$$ 🏨 **Le Meridien Changi.** Aside from its location 10 minutes from the airport, this hotel has no particular merits, except for golfers. Some rooms are designed for the physically challenged. ⊠ *1 Netheravon Rd., 508502,* ☎ *542–7700,* ₣ₐₓ *542–5295. 280 rooms. Restaurant, coffee shop, pool, golf privileges, exercise room, bicycles, baby-sitting, business services. AE, DC, MC, V.*

$$ 🏨 **Peninsula Hotel.** Near the Padang and between the fashionable Orchard Road and commercial district areas, this hotel offers the basic creature comforts. The lobby is small and nondescript. The fairly spacious guest rooms are clean, and those on the 17th floor and up have good views. There's no on-site restaurant, but a coffee shop serves the basics, and there are several reasonably priced restaurants nearby. ⊠ *3 Coleman St., 179804,* ☎ *337–2200,* ₣ₐₓ *339–3847. 299 rooms, 8 suites. Coffee shop, in-room safes, minibars, room service, pool, exercise room, nightclub. AE, DC, MC, V.*

$$ 🏨 **Plaza Hotel.** The rooms in this Little Araby hotel include IDD phones, coffee- and tea makers, and sensor-touch bedside control panels. Service is friendly, though a bit laid-back. The three on-site restaurants offer Cantonese and Thai cuisine, Western and regional fare, and spicy Oriental-style steaks. With a full house, the hotel can be quite lively. There's entertainment in the evenings; if you want to be the evening's entertainment, check out the 18-room Singsation karaoke club. ✉ *7500A Beach Rd., 199591,* ☎ *298–0011,* ℻ *296–3600. 350 rooms. 2 restaurants, 2 bars, refrigerators, pool, steam room, exercise room, business services. AE, DC, MC, V.*

$$ 🏨 **Rasa Sentosa.** A vast, arc-shape building facing the sea, this Sentosa Island resort getaway is popular with both conventions and Singaporean families escaping to the beach for the weekend (room rates are lower during the week). The motel-like rooms are small though all have balconies; ask for a room facing the water, otherwise your view will merely be of a grassy knoll. The main restaurant serves Cantonese fare, and the café dishes up Western and Asian food. Children love this place for its pool with water slides, its playground, its nursery, and its video-games room. Adults appreciate the many recreational activities, including rock-wall climbing, golf, and windsurfing. Travelers with disabilities will find that the hotel caters to their needs as well. You can get to the island on a free shuttle bus from the Shangri-La hotel, which owns this resort. ✉ *101 Siloso Rd., Sentosa Island 098970,* ☎ *275–0100, 0181/747–8485 (reservations in the U.K.), or 800/942–5050 (reservations in Canada and the U.S.);* ℻ *275–0355. 459 rooms. 3 restaurants, bar, lobby lounge, pool, massage, health club, Ping-Pong, windsurfing, boating, recreation room, video games, nursery, playground. AE, DC, MC, V.*

$$ 🏨 **Seaview Hotel.** Off the East Coast Parkway, midway between Changi Airport and Singapore city, this high-rise hotel is more convenient for travelers in transit than for those here to see the sights. Guest rooms offer the basic amenities, and there are restaurants and shops on the premises and in the area. The nearby East Coast Park offers many outdoor activities, including water-sports facilities. ✉ *26 Amber Close, 439984,* ☎ *345–2222,* ℻ *345–1741. 435 rooms. 2 restaurants, bar, coffee shop, room service, pool, nightclub. AE, DC, MC, V.*

$$ 🏨 **Traders Hotel.** For value (try to take advantage of the frequent pro-
★ motional rates) and service, this hotel is hard to beat. It has all the necessary comforts—including those for travelers with disabilities—but no frills. There's only one coffee shop for dining and no fancy room service, but scores of restaurants and a supermarket are just steps away; the Orchard Road area is also nearby. Rooms are comfortable, with writing desks and plenty of light from the bay windows. There are spacious gardens and a pool. ✉ *1A Cuscaden Rd., 249716,* ☎ *738–2222, 0181/747–8485 (reservations in the U.K.), or 800/942–5050 (reservations in Canada or the U.S.);* ℻ *831–4314. 543 rooms. Coffee shop, pool, exercise room, business services, meeting rooms. AE, DC, MC, V.*

$$ 🏨 **York Hotel.** Near busy Orchard Road, this classic European hotel is a quiet oasis. The tower has only suites, and the poolside wing has split-level cabanas and rooms surrounding a garden. All guest quarters have two queen-size beds. The White Rose Cafe serves Asian and Western fare. ✉ *21 Mt. Elizabeth, 228516,* ☎ *737–0511,* ℻ *732–1217. 335 rooms, 69 suites. 2 restaurants, bar, pool, beauty salon, sauna, exercise room. AE, DC, MC, V.*

$ 🏨 **Hotel Royal.** This modest hotel has the standard amenities and in-room IDD phones. On the premises is an international forwarding service that can be useful for anyone—especially shoppers—who wishes to send excess baggage back home. The hotel is near Newton Circus and a 20-minute walk from Orchard Road. ✉ *36 Newton Rd., 307964,* ☎ *253–4411,* ℻ *253–8668. 331 rooms. 3 restaurants, coffee shop, minibars, refrigerators, pool, meeting rooms, travel services. AE, DC, MC, V.*

$ ⊞ **Inn at Temple Street.** One of the latest additions to Chinatown's unique
★ boutique hotel scene, the Inn at Temple Street opened in early 1998
and occupies five beautifully restored shophouses. The attractive Peranakan decor—a fusion of 19th-century European, Chinese, and Malay
furnishings and color schemes—reminds you of the neighborhood's rich
cultural traditions. Ask for a room with a view of the street below, which
is slated to become a pedestrian mall. ⊠ *36 Temple St., 058581,* ☎
221–5333, FAX *225–5391. 42 rooms. Coffee shop, bar, in-room safes,
refrigerators. AE, DC, MC, V.*

$ ⊞ **Ladyhill Hotel.** The Ladyhill emphasizes home comforts and relax-
★ ation. In the main building are the intimate Swiss-style restaurant Le
Chalet, a cozy split-level bar (a Filipino band plays here in the evening)
and standard guest rooms. Superior rooms in the surrounding cottages
are spacious enough for an extra bed—perfect for families. The Ladyhill is in a residential area a good 10-minute walk uphill from Orchard Road (a hotel bus shuttles the weary back and forth). ⊠ *1
Ladyhill Rd., 258670,* ☎ *737–2111,* FAX *737–4606. 171 rooms.
Restaurant, bar, coffee shop, pool, nightclub, meeting rooms. AE, V.*

$ ⊞ **Metropole Hotel.** This very modest, very basic hotel near Raffles City
has simply furnished rooms. Rare in budget lodgings, you'll find both
a helpful staff and room service. ⊠ *41 Seah St., 188396,* ☎ *336–3611,*
FAX *339–3610. 54 rooms. Restaurant, coffee shop, room service. AE,
DC, MC, V.*

$ ⊞ **Metropolitan YMCA, Tanglin Centre.** A 10-minute walk to Orchard
Road, this YMCA (which admits women) has rooms with air-conditioning and private baths. There are even a few suites. The budget restaurant offers wholesome English breakfasts, as well as Chinese, Malay,
Nonya, and Western meals. ⊠ *Tanglin Centre, 60 Stevens Rd., 257854,*
☎ *737–7755,* FAX *235–5528. 93 rooms. Coffee shop, pool, exercise
room, meeting rooms. AE, DC, MC, V.*

$ ⊞ **Regalis Court.** This charming, 43-room, boutique hotel—which
★ opened in mid-1997—once housed the Singapore Ballet Academy of
British colonial days. The rooms have a Peranakan-inspired decor (earth
tones, reds, and browns) with classical European touches and such
novel items as reproductions of clunky black telephones and old alarm
clocks. You can open your windows (be sure to ask for a room that has
them) to the quiet residential neighborhood, and a Continental breakfast is included in the room rate. Only a few minutes' walk to Orchard
Road, the hotel is not well known and attracts savvy independent travelers from around the globe. Check out the Indonesian Rajah Inn (☞
Dining, *above*) restaurant for inexpensive, tasty dishes. ⊠ *64 Lloyd Rd.,
239113,* ☎ *734–7117,* FAX *736–1651. 43 rooms. Restaurant, breakfast room, in-room safes, no-smoking rooms. AE, DC, MC, V.*

$ ⊞ **RELC International Hotel.** This is less a hotel than an international
★ conference center often used by Singapore's university for seminars.
However, the upper floors contain bargain guest rooms that are large
and basically comfortable and have plenty of light. The building is in
a residential neighborhood, up a hill beyond the Shangri-La hotel, a
10-minute walk to the Orchard and Scotts roads intersection. Because
of its good value, it's often booked, so reservations well in advance
are strongly advised. Breakfast is included, and there are coffeemak-
ers in the rooms. ⊠ *30 Orange Grove Rd., 258352,* ☎ *737–9044,* FAX
733–9976. 128 rooms. Coffee shop, coin laundry. AE, DC, MC, V.

$ ⊞ **Royal Peacock.** Living up to its name, this brightly painted shop-
house boutique hotel opened in 1997 on the once notorious Keong Saik
Road (it was known for its red lanterns and ladies of the night, who
are still here but are in state-controlled brothels). The standard rooms
don't have windows, so ask for a deal on a superior or deluxe room
(listed at S$180). Breakfast and coffee and tea fixings are included in

all prices. The hotel is within the central business district in Chinatown, and it has facilities for travelers with disabilities. ✉ *55 Keong Saik Rd., 089518,* ☎ *223–3522,* FAX *221–1770. 76 rooms. Bar, café, minibars, business services. AE, DC, MC, V.*

$ 🏨 **Transit Hotel.** At last: a lodging truly geared to bleary-eyed travelers en route to still another destination. This new hotel is *inside* Changi Airport on Level 3 of the departure lounge in Terminal 1. (Note: if you stay here, you don't go through immigration control.) Rooms are clean, fresh, and basic. Rates are for six-hour periods—a double is S$56—and include use of the swimming pool, sauna, and fitness center. Nonguests may also use the pool (S$10), the sauna and showers (S$10), or just the shower (S$5). ✉ *Terminal 1, Changi Airport,* ☎ *543–0911, 0800/96–3562 (reservations in the U.K.), or 800/690–6785 (reservations in the U.S.);* FAX *545–8365. Pool, sauna, health club, nursery. AE, DC, MC, V.*

$ 🏨 **YMCA International House.** This well-run YMCA at the bottom of Orchard Road offers hotel-like accommodations for men and women—with double (S$105) and single (S$90) rooms—as well as dormitory-style quarters (S$25); S$5 will buy you temporary YMCA membership. All rooms have private baths, color TVs, and IDD phones. In addition to an impressive gym, you'll find a rooftop pool and squash and badminton courts. There's also a McDonald's at the entrance. ✉ *1 Orchard Rd., 238824,* ☎ *336–6000,* FAX *337–3140. 111 rooms. Pool, exercise room, squash. AE, DC, MC, V.*

Bintan Island, Indonesia

Bintan's resorts dot wide sandy beaches on the northern coast. Each hotel has a wide range of restaurants, bars, and other facilities. Since there are really only six establishments (the hotels in Tanjung Pinang, the island's main city, are substandard), book as far in advance as possible. On weekends Singaporeans and expats take full advantage of the island's clean waters, just 45 minutes from one of the world's busiest ports.

The resorts accept Singapore dollars for rooms and for meals (price categories assigned below are based on Singapore dollars), though credit card purchases for other items may be charged in Indonesian rupiahs at, no doubt, a better rate of exchange. The newest resorts, such as Club Med and Sol Elite Bintan, have been offering promotional specials, so always ask about discounts when booking. All resorts have their marketing offices in Singapore, and it's best to make reservations before arriving on Bintan; for more information contact **Bintan Resort Management** (☎ 543–0039). If, for some reason, you need to dial an establishment directly, the country code for Indonesia is 62, and the area code for Bintan is 771.

At press time, plans for shuttle bus service between the resorts were afoot. If, however, you have to rely on a taxi to get around, you must book it in advance from a car rental agency at the ferry terminal. Ask the front desk staff of your hotel to help with the arrangements. Although most people come here to relax or frolic in a beach resort environment, consider taking a guided day trip outside of your resort; it will definitely enhance your Indonesian experience (☞ Tour Operators *in* Singapore A to Z, *below*).

$$$$ 🏨 **Banyan Tree Bintan.** You'll find romance, luxury, and top-notch ser-
★ vice during a stay here. Accommodations are in private, Balinese-style villas that stand on stilts and overlook a horseshoe-shape bay. Fifty-five villas have a whirlpool tub on a deck that faces the South China Sea. The more luxurious Pool Villas also have either a private swimming pool or plunge pool, two bedrooms with king-size beds, a bath-

room with a sunken bath, a spacious dressing room, and a kitchen (though you can make your own meals, most people just ask for a staff chef to drop by and whip up a special meal or two; there's no grocery store nearby). Rooms have green and brown color schemes, Indonesian pottery, elevated beds that are draped with mosquito netting, and sea views—truly idyllic. ⊠ *Site A4, Lagoi, Tanjong Said,* ☎ *462–4800 (in Singapore) or 771/26918 (in Bintan),* FAX *462–2800 (in Singapore) or 771/81348 (in Bintan). 74 villas. 2 restaurants, 2 pools, outdoor hot tub, spa, 18-hole golf course, 2 tennis courts, beach, dive shop, dock, snorkeling, windsurfing, fishing, meeting rooms. AE, MC, V.*

$$$ 🏨 **Club Med Ria Bintan.** This resort opened in late 1997 with all the amenities of a luxury Club Med, including many, many water and land activities—there's even a circus school for children, complete with a trapeze that gives parents heart palpitations. The resort is popular with Europeans, Japanese families, and Club Med junkies from around the world, so its staff members are multilingual. You might feel as if you're on the French Riviera: there are numerous chaises longues around the pools and on the private beach; the TV in your room has French satellite television; and wines served at meals are distinctly French. Among the facilities are an excellent children's activity center and a well-equipped exercise room and spa. The general feeling here is that you never need to leave the resort for anything; everything is terribly well organized (great if you want to be involved, not so great if you're seeking solitude). The comfortable rooms have balconies (the sunset views are terrific) and well-equipped baths. ⊠ *North coast,* ☎ *738–4222 (in Singapore),* FAX *738–0770 (in Singapore). 307 rooms. 4 restaurants, bar, 2 pools, spa, 2 tennis courts, aerobics, health club, beach, water slide, cabaret, dance club, baby-sitting, children's programs, nursery, playground, coin laundry, meeting rooms. AE, MC, V. FAP.*

$$–$$$ 🏨 **Hotel Sedona.** Japanese visitors and locals alike are drawn to this enormous villa complex. Amenities include two pools—one of them *very* large—water sports facilities, a spa, a mah-jongg hall, tennis, golf, karaoke, and a children's center. Although right next to the beach, this hotel isn't as aesthetically appealing or relaxed as some of the other resorts. Still, it *is* a golfer's paradise with two 18-hole courses—one designed by Jack Nicklaus, the other by Ian Baker-Finch—that have driving ranges and putting greens. The stunning view of the Nicklaus course from the golf club's alfresco café is itself inspiring. The rest of the grounds are equally well landscaped; you can rent a bicycle for an hour or two and take a tour of them. Rooms and suites are clean and well kept, if a bit stark in their furnishings; the Sedona Club Suites have huge balconies and sunken tubs. You won't lack for a place to eat: there are seven on-site restaurants that offer a variety of cuisines. ⊠ *Pasir Panjang Beach, north coast,* ☎ *223–3223 (in Singapore); 771/91388 (in Bintan),* FAX *421–7878 (in Singapore); 771/91399 (in Bintan). 401 rooms, 15 suites. 7 restaurants, 2 pools, massage, spa, 2 driving ranges, 2 18-hole golf courses, 2 putting greens, 4 tennis courts, health club, Ping-Pong, volleyball, beach, snorkeling, water slide, windsurfing, jet skiing, fishing, bicycles, billiards, dance club, video games, baby-sitting, children's programs, playground, laundry service, business services, meeting rooms, travel services. AE, DC, MC, V.*

$$ 🏨 **Sol Elite Bintan.** Another new addition to Bintan's north coast is the sprawling Sol Elite, one of the Spanish-run Sol Melia properties. Rooms are bright, clean, and relatively spacious; those facing the sea have balconies. For about S$100 more a night, you can stay in one of the two- to four-bedroom villas. The public areas are well maintained and cheery; the buildings are painted in dazzling primary colors. To get away from it all, head for the beach; most guests opt for the pool area so it's often deserted. Organized activities include staff-led lawn games and instruction on how to properly open a coconut. Buffet breakfast in El Patio coffee shop is included in the rates, and the lively Cantores Karaoke Lounge is one of Bintan's few nightspots. ⊠ *Nirwana Gardens,* ☎ *334–3332 (in Singapore); 771/311–798 (in Bintan),* FAX *334–2065 (in Singapore). 245 rooms, 14 villas. 2 restaurants, 2 bars, pool, croquet, volleyball, beach, snorkeling, nightclub, video games, playground, business services, meeting rooms, travel services. AE, DC, MC, V. BP.*

$–$$ 🏨 **Mayang Sari.** Set on a bay with an exquisite palm-lined beach, the relaxed, friendly Mayang Sari is a quiet retreat—the perfect place to read a novel or go beachcombing. The chalet-style cabins have high ceilings, Indonesian teak furnishings, large beds, and private verandas. This, Bintan's first resort property, is reminiscent of what Bali might have been like in the 1960s: tall palm trees lining the beach, friendly service, decent prices, gentle breezes. The on-site Mayang Terrace restaurant serves delicious Indonesian dishes at affordable prices. The gift shop seems to have sporadic opening hours, but again, the price of the goods makes it worth checking out. ⊠ *Northwest coast at Tanjong Tondang,* ☎ *732–8515 (in Singapore); 771/92580 (in Bintan),* FAX *732–3959 (in Singapore); 771/92576 (in Bintan). 56 beach and garden cabins. Restaurant, 2 bars, beach, recreation room, baby-sitting, laundry service, meeting room. AE, MC, V.*

$ 🏨 **Mana Mana.** College students and other young Europeans and Australians flock to this resort because of its affordable rates; water-sports enthusiasts of all ages are drawn by the facilities at its beach club. Accommodations are in small, no-smoking huts with TVs and baths (shower only). Most of the cabins are in a garden setting; only the lobby and alfresco restaurant-bar front the beach. The on-site gift shop stocks souvenirs, clothing, knapsacks, and jewelry, but the prices are on the high side. ⊠ *North coast,* ☎ *346–1984 (in Singapore),* FAX *440–3132 (in Singapore). 50 rooms in 25 huts. Restaurant, bar, beach, snorkeling, windsurfing, boating. AE, MC, V.*

NIGHTLIFE AND THE ARTS

Eating out once consumed so much of Singaporeans' time and money that there were few other forms of entertainment. Now, entering a new century and relatively unfazed by the Southeast Asian economic crisis of the late '90s, the city just keeps adding activities to keep its mostly under-30 population entertained. The Singapore Tourism Board (☞ Singapore A to Z, *below*) has monthly listings of events. You can also find schedules for major performances in the local English-language newspaper, the *Straits Times,* or in the free weeklies *I.S.* and *This Week Singapore,* available at most hotel reception desks.

Tickets to events are available at box offices or through **SISTIC,** a ticketing service that operates Monday–Saturday 10–10 and Sunday and holidays noon–10. There are offices at Scotts Shopping Centre, Raffles City, Specialists Centre, Suntec City Mall, Parco Bugis Junction, and Takashimaya (☞ *also* Shopping, *below*). You can also call the company's hot line (☎ 348–5555) and reserve tickets for a S$3 service charge.

Nightlife

Several areas of town come alive at night. Bugis Street, once a bawdy area, has been sanitized with boutique shopping, cafés, bars, and the only air-conditioned outdoor mall in Asia. More authentic is Chinatown's Tanjong Pagar, where shophouses have been turned into hotels, stores, restaurants, teahouses, and bars. On the Singapore River, you'll find similar offerings in former godowns and shophouses at Clarke

Quay and Robertson Quay. Wet your whistle with a beer or a glass of wine on a tongkang before taking a walk along Boat Quay, which was developed with less stringent government supervision. Here you can enjoy the natural flavor of Singapore with an interesting mix of reasonably priced restaurants and bars. Though not very lively, Chinatown's Duxton Hill does have two or three jazz bars.

Trendy, glitzy music and dance clubs that have everything from jazz to disco are popular with the young and the restless. The distinction between a disco and a place with live music and a dance floor has become blurred; one thing both places share is a decibel level that allows for only snatches of conversation. You'll also usually find a cover charge or a "first-drink" charge (cover plus one free drink) of about S$15 weeknights and S$25 weekends. Certain places allow women in for free or at a reduced rate.

Older Singaporeans often prefer nightclubs with floor shows and hostesses, also called "public relations officers" or PROs. Depending on the establishment, "booking the hostess" requires either a flat hourly fee or a gratuity at the end of the evening. (Be forewarned that some hostesses may be prostitutes with their *mamasans,* or madams, urging them to go after your wallet.) It's also common practice to buy a bottle of brandy (for as much as S$300), which some consider a high-status drink (whereas whiskey is "bad smelling and shows poor taste"). You are under no obligation to select a hostess or buy a bottle of brandy, however.

The truly risqué disappeared long ago from Singapore. Prostitution is legal only in certain areas, such as parts of Geylang, which has red-light districts. Brothels are numbered with large, backlit signs, and some hotels rent rooms in two-hour time slots. With typical Singaporean efficiency, prostitutes are registered and are subject to regular medical checks.

Bars and Pubs

Brewerkz. Beer lovers need look no farther than this large pub on Riverside Point, across from the restaurants and shops of Clarke Quay. Brewmaster Scott Robinson offers seven ales and bitters (the most popular is the India Pale Ale) and chef James Chew serves an eclectic selection of Eastern and Western favorites (the kitchen is open from noon to midnight). The best buy is the set lunch menu (about S$15); unbelievably for Singapore, the price includes two glasses of beer and coffee or tea. Check out the Cigar Divan Room, and the large interior room, which rebroadcasts NFL and NBA games. ⊠ *No. 01-05/06 Riverside Point, 30 Merchant Rd.,* ☎ *438–7438.* ⊙ *Sun.–Thurs. noon–1* AM; *Fri.– Sat. noon–3* AM.

Father Flanagan's. This Irish pub in the Chijmes complex gets its fair share of homesick Dubliners, but the good pub grub and variety of brews make it popular with the local business crowd, too. ⊠ *Chijmes complex (lower level), 30 Victoria St.,* ☎ *333–1418.* ⊙ *Sun.–Tues. noon to midnight; Wed.–Thurs. noon–1* AM; *Fri.–Sat. noon–2* AM.

Hard Rock Cafe. Hamburgers and light fare are served at this pub-café, and a live band plays in the evenings. It's much like other establishments in the chain, with a casual, festive, atmosphere; plenty of rock memorabilia; a bar; booth tables; pool tables; and souvenir shops so you can get your Hard Rock Singapore T-shirt. ⊠ *No. 02–01 HPL House, 50 Cuscaden Rd.,* ☎ *235–5232.* ▣ *On evenings with live bands: 1st drink S$12.* ⊙ *Weekdays 11* AM*–2* AM, *weekends 11* AM*–3* AM.

Ice Cold Beer. Expats tend to gather at this lively pub on a small pedestrian street off Orchard Road. Beers from around the world dominate, ranging from S$5 specials to S$14 a pop, and good hot dogs are available for S$5. There's never a cover charge; the music tends to be rock from the '70s and '80s. Happy hour is from 5 to 9 Monday through Saturday; it turns into "happy day" on Sunday. ⊠ *5 Emerald Hill Rd.,* ☎ *735–9929.* ⊙ *Daily 5 PM–2 AM.*

Moods. This pub attracts a local university crowd, even though it's in the heart of the Orchard and Scotts roads' shopping area, behind the Royal Crowne Plaza Hotel. It's a good place to stop when you're tired of seeing all those other tourists and expats. ⊠ *No. 01-02 Scotts Walk, 25 Scotts Rd.,* ☎ *734–8098.* ⊙ *Nightly 5 PM–1 AM.*

Muddy Murphy's. A longtime favorite, due to its wine and cheese promotions, weekly Sunday brunches, and excellent Irish bands, "Muddy's" is in the heart of the shopping belt. Here's a place to wind down when your feet won't take you any farther. ⊠ *No. B1-01/06 Orchard Hotel Shopping Arcade, 442 Orchard Rd.,* ☎ *735–0400.* ⊙ *Mon.–Sat. 8 PM–1 AM; Sun. 3 PM–1 AM.*

Pop Cat. A pub with a difference: this is 1950s kitsch, Chinatown style. Wacky theme bashes, such as "Squirt" (a water pistol shootout), are regular events. The music is eclectic—anything from Japanese pop to jazz to cutting edge. Creative and entertainment types tend to hang out here. ⊠ *42/42A Pagoda St.,* ☎ *226–6229.* ⊙ *Weekdays 11 AM–midnight; Sat. 11 AM–1 AM.*

Que Pasa. For wine lovers, this friendly pub is a sure bet. Small and intimate, it has a mix of local and expat twenty- to thirtysomething customers. ⊠ *7 Emerald Hill Rd.,* ☎ *235–6626.* ⊙ *Nightly 5 PM–2 AM.*

Riverbank Restaurant & Pub. This riverside terrace is a great place to start your evening. Wander in here, watch others as they wander around Boat Quay, and then wander on out for some casual barhopping. ⊠ *Boat Quay,* ☎ *538–1135.* ⊙ *Nightly 6 PM–2 AM.*

Wild West Tavern. One of Clarke Quay's plethora of restaurants and bars, this is less pricey than most and quite appealing for a beer and a chat. As the name may imply, expect an authentic Hollywood-style saloon—but without the cowboys. ⊠ *12 Clarke Quay,* ☎ *334–4180.* ⊙ *Nightly 4 PM–midnight.*

Comedy Club

Boom Boom Room. Two years ago, you wouldn't find the delightful unsavoriness of old Bugis Street here, but this comedy house has gotten a bit more daring in its twice-nightly shows. A basic knowledge of the local "Singlish" would certainly help in understanding many of the jokes. Be prepared for cross-dressing and jibes aimed at individuals in the audience. A DJ spins disks between shows. ⊠ *Bugis Village,* ☎ *339–8187.* ▤ *S$15 and up.* ⊙ *Tues.–Sun. 8 PM–2 AM.*

Discos and Dance Clubs

Caesars. The decor and the waitresses clad in lissome togas give this disco an air of decadent splendor. DJ-spun music plus imported live bands make it a hot venue for entertainment. ⊠ *No. 02–04 Orchard Towers (front block), 400 Orchard Rd.,* ☎ *235–2840.* ▤ *1st drink Sun.–Thurs. S$15, Fri.–Sat. S$24.* ⊙ *Sun.–Thurs. 8 PM–2 AM, Fri.–Sat. 8 PM–3 AM.*

Europa Music Bar. It's easy to have fun at this busy club where young Singaporeans let down their hair. There are stage shows as well as contests and prizes for the serious drinking crowd. ⊠ *No. B1–00 International Building, 360 Orchard Rd.,* ☎ *235–3301.* ▤ *Cover charges vary.* ⊙ *Weeknights 6 PM–1 AM, weekends 6 PM–2 AM.*

Fire. One of Singapore's steady favorites, Fire has live music danced to by a lively (very young and local) crowd. Drinks are paid for by coupons, so work out the cost before making the purchase. Upstairs, would-be artists sing their lungs out in 12 computerized karaoke rooms. ⊠ *No. 04-19 Orchard Plaza, 150 Orchard Rd.,* ☎ *235–0155.* ⊙ *Nightly 9 PM–2 AM.*

Heaven. Opened in 1998, Heaven should be around for a while, owing to the good reputation of its sister club in Kuala Lumpur. Although not as mammoth as Zouk or Venom (☞ *below*), Heaven's clever interiors, VIP Lounge, and varied mix of tourists and locals almost ensure its success. Women (who must be 21 to enter) don't pay a cover charge, and they receive two free drinks after 10:30 PM on Tuesday and Thursday; men have to pay a first-drink charge and must be at least 23 to get in. The music ranges from soul to "garage" to "happy house." ⊠ *No. 01-01A Orchard Parade Hotel, 1 Tanglin Rd.,* ☎ *732–7808.* 🎟 *1st drink S$18; S$25 on weekends.* ⊙ *Nightly 8 PM–3 AM.*

The Jump. By day, it's a Tex-Mex American style restaurant; at night, it turns into a busy disco featuring retro tunes for the over-25 set. (Your ID may be checked to make sure you fall into this age bracket.) The long lines and ubiquitous cover charges don't deter the yuppies who frequent this spot. ⊠ *Chijmes complex (interior courtyard), 30 Victoria St.,* ☎ *338–9388.* 🎟 *Fri.–Sat. S$20 men, S$15 women.* ⊙ *Sun.–Wed. noon–1 AM; Thurs.–Sat. noon–3 AM.*

Neo Pharoahs. Housed in a quaint, three-story shophouse, this dance club is more personal than the larger, warehouse-style discos. The third-floor main dance hall has British house music; the ground and second floors have a combination of acid jazz, R&B, and '70s and '80s funk. The place attracts a mix of expats and locals, mostly in their mid-20s to mid-40s. ⊠ *56 Cairnhill Rd.,* ☎ *736–3098.* 🎟 *Cover charges vary.* ⊙ *Weeknights 8 PM–1 AM, weekends 8 PM–2 AM.*

Pleasure Dome. Upscale and expensive with decent live bands, private rooms, and a Members' Lounge, this club is always busy with the young and well-to-do. The adjoining wine and cigar bar, **Le Château,** is great place to chill when the crowd gets too noisy. The cover charge varies, but expect to pay at least S$20, and don't bother going if you're under 25. ⊠ *No. B1-02 Specialists Shopping Centre, 277 Orchard Rd.,* ☎ *834–1221.* ⊙ *Weeknights 6 PM–1 AM, weekends 6 PM–2 AM.*

Sparks. An offshoot of the popular Fire disco, this club has karaoke rooms, live music, and laser shows. It's on the seventh floor of the upscale Takashimaya where, so it would seem, the revelers have just made purchases. Foreign dance bands often stop here for one-night shows. ⊠ *Ngee Ann City, Tower B, Level 7,* ☎ *735–6133.* 🎟 *Cover charges vary, but start at S$12 weeknights and S$20 weekends.* ⊙ *Mon.–Sat. 8 PM–2 AM.*

Venom. This lavish, 10,000-square-ft penthouse disco used to be Studebaker's, and it re-opened in 1998 to rave reviews after an S$1.4-million renovation. All the praise must have gone to the staff's collective head, as attitude reigns supreme here. Security guards, cell phones in hand, try to give the impression celebrities are always in the house. Don't bother coming unless you're decked out in the latest Italian designer fashions. ⊠ *Pacific Plaza Penthouse, 12th floor, 9 Scotts Rd.,* ☎ *734–7677.* 🎟 *S$20 weeknights, S$25 Fri.–Sat. and eve of public holidays.* ⊙ *Tues.–Sun. 6 PM–2 AM.*

Zouk, Velvet Underground, and Phuture. You'll need a taxi to get here and back, but every cabbie knows where it is. A huge dance emporium that's remained open for more than two years, Zouk is an institution of sorts. Sprawling and mammoth, it's really three clubs in one: a younger set flocks to Zouk itself; a more sophisticated crowd fills Velvet, the place for true disco divas; and experimental music lovers head for Phuture. Visiting DJs from around the world serve as hosts, and the club consistently gets rave reviews from pop culture critics in the

United Kingdom. When the lights come up at 3 AM, the crowd swiftly disappears into the dozens of waiting taxis outside. ⊠ *17 Jiak Kim St.*, ☎ *738–2988.* ⊡ *Men S$28–S$35, women S$20–S$25; cover includes 2 drinks.* ☽ *Wed.–Sun. 6 PM–3 AM.*

Music Clubs

JAZZ

Bar & Billiard Room. Light acoustic jazz is offered from Monday through Saturday in Singapore's best known hotel. There's no cover charge. ⊠ *Raffles Hotel, 1 Beach Rd.,* ☎ *331–1746.* ☽ *Daily 11:30 AM–12:30 AM; live music begins at 8:30 PM.*

The Bar at the Regent. Jazz duos and trios often perform at this Four Seasons Hotel sister property. Your only cost will be your bar tab. ⊠ *The Regent Singapore, 1 Cuscaden Rd.,* ☎ *733–8888.* ☽ *Daily 4 PM–1 AM.*

Harry's Quayside. This is a comfortable place to hang out and listen to a mix of jazz, blues, and old-time rock. Occasionally the live band, which starts performing at around 9:30 PM, gets carried away and turns the show into a good old-fashioned jam session. Food is served upstairs, and there are fine waterfront views. ⊠ *28 Boat Quay,* ☎ *538–3029.* ☽ *Sun.–Thurs. 11 AM–midnight; Fri.–Sat. 11 AM–2 AM.*

Saxophone. At this club, which has both jazz and popular rock, the volume is loud and the space is compact (read: standing room only). However, there's a terrace outside where you can sit and still hear the music. Saxophone was a pioneer of the Singapore jazz scene, and the customers keep coming, so the sound must be right. ⊠ *23 Cuppage Terr.,* ☎ *235–8385.* ☽ *Tues.–Sun. 6–1.*

Somerset Bar. The jazz and contemporary music played here has attracted a loyal following. With a larger space than the Saxophone, it offers room to sit and relax, making it popular with an older crowd. There's a happy hour from 5 PM to 7 PM nightly. ⊠ *Westin Plaza (3rd floor), 4 Stamford Rd.,* ☎ *338–8585.* ☽ *Nightly 5 PM–2 AM; music starts around 9 PM.*

ROCK

Anywhere. Crowds gather, especially on weekends, in this smoke-filled room to hear decent live music. If you're in your forties and divorced, you'll feel at home. ⊠ *No. 04–08 Tanglin Shopping Centre, 19 Tanglin Rd.,* ☎ *734–8233.* ⊡ *1st drink: Sun.–Thurs. S$12, Fri.–Sat. S$18.* ☽ *Sun.–Thurs. 8 PM–2 AM, Fri.–Sat. 8 PM–3 AM.*

Crazy Elephant. Billed as Singapore's "only rock-and-roll blues bar," jam sessions are held every here Sunday, and a live band appears every night except Monday. Cover charges vary. ⊠ *No. 01–07 Clarke Quay,* ☎ *337–1990.* ☽ *Weeknights 5 PM–1 AM, weekends 5 PM–2 AM.*

Roomful of Blues. Blues lovers and local musicians flock to this club—really a combination café and high-tech studio—in a neighborhood northeast of the city. The music is eclectic ('70s funk, rock, R&B, punk, heavy metal), and local bands play on Saturday nights. Dress is very casual. ⊠ *Macpherson Rd.,* ☎ *289–6718.* ☽ *Daily 10 AM–midnight.*

WORLD MUSIC

Fabrice's World Music Bar. Hopping, busy, crowded—this bar is true to its name, with live Latin, African, European, and American music. It opens in the evening with "early sessions"; the wilder music and raucous crowds fill the room later in the night. Cover charges vary. ⊠ *Marriott Hotel (basement level), 320 Orchard Rd.,* ☎ *738–8887.* ☽ *Nightly 8 PM–2 AM.*

Nightclubs

Apollo Theatre Restaurant and Nightclub. This club is very popular with Chinese businessmen, who come here to be entertained by a steady stream of Chinese singers and hostesses and to enjoy the Hunanese cuisine. ⊠ *Apollo Singapore Hotel, 405 Havelock Rd., 17th floor,* ☎ *235–7977.* ⊠ *Brandy S$270; hourly hostess fee S$25.* ⊙ *Nightly 8 PM–2 AM.*

Lido Palace Niteclub. Promoting itself as the "palace of many pleasures," this lavish establishment offers Chinese cabaret, a band, a DJ-spun disco, hostesses, karaoke, and—for those who wish to dine—Cantonese cuisine. ⊠ *Concorde Hotel, 317 Outram Rd., 5th floor,* ☎ *732–8855.* ⊠ *1st drink S$30.* ⊙ *Nightly 9 PM–3 AM; shows at 9:30 and 12:30.*

Neptune. At this sumptuous two-story club, designed as an Oriental pavilion, you can dine on Cantonese food or take a seat in the gallery for nondiners. Local, Taiwanese, and Filipino singers entertain in English and Chinese; occasionally a European dance troupe is added to the lineup. For the most fun, go with a group. The club is operated by the Mandarin Hotel, so call ahead to be sure it's not already booked for private functions. (It's also the only nightclub in Singapore that has a license allowing it to feature the occasional topless cabaret show.) ⊠ *Overseas Union House, 7th floor, Collyer Quay,* ☎ *224–3922 or 737–4411.* ⊠ *Drink minimum S$8; with dinner, drink minimum S$15.* ⊙ *Nightly 8 PM–2 AM.*

The Arts

Each year sees more arts events—particularly orchestral and dramatic performances—added to Singapore's cultural calendar. The many sporadic Chinese, Indian, and Malay happenings and festivals add further color. Springtime is especially busy with such well-attended events as an international film festival; a comedy festival; WOMAD (World of Music, Arts, and Dance); the Festival of Arts; and performances by Theatreworks, the Singapore Dance Theatre, and the Singapore Symphony Orchestra.

Some of the best performances take place at the **Victoria Theatre and Memorial Hall** (⊠ 11 Empress Pl., ☎ 339–6120 for information or 338–8283 for bookings), two adjoining buildings at the Padang. These Victorian structures are home to the 85-member Singapore Symphony Orchestra, which is renowned for its large repertoire of well-known classics and works by Asian composers. Other performances here include those by music and dance groups from all over Southeast Asia and by Singapore's various theatrical and operatic societies. You'll also find Chinese opera and Indian classical dance presentations.

Singapore hopes that **The Esplanade—Theatres on the Bay** (⊠ The Esplanade Co. Ltd., 60 Raffles Ave., ☎ 337–3711), which was under construction at press time and was due to open in 2001, will become as famous a landmark as Sydney's Opera House. In 1998, impressive construction works for this complex were well underway alongside Marina Bay and next to both the central business district and the colonial district. The Esplanade is slated to contain the 2,000 seat **Lyric Theatre** and the 1,800 seat **Concert Hall,** which will have a 39-ft-high pipe organ with 4,489 pipes and the necessary acoustics to match. Also planned are three smaller studios and numerous outdoor performance spaces. In keeping with Singapore's two obsessions—shopping and eating—expect to see a retail complex and food and beverage outlets.

Indian music, drama, and dance performances are staged during major festivals at the more important temples, including the **Sri Mariamman Temple** (⊠ 244 South Bridge Rd., ☎ 223–4064) and the **Chettiar Temple** (⊠ 14 Tank Rd., ☎ 737–9393). Themes are from the ancient epics—tales of gods, demons, and heroes. For more information, contact the **Hindu Endowment Board** (☎ 373–4590).

At **The Substation** (✉ 45 Armenian St., ☎ 337–7535 for information; 337–7800 for tickets) you'll find all of the arts combined. Actors, artists, and musicians do what they do best at this theater-gallery-restaurant and often gather for alfresco cover drinks (daily from noon to 8:30 PM).

Dance

Periodic performances by companies such as the **Singapore Dance Theatre** (✉ Fort Canning Centre, 2nd floor, Cox Terr., ☎ 338–0611) are given in Fort Canning Park. Take along a picnic to enjoy before the show, which will start at about 7 PM or so.

The **Kala Mandhir Temple of Fine Arts** (☎ 339–0492) and the **Nrityalaya Aesthetics Society** (☎ 336–6537) are Indian dance schools that perform regularly throughout the year at different venues. **Sriwana** (✉ No. 02-494 Block 125, 11 Tampines St., ☎ 783–2434) is recognized for its innovative presentations of traditional Malay dances.

Music

ORCHESTRAS

The **Singapore Symphony Orchestra** gives concerts on Friday and Saturday evenings twice a month at the Victoria Concert Hall. Tickets cost S$8–S$80 and are available at the box office (Monday–Saturday 10–6 and up to 8:30 on the night of a concert) or through SISTIC (☞ *above*). You should also check local listings for performances by the following noteworthy groups: **Singapore Chinese Orchestra** (✉ People's Association, Room 5, Block B, 9 Stadium Link, ☎ 344–8777); the **Singapore Youth Orchestra** (✉ ECA Branch, No. 02-03, Block 2, 51 Grange Rd., ☎ 831–9606); and the **Singapore Lyric Theatre** (✉ No. 03-06 Stamford Arts Centre, 155 Waterloo St., ☎ 336–1929), which specializes in opera.

CHINESE OPERA

The dramatic *wayangs* (Chinese operas) reenact Chinese legend through powerful movement, lavish costumes, outrageous masks, and heavy makeup. Performances are held on temporary stages set up near temples, in market areas, or outside apartment complexes. They're staged all year, but most frequently in August and September, during the Festival of the Hungry Ghosts. Street performances—such as those at Clarke Quay held on Wednesday and Friday at 7:45 PM—are free. You'll need to buy tickets to shows by the **Chinese Theatrical Circle** (☎ 235–2911) and other groups that perform at different venues, including the Victoria Theatre and Memorial Hall, throughout the city.

The wayangs are full of action. Gongs and drums beat, devils leap, maidens weep, and heroes reap the praise of an enraptured audience. The characters are fancifully weird—take a look behind the stage and watch the actors apply their makeup—and gorgeously costumed. With Chinese TV programming mostly in Mandarin, street wayangs—spoken in dialect, though totally different from the conversational dialect—have become popular with the older generation, who rarely have a chance to be entertained in their own language. Do try to seek out a wayang. It's an experience you won't soon forget. And don't be bashful about asking a fellow spectator who the characters portrayed are.

Theater

The Necessary Stage (☎ 738–6355) performs highly experimental works and is an established and respected company. In 1998, the bilingual (Mandarin and English) **Practice Theatre Ensemble** (☎ 337–2529) was very involved with an Asian version of *King Lear* that was staged in Japan.

The **Singapore Repertory Theatre** (SRT; ⊠ Telok Ayer Performing Arts Centre, 182 Cecil St., ☎ 221–5585), is the country's most popular troupe, staging local and international plays and musicals. (*The Golden Child*, by local playwright David Hwang, for example, went from here to Broadway.)

OUTDOOR ACTIVITIES AND SPORTS

Despite the heat, Singapore is one of the best cities in Asia for outdoor activities, for it's one of few that are not polluted. The government has taken care to set aside a significant portion of the island for recreation, so you can go waterskiing or scuba diving, take a jungle hike, or play beach volleyball. Virtually all Singapore hotels have swimming pools, and there are 19 public swimming complexes, some of which are superb. Be sure to drink lots of water, and try to schedule the most strenuous activities for early morning or late afternoon.

Beaches and Parks

Bintan Island, Indonesia. Whether you're in Singapore for business or pleasure, you may be able to slip in a quick side trip to Indonesia—it's that close. Bintan Island, which is just only 45 minutes by ferry away from Singapore's east coast, has recently become a resort haven. You can frolic on its beaches, golf its courses, and experience Indonesian cuisine and culture.

East Coast Park. This park stretches for 8 km (5 mi) on reclaimed land between the road to the airport and the seashore. Here you'll find well-planned recreational facilities, including an excellent beach and a watersports lagoon where you can rent sailboards, canoes, and sailboats. If you prefer swimming in a pool, the **Aquatic Centre** has four—including a wave pool—as well as a giant water slide called the Big Splash. "Holiday chalets" set among the palm trees beside the beach can be rented by the day. Restaurants and changing facilities are available.

Nearby Islands. The islands of **Kusu** and **St. John's** (☞ *also* Exploring, *above*) have reasonable small beaches and swimming facilities. On weekends, they're crowded with locals.

Sentosa Island. Billed as Singapore's leisure resort, Sentosa offers a range of recreational facilities in addition to its museums, waxworks, fountains, and other attractions (☞ *also* Exploring, *above*). There's a reasonable beach and a swimming lagoon, with changing and refreshment facilities, as well as rowboats, sailboards, and canoes for rent. You can camp here, play golf or tennis, bike, roller skate (the rink is said to be the largest in Southeast Asia and skate rentals are only S$2 per hour), or join the beach volleyball games. The island gets very crowded on weekends.

Participant Sports

Archery

The **Archery Association of Singapore** (⊠ 5 Binchang Walk, ☎ 258–1140), founded in 1967, has 18 affiliated clubs, most of which welcome enthusiasts. The range at 131 Portsdown Road is open daily and offers day and night (floodlit) shooting. The fee is S$25 for visitors.

Bicycling

Look for signs that point to one of the many **bicycle kiosks** dotting designated bike paths. You can rent bikes for about S$3–S$8 an hour, with a deposit of S$20–S$50. There are many such kiosks in East Coast Park, Sentosa Island, Pasir Ris, Bishan, and Pulau Ubin (an island on Singapore's northeast coast). Cycling through the beaches and parks along the highway to the airport is a very pleasant way to sightsee.

Bowling

There are a number of bowling centers in Singapore; the cost per string is about S$2.80 on weekdays before 6 PM, S$3.90 on weekends and after 7 PM weekdays. For general information contact the **Singapore Tenpin Bowling Congress** (☎ 440–7388). **Leisure Bowl** (✉ Leisure-Dome, 5 Stadium Walk, Kallang Park, ☎ 345–0545) has 30 lanes. Other alleys include **Jackie's Bowl** (✉ 452B East Coast Rd.) and **Plaza Bowl** (✉ Textile Centre, 8th floor, Jalan Sultan, ☎ 292–4821).

Fitness Facilities

HOTELS

If you absolutely *have* to work out in a gym, consider a stay at one of these hotels with fabulous fitness facilities. Because most hotel clubs offer annual memberships to Singaporeans, you'll find the facilities busy early in the morning, at midday, and early in the evening.

Four Seasons (✉ 190 Orchard Blvd., ☎ 734–1110). Tennis lessons are offered by Peter Burwash International pros on indoor, air-conditioned courts. You'll also find two pools (one for adults only), a fully equipped fitness center, massage, a golf simulator, saunas, and steam rooms. Continental breakfast is served free to members; hotel guests must pay S$18 plus tax.
Marina Mandarin (✉ 6 Raffles Blvd., ☎ 338–3388). If you're a guest here, you can play a couple games of squash or tennis and then take a dip in the outdoor pool. Or you can head for the gym—which has Nautilus-type equipment, a Universal gym, free weights, and treadmills—before relaxing in the steam room or sauna. If you need still more relaxation, massage therapy is an option, too.
Oriental (✉ 5 Raffles Blvd., ☎ 338–0066). Here you'll find a jogging track, tennis and squash courts, and a splendid outdoor pool with an underwater sound system and a view of the harbor. The fifth-floor health club includes a hot tub, massage, steam and sauna rooms for men and for women, free weights, a Universal gym, stationary bikes, and treadmills. Runners should try the waterfront path across the street from the hotel; maps are provided in your room.
Ritz-Carlton (✉ 7 Raffles Ave., ☎ 337–8888). The health and fitness club here is so exclusive that it has the highest-priced membership for locals in Singapore: S$25,000 plus annual fees. If you're a hotel guest, take advantage of being able to use the state-of-the-art gymnasium, the pool and outdoor Jacuzzi, the sauna, and the steam facilities for free.
Shangri-La (✉ 22 Orange Grove Rd., ☎ 737–3644). Here the amenities include a good-size outdoor pool and a smaller indoor one; a modern health club with a Universal gym, stationary bikes, treadmills, and other equipment; tennis and squash courts; and a three-hole golf course, where you can jog in the early morning. The site also has spacious, separate, "wet" areas—which include saunas, steam rooms, and Jacuzzis—for men and women.

YMCAS/YWCAS

The following YMCA/YWCA complexes have fitness facilities and offer temporary memberships: **Metropolitan YMCA** (✉ 60 Stevens Rd., ☎ 737–755) **Metropolitan YMCA International Centre** (✉ 70 Palmer Rd., ☎ 222–4666), **YWCA Fort Canning** (✉ 6 Fort Canning Rd., ☎ 338–4222), and the **YMCA International House** (✉ 1 Orchard Rd., ☎ 336–6000).

Flying

The **Republic of Singapore Flying Club** (✉ East Camp Building, 140B Seletar Airbase, ☎ 481–0502 or 481–0200) offers visiting membership to qualified pilots and has aircraft available for hire (approximately S$270 per hour plus S$65 per hour for a temporary one-month membership).

You can't fly solo unless you have a Singapore license. A piloted ride for up to three people can be arranged for about S$270 an hour.

Golf

Some of the top hotels will make arrangements for their guests to golf at local courses. This can include making all the necessary bookings, including equipment reservations, at the club of your choice and arranging for a limousine to take you there. You might check before leaving home to see whether your club has any reciprocal arrangements with a Singapore club. Several excellent Singapore courses accept nonmembers, though some limit this to weekdays. Most clubs are open daily 7–7; some offer night golfing until 11. Driving ranges offer you the chance to practice your drives for as little as S$2 for 50 balls.

Changi Golf Club. This hilly nine-hole course on 50 acres is open to nonmembers on weekdays. ⊠ *345 Netheravon Rd.,* ☎ *545–5133.* ☜ *Greens fee: S$49. Caddy fee: S$15.*

Jurong Country Club. Here you'll find an 18-hole, par-71 course on 120 acres, as well as a driving range. Half the holes are on flat terrain; the other nine are on small hills. ⊠ *9 Science Centre Rd.,* ☎ *560–5655.* ☜ *Greens fee: S$123.60 weekdays, S$185.40 weekends and holidays. Caddy fee: S$25.75.*

Keppel Club. This 18-hole course close to the city also has a driving range. ⊠ *Bukit Chermin,* ☎ *273–5522.* ☜ *Greens fee: S$123.60 Tues.–Fri., S$185.40 weekends and holidays. Caddy fee: S$40. Closed Mon.*

Seletar Country Club. Laid out in 1932 by the Royal Air Force, this is considered the best nine-hole course on the island. ⊠ *Seletar Airbase,* ☎ *481–4745.* ☜ *Greens fee: S$45 Tues.–Fri., S$60 weekends and holidays. No caddies; trolley fee: S$4. Closed Mon.*

Sembawang Country Club. Because of its hilly terrain, this 18-hole, par-70 course is known as the "commando course." There are also squash courts available. ⊠ *Km 17, Sembawang Rd.,* ☎ *257–0642.* ☜ *Greens fee (includes cart): S$113.30 weekdays, S$139.05 weekends and holidays. No caddies.*

Sentosa Golf Club. Here you can play on the 18-hole **Tanjong course** on the southeastern tip of the island or the 18-hole **Serapong course.** At both courses visitors can only play weekdays. ⊠ *Sentosa Island,* ☎ *275–0022.* ☜ *Greens fees (includes cart): Tanjong S$164.80; Serapong S$123.60–S$144.20. No caddies.*

Running

Singapore is a great place for runners: there are numerous parks, and a number of leading hotels offer jogging maps. Serious runners can tackle the 10-km (6.2-mi) **East Coast Parkway track,** then cool off with a swim at the park's sandy beach. One of the most delightful places to run is the **Botanic Gardens** (off Holland Road and not far from Orchard Road), where you can jog on the paths or on the grass until 11 at night. The best time to run in Singapore is in the morning or evening; avoid the midday sun. It's safe for women to run alone. Remember to look right when crossing the road—in the British manner, driving is on the left. Several full or half-marathons are organized in Singapore during the year.

Sailing

Folks at the **Changi Sailing Club** (⊠ Netheravon Rd., ☎ 545–2876) can provide general information about sailing. You can rent Sunfish and sailboards at the **Europa Sailing Club** (⊠ 1210 East Coast Pkwy., ☎ 449–5118). Sailboat rentals are also available on **Sentosa Island** (☞ Beaches and Parks, *above*).

Scuba Diving

The most interesting (and cleanest) diving is found off the coasts of nearby islands, though the currents are treacherous. The cost can run anywhere from S$380 to S$600, including scuba equipment. For information on local opportunities, contact **Marsden Bros.** (☎ 778–8287) or **Pro Diving Services** (☎ 291–2261). **Scuba Corner** (⊠ No. 02-47 Millennia Walk, 9 Raffles Blvd., ☎ 338–6563) is a dive shop that runs trips to the outer islands.

Tennis, Squash, and Racquetball

Several hotels have their own tennis and squash courts (☞ Fitness Facilities, *above*), and there are a few public squash and racquetball courts as well. One public court complex is **Kallang Squash and Tennis Centre** (⊠ National Stadium, ☎ 440–6839), where courts cost around S$10 an hour, depending on the time of day. At the **Singapore Tennis Centre** (⊠ 1020 East Coast Pkwy., ☎ 442–5966) court costs range from S$7 to S$12 an hour. The **Tanglin Tennis Courts** (⊠ Minden Rd., ☎ 473–7236) charges S$3.50 an hour during the day and S$9.50 in the evenings.

Waterskiing

The center of activity is Ponggol, a village in northeastern Singapore. **Ponggol Water Ski Centre** (⊠ 17th Ave., ☎ 386–3891) is open daily 9–5:30 and charges S$60 an hour weekdays, S$70 an hour on weekends for a boat with ski equipment. Some of the local boats are for hire at considerably lower rates—about S$40 an hour. Negotiate directly, and make sure the proper safety equipment is available. Another popular place to water-ski is along the Kallang River, where world championships have been held. For rentals, try **Bernatt Boating and Skiing** (⊠ 53 Jalan Mempurong, ☎ 257–5859). Rentals are usually S$70 an hour on weekdays, S$75 on weekends.

Windsurfing

At the **Europa Sailing Club** (☞ Sailing, *above*) sailboards rent for S$20 for two hours, S$10 per hour thereafter. Half-day lessons are available weekdays 2–6 for S$90, with a minimum of three people per class, and subject to the availability of instructors. Windsurfing is available on **Sentosa Island** (☞ Beaches and Parks, *above*) from 9:30 to 6:30.

Spectator Sports

In addition to the sports listed below, golf, tennis, cycling, auto racing, swimming, badminton, and squash competitions are held from time to time. Some of these attract top professionals from abroad, and it may be easier to see these top athletes here than in countries where competitions are more heavily attended. A number of unique happenings—such as dragon-boat races and a kite-flying festival—are also organized annually. Most events are detailed in the newspapers. You can also get information from the **National Sports Council** (☎ 345–7111, ext. 663).

Cricket

From March through September, matches take place on the Padang grounds in front of the old **Cricket Club** (☎ 338–9271) every Saturday at 1:30 PM and every Sunday at 11 AM. Entrance to the club during matches is restricted to members, but you can watch from the sides of the playing field.

Horse Racing

You'll find on-site racing as well as live telecasts of Malaysian races at the **Singapore Turf Club.** There's a strict dress code: shorts, sleeveless

T-shirts, and sandals aren't allowed in the public stands; smart casual is the the way to go in the air-conditioned members enclosures (which foreigners need a passport to enter). ⊠ *Head Office: Bukit Timah Race Course,* ☎ *460–3400.* 🎟 *Public stands S$5.15 and S$10.30; members enclosures, S$20.60.* ⊙ *Weekends 1:30* PM*–6* PM.

Polo

The **Singapore Polo Club** (⊠ Thomson Rd., ☎ 256–4530) has both local and international matches. Spectators are welcome to watch Tuesday, Thursday, Saturday, and Sunday matches, which are played in the late afternoon.

Rugby

Rugby is played on the **Padang** grounds in front of the Singapore Cricket Club. Kickoff is usually at 5:30 PM on Saturday from September through March.

Soccer

Soccer is the major sport of Singapore; important matches take place in the **National Stadium** at Kallang. Details are published in the daily papers, and ticket reservations can be made through the National Sports Council (☞ *above*). The main season is September through March.

Track and Field

In recent years, most Asian countries have become keen on track-and-field events. Singapore has the **National Stadium** at Kallang for major events as well as nine athletic centers with tracks. International meets are usually detailed in the daily press and arouse considerable nationalistic feeling. For information and details on how to book seats for major meets, call the National Sports Council (☞ *above*).

SHOPPING

With an incredible range of goods—brought in from all over the world and sold in an equally incredible number (and variety) of shops—Singapore is truly a shopping fantasyland. Unfortunately, the bargains for which the city was once famous no longer exist. Though you can still find deals on handcrafted rosewood furniture, Chinese objets d'art, and carpets, prices for most items are the same as or higher than those in the United States. You should know the costs of goods you intend to buy—especially photographic and electronic items—at home. Though prices don't vary much from shop to shop, compare a few shops to feel secure about your price.

If you have (or wish you had) the money to spend on haute couture, head over to the Orchard and Scotts roads area to browse in the boutiques of the Hilton International arcade—which leads to the Four Seasons Hotel arcade—where every designer imaginable has a store. A 10-minute walk farther up Orchard Road takes you to the Tanglin Shopping Centre with its distinctive gift shops. For truly singular gifts check out the shops around Temple Street and Sago Street in Chinatown, where you'll find such things as Chinese herbal medicines, paper funerary items, and religious sculptures.

Stop into at least one of the Watson's drugstores scattered throughout the city. You'll find bags of prawn chips from Indonesia, tapioca chips from Malaysia, and bar snacks or lobster balls from Singapore; cookies from Australia; mints from England; and candied jellies from Japan. All make great gifts (if they're not eaten before you get them home).

For small, inexpensive souvenirs, take the MRT to the Bugis stop. On one side of Victoria Street is the Parco Bugis Junction—an air-conditioned, semioutdoor, multilevel shopping center. On the other side are an array of market stalls that sell everything from fake designer watches at S$18 each to silk boxer shorts and scarves (three for S$10). "Dollar" stores abound here, and they're full of such inexpensive and indispensable consumer goods as cans of "prickly heat" talcum powder (three for S$1) or packages of one-use, throwaway underwear (S$3 for five pairs).

For real deals, savvy locals flock to the weekly garage sales—usually held by expats leaving the country—advertised in the Saturday classifieds of the *The Straits Times*. At these, furniture and goods are sold at bargain-basement prices by people who literally can't take it with them.

Shopping Essentials

Bargaining

Although department stores, chain stores, and some independent stores do not offer discounts—their items are tagged with fixed prices—bargaining is common in Singapore. Shops that are reluctant to offer discounts usually have a FIXED-PRICE STORE sign in their windows (price tags may have the same message). If you don't like to bargain, stick to the department stores, which usually have the lowest initial ("first") price. If you don't mind bargaining, visit a department store first to get an idea of established prices, and then shop around.

Price tags in places that allow bargaining may say "recommended price." Local shops in upscale complexes or malls tend to give a 10%–15% discount on clothes. However, at jewelry stores, the discount can be as high as 40%–50%; carpet dealers also give hefty reductions. At less-upscale complexes, the discounts tend to be greater. Stalls and shops around visitor attractions have the highest initial asking prices, so bargaining here yields deep discounts

Everyone has his or her own method of bargaining, but in general, when a vendor tells you a price, ask for the discounted price, then offer even less. The person will probably reject your offer but come down a few dollars. With patience, this can continue and earn you a few more dollars off the price. If you don't like haggling, walk away after hearing the discounted price. If the vendor hasn't hit bottom price, you'll be called back.

Complaints

To avoid even having to worry about problems with goods or services, look for shops that have the Singapore Tourism Board's gold circular logo in their windows. This indicates that the retailer has been distinguished for excellent service and fair pricing among other things. Members need to be approved by the Consumers Association of Singapore (✉ No. 04-3625, 164 Bukit Merah Central, 150164, ☎ 270–4611) and the tourist board (☞ Visitor Information *in* Singapore A to Z, *below*). If you do end up with complaints about either a serious disagreement with a shopkeeper or defective merchandise, lodge them with the tourist board; rest assured that staff members will follow up on them. The consumers association can also help. If you encounter retailer malpractice, you can get full redress through the Small Claims Tribunals—something retailers dread, because the tourist board publishes the names and addresses of miscreants ordered to make redress to visitors.

Electrical Goods

Singapore's current is 220–240 volts at 50 cycles, like that in Australia and Great Britain. Canada and the United States use 110–120 volts at

60 cycles, so before you buy appliances, verify that you can get special adapters, if required, and that these will not affect the equipment's performance. These days, most electrical goods sold are 110–220 volts compatible. Check the sticker on the apparatus you are about to buy.

Guarantees and Receipts

Make sure you get international guarantees and warranty cards with your purchases. Check the serial number of each item against its card, and don't forget to mail the card in. Sometimes guarantees are limited to the country of purchase. If the dealer cannot give you a guarantee, he's probably selling an item intended for the domestic market in its country of manufacture; if so, he has bypassed the authorized agent and should be able to give you a lower price. Though your purchase of such an item isn't illegal, you have no guarantee. If you decide to buy it anyway, be sure to check that the item is in working order before you leave the shop.

Be sure to ask for receipts, both for your own protection and for customs. Though shopkeepers are often amenable to stating false values on receipts, customs officials are wary and knowledgeable.

How to Pay

All department stores and most shops accept credit cards—American Express, Diners Club, MasterCard, and Visa—and travelers checks. Many tourist shops also accept foreign currency; just be sure to check the exchange rates before agreeing to any price—some store owners try to skim extra profit by giving an unfair rate of exchange. Retailers work at a low profit margin and depend on high turnover; they assume you will pay in cash. Except at the department stores, paying with a credit card will mean that your "discounted price" will reflect the commission the retailer will have to pay the credit card company.

Imitations

Copyright laws passed in early 1987 impose stern penalties on the selling of pirated music recordings and computer software. However, Singapore still has a reputation for pirated goods. If you're buying a computer, for example, some stores are quite amenable to loading it with all the software you want. Pirated CDs and video laser discs can be found at certain market stalls, as can incredibly authentic-looking wristwatches from every designer on the globe. The greatest of the fakes is the "solid gold" Rolex, which comes complete with serial number for less than S$100. It looks so good you could have a problem at customs—though you're more likely to have a customs problem (either in Singapore or at home) if it's discovered that you've purchased a counterfeit item.

Shipping

All stores that deal with valuable, fragile, or bulky merchandise know how to pack well. Ask for a quote on shipping charges, which you can then double-check with a local forwarder. Check whether the shop has insurance covering both loss and damage in transit. You might find you need additional coverage. If you're sending your purchases home by mail, check with **Singapore Post** (☎ 800/222–5777), the national postal service, about regulations.

Touts

Touting—soliciting business by approaching people on the street with offers of free shopping tours and special discounts—is illegal (maximum fines are S$5,000, and prison sentences of up to six months are possible). Nevertheless, it continues inside one or two shopping centers, especially Lucky Plaza. Each center has its band of men looking for people to interest in their special stash of fake designer watches.

The touts at the top of Tanglin Road can be particularly bothersome. Some taxi drivers tout as well. Avoid all touts and the shops they recommend; a reputable shop doesn't need them. The prices will end up being higher—reflecting the tout's commission—and the quality of the goods possibly inferior.

Shopping Districts

Throughout the city are complexes full of shopping areas and centers. Many stores will have branches that carry much the same merchandise in several of these areas.

Orchard Road

The heart of Singapore's preeminent shopping district, Orchard Road is bordered on both sides by tree-shaded, tiled sidewalks lined with modern shopping complexes and deluxe hotels that house exclusive boutiques. Also considered part of this area are the shops on Scotts Road, which crosses Orchard, and two shopping centers—**Supreme House** on Penang Road and **Singapore Shopping Centre** (which was under renovation at press time).

Orchard Road is known for fashion and interior design shops, but you can find anything from Mickey Mouse watches to Chinese paper kites and antique Korean chests. The interior-design shops have unusual Asian bric-a-brac and such original items as a lamp stand made from old Chinese tea canisters or a pair of bookends in the shape of Balinese frogs. Virtually every Orchard Road complex, with the exception of the Promenade, has a clutch of department stores selling electronic goods, cigarette lighters, pens, jewelry, cameras, and so on. Most also have money changers, a few inexpensive cafés, and snack bars.

Though there's reference to an "Orchard Road price," which takes into account the astronomical rents some shop tenants have to pay, the department stores have the same fixed prices here as at all their branches. Small shops away from the center may have slightly cheaper prices.

Chinatown

Once Singapore's liveliest and most colorful shopping area, Chinatown lost a great deal of its vitality when the street stalls were moved into the **Kreta Ayer Complex** off Neil Road, **Chinatown Point** off Trengganu Street, and the **People's Park Complex** on Eu Tong Sen Street. Still, this neighborhood is fun to explore. The focus is on the Smith, Temple, and Pagoda street blocks, but nearby streets—Eu Tong Sen Street, Wayang Street, and Merchant Road on one side and Ann Siang Hill and Club Street on another—can yield some interesting finds.

Chinese kitchenware can be fascinating, and Temple Street has an abundance of unusual plates, plant pots, teapots, lacquered chopsticks, and so on. Paraphernalia for Chinese funerals is particularly prevalent around Sago Street. Nearby Sago Lane was lined, not so long ago, with "death houses," where elderly people went to await death. This may sound gruesome, but funerary items are among the most creative examples of folk art in the world. They include paper replicas of life's necessities, to serve the dead in their afterlife. There are some famous craftsmen on Ann Siang Hill. Just around the corner, on Club Street, are several wood-carvers who specialize in creating idols of Chinese gods. On Merchant Road, a vendor of costumes for Chinese operas welcomes customers. And on Chin Hin Street, you can buy fragrant Chinese tea direct from a merchant.

South Bridge Road in Chinatown is the street of goldsmiths. Dozens of jewelers here specialize in 22K and even 24K ornaments in the characteristic orange color of Chinese gold. Each assistant, often shielded by a metal grill, uses an abacus and a balance to calculate the value of the piece you wish to buy. You must bargain here. South Bridge Road is also home to many art galleries.

Little India

Serangoon Road is affectionately known as Little India. For shopping purposes, it begins at the **Zhujiao Market,** better known as the KK Market, on the corner of Serangoon and Buffalo roads. Some of the junk dealers and inexpensive-clothing stalls form a bazaar known as Mustafa Centre. This is a fun place to poke about and look for bargains.

All the handicrafts of India can be found on Serangoon Road: intricately carved wood tables, shining brass trays, hand-loomed table linens, fabric inlaid with tiny mirrors, brightly colored pictures of Hindu deities, and garlands of jasmine for the gods. And the sari shops! At dozens of shops here you can get the 6½ yards of voile, cotton, Kashmiri silk, or richly embroidered Benares silk required to make a sari. For the variety, quality, and beauty of the silk, the prices are very low. Other Indian costumes, such as long or short *kurtas* (men's collarless shirts) and Punjabi trouser sets, are unusual and attractive buys. Should you overspend and find yourself with excess baggage, there are several luggage shops on Serangoon Road where you can buy an old-fashioned tin trunk big enough to hide a body in.

Arab Street

The Arab Street shopping area really begins at Beach Road, opposite the Plaza Hotel. This old-fashioned street is full of noteworthy buys. A group of basket and rattan shops first catches your eye. There are quite a few jewelers here, and even more shops selling loose gems and necklaces of garnet and amethyst beads. The main business is batiks (textiles bearing hand-printed designs) and lace.

Brassware, prayer rugs, carpets, and leather slippers are sold in abundance on Arab Street and its side streets, which have appealing names such as Muscat Street and Baghdad Street. Two noteworthy complexes in the vicinity are Beach Road's **Golden Mile Food Centre,** which is devoted to good food on the lower floors and junk and antiques on the top floors, and Jalan Sultan's **Textile Centre,** which offers a wide variety of batiks.

Katong

The quiet east-coast suburb of Katong, just 15 minutes from town via the Pan Island Expressway, has old-fashioned shophouses along its main street, some selling inexpensive children's clothes and one dealing in antiques. Off the main road is the even more old-fashioned Joo Chiat Road, which gets more and more interesting as it approaches Gelang Road. Its shops sell Chinese kitchenware, antiques, baby clothes, and lots of offbeat items.

Holland Village

Holland Village, 10 minutes west of town by taxi, is a bit of a yuppie haunt, but it's the most rewarding place to browse for unusual and inexpensive Asian items, large and small. Many shops here specialize in Korean chests. Behind the main street is Lorong Mambong, a street of shophouses jammed with baskets, earthenware, porcelain, and all sorts of things from China and Thailand. One complex to look for in this area is the **Holland Village Shopping Centre** on Holland Avenue. A 10-minute walk along Holland Avenue from Holland Village is **Cold Storage Jelita,** which also has several shops.

Centers and Complexes

Shops in multilevel buildings and shopping complexes are often listed with a numerical designation such as "No. 00-00." The first part of this number indicates what floor the shop is on. The second part indicates its location on the floor. When the phone number of an individual shop is not given in this section, you'll find it listed with the shop under a specific merchandise category, below.

Centrepoint (✉ 176 Orchard Rd.). This spacious and impressive center has the **Robinsons** department store as its anchor tenant. One of the liveliest complexes, Centrepoint also has jewelry, silverware, and fashion shops; furniture stores that sell Philippine bamboo and Korean chests; and a large basement supermarket.

Delfi Orchard (✉ 402 Orchard Rd.). Delfi is full of wedding boutiques, art galleries, and jewelry shops. **Waterford Wedgwood** and **Royal Selangor Pewter** are also here, along with a well-stocked golf shop.

Far East Plaza (✉ 14 Scotts Rd.). This center is where the young and trendy gather to see and be seen. The shops are geared to them, and there's a bargain-basement atmosphere about the place. A forecourt offers fast-food restaurants (including a McDonald's and Canadian Pizza—the best in the city), outdoor tables, and entertaining people-watching.

Forum Galleria (✉ 583 Orchard Rd.). Here you'll find a huge **Toys 'R' Us**, as well as an assortment of boutiques, including **Guess! Kids**.

Funan Centre (✉ 109 North Bridge Rd.). Next to the Peninsula Hotel on North Bridge Road and High Street, this shopping center will thrill computer and information-technology lovers.

The Heeren Shops (✉ 260 Orchard Rd.). This new complex at Orchard and Grange roads houses a huge **HMV** music store; **True Colours**, a futuristic makeup boutique; **Electric City**, an electronics superstore; and a branch of the popular Nonya restaurant, **The Blue Ginger**.

Hilton Shopping Gallery (✉ 581 Orchard Rd.). Most of Singapore's upscale hotels have a boutique or two in their lobbies, but the Hilton has an extensive shopping arcade full of them. It is home to several top names—**Giorgio Armani, Matsuda, Valentino**—and, through a boutique called **Singora**, many other Italian and French fashion houses. Among its other top-flight tenants are **Gucci, Davidoff, Dunhill, L'Ultimo**, and **Louis Vuitton**. This gallery leads to a similar arcade with still more expensive boutiques that's attached to the Four Seasons.

Liang Court Complex (✉ 177 River Valley Rd.). Liang Court is off the beaten track but only five minutes by cab from Orchard Road and worth the drive. The department store **Daimaru** is here; half of its floor space has been transformed into selected designer boutiques, such as **Dunhill**, and areas that sell books, silk, pearls, and other specialty items.

Lucky Plaza (✉ 304 Orchard Rd.). This plaza has gone downhill as its shops have moved to trendier, newer buildings. What stores remain are geared toward tourists. Plan to bargain furiously, particularly with the many jewelers who are, it seems, involved in a perpetual price-cutting war.

Marina Square. Part of an elegant complex that begins east of the Nicholl Highway downtown (a five-minute walk from the Raffles City MRT station), it includes Millennia Walk (look up to admire the architecture) and houses **Metro**, a large department store that has great sales; DFS, a massive duty-free shop; two cineplexes for film buffs; and about 200 small shops, including the English store **Mothercare**.

Ngee Ann City (✉ 391 Orchard Rd). Although the Japanese store **Takashimaya** takes up most of this complex, you'll find a number of small boutiques as well.

Orchard Point and Orchard Plaza (✉ No. 220 and No. 150 Orchard Rd.). These side-by-side centers don't have the popular appeal of some other complexes but will reward dedicated shoppers with good finds. Reptile bags can be found in the basement shops of Orchard Point. (Note that Orchard Plaza houses several brothels; you might want to avoid it at night.)

Palais Renaissance (✉ 390 Orchard Rd.). Across the road from the Hilton hotel is this new high-fashion center. Targeted at those who seek status labels at high prices, the Palais Renaissance is chic, opulent, and overpriced. It's a delight to wander through regardless of whether you're well heeled or not. Here **Prada, DKNY, Gianni Versace,** and **Krizia** compete as much in the design of their stores as in the design of their merchandise. Perfumes, jewelry, and travel accessories are also expensively represented in this extravagant marbled emporium.

The Paragon (✉ 290 Orchard Rd.). The glossy Paragon has more than 15 men's fashion boutiques and counts **Gucci** and **Sonia Rykiel** among its more popular tenants. It also has the **Metro** department store.

Parco Bugis Junction (✉ 230 Victoria St.). Linking the Hotel Inter-Continental and the Bugis MRT station, this shopping center has the Japanese department store **Seiyu** as its major tenant. It also houses a host of boutiques, restaurants, cafés, a cineplex, and the **Amusement Wonder Park Namco.** Bargain hunters might want to stop by the *pasar malam* (night market) at Bugis Village.

Parkway Parade (✉ 80 Marine Parade Rd.). This excellent and very attractive center is on Marine Parade Road, 15 to 20 minutes east of town by expressway. On weekdays you can shop here in peace and quiet; on weekends, it's uncomfortably crowded. The focus is on up-to-date and affordable fashions. Things get started around noon.

People's Park Complex and Centre (✉ Eu Tong Sen St.). Though not new and glossy, this Chinatown center has an international reputation and is always entertaining. Everything is sold here: herbs, Chinese medicines, cameras, stereo equipment, clothes, luggage. Shopkeepers are much more aggressive here than in town, and if you haven't done your homework, you can get taken.

The Promenade (✉ 300 Orchard Rd.). The elegant architecture (there's a spiral walkway with a gentle slope instead of escalators) here is matched by the elegance of the tenants. Its fashion stores carry some of the hottest names, including **Charles Jourdan, Dolce&Gabbana,** and **Issey Miyake.** Home-decor shops sell superb Asian odds and ends.

Raffles City and Raffles Hotel Arcade. Bordered by Stamford, North Bridge, and Bras Basah roads, this complex has a confusing interior. If you get lost, you're sure to come across many shopping finds, some of them in the Japanese department and grocery store **Sogo.** You'll also find several fashion boutiques, the **Times** bookshop, and a post office branch. Across the road is the Raffles Hotel Arcade, whose 60 boutiques sell high fashion and art. There's also a tourist board office here.

Scotts Shopping Centre (✉ 6–8 Scotts Rd.). One of the best places in Singapore for affordable fashion that stops just short of haute couture, Scotts also has a basement food court with local and delicatessen food, plus activities and demonstrations to keep shoppers entertained.

Shaw House (✉ 350 Orchard Rd.). **Isetan,** a large Japanese department store, is the major anchor in this complex. The **Kinokuniya** bookstore is excellent for volumes on Japan. **Etienne Aigner** is a good place for leather items.

Specialists Centre (✉ 277 Orchard Rd.). This center is the home of the **John Little** department store, better known as JL, and assorted boutiques.

Stamford Court and Stamford House. This corner of North Bridge and Stamford roads has more speciality shopping centers than any other section of downtown Orchard Road. Check out the fine array of furniture and home decor stores here, as well as antiques, sculpture, fine art, and gift shops.

Suntec City Mall. At the corner of the Nicholl Highway and Raffles Boulevard in the Marina Bay area, this large complex is divided into four zones: the Tropics (lifestyle products and services), the Entertainment Centre (housing the French superstore **Carrefour**), the Fountain Terrace (an array of restaurants, pubs, and a food court), and the Galleria (high-end boutiques). You could shop and dine here and not even bother seeing the rest of Singapore.

Tanglin Shopping Centre. This center, where Orchard Road meets Tanglin Road, has a good selection of antiques shops, especially in a small, self-contained section at ground level. **Moongate** is one of Singapore's oldest dealers in fine antique porcelain. **Antiques of the Orient** is the only shop in town that specializes in antique maps. The contemporary interior-design shops, as well as the food court in the basement, are excellent, too.

Wisma Atria (✉ 435 Orchard Rd.). Come here if only to see the aquarium that wraps around the elevator. If you want to shop as well, this center has such grand names in fashion as **Dior** and **Fendi**. You'll also find the **Isetan** department store.

Department Stores

Singapore has one homegrown chain—**Metro**—that offers a wide range of affordable fashions and household products. When shopping for locally designed and manufactured fashion as well as brands such as Esprit, Metro is the best bet. The designs are up-to-the-minute, and the prices are good by local standards and unbelievably good by international standards. Look for Metros in Far East Plaza, Marina Square, and the Paragon.

Locally owned **Tang's** (✉ 320 Orchard Rd., ☎ 737–5500), also known as Tang's Superstore or C. K. Tang's, is next to the Marriott Hotel. It looks upscale, but it has some of the best buys in town. Its fashions are, at best, improving, but its accessories are excellent—especially the costume jewelry—and its household products are unsurpassed.

Two Chinese department stores under different ownership, but with the same name, **Overseas Emporium,** are in the People's Park Complex (☎ 535–0555) and the People's Park Centre (☎ 535–1948). Both offer basically the same goods: Chinese silk fabric, silk blouses, brocade jackets, crafts, children's clothes, and china.

Singaporeans enjoy Japanese department stores. **Isetan**—in Wisma Atria (☎ 733–7777), Shaw House (☎ 733–1111), and Parkway Parade (☎ 345–5555)—always has good specials, and the fashion departments for men and women are well stocked. **Daimaru** (☎ 339–1111), in Liang Court, has some very unusual goods. **Sogo** (☎ 339–1100) opened in Raffles City as did **Seiyu** in the Parco Bugis Junction Complex (✉ 230 Victoria St., Bugis MRT, ☎ 223–2222).

The English **Robinsons** (☎ 733–0888), in Centrepoint, is Singapore's oldest department store. It recently shed its fuddy-duddy image and rethought its pricing and is once again one of the best. **John Little** (☎ 737–2222), at the Specialists Centre, has a full range of offerings but is now targeting the young and trendy. There are still good sales here, however. The **Marks & Spencer** in the basement of Lane Crawford at the corner of Scotts and Orchard is the biggest of several outlets in town.

Markets

Stalls crowding upon stalls in covered, open spaces of the city's **food markets** make for a hectic, colorful scene. The range of foodstuffs is

Babazar, **23**
Centrepoint, **22**
Chinatown Point, **33**
Cuppage Centre, **24**
Delfi Orchard, **4**
Far East Plaza, **11**
Forum Galleria, **7**
Funan Centre, **35**
Golden Mile Food Centre, **43**
The Heeren Shops, **19**
Hilton Shopping Gallery, **8**
Holland Village Shopping Centre, **1**
Keng of Tong Mern Sern, **29**
Kreta Ayer Complex, **34**
Liang Court Complex, **30**
Liat Towers, **9**
Lucky Plaza, **14**
Mandarin, **18**
Marina Square, **42**
Millennia Walk, **38**
Ngee Ann City, **20**
Orchard Plaza, **26**
Orchard Point, **25**
Orchard Towers, **6**
Palais Renaissance, **5**
The Paragon, **17**
Parco Bugis Junction, **45**
Parkway Parade, **41**
People's Park Centre, **31**
People's Park Complex, **32**
The Promenade, **16**
Raffles City, **37**
Raffles Hotel Arcade, **39**
Scotts Shopping Centre, **12**
Shangri-La, **3**
Shaw House, **10**
Singapore Shopping Centre, **28**
Specialists Centre, **21**
Stamford Court/Stamford House, **36**
Suntec City Mall, **40**
Supreme House, **27**
Tanglin Shopping Centre, **2**
Tang's, **13**
Textile Centre, **44**
Wisma Atria, **15**
Zhujiao Centre, **46**

Singapore Shopping Complexes and Markets

NEWTON

Nassim Rd.

Claymore Hill

Scotts Rd.

Cairnhill Rd.

Clemenceau Ave.

Cavenagh Rd.

Tanglin Rd.

Bideford Rd.

ORCHARD

Orchard Blvd.

One Tree Hill

Paterson Rd.

Orchard Rd.

ORCHARD ROAD

Grange Rd.

Grange Rd.

Exeter Rd.

SOMERSET

River Valley Rd.

River Valley Rd.

Zion Rd.

Kim Seng Rd.

River Valley Rd.

Singapore River

Alexandra Rd.

Havelock Rd.

Havelock Rd.

TIONG BAHRU

Tiong Bahru Rd.

Outram Park

Henderson Rd.

Outram Rd.

OUTRAM PARK

N

Jalan Bukit Merah

Craig Rd.

0   1000 meters
0   1000 yards

Neil Rd.

Cantonment Rd.

Bahru   Rd.

Spottiswoode Park

Keppel Rd.

KEY

AE American Express Office
North-South MRT line
East-West MRT line
Railroad lines
Subway stop

Keppel Rd.

Empire Dock

staggering, and some of the items may turn your stomach. The live animals eyed by shoppers will tug at your heartstrings. Usually a food
market is divided into two sections: the dry market and the wet market, which has squirming fish, crawling turtles, strutting chickens, and
cute rabbits that are sold for the pot (the floors are continually sluiced
to maintain hygiene). The wet market at the **Chinatown Point** is the
most fascinating; the dry market at **Cuppage Centre** (on Cuppage Rd.,
off Orchard Rd.), where the flower stalls are particularly appealing,
is a better choice for the squeamish.

The old-style street bazaars are all gone now, but in the **Sungei Road**
area, site of the once-notorious Thieves Market, a few street vendors
creep back each weekend. The stalls sell mainly inexpensive shirts, T-
shirts, children's clothes, and underwear, as well as odds and ends such
as inexpensive watches, costume jewelry, and sunglasses. A few sell plastic household items.

The **Kreta Ayer** complex in Chinatown may be modern, but it has all
the atmosphere of a bazaar. All the street vendors from Chinatown were
relocated here. The shops sell cassette tapes, clothing from China,
toys, and a lot of gaudy merchandise.

Some of Chinatown's elderly junk peddlers refuse to leave the streets.
In the afternoon, they line up along **Temple Street** and lay out a strange
variety of goods—old bottles, stamps, bits of porcelain or brass, old
postcards, and the like—on cloths.

Shops and stalls also cluster at the **Bugis Street** mall and at **Telok Ayer,**
but some merchandise tends to be overpriced. Since 1996, several "dollar stores" have opened at Bugis, where items—from Indonesia, Malaysia,
Korea, Thailand, and other parts of Asia—that you never thought
you'd ever need are for sale. They are great shops for those on a budget who have to pick up several souvenirs for the folks back home.

Specialty Shops

Antiques and Curios
Most antiques stores have a variety of small items—porcelain, brassware, idols, and so on—as well as Chinese furniture, which may be of
blackwood inlaid with mother of pearl, or namwood stained red with
elaborate carvings picked out in gold. Falling halfway between souvenir shops and antiques stores, curio shops sell a fascinating variety
of goods, mainly from China. Reverse-glass paintings, porcelain vases,
cloisonné, wood carvings, jewelry (agate, jade, lapis lazuli, malachite),
ivory carvings, embroidery, and idols represent just a fraction of their
treasures. Note that some curio dealers style themselves as antiques shops,
as do some vendors who sell rosewood items or reproduction furniture. (Strictly speaking, antiques in Singapore are defined as items that
are more than 80 years old.)

If you don't have time to step outside of the Orchard Road shopping
mecca, good places to see genuine antiques are the Tanglin Shopping
Centre's **Antiques of the Orient** (☎ 734–9351), which specializes in
maps, ceramics, and furniture; **Moongate** (☎ 737–6771), which sells
porcelain; and **Tatiana** (☎ 235–3560), which carries primitive art and
antique Indonesian batik and ikat (a woven fabric of tie-dyed yarns).

Off Orchard Road on Cuppage Road is a row of restored shophouses.
Here, **Babazar** (✉ 31A–35A Cuppage Terr., ☎ 235–7866) is full of
wonderful jewelry, furniture, clothes, art, knickknacks, and antiques.
Keng of Tong Mern Sern (✉ 226 River Valley Rd., ☎ 734–0761), near

the Chettiar Temple, is a rabbit warren full of antiques. The store's sign says, WE BUY JUNK, WE SELL ANTIQUES.

For curios, try **Lim's Art & Crafts** (✉ Top floor, ☎ 735–2966) in the Scotts Shopping Centre. For museum-quality Asian antiques, visit the **Paul Art Gallery** in Holland Park (✉ 68 Greenleaf Rd., ☎ 468–4697). In the east end, about a 20-minute walk on Sims Avenue from the Kallang MRT, is **Poh Antiques and Junks** (✉ 139 Sims Ave., ☎ no phone), which has Buddhist and Hindu sculptures as well as assorted kitsch from this century. It opens when the owner feels like opening—but even if it's closed when you get there, Sims Avenue around Geylang and Lorong 9 is an interesting neighborhood in which to stroll.

Art

Singapore has more than its share of fine artists. Established names—Chen Wen Hsi for Chinese brush painting, Thomas Yeo for abstract landscapes, and Anthony Poon for contemporary graphics—fetch high prices. Among the artists who are gaining recognition are Wan Soon Kam, Ng Eng Teng (a sculptor who re-creates the human figure in cement, stoneware, and bronze), James Tan (known for his traditional and abstract Chinese brush paintings), and Teng Juay Lee (who specializes in orchids). Nostalgic scenes of the Singapore of yesteryear are captured in watercolors and oils by artists such as Gog Sing Hoi, Ang Ah Tee, and Ong Kim Seng, known for his scenes of the Singapore River and Chinatown. Some delightful paintings can be had for as little as S$300.

For a range of art, try **Art Forum** (✉ 56 Monk's Hill Terr., ☎ 737–3448), but call before visiting. There are also many galleries on South Bridge Road in Chinatown. If you wish to see Chinese calligraphy in the works, Yong Cheong Thye practices his art at the **Yong Gallery** (✉ 17 Erskin Rd., ☎ 226–1718) in Chinatown.

Other galleries include: **Cicada Gallery of Fine Arts** (✉ 31 Ann Siang Rd., ☎ 225–6787), **Opera Gallery** (✉ No. 02-12H, 391 Orchard Rd., ☎ 735–2618), **Plum Blossoms Gallery** (✉ Raffles Hotel, 1 Beach Rd., ☎ 334–1198), and **Shenn's Gallery** (✉ 37 Blair Rd., ☎ 223–1233).

Batik

A traditional craft item of Singapore, Malaysia, and Indonesia, batik is now also important in contemporary fashion and interior design. **Blue Ginger Design Centre** (✉ 1 Beach Rd., ☎ 334–1171) and **Design Batik** (✉ 1 Beach Rd., ☎ 776–4337), both at the Raffles Hotel, sell clothes and fabrics in modern designs. Blue Ginger is especially innovative, and has opened a branch at the Merchant Court Hotel (✉ 20 Merchant Rd., ☎ 536–4986). **Tang's** department stores (☞ *above*) sell inexpensive batik products, including a good range of men's shirts. Traditional batik sarong lengths can be bought in the shops on Arab Street and in the **Textile Centre** on Jalan Sultan.

Cameras

Photographic equipment may not be the bargain it once was, but the range of cameras and accessories available can be matched only in Hong Kong. It's especially important that you establish the price at home before buying here. Film and film processing remain excellent buys. All department stores carry cameras, and there are so many in Lucky Plaza that you can do all your comparison shopping in one spot.

For personalized service try **Cathay Photo** (☎ 339–6188) on the second floor of Marina Square. For camera repairs, **Goh Gin Camera Service Centre** (✉ 150 Orchard Rd., Orchard Plaza, ☎ 732–6155) may be able to help.

Carpets

Carpets are very attractively priced in Singapore. Afghan, Pakistani, Persian, Turkish, and Chinese carpets—both antique and new—are carried by reputable dealers. Carpet auctions, announced in the newspapers, are good places to buy if you know your stuff. In shops, it's acceptable to bargain—in fact, it's integral to the rather lengthy proceedings.

Good shops include: **Amir & Sons** (⊠ No. 03–01, ☎ 734–9112) in Lucky Plaza, **Hassan's** (⊠ No. 03–01, ☎ 737–5626) in the Tanglin Shopping Centre, and **Qureshi's** (⊠ No. 05–12, ☎ 235–1523) in Centrepoint.

Clothing

CASUAL OUTFITS

In department stores and small boutiques all over the island—but especially on Orchard Road—locally made women's fashions and Japanese imports sell for a song. Brands such as Chocolate and Ananas offer colorful, reasonably made, very fashionable garments. Two of the better-known chain stores are the **East India Company** (⊠ 11 Stamford Rd., ☎ 336–0448) and the **British India Company** (⊠ 11 Stamford Rd., ☎ 334–6806), both of which are in the Capitol Building. **Trend** (☎ 235–9446) is a popular Centrepoint boutique.

Shoes are good buys, too, especially in the Metro and Tang's department stores (☞ Department Stores, *above*), but sizes here are smaller than in the West, and some women may have a problem getting the right fit.

HIGH FASHION

Singapore has its own designers, including London-based Benny Ong, who sells through Tang's and China Silk House (☞ Silk, *below*) and Song & Kelly, a Singaporean/British couple who are winning raves internationally. You should also look for the designs of Jut Ling, Thomas Wee, and Celia Loe in the more upscale department stores and boutiques. For European couture, check the arcades of the Hilton International and the Mandarin, as well as the more fashionable shopping centers, especially the Palais Renaissance.

Boutiques that carry a number of designers include **Club 21** (☎ 738–8778), which has men's and women's fashions and is in the Four Seasons arcade; **Glamourette** (☎ 737–5939) in the Promenade; and **Link** (☎ 736–0645) in the Palais Renaissance.

Men's fashions are represented by **Hermès** (⊠ 541 Orchard Rd., ☎ 734–1353) in Liat Towers, **Mario Valentino** (☎ 338–4457) in Marina Square, and **Ralph Lauren** (☎ 738–0298) in Takashimaya.

Jewelry

Singapore is a reliable place to buy jewelry, and there are so many jewelers that prices are competitive. Never accept the first price offered, no matter how posh the store. (All jewelers give enormous discounts, usually 40% or more, but some, especially in hotels, don't mention this until pressed.) The Singapore Assay Office hallmarks jewelry, though the procedure is time-consuming and not many jewelers submit to it unless required for export.

In Chinatown, particularly along South Bridge Road and in People's Park, there are dozens of jewelers who sell 22K gold. Many of these are old family firms, and prices are calculated by abacus based on the weight of the ornament and the prevailing price of gold. The bargaining procedure can take quite some time. On Orchard Road, the jewelry shops are often branches of Hong Kong firms or are local firms modeled along the same lines. They sell 18K set jewelry, often in Italian designs, as well as loose investment stones.

Cartier has shops in Takashimaya (☎ 734–2427) and in Millennia Walk in Marina Square (☎ 339–3294). One of the many small jewelers in Takashimaya is the **Hour Glass** (☎ 734–2420), which carries a large selection of designer watches. **Je T'Aime** (☎ 734–2275) in Wisma Atria is a reputable firm. **Larry's** (☎ 732–3222), with branches in Raffles City and other malls, is a popular store. You'll find the antique silver and gold jewelry of the Straits Chinese at **Petnic's** (✉ 41A Cuppage Rd., ☎ 235–6564). **Tiffany & Co.** recently opened a two-story store at Ngee Ann City (☎ 735–8823).

Luggage and Accessories

Luggage is a bargain in Singapore, and every complex contains several stores that carry designer names including Charles Jourdan, Dunhill, Etienne Aigner, and Louis Vuitton. Department stores also carry such brands as Samsonite and Delsey. The **Escada** boutique (☎ 336–8283) at the Promenade and the Millennia Walk has a range of accessories and custom-made luggage.

Pewter and Dinnerware

Malaysia is the world's largest tin producer, and pewter is an important craft item in the region. Modern pewter items are heavily influenced by Scandinavian design. Items range from jewelry and tiny figurines to coffee and tea sets. Sake sets, bowls, vases, ornamental plates, clocks, and traditional beer tankards are also available. Some items are specifically aimed at the tourist trade, such as Raffles plates and Chinese zodiac plaques.

For dinnerware, **Christofle** (☎ 733–7257) has a boutique in the Hilton. **Royal Selangor Pewter** (✉ Main office: 32 Pandan Rd., ☎ 268–9600), the largest pewter concern in Singapore, has a great product range displayed at the showrooms in the Paragon, Delfi Orchard, Clarke Quay, Raffles Hotel, Marina Square, and Raffles City. Also try the **Waterford Wedgwood Shop** (✉ No. 01–01 Delfi Orchard, ☎ 734–8375).

Silk

Chinese silk is easy to find in Singapore. All the emporiums have special departments that sell the fabric or clothes (tailored and ready-to-wear) made from it. **China Silk House,** which has outlets in the Tanglin Shopping Centre (☎ 235–5020) and in Centrepoint (☎ 733–0555), has a wide range of fabrics in different weights and types. You'll also find silk clothing, including a line designed for the shop by Benny Ong.

For Indian silk in sari lengths check out the many shops in the Serangoon Road area. You pay only a fraction of what it would cost elsewhere to buy the 6 meters (6.5 yards) of silk—which could be the thin Kashmiri type or the heavier, embroidered Benares type—required to make a sari. The major store for Indian textiles is **P. Govindasamy Pillai** (PGP; ✉ Campbell La., ☎ 297–5311). To enter it, you must first walk into Kuna's Handicraft Shop, which will lead you to the PGP Supermarket and the sari shop upstairs.

Thai silk, in different weights for different purposes, comes in stunning colors. Specialty shops sell it by the meter or made up into gowns, blouses, and dresses. The **Siam Silk Company** (✉ 87 Tanjong Pagar Rd., ☎ 323–4800) is a good place to look.

Tailoring

There are tailors and tailors—what you end up with depends on how well you choose. Tailors who offer 24-hour service rarely deliver, and their quality is often suspect. Another indication of danger is not seeing a tailor on the premises. Anyone can set up shop as a tailor by filling a store with fabrics and then subcontracting the work; the results from such places are seldom felicitous. Allow four to five days for a good job. **Justmen** (☎ 737–4800) in the Tanglin Shopping Centre is one of a number of excellent men's tailors. For women, shops such as the Tanglin branch of **China Silk House** (☞ Silks, *above*) offer good tailoring.

SINGAPORE A TO Z

Arriving and Departing

By Airplane

AIRPORTS

The major gateway to Singapore is **Changi International Airport** (☎ 541–9828), which is on the eastern end of the island. The AIRBUS (S$5) runs to and from all major hotels 6 AM–midnight. Under normal traffic conditions, the trip the airport by taxi takes 20 to 30 minutes. Fares from S$13 to S$20, plus a S$3 airport surcharge (not applicable for trips *to* the airport, but be wary of taxi drivers who try imposing this charge anyway). Other surcharges apply when baggage is stored in the trunk or when more than two adults travel in the same cab.

CARRIERS

Singapore Airlines (☎ 223–8888), the national carrier, offers direct, one-stop flights from Los Angeles and New York to Singapore. **United** (☎ 220–0711), has direct one-stop flights from Los Angeles, San Francisco, and Seattle, and connecting flights (one stop, with a change in Tokyo) from New York and Chicago.

Among the many other airlines that serve Singapore are: **Air New Zealand** (☎ 535–8266), **British Airways** (☎ 839–7788), **Cathay Pacific Airways** (☎ 533–1333), **China Airlines** (☎ 737–2211), **Garuda Indonesian Airways** (☎ 250–2888), **Japan Airlines** (☎ 221–0522), **Korean Air** (☎ 534–2111), **Northwest Airlines** (☎ 336–3371), **Malaysia Airlines** (☎ 336–6777), **Qantas** (☎ 839–7788), and **Thai Airways International** (☎ 224–9977).

FLYING TIMES

Flying west, Singapore is 22 hours from Chicago, 18 hours from Los Angeles, 17 hours from Vancouver, 10½ hours from Auckland and Christchurch, and 8 hours from Sydney. The flying time east from New York is 19 hours; from London it's 13 hours.

By Boat

There are currently two cruise lines whose ships stop in Singapore en route to points in Malaysia, Indonesia, and Thailand: **Star Cruises** (✉ No. 21-01, Ngee Ann City, Tower B, 391B Orchard Rd., ☎ 733–6388) and **Sun Cruises** (✉ No. 05-02 Lucky Plaza, 304 Orchard Rd., ☎ 830–8800).

Ferrylink (☎ 545–3600 or 733–6744) plies between Changi Point in Singapore and Tanjong Belungkor in the eastern corner of Johor and other places on the coast of peninsular Malaysia. Most check-ins are an hour before sailing time. From Singapore's Tanah Merah Ferry Terminal, **Auto Batam Ferries & Tours** (☎ 542–7105 or 345–1210) offers a four-hour trip to the scuba divers' favorite Malaysian island, Tioman, at 8:30 AM, for about S$160 round-trip. From the same ferry terminal, regular ferries go to the two closest Indonesian islands, Batam and Bintan (☞ *also* Getting Around, *below*).

By Bus

Air-conditioned buses are a convenient way to travel between Singapore and three main destinations in Malaysia. The nearest city to Singapore is Johor Bahru (everyone calls it "JB"). The **Singapore-Johor Bahru**

Express (☎ 292–8149) runs every seven minutes from 6:30 AM to midnight; the cost is only S$2.10 one way. The **Kuala Lumpur–Singapore Express** (☎ 292–8254) leaves daily at 9 AM, 1 PM and 10 PM from Singapore, at S$25 one way, and takes about six hours. The **Malacca–Singapore Express** (☎ 293–5915) takes about 4½ hours, costs S$11 one way, and leaves at 8 AM, 9 AM, 10 AM, 11 AM, 2 PM, 3 PM and 5 PM.

By Car
If you're driving from Malaysia, your Malaysian-registered car must have a valid VEP (Vehicle Entry Permit) during its stay in Singapore. Upon entering Singapore, you can apply for up to five days of VEP at the Land Transport Authority (LTA; ☎ 800/553–5229) booths at Woodlands Checkpoint or Changi Ferry Terminal. Further extensions can be made at the LTA on Sin Ming Drive and at designated post offices. Each car is allowed one free VEP per year for admission and stay during the following times: weekdays 7 PM to 2 AM, Saturday after 3 PM, and all day on Sunday and public holidays. (For more information on driving, ☞ Getting Around, *below*).

By Train
There are regular trains between Singapore and key cities and towns on the western seaboard of Peninsular Malaysia, including Kuala Lumpur (called "KL") and JB. There are three daily departures to JB; the trip takes about an hour and costs roughly S$3. The air-conditioned express train to KL also leaves three times daily. The trip takes about six hours, and the first-class one-way fare is S$60. For further information, call the **Singapore Train Station** (☎ 222–5165).

E&OE Services (☎ 392–3500 or 323–4390), the company that operates the *Venice Simplon–Orient Express,* runs the deluxe *Eastern & Oriental Express;* it travels between Singapore and Bangkok once a week and stops in Butterworth, Malaysia, permitting an excursion to Penang. The 1,943-km (1,200-mi) journey takes 41 hours and includes two nights and one full day on board. The cabin decor is modeled on the Josef von Sternberg–Marlene Dietrich movie *Shanghai Express.* Fares, which vary according to cabin type and include meals, start at S$2,140 per person one way.

Getting Around

By Bicycle-Rickshaw
Once a major way to get around the city, rickshaws are now driven mostly by elderly Chinese, and there are only a few dozen left. You're most likely to find them on Orchard Road in front of the National Museum and at Bugis Junction. Bargain for the fare; you really shouldn't pay more than S$15 for a 45-minute ride. The best time to take a rickshaw ride is early evening, after rush hour.

By Boat
Harbor cruises and ferries to Singapore's outer islands, Malaysia, and the Indonesian Riau islands depart from two locations: the **Singapore Cruise Centre** (✉ World Trade Centre, ☎ 270–3918), a 10-minute drive from the city center, and the **Tanah Merah Ferry Terminal** (✉ Changi Rd., ☎ 345–1210) on Singapore's east coast.

TO SENTOSA ISLAND
Daily ferries ply between the Jardine Steps of the World Trade Centre and Sentosa Island every 15 minutes starting at 9:30 AM; the crossing takes four minutes, and the one-way fare is S$1.30. The last ferry back from Sentosa departs at 9 PM Monday through Thursday; Friday through Sunday and holidays, there are two extra return ferries—one at 11:15 PM, the other at midnight.

Monday through Saturday, two ferries—one at 10 AM and another at 1:30 PM—leave for Kusu from the Singapore Cruise Centre at the World Trade Centre; on Sunday and holidays there are six ferries, with the first departing at 6 AM and the last at 8 PM. The trip takes about 30 minutes and costs S$6.20 each way. The same ferries that go to Kusu run to St. John's, a trip that takes a little over an hour and costs S$6.20.

Bumboats are motorized launches that serve as inexpensive taxis. Sailors use them to shuttle between Singapore and their ships, but you can hire a bumboat for a trip to Pulau Ubin. Take SBS bus 2 from the Tanah Merah MRT station to Changi Point. Then take a bumboat (S$1.50) from the Changi Jetty nearby. To reach Sisters Island, hire a water taxi (S$50 an hour) at the Jardine Steps or Clifford Pier. (Note that water taxis are larger than bumboats and can comfortably accommodate six people.)

Ferries directly to any of the resorts on Bintan leave regularly from Singapore's Tanah Merah Ferry Terminal. The round-trip fare for the 45-minute trip to the island is S$45. Do not go without a hotel reservation and arrangements for land transfer, and remember to bring your passport. Regular ferries to Bintan's main town, Tanjung Pinang, also depart from the Tanah Merah terminal; the trip takes 1½ hours and costs about S$58 round-trip. Companies that offer service include **Auto Bataam Ferries** (☎ 542–7105) and **Bintan Resort Ferries** (☎ 345–1210).

By Bus

During rush hours, buses can be quicker than cabs (and they're always cheaper); there are special lanes along the main roads, and service is frequent—usually every 5 to 10 minutes. The excellent *TransitLink Guide,* available for S$1.40 at any bookstore or subway (MRT) station, pinpoints major stops. Fares range from S$.60 to S$1.20 for buses without air-conditioning and from S$.70 to S$1.50 for those with it. Bus numbers are clearly marked, and most stops have a list of destin·tions with the numbers of the buses that serve them. Deposit exact change, and remember to collect your ticket. Most buses run from 6 AM until around midnight; a few run all night. To reach Sentosa Island by bus, first take one to the World Trade Centre—number 10, 97, 100, or 125 from Shenton Way, or number 65 or 143 from Orchard Road—and transfer there onto a shuttle across the causeway. The S$6 round-trip fare includes admission to the island. Shuttles operate weekdays 7 AM–11 PM (till midnight on weekends).

The Singapore Explorer Bus Ticket (available at major hotels, travel agents, money changers, and convenience stores) lets you travel on any bus operated by Singapore Bus Service (SBS, the red-and-white buses) or Trans Island Bus Service (TIBS, the orange-and-yellow buses). You may embark and disembark as frequently as you like, flashing your pass as you board. A one-day pass costs S$5 and a three-day pass costs S$12.

The Singapore Trolley bus plies between the Orchard Road shopping belt, the colonial district, the Singapore River, Chinatown, the Raffles Hotel, Boat Quay, Clarke Quay, the Marina, and Suntec City. It's expensive (S$9), but it does make 22 stops, and your ticket is good for a full day of unlimited travel. You can buy it (you'll need exact change) when you board or from your hotel concierge.

For all information on bus travel within Singapore, contact the **Singapore Bus Service Passenger Relations Center** (☎ 800/287–2727) or **Singapore Explorer** (☎ 338–6833).

By Cable Car

You can catch a cable car to Sentosa Island from one of two terminals on the Singapore side: the **Cable Car Towers** (☎ 270–8855), next to the World Trade Centre, and the **Mt. Faber Cable Car Station** (☎ 275–0248). The trip from Cable Car Towers starts at the edge of the sea and is shorter than that from Mt. Faber. However, the trip from Mt. Faber offers better views. There's no bus to the Mt. Faber Cable Car Station, and it's a long walk up the hill, so a taxi is the best way to get there. The Cable Car Towers station is accessible by bus: from Orchard Road, take Bus 10 or 143; from Collyer Quay, Bus 10, 20, 30, 97, 125, or 146. Cable cars run regularly Monday–Saturday 8:30 AM–9 PM and Sundays and holidays 9–9; fares are S$6.90 round-trip, S$5.90 one way.

By Car

With the amount of road rules, regulations, tariffs, tolls, and permit requirements that seem to change and expand in Singapore every year, you'd be advised to stick to public transportation. Road congestion (particularly to and from Malaysia) can be harrowing during rush hours and on weekends and holidays. Highway names, tariffs, and all licensing schemes are abbreviated, and this can cause great confusion.

To even out traffic flow into the Central Business District (CBD), all cars entering during the restricted hours of 7:30 AM to 7 PM are required to display a valid ALS (Area Licensing Scheme) license. At ALS checkpoints, a yellow light indicates that a part-day license is required; blue and yellow lights indicate that a full-day license is required.

To relieve congestion during morning peak hours along the expressways, all cars passing through RPS checkpoints (Road Pricing Scheme), must display a valid ALS or RPS license. Gantries are located at East Coast Parkway (ECP) between Fort Road junction and Rochor Road exit; the entry to the ECP from Ophir Road towards Jurong; the Pan-Island Expressway (PIE) towards Jurong near Kallang Way; the entry into the PIE from Kallang Way Central Expressway (CTE) toward the city between Braddell Road and PIE; and the CTE toward the city between Bukit Timah Road and Balestier Road.

One-day ALS and RPS licenses cost S$3 and are available at gas stations, ALS/RPS booths, post offices and 7-Eleven stores.

EMERGENCY ASSISTANCE

The **Automobile Association of Singapore** (AAS; ☎ 748–9911) 24-hour emergency road service.

GASOLINE

Unleaded gas starts at S$1.25 per liter in Singapore. A government ruling requires any car passing the Causeway out of Singapore to drive with at least three-quarters of a tank of gas or be fined; the republic's huge losses in revenue as a result of Singaporeans driving to Malaysia to fill up cheaply led to this unpopular ruling.

PARKING

For visitors, there are two ways of parking: coupon parking and paid parking. Where required, parking coupons should be displayed on the dashboard. Denominations of parking coupons are S$0.45, S$0.90, S$1.80, and S$2 (for overnight parking). Generally, parking rates are S$0.45 per half hour outside the CBD, and S$0.90 per half hour within it. Parking coupons are available from gas stations, post offices, shopping centers, and some shops.

Paid parking is practiced in almost all shopping centers, buildings, and some public parking areas. You basically pay for the amount of time your car is parked. Some shopping centers offer a rebate on your parking charges, as do some hotels.

RENTAL AGENCIES

Rates in Singapore begin at S$65 a day and S$392 a week for an economy car with unlimited mileage. This doesn't include tax on car rentals, which is 3%. The major car-rental companies represented here are Avis, Budget, Hertz, and Sintat. Should you want to look up firms in the Singapore Yellow Pages, check under "Motorcar Renting and Leasing." The following are some local branches of international agencies: **Avis** and **National** (✉ Changi Airport, ☎ 543–2331 or 542–8855; ✉ Boulevard Hotel, 200 Orchard Blvd., ☎ 737–1668), **Budget** (✉ Pan Pacific Hotel, ground floor, ☎ 334–0019), **Hertz** (✉ Changi Airport, Terminal 2, ☎ 542–5300; ✉ Tudor Court Shopping Gallery, 125 Tanglin Rd., ☎ 800/734–4646), and **Sintat** (✉ Changi Airport, Terminal 1, ☎ 542–7288; ✉ 60 Bendemeer Rd., ☎ 295–2211 or 295–6288).

ROAD CONDITIONS

For the most part, road conditions are quite good, especially on the expressways. Some streets have fairly deep ditches and may not be well-lit in the evenings.

RULES OF THE ROAD

Driving is on the left-hand side of the road in both Singapore and Malaysia. A valid driving license from your country of residence or a valid International Drivers Permit is required. Parking coupons (☞ Parking, *above*) should be displayed on the dashboard. The speed limit is 50 kph (31 mph) in residential areas and 80 kph (50 mph) on expressways. Speed cameras are installed throughout the island; fines are comparable to those in, say, New York City or Toronto. Bus lanes or extreme left lanes marked by unbroken yellow lines should not be used by cars during the following hours: weekdays 7:30 AM–9:30 AM and 4:30 PM–7 PM, Saturday 7:30 AM–9:30 AM and 11:30 AM–2 PM.

By Subway

The subway, or MRT, consists of two lines that run north–south and east–west and cross at the City Hall and Raffles Place interchanges. The system includes 42 stations along 67 km (42 mi). All cars and underground stations are air-conditioned, and the trains operate between 6 AM and midnight daily. Like everywhere else in Singapore, there are rules. Durians, the infamous "smelly" fruit of Singapore, aren't allowed on the trains or buses. There are signs posted at all stations listing the fines that can be levied if you are caught smoking, eating, drinking, or littering.

You can buy tickets from booths or vending machines in the stations. Large maps showing the station locations and the fares between them hang above each vending machine. There's a S$2 fine for underpaying, so make sure you buy the right ticket for your destination. The magnetic tickets are inserted in turnstiles to let you on and off the platform. Fares start at S$.70 for about two stations; the maximum fare is S$1.60. The fare between Orchard Road Station and Raffles Place Station (in the business district) is S$.70. The TransitLink fare card, a prepaid mass-transit ticket, lets you travel on trains and on many buses; the fare for each trip is deducted from the balance on the card. You put from S$12 to S$52 (including a S$2 deposit) on the card, which is available at TransitLink sales offices in MRT stations and at bus interchanges. Any unused fare and the deposit can be refunded at TransitLink offices.

For more information contact: **TransitLink** (☎ 800/779–9345), **Singapore Bus Services** (☎ 800/287–2727), or **Singapore MRT Ltd.** (☎ 800/336–8900).

By Taxi

There are more than 15,000 strictly regulated, metered taxis in Singapore. The starting fare is S$2.40 for the first km (0.9 mi) and S$.10 for each subsequent 240 meters (900 ft). After 10 km (6 mi) the rate increases to S$.10 for every 225 meters (820 ft). Every 30 seconds of waiting time carries a S$.10 charge. You can catch cabs at stands or by hailing them from any curb not marked with a double yellow line. Radio cabs are available 24 hours (☎ 481–1211). Often, it's almost impossible to get through to reserve a cab, so it's better to just hail one or take the bus. A driver showing a red disk in the window is returning to his garage and can pick up passengers going only in his direction. Drivers don't expect tips.

Be aware of several surcharges that may apply. A S$3.20 charge is added for taxis booked by phone (there's an additional S$2 surcharge for every booking half an hour or more in advance). Trips made between midnight and 6 AM have a 50% surcharge, and rides from, *not to*, the airport carry a S$3 surcharge. Unless a taxi displays a yellow permit, a S$1.50 surcharge is added to fares from the CBD between 4 and 7 PM on weekdays and noon and 3 PM on Saturdays. To the CBD, there's a S$3 surcharge for the purchase of an Area License, which is needed to enter the Restricted Zone between 7:30 AM and 6:30 PM weekdays, between 7:30 AM and 2 PM Saturday, and on the eve of five major holidays. You don't pay the fee if the taxi already has the sticker. A $1 surcharge is added for all trips in London cabs and station-wagon taxis; an extra 10% of the fare is charged for payment by credit card. On trips to Sentosa Island there's a S$3 toll in addition to the fare, but only between 7 AM and 10 PM; cabs may drop or collect you only at the three island hotels.

Contacts and Resources

Customs and Duties

ON ARRIVAL

Duty-free allowances include 1 liter each of spirits, wine, and beer (applies to visitors over 18); all personal effects; and less than S$50 in foodstuffs such as chocolates, biscuits, and cakes. The following imports are prohibited: drugs; pornography (including such publications as *Playboy* and *Playgirl*); seditious and treasonable materials; toy coins and currency notes; cigarette lighters of pistol/revolver shapes; reproductions of copyrighted publications, videotapes, records, or cassettes; duty-free cigarettes; and chewing gum in amounts deemed large enough for resale. Special import permits are required for animals, live plants, meats, arms, and controlled drugs. (Penalties for drug abuse are very severe in Singapore and rigidly enforced.) Customs is also extremely strict regarding the import of any form of arms, including such items as ceremonial daggers purchased as souvenirs in other countries. These are held in bond and returned to you on your departure. There are no import (or export) restrictions or limitations on the amount of cash, foreign currencies, checks, and drafts.

ON DEPARTURE

Export permits are required for arms, ammunition, explosives, animals, gold, platinum, precious stones and jewelry, poisons, and medicinal drugs. The export of narcotics is punishable by death under Singapore law.

Electricity

The electrical current in Singapore is 220 volts, 50 cycles alternating current (AC), like that in Australia and Great Britain. If you're a resident of North America, bring an adapter and converter; if your appliances are dual voltage, bring just an adapter. Wall outlets take a variety of plug styles, including plugs with two round oversize prongs and plugs with three prongs. Many hotels lend guests adapters and converters.

Embassies and Consulates

Most countries maintain a diplomatic mission in Singapore. Call ahead to confirm hours. If you hope to obtain visas for neighboring countries, be aware that the visa-application process at Singapore consular offices may take several days.

Australia (✉ 25 Napier Rd., ☎ 737–9311). **Canada** (✉ 80 Anson Rd., ☎ 325–3200). **New Zealand** (✉ No. 15/06-10, Tower A, 391A Orchard Rd., ☎ 235–9966). **United Kingdom** (✉ 100 Tanglin Rd., ☎ 473–9333). **United States** (✉ 27 Napier Rd., ☎ 476–9100).

Emergencies

Ambulance and fire: ☎ 995. **Police:** ☎ 999.

Hospitals and doctors: Most hotels have their own doctor on 24-hour call. **Alexandra Hospital** (✉ Alexandra Rd., ☎ 473–5222); **Raffles Medical Group** (✉ 182 Clemenceau Ave., ☎ 331–5888 24-hour clinic/emergency center; 334–3333 SurgiCentre) has 29 clinics and operates the Raffles SurgiCentre, a private hospital on Clemenceau Avenue near the Dhoby Ghaut MRT station; **Singapore General Hospital** (✉ Outram Rd., ☎ 222–3322).**Pharmacies:** Some pharmacies are open until 10 PM, although most close at 6 PM. For more information, contact the Singapore Tourism Board (☞ Visitor Information, *below*).

Sentosa Island Ranger Station: ☎ 279–1155.

English-Language Bookstores

Since English is the lingua franca, all regular bookstores carry English-language books, and there are bookstores (or at least newsstands) in most of the larger shopping centers and major hotels, though selections are often limited. Should you have trouble finding a book, try the **Times Bookstore** (☎ 284–8844 main office), which will tell you whether any of its branches carries the title.

S: ·gapore has a policy of censorship. Certain books and magazines are banned from being sold or even owned. Only one serious English-language newspaper, the *Straits Times,* is published in Singapore. It concentrates on local news but has international coverage as well. Editorially, it speaks for the ruling People's Action Party, and its reporting is highly biased.

Health and Safety

FOOD AND DRINK

Tap water is safe, and every eating establishment—from the most elegant hotel dining room to the smallest sidewalk stall—is regularly inspected by the very strict health authorities.

OTHER PRECAUTIONS

Singapore is a safe place in which to walk around unaccompanied at night. Like everywhere else, however, precautions should be taken after midnight, when subway and bus service stops. Taxis can be flagged, but you'll see more of them in the city center than in the suburbs. During the day, although everyone seems to jaywalk, you do so at your own risk; Singapore drivers don't slow down or stop to let you cross the street. Women aren't normally harassed, but conservative attire is recommended in neighborhoods such as Little India and the Arab District—more out of deference for conservative religious customs than for reasons of personal safety.

Be aware that although you will see garbage on the streets in certain sections of the city, littering is against the law and can nab you a

S$500 fine—don't expect special treatment just because you're a visitor. Similarly, consuming food or drink or smoking on the transit systems (this includes subway platforms) is not allowed. Although chewing gum is not sold anywhere, you may bring it in for personal use—just dispose of it properly!

The rights of gays and lesbians aren't protected in Singapore, so employment and housing discrimination isn't uncommon. There is no gay "neighborhood" per se, although a couple of gay and lesbian bars do exist, unadvertised as such. You may see a nightclub or disco listing in one of the entertainment weeklies mentioning "boys' night," which usually means gays are welcome and will be in the majority. "Women's night" may mean that lesbians are welcome (although "ladies' night" would mean that heterosexual women get in free or receive discounted drinks). It may be confusing, but a sympathetic STB employee should be able to steer you in the right direction. Be discreet, as the "don't ask, don't tell" attitude seems to prevail.

When swimming the waters of Singapore's offshore islands, be aware not only of the water quality but also of the strong undercurrents in some places. If you plan to visit Bintan Island, Indonesia, you'll need to take precautions against malaria. Check with your doctor about medication before you leave home and pack plenty of bug spray. Note, however, that resorts on the island will have netting, insect repellent, and mosquito coils.

Language, Culture, and Etiquette

Singapore is a multiracial society with four official languages: Malay, Mandarin, Tamil, and English. The national language is Malay, but the lingua franca is English. It's used in administration, it's a required course for every schoolchild, and it's used in entrance exams for universities. Hence, virtually all Singaporeans speak English with varying degrees of fluency. Mandarin is increasingly replacing the other Chinese dialects. However, many older Chinese do not speak Mandarin and communicate in "Singlish," a Singaporean version of English that has its own grammar.

You'd do well to bring along a stash of business cards—it seems like everyone exchanges them, even people who are on vacation. It's proper to offer your business card using both hands with the card facing the recipient. Likewise, when a card is offered to you, accept it in both hands and make a point to read the card. This shows your respect for the person's title and position.

Don't use your left hand for shaking or giving something to a Malay or an Indonesian, as both countries are predominantly Muslim. It's also improper for a male to kiss a female acquaintance on the cheek; and a man shouldn't offer his hand to most women until she has offered hers first. Do not be surprised or shocked to see members of the same sex hold hands, link arms, or act affectionate with one another. This is purely social behavior, not sexual.

If you're invited for dinner by Chinese friends or business acquaintances, it's proper etiquette to leave some food on the plate or in the bowl, to indicate your host has been so generous with ordering or preparing the food, you cannot eat any more. It is common for non-Asians to ask for a knife and fork instead of chopsticks. Tea is generally served at the beginning and probably throughout the meal, and it's good form to drink or at least sip the tea.

Mail

POSTAL RATES

Most hotels sell stamps and mail guests' letters. You can buy postage, stationery, and certain types of driving permits at some post offices. Postage on local letters up to 20 grams (0.8 ounces) is S$0.22. Airmail takes about seven business days to reach North America and Great Britain. An airmail postcard costs S$0.50; larger cards are S$1. A letter up to 20 grams is S$.35 to Malaysia or Brunei, S$.40 to other foreign countries. Printed aerogram letters (available at most post offices) are S$.45. Note that delivery of small packets, printed paper, and parcels (both international and domestic mail) isn't regulated; service for such items is provided by several courier companies as well as Singapore Post.

RECEIVING MAIL

If you know which hotel you'll be staying at, have mail sent there marked "Hold for Arrival." American Express cardholders or traveler's-check users can have mail sent care of **American Express International** (⊠ The Concourse, No. 18-01/07, 300 Beach Rd., 199555, ☎ 299–8133). Envelopes should be marked "Client Mail." For more postal information, contact the General Post Office (GPO; ⊠ No. 05-12750 Chai Chee Industrial Park, Chai Chee Rd., 469000, ☎ 448–7733). The new GPO is in the suburbs; a phone inquiry is your best bet.

WRITING TO SINGAPORE

In 1997, Singapore began using a six-digit postal code; it's important to include this on any correspondence. Addresses can be written either with the number and street following the name of the person or company, with the second or third line being used for the name of the building: "XYZ Sales Office, No. 16-00 Cable Car Towers, 3 Maritime Square, Singapore 099254" or "ABC Cable Car (Pte) Ltd., 333 Orchard Rd., No. 03-10 Mandarin Hotel Shopping Arcade, Singapore 238867." Note that in the last address, "03-10" refers to the third floor, office number 10; the abbreviation "Pte" (which is used in many business names) indicates that a company is owned privately rather than by the government.

Money Matters

COSTS

Singapore ranks up there with other world capitals as far as expenses go. Although a gastronomical delight still costs a little less than you would pay in Paris, hotel room prices are in the New York and London ranges. You can keep costs down by eating at hawker food centers, especially those in the major shopping malls, and by using public transportation. Many hotels offer special promotional rates, corporate rates, or weekend rates; always ask about such deals before booking.

Sample Prices: In moderately priced restaurants, expect to pay: cup of coffee, S$2.50–S$3; bottle of beer, S$6–S$9; soft drink, S$2.50; bottle of house wine, S$30; sandwich, S$5. Transportation costs are about: 2-km (1-mi) taxi ride, S$4; city bus ride, S$.70. Museum entrance is generally S$3.

CURRENCY

The local currency is the Singapore dollar (S$), which is divided into 100 cents. Notes in circulation are S$1, S$2, S$5, S$10, S$20, S$50, S$100, S$500, S$1,000, and S$10,000. Coins: S$.01, S$.05, S$.20, S$.50, and S$1. At press time, the exchange rate was S$1 to the Australian dollar, S$1.08 to the Canadian dollar, S$.84 to the New Zealand dollar, S$1.68 to the U.S. dollar, and S$2.87 to the pound sterling.

SERVICE CHARGES, TAXES, AND TIPPING

There's a 3% sales tax, called the GST. You can get the tax refunded at the airport as you leave the country for purchases of more than S$300 made at a store or retail chain displaying the Tax Free for Tourists sticker. (Ask for a Tax Free Shopping Cheque to be completed, and show the goods and the checks at the airport departure terminal for customs inspection. You can cash the checks at the Cash Refund Counters in Changi Airport; opt for a bank check via mail; or ask for a refund to a specific credit card, although a surcharge may be levied for this). This government tax is also added to restaurant and hotel bills, as is a 10% service charge (except by hawker stalls and small restaurants). You're also subject to a S$15 airport departure tax (for travelers to Malaysia, the tax is S$5), which—if it's not already included in the price of your ticket—is payable at the airport (to save time and avoid standing in line, buy a tax voucher at your hotel or any airline office).

Tipping isn't customary in Singapore. It's prohibited at the airport and discouraged in hotels (except for bellboys, who generally receive S$1 per bag) or restaurants that levy the 10% service charge. Unlike in other countries, wait staffs don't receive a percentage of this service charge, except in the more progressive establishments, which need to retain the best waiters and waitresses. Hence, after experiencing some Singapore service you may begin to wish that tipping was the norm. Taxi drivers don't receive tips from Singaporeans, some of whom become upset when they see tourists tip.

Opening and Closing Times

Businesses are generally open weekdays 9 or 9:30 to 5 or 5:30; a few are also open on Saturday morning. In general, **banks** have hours weekdays 10–3 and Saturday 9:30–11:30 AM. However, branches of the Development Bank of Singapore stay open until 3 PM on Saturday, and the bank at Changi Airport is open whenever there are flights. Many **museums** close on Monday; otherwise, they're generally open 9 to 4:30 or 5:30. Registered pharmacists work 9–6, though some **pharmacies** in the major shopping centers stay open until 10 PM. Of the 87 **post offices** on the island, most of them are open weekdays 8:30–5 and Saturday 8:30–1. The branches at the airport post office and in Takashimaya are open daily 8–8. **Shop** opening times vary. Department stores and many shops in big shopping centers are generally open daily from about 10 AM to 9 PM (sometimes later on weekends); smaller shops tend to close on Sunday.

NATIONAL HOLIDAYS

Singapore has 10 public holidays: New Year's Day (Jan. 1), Hari Raya Puasa (Jan. 19, 1999; Jan. 8, 2000), Chinese New Year (Feb. 16 &17, 1999, Feb. 5 &6, 2000), Good Friday (Apr. 2, 1999; Apr. 21, 2000), Hari Raya Haji (Mar. 28, 1999; Mar. 16, 2000), Labor Day (May 1), Vesak Day (May), National Day (Aug. 9), Deepvali (Oct.–Nov.), Christmas (Dec. 25).

Passports and Visas

Visas aren't required for stays of up to 14 days for Canadian, U.K., U.S., Australian, and New Zealand citizens. You may automatically be given a 30-day social visit pass upon your arrival if you come from any of these countries; if you arrive in Singapore from Malaysia, Indonesia, or Thailand, your passport may only be stamped for 14 days. If you require a longer stay, you may apply to **Singapore Immigration** (⌧ 10 Kellang Rd., ☎ 800/391–6400) after your arrival. Women who are in an advanced state of pregnancy (six months or more) should make prior application to the nearest Singapore overseas mission or the Singapore Immigration Department.

To visit Bintan Island, Indonesia, citizens of Great Britain, Canada, the United States, Australia, and New Zealand require only passports for stays of less than one month.

Telephones

CALLS TO SINGAPORE

To call Singapore from overseas, first dial the country code, 65, then the number (Singapore has no area codes). The country code for Indonesia is 62; the area code for Bintan is 771.

LOCAL CALLS

From a pay phone, the cost is S$.10; insert a coin and dial the seven-digit number. Hotels charge anywhere from S$.10 to S$.50 a call. (There are free public phones at Changi Airport, just past immigration.) Many pay phones only accept cards; the coin-operated phones are smaller and frequently found in shopping malls and at information desks. Phone cards (☞ *below*) in a variety of denominations are sold at most kiosks, newsstands, and gift shops. For directory assistance, simply dial 100.

LONG-DISTANCE AND INTERNATIONAL CALLS

To make direct overseas calls dial 011 and then the country code and the number; if you'd like operator assistance, dial 104. To avoid hefty hotel service charges, use the SingTel (Singapore Telecom; ☎ 288–6633) phone card if you plan to make lots of long-distance calls during your stay. The cards are available in denominations of S$2, S$5, S$10, S$20, and S$50 and permit you to make both local and overseas calls. The price of each call is deducted from the card total, and your balance is roughly indicated by the punched hole in the card. Phone cards are available from post offices, some newsstands, SingTel customer services outlet, and drugstores.

To save money on calls to North America or the United Kingdom, use international Home Countries Direct phones—USA Direct or UK Direct. These put you in touch with either an American or a British operator, who places your call, either charging your phone credit card or making the call collect. You'll find these phones at many post offices in the city center. You can also use pay phones by first depositing the S$.10 and then dialing 8000–111–11 to reach a U.S. operator or 8000–440–440 for a British operator. Note also that some public phones at the airport and many at city post offices accept Diners Club, MasterCard, and Visa.

Tour Operators

A wide range of sightseeing tours covers the highlights of Singapore and are a good introduction to the island. Tours can take two hours or the whole day, and prices range from S$28 to S$80. Most are operated in comfortable, air-conditioned coaches with guides and include pickup and return. Tour agencies can also arrange private-car tours with guides; these are considerably more expensive. There's no need to book tours in advance of your visit; they can be easily arranged through the tour desks in hotels. Also, if you're only in Singapore on a six-hour stopover, the tourist board offers free city tours from Changi Airport. See the STB Desk at the airport.

The following companies are recommended: **Gray Line Tours** (☎ 331–8244), **Holiday Tours** (☎ 738–2622), **Malaysia and Singapore Travel Centre** (☎ 737–8877), **RMG Tours** (☎ 220–1661), and **Singapore Trolley** (☎ 339–6833).

Singapore Sightseeing Tour East (☎ 332–3755) has day trips that start and end at Clarke Quay. The "Round Island with Tiger Balm Gardens" excursion includes stops at the Kranji War Memorial and the replica of the Prison Chapel and Museum of Changi Prison. If you want to see the chapel and museum, but don't want to take a full-day trip, try the "Heartlands" half-day tour (S$27 per person) offered by Holiday Tours (☞ *above*).

Although it's easy to get around Sentosa Island on your own, **Sentosa Discovery Tours** (☎ 277–9654 or 275–0248) offers three-hour guided trips that cover the major attractions. The tours commence every 3½ hours, beginning at 9:30 AM; tickets cost S$39.

If your itinerary includes a trip to Bintan Island, Indonesia, book a day with **Riau Island Adventures** (☎ 270–9937 or 270–3397). You can make reservations before leaving Singapore or through the concierge at your resort on Bintan. The company's "Pinang–Penyengat Adventure Cruise" takes you from your hotel by car or bus to Busung, where a traditional Indonesian fishing boat sails you to the bustling old town of Tanjung Pinang. Here, accompanied by a guide, you can shop in the lively marketplace. An hour or so later, you're back on the boat for a traditional Indonesian lunch and a short ride to Pulau Penyengat. As no cars are allowed on this island, you'll be given a bicycle to see the sights. Bring lots of film, sunblock, and water. During the slow cruise back to Busung, you can take a dip in the "swimming net" that's lowered over the side of the boat into the water. The S$100 per person cost for this tour includes lunch and all transportation.

Travel Agencies

BnE Travel Consultants Pte Ltd (✉ No. 05-21, Parklane Shopping Mall, 35 Selegie Rd., 188307, ☎ 339–2123) is well versed in day tours, short side trips from Singapore, and international bookings. (Ask to speak with Mr. Chia and mention the Fodor's Guide.) Many other agencies offer three- and four-day hotel and air excursions to neighboring countries, but you must shop around for the best deal.

Visitor Information

Before leaving home, contact the **Singapore Tourism Board (STB)** in the United States (✉ 590 5th Ave., 12th floor, New York, NY 10036, ☎ 212/302–4861, FAX 212/302–4801, www.singapore-usa.com; ✉ Two Prudential Plaza, 180 N. Stetson Ave., Suite 1450, Chicago, IL 60601, ☎ 312/938–1888, FAX 312/938–0086; ✉ 8484 Wilshire Blvd., Suite 510, Beverly Hills, CA 90211, ☎ 213/852–1901, FAX 213/852–0129); in **Canada** (✉ The Standard Life Centre, 121 King St. W, Suite 1000, Toronto, Ontario M5H 3T9, ☎ 416/363–8898, FAX 416/363–5752, www.singapore-ca.com); in the United Kingdom (✉ Carrington House, 126-130 Regent St., 1st floor, London W1R 5FE, ☎ 0171/437–0033, FAX 0171/734–2191); in **Australia** (✉ 8th floor, St. Georges Ct., 16 St. Georges Terr., Perth, WA 6000, ☎ 8/9325–8511, FAX 8/9221–3864; ✉ Level 11, AWA Building, 47 York St., Sydney, NSW 2000, ☎ 2/9290–2888 or 2/9290–2882, FAX 2/9290–2555); or in **New Zealand** (✉ 43 High St., 3rd floor, Auckland, ☎ 9/358–1191, FAX 9/358–1196).

In Singapore, the **STB** (✉ Tourism Court, 1 Orchard Spring La., Singapore 247729, ☎ 736–6622 or 800/738–3778, www.stb.com.sg; ✉ No. 02–34 Raffles Hotel Arcade, 328 North Bridge Rd., 189673, ☎ 800/334–1335 or 800/334–1336) has a couple of locations with staff members ready to answer any questions you may have and to attend to legitimate complaints. The offices are open daily from 8:30 AM to 7 PM. If you're planning a trip to Bintan Island contact the **Indonesian Tourist Promotion Office** (✉ No. 5–07 Ocean Building, 10 Collyer Quay, Singapore 039192, ☎ 534–2837) for tourist, passport and visa, health, and currency information.

When to Go

With the equator only 129 km (80 mi) to the south, Singapore is usually either hot or very hot. The average daily temperature is 80°F (26.6°C); it usually reaches 87°F (30.7°C) in the afternoon and drops to a cool 75°F (23.8°C) just before dawn. The months from November through January, during the northeast monsoon, are generally the coolest. The average daily relative humidity is 84.5%, though it drops to 65%–70% on dry afternoons.

Rain falls year-round, but the wettest months are November through January. February is usually the sunniest month; December, the most inclement. Though Singapore has been known to have as much as 512.2 mm (20 in) of rainfall in one 24-hour period, brief, frequent rainstorms are the norm, and the washed streets soon dry in the sun that follows.

CLIMATE

Jan.	86F	30C	May	89F	32C	Sept.	88F	31C
	74	23		75	24		75	24
Feb.	88F	31C	June	88F	31C	Oct.	88F	31C
	74	23		75	24		74	23
Mar.	88F	31C	July	88F	31C	Nov.	88F	31C
	75	24		75	24		74	23
Apr.	88F	31C	Aug.	88F	31C	Dec.	88F	31C
	75	24		75	24		74	23

FESTIVALS AND SEASONAL EVENTS

With so many different cultural and religious groups, Singapore is a city of festivals, from the truly exotic to the strictly-for-tourists. The dates and seasons of many of them vary from year to year according to the lunar calendar; contact the STB (☞ Visitor Information, *above*) for details.

Dec.–Jan.: **Ramadan** is the month of daytime fasting among the city's Muslim population. After sunset, stalls on Bussorah Street and around the Sultan Mosque sell a variety of dishes, including Malay rice cakes wrapped in banana leaves, and fragrant puddings.

Jan.–Feb.: **Thaipusam** celebrates the victory of the Hindu god Subramaniam over the demon Idumban. After nightlong ritual purification and chanting, penitents enter a trance and pierce their flesh with knives, steel rods, and fishhooks, which they wear during the festival's spectacular 8-km (5-mi) procession. The procession begins at the Perumal Temple on Serangoon Road, passes the Sri Mariamman Temple on South Bridge Road, and ends at the Chettiar Temple, where women pour pots of milk over the image of Lord Subramaniam. The lunar New Year celebration known as the **Chinese New Year** lasts for 15 days, and most shops and businesses close for about a week. The end of the Chinese New Year is marked by the **Chingay Procession.** Chinese, Malays, and Indians all get into the act for this event. Accompanied by clashing gongs and beating drums, lion dancers lead a procession of stilt-walkers, swordsmen, warriors, acrobats, and characters from Chinese myth and legend. A giant dragon weaves through the dancers in its eternal pursuit of a flaming pearl. Check local newspapers for the parade route, which varies from year to year.

Mar. or Apr.: On the **Birthday of the Saint of the Poor,** the image of Guang Ze Zun Wang is carried from the White Cloud Temple on Ganges Avenue around the neighborhood and back to the temple through streets thronged with devotees. Spirit mediums—their cheeks, arms, and tongues pierced with metal skewers—join the procession.

Apr.: Songkran (April 18) is a traditional Thai water festival that marks the beginning of the year's solar cycle. In Singapore's Thai Buddhist temples, images of Buddha are bathed with perfumed holy water, caged birds are set free, and blessings of water are splashed on worshipers and visitors. The liveliest (and wettest) celebrations are at the Ananda Metyrama Thai temple on Silat Road and the Sapthapuchaniyaram Temple on Holland Road.

May: Vesak Day commemorates the Buddha's birth, Enlightenment, and death. It is the most sacred annual festival in the Buddhist calendar. Throughout the day, starting before dawn, saffron-robed monks chant holy sutras in all the major Buddhist temples and captive birds are set free. Many temples offer vegetarian feasts, conduct special exhibitions, and offer lectures on the Buddha's teachings. Visitors are permitted at any temple; particularly recommended are the Kong Meng San Phor Kark See temple complex on Bright Hill Drive and the Temple of 1,000 Lights on Race Course Road. Candlelight processions are held at some of the temples in the evening.

June: Festival of Arts is an annual international event that features both Asian and Western attractions—concerts, plays, films, Chinese opera—with local and visiting performers. Performances take place throughout the city.

Aug.: National Day, the anniversary of the nation's independence, is a day of processions, fireworks, and dancing. The finest view is from the Padang, where the main participants put on their best show.

Sept.: The Mooncake Festival, a traditional Chinese celebration, is named for special cakes—found for the most part only during this festival—that are the subject of legend. The festival is held on the night of the year when the full moon is thought to be at its brightest. There are lantern-making competitions and special entertainments, including lion and dragon dances. (Locations are published in local newspapers.) Mooncakes—sweet pastries filled with red-bean paste, lotus seeds, nuts, and egg yolks—are eaten in abundance.

Sept.–Oct.: During the nine-day Navarathri Festival, Hindus pay homage to three goddesses. The first three days are devoted to Parvati, consort of Shiva the Destroyer. The next three are for Lakshmi, goddess of wealth and consort of Vishnu the Protector. The final three are for Sarawathi, goddess of education and consort of Brahma the Creator. On all nights, at the Chettiar Temple on Tank Road, there are performances of classical Indian music, drama, and dance from 7 to 10 PM. On the last evening the image of a silver horse is taken from its home in the Chettiar Temple and paraded around the streets. Thousands take part in the procession, best seen at the Sri Mariamman Temple.

Oct.–Nov.: During the Pilgrimage to Kusu Island, more than 100,000 Taoist believers travel to the temple of Da Bo Gong, the god of prosperity. If you want to join in, take one of the many ferries that leave from Clifford Pier.

Nov.: Merlion Week is Singapore's version of Carnival, with food fairs, fashion shows, masquerade balls, and fireworks displays. The events start with the crowning of Miss Tourism Singapore and end with the international Singapore Powerboat Grand Prix.

Nov.–Dec.: Being a multicultural society, Singapore has taken Christmas to heart—and a very commercial heart it is. All the shops are deep in artificial snow, and a Chinese Santa Claus appears every so often to encourage everyone to buy and give presents, which they do with zest. A lighting ceremony takes place on Orchard Road during the last 10 days of November.

6 Thailand

A dynamic economy and an energetic people whose traditions are rooted in centuries of culture make Thailand the fulcrum of Southeast Asia. No other country in the region has so well combined a rush toward industrialization with a genuine reverence for heritage. Pristine mountain jungles and idyllic virgin beaches contrast with sleazy beach resorts and red-light districts, and amid the sensory kaleidoscope of the capital peaceful temple complexes and wonderful hotels are islands of calm.

By Nigel Fisher

THE KINGDOM OF THAILAND is unique among Southeast Asian nations in having developed its culture independently of Western colonialism. Thailand's origins may reach as far back as 5,600 years to the world's oldest Bronze Age civilization. Much later, from the 6th to the 13th centuries, known as the Dvaravati period, people from the southern Chinese province of Yunnan moved into the fertile basin of the Chao Phraya River. The Sukhothai period began when two Siamese chieftains banded together, captured the Khmer outpost of Sukhothai, and established the first Thai kingdom in 1238. Early in the Sukhothai period, Thailand's first great king, Ramkhamhoeng, came to power. Not only was he an outstanding warrior, but he made two lasting and significant contributions to Thai culture. He revised and adapted the Khmer alphabet to the requirements of the Thai language, and he invited Ceylonese monks to purify the Khmer-corrupted Theravada (sometimes called Hinayana) Buddhism and establish the religion in a form that is, for the most part, still practiced today.

By 1350, Sukhothai's strength had waned sufficiently for the rising and dynamic young state of Ayutthaya to usurp the reins of power. For four centuries and 33 kings, Ayutthaya was the heart and brain of Thailand. In the 1650s, the city's population exceeded that of London and—according to many foreign travelers—with its golden spires, waterways, and roads, it was the most glorious capital not just in Asia, but in all the world.

In 1766 the Burmese attacked the city. After a 15-month siege, they finally captured Ayutthaya and plundered it. Golden Buddhas were melted down, treasuries ransacked, and buildings burned. Thais who were unable to escape were killed or sent into slavery; by the time the Burmese left, Ayutthaya's population had dropped from 1 million to 10,000.

Under General Taksin, the Thais regrouped, established a capital on the Chao Phraya River at Thonburi (opposite present-day Bangkok), and set about successfully expelling the Burmese from Thailand. In 1782, Chao P'ya Chakri, a supporter of General Taksin, who had briefly been crowned king, became the first king of the current Chakri dynasty. (The present monarch, King Bhumibol Adulyadej, is the ninth in the line.) One of the first acts of P'ya Chakri, or Rama I (all kings of the Chakri dynasty are given the title Rama), was to move the Thai capital to Bangkok.

During the past 200 years, Thailand has had two prime concerns: staving off foreign encroachment on its sovereignty and restructuring its society to meet the demands of modern industrialism. Despite the economic crisis and devaluation of its currency in 1998, Thailand has managed to succeed quite well with both.

Western powers were first welcomed when they arrived in 1512, but the French (from whom the Thai word *farang,* meaning foreigner, is derived) tried to overthrow the legitimate government and install a puppet regime. The result was that the Thais not only threw out the French, but also closed their doors to all outsiders until the middle of the 19th century. When the West again threatened Thailand's sovereignty, King Mongkut (Rama IV, 1851–68) kept the colonial forces at bay through a series of adroit treaties. His efforts were continued by King Chulalongkorn (Rama V, 1868–1910). Thai independence was eventually secured by the cession to the British of a little of what is now Malaysia and to the French of a little of Cambodia.

Thailand

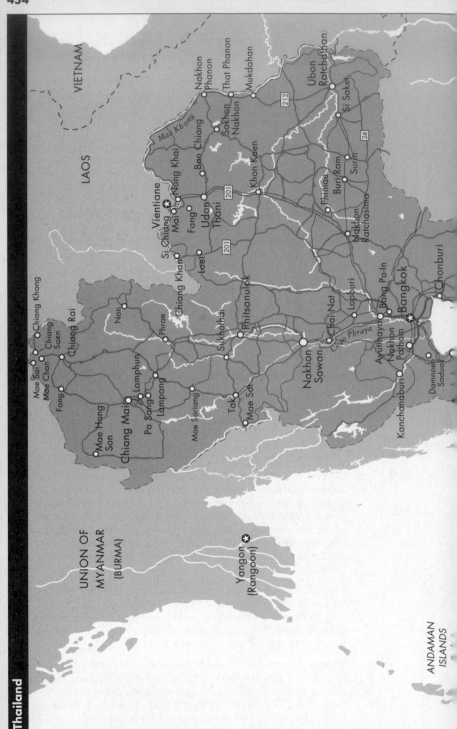

VIETNAM

LAOS

Mae Khong

Nakhon
Phanon

That Phanon

Mukdahan

212

Ubon
Ratchathani

Si Saket

Sakhon
Nakhon

Ban Chiang

Vientiane

Nong Khai

24

Udon
Thani

Khon Kaen

201

Si Chiang
Mai

Fang

Phimai

Buri Ram

Surin

Chiang Khan

Loei

201

Nakhon
Ratchasima

Chiang Khong

Nan

Chiang
Saen

Chiang Rai

Chiang Rai

Phrae

Chiang Rai

Sukhothai

Phitsanulok

Chai Nat

Lopburi

Bang Pa-In

Bangkok

Chonburi

Mae Sai

Mae Chan

Fang

Lamphun

Lampang

Chao Phraya

Nakhon
Sawan

Ayutthaya

Mae Hong
Son

Chiang Mai

Pa Sang

Mae Sariang

Tak

Mae Sot

Nakhon
Pathom

Damnoen
Saduak

Kanchanaburi

UNION OF
MYANMAR
(BURMA)

Yangon
(Rangoon)

ANDAMAN
ISLANDS

CAMBODIA

VIETNAM

Phnom Penh

Chantaburi

Trat

Rayong

Pattaya

Ko Chang

Ko Samet

Gulf of Thailand

MALAYSIA

Saduck

Petchaburi

Cha Am

Hua Hin

Ko Phai

Prachuap Khiri Khan

Ko Tao

Ko Pha Ngan

Ko Samui

Nakhon Si Thammarat

Thung Song

Songkhla

Pattani

ISTHMUS OF KRA

Chumphon

Ataihong Marine N.P.

Surat Thani

Trang

Hat Yai

Satun

Langkawi

Ranong

Phang Nga

Krabi

Phuket

SEE INSET

Andaman Sea

Similan Islands

ISLANDS (India)

Thap Put

Ao Luk Nua

Khlong Sai

Thung

Krabi

Khlong Chon

Phang Nga

Laem Sak

Ao Luk

Chong Phli

Ao Nang

Thung Maphrao

Phang Ngo

Khok Kloi

Phang Nga Bay

Suan Maphrac

Muang Mai

Phak Chit

Thalang

Lum Fuang

Sapam

Phuket

Ko Phuket

Kata

Phuket Bay

Phi Phi Islands

402

4

4

N

100 miles

150 km

Thailand's other concern was adapting to modern social pressures. Under King Chulalongkorn, slavery was abolished, hospitals and schools were established, and some upper-class Thais received a European education so they could replace Western advisers. Under King Prajadhipok (Rama VII, 1925–35), the world's economic depression brought its share of discontent to Thailand. The pressure for sweeping reform ended in 1932 with the military demanding the establishment of a constitutional monarchy on lines similar to that of Great Britain. Since then, quasimilitary governments and a strong bureaucracy have administered the country. Changes in government have been by coup as often as by election. Despite such occasional upheavals, the nation's policies have been remarkably consistent in fostering the expansion of the industrial economy. But in their increasing affluence, Thais are developing a desire for pluralistic representation and accepting less the dictates of unelected officials.

Throughout all this, the monarchy, which has enormous respect at all levels of society, has been a powerful stabilizing influence (it is an indictable offense to show disrespect for the monarch). The much-loved king is seen as the father of the nation, and the queen has won the heart of every Thai. This trust and respect for the royal family had a calming effect during the democracy demonstrations that brought down the military-backed government in 1992, and in the time of the economic woes of 1998. They bind Thai society and permit the nation, unlike any other in Asia, to progress peacefully into the 21st century.

Pleasures and Pastimes

Architecture

No country is an island free from external influence, and over its 1,000-year history Thailand, though staving off modern colonial rule, has been the beneficiary of many architectural and artistic styles. It is graced with the leavings of the early Lanna culture, of the Khmer empire, and with the classic Thai architecture of its Buddhist temples.

Beaches

Thailand's two shorelines, along the Gulf of Thailand and the Andaman Sea, lie slowly steaming below the Tropic of Cancer, a sun-worshiper's dream come true. The beaches come in every flavor: there are lively scenes with bars, discos, and Jet Skis; quiet coves with luxury hotels; islands with thatched bungalows; resorts for families; and stretches of sands with no footprints at all.

Dining

Food to the Thais is a consuming passion: they constantly eat and snack except when they're actually asleep. Throughout the day, a succession of corner food carts replaces one another, each vendor stirring up a different tasty morsel, depending on the time of day. The range of Thai cuisine is vast; no restaurant worth its salt has fewer than 100 dishes on its menu. There are regional differences and specialties and, of course, seasonal delights. Thais know that eating out can be cheaper than eating in, and that inexpensive restaurants often serve food that's as good as, and sometimes better than, the fare at fancy places. The best roast duck in Bangkok, for instance, comes from a tiny hole-in-the-wall and costs *very* little, rice included. And though some Thai food is as hot as the fires of hell, an equal number of dishes are mild—and the hot ones can be tempered. Thai food can easily become your passion too, if not second to none at least second to one.

Price categories throughout the chapter are based on the following ranges:

CATEGORY	COST*
$$$$	over B800 (over US$20)
$$$	B400–B800 (US$10–US$20)
$$	B160–B400 (US$4–US$10)
$	under B160 (under US$4)

*per person, including service charge; a 8% government tax (VAT) is added
to restaurant bills*

Lodging

In no other country does the visitor have such a range of accommodation. On one of the finest beaches in the world, a few dollars can get you a bed cocooned in a mosquito net, in a wood hut under a thatched roof. On another beach of equal perfection you can dwell in such luxury and beauty that five-star hotels on the French Riviera pale in comparison. Though you could become jaded, taking such luxury for granted, you'll not forget the smiling attentive service. In the "smaller" provincial capitals, a clean air-conditioned room with private bath should be your expectation. If you spend only $15–$20, you'll get a smaller room with flaking plaster, gurgling plumbing, and instead of air-conditioning a rhythmically wobbling fan.

Price categories throughout the chapter are based on the following ranges:

CATEGORY	COST*
$$$$	over B6,400 (over US$160)
$$$	B4,000–B6,400 (US$100–US$160)
$$	B2,400–B4,000 (US$60–US$100)
$	B800–B2,400 (US$20–US$60)
¢	under B800 (under US$20)

per double room, including service and tax

Massage

Every visit to Thailand should include a massage or two—and they come in many different varieties. Aside from those that promise lots of bubbles, soap, and full body contact, they range from gentle kneading of the muscles to joint-breaking pulls. The most famous place for a massage is Bangkok's Wat Po; you'll get the most expensive one at Bangkok's Oriental Hotel, the most gentle and soothing at Bangkok's Regent hotel. Those offered at the beach resorts tend to be a cross between soothing and traditional. The traditional massage (*nuat boroan*) aims to release blocked channels of energy and uses methods similar to Shiatsu and reflexology. Joint pains and headaches can be eased, but it's also invigorating.

Shopping

You can get hooked on shopping in Thailand—everything is for sale and there are so many places to look. Bangkok has fancy shopping centers and department stores, antiques and crafts shops, markets and street vendors. There are watches with recently affixed "Rolex" or "Cartier" trademarks and T-shirts with a crocodile slightly askew. Negotiated prices are irresistibly low. In many large cities and resorts, visiting the Night Market is part of an evening's entertainment. Except for imported electronics and luxury goods, Thailand's prices, though not duty-free, are considerably lower than Singapore's or Hong Kong's.

Trekking

The forested hills north and west of Chiang Mai would make for good trekking just for their misty, rugged beauty. But here you can take treks of a day or longer to visit isolated villages that are home to the hill tribes, ethnic groups who migrated from Burma and China, and who have kept their traditions over the last two centuries.

Exploring Thailand

It is in Bangkok that we begin, as do most visitors to Thailand. The capital city, equidistant from the country's four corners, is in position to become the hub of Southeast Asia. A number of points of interest lie within a day's striking distance of Bangkok. To the west, through forested hills close to the Burmese border, flows the River Kwai, known for its infamous bridge. North up the Chao Phraya River stand the ruins of Ayutthaya, the ancient, glorious capital, and the Khmer-influenced buildings at Lopburi. To the southwest are the floating market at Damnoen Saduak and Nakhon Pathom, where Buddhism first found a home in Thailand. And down both sides of the Gulf of Thailand lie convenient beach resorts.

The vast middle of Thailand stretches from the Burmese border to those of Laos and Cambodia. In the Central Plains stand the restored and partially rebuilt palaces and temples of Thailand's first capital, Sukhothai, and its satellite town, Sri Satchanalai. An hour east of Sukhothai is the busy transportation hub of Phitsanulok, and east of there lies the vast agricultural Northeast, often referred to as the "I-san." Along I-san's southern border are scattered grand sanctuaries and palaces left behind by the 13th-century Khmer empire.

The unofficial capital of Northern Thailand is Chiang Mai, whose cultural traditions matured apart from those of the central region. Its temple architecture stems from the Lanna kingdom, which preceded the Thai nation; its food is zestier; its language is slower; and its rivers are faster flowing. Northern Thailand is hilly, forested, and has stretches of no-man's-land on the Burmese border where the opium poppy grows. Throughout these forests live seven ethnic groups known collectively as the Hill Tribes. Today they maintain a village life independent of mainstream Thailand.

Beach resorts line the skinny peninsula stretching south from Bangkok to the Malaysia border. For now, three areas: Phuket, on the Andaman Sea; Krabi on the western shore facing it; and Ko Samui, an island in the Gulf of Thailand, have exploited nature's potential, but on these long coastlines the possibilities are endless.

Great Itineraries

IF YOU HAVE 7 DAYS

Spend your first two days in **Bangkok.** Start your first day with the most famous of all Bangkok sights, the Grand Palace, then go on to the gorgeously ornate Wat Phra Keo and Bangkok's oldest and largest temple, Wat Po. Explore Chinatown and visit Wat Traimitr, the Temple of the Golden Buddha. At the Chao Phraya, catch a river bus to the Oriental Hotel and have a cup of tea. In the evening, walk bustling Silom Road to check out the vendor stalls and catch a dinner show of Thai dancing. Next day, go to Wat Benjamabophit, which contains Bangkok's much-photographed Marble Temple. Spend the afternoon in the National Museum to gain an overview of Thai history and art. In the evening explore Bangkok's nightlife.

On the third day go to **Ayutthaya,** the glorious former capital. If you intend to head south to a beach resort next, travel to Ayutthaya by bus and return to Bangkok the same day by boat down the Chao Phraya River. For your remaining four days, enjoy sun, sea, and sand at a resort on **Phuket** or **Ko Samui,** both of which are short flights from Bangkok.

If you would rather spend your final days seeing more of Thailand's history and landscape, use your fourth day to continue north by train or bus to **Chiang Mai.** On the fifth day explore the wats of the inner city and in the afternoon check out the craft stores along Sankamphaeng Road. In the evening have a Thai massage, followed by a *khantoke* (northern Thai) dinner and cultural show. On the sixth day rise early and go to Wat Phrathat Doi Suthep, a temple on a mountain overlooking Chiang Mai. In the afternoon see Wat Chedi Yot and the **National Museum.** For the evening's entertainment go to the Night Bazaar. On your final day take an excursion south to the ancient wats at **Lamphun,** and buy cottons at **Pa Sang.**

IF YOU HAVE 10 DAYS

Spend your first two days in **Bangkok** and your third in **Ayutthaya.** Beach lovers can then head south to spend the remainder of their trip at southern beach resorts. If you go overland, break the 12- to 14-hour trip to **Ko Samui** or the Andaman Sea Resorts—**Phuket, Krabi,** and **Ko Phi Phi**—with a night or two at the adjoining Gulf Coast resort towns of **Hua Hin** and **Cha' Am;** or fly straight to Phuket and make the six-hour land/boat crossing to Ko Samui.

If you head north from Ayutthaya on your fourth day, spend the fifth and sixth days covering the major sights of **Chiang Mai**—not forgetting to shop and have a massage. On the seventh day fly to **Mae Hong Son** and make a three-day, two-night trek among the hill tribes. Or travel by raft to **Chiang Rai,** and spend the remaining days relaxing in nearby **Sop Ruak** and exploring the **Golden Triangle.**

IF YOU HAVE 14 DAYS

With a full two weeks you have plenty of options. After spending your first three days in and around **Bangkok,** you could devote your time to some of Thailand's less-developed paradises, like the Gulf Coast's **Ko Chang;** or **Ko Pha Ngan and Ko Tao,** north of Ko Samui; or **Ao Nang,** near Krabi, on the Andaman Sea. You could also combine the best of both worlds: travel north from Bangkok to Ayutthaya and Chiang Mai during the first week, then fly south to **Phuket** or another of the southern resorts for the latter half of your trip.

To see more of Thailand's heartland, however, visit the central plains and I-san. After visiting Ayutthaya and returning to Bangkok by boat, take the night train or an early morning flight to **Nakhon Ratchasima,** or Korat, which you'll use as your base for the fourth and fifth days. Take a day trip to **Prasat Hin Phimae** to visit the late-11th-century Khmer sanctuary. In the evening be sure to go to Korat's Night Bazaar. On the fifth day take a car or bus to **Prasat Him Khao Phanom Rung,** a supreme example of 12th-century Khmer architecture. On the sixth day either take a direct bus or fly via Bangkok to **Phitsanulok** and spend the night there. On the seventh and eighth days visit **Old Sukhothai,** then continue north to explore Chiang Mai and its surroundings for the rest of the trip.

When to Tour Thailand

November through March is the best time to be in Bangkok. The city is at its coolest—85°—and driest. The Andaman Sea (Phuket, Krabi, and environs) has two seasons. From May through October (monsoon season), hotel prices are considerably lower, but rough seas can make some beaches unsafe for swimming. The peak season is the dry period, from November through April. The rains hit Ko Samui from late October through December, when prices drop by as much as 40%, and its peak season runs from January through early July.

The central and northern part of Thailand has three seasons. The best time to visit is winter. From November to March the weather is cool in the hills at night. The region is hottest and driest from March to May—rather unbearably hot on the plains—and the rainy season, from June to October, makes unpaved roads difficult, especially during September.

Numbers in the text correspond to numbers in the margin and on the maps.

BANGKOK

A foreigner's reaction to Bangkok is often as confused as the city's geography. Bangkok has no downtown, and the streets, like the traffic, seem to veer off in every direction. The oldest quarter clusters along the eastern bank of the Chao Phraya River, which snakes between Bangkok and Thonburi, where the capital was first established after the fall of Ayutthaya in 1767. There's even confusion about the city's name. Though to Thais it is Krung Thep, the City of Angels, foreigners call it Bangkok. When King Rama I moved his capital in 1782 from Thonburi across the Chao Phraya, he chose a site that foreign vessels knew from their navigational charts as the village of Bangkok. This settlement—dominated by the Royal Palace and bordered by the Chao Phraya and semicircular *klongs* (canals)—is called Ratanakosin and is today a jumble of streets that lead to palaces, government buildings, temples, and museums.

In the last 20 years, this city has changed enormously. Before the Vietnam War, and before Bangkok became *the* R&R destination for American servicemen, it had a population of 1.5 million. Then, as U.S. dollars attracted the rural poor and development began, it grew to 8 million, 40 times the size of any other city in Thailand. Nowadays, space in which to live and breathe is inadequate. Air pollution is among the worst in the world (policemen directing traffic are now required to wear masks). Building is going on everywhere; Bangkok is often described as the world's largest construction site. Constant traffic jams the streets and *sois* (side streets and alleys), and no cure is in sight. Despite new expressways and an overhead electric train that may be completed, at long last, by the year 2000, it seems unlikely that improvements to Bangkok's infrastructure can catch up with the increasing demands of the 21st century.

Yet, while hurtling headlong into the modern world, Bangkok strangely gives you a sense of history and timelessness, perhaps because King Rama I set out to build a city as beautiful as old Ayutthaya before the Burmese sacked it. Bangkok's contrasts require an adjustment on your part, but amid the chaos you soon come to appreciate the gentle nature of the Thais and their genuine respect for other people.

Exploring Bangkok

Because confusion is part of Bangkok's fascination, learning your way around is a challenge. It may help to think of Bangkok as an isosceles triangle with the base abutting the S curve of the Chao Phraya and the apex, pointing east, ending down Sukhumvit Road, somewhere around Soi (lane) 40.

Sukhumvit, at the apex of this conceptual triangle, was once a residential neighborhood. In the last decade, it has developed into a district of hotels, shops, nightclubs, and restaurants while retaining some of its warm, residential atmosphere. In this area, the new Bangkok Conference Centre is attracting more hotels and commercial enterprises. Indeed, ever since Ramkhamhaeng University opened in the 1970s, Bangkok has sprawled even farther east. Now the area known as Bangkapi has become a satellite town, attracting industry and residential complexes.

Westward, toward the Chao Phraya, you come to spacious foreign embassy compounds, offices of large corporations, and modern international hotels. To some this is Bangkok's center, symbolized by the Erawan shrine, where everyday Thais pay respect and traditional dancers perform. Slightly farther west, stores, offices, and more hotels are more closely packed. Now you reach the older sections of Bangkok. On the southern flank runs Silom Road, a shopping and financial district; Suriwongse Road, with more hotels, parallels it; and between them lies the entertainment district of Patpong. Continue farther and you reach the riverbank and three of the leading hotels: the Sheraton Orchid, the Oriental, and the Shangri-La.

Going west along Rama I Road in the center of the triangle, you pass the Siam Square shopping area and the National Stadium. Continue south toward the Hualamphong Railway Station, and between it and the river lies Chinatown, a maze of streets containing restaurants, goldsmiths, small warehouses, and repair shops.

In the northern part of the triangle, moving westward, you pass through various markets before reaching Thai government buildings, the Victory Monument, Chitlada Palace, the Dusit Zoo, the National Assembly, the National Library, and, finally, the river. Slightly south of this route, you can go west from the Democracy Monument to the National Museums and Theatre near the river, and then south to the Grand Palace, and Wat Phra Keo (the Temple of the Emerald Buddha).

Knowing your exact destination, its direction, and approximate distance are important in negotiating tuk-tuk fares and planning your itinerary. (But note that many sights have no precise written address.) Crossing and recrossing the city is time-consuming; many hours can be spent in frustrating traffic jams. Above all, remember that Bangkok is enormous and distances are great; it can take a half hour or more to walk between two seemingly adjacent sites.

Old Bangkok Along the Chao Phraya

Bangkok's major sightseeing attractions—the state palace and many of the famous, highly revered temples—are within a short distance of the Chao Phraya River in the part of Bangkok that was founded in 1782. Chinatown is also here. On the tour described below you'll experience one of Bangkok's greatest pleasures—after getting good and hot from looking at a temple or two, you'll be refreshed by crossing the cool Chao Phraya on a ferryboat before tackling another.

A GOOD TOUR

Start at the **Grand Palace** ①, Bangkok's major landmark, and go on to the adjoining **Wat Phra Keo** ② (Temple of the Emerald Buddha). Walk south from the Grand Palace on Sanamchai Road (or take a taxi) to **Wat Po** ③ (or Wat Phra Jetuphon) with its Temple of the Reclining Buddha. From Wat Po, walk west to the river and then north (toward the Grand Palace) about 250 yards to the Tha Thien jetty, to take the ferry across to **Wat Arun** ④, the Temple of the Dawn. Return by the same ferry to the eastern shore and take a tuk-tuk to **Chinatown.** Get out at Pahurat Road, and as you take in the sights, walk east, then zigzag left to Yaowarat Road, and continue east until it leads into Charoen Krung. There, on the opposite corner stands **Wat Traimitr** ⑤ (Temple of the Golden Buddha).

TIMING

This is a full day's sightseeing. Ideally, you would begin early in the morning, take a break for lunch to escape the heat of midday, and end the excursion in the late afternoon. Most sites are open every day 8–5, but the Grand Palace and Wat Phra Keo are open daily 8:30–11:30 and

Exploring Bangkok

TO DON MUANG AIRPORT

i Rd.

Klong Samsen

Rajvithi Rd.

Rama 6 Rd.

Phayathai Rd.

Victory Monument

Sri Ayudhaya Rd.

TO AIRPORT

Dindaeng Rd.

Rajaprarop Rd.

Express Way

Phraram Kao (Rama 9)

Rajadapisek Rd.

Royal City Ave. (RCA)

KEY

AE American Express Office

— Rail Lines

- - - River Bus

— Expressways

0   500 yards

0   500 meters

16

Phetchburi Rd.

AE

17

Pharam Nung (Ruma 1 Rd.)

National Stadium

Phayathai Rd.

Siam Square

Pratunam Market

Klong San Sab

New Phetchburi Rd.

World Trade Centre

Ploenchit Rd.

British Embassy

Soi 11

Soi 13

Soi 15

Rajdamri Rd.

Henri Dunant Rd.

Regent Hotel

Witthayu (Wireless Rd.)

Sarasin Rd.

American Embassy

S. 21 Soi Asoke

Soi 23

Sci 31

Sukhumvit Rd.

Soi 39

Phraram See (Rama 4 Rd.)

LUMPHINI PARK

iphraya Rd.

Suriwongse Rd.

Patpong 1

Patpong 2

Silom Rd.

N. Sathorn Rd.

S. Sathorn Rd.

Soi Suanplu

Rd.

Express Way

Soi 20

Soi 24

Soi 26

TO EKKAMAI BUS TERMINAL

Phraram See (Rama 4 Rd.)

Aj-Narong

Immigration Office

Rd.

18 **19**

N

1–3:30. You might spend as much as 90 minutes at each. Wat Po, which opens at 7 AM, will only take a half hour, unless you have an hour-long massage. Allow time to climb the prang (tower) at Wat Arun (unless you suffer from vertigo). Chinatown is a maze of streets and markets, so two hours wandering through here can pass by quickly, though non-shoppers may find 30 minutes sufficient. During Chinese New Year much of Chinatown closes down. Wat Traimitr can be a 15-minute stop, or you might like to sit there a while and restore your spirit.

SIGHTS TO SEE

Chinatown. With its tall buildings, Chinatown used to be Bangkok's prosperous downtown, but, as the city grew, new, taller office buildings sprang up farther east, and the neighborhood lost some of its bustle and excitement. Red lanterns and Chinese signs still abound, and modest restaurants line the streets. Pahuraht Road is full of textile shops, with nearly as many Indian dealers here as Chinese, and Yaowarat Road, the main thoroughfare, is crowded with gold and jewelry shops. The Thieves Market, at the northwest end of Yaowarat Road, was once a place for antiques bargains but is still fun to browse through, though it has become more utilitarian in its wares.

❶ **Grand Palace.** In 1782, when King Rama I moved the capital from Thonburi, across the Chao Phraya, he built this palace and walled city, which subsequent Chakri monarchs enlarged. The compound is open to visitors, but all the buildings, which are used only for state occasions and royal ceremonies, are not. The official residence of the king—he actually lives at Chitlada Palace in north Bangkok—is the Chakri Maha Prasart palace, whose state function rooms are sometimes open to visitors. The Dusit Maha Prasart, on the right, is a classic example of palace architecture, and Amarin Vinichai Hall, on the left, the original audience hall, is now used for the presentation of ambassadors' credentials. Note the glittering gold throne. ✏ *Admission.* ⊙ *Daily 8:30–11:30 and 1–3:30.*

❹ **Wat Arun.** Wat Arun means "Temple of the Dawn," and at sunrise, it is inspiring. It is even more marvelous toward dusk, however, when the setting sun casts its amber tones. The temple's architecture is symmetrical, with a square courtyard containing five Khmer-style prangs (stupas)—the central prang (282 ft) surrounded by its four attendant prangs in the corners. All five are covered in mosaics of broken Chinese porcelain. The energetic climb the steep steps of the central prang for the view over the Chao Phraya, and the less ambitious linger in the small park by the river, a peaceful spot where you can take in the sights and smells and watch the sun go down. ✉ *West side of Chao Praya.* ✏ *Admission.* ⊙ *Daily 8–5:30.*

★ ❷ **Wat Phra Keo** (Temple of the Emerald Buddha). No building within the Royal Palace compound excites such awe as the adjoining royal chapel, the most sacred temple in the kingdom. No other wat in Thailand is so ornate and so embellished with murals, statues, and glittering gold. As your wat experience grows, you may decide that you prefer the simplicity of some other wats, but you'll never quite get over Wat Phra Keo's elaborate richness.

As you enter the compound, take note of the 20-ft-tall helmeted and tile-encrusted statues in traditional Thai battle attire standing guard and surveying the precincts. They set the scene—mystical, majestic, and awesome. Turn right as you enter, and notice along the inner walls the lively murals (recently restored) depicting the whole *Ramayana* epic (*Ramakien* in Thai).

The main chapel, with its gilded, glittering, three-tier roof, dazzles your eyes. Royal griffins stand guard outside, and the perfect symmetry of the shining gold stupas in the court establish a feeling of serenity. Inside sits the Emerald Buddha. This most venerated image of the Lord Buddha is carved from one piece of jade 31 inches high. No one knows its origin, but history places it in Chiang Rai in 1464. From there it traveled first to Chiang Mai, then to Lamphun, and finally back to Chiang Rai, where the Laotians stole it and took it home with them. Eventually, the Thais sent an army into Laos to get it back, and it reached its final resting place when King Rama I built the chapel. The statue is high above the altar and visitors can see it only from afar. Behind the altar and above the window frames are murals depicting the life and eventual enlightenment of the Lord Buddha.

At the back of the royal chapel you'll find a scale model of Angkor Wat. As this complex, in Cambodia, is difficult to reach nowadays, this is a chance to sense the vastness of the old Khmer capital. 🔲 *Admission.* ⊙ *Daily 8:30–11:30 and 1–3:30.*

Just east of the Grand Palace compound is the **City Pillar Shrine**, containing the foundation stone (Lak Muang) from which all distances in Thailand are measured. The stone is believed to be inhabited by a spirit that guards the well-being of Bangkok.

★ ❸ **Wat Po, or Wat Phra Jetuphon** (Temple of the Reclining Buddha). The largest temple in Bangkok, Wat Po is famous, in part, for housing the largest—151 ft—reclining Buddha in the country. Especially noteworthy are his 10-ft feet, inlaid in mother-of-pearl with the 108 auspicious signs of the Lord Buddha.

Walk beyond the chapel containing the Reclining Buddha and enter Bangkok's oldest open university. A hundred years before Bangkok was established as the capital, a monastery was founded to teach classical Thai medicine. The school still gives instruction in the natural methods of healing. Around the walls are marble plaques inscribed with formulas for herbal cures, and stone sculptures squat in various postures demonstrating techniques for relieving pain.

The monks still practice ancient cures, and the **massage school of Wat Pho** has become famous. The massage (B200) lasts one hour, growing more and more pleasurable as you adjust to it. Masseurs and masseuses are available daily 8–6.

Don't be perturbed by the tall statues that good-naturedly poke fun at farangs (Westerners). Referred to as Chinese rock sculptures, these gangling twice life-size figures depict the most evil demons, which scare away all other evil spirits. With their top hats, they look farcically Western and, in fact, were modeled after the Europeans who plundered China during the Opium Wars.

These statues guard the entrance to the northeastern quarter of the compound and a very pleasant three-tier temple containing 394 seated Buddhas. Usually, a monk sits cross-legged at one side of the altar, making himself available to answer questions (in Thai). On the walls, bas-relief plaques salvaged from Ayutthaya depict stories from the *Ramayana*. Around this temple area are four tall *chedis* (Thai-style pagodas where holy relics are kept), decorated with brightly colored porcelain, each representing one of the first four kings of the Chakri (present) dynasty. 🔲 *Admission.* ⊙ *Daily 7–5.*

NEED A BREAK?	When you're ready for refreshment, try the pleasant **snack bar** in the northeastern part of the compound, where the fare includes delicious chilled coconut milk.

★ ❺ **Wat Traimitr** (Temple of the Golden Buddha). The main temple of Wat Traimitr has little architectural merit, but off to the side, next to the money-changing wagon, is a small chapel containing the world's largest solid-gold Buddha, cast about nine centuries ago. Weighing 5½ tons and standing 10 ft high, the statue gleams with such richness and purity that even the most jaded are inspired by its strength and power (and value). The statue, sculpted in Sukhothai style, is believed to have been brought first to Ayutthaya. When the Burmese were about to sack the city, it was covered in plaster, and two centuries later, still in plaster, it was regarded as just another statue. When it was being moved to a new temple in Bangkok in the 1950s it slipped from the crane, and leaving the statue in the mud, the workmen called it a day. First thing in the morning, a temple monk, who had dreamed that the statue was divinely inspired, went to see the Buddha image. Through a crack in the plaster he saw the glint of yellow, and opening the plaster farther, he discovered that the statue was pure gold. ▨ *Admission.* ⊙ *Daily 9–5.*

Museums and Wats

Slightly inland from the river and north of the Grand Palace stands a cluster of cultural and government buildings. The neighborhood, in itself not particularly attractive, is made less appealing by the jammed traffic on weekdays, but you must not miss the National Museum, with Thailand's most valued historic treasures and a great collection of Southeast Asian art. There are also two unusual temples a little farther east.

A GOOD TOUR

The **National Museum** ⑥ should be seen early in your visit. It really helps in understanding Thai history, art, and architecture. Next door, in the **National Theatre** ⑦, classical Thai dance and drama performances are held (☞ Nightlife and the Arts, *below*). Next visit the **National Art Gallery** ⑧, opposite the theater, which has exhibits of modern and traditional Thai art. Next, take a ferry across the Chao Phraya (one of Bangkok's great pleasures) to visit the **Royal Barges** ⑨, and come back the same way. You can walk or take a tuk-tuk east, past the National Museum and the Democracy Monument, to **Wat Rachanada** ⑩ (the Temple of the Metal Castle), and then walk east, across Maha Chai Road, to **Wat Saket** ⑪ (the Temple of the Golden Mount), a notable landmark of the old city.

TIMING

This route is fairly compact. The museums are close together, and though it's not more than a 15-minute walk, you'll probably take a tuk-tuk or taxi to Wat Rachanada. Wat Saket is just a block away. Allow a good two or three hours at the National Museum and just under an hour at the National Art Gallery. Both are closed on Monday, Tuesday, and public holidays; go to the National Museum on Wednesday or Thursday morning for the free lecture tour in English. Then, after lunch, visit Wat Rachanada and Wat Saket. It will take at least an hour by taxi from the Sukhumvit area to reach the National Theatre, and 40 minutes from the Silom Road area via the river bus.

SIGHTS TO SEE

❽ **National Art Gallery.** Opposite the National Theatre, the National Art Gallery exhibits both modern and traditional Thai art. ✉ *Chao Fa Rd.,* ☎ *02/281–2224.* ▨ *Admission.* ⊙ *Tues.–Thurs. and weekends 9– noon and 1–4.*

★ ❻ **National Museum.** By far the best place to acquaint yourself with Thai history and art is at the extensive National Museum, which has one of the world's best collections of Southeast Asian art in general, and

Buddhist and Thai art in particular. Most of the great masterpieces of the Sukhothai and Ayutthaya periods and works from the northern provinces have found their way here, leaving up-country museums rather bare of fine Thai art. Here you'll have a good opportunity to trace Thailand's long history, beginning with the ceramic utensils and bronzeware of the Ban Chiang civilization (3000–4000 BC). The main building was built in 1783 as a palace for surrogate kings (a position abolished in 1874). You might go first to the artifact gallery, at the left of the ticket counter, for a historical overview. Afterward, explore the galleries that portray the Dvaravati and Khmer periods of more than 1,000 years ago. These will prepare you for the different styles of Thai art, from the Sukhothai period (1238–mid-14th century) on. ☎ 02/224–1333 ⌨ *Admission.* ☉ *Wed.–Sun. 9–noon and 1–4. Cafeteria. Free 90-min orientation tours in English by specialists start at the bookshop 9:30 AM Wed., Thurs.*

❼ National Theatre. Next door to the National Museum is the National Theatre, where classical Thai dance and drama can be seen on the last Friday and Saturday of each month (☞ Nightlife and the Arts, below). ✉ *Na Phra That Rd.,* ☎ *02/224–1342 for information on scheduled programs.*

❾ Royal Barges. These splendid ceremonial barges are berthed in a shed on the Thonburi side of the Chao Phraya River. The beautifully crafted boats, carved in the early part of this century, take the form of famous mythical creatures of the *Ramayana.* The most impressive is the red-and-gold royal flag barge, *Suphannahongse* (Golden Swan), used by the king on special occasions. Carved from a single piece of teak, it measures about 150 feet and weighs more than 15 tons. Fifty oarsmen propel it along the Chao Phraya River, not counting two coxswains, the flag wavers, and the rhythm-keeper. ⌨ *Admission.* ☉ *Daily 8:30–4:30.*

❿ Wat Rachanada (Temple of the Metal Castle). Across from Wat Saket, Wat Rachanada intentionally resembles the mythical castle of the gods. According to legend, a wealthy and pious man built a fabulous castle, Loha Prasat, according to the design laid down in Hindu mythology for the disciples of the Lord Buddha. Wat Rachanada, built in metal, is meant to duplicate that castle and is the only one of its kind remaining. In its precincts are stalls selling amulets that protect the wearer from misfortune—usually of the physical kind, though love amulets and charms are also sold. They tend to be rather expensive, but that's the price of good fortune. ⌨ *Admission.* ☉ *Daily 8–6.*

⓫ Wat Saket (Temple of the Golden Mount). East of the Democracy Monument you'll find Wat Saket, a notable landmark of the old city and, for a long time, the highest building around. King Rama III started the building of this mound and temple, which were completed by Rama V. To reach the gold-covered chedi, you must make an exhausting climb up 318 steps winding around the mound. Don't even attempt it on a hot day, but on a cool, clear day, the view from the top is worth the effort. Every November, at the time of the Loi Kratong festival, the compound is the site of Bangkok's largest temple fair (*ngan wat*), with food stalls, stage shows, and merrymaking. ⌨ *Admission.* ☉ *Daily 8–5.*

Scattered Bangkok

One of the delights of Bangkok is that it sprawls, seemingly without rhyme or reason, in delightful chaos. Neighborhoods as we know them in the West do not exist. Once you leave the Chao Phraya River, you are in a mix of the old and the new; the glitz of new wealth juxtaposed with the simplicity of poverty. Temples, factories, palaces, office buildings, and private houses may all be found on one block. The negative is that getting from one major sight to another takes time, usually spent in stalled traffic.

A GOOD TOUR (OR TWO OR THREE)

It makes sense to treat the widely spaced sights in Scattered Bangkok as a smorgasbord from which to select a sight or two when you're nearby. You might go first to one of Bangkok's most photographed wats, northeast of the Democracy Monument, the **Wat Benjamabophit** ⑫ (Marble Temple). Then it's a short tuk-tuk ride to **Vimarnmek Palace** ⑮, the largest teak structure in the world, and on your way there, you'll probably pass by **Chitlada Palace** ⑬, one of the king's residences, on the right. On the other side of the road is the **Dusit Zoo** ⑭ (Khao Din Wana). West of the Dusit Zoo is **Banglampoo,** where the backpackers gravitate, a fascinating sight, and an eye-opener to what Western culture can produce. The **Suan Pakkard Palace** ⑯ is on the south side of Ayutthaya Road, between Phayathai and Ratchaprarop roads); its five traditional Thai houses make a nice contrast to Vimarnmek Palace. Compare that royal setting also with **Jim Thompson's House** ⑰ off Rama I Road, just west of Siam Square, a resurrected Thai residence that he constructed from six houses brought from up-country.

SIGHTS TO SEE

Banglampoo. Backpackers from around the world gather in this section, just north of where Ratchawithi Road crosses the Chao Phraya river at Krunthun Bridge. It's not really Bangkok; it's a human zoo, and Thais, we are told, sometimes go there to look at strange Westerners. It's a source for the latest in travel tips, however, and many agencies there can book inexpensive travel and tours. The main thoroughfare, Khao Sahn Road, is full of cafés, secondhand book stalls, and inexpensive shops. In the evening, the streets are full of stalls and food stands catering to young Westerners on their not-so-grand tour. Off Khao Sahn Road, hundreds of small guest houses rent tiny rooms for around B150 to B300 a night. Ironically, some prices are inflated: the Bangkok Post, normally B20, often costs B25 here.

⑬ **Chitlada Palace.** When in Bangkok, the king resides at the Chitlada Palace, which covers the whole block across from the Dusit Zoo. The public is not permitted, and you are only able to see high walls and the honor guards as you drive by.

⑲ **Crocodile Farm and Zoo.** This enormous zoo and amusement ground, with stalls, food stands, and animals, is in downtown Samut Prakan. Crocodile-wrestling shows and elephant acrobatics are staged throughout the day, and, though nothing unusual, they're lighthearted fun, especially for children. You may be photographed for a fee with your arm around a tiger (who appears drugged). Take air-conditioned Bus No. 7, 8, or 11, or Micro Bus 13. Annoyingly, foreigners pay six times as much as Thais to enter the park. ⊠ *555 Moo 7 Taiban Rd., Samut Prakan,* ☎ *02/703–4891.* ☒ *Admission.* ☉ *Daily 7–6.*

⑭ **Dusit Zoo.** When you are exhausted by Bangkok's traffic and want to rest in a pleasant expanse of greenery, pay a visit to the Dusit Zoo (Khao Din Wana). Children can ride elephants (not the white ones, which are of "royal blood"), and you can sit at one of the cafés under the shade of a tree. ☎ *02/281–0021.* ☒ *Admission.* ☉ *Daily 8–6.*

⑰ **Jim Thompson's House.** This wonderful compound of traditional architecture and Southeast Asian furnishings, a virtual museum, is popular with Westerners. American Jim Thompson, once an architect in New York, joined the OSS in World War II and went to Asia. After the war, he stayed on and took it upon himself to revitalize Thailand's moribund silk industry. His project and product met with tremendous success, which in itself would have made him into a legend. In 1967 Thompson went to the Malaysian Cameron Highlands for a quiet holiday and was never heard from again.

Thompson imported parts of up-country buildings, some as old as 150 years, to construct his compound of six Thai houses. Three are exactly the same as their originals, including details of the interior layout. With true appreciation and a connoisseur's eye, Thompson then furnished them with what are now priceless pieces of Southeast Asian art. The entrance is easy to miss: at the end of an unprepossessing lane, leading north off Rama I, west of Phayathai Road, the house is on your left. ⊠ *Soi Kasemsong 2,* ☎ *02/215–0122.* ▣ *Admission.* ☉ *Mon.– Sat. 9–4:30.*

⑱ Muang Boran (Ancient City). About an hour's driving time (20 km/12 mi) southeast of the city is an amazing park roughly shaped like the map of Thailand. You enter at the country's southern tip and find throughout the park, placed more or less as in geographical reality, 108 replicas of Thailand's most important architectural sites and monuments. You really need wheels—the area is too vast to cover on foot. Small, discreetly placed restaurant areas are scattered throughout the grounds, and crafts are sold in a "traditional Thai village" and elsewhere. Allow a good four hours to cover most of the sites. Rather than eat in the park, you may want to go 5 km (3 mi) farther south on Old Sukhumvit Road to Bang Pu's restaurant (☎ 02/323–9590) by the sea, for excellent, inexpensive seafood. By car, take the Samrong–Samut Prakan expressway and turn left at the Samut Prakan intersection to the old Sukhumvit Road on the way to Bang Pu. At km 33, Muang Boran is on your left. Or, take air-conditioned bus No. 11 and get off at Pak Nam to transfer to a small bus, No. 36, which passes in front of the city. You can take a tour arranged by your hotel, or, better yet, four can hire a car and driver for about B1,000. ⊠ *Old Sukhumvit Rd., Samut Prakan,* ☎ *02/323–9252.* ▣ *Admission.* ☉ *Daily 9–5.*

♦ Pasteur Institute (Red Cross Snake Farm). Not only children will find the Red Cross Snake Farm of interest. In 1923, the Thai Red Cross established this farm, where venom is milked and stored as the antidote for people kissed by poisonous snakes. This facility at the top end of Suriwong Road (corner of Rama IV and Henri Dunant) was the second in the world (the first was in Brazil). There are slide shows before the milking sessions, at 10:30 AM and 2 PM on weekdays. You can watch the handlers work with deadly cobras, kraits, and pit vipers, and even get typhoid, cholera, and smallpox vaccinations here. ⊠ *1871 Rama IV Rd.,* ☎ *02/252–0161.* ▣ *Admission.* ☉ *Weekdays 8:30–12, 2–4.*

★ ⑯ Suan Pakkard Palace. This palace is traditional Thai. Five antique teak houses, built high on columns, complement the perfectly kept, undulating lawns, and the shimmering lotus pools and lush shrubbery. The serene atmosphere makes Suan Pakkard one of the most relaxing places in which to absorb Thai culture. The center of attraction, the Lacquer Pavilion, at the back of the garden, contains gold-covered paneling with scenes from the life of Buddha, and the other houses display porcelains, Khmer stone heads, old paintings, and statues of Buddha. ☎ *02/245–4934.* ▣ *Admission.* ☉ *Mon.–Sat. 9–4.*

⑮ Vimarnmek Palace. This is the largest teak structure in the world, built in 1900 by King Rama V on his return from Europe, as a four-story suburban palace. Now, with the capital's growth, it's in the center of administrative Bangkok, next to the National Assembly building. The palace fits its name, "Castle in the Clouds," its extraordinary lightness enhanced by a reflecting pond. King Rama's fascination with Western architecture shows in its Victorian style, but the building retains an unmistakably Thai delicacy. Most of the furnishings were either bought in the West or given by European monarchs. Some are exquisite—porcelain, handcrafted furniture, and crystal—and some have novelty value, like the first typewriter brought to Thailand. Exhibitions of Thai dancing take place daily at 10:30 and 2. ☎ 02/281–5169. 🎟 *Admission.* ⊙ *Daily 9:30–3:15.*

★ ⑫   **Wat Benjamabophit** (Marble Temple). Bangkok's most photographed wat, built in 1899, is where Thailand's present king came to spend his days as a monk before his coronation. Statues of Buddha line the courtyard, and the magnificent interior has cross beams of lacquer and gold, but Wat Benjamabophit is more than a splendid temple. The monastery is a seat of learning that appeals to Buddhist monks with intellectual yearnings. 🎟 *Admission.* ⊙ *Daily 7–5.*

Dining

Thais are passionate about food—finding the out-of-the-way shop that prepares some specialty better than anyplace else, then dragging groups of friends to share the discovery, is a national pastime. The aroma of cooking is everywhere and the tastes of Thai food are all around you, day and night, since Thais always seem to be eating.

Until your digestion adjusts to the food, steer clear of the stands in markets and at roadsides. Most of these are safe, but as a general rule, you should stick to cooked food. The clean, well-maintained food shops on major roads and in shopping centers rarely cause problems and will give you a chance to taste authentic versions of popular Thai dishes at very low prices.

Though Bangkok's water is potable, it's best for visitors to drink bottled. Clear ice cubes with holes through them are made with purified water, and most restaurants use them.

Restaurants usually stop serving dinner at 10:30 PM, but you will find many local restaurants stay open until midnight and later. For price categories, *see* Pleasures and Pastimes, *above.*

Chinese

$$$ ✕ **Mayflower.** Captains of industry, royalty, and heads of state are counted among the regular customers of the five stylishly opulent private rooms and main dining area of the Mayflower. The carved wood screens and porcelain vases set a tone of simple-but-luxurious refinement perfectly in keeping with the outstanding Cantonese food. In order to provide the best service possible, a computerized record is kept of the guests—of their food preferences, the size of their families, important anniversaries, etc. Tables are set with chopsticks and spoons, but knives and forks are available. Two of the best items on the menu are the piquant abalone-and-jellyfish salad, and the Drunken Chinese Chicken—steamed, skinned, and boned chicken doused with Chinese liquor and served with two sauces, one sweet and one spicy. The shark's-fin soup and the dim sum are also worth sampling. An excellent wine list assumes price is no object. Waitresses wear slinky silk dresses slit to the hip. Two- to three-day advance notice is required for private rooms. ✉ *Dusit Thani Hotel, Rama IV Rd.,* ☎ *02/236–0450. Reservations essential. AE, DC, V.*

$$$ ✕ **Royal Kitchen.** Perhaps the most elegant of Bangkok's many Chi-
★   nese restaurants, the Royal Kitchen consists of a number of small, atmospherically decorated dining rooms where everything, right down to the silver chopsticks, has been carefully considered. The menu is a

reference resource for southern Chinese delicacies, including such offerings as *mieng nok,* with finely minced, seasoned pigeon served on individual fragrant leaves. At lunchtime, dim sum is served, and it, too, is probably Bangkok's best, as beautiful to look at as it is subtle in taste. ✉ *N. Sathorn Rd., opposite YWCA and Thai Oil,* ☎ *02/234–3063. Reservations essential. Jacket and tie. AE, DC, MC, V.*

$$–$$$ ✕ **Hok Thean Lauo.** A shuttle boat runs guests across the Chao Phraya from the River City Shopping Centre to one of Bangkok's top Cantonese restaurants. The decor includes Chinese lanterns, but it's best to sit at a table by the window, watching the streams of rice barges labor up and down the river. Hok Thean Lauo is known for its dim-sum lunches, especially on Sunday. Waiters continually pass your table offering you small baskets of delicacies. If you're not selective, you'll probably spoil your appetite for the next two days. ✉ *762 Ladya Rd., Klongsam,* ☎ *02/437–1121. Reservations essential Sun. AE, DC, MC, V.*

$$ ✕ **Shangrila.** The menu has a wide range of dishes, from Peking duck
★ to thinly sliced pork with garlic, but it is hard to pass up the house's marvelous selection of dim-sum dishes. Waiters will help you choose, but it is difficult to make a mistake. Service is pleasantly attentive even when a high-powered politician comes in and is fawned over. The restaurant's split level and small size make it a more comfortable Chinese place than many in this neighborhood, and the bright white tablecloths and gleaming glassware give an upbeat note to the dining experience. ✉ *154/4-7 Silom Rd.,* ☎ *02/234–9147/9. AE, DC, MC, V.*

$$ ✕ **Tien Tien.** During the day Patpong is just an average soi with shops and restaurants, and Tien Tien has been here for years catering to a busy business lunch trade. Dinner is good, too, if you happen to be in the neighborhood, but the decor doesn't get much beyond white tablecloths and some red walls. The roast pork is superb: have it any which way you want, but it is so juicy and tender that perhaps simply with steamed rice is sufficient. The Peking duck is also a must; its skin is crisp and the pancakes light and fluffy. The rest is up to you, be it tiger prawns or a selection of dim sum. ✉ *105 Patpong, Silom Rd.,* ☎ *02/ 234–8717. MC, V.*

$ ✕ **Coca Noodles.** This giant, raucous restaurant is as high spirited as any in town. On evenings and weekends, it is full of Chinese families eating a daunting variety of noodle dishes with noisy gusto. Both wheat- and rice-based pastas are available in abundance, in combination with a cornucopia of meats, fish, shellfish, and crunchy Chinese vegetables. Try some of the green, wheat based noodles called *mee yoke,* topped with a chicken thigh, red pork, or crabmeat. Also, on a gas ring built into the table, you can prepare yourself an intriguing Chinese variant of sukiyaki. ✉ *In Siam Square Shopping Center facing 461 Henri Dunant Rd.,* ☎ *02/251–6337 or 02/251–3538. Another branch at* ✉ *Suriwongse Rd.,* ☎ *02/236–0107. No credit cards.*

$ ✕ **Prachak.** This simple, no-nonsense, tile-floor and bare-walls restau-
★ rant serves superb roast duck (*ped*), for which it is famous, and red pork (*moo daeng*). Families from wealthy neighborhoods send their maids here to bring back dinner, and by 6 PM there's often no duck or pork left. Nobody comes here for decor, though improvements were made, with air-conditioning, in 1997. It may even strike you as being a little grungy, but whenever we are in the neighborhood we grab a quick meal here and never have any problems. Our problem is in *finding* this "hole-in-the-wall" restaurant. It is across from Bangrak Market (beside the Shangri-La hotel), diagonally across the road from a 7-Eleven store. Two can dine well for $6. The present owner, grandson of the founder, speaks just a little English. ✉ *1415 Charoen Krung (New Road), Silom Bansak,* ☎ *02/234–3755. Reservations not accepted. No credit cards.*

Bangkok Dining and Lodging

Dining

The Atlanta, **50**
Baan Kahanitha, **60**
Ban Chiang, **23**
Ban Khun Phor, **31**
Banana Leaf, **36**
Cabbages &
Condoms, **55**
Coca Noodles, **32**
The Front Page, **41**
Genji, **45**
Harmonique, **18**
Himali Cha Cha, **16**

Hok Thean Lauo, **7**
Kaloang Seafood, **1**
Le Dalat, **59**
Le Normandie, **10**
Lemongrass, **64**
Mayflower, **37**
My Choice, **67**
Nai Sow, **6**
Pan Pan, **46, 62**
Prachak, **15**
The Regent Grill, **42**
River City Bar B-Q, **11**

Royal Kitchen, **39**
Sala Rim Naam, **8**
Salathip, **14**
Sara-Jane's, **47**
Saw Ying Thai, **4**
Seafood Market, **63**
Shangrila, **25**
Soi Polo Fried
Chicken, **48**
Spice Market, **42**
Sweet Basil, **66**
Thai Room, **34**
Thong Lee, **61**

Tien Tien, **35**
Ton Po, **3**
Yok Yor, **2**

Eclectic

$ ✕ **The Front Page.** This cozy British-style pub and restaurant is a convenient social spot if you are at the upper end of Silom or Sathorn roads. (It's between the two, one block in from Rama IV.) It used to be the hangout for the *Bangkok Post* until the newspaper moved offices; now it attracts local expats and Thais for its convivial atmosphere. You sit either at the bar or at tables, and the food is mostly Western, from hamburgers to steak, but there are simple Thai dishes as well. On weekends, a trio plays jazz until shortly after midnight. ✉ *14/10 Soi Saladeang Rama IV,* ☎ *02/234–8134. MC, V.*

$ ✕ **Sara-Jane's.** Sara, formerly of Massachusetts, married a Thai 20 years ago and started a restaurant in 1986. In 1998 her success led to the opening of a new restaurant just down from the American Embassy. In the ground-floor shopping mall of a large office building, Sara-Jane's open dining room has sparse decor. It is designed to accommodate lots of people for lunch, though many also stop off for dinner. The menu celebrates I-san food, with many types of salad served with *larb*—a mince made from pork, chicken, tuna, or other meat and fish. One favorite is *yam pla dook foo,* a crisp, golden, fried fish with a mango topping. For those who want European fare, Sara-Jane also offers Italian food, with a good representation of pasta dishes. ✉ *Ground floor, Sindhorn Tower 1, 130-132 Wireless Rd.,* ☎ *02/650–9992. No credit cards.*

$ ✕ **Thai Room.** This time capsule has remained the same since it opened during the Vietnam War, in 1966, when it was packed in the evening with GIs on R&R. Not a molecule of the decor has changed since then, and it is not unusual to see a veteran of that war quietly reminiscing. Around him, however, will be local residents and tourists in from the tawdry riot of Patpong. The Mexican food is a peculiar hybrid of Mexican and Thai cuisines, and the result is not unpleasing. Some of the Italian items, like the eggplant parmigiana, are very good by any standard, and the Thai food can be excellent. Local clients feel great affection for this one-of-a-kind restaurant, which stays open until midnight. ✉ *30/37 Patpong 2 Rd. (between Silom and Suriwongse Rds.),* ☎ *02/233–7920. Reservations not accepted. AE, DC, MC, V.*

French

$$$$ ✕ **Le Normandie.** This legendary restaurant perched atop the Oriental Hotel commands a panoramic view across the Chao Phraya River. Michelin three-star chef Georges Blanc is the restaurant's permanent consultant and, periodically, the most highly esteemed chefs in France are persuaded to take over in the kitchen. These artists usually import ingredients from home, and at such times the restaurant's patrons enjoy what is literally the finest French food in the world. Even when no superstar chef is on the scene, the cuisine is unforgettable, with the menu often including rare dishes taught to Le Normandie's master chef by the visiting chefs. ✉ *48 Oriental Ave.,* ☎ *02/234–8690. Reservations essential. Jacket and tie. AE, DC, MC, V. No lunch Sun.*

$$$$ ✕ **The Regent Grill.** This is a strikingly designed, high-fashion French restaurant. On the menu from time to time appear such memorable dishes as fresh goose liver in raspberry vinegar (which can be specially ordered a day or so in advance). Excellent endive salads and lobster dishes, one with a subtle goose-liver sauce, are regularly featured. Formerly Le Cristal, the restaurant has been enlarged to encompass a terrace overlooking the imaginatively landscaped grounds of the Regent of Bangkok Hotel, and it is now putting more emphasis on grilled dishes. ✉ *155 Rajadamri Rd.,* ☎ *02/251–6127. Reservations essential. Jacket and tie. AE, DC, MC, V. No dinner weekdays.*

Indian

$$ ✕ **Himali Cha Cha.** We are sad to report that Cha Cha, the chef who was once Nehru's cook, died in 1996. His recipes, however, are now prepared with matching ability by his wife, who serves up the northern Indian cuisine in a pleasantly informal setting with the usual Mogul decor. The quality of the food, which has kept the place a favorite for a decade, remains top-notch. The tandoori chicken is locally famous, and the daily specials, precisely explained, are usually to be recommended. Always good are the breads and the fruit-flavored *lassis* (yogurt drinks)—especially the mango ones. ✉ *1229/11 New Rd.,* ☎ *02/235–1569. AE, DC, MC, V.*

Italian

$$ ✕ **Pan Pan.** The two branches of this Italian food-and-ice-cream chain are enormously popular. They are pleasingly decorated with Italian kitchen items and spices, and the relaxed feeling in both places invites intimate talk. The long list of generous and delicious pasta dishes includes linguine with a sauce of salmon, cream, and vodka that is a taste of high-calorie heaven, and "Chicken Godfather," with a cream-and-mushroom sauce, which is similarly disappointment-proof. But save room for the ice cream, which is of the thick, dense Italian type. The branch on Sukhumvit Road offers an antipasto buffet and a large selection of extremely rich desserts. ✉ *6–6/1 Sukhumvit Rd., near Soi 33,* ☎ *02/258–9304 or 02/258–5071;* ✉ *45 Soi Lang Suan, off Ploenchit Rd.,* ☎ *02/252–7104. AE, DC, MC, V.*

Japanese

$$$ ✕ **Genji.** Bangkok has many good Japanese restaurants, although a number of them give a chilly reception to outsiders. Genji is a happy exception. The fact that it's in a large international hotel shouldn't deter even culinary purists—there is an excellent sushi bar and several small, private rooms. Try especially the succulent grilled eel. Set menus for lunch and dinner are well conceived, and Japanese breakfasts are also served. ✉ *Hilton International, 2 Wireless Rd.,* ☎ *02/253–0123. Reservations essential. AE, DC, MC, V.*

Thai

$$$ ✕ **Lemongrass.** Elegance and a certain adventurousness have made this restaurant a favorite with Thais and resident Westerners. Embellished with Southeast Asian antiques, the dining rooms and the garden have plenty of atmosphere. Over the years the cuisine has become more geared to the softer palate of Westerners than to that of Thais, which can make this restaurant a good introduction to Thai cooking. Be sure to try a glass of *nam takrai,* the cold, sweet drink brewed from lemongrass. ✉ *5/1 Sukhumvit Soi 24,* ☎ *02/258–8637. AE, DC, MC, V.*

$$$ ✕ **Sala Rim Naam.** Definitely an upscale restaurant for visitors, and
★ with style to spare. This elegant *sala* (room), across the river from the Oriental Hotel, realizes many of the images that come to mind with the word *Siam.* Here some dishes are so beautifully presented that eating them feels like vandalism. Try some of the hot-and-sour salads, particularly the shrimp version called *yam koong.* Make reservations for 7:30 PM, and plan to stay afterward for the excellently staged Thai dancing. Lunch at the Sala Rim's excellent buffet is always less crowded and, during the hot season, special and rarely found light Thai recipes called *Khon Chere* are offered. ✉ *Use free boat from Oriental Hotel,* ☎ *02/437–6211. Reservations essential weekends and Oct.–late-Feb. AE, DC, MC, V.*

$$$ ✕ **Salathip.** Built as a Thai pavilion, with a veranda facing the Chao Phraya River, the restaurant provides an ambience that guarantees a romantic evening. Be sure to reserve a table outside. Though the food may not have as much hot chili as some like, it hasn't been adulterated to suit Western tastes. On Sunday night, there's possibly the best buffet in Bangkok, where you can sample some of the finest Thai cuisine there is. ⊠ *Shangri-La Hotel, 89 Soi Wat Suan Phu, New Rd.,* ☎ *02/236–7777. Reservations essential for veranda. AE, DC, MC, V. No lunch.*

$$$ ✕ **Seafood Market.** This vast restaurant still feels like the fish supermarket it used to be. You take a cart and choose from an array of seafood—crabs, prawns, lobster, clams, oysters, flat fish, snapperlike fish, crayfish—and vegetables. The waiter takes it away and cooks it any way you like. Typically your eyes are bigger than your stomach, so select with prudence, not gusto. Though the fluorescent lighting gives it the ambience of a giant canteen, people pack the tables because the prices are reasonable and the fish is fresh. Beware of Johnny-come-latelies who also call themselves Seafood Market and pay taxi and tuk-tuk drivers to divert you to their establishments. ⊠ *388 Sukhumvit Rd., Soi 24,* ☎ *02/258–0218. Reservations not accepted. AE, DC, MC, V.*

$$ ✕ **Baan Kahanitha.** Half the pleasure of eating here is in the ambience and attentive service. Wood paneling, old Thai prints, blooming orchids, antique copper, and tableware from Thai kilns create just the right mood for a relaxing evening. The food is strictly Thai, explained well in the English menu and by the English-speaking waiters. The taste is excellent and dishes have not been compromised to appeal to the restaurant's Western clientele. The fried soft-shell crabs in a hot and sour sauce are divine and the *tom kha gai* soup is wonderfully rich, with just enough lime and lemongrass. ⊠ *3/1 Sukhumvit 23, Soi Prasan,* ☎ *02/258–4181. MC, V.*

$$ ✕ **Ban Chiang.** The decor here is turn-of-the-century Bangkok, and the painted walls are adorned with prints, photographs, and a pendulum clock. The extensive menu can be quite spicy: for example, the roast-duck curry and the shrimp-and-vegetable herb soup. The fried fish cakes and the grilled prawns are milder, as is the chicken marinated in coconut milk and baked in pandanus leaves. The service is not a strong point, and you need to know your way around a Thai menu to order a balanced set of dishes. ⊠ *14 Srivieng Rd.,* ☎ *02/236–7045. MC, V.*

$$ ✕ **Ban Khun Phor.** If you're in the area of Siam Square, try this popular bistro diagonally across from the Novotel. The wooden tables mix with European Victoriana and Thai artifacts. The menu is varied, with such standard favorites as *tom kha gai* (lemongrass coconut soup with chicken), roast duck with red curry, and even spicy stir-fried boar's meat. The best dish is the spicy crab soup. ⊠ *458/7–9, Soi 8, Siam Sq.,* ☎ *02/250–1733. Reservations not accepted. MC, V.*

$$ ✕ **Harmonique.** You can eat on the terrace or on the ground floor of this small house near the river. The decoration, from flowers tumbling out of vases to chests scattered with bric-a-brac, gives the feeling of casual ease that you could expect in Western Europe, but here it is, down a small soi off Charoen Krung (New Road) just left of the General Post Office. The menu for a Thai restaurant is quite small, but what there is is made with care. Foreign tourists come here from the Oriental and Royal Orchid Sheraton and are ably assisted by Madame in selecting the right courses, At a recent dinner we had crisp fish sautéed in garlic, a mild crab curry, and Chinese cabbage topped with salted fish. All were excellent. ⊠ *22 Charoen Krung 34,* ☎ *02/237–8175. AE.*

$$ ✕ **Cabbages & Condoms.** Don't be misled by the restaurant's name or disconcerted by the array of contraceptive devices for sale. C&C is a fund-raiser for Thailand's birth-control program, the Population & Community Development Association. Once you accept this strange association, you'll find the Thai food here excellently prepared, with such dishes as chicken wrapped in a pandanus leaf, crisp fried fish with chili sauce, and shrimp in a mild curry sauce. There's a simply decorated dining room and a pleasant garden with bench tables under shady trees—one of the few places in Bangkok to sit outside without noise and air pollution. ✉ *10 Sukhumvit Soi 12,* ☎ *02/251–0402. AE, DC, MC, V.*

$$ ✗ **Kaloang Seafood.** This local favorite is a little off the beaten track, but it's worth the effort if you want the genuine flavor of riverside Bangkok and good seafood as well. Beginning at the National Library, the soi leading down to the place is charmingly ethnic, and the restaurant itself is open, built on a ramshackle pier. Fans and the breeze off the river keep things comfortably cool most evenings. The more observant customer will notice right away that almost all the waiters/waitresses are transvestites. Service is friendly and competent, if initially somewhat disconcerting. The grilled seafood platter is both generous and cheap, and the grilled giant river prawns are also a bargain. Try the *yam pla duk foo* (puffed and deep-fried catfish with peanuts, green mango, lime, and chilies). It is rather spicy, but it complements cold beer as few things in this world do. ✉ *2 Sri Ayutthaya Rd.,* ☎ *02/281–9228. AE, DC, MC, V.*

$$ ✗ **My Choice.** At its new location (it was on Soi 33) middle-class Thais with a taste for their grandmothers' traditional recipes flock to this this restaurant all day. The *ped aob,* a thick soup made from beef stock, is particularly popular, but foreigners may prefer the *tom kha tala,* a hot-and-sour dish with shrimp, served with rice. The interior is plain, with Formica tables; it's better outside. ✉ *Soi 36 Sukhumvit,* ☎ *02/258–6174. AE, DC, MC, V.*

$$ ✗ **River City Bar B-Q.** As you're seated on the roof of the River City Shopping Centre, the waiter brings a burner and hot plate, and a mound of different meats and vegetables. You use your chopsticks to grill the food. Order some appetizers to nibble on while dinner is cooking—the northern Thai sausage is excellent. Request a table at the edge of the roof for a romantic view of the Chao Phraya River. ✉ *5th floor, River City Shopping Centre,* ☎ *02/237–0077, ext. 240. MC, V.*

$$ ✗ **Spice Market.** Here is Thai home cooking as it was when domestic
★ help was cheap. The decor re-creates a once-familiar sight—the interior of a well-stocked spice shop, with sacks of garlic, dried chilies, and heavy earthenware fish-sauce jars lined up as they were when the only way to get to Bangkok was by steamer. The authentic recipes are tempered to suit the tender mouths of Westerners, but you may ask for your dishes to be prepared full-strength; a chili logo on the menu indicates peppery dishes. The curries are superb, and there is a comprehensive selection of old-fashioned Thai sweets. From mid-January to the end of March, try the *nam doc mai* (Thai mango) with sticky rice and coconut milk; knowledgeable foreigners arrange trips to Bangkok at this time of year just for this dessert. ✉ *Regent of Bangkok Hotel, 155 Rajadamri Rd.,* ☎ *02/251–6127. Reservations essential. AE, DC, MC, V.*

$$ ✗ **Ton Po.** This is open-air riverside dining without tourist trappings.
★ Ton Po (Thai for the Bo tree, of which there is a large, garlanded specimen at the entrance) has a wide, covered veranda on the Chao Phraya. To get the breeze that blows even in the hottest weather, try to wangle a riverside table. Many of the dishes are well known, and none more so than the *tom khlong plaa salid bai makhaam awn,* a delectable, very hot and sour soup made from a local dried fish, chili, lime juice, lemongrass, young tamarind leaves, mushrooms, and a full frontal assault of other herbal seasonings. Less potent but equally good are the *kai haw bai toei* (chicken wrapped in fragrant pandanus leaves and grilled) and *haw moke plaa* (a type of curried fish custard, thickened with coconut cream and steamed in banana leaves). ✉ *Phra Atit Rd,* ☎ *no phone. Reservations not accepted. AE, DC, MC, V.*

$-$$ ✕ **Yok Yor.** At dinner recently aboard a grounded vessel on the Chao Phraya, reached by a gangplank, we saw not a single Westerner, and little English was spoken. The well-cooked Thai food was served with dispatch, and the cool darkness of the river lent a romantic aura to the exotic scene. There's live music from 6 PM on, and Japanese, Chinese, and some European dishes are also served. The management also runs a dinner/music cruise along the Chao Phraya every night (8:30–10:30; B70 plus cost of food), aboard a 400-seat boat. ✉ *Wisutikasat Rd. at Yok Yor Pier (next to Bank of Thailand, ☎ 02/281–1829 or 02/282–7385. No credit cards.*

$ ✕ **The Atlanta.** It is not often that we recommend a coffee shop in a budget hotel, but the Thai cooking here is surprisingly good and very inexpensive, thanks to the reclusive innkeeper, Charles Henn, a food fanatic. The menu, which explains the ingredients and their origin, makes interesting, amusing reading. Don't pass up the *tom yam khung* soup here—it's especially smooth. The restaurant has just been renovated. Classical jazz is played at dinner, followed by a movie of some repute. New vegetarian dishes are being added every week to the menu, which, if Henn has his way, will soon be recognized as the best in Bangkok. ✉ *Sukhumvit 78 Soi 2, ☎ 02/252–1650 or 02/252–6069. No credit cards.*

$ ✕ **Banana Leaf.** This is not only the best restaurant of this shopping complex, but it's worth making tracks for if you are in the vicinity of upper Silom Road—the people lining up to get in aren't coming for the decor. It's just bare, painted walls, but the harried waiters and waitresses give quick, friendly service, and there's delicious Thai food at low prices. Try the baked crab with glass noodles, hen's fingers salad, spicy papaya salad, grilled black band fish, or grilled pork with a coconut milk dip. ✉ *Basement level, Silom Complex, Silom Rd., ☎ 02/231–3124. No credit cards.*

$ ✕ **Nai Sow.** We searched for the best *tom yum khung* (hot and sour soup with prawns) and found it here, a Chinese-Thai restaurant next door to Wat Plaplachai in Chinatown. Chefs come and go, but the owner, who never divulges his recipes to his chefs, makes the essential mixture—which includes the fatty juices from the prawns—in secret. The result is a smooth, scintillating tom yum khung. Other equally tasty dishes range from curried Thai beef to a mix of sweet and sour mushrooms. For an unusual—and delicious—dessert, finish with the fried taro. Forget decor: Round tables and chairs are about the only furnishings. You come here to eat and talk, not for the ambience. ✉ *3/1 Maitrichit Rd., ☎ 02/222–1539. Reservations not accepted. MC, V.*

$ ✕ **Saw Ying Thai.** This place has been open for almost 60 years, and among its extremely devoted clientele many have been regulars for decades. It is rare to find a tourist here, and even long-term expatriate customers are few. The menus on the wall are in Thai only, and none of the staff speaks English, so try to bring a Thai friend. Be sure to order the *kai toon*, a chicken soup with bamboo sprouts; also memorable are *plaa du thawd krawb phad phed,* crisp-fried catfish stir-fried with curry spices and herbs, and *khai jio neua puu,* an omelet full of crabmeat. Recently, it has been spiffed up, and the out-of-date posters on the walls are gone, but the charm remains the same. This restaurant would rate a star if it were more accessible in language or location. ✉ *Corner of Bamrungmuang and Tanao Rds., ☎ no phone. Reservations not accepted. No credit cards.*

$ ✕ **Soi Polo Fried Chicken.** Although its beat-up plastic tables, traffic
★ noise, and lack of air-conditioning make this small place look like a sure thing for stomach trouble, it is one of the city's most popular lunch spots for nearby office workers. The reason: its world-class fried chicken flavored with black pepper and plenty of golden-brown, crisp-fried garlic. The chicken should be sampled with sticky rice and per-

haps a plate of the restaurant's excellent *som tam* (hot-and-sour raw papaya salad, a hydrogen bomb of a hot coleslaw from the northeast). Try to get there a bit before noon, or landing a table will be a problem. ⊠ *Walk into Soi Polo from Wireless Rd. (the restaurant is the last of the shops on your left as you enter the soi),* ☎ *no phone. Reservations not accepted. No credit cards. No dinner.*

$ ✕ **Thong Lee.** This small but attractive shop-house restaurant has an air-conditioned upstairs dining area. Although prices are very low, Thong Lee has a devoted upper-middle-class clientele. The menu is not adventurous, but every dish has a distinct personality—evidence of the cook's artistry and imagination. Almost everyone orders the *muu phad kapi* (pork fried with shrimp paste); the *yam hed sod* (hot-and-sour mushroom salad) is memorable but very spicy. ⊠ *Sukhumvit Soi 20,* ☎ *no phone. Reservations not accepted. No credit cards.*

Vietnamese

$$–$$$ ✕ **Sweet Basil.** It is worth making the long trek down Sukhumvit to
★ Soi 62 (Ekimae) for the splendidly presented Vietnamese fare, in a fresh setting of crisp white tablecloths, glistening silver and glassware, and ferns and flowers. The cooking is professional—try the *bo la lat* (brochettes of beef wrapped in a pungent leaf) and the *ban cuon tom* (dumplings stuffed with shrimp and mushrooms), or the more usual but delicious salads and crunchy *cha gio* (spring rolls with a sweet, tangy sauce). This is a smart restaurant where you find Thais dressing up for a special meal. ⊠ *23 Soi 62,* ☎ *02/176–5490. Reservations essential. AE, DC, MC, V.*

$$ ✕ **Le Dalat.** This very classy Vietnamese restaurant, once a private house,
★ consists of several intimate and cozily decorated dining rooms. Much Vietnamese cuisine is based on flavor juxtapositions striking to the Western palate, and here it's all served up with style. Try *naem neuang,* which requires you to take a garlicky grilled meatball and place it on a round of *mieng* (edible thin rice paper wrapper), then pile on bits of garlic, ginger, hot chili, star apple, and mango, spoon on a viscous sweet-salty sauce, and wrap the whole thing up in a lettuce leaf before eating. The restaurant has become a favorite with Bangkok residents. ⊠ *51 Sukhumvit Soi 23, opposite Indian Embassy,* ☎ *02/260–1849. Reservations essential. AE, DC, MC, V.*

Lodging

The economic and currency crisis of 1998 has had the effect of lowering the prices in dollars or sterling at hotels whose clientele is mostly Thais and other Asians. Those hotels with mostly an American or European clientele (especially the luxury hotels) raised their prices to offset the devaluation of the baht. But by the end of 1988 even hotels that quote prices in baht started to raise their rack rates. Nevertheless, prices fluctuate enormously, but if business is down, huge discounts are offered. The best bargains are probably found in the $$–$$$ categories.

That said, Bangkok hotel prices are still lower than those in Singapore and Hong Kong and are not expensive by European standards. Rates at wonderful deluxe hotels are about the equivalent of $250 for a double. Those in the $80–$100 range also have fine service, excellent restaurants, health centers, and facilities for businesspeople. For $40 to $50, you can find respectable lodgings in a hotel with an efficient staff. Rooms in small hotels with limited facilities are available for around $10, and, for those willing to share a bathroom, guest houses are numerous.

The four main hotel districts are next to the Chao Phraya and along Silom and Suriwongse roads; around Siam Square; in the foreign-embassy neighborhood; and along Sukhumvit Road. Other areas, such as Khao San Road for inexpensive guest houses favored by back-packers, and across the river, where modern high-rise hotels are sprouting up, are not included in the following list. For price categories, see the price chart at the start of this chapter.

$$$$ 🏨 **Dusit Thani.** This low-key 23-story hotel with distinctive, pyramid-style architecture is the flagship property of an expanding Thai hotel group. An extensive shopping arcade, a Chinese restaurant, and an elegant Thai restaurant occupy the street level. One floor up, the lobby, reception area, and a delightful sunken lounge look out over a small garden. The pool area, a central courtyard filled with trees, is a peaceful oasis amid Bangkok's frenzy. (But be aware that the construction of a subway and the attendant traffic diversion, begun in late 1998, will make the neighborhood a mess for two years.) Guest rooms are stylishly furnished in pastels; the higher floors have a panoramic view. The Dusit Thani is particularly noted for the spaciousness of its Landmark suites, their concierge service, and for the attention paid to every possible need. On request, a fax machine is installed in your room. The 30 very special Thai Heritage suites are furnished in classical Thai tradition with handcrafted furniture, but the standard rooms are due for refurbishing. The service, as in many deluxe hotels in Bangkok, is not up to past standards, but it still rates as one of the best hotels in Southeast Asia. ⊠ *Rama IV Rd., 10500,* ☎ *02/236–0450, 800/223–6800, 212/838–3110 in N.Y.,* ℻ *02/237–5837. 510 rooms and 15 suites. 7 restaurants, bar, coffee shop, in-room VCRs, pool, health club, shops, nightclub, business services, meeting rooms. AE, DC, MC, V.*

$$$$ 🏨 **Grand Hyatt Erawan.** The Grand Hyatt is built on the site of the old Erawan Hotel, next to the much-revered Erawan shrine. The typically Hyatt lobby is a stylish four-story atrium with a domed, stained-glass roof—decorated with an extensive art collection. Service is swift and efficient. Guest rooms are large, with window bays for a desk and a couple of chairs. The wood floors are strewn with area rugs, and each room has original art. Messages are displayed on a television monitor, and the bathrooms have separate showers, oversize tubs, and dressing areas. The three Regency floors offer concierges and other services. The rooms with the best view look over Lumphini Park and the racetrack, though the traffic on Rajdamri Road can be heard. When the new overhead electric train is completed (circa 2000), noise in the lower-floor rooms may become a nuisance. Restaurants abound. The Italian fare at Spasso, developed by a Milanese chef, is especially creative and a lunch here is recommended whether you stay in the hotel or not. The pool terrace is covered with ferns and plants that shade you from reflected brilliance, and a trained physical therapist manages the elaborate health club. ⊠ *494 Rajdamri Rd., 10330,* ☎ *02/254–1234, 800/233–1234 U.S. reservations,* ℻ *02/253–5856. 389 rooms and suites. 3 restaurants, bar, pool, 2 tennis courts, health club, squash, business services, meeting rooms. AE, DC, MC, V.*

$$$$ 🏨 **Landmark Hotel.** Though it calls itself high-tech, the Landmark's generous use of teak in its reception areas creates an ambience suggestive of a grand European hotel. Guest rooms, unobtrusively elegant, are geared to the international business traveler, with good desks and TV/video screens that can tune in to information banks linked to the business center. With a staff of 950, service is swift and attentive. The hotel's elegant Hibiscus restaurant has a view of the city to accompany its European fare, and a jazz trio accompanies drinks and light meals in the Huntsman Pub. ⊠ *138 Sukhumvit Rd., 10110,* ☎ *02/254–0404,* ℻ *02/253–4259. 395 rooms and 55 suites. 4 restaurants, coffee shop, snack bar, pool, sauna, health club, 2 squash courts, shops, business services, meeting rooms. AE, DC, MC, V.*

$$$$ ✈ **Oriental Hotel.** The Oriental has set the standard for which all other
★ Bangkok hotels strive. Part of its fame stems from its past famous
guests, and today's roster features heads of state and film personal-
ities. The location on the Chao Phraya is unrivaled; the original
building, now the Garden Wing, has been refurbished, and the rooms
here—and the main building's luxury suites—are the hotel's best.
Among its well-known restaurants are China House, Sala Rim Naam
across the river, renowned for its Thai food, and Le Normandie, the
best French restaurant in Bangkok. In addition, the hotel has a riverside barbecue every night. The Oriental radiates elegance and provides superb service, though in recent years some of the crispness and
panache have disappeared, perhaps because the staff is continually
wooed away by other hotels. You can attend a Thai cooking school
here, afternoon seminars explaining Thai culture, and, more recently,
a smart spa across the river (next to the Sala Rim), where you can
indulge in all sorts of luxurious treatments. The hotel, in conjunction with the Royal Orchid Sheraton and the Shangri-La, has a helicopter service ($200) to and from the airport. ✉ *48 Oriental Ave.,
10500,* ☎ *02/236–0400, 71/537–2988 reservations in the U.K.,
800/223–6800 in the U.S.;* FAX *02/236–1937. 398 rooms. 8 restaurants, 2 tennis courts, health club, jogging, 2 squash courts, nightclub, business services. AE, DC, MC, V.*

$$$$ ✈ **The Regent.** Long one of Bangkok's leading hotels, the Regent is in
★ the embassy district, which is now the geographical center of the city.
You enter from palatial steps into a formal lobby where local society
meets for morning coffee and afternoon tea, and where Thai classical
art adds serenity to sophisticated luxury. Service is exemplary. Off a
delightful courtyard there are shops and restaurants, including the
popular Spice Market. In 1996 a $15-million refurbishment program
eliminated some rooms to make the remaining ones larger and give each
a separate shower. They are decorated in timeless good taste, with Thai
silk upholstery. Our favorite rooms overlook the racetrack, but choose
one on a high floor, since the new elevated electric train blocks the view
for rooms on the first three floors. There are also four "cabana rooms,"
whose private patios look onto a small garden with a lotus pond. In
the new concierge club lounge (extra charge), there's an extensive library, concierge services, excellent breakfasts, and complimentary hors
d'oeuvres. Be sure to have the Regent's fragrant-oil massage. ✉ *155
Rajdamri Rd., 10330,* ☎ *02/251–6127,* FAX *02/253–9195. 363 rooms.
3 restaurants, pool, massage, health club, shops, business services.
AE, DC, MC, V.*

$$$$ ✈ **Royal Orchid Sheraton.** Of the hotels offering riverfront luxury this
28-story palace is more oriented toward tour groups than its neighbors, the Oriental and the Shangri-La. All rooms face the river and are
well appointed—the namesake flowers are everywhere. The decor of
the public rooms, low-key peaches and creams, are soothing to the eye
but a little wishy-washy and boring. Standard rooms tend to be long
and narrow, with a slightly cramped feeling, but if you go for a deluxe
room, you'll be paying the same price as if you were staying at the Oriental or Shangri-La. The restaurants are almost too numerous to mention, but the Thai Thara Thong is memorable, with subtle classical music
accompanying your meal. You could equally well choose Japanese, Indian, or Italian cuisine. A glassed-in bridge leads to the River City Shopping Centre next door. ✉ *2 Captain Bush La., 10500,* ☎ *02/266–0123
or 02/237–0022,* FAX *02/236–8320. 771 rooms. 9 restaurants and
bars, wading pool, 2 tennis courts, health club, shops, business services,
meeting rooms, helipad. AE, DC, MC, V.*

$$$$ ✈ **Shangri-La Hotel.** For decades the Oriental could safely claim to be
Bangkok's finest hotel; then came the challenge by a spate of new ho-

tels, of which the Shangri-La was one of the first and best. The initial enthusiasm has passed—it's looking a little tired these days, the smiles seem permanently fixed, and the fairly large guest rooms, decorated in pastels, are showing signs of age. The staff is nevertheless professional and efficient, and the spacious marble lobby with crystal chandeliers is a relief from the congestion of Bangkok. The lobby lounge, with its floor-to-ceiling windows, offers a marvelous panorama of the Chao Phraya River. The gardens are an oasis whose peace is interrupted only by the riverboat traffic. In the opulent Krungthep Wing, a separate tower across the gardens, all guest rooms have fax outlets and balconies overlooking the river. ⊠ *89 Soi Wat Suan Phu, New Rd., 10500,* ☎ *02/236–7777,* 𝔽𝔸𝕏 *02/236–8579. 801 rooms and 65 suites. 13 restaurants and bars, 2 pools, 2 tennis courts, health club, squash, shops, business services. AE, DC, MC, V.*

$$$$ ▦ **Sheraton Grande Sukhumvit.** Bangkok's second and newest Sheraton opened in late 1996 and soars 33 floors above the business/shopping/embassy area. The light-flooded guest rooms, on the upper floors, are a far cry from typical boxlike hotel rooms; each has a spacious bathroom angled off the bedroom, and the entrance hall and walk-in wardrobe have interesting diagonals. In these "Deluxe" rooms, a 24-hour butler service will bring you coffee or iron your dress at the push of a button. You'll never go hungry here: the street-level entrance has Riva's, a restaurant and bar offering live music and California cooking; off the marble lobby on the first floor, the Orchid Café provides an international buffet; on the second floor you can choose Italian (Rossini's) or Chinese, or have tea in a lounge or cocktails in a rotunda; and on the third floor, the health club and the deep-blue, serpentine swimming pool are laid out in an Oriental garden, which is also the setting for the Thai restaurant and in the winter (dry) months a barbecue. ⊠ *250 Sukhumvit Rd., 10110,* ☎ *02/653–0333,* 𝔽𝔸𝕏 *02/653–0400. 445 rooms. 4 restaurants, pool, health club, business services. AE, DC, MC, V.*

$$$$ ▦ **Sukhothai.** On six landscaped acres off Sathorn Road (a high-traffic area with no tourist attractions), this 1991 hotel attempts to recapture the glory of Thailand's first kingdom in its architecture and ambience, but it does not quite succeed. It does, however, offer quiet; the clutter and chaos of Bangkok seem a world away from its numerous courtyards. The hotel's Thai restaurant is attractively set in a pavilion in an artificial lake, but for all its elegance, it feels a bit stiff and pretentious. Public areas have stern pillars, sharp right angles, and prim little tables laid for tea. The dining room for Continental and grilled fare is comfortable, but prices are high. Standard rooms are spacious but not exceptionally well furnished. The one-bedroom suites ($400) have splendid, oversize, teak-floor bathrooms with "his and her" washbasins and mirrors. Most of the guest rooms face one of the pond-filled courtyards. ⊠ *13/3 South Sathorn Rd., 10120,* ☎ *02/287–0222,* 𝔽𝔸𝕏 *02/287–4980. 212 rooms, including 76 suites. 2 restaurants, pool, massage, sauna, tennis court, health club, squash. AE, DC, MC, V.*

$$$–$$$$ ▦ **J. W. Marriott Hotel.** The last thing Bangkok needed in late 1997 was a new luxury hotel, but it got this one, and though normally it would be in the $$$$ price category, it has priced itself lower to win some business. Other than being sparkling new with all modern technological conveniences, such as two telephone lines per room and a separate shower stall in the bathrooms, the Marriott does not stand out. Rooms are standard, though a firm king-size bed makes for good sleeping. It's worth an extra B800 to stay on the Executive Floors, 16 through 24. Although the rooms are the same as others, guests check in and out in the executive lounge and are offered complimentary breakfast, afternoon tea, and evening cocktails. The fitness center is

superb, with saunas and the latest equipment for retooling the body. Restaurants include the Cantonese Man Ho, which has private alcoves and, for parties of more than six, a separate lounge area adjacent to the table; the White Elephant Thai restaurant, and the informal JW's California, with an open kitchen and Pacific Rim cuisine. ⊠ *4 Sukhumvit, Soi 2, 10110,* ☎ *02/656–7700,* ℻ *02/656–7711. 446 rooms. 3 restaurants, bar, pool, sauna, health club, business services, meeting rooms. AE, DC, MC, V.*

$$$ 🏨 **Amari Airport Hotel.** If you need to stay within walking distance of the airport, this is your only option, and a convenient one at that. A covered passageway leads from the International Terminal to the hotel. The hotel is modern and utilitarian, with a helpful staff. In contrast to the exotic surroundings of Thailand, however, it is a bit boring. Rooms are functional and efficient. The daytime (8 AM–6 PM) rate for travelers waiting for connections is B600 for stays up to three hours, and video screens in the public rooms display the schedules of flight arrivals and departures. ⊠ *333 Chert Wudhakas Rd., Don Muang 10210,* ☎ *02/566–1020,* ℻ *02/566–1941. 440 rooms. 2 restaurants, coffee shop, pool, nightclub, meeting rooms. AE, DC, MC, V.*

$$$ 🏨 **Ambassador Hotel.** This hotel, with three wings of guest rooms, a complex of restaurants, and a shopping center, is virtually a minicity, which perhaps explains the impersonal service and limited helpfulness of the staff. Milling convention delegates contribute to the businesslike atmosphere. Guest rooms are compact, decorated with standard pastel hotel furnishings. There is plenty to keep you busy at night: the Dickens Pub garden bar, the Flamingo Disco, and The Club for rock music. The 5,000-room Ambassador City on Jontien Beach, Pattaya, is a sister hotel. ⊠ *171 Sukhumvit Rd., Soi 11–13, 10110,* ☎ *02/254–0444,* ℻ *02/253–4123. 1,050 rooms, including 24 suites. 12 restaurants, coffee shop, snack bar, pool, massage, 2 tennis courts, health club, business services, meeting rooms. AE, DC, MC, V.*

$$$ 🏨 **Montien.** This hotel across the street from Patpong, convenient to the corporations along Silom Road, has been remarkably well maintained over its two decades. The concierge is particularly helpful. The guest rooms are reasonably spacious, though not decoratively inspired. They do, however, have private safes. Prices are slightly higher than you would expect, but the hotel will give discounts. It's also the only hotel with in-house fortune-tellers who will read your palm or your stars for B250. ⊠ *54 Suriwongse Rd., 10500,* ☎ ℻ *02/234–8060. 500 rooms. 2 restaurants, coffee shop, pool, nightclub, business services, meeting rooms. AE, DC, MC, V.*

$$$ 🏨 **Narai Hotel.** Conveniently located on Silom Road near the business, shopping, and entertainment areas, this friendly, modern hotel offers comfortable, utilitarian rooms, many decorated with warm, rose-color furnishings. At the low end of this price category, the hotel is a good value, given its cheerful rooms and high level of service. The most distinguishing feature is Bangkok's only revolving restaurant, La Rotonde Grill, on the 15th floor. ⊠ *222 Silom Rd., 10500,* ☎ *02/257–0100,* ℻ *02/236–7161. 500 rooms, including 10 suites. 3 restaurants, coffee shop, pool, health club, nightclub, business services. AE, DC, MC, V.*

$$$ 🏨 **Siam Inter-Continental.** In the center of Bangkok on 26 landscaped acres, the Siam Inter-Continental has a soaring pagoda roof. Its modern Thai architecture, lofty lobby, and feeling of space make this hotel stand out from all others in Bangkok. Each of the air-conditioned rooms is stylishly decorated with teak furniture, a trim, upholstered wing chair and love seat, and a cool, blue color scheme. Especially attractive are the teak-paneled bathrooms with radios, telephones, and hair dryers. ⊠ *967 Rama I Rd., 10330,* ☎ *02/253–0355,* ℻ *02/253–2275.*

411 rooms and suites. 4 restaurants, 2 bars, pool, driving range, putting green, health club, jogging track, meeting rooms. AE, DC, MC, V.

$$ ⛨ **Bel-Air Princess.** Two hundred yards down Soi 5 from bustling Sukhumvit is this quiet, well-managed hotel. It gets its fair share of tour groups, but for the most part the lobby and lounge area are cool and peaceful, and the downstairs restaurant is a good place to relax over a light meal. Northern Indian cooking, lightly spiced for Western taste, is served in the formal restaurant, the Tiffin Room. The spacious, carpeted guest rooms, with two queen-size beds or one king, are large enough for a round table and chairs as well as the standard TV-cabinet/desk. Personal safes, in-house movies, hair dryers, and tea/coffeemakers are pluses, and the bowl of fruit on each landing is a nice touch. Choose a room at the back of the hotel overlooking Soi 7 and beyond for the most light and a sprawling view. ⊠ 16 Sukhumvit Rd., Soi 5, 10110, ☎ 02/253–4300, ⅻ 02/255–8850. 160 rooms. 2 restaurants, bar, pool, health club. AE, DC, MC, V.

$$ ⛨ **Century Hotel.** This location in the northern part of downtown is convenient to the airport. The rooms, though neat and clean, are small and dark. The coffee shop–bar is open 24 hours, a plus for travelers with early morning flights. ⊠ 9 Rajaprarop Rd., 10400, ☎ 02/246–7800. 240 rooms. Bar, coffee shop, pool. AE, DC, MC, V.

$$ ⛨ **City Lodge.** There are two City Lodges off Sukhumvit, one on Soi 9 and this, which is a tad better, on Soi 19. Both are part of the Amari group of hotels, but designed for the frugal traveler. The compact rooms are charmless: utilitarian and functional, designed for efficiency of space. Business services are minimal, but you can use those at the nearby sister hotel, the Amari Boulevard (as well as its swimming pool). The coffee-shop restaurant specializes in Italian recipes at dinner. ⊠ Sukhumvit Soi 19, 10110, ☎ 02/254–4783, ⅻ 02/255–7340. 35 rooms. Restaurant. AE, DC, MC, V.

$$ ⛨ **Grand China Princess.** One good reason for staying in Chinatown is that it's the center of old Bangkok, with lots of exotic turn-of-the-century Asian ambience. Another reason is this hotel, which opened in October 1993. It occupies the top two-thirds of a 25-story tower from which the guest rooms have panoramic views of the city. Room 2202, for example, gives you a wonderful sight in the morning of the Temple of the Dawn, the Golden Mount, and Wat Tuk in one sweep of the eyes. Since the rooms form a segment of a circle, they are not rectangular; the window wall is narrower than the back wall, so the side walls seem to converge. The furnishings are unexciting but functional, and all the rooms have safes and satellite television. The bathrooms are on the small side. Service is wonderfully friendly, and the reception floor (10th) has a welcoming bar, lounge, and coffee shop. Carpeted in a huge lotus design, with dark teak furniture, the restaurant, Siang Ping Loh (Cantonese and Szechuan fare), is well worth a visit in its own right. ⊠ 215 Corner of Yaowaraj and Ratchawongse Rd., Samphantawongse, 10100, ☎ 02/224–9977, ⅻ 02/224–7999. 155 rooms. Restaurant, coffee shop, health club, business services. AE, DC, MC, V.

$$ ⛨ **La Residence.** You would expect to find this small town-house hotel on the Left Bank of Paris, not in Bangkok. Though it's a little overpriced, La Residence suits the frequent visitor to Bangkok who wants a low-key hotel. The staff members, however, can be abrupt at times. The guest rooms are small, but the furnishings—pale wood cabinets, pastel draperies—give them a fresh, airy feel. The restaurant, which serves Thai and European food, also serves as a sitting area for guests. ⊠ 173/8–9 Suriwongse Rd., 10150, ☎ 02/233–3301. 23 rooms. Restaurant, laundry service. AE, DC.

$$ ⛨ **Manohra Hotel.** An expansive, spotless marble lobby characterizes the pristine efficiency of this hotel between the river and Patpong. Rooms

have pastel walls, rich patterned bedcovers, and dark-green carpets. There is a roof garden for sunbathing, and for evening action, there is the Buccaneer Night Club. A word of caution: If the Manohra is fully booked, the staff may suggest its new sister hotel, the Ramada (no relation to the American-managed Ramada), on New Road. Unless you are desperate, decline: it is overpriced and has small, poorly designed rooms. The Manohra, on the other hand, is attractive and well run, with a helpful, friendly staff. ⊠ *412 Suriwongse Rd., 10500,* ☎ *02/234–5070,* FAX *02/237–7662. 230 rooms. 2 restaurants, coffee shop, indoor pool, nightclub, meeting rooms. AE, DC, MC, V.*

$$ ⊡ **Park Hotel.** After its 1992 renovation, the hotel has a fresh crispness to it not often found in this price category. The lobby area, lounge, and bar are far from being designer decorated, but there is adequate room for checking in and comfortable seating. And there is a small pool in the garden. Ample light makes the guest rooms cheerful, and bathrooms are small and clean. The deluxe doubles have space for a desk. ⊠ *Sukhumvit Soi 7, Sukhumvit Rd., 10110,* ☎ *02/255–4300,* FAX *02/255–4309. 139 rooms. Restaurant, bar, coffee shop, pool, travel services. MC, V.*

$$ ⊡ **Silom Plaza Hotel.** This hotel in the shopping area on Silom Road has an open lobby area with a lounge. The compact rooms have modern decor in soft colors; the more expensive ones have river views. The hotel caters to business travelers who want to be close to Silom Road. Service is quick. The facilities are limited, but all the entertainment you could wish for is nearby. ⊠ *320 Silom Rd., 10500,* ☎ *02/236–0333,* FAX *02/236–7562. 209 rooms. Restaurant, coffee shop, indoor pool, sauna, health club, meeting rooms. AE, DC, MC, V.*

$$ ⊡ **Silom Village Inn.** Clean, neat, and friendly, with extremely reasonable
★ prices (about B1,000, with the invariable discount) describes this small hotel. The king-size beds leave just enough space for a desk and a couple of chairs. Bathrooms are new and functional. Choose a room at the back of the hotel to avoid the Silom street noise. The staff in the small reception lobby is helpful and reliable at taking messages. A small restaurant is good for breakfast and snacks and also serves Italian food, but the Seafood Village Plaza next door is tempting. ⊠ *Silom Village Trade Centre, 286 Silom Rd., 10500,* ☎ *02/635–6810/7,* FAX *02/635–6817. 34 rooms. Restaurant. AE, DC, MC, V.*

$$ ⊡ **Swiss Lodge.** This small hotel off Silom Road near the Dusit Thani is the closest equivalent to a boutique hotel in Bangkok. Rooms are furnished in light colors giving a crisp, fresh look, single rooms are really the size of small doubles. Doubles are a bit larger, so as to fit in king-size beds. All rooms have built-in safe-deposit boxes, bathrobes, and ample work space, and the telephone line can be transferred to your computer. Bathrooms are compact, but fully equipped. Half of the guestroom floors are designated no smoking. A very small outdoor pool and sundeck are on the fifth floor, and a helpful business center has computer facilities and a small meeting room for up to six people. The second floor has a bar lounge, a clublike place to repair to after tromping Bangkok's streets. On the ground floor is a coffee-shop-style dining room serving Thai and Continental food. ⊠ *3 Convent Rd., 10500,* ☎ *02/233–5345,* FAX *02/236–9425. 57 rooms. Restaurant, pool, business services. AE, DC, MC, V.*

$$ ⊡ **Tara Hotel.** Built in 1989, the Tara is in the developing restaurant-
★ and-nightlife section of Sukhumvit Road. Guests register in a check-in lounge, where tea or coffee is served while the formalities are completed. The lobby is spacious, lined with teakwood carving. Guest rooms, which are on the small side, are decorated with pastels; many overlook the eighth-floor terrace garden with swimming pool. ⊠ *Sukumvit Soi 26, 10110,* ☎ *02/259–0053,* FAX *02/259–2900. 200*

rooms and 20 suites. Restaurant, coffee shop, pool, meeting room. AE, DC, MC, V.

$$ ⊞ **Tower Inn.** For a reasonably priced room, centrally located, consider the Tower Inn. The hotel's name is appropriate; it is a tall skinny building on Silom Road near the Thai International Airways office. The top floor has a health club and swimming pool, from which you can glimpse the Chao Phraya River. The reception desk, a bar, and a small lounge are on the ground floor, and the coffee shop (Thai and Continental food) is on the second floor. The rooms are as spacious as those at the Shangri-La, with plenty of light flooding in from picture windows. The furnishings, mind you, are ordinary and utilitarian—two queen-size beds and a cabinet that holds the television and serves as a desk. The bathroom is smallish—not one to linger in. You can usually negotiate a 30% discount with no trouble at all, which brings the room rate down to B1,335 ($53). ⊠ *533 Silom Rd., 10500,* ☎ *02/237–8300,* FAX *02/237–8286. 150 rooms. Restaurant, pool, health club, travel services. AE, DC, MC, V.*

$ ⊞ **The Executive House.** Though it offers only limited services, this hotel's reception staff will sometimes help with travel questions, and the coffee shop will deliver food to your room until midnight. The rooms are spacious for the price, the air-conditioning works, and, even if the decor is drab and a bit run-down, the rooms on the upper floors have plenty of light. The penthouse rooms—on the 15th–18th floors—are flooded with light. Currently, the 15th floor has the freshest rooms. Rooms with a river view are B200 more than those with a city view. Over the last few years, room prices have steadily increased, with no improvement in facilities, and the lack of tourist services makes this hotel more suited for visitors already familiar with Bangkok. The hotel is next to the Manohra Hotel, down a short driveway. ⊠ *410/3–4 Suriwongse Rd., 10500,* ☎ *02/235–1206,* FAX *02/236–1482. 120 rooms. Coffee shop. MC, V.*

$ ⊞ **First House.** Tucked behind the Pratunam market on a soi off Phetchburi, the First House offers excellent value for a full-service hotel in this price range. The small lobby–sitting area serves as a meeting place where guests can read the complimentary newspapers. Off to the left, the Saranyuth coffeehouse-restaurant, open 24 hours, serves Thai and Western dishes. The compact rooms are carpeted and amply furnished but so dark as to be depressing during the day. Bathrooms are clean, though patches of rough plaster and drab fixtures don't encourage leisurely grooming. But the reasonable rates, the security, and the helpfulness of the staff all contribute to making this hotel worth noting. ⊠ *14/20–29 Phetchburi Soi 19, Pratunam, 10400,* ☎ *02/254–0303. 84 rooms. Coffee shop, travel services. AE, DC, MC, V.*

$ ⊞ **New Trocadero.** This hotel, between Patpong and the Chao Phraya River, has been a Westerner's standby for six decades. Its smallish rooms, recently refurbished, have queen-size-plus beds and clean bathrooms. Service is friendly, and there's a helpful travel-tour desk in the lobby. The New Trocadero is associated with two adjacent, very similar hotels, the Peninsula and the Fuji. ⊠ *343 Suriwongse Rd., 10500,* ☎ *02/234–8920,* FAX *02/236–5526. 130 rooms. Coffee shop, pool, travel services. AE, DC, MC, V.*

$ ⊞ **Stable Lodge.** Down a small, partly residential street off Sukhumvit Road, this small hotel seems more like a guest house; videos are shown in the lounge in the evening. Since the new owners acquired the property (formerly Mermaid's), prices have climbed to around B1,000, but we still recommend it. It is quiet; rooms are clean and neat with queen-size beds. The more expensive rooms have private balconies and those at the back are the quietest. A pool in the garden is an added attraction. The coffee shop serves Thai and Western food all day and a garden barbecue at night. ✉ *39 Sukhumvit Soi 8, 10110,* ☎ *02/653–0017,* FAX *02/253–5125. 40 rooms, most with private baths. Restaurant, pool. AE, MC, V.*

¢ 🏨 **The Atlanta.** Charles Henn, a part-time professor, caters to visit-
★ ing academics and scholars, mature frugal travelers who often return again and again. The dining room and lobby lounge are straight out of the 1950s, with leatherette banquettes and a circular sofa; it's often used for fashion shoots. The accommodations are simple and with-out TV, but they're clean and very spacious for the rock-bottom rates. (Many rooms were repainted in 1996; some in 1998.) Some rooms have air-conditioning, some have fans and ventilators, and some have balconies; most have personal safes (some big enough for lap-top computers), and some have universal electric receptacles. Ask for a room on the quiet side. The hotel's big plus is the just-renovated dining room, where classical music is heard before 5 PM, jazz is played thereafter, and a movie from Henn's sophisticated videotape collection is shown after dinner. The menu, which explains the in-gredients of each dish, makes interesting reading (Henn is a food critic), and the Thai food is superb, with a wide vegetarian selection. In the crass glitter of modern Bangkok, the Atlanta is an oasis for the ed-ucated traveler—and one of the best values in town. ✉ *78 Sukhumvit Soi 2, 10110,* ☎ *02/252–1650 or 02/252–6069,* FAX *02/656–8123 or 02/255–2151. 59 rooms. Restaurant, pool, travel services. No credit cards.*

¢ 🏨 **River City Guest House.** It's a shame this small hotel, a block from the water's edge, has no view of the river. But then if it had, the price of a room would probably quadruple. As it is, B500 gives you a mod-est air-conditioned room with a double bed, and a table and chair. The small bathrooms have showers with hot and cold water, with exposed plumbing for decoration! Ask for a room with a window. The trick is to find the hotel: walk upriver from the Sheraton, past the River City Shopping Centre, and as the soi bends to the right, the hotel is on the right. This location gives you easy access to the marvelous sois of Chi-natown and the river ferries, and puts you within walking distance of Suriwongse and Silom roads. ✉ *11/4 Soi Rong Nam Khang 1, Chareon Krung Rd. (Soi 24), 10100,* ☎ *02/235–1429,* FAX *02/237–3127. 17 rooms with bath or shower. Coffee shop. MC, V.*

¢ 🏨 **River View Guest House.** Down a tiny soi on the edge of Chinatown and just one house in from the Chao Phraya River, this family-run hotel is unique for being a budget hotel with river views. The rooms are shabby, no doubt about it, but they are kept clean. The river-view rooms are fan-cooled and without a full bathroom (B450), while the rooms with only a limited view of the river have air-conditioning and a bath (B700). Tiny rooms with shared bathrooms cost only B150. The cof-fee shop, on the eighth floor, has a most spectacular view, since this is where the Chao Phraya makes a turn. This hotel is not for everyone. The location is ethnic and the hotel could use a bundle of money to refurbish it, but for those still reading Joseph Conrad, it fulfills the imag-ination. The easiest way to find it is to walk upriver from the Shera-ton Orchid, keeping as close to the river as you can. After about 1,000 yards, you'll see the guest house's sign pointing down a soi on the left. ✉ *768 Soi Panurangsri, Songvad Rd., 10100,* ☎ *02/234–5429,* FAX *02/ 236–6199. 37 rooms, half with bath. Restaurant. V.*

In the neighborhood of Khao San Road, there are hundreds of small guest houses where the price of a room and shared bath is about B60. The **C&C Guest House** (✉ 12 Wisut Kasat Rd., Bang Khunprom, 10200, ☎ 02/282–4941) is near Wat In and has clean rooms, a cof-fee lounge, a small garden, and a friendly staff. The same can be said for the **Shanti Lodge** (⊠ 37 Sri Ayutthaya, 10200, ☎ 02/281–2497), behind the National Library.

Nightlife and the Arts

The English-language newspapers, the *Bangkok Post* and *The Nation,* have good information on current festivals, exhibitions, and nightlife. TAT's weekly *Where* also lists events.

Nightlife

A recent law requires that bars and nightclubs close at 2 AM, but Bangkok never sleeps, and many restaurants and street stalls stay open for late-night carousing. Unfortunately, tourism has propagated the most lurid forms of nightlife geared to the male tourist. Live sex shows, though officially banned, are still found in Patpong and other areas. Expect to be ripped off if you indulge. A classic trick is for the hustler outside to promise you B60 beer and no cover charge, but when the bill comes, the beer is perhaps B200 and the service charge is B500. When you dispute the charge, large burly men appear, and if you then pay with a credit card, the establishment secretly makes several imprints, which it later fills in, forging your signature.

BARS

Just beyond Soi Cowboy in the curving side streets (Soi 23 to Soi 31) off Sukhumvit are several small, pleasant bars, often with a small live band playing jazz or country music. **Rang Phah** (⊠ 16 Sukhumvit 23 Soi, ☎ 02/258–4321) is also a restaurant with excellent Thai food, and you can sit in the garden outside the marvelous Thai house and drink, eat a little, and gaze at the stars. **September** (⊠ 120/1 Sukhumvit 23, ☎ 02/258–5785), which serves food as well as drink, is designed in a Victorian Thai style with a heavy teak bar. **Fred and Barts** (⊠ 123/1 Sukhumvit, ☎ 02/258–4541), a modern bar with stainless-steel furnishings, has enthusiastic hostesses. The friendly and cozy **Drunken Duck Pub** (⊠ 59/4 Soi 31, Sukhumvit Rd., ☎ 02/258–4500) has a three-piece band playing popular jazz. A country-and-western band plays at **Trail Dust** (⊠ 43/2 Sukhumvit 31, ☎ 02/258–4590), a large tavern with tables both in its patio garden and inside.

Friendly pubs and cafés, popular with yuppie Thais and expats, can be found along Sarasin Road (north of Lumphini Park). **Brown Sugar** (⊠ 231/20 Soi Sarasin, ☎ 02/250–0103) has a clutter of small rooms humming with animated conversation. The **Old West Saloon** (⊠ 231/17 Soi Sarasin, ☎ 02/252–9510) re-creates the atmosphere of America's Old West aided by a four-piece band and a happy hour. The **Burgundy Pub** (⊠ 231/18 Soi Sarasin, ☎ 02/250–0090) is good for conversation and relaxation—it's a good place to meet local yuppie Thais, but the price of a beer is more than double that at the Old West Saloon next door. **The Hemingway Bar & Grill** (⊠ 159/5 Sukhumvit, Soi 55, ☎ 02/392–3599) is popular with Thais and expats for an evening of fellowship in log cabin–style ambience. Those who want Western food and live music will always gravitate to the **Hard Rock Cafe** (⊠ Siam Sq., ☎ 02/251–0792). An oasis in Patpong is the British-style **Bobbies Arms** (⊠ Car Park Blvd., second level, Patpong 2 Rd., ☎ 02/233–6828), where you can get a decent pint of beer (chilled) with convivial chatter and pub grub. On weekends, a live band plays and various excuses are made for a party—anything from St. Patrick's Day to St. George's Day.

At **Summertime** (⊠ 133/19 Kesorn Rd., Rajprasong, near the Erawan Hyatt, ☎ 02/253–7604), with a solid-mahogany bar and Italian food, the collectibles on the walls are for sale. The seafood restaurant **Moon**

Shadow (⊠ Kesorn R., Rajprasong [across from Summertime], ☎ 02/ 253–7553) features live jazz in an upstairs lounge and serves excellent fish in a publike setting. **Witch's Tavern** (⊠ Soi Thonglor, Sukhumvit Rd., ☎ 02/391–9791) offers classical jazz in a cozy Victorian atmosphere where you can order just a beer or hearty English fare.

Only in Bangkok would you ever find a phenomenon like **Royal City Avenue** (called "RCA" or, by some, "RC Awaiti," which means RC Hell). By about 11 PM this strip, completely deserted by day, used to be thronged with thousands of young Thais walking up and down enticed to alight at one of the 160 bars lining the avenue and blaring loud music. In 1996, the police started swooping down on underage Thais and cracking down on the nightswingers popping ecstasy pills. Then came the economic crisis of 1998. The result is that RCA has lost its wild gaiety. Though many bars have closed up, there are still scores of drinking and music joints. No one bar appears different from the others, except the **The Old Dragon,** or Old Leng, a resurrected 100-year-old storehouse full of oddities out of the past—from wooden cinema seats to etchings of Chinese characters on old mirrors. Vorapoj Praponphan, the owner, says that except for the music machines, the cash register, and most of the guests, nothing in the place is younger than 50 years. Food is a mix of Chinese and Thai (snacks are also available), and though the menu is in Thai, Nutty, the hostess, bubbles along in English. ⊠ 29/78–81 Royal City Ave., ☎ 02/203–0972. ⊙ Daily 6 PM–2 AM. MC, V.

CABARET

Most of the nightlife will be found on three infamous side streets that link Suriwongse and Silom roads. **Patpong 1 and 2** are packed with go-go bars with hostesses by the dozen. The obscene club acts are generally found one flight up and, despite promises to the contrary by touts, usually require a hefty cover charge. **Patpong 3** caters to homosexuals. Patpong is quite safe and well patrolled by police, and it even has a night market where Thai families shop. **Soi Cowboy,** off Sukhumvit Road at Soi 21, is less raunchy; a quieter version of Patpong. Here the bars are considerably tamer, either with some go-go dancers who'll assist in pouring your beer (B55) or bars where a quiet beer with or without a temporary companion is as risqué as it gets. **Nana Plaza,** at Soi 4 off Sukhumvit Road, is another party area, with 20 bars that cater mostly to the spirited male. The bars on the gallery upstairs have the more fleshy shows. The largest troupe of performing transvestites is reputed to be on stage at the **Calypso Garden** (⊠ 688 Sukhumvit Rd., between Soi 24 and 26, ☎ 02/258–8987) with nightly shows at 8:15 and 10. For less ribald entertainment with live bands and internationally known nightclub artists, try the **Tiara** penthouse restaurant at the Dusit Thani Hotel (☞ Lodging, above).

CULTURAL SHOWS

Silom Village (⊠ 286 Silom Rd., ☎ 02/234–4448), open 10 AM–10 PM, may be rather touristy, but it appeals also to Thais. The block-size complex has shops, restaurants, and performances of classical Thai dance. At a couple of the restaurants, chefs cook tasty morsels in the open—you select what suits your fancy or order from a menu. The best cultural show is at **Ruan Thep** (☎ 02/234–4581). Dinner starts at 7 and showtime is at 8:20. Dinner and a show costs B350; the show only is B200.

DINNER CRUISES

These two-hour evening cruises on the Chao Phraya River are strictly for tourists, except the one run by **Yok Yor** (☞ Dining, above), which is likely to be all Thai. Boats like the **Wan Foh** (☎ 02/433–5453)—built to look like a traditional Thai house—start at the Mae-Nam Building near the Shangri-La Hotel. A Western/Thai dinner is served and the difference between one ship and another is marginal. Your hotel staff will make reservations. The cost is B750 per person. **The Horizon** (Shangri-La Hotel, ☎ 02/236–7777; departures at 7:30 PM) also offers a very civilized cruise on the river while serving its guests dinner.

DISCOS

Most of the large hotels have their own disco/nightclubs. One of the best known is **Diana's** at the Oriental (☞ Lodging, *above*), said to be Bangkok's most extravagant club. Continuously popular since it was sparklingly refurbished is **Bubbles** (Dusit Thani Hotel, ☎ 02/233–1130), which attracts the Thai BMW set. If you're looking for the hot disco and pub center, head for **Silom Plaza** (✉ 320/14 Silom Rd., nearly opposite Patpong, ☎ 02/234–2657), where discos, such as the **Virgin,** and bars thumping out loud stereo music line the courtyard, and you can drink and eat at tables outdoors while watching the swinging young Thais.

The Arts

CLASSICAL THAI DANCE

Thai classical dance is the epitome of grace. Themes for the dance drama are taken from the *Ramayana* (*Ramakien* in Thailand). A series of controlled gestures uses eye contact, ankle and neck movements, and hands and fingers to convey the stories' drama. It is accompanied by a woodwind called the *piphat,* which sounds like an oboe, and percussion instruments.

In 1994, dance drama received a shot in the arm, with support from private industry and the donation by King Rama VII of the **Chalernkrung Royal Theatre** (✉ 66 New Rd., ☎ 02/222–0434). A troupe of 170 dancers now performs the Khon Masked Dance, with stunning light effects and high-tech sophistication. English translations are printed in the programs and on screens above the stage. Performances are held Tuesday and Thursday at 8 PM; your hotel can make seat reservations.

Various restaurants offer a classical dance show with dinner. **Baan Thai** (✉ Soi 22, Sukhumvit Rd., ☎ 02/258–5403) is a popular one for those staying at hotels in the eastern part of Bangkok. The **Sala Rim Naam** (✉ Oriental Hotel, 489 Charoen Nakom Rd., ☎ 02/437–6211) puts on a good show and their buffet of Thai food is excellent. At the **National Theatre** (✉ Na Phra That Rd., ☎ 02/221–5861 or 02/224–1342), performances are given most days at 10 AM and 3 PM, and special performances are held also on the last Friday of each month at 5:30 PM.

Outdoor Activities and Sports

Participant Sports

GOLF

There are good golf courses in and around Bangkok, and although weekend play requires advance booking, tee times are usually available during the week. Greens fees are approximately B700 weekdays and B1,350 on weekends. **Krungthep Sports Golf Course** (✉ B.P. 522, 10 Huamark, ☎ 02/374–0491) is attractively laid out with fairways flanked by bougainvillea and pine trees, and elevated greens surrounded by sand traps. The **Navatanee Golf Course** (✉ 22 Mul Sukhaphiban 2 Rd., Bangkapi, ☎ 02/374–6127), designed by Robert Trent Jones, is thought to be the most challenging. The **Rose Garden Golf Course** (✉ 4/8 Soi 3 Sukhumvit, ☎ 02/253–0295) is a pleasant, undemanding course.

JOGGING

For a quick jog, the small running track at many hotels may be the best bet. In all city parks, stay off the grass; don't run in the parks at night, but you can run alone safely during the day. The **Siam Inter-Continental Hotel's** jogging track in its parkland gardens is one of the most attractive. **Lumphini Park,** whose pathways are paved, is about 2 km (1¼ mi) around and is popular with serious joggers. **Chatuchak Park's** loop is 4 km (2½ mi) but it is north of the city. **Sanam Luang,** in front of the Grand Palace, is also a popular park for runners. A **Clark Hatch Athletic Club** has opened in the new Thaniya Plaza (⊠ Silom Rd., ☎ 02/231–2250). The **Grand Hyatt Erawan** has the best health-and-fitness facility of any Bangkok hotel.

MASSAGES

The massage (B150) given at the famous **Wat Po school** is the best bargain and an experience not to be missed. A very gentle massage in very genteel surroundings may be had at the new **Health and Beauty Center** (☎ 02/236–0400) in the Oriental Hotel. Here in wood-paneled sophistication you can get facials, hydrotherapy, mud and seaweed wraps, and herbal treatments—from the "Jet Lag Solution" at B3,000 to a full day's pampering for $200. A most relaxing massage, with oils, is available at the **Regent Hotel** (☎ 02/251–6127).

Spectator Sports

HORSE RACING

Horse racing is a popular pastime in Bangkok, where each meeting has up to 12 races, and public betting is permitted. The **Royal Bangkok Sports Club** (☎ 02/251–0181) and the **Royal Turf Club** (☎ 02/280–0020) hold races on alternating Sundays.

THAI BOXING

The national sport of Thailand draws an enthusiastic crowd in Bangkok, where the bouts are the real thing, unlike some Thai boxing shows you may see in tourist resort areas. Understanding the rules is close to impossible; it's fast and furious, and the playing of traditional music heightens the drama. Though you will be out of your element, try to catch a match or two at one of the **two main stadiums.** Bouts begin at 6 PM, on Sunday at 1 PM; tickets (B100–B500) may be bought at the gates. *Lumphini:* ⊠ *Rama IV Rd.,* ☎ *02/251–4303, Tues., Fri., Sat., Sun.; Ratchadamnoen:* ⊠ *Ratchadamnoen Nok Rd. near TAT office,* ☎ *02/ 281–4205, Mon., Wed., Thurs.*

Shopping

Browsing through the markets is fascinating, even if you're not in a buying mood. Everything (some say everyone) is for sale—from fake Rolex watches for the equivalent of a few bucks to Paris originals costing thousands. And aside from the wonderfully cheap mass-produced knockoffs of international brands, you'll find good-quality merchandise and crafts made in Thailand: jewelry, silks, silverware, leather, and Oriental antiques are just some examples.

Districts

The main shopping areas are along Silom Road and at the Rama IV end of Suriwongse for jewelry, crafts, and silk; along Sukhumvit Road for leather goods; along Yaowarat in Chinatown for gold; and along Silom Road, Oriental Lane, and Charoen Krung Road for antiques. The Oriental Plaza and the River City Shopping Centre next to the Sheraton Orchid Hotel have shops with collector-quality goods; the shops around Siam Square and at the new World Trade Centre attract middle-income Thais and foreigners. Peninsula Plaza, across from the Regent Hotel, has very upscale shops, and the newest and glitziest complex is Thaniya Plaza, between Silom and Suriwongse roads, near Patpong. If you're knowledgeable about fabric and cut, you can find bargains

at the textile merchants and tailors who compete along Pahurat Road
in Chinatown and Pratunam off Phetchburi Road.

DUTY-FREE SHOPPING

Despite protests from shopkeepers, **TAT** (Tourist Authority of Thailand)
has a duty-free shop that carries all sorts of merchandise. Clerks speak
English and other languages, but prices are not low, and you miss out
on the cultural experience of shopping in a foreign country. Purchasers
need their passports and airline tickets and must order their goods not
less than eight hours before leaving the country. ⊠ *World Trade Center, 4 Rajdamri Rd., 7th floor, Patumwan, 10330,* ☏ *02/263–8550.*
🕓 *Daily 10–9.*

Markets

Bangkok's largest market, where you can buy virtually anything, is the
Chatuchak Weekend Market, up near the Northern Bus Terminal
(Morsit). If you want cheap chinaware or a tough pair of boots, come
here. Sometimes you'll find great fashion buys, for example, items made
from *mudmee* silk (Ikat weave; whose thread is tie-dyed before weaving) that would sell in America for five times the price. Even if you don't
buy, a visit will open your eyes to exotic foods, flowers, and Thai life.
This popular market has begun to open Friday evenings. ⊠ *Chatuchak
Park, Paholyothin Rd. opposite Northern Bus Terminal.* 🕓 *Fri. 5 PM–
9 PM; weekends 9–9.*

Bargain lovers should sift through the merchandise at **Pratunam Market** (⊠ Corner of Phetchburi and Rajaprarop Rds., near the Indra Regent Hotel). Hundreds of stalls and shops jam the sidewalk daily; the
stacks of merchandise consist mainly of inexpensive clothing—jeans
for $5 and shirts for $4. It's a good place to meet Thais, who come in
the evening after the movies, to shop and eat tasty, inexpensive Thai
and Chinese street food.

A lively market for goods that are cheap—but prices are inflated for
the tourist—is in **Patpong 1.** You'll see locals buying here too, between
5 and 8 every evening. Along **Silom Road,** stalls are set up in the afternoon and evening to sell tourists everything from "Rolex" watches
to leather belts and knockoff designer shirts. Prices are high and require serious negotiation. Between Yaowarat and Charoen Krung
(New Road) in Chinatown lies the so-called **Thieves Market** (Nakorn
Kasem), an area of small streets with old wood houses, where you can
buy all sorts of items, from hardware to porcelains. Bargains are hard
to find nowadays, but these small, cluttered streets are fascinating to
walk through, and, who knows, a porcelain vase may take your fancy.
Bargain hard! **Soi Sampeng** (⊠ Parallel to Yaowarat Rd.), has toys,
household goods, clothes, and lots of fabrics—it is Bangkok's best known
and oldest textile center. **Pahurat Cloth Market** (⊠ Off Yaowarat Rd.),
which is operated mostly by Indians, is known for its bargain textiles,
batiks, and buttons. An auctioneer with a microphone announces that
everything at a particular stall is to be sold at half price, and the shoppers surge over to bid. **Ta Phra Chan** (⊠ Near Wat Phra Keo), where
the Weekend Market was held before it moved, still has booths selling antiques and assorted goods. At the corner of **Wat Mahathat,** the
sidewalk stands sell amulets and good-luck charms. More antiques (both
old and new) are found on **Ta Chang Road,** where there's also jewelry
made by Thailand's northern hill tribes.

Specialty Stores

ART, CRAFTS, AND ANTIQUES

Suriwongse Road, Charoen Krung Road, and the Oriental Plaza (across
from the Oriental Hotel) have many art and antiques shops. Good qual-

ity artifacts are found in the shops at the **River City Shopping Centre,** next to the Royal Orchid Sheraton Hotel. **Peng Seng** (✉ 942 Rama IV, at the intersection of Suriwongse Rd., ☎ 02/234–1285) is one of the most respected dealers in antiquities in Bangkok. The price may be high, but the article is likely to be genuine. **Rasi Sayam,** in an old teak house in a garden (✉ 32 Sukhumvit Soi 23, ☎ 02/258–4195) has a wonderful collection of fine Thai crafts of all sorts.

Don't miss **123 Baan Dee** (✉ 123 Fuengnakorn Rd., ☎ 02/221–2520) in the old town, in a prizewinning restoration of a small teak house. Antique silks, ceramics, beads, pictures, and other fascinating artifacts abound on two floors, and there's a small ice-cream parlor in back. Note that Thai antiques and old images of Buddha need a special export license.

CLOTHING AND FABRICS

Thai silk gained its world reputation only after World War II, when technical innovations were introduced. Two other fabrics are worth noting: mudmee silk, produced in the northeast, and Thai cotton, which is soft, durable, and easier on the wallet than silk.

The Jim Thompson Thai Silk Company (✉ 9 Suriwongse Rd., ☎ 02/234–4900), begun by Jim Thompson, is a prime place for silk by the yard and for ready-made clothes. There is no bargaining and the prices are high, but the staff is knowledgeable and helpful. A branch store has opened in the Oriental Hotel's shopping arcade. **Choisy** (✉ 9/25 Suriwongse, ☎ 02/233–7794) is run by a French woman who offers Parisian-style ready-to-wear dresses in Thai silk. **Design Thai** (✉ 304 Silom Rd., ☎ 02/235–1553) has a large selection of silk items in all price ranges—a good place for that gift you ought to take home (you can usually manage a 20% discount here).

Napajaree Suanduenchai studied fashion design in Germany, then started the **Prayer Textile Gallery,** where for 32 years she has made (and now her daughter makes) stunning ethnic and traditional clothes in naturally dyed silks and cottons and in old fabrics from the north, Laos, and Cambodia. (✉ Phayathai Rd., near Siam Square, ☎ 02/251–7549). For factory-made clothing, visit the **Indra Garment Export Centre** (✉ Rajaprarop Rd., behind the Indra Regent Hotel), where hundreds of shops sell discounted items, from shirts to dresses.

The custom-made suit in 48 hours is a Bangkok specialty, but the suit often hangs on the shoulders just as one would expect from a rush job. If you want an excellent cut, give the tailor more time. The best in Bangkok is **Marco Tailor** (✉ 430/33 Siam Sq., Soi 7, ☎ 02/252–0689), where, for approximately B10,000, your suit will equal those made on Savile Row.

JEWELRY

The **Narayana-Phand** government store (✉ 295/2 Rajaprarop, Payatai, ☎ 02/245–3293) has a selection of handcrafted jewelry; but prices are not negotiable. **Polin** (✉ 860 Rama IV Rd., ☎ 02/234–8176), close to the Montien Hotel, has jewelry of interesting design. The **A. A. Company** (✉ Siam Centre, ☎ 02/251–7283), across from the Hotel Siam Inter-Continental, will custom-make jewelry if you have three days to wait or are returning to Bangkok.

A long-established jewelry firm is **Johny's Gems** (✉ 199 Fuengnakorn Rd., ☎ 02/224–4065). If you telephone, he'll send a car to pick you up (a frequent practice among the better Bangkok stores), or you can walk to the shop if you are in the vicinity of Wat Phra Keo.

LEATHER

Leather is a good buy in Bangkok, with possibly the lowest prices in the world, especially for custom work. Crocodile leather is popular, but be sure to obtain a certificate that the skins came from a domestically raised reptile; otherwise U.S. Customs may confiscate the goods. For shoes, try **River Booters** at the River City Shopping Centre (☎ 02/235–2966).

PRECIOUS METALS

Anan Bronze (✉ 157/11 Phetchburi Rd., ☎ 02/215–7739) should have something to suit your fancy. The store will arrange shipping. **S. Samran** (✉ 302/8 Phetchburi Rd., ☎ 02/215–8849) has a good selection at fair prices and is reliable for shipping purchases home.

Bangkok Essentials

Arriving and Departing

BY AIRPLANE

At **Don Muang Airport international terminal,** next to the domestic terminal, you'll find an array of desks where you can arrange for taxis into Bangkok and transport to other destinations; a reservation desk for Bangkok hotels (no fee); and a **TAT** desk with free brochures and maps (☎ 02/523–8972). Both terminals have luggage-checking facilities (☎ 02/535–1250).

There is a tax of B500 for international departures and B30 for domestic departures.

Thai Airways International (✉ 485 Silom Rd., ☎ 02/280–0060) is the national airline, and most of its flights come in and out of Don Muang. It has direct flights from the west coast of the United States and from London, and it also flies daily to Hong Kong, Singapore, Taiwan, and Japan. Service has gone down recently.

The U.S. carrier with the most frequent flights is **Northwest Airlines** (✉ 153 Rajdamri Rd., Peninsula Shopping Plaza, 4th floor, ☎ 02/254–0789). It has direct service through Tokyo (with a minimal stopover) from New York, Detroit, Seattle, Dallas, San Francisco, and Los Angeles. Incidentally, this airline's seats recline more than most, making sleeping much easier. Northwest also has a round-Asia fare, in conjunction with local airlines, which lets you hop from one capital to another. **Singapore Airlines** flies to Bangkok from Singapore. **British Airways** flies nonstop to Bangkok from London. In total, 35 airlines serve Bangkok, and more are seeking landing rights.

A word of caution: the airport has more than its share of hustlers out to make a quick baht, who often wear uniforms and tags that make them seem official. They will try to get you to change your hotel to one that pays them a large commission, perhaps claiming your intended hotel is overbooked. They will hustle you into overpriced taxis or limousines. Do not get taken in.

BETWEEN THE AIRPORT AND TOWN

By Bus: New in 1996, an airport bus service that costs B70 runs approximately every 30 minutes between Don Muang and three sectors of downtown Bangkok. A1 travels to Rajdamri and Silom roads. A2 covers the central area that includes the Victory Monument and Chinatown. A3 goes down Sukhumvit. A detailed listing of each route is available from the airport TAT office and at the bus stop outside the arrivals hall. You can also catch local air-conditioned buses on the main road that passes the airport. Cost: B15.

By Helicopter: Anyone who will pay a fare that's the equivalent of about $200 is welcome aboard the helicopter that lands at the Shangri-La

Hotel, but the new expressways have greatly diminished the need for the service.

By Taxi: Don Muang is 25 km (15 mi) from the city center. The highways are often congested, and the trip can take from 30 minutes to more than an hour. State your destination at the counter on the curb (at either terminal) and obtain a voucher; a driver will lead you to the taxi. The fare on the meter (be sure that the meter is turned on) for downtown Bangkok depends on the exact destination and, to some extent, the time of day. Count on B200–B250 plus a B50 expressway toll charge and a B50 airport surcharge. Taxis to the airport from downtown Bangkok do not have the airport surcharge, and will cost approximately B150.

By Train: The **Bangkok Airport Express** trains make the 35-minute run every 90 minutes from 8 AM to 7 PM. Check the schedule at the tourist booth in the arrival hall. The fare is B100. You can also take the regular trains from 5:30 AM to 9 PM. The fare is B5 for a local train, B13 for an express, but the train is rarely convenient since it leaves you in a part of Bangkok where there are few hotels.

BY BUS

Bangkok has three main bus terminals. **Northern/Northeast Bus Terminals,** called Morsit (⊠ Paholyothin Rd., next to Chatuchak Park, ☎ 02/272–0296 or 02/279–6222), serves the I-san (Terminal 1) and Chiang Mai and the north (Terminal 2). **Southern Bus Terminal** (⊠ Pinklao-Nakomchaisri Rd., Talingchan, ☎ 02/435–1199), in Thonburi, is for Hua Hin, Ko Samui, Phuket, and points south. **Eastern Bus Terminal** (called Ekkamai) (⊠ Sukhumvit Rd., Soi 40, Ekkamai, ☎ 02/391–2504 or 02/392–2391), is for Pattaya, Rayong, and Trat province.

BY TRAIN

Hualamphong Railway Station (⊠ Rama IV Rd., ☎ 02/223–0341), the city's main station, serves mostly long-distance trains. **Bangkok Noi** (⊠ Arun Amarin Rd., ☎ 02/411–3102) on the Thonburi side of the Chao Phraya River, is used by local trains to Hua Hin and Kanchanaburi.

Getting Around

In about year 2000 two routes of the new Skyway train should be operating: one going up Silom, along Rajdamri and on to northern downtown; the other going along Sukhumvit and Rama I Road to the Democracy Monument. This will be Bangkok's first attempt at rapid inner-city transport and may speed up some travel, but meanwhile the horrendous traffic is made even worse by the ongoing construction. Allow twice the normal travel time during rush hours, 7–10 AM and 4–7 PM.

BY BOAT

Water taxis and ferries ("river buses") ply the Chao Phraya River. The taxis are long-tailed boats (so called for the extra-long propeller shaft that extends behind the stern) that you can hire for about B400 an hour. The river-bus fare is based on zones, but B5 will cover most trips that you are likely to take. At certain ferry piers (*tha*) you will also pay a B1 jetty fee. The jetty adjacent to the Oriental Hotel is a useful stop. In about 10 minutes and half a dozen stops, you can get to the Grand Palace, or to the other side of Krungthon Bridge in about 15 minutes. It is often the quickest way to travel north–south.

BY BUS

Though buses can be very crowded, they are convenient and inexpensive. For a fare of only B3.50 (any distance) on the ordinary non-air-conditioned buses and B6 to B16 on the less frequent air-conditioned ones, you can go virtually anywhere in the city. A new addition is Micro Buses, which are smaller, air-conditioned, do not permit standing passengers, and charge B20 for any distance. Buses operate from 5 AM to around 11 PM. The routes are confusing, but usually someone at the bus stop will know the number of the bus you need to catch. You can pick up a route map at most bookstalls for B35. Be alert for purse snatchers on the buses.

BY MOTORBIKE

At the head of many sois you will often find a gang of motorbikers. These "soi boys" began by taking passengers down the sois, but their operations have expanded to take you anywhere in Bangkok. The physical risk and discomfort limit their desirability, but, if you are late for a date, they are the fastest means of transport in congested traffic. Ask for a helmet. Fares, negotiated, are about the same as, and perhaps a little less than, taxi fare. This is because they are permitted to pick up passengers only at their soi and therefore must return passengerless.

BY SAMLOR

These unmetered three-wheeled polluters, called tuk-tuks, are slightly cheaper than taxis and are best used for short trips in congested traffic. But the drivers are tough negotiators, and unless you are good at bargaining you may well end up paying more than for a metered taxi.

BY TAXI

Nowadays most taxis are metered, and you should take only these. The tariff for the first 2 km (1.2 mi) is set at B35 and then increases a baht for about every 50 meters. If the speed drops to under 6 kph, there is a surcharge of one baht per minute. A typical journey of about 5 km (3 mi) runs about B60.

Contacts and Resources

EMERGENCIES

General emergencies (☎ 1699). **Ambulance** (☎ 02/246–0199). **Fire** (☎ 199). **Police** (☎ 191).

You're advised to contact the **Tourist Police** (✉ Unico House, Ploenchit Soi Lang Suan, ☎ 02/221–6209) rather than the local police. There are tourist police mobile units at critical tourist areas, such as at Patpong in the evening.

ENGLISH-LANGUAGE BOOKSTORES

The English-language dailies, the *Bangkok Post* and *The Nation*, are available at newsstands.

Asia Books has a wide selection of books and magazines at branches throughout the city. Two convenient locations are: ✉ 221 Sukhumvit Rd., Soi 15, ☎ 02/252–7277, and in the ✉ Peninsula Plaza, adjacent to the Regent Hotel, ☎ 02/253–9786. DK Books or, more properly, **Duang Kamol Bookshop,** has stores in most neighborhoods (largest branch: ✉ 244–6 Siam Sq., ☎ 02/251–6335).

GUIDED TOURS

Numerous tours cover Bangkok and its environs. With slight variation, they cover the following itineraries.

Grand Palace and Emerald Buddha Tour. Because you can easily reach the palace by yourself and hire a guide on the spot, you may want to visit these sights independently.

City and Temples Tour. In half a day, you can visit some of Bangkok's most famous temples: Wat Po with the Reclining Buddha; Wat Benjamabophit, famous for its marble structure; and Wat Traimitr, with the five-ton golden Buddha. This tour does not include the Grand Palace.

Thai Dinner and Classical Dance. This evening tour includes a buffet-style Thai dinner with a show of classical dancing. You can manage it just as well on your own.

HOSPITALS

Chulalongkorn Hospital (✉ Rama I Rd., ☎ 02/252–8181), **Police Hospital** (✉ Rajdamri Rd., ☎ 02/252–8111). **Bangkok Christian Hospital** (✉ 124 Silom Rd., ☎ 02/233–6981/9). **The Bangkok Nursing Home** (✉ 9 Convent Rd., ☎ 02/233–2610/9). **Bangkok Adventist Hospital** (✉ 430 Phitsanulok Rd., ☎ 02/281–1422). **Nonthavej Hospital,** out toward Don Muang Airport (✉ 30/8 Ngam-wongwan Rd., Bangkhen Nonthaburi, ☎ 02/951–8575), has qualified doctors and an excellent staff accustomed to patients from overseas.

Bangkok has a number of dental clinics, among them **Ambassador Dental Clinic** (✉ 171 Sukhumvit Soi 11, Ambassador Plaza, ☎ 02/255–2279) and **Thaniya Dental Center** (✉ 4th floor, Thaniya Plaza, 52 Silom Rd., ☎ 02/231–2100). If you want a private dentist, see **Khun Phira Sithiamnuai** (✉ 97/69 Sukhumvit 24, ☎ 02/661–1156), who did his training and internship in Massachusetts.

LOST CREDIT CARDS

To report lost or stolen credit cards: **American Express** (☎ 02/273–3660); **Diners Club** (☎ 02/238–3660); **MasterCard** and **Visa** (☎ 02/246–0300).

PHARMACIES

There is no shortage of pharmacies in Bangkok. Compared with the United States, fewer drugs require prescriptions, but if you need one, the prescription must be written in Thai. Be aware that over-the-counter drugs are not necessarily of the same chemical composition as those in the United States. **Foodland Supermarket Pharmacy** (✉ No. 9 Patpong II Rd., ☎ 02/234–4559; ✉ 1413 Sukhumvit Soi 5, ☎ 02/254–2247) stays open all night. The ubiquitous **7-Eleven, AM/PM,** and other 24-hour stores carry some sundries and nonprescription medications.

TELEPHONE

Telephone information from an English-speaking operator is available by dialing 13.

TRAVEL AGENCIES

In virtually every major hotel, a travel desk books tours in and around Bangkok. Smaller travel agencies sometimes do not live up to their promises, and so for significant purchases, you may want to use a large, established agency such as **Diethelm** (✉ 544 Phoenchit Rd., ☎ 02/252–4041) or **World Travel Service** (✉ 1053 New Charoen Krung Rd., ☎ 02/233–5900).

Bangkok used to be the world's leading center for discounted airline tickets. The prices are not as competitive as they used to be, but agencies still offer some good prices, usually on lesser-known airlines. Be sure to read the restrictions on the ticket carefully before you part with any money. It's safer to buy open tickets than those naming a specific flight and time.

VISITOR INFORMATION

The **Tourist Authority of Thailand (TAT)** (✉ Le Concord Building, 202 Ratchadaphisek Rd., Huay Kwang, 10320, ☎ 02/694–1222, FAX 02/694–1220) tends to have more in the way of colorful brochures than hard information, but it can supply useful material on national parks and various routes to out-of-the-way destinations. A "tourist hot line" (dial 1155), providing information on destinations, accommodations, festivals, arts, and culture, operates 8:30–4:30. You may also use the hot line to register complaints or request assistance. There is also a TAT branch at the international terminal at Don Muang Airport (☎ 02/523–8973), open 8 AM–midnight. TAT has begun a mail drop service, similar to poste restante, which will accept parcels, letters, and fax messages for pickup at $1 per transaction (✉ 4 Ratchadamnoen Nok Av., Pom Prap 10100, ☎ 02/282–0071, FAX 02/282–9775).

SIDE TRIPS OUT OF BANGKOK

Though the fascination of Bangkok never really dulls, there comes a time when you want to escape the clouds of pollution and find fresher fields. Sophisticated seaside resorts at Cha' Am and Hua Hin are a few hours away, pristine beaches on Ko Samet and Ko Chang, a day's journey. But exotic markets in Damnoen Saduak, religious centers at Nakhon Pathom, Kanchanaburi's forested jungles laced with waterfalls, ancient temples and palaces in Ayutthaya and Lopburi can all be seen on day trips from the City of Angels.

West of Bangkok

Don't bother visiting the floating market in Bangkok; head out through rice paddies and water buffalo to Damnoen Saduak in the province of Rajburi, where the colorful scene is a photographer's fantasy. Around Nakhon Pathom the country has been settled for millennia—the city was founded before the time of Christ. Kanchanaburi Province, farther west, is so full of lush tropical beauty that you may want to go hiking and thoroughly explore its gorges and waterfalls, or even take an overnight rafting trip.

Damnoen Saduak

❶ *109 km (65 mi) southwest of Bangkok.*

At Damnoen Saduak, hire a *ruilla pai* (sampan) for about B300—it's hard to negotiate a much lower rate. Then, for an hour or more, lazily travel the canal and witness true gridlock—a mess of boats, each trying to shove its way along the klong. The traffic jams of sampans, with vendors selling fresh vegetables, meats, and clothes, are a memorable sight. Farmers' wives dressed in baggy pants, long-tail shirts, and straw hats sell produce from their sampans, paddling back and forth, or rather pushing and barging their way through the congestion. Other women, cooking tasty treats on their little stoves, sit ready to ferry sustenance to the hungry, in other boats or on the shore. It's an authentic and colorful slice of Thai life.

If you want to rest, a wharf alongside the klong has tables and chairs. Buy your drinks from the stall and your food from any one of the ruilla pai. By 11 AM, you will have seen the best of Damnoen Saduak; any longer and the novelty of exotica wears thin and the irritation of the vendors' commercialism sets in.

Nakhon Pathom

❷ *56 km (34 mi) west of Bangkok.*

Nakhon Pathom is reputed to be Thailand's oldest city, dating from 150 BC. Its main attraction is **Phra Pathom Chedi,** the tallest Buddhist monument in the world—at 417 ft, it stands a few feet higher than the Shwe

Around Bangkok

Dagon Chedi of Burma. The first chedi on this site was erected in the 6th century, but the large chedi you see today, built in 1860, encases the ruins of the original. It also marks the first center of Buddhist learning on the Thai peninsula, established here about 1,000 years ago.

The man responsible for reconstructing the chedi was King Monghut, who, when he was a monk, saw the Phra Pathom Chedi as crucial to the establishment of Buddhism in Thailand. Believing that the chedi, then in a state of disrepair, contained Buddha's holy ashes, he ordered that it be incorporated into the new one. In the outer courtyard are four *viharn* (halls) facing in different directions and containing images of Lord Buddha in various postures. The terraces around the temple complex are full of fascinating statuary, including a Dvaravati-style Buddha seated in a chair, and the museum contains some interesting Dvaravati (6th–11th century) sculpture. Occasionally, classical Thai dances are performed in front of the temple, and during the Lai Krathong festival, bazaars and a fair are set up in the adjacent park. ۞ *Museum: Wed.–Sun. 9–noon and 1–4.*

Sanan Chan Palace, just west of Phra Pathom Chedi, was built during the reign of King Rama IV. The palace is closed to the public, but the surrounding park is a lovely place to relax in cooling shade between Damnoen Saduak and Bangkok.

Rose Garden

۞ *25 km (15 mi) east of Nakhon Pathom, 32 km (19 mi) west of Bangkok.*

On the Bangkok Road out of Nakhon Pathom is the **Rose Garden,** a complex that replicates a Thai village. Amid flowering gardens of 20,000 rosebushes, there are traditional Thai houses and a stage where a "cultural show" of dance, Thai boxing, sword fighting, and a wedding ceremony are performed at 2:15 and 3:15. The park also contains a hotel, restaurants, swimming pools, and other playground activities. The B250 admission price is fairly steep, but you can while away a few pleasant hours, especially with children, in this somewhat sterile re-creation of Thailand. There is, in fact, a daily afternoon tour out of Bangkok. ⊠ *195/15 Soi Chokchai Chongchamron, Rama III Rd. (Bangkok booking office),* ☎ *02/2953261.* ☜ *Admission.* ⊘ *Daily 10–7.*

🐘 Next door to the Rose Garden and equally commercial are the elephant roundups and crocodile shows at the neighboring **Samphran Elephant Ground & Zoo.** Commercial or not, sometime during your visit to Thailand you should attend an elephant show, and this is a good one. Though there is lots else to see, it is the elephants that steal the day. A score of these great pachyderms haul logs, play football, and dance on their hind legs. The finale is a mock battle on elephant-back reenacting the Yutha Harti, the battle between King Naresuan and the Burmese prince in the 18th century. During the 40-minute show a soundtrack explains the role of elephants in Thai history. ⊠ *Km 30, Petchkasem Rd.,* ☎ *034/311971, 02/2841873 for reservations.* ☜ *Admission.* ⊘ *Daily 10–4.*

Kanchanaburi

❸ *140 km (87 mi) west of Bangkok.*

The movie *The Bridge Over the River Kwai,* adapted from Pierre Boulle's novel, gave the area of Kanchanaburi a certain fame—or, more accurately, the Japanese gave it the dubious distinction of being the site of the Death Railway. Even if this were not so, Kanchanaburi Province would attract tourists. Lush tropical vegetation and rivers with waterfalls and gorges make it one of the most beautiful national parks in Thailand. The small, sleepy town has little architectural merit, but its location, where the Kwai Noi and Kwai Yai rivers meet to form the Mae Khlong River, is splendid. A reconstruction of the now-famous bridge (it was successfully bombed by the Allies toward the end of the war) stands just north; take Saeng Chuto Road, the main street.

One may forgive, but one cannot forget, the inhumanity that caused the death, between 1942 and 1945, of more than 16,000 Allied prisoners of war and 49,000 impressed Asian laborers. They were forced by the Japanese, under abysmal conditions, to build a railway—the **Death Railway**—through the jungle from Thailand into Burma. One person died for every railway tie on the track.

In two Allied cemeteries are buried the remains of 8,732 POWs. At **Kanchanaburi War Cemetery,** with row upon row of neatly laid-out graves, the 6,982 American, Australian, British, and Dutch prisoners of war are remembered at a commemorative service every April 25. After the cemetery, take the next road to the left and make a right at the T junction. Be sure to read the plaque on the **Japanese War Memorial Shrine** at the junction—it has an English translation.

Just up the street from the Japanese War Memorial, the road opens out to a plaza, with restaurants, souvenir shops, and jewelry stores, and **the bridge** is on the left. Built with forced labor toward the end of the war, the bridge has steel girders, the center spans of which were knocked out by Allied bombs and replaced after the war with girders made in Japan. The other steel spans are the original ones. You can walk across the bridge. The wooden bridge associated with the movie was 2–3 km (1–2 mi) downstream.

Upriver, on the road leading back to town from the bridge, is the **JEATH War Museum** (JEATH is an acronym for Japan, England, America, Australia, Thailand, and Holland). Founded by a monk from the adjoining temple, the museum consists of a reconstructed bamboo hut—the type used to house the POWs—and a collection of utensils, railway spikes, clothing, aerial photographs, newspaper clippings, and illustrations designed to show the conditions the POWs lived under during the construction of the Death Railway. 🖾 *Admission.* 🕑 *Daily 8–5.*

A quiet and sadly serene Allied burial ground, the **Chong-Kai War Cemetery,** lies across the river. The simple crosses of the Commonwealth soldiers, so neatly planted and organized, make the scene even more poignant. To get there, take the ferry from the pier below the park off Patana Road.

Walk inland from Chong-Kai about 1 km (½ mi) to find **Wat Thum Khao Pun,** one of the best cave temples in the area. A small temple stands outside and a guide entices you into the cave, where calm images of Buddha sit between the stalagmites and stalactites.

Erawan Waterfall

❹ *65 km (40 mi) northwest of Kanchanaburi (Rte 3199).*

If you want to visit some of the spectacular countryside of Kanchanaburi Province, the Erawan Waterfall, perhaps the most photographed in Thailand, is worth the trip. It is in the beautifully forested Khao Salop National Park and is at its best in early autumn. You can take a tour bus from Kanchanaburi or the public bus (No. 8170), which leaves every hour for the 90-minute journey. It's a 1½-km (1-mi) walk or taxi ride to the foot of the falls. Allow two hours to climb up all seven levels of the falls, and wear tennis shoes or similar footwear. The rock at the top is shaped like an elephant; hence the name Erawan, which means elephant in Thai.

Five kilometers (3 miles) up the road from the Erawan Waterfall is the 300-ft **Sri Nakharin Dam,** with its power station and vast reservoir. A tour boat makes a two-hour excursion from here on the reservoir to the **Huay Khamin Falls.**

OFF THE BEATEN PATH

SAI YOK NOI – The most memorable trip out of Kanchanaburi is to this waterfall (also called Kao Phang), because you travel the 77 km (46 mi) on the Death Railway (notice the wood crosses at the side of the track). The train leaves each day at 10:33 AM, passing through lush jungle landscape and by rushing waterfalls as it clings to the mountainside on a two-hour run that is not for the faint-hearted. From Nam-Tok, the last stop, it's a 1½-km (1-mi) walk to Sai Yok Noi. This waterfall, a lot smaller than the Erawan falls, offers pools for swimming during the rainy season (May–Aug.), the best time to visit. On weekends the area is packed with Thai families. The bus back to Kanchanaburi takes half the time of the train, with half the strain on the nervous system.

Dining and Lodging

Most of the restaurants for tourists are near the River Kwai Bridge or farther downstream where the Kwai Noi and Kwai Yai join to form the Mae Klong. Most hotels are also along the riverbanks. A few of the resorts also offer thatched bungalows on the river. These raft houses have river views by day, but tend to be hot and muggy at night. Most foreign visitors visit Kanchanaburi on day trips, so the hotels are designed primarily for Thai families.

$ ✕ **Pae Karn Floating Restaurant.** For authentic Thai food, try this little restaurant. You'll find it on a floating dock at the river's edge just at the confluence of the Kwai Noi and Kwai Yai rivers. The food is better than in the tourist restaurants around the bridge, but the decor amounts to no more than plain walls and a few tables. ✉ *Song Kwai Rd.,* ☎ *034/513251. No credit cards.*

$ ✕ **River Kwai Floating Restaurant.** The most attractive—and crowded— open-air restaurant is this one to the right of the bridge. Fish dishes, either cooked with Thai spices or lightly grilled, dominate the menu. The specialty is *yeesok,* a fish found in the Kwai Yai and Kwai Noi rivers. Try to arrive before the tour groups, and request a table alongside the river. ✉ *River Kwai Bridge,* ☎ *034/512595. No credit cards.*

$$ ✕📷 **River Kwai Village.** Nestled in the heart of the jungle in the River Kwai Valley, this resort village consists of five one-story log cabins and a few guest rooms on rafts. All non-raft rooms have air-conditioning and are simply furnished, with teak and colored stones embedded in the walls. The cafeteria-style restaurant offers a combination of Thai and Western dishes, but it's more fun to eat at the casual restaurant on one of the anchored floating rafts. The resort will supply transportation from Bangkok and arrange tours of the area. ✉ *72 Moo 4, Tambon Thasao, Amphoe Sai Yok, Kanchanaburi 71150,* ☎ *034/ 591055,* FAX *034/591054. 60 rooms and 7 raft houses. 2 restaurants, pool, meeting rooms, travel services. AE, DC, V.*

$$$ 📷 **Felix River Kwai Resort.** This luxury hotel, completed in 1992, was first managed by Sofitel and then by a Thai group. It is still going through growing pains, but it does have a tranquil setting along the bank of the river in sight of the bridge. Polished wood floors and wicker headboards give a cool country airiness to the rooms. Each has two queen beds or one king, as well as a private safe and four-channel cable TV. A large free-form pool amid the tropical plants sets the scene, and this relaxing hotel is within walking distance to most of Kanchanaburi's attractions. ✉ *9/1 Moo 3, Tambon Thamakham, Kanchanaburi 71000,* ☎ *034/515061, 02/255–3410 Bangkok reservations,* FAX *034/51095. 150 rooms. Restaurant, pool, massage, health club. AE, DC, MC, V.*

$$–$$$ 📷 **The Pavilion Rim Kwai Thani Resort.** Between downtown Kanchanaburi and the Erawan Waterfall, this new resort caters to the upscale Bangkokian who wishes to retreat into the country and still have his creature comforts. Lush tropical grounds surround the hotel, and the infamous River Kwai flows serenely past. Guest rooms are sparsely furnished, which, along with the shining wood floors, gives a fresh, sparkling ambiance. The large dining room serves Thai and Western dishes. ✉ *79/2 Moo 4, Km 9 Ladya-Erawan Rd., Tambon Wangdong, Kanchanaburi 71190,* ☎ *034/515772,* FAX *034/515774. 200 rooms. Restaurant, pool, 2 tennis courts, exercise room. AE, MC, V.*

$$ 📷 **Kwai Yai Garden Resort.** This small resort 15 minutes by ferry from the Tha Kradan Pier offers thatched bungalows, a few raft houses, a small restaurant, and a friendly staff. ✉ *125 Moo 2, Tambon Thamakham, Kanchanaburi 71000,* ☎ *034/513611, 02/5135399 Bangkok reservations. 12 rooms and 4 rafts. Restaurant, bar, travel services. MC, V.*

$$ 📷 **River Kwai Hotel.** Across the bridge on the banks of the Kwai Yai, this hotel is a small complex of thatched bungalows, including some on rafts. The dining room and lounge, on one raft, offer a picturesque view of the bridge. ✉ *284/4–6 Saengchuto Rd., Kanchanaburi 71000,* ☎ *034/511184,* FAX *034/511269. 77 rooms and 9 raft houses. Restaurant, travel services. MC, V.*

Outdoor Activities and Sports

RAFTING

Rafting trips on either the Kwai Yai or Mae Khlong rivers, which take at least a full day, let you experience the tropical jungle in a leisurely way. The rafts, which resemble houseboats, are often divided into sections for eating, sunbathing, and diving. When swimming, be careful—the currents can have a whirlpool effect that will suck a swimmer down. For one-day rafting trips, the cost is approximately B300. Longer trips are also offered. Make advance reservations through the TAT office or a travel agent. If you book through a responsible travel agent, you may have to pay a bit more, but you'll also be more likely to get a raft in good condition and a skipper familiar with the currents.

Shopping

Blue sapphires from the Bor Ploy mines, 45 km (28 mi) north of Kanchanaburi, are generally a good buy, but prices are marked up at the shops in the plaza before the bridge. You're better off buying the sapphires at the small shops in the center of town.

North from Bangkok

Ayutthaya became the kingdom's seat of power in 1350, and toward the end of the 16th century, Europeans described the city, with its 1,700 temples and 4,000 golden images of Buddha, as more striking than any capital in Europe. Certainly the Ayutthaya period was also Thailand's most glorious. In 1767, the Burmese conquered Ayutthaya and destroyed the temples with such vengeance that little remained standing. The city never recovered, and today it is a small provincial town with partially restored ruins. The site is particularly striking at sunset, when the silhouetted ruins glow orange-brown and are imbued with a melancholy charm.

People visit these sites on excursions from Bangkok or on the way to Thailand's northern provinces. Try to get an early start for Ayutthaya to see as much as possible before 1 PM, when the heat becomes unbearable. Then take a long lunch and, if you have time, continue into the late afternoon and catch the sunset before you leave. Most people, though, find that a morning is sufficient. For a three-hour tour of the sights, tuk-tuks can be hired for approximately B450; a four-wheel *samlor* (small bicycle cab) costs about B700. English-speaking guides can be hired around the station. A popular excursion to Ayutthaya from Bangkok, run by the Oriental and Shangri-La hotels, takes you by cruise boat one way and bus the other. (To go by bus and come back by boat is the better of the two.) A tour of a couple of Ayutthaya's sights and of the Bang Pa In Palace is included, along with lunch on the cruise boat. It makes for a hassle-free day, and the boat trip is wonderful, but it gives you very little time actually visiting what you spend most of the day traveling to see.

Ayutthaya

5 *72 km (45 mi) north of Bangkok.*

Ayutthaya lies within a large loop of the Chao Phraya River, where it meets the Pa Sak and Lopburi rivers. To completely encircle their capital by water, the Thais dug a canal along the northern perimeter, linking the Chao Phraya to the Lopburi. Although the new provincial town of Ayutthaya, including the railway station, is on the east bank of the Pa Sak, most of Ayutthaya's ancient temples and ruins are on the island. An exception is Wat Yai Chai Mongkol (a B20 tuk-tuk ride southeast of the railway station).

Wat Yai Chai Mongkol was built in 1357 by King U-Thong for meditation. After King Naresuan defeated the Burmese by killing the
Burmese crown prince in single-handed combat on elephants in 1582,
he enlarged the temple. The complex was totally restored in 1982, and
with the neatly groomed grounds, smart new monks' quarters, and the
contemporary images of Buddha lining the courtyard, it looks a little
touristy, an impression not helped by several souvenir shops, a beverage stand, and a host of tour buses from Bangkok. Notice how the chedi
is leaning; it was restored without replacing the foundations and is,
under the increased weight, sinking. Linger a while to pay your respects
to the Reclining Buddha, and be sure to enter the new sala to look at
a painting (1988) of the battle in which the Thai king lopped off the
head of the Burmese prince. (Thai soldiers are dressed in red uniforms.) The picture actually gives a good rendition of how duels were
fought on elephants. ⌧ *Admission.* ⊙ *Daily 8–5.*

★ The road continues to **Wat Phanan Choeng,** a small temple on the banks
of the Lopburi, which predates Ayutthaya's flowering. In 1324, one
of the U-Thong kings, who had arranged to marry a daughter of the
Chinese emperor, came to this spot on the river; instead of entering the
city with his fiancée, he arranged an escort for her. But she, thinking
that she had been deserted, threw herself into the river in despair and
drowned. The king tried to atone for his thoughtlessness by building
the temple. The story has great appeal to Thai Chinese, many of whom
make romantic pilgrimages here. ⌧ *Admission.* ⊙ *Daily 8–6.*

Returning to the main road, go left and cross over the bridge to the is-
land. Continue on Rojana Road for about 1½ km (1 mi) to the **Chao
Phraya National Museum.** Though Ayutthaya's best pieces are in
Bangkok's National Museum, a guided visit here can highlight the evo-
lution of Ayutthaya art over four centuries. ⌧ *Admission.* ⊙ *Wed.–
Sun. 9–noon and 1–4.*

Just beyond the Chao Phraya National Museum, turn right onto Si Samphet Road. Pass the city hall on the left and continue for 1 km (½ mi)
to **Wat Phra Si Samphet,** easily recognizable by the huge parking lot.
The shining white marble temple south of Wat Phra Si Samphet not
only looks modern, it is. Built in 1956, **Viharn Phra Mongkol Bopitr**
houses a large bronze image of Buddha, one of the few that escaped
the destruction wrought by the Burmese.

Wat Phra Si Samphet was the largest wat in Ayutthaya and the temple
of the royal family. Built in the 14th century, in 1767 it lost its 50-ft
Buddha, Phra Sri Samphet, to the Burmese, who melted it down for
its gold—374 pounds' worth. The chedis, restored in 1956, survived
and are the best examples of Ayutthaya architecture. Enshrining the
ashes of Ayutthaya kings, they stand as eternal memories of a golden
age. The architectural design of Wat Phra Si Samphet was used in the
construction of the temple (Wat Phra Keo) at Bangkok's Royal Palace.
Beyond these monuments is a grassy field where the royal palace once
stood. The field is a cool, shady place in which to walk and picnic. The
foundation is all that remains of the palace that was home to 33 kings.
⊙ *Daily 8–5.*

Before you leave, visit some of the stalls in the **market** behind the souvenir stands; you'll find a marvelous array of vegetables, fruits, and
other foods. After wandering around, stop at the café at the viharn end
of the market for refreshments—try the chilled coconut in its shell.

From the large coach park, Naresuan Road crosses Si Samphet Road
and continues past a small lake to nearby **Wat Phra Mahathat,** on the
corner of Chee Kun Road. Built in 1384 by King Ramesuan, the

monastery was destroyed by the Burmese, but a buried treasure chest was found during a 1956 restoration project. The chest contained a relic of Lord Buddha, golden Buddha images, and other objects in gold, ruby, and crystal that are now housed in Bangkok's National Museum. If you climb up what is left of the monastery's 140-ft prang (Khmer-style pagoda with an elliptical spire), you'll be able to envision just how grand the structure must have been. You can also admire the neighboring **Wat Raj Burana**, built by the seventh Ayutthaya king in memory of his brother.

Continue east on Naresuan Road, now called Chao Phnom Road, to the Pa Sak River. Either go left up U-Thong Road to **Chandra Kasem Palace,** or go right to the bridge. The reconstructed 17th-century palace is Ayutthaya's second national museum.

For an educational overview of the 400 years of the Ayutthaya period, stop in at the new **Ayutthaya Historical Study Centre,** near the Teacher's College and the U-Thong Inn. Financed by the Japanese government, the center functions as a place of national research and as a museum. Models of the city as a royal capital, as a port city, as an administrative and international diplomatic center, and as a rural village depicting lifestyles in the countryside are displayed. ✉ *Rotchana Rd.,* ☎ *035/ 245124.* 💰 *Admission.* ⊙ *Tues.–Sun. 9–4:30.*

About 5 km (3 mi) north of Ayutthaya is the **Elephant Kraal,** Thailand's only intact royal kraal, last used during King Chulalongkorn's reign in 1903. A stockade of massive teak logs, it held wild elephants to be trained for martial service.

Dining and Lodging

Romantics may want to stay in Ayutthaya to see the ruins at night. Since most tourists arrive from Bangkok around 10 AM and depart at 4 PM, those who stay are treated to genuine Thai hospitality. Don't expect luxury, however; Ayutthaya boasts only modest though comfortable hotels and simple Thai restaurants.

$$ ✕ **Pae Krung Kao.** If you want to dine outdoors on Thai food and watch the waters of the Pa Sak, this is the better of the two floating restaurants near the bridge. You can also come here for a leisurely beer. ✉ *4 U-Thong Rd.,* ☎ *035/241555. No credit cards.*

$ ✕ **Tevaraj.** For good Thai food that does not spare the spices, head for this unpretentious restaurant behind Ayutthaya's railway station. The restaurant is short on decor, but the fish dishes and the *tom kha* (soup made with coconut milk) are excellent. ✉ *74 Wat Pa Kho Rd.,* ☎ *no phone. No credit cards.*

$$$$ ✕🛏 **The Manohra Song.** The 60-ft wreck of an old teak rice barge has, with the help of lots of taste and money, been brought back to life as a luxury cruiser on the Chao Phraya. For a day and a half eight passengers are pampered by a chef and their own guide, amid mahogany and silks, antique furnishings, and the artifacts of ease, as they watch the world drift by between Bangkok and Ayutthaya. ✉ *Manohra Cruises, 257/1–3 Charoen Nakorn Rd., Thonburi 10600,* ☎ *02/476– 0021/2,* 📠 *02/4761120 or 02/460–1805. 4 suites. AE, MC, V. AP.*

$$ 🛏 **Krungsri River Hotel.** For a long time the U-Thong Inn was the only reasonably smart hotel in Ayutthaya, but it had its drawbacks. It was on the edge of town and crowded with Japanese businessmen attending to the factories nearby. The Krungsri is a welcome addition and it is conveniently close to the train station. The spacious marble-floor lobby is refreshingly cool after the outside heat, and the rooms, albeit not special in any way, are clean, fresh, and furnished with modern amenities. For atmosphere, choose a room overlooking the river. Because Ayutthaya has few overnight visitors, try to negotiate a discount from the published room rate. ✉ 27/2 Rojana Rd., 13000, ☎ 035/242996, FAX 035/242996. 200 rooms. Restaurant. MC, V.

Bang Pa-In

❻ *20 km (12 mi) south of Ayutthaya.*

A popular attraction outside Ayutthaya is the Bang Pa-In Summer Palace, within well-tended gardens in an architectural complex of striking variety. The original palace, built by King Prusat (ruled 1630–55) on the banks of the Pa Sak, was used by the Ayutthaya kings until the Burmese invasion. After being neglected for 80 years, it was rebuilt during the reign of Rama IV (1851–68) and became the favored summer palace of King Chulalongkorn (Rama V, 1868–1910) until tragedy struck. Once, when the king was delayed in Bangkok, he sent his wife ahead on a boat, which capsized, and she drowned. She could easily have been saved, but because a royal person was sacrosanct she could not be touched by a commoner on pain of death. The king could never forgive himself. He built a pavilion in her memory; be sure to read the touching inscription engraved on the memorial.

King Chulalongkorn was fascinated by Europe and its architecture, and many Western influences are evident here. The most beautiful building, however, is the **Aisawan Thippaya,** a Thai pavilion that seems to float on a small lake, its series of staggered roofs leading to a central spire. It has been dismantled and taken to represent the country at worldwide expositions.

Phra Thinang Warophat Phiman, nicknamed the Peking Palace, stands to the north of the Royal Ladies Landing Place in front of a stately pond. The replica of a palace of the Chinese imperial court, it was built from materials custom-made in China—a gift from Chinese Thais eager to win the favor of the king. It contains a collection of exquisite jade and Ming-period porcelain.

T ke the cable car across the river to the unique wat south of the palace grounds. King Chulalongkorn built this Buddhist temple, **Wat Nivet Thamaprawat,** in Western Gothic style. Complete with a belfry and stained-glass windows, it looks as much like a Christian church as a wat. ✉ *Admission to Bang Pa-In Palace Complex.* ☉ *Tues.–Thurs. and weekends 8–3.*

The **Bang Sai Folk Arts and Craft Centre** was set up by the queen in 1976 to train and employ families with handicraft skills. Workers at the center demonstrate the techniques and make and sell products that are sold throughout Thailand at the Chitrlada handicraft shops. The crafts on sale include fern-vine basketry, wood carvings, dyed silks, and handmade dolls. The park is a pleasant place for a picnic, although it is crowded on weekends with Thai families. It also has a small restaurant. ✉ *24 km (14½ mi) south of Bang Pa-In on the Chao Phraya River,* ☎ *035/366–6092.* ✉ *Admission. Closed Wed.*

Lopburi

❼ *75 km (47 mi) north of Ayutthaya, 150 km (94 mi) north of Bangkok.*

Lopburi is one of Thailand's oldest cities: the first evidence of its habitation dates from the 4th century. After the 6th century, its influence grew under the Dvaravati rulers, who dominated northern Thailand until the Khmers swept in from the east. From the beginning of the 10th century until the middle of the 13th, when the new Thai kingdom drove them out, the Khmers controlled the region from Lopburi, as the chief provincial capital. During the Sukhothai and early Ayutthaya periods, the city's importance declined until, in 1664, King Narai made it his second capital—to escape the heat and humidity of Ayutthaya. He employed French architects to build his palace; consequently, Lopburi is a strange mixture of Khmer, Thai, and Western architecture.

Lopburi is relatively off the beaten track for tourists. Few foreigners stay overnight, but there is one reasonable hotel, the Lopburi Inn. You can travel up to Phitsanulok or return to Ayutthaya or Bangkok. Perhaps the rarity of foreigners explains why the locals are so friendly and eager to show you their town—and to practice their English! Bicycle samlors are available, but most of Lopburi's attractions are within easy walking distance.

Wat Phra Si Mahathat, built by the Khmers, is at the back of the railway station. It underwent so many restorations during the Sukhothai and Ayutthaya periods that it's difficult to discern the three original Khmer prangs—only the central one has survived intact. Several Sukhothai- and Ayutthaya-style chedis are also within the compound. ▨ *Admission.* ⊙ *Daily 8:30–4:30.*

Walk diagonally through Wat Phra Si Mahathat to **Narai Ratchaniwet Palace.** The preserved buildings, which took from 1665 to 1677 to complete, have been converted into museums. Surrounding the buildings are castellated walls and triumphant archways grand enough to admit an entourage mounted on elephants. The most elaborate structure is the **Dusit Mahaprasat Hall,** built by King Narai to receive foreign ambassadors. The roof is gone, but you'll be able to spot the mixture of architectural styles: the square doors are Thai and the dome-shape arches are Western.

The next group of buildings in the palace compound—the **Chan Phaisan Pavilion** (1666), the **Phiman Monghut Pavilion** (mid-19th century), and the row of houses once used by ladies of the court—are now all museums. The ladies' residences now house the **Farmer's Museum,** which exhibits regional tools and artifacts seldom displayed in Thailand. ▨ *Admission.* ⊙ *Wed.–Sun. 9–noon and 1–4.*

North across the road from the palace (away from the station), you'll pass through the restored **Wat Sao Thong Thong.** Notice the windows of the viharn, which King Narai changed in imitation of Western architecture. Beyond Wat Sao Thong Thong and across another small street is **Vichayen House,** built for Louis XIV's personal representative, De Chaumont. The house was later occupied by King Narai's infamous Greek minister, Constantine Phaulkon, whose political schemes eventually caused the ouster of all Westerners from Thailand. When King Narai was dying in 1668, his army commander, Phra Phetracha, seized power and beheaded Phaulkon. In the attack, the Vichayen House and its ancillary buildings, including a Roman Catholic church, were nearly destroyed. ▨ *Admission.* ⊙ *Wed.–Sun. 9–noon and 1–4.*

Walk east on the road between Wat Sao Thong Thong and Vichayen House to **Phra Prang Sam Yot,** a Khmer Hindu shrine and Lopburi's primary landmark. The three prangs symbolize the sacred triad of Brahma, Vishnu, and Siva. King Narai converted the shrine into a Buddhist temple, and a stucco image of the Lord Buddha sits serenely before the central prang once dedicated to Brahma.

About 250 yards down the street facing Phra Prang Sam Yot and across the railway tracks is the **San Phra Kan shrine.** The respected residents of the temple, Samae monkeys, often perform spontaneously for visitors. These interesting animals engage in the human custom of burying their dead.

Dining and Lodging

Accommodations in Lopburi are used mostly by Thai traveling salesmen. Except for the hotel dining rooms, Lopburi restaurants are sidewalk cafés serving Thai and Chinese food. Menus are written in Thai, but you point to what you want in the glass cases at the front of the restaurant.

$$ ⊞ **Lopburi Inn.** This is the only hotel in Lopburi with air-conditioning and modern facilities. Even so, don't expect your room to have much more than a clean bed and a private bath. The dining room serves Thai and Chinese food, and the hotel has achieved a certain fame by having an annual dinner party for the town's resident monkeys. ✉ *28/9 Narai Maharat Rd.,* ☎ *036/412300,* 🖷 *036/411917. 142 rooms. Restaurant, coffee shop. DC, V.*

The Western Gulf Coast

In the 1920s the royal family built a palace at Hua Hin on the west shore of the Gulf of Thailand. The royal entourage would travel from Bangkok on special trains, and high society followed. Those were Hua Hin's glory days. After World War II, Pattaya's star ascended, and Hua Hin became a quiet town once more, but Pattaya's seedy reputation has caused Thais and foreign visitors to reconsider Hua Hin and its near neighbor Cha' Am as desirable beach resorts close to the capital. In the last several years, the area has enjoyed a building boom. Now the coastline is dotted with high-rise hotels and weekend condominiums.

This is a low-key destination, where nightlife is restricted mostly to the hotels. During the day, Hua Hin is a busy market town, but most tourists are at the beach. They come into town in the early evening to wander through the bazaars before dinner. There is no beachfront road to attract boisterous crowds, so stretches of beach remain deserted. They have gently sloping drop-offs, and the waters are usually calm. The only drawback is the occasional invasion of jellyfish—check for them before you plunge in. As a foreign visitor, you will probably stay in a hotel in Hua Hin rather than in a self-contained resort, where you will need a car or taxi to take you into town.

Hua Hin

❽ *189 km (118 mi) south of Bangkok.*

On the east side of the highway at the northern boundary of Hua Hin stands the royal summer palace, where the king and queen spend the month of April and celebrate the anniversary of their royal wedding. The palace was completed in 1928 by King Rama VII, who named it Klai Kangwol ("far from worries"). Four years later, while he was staying at Klai Kangwol, the army seized control in Bangkok, demanding that he relinquish absolute power in favor of a constitutional monarchy. He agreed, and the generals later apologized for their lack of courtesy.

The highway to the southern provinces passes through the center of Hua Hin. In fact, it's the town's main street, with shops and cafés lining the sidewalk; a congested street of market stalls and buses runs parallel to it. The **Chatchai street market** is fun to walk through. In the morning it sells meats and vegetables; then, from early evening, all sorts of wares, from food to trinkets. Toward the southern end of town, across the tracks from the quaint wooden railway station lies the respected **Royal Hua Hin Golf Course** (☎ 032/512475 and 02/2411360). Nonmembers can play the par-72 course for B600–B1,000; you can rent clubs, and there's a coffee lounge for refreshments. Tourist shops and moderately priced hotels line both sides of Damnernkasem Road, leading to the **public beach.**

On your way to the beach, keep your eyes open for **Naresdamri Road,** just before the Sofitel, where Damnernkasem Road becomes closed to traffic. Several small restaurants here are excellent places to keep in mind for dinner. Most have their offerings displayed on slabs of ice. You choose the fish, negotiate a fair price, and then take a table and order any other dishes and drinks you want. Down Naresdamri Road toward the water, past numerous inexpensive guest houses, is **Fisherman's Wharf.** It's alive with activity in the morning, when the catch comes in.

Near the end of the street on the right-hand side, you will see the **Sofitel Central Hua Hin Resort,** formerly the Royal Hua Hin Railway Hotel, which put up royalty and Thailand's elite during the town's heyday. The magnificent Victorian-style colonial building was portrayed as the hotel in Phnom Penh in the film *The Killing Fields.* Be sure to wander through the well-tended gardens and along the verandas of the hotel.

If you look south along the coast, you'll see a small headland, **Khao Takiab,** and a small island, **Ko Singto.** You can reach the headland by *songthaew* (small trucklike jitney), but the best way to get there is to hire a pony and trot along the beach. The 7-km (4-mi) stretch passes hotels and villas, and then becomes virtually deserted, and you eventually reach the beach of Khao Takiab, where, unfortunately, three tall condominiums have been built. At the end of the beach, where restaurant stalls abound, dismount for the steep climb past a large statue of the Lord Buddha to the small Buddhist monastery—the views are worth the climb. Then, if you can, rent a fishing boat at the base of Khao Takiab to cross over to Ko Singto, where you are guaranteed a catch within an hour.

OFF THE
BEATEN PATH

KHAO SAM ROI YOD NATIONAL PARK – The rice fields, sugar palms, pineapple plantations, and crab farms that make up this park are about 40 km (25 mi) south of Hua Hin. The plains of the park were depicted in the movie *The Killing Fields* as the site of Pol Pot's murderous schemes of reeducation. The charming fishing village of **Wang Daeng** is typical of coastal Thailand 20 years ago, and south of Wang Daeng, the countryside is even more magnificent, with jungle-clad hills and a curving shoreline. Try to get as far south as the picturesque fishing village of **Ao Noi.** Beyond that is the pleasant, sleepy town of **Prachuap** (about 90 km/56 mi south of Hua Hin), which has little appeal for the tourist except for staggering panoramic views from the hills at the back of its bay.

Dining and Lodging

The restaurants along Naresdamri Road in Hua Hin offer a warm ambience and good value, especially for fresh seafood. For Western food, it's best to eat at one of the major hotels, but for Thai holiday weekends, reservations must be made in advance. During peak season—October through mid-March—the prices at hotels are nearly double those in the off-season.

$$$ ✕ **Fisherman's Seafood Restaurant.** The nautical decor sets the tone of the Royal Garden Resort's restaurant, which serves excellently prepared gulf seafood—clams, lobsters, mussels, sea-tiger prawns, and crabs. Depending on your taste, these can be cooked with Thai spices (such as lobster with garlic and peppers) or simply grilled. ✉ *107/1 Phetkasem Rd.,* ☎ *032/511881. AE, DC, MC, V.*

$$ ╳ **Sang Thai.** For interesting seafood dishes—from grilled prawns with bean noodles to fried grouper with chili and tamarind juice—this open-air restaurant down by Fisherman's Wharf has been consistently popular with Thais. Certainly, the extensive menu is appealing, but you need to close your eyes to the ramshackle surroundings and floating debris in the water. Don't miss the *kang* (mantis prawns). ⊠ *Naresdamri Rd.,* ☏ *032/512144. DC, MC, V.*

$–$$ ╳ **Chao Lay.** Of the many outdoor pier restaurants, this one is consistently good. The fish is fresh, the cooking exact, and the service friendly (many of the staff speak English). The pier stretches out into the sea a little farther than at the other restaurants, which seems to allow for more cooling breezes. There is an ample selection of dishes, from spicy to tame, from prawns to snapper, and from hot pork curry to mild chicken in coconut milk. ⊠ *15 Naresdamri Rd.,* ☏ *032/513–436. No credit cards.*

$$$$ ⌂ **Royal Garden Resort.** Adjacent to the Sofitel, this hotel has accommodations and service equal to those of its neighbor, but because it doesn't have the colonial ambience, the rates are a few hundred baht less. The hotel tends to draw a younger set, attracted by the nightclub and the proximity to the beach. Guest rooms are decorated with modern, unimaginative furniture. The Market Seafood Restaurant is less elegant than Sofitel's Salathai, but it serves better food. The Jungle is Hua Hin's hottest disco. ⊠ *107/1 Phetkasem Rd., Hua Hin 77110,* ☏ *032/511881, 02/255–8822 Bangkok reservations,* ℻ *032/512422. 215 rooms. 2 restaurants, bar, coffee shop, pool, 4 tennis courts, snorkeling, boating, nightclub, playground. AE, DC, MC, V.*

$$$$ ⌂ **Sofitel Hua Hin Resort.** Even if you don't stay here, the Old World
★   charm of this tastefully renovated hotel is worth a visit. Wide verandas fan out in an arc, following the lines of the wooden building, and open onto gardens leading down to the beach. The gardens are splendidly maintained by 30 gardeners, with scores of different plants plus topiary figures that look like shadows in the night. The lounges around the reception area are open to the sea breezes, and the airiness revives memories of Somerset Maugham. The best guest rooms are those on the second floor with sea views. The units in an annex across the street, run by Sofitel's sister company Mercure, are less attractive but also less expensive. ⊠ *1 Damnernkasem Rd., Hua Hin 77110,* ☏ *032/ 512021, 02/233–0974 Bangkok reservations,* ℻ *032/511014. 154 rooms. 2 restaurants, bar, coffee shop, pool, 4 tennis courts, snorkeling, boating, nightclub, meeting rooms. AE, DC, MC, V.*

$$$–$$$$ ⌂ **Dusit Resort & Polo Club.** Although this resort opened in early 1991,
★   the polo grounds and riding stables have yet to be added. Perhaps not so many guests will be playing polo, but the game establishes the tone—smart, exclusive, and luxurious. The spacious lobby serves as a lounge for afternoon tea and evening cocktails, drunk to the soft tunes of the house musicians. Beyond the ornamental lily pond out front is the swimming pool with bubbling fountains, and beyond that is the beach. The main dining room serves Thai, Chinese, and European fare. Off to the left is the San Marco, an alfresco Italian restaurant; to the right is the Benjarong, in a traditional Thai-style pavilion. All the guest rooms have private balconies and a pool or sea view: there's shuttle service to Hua Hin and car service to Bangkok. ⊠ *1349 Petchkasem Rd., Cha' Am, Petchburi 76120,* ☏ *032/520009, 02/636–3333 Bangkok reservations,* ℻ *032/520296. 308 rooms and suites. 5 restaurants, 2 bars, in-room safes, pool, wading pool, 5 tennis courts, steam room, exercise room, squash, boating, parasailing, waterskiing, meeting rooms. AE, DC, MC, V.*

$$$–$$$$ ⊞ **Melia Hua Hin.** In some people's view, this 15-story monster of a hotel has no right to be in small, charming Hua Hin. But it does offer great rates during the off-season, as low as 1,000 baht a night, and for a five-star hotel that is a bargain. In-season rates are a little lower than the Sofitel's. The Melia is a mass-market hotel, popular with many European tour groups. Its rooms are spacious (a minimum of 42 square meters/450 square ft), modern, and functional. The lagoonlike pool dominates the garden and the small sandy beach shares its limited space with vendors and tourists from other hotels. ⊠ *33 Naresdamri Rd., 77110,* ☎ *032/511612,* FAX *032/511135. 297 rooms. 3 restaurants, pool, 2 tennis courts, health club, squash, dance club, meeting rooms. AE, DC, MC, V.*

$$$ $$$$ ⊞ **Regent Cha' Am.** This modern beach resort has everything from water sports to gourmet dining to shopping arcades. The Lom Fang restaurant, overlooking the lake at the back, serves excellent fish with a spiced-curry-and-lime sauce. The more formal restaurant, the Tapien Thong Grill Room, offers seafood and steak. Some guest rooms are in bungalows, a number of which face the beach (No. 309 looks onto the sea and is away from the main building), while others are housed in one of two 12-story buildings set back from the beach. Gardens separate the bungalows, the main building, two large outdoor pools, and two smaller outdoor pools. In the evening, a small group sings Western songs in Thai. The hotel has its own car service from Bangkok. ⊠ *849/21 Cha' Am Beach, Petchburi,* ☎ *032/471480, 02/251–0305 Bangkok reservations,* FAX *032/471492, 02/253–5143 Bangkok reservations. 400 rooms. 3 restaurants, coffee shop, 4 pools, snorkeling, boating, nightclub. AE, DC, MC, V.*

$$$ ⊞ **The Pran Buri Beach Resort.** This isolated holiday complex south of Hua Hin offers a collection of small bungalow units along the shore. The first row, facing the beach, is obviously the best. Though simply furnished, guest rooms have their own terraces and minibars, telephones, and TV with in-house VCR. The main lodge contains the bar/lounge and dining room, where Thai, Chinese, and Western food is served. The atmosphere is laid-back, casual, and fun. ⊠ *9 Parknampran Beach, Prachuapkhirikhan 77220,* ☎ *032/621701, 02/233–3871 Bangkok reservations,* FAX *02/235–0049. 60 rooms. Restaurant, bar, pool, 2 tennis courts, health club, snorkeling, boating, meeting rooms. AE, DC, MC, V.*

$ ⊞ **Jed Pee.** This hotel, centrally located on the main tourist street, has bungalow cottages in its courtyard. Rooms have huge beds and not much else, but the price is right. The terrace restaurant facing the street stays open late and is a popular spot from which to watch the parade of vacationers walking past. ⊠ *17 Damnernkasem Rd., Hua Hin 77110,* ☎ *032/512381,* FAX *032/53063. 44 rooms. Restaurant/coffee shop. MC, V.*

$ ⊞ **Sirin.** At approximately 1,500 baht during the high season, this safe, ordinary hotel is a bargain. It's on the main tourist avenue, a block from the beach, and the staff is happy to assist you. The air-conditioned rooms are plain but clean and light, and the bathrooms are reasonably large. The dining room serves as a place to rest up as well as to eat, though for dinner you will probably want to go out. ⊠ *18 Damnernkasem Rd., 77110,* ☎ *032/511150 or 032/512045,* FAX *032/513571. 35 rooms. Restaurant. AE, DC, MC, V.*

¢ ⊞ **All Nations.** Of the backpacker hangouts in Hua Hin, this is about the best. You'll find local expats coming by for a drink or breakfast. Rooms are clean, and while none has private bathrooms, there is a large bathroom on each floor, with only two or three rooms per floor. The expat owner has set up a computer corner where guests (and nonguests) can, for a fee, access E-mail. ⊠ *10–10/1 Dechanuchit Rd., Hua Hin*

77110, ☎ 032/512747, ℻ 032/53474. *11 rooms. Restaurant, bar. No credit cards.*

The Eastern Seaboard

As the Bangkok metropolitan area becomes more and more congested, the Eastern Seaboard is growing rapidly, with most of the economic development around Chonburi and Rayong. The coast, and chiefly the resort of Pattaya, has been the attraction, with its water sports, fairgrounds, and nightlife, but Pattaya has so exemplified the seedier aspects of tourism and so rapidly outpaced its infrastructure that many travelers continue into Chantaburi and Trat provinces as far as the Cambodian border. Not all the coastline is particularly attractive, and cultural sites are few and far between, but there are fishing villages along the way, a few decent beaches, delightful islands offshore, and provincial capitals inland for supplies. Except for buying gemstones in Chantaburi and Trat, tourists come for beach pleasures. The following destinations are arranged in order of their proximity to Bangkok.

Pattaya

9 *147 km (88 mi) southeast of Bangkok.*

Four decades ago, Pattaya was a fishing village on an unspoiled natural harbor. Discovered by affluent Bangkok residents, it became a weekend playground, replacing the southwest coast as a vacation destination. Then came the Vietnam War, when thousands of American soldiers sought release and recreation. With air and naval bases nearby, U.S. servicemen hit the beaches at Pattaya in droves, and the resort became a boomtown of uncontrolled development.

Pattaya's unbridled sex trade, its crowds, and its water pollution began to erode its appeal, and business dropped off. Now, after a few years in the doldrums, Pattaya is getting busier, with conventioneers and many tourists from Eastern Europe. Pattaya has something tacky for everyone, the most obvious being its many bars and nightclubs catering to foreign males. Conveniently located on the side streets are dozens of clinics to treat venereal diseases. The highway from Bangkok is congested; on weekends the two-hour trip often takes four. Raw sewage still seeps into the once-crystal-clear bay, though the government and private enterprise have started a cleanup process with water- and sewage-treatment plants. Perhaps by the year 2000, all the hotels will be connected and the water may be safe once more for marine and human life. But another problem now faces Pattaya: foreign underworld gangs, generally referred to by Thais as the "Mafia," are a law unto themselves, with the Russian mafia coming out on top. General Chavalit, a former prime minister, recently admitted that Thailand's first international resort is a "social wart."

If Pattaya were anywhere else but Thailand, it would be positively distasteful. But it *is* in Thailand, and somehow what is gross is made acceptable by the smiling Thais. Pattaya is Thailand's total beach resort, offering everything from deep-sea fishing to golf, from windsurfing to elephant kraals.

Pattaya can be divided into three sections: the northernmost, Naklua Beach, still attracts locals but has recently expanded, with bars and restaurants that cater to foreigners—particularly Germans and some backpackers. On a small promontory south of the Dusit Resort Hotel is the picturesque curving bay of Pattaya, along which runs Beach Road, lined with palm trees on the beach side and modern resort hotels on the other. At the southern end of the bay is the fun part of town—bars, nightclubs, restaurants, and open-front cafés dominate both Sunset Avenue (the extension of Beach Rd.) and the side streets.

Parallel to Beach Road runs Pattaya 2 Road, the main commercial street, which becomes more crowded with traffic and shops the farther south you go. Continuing through town, Pattaya 2 Road climbs a hill leading past Buddha Park on the left and then descends to quieter Jontien Beach, which has attracted condominium developers and hotels along its stretch of white sand.

Tourist attractions abound in Pattaya. The number of open-air bars will astound you. Massage parlors line Pattaya 2 Road. And there are a dozen or so attractions designed for families. One such diversion in Pattaya is elephants. Since teak logging was restricted, these noble beasts suffer from high unemployment, and only an estimated 4,000 of them live in Thailand now. At the **Elephant Kraal,** 14 pachyderms display their skill at moving logs in a two-hour show, twice daily. There are also demonstrations by war elephants, an enactment of ceremonial rites, and the capture of a wild elephant. Everything is staged, but it's always fun to see elephants at work and at play. ⊠ *On main hwy., 5 km (3 mi) from Pattaya,* ☎ *038/249818. Tickets and transport:* ⊠ *Tropicana Hotel Elephant Desk, Pattaya 2 Rd.,* ☎ *038/428158.* ⌨ *Admission.* ⊙ *Shows daily at 2:30 and 4:30.*

Nong Nuch Village offers a general overview of Thai culture with a folk show, an exhibition of monkeys picking coconuts, elephants bathing, and a small zoo and aviary. Two restaurants, one Thai and one Western, serve refreshments on rolling grounds covered with coconut plantations. Despite its touristy nature, the village provides a pleasant break from sunbathing on the beach, particularly if you're traveling with children. Hotels will arrange transportation for morning and afternoon visits, since it is 15 km (9 mi) south of Pattaya, at the 163-km marker on Highway 1. Or you can contact the office in Pattaya opposite the Amari Nipa Resort on Pattaya Klang Road (☎ 038/429321). ⊠ *163 Sukhumvit Hwy., Bang Saray,* ☎ *038/709358.* ⌨ *Admission.* ⊙ *Daily 9–5:30; folk show daily 10 AM and 3 PM.*

Among the plenitude of commercial attractions are **Ripley's Believe It or Not Museum** (⊠ Royal Garden Plaza, 218 Beach Rd., South Pattaya, ☎ 038/710294), which offers an adventure through 10 themed galleries that lasts about an hour, and the **Million Years Stone Park and Crocodile Farm** (⊠ 22/1 Mu, Nongplalai, Banglamung, ☎ 038/422957) which has gigantic, grotesque-shape rocks decorating a large garden, and a man-catching-crocodile show performed every hour from 10 am to 5 pm. The **Pattaya Monkey Training Centre** (⊠ 151 Km., Soi Chaiyapruk, Sukhumvit Rd., ☎ 038/756367) has shows at 9, 11, noon, 1, 2, and 5. The pig-tailed monkeys, who live about 40 years, are trained for harvesting coconuts, a 12-month course, but are also taught a few other entertaining tricks. If you want to let your child catch a tiger by the tail, then a visit to the **Sri Racha Tiger Zoo** (⊠ 341 Mu 3, Nongkham, Sri Racha, ☎ 038/29556) may be warranted. Then there is the **Bottle Museum,** which is quite special. Pieter Beg de Leif, a Dutchman, has devoted 14 hours a day for the last 17 years to creating more than 300 miniatures in bottles—tiny replicas of famous buildings and ships. ⊠ *79/15 Moo 9, Sukhumvit Rd.,* ☎ *038/422957.* ⌨ *Admission.* ⊙ *Daily 10–9.*

Dining and Lodging

$$$ ✕ **Bruno's.** The former manager at the Royal Cliff Beach has taken over Dolf Riks, for many years a Pattaya institution. Bruno promises to keep the same warm, friendly atmosphere; you'll still be able to chat at the bar and dine on top-quality food. The difference will be in the cooking. Riks was Indonesian influenced; Bruno's will use Swiss recipes. ⊠ *463/28 Sri Nakorn Centre, N. Pattaya (turn down cul-de-sac beside Pattaya Bowl)*, ☎ *038/428269. AE, DC, MC, V.*

$$$ ✕ **Buccaneer Terrace.** The view of the bay from this rooftop restaurant in the Nipa Lodge Hotel is its prime attraction, although it also offers a good choice of fresh seafood and grilled steaks. ⊠ *Beach Rd.,* ☎ *038/428195. AE, DC, MC, V.*

$$$ ✕ **Peppermill Restaurant.** Tucked away next to P. K. Villa, this distinctly French restaurant takes a classical approach to dining, with an emphasis on flambéed dishes. More creative dishes such as fresh crab in a white-wine sauce and poached fillet of sole with a lobster tail are also served. Dinner is a special occasion here, particularly if complemented by a good bottle of wine from the respectable cellar. ⊠ *16 Beach Rd.,* ☎ *038/428248. AE, DC, MC, V. No lunch.*

$$$ ✕ **San Domenico.** The Roman owner of this restaurant halfway between Pattaya and Jontien prides himself on pasta dishes and ice cream, and you might want to try his filling pizzas, excited by Thai spices, or the buffet (B300). Be sure to have the Italian ice cream that made this place an instant success. ⊠ *Jontien Rd., S. Pattaya,* ☎ *038/426871. MC, V.*

$$ ✕ **Angelo's.** For Italian food, this is a good choice. It's owned by a Milanese who presides over the dining room, and his Thai wife, the chef. Her fortes are lasagna and a wonderful fish casserole. ⊠ *N. Pattaya Rd.,* ☎ *038/429093. MC, V.*

$$ ✕ **Nang Nual.** Next to the transvestite nightspot, Simon Cabaret, this restaurant is one of Pattaya's better places for seafood, cooked Thai-style or simply grilled. A huge array of fish is laid out as you enter the restaurant. Point out what you want and say how you want it cooked. There's a dining room upstairs, but you may want to eat on the patio overlooking the sea. For carnivores, the huge steaks are an expensive treat. Photographs of the finished products will overcome any language barrier. Similar dishes are found at Nang Nual's Jontien Beach branch, near the Sigma Resort. ⊠ *214–10 S. Pattaya Beach Rd.,* ☎ *038/ 428478. AE, MC, V.*

$$ ✕ **PIC.** Though the restaurant seems designed to appeal only to Westerners, Thais come here as well. You dine in classic teak pavilions on a wide range of Thai dishes like delicious deep-fried crab claws and spicy eggplant salad. The food can be spicy or mild, and if you are averse to chilies, try the succulent white snapper on vegetables, scented with ginger and salted prunes. ⊠ *Soi 5, Beach Rd.,* ☎ *038/428387. AE, DC, MC, V.*

$$ ✕ **Tak Nak Nam.** This floating restaurant in a Thai pavilion at the edge of a small lake has an extensive menu of Chinese and Thai dishes. Live classical Thai and folk music is played while you dine on such specialties as steamed crab in coconut milk or blackened chicken with Chinese herbs. ⊠ *252 Pattaya Central Rd., next to Pattaya Resort Hotel,* ☎ *038/429059. MC, V.*

$ ✕ **Sportsman Inn.** If you want some down-home English cooking, this is the best spot in Pattaya. The steak-and-kidney pie, bangers and chips, fish-and-chips, and such are well prepared, as testified to by the many expats who get their daily sustenance here. ⊠ *Soi Yod Sak (Soi 8),* ☎ *038/361548. No credit cards.*

$$$$ 🏨 **Royal Cliff Beach Hotel.** Pattaya's most lavish hotel, 1½ km (1 mi) south of town on a bluff jutting into the Gulf, is a self-contained resort with three wings. The 84 one-bedroom suites in the Royal Wing (double the price of standard rooms in the main building) have butler service, breakfast in the room at no charge, and reserved deck chairs. The Royal Cliff Terrace wing has two-bedroom and honeymoon suites with four-poster beds. The swimming pool sits on top of a cliff over-

looking the sea. ⊠ *Jontien Beach, Pattaya, Chonburi,* ☎ *038/250421, 02/282–0999 Bangkok reservations,* FAX *038/250511. 700 rooms and 100 suites. 4 restaurants, 3 pools, sauna, miniature golf, 2 tennis courts, jogging, squash, 2 private beaches, windsurfing, boating, shops. AE, DC, MC, V.*

$$$ ☎ **Dusit Resort.** On a promontory at the northern end of Pattaya
★ Beach, this large hotel offers superb sea views. The beautifully laid-out grounds with two pools that run around the promontory add to the pleasure. Though the rooms are in need of some cheerful refurbishing, they have large bathrooms, balconies, oversize beds, and sitting areas. The Landmark Rooms are larger and have extensive wood trim. The Empress restaurant serves sophisticated Cantonese fare against the panoramic backdrop of Pattaya Bay. This retreat from the Pattaya tourists is only a B5 songthaew ride from all the action. ⊠ *240/2 Pattaya Beach Rd., Pattaya, Chonburi 20260,* ☎ *038/425611, 02/236–0450 Bangkok reservations,* FAX *038/428239. 500 rooms and 28 suites. 4 restaurants, 2 pools, massage, sauna, 3 tennis courts, health club, Ping-Pong, squash, windsurfing, boating, shops, billiards. AE, DC, MC, V.*

$$$ ☎ **Montien.** Though not plush, this hotel has a central location and a design that takes advantage of the sea breezes. With the hotel's generous off-season discounts, a room with a sea view can be one of the best values in town. The air-conditioned section of the Garden Restaurant has a dance floor and stage for entertainment. ⊠ *Pattaya Beach Rd., Pattaya, Chonburi 20260,* ☎ *038/428155, 02/233–7060 Bangkok reservations,* FAX *038/423155. 320 rooms. 2 restaurants, bar, coffee shop, snack bar, pool, 2 tennis courts, meeting rooms. AE, DC, MC, V.*

$$$ ☎ **Royal Garden Resort.** This modern resort in downtown Pattaya, a block from the beach, gives the feeling of great space by having both a large, open lobby and lounge, and a garden full of trees with a pool in its center. The carpeted bedrooms are standard: furnished in light colors, with enough room for a coffee table and two chairs; a balcony looks over the pool and garden to the sea. Next door is the Royal Garden Plaza, a shopping and entertainment complex, where the whole family can while away the time. ⊠ *218/2–4M, 10 Beach Rd., 20260,* ☎ *038/412120,* FAX *038/429926. 300 rooms. 2 restaurants, bar, pool, beauty salon, 4 tennis courts, health club, business services, meeting rooms, travel services. AE, DC, MC, V.*

$–$$ ☎ **Palm Lodge.** This started as a no-frills hotel, but its central yet quiet location has prompted the owners to expand and improve the facilities. Now the hotel offers modern rooms with televisions and minibars. Bathrooms are tiled and clean. The outdoor pool is smallish but pleasantly laid out in a shady garden and, anyway, the sea is just across the road. ⊠ *Mu 9, Beach Rd., Pattaya, Chonburi 20260,* ☎ *038/428780,* FAX *038/421779. 80 rooms. Coffee shop, pool, laundry service. MC, V.*

$ ☎ **Chris Guest House.** Owned by an Englishman, this small hotel offers clean, inexpensive (B500), air-conditioned rooms with private baths—ask for a new rather than an old room. The friendly atmosphere makes this the top choice in the budget category. On the ground floor there's an open-front lounge/restaurant/bar where old roués gather at a round table chaired by Chris to review the world of lust, sex, and sin. Though it's only half a block from the sea, it is nevertheless quietly secluded, with its own small garden down a small soi. ⊠ *185 Soi 13, Pattaya Beach Rd., Pattaya, Chonburi 20260,* ☎ *038/429586,* FAX *038/423653. 15 rooms. Restaurant, bar. No credit cards.*

$ ☎ **Diamond Beach Hotel.** In the heart of Pattaya's nightlife section amid discos and cafés, this hotel is a bastion of sanity. Rooms are clean, and security guards make female guests feel safe. The staff, however, is not particularly friendly or helpful—perhaps that's why you can often find a room here when other hotels are full. ⊠ *373/8 Pattaya Beach*

Rd., Pattaya, Chonburi 20260, ☎ *038/428071,* FAX *038/424888. 126 rooms. Restaurant, massage, travel services. No credit cards.*

Nightlife and the Arts

Entertainment in Pattaya revolves around the hundreds of bars, bar/cafés, discos, and nightclubs. Bars and clubs stay open past midnight, and some are open much later. Discos usually have a cover charge of B100, and drinks cost about B50. Drinks for any hostess who joins you are B100. Pattaya is obviously confronted with the catastrophic AIDS problem and, added to this stigma, there has been a rash of drug-related killings. Caution is advised for night revelers! One popular nightspot is the **Pattaya Palladium** (☎ 038/42922), which bills itself as the largest disco in Southeast Asia. The **Marina Disco** in the Regent Marina Hotel (✉ S. Pattaya Rd., ☎ 038/429568) has a laser light show, live entertainment, and three DJs who keep the activity going until the wee hours of the morning. A popular transvestite show is presented at **Tiffany's** (✉ Pattaya 2 Rd., ☎ 038/429642).

Outdoor Activities and Sports

BUNGEE JUMPING

If you are one to take a fall, try **Kiwi Thai Bungee Jump,** off the main road to Jontien Beach. You are hoisted in a metal cage to a height of 150 ft and then you jump. Just remember to attach your rubber harness first! ✉ *Road to Jontien Beach,* ☎ *038/250319.* ⏺ *Daily 1–9.*

GOLF

Thailand's longest course (6,800 yards), the **Royal Thai Navy Course** (✉ Phiu Ta Luang Golf Course, Sattahip, Chonburi, ☎ 02/466–1180, ext. Sattahip 2217), is 30 km (18 mi) from Pattaya. With rolling hills and dense vegetation, it's considered one of the country's most difficult. The **Siam Country Club** (✉ Pattaya, Chonburi, ☎ 038/418002), close to Pattaya, offers a challenging course with wide fairways but awkward water traps and wooded hills. **Panya Resort Country Club** (✉ Pattaya, ☎ 038/239400) boasts three par-72 courses, where clubs can be rented and greens fees are B500 (B750 on weekends).

WATER SPORTS

All kinds of water sports are available, including windsurfing (B200 per hr), waterskiing (B1,000 per hr), and sailing on a 16-ft Hobie catamaran (B500 per hour). Private entrepreneurs offer these activities all along the beach, but the best area is around the **Sailing Club** on Beach Road. Jet skiing and parasailing are dangerous and shouldn't be tried for the first time here. Be on the lookout for unscrupulous operators who rent a defective machine and hold the customer responsible for its repair or loss. The operators of parasailing boats tend to be inexperienced, making sharp turns or sudden stops that bring the parachutist down too fast. The water near shore is too polluted for diving and snorkeling.

En Route   Take highway H3 south for about 20 km (12 mi), and turn right at the 165-km marker for **Bang Saray.** The village consists of jetties, a fishing fleet, a small temple, and two narrow streets running parallel to the bay. Fully equipped game-fishing craft are tied up to the jetty, and photos to prove fishermen's stories are posted in the area's two hotel bars, Fisherman's Lodge and Fisherman's Inn. It costs about B2,500 to charter one of the faster fishing boats for the day. If you just want to soak up the scene, stop next to the main jetty at the Ruam Talay Restaurant. Windsurfers can be rented at the beach, just north of the bay at the Sea Sand Club. H3 goes through Sattahip, a Thai naval base. Avoid it by taking bypass H332, which passes through countryside full of coconut groves and tapioca plantations to **Rayong** (50 km/31 mi east of Sattahip), a booming market town famous for seafood and nam plaa, the fermented fish sauce Thais use as salt. In the last five years, this area has become a center of economic growth, with corporations building factories here. About 20 km (12 mi) east of Rayong is the small village of **Ban Phe,** whose beaches and self-contained family resorts attract Thai families. Ban Phe is the jumping-off point for Ko Samet.

Ko Samet

⑩ *30 mins by ferry from Ban Phe (223 km/139 mi southeast of Bangkok).*

Two ferries from Ban Phe make the crossing to Ko Samet (fare: B20): one goes to Na Duan on the north shore, the other to An Wong Duan halfway down the eastern shore. All the island's beaches are an easy walk from these villages. Indeed, from the southern tip to the north is about a three-hour, comfortable walk. Ko Samet is known for its beaches; its other name is Ko Kaeo Phitsadan ("island with sand like crushed crystal"), and its fine sand is in great demand by glassmakers. The island has many bungalows and cottages, with and without electricity. Make sure that yours has mosquito netting: come dusk, Ko Samet's mosquitoes take a fancy to tourists.

Lodging

¢ ⊞ **Lung Dumhut.** At the southern end of the eastern shore, in a small beach community, this collection of budget bungalows is a friendly place to stay. The helpful owner speaks English well. The small restaurant produces simple Thai and Western food, the fan-cooled rooms have small single beds and mosquito netting, and the shower is one where you ladle water over yourself. ⊠ *Sangtean Beach,* ☎ *038/651810. 15 rooms share communal baths. Restaurant. No credit cards.*

Chantaburi

100 km (62 mi) east of Rayong; 180 km (108 mi) from Pattaya.

Buses from both Rayong and Ban Phe make the 90-minute journey to Chantaburi. Much of the jewelry that is sold in Pattaya contains gemstones from the open-pit mines here. Star sapphires and rubies are the two most popular stones. It is fascinating to walk along Gem Street, in the center of town: here, in small storefronts, you see traders sorting through gems and making deals that are in the hundreds of thousands of baht. You can also take a tour of the mining area and see the 30-ft holes where the prospectors dig. The province of Chantaburi has few beach resorts of note, and those cater mostly to Thais. Laem Sadet, 18 km (11 mi) from Chantaburi, is the most popular, and its accommodations range from small bungalows to low-rise hotels.

Lodging

$$ ⊞ **KP Grand Hotel.** This is the smart business hotel in the town of Chantaburi. The 18-story building has no charm, but it does have modern facilities, large guest rooms with two single beds or a king, and attentive service. It's on the eastern side of town, but within walking distance of Gem Street. ⊠ *35/200-201 Theerat Rd., 22000,* ☎ *039/ 323201,* ℻ *039/323214. 200 rooms. 2 restaurants, bar, pool, health club, meeting rooms. AE, DC, MC, V.*

En Route Beyond Chantaburi lies Trat, Thailand's easternmost province. Hemmed in by the Khao Banthat mountain range, the region is waiting to be discovered by tourists. The provincial capital, **Trat,** two hours plus from Chantaburi, is a small town whose interest is as a market and transport center. For travelers, it is where the buses arrive from and depart for Bangkok, and where the songthaews leave for the 20-minute trip to Laem Ngop, the port for ferries to Ko Chang.

Ko Chang

★ ⑪　*1 hr by ferry from Laem Ngop, which is 15 km (9 mi) southwest of Trat; Trat is 400 km (250 mi) southeast of Bangkok.*

Ko Chang is the largest and most developed of the 52 islands that compose Mu Ko Chang National Park, many of them not much more than hummocks protruding from the sea. These islands are being discovered by Westerners and local tourists, and they have not yet been spoiled by the honky-tonk commercialism found in Pattaya, Phuket, and Ko Samui. That also means that their infrastructure is basic and accommodations rustic. You can book lodgings on these islands in Laem Ngop, where you buy your ferry ticket. Most of the tourists who make the trip here (a good eight hours from Bangkok) are backpackers and young Thais looking for inexpensive vacations.

Ko Chang's best beaches are on the western shore. First comes Haad Sai Khao (White Sand Beach), which attracts mostly tattooed backpackers who pay B100 a night for a cot in huts crammed together along the narrow beach. Next in line is Haad Khlong Phrao, which has a long, curving beach of pale golden sand. Accommodations here are spaced farther apart and tend to be larger and more expensive. Farther down and at the end of the only road on the island is Haad Kai Bae. Here, the beach, with both sand and pebbles, has a very gentle dropoff—safe for nonswimmers. A couple of small, uninhabited islands offshore make the views from here attractive, and accommodations range from a few air-conditioned bungalows to small huts.

Ko Mak, one of the largest of the other islands, has a small village and a couple of basic resorts with bungalows. One of the most beautiful islands is tiny **Koh Wai** (three hours by ferry from Laem Ngob), resplendent with idyllic beaches, tropical flora, and fantastic coral reefs. **Ko Ngam,** also small, is shaped like a butterfly and has waters of different hues. **Ko Kradat** has little development except for one bungalow resort. **Ko Kut,** the second largest of the Ko Chang group, is mountainous, with lush tropical foliage.

Lodging

Booking agents at travel agencies in Laem Ngob port can make reservations for you on the Ko Chang islands.

$$$　🏠 **Ko Chang Resort.** This was one of the first comfortable resorts to be built on Ko Chang. It is a self-contained complex on the edge of the bay, with clean, rustic bungalows around a reception lounge and dining room. The rate for the air-conditioned units is fairly steep, and the small ones are very cramped. The advantage of the resort is that you can make the booking in Bangkok, and it has its own boat service to the island. ✉ *Ko Chang, Trat 23120,* ☎ *01/211–3834, 02/276–1233 Bangkok reservations,* ℻ *02/276–6929. 45 rooms. Restaurant. MC, V.*

$–$$$　🏠 **Sea View Resort.** Your option is either a small fan-cooled thatched bungalow just back from the sands of Kai Bae Beach or a larger air-conditioned unit with a private bath 100 yards inland on a slight rise. The resort is at the far end of the beach and is therefore quieter than the others. Its pluses are an attractive terrace restaurant and a very gentle, sloping, sandy beach—too gentle for many. ✉ *Ko Chang, Trat 23120,* ☎ *01/321–0055, 02/276–1233 Bangkok reservations,* ℻ *02/276–6929. 32 rooms. Restaurant. MC, V.*

¢–$$ 🏠 **Kae Bae Hut Bungalows.** Accommodations run the gamut from
★ tiny B50 bungalows back from the beach to much larger ones with
air-conditioning and private baths facing the beach. Because it's near
the center of Kae Bae Beach, guests can wander over to nearby restau-
rants for meals and entertainment. But, in fact, the food here is the
best on the beach and the staff is the friendliest. ⊠ *Ko Chang, Trat
23120,* ☎ *01/329–0452. 25 rooms. Restaurant, dive shop. No credit
cards.*

Side Trips out of Bangkok Essentials

Arriving and Departing

Ayutthaya, Bang Pa-In, and Lopburi
BY BOAT

Though you can reach Ayutthaya by rail or road, the nicest way to get
there (at least one-way) is by boat along the Chao Phraya River (☞
Tour Operators, *below*). Boats also make the 40-minute trip down the
Chao Phraya from Ayutthaya; the fare is B150.

BY BUS

Buses leave Bangkok's **Northern Terminal** every 30 minutes between 6
AM and 7 PM for Ayutthaya and Lopburi. Minibuses leave Ayutthaya's
Chao Prom Market for Bang Pa-In frequently, starting at 6:30 AM, for
the 50-minute trip (B10).

BY TRAIN

Between 4:30 AM and late evening, trains depart frequently from
Bangkok's **Hualamphong station,** arriving in Ayutthaya 80 minutes later.
Since Don Muang Airport lies between the two cities, many travelers
en route from Chiang Mai visit Ayutthaya and then stop off at the air-
port to fly to their next destination. Trains from Bangkok regularly make
the 70-km (42-mi) run to Bang Pa-In railway station, from which a
minibus runs to the palace. Three morning and two afternoon trains
depart from **Hualamphong station** on the three-hour journey to Lop-
buri. The journey from Ayutthaya takes just over an hour. Trains back
to Bangkok run in the early and late afternoon.

Damnoen Saduak, Nakhon Pathom, and Kanchanaburi
BY BUS

Public buses, some air-conditioned, leave from the **Southern Bus Ter-
minal** every 20 minutes from 6 AM. The fare is B30; B50 air-conditioned.
From the bus station, walk along the canal for 1½ km (1 mi) to the
floating market or take a taxi boat at the pier for B10. Buses leave from
the same terminal for the 2½-hour trip to Kanchanaburi every half hour.
Buses also run to Nakhon Pathom from Damnoen Saduak.

BY TAXI

You can arrange to be picked up by a private car or taxi, which is
far superior to a tour bus because you can reach the Damnoen Sad-
uak market by 9 AM, before the tours arrive. Speak to your concierge,
who will usually have a good resource. The cost for two people will
be no more than the tour-bus fare. The round-trip fare from Bangkok
to Damnoen Saduak can be as low as B1,300. If you keep the car to
visit both Nakhon Pathom and Kanchanaburi, the cost will be about
B1,800.

BY TRAIN

Trains from the Bangkok Hualamphong and Bangkok Noi stations stop
in Nakhon Pathom. There is no train to Damnoen Saduak. The train
for Kanchanaburi leaves from the **Bangkok Noi Station** at 8 AM and 1:55

PM. The State Railway of Thailand also runs a **special excursion train** (B75) on weekends and holidays; it leaves Hualamphong Station at 6:15 AM and returns at 7:30 PM, stopping at Nakhon Pathom, the River Kwai Bridge, and Nam-Tok, from which point minibuses take you to Khao Phang Waterfall. Buy your ticket in advance (☎ 02/223–3762).

Hua Hin/Cha'Am

BY AIRPLANE

Bangkok Airways (☎ 02/253–4014) serves Hua Hin from Bangkok with a daily 25-minute evening flight. Take a taxi from the airport, or ask your hotel to meet you.

BY BUS

Buses, air-conditioned and non-air-conditioned, leave Bangkok's **Southern Bus Terminal** every half hour during the day for the three-hour trip to **Hua Hin's terminal** (✉ Srasong Rd., ☎ 032/511654).

BY CAR

A few hotels, such as the Regent and Dusit Thani, run minibuses between their Bangkok and Cha' Am/Hua Hin properties for a flat fee of B450. Nonguests may use these. Otherwise, you can hire a car and driver for approximately B2,500 to or from the Bangkok airport.

BY TRAIN

The train from the Bangkok Noi station in Thonburi takes four long hours to reach Hua Hin's delightful wooden **train station** (✉ Damnernkasem Rd., ☎ 032/511073).

Pattaya and Ko Samet

BY AIRPLANE

Bangkok Airways runs twice-daily flights from Ko Samui, which land at U-Tapao Airport, 50 km (30 mi) east of Pattaya. **Silk Air** has flights between Singapore and Pattaya every Tuesday, Wednesday, Friday, and Saturday.

BY BUS AND LIMOUSINE

Buses depart every half hour from Ekkamai, Bangkok's **Eastern Bus Terminal,** and its **Northern Terminal,** arriving at Pattaya's **bus station** (✉ North Pattaya Rd., ☎ 038/429877). The fare is B66 per person. From the bus station, songthaews will take you into downtown Pattaya for B20—tell the driver where you want to go. A bus runs between Don Muang Airport and Pattaya (B120) every two hours 7 AM–5 PM, and direct buses run between Korat and Pattaya from the northern bus station on Central Pattaya Road.

Most hotels in Bangkok and Pattaya have a travel desk that works directly with a minibus company. Minibuses leave approximately five times a day and cost B200 per person. An Avis minibus that departs from Bangkok's Dusit Thani Hotel for its property in Pattaya is open to nonguests as well.

Direct buses make the three-hour drive between Pattaya's hotels and Bangkok's Don Muang Airport every two or three hours from 6 AM to 9 PM. **Thai Limousine Service** (ticket desk at airport, or in Pattaya, ☎ 038/421421) has the cleanest, most reliable air-conditioned buses. The cost is B200.

For Ko Samet, buses leave frequently from the **Eastern Bus Terminal** for Ban Phe to connect with the ferry. From Pattaya, try the **Malibu Travel Centre** (✉ Post Office La., Pattaya, ☎ 038/423180), which has daily 8 AM departures for B120, or you can take the local bus or a car to Ban Phe.

Taxis to Pattaya from either Don Muang Airport or downtown Bangkok will ask B2,500, which can be quickly renegotiated to B1,800 or less. Coming back costs about B1,000.

Ko Chang

BY BUS

For the various islands of the Ko Chang group, take a bus from **Ekka-mai** (Eastern Bus Terminal), for the five-to-six-hour trip to Trat, where you pick up a songthaew for the 20-minute run to Laem Ngob and the ferries. Schedules vary, but if you can get to Laem Ngob by 1 PM (take the first bus, at 6 AM), you should find a ferry that afternoon going to Ko Chang, the big island, or another of your choice. The last bus out of Bangkok is at 11 PM, which gets you to Trat at 4 or 5 AM, in time for coffee at the market before a songthaew, usually loaded with housewives and vegetables, leaves for Laem Ngob to connect with the 7 AM ferry.

Getting Around

Ayutthaya

For a three-hour tour of the sites, tuk-tuks can be hired within the city for about B400.

Hua Hin/Cha'Am

Local buses make it easy to travel between Cha' Am and Hua Hin, as well as to points south of Hua Hin. Taxis are available, but samlors are more convenient for short distances. You can walk to most of the sights in town, but if you are staying at a resort hotel in Cha' Am, use the hotel shuttle bus or take a taxi. Tours to nearby attractions are arranged through your hotel.

Kanchanaburi

Attractions around Kanchanaburi are accessible both on foot and by samlor. Buses leave from the town's **terminal** (⊠ Saeng Chuto Rd., ☎ 034/511387) every half hour for most of the popular destinations.

Pattaya

Songthaews cruise the two main streets, parallel to the beach. The fare is B5 in town, and B10 between Naklua and Pattaya; for the Royal Cliff Resort, the fare is about B50, and to Jontien Beach, it's at least B100. Sedans and Jeeps can be rented for B700–B900 a day, with unlimited mileage. **Avis** (⊠ Dusit Resort Hotel, Pattaya, ☎ 038/429901) offers insurance, though not all rental companies do. Motorbike rental costs about B250 a day.

Contacts and Resources

Emergencies

Tourist Police: Ayutthaya (☎ 035/242352); **Cha'Am** (☎ 032/471005); **Hua Hin** (☎ 032/515995); **Pattaya** (⊠ Pattaya 2 Rd., ☎ 038/429371, 1699 for emergencies).

Hospital or Ambulance: Hua Hin (⊠ Phetkasem Rd., ☎ 032/511743); **Pattaya** (☎ 191); **Rayong**'s hospital has a malaria clinic.

Tour Operators

Tours of Ayutthaya and Bang Pa-In take a full day. You may travel the 75 km (46 mi) both ways by coach or in one direction by cruise boat and the other by coach. The best combination is to take the morning coach to Ayutthaya for sightseeing before the day warms up, and return downriver. The most popular trip is aboard the *Oriental Queen*, managed by the Oriental Hotel (☎ 02/236–0400, ext. 3133); the cost is B900. The *Ayutthaya Princess* (☎ 02/255–9200), a new boat whose exterior resembles a royal barge, offers the same itinerary for the same fare, leaving from the Shangri-La and the Royal Orchid Sheraton piers. You can also book either of these cruises with any travel agent.

The **Chao Phraya Express Boat Co.** (✉ 2/58 Aroon-Amarin Rd., Maharat Pier, Bangkok, ☎ 02/222–5330) runs a Sunday excursion to Bang Pa-In Summer Palace for Thais, which leaves the pier at 8:30 AM and arrives in time for lunch. On the downriver trip, it stops at the Bang Sai Folk Arts and Craft Centre and arrives in Bangkok by 5:30 PM.

All the major hotels have arrangements with a tour operator who organizes morning trips to Damnoen Saduak, sometimes combined with the Rose Garden, or Kanchanaburi and the bridge over the River Kwai. These tours collect you from your hotel at about 8 AM and cost about B700. Usually a full day is necessary to visit the Allied war cemeteries and the infamous bridge, and to tour the lush tropical countryside. If you wish to take a minibus tour, having reached Kanchanaburi under your own steam, daily guide services are available from **B. T. Travel** (✉ Saeng Chuto Rd., Kanchanaburi, ☎ 034/511967), next door to the TAT.

Visitor Information

Hua Hin Tourist Information Center (✉ 114 Phetkasem Rd., near the railway station, ☎ 032/512120), open daily 8:30–4:30. Kanchanaburi **Tourist Authority of Thailand** (TAT) (✉ Saeng Chuto Rd., Kanchanaburi, ☎ 034/511200). Pattaya **TAT** (✉ 382/1 Beach Rd., S. Pattaya, ☎ 038/428750), open daily 9–5. The tourist office is planning a move in 1999 to the southern end of Pattaya 2 Road and not far from the Royal Cliff Resort—very out of the way and inconvenient for tourists.

NORTHERN THAILAND

Northern Thailand is a scene of untutored peoples and traditional cultures meeting the modern age. Chiang Mai is for travelers the gateway to the region: Many stay for a month or longer, making excursions and returning to rest. Guest houses and sophisticated hotels accommodate them, and well-worn tracks lead into the tribal villages. The opium trade still flourishes, flowing illegally into southern Thailand en route to the rest of the world. For the tourist, however, the attractions are trekking in forested hills laced with rivers, the cultures of the hill tribes, and the cool weather. (Those who also seek the poppy often find themselves languishing in a Chiang Mai prison.)

The hill tribes around Chiang Mai have been visited so frequently that they have lost some of their character. You need to go farther afield, to areas around Tak, near the Burmese border, and Nan to the east, to find villages untainted by commercialism. Even Mae Hong Son, west of Chiang Mai, known for its sleepy pace and the regular gathering of hill tribes, is developing its tourist trade. Two paved highways from Chiang Mai, and daily flights have opened up the region.

The Golden Triangle (Sop Ruak in Thai), the area where Thailand, Laos, and Burma (Myanmar) meet, has long captivated the Western imagination. The opium poppy still grows here, albeit on a much diminished scale, and the hill tribes that cultivate it are semiautonomous, ruled more by warlords than by any national government. Today, the tribes of Laos and Burma retain their autonomy, but Thailand's corner of the Golden Triangle has become a tourist attraction, with the tribes caught up in the tide of commercialism. Chiang Rai is the closest city. In 1990 it had only one luxury hotel; now there are at least three re-

Northern Thailand

sort complexes, and two more have been built up where the rivers converge, overlooking Laos and Burma.

Chiang Mai and West to the Border

Most visitors fly to the walled, moated city of Chiang Mai from Bangkok (though many are discovering the pleasant overnight train) and make short excursions to the smaller towns south and southeast; we cover those spots in that order. Then, if there's time, people drive or fly west to Mae Hong Son. They come to see Chiang Mai's ancient buildings and stay to take advantage of its wonderful shopping. In Mae Hong Son the draw is, first of all, the nearby hill-tribe villages.

Chiang Mai

❶ *696 km (430 mi) north of Bangkok.*

Chiang Mai's rich culture stretches back 700 years, to the time when several small tribes, under King Mengrai, banded together to form a new "nation" called Anachak Lanna Thai. They first made Chiang Rai (north of Chiang Mai) their capital, but in 1296 they moved it to the fertile plains between Doi Suthep mountain and the Mae Ping River and called it Napphaburi Sri Nakornphing Chiang Mai.

Lanna Thai eventually lost its independence to Ayutthaya and, later, Burma. Not until 1774—when General Taksin (king before Rama I) drove the Burmese out—did the region revert to Thailand. After that, it developed independently of southern Thailand. Even the language is different, marked by a relaxed tempo. In the last 50 years communications have opened up between Bangkok and Chiang Mai; the small, provincial town has exploded beyond its moat and gates, and some of its innocence has gone.

Chiang Mai

KEY

––––– Rail Lines

```
0        550 yards
0        500 meters
```

N

Chiang Mai Tribal
Museum, **7**
National Museum, **6**
Phuping Palace, **3**
Wat
Chaimongkol, **11**
Wat Chedi Luang, **9**
Wat Chedi Yot, **5**

Wat Chiang Man, **10**
Wat Phra Singh, **8**
Wat Phrathat Doi
Suthep, **2**
Wat Suan Dok, **4**

Chiang Mai can be explored easily on foot or by bicycle, with the occasional use of buses, tuk-tuks, or taxis for getting to attractions outside the center.

② **Wat Phrathat Doi Suthep** is perched high up—3,542 ft—on Doi Suthep, a mountain 16 km (10 mi) northwest of Chiang Mai, overlooking the city. It is a 30-minute drive—you can take a bus from Chuang Puak Gate on the north side of the city—and then a cable-car ride or a steep climb up 290 steps beside a marvelous balustrade. This stone railing, added in 1577, is in the form of *nagas* (mythical snakes that control the irrigation waters in the rice fields), inlaid with scales of brown and green tiles. It leads to the *chedi,* the pagoda where holy relics are kept.

A special relic here makes Wat Phrathat one of the four royal wats: in the 14th century, when a relic of the Lord Buddha was being installed at Wat Suan Dok, it split into two. So a white elephant was sent to find a new location for the second piece. The animal stomped his way up Doi Suthep, circled three times in a counterclockwise direction and knelt down, marking the chosen spot. A chedi was built, then later enlarged and followed by other shrines to make a large and glorious complex. Of particular note are the murals that depict scenes from the life of the Lord Buddha.

③ **Phuping Palace,** the summer residence of the Thai royal family, is across a valley from Wat Phrathat. Though the palace may not be visited, the gardens are open on Friday, Sunday, and public holidays, unless any of the royal family is in residence. The blooms are at their best in January.

④ **Wat Suan Dok,** on Suthep Road, one of the largest of Chiang Mai's temples, is said to have been built on the site where bones of Lord Buddha were found. Some of these relics are reportedly housed in the chedi; the others went to Wat Phrathat on Doi Suthep. At the back of the viharn is the *bot* (main chapel) housing Phra Chao Kao, a superb bronze Buddha cast in 1504. Chiang Mai aristocrats are buried in stupas in the graveyard.

On the Superhighway, between its intersection with Huay Kaew Road and Highway 107, stands Wat Photharam Maha Viharn, more commonly known as **⑤** **Wat Chedi Yot** (Seven-Spired Pagoda). Built in 1455, it is a copy of the Mahabodhi temple in Bodh Gaya, India, where the Lord Buddha achieved enlightenment; the seven spires represent the seven weeks that he subsequently spent there. The sides of the chedi have marvelous bas-relief sculptures of celestial figures.

⑥ From Wat Chedi Yot you can walk to the **National Museum,** a northern Thai-style building containing many statues of Lord Buddha and a huge Buddha footprint of wood with mother-of-pearl inlay. The upper floor's archaeological collection includes a bed with mosquito netting used by an early prince of Chiang Mai. The museum has been closed for renovations, but a few galleries are now open and it may be fully open in late 1999. 🔼 *Admission.* ☉ *Weekdays 8:30–noon and 1–4:30.*

⑦ After the National Museum you'll need a tuk-tuk to go up Chang Puak Road to Rachanangkla Park, where the new **Chiang Mai Tribal Museum** has opened. Until 1998, more than 1,000 pieces of traditional crafts from the hill tribes, collected over the past 30 years, had been hidden away in a small museum at Chiang Mai University. Now this fine collection is interestingly displayed in its own new contemporary building by the lake in the park: farming implements, colorful embroidery, weapons, hunting traps, a variety of drums and musical instruments, among other things. ✉ *Rachanangkla Park, Chang Puak Rd.,* ☎ *053/ 221933.* 🎫 *Admission.* 🕙 *Mon.–Sat. 8:30–4.*

Chiang Mai's city walls contain several important temples—all in walking distance of one another. At the junction of Ratchadamnoen and Singharat roads, in the middle of town, stands Chiang Mai's prin-⑧ cipal monastery, **Wat Phra Singh,** containing the Phra Singh Buddha image. The serene and benevolent facial expression of this statue has a radiance enhanced by the light filtering into the chapel. Be sure to note the temple's facades of splendidly carved wood, the elegant teak beams and posts, and the masonry. In a large teaching compound, student monks often have the time and desire to talk.

On Phra Pokklao Road, just before it crosses Rajmankha Road, stands ⑨ **Wat Chedi Luang.** In 1411, a vision commanded King Saen Muang Ma to build a chedi "as high as a dove could fly." He died before it was finished, as did the next king, and, during the next king's reign, an earthquake knocked down 100 ft of the 282-ft chedi. It is now a superb ruin. Don't miss the naga balustrades at the steps to the viharn—considered the finest of their kind.

⑩ **Wat Chiang Man,** Chiang Mai's oldest (1296) monastery, typical of northern Thai architecture, has massive teak pillars inside the bot. Two important images of the Buddha sit in the small building to the right of the main viharn. Officially, they are on view only on Sunday, but sometimes the door is unlocked.

Each of Chiang Mai's multitude of temples has merit, but the temple that counts is the one that inspires you. One that may, for example, is ★⑪ **Wat Chaimongkol,** along the Mae Ping River, near the Chiang Mai Plaza Hotel. It's small, with only 18 monks in residence, and foreigners rarely visit. Though the little chedi is supposed to contain holy relics, its beauty lies in the quietness and serenity of the grounds.

☾ If you have not seen an "elephant camp" elsewhere, visit the **Elephant Training Centre** about 20 km (12 mi) northwest of Chiang Mai at Mae Sa. As commercial and touristy as it is, elephants are so magnificent that the show (80 baht) cannot fail to please. Action begins at 9:40 AM, when the mahouts bring their beasts to the river for a thorough wash down. The elephants frolic in the water, loving every moment of it. They then stage a dull demonstration of dragging in 20-ft teak logs and nudging them into a pile. At the end of the show, the audience feeds bananas to the performers, and you can ride an elephant around the camp or take a one-hour trek through the forest. Lunch at the **Mae Sa Valley Resort** (✉ in the valley, ☎ 053/291051, 🖷 053/290017), which has well-appointed thatched cottages in beautiful gardens, where they grow their own vegetables. Ask the owner for the honey-cooked chicken with chili.

Dining

All the top hotel dining rooms serve good Continental and Thai cuisines, but for the best Thai food, go to Chiang Mai's restaurants. Several good bistro-style restaurants that serve northern Thai cuisine are across from the Rincome Hotel on Nimanhaemin Road, about 1½ km (1 mi) northwest of downtown. Also try the food at the Anusan Market.

$$–$$$ ✕ **Baen Suan.** This delightful restaurant off the San Kamphaeng Road (the shopping/factory street) is a B40 tuk-tuk ride from downtown. The northern-style teak house sits in a peaceful garden, and the excellently prepared food is from the region. Try the hot Chiang Mai sausage (the recipe originally came from Burma), broccoli in oyster sauce, green curry with chicken, and a shrimp-and-vegetable soup. ✉ *51/3 San Kamphaeng Rd.,* ☎ *053/242116. Reservations essential. No credit cards.*

$$–$$$ ✕ **The Gallery.** North along the Mae Ping from the Riverside and the Good View is the third in a line of pleasant, shaded, waterside restaurants. This one is also an art/antiques gallery with a wide variety of upscale artifacts and gifts—even furniture. The terraces down toward the river have a secluded feeling, and the food is fine. ✉ *25–29 Charoen Rat Rd.,* ☎ *053/248601. AE, DC, MC, V.*

$$ ✕ **Arun Rai.** This is the best-known restaurant in Chiang Mai for northern Thai cuisine. Its success has inspired the owner to roof half of his space, but you still should not expect great ambience; the focus is on the food. Try the papaya salad, *tabong* (boiled bamboo shoots fried in batter), *sai oua* (pork sausage with herbs), or the famous frog's legs fried with ginger. The menu is available in English. The Arun Rai often has the delicacy *rod fai* (fried banana worms), which you may want to try. ✉ *45 Kotchasarn Rd.,* ☎ *053/276947. Reservations not accepted. No credit cards.*

$$ ✕ **The Good View.** Of the three terraced restaurants in a row along the Mae Ping River, this one, in the middle, is the prettiest and the quietest, and it does have a wonderful view. You can sit on the shaded deck just outside the restaurant or down toward the water on varying levels. A broad menu should satisfy all comers. ✉ *13 Charoen Rat Rd.,* ☎ *053/302764. MC, V.*

$$ ✕ **Hong Tauw Inn.** This relaxing, intimate restaurant has the atmosphere of a Thai bistro, where you can linger, trying dishes from northern Thailand and from the central plains. There is an English menu, and the owner speaks English fluently. Excellent Thai soups, sai oua, crispy *pla mee krob* (fried fish with chili), and *nam phrik ong* (minced pork with chili paste and tomatoes) are among the popular dishes. ✉ *Across from Rincome Hotel, 95/17–18 Nantawan Arcade, Nimanhaemin Rd.,* ☎ *053/218333. MC, V.*

$$ ✕ **Huen Phen.** The small rooms in this delightful restaurant, once a
★ private home, are full of old handicrafts which, if not antiques, are wonderful decorative artifacts. Be sure to browse through each dining room, both upstairs and downstairs, before settling in to study the extensive menu. The *kaeng hang lae* (northern pork curry) with *kao neeu* (sticky rice) is a top specialty; *larb nua* (spicy ground beef fried with herbs) and deep-fried pork ribs are two more good dishes to try. ✉ *112 Rachamongka Rd., Phrasing,* ☎ *053/277103. MC, V.*

$$ ✕ **Kaiwan.** Not many Westerners come here, but the food is held in high
★ esteem by Thais. The best place to sit is upstairs at one of the picnic tables under the stars. For a not-so-spicy beef curry, try *kaeng mat su man*, and for a zesty fried fish, go for the *pla tot na phrik*. ✉ *181 Nimanhaemin Rd., Soi 9, near the Rincome Hotel,* ☎ *053/221147. MC, V.*

$$ ✕ **Len Pae.** If you have made the shopping trip along Chiang Mai-Sankamphang Road and want a relaxing lunch, this floating restaurant on an artificial lake is the spot. The lake and the water sprays create a gentle breeze and keep the temperature down. The best tables are those on the piers extending into the lake. The fare is northern Thai with a variety of spicy sausages, fried freshwater fish with chili, as well as less-spicy Chinese food. ✉ *114 Moo 2 Sanklang, Chiang Mai-Sankamphang Rd.,* ☎ *053/338641. No credit cards.*

$$ ✕ **Nang Nuan.** Though this large restaurant has tables indoors, it's pleasant to sit on the terrace facing the Mae Nam Ping. Because it's 3 km (2 mi) south of Chiang Mai, you'll need to take a tuk-tuk or taxi, but the *tom kha gai* (chicken soup with coconut milk) and the *yam nua* (beef salad) are worth the trip. Grilled charcoal steaks and fresh seafood (displayed in tanks) are also on the menu. ✉ *27/2 Ko Klang Rd., Nonghoy,* ☎ *053/281955. AE, DC, MC, V.*

\$\$ ✕ **Riverside.** In a 100-year-old teak house on the bank of the Mae Nam Ping, this restaurant serves primarily Western food given zest by the Thai chef. The owner is John Vloet, a Dutchman. The casual, conversation-laden atmosphere attracts young Thais and Westerners, and with lots of beer flowing, the food gets only partial attention. The choice tables are on the deck jutting out over the river, with views of Wat Phrathat on Doi Suthep in the distance. There's live light jazz and popular music after 7 PM. ✉ *9–11 Charoen Rat Rd.,* ☎ *053/243239. Reservations not accepted. No credit cards.*

\$\$ ✕ **Whole Earth.** On the road leading to the Chiang Plaza Hotel, this long-established restaurant serves delicious vegetarian and health foods and a few nonveg dishes for the indulgent, such as *kai tahkhrai* (fried chicken with lemon and garlic). Many are Indian dishes—try the eggplant marsala. On the second floor of an attractive, old Thai house in a garden, the inside dining room is air-conditioned, and the balconies take full advantage of any breezes (but you should ask for a mosquito coil under your table). The service is sometimes slow. ✉ *88 Sridonchai Rd.,* ☎ *053/282463. Reservations not accepted. No credit cards.*

\$ ✕ **Supotana Kaun.** For this superb northern Thai food you must travel
★   7 km (4.3 mi) north on the Chiang Dao road (Hwy. 107) and also put up with traffic noise, zero decor, and crates of empty bottles lying around. What you are about to eat is worth all this. A recent meal here included the house specialty, a light, airy omelet, the like of which we've never tasted; *phad thai* (stir-fried noodles) so crisp and delicate it melted in our mouths; fish with a hot-and-sour sauce; and "1,000-year-old eggs" (actually eggs buried in mud for three months, which the Thai call *kai yean ma,* which means eggs washed in horse's urine!). ✉ *Chiang Dao Rd., at traffic light where road from Chiang Mai Sports Complex joins from left,* ☎ *053/210980. No credit cards.*

Lodging

With Chiang Mai on every tourist's itinerary, hotels of every persuasion flourish, and construction is ongoing. Some hotels add a surcharge in January and February, which brings prices here close to those at Bangkok hotels. Lodgings cluster in four districts. The commercial area, between the railway station and the old city walls, holds little interest for most tourists. The area between the river and the old city has the largest concentration of hotels and is close to most of the evening street activity. Within the city walls small hotels and guest houses offer simple, inexpensive accommodations, centrally located. The west side of town, near Doi Suthep, has attracted the posh hotels; it's quieter but also farthest from points of interest. Taxi and tuk-tuk drivers will try to get you to change your hotel for the one that they recommend (which gives them a commission), and hotels that don't pay them off (the River View Lodge and Gap's House are two) often have their clients misrouted!

\$\$\$\$ ▦ **Regent Chiang Mai.** In the lush Mae Rim Valley, 20 minutes north
★   of Chiang Mai, the most attractive hotel in northern Thailand nestles in 20 acres of landscaped gardens amid lakes, lily ponds, and terraced rice paddies. An arc of 16 two-story buildings in traditional Lanna style contains the suites, each with its outdoor *sala* (Thai gazebo) just perfect for breakfast and cocktails. Rooms are furnished with rich Thai cottons and Siamese art; floors are polished teak. Huge bathrooms overlook a garden. The main restaurant, Sala Mae Rim, serves beautifully presented Thai dishes and offers splendid sweeping views of the valley. Another restaurant beside the pool is popular for light meals. Once you're here, you're tempted not to leave; even catching the shuttle bus to Chiang Mai center seems too much effort, and therein lies its disadvantage: you are isolated from the rest of the world. ✉ *Mae*

Rim-Samoeng Old Rd., 50180, ☎ *053/298181,* ℻ *053/298189. 67 suites. 2 restaurants, bar, pool, 2 tennis courts, health club. AE, DC, MC, V.*

$$$ ⊞ **Chiang Mai Orchid Hotel.** This is a grand hotel in the old style, with teak pillars in the lobby. Rooms are tastefully furnished and trimmed with wood. You can choose among the formal Continental restaurant, Le Pavillon; the Japanese restaurant; or the informal Thai coffee shop; you'll find entertainment in the lobby bar or the cozy Opium Den. The Honeymoon Suite, we are told, is often used by the Crown Prince. The hotel is a 10-minute taxi ride from Chiang Mai center. ✉ *100–102 Huay Kaeo Rd., 50000,* ☎ *053/222099, 02/2453973 Bangkok reservations,* ℻ *053/221–625. 260 rooms and 7 suites. 3 restaurants, 2 ㏌rs, pool, beauty salon, sauna, health club, business services, meeting room. AE, DC, MC, V.*

$$$ ⊞ **Imperial Mae Ping Hotel.** This high-rise hotel is making a splash for itself in the center of town. Festoons of lights sweep down from the building's towering heights to the vast courtyard and gardens below. Here, in the outdoors, buffet dinner is served and, in the beer garden, Filipino bands drown out any street noises. Shows of classical and hilltribe dancing are performed at the far end of the garden. Inside the hotel, aside from the large lobby and a coffee shop, are three more restaurants—European, Chinese, and Japanese. With 371 rooms to fill, the Imperial caters to package tours, particularly Japanese, but the modern, functional bedrooms are well kept and the staff is surprisingly eventempered. ✉ *153 Sridonchai Rd., Chang Klan 50100,* ☎ *053/270160, 02/261–9460 Bangkok reservations,* ℻ *053/270181. 371 rooms. 4 restaurants, bar, beer garden, pool, meeting rooms. AE, DC, MC, V.*

$$$ ⊞ **Royal Princess.** Formerly the Dusit Inn and still part of the chain, this hotel is ideal if you'd like to step out the front door into the bustle of Chiang Mai's tourist center. The famous Night Bazaar is a block away, and street vendors are even closer. The rooms' lack of natural light makes them seem a little dreary, but the staff is well trained and helpful, the lobby is pleasant, the cocktail lounge has a pianist in the evenings, and the Jasmine restaurant serves the best Cantonese fare in Chiang Mai. ✉ *112 Chang Rd., 50000,* ☎ *053/281033, 02/233–1130 Bangkok reservations,* ℻ *053/281044. 200 rooms. 2 restaurants, pool, airport shuttle, meeting room. AE, DC, MC, V.*

$$ ⊞ **Chiang Inn.** Behind the Night Bazaar, the centrally located Chiang Inn has offered well-kept guest rooms since 1980. As the hotel is set back from the street, the rooms are quiet (the higher the better). They are reasonably spacious and are done in local handwoven cottons. La Grillade serves Thai-influenced French cuisine in a formal atmosphere, and the more casual Ron Thong Coffee House serves Thai and Western dishes. The hotel is usually swamped with tour groups, and its facilities are geared to that kind of traffic. ✉ *100 Chang Khlan Rd., 50000,* ☎ *053/270070, 02/251–6883 Bangkok reservations,* ℻ *053/274299. 170 rooms and 4 suites. 2 restaurants, pool, dance club, meeting room, travel services. AE, DC, MC, V.*

$$ ⊞ **River View Lodge.** Facing the Mae Nam Ping across a grassy lawn,
★ this lodge is an easy 10-minute walk from the Night Bazaar. Some seasoned travelers say it's the best place to stay in the city. The rooms are tastefully done with wood furniture crafted in the region and terra-cotta floor tiles; the more expensive ones have private balconies overlooking the river. Though neither elegant nor luxurious, there's a restful simplicity here that's a far cry from the standard uniformity in most of the city's high-rise hotels. The small restaurant is better for breakfast than for dinner, and the veranda patio overlooking the pool and river is good for relaxing with a beer or afternoon tea. The owner speaks nearly fluent English and will assist in planning your explorations. ✉

25 Charoen Prathet Rd., Soi 2, 50000, ☎ *053/271109,* FAX *053/279019. 36 rooms. Restaurant, pool. AE, DC, MC, V.*

$$ ⊡ **Zenith/Suriwongse.** This hotel around the corner from the Royal Princess, near the Night Bazaar, has recently undergone a refurbishment that brings it up to first-class standards. Its association with the French hotel chain attracts European tour groups, and the staff makes a game attempt to speak French, with some English words and a Thai accent! The rooms, redone in pastels, are bright and cheery, and the hotel compares favorably with the Royal Princess. ⊠ *110 Chang Khlan Rd., 50000,* ☎ *053/270051, 02/251–9883 Bangkok reservations, 800/221–4542 U.S. reservations,* FAX *053/270063. 166 rooms and 4 suites. Restaurant, coffee shop, travel services, airport shuttle. AE, DC, MC, V.*

$–$$ ⊡ **Galare Guest House.** On the Mae Ping riverfront, this guest house
★   has many advantages: its good location, within five minutes' walk of the Night Bazaar; friendly service; small but clean rooms with air-conditioning and fans; a shady garden in which to relax, and a restaurant facing the river. It offers more charm and personal service than many of the other city hotels, and it is the best value in town. ⊠ *7 Charoenprathet Rd. Soi 2, 50100,* ☎ *053/818887,* FAX *053/279088. 35 rooms. Restaurant. MC, V.*

$–$$ ⊡ **Grand Apartments.** This new building in the old city offers air-conditioned rooms by the day or by the month, which makes it useful for an extended stay at very reasonable rates (B4,000 per month). The rooms are efficient and clean, and guests have access to telex, fax machines, and a laundry room. ⊠ *24/1 Prapklao Rd., Chang Puak Gate, 50000,* ☎ *053/217291,* FAX *053/213945. 36 rooms. Café. MC, V.*

$–$$ ⊡ **River Ping Palace.** The complex of Siamese buildings at this little guest house shows you what Chiang Mai was like 50 years ago. It's owned by a Frenchman and his Thai wife and served by a welcoming staff. Food is served at any time in the pleasant open-air restaurant that's also a sitting area. The wooden structures have smallish rooms decorated with old Thai furnishings and artifacts—very personal, if a bit fussy. The best room, No. 3, costs B1,600; in the smaller ones (B1,200) there's very little space around the double bed. Another drawback is that it's a B30 tuk-tuk ride south of the Night Bazaar. ⊠ *385/2 Charoen Phrathat Rd., Chang Klan 50100,* ☎ *053/274932,* FAX *053/204281. 5 rooms, most with bath. Restaurant. MC, V.*

$ ⊡ **Roong Ruang Hotel.** You step into the treed courtyard of this little garden hotel right off Tha Pae Road, where lots of the action is. Two-story wings with overhanging eaves and galleries for sitting flank the courtyard, where motorbikes and a few cars can be parked. All the rooms have hot water and satellite TV; some have fans (B350) and some are air-conditioned (B450). The owner, who speaks English, owns the neighboring cybercafe and will order breakfast if you want it ⊠ *398 Tha Pae Rd., 50000,* ☎ *053/234746 and 053/232017,* FAX *053/252409. 25 rooms. No credit cards.*

¢   ⊡ **Gap's House.** Thais don't stay here; they like modern concrete hotels, whereas this collection of traditional wood houses is like a tiny shady village within the walls of old Chiang Mai. No. 5 overlooks a jungle-like plant nursery and tiny fenced vegetable garden; one room has a fishpond, another an old Thai bed on its veranda. A lively rooster and a bilingual mynah bird add to the rural atmosphere, and antique bric-a-brac is scattered around the open breakfast/sitting area. It is what Westerners come to see in Thailand, but discover increasingly hard to find, and it is the personal domain of Mr. Gap, who likes you or not, immediately. The rooms are furnished with an odd assortment of antiques, and this gives a homey, well-worn feel. Bathrooms are basic, with cement floors and rudimentary showers. Breakfast comes with the room; treks or excursions can be arranged; and the garden bar is often full of happy travelers swapping stories. English is spoken here, but don't speak it too loudly or get rowdy: Gap might throw you out! ⊠ *3 Soi 4 Ratchadumnern Rd., 50200,* ☎ *053/278140. 18 rooms. Bar. MC, V.*

¢ 🖭 **Lai Thai.** On the edge of the old city walls, a 10-minute walk from the Night Bazaar, this friendly guest house offers rooms around a garden courtyard and a casual open-air restaurant that serves Thai, European, and Chinese food. The rooms are either air-conditioned or cooled by overhead fans. Bare, polished floors and simple furniture give them a fresh, clean look. Those at the back are quietest. ⊠ *111/4–5 Kotchasarn Rd., 50000,* ☎ *053/271725,* FAX *053/272724. 120 rooms. Restaurant, motorbikes, coin laundry, travel services. MC.*

Nightlife and the Arts

Chiang Mai is a good place to try a **traditional Thai massage.** The Indian art has been practiced since the time of Buddha, and it is believed to ameliorate problems ranging from epilepsy to backaches and simple tension. The cost is B200 for a simple hour massage and B400 for a two-hour rubdown. **Petngarm Hat Wast** at the Diamond Hotel (⊠ 33/10 Charoen Prathet Rd., Chiang Mai, ☎ 053/270080) offers a range of traditional and herbal massages. Good massages with or without herbs are also given at **Suan Samoon Prai** (⊠ 105 Wansingkham Rd., ☎ 053/252716).

No first visit to Chiang Mai should omit a **khantoke dinner,** whose menu is usually sticky rice, which you mold into balls with your fingers; delicious *kap moo* (spiced pork skin); a super-spicy dip called *nam phrik naw,* with onions, cucumber, and chili; and *kang ka,* a chicken-and-vegetable curry—all accompanied by Singha beer. Frequently the khantoke dinner includes performances of Thai and/or hill-tribe dancing. An evening's diversion usually starts at 7, costs about B650 for two, and requires reservations.

One much-publicized "dinner theater" puts on a repertory of dancing and a khantoke dinner at the back of the **Diamond Hotel** (☎ 053/272080). Tour groups come here because there are good explanations of the symbolism in the dancing. The **Old Chiang Mai Cultural Centre** (⊠ 185/3 Wualai Rd., ☎ 053/275097), designed like a hill-tribe village, has nightly classical Thai and authentic hill-tribe dancing, after a khantoke dinner. The best place in the center of Chiang Mai to eat a khantoke dinner and see hill-tribe and classical Thai dances is the **Khum Kaew Palace** (⊠ 252 Pra Pok Klao Rd., ☎ 053/214315). The symbolism of each dance is explained in Thai and English. The building is a distinctive traditional northern Thai house, where you sit cross-legged on the floor or at long tables.

At **The Hill** (⊠ 92–93 Bumrungburi Rd., ☎ 053/277968), in a large, mostly covered courtyard, Thais while away the evening listening to a live band (mostly with Thai vocalists). The cement floors are scattered with bench tables, a wooden bridge crosses a stream that divides the cavernous area, and a balcony attracts the more demonstrative couples. The focus is an artificial hill, with rocks and ferns, where the entertainers perform. You buy tickets at a kiosk, then collect your food, beer, and soft drinks from stands (bring your own bottle and pay a corkage fee if you want the hard stuff).

Tour buses deposit middle-aged Westerners at the **Blue Moon** (⊠ 5/3 Moon Muang Rd., ☎ 053/278818) for a very routine performance of a dance show that includes a troupe of transvestites.

For more mundane evening entertainment, aside from the "love palaces," of which Chiang Mai has its share, there are several pub restaurants. The **Riverside** (☞ Dining, *above*) is one of the most popular, especially for its location next to the Mae Ping River and the small bands that drop in to perform throughout the evening. For a casual evening, with a jazz trio, drop in at the European-style **Bantone** (⊠ 99/4 Moo 2, Huay Kaew Rd., ☎ 053/224444).

At the **Cozy Corner** (⊠ 27 Moon Muang Rd., ☎ 053/277964), the pub atmosphere, chatty hostesses, and beer garden with a waterfall are all popular with the patrons, who come for hamburgers and beer. For those who want to visit each branch of the famous chain, there is a **Hard Rock Cafe** (⊠ 66/3 Loi Kroh Rd., near Thape Gate, ☎ 053/206103). Described by *Newsweek* as "one of the world's best bars," **The Pub** (⊠ 189 Huay Kaew Rd., ☎ 053/211550) can get a little crowded. Still, for draft beer, good grilled steak, and a congenial atmosphere, this place is hard to beat. **Bubbles** (☎ 052/270099), in the Pornping Tower Hotel, is a lively disco for the young at heart. At the Chiang Mai Orchid Hotel, **Club 66** (☎ 053/222099) aspires to being sophisticated to attract a more stylish crowd. **The Domino Bar** (⊠ 47 Moon Muang Rd., ☎ 053/278503), an English-style pub with snacks, is a meeting place where you may leave messages for fellow travelers.

Shopping

Always negotiate prices. Even if merchandise is priced, there is room for negotiation. Most shops honor major credit cards, and a further discount for cash is often possible. You will surely spend some time along the **Golden Mile,** a 16-km (10-mi) stretch of the road that runs east to San Kamphaeng. On both sides, large emporiums sell silver, ceramics, cottons and silks, wood carvings, hill-tribes' crafts and artifacts, lacquerware, bronzeware, and hand-painted umbrellas. At factory workshops you can watch the goods being made, which is alone worth the trip. The taxi drivers know the stores and any of them will happily spend a couple of hours taking you around for the giveaway rate of about B50 to B100. The driver receives a commission each time he brings tourists to a store, whether they buy or not. (Regular stores give him B10; jewelry stores give him B50.)

The **Chiang Inn Plaza,** across from the Chiang Inn in the center of town, is a modern shopping center where you can buy well-crafted goods from northern Thailand. At the **Rimping Superstore Chotana** (⊠ 171 Chang Puak Rd., ☎ 053/210377), established retailers sell quality goods at fixed prices.

One of Thailand's most exciting markets, the **Night Bazaar** is a congestion of stalls selling anything from intricately woven Burmese rugs to designer-label shirts made in Thailand. The clothing can be very inexpensive, and, at times, good quality. Some objets d'art are instant antiques, but there's the real thing, too. Try **Lanna Antiques,** booth No. 2 on the second floor, for a good selection. The bazaar is shopper's heaven for crafts made in the rural villages throughout Myanmar, Laos, and northern Thailand—but inspect the goods thoroughly. The back of the stalls opens up into a sort of courtyard, with restaurants and some good hill-tribe products. The **Anusan Night Bazaar,** down the main street, past the Princess Hotel, sells goods for locals, but it has mostly food outlets for tasty, inexpensive Chinese and Thai fare.

Lamphun

 26 km (16 mi) south of Chiang Mai.

It's a pleasant day's trip to drive south on Highway 106, a lovely shady road lined by 100-ft rubber trees, past Lamphun, as far as Wat Phra Baat Takpa. A few miles south of Chiang Mai, before you reach Lamphun, a small road marked by a Shell station on the corner leads west to **Wat Chedi Liem,** a five-tier wat built by King Mengrai in the 13th century, and probably copied from Wat Chama Devi in Lamphun.

Approximately 3 km (2 mi) past this monastery, on a small island in the Mae Nam Ping, is the **McKean Leprosarium,** which since 1908 has treated leprosy sufferers and is internationally recognized as the model of a self-contained community clinic. Don't worry about catching the disease—visitors are perfectly safe. The community itself is inspiring: some 200 patients have their own cottages on 160 secluded acres, which also contain medical facilities, occupational therapy workshops, stores, and a church. A visit here is an ennobling experience. ✉ *Donations requested.* ⊙ *Weekdays 8–noon and 1–4, Sat. 8–noon.*

Lamphun claims to be the oldest existing city in Thailand (but so does Nakhon Pathom). Originally called Nakorn Hariphunchai, it was founded in AD 680 by the Chamdhevi dynasty, which ruled until 1932. Unlike Chiang Mai, with its rapid growth, Lamphun remains a sleepy town, consisting of a main street with stores, several food stalls, and not much else. The town is known for its *lamyai* (longan) fruit, a sweet cherry-size fruit with a thin shell. In the nearby village of Tongkam, the "B10,000 lamyai tree" nets its owner that sum in fruit every year. Buy yourself a jar of lamyai honey; you'll be in for a treat.

Lamphun's architectural prizes are two temple monasteries. Two kilometers (1¼ miles) west of the town's center is **Wat Cham Devi**—often called Wat Kukut (topless chedi) because the gold at its top has been removed. You'll probably want a samlor to take you down the narrow residential street to the wat. Since it is not an area where samlors generally cruise, it's a good idea to ask the driver to wait for you.

Despite a modern viharn at the side of the complex, the beauty of this monastery is in its weathered look. Suwan Chang Kot, to the right of the entrance, is the most famous of the monastery's two chedis. Built by King Mahantayot to hold the remains of his mother, the legendary Queen Cham Devi, first ruler of Lamphun, the five-tier sandstone chedi is square; on each of its four sides, and on each tier, are three Buddha images. The higher the level, the smaller the images. All are in the Dvaravati style—8th and 9th centuries—though many have obviously been restored. The other chedi was probably built in the 10th century, though most of what we see today is the work of King Phaya Sapphasit in the 12th century.

Lamphun's second major attraction, **Wat Phra That Hariphunchai,** is dazzling. Enter the monastery from the river, through a parking lot lined with stalls selling food, clothing, and mementos. Go through the gates, guarded by ornamental lions, and you'll encounter a three-tier, sloping-roof viharn, a replica (built in 1925) of the original, which burned in 1915. Inside, note the large Chiang Saen–style bronze image of Buddha, Phra Chao Thongtip, and the carved *thammas* (Buddhist universal principals) to the left of the altar.

Leave the viharn by walking to the right past what is reputedly the largest bronze gong in the world, cast in 1860. The 165-ft Suwana chedi, covered in copper plates and topped by a golden spire, dates from 847. A century later, King Athitayarat, the 32nd ruler of Hariphunchai, raised its height and added more copper plating to honor the relics of Lord Buddha inside. On top of the chedi, he added a nine-tier umbrella, gilded with 14 pounds of pure gold. The monk who brought the relics from India is remembered by a gold statue in a nearby chamber. He's also remembered for his potbelly—legend has it that he made himself obese so his youthful passion for women wouldn't interfere with his concentration on Buddha's teachings.

At the back of the compound—which leads to a shortcut to the center of town—there's another viharn with a standing Buddha, a sala housing four Buddha footprints, and the old museum. The new museum, just outside the compound, has a fine selection of Dvaravati stucco work and Lamma antiques. 🎫 *Admission.* ⊙ *Museum: Wed.–Sun. 8:30–4.*

NEED A BREAK?	For lunch or a cold drink, go back through Wat Hariphunchai to the main road along the Kwang River and choose any one of the string of cafés.

Pa Sang

⑬ *12 km (7½ mi) south of Lamphun, 38 km (19 mi) south of Chiang Mai.*

Many visitors go to Pa Sang, down Highway 106 from Lamphun, to shop for locally produced cotton goods with traditional designs and to watch the weaving. Songthaews (fare is B10) ply the route all day. Although in recent years the better stores have moved to Chiang Mai, and the selection has diminished, you can find both yard goods and clothing, and the prices here are good: a shirt with a batik pattern is about B100, while dresses run about B175. More contemporary clothing and household items may be found at **Nandakwang Laicum,** on the right-hand side as you enter town.

Five kilometers (3 miles) south of Pa Sang on Highway 106 is **Wat Phra Bhat Takpa,** commonly known as the Temple of Buddha's Footprint. The energetic may mount the 600 steps to the chedi at the top of the hill, but the main attraction is the two huge imprints of the Lord Buddha's foot, indented in the floor, inside the temple at the right of the car park. As you enter, buy a piece of gold leaf (B20), which you can paste in the imprint and make a wish.

Lampang

⑭ *65 km (40 mi) southeast of Lamphun, 91 km (59 mi) southeast of Chiang Mai.*

During the reign of Rama VI, carriage horses were imported from England. The charming image of horse-drawn carriages in the town's quaint streets is still promoted by tourism officials, but the 20th century has come to Lampang, and a superhighway connects it to Chiang Mai and Bangkok. Concrete houses and stores have replaced the wooden buildings, cars and buses have taken over the streets, and only a few horses remain. Though today the busy metropolis on the Wang River has lost some of its charm, its wats, shops, and the few old-style wooden houses are sufficiently pleasant that you may wish to spend the night. Hotels in Lampang are the best that you will find between Chiang Mai and Phitsanulok.

Despite its rush into the 20th century, Lampang has some notable Burmese architecture remaining. Opposite the Thai International Airways office is **Wat Phra Fang,** easily recognizable by the green corrugated-iron roof on the viharn and the tall white chedi, decorated with gold leaf, at the top. Surrounding the chedi are seven small chapels, one for each day of the week. Inside each chapel is a niche with images of the Lord Buddha.

A well-preserved example of Lampang's Burmese architecture is **Wat Sri Chum.** Pay particular attention to the viharn: the eaves have beautiful carvings, and its doors and windows have elaborate decorations. Inside, gold-and-black lacquered pillars support a carved-wood ceiling, and to the right is a bronze Buddha cast in the Burmese style. Red-and-gold panels on the walls depict country temple scenes.

North of town, on the right bank of the River Wang, is **Wat Phra Kaeo Don Tao,** whose dominating visual element is the tall chedi, built on a rectangular base and topped with a rounded spire. Of more interest, however, are the Burmese-style shrine and the adjacent Thai-style sala. The 18th-century shrine has a multitier roof rising to a point. Inside, the walls are masterfully carved and inlaid with colored stones; the ornately engraved ceiling is inlaid with enamel. The Thai sala, with the traditional three-tier roof and carved-wood pediments, houses a Sukhothai-style reclining Buddha.

Legend suggests that the sala was also home to the famous **Emerald Buddha** (Phra Keo). In 1436, when King Sam Fang Kaem was transporting the statue from Chiang Rai to Chiang Mai, his elephant reached Lampang and refused to go any farther. The statue remained here for the next 32 years, until the succeeding king managed to get it to Chiang Mai.

If you are driving to Chiang Mai or you want a tranquil rural escape, stop on the north side of town at **Wat Chedi Sao,** a charming, peaceful monastery named after its 20 small white chedis.

Wat Phra That Lampang Luang, south of Lampang, is one of the most venerated temples in the north. You'll spot the chedi towering above the trees, but the viharn to the left is the most memorable. The carved wood facade and two-tier roof complement its harmonious proportions; note the painstaking workmanship of the intricate decorations around the porticoes. The temple compound was once part of a fortified city, which has long since disappeared. It was founded in the 8th century by the legendary Princess Chama Dewi of Lopburi and destroyed about 200 years ago by the Burmese. The temple museum has excellent wood carvings, but its treasure is a small emerald Buddha, which some claim was carved from the same stone as its counterpart in Bangkok. ▣ *Admission.* ⊙ *Tues.–Sun. 9–4. Closed Mon.*

Dining and Lodging

$$$ ✕ **Krua Thai.** For a stylish Thai meal, take a samlor to this popular restaurant in a northern-Thai–style house. Locals gather here in the many small, heavily timbered dining rooms to eat the mostly spicy Northern Thai food, but there are some Chinese dishes to offset the heat of chilies. ▣ *Paholyothin Rd.,* ☎ *054/226766. MC, V.*

$$ ✕ **Baan Rim Nam.** The name means "home by the river," and that is exactly what this traditional wood house was before it became a wonderful, atmospheric restaurant. The menu offers good Thai food (not too spicy for foreigners) and international dishes. ▣ *328 Thip Rd.,* ☎ *054/322501. MC, V.*

$ ✕ **U-Ping.** The fun local place to eat is this open-sided restaurant on the main street across from the access road to the Thip Chang hotel. Sports fans gather here to dine on the varied and well-prepared Thai food, and drink the evening away while watching local and international matches on the half dozen television sets suspended from the ceiling. ▣ *Thakraw Noi Rd.,* ☎ *054/226824. No credit cards.*

$$ ▥ **Thip Chang.** This hotel has aged badly and is in need of a complete overhaul. Stay here only if the Wienthong Hotel is full. Most rooms have two double beds, a coffee table, and a couple of chairs. A few of the staff members speak some English, but often not with a smile. The coffee shop stays open until 1 AM, and the restaurant serves respectable Western, Thai, and Chinese food. It is sometimes fully booked by tour groups. ▣ *54/22 Thakraw Noi Rd., Lampang 52000,* ☎ *054/226501,* FAX *054/225362. 120 rooms. Restaurant, bar, coffee shop, pool. AE, MC.*

$$ ⊞ **Wienthong Hotel.** Currently the best hotel in Lampang, the Wienthong has the most comfortable rooms and public areas. Rooms are kept clean and fresh, despite the continual flow of tour groups. The restaurant is the best in town for Western food. ✉ *138/109 Paholyothin Rd.,* ☎ *054/225801,* FAX *054/225803. 178 rooms. Restaurant. AE, MC, V.*

¢ ⊞ **No 4 Guest House.** An old Thai-style teak house with a garden. The friendly owner teaches English at the local school. ✉ *54 Pamai Rd., Vieng Nuea, Lampang,* ☎ *no phone. 25 rooms with shared bath. Breakfast room. No credit cards.*

Shopping

Lampang is known for its blue-and-white pottery. Buy it at shops in the city center, or visit any of the 60 factories in town. The ware is sold in Bangkok and Chiang Mai with hefty markups, so do your shopping here. Generally, a samlor driver will take you to these factories for a few baht, because if you buy something he'll receive a commission. **Ku Ceramic** (✉ 167 Mu 6, Phahonyothin Rd., ☎ 054/218313) has a good selection.

Doi Inthanon National Park

57 km (36 mi) southwest of Chiang Mai.

Doi Inthanon comprises Thailand's highest mountain (8,464 ft), the habitat of many species of plants, animals, and birds. From the park entrance on the main road, you can either drive the steep, 48-km (30-mi) toll road to the top or take a minibus from Chom Thong, beyond the park's turnoff. It's a good idea to rent a minibus if you wish to see the Mae Ya waterfall, because the road there, consisting of 12 km (7½ mi) of unpaved tracks, can be impassable. An easier waterfall to reach is Mae Klang, which has three tiers of falls. The turnoff is 6 km (3½ mi) from the entrance.

Mae Hong Son

⑮ *270 km (169 mi) northwest of Chiang Mai via Pai, 368 km (230 mi) via Mae Sariang, 924 km (574 mi) north of Bangkok.*

Just inside the Burmese (Myanmar) border, this sleepy market town where villagers trade vegetables and wares is like the Chiang Mai of 30 years ago, but it is developing quickly. Already it has two comfortable hotels, several small resorts, and at least a dozen guest houses. Mae Hong Son means "province of the three mists," and it seems as if the outside world does not exist. Tourists usually spend a night, or two at the most, here, though a few foreign travelers have embraced the gentle pace and stayed a month or more. It is a favored base for those wishing to trek through the jungles to less commercialized hill-tribe villages. A word of warning: in spring, around late March and April, the surrounding hills are often alight with brush fires set by farmers to clear the land. It can make breathing unpleasant and often prevents the scheduled Thai International Airways planes from landing at Mae Hong Son.

If you take a 15-minute walk up the winding stepped path to the top of Doi Kong Mu, Mae Hong Son's highest hill, you will be rewarded first by restful views as you sit in the small shaded pavilion, then by the marvelously varied structures of **Wat Phra That Doi Kong Mu,** a gleaming white temple inhabited by wonderful white plaster demons with gaping scarlet mouths. A kiosk sells bottled water and film. In town, after you stroll around the lake and look at the two temples, there is little to do but have coffee or eat at one of the restaurants on the main street and observe daily life. A few stores sell hill-tribe jewelry and textiles and a few garments, but the merchandise is more of the souvenir variety than art. (Art objects are bought by dealers directly from the villages and shipped to Chiang Mai or Bangkok.) In the morning the local market has a colorful array of fruits, vegetables, and people.

Aside from the lush countryside, waterfalls, and caves around Mae Hong Son, the tourist lure is **visiting hill-tribe villages,** especially those of the Karen Long Necks. Photographs and postcards of the Karen Long Necks (also called Padong), whose women wear copper bands around their necks, making them exceptionally long, are often used as bait for visits to northern Thailand, but most of the Karen Long Necks are in Myanmar—an estimated 3,000 families. In Thailand there are three villages, all outside Mae Hong Son, with a total of 36 Long Neck families, all of whom are accustomed to posing for photographs. There is a B300 fee for entering the village; half of the tax goes to the village, the other half to the local warlord, who uses the money to fund his army. With as many as 150 tourists a day in the peak season, a village can make good money by exhibiting their long-neck women.

Long Neck Karens have a legend that their ancestors were descended from the god of wind and a female dragon, and it is thought that the women extend their necks to imitate the dragon. Perhaps it is more true that the copper bands are a sign of wealth. The girls start to wear bands at six, adding another every three years until they are 21. They are never removed, even after death, except for cleaning, or in the case of adultery, when the woman's relatives, out of shame, will forcibly remove them.

The easiest village to reach is the one with six families, upriver from Mae Hong Son beyond the village of Nam Pieng Din. By arrangements made through your hotel or a local guide, you travel by boat, with a guide, for the 90-minute trip. Cost is approximately B1,300.

The second village, near the Shan village of Nai Soi, has 15 ladies. Getting there is a two-hour, four-wheel drive journey, followed by a 30-minute hike (or an experienced rider traveling with a guide can go by motorbike, over a rough trail and a swinging bridge). The cost is B1,500.

The third village, at Huey Santea, has 15 Long Necks, whose families arrived only in 1995, fleeing from factional fighting in Myanmar. This one is relatively easy to reach by a 50-minute drive in the dry season, but if it rains, the track becomes extremely muddy and waters must be forded. The cost is B1,000.

Within a three-hour drive of Mae Hong Son, the Shans, Lanna Thais, Karens, and Hmongs (Meo) also have villages, which are usually visited on guided treks of three or more days. You can leave the choice of village up to the guide—each has his favorites—but you should ask him whether he speaks the village language and discuss fully with him what is planned and how strenuous the trek is. Since guides come and go, and villages tend to change in their attitude toward foreigners, what is written today is out of date tomorrow (☞ Outdoor Activities and Sports, *below).*

Dining and Lodging

$–$$ ✕ **Bai Fern.** For food and music together this is the most popular restaurant in town, both with Thais and foreigners. The room is large, with paneled walls and teak columns—it's usually full of customers, and there's a relaxed and friendly atmosphere. Subdued lights and whirling fans add to the festive mood. A band plays Thai Western songs that harmonize with the clatter of plates. The staff is surprisingly helpful, anxious for you to enjoy the food. Most of the menu is Thai, and spicy dishes are adapted to Western tastes on request. ⊠ *87 Khun Lum Praphas Rd.,* ☎ *053/611374. MC, V.*

$ ✕ **Kai-Mook.** Just off the main street, this is the best restaurant for al-
★ fresco dining and excellent northern Thai cooking. Of the 10 or so restau-
rants along this street, Kai-Mook has the freshest and tastiest food. ⊠ *71 Khun Lum Praphas Rd.,* ☎ *053/612092. No credit cards.*

$$–$$$ 🏨 **Rooks Holiday Hotel and Resort.** This former Holiday Inn, about 1½ km (1 mi) out of town off the main road to Khun Yuam, bustles with tour groups coming and going; activity focuses around the pool in the daytime and in the disco at night. Rooms are standard, boring, slightly depressingly furnished in blue, and well worn but clean. The best of them have private balconies that look out over the gardens and the pool. Service is a little sloppy, but many of the staff speak English. ⊠ *114/5–7 Khun Lum Praphas Rd., Mae Hong Son 58000,* ☎ *053/ 611390,* 𝐅𝐀𝐗 *053/611524. 144 rooms. Restaurant, pool, nightclub, travel services. AE, DC, MC, V.*

$$ 🏨 **Tara Mae Hong Son.** This hotel is slightly less expensive than the
★ Rooks Holiday Hotel and considerably more attractive. Its classic northern Thai architecture, with the huge lobby reception area and broad open porches, gives it an airy feeling. The restaurant, which serves good Thai food—both northern and Bangkok—has a glassed-in section for chilly mornings and evenings. It faces the lush terraced valley, as does the beautifully landscaped pool. The decor emphasizes wood with highly polished floors and bamboo chairs and tables. The service is en-thusiastic and helpful. The hotel is 3 km (2 mi) out of town, slightly beyond Rooks. ⊠ *149 Moo 8 Tambon Peng Moo, Mae Hong Son 58000,* ☎ *053/611473, 02/254–0023 in Bangkok,* 𝐅𝐀𝐗 *053/611252. 104 rooms. Restaurant, pool, travel services. AE, DC, MC, V.*

$–$$ 🏨 **Rim Nam Klang Doi.** On the Pai River, 5 km (3 mi) out of town, this is one of the better rural resorts and offers good value. Many of the rooms look out onto the river; others have views of the tropical landscaped grounds. The preferred rooms are fan-cooled with a private hot-water shower—you really don't need the more expensive air-conditioned rooms. A minivan shuttles you to town or back for B100. ⊠ *Ban Huay Dua,* ☎ *053/612142,* 𝐅𝐀𝐗 *053/612086. 34 rooms. Restaurant. MC, V.*

$ 🏨 **Piya Guest House.** This is the most comfortable guest house in the area, with the best location, facing serene Jong Kham lake in the cen-ter of Mae Hong Son. The owner, Piya Grongpherpoon, has let the fan-cooled rooms around the courtyard deteriorate slightly (but they cost only 250 baht) and paid more attention to the air-conditioned rooms (each with a clean private bath) that face the garden and cost 550 baht. Outside tables at the restaurant face the lake; those inside share space with a pool table. ⊠ *1 Soi 6, Khun Lum Praphat Rd., Mae Hong Son 58000,* ☎ *053/611260,* 𝐅𝐀𝐗 *053/612308. 11 rooms, most with bath. Restaurant. No credit cards.*

¢ 🏨 **Jean's Guest House.** This is truly a basic, bungalow guest house where a tiny room with a fan goes for B100. The advantage of staying here is that Jean speaks fluent English and can often serve as a good resource for finding local guides. ⊠ *6 Prachautith Rd., Mae Hong Son 58000,* ☎ *053/611662. 9 rooms. No credit cards.*

Outdoor Activities and Sports

TREKKING

In the 1960s a few intrepid travelers in northern Thailand started wan-dering the hills and staying at the villages; by 1980, tour companies were organizing groups with a guide and sending them off for three- to seven-day treks. Days are spent walking forest trails between villages, where nights are spent as paying guests. Accommodation is in huts, and at best a wooden platform with no mattress is provided. Food is likely to be a bowl of sticky rice and stewed vegetables. It can become very cold at night; so take warm clothes as well as sturdy hiking shoes. Also take insect repellent, against mosquitoes, and perhaps some disinfectant soap, in case the huts are grubby. Otherwise, travel light.

The level of difficulty varies: you might traverse tough, hilly terrain for several hours, or travel by Jeep and then take an easy 30-minute walk to a village. Perhaps a ride on an elephant or a half day on a raft is thrown in to give the sense of adventure.

Typically, the easier the trek the more commercial the village; the search is for one that has not been saturated with Westerners, but they are becoming fewer and fewer. Because areas quickly become overtrekked and guides come and go, the only way to select a tour is to talk to other travelers and try to get the latest information. What was good six months ago may not be good today.

Unless you speak some Thai, know the local geography, and understand something of the native customs, don't go alone: you risk being robbed or worse by bandits. It's best to use the services of a certified guide. Since the guide determines the quality of the tour, it's important to pick one who's familiar with the local dialects and languages spoken and who knows which villages are the least tourist-ridden. He should also speak English well. It is also imperative that you discuss the villages and route; that way you'll at least seem to know the ropes. You usually can tell whether the guide is knowledgeable and respects the villagers, but question him thoroughly about his experience before you sign up.

Chiang Rai and the Golden Triangle

Chiang Rai's raison d'être is as a base for visiting tribal villages and for exploring the Golden Triangle. This area, remarkable for its natural beauty and friendly inhabitants, is relatively easy to explore on your own. The following itinerary goes from Chiang Rai to Chiang Saen and up to the apex of the triangle, Sop Ruak. Then going west along the Burmese border, it continues to Mae Sai and back to Chiang Rai. You can hire a taxi or take a public bus, though many people rent Jeeps or motorbikes.

Chiang Rai

16 *180 km (112 mi) northeast of Chiang Mai, 780 km (485 mi) north of Bangkok.*

King Mengrai, who founded the Lanna kingdom, built Chiang Rai in 1256. According to legend, a runaway royal elephant stopped to rest on the banks of the Mae Kok River. Considering this an auspicious sign, King Mengrai placed his capital where the elephant stopped. In the 15th century the area was overrun by the Burmese, who stayed until 1786. Architecturally, little can be said for this city of two-story concrete buildings. Most of the famous old structures are gone: Wat Phra Keo once housed the Emerald Buddha that is now in Bangkok's Royal Palace, and a precious Theravada Buddha image in the 15th-century Wat Phra Singh has long since disappeared. Today, Chiang Rai is a market town that works during the day and is fast asleep by 10 PM, though a recently established night bazaar, just off Phahalyothin Road, provides crafts stalls and open-air dining.

The Akha, Yao, Meo, Lisu, Lahu, and Karen tribes all live within Chiang Rai province. Each has a different dialect, different customs, handicrafts, costumes, and a different way of venerating animist spirits. Only in the past two decades have the tribes been confronted with the 20th century. Now, the villagers are learning to produce their handicrafts commercially for eager buyers in exchange for blue jeans and other commodities. You can visit some villages on day trips or make two- to five-day guided treks to the more remote ones (☞ Outdoor Activities and Sports, *above*).

Dining and Lodging

$ ✕ **Honarira.** If you decide not to dine at the night bazaar, then this restaurant is Chiang Rai's best for a casual outdoor meal under an umbrella of small trees. The menu (also in English) is a mix of northern and mainstream Thai, so you might start with some spicy sausages and follow with *pla tod chon* (deep fried serpent-head fish) and red curry beef. You'll have no trouble finding something to your taste among the 50 or so dishes on the extensive menu. ⊠ *402/1-2 Banphaprakan Rd.,* ☎ *053/715722. No credit cards.*

$$$–$$$$ ⌂ **Dusit Island Resort.** Sitting on an island in the Kok river, the Dusit Is-
★   land has the best location in Chiang Rai. The hotel, on 10 acres, has all the amenities of a resort, including the largest outdoor pool in the north, plus quick access to town. The building's three wings give all the guest rooms a stunning view of the river, especially Suite 833. Furnished in a modern rendition of traditional Thai, the spacious rooms have private safes and large marble baths. The formal dining room offers Western cuisine and a panoramic view; a Chinese restaurant serves Cantonese food; and the Island Cafe, where a buffet breakfast is served, has rather disappointing Thai and Continental food all day. If you arrive in Chiang Rai by river, the boatman can drop you off at the hotel's pier, except in periods of low water. ⊠ *1129 Kraisorasit Rd., Chiang Rai 57000,* ☎ *053/715777, 02/238–4790 Bangkok reservations,* FAX *053/715801 or 02/238–4797. 271 rooms. 3 restaurants, 4 bars, pool, beauty salon, massage, 2 tennis courts, health club, shops, nightclub, meeting rooms, shuttle to town and airport, car rental. AE, DC, MC, V.*

$$$ ⌂ **Little Duck Hotel.** The first luxury resort in Chiang Rai, this hotel screams modernity. Guests are often conventioneers, who mill around the huge lobby, far removed from the world outside. The rooms are b. ight and cheery, with light-wood fixtures and large beds. Service is brisk and smart, and the travel desk is ready to organize excursions into the neighboring hills. ⊠ *450 Super Highway Rd., Amphoe, Muang, Chiang Rai 57000,* ☎ *053/715620, 02/255–5960 Bangkok reservations,* FAX *053/712639. 350 rooms. 2 restaurants, coffee shop, pool, tennis court, meeting rooms, travel services. AE, DC, MC, V.*

$$–$$$ ⌂ **Rimkok Resort.** This hotel, in extensive grounds, opened in early 1991. Because it's across the Mae Kok river, a 10-minute drive from town, the hotel has more appeal for tour groups than for independent travelers. The main building is designed in modern Thai style with palatial dimensions—a long, wide lobby lined with boutiques leads to a spacious lounge and dining area. Guest rooms are in wings on both sides, and most have views of the river from their picture windows. ⊠ *6 Moo 4 Chiang Rai Tathorn Rd., Rimkok Muang, Chiang Rai 57000,* ☎ *053/716445, 02/279–0102 Bangkok reservations,* FAX *053/715859. 248 rooms. 4 restaurants, bar, pool, shops, meeting rooms, car rental. AE, DC, MC, V.*

$$–$$$ ⌂ **Wiang Inn.** In the heart of town, this comfortable, well-established hotel has a small outdoor pool, a pleasant sitting area, and a restaurant with Chinese, Thai, and Western food. Spacious bedrooms, now slightly worn, made this the top hotel in Chiang Rai until the two resort hotels opened, around 1990; it is still the best hotel within the town itself. ⊠ *893 Phaholyothin Rd., Chiang Rai 57000,* ☎ *053/711543,* FAX *053/711877. 260 rooms. Restaurant, pool, health club, nightclub, travel services. AE, DC, V.*

$ ⛭ **Golden Triangle Inn.** Don't confuse this guest house with the resort at Bop Sop Ruak. It is a backpackers' base for trips into the hills. Rooms have private bathrooms and are either air-conditioned or fan-cooled. The restaurant/lounge offers Thai and Western fare. The owners arrange trips to Chiang Khong, where they have another guest house. ⌧ *590 Phaholyothin Rd., Chiang Rai 57000,* ☎ *053/711339,* FAX *053/ 713363. 20 rooms. No credit cards.*

Chiang Saen

⓱ *59 km (37 mi) northeast of Chiang Rai, 239 km (148 mi) northeast of Chiang Mai, 935 km (581 mi) north of Bangkok.*

An hour outside Chiang Rai, on the banks of the Mae Khong River, is Chiang Saen, a small, one-street town that in the 12th century was home to the future King Mengrai. Only fragments of the ancient ramparts survived destruction by the Burmese in 1588, and the remainder was ravaged by fire in 1786, when the last Burmese were ousted.

Only two ancient chedis remain standing. Just outside the city walls is the oldest, **Wat Pa Sak,** whose name (*sak* means teak) reflects the fact that 300 teak trees wre planted around it. The stepped pyramid, which narrows to a spire, is said to enshrine holy relics brought here when the city was founded. Inside the walls stands the imposing octagonal 14th-century chedi, **Wat Luang.**

Next door to Wat Luang stands the **National Museum,** which houses artifacts from the Lanna period (Chiang Saen style), as well as some Neolithic finds. The museum also has a good collection of carvings and traditional handicrafts from the hill tribes, and some Burmese lacquerware. ▦ *Admission.* ☉ *Wed.–Sun. 9–4.*

Lodging

¢ ⛭ **Chiang Saen Guest House.** One of several guest houses in this area, the Chiang Saen was among the first on the scene and is still a gathering point for travelers. Rooms are clean and simple, and guests can eat and socialize in the dining room. The helpful owner is well informed on trips in the area. ⌧ *45 Tambon Wiang, Amphoe Chiang Saen, Chiang Rai 57150,* ☎ *053/650146. 10 rooms and 3 bungalows. No credit cards.*

OFF THE
BEATEN PATH

CHIANG KHONG – The recently paved road east out of Chiang Saen parallels the Mae Khong en route to **Chiang Khong,** with magnificent views of the river and Laos on the other side. Not too many tourists make the journey to villages like this, and the local tribes—Hmong and Yao—seem little affected by visitors. Across the river is the Laotian town of Ban Houie Sai, from which beautiful antique Lao textiles and silver jewelry are smuggled to Thailand. Only locals are permitted to cross the river here; they bring back tiger skins and deer antlers in exchange for salt, sugar, and soap. From Chiang Khong, you could drive directly back to Chiang Rai, but retracing your steps north from Chiang Khong will give you a different view of the wild, rugged, and beautiful scenery along the Mae Khong that is actually more dramatic than that around the Golden Triangle.

Sop Ruak (The Golden Triangle)

⓲ *8 km (5 mi) north of Chiang Saen.*

Turning left (north) at the T junction in Chiang Saen will take you to **Ban Sop Ruak,** the village in the heart of the Golden Triangle where the opium warlord Khun Sa once ruled. A decade ago, Thai troops forced him back to Burmese territory, but visitors still flock here to see this notorious region, and the village street is lined with souvenir stalls to lure them from their buses. Some of the best views over the confluence of the Mae Sai, Mae Ruak, and Mae Khong rivers, and into the lush hills of Myanmar and Laos, are from the new **Golden Triangle Resort Hotel.** Even if you are not staying at the hotel, pay a visit to check out the view. Another good viewing point is the pavilion along the path leading from behind the police station.

Lodging

$$$ 🏨 **Le Meridien Baan Boran Hotel.** This distinctive resort hotel, on a
★ hill off the Mae Sai road 12 km (7 mi) out of Chiang Saen, looks out over the confluence of the Ruak and Mae Khong rivers to the mysteries of Myanmar and Laos. All the hilltop guest rooms share the hotel's panoramic views. They have corner table/desks, couches, coffee tables, and picture windows opening onto balconies. Bedside panels hold controls for the television and lights. The central building houses the Yuan Lue Lao restaurant, serving Thai and Western fare, and in high season the more formal Suan Fin offers elaborate Thai and European dishes. People meet in the evening in the cocktail bar and the Opium Den bar. ✉ *Chiang Saen, Chiang Rai 57150,* ☎ *053/784084 or 02/ 653–2201 Bangkok reservations,* ℻ *053/784090 or 02/653–2208. 106 rooms and 4 suites. 2 restaurants, 2 bars, in-room safes, pool, 2 tennis courts, health club, squash, meeting room, travel services, airport shuttle, car rental. AE, DC, MC, V.*

$$–$$$ 🏨 **Imperial Golden Triangle Resort Hotel.** The views of the forested hills across the rivers are splendid from this resort. The architecture is northern Thai, with plenty of wood throughout. The superior ("executive") rooms have private balconies overlooking the Golden Triangle; third-floor rooms have the best view. The hotel has an elegant dining room called the Border View, but it's more fun sitting out on the deck, sipping Mae Khong whiskey and imagining the intrigues in the villages across the border. Classical Thai dances are performed in the evening. ✉ *222 Baan Sobruak, Chiang Saen, Chiang Rai,* ☎ *053/ 784001 or 02/261–9000 Bangkok reservations,* ℻ *053/784006 or 02/ 261–9518. 74 rooms. 2 restaurants, pool, travel services. AE, DC, MC, V.*

Mae Sai

⑲ *25 km (15 mi) west of Ban Sop Ruak, 60 km (36 mi) north of Chiang Rai.*

By minibus—or your car or motorbike—from Ban Sop Ruak you can travel west on a semipaved, dusty, but easy road to Mae Sai, along what's now called the Mae Sai river. Mae Sai is a border market town where merchants trade goods with the Burmese from Tha Kee Lek village. For the best view across the river into Myanmar, climb up to **Wat Phra That Doi**—the 207-step staircase starts from behind the Top North Hotel.

Non-Thais may cross the river to visit **Tha Kee Lek** on a one-day visa, obtainable at the bridge for $10. On the far side of the river you'll find a smaller version of Mae Sai selling the same goods. For $30 plus a mandatory purchase of $100 worth of Myanmar's Foreigner Exchange Certificates, you can get a three-night visa that lets you travel north to **Kengtung,** a quaint town with British colonial structures alongside old Buddhist temples. The trip on the unpaved road (163 km/101 mi) takes four to five hours in the dry season and up to eight from June through November.

Dining and Lodging

$ × **River Side Restaurant.** With its open terrace above the Mae Sai, over-looking Myanmar, this restaurant makes a good choice for relaxing. You'll also enjoy the Thai food; if you are not hungry, just admire the view with a Singha beer. ⊠ *Paholyotin Rd.,* ☎ *053/731207. No credit cards.*

$$ 🏨 **Wang Thong.** Cashing in on the relaxing of trade restrictions with Myanmar, this new hotel on the banks of the Mae Sai opened in 1993. Choose a guest room on the river side, and you can spend the day idly watching the flowing waters and the flowing pedestrian traffic across the bridge. The hotel is designed for upscale business travelers. Its rectangular rooms are modern and functional, and though the restaurant offers no-more-than-average fare, it has Western dishes as well as Thai and Chinese. ⊠ *299 Paholyotin Rd., Mae Sai, Chiang Rai,* ☎ *053/ 733388,* 🖷 *053/733399. 148 rooms. Restaurant, coffee shop, pool. MC, V.*

$ 🏨 **Mae Sai Guest House.** This is ranked by backpackers as the best guest house in Mae Sai. On the river, 1 km (½ mi) west of the bridge, it has clean bungalows and some river views. A small garden area surrounds the bungalows, and the office building contains a casual dining area. ⊠ *688 Wiengpangkam, Mae Sai, Chiang Rai,* ☎ *053/732021. 20 cottages with communal showers. No credit cards.*

$ 🏨 **Northern Guest House.** When the Mae Sai Guest House is full, this is a good second choice. It's on the way back to town from the Mae Sai, and it has small (there's just enough room for a bed) but clean bungalows. A few have their own shower and toilet. The veranda-style dining room is pleasant in the evenings, and the Mae Sai flows at the edge of the garden. The owner is helpful and always eager to please. ⊠ *402 Tumphajom Rd., Mae Sai, Chiang Rai,* ☎ *053/731537. 26 cottages, a few with bath. Dining room. No credit cards.*

Shopping

Thais take across household goods and consumer products, and the Burmese bring sandalwood, crafts, raw jade, and rubies. Though you may want to put a foot into Myanmar, the prices and quality of the goods will not be better than in Mae Sai, where prices are better than in Chiang Mai. A good store is **Mengrai Antique** (⊠ close to the bridge, ☎ 053/731423). On the east side of Phaholyothim Road, opposite the Tourist Police, is the **Thong Tavee Jade** factory. Mae Sai is also justifiably proud of its oh, so sweet strawberries, which come to perfection in December or January.

Cheng Dao Cave

5 km (3 mi) from Mae Sai.

From Mae Sai, it is a 1½-hour local bus ride back to Chiang Rai, or you can take an air-conditioned express bus to Chiang Mai (via Chiang Rai) that takes about five hours. If you are traveling back to Chiang Rai by car or motorbike, drive to the **Cheng Dao Cave Temple,** known for its Buddha carvings and monstrous stalactites. Farther up the dirt road you come to the **Monkey Temple,** where playful monkeys will snatch anything that sparkles.

OFF THE
BEATEN PATH

DOI TUN – Just south of Mae Chan, between Mae Sai and Chiang Rai, look for the right-hand turnoff for Highway 149, a steep, rough road that runs 17 km (11 mi) up to **Phra That** on Doi Tun, one of the highest peaks in northern Thailand. En route, stop at the Akha Guest House to inquire about road conditions to the top. The drive is awe-inspiring; at the summit, mist cloaks monks chanting at the temple, which was built in 911.

This has become one of the area's most revered shrines. If you don't feel like driving, you can arrange in Mae Chan for a car to take you.

Nan

20 *270 km (167 mi) southeast of Chiang Rai, 318 (197 mi) km east of Chiang Mai.*

Near the Laos border lies the city of Nan, a provincial capital whose records establish that it was founded in 1272 by the court of Laos—though according to local legend, the Lord Buddha, passing through Nan valley, spotted an auspicious site for a temple to be built. By the late 13th century Nan was brought into the fold of Sukhothai but, in fact, it maintained a fairly independent status into the 20th century. Only in the last two decades has a modern road been cut from Phrae to bring this region into closer communication with Bangkok authority. Nan province is rich in teak plantations and fertile valleys which, aside from rice, produce superb oranges. The most popular time to visit Nan is in October during the traditional boat races.

To get a sense of the art of the region visit the **National Museum** housed in the former palace of the Nan royal family. The collection has a good array of wood and bronze Buddha statues, textiles, musical instruments, ceramics, and other works of Lanna art, all of which are explained in English. ⊠ *Phalong Rd.* ⊡ *Admission.* ⊘ *Wed.–Sun. 9–12, 1–5.*

★ The most astounding temple in Nan is the beautiful **Wat Pumin** and its murals. The cruciform bot, built in 1596, is small and, in that sense, quite intimate. You climb a flight of steps flanked by two superb nagas, their heads guarding the north entrance and their tails the south. The temple was extensively renovated in 1865 and 1873, and at the end of the 19th century murals were painted on the inner walls. These delightful illustrations picture everyday life and a commoner's view of the world. Fascinating images range from the traumas of Buddhist hell and men with oversize testicles to a starving farang clasping a tool for premasticating food; from hunting scenes to views of courtly life. These are simple murals totally unlike the sophisticated art found in Bangkok's Grand Palace. The unknown artist is presumed to be from southern Yunan. The bot's central images are also quite unusual—four Sukhothai Buddhas in the vanquishing Mara position, facing the cardinal compass points. ⊠ *Phalong Rd.*

Nan is dotted with wats. **Wat Hua Wiang Tai** on Sumonthewarat Road is the gaudiest, with a nag running along the top of the security wall and lively murals painted on the viharn's exterior. **Wat Suan Tan** in Tambon Nai Wiang district has a 15th-century bronze Buddha image and is the scene for fireworks during Songkran. **Wat Ming Muang** on Suriyaphong contains the city pillar (lak muang). **Wat Chang Kham** on Suriyaphong has a large chedi supported by elephant buttresses. The town of Nan itself is small; everything is within walking distance, and daily life centers on the morning and evening markets. The Nan river, which flows past the eastern edge of town, is ignored by the tourist industry, except for a couple of riverbank restaurants whose food is rather overpriced.

Lodging

$–$$ ⊡ **Dhevaraj.** This, the first international hotel in Nan, has been modernized to become the hotel of choice. While the Park Hotel is more recent and benefits from a swimming pool, it is a good mile out of town and has a deserted, empty feel unless a tour group has descended on

it. Dhevaraj, on the other hand, is in the center of town across from
the market and is a meeting point for locals as much as tourists. A coffee shop is open from 6 AM to midnight and the courtyard dining room
serves dinner in a romantic setting. Rooms were refurbished in 1995
and are still quite respectable, including the small but modern bathrooms. ⊠ *T44 Sumonthevaraj Rd., 50000,* ☎ *054/710094,* FAX *054/
710212. 154 rooms with bath. 2 restaurants. MC, V.*

$ 🏨 **Nanfah Hotel.** This old wooden Chinese hotel, a relic of the past,
is worth a visit, even if you are disinclined to stay in its rather dark,
bare rooms with their dated bathrooms. A live band plays in the
lounge/restaurant at nighttime. That, of course, does not help those
trying to sleep in the rooms above, but rooms at the back of the hotel
are quiet. The wide-planked floors are of a bygone age and a balcony
overlooks the street, a delight of an era that had never heard the automobile. Marvelous antiques are scattered around the hotel, and the young
female owner, who also has the souvenir/artifact shop in the lobby, is
a delightful host. ⊠ *438 Sumontewaraj Rd., 55000,* ☎ *054/772640.
14 rooms with shower. No credit cards.*

Phrae

㉑ *235 km (145 mi) south of Chiang Rai, 201 km (125 mi) southeast of
Chiang Mai, 118 km (73 mi) southwest of Nan.*

Phrae (pronounced "prayer") is off the main tourist beat, a market town
in a narrow rice valley on the road to Nan. The town's recorded history starts in the 12th century, when it was called Wiang Kosai, the
Silk Cloth City. It remained an independent kingdom until the Ayutthaya period. Remains of these former times are seen in the crumbling
city walls and moat, which separate the old city from the new commercial sprawl. On the northeastern edge of town stands **Wat Chom
Sawan,** a beautiful monastery built during the reign of King Rama V
(1868–1910) and designed by a Burmese architect. The bot (ordina-
tion hall) and viharn (assembly hall) are combined to make one giant
sweeping structure. Phrae's oldest building is **Wat Luang,** near the city
wall and moat. Though it was founded in the 12th century, renovations and expansions completely obscure the original design, and the
only original section is a Lanna chedi with primitive elephant statues.
A small museum on the grounds contains sacred Buddha images,
swords, and texts; a monk will take you around, but his explanations
are likely to be only in Thai.

On a hilltop in Tambon Pa Daeng, 10 km (6 mi) southeast of town,
stands another ancient wat, **Wat Phra That Cho Hae.** It was built in the
late 12th century, and its 108-ft chedi is coated in gold sheet. The chedi
is linked to the viharn, a later construction, which contains a series of
murals depicting scenes from the life of Buddha. Cho Hae is the name
given to the cloth woven by the local people, and in the fourth lunar
month (June) the chedi is wrapped in this cloth and an annual fair is
held. Two kilometers (1 mile) from Wat Cho Hae there's another
smaller wat, **Wat Phra That Chom Chang,** which is quite famous; its
chedi is said to contain a strand of Lord Buddha's hair.

About 9 km (6 mi) west of Phrae's center, in the hamlet of Tambon Pa
Maet, on highway 1023 is a house, **Ban Prathap Chai,** that's billed as
one of the largest teak structures in the world. Although that may be
an exaggeration, it is constructed from 130 huge teak posts, and the
rooms inside are a beautiful example of traditional Thai housing.
Much of the compound is given over to shops, some of which have
weaving and crafts of good quality.

Lodging

$ $$ Ⓜ **Nakorn Phrae Tower Hotel.** Although Phrae is not a tourist town, you'll find hereall the creature comforts one might expect in the leading hotel of a provincial capital. Bedrooms have either two queen-size beds or a king and are furnished with chairs, desks, minibars, and TVs. Bathrooms are small, tiled, and functional. The restaurant serves Thai, Chinese, and Western fare, and you can have drinks in the lounge or at a small bar. ⊠ *3 Muanghit Rd., 54000,* ☎ *054/521321,* 𝔽𝔸𝕏 *054/523503. 139 rooms. Restaurant, bar, meeting rooms. AE, DC, MC, V.*

Northern Thailand Essentials

Arriving and Departing

The State Railway links Chiang Mai to Bangkok and points south but goes no farther north. As the trip from Bangkok takes about 13 hours and there's little to see but paddy fields, overnight sleepers are the best trains to take, and they are very comfortable. On most routes buses are faster and cheaper than trains, but if time is short, take a plane. Don't leave your valuables unattended on either bus or train. Petty thievery is common.

Chiang Mai and Nearby; Mae Hong Son

BY AIRPLANE

In peak season, flights to **Chiang Mai** are heavily booked. The airport is about 10 minutes from downtown, a B80 taxi ride. **Thai Airways International** (☎ 02/234–3100 in Bangkok) has 10 or more flights daily from Bangkok (about one hour; B1.700), and direct daily flights from Phuket. **Bangkok Airways** (☎ 02/281519) flies daily from Bangkok, with a stopover in Sukhothai. **Silk Air** has direct flights from Singapore, and **Air Mandalay** (☎ 053/818049) flies three times a week from Mandalay (book through a travel agent). **Thai Airways International** has one daily flight between Bangkok and **Lampang** and several flights a day between Bangkok and **Mae Hong Son.** It also flied twice daily between Chiang Mai and Mae Hong Son (book these popular flights in advance; the cost is amazingly low—B345 one way). **Note:** In March and April, smoke from slash-and-burn fires frequently prevents planes from landing at Mae Hong Son airport.

BY BUS

The trip between Bangkok and **Chiang Mai** takes about 11 hours and costs approximately B300. Privately run air-conditioned buses (the preferred choice) cost about B470. State-run buses leave from Bangkok's **Northern Terminal** (⊠ Phahonyothin Rd., ☎ 02/279–4484). Some of the private buses use Bangkok's Banglampoo section of town as the drop-off and pick-up point. Chiang Mai's **Arcade bus terminal** (☎ 053/274638 or 053/242664) serves Bangkok, Mae Hong Son, Chiang Rai, and Chiang Rai province; the **Chiang Phuak terminal** (☎ 053/211586) serves Lamphun, Fang, Tha Ton, and destinations within Chiang Mai province.

The easiest way to reach **Lamphun** from Chiang Mai is to take the minibus songthaew (B10), which leaves about every 20 minutes from the TAT office on Lamphun Road. An express bus to **Mae Hong Son** leaves **Chiang Mai Arcade Station** (☎ 053/242664) in the morning for the five- to six-hour trip (B175). Both air-conditioned and non-air-conditioned buses connect **Lampang** to Thailand's north and northwest and to Bangkok. The bus station is 3 km (2 mi) away—take a samlor into town—but the ticket offices are in Lampang.

BY CAR

The road to **Mae Hong Son** from Chiang Mai has 1,273 arm-wrenching bends but is also very scenic; the northern route through Pai (4 hours) is shortest and most attractive; the southern route—Highway 108 through Mae Sariang—is easier driving but takes about two hours longer.

BY TRAIN

Trains for the north depart from Bangkok's **Hualamphong Railway Station** and arrive in **Chiang Mai** (✉ Charoenmuang Rd., ☎ 053/245563). Overnight sleepers leave at 6 PM and 7:40 PM, arriving at 7:05 AM and 7:55 AM. The return train leaves at 5:15 PM and arrives in Bangkok at 6:25 AM. (Departure times are subject to minor changes.) The overnight trains are invariably well maintained, with clean sheets on the rows of two-tier bunks. The second-class carriages, either fan-cooled or air-conditioned, are comfortable (fare approximately B625). First class (two bunks per compartment) is twice the price. The **Nakhonphing Special Express** (no first class) leaves Bangkok at 7:40 PM and arrives at Chiang Mai at 8:25 AM (return trip departs at 9:05 PM and arrives in Bangkok at 9:40 AM). The tuk-tuk fare to the center of town ranges from B20 to B30. The train to **Lampang** from Chiang Mai takes approximately 2½ hours; from Bangkok, it takes 11 hours, and from Phitsanulok, five hours.

Most Bangkok–Chiang Mai trains stop at Phitsanulok and at Lamphun, where a bicycle samlor can take you the 3 km (2 mi) into town for B30.

Chiang Rai

BY AIRPLANE

Thai Airways International offers two nonstop flights daily from Bangkok (B1,820) and two from Chiang Mai (B230). Taxis meet incoming flights, but most tourist hotels have their own shuttle vans waiting for guests.

BY BUS AND BOAT

Buses run throughout the day from the **Chiang Mai Arcade Bus Station** (☎ 053/242664). The express takes 2½ hours and costs about B80; the local takes 3½ hours and is even cheaper.

The most exciting way to reach Chiang Rai is on a combination bus and boat trip. You leave Chiang Mai at 6:30 AM for a four-hour trip on a local bus to Tha Thon, north of Fang (or you can hire a car and driver for about B1,200 and leave your Chiang Mai hotel at 8 AM). In Tha Thon, after lunch at the restaurant opposite the landing stage, you leave on a long-tail boat at 12:30 PM (buy your ticket at the kiosk). These public boats hold about 12 passengers, sitting in the bottom, and the fare is B160 per person. You may hire your own boat for B1,600, which you will have to do if you arrive after 12:30 PM. The trip down the Mae Kok River to Chiang Rai takes five hours, going through rapids and passing a few hill-tribe villages. Bring bottled water, an inflatable cushion, and a sun hat. The more adventurous can travel by unmotorized raft (best during October and November, when the water flows quickly), staying overnight in small villages on the three-day journey.

Getting Around

Chiang Mai and Nearby

Compact **Chiang Mai** can be explored easily on foot or by bicycle, with the occasional use of public or other transport for temples, shops, and attractions out of the city center. A car, with a driver and guide, is the most convenient way to visit the five key temples outside Chiang Mai, the elephant camp, the hill-tribe villages, and the Golden Mile craft factory/shopping area. If you hire a taxi for a day (B1,000–B1,400, depending on mileage), negotiate the price in advance or, better yet, arrange it the evening before and have the driver collect you from your hotel in the morning. Do not pay until you have completed the trip. More and more tourists are renting four-wheel-drive vehicles. Driving is easier than it may first appear, though pedestrians and unlighted vehicles make it hazardous at night. Two major car rental agencies in Chiang Mai are: **Hertz** (⊠ 90 Sridornchai Rd., ☎ 053/279474) and **Avis** (⊠ Chiang Mai Airport, ☎ 053/201574).

Motorcycles are popular. Rental agencies are numerous, and most small hotels have their own agency. Shop around to get the best price and a bike in good condition. Remember that any damage to the bike that can be attributed to you will be, including its theft. Most trips in a **tuk-tuk** within Chiang Mai should cost less than B30. **Songthaews** (red minibuses) follow a kind of fixed route, but will go elsewhere at a passenger's request. Name your destination before you get in. The cost is B5.

In the small town of **Lamphun** all the sights are within a B20 bicycle samlor ride.

Chiang Rai
Taxis and **bicycle samlors** are always available in Chiang Rai and in the surrounding small towns. **Buses** depart frequently for nearby towns (every 15 minutes to Chiang Saen or to Mae Sai, for example), or you can commission a taxi for the day.

Lampang
Horse-drawn carriages are available for tourists at a rank outside the government house, although some are usually waiting at the train station. The price for a 15-minute tour of central Lampang is B30. The hourly rate is approximately B100. The easiest and least expensive way to get around, however, is by **samlor.**

Mae Hong Son
Mae Hong Son is very small; everything is within walking distance, although you may need a **tuk-tuk** or **taxi** to take you into town from your hotel. It is usual to take trips to the outlying villages and sights with a **guide and chauffeured car.** Should you **hire a Jeep,** be sure that its four-wheel drive is in working order. Less expensive, if you want to explore on your own, are **motorbikes,** which can be rented from one of the shops along the town's main street. Be careful: the main roads have gravel patches, the side roads are rutted and, in the rainy season, you must also contend with mud.

Contacts and Resources

Emergencies
Chiang Mai and Nearby. Police and ambulance (☎ 191). **Tourist Police** (⊠ 105/1 Chiang Mai–Lamphun Rd., ☎ 053/248974 or 1699). There are also **tourist police boxes** (⊠ in front of the Night Bazaar and in the airport). **Lanna Hospital** (⊠ 103 Superhighway, ☎ 053/211037).

Chiang Rai. Police (☎ 053/711444). **Chiang Rai Hospital** (☎ 053/711300). **Over Brook Hospital** (☎ 053/711366).

Mae Hong Son. Thai **Tourist Police** (⊠ Rajadrama Phithak Rd., ☎ 053/611812).

Tour Operators
Every other store in Chiang Mai seems to be a tour agency, so you'd be wise to pick up a list of TAT-recognized agencies before choosing

one. Also, each hotel has its own travel desk and association with a tour operator. Since it is the guide who makes the tour great, arrange to meet yours before you actually sign up. This is particularly important if you are planning a trek to the hill-tribe villages. Prices vary quite a bit, so shop around, and carefully examine the offerings. Unreliable tour operators often set up shop on a Chiang Mai sidewalk and disappear after they have your money, so *use* your TAT-approved list. **Top North** (⊠ 15 Soi 2, Moon Muang Rd., ☎ 053/278532) and **Summit Tour and Trekking** (⊠ Thai Charoen Hotel, Tapas Rd., ☎ 053/233351) offer good tours at about B350 a day (more for elephant rides and river rafting), and **World Travel Service** (⊠ Rincome Hotel, Huay Kaeo Rd., ☎ 053/221–1044) is reliable.

The four major hotels in Chiang Rai and the Golden Triangle Resort in Chiang Saen organize minibus tours of the area. Their travel desks will also arrange treks to the hill-tribe villages with a guide. Should you prefer to deal directly with a tour/travel agency, try **Golden Triangle Tours** (⊠ 590 Phahotyothin Rd., Chiang Rai 57000, ☎ 053/711339).

Travel Agencies

In Chiang Mai, **ST&T Travel Center** (⊠ 193/12 Sridonchai Rd., ☎ 053/251922), on the same street as the Chiang Plaza Hotel, is good for plane, train, or bus tickets. Contact **Thai International Airways** (⊠ Phra Poklao Rd., ☎ 053/241044) to arrange domestic and international bookings.

Visitor Information

In Chiang Mai you'll find an office of the **Tourist Authority of Thailand** (TAT) (⊠ 105/1 Chiang Mai-Lamphun Rd., ☎ 053/248604) on the far side of the river.For information in Chiang Rai try the **Tourist Information Center** (⊠ Singhakhlai Rd., ☎ 053/711433).

THE CENTRAL PLAINS AND I-SAN

While Bangkok is the economic heart of Thailand, and the south its playground, the soul of the country may be said to live in the vast central area that stretches from the Myanmar border to Cambodia. Here are the rice fields worked by farmers and water buffalo who toil in the age-old way. In the western part of this region, at Sukhothai, Thailand's first kingdom was established when the Khmer empire was defeated. The eastern part, known as the I-san, close to Cambodia and the Khmer capital of Angkor Wat, was slower in being absorbed into the new Thai nation. With its many Khmer ruins it represents a different aspect of Thailand; other parts of it were strongly influenced by the culture of the land that is now Laos.

The shift of power, first to Ayutthaya and then to Bangkok, left both the western and eastern regions of this central area to become rural backwaters. Modern international hotels are few and far between, yet some of Thailand's most fascinating historic sites are here. Sukhothai takes first place, since it was the nation's first capital, but there are other architectural treasures that span half a millennium of Thai history.

Central Plains

The early history of Thailand lies in the plains due north of Bangkok, where the Thai nation was founded at Sukhothai in 1238. After 112 years the seat of government was transferred briefly to Phitsanulok, then south to Ayutthaya. In recent times, Phitsanulok has grown into a major provincial capital, while Sukhothai has become a small farming community. Fortunately, the wats and sanctuaries of Old Sukhothai were largely spared destruction, and their careful restoration shows us the classical art of early Thailand.

Phitsanulok

❶ *377 km (234 mi) north of Bangkok.*

For a brief span, Phitsanulok was the capital of Siam, after the decline of Sukhothai and before the consolidation of the royal court at Ayutthaya in the 14th century. Farther back in history, before the Kwae Noi River changed its course, Phitsanulok was a Khmer outpost called Song Kwae—now only an ancient monastery remains. The new Phitsanulok, which had to relocate 5 km (3 mi) from the old site, is a modern provincial administrative seat with few architectural blessings. Two outstanding attractions, however, merit a visit: Phra Buddha Chinnarat and the Pim Buranaket Folklore Museum. Phitsanulok is also the closest city to Sukhothai with modern amenities and communications, which makes it a good base for exploring the region.

A major street runs from the railway station to the Kwae Noi River. The newer commercial and office area is along this street and a little farther south, around the TAT office. North of this main street are the market and **Wat Phra Si Ratana** (commonly known as Wat Yai), where the treasured statue of Lord Buddha sits in majesty. Take a samlor to Wat Yai from the railway station or your hotel, but pay no more than B20. The temple is close to the river, on the city side of Naresuan Bridge.

Built in 1357, Wat Yai has developed into a large monastery with typical Buddhist statuary and ornamentation. Particularly noteworthy are the viharn's wooden doors, inlaid with mother-of-pearl at the behest of King Boromkot in 1756. Behind the viharn is a 100-ft prang that you can climb, though you cannot see the Buddha relics, supposedly resting in a vault.

All this is secondary, however, to what many claim is the world's most beautiful image of the Buddha, **Phra Buddha Chinnarat** cast during the late Sukhothai period. The statue, in the position of subduing evil, was covered in gold plate by King Eka Thossarot in 1631. According to folklore, the king applied the gold with his own hands. The statue's grace and air of humility have an overpowering serenity. The black backdrop, decorated with gilded angels and flowers, further increases its strength. It's no wonder that so many copies of this serene Buddha image have been made, the best known of which resides in Bangkok's Marble Temple. The many religious souvenir stands surrounding the bot make it hard to gain a good view of the building itself, but the bot has a fine example of the traditional three-tier roof, with low sweeping eaves. This design has the effect of diminishing the size of the walls, accentuating the nave, and emphasizing the image of the Lord Buddha. 🔲 *Free.* ⏱ *Daily 8–6.*

From Wat Yai, walk south along the river, where numerous tempting food stalls line the bank, particularly in the evening. On the far side of the bank you'll see many houseboats, which are popular among the Thais, who have an affinity for rivers and fish. Disregarding the Naresuan Bridge, some Thais still paddle across in sampan ferries. Two blocks after the post office and communications building—from which you can make overseas calls—you come to a small park. Turn left and the railway station is straight ahead.

Phitsanulok also has an unheralded museum that alone justifies a visit to the city. The **Pim Buranaket Folkcraft Museum** (Sergeant-Major

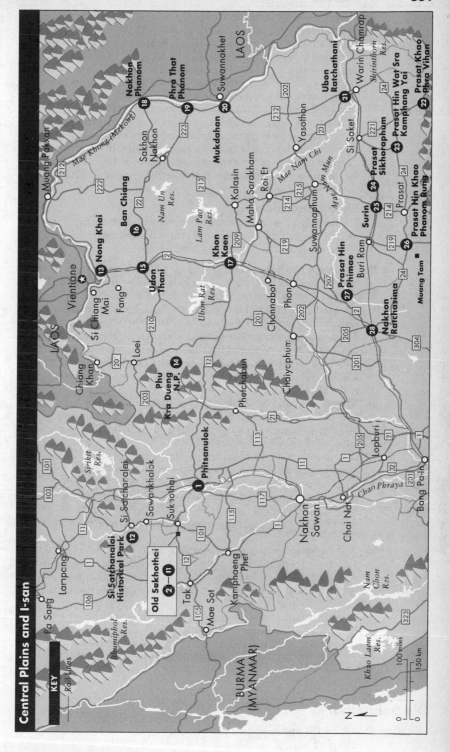

Central Plains and I-san

KEY

Rail Lines

Thawee Folk Museum) is about a 15-minute walk south of the railway station, on the east side of the tracks. In the early 1980s, Sergeant-Major Khun Thawee traveled to small Thai villages collecting the traditional tools, cooking utensils, animal traps, and crafts that are rapidly disappearing, and crammed them into a traditional Thai house and barn. For a decade nothing was properly documented; visitors stumbled through tiger traps and cooking pots. Then Khun Thawee's daughter graduated from college and came to the rescue: The marvelous artifacts are now systematically laid out, and the displays show how the items were used—from the simple wood pipes hunters played to lure their prey to elaborately complex rat guillotines. It's best to have the daughter or her assistant explain the ingenuity of the contraptions and the cultural norms embedded in the household implements. ▨ *Donations requested.* ⊗ *Daily 9–5.*

Dining and Lodging

Phitsanulok lacks fine dining establishments, and most travelers eat at their hotels, but the food sold from the stalls and carts along the river by Naresuan Bridge is tasty and hard to resist.

\$\$ ▦ **Amarin Nakhon.** Centrally located and only two blocks from the train station, this hotel offers all the basic creature needs at a good price. The hotel had a little face-lift in 1998, which made it more cheerful. The staff is helpful and the rooms are clean. Each has two queen-size beds, leaving little space for other furniture. The coffee shop stays busy 24 hours a day, serving late-night customers from the hotel's basement disco. U.S. Army personnel use this hotel during visits to the Thai military base on the outskirts of town. ✉ *3/1 Chao Phraya Rd.,* ☎ *055/ 258588,* 🄵🄰🄷 *055/258945. 130 rooms. Restaurant, coffee shop, dance club. AE, DC, MC, V.*

\$\$ ▦ **Pailyn Hotel.** Phitsanulok has sprouted several new hotels in the late 1990s and this is the best, if only because it's downtown, within walking distance of most of the city's attractions. Rooms are quite large, with picture windows—choose a higher floor with a view of the Nan River. Furnishings are in pastels and the larger rooms have two queen beds. The large lobby and coffee shop can be a scene of great activity in the mornings as tour groups depart, and in the evening the disco attracts locals and tourists alike. ✉ *36 Baromatrailokart Rd., 65000,* ☎ *055/253411, 02/215–7110 Bangkok reservations,* 🄵🄰🄷 *055/ 258185. 125 rooms. 2 restaurants, dance club, meeting rooms. AE, DC, MC, V.*

\$–\$\$ ✗▦ **Rajapruk Hotel.** Of the modest hotels in town, this one is quieter and more refined, and has newer furnishings. The owner's wife is American, and many staff members speak a few English words. Guest rooms are decorated with wood and warm colors that accentuate the hotel's feeling of intimacy. The small restaurant off the lobby is good for light meals; a formal restaurant serves Thai and Chinese food. The hotel's main drawback is its location, away from the town center on the east side of the railroad tracks. ✉ *99/9 Pha-Ong Dum Rd.,* ☎ *055/ 258477, 02/251–4612 Bangkok reservations,* 🄵🄰🄷 *055/251395. 110 rooms. Restaurant, coffee shop, pool, beauty salon, nightclub, car rental. AE, DC, MC, V.*

Old Sukhothai

❷ *56 km (35 mi) northwest of Phitsanulok, 427 km (265 mi) north of Bangkok.*

An hour from Phitsanulok by road, Sukhothai has a unique place in Thailand's history. Until the 13th century, most of Thailand consisted of many small vassal states under the suzerainty of the Khmer Empire in Angkor Wat. But the Khmers had overextended their resources, allowing the princes of two Thai states to combine forces. In 1238 one of the two princes, Phor Khun Bang Klang Thao, marched on Sukhothai, defeated the Khmer garrison commander in an elephant duel, and captured the city. Installed as the new king of the region, he took the name Sri Indraditya and founded a dynasty that ruled Sukhothai for nearly 150 years. His youngest son became the third king of Sukhothai, Ram Khamhaeng, who ruled from 1279 to 1299 (or possibly until 1316), and through military and diplomatic victories expanded the kingdom to include most of present-day Thailand and the Malay peninsula.

The Sukhothai (Sukhothai means "the dawn of happiness") period was relatively brief—a series of only eight kings—but it witnessed lasting accomplishments. The Thais gained their independence, which has been maintained to the present day despite the empire building of Western powers. King Ram Khamhaeng formulated the Thai alphabet by adapting the Khmer script to suit the Thai tonal language; Theravada Buddhism was established and became the dominant national religion; and, toward the end of the Sukhothai dynasty, a distinctive Thai art flourished that was so wonderful the period is known as Thailand's Golden Age of Art.

By the mid-14th century, Sukhothai's power and influence had waned, permitting its dynamic vassal state, Ayutthaya, to become the capital of the Thai kingdom. Sukhothai was gradually abandoned to the jungle, and a new town of Sukhothai grew up 10 km (6 mi) away. In 1978, a 10-year restoration project costing more than $10 million saw the creation of the Sukhothai Historical Park. New Sukhothai, where all intercity buses arrive, is a small, quiet market town where most inhabitants are in bed by 11 PM. The vast historical park (70 square km/27 square mi) has 193 historic monuments, of which about 20 can be classified as noteworthy and six have particular importance.

The bus will drop you on the main street, about 500 yards from the museum, just before the park entrance. You should start with the museum, but first you'll probably want to rent a bicycle from a store along the main street.

❸ Most of the significant pieces of Sukhothai art are in Bangkok's National Museum, but the **Ramkhamhaeng National Museum** has a sufficient sampling to demonstrate the gentle beauty of this period. The display of historic artifacts helps visitors form an image of Thailand's first capital city, and a relief map gives an idea of its geographic layout. ▨ Admission. ☉ Wed.–Sun. 9–noon and 1–4.

The restaurant across the street from the museum is your last chance for refreshment until you reach the food stalls at the center of the Historic Park. It's a good idea to take a bottle of water with you into the park—cycling in the sun is hot work. The park's main entrance is at the east end of the main street, and the terminus for the tourist tram is at this entrance. The admission ticket does not permit reentry.

❹ For the modern Thai, Sukhothai represents the utopian state, in which man is free, land is plentiful, and life is just. The spiritual center of this utopia is magical **Wat Mahathat.** Sitting amid a tranquil lotus pond, it is the largest and most beautiful monastery in Sukhothai. Enclosed in the compound are some 200 tightly packed chedis, each containing the funeral ashes of a nobleman, and towering above them, a large central chedi, notable for its bulbous, lotus-bud prang. Around the chedi are friezes of 111 Buddhist disciples, hands raised in adoration, walking around the base. Probably built by Sukhothai's first king, Wat Mahathat owes its present form to a 1345 remodeling by King Lö Thai,

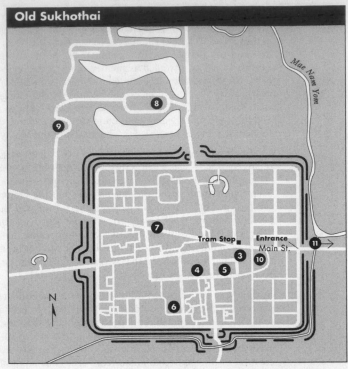

who erected the lotus-bulb chedi to house two important relics—the Hair Relic and the Neck Bone Relic—brought back from Ceylon by the monk Sisatta. This Singhalese chedi became the symbol of Sukhothai. Copies of it were made in the principal cities of its vassal states, signifying a magic circle emanating from Sukhothai, the spiritual and temporal center of the empire.

The image of Sukhothai's government is that of a monarchy that served the people, stressing social needs and justice. Slavery was abolished, and people were free to believe in their local religions, Hinduism and Buddhism (often simultaneously), and to pursue their trade without hindrance. In the 19th century, a famous stone inscription of King Ram Khamhaeng was found among the ruins of the **Royal Palace** across from Wat Mahathat. Sometimes referred to as Thailand's Declaration of Independence, the inscription's best-known quote reads: "This Muang Sukhothai is good. In the water there are fish, in the field there is rice. The ruler does not levy tax on the people who travel along the road together, leading their oxen on the way to trade and riding their horses on the way to sell. Whoever wants to trade in elephants, so trades. Whoever wants to trade in horses, so trades." No other political platform appeals to the Thais as much as this one.

Possibly the oldest structure of Sukhothai is **Wat Sri Sawai.** The architectural style is Khmer, with three prangs—similar to those found in Lopburi—surrounded by a laterite wall. (Laterite, made from red porous soil that hardens when exposed to air, is the building material used most in Sukhothai.) The many stucco Hindu and Buddhist images and scenes suggest that Sri Sawai was probably first a Hindu temple, later converted to a Buddhist monastery, and that Brahmanism probably played an important role throughout the Sukhothai period.

❼ Another one of Sukhothai's noteworthy attractions is the striking and peaceful **Wat Sra Sri,** which sits on two connected islands encircled by a lotus-filled lake; the rolling, verdant mountains beyond add to the monastery's serenity. The lake, called Traphong Trakuan Pond, supplied the monks with water and served as a boundary for the sacred area. In classical Sukhothai style, a Singhalese chedi dominates six smaller chedis. A large, stucco, seated Buddha looks down a row of columns, past the chedis, and over the lake to the horizon.

Even more wondrous is a **walking Buddha** by the Singhalese-style chedi. The walking Buddha is a Sukhothai innovation and the most ephemeral of Thailand's artistic styles. The depiction of Buddha is often a reflection of political authority and is modeled after the ruler. Under the Khmers, authority was hierarchical, but the kings of Sukhothai represented the ideals of serenity, happiness, and justice. The walking Buddha is the epitome of Sukhothai's art: Lord Buddha appears to be floating on air, neither rooted on this earth nor placed on a pedestal above the reach of the common people. Later, after Ayutthaya had become the capital, statues of Buddha took on a sternness that characterized the new dynasty.

❽ Just beyond the northern city walls is **Wat Phra Phai Luang,** second in importance to Wat Mahathat. This former Khmer Hindu shrine was also converted into a Buddhist temple. Surrounded by a moat, the sanctuary is encircled by three laterite prangs, similar to those at Wat Sri Sawai—the only one that's intact is decorated with stucco figures. In front of the prangs are the remains of the viharn and a crumbling chedi with a seated Buddha on its pedestal. Facing these structures is the *mondop* (square structure with a stepped pyramid roof, built to house religious relics), once decorated with standing Buddha images in four different poses. Most of these are now too damaged to be recognizable; only the reclining Buddha still has a definite form.

❾ The **Wat Si Chum,** southwest of Wat Phra Phai Luang, is worth visiting for its sheer size. Like other sanctuaries, it was originally surrounded by a moat. The main sanctuary is dominated by Buddha in the Mara posture. The huge stucco image is one of the largest in Thailand, measuring 37 ft from knee to knee. Enter the mondop through the passage inside the left inner wall. Keep your eyes on the ceiling: more than 50 engraved slabs illustrate scenes from the *Jataka* (stories about the previous lives of Lord Buddha).

❿ On the east side of the park, the most notable temple is **Wat Traphang Thong Lang.** The square mondop is the main sanctuary, the outer walls of which boast beautiful stucco figures in niches—some of Sukhothai's finest art. The north side depicts episodes of Buddha returning to preach to his wife; on the west side, Buddha is preaching to his father and relatives. Note the figures on the south wall, where the story of Buddha is accompanied by an angel descending from Tavatisma Heaven.

⓫ Also on the east side of the park is **Wat Chang Lom.** The Ceylonese-style bell-shape chedi is raised on a square base atop now-damaged elephant buttresses (a few of the elephants have been reconstructed). In front of the chedi is a viharn and solitary pillars; the remains of nine other chedis have been found within this complex.

Dining and Lodging

Sukhothai has no smart restaurants, but there are many inexpensive cafés and food stalls. Most visitors stay in New Sukhothai, where there's some evening entertainment and where across from the long distance bus stop, there are a number of good Thai food stalls/restaurants in the open marketplace. For the best coffee in the province as well as an attractive rustic decor, visit the **Dream Coffee Shop** across from the Sawat Phong Hotel on Singhawat Road.

$$ ✕⌑ **Northern Palace.** The best of New Sukhothai's indifferent lodgings is this small, modern hotel on the Phitsanulok road, close to the town center. Rooms have twin beds and are furnished in light colors and kept clean. The staff speaks a little English, and the bar and dining room serves as an evening gathering spot—often with live music—for locals and foreigners. The dining room offers mostly Chinese and Thai food. ⌑ *43 Singhawat Rd., 64000,* ☎ *055/612081,* FAX *055/612038. 81 rooms. Restaurant, pool, nightclub. MC, V.*

$–$$ ✕⌑ **Thai Village House.** This compound of thatched bungalows is usually stuffed with tour groups. Consequently, the staff is impersonal and unhelpful. The hotel's advantage is its location—a five-minute bicycle ride from the Historical Park. Guest rooms (most are air-conditioned) have two queen-size beds and little else except for private bathrooms. The open-air dining room is pleasantly relaxing when tour groups aren't around. ⌑ *214 Jarodvithitong Rd., Muang Kao, 64000,* ☎ *055/611049 or 055/612075,* FAX *055/612583. 123 rooms. Restaurant, shops. MC, V.*

$$ ⌑ **Pailyn Sukhothai Hotel.** This modern building, opened in 1991, tries to incorporate Thai architecture, but the result is characterless. Nevertheless, it has the most creature comforts of any hotel in the area and most of the better tour groups stay here. It has a shuttle to the historic area. The big negative is that it's off by itself between Old and New Sukhothai, with no place of interest in the vicinity. ⌑ *Jarodvithithong, 64210,* ☎ *055/613310, 02/215–5640 Bangkok reservations,* FAX *055/613317. 238 rooms. 3 restaurants, pool, massage, sauna, health club. MC, V.*

$ ⌑ **Anasukho.** In a small Thai house down a narrow soi on the south side of the river, this guest house is run by a friendly Thai couple. The wood floors and beams and the small garden add to the feeling that this could be your home away from home. No food is served, but tea and coffee are always available. ⌑ *234/6 Jarodwitheethong Rd. and Soi Panison, Sukhothai 64000,* ☎ *055/611315. 3 rooms with shared bath. No credit cards.*

$ ⌑ **River View Hotel.** Steps away from the private bus terminal in the center of the new town, this very basic and rather institutional hotel is currently the best and most convenient budget choice. (Neighboring Chinawat has deteriorated in the last couple of years.) The air-conditioned rooms are mopped clean, and each has a private shower. There is a restaurant, but I would not bother with it—eat in the market across the street. ⌑ *92 Nikorn Kasem Rd., 64000,* ☎ *055/61156,* FAX *055/613373. 32 rooms. Dining room. No credit cards.*

Si Satchanalai Historical Park

⓬ *57 km (35 mi) north of Sukhothai.*

With its expanse of mown lawns, Sukhothai Historical Park is sometimes criticized for being too well groomed—even the ruins are neatly arranged. Si Satchanalai is less so; it remains a quiet place with a more ancient, undisturbed atmosphere spread out on 228 acres on the right bank of the Mae Yom River. Si Satchanalai may be reached either as part of a tour from Sukhothai—Chinawat Hotel offers a day minibus tour—or by local bus. If you go by bus, you should get off in Sawankhalok, and from there, take a taxi to get to the historical park and to go from one site to another. Accommodations near the park are only expensive bungalow-type guest houses.

Si Satchanalai, a sister city to Sukhothai, was usually governed by a son of Sukhothai's reigning monarch. Among its many monuments are two to search out: **Wat Chang Lom,** at the right of the entrance, shows strong Sri Lankan influences, with its 39 elephant buttresses. The main chedi, completed by 1291, is said to contain relics of the Lord Buddha, and as you climb the stairs, you will move from earthy concerns to the spiritual realm, where you'll find seated images of Buddha. The second important monument, **Wat Chedi Jet Thaew,** south of Wat Chang Lom, has seven rows of lotus-bud chedis, in a ruinous state, that contain the ashes of members of Si Satchanalai's ruling family.

I-san

The sprawling northeast plateau, known as I-san, is rarely visited by tourists. Comprising one third of Thailand's land area, 17 provinces, and four of the kingdom's most populous cities, the Northeast is also the least-developed area and the poorest. Life, for the most part, depends upon the fickleness of the monsoon rains; work is hard and scarce. For many, migration to Bangkok has been the only option. Most tuk-tuk drivers in Bangkok are from I-san, and the bars of Patpong are filled with its daughters, sending their earnings back to their parents.

The people of the Northeast, burned by the scorching sun and weathered by the hard life, are straightforward and direct, passionate and obstinate. Their food is hot and spicy, their festivals are robust, and their regional language reflects their closeness to Laos. I-san's attractions are: the Khmer ruins, which have been only partially restored; national parks; the Mae Khong river; and the traditional rural way of life. And while there are hotels in every town, and an efficient bus service reaches the smallest of hamlets, the plain accommodations lack sophisticated amenities.

Travelers in Bangkok who are short on time may want to limit their visit to Nakhon Ratchasima (Korat), only four hours away by train, which can serve as a base for trips to the nearby Khmer ruins at Phimae and Buri Ram, and, perhaps, the Khao Yai National Park. Our itinerary begins in the far north at Nong Khai on the Mae Khong, then loops west via Loei and the national park, to Udon Thani and Khon Kaen, then back to the Mae Khong at Nakon Phanom. Next it roughly follows the Mae Khong south along the Laotian border to Ubon Ratchathani before turning west along the Mun River and the Kampuchean border, through an area full of Khmer ruins back to Korat.

The new bridge into Laos at Nong Khai has stimulated local trade, and shoppers will find interesting goods there and also at Mukdahan. Some of the handmade lace or the tie-dyed mudmee cottons may tempt you, as may even such oddities as large washbowls made of aluminum from downed U.S. aircraft. Nong Khai is also a good source for silver. For silk, try Udon Thani, the nearby silk-weaving villages, and, farther south, Khon Kaen.

Nong Khai

⑬ *615 km (381 mi) northeast of Bangkok, 356 km (221 mi) north of Korat.*

The delight of Nong Khai is its frontier-town atmosphere: because Laos has been closed to the world for so long, you feel as if you're at the end of the line. However, times are changing. Laos is opening up, seeking cooperation with Thailand as well as encouraging tourist travel. In 1994, the Friendship Bridge across the Mae Khong opened, joining Nong Khai and Vientiane in a sweeping arc. Previously the only connection was a scurry of ferries from Tha Sadet, the boat pier, which has a small immigration and customs shed. Now the traffic crosses the river, switching on the Laotian side so drivers can change from driving on the left-hand side—as in Thailand—to the right-hand side, as in Laos. Non-Thais need Laotian visas, which can be obtained in Nong Khai, but you need to show that you have a return ticket and ample funds to support yourself in Laos. The opening of this bridge was expected to facilitate border traffic and cause a surge in tourism. It has not. Immigration officials still take a long time to check all papers, tourists are staying away, and hotels are suffering, with occupancy rates a feeble 30%.

Fanning out from Tha Sadet, the boat pier, on Rim Khong Road, are market stalls with goods brought in from Laos. On Nong Khai's main street, Meechai Road, the old wooden houses—for example, the governor's residence—show French colonial influences from Indochina. **Wat Pho Chai,** the best-known temple, houses a gold image of Buddha, Luang Pho Phra Sai, that was lost for many centuries in the muddy bottom of the Mae Khong. Its rediscovery, part of the local lore, is told in pictures on the temple's walls. **Village Weaver Handicrafts,** next to the temple, employs 350 families in the production of indigo-dyed mudmee cotton. You may want to take a B50 tuk-tuk ride 5 km (3 mi) along the Nong Khai–Phon Pisai Road west of town to visit **Wat Khaek** (also called Sala Kaew Koo), something of an oddity created by Luang Pu, a monk who believes that all religions should work together. The temple's gardens are a collection of bizarre statues representing gods, goddesses, demons, and devils from many of the world's faiths, though the emphasis is on the Hindu gods.

Lodging

$$ 🏨 **Mekong Royal.** The gleaming white building standing back from the river 2 km (1 mi) out of town was built on the unfulfilled promise that the Friendship Bridge would bring tourists by the busload to Nong Khai. While the furnishings and architecture may not enthrall you, the rooms are spacious, amenities are new, and most of the rooms have great views over the Mae Khong into Laos. Best of all is the large pool, so refreshing in the blistering heat of the I-san. The hotel is a member of the Holiday Inn chain. ✉ 222 Jomanee Beach, 43000, ☎ 042/420024, 02/272–0087/9 Bangkok reservations, FAX 042/421280, 02/272–0090 in Bangkok. 198 rooms. Restaurant, pool, meeting rooms. AE, DC, MC, V.

$–$$ 🏨 **Chiang Khan Hill Resort.** On 2 acres atop the banks of the Mae Khong,
★   commanding marvelous views of a series of rapids and of the Laotian countryside, this resort is worth a trip in its own right. Rooms are in octagonal bungalows, the choicest being the ones with a clear view of the river. Room No. 7 is one of these, with a king-size bed, a coffee table and comfortable chairs by the window, and a small but modern bathroom. There's an excellent open-air restaurant where the deep-fried shrimp cakes are crispy and delicious, the *somtan* (a relish) tingles with lime, and the chicken dishes are made from free-range birds. ✉ Kaeng Khut Khu, 28/2 Mu 4, Chiang Khan, ☎ 042/821285, FAX 042/821414. 40 rooms. Restaurant. MC, V.

$ 🏨 **Phanthawi.** This is Nong Khai's downtown business hotel. Don't expect more than clean rooms with either air-conditioning or fans. The beds suffice rather than being really comfortable, and the furnishings are sparse. The restaurant, on the open-fronted ground floor, serves also as a sitting area. The staff speaks limited English, but enough to direct guests to the appropriate bus stations. ✉ Haisoke Rd., 43000, ☎ 042/411568. 67 rooms. Restaurant. MC, V.

En Route   There is a marvelous **scenic trip** west along the Mae Khong, on the old dirt road with your own wheels, or on Highway 211, by bus, to **Si Chiang Mai,** 50 km (31 mi) from Nong Khai. This sleepy backwater is famous for producing spring-roll wrappers—everywhere you'll see the white translucent rice flour spread out on mats to dry. Just out of Si Chiang Mai at road marker 83 you come to **Wat Hin Maak Peng,** a meditation temple run by *mae chee,* Buddhist nuns, and farther on you'll come to **Than Thon waterfall,** a series of rapids in a stream, where Thais take delight in picnicking and bathing. After another waterfall at **Sangkhom,** you cross into Loei province and soon reach the town of **Chiang Khan,** where the road turns south to **Loei,** the provincial capital, a major stop on bus routes in all directions.

Phu Kra Dueng National Park

⑭ *70 km (42 mi) south of Loei, off the Loei–Khon Khaen highway.*

Loei province's key attraction is Phu Kra Dueng National Park, a lone, steep-sided mountain topped by a 60-square-km (23-square-mi) plateau nearly a mile above sea level. It's wonderfully cool up here, and the profusion of flowers during March and April is brilliant. You reach the plateau by a 9-km (5½-mi) hike through lightly forested fields of daisies, violets, orchids, and rhododendrons, and on top there are well-marked trails to scenic overlooks at the edge of the escarpment. The park is closed during the rainy season, July through October.

Udon Thani

⑮ *564 km (350 mi) northeast of Bangkok, 51 km (32 mi) south of Nong Khai.*

As a major U.S. Air Force base during the Vietnam War, Udon Thani grew in size and importance and, though diminished, the American military presence remains in a few glitzy bars and in half Thai–half Western young people. A popular hangout for them is the Charoen Hotel on Pho Si Road, where pop singers perform nightly. Tourists come to Udon Thani chiefly as a place to stay while visiting Ban Chiang. The town is known for its *kai yang*(roast chicken), the best of which can be found at the stalls on the corner of Phrajak and Mukkhamontri roads. There is a Western-style shopping center at Jaroensri at the junction of Pho Si and Tahaan roads. At the **Udon Cultural Center** of Udon Teacher's College (Tahaan Road, away from the clock tower), an exhibit of photographs and artifacts illustrates daily life and the regional folk crafts. To buy silk, go to **Ban Na Kha,** a village of silk weavers, about 14 km (8 mi) north on the Nong Khai road.

Ban Chiang

⑯ *60 km (36 mi) east of Udon Thani.*

The chief attraction near Udon Thani is Ban Chiang, where archaeological finds of "fingerwhorl" pottery, skeletons, jewelry, and flint and iron weapons suggest a civilization here more than 7,000 years ago. UNESCO declared it a Heritage Site in 1992. The pottery in particular—red-on-cream with swirling geometric spirals—indicates that this civilization was ahead of its time in cultural development, and even more intriguing is that copper bells and glass beads found here are similar to some found in North and Central America. This poses the question: did Asians trade with Americans 7,000 years ago, or even migrate halfway around the world? You can reach Ban Chiang from Udon Thani on the local bus, or take a car and driver for approximately B600. The excavation site is a short walk away at **Wat Pho Si Mai.** The larger of the two museums in the center of the village has English explanations. ▦ *Admission.* ☉ *Wed.–Sun., 9:30–4:30.*

One hour by bus northwest of Udon Thani there is a 1,200-acre mountain park at **Ban Phue,** where you can rent a motorbike (B40) to get to the
top of the mountain, 8 km (5 mi) away. The park is covered with rocks of
all sizes, some shaped into Buddhist and Hindu images. **Wat Phra Buddha Baht Bua Bok,** at the top of the hill, is named after the replica of Buddha's footprint at its base; its 131-ft pagoda copies the style of the
revered Wat That Phanom, farther to the east. Take the path to the right
of the temple, and within a km (½ mi), you'll reach a **cave** with a series of
stick-figure and silhouette paintings thought to be 4,000 years old.

Khon Kaen

⑰ *110 km (68 mi) south of Udon Thani, 449 km (278 mi) northeast of
Bangkok.*

South of Udon Thani on the road to Nakhon Ratchasima lies Khon
Kaen, a rapidly developing town that holds a silk fair in December. This
area is known for mudmee silk; in fact, if you are in the neighborhood, you should make the 50-km (30-mi) trip south to the village
of Chonnabot to see the silk being processed, from the cocoon through
the spinning and dying to the weaving on hand looms. If you don't
have time to make the trip, visit **Rin Thai Silk** (☒ 412 Namuang Rd.,
☎ 043/220705, 043/221042), a fascinating emporium that carries
mudmee silks and cottons, both new and old; ready-to-wear items; and
local goods, all at reasonable prices.

Lodging

$$–$$$ 🏨 **Sofitel Raja Orchid.** This splendid 25-story hotel (built in 1996) dom-
inates the skyline of Thailand's third largest city. The soaring lobby is
centered by a gorgeous stylized lotus, symbol of the I-san, sculpted of
glass and copper, silver and gold, rising like a huge Christmas tree from
a marble pool. Carved woods and handwoven silks add to the luxury,
as does the five-bedroom Royal Suite, with its own helipad. You can try
Thai, Chinese, Vietnamese, or international cuisine in the sleek restaurants, and in the Underground entertainment complex you can drink beer
at the Kronen Brauhaus microbrewery, air your lungs at Studio 1 Karaoke,
or dance in the dazzling lights at the Wow! Fun House. ☒ 9/9 Pracha-
sumran Rd., 44000, ☎ 043/322155, 800/221–4542 reservations in the
U.S., ☒ 043/322150. 300 rooms. 5 restaurants, 3 bars, pool, health club,
dance club, business center, meeting rooms. AE, DC, MC, V.

Nakhon Phanom

⑱ *740 km (459 mi) northeast of Bangkok, 252 km (156 mi) east of Udon
Thani.*

Approximately three hours east of Udon Thani by bus is Nakhon
Phanom, on the banks of the Mae Khong, a sleepy market town with
the best hotel in the area, where you should spend the night.

Lodging

$$–$$$ 🏨 **Mae Nam Khong Grand View.** The most expensive of Nakhon
Phanom's hotels is a modern construction along the river. The concrete
structure is not pleasing to the eye, but the carpeted guest rooms are
spacious and the tiled bathrooms modern and clean. The restaurant
serves both Thai and Western menus, and a live band plays in the
nightclub on weekends. ☒ 527 Sunthon-Wichit Rd., ☎ 042/513564,
☒ 042/511037. 116 rooms. Restaurant, nightclub. AE, MC, V.

$–$$ 🏨 **Si Thep Hotel.** This hotel is a good alternative if you don't want to
pay luxury prices. The property is about 400 yards from the Mae Khong
river, back from a side street off the main road, so all the rooms are

quiet. Rooms are standard and the well-used furnishings are slightly depressing, but all is clean, including the bathrooms. The restaurant has a terrace if you want the evening air instead of air-conditioning. ✉ *708/11 Si Thep Rd.,* ☎ *042/512395,* FAX *042/511346. 87 rooms. Restaurant. MC, V.*

Phra That Phanom

19 *50 km (31 mi) south of Nakhon Phanom.*

Take the bus from Nakhon Phanom that goes through to Mukdahan to get to Phra That Phanom, northeast Thailand's most revered shrine. No one knows just when Phra That Phanom was built, though archaeologists trace its foundations to the 5th century. The temple has crumbled and been rebuilt several times—it now stands 171 ft high, with a decorative tip of gold weighing 22 pounds. Though it's impressive, you may be equally moved by the small museum to the left of the grounds that houses its ancient bells and artifacts. Once a year droves of devotees arrive to attend the Phra That Phanom Fair during the full moon of the third lunar month, and the village becomes a minimetropolis, with stalls of market traders and makeshift shelters for the pilgrims.

Ten kilometers (6 miles) back toward Nakon Phanom is the small village of **Renu Nakhon** which, along the main street, has a row of showrooms and cottage industries similar to those at San Kamphaeng in Chiang Mai. They produce and sell an extensive range of products, including cotton and silk dresses, quilted blankets, and ceramics.

Mukdahan

20 *40 km (24 mi) south of Phra That Phanom.*

Mukdahan on the Mae Khong, Thailand's newest provincial capital, is opposite the Laotian town of Suwannakhet. It bustles with vendors in stalls and shops all along the riverfront, selling goods brought in from Laos—a fascinating array of detailed embroidery, lace, lacquered paintings, trays, and bowls, cheap cotton goods, and a host of souvenir items. Time out from shopping can be spent promenading along the riverfront, stopping occasionally to sample Thai and Laotian delicacies from one of the numerous food stalls.

Lodging

$$ 🏨 **Mukdahan Grand Hotel.** The only Western-style hotel in town is this modern concrete building. The staff is welcoming and helpful, though little English is spoken. Rooms are plain, but adequately furnished with twin- or king-size beds, and a table and chairs. The restaurant serves a buffet breakfast, and Thai and Western dishes for lunch and dinner. ✉ *70 Songnang Sanid Rd., 49000,* ☎ *042/612020,* FAX *042/612021. 200 rooms. Restaurant. AE, MC, V.*

Ubon Ratchathani

21 *181 km (112 mi) south of Mukdahan, 227 km (141 mi) east of Surin.*

A three-hour bus ride south from Mukdahan takes you to Ubon Ratchathani, southern I-san's largest city. Its best-known tourist attraction is the Buddhist-inspired Candle Procession in late July, when huge wax sculptures are paraded through town. At other times, especially after the rainy season, locals make for **Haad Wat Tai Island** in the middle of the Mun River, a site for food stalls. It's connected to the shore by a rope bridge (1 baht) that sends shivers of apprehension through those who cross. Try the local favorites: *pla chon,* a fish whose name is often translated as "snakehead mullet," or, if your stomach is feeling conservative, the ubiquitous kai yang. Temple enthusiasts should visit both the Indian-style pagoda **Wat Nong Bua** and the **Wat Maha Wanaram** (Wat Pa-Yai), which houses a revered Buddha image named Phra Chao Yai Impang, believed to have magical powers.

Lodging

$$ 🏨 **Patumrat Hotel.** Though the nearby Regent Palace is the newest four-star hotel in town, the Patumrat's service and personality guarantee its position as Ubon's leading hotel. Its drawback, as is the Regent's, is the location, a 20-minute walk from the center of town. ⌧ *173 Chayangkun Rd., 34000,* ☎ *045/241501,* 🖷 *045/243792. 137 rooms. Restaurant, coffee shop. AE, DC, MC, V.*

$ 🏨 **Rajthani Hotel.** This convenient, modest hotel used by Thai business travelers and tourists is downtown on the main street. The uncarpeted rooms are simply furnished but clean, and the bathrooms have hot and cold water. The clerks at the reception desk are friendly but not able to provide much tourist information. ⌧ *297 Khuan Thani Rd., 34000,* ☎ *045/244388,* 🖷 *045/243561. 100 rooms. Restaurant. No credit cards.*

$ 🏨 **Sri Kamol Hotel.** This clean, modern hotel in the center of town, a five-minute walk from the TAT office, has carpeted rooms with twin- or king-size beds. The furnishings are standard—there's a table with two chairs and a minibar with a small television on top. The staff is welcoming, and a few of them speak English well. You can often negotiate a discount of 25% on the price of a room. ⌧ *26 Ubonsak Rd., 34000,* ☎ *045/ 255804,* 🖷 *045/243793. 82 rooms. Restaurant. No credit cards.*

Si Saket

40 km (24 mi) west of Ubon Ratchathani, 571 km (357 mi) northeast of Bangkok.

With the exception of a brand new Buddhist temple, said to be one of the grandest in the Northeast, the town of Si Saket is known more for its pickled garlic, pickled onion, somtam, and, of course, kai yang than its architecture. But in early March, when the colorful lamduan flower blooms, the town comes alive in a riot of yellows and reds, and locals celebrate with the three-day Lamduan Festival.

Prasat Khao Phra Vihan

㉒ *125 km (86 mi) southeast of Si Saket.*

Both Thailand and Cambodia claim that Prasat Khao Phra Vihan is on their soil, and the World Court awarded it to Cambodia—but because access from that side requires scaling a cliff, you get to the site from Thailand! The temple is on the outskirts of Guntharalak. Although the 12th-century sandstone laterite ruins are in a state of neglect, enough remains in this commanding location to let your imagination fly back nine centuries to when the Khmer ruled much of southeast Asia. Because brigands and disbanded soldiers still (mid-1998) cause security problems, the area is closed, preventing access to the site. When conditions improve, you can go by car or by bus from Si Saket down Highway 221 to Guntharalak. If you can't visit this site, you can see a replica in miniature at Muang Boran, the "Ancient City" south of Bangkok (☞ Scattered Bangkok, *above*).

Prasat Hin Wat Sra Kamphang Yai

㉓ *40 km (25 mi) south of Si Saket.*

Prasat Hin Wat Sra Kamphang Yai (Stone Castle), just outside Ban Sa Kampang, is in better condition than many of the other Khmer sanctuaries in I-san. Thailand's Department of Fine Arts has restored it, re-creating what has been lost or stolen over the last 900 years. Particularly marvelous are the lintels of the middle stupa, which depict the Hindu god Indra riding the Erawan (elephant). The main gate, inscribed with Khom letters, is estimated as 10th century and built during the reign of King Suriyaworamann. The temple behind the prasat is a Thai addition, with walls covered with pictures illustrating Thai proverbs.

Prasat Sikhoraphum

㉔ *85 km (52 mi) west of Si Saket, 40 km (24 mi) east of Surin.*

On the main road west, between Si Saket and Surin, you come to Prasat Sikhoraphum, a five-prang Khmer pagoda built in the 12th century. The central, main structure has wonderfully engraved lintels of Shiva, as well as depictions of Brahma, Vishnu, and Ganesa. Shoppers may want to detour south to **Ban Butom,** 12 km (7½ mi) before Surin, where the villagers make straw baskets that are sold in Bangkok. They'll be happy to demonstrate their skill and sell you their wares.

Surin

㉕ *227 km (141 mi) west of Ubon Ratchathani, 190 km (120 mi) east of Korat.*

Surin is famous for its annual elephant roundup in the third week of November. The roundup is essentially an elephant circus, albeit an impressive one, where elephants perform tricks in a large arena and their mahouts reenact scenes of capturing wild elephants. At other times, if you want to see elephants, you must travel to **Ban Ta Klang,** a village 60 km (37 mi) north of Surin, off Highway 214. After 36 km (22 mi), at Ban Krapo, take a left and go another 24 km (15 mi) to Ban Ta Klang. This is the home of the Suay people, who migrated from southern Cambodia several centuries ago and whose expertise with elephants is renowned. Until recently, teams of Suay would go into Cambodia to capture wild elephants and bring them back for training. But civil turmoil in Cambodia and the elephants' vast appetites have led to their replacement by heavy machinery—the beasts and their mahouts have become little more than a tourist attraction here and throughout Thailand. Many an elephant and his mahout travel now to Bangkok and even as far as Phuket, where tourists pay B20 to feed the animal a banana or B400 to take an hour's ride.

Recently, TAT and Thai Airways International have contributed to an Elephant Study Center in Ban Ta Klang. (A mobile medical unit there provides basic treatment, so the animals won't have to go to the elephant hospital in Lampang.) Elephant shows are given on weekends at the newly built arena. Tentatively, performances are scheduled during the winter months for 9:30 AM on Saturday, though times do change (we caught a show on a Saturday afternoon), so inquire first (☎ 044/512925 or 044/516053).

On your return south from Ban Ta Klang, 15 km (10 mi) before Surin, a small road leads off to the left to **Ban Choke,** a village once famous for its excellent silk where now silver jewelry is also made. You can find bargains in bracelets and necklaces with a minimal amount of negotiation.

Lodging

$$　**🏨 Tharin Hotel.** Surin's newest (and only high-rise) hotel (1990) is about a 10-minute walk from the center of town. The lobby and public reception areas are kept shining, and light flooding in through tall glass windows reflects off the polished marble. Rooms are done in light pastels or burnt browns, and have wall-to-wall carpeting, TV, telephones, a table, and two chairs. Bathrooms are large. Ask for a corner room and you'll have good city views and lots of light. In the evenings, the Darling Cocktail Lounge attracts local swells, and the disco swings on weekends. ⊠ *60 Sirirat Rd., 32000, ☎ 045/514281, FAX 045/511580. 160 rooms and 35 suites. Restaurant, bar, coffee shop, sauna, nightclub, meeting rooms. AE, MC, V.*

$ 🏨 **Petchkasem Hotel.** Though the newer Tharin Hotel has smarter creature comforts, the Petchkasem is in the center of town between the bus and railway station. The carpeted guest rooms have air-conditioning, refrigerators, color TV, and not much else. The lobby area is a pleasant sitting area, and the staff is helpful. In the evening, charming hostesses serve drinks in the relaxing ambience of the Bell Cocktail Lounge. ⊠ *104 Jitbamroong Rd., 32000, ☎ 045/511274, FAX 044/ 511041. 162 rooms. Restaurant, lobby lounge, pool, nightclub, meeting rooms. AE, MC, V.*

¢   🏨 **Pirom Guest House.** The owners, who speak English well, make this a choice place to stay if you don't mind very basic accommodation. The Piroms are enthusiastic about the I-san and its traditions and love to explain the region to their guests. Mr. Pirom often arranges tours to off-the-beaten-track villages. They have only five small, fan-cooled rooms (no private baths) in the old-fashioned teak house, but most of your time will be spent in the garden or in the small, homey dining room. The guest house is two blocks west of the market. (The Piroms may move into a newer, larger house in 1999, but they will keep the same telephone number.) ⊠ *242 Krungsrinai Rd., 32000, ☎ 044/ 515140. 6 rooms. Breakfast room. No credit cards.*

Buri Ram

98 km (60 mi) west of Surin, 349 km (220 mi) northeast of Bangkok.

The provincial capital of Buri Ram, less than an hour west of Surin by train or bus, is a rather uninteresting town with little reason for an overnight stay, but, being on the railway line, it is the gateway for those visiting the nearby prasats by public transport. People traveling by car generally use Korat as their base.

Prasat Hin Khao Phanom Rung

㉖   *60 km (34 mi) south of Buri Ram, 65 km (39 mi) west of Surin, 90 km (54 mi) east of Korat.*

The restored hilltop sanctuary of Prasat Hin Khao Phanom Rung is 7 km (4½ mi) by bus or taxi from the village of Nang Rung. It is a supreme example of Khmer art, built in the 12th century under King Suriyaworamann II, one of the great Khmer rulers, and restored in the 1980s at a cost of $2 million. It's one of the few Khmer sanctuaries without later Thai Buddhist additions. The approach to the prasat sets your heart thumping—you cross an imposing naga bridge and climb majestic staircases to the top, where you are greeted by the magnificent Reclining Vishnu lintel. This lintel, spirited away in the 1960s, reappeared at the Chicago Art Institute, and after 16 years of protests and negotiations, was finally returned to its rightful place in Thailand. Step under the lintel and through the portal, and you are within the double-walled sanctuary. Intricate carvings in a style similar to those found in Lopburi cover the interior walls, and in the center of the prasat stands the great throne room dedicated to Brahma Lord Siva.

Scattered in the area are other Khmer prasats in various stages of ruin, overgrown by vegetation, with their millennial stones lying where they have fallen. One of these has been rescued from nature's consumption and prettified by Thailand's Department of Fine Arts. **Prasat Muang Tam** (15 minutes by car south of Phanom Rung; no public bus makes this trip), estimated to be 100 years older than its neighbor, started off as a Hindu sanctuary in the 10th century. Its main building symbolically represents the universe, with lesser towers emanating from the center. Today four towers remain, which contain some marvelous Hindu carving of Shiva and his consort Uma, Varuna on a swan, Krishna with cows, and Indra on the elephant Erawan. The complex is flanked by ceremonial ponds, with five-headed nagas lying alongside.

Prasat Hin Phimae

🕗 *58 km (36 mi) north of Korat; buses leave for Phimae every 15 mins between 6 AM and 6 PM for the 1¼-hr trip.*

Prasat Hin Phimae, the other great Khmer structure of the Northeast (along with Phanom Rung) was probably built sometime in the late 11th or early 12th century, and though the ruins have been restored, they have not been groomed and manicured. Entering the prasat through the two layers—the external sandstone wall and the gallery—is to step back eight centuries, and by the time you reach the inner sanctuary, you're swept up in the creation and destruction of the Brahman gods engraved on the lintels. Gate towers (*gopuras*) at the four cardinal points guard the entrances, with the main one facing south, the route to Angkor. The central white sandstone prang, 60 ft tall, flanked by two smaller buildings, one in laterite, the other in red sandstone, makes an exquisite combination of pink and white against the darker laterite, especially in the light of early morning and late afternoon. The principal prasat is surrounded by four porches, whose external lintels reflect scenes from the Ramayana and depict the Hindu gods. Inside, the lintels portray the religious art of Mahayana Buddhism.

Though I-san covers a third of Thailand, only recently has it been given any attention (however small), for its heritage as part of the Khmer empire. In the 1990s with the support of Princess Maha Chakri Sirindhorn, the excellent **Phimae National Museum** was founded. Its two floors contain priceless treasures from the early settlers of I-san and from the Dvaravatia and Khmer civilizations—notably great works of Khmer sculpture. The museum's masterpiece is a stone statue of King Jayavarman VII of Anghor Thom, found at Phimae. More boundary stones, lintels, and friezes are stacked outside in the garden, and though less interesting to the casual visitor, they are definitely worth a walk past. ⊠ *Tha Songkran Rd.,* ☎ *044/471167.* 🖼 *Admission.* ⊘ *Tues.–Sun. 9–4.*

You may want to drive about 2 km (1¼ mi) from the ruins to see **Sai Ngam,** the world's largest banyan tree, whose mass of intertwined trunks supports branches that cast a shadow of nearly 15,000 square ft. Some say that it is 3,000 years old. On weekends, the small nearby park has stalls selling *patnee* (noodles) and fried chicken for picnics.

Lodging

$ 🏨 **Phimae Hotel.** Phimae has limited tourist facilities and only very basic hotels, of which the Phimae is about the best, but that is not saying much. Though the rooms are clean, and so are the sheets, that typical musty odor of neglected up-country hotels pervades. Only a bottom sheet is provided, along with a blanket, which, with the air-conditioning, you'll need. You may want to request two extra sheets and place the well-used blanket between them, which covers the blanket and feels more comfortable against your skin. (In these older up-country hotels the hotel management always supplies the sheets without cost or question.) ⊠ *305/1–2 Haruthairom Rd., 30100,* ☎ *044/471306,* FAX *044/ 471918. 40 rooms. No credit cards.*

Nakhon Ratchasima

㉘ *54 km (34 mi) southwest of Phimae, 259 km (160 mi) northeast of Bangkok.*

Most tourists use Nakhon Ratchasima (Korat) as a base for visiting Phimae and Buri Ram. It is I-san's major city, with a population of over 200,000, and it is considered the gateway to the Northeast. You will probably not want to spend many daytime hours here, but between 6 and 9 PM, head to the **Night Bazaar** in the center of town. A block-long street is taken over by food stands and shopping stalls and is crowded with locals in a festive atmosphere.

A side trip to **Pak Thongchai Silk and Cultural Center,** 32 km (20 mi) south of Korat, offers a chance to see the complete silk-making process, from the raising of silk worms to the spinning of thread and weaving of fabric. You can also buy silks at some 70 factories in the area. Try the **Srithai Silk** showroom (⊠ 333 Subsiri Rd., ☎ 044/441588) in Pakthongchai. For ceramics, drive out to the village of **Ban Kwian,** 15 km (10 mi) southwest of Korat. The rust-color clay here has a tough, ductile texture and is used for reproductions of classic Thai designs.

Korat also serves as a base for a trip to **Khao Yai National Park,** southwest of town, which covers 2,168 square km (833 square mi) in four provinces, providing fresh air, hiking, and four golf courses for Thais from Bangkok.

From Korat, Thailand is your oyster. Bangkok is four hours away by train, via Ayutthaya and Don Muang Airport, and there are direct buses to Bangkok (256 km/159 mi), Pattaya (284 km/176 mi), Rayong (345 km/214 mi), Chiang Rai (870 km/539 mi), Chiang Mai (763 km/473 mi), and Phitsanulok (457 km/283 mi).

Lodging

$$–$$$ 🏨 **The Royal Princess.** This is the newest (1994) hotel in town, and it perhaps has just the edge over the Sima Thani. The expansive lobby gives way to a comfortable lounge—two army officers were snoozing in it during our last visit. The staff is efficiently professional and helpful. The coffee shop looks out onto a small garden and rectangular pool, and the surrounding concrete buildings create a strong glare in the noonday sun. The large rooms are furnished in pastels, and most have queen-size beds. The formal restaurant serves the best Cantonese food in town. The hotel's drawback, like that of the Sima Thani, is that it's 3 km (2 mi) from downtown. ⊠ *1/37 Surenarai Rd., 30000,* ☎ *044/256629,* FAX *044/ 256601. 186 rooms. Restaurant, coffee shop, pool, 2 tennis courts, health club, business services, meeting rooms. AE, DC, MC, V.*

$$–$$$ 🏨 **Sima Thani Hotel.** Opened in April 1992 on the outskirts of Korat (a B40 tuk-tuk ride from the Night Bazaar), this sparkling hotel is well-accustomed to tourists and businessmen and its outdoor buffet is the best place to dine. It is designed around a hexagonal atrium lobby. Furnishings in the guest rooms are not inspired but are comfortably unobtrusive. Each room has two queen-size beds, a table and chairs, and a good working desk (except for an inadequate reading lamp). Bathrooms come with hair dryers, telephones, and toiletries. The coffee-shop dining room is open 24 hours, the Chinese restaurant is Cantonese, and best of all is the extensive evening buffet outdoors, with musicians and classic I-san dancers every night except Monday. Most of the staff knows some English, and service is extremely professional. ⊠ *Mittraphap Rd., Tambon Nai Muang, 30000,* ☎ *044/243812,* FAX *044/251109. 135* *rooms. Restaurant, coffee shop, piano bar, pool, massage, health club, meeting rooms. AE, DC, MC, V.*

$ ▣ **Chansurang.** In the heart of town, minutes away from the Night Bazaar, this was once Korat's main hotel. It then deteriorated, but recent renovations have smartened up the rooms and added modern amenities. The lobby area has been redesigned, and the reception staff gives clients a warm welcome. The restaurant serves Thai dishes, including I-san specialties, and Western food. ✉ *2701/2 Mahadthai Rd., 30000,* ☎ *044/ 257060,* ℻ *044/252897. 157 rooms. Restaurant, pool. MC, V.*

The Central Plains and I-san Essentials

Arriving and Departing

I-san

BY AIRPLANE

All air traffic to the Northeast radiates from Bangkok, with daily flights on **Thai Airways International** between the capital and Khon Kaen, Udon Thani, Nakhon Phanom, Ubon Ratchathani, and Korat.

BY BUS

Many of the towns in the Northeast are served by direct air-conditioned and non-air-conditioned buses from Bangkok's Northern Bus Terminal on Phahonyothin Road. The fares are slightly lower than those for the train. From Phitsanulok there is daily service to Loei and then on to Khon Kaen and Nong Khai. There are also daily direct buses that connect Chiang Mai and the major provincial capitals in the Northeast.

BY TRAIN

Northeastern Railways has frequent service from Bangkok to Nakhon Ratchasima, where the line splits. One route runs east, stopping at Buri Ram, Surin, and Si Saket before terminating at Ubon Ratchathani; the other line goes north, stopping at Khon Kaen and Udon Thani before arriving at Nong Khai. Both routes have daytime express and local trains and an overnight express train with sleeping cars. The Ubon Ratchathani sleeper leaves Bangkok at 9 PM to arrive at 7:05 AM and departs from Ubon Ratchathani at 7 PM to arrive in Bangkok at 5:20 AM. The Nong Khai sleeper departs from Bangkok at 10:30 PM to arrive at 7:30 AM and on the return trip leaves Nong Khai at 7 PM to be back in Bangkok at 6 AM.

Phitsanulok

BY AIRPLANE

With three direct flights each day, **Thai Airways International** connects Phitsanulok with Bangkok (B920) and Chiang Mai (B650). Taxis meet incoming flights.

BY BUS

Buses run frequently to Phitsanulok from Chiang Mai, Bangkok, and Sukhothai. Bus service also connects Phitsanulok to eastern Thailand. Long-distance buses arrive and depart from the intercity bus terminal, 2 km (1¼ mi) northeast of town.

BY TRAIN

Phitsanulok is about halfway between Bangkok and Chiang Mai. On the rapid express, it takes approximately six hours from either city. Some trains between Bangkok and Phitsanulok stop at Lopburi and Ayutthaya, enabling you to visit these two historic cities en route. A special express train between Bangkok and Phitsanulok takes just over five hours. Tickets for this service, which cost 50% more than those for regular second-class travel, may be purchased at a separate booth inside the Bangkok and Phitsanulok stations; reservations are essential.

Sukhothai

BY AIRPLANE

Bangkok Airwaysoperates a daily direct flight to Sukhothai from Bangkok and Chiang Mai. The airport, between Sukhothai and Si Satchanalai, is a 35-minute ride from Sukhothai. Alternatively, you can use **Thai International** into Phitsanulok and take an hour-long bus or taxi ride to Sukhathai.

BY BUS

Buses depart from Phitsanulok's intercity bus terminal, located on the northeast edge of town. The Sukhothai bus, however, makes a stop just before the Naresuan Bridge. These buses end their journey in New Sukhothai; you can take the minibus at the terminal to Old Sukhothai. Buses go directly to Sukhothai from Chiang Mai's **Arcade Bus Station** (☎ 053/242664); the trip takes five hours and costs B100. The bus trip from Bangkok's **Northern Bus Terminal** (☎ 02/279–4484) takes seven hours and costs B140.

Getting Around

I-san

BY BUS, BICYCLE, AND CAR

Between cities, there are buses throughout the day, from about 6 AM to 7 PM. In towns, the bicycle samlors and songthaews are plentiful. Rental cars, with or without a driver, are available in the provincial capitals.

Phitsanulok

Most sights in Phitsanulok are within walking distance, but bicycle samlors are easily available. Bargain hard for a proper fare—most rides are about B20. Taxis are available for longer trips; you'll find a few loitering around the station.

Sukhothai

Bicycle samlors are ideal for getting around New Sukhothai, but take either a taxi (B120) or a local bus (B5) to travel the 10 km (6 mi) from New Sukhothai to Old Sukhothai (Muang Kao) and the Historical Park. Buses depart from the local terminal, located 1 km (½ mi) on the other side of Prarong Bridge.

The best means of transportation around the Historical Park is a rented bicycle (B30 for the day). If you don't have much time, you can hire a taxi from New Sukhothai for B300 for a half day. The drivers know all the key sights. Within the park, a tourist tram takes visitors to the major attractions for B20.

Contacts and Resources

Emergencies

NAKHON RATCHASIMA

Emergency number (☎ 191). **Police** (☎ 044/242010). Maharat Hospital (⊠ Chang Phuak Rd., ☎ 044/254990).

NONG KHAI

Police (☎ 042/411020). **Nong Khai Provincial Hospital** (⊠ Meechai Rd., ☎ 042/411504).

PHITSANULOK

Police (☎ 055/240199). **Phitsanuwej Hospital** (⊠ Khun Piren Rd., ☎ 055/252762).

SUKHOTHAI

Police (☎ 055/611199). **Sukhothai Hospital** (☎ 055/611782).

UBON RATCHATHANI

Police (☎ 045/254216). **Rom Gao Hospital** (✉ Auparat Rd., ☎ 045/254053).

Visitor Information

I-SAN

Tourism Authority of Thailand/Tourist Police (✉ 2102–2104 Mittraphap Rd., Nakhon Ratchasima 30000, ☎ 044/243427; ✉ 264/1 Khuan Thani Rd., Ubon Ratchathani 34000, ☎ 038/377008).

PHITSANULOK/SUKHOTHAI

TAT/Tourist Police (✉ 209/7–8 Boromtrailokanat Rd., Phitsanulok 65000, ☎ 055/252742), open weekdays 9–4:30.

THE SOUTHERN BEACH RESORTS

The resorts of southern Thailand's long peninsula are pure hedonism. Everything is here for the wanting, from five-star luxury hotels to dirtcheap bungalows, from water sports to golf, from sleazy bars to elegant dining rooms, from beaches washed by azure waters to verdant hills, from exotic fruit to bountiful seafood and, we regret to say, pizza and hamburgers. The Andaman Sea and the Gulf of Siam have become international playgrounds.

Phuket

Backpackers discovered Phuket in the early 1970s. The word got out about its long, white, sandy beaches and cliff-sheltered coves, its waterfalls, mountains, clear waters, scuba diving, fishing, seafood, and fiery sunsets—with rainbow colors shimmering off the turquoise Andaman Sea. Entrepreneurs built massive developments, at first clustering around Patong, and then spreading out. Most formerly idyllic deserted bays and secluded havens now have at least one hotel impinging on their beauty, and hotels are still being built despite a shortage of trained staff and an overburdened infrastructure. Prices have escalated to a point where staying here costs about half as much again as in Bangkok. Even the local Director of Tourism admits that Phuket has become overpriced. Charter flights continue to bring tourists from Europe, especially Germany, and during the peak season Phuket's 20,000 hotel rooms are jammed to capacity. Phuket's popularity still continues, perhaps because it is large enough (so far) to absorb the influx, though more and more visitors are cutting their visits short and moving to less commercial pastures.

Shaped like a teardrop pendant with many chips, Phuket is linked to the mainland by a causeway. Its indented coastline and hilly interior make the island seem larger than its 48-km (30-mi) length and 21-km (13-mi) breadth. Before the tourists came, Phuket was already making fortunes out of tin mining (it is still Thailand's largest tin producer) and rubber plantations. Although the west coast, with its glittering sand beaches, is committed to tourism, other parts of the island still function as normal communities, largely untainted by the influx of foreign vacationers. Typically, tourists go directly to their hotels on arrival, spend most of their vacation on the beach, and make only one or two sorties to visit other parts of the island. Hence, the sights and places (mostly beaches) are listed in a counterclockwise itinerary, beginning with Phuket Town, the provincial capital and only real town on the island.

Phuket Town

❶ *862 km (539 mi) south of Bangkok.*

About one-third of the island's population lives in Phuket Town, the provincial capital, but very few tourists stay here. The town is busy, and drab modern concrete buildings have replaced the old Malay Colonial–type architecture. A few hours of browsing through the tourist shops are not wasted, however. Most of the shops and cafés are along Phang-Nga Road and Rasda Road. By bus, you arrive in Phuket on the eastern end of Phang-Nga Road.

Phuket Town's main street (and where many hotel shuttles drop you off) is Rasda Road, and the sidewalk tables in front of the **Thavorn Hotel** provide a good place to do a little people-watching while sipping a cold beer. Going east from there along Rasda Road, an immediate right puts you on Phuket Road, with, on the left, the **TAT office** and the **Tourist Police.** West on Rasda Road after the traffic circle (Bangkok Circle) you come to Ranong Road, with, on the left, the **local market,** Phuket Town's busiest and most colorful spectacle—a riot of vegetables, spices, meats, sellers and buyers, and rich aromas. On the next block of Ranong Road you come to the **Songthaew Terminal,** where you get the minibus to Patong, Kata, Kamala, Karon, Nai Harn, and Surin beaches. Songthaews for Rawai and Nai Harn beaches stop at Bangkok Circle. The **Provincial Town Hall,** diagonally across town from the market, was used as the French Embassy in the movie *The Killing Fields.*

2 Perhaps the most relaxing way to see Phuket is from the top of **Khao Rang** (Rang Hill) northwest of town. The elevation permits a view of both Phuket Town and the island's interior.

Lodging

$$$ 🏨 **Metropole.** If you come to Phuket Town on business, you should stay at the best and newest hotel—the Metropole. A sparkling, crisp, marble lobby greets you; there's a spacious lounge bar for cool comfort during the day, and a karaoke bar for fun at night. The very handsome Chinese restaurant, the Fortuna Pavilion, offers a dim sum lunch. For Western food in a steak-house atmosphere, try the Metropole Café. Guest rooms are bright, with picture windows and furnishings in pastel colors. ✉ *1 Soi Surin, Montri Rd., Phuket Town 83000,* ☎ *076/214022,* 📠 *076/215990. 248 rooms. 2 restaurants, lobby lounge, pool, health club, business services, meeting rooms. AE, DC, MC, V.*

Thai Cultural Village

3 *5 km (3 mi) north of Phuket Town.*

The Thai Cultural Village, north of Phuket Town, has a 500-seat amphitheater, where it presents various aspects of southern Thai culture: classical Thai dance, shadow puppet shows, Thai boxing exhibitions, sword fighting, an "elephants-at-work" show, and more. ✉ *Thepkasati Rd.,* ☎ *076/214860.* 🎟 *Admission.* ⊙ *Show times: 10:15, 11, 4:45, 5:30.*

Heroines Monument

4 *12 km (7 mi) north of Phuket Town.*

On the airport highway at a crossroads, you'll notice a statue of two women, the *Heroines Monument.* In 1785 these women rallied the Thais to ward off a siege by the Burmese, who had sacked Ayutthaya four years earlier.

The **National Museum,** nearby, has exhibits displaying the way of life and history of Phuket, including dioramas of the heroines. ☎ *076/ 311426.* 🎟 *Admission.* ⊙ *Wed.–Sun. 10–4.*

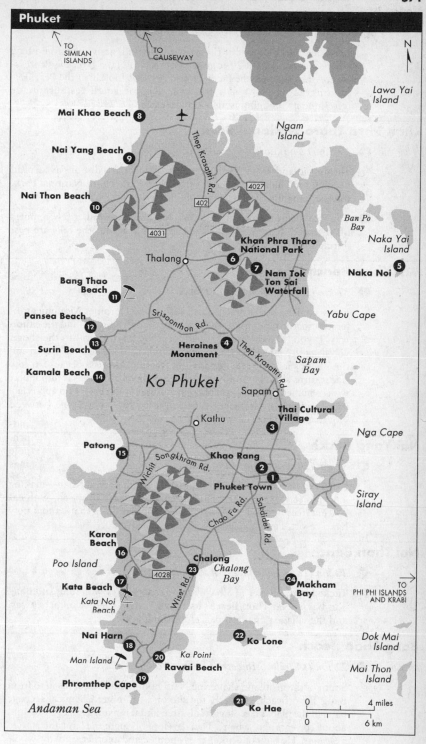

Phuket

TO SIMILAN ISLANDS

TO CAUSEWAY

N

Lawa Yai Island

Mai Khao Beach ⑧

Ngam Island

Nai Yang Beach ⑨

4027

Ban Po Bay

Naka Yai Island

402

Nai Thon Beach ⑩

Thep Krasattri Rd.

4031

Khan Phra Tharo National Park ⑥

Thalang

⑦ Nam Tok Ton Sai Waterfall

Naka Noi ⑤

Bang Thao Beach ⑪

Srisoonthon Rd.

Yabu Cape

Pansea Beach ⑫

Heroines Monument ④

Sapam Bay

Surin Beach ⑬

Thep Krasattri Rd.

Kamala Beach ⑭

Ko Phuket

Sapam

Thai Cultural Village ③

Nga Cape

Kathu

Patong ⑮

Wichit Songkhram Rd.

Khao Rang

② ①

Phuket Town

Siray Island

Chao Fa Rd.

Sakdidet Rd.

Karon Beach ⑯

Poo Island

Chalong ㉓

Chalong Bay

4028

Wiset Rd.

㉔ Makham Bay

TO PHI PHI ISLANDS AND KRABI

Kata Beach ⑰

Kata Noi Beach

Nai Harn ⑱

Ka Point

㉒ Ko Lone

Dok Mai Island

Man Island

⑳ Rawai Beach

⑲ Phromthep Cape

Mai Thon Island

Andaman Sea

㉑ Ko Hae

0   4 miles

0   6 km

Naka Noi

⑤ *26 km (16 mi) northeast of Phuket Town.*

By taking the road east at the crossroads you'll arrive at Ban Po Bay, where you can take a 20-minute boat ride to Naka Noi, the Pearl Island. After you tour the facilities and perhaps look in at the Pearl Extracting Show at 11 AM, you can visit the small restaurant for refreshments. Lodging is also available (☎ 076/213723).

Khan Phra Tharo National Park

⑥ *19 km (12 mi) north of Phuket Town.*

Turning inland from Ban Po on the small, partially unpaved road heading for Thalang, you'll traverse Khan Phra Tharo National Park, the last remaining virgin forest on Phuket.

⑦ You may want to stop at **Nam Tok Ton Sai Waterfall,** a few minutes off the road. It's a popular picnic spot all year, but the falls are best during the rainy season.

Mai Khao Beach

⑧ *37 km (23 mi) northwest of Phuket Town.*

From Thalang, a few miles northwest of the Heroines Monument intersection, the main road continues north to the airport and the causeway. If you take the airport road west for 5 km (3 mi) to the shore, you'll get to Mai Khao Beach. This is Phuket's northernmost beach and the island's largest, often ignored by Western tourists because at low tide it turns slightly muddy, and its steep drop-off makes it unpopular with swimmers. The absence of farangs attracts the Thais, who appreciate its peacefulness. Giant sea turtles like it, too: they come between November and February to lay their eggs.

Nai Yang Beach

⑨ *34 km (20 mi) northwest of Phuket Town.*

Nai Yang Beach is really a continuation south of Mai Khao—making a 10-km (6-mi) stretch of sand. It curves like a half-moon, with casuarina trees lining the shore. It is also popular with Thais, and it now has a resort, Pearl Village.

Nai Thon Beach

⑩ *30 km (18 mi) northwest of Phuket Town.*

Tucked in the center of a headland that separates Nai Yang and Bang Tao Bay is Nai Thon Beach. Its rough waters keep swimmers away, and the village remains a peaceful fishing port.

Bang Thao Beach

⑪ *22 km (14 mi) northwest of Phuket Town.*

South of the headland sheltering Nai Thon, the shore curves in to form Bang Thao Beach, formerly the site of a tin mine. Chemical seepage had left the place an ecological disaster, and it remained an eyesore until about 10 years ago, when a Thai developer bought the land and started a cleanup. He built one hotel, then another, and another, until the whole bay became a resort area with five major hotels offering, in total, 2,000 rooms and 27 restaurants. All the hotels—the Banyan Tree, Dusit Laguna, Laguna Beach Club, Sheraton Grande Laguna, and Allamanda—cater to the affluent tourist. A free shuttle service travels between them, guests can use the pool facilities of any hotel in the group, and a cross-dining plan permits guests of any one hotel to dine at any other and simply sign the check. The Dusit and the Sheraton have the best beaches.

Dining and Lodging

$$$$ ✕⌦ **Banyan Tree Phuket.** Of the five resort hotels at Laguna Beach on Bang Thao Bay, this is the most exclusive—and expensive. Built along classical European lines, but with teak floors and Thai fabrics, it gives a sense of entering a hedonistic Greek compound. Indeed, many guests come for the rejuvenation treatments that include herbal massages, special diets, and exercise. When not being pampered at the spa center, you can stay in your private villa—a secluded enclave whose bathroom, with an extra outdoor shower, is as big as the spacious bedroom. The king-size bed is enthroned on a raised platform and, lying on it wrapped in your toga, you look out onto your private garden. At the end of the garden there's a open-sided gazebo where, if the mood takes you, a masseuse will come and perform miracles on your body. Thirty-four of these villas have their own 9-by-3-meter pools (B5,000 extra). Should you tire of the hotel's two restaurants, you can join the hoi polloi at any of the 28 restaurants at the other Laguna Beach hotels and bill your meals to your room. One negative to staying at this resort is the mosquitoes: they nibble at your ankles when the sun goes down. ⊠ *33 Moo 4 Srisoonthorn Rd., Cherngtalay, Thalang, Phuket 83110,* ☎ *076/324374,* ℻ *076/324356. 98 villas. 2 restaurants, pool, massage, spa, 18-hole golf course, 5 tennis courts, health club, squash. AE, MC, V.*

$$$ ✕⌦ **Dusit Laguna.** Facing a mile-long beach and flanked by two lagoons, this resort hotel is part of the Laguna Beach complex. The hotel rooms, with picture windows opening onto private balconies, have pastel decor and commodious bathrooms. The hotel is popular with upscale Thais seeking refuge from the more commercial areas of Patong and with foreigners who want to stay in a sedate, quiet resort yet like to be near a more lively hotel (the Sheraton) when the mood strikes. There's barbecue dining on the terrace and, after dinner, dancing to the latest sounds. European fare is served at the Junkceylon; Thai cuisine, to the tune of traditional Thai music, is served in the Ruen Thai restaurant. Evening entertainment changes nightly and may consist of a song-and-dance troupe of transvestites or classical Thai dance. The cross-dining plan with the other four resorts in the Laguna complex extends your choices of where to eat and be entertained. ⊠ *390 Srisoonthorn Rd., Cherngtalay District, Thalang, Phuket 83110,* ☎ *076/324320, 02/236–0450 Bangkok reservations,* ℻ *076/324174. 233 rooms and 7 suites. 4 restaurants, pool, putting green, 2 tennis courts, windsurfing, boating, meeting rooms, travel services. AE, DC, MC, V.*

$$$ ✕⌦ **Sheraton Grande Laguna.** The Sheraton Grande Laguna, built around a lagoon, is part of the Laguna Beach group. Guests can dine at a range of restaurants, the best of which is the Marketplace, a group of food stands that present a sampling of Asian foods, from grilled native lobster to Mongolian hot pot. There are several other casual restaurants; the more formal Tea House for Chinese seafood; and, for Thai food, the Chao Lay, built on stilts over a lagoon. The beach is just across a grassy lawn, and a 323-meter-long, narrow pool meanders through the hotel complex before opening up into two larger, swimmable pools. The wonderfully spacious rooms are furnished minimally and decorated with indigenous art. All have small private balconies. Bathrooms have a sunken tub that looks appealing but takes forever to fill, so you tend only to use it for a shower. For a large hotel

the service is swift and polite. For more privacy and personal attention, rent one of the 85 one- or two-bedroom "villa suites" in a separate enclave with its own pool, and receive a complimentary breakfast as well as evening cocktails. ⊠ *Bang Thao Bay, 10 Moo 4 Srisoonthorn Rd., Cherngtalay, Thalang, Phuket 83110, ☎ 076/324101, FAX 076/324108. 343 rooms including villa suites. 5 restaurants, 2 pools, 18-hole golf course, 4 tennis courts, windsurfing, boating, nightclub. AE, DC, MC, V.*

Pansea Beach

★ ⑫ *21 km (12 mi) northwest of Phuket Town.*

South of Bang Thao, in a small bay sheltered by a headland, stretches Pansea Beach, virtually a private enclave for two splendid hotels.

Dining and Lodging

$$$$ ✕▦ **Amanpuri.** For taste and elegance, there is no finer place in Thailand—nor is any place quite as expensive. The most basic accommodation costs $370, but a room with a better view—for example No. 105, costs $850. The main building, completely open, with polished floors, modern bamboo furniture, and pitched, thatch roofs, looks over a serene, black-lined swimming pool surrounded by tall palms. The pool is above a sweeping staircase leading down to the secluded beach. Guests stay in individual pavilions, staggered up the hillside and reached by an elevated boardwalk, whose style is distinctly Thai, with broad eaves and swooping roofs. Each suite has a private sundeck with a gazebo; the furnishings are handcrafted of local woods. A split-level bar perched on the hill affords a romantic view of the sunset across the Andaman Sea, and in the beautiful dining room the culinary delights prepared by an enthusiastic French chef (with an Italian touch) will tempt you to return. Try the fresh fish on a bed of vegetables, topped with a sauce sparked by fresh ginger and lemongrass. Thirteen privately owned villas, each with several bedrooms and a pool, are also rented out. ⊠ *Pansea Beach, Cherngtalay, Phuket 83110, ☎ 076/324–333, 02/287–0226 B ngkok reservations, 800/447–7462 in U.S., FAX 076/324100. 40 pavilions and 30 villas. 2 restaurants, bar, pool, 2 tennis courts, windsurfing, boating, shops, travel services. AE, V.*

$$$$ ▦ **Chedi.** There's a special ambience and superior service here, with a
★ feeling that it is an exclusive resort without being overly formal and stiff. As you enter the lobby, you are greeted by a sweeping view of the Andaman Sea and a hexagonal pool, with gardens below that abut the sands of the virtually private beach. Although all the chalets along the hillside face the sea, it is hidden from most of them by swaying palms. One that does have a sea view is No. 106. Each chalet has its own sundeck; inside it's quite compact but pleasantly uncluttered and accentuated by shining wood floors and woven palm walls. The bathrooms, a bit skimpy, have only showers and no baths. The Chedi used to be a bargain but the rates have steadily climbed to around $220—still, that is $150 cheaper than the next-door Amanpuri. ⊠ *118 Moo 3, Pansea Beach, Cherngtalay, Phuket 83110, ☎ 076/324017, FAX 076/324252. 105 rooms. Restaurant, outdoor café, pool, 2 tennis courts, windsurfing, boating, business services, meeting rooms. AE, DC, MC, V.*

Surin Beach

⑬ *20 km (12 mi) northwest of Phuket Town.*

Surin Beach, adjoining Pansea Beach to the south, has a long stretch of golden sand, but it is not good for swimming because of strong currents. On the headland south of Surin you'll find several small, intimate, and romantic coves. Each requires a climb down a cliff, where, with luck, the tiny beach surrounded by palms and rocks is your personal haven. One particularly peaceful cove is **Laem Sing.**

Kamala Beach

⑭ *18 km (11 mi) west of Phuket Town.*

South of a small headland below Surin Beach you come to Kamala Beach, a small curving strip of sand with coconut palms and a few bungalows, a resort hotel, and a delightful, tiny, open-air restaurant called the White Orchid. Beyond this little restaurant a small dirt road leads over a rugged cliff to Patong—passable, but very tricky and not advised even if you are an experienced dirt track motorcyclist. It's best to drive back to the main road that sweeps its way down the west coast.

Dining

$ ✕ **White Orchid.** My favorite place to eat in Phuket, by far, will not
★ be everybody's choice. At the far end of the Kamala Bay Terrace Resort, beyond the Kamala Hotel, where the road peters out to a rutted track, is Eed's little restaurant, with six or seven tables under a thatched cover and two more sitting under palm trees at the water's edge. The menu is limited to what Eed bought that day in the market. If she has the tiger prawns, be sure to have those, and start with her spring rolls—but if you fancy a steak, she may have just what you want. Although most of what she and her sister cook is Thai, she does a couple of Western dishes as well. All is clean, and Eed will prepare the food according to your taste. Best of all, not only is she warm and welcoming, but she speaks English and French—yes, I'm a little bit in love with Eed. ✉ *Kamala Bay,* ☎ *no phone. No credit cards.*

$ ⌂ **Seaside Inn.** A line of bungalows facing a courtyard constitutes this 1998 motel-like inn, in the center of Kamala village, just across the road from the beach. The owner is helpful and enthusiastic, and the air-conditioned rooms are modern and clean, with tiled floors. The queen-size beds have firm mattresses, the minibar supports the TV, and there is a small kitchenette for preparing simple meals. The large bathrooms have hot and cold water, and the accommodation here is a bargain at B1,000—far below the prices generally charged on Phuket. ✉ *88/6 Moo 3, Rimhad Rd., Kamala Beach, Phuket 83000,* ☎ FAX *076/270894. 14 rooms. No credit cards.*

Patong

⑮ *13 km (8 mi) west of Phuket Town.*

Patong is Phuket's mini Pattaya, complete with German restaurants, massage parlors, hustlers selling trinkets, and places like Tatum's, a combined coffeehouse, disco, and go-go dance floor. The 90 lodgings, ranging from deluxe hotels to small cottages, with more than 6,000 double rooms, attest to Patong's popularity among the charter groups flying into Phuket. From about 7 PM on, the main street is lined for about 3 km (2 mi) with stalls selling everything from T-shirts to watches. Down the side streets restaurants offer seafood and Western-style food, and beyond these, one bar crowds out another. Special buses bring hotel guests to Patong for the evening, allowing time for dinner, shopping, and a turn around the café bars, which are full of hostesses of both sexes.

Dining and Lodging

$$ ✕ **Baan Rim Pa.** For classical Thai cooking, come to this restaurant on the cliff at the north end of Patong Beach. The large, open terrace is one of the most attractive settings on Phuket, and the food is pret-

tily presented in traditional style. In fact, the head chef started the Thai Cooking School and has constructed set menus to make ordering simpler for non-Thais. Therein lies the warning: if you like hot and spicy Thai fare, you may be disappointed. ⊠ *100/7 Kalim Beach Rd., Patong,* ☎ *076/340789. AE, MC, V.*

$$ ✕ **Chao Lay at Coral Beach Hotel.** Perched on a bluff overlooking the Andaman Sea and the beach, the Chao Lay open-front restaurant is an ideal spot to enjoy fantastic views and Thai cooking. Dishes include tom kaa gai, *mee krob* (crispy fried noodles with shrimp), spring rolls, and grilled seafood. ⊠ *104 Moo 4, Patong Beach,* ☎ *076/321106. Reservations essential. AE, DC, MC, V.*

$$ ✕ **Mallee's Seafood Village.** An array of international dishes is offered at this restaurant in the center of Patong. Two Thai dishes worth trying are the charcoal-grilled fish in banana leaves and the steamed fish in a tamarind sauce. If you want Chinese food, try the shark steak in a green-pepper sauce; for European fare, consider the veal sausage with potato salad. On the other hand, you may simply want to sit at one of the sidewalk tables and indulge in pancakes with honey. ⊠ *94/4 Taweewong Rd., Patong,* ☎ *076/321205. AE, DC, MC, V.*

$$$ ✕🏠 **Diamond Cliff Hotel.** North of town, away from the crowds, this is one of the smartest and most architecturally pleasing resorts in Patong. The beach across the road has mammoth rocks that create the feeling of several private beaches. The swimming pool is built on a ledge above the main part of the hotel, providing an unobstructed view of the coast and the Andaman Sea. Rooms are spacious, full of light, and decorated in pale colors to accentuate the open feel of the hotel. Dining is taken seriously, with the fresh seafood cooked in European or Thai style. Guests may dine indoors or on the restaurant's terrace looking out to sea. ⊠ *61/9 Kalim Beach, Patong, Kathu District, Phuket 83121,* ☎ *076/340501, 02/246–4515 Bangkok reservations,* FAX *076/340507. 140 rooms. Restaurant, bar, lobby lounge, pool, boating, travel services. AE, MC, V.*

$$ 🏠 **Paradise Resort.** Of many similar moderately priced hotels in Patong, this one on the strip facing the beach has more appeal than those in the thick of the restaurants, shops, and bars. The Paradise has reasonably large rooms and clean bathrooms, a pool, and a coffee shop/dining room for light Thai and Western fare. ⊠ *93 Taweewong Rd. (next to the Holiday Inn), Patong 83121,* ☎ *076/340172,* FAX *076/295467. 16 rooms. Restaurant, pool, travel services. MC, V.*

$$ 🏠 **Phuket Cabana.** This hotel's attraction is its location, in the middle of Patong, facing the beach. Laid-back and casual describes guests as well as staff, but the basic resort amenities are here, with a good tour desk and a reputable dive shop to arrange outings. Modest rooms are in chalet-type bungalows furnished with rattan tables and chairs. The Charthouse restaurant serves grilled Western food and a modest selection of Thai dishes. ⊠ *80 Taweewong Rd., Patong Beach, Phuket 83121,* ☎ *076/340138, 02/278–2239 Bangkok reservations,* FAX *076/ 340178. 80 rooms. Restaurant, pool, dive shop, travel services, airport shuttle. AE, MC, V.*

Karon Beach

🔟 *20 km (12 mi) southwest of Phuket Town.*

Karon Beach, south of Patong, is divided into two areas. Karon Noi, a small bay surrounded by verdant hills, is truly beautiful but virtually taken over by Le Meridien Hotel, a huge resort with a meandering swimming pool, and many restaurants and shops, ever processing the next batch of vacationers. Occasionally, cruise ships anchor offshore, doubling the crowds. Because of its good swimming and surfing, the other part, Karon Yai, is becoming increasingly popular, and several hotels and a minitown have sprung up, although perhaps because of all this new building, it lacks an identity and seems to be only a strip of beach with hotels.

Dining and Lodging

$$ ✕ **On the Rock.** This 100-seat restaurant on three levels, perched on the rocks overlooking Karon Beach, has a wonderfully romantic setting surrounded by tropical plantings. Three baby reef sharks lazily glide in an aquarium tank, glancing at the diners. Seafood is the specialty: try the *her thalee kanom khrok* (mackerel with fresh tomato and onion) and the *pla goh tod na phrik* (snapper in a pepper and chili sauce) with rice. Those not partial to this Thai fare can choose Italian pasta dishes. ✉ *Marina Cottages, south end of Karon Beach,* ☎ *076/381625. AE, MC, V.*

$$$$ 🏨 **Le Meridien.** This self-contained resort occupying a small bay is designed to keep you so fully occupied that you never need to bother with the rest of Phuket. The U-shape bay is good for the water sports, though it limits strolling on the beach. Most of the hotel guest rooms, which are furnished in rattan and teak, have lovely views of the sea. The focus of the guests (mostly on packaged holidays from Europe), seems, however, to be on the two large swimming pools, complete with an island planted with palm trees. The complex, on 48 acres with 400 rooms, long passageways, and multiple shops, restaurants, and bars, has the feel of an international vacation camp, but if you're looking for one place to meet all your holiday needs, Le Meridien could be your answer. ✉ *Karon Beach, Box 277, Phuket 83000,* ☎ *076/340480,* FAX *076/340479. 470 rooms. 7 restaurants, 3 bars, 2 pools, 4 tennis courts, health club, squash, meeting rooms. AE, DC, MC, V.*

$–$$ 🏨 **Marina Cottages.** The 50 small cottages here, straddling the divide
★ between Karon and Kata beaches, all have verandas with views of either the ocean or palm trees. Those closer to the beach are more spacious than those up the hill, but all have air-conditioning, tiled floors, balconies, and private bathrooms. The pool, nestled among rock outcroppings, is surrounded by tropical foliage. ✉ *Box 143, Phuket 83000,* ☎ *076/330625,* FAX *076/330516. 104 rooms. 2 restaurants, pool. AE, MC, V.*

Kata Beach

�🄸 *22 km (13 mi) southwest of Phuket Town.*

Kata Beach is the next beach south of Karon Beach. The sunsets are as marvelous as ever, but the peace and quiet are fading fast. Club Méditerranée has moved in, but there are still stretches of sand with privacy, and the center of town has only a modest number of bars. Nearby, on Kata Noi Beach (*noi* means small) in the shelter of a forest-clad hill, a few inexpensive bungalows share the quiet beach with the Kata Thani Hotel, popular with tour groups.

Dining and Lodging

$$$ ✕🏨 **Boathouse Inn & Restaurant.** With all 33 rooms looking onto Kata
★ Beach, an excellent Thai restaurant facing the Andaman Sea, and a relaxing beach bar, this small hotel is a very comfortable retreat. The Thai-style architecture adds a traditional touch to the otherwise modern amenities, such as bedside control panels and a Jacuzzi pool. Guest rooms are furnished in reds and browns and have individually controlled air-conditioning, private safes, and bathrooms with baths and massage showers. Though the restaurant is air-conditioned, it's best to sit on the veranda listening to gentle music from a small band. Try the *kung thot keeow:* fried shrimp paste with green curry, full of herbs and spices, garnished

with basil leaves and strips of red chili, and served on thin, crisp pastry shells. ✉ *2/2 Patak Rd., Kata Beach, Phuket 83100, ☎ 076/330015, 02/253–9168 Bangkok reservations, 800/526–6566 U.S. reservations, 071/537–2988 U.K. reservations,* FAX *076/330561. 33 rooms. Restaurant, bar, beauty salon, travel services. AE, DC, MC, V.*

$ ✕🅣 **Friendship Bungalows.** A four-minute walk from the beach, two rows of single-story buildings contain modest, sparsely furnished, but spotlessly clean rooms, each with its own bathroom (there is usually hot water). The owners are extremely hospitable and encourage guests to feel at home. The small restaurant/bar on a terrace offers good Thai food; Western food is also available. What you leave will probably be enjoyed by the two monkeys on the restaurant's wall that play there all day. ✉ *6/5 Patak Rd., Kata Beach, Phuket 83130, ☎ 076/330499. 30 rooms. Restaurant. No credit cards.*

$ 🅣 **Mountain View.** Room prices on Phuket have been on the rise of late, so we were pleased to find this reasonable three-story hotel at the south end of Kata Noi beach. Though the facilities are minimal, it is right across the street from the beach. Rooms are spare, and, after their new coat of paint, look fresh and clean. ✉ *4/7 Kata Noi, Phuket 83130, ☎ 076/330565,* FAX *076/330567. 33 rooms. Restaurant, bar. MC, V.*

Nai Harn

★ ⑱ *18 km (11 mi) southwest of Phuket Town.*

The road south of Kata cuts inland across the hilly headland to drop into yet another gloriously beautiful bay, Nai Harn. Protected by Man Island, this deep bay has been a popular anchorage for international yachtsmen. On the north side, a huge, white-stucco, stepped building, the Phuket Yacht Club, rises from the beach in stark contrast to the verdant hillside. From the Yacht Club's terrace, the view of the sun dropping into the Andaman Sea is superb. The beach is good for sunning and swimming in the dry season, but beware of the steep drop-off.

Dining and Lodging

$$$$ ✕🅣 **Royal Meridien Phuket Yacht Club.** Set in a picturesque, westward-facing bay, this stepped, modern, luxury hotel (now managed by Meridien) looks like an ambitious condominium complex. The architecture aside, its comfort, service, amenities, and secluded location make it extremely pleasant, though we hope some refurbishment is to come. Make a point of dining in the Chart Room, the open-sided restaurant that overlooks the bay (try the baked fresh fish stuffed with prawns in a tasty mixture of Thai spices). The guest rooms are large and have separate sitting areas and private balconies overlooking the beach and the islands (balconies on upper floors are completely hidden from other eyes). ✉ *Nai Harn Beach, Phuket 83130, ☎ 076/381156, 02/251–4707 Bangkok reservations, 071/537–2988 in U.K., 800/526–6566 in U.S.;* FAX *076/381164. 100 rooms and 8 suites. 2 restaurants, bar, pool, 2 tennis courts, health club, windsurfing, boating, travel services. AE, DC, MC, V.*

Phromthep Cape

⑲ *18 km (11 mi) southwest of Phuket Town.*

From the cliff top at Phromthep Cape, the southern point of Phuket Island, the panorama includes Nai Harn Bay, the island's coastline, and the far-off horizon of the Andaman Sea. At sunset, the view is supreme. This evening pilgrimage has become so popular that policemen organize parking, and a row of souvenir stands lines the parking lot. But once you get away from the congestion, you can enjoy the colors of the setting sun in contemplative solitude.

Rawai Beach

20 *16 km (10 mi) southwest of Phuket Town.*

Around the corner from Phromthep, facing south, is Rawai Beach, whose shallow, muddy beach is not so attractive, but whose shoreline, with a fishing village set in a coconut grove, has the charm you may have expected to find in Phuket.

At the southern end of Rawai Beach lies **Chao Le** a small gypsy village, whose inhabitants are descendants of the original tribes living on Phuket. Called Chao Nam (Water People) by the Thais, they tend to shy away from the modern world, preferring to stay among their own. They are superb swimmers, able to fish at 90 ft in free dives. One of the three tribes of the Chao Nam is believed to have been the sea gypsies who pirated 17th-century trading ships entering the Burmese-Singapore waters. Of the three Chao Nam villages on Phuket, the one at Rawai Beach is the easiest to visit.

East of Rawai on **Ka Point,** most of the promontory is owned by the huge Mercure Hotel Phuket Island Resort, which is virtually a small township now run by a French company, with several restaurants, two swimming pools, and a minibus to take guests from one facility to another.

Ko Hae

21 *8 km (5 mi) offshore from Chao Le.*

Cruise boats leave Rawai and Chalong, farther up the coast, for popular Ko Hae (Coral Island), 30 minutes from shore, which has clear water for snorkeling and superb beaches for sunbathing. There is a café on the island and a resort with 40 bungalows.

Ko Lone

22 *6 km (4 mi) north of Ko Hae.*

North of Ko Hae is Ko Lone, another island reached by boat from Rawai or Chalong, with a 30-room resort on its northern shore. Hiring a boat for half a day costs B800.

Chalong

23 *11 km (7 mi) south of Phuket Town.*

South of Phuket Town lies the huge, horseshoe-shape Chalong Bay, whose entrance is guarded by Ko Lone and whose waters are the temporary resting place for yachts making passage from Europe to Asia. Commercial fishing boats also anchor here, and you can catch a boat to Ko Hae and Ko Lone from the jetty. The town of Chalong has several good, inexpensive, outdoor seafood restaurants—try Kan Eang for delicious crabs and prawns. Boats also make the short run over to Ko Raya, a small, tranquil horseshoe-shape island where Jet Skis are banned. The island has a couple of spotless beaches, Ao Tok (best for sunsets) and Ao Siam. Should you wish to spend the night, five small resorts can accommodate you at prices ranging from B500 to B1,000. Book through Pal Travel Services (☎ 076/340551, ext. 1150).

A bit inland from Chalong Bay you'll find **Wat Chalong,** the largest and most famous of Phuket's 20 Buddhist temples—all built since the

19th century. It enshrines the gilt statues, wrapped in saffron robes, of two revered monks who helped quell an 1876 rebellion.

Dining

$$ ✕ **Jimmy's Lighthouse Bar and Grill.** This pub/restaurant, formerly called Latitude 8, is still a hangout for sailors, but many of the sailing crowd now go next door to the marina, and the crowd that gathers here is partly tourists. The food, both Thai and Western, has improved, though, so it's good both for lunch and dinner. ✉ *45/33 Chao Fa Rd., Chalong,* ☎ *076/381709. No credit cards.*

$$ ✕ **Kan Eang.** There are now two Kan Eang restaurants in Chalong. Thais make a point of going to Kan Eang 1; the food is more authentic and spicier than at nearby Number 2. At Number 1, choose a table next to the sea wall under the coconut palms, and order seafood. Choose spicy dishes carefully, and be sure that your waiter understands whether you want Thai *pet* (spicy hot) or to farang taste. Include the succulent and sweet crabs in your order. ✉ *Chalong,* ☎ *076/381323. AE, MC, V.*

Makham Bay

㉔ *11 km (6 mi) east of Chalong Bay, 9 km (5 mi) south of Phuket Town.*

East of Chalong Bay lies a peninsula with the town of Makham Bay, the place to catch the ferryboat to the Phi Phi Islands and then on to Krabi.

OFF THE BEATEN PATH

THE SIMILAN ISLANDS – With some of the world's most interesting marine life, these islands off the west coast in the Andaman Sea are renowned for snorkeling and diving. No hotels are permitted, though there are camping facilities. The underwater sights rival those of the Seychelles and the Maldives, and visibility ranges from 60 to 120 ft. You'll dive in water 10 ft deep down to about 120 ft. The most comfortable way to visit the islands is to take a cruise boat with a sleeping cabin from Phuket. An alternative is to travel north of Phuket to the mainland and up the coast to Tha Talamu in Phang Nga Province, from where boats make the 70-minute run out to the islands on day trips. Several hotels have opened to accommodate tourists. Two of the more comfortable are **Kao Lak Laguna** (✉ 27/3 Mu 1, Bangaisri, Phang Nga 82210, ☎ 01/229–2135, ℻ 01/229–2274) and **Similana Resort** (✉ 4/7 Mu 1, T. Kuk-Kuk, Takuapa District, Phang Nga 82190, ☎ 01/229–2337) which has a delightful private beach. Both hotels charge around B2,500 for a double room in high season.

Ko Phi Phi

In Phuket Bay, 90 mins southeast of Phuket Town; 2 hrs southwest of Krabi.

The Phi Phi Islands used to be idyllic retreats, with secret silver-sand coves, unspoiled beaches, and limestone cliffs that drop precipitously into the sea. But their proximity to busy Phuket and the easy 90-minute journey by ferry from Makham Bay have meant that tourists coming to escape Phuket's commercialism bring that very commercialism with them. Ko Phi Phi became in some ways the poor man's Phuket, with very modest bungalow accommodations for the tattooed budget traveler, but in the late 1990s the cheap bungalows on the better beaches gave way to more expensive accommodations and the backpacker lodging was pushed to the outskirts of the main shopping street. This street, crowded with gift shops, travel agencies, and inferior restaurants, is extremely tacky, but even so it draws tourists in droves, and in high season, Ko Phi Phi is a zoo.

Of the two main islands, **Phi Phi Don and Phi Phi Lae,** only Don is inhabited. It's shaped like a butterfly, with two hilly land portions linked by a wide sandbar, 2 km (1¼ mi) long. Most accommodations and the main mall with its shops and restaurants are on this sandbar, where boats come into a village called **Ton Sai.** No vehicles are allowed on the island; you can disembark at the hotels, on the north cape, if you wish. In the evening, visitors stroll up and down the walkway along the sandbar, where small restaurants display the catch of the day on ice outside. Later in the evening, bars and discos keep the young from their beds. Away from Ton Sai, Ko Phi Phi quiets down where travel is either by serious hiking or by boat, and here you will find some very high-priced resorts, such as the P. P. Palm, in an oasis of greenery fronting a beach.

The most popular way to explore is by either a cruise boat or a long-tailed boat that seats up to six people. One of the most visually exciting trips is to **Phi Phi Lae.** The first stop is **Viking Cave,** a vast cavern of limestone pillars covered with what look like prehistoric drawings but are actually only a few centuries old, depicting Portuguese or Dutch cutters. The boat continues on, gliding by cliffs rising vertically out of the sea, for an afternoon in **Maya Bay.** Here the calm, clear waters, sparkling with color from the live coral, are ideal for swimming and snorkeling. You can take a worthwhile 45-minute trip by long-tailed boat to **Bamboo Island,** which is roughly circular, with a superb beach around it. The underwater colors of the fish and the coral are brilliant. The island is uninhabited, but you can spend a night under the stars if you like.

Dining and Lodging

Restaurants on Phi Phi consist of a row of closely packed one-room cafés down the narrow mall. The menus offer mostly fish dishes—you choose your fish from the ice bin outside, and the chef cooks it according to your instructions. Prices are well under B200 for two people, including a couple of Singha beers. The open-air restaurants to the left of the pier cost more, but the food is essentially the same. The two more luxurious accommodations are off by themselves, 15 minutes by boat or a stiff 45-minute hike from the isthmus.

$$$–$$$$ ✕🏠 **P. P. Palm Beach Travelodge Resort.** This isolated retreat built on a terrace at the north end of the island has standard double rooms, and larger deluxe rooms in bungalows with sea views at twice the price. All rooms are air-conditioned and have small refrigerators and color TV. A new management is in the process of refurbishing all the rooms with the intention of making this the most exclusive resort on Ko Phi Phi. The terraced restaurant, serving Thai and European cuisines, has splendid views of the sea, and the fish is absolutely fresh. ✉ *Cape Laemthong, Phi Phi, 81000,* ☎ *01/229–1052 reservations on Phi Phi, 076/214654 reservations in Phuket,* FAX *01/229–1922. 100 rooms. Restaurant, snorkeling, windsurfing, boating, travel services. AE, V.*

$$–$$$ 🏠 **PP Princess.** In the center of the isthmus, this complex of bungalows in a coconut grove looks a little like a modern housing development, but its air-conditioned units with shiny wood floors are spacious and comfortable. The main building houses a restaurant and a huge lobby where guests, sometimes arriving in large groups, are processed before being shunted off to their bungalows. The complex faces Lohdalum Bay, though only a few bungalows have views. ✉ *Lohdalum Bay, Phi Phi, 81000,* ☎ *075/612188 or 01/723–0495 reservations in Krabi.,* FAX *075/620615. 60 rooms. Restaurant, bar, dive shop. AE, DC, MC, V.*

$$ 🛏 **Cabana Hotel.** Facing the sea amid coconut palms, this newly renovated property offers smart accommodations in the center of Phi Phi at Ton Sai Village, just five minutes from the ferry docks. Rooms are either in the hotel (built 1997) around the swimming pool or in small wood bungalows with a more rustic flavor—the ambience is set by the cane furniture. All have air-conditioning. The outdoor restaurant, like most other restaurants on the island, specializes in fish. ✉ *Ton Sai Beach, Phi Phi, 81000,* ☎ *075/620634,* 𝔽𝔸𝕏 *075/612132. 100 rooms. Restaurant, pool. AE, DC, MC, V.*

$$ 🛏 **Pee Pee Island Village.** This hotel on the north cape offers modest accommodations in small thatched bungalows. It provides the same water sports and tours as its neighbor, P. P. International, but the service is more casual and the atmosphere more laid-back—and less expensive. Views from the hotel are less impressive, however, although guests do have panoramas of the sea and palm-clad hills. ✉ *Cape Laemthong, Phi Phi, 81000,* ☎ *02/277–0038 Bangkok reservations, 076/215014 in Phuket. 65 rooms. Restaurant, snorkeling, boating, travel services. AE, V.*

$ 🛏 **Pee Pee Resort.** This hotel consists of two rows of tiny, thatched, palm-woven huts facing the beach, each with its own Asian-style toilet. A mosquito net is supplied. A small café, attractively located on a small headland, offers basic Thai food. ✉ *250 yards east of ferry dock, Ton Sai, Phi Phi 81000,* ☎ *no phone. 40 rooms. No credit cards.*

Krabi

867 km (538 mi) south of Bangkok, 180 km (117 mi) southeast from Phuket, 43 km (27 mi) by boat east of Ko Phi Phi.

Krabi, the provincial capital of the region, lies across Phuket Bay on the mainland. Once a favorite harbor for smugglers bringing alcohol and tobacco from Malaysia, it has become a fishing port and gateway to the province's islands, particularly Ko Lanta and Ko Phi Phi, and the famous beaches at and around Ao Nang. It is a pleasant, low-key town, but most visitors stop here only to do some shopping, cash traveler's checks, arrange onward travel, and catch up on the news at one of the restaurants on Uttarakit Road. With the opening of an airport in 1999, however, one can expect Krabi to mushroom in size and increase its tourist infrastructure.

Between Krabi and Ao Nang Beach lies **Susan Hoi** (Shell Cemetery Beach), aptly named for the 75-million-year-old shells that have petrified into bizarre-shape rock slabs.

Dining and Lodging

$$ ✕ **Isouw.** This floating restaurant just across from the night market can be a cool place in which to sit, enjoy lunch, and watch the river traffic. It specializes in grilled fish with sweet-and-sour sauce, and the mee krob here has an abundance of fresh, sweet shrimp. ✉ *Krabi,* ☎ *075/611956. Reservations not accepted. No credit cards.*

$–$$ 🛏 **Thai Hotel.** This new hotel ranks as Krabi town's best, though it is primarily for the business traveler rather than the tourist. If you have missed your connections, it serves a purpose for an overnight in Krabi, and the location is convenient—just a block in from the pier. Rooms are uniform and have a two-tone dark blue and pale blue color scheme. Many have a queen-size bed and a single, just in case you bring your mother-in-law. Bathrooms are modern and functional. ✉ *7 Issara Rd., Krabi 81000,* ☎ *075/611122,* 𝔽𝔸𝕏 *075/612556. 82 rooms. Restaurant. MC, V.*

$ 🛏 **Grand Tower Hotel.** This modern five-story guest house is extremely popular with backpackers of all ages. The rooms are large and clean and the bathrooms are modern. All are fan-cooled. The café serves basic

Western fare, and the tour desk is knowledgeable. Many of the long-distance private bus companies stop here. ⊠ *73/1 Uttarakit Rd., Krabi,* ☎ *075/621456,* ℻ *075/621457. 27 fan-cooled rooms with baths. Restaurant, travel services. MC, V.*

Ao Nang

★ *20 km (12 mi) from Krabi Town.*

Ao Nang, less than 20 minutes (a B20 songthaew ride) by road from Krabi, is in the process of being discovered by land speculators. In the early 1990's it was just being discovered by the backpackers. Already, smart modern hotels have replaced most of the thatched bungalows, and the rutted roads are paved; we can expect further growth when the Krabi airport opens in 1999. But even with the development, the fine beaches here are some of Thailand's most attractive and the fascination of the 83 offshore islands and limestone karsts will always remain. Days are spent on the beach or exploring the islands by boat, dipping into the water, snorkeling or scuba diving, particularly around Turtle Island and Chicken Island. Long-tail boats for hire line the beaches, for trips to other islands or to other beaches along the coast.

Around a headland farther on from Ao Nang Bay is **Haad Noppharat Thara,** another beach, less populated than Ao Nang, that's famous for its rows of casuarina trees. You can walk out to the little rocky island at low tide, but don't linger there too long. When the tide comes in, so does a current. For total seclusion, hire a long-tailed boat to take you (15 minutes) to the offshore islands. You can also take a boat back toward Krabi to the beaches of Nam Mao and Railay (the shuttle boat between Ao Nang and Railay costs B30). You can stay at Railay, in the luxury Dusit Rayavadee or in a backpacker-type bungalow, and have a meal in a restaurant or two.

Dining and Lodging

$$$$ ✕▥ **Dusit Rayavadee.** A true retreat, marvelously laid out on 26 land-
★ scaped acres, this resort is on the mainland but is accessible only by boat (20 minutes from Krabi Town or 10 minutes from Ao Nang Bay). Its gardens and coconut groves lead down to white-sand beaches on three sides. This privacy comes dearly: prices start at $330. The modern Thai-style pavilions are circular, with spacious living rooms downstairs and curving staircases to the magnificent bedrooms and sumptuous bathrooms with huge round tubs. The use of highly polished wood and tile floors adds to the cool luxury. Because nearly all the pavilions are between the two beaches that flank the headland, you are never more than a five-minute walk from a beach—you can hear but not see the waves roll in. Krua Pranang, the memorable Thai restaurant in a breezy pavilion one floor up, serves food as exciting as it is delicious. For an appetizer, try the *mieng kana* (Chinese broccoli leaves filled with lime, chili, shallots, and ginger) or the fried sweetened beef and papaya salad served with steamed rice. For entrées, the steamed fish with pickled plum and the tom kha gai are two tasty choices. If you plan to arrive at the hotel directly from Bangkok, you will need to fly into Phuket by 3:30 PM, have a hotel car take you the two hours to a ferry landing, and then take a 10-minute boat ride to the Dusit property. ⊠ *67 Mu 5, Susan Hoy Rd., Tambol Sai Thai, Krabi 81000,* ☎ *075/ 620740, 02/236–0450 Bangkok reservations,* ☎ *800/223–6800 in U.S;* ℻ *075/620630. 98 pavilions. 2 restaurants, bar, snack bar, in-room safes, in-room VCRs, pool. AE, DC, MC, V.*

$$$ ✕▥ **Krabi Resort.** What was once a small collection of thatched cottages on Ao Nang has now mushroomed into a large resort. Rows of attractive wood bungalows are staggered back from the beach. (The first

two rows closest to the beach command a 15% higher price tag, at B3,000.) Furnishings are wood and wicker. Comfortable, nothing fancy. A concrete two-story building at the back of the property offers 40 standard hotel rooms for the same price as the bungalows in the last two rows. There is also a pool in the garden, though the beach has greater attraction. The restaurant is alongside the beach adjoining several other dining establishments, all of which specialize in local seafood. ⊠ *Ao Nang. Reservations:* ⊠ *55–57 Pattana Rd., Amphoe Muang, Krabi 81000,* ☎ *075/637030, 02/637057 Bangkok reservations,* 𝖥𝖠𝖷 *075/ 637057. 103 rooms. Restaurant, pool, boating, nightclub. DC, MC, V.*

$$ ✕⊡ **Emerald Bungalows.** On the quiet, sandy beach of Haad Noppharat, just north of Ao Nang, this hotel offers a choice of bungalows with private baths. Those facing the beach are the best and most expensive (B900). The restaurant serves seafood and Thai dishes and is the place for socializing and reading. ⊠ *Haad Noppharat Beach, Moo 4, Tambol Ao Nang. Reservations:* ⊠ *2/1 Kongca Rd., Krabi 81000,* ☎ *075/ 611106. 36 rooms. Restaurant. No credit cards.*

$–$$$ ⊡ **Ao Nang Villa.** At the other end of the beach from the Krabi Resort stands the new version of the Ao Nang Villa: in place of the bungalows there is now a three-story hotel facing the beach, which curves around a good-size swimming pool and gardens. All rooms have balconies facing the pool. The restaurant pavilion, in gardens of its own next door, serves dinner both under its roof and on the surrounding lawn. The good news is that a few twin-bedded bungalows (B550) still remain, kept only for those in the know. These are fan-cooled and smallish, but with private bathrooms (cold water only) and full access to all the hotel's amenities, they are a great bargain. ⊠ *113 Ao Nang Beach, Krabi 81000,* ☎ *075/637270,* 𝖥𝖠𝖷 *075/637274. 80 rooms. Restaurant, pool, tennis court. MC, V.*

$ ⊡ **Jinda Guest House.** Inexpensive bungalows that appeal to the budget traveler are hard to find in Ao Nang. But there are four guest houses in a row up the main street, 200 yards from the beach. There isn't much difference among them; they all charge B200 for a fan-cooled room and shared bathroom. You may want to try the Jinda first, since breakfasts here are quite reasonable and the owner speaks a little English. ⊠ *Moo 2, Ao Nang, Krabi 81000,* ☎ *01/607–8556. 9 rooms with shared bath. No credit cards.*

$ ⊡ **Railay Bay Bungalows.** This is one of a couple of modest resorts facing the same pretty beach as the Dusit Rayavadee. (Cocos, the cheapest, with tiny units and shared baths, gets an active, friendly, young, backpacking clientele.) The Railay Bay's bungalows start at B400 for a small fan-cooled unit that's back from the beach and go up to B700 for a larger unit closer to the water. There is even one air-conditioned bungalow at B1,600. The two tightly packed rows of bungalows are perpendicular to the beach, extending inland from the beachfront restaurant, which serves inexpensive seafood, Thai dishes, and European breakfasts. ⊠ *Railay Beach, Ao Nang, Krabi 81000,* ☎ *01/228– 4112,* 𝖥𝖠𝖷 *01/228–4516. 30 rooms. Restaurant. No credit cards.*

Phang Nga Bay

★ *100 km (62 mi) north of Phuket, 93 km (56 mi) northwest of Krabi.*

Phang Nga Bay, made famous by the James Bond movie *The Man with the Golden Gun,* lies at the top of Phuket Bay. There are little islands to explore, offshore caves, and karst formations—outcroppings of limestone rising 900 ft straight up from the sea—a splendid sight. You really need a full day to see everything and to appreciate the sunsets, which are particularly beautiful on **Ko Mak.**

The best, really the only, way to visit this bay is by boat. A number of agencies on Phuket run half-day trips, or you can hire a boat locally. Most tourists don't arrive from Phuket until 11 AM. If you can get into the bay before then, it will be more or less yours to explore, with a boatman as your guide. To make an early start, you may want to stay overnight (☞ Dining and Lodging, *below*).

The key sights to visit are **Ko Panyi**, with its Muslim fishing village built on stilts; **Ko Phing Kan**, now known as James Bond Island; **Ko Tapu**, which looks like a nail driven into the sea; **Tham Kaeo grotto**, an Asian version of Capri's Blue Grotto; and **Tham Lot**, where a large cave has been carved into an archway large enough to allow cruise boats to pass through.

Dining and Lodging

$$ ╳🖬 **Phang Nga Bay Resort.** This modern hotel's raison d'être is as a base for exploring the bay, and you can hire a boat here to do so. It's on an estuary 1½ km (1 mi) from the coast, and it does not have panoramic views, but the rooms are comfortable and modern, the bathrooms are clean and large, and the dining room serves reasonable Chinese, Thai, and European food. ✉ *20 Thaddan Panyee, Phang Nga 82000,* ☏ *076/411067, 02/259–1994 Bangkok reservations,* FAX *076/ 411057. 88 rooms. Restaurant, coffee shop, pool, 2 tennis courts. AE, MC, V.*

Ko Samui

500 km (310 mi) south of Bangkok, 30 km (18½ mi) by boat east of Surat Thani.

In the southern Gulf of Thailand lies Ko Samui, the world's coconut capital, discovered by backpackers several years ago, and now regarded as an alternative to Phuket. Already too commercial for some people, it still has far fewer hotels, restaurants, and café/bars than Phuket, and it is a haven of tranquility compared with seedy Pattaya. The island's best food, both Thai and Western, is found at the major hotels; the greatest number of local restaurants are in **Chaweng**, but little distinguishes one from another. Just look to make sure that the seafood is fresh. The TAT has a list of guest houses on the islands, and most travel agencies can make reservations at some of them and at the hotels.

Ko Samui is half the size of Phuket, and could be easily toured in a day. But tourists come for the sun and beach, not for sightseeing, and they usually stay put. We cover the island clockwise. The best beaches, with glistening white sand and clear waters, are on the east coast; the others have either muddy sand or rocky coves. Already the waters around Ko Samui are less clear than they were years ago. The sea surrounding the smaller islands nearby is still crystal clear, however, and the tiny islets of the **Angthong Marine National Park** (☞ *below*) are superb for snorkeling and scuba diving.

New Port

❶ The car ferry from Don Sak on the mainland arrives at **New Port**, 6½ km (4 mi) south of Na Thon, the main town. Unless a hotel van is waiting for you, take a songthaew first to Na Thon, and then another to reach your final destination.

Na Thon

❷ Compared with the other sleepy island villages, **Na Thon** is a bustling town. The passenger ferry from Surat Thani docks here; shops, travel agencies, and restaurants line the waterfront, and local businesses and

Ko Samui

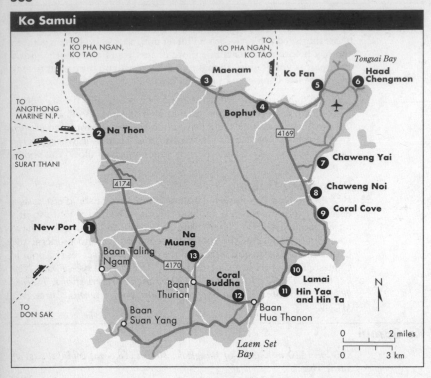

TO
KO PHA NGAN,
KO TAO

TO
KO PHA NGAN,
KO TAO

Tongsai Bay

Maenam ③

Ko Fan ⑤

Haad ⑥
Chengmon

TO
ANGTHONG
MARINE N.P.

Bophut ④

Na Thon ②

4169

Chaweng Yai ⑦

TO
SURAT THANI

4174

Chaweng Noi ⑧

Coral Cove ⑨

New Port ①

Na
Muang

Baan Taling
Ngam

4170 ⑬

N

Coral
Buddha

Baan
Thurian ⑫

Lamai ⑩

⑪ Hin Yaa
and Hin Ta

TO
DON SAK

Baan
Suan Yang

Baan
Hua Thanon

| 0 | | 2 miles |
| 0 | | 3 km |

*Laem Set
Bay*

banks are on the parallel street one block back. Though Na Thon has a hotel, tourists seldom stay in town.

Maenam

③ On the north coast east of Na Thon, the first major tourist area is **Mae-nam.** Its long, curving, sandy beach shaded by trees is lapped by gentle waters that are great for swimming. Inexpensive guest houses and the new luxury Santiburi resort hotel share the 5-km (3-mi) stretch of sand.

LODGING

$$$$ 🖬 **Santiburi.** This resort set on 23 acres of lush, tropical gardens par-
★ alleling the beach is an exclusive hideaway. The standard suites are private bungalows with highly polished wood floors, even in the huge bathrooms, which have two black washbasins, black oval bathtubs, and separate black-tile shower stalls—a typical case of modern Thai opulence. The contemporary Thai furnishings give a warm, open feel that's enhanced by a glass panel between the living room and bedroom. Sliding doors to the patio add more openness, though at the expense of privacy. Each bungalow has its own TV, VCR, and CD player, with free CDs and videotapes. Ask for a bungalow close to the palm-shaded beach. The main building, a modern Thai pavilion overlooking the oval swimming pool, has European and Thai restaurants—the Sala Thai has superb dishes, and guests amble up to the beach bar for informal meals. With a new general manager in place, the staff is wonderfully friendly. From this secluded oasis you can walk to the main road and take a songthaew to any place on the island. ⊠ 12/12 Moo 1, Tambol Maenam, Ko Samui 84330, ☎ 077/425031, 02/238–4790 Bangkok reservations, 800/223–5652 in U.S.; 📠 077/425040. 75 suites. 2 restaurants, snack bar, pool, 2 tennis courts, health club, squash, boating. AE, DC, MC, V.

Bophut

4 A small headland separates Maenam from the next bay, **Bophut.** The beach is quite narrow at Bophut, but still plenty wide enough to laze and jog. During rainy season the runoff waters make the sea slightly muddy, but otherwise this village community is a low-key resort in contrast to the burlesque of Chaweng beach. Hotels and guest houses range from backpacker hangouts to fancier three-star hotels, and a line of pleasant restaurants face the seafront. Stay here if you want to avoid the congestion of tourists and commercialism of the east coast of Samui; generally, you'll find prices here less than in Chaweng or Lamai. Bophut also serves as a staging point for the high-speed boats that go over to Ko Tao every morning at about 8:30.

DINING AND LODGING

$–$$ ✕ **La Sirene.** For a touch of French cooking, try this small bistro on the waterfront with its Provençal air—the owner comes from Nice. A four-course menu beginning with some homemade pâté followed by medallions of beef or pork in a mustard sauce, and then salad and a dessert runs about B220. A la carte dishes, including Thai ones, are also offered. A few tables are inside under cover, but the delight is to sit on the deck overlooking the boats moored a few yards offshore. ✉ *65/1 Bophut Beach,* ☎ *077/425301. No credit cards.*

$ ✕ **Happy Elephant.** Owner Khun Sasothon displays the day's specialty, seafood, on ice in front of his Thai restaurant. Choose the fish that you would like—try it baked in foil over charcoal—have a drink at the bar, and then, when dinner is ready, sit outside on the deck above the beach and dine under the stars, watching the twinkling lights of Ko Pha Ngan across the sea. Other dishes are also served—strongly recommended is the *tom yam pla nam sai* (clear spicy soup with fish). ✉ *79/1 Moo 1, Bophut Beach,* ☎ *077/245347. No credit cards.*

$ ☷ **The Lodge.** Looking a bit like an English roadside inn, this small, two-story, vine-clad hotel has clean, modern rooms, all facing the sea. The spacious air-conditioned rooms have minimal but adequate furnishings and wood floors, with ceiling fans and lockboxes. Bathrooms have both showers and tubs, with hot and cold water. The TV has CNN, and best of all, each room has a balcony. At about B1,000, The Lodge is very good value. ✉ *91/1 Moo 1, Bophut Beach, Ko Samui 84140,* ☎ *077/ 425337,* Ⅲ *077/425336. 10 rooms. Restaurant, bar. No credit cards.*

$ ☷ **Smile House.** Just across the road from the beach, facing the sea, you'll find a group of thatched cottages around a swimming pool in a grove of palm trees. All have neat rattan furniture; some are fan-cooled, and others have air-conditioning, refrigerators, and tubs. ✉ *Bophut Beach, 84140,* ☎ *077/425461,* Ⅲ *077/425239. 18 rooms. Restaurant, bar. No credit cards.*

Ko Fan

5 On the north shore near the northeast tip, you come to **Ko Fan,** a little island with a huge sitting Buddha image covered in moss. Try to visit at sunset, when the light off the water shows Big Buddha at its best. Back across the causeway, on the beach facing the seated Buddha, there are a number of guest houses and bungalows frequented by backpackers who find Bophut too noisy and expensive.

Chengmon

6 Continue east along the north coast to **Haad Chengmon** (*haad* means beach), which is dominated by the headland Laem Rumrong. This is the end of the road for the few songthaews that take this route, and few tourists come here. Several guest houses and an upscale resort are scattered along the shoreline, but you can still find peace and tranquility.

$$$$ ✕🏨 **Tongsai Bay Hotel.** The Tongsai Bay is an elegant resort retreat whose service is not as good as it should be for the price. Set on 25 acres stepped up from the bay, it has whitewashed, red-tile hillside cottages, with balconies looking out to sea (when the view is not blocked by foliage), and 24 rooms in the three-story main building. The cottage rooms are stylishly furnished, and some of the split-level rooms incorporate the natural rock, but they are too closely clustered together. The dining room has beautiful views; reserve a table on the terrace. Ko Samui is known for huge succulent oysters and king prawns, and Tongsai gets the best. The duck in tamarind sauce is also excellent. A shuttle will take you to Na Thon and Chaweng. ✉ *Tongsai Bay, Ko Samui,* ☎ *077/421451, 02/254–0023 Bangkok reservations,* 🖷 *077/421462, 02/253–3190 Bangkok reservations. 80 rooms. Restaurant, bar, pool, 2 tennis courts, windsurfing, boating. AE, DC, MC, V.*

$$$ 🏨 **Boat House Hotel.** This imaginative property across the bay from Tongsai comprises 34 rice barges converted into duplex suites. The whale-like boats in tightly packed rows 100 yards in from the shore look like a Jonah's nightmare, but on board, they're superb. Each has an enclosed upper deck with a lounge and wet bar and, below, a large bathroom with a grand oval tub, a dressing room/sitting area, and the bedroom. The hulls are original; the uncluttered interiors and upper decks are new, with highly polished teak and mahogany beams and paneling. The double beds are just a foot off the floor, while high above are suspended fishing nets. Very nice! Another 176 rooms were built in two wings between the barges and the road. They're less expensive (B3,200 versus B5,400 for a barge suite) but have no sea view. Coral reefs are exposed at low tide, but the swimming is safe and in sheltered waters. The hotel is a little off the beaten track. ✉ *Chengmon Beach, Ko Samui, Surat Thani 84140,* ☎ *077/421451, 02/254–0023 Bangkok reservations,* 🖷 *077/421462. 34 boat suites, 176 rooms. 2 restaurants, pool, 4 tennis courts, windsurfing, boating, travel services. AE, DC, MC, V.*

Chaweng

If you have your own transportation—and don't mind bumping over rutted, unpaved surfaces—the road continues around the peninsula for 6 km (3¾ mi) to Chaweng Beach (also served by the northern songthaew route from Bophut). Of the 11 beach areas of Ko Samui, Chaweng has the finest glistening white sand. But it is also the most congested, crammed with guest houses, hotels, shops, restaurants, and tourists. All this commercial activity enlivens both sides of the one unpaved road, a block in from the beach. It might be seen as a miniature version of Patong Beach on Phuket, but in contrast to the tacky, neon-lighted crass commercialism there, the chaotic Wild West mishmash of buildings and shacks on Chaweng's strip is more fun and more Thai.

❼ **Chaweng Yai** (*yai* means large), the northernmost section, is separated from Chaweng Noi (*noi* means little) by a small point, Laem Koh Faan. Chaweng Yai is divided by a reef into two sections, of which the northern one is a quiet area popular with backpackers. The southern, or main, part is crowded with hotels; tanned, scantily clad youths; and bulbous-breasted German *hausfrauen*. (Thais find it offensive that Western women sunbathe topless, and while they usually say nothing, they give a scornful smile.) Here you will find anything you want, from water-scooter rentals to money changers and nightclubs, like the currently popular **Reggae Pub** (☎ 077/422331), with its many bars and dance floors.

❽ South of this busy beach is **Chaweng Noi,** which is not as fully developed and whose beach has more lively waves. The salt air has yet to be tainted by the odor of suntan oil, but there are many hotels and more on the way.

DINING AND LODGING

$ ✕ **Nakorntorung.** There are prettier places to dine than this open-sided restaurant with concrete floor, Formica-topped tables, and toilet rolls for napkins, but it is hard to find better seafood, Thai curries, and soups. That's why the locals come here, as does a smattering of Westerners who recognize good food and are not put off by the service—the staff is friendly and helpful, just slow. The restaurant is on the main street in the southern part of town diagonally across from the Beachcomber Resort. ✉ *2 Chaweng Beach Rd., Chaweng,* ☎ *077/422500. No credit cards.*

$$$ ▦ **The Imperial Samui.** This resort property is attractively laid out at the top of a landscaped garden terrace with steps leading down to the beach. Guest rooms, which fan out from the main building, are standard, with modern furnishings and little appeal except for the view of the beach. One disadvantage is that wherever you go on the property, you must go up or down steps. Attention is focused on the swimming pool, which contains a small island, complete with three coconut trees. The hotel is at the south end of Chaweng Noi, where the beach isn't crowded and the sea is clean. The restaurant tends to serve too many boring, although bountiful, buffets. ✉ *Chaweng, Ko Samui 84140,* ☎ *077/421390, 02/254–0023 Bangkok reservations,* ℻ *02/253–3190. 77 rooms. Restaurant, bar, pool, windsurfing, boating. AE, DC, MC, V.*

$$ ▦ **Amari Palm Reef Hotel.** This 1993 hotel with an enthusiastic staff is on the part of Chaweng Beach (Chaweng Yai) that's too shallow for swimming; you must walk 500 yards south for that. The hotel has a swimming pool with a swim-up bar. The dining room (mostly Western fare) is one floor up, with a view; the Thai restaurant is in a wood-paneled room to the rear. Half the rooms, in two wings that look onto the pool and garden, are simply functional, with small bathrooms and showers only. The more attractive accommodations are across the road from the beach. They're Thai-style cottages, in small compounds of teak bungalows, like a traditional Thai village. Mattresses are on low platforms above the polished mahogany floor. Large cottages have sleeping lofts, air-conditioning, and small terraces. ✉ *14/3 Moo 2, Tambon Boput, Chaweng Ko Samui 84140,* ☎ *077/422015, 02/251–4727 Bangkok reservations,* ℻ *077/422394. 104 rooms. 2 restaurants, bar, 2 pools, 2 tennis courts, squash. MC, V.*

$$ ▦ **Central Samui Hotel.** The Central Samui, set back from the beach, may not be quite as smart as its neighbor, the Imperial Samui, but it costs less. Guest rooms come with fans or, for a few more dollars, air-conditioning. Equipment for water sports is available, and the restaurant offers views over the gulf. ✉ *Chaweng Noi Beach, Ko Samui 84140,* ☎ *077/421384,* ℻ *077/421385. 50 rooms. Restaurant, bar, coffee shop, windsurfing. AE, MC, V.*

$–$$ ▦ **Fair House.** This hotel right on the beach at Chaweng Noi used to have small, simple bungalows with air-conditioning. Only a couple of these are left, and a modern resort has been constructed, separated from the beach by a swimming pool. Furnishings are simple but adequate—queen-size or twin beds, two cane chairs, a small coffee table, and a television on the minibar. The shower has hot and cold water. The open-front dining room has broad sea views, and the Thai cuisine—with a few Western dishes—is remarkably good. ✉ *Chaweng, Ko Samui 84140,* ☎ *077/ 422327,* ℻ *077/422255. 36 rooms. Restaurant, bar, pool. MC, V.*

$ ▦ **Montien.** Decent-size bungalows here, each with a patio given privacy by tropical foliage, line up perpendicular to the beach. The ambience is spare, but there's an attractive cluster of lights in the ceiling, and well-placed bedside lights make for easy reading. A separate washbasin just outside the bathroom is convenient, and there's a hot and cold shower. At B1,200 the Montien is a good buy, especially if you want to be in the heart of Chaweng's action. ✉ *5 Moo 2, Chaweng, Ko Samui 84140,* ☎ *077/422169,* FAX *077/422145. 25 rooms. Restaurant, bar. MC, V (adds 5% to bill).*

$ ⊡ **O. P. Bungalow.** Among the inexpensive bungalow hotels that line the middle part of Chaweng Beach where it's protected by a reef, this quiet property is efficiently run, and it has clean, simple rooms with hot-water showers. The narrow property has four rows of cottages stretching back from the beach to the road (rates are higher close to the beach). The rooms have tile floors and most have twin beds (with a few doubles). Room 502, with a double (and close to the beach), is a good one to ask for. An open-sided coffee shop down at the beach has reasonably priced Thai and Chinese food. ✉ *111 Chaweng Beach Rd., Chaweng, Ko Samui, Surat Thani 84320,* ☎ *077/422424,* FAX *077/ 422425. 38 rooms. Restaurant. No credit cards.*

Coral Cove

❾ Beyond the Imperial Samui Hotel is **Coral Cove,** popular among scuba divers. But you don't have to be a diver to enjoy the underwater scenery: just walk waist-high into the water and look through a mask to see the amazing colors of the coral. For a Thai seafood lunch, walk up the rocks to Coral Cove Bungalows, where you also can rent snorkeling equipment.

Lamai

A rocky headland separates Chaweng from Ko Samui's second most **❿** popular beach, **Lamai.** It lacks the glistening white sand of Chaweng, but its clear water and rocky pools made this attractive area the first to be developed on Ko Samui (investors only later shifted their get-rich plans to Chaweng). Lamai has more of a steeply shelving shoreline than Chaweng, so few families come here, but it does make the swimming better. Lamai has a different feel from Chaweng; it's not so honky-tonk or congested, though there are plenty of restaurants and bars and enough shops to stir your acquisitive instincts.

Every visitor to Ko Samui makes a pilgrimage to Lamai for yet another reason: at the point marking the end of Lamai beach stand two rocks, **⓫** named **Hin Yaa** (Grandmother Rock) and **Hin Ta** Grandfather Rock). Erosion has shaped the rocks to resemble weathered and wrinkled intimate private parts. It is nature at its most whimsical.

LODGING

$ ⊡ **Golden Sand Beach Resort.** The open lobby and reception area of this hotel are off Lamai's main street. Guest rooms, in two-story buildings, angle out from the reception room and overlook a palm-fringed garden. While the rooms are small, most have air-conditioning (a few less expensive ones are fan-cooled) and each has its own balcony and private bathroom with a shower. The most expensive rooms have a sea view. The coffee shop offers Thai, Chinese, and Western fare, and a beach bar stays open late serving refreshments. ✉ *124/2 Lamai Beach, Ko Samui, Surat Thani 84310,* ☎ *077/424031,* FAX *077/424430. 82 rooms. Coffee shop, bar. MC, V.*

Baan Hua Thanon

At this small Chinese fishing village, the road that forks inland (the di-**⓬** rect route to Na Thon) leads to the **Coral Buddha,** a natural formation carved by years of erosion. Beyond the Coral Buddha, toward Na Thon, lies the village of Baan Thurian, famous for its durian trees, where a track to the right climbs up into jungle-clad hills to the island's best **⓭** waterfall, **Na Muang.** The 105-ft falls are spectacular—especially just after the rainy season—as they tumble from a limestone cliff to a small pool. You can bathe in the pool, getting cooled by the spray and warmed by the sun. For a thrill, swim through the curtain of falling water; you can sit on a ledge at the back to catch your breath.

Laem Set Bay

This small rocky cape on the southeastern tip of the island is away from the crowds. It's a good 3 km (2 mi) off the main circle road, and without your own transport, it's hard to reach, but it's worth the effort to get there to have a meal at the Laem Set Inn (☞ *below*). You may also want to visit the nearby **Samui Butterfly Garden.** Two acres of meandering walks enclosed by nets take you through kaleidoscopic clouds of butterflies. ⊙ *Daily 10–4.*

DINING AND LODGING

$–$$$$ ✕🏨 **Laem Set Inn.** British owner David Parry and his Thai wife have made a unique retreat here, with widely varying rates. The buildings are reconstructions of traditional Thai houses or genuine old houses they saved from destruction. The top-priced Kho-Tan suite (two bedrooms, B9,250), an old rosewood house found on nearby Kho-Tan and reassembled here overlooking the sea, even has its own pool. Another suite was made from the old Ko Samui post office. The small, thatched cottages (B1,250) with woven bamboo walls are more modest, with small bathrooms and showers only, but they have lofts for a child or for storage. Dining is given serious attention, and the kitchen has won accolades from the international press. The beach is a mix of sand and coral, with a picturesque sprinkling of rocks. The inn provides kayaks, snorkeling equipment, and mountain bikes at no charge. ⊠ *110 Moo 2, Hua Thanon, Ko Samui, Surat Thani 84310,* ☎ *077/424393, 077/ 233300,* 🖷 *077/424394. 16 rooms. Restaurant, pool, snorkeling, boating, bicycles. MC, V.*

Baan Taling Ngam

Although the south and west coasts are less developed, their beaches, in general, are not so golden, the water not so clear, and the breezes not so fresh. But there is one very good reason for coming to the west coast, and that is a luxury hotel directly west of the village of Baan Taling Ngam, on a pretty stretch of shore with magnificent views.

DINING AND LODGING

$$$$ ✕🏨 **Le Royal Meridien Baan Taling Ngam.** The name of this luxury hotel, now under Meridien management, means "home on a beautiful cliff," which eminently suits the small and appealing hotel set dramatically on a 200-ft cliff facing west across the sea. Sunsets are phenomenal—be sure you come for a sundowner at least once. The equally stunning swimming pool is set so that its water, flowing over one side, seems to disappear over the cliff. The 42 guest rooms are built into the cliffside, and each has a private terrace. The contemporary furnishings are given warmth by a generous use of wood paneling. Seven suites and a pool down by the beach are reached by golf carts, and above the main building there are 33 private, two-bedroom villas that the hotel leases for hideaways. You dine elegantly on Thai and European fare at the Lom Talay, while seafood is served at the more casual Promenade. Baan Taling Ngam is secluded, but some may find it inconveniently far from most of the island's attractions—you'll need transportation whenever you leave the property. ⊠ *295 Moo 3, Baan Taling Ngam, Ko Samui 84140,* ☎ *077/423019, 0800/40–40–40 U.K. reservations, 800/225–5843 U.S. reservations,* 🖷 *077/423220. 42 rooms, 7 suites, 33 villas. 2 restaurants, pool, 2 tennis courts, health club, travel services. AE, DC, MC, V.*

ANGTHONG MARINE NATIONAL PARK – You should take one full day for a trip out to the 40 islets that make up the Angthong Marine National Park, which covers some 250 square km (90 sq mi). The water, the multicolor coral, and the underwater life are superb, and the rocky islets form weird and wonderful shapes. Boats leave Na Thon daily at 8:30 AM for snorkeling and scuba diving; the cost is B250; the trip takes about one hour.

Ko Pha Ngan

12 km (7.5 mi) by boat north of Ko Samui.

Since Ko Samui is no longer off the beaten track, travelers looking for the simple beach life now head for Ko Pha Ngan, which is at the turning point of its development. A decade ago, the few international wanderers stayed in fishermen's houses or slung hammocks on the beach. Now guest bungalows, cheap and simple, have sprung up on most of the best beaches, and investors are buying up beach properties. Land worth a million baht three years ago can bring as much as 45 million baht today. For now, though, the lack of transportation to and on the island limits Ko Pha Ngan's development, and one of the world's most idyllic places has yet to be spoiled.

Since the island's unpaved roads twist and turn, it's easier to beach-hop by boat. In fact, if you want to find the beach that most appeals to you, take a boat trip around the island on the ferries—it takes about nine hours with stops along the way. The southeast tip of the island is divided by a long promontory into **Haad Rin West** and **Haad Rin East,** the island's most popular and crowded areas, sometimes referred to as the backpackers' ghetto. Boats from **Thong Sala,** the major town, take 40 minutes to reach Haad Rin East; their departure is timed to meet arriving passengers from the interisland boat.

If Haad Rin is too crowded, catch the onward boat up the east coast to **Haad Tong Nai Pan,** a perfect horseshoe bay divided by a small promontory. On the beach of the southern and larger half are several guest houses and a couple of small restaurants. The northern bay, **Tong Nai Pan Noi,** is the smaller and quieter of the two. Perhaps it has a few more years before being developed, but for now it's a beach-comber's paradise. Telephone cables have yet to link it with the world, and though there is a road, no self-respecting kidney will take the incessant bouncing of the four-wheel-drive vehicle negotiating its curves and ruts. Glistening white sand curves around the turquoise waters of this half-moon bay, and coconut trees behind the beach hide the small houses of the villagers. At the ends of the bay are two small resorts.

Dining and Lodging

$ ✕ **Pannoi's.** The owner of this local restaurant goes fishing in the evening for tomorrow's menu. The guests, barefoot and shirtless, sit at rough-hewn wood tables set in the sand. A meal may consist of tender and succulent *ma pla* (horsefish, much like snapper) and a plateful of barbecued prawns with garlic and pepper. ⊠ *Haad Tong Nai Pan Noi,* ☎ *no phone. No credit cards.*

$–$$ ✕🏨 **Panviman Resort.** This resort has thatched cottages and stone-and-
★ stucco bungalows, some cooled by fan and others by air-conditioning. Each bungalow has a balcony, a large bedroom, and a spacious bathroom with a cold-water shower. During the day, electricity is turned off and the rooms become stifling, but who wants to be inside? Outside, a breeze blows in from the sea. There are also twin-bed, fan-cooled hotel rooms (half with ocean views) that cost B1,200. The circular wood restaurant, cooled by the breezes blowing over the promontory, serves West-

ern food, but the Thai dishes are better and more extensive. Ask for a light hand in the chili department. Guests gather here to watch the nightly video. ✉ *Haad Tong Nai Pan, Ko Pha Ngan,* ☎ ᶠᴬˣ *077/377048,* ☎ *02/587–8491 Bangkok reservations,* ᶠᴬˣ *02/587–8493 in Bangkok. 10 bungalows, 15 hotel rooms, 15 cottages. Restaurant. MC, V.*

$ 🏠 **Tong Tapan Resort.** These small thatched cottages on stilts perched on the side of the hill are home to international backpackers. ✉ *North end of Haad Tong Nai Pan Noi,* ☎ *no phone. No credit cards.*

Ko Tao

47 km (29 mi) by boat north of Ko Pha Ngan.

Small Ko Tao is an island 4 km (2 mi) wide and 8 km (5 mi) long, with unpaved roads. Only five years ago the island was likened to a second home for Robinson Crusoe. Now it is inundated with tattooed backpackers, hanging out and dreading the day when they might have to go to work. It's now on the scheduled route of ferries out of Ko Pha Ngan and Ko Samui, and two boats a day make the three-hour (express boat) or six-hour (regular ferry) run between Ko Tao and Chumphon on the mainland. The island used to make its living from coconuts, but tourism is taking over despite the rugged interior and few beaches, and more than two dozen small bungalow developments offer basic accommodation. Since the peace and quiet has gone, the main reason to come here, if you're not joining the deadbeats, is the snorkeling. In fact, speedboats now leave from Ko Samui's Bophut pier at 8:30 AM, taking snorkelers on day trips to Ko Tao (about B1,300) and to neighboring Ko Nang Yuan.

Ko Nang Yuan is a teeny island, or rather three islands linked by a sandbar, where the snorkeling is excellent. It's 15 minutes off the north coast of Ko Tao, and it tends to be flooded with visitors arriving on the 10 AM ferry who depart at 4 PM. The only residents on the island are guests at the Ko Nang Yuan Dive Resort (☎ 01/229–5085, ᶠᴬˣ 01/229–5212) which has simple rooms at B80 and more spacious ones with air-conditioning at B2,500. It's the only lodging on the island, so before the last ferry leaves, make sure you can stay there.

Most of the bungalows on Ko Tao are on **Haad Sai Ri,** a sweeping crescent beach north of **Ban Mae Hut,** the village where the ferries dock. One of the better places is Sea Shell Bungalows (☎ 01/229–4621) Rooms here (B800) are fan-cooled and have private bathrooms. On the south shore of the island at Haad Chalok Kao, the Ko Tao Cottage International Dive Resort (☎ 01/229–3662, ᶠᴬˣ 01/229–3751) has fan-cooled bungalows for less than B1,000 a night. If both these are full, go to the Ko Tao Tourism Center, a commercial travel office, and ask the owner, Khun Aka, to find you a bungalow. This office is to the right as you exit the ferry terminal building and about 165 yards up the dirt road.

Chumphon

400 km (240 mi) south of Bangkok, 50 km (21 mi) by boat east of Ko Tao.

Chumphon is often seen as the gateway to the south since trains and buses connect it to Hua Hin and Bangkok in the north, to Surat Thani and Phuket farther south, and to Ranong to the southwest. Ferries to Ko Tao dock at Pak Nam at the mouth of the Chumphon River, 11 km (7 mi) southeast of town. Most boat services run a free shuttle between the docks and the city. Songserm Travel (✉ 66/1 Thatapao Hotel, Chumphon, ☎ 077/502764) coordinates its ferry with its bus service to and from Bangkok.

You'll find there is little of specific interest in Chumphon, but people here are very friendly (especially after the commercialism of Ko Tao). If you are overnighting here or have a couple of hours before catching onward transportation, visit the Night Market. If you have more time, just north of Chumphon there's an excellent beach, **Ao Thong Wua Laen,** with a superb hotel. (You can catch a songthaew [B25] on the street across from the bus station or take the hotel's minivan [B120]; ☞ Dining & Lodging, *below*). The curving beach is 3 km (2 mi) of white-yellow sand with a horizon dotted by small islands famous as the nesting place of swifts. Swifts make those homes that the Chinese like to serve as bird's nest soup. Never venture onto these islands—they are patrolled by armed guards who will shoot you on sight to protect the fortune of the concessionaire. Just offshore is, however, safe. Dive boats go out to nearby reefs where there is some spectacular coral.

There are several restaurants and guest houses along Thong Wua Laen beach as well as picnic and camping spots. But even on national holidays the beach is far from crowded. This paradise has yet to be overrun by either Thais or farangs. Perhaps that is why the local people are so friendly.

Dining and Lodging

$–$$ 🏠 **Chumphon Cabana Resort.** This excellent resort at the south end of Thong Wua Laen beach consists of 40 bungalows hidden in lush foliage and another 100 hotel rooms in three low-rise buildings. Each of the hotel rooms has a private balcony. Furnishings are simple but pleasant, and the bamboo-walled bungalows are especially romantic. The public areas are open-sided and spacious, but most guests, when not out diving or getting some sun, sit around the airy, open restaurant beside the beach. The staff is super friendly and, even if you are not staying at the hotel, will help you make travel arrangements. The hotel also should be commended for building an ecologically friendly hotel (and spending a few extra million) with an infrastructure designed to protect the environment. A PADI registered dive shop is attached to the hotel. ✉ *69 Moo 8, Saplee, Pathui, Chumphon 86230,* ☎ *077/560245 through 9,* 𝔽𝔸𝕏 *077/560247;* ☎ 𝔽𝔸𝕏 *02/427–0122 Bangkok reservations. 140. Restaurant, dive shop, meeting rooms. MC, V.*

¢   🏠 **Marokot.** This is not the most luxurious or the most prestigious hotel in Chumphon, but the rooms are clean, the air-conditioning is efficient, the queen-size beds are firm and comfortable, and the bathrooms have hot and cold water. The staff is very helpful and the hotel's location is a short walk from Songserm's bus and ferry pickup point, the city bus terminal, and the Night Market. Best of all, the price for a room is only B300. ✉ *102–112 Thannon Songkla, 86000,* ☎ *077/503628,* 𝔽𝔸𝕏 *077/ 570196. 46 rooms, most with air-conditioning. No credit cards.*

Southern Beach Resorts Essentials

Arriving and Departing

Ko Pha Ngan and Ko Tao

BY BOAT

From Surat Thani, **Songserm** express boats (☞ Travel Agencies, *below*) depart for Thong Sala on Ko Pha Ngan at 7 AM, 9 AM, and 2 PM (sometimes more often), stopping en route at Na Thon on Ko Samui. From Chumphon on the mainland, two ferries (one Songserm express taking just over two hours and one slow boat taking just over six hours) travel daily to Ko Tao and on to Ko Pha Ngan and Ko Samui. From

Ko Samui, you can also take a small ferryboat from Bophut to Haad Rin at about 10 AM, and in good weather (but not when the seas are high), a long-tailed boat ferry leaves Maenam for Haad Tong Nai Pan at about 9 AM. A speedboat seating a score of passengers departs for Ko Tao every morning from Bophut at 8:30.

BY TRAIN

The State Railway offers a combined ticket that takes you by train to Chumphon and by ferry to Ko Tao and Ko Pha Ngan.

Ko Phi Phi

BY BOAT

Boats leave Makham Bay on Phuket twice a day (9:30 and 1) for the two-hour journey; those run by **Songserm Travel Center** are the best. Two to four ferries a day make the two-hour trip between Krabi and Phi Phi Don.

Ko Samui

BY AIRPLANE

Ko Samui's small airport, on the island's northeast tip, is served by **Bangkok Airways,** which runs five very expensive flights daily between Bangkok and Ko Samui (B3,950 one way), between Phuket and Ko Samui (B2,550 one way), and between Singapore and Ko Samui. Reservations are crucial during peak periods. **Thai Airways International** flies to Surat Thani on the mainland, from which you must transfer to Ko Samui. Taxis meet arrivals; their price is fixed—with little room for negotiation—for trips to various parts of the island. The most common price is B200. Some hotels have a limo/van service at the airport, but these cost the same as a taxi. Songthaews sporadically go between the airport and Na Thon, for B30.

BY BOAT

From Surat Thani (☞ *below*), two ferries cross to Ko Samui. The **Songserm** passenger boat leaves several times a day for Na Thon from its terminal 8 km (5 mi) out of town (a Songserm bus collects passengers from the row of travel agencies on the Surat Thani waterfront). Half the ferry ride is down the river's estuary and the other half across open water, taking, in all, about two hours, after which the ferry goes on to Ko Pha Ngan. The other ferry, which takes cars and cargo, leaves from Donsak at the mouth of the river, 45 minutes by bus from Surat Thani, and lands at New Port. This ferry takes about 90 minutes. Combined bus-ferry tickets are available from one of the many tour/bus companies in Surat Thani. The last ferry to Ko Samui leaves around 4 PM, and the last ferry from Ko Samui departs at 3 PM. Times vary, so be sure to check the schedule.

BY TRAIN, BUS, AND FERRY

The State Railway of Thailand sells a combined ticket that includes rail fare, a berth in air-conditioned second class, bus connection, and the ferry ride, for B610. Passengers arrive at Ko Samui at about 10 AM the following day.

Krabi and Ao Nang

BY BOAT

Two to four ferries a day make the two-hour run between Krabi and Phi Phi. Bookings can be made on Phi Phi Don; the fare is B160. Ferries also go once a day between Ko Phi Phi and Ao Nang.

BY BUS

Air-conditioned buses depart from Bangkok's Southern Bus Terminal at 7 PM and 8 PM for the 290-km (180-mi) journey (B290) to Krabi.

If you book accommodations in Krabi, transportation to Ao Nang will probably be arranged for you, or you can take a songthaew from Krabi for B20.

Phang Nga Bay

First get yourself to the one-horse town of Phang Nga, served by a frequent buses from Krabi and Phuket, then take a songthaew 10 km (6¼ mi) to the bay. At the bay, hire a long-tailed boat to tour the islands.

Phuket

BY AIRPLANE

Thai Airways International has daily 70-minute flights from Bangkok and 30-minute flights from Hat Yai. The airline also has direct flights from Chiang Mai, from Penang (Malaysia), and from Singapore. **Bangkok Airways** now offers two flights daily between Chiang Mai and Phuket and between Phuket and Ko Samui.

Phuket's airport is at the northern end of the island. Most of the hotels are on the west coast, and many send minivans to meet arriving planes. These are not free—just convenient. For Phuket Town (32 km/20 mi southeast of the airport) or Patong Beach, take a Thai Airways minibus—buy the ticket (B80 and B120, respectively) at the transportation counter in the terminal. Songthaews run sporadically between the airport and Phuket Town for B30.

BY BUS

Non-air-conditioned buses leave throughout the day from Bangkok's Southern Bus Terminal. One air-conditioned bus leaves in the evening. Tour companies also run coaches that are slightly more comfortable, and often the price of a one-way fare includes a meal. The bus trip from Bangkok to Phuket takes 12–13 hours. A bus plies between Phuket and Surat Thani with timed connections for the Ko Samui ferry. There's also service between Phuket and Trang, Hat Yai, and Satun.

BY TRAIN AND BUS

The closest train station is at Surat Thani (☞ *below*), where trains connect to Bangkok and Singapore. A bus service links Phuket with Surat Thani. Traveling time between Phuket and Bangkok is five hours on the bus plus 11 hours on the overnight train. The State Railway of Thailand, in conjunction with **Songserm Travel,** issues a combined train and bus ticket. **Panthip Tour** also runs a daily bus between Phuket and Surat Thani, with ferry connections to Ko Samui.

Surat Thani

BY BUS

This town, at the crossroads of railway and bus lines, is the jumping-off place for many southern beach resorts. The buses from Bangkok's Southern Bus Terminal cost less than the train (about B255 for air-conditioned buses), but they are also less comfortable. Private tour companies use more comfortable, faster buses. Express buses also go to Surat Thani from Phuket (5 hrs), from Krabi (4 hrs), and from Hat Yai (7 hrs).

BY TRAIN

Many express trains from Bangkok's Hualamphong railway station stop at Surat Thani on their way south. The journey takes just under 12 hours, and the best trains are the overnighters that leave Bangkok at 6:30 PM and 7:20 PM, arriving in Surat Thani soon after 6 AM. First-class sleeping cabins are available only on the 7:20 PM train. Two express trains make the daily run up from Trang and Hat Yai in southern Thailand.

Getting Around

Ko Pha Ngan

The twisting, rutted, unpaved roads should be avoided, but from Thong Sala, long-tailed-boat ferries travel to all the bays on the island.

Ko Phi Phi

On these pedestrian islands the way to get around is on foot or by cruise boat or long-tail boat.

Ko Samui

BY BUS

Na Thon on the west coast is the terminus for songthaews, which take either the north route around the island via Chengmon to Chaweng on the east coast, or the southern route along the coast to reach Lamai. Between Chaweng and Lamai you change songthaews at a transfer point for either the northern or southern route. The fare from Na Thon to Chaweng, the most distant point, is B30. Songthaews for the northern trip start from the waterfront north of the pier; those on the southern route start from south of the pier.

After about 6 PM songthaews become private taxis, and fares need to be established before setting out. During the day, songthaews may be rented as private taxis. The trip from Na Thon to Chaweng, for example, costs B250.

BY RENTAL CAR AND SCOOTER

If you want to explore Ko Samui, it's best to rent your own transportation. Jeeps are expensive (around B1,200 plus B175 for the Collision Damage Waiver), but they're the safest, although most people choose motor scooters (about B175 per day), which can be rented at most of the resorts. Gravel, potholes, and erratic driving make riding dangerous, and each year some travelers return home with broken limbs, though crash helmets are now mandatory. Some never return at all.

Phuket

BY BUS

Songthaews, the minibuses that seat 10 people, have no regular schedule, but all use Phuket Town as their terminal. Songthaews leave from Rangong Road near the day market and Fountain Circle, to ply back and forth to most beaches, and a few make the trip to the airport. If you want to get from one beach to another, you will probably have to go back into Phuket Town and change songthaews. Fares range from B20 to B40.

BY RENTAL CAR AND SCOOTERS

Your own transport, of course, is most convenient for exploring. Driving poses few hazards except for motor scooters. Potholes and loose gravel can cause a spill, and some minor roads are not paved. Crash helmets are required by law. Many hotels have rental desks, but their prices are 25%–40% higher than those outside the hotel, especially in Phuket Town, where a scooter costs B150 a day and a Jeep is B750.

BY TAXI

Fares are, to a large extent, fixed between different destinations. If you plan to use taxis frequently, get a list of fares from the TAT office because drivers are not above charging more. A trip from Phuket Town to Patong Beach is B140 and to Bang Tao is B200.

Contacts and Resources

Airlines

KO SAMUI

Bangkok Airways (☎ 077/425012, 02/2293456 in Bangkok). **Thai Airways International** (☎ 077/273355).

PHUKET

Bangkok Airways (✉ Yaowarat Rd., Phuket Town, ☎ 076/212341) and **Thai Airways International,** (✉ 78 Ranong Rd., Phuket Town, ☎ 076/211195 domestic, 076/212499 international).

Car and Scooter Rentals

KO SAMUI

Avis (✉ Santiburi Hotel, ☎ 077/425031; ✉ Imperial Tongsai Bay Hotel, ☎ 077/421451; and at the airport). **Hertz** is represented at the airport and at most of the luxury resorts.

PHUKET

At **Pure Car Rent** (✉ 75 Rassada Rd., Phuket Town, ☎ 076/211002), prices for a Jeep start at B770 per day, plus a CDW of B120 per day. Motor scooters begin at B150 a day. The larger, 150-cc scooters are safer. **Avis** (☎ 076/327358), **Budget** (☎ 076/205396), and **Hertz** (☎ 076/321190) have offices at the airport, as well as at some hotels.

Emergencies

KO SAMUI

General emergencies (☎ 1699). **Tourist Police** (☎ 077/421281 in Na Thon). **Hospital** (☎ 077/421230); also **Surat Thani Hospital** (☞ *below*).

PHUKET

General emergencies (☎ 1699). **Ambulance** (☎ 076/212297). **Police** (☎ 076/212046). **Tourist Police** (☎ 076/212468).

SURAT THANI

Tourist Police (☎ 077/281300 or 1699). **Surat Thani Hospital** (✉ Surat-Phun Phin Rd., ☎ 077/272231).

Guided Tours

PHUKET

A half-day Phuket **sightseeing tour** includes Wat Chalong, Rawai Beach, Phromthep Cape, and Khao Rang. Other half-day tours take in the Thai Cultural Village and the cultured-pearl farms on Naka Noi Island. Make arrangements at your hotel.

A full-day **boat tour** goes from Phuket to Phang Nga Bay and other islands. **World Travel Service** (☞ Travel Agencies, *below*) runs a comprehensive tour to Phang Nga Bay. Another full-day tour visits the Phi Phi Islands for swimming and caving. The daylong Ko Hav (Coral Island) tour takes you snorkeling and swimming.

SIMILAN ISLANDS

Full-day cruises to the Similan Islands, costing B1,500, are run by **Songserm Travel Center** (☎ 076/222570 in Phuket; ☞ *below*). The boat trip takes about 10 hours from Phuket, and about four hours from Thap Lamu Port, on the west coast two hours north. **Marina Divers** (✉ Karon Villa Hotel, Karon Beach, Phuket, ☎ 076/381625) runs diving trips to the Similan islands. The **Siam Cruise Co.** (✉ 33/10–11 Chaiyod Arcade, Sukhumvit Soi 11, Sukhumvit Rd., Bangkok 10110, ☎ 02/255–8950), operates two- and three-night cruises to the Similans on the luxury cruise ship *Andaman Princess*. **PIDC Divers** (✉ 1/10 Viset Rd., Chalong Bay, Phuket, ☎ 076/381219), operates the 66-ft MV *Andaman Seafarer* for four- and six-day live-aboard dive excursions that cost approximately $520 and $720, respectively.

Travel Agencies

Chok Anan (✉ Ratchadamnoen Klang Ave., ☎ 02/281–2277) runs buses to Surat Thani.

Songserm Travel Center (✉ 121/7 Soi Chapermla, Phyathai Rd., Bangkok 10400, ☎ 02/252–9654 and 02/251–8994).

KO SAMUI

Songserm Travel Center (✉ 64/1-2 Na Thon, ☎ 077/421316). Also in Ko Pha Ngan (☎ 077/281639).

KRABI

Chan Phen Tour (✉ 145 Uttarakit Rd. ☎ 075/612404, FAX 075/612629). **Lao Ruam Kij** (✉ 11 Khongka Rd., ☎ 075/611930). There are also many other travel shops on Uttarakit Road.

Travel Accommodation Center (✉ Seafood Village, Ao Nang ☎ 075/637311, FAX 075/637311) is extremely knowledgeable and helpful in finding lodging on all the east coast, including Phuket.

PHUKET

World Travel Service (✉ Hotel Phuket Merlin, Phuket Town, ☎ 076/212866, ext. WTS, and ✉ Phuket Yacht Club, ☎ 076/214020, ext. WTS); **Songserm Travel Center** (✉ 51 Satoon Rd., Phuket Town 83000, ☎ 076/222570, FAX 076/214391). **Panthip Tour** (☎ 076/210425).

SURAT THANI

Songserm Travel Center (☎ 077/272928).

Visitor Information
KO SAMUI

TAT (☎ 077/421281 in Na Thon).

KRABI

TAT (✉ Uttarakit Rd., ☎ 075/612740).

PHUKET

TAT (✉ 73–75 Phuket Rd., near bus terminal, Phuket Town, ☎ 076/212213). The TAT desk at Phuket airport offers limited help.

SURAT THANI

The **TAT** office (✉ 5 Talat Mai Rd., Surat Thani 84000, ☎ 077/281828) also handles Ko Phi Phi, Ko Pha Ngan, and Ko Tao, which have no proper representative.

THAILAND A TO Z

Arriving and Departing

By Airplane
AIRPORTS

The major gateway to Thailand is Bangkok's **Don Muang International Airport** (☎ 02/535–2081).

CARRIERS

In total, 35 airlines serve Bangkok, and more are seeking landing rights. The U.S. carrier with the most frequent flights is **Northwest Airlines** (☎ 800/447–4747). It has direct service through Tokyo (with a minimal stopover) from New York, Detroit, Seattle, Dallas, San Francisco, and Los Angeles. Incidentally, this airline's seats recline more than most, and it has the best connections into SE Asia. Northwest also has a round-Asia fare, in conjunction with local airlines, which lets you hop from one capital to another.

To fly from the West Coast, contact **Cathay Pacific** (☎ 800/223–
2742), **Thai Airways International** (☎ 800/426–5204), **Northwest Airlines** (☎ 800/447–4747), and **United Airlines** (☎ 800/241–6522).

For departures from the East Coast, contact **All Nippon Airways** (☎ 800/
235–9262), **Asiana Airlines** (☎ 800/227–4262), **China Airlines** (☎ 800/
227–5118), **EVA Air** (☎ 800/695–1188), **Gulf Air** (☎ 800/553–2824),
Japan Airlines (☎ 800/525–3663), **Korean Air** (☎ 800/438–5000),
Northwest Airlines (☞ *above*), and **Singapore Airlines** (☎ 800/742–3333).

Daily departures to Thailand from London are scheduled aboard
British Airways (☎ 0181/897–4000 or 0345/222111 outside London),
Qantas (☎ 0345/747767 or 0800/747767), and **Thai Airways** (☎
0171/499–9113). From Australia, you can fly **British Airways, Qantas,** and **Thai Airways International.**

FLYING TIMES
Bangkok is 18 hours from Seattle and Vancouver, 17 hours from San
Francisco, 20 hours from Chicago, and 22 hours from New York and
Toronto; 11 hours from London, 10 hours from Sydney. Add more time
for stopovers and connections, especially if you are using more than
one carrier.

Getting Around

By Airplane
The major domestic carrier is **Thai Airways International** (✉ 485 Silom
Rd., Bangkok, ☎ 02/280–0060). Its planes connect Bangkok with all
major cities and tourist areas in Thailand, except Ko Samui. **Bangkok
Airways** (☎ 02/229–3434), has several daily flights between Bangkok
and Ko Samui, using 40-seat planes. It also flies daily between Ko Samui
and Phuket and three times a week from Bangkok to Chiang Mai via
Sukhothai. Its fares are higher than those of Thai Airways.

On popular routes during peak times, flights are often fully booked.
Make reservations well in advance, reconfirm flights when you arrive
in Thailand, and get to the airport well before departure time—the airlines have started giving away the seats of late passengers to standby-
ticket holders. Thai Airways has a good on-time record, but during the
rainy season there may be delays.

AIR PASSES
The Thai Airways **Discover Thailand Pass** ($259 for four internal
flights) must be purchased outside Thailand. Virtually all planes go
through Bangkok, except for the daily nonstop service between Chiang Mai and Phuket. And be aware, for example, that if you fly from
Chiang Mai to Surat Thani, you must change planes in Bangkok and
thus use two of your flights.

By Bicycle Rickshaw
For short trips, bicycle rickshaws are a popular, inexpensive form of
transport. They become expensive for long trips. Fares are negotiated.
It is imperative to be very clear with these drivers about what price is
agreed upon. They have a tendency to create a misunderstanding leading to a nasty scene at the end of the trip.

By Bus
Long-distance buses are cheaper and faster than trains and reach every
corner of the country. A typical fare for the nine-hour trip between Chiang Mai and Bangkok is B500. The level of comfort depends on the
bus company. Air-conditioned buses are superior, but is always turned
on so high you'll want an extra sweater. The most comfortable buses,
run by private companies, usually serve only resort destinations.

By Car

Cars are available for rent in Bangkok and in major tourist destinations, but the additional cost of hiring a car and driver is small and the peace of mind great. If a foreigner is involved in an automobile accident, he or she—not the Thai—is likely to be judged at fault.

In Chiang Mai, Ko Samui, Pattaya, and Phuket, hiring a Jeep or motorcycle is convenient, but be aware that motorcycles skid easily on gravel roads. A sign in Ko Samui posts the year's count of foreigners who never made it home from their vacation! Crash helmets are now required by law.

GASOLINE

A liter of gasoline costs approximately B12.50. Many gas stations stay open 24 hours and have clean toilet facilities. Many, too, have minimarkets that sell snacks, beer, and whiskey.

PARKING

In cities, the larger hotels, restaurants, and department stores have garages or parking lots. Rates vary, but count on B10 an hour. If you purchase anything parking is free, but you must have your ticket validated.

RENTAL AGENCIES

Rates from international franchises begin at $39 a day and $336 a week for an economy car with unlimited mileage, not including tax (7%) or the Collision Damage Waiver (about $10 a day). With a significant surcharge over the basic cost, Avis permits one-way rentals with drop-offs in most major cities. It is better to rent your car in Thailand, as you can usually get a discount and can rent from small local agencies for about $20 a day, including insurance.

The major companies represented in Thailand are **Avis** (☎ 800/331–1084, 800/879–2847 in Canada) and **Hertz** (☎ 800/654–3001, 800/263–0600 in Canada, 0345/555888 in the U.K.).

ROAD CONDITIONS

The major roads in Thailand tend to be very congested, and street signs are often in Thai only. But the limited number of roads and, with the exception of Bangkok, the straightforward layout of cities combine to make navigation relatively easy. Driving at night in rural areas, especially north and west of Chiang Mai and in the south beyond Surat Thani is not advised, as highway robberies have been reported.

RULES OF THE ROAD

If your current driving license is not written in English, an international driving license is required. Driving is on the left; speed limits are 60 kph (37 mph) in cities, 90 kph (56 mph) outside, and 130 kph (80 mph) on expressways.

By Samlor

Usually called tuk-tuks for their spluttering sound, samlors are three-wheel cabs that are slightly less expensive than taxis and, because of their maneuverability, the most rapid form of travel through congested traffic. All tuk-tuk operators drive as if your ride will be their last, but, in fact, they are remarkably safe. Tuk-tuks are not very comfortable, though, and they subject you to the polluted air, so they're best used for short journeys.

By Taxi

Most Bangkok taxis now have meters installed, and these are the ones tourists should take. In other cities, fares are still negotiated. Taxis waiting at hotels are more expensive than those flagged down while cruising. Never enter the taxi until the price has been established. Most taxi drivers do not speak English, but all understand the finger count. One finger means B10, two is for B20 and so on. Ask at your hotel what the appropriate fare should be. Never pay more than what the hotel quotes, as they will have given you the high price. If in doubt, accept 65%–75% of the cabbie's quote.

With any form of private travel, never change your initial agreement on destination and price unless you clearly establish a new "contract." Moreover, if you agree to the driver's offer to wait for you at your destination and be available for your onward or return journey, you will be charged for waiting time, and, unless you have fixed the price, the return fare can be double the outbound fare.

By Train

The State Railway of Thailand has three lines, all of which terminate in Bangkok. The Northern Line connects Bangkok with Chiang Mai, passing through Ayutthaya and Phitsanulok; the Northeastern Line travels up to Nong Khai, near the Laotian border, with a branch that goes east to Ubon Ratchathani; and the Southern Line goes all the way south through Surat Thani—the stop for Ko Samui—to the Malaysian border and on to Kuala Lumpur and Singapore, a journey that takes 37 hours. (There is no train to Phuket, though you can go as far as Surat Thani and change to a scheduled bus service.) For information on schedules and passes, call the **Bangkok Railway Station,** Advance Booking Office (☎ 02/223–3762 or 02/223–0341).

Most trains offer second- and third-class seats, and some of the overnight trains to Chiang Mai, to the northeast, and to the south have first-class sleepers with two berths per compartment. Second-class sleepers have multiple couchettes, with sheets and curtains for privacy, and are surprisingly comfortable. They cost about half the price of first-class, and most Western travelers choose them. Do not leave valuables unguarded on these overnight trains.

Fares are reasonable. An air-conditioned, second-class couchette, for example, for the 14-hour Bangkok–Chiang Mai journey costs B625; first class is B1,190. Reservations are strongly advised for all long-distance trains.

RAIL PASSES

The State Railway of Thailand offers two types of rail passes. Both are valid for 20 days of unlimited travel on all trains in either second or third class. The **Blue Pass** costs B1,500 and does not include supplementary charges such as air-conditioning and berths; for B3,000, the **Red Pass** does.

You need to book seats ahead even if you are using a rail pass; reservations are required on some trains, and they're a good idea in summer on popular routes.

Contacts and Resources

Customs and Duties

If you are bringing any foreign-made equipment from home, such as cameras, it is wise to carry the original receipt with you or register it with U.S. Customs before you leave (Form 4457). Otherwise, you may end up paying duty on your return.

One quart of wine or liquor, 200 cigarettes or 250 grams of smoking tobacco, and all personal effects may be brought into Thailand duty-free. Visitors may bring in any amount of foreign currency; amounts taken out may not exceed those declared upon entry. Narcotic drugs, pornographic materials, and firearms are strictly prohibited.

The export of more than B50,000 in Thai currency is prohibited, as is the export of antiquities or Buddha images without a permit. The antiques store can arrange the formalities.

Electricity

Some new U.S.-purchased electrical equipment has a built-in transformer; older items will need a converter and an adapter. The electrical current in Thailand is 220 volts, 50 cycles alternating current (AC); wall outlets take either plugs with two flat prongs, like those in the United States, or Continental-type plugs, with two round prongs.

Embassies and Consulates

Most nations maintain diplomatic relations with Thailand and have embassies in Bangkok; a few have consulates also in Chiang Mai. Should you need to apply for a visa to another country, the consulate hours are usually 8–noon.

In **Bangkok**: Australian Embassy (⊠ 37 Sathorn Tai Rd., ☎ 02/287–2680); British Embassy (⊠ 1031 Wireless Rd., ☎ 02/253–0191); Canadian Embassy (⊠ Boonmitr Bldg., 11F, 138 Silom Rd., ☎ 02/237–4125); New Zealand Embassy (⊠ 93 Wireless Rd., ☎ 02/251–8165); United States Embassy (⊠ 95 Wireless Rd., ☎ 02/205–4000).

In **Chiang Mai**: U.S. Consulate (⊠ 387 Wichayanom Rd., ☎ 053/252629). U.K. Consulate (⊠ 3rd floor, IBM Building, 139/2 Huay Kaew Rd., ☎ 053/203–405).

Health and Safety

FOOD AND DRINK

In Thailand, the contamination of drinking water, fresh fruit, and vegetables frequently causes traveler's diarrhea. Stay away from ice (unless it was made from bottled water), uncooked food, and unpasteurized milk and milk products; drink only water that has been bottled or boiled for at least 20 minutes.

If you plan to visit rural areas, where there's questionable sanitation, you'll need a vaccination as protection against hepatitis A. Take extra precautions against malarial mosquitoes, in both Ko Samet and northern Thailand. The U.S. Centers for Disease Control recommend chloroquine (analen) as an antimalarial agent. In areas with malaria and dengue, also carried by mosquitoes, take mosquito nets, wear clothing that covers the body, apply repellent containing DEET, and use a spray against flying insects in living and sleeping areas.

OTHER PRECAUTIONS

Be aware that high percentages of bar girls in Thailand are HIV positive if not actively infected with AIDS, and that associating with them is extremely risky.

Thais are seldom violent against farangs, and you can feel secure walking at night. You may be charged too much or cheated in various ways (we mention a few imaginative scams), and the current economic crisis may cause more theft than usual from tourists, but your life and limb won't be in danger, except perhaps from speeding vehicles.

Language, Culture, and Etiquette

Thai is the national language, a tonal language that uses the Khmer script. What may sound to a foreigner as "krai kai kai kai" will mean to a Thai, said with the appropriate pitch, "who sells chicken eggs?" In polite conversation, males use the word "krap" to end a sentence or to acknowledge what someone has said. Females use "ka." It is easy to learn a few phrases, such as "sawahdee krap" or "sawahdee ka" (good day) and "khop khun krap" or "khop khun ka" (thank you).

With the exception of taxi drivers, Thais who work with travelers generally speak enough English for basic communication.

Thais believe in accommodation rather than confrontation. Demands, displays of anger, and any behavior that upsets harmony are frowned upon. Though you might see two grown men holding hands (an ordinary custom), publicly shown affection, hetero- or homosexual, is out of place, as is nudity. There are few respectable venues for gays and lesbians to meet and socialize, and the prevalence of AIDS makes the raunchy ones dangerous. Discretion is the order or the day—and night.

Mail

POSTAL RATES

The airmail postcard rate to the United States and Canada is B13; to the United Kingdom, Australia, and New Zealand, B9. Airmail letters cost B19 to the United States and Canada; B15 to the United Kingdom, Australia, and New Zealand. Allow about two weeks.

RECEIVING MAIL

You may have mail sent to you "poste restante." Usually there is a B1 charge for each piece collected. You may also have mail sent post restante to the Tourist Authority of Thailand (TAT) office (⌧ 4 Ratchadamnoen Nok Av., Pomprap, Bangkok 10100, ☎ 02/282–0071) for a nominal charge.

WRITING TO THAILAND

Thais put their last name first, so be sure to write the recipient's surname in capital letters and underline it. The elements of an address may include a building, then a street and a soi (a street, or alley, running off a main road), both with numbers, and a suburb or city district.

Money and Expenses

COSTS

The cost of visiting Thailand is very much up to you. It is possible to live and travel quite inexpensively if you do as Thais do—eat in local restaurants, use buses, and stay at non-air-conditioned hotels. Once you st rt enjoying a little luxury, prices jump drastically. For example, crossing Bangkok by bus is a 10¢ ride, but by taxi the fare may run to $10.

Sample Prices. Continental breakfast at a hotel, $8; large bottle of beer at a hotel, $6 (in a local restaurant, under $2); bottles of water start at 15¢; a bowl of noodles with slices of pork at a street stall, 50¢; a meal in a local restaurant, $4 for two (two or three dishes plus a bowl of rice); a similar meal in a smartish restaurant, $13; 2-km (1-mi) taxi ride, $1.50; local bus ride, 8¢–12¢; museum entrance, 50¢–$2.

CURRENCY

The basic unit of currency is the baht. There are 100 satang to one baht. There are five different bills, each a different color: B10, brown; B20, green; B50, blue; B100, red; B500, purple; and B1,000, silver. Coins in use are 25 satang, 50 satang, B1, B5, and B10. One-baht coins and B5 coins both come in different sizes and can be easily confused—get the feel of them quickly. The B10 coin has a gold-colored center surrounded by silver.

All hotels will convert traveler's checks and major currencies into baht, though exchange rates are better at banks and authorized money changers. The rate tends to be better in Bangkok than up-country and is better in Thailand than in the United States.

At press time, the exchange rate was B24 to the Australian dollar, B27 to the Canadian dollar, B20 to the New Zealand dollar, B40 to the U.S. dollar, and B63 to the pound sterling.

To report lost or stolen credit cards, contact the following: **American Express** (☎ 02/273–3660). **Diners Club** (☎ 02/238–3660). **MasterCard or Visa** (☎ 02/246–0300).

SERVICE CHARGES, TAXES, AND TIPPING

A 7% Value Added Tax is built into the price of all goods and services, including hotel stays and restaurant meals, and it is essentially nonrefundable. The top hotels are beginning to include a service charge in their bills, including their restaurant bills, but otherwise, tips are left up to you. In Thailand, tips are generally given for good service, except when a price has been negotiated in advance. A taxi driver is not tipped unless hired as a private driver for an excursion. With metered taxis in Bangkok, however, the custom is to round the fare up to the nearest 5 baht. Hotel porters expect at least a B20 tip, and hotel staff who have given good personal service are usually tipped. A 10% tip is appreciated at a restaurant when no service charge has been added to the bill.

Opening and Closing Times

Thai and foreign **banks** are open weekdays 8:30–3:30, except for public holidays. Most **commercial concerns** in Bangkok operate on a five-day week and are open 8–5. **Government offices and post offices** are generally open 8:30–4:30 with a noon–1 lunch break. Many **stores** are open daily 8–8. Museums tend to close on Monday, otherwise they are open 9–4.

NATIONAL HOLIDAYS

New Year's Day (January 1); Chinese New Year (two days, starts February 16 in 1999 and February 5 in 2000); Magha Puja (on the full moon of the third lunar month, March 1 in 1999 and February 19 in 2000); Chakri Day (April 6); Songkran (April 13–15); Coronation Day (May 5); Visakha Puja, May, on the full moon of the sixth lunar month; Queen's Birthday (August 12); King's Birthday (December 5). Government offices, banks, commercial concerns, and department stores are usually closed on these days, but smaller shops stay open.

Passports and Visas

Australian, Canadian, New Zealand, U.K., and U.S. citizens need only a valid passport to enter Thailand for stays of up to 30 days. The **Immigration Division** (✉ Soi Suan Phlu, Sathorn Rd., Bangkok, ☎ 02/286–9176) issues Thai visa extensions, but if you overstay by a few days, don't worry; you'll simply pay a B100 per diem fine as you go through emigration on departure.

Telephones

CALLS TO THAILAND

To call Thailand from overseas, dial the country code, 66, and then the area code, omitting the first 0.

LOCAL AND LONG-DISTANCE CALLS

Public telephones are available in most towns and villages and take B1 coins or both B1 and B5 pieces. Long-distance calls can only be made on phones that accept both B1 and B5 coins. For a long-distance call in Thailand, dial the area code and then the number.

To make overseas calls, you should use either your hotel switchboard—Chiang Mai and Bangkok have direct dialing—or the overseas telephone facilities at the central post office and telecommunications building. You'll find one in all towns. For assistance, dial 100/233–2771. For local telephone inquiries, dial 100/183, but you will need to speak Thai. In Bangkok, you can dial 13 for an English-speaking operator.

When calling the States, you can dial the following **access numbers** to reach a U.S. long-distance operator: AT&T (☎ 0019–991–1111; MCI (☎ 001–999–1–2001); Sprint (☎ 001–999–13–877). Many hotels block these access numbers and charge as much as 400% more than a calling card for calls placed from your room. If the hotel operator claims that you cannot use any phone card, ask to be connected to an international operator, who will help you to access your phone card, or try calling your phone company collect. If collect calls are also blocked, call from a pay phone in the hotel lobby. Some locations in Bangkok have AT&T USADirect phones, which connect you directly with an AT&T operator. You can also use those public phones which accept both B1 and B5 coins to reach a U.S. operator; your coin will be returned after the call.

Visitor Information

Contact the offices of the **Tourism Authority of Thailand** (TAT, ⊠ 5 World Trade Center, Suite 3443, New York, NY 10048, ☎ 212/432–0433, ℻ 212/912–0920; ⊠ 303 E. Wacker Dr., Suite 400, Chicago, IL 60601, ☎ 312/819–3990, ℻ 312/565–0359; ⊠ 611 North Larchmont Blvd., 1st fl., Los Angeles, CA 90004, ☎ 213/461–9814, ℻ 213/461–9834). Inquiries from Canada should be directed to the Chicago office. In the U.K., contact the **Thailand Tourist Board** (⊠ 49 Albemarle St., London W1X 3FE, ☎ 0171/499–7679).

Australians and New Zealanders should contact the Sydney **TAT office** (⊠ Level 2, National Australia Bank House, 255 St. George St., 20000, NSW, ☎ 2/9247–7549).

When to Go

Thailand has two climatic regions: tropical savannah in the northern regions and tropical rain forest in the south. The three seasons run from hot (March through May) to rainy (June through September) to cool (October through February). Humidity is high all year, especially during the hot season. The cool season is pleasantly warm in the south, but in the north, especially in the hills, it can be quite chilly. The cool season is the peak season. Prices can be twice as high then as in the low seasons, yet hotels are often fully booked.

CLIMATE

Following are average temperatures for Bangkok. The north will generally be a degree or two cooler.

Jan.	89F	32C	May	93F	34C	Sept.	89F	32C
	68	20		77	25		75	24
Feb.	91F	33C	June	91F	33C	Oct.	88F	31C
	72	22		75	24		75	24
Mar.	93F	34C	July	89F	32C	Nov.	88F	31C
	75	24		75	24		72	22
Apr.	95F	35C	Aug.	89F	32C	Dec.	88F	31C
	77	25		75	24		68	20

FESTIVALS AND SEASONAL EVENTS

The festivals listed below are national and occur throughout the country unless otherwise noted. Many events follow the lunar calendar, so dates vary from year to year.

Jan.: New Year celebrations are usually at their best around temples. In Bangkok, special ceremonies at Pramanae Ground include Thai dances.
Feb.: Magha Puja commemorates the day when 1,250 disciples spontaneously heard Lord Buddha preach the cardinal doctrine on the full moon of the third lunar month.

Apr.: Songkran marks the Thai New Year and is an occasion for setting caged birds and fish free, visiting family, dancing, and water-throwing, in which everyone splashes everyone else in good-natured merriment. The festival is at its best in Chiang Mai, with parades, dancing in the streets, and a beauty contest.

May: On the full moon of the sixth lunar month, the nation celebrates the holiest of Buddhist days, **Visakha Puja**—commemorating Lord Buddha's birth, enlightenment, and death. Monks lead the laity in candlelighted processions around their temples.

Aug.: On the 12th, **Queen Sirikit's birthday** is celebrated with religious ceremonies at Chitlada Palace, and the city is adorned with lights galore.

Nov.: Held on the full moon of the 12th lunar month, **Loi Krathong** is the loveliest of Thai festivals. After sunset, people make their way to a body of water and launch small lotus-shape banana-leaf floats bearing lighted candles, to honor the water spirits and wash away the sins of the past year. Of all Bangkok's fairs and festivals, the **Golden Mount Festival** is the most spectacular, with sideshows, food stalls, bazaars, and large crowds of celebrants.

Dec.: On the 5th, the **King's birthday,** a trooping of the colors is performed in Bangkok by Thailand's elite Royal Guards.

7 Vietnam

The midday downpour is a given. The lush green of the landscape is only one sign that you're in monsoon country. Another is the relentless flooding. But these are conditions the Vietnamese have learned to abide, even to revere. For thousands of years, they have followed the dictates of the predictable climate, obediently plowing, planting, and harvesting when the weather tells them to. Foreign oppressors may come and go, but the rhythmic cycle of the seasons endures.

VIETNAM IS A COUNTRY ON THE MOVE. The introduction of economic reforms—known as *doi moi,*
meaning "new change"—more than a dozen years
ago acted as a catalyst, releasing the energies of the nation left behind
after decades of war and isolation. Now wherever you travel in Vietnam—in the towns, the cities, and the countryside—you will see people on the go.

From the rows of *pho* (noodle soup) stalls lining the sidewalks to the
numerous vendors selling postcards to the huge neon signs advertis-
ing Western chic, it is apparent that the drive to make it in this new
era cuts across social boundaries. Billboards hawking everything from
Lifebuoy soap and Heineken beer to the newest luxury apartments tower
above streets jammed with motorbikes, bicycles, and more and more
cars. It seems as if, once the sun rises, the entire population is up
within an hour rushing headlong into another day.

It is especially in the main cities—Hanoi, Haiphong, Danang, and most
of all Ho Chi Minh City (formerly Saigon)—that you see this headlong
rush. But travel just 16 km (10 mi) into the countryside and you still
see farmers sowing rice with water buffalo, and duck herders wooing
their flocks across roads where the only hazards are passing bicycles.
These scenes are no less exhilarating than those in the booming cities.

For Vietnam is a country of stunning beauty, its pristine coastline of
golden beaches stretching 3,225 km (2,000 mi) from tip to tail along
the South China Sea. To the north, Vietnam borders China along the
rugged Hoang Lien mountain chain (the Tonkinese Alps), a breathtaking
landscape of deep valleys and tall, mysterious peaks shrouded in mist.
Down the country's enormous arched spine are forest-covered highlands, which can be as deliciously cool as a European spring. These
mountains, as well as those in the north, are home to Vietnam's 53
ethnic minority groups—the Black Tai, Flower H'mong, Ede, and
Muong, among others—whose traditional way of life is today under
siege by the forces of development: some have been removed from their
land to make way for power stations and the ever-encroaching Kinh
majority. Change has been thrust on others by severe deforestation of
much of the highlands and mountains. The majority of Vietnamese,
however, live along the coast and in the country's two major deltas—
the Red River Delta in the north and the Mekong Delta in the south.
Here the land fans out into patchworks of vivid-green, wet rice paddies, fruit orchards, and fishing hamlets—inhabited as they have been
for hundreds of generations by farmers and fishermen.

In the midst of this beautiful country, stark reminders of the high price
paid by the Vietnamese people for their independence are never far away.
Although few visible signs of the damage sustained by Vietnam remain,
every town has its monument to war, be it a captured American jet fighter
or a victorious North Vietnamese tank. And dotting the cities and countryside are huge Soviet-style memorials recording the millions that
died in the country's most recent struggle against outside forces.

For 2,000 years the country has been fending off foreign invaders, most
notably the Chinese, Japanese, French, and Americans. The Chinese
were the first to invade, and by the time they were finally driven out
by Ngo Quyen in AD 938 they had ruled the country for a millennium.
During the following centuries the Vietnamese migrated south in ever
increasing numbers, battling with the kingdoms of Champa and Angkor
as they went. These expansionist ambitions led to conflicts between
competing Vietnamese lords—the Nguyen and the Trinh.

The French entered the scene at the beginning of the 19th century by invitation of the Nguyen lords, who sought assistance in crushing a rebellion, and by the mid-19th century, the French had taken over by force, annexing large parts of Vietnam to create the colony of Cochin China and protectorates of Annam and Tonkin. The Japanese occupation during World War II interrupted the French hegemony, briefly. With Japan's surrender, the French returned to rule Vietnam, but not without conflict: Ho Chi Minh had declared Vietnamese independence in 1945, and by 1946 anti-French sentiment developed into the French-Indochina War.

The French were soundly defeated by General Vo Nguyen Giap and the Viet Minh at Dien Bien Phu in 1954, and the country was split in two under the Geneva Accords that same year. Cold War concerns drew the American military into Vietnam, which led to full-scale U.S. involvement in the Vietnam War. But American firepower only reinforced the conviction among many North Vietnamese that they would not be defeated. And the 1968 Tet Offensive was the turning point. Though the collective push by northern forces and the Communist Viet Cong in the south was eventually rebuffed, American sentiment turned against intervention and favored withdrawal. By 1973 most U.S. troops had left the country, and the Saigon regime fell in 1975.

But strife did not end there for the Vietnamese. Following Khmer Rouge border incursions in 1978, Vietnam "volunteers" invaded Cambodia late in that year and within a few weeks reached Phnom Penh, effectively ending the "killing fields" of Pol Pot. (Hanoi set up a de facto Vietnamese occupational government which ruled Cambodia until 1989.) In response to Vietnam's expansionist foray, the Chinese invaded northern Vietnam in 1979, devastating much of the countryside and leveling many towns and villages near the border. But the Vietnamese quickly repulsed the Chinese and for the first time in decades lived in relative peace. They were not, however, without a new set of visitors: the Soviets.

Now that that dismal era has ended and the thousands of Soviet advisors have departed, what becomes evident is the amazing resilience of the Vietnamese people. When you visit Vietnam, you can't help marveling at their endurance. Slender, silk-clad women bear yokes hung with baskets of rice weighing several times their own weight; they build roads, protected only by a conical hat and a perfectly white handkerchief tied over nose and mouth.

And in the cities, you have to admire their panache—well-primped teenage girls ride the backs of their friends' Hondas, wearing spaghetti-string halter tops, eye-popping bell-bottoms, and five-inch chockablock heels. Do not be surprised to encounter a pair of bareheaded men careening on a motorbike through city traffic at the height of a midday downpour, the driver tooting his horn with a soggy cigarette in his mouth, his companion, arms outstretched, balancing a large pane of glass on his knees. That mixture of practicality and bravado, in some ways the essence of Vietnam, is what's taking the country into the future.

Pleasures and Pastimes

Beaches

Unlike Thailand and other Southeast Asian countries, Vietnam's beach culture is still underdeveloped. Although there are incredible coral reefs, sea life, and surf (Danang was the site of an international surfing competition in 1994), there are few places that rent gear or give lessons. However, some towns along the coast—especially Nha Trang, which does have a few dive shops, and China Beach near Danang, for instance—are beginning to grow.

Dining

Seafood is delicious, abundant, and cheap all over Vietnam, particularly in coastal towns like Nha Trang, Danang, and Halong Bay. But the dish that reigns supreme is pho, the ubiquitous noodle soup that can safely be called Vietnam's national dish. In addition to pho, noodles, and spring rolls (called *nem* in the north, and *cha goi* in the south), rice (*com*) is another staple, served with anything and everything. Beef, pork, and chicken are generally of high quality in the cities, but out in the provinces they can be tough. Dog meat isn't as inexpensive or plentiful as you might think; just watch out for dishes that contain *"thit cho."* Instead of soy sauce, the seasoning of choice is *nuoc mam,* inadequately translated as fish sauce, a clear amber liquid pressed out of large barrels of anchovies and salt.

To taste pho and other favorites, you only need to step out of your hotel and into the streets. The best meals in Vietnam aren't usually found in elegant restaurants or hotel dining rooms but at stalls on every street corner and in the marketplace. Family-run restaurants and cafés everywhere serve seafood, delicious and curious meats, and tasty *an chay* (vegetarian dishes). A number of upscale Vietnamese and international restaurants have opened in Ho Chi Minh City and Hanoi, but finding top-notch Western food elsewhere is difficult. Cities like Haiphong, Danang, and Nha Trang are entering the realm of international cuisine with varying degrees of success.

CATEGORY	COST*
$$$$	over $25
$$$	$15–$25
$$	$7–$15
$	$2–$7
¢	under $2

per person for a three-course dinner, including 10% tax and 5% service but not drinks

Lodging

Graham Greene did much to romanticize hotel life in Vietnam in *The Quiet American*. But aside from the Continental Hotel in Ho Chi Minh City, immortalized in Greene's book, and a handful of other older institutions, including the Sofitel Metropole in Hanoi, hotels in Vietnam have little Old World charm or mystery. The focus today is on newness; the vast majority of joint-venture, international-standard hotels are less than five years old. And unfortunately many of the older hotels that have survived the wrecking ball have fared poorly from years of neglect, bad management, and lack of funds.

Until a few years ago hotels in Vietnam were not renowned for good service. This has changed over the past couple of years because of the influx of foreign tourists and the increasing number of international hotel chains, although service in many of the state-run hotels still leaves a lot to be desired. Resorts have been developed along the coast—the best so far near Phan Thiet, Nha Trang, and on China Beach near Danang—and in the mountain town of Dalat.

Besides surprisingly pricey international properties, Vietnam has a selection of midsize, mid-level hotels and guest houses, especially in cities and popular tourist areas, that are generally state-run and are acceptable for a night's sleep. "Minihotels" are usually a better option. These privately owned, often family-run operations range from utilitarian to plush; they usually provide friendly service, spotless if basic

Vietnam

rooms, IDD phones, private bathrooms, air-conditioning, and a homey environment. In small towns or rural areas off the beaten track, expect much more basic digs.

The rates quoted below are for accommodations in summer. Reservations are recommended during July and August and particularly during Tet, the lunar new year (January or February); prices often go up at that time. Rates sometimes include breakfast. Many of the larger, international hotels, particularly in Hanoi, aren't always fully booked and should be ready to give you a better room rate than listed.

CATEGORY	COST*
$$$$	over $200
$$$	$100–$200
$$	$50–$100
$	$25–$50
¢	under $25

*All prices are for a standard double room, including 10% tax and 5% service.

Shopping

There is plenty to buy in Vietnam, though perhaps not of as high quality as elsewhere in Southeast Asia. Custom-made clothing, unique handicrafts such as delicate blue-and-white ceramics, elegant black-and-red lacquerware, colorful textiles made by ethnic minority groups, and intricate woodcarvings can be found at rock-bottom prices. In addition, Vietnam—particularly Hanoi—has a booming contemporary arts scene, though paintings can get pricey. Bargaining is virtually mandatory in all but the most exclusive shops.

Exploring Vietnam

The best way to see Vietnam is to use the major cities as your base for trips into the outlying regions. Begin in Hanoi, the capital, and travel north to south, against the tourist tide, for less crowding and more choice. Hanoi is the most sober and ideologically driven of Vietnam's cities, but the French influence still reverberates, and you'll enjoy this beautiful tree-shaded town. Trips out of Hanoi include two-day boat excursions through the limestone archipelagoes of Halong Bay and trekking tours through breathtaking scenery in the Hoang Liem Mountains, where, in towns like Sapa, ethnic minorities persist.

South along the coast, Hue is perhaps the country's most culturally attractive city. Its wide boulevards lead to the vestiges of the imperial city, where elite mandarins ruled, and the romantic Perfume River takes you out of town to their remarkable, mysterious tombs. South of working-class Danang, site of the lovely Cham Museum of Art, lie spectacular stretches of coastline, such as "China Beach," and Hoi An, a delightful centuries-old port town that has emerged as one of Central Vietnam's "must-sees." This living, working museum is blessed with a beautiful beach and estuary, a remarkably intact historic center, and nearby Cham ruins. The south-central coast (the area around Nha Trang) is also known for its beaches and ruins. From Hoi An or Nha Trang you can visit the resort town of Dalat and take a trip through the Central Highlands up the spine of the country to the mountain towns of Pleiku and Kontum. Like the northern Alps, these towns are surrounded by spectacular mountains and rivers and populated by ancient Malayo-Polynesian hill tribes who still use working elephants.

Ho Chi Minh City, still called Saigon by people who live in it, is the engine of Vietnam, with a population of over 6 million. An exuberant mix of the old and the new, the crass and the sophisticated, it betrays its thoroughly Western heritage as the former capital of French Cochin

China and of South Vietnam. From the city you can head to the Mekong Delta on day trips or longer, cruising by palm-lined hamlets and punting through magnificent, ancient mangrove forests.

Great Itineraries

Even under the most stringent time constraints, touring just the two major cities would not only be unsatisfying, but would misrepresent the country as a whole. Therefore, we try here to combine city and country, while allowing for limited time.

IF YOU HAVE 3 DAYS

Spend one or two days in Ho Chi Minh City, using it as a base for a day trip either to the Cu Chi Tunnels and the Cao Dai Holy See in Tay Ninh, or through the Mekong Delta on a boat. Another option is to spend a day and a half in Hue and a day and a half in Hoi An, which is a three-hour car trip from Hue. You could also easily spend your time in Hanoi, with an overnight trip to Halong Bay, Vietnam's premier natural wonder.

IF YOU HAVE 7–10 DAYS

Spend one day in Ho Chi Minh City, taking a day trip to the Cu Chi Tunnels and the Cao Dai Holy See in Tay Ninh, or into the Mekong Delta. Fly to Hue for two days; tour the ancient citadel and the Nguyen dynasty tombs and pagodas. A trip to the perfectly preserved 18th-century city of Hoi An is well worthwhile. Fly or take an overnight train to Hanoi. From Hanoi you could take a day trip to the Perfume Pagoda or make an overnight excursion to Halong Bay.

WHEN TO TOUR VIETNAM

Vietnam's microclimates can make it hot and dry in one area while it's monsoon season in another. March–April and October–November have the best weather in the largest number of regions. Weather in the north is finest around August to December, and it rains for much of the rest of the year although not as heavily as in the south. It can get quite chilly there January–March. Dry season in the south (about November–June) is best; during the monsoons much of the Mekong Delta and Central Highlands are impassable. (☞ When to Go *in* Vietnam A to Z, *below*.)

Numbers in the text correspond to numbers in the margin and on the maps.

HANOI

By Michael Mathes and Felicity Wood

658 km (408 mi) north of Hue, 763 km (473 mi) north of Danang, 1,710 km (1,060 mi) north of Ho Chi Minh City.

Hanoi, the self-appointed stronghold of "true" Vietnamese, anti-imperialist culture, has learned to covet satellite TV and blue jeans. The country's leaders let in a flood of overseas investment from Hong Kong, Malaysia, Singapore, Taiwan, and even the United States and Australia, and now the capital of the Socialist Republic of Vietnam relishes its newfound economic liberalization despite itself. Although Western fashions, music, and food have managed to elbow their way into the once-impenetrable north, Hanoi is appealing because it retains its ancient culture, French colonial architecture, broad tree-lined boulevards, and beautiful lakes.

The city dates to the 7th century, when Chinese Sui dynasty settlers occupied the area and set up a capital called Tong Binh. In 1010 King Ly Thai To is said to have seen a golden dragon ascending from Hoan Kiem Lake. The dragon is a traditional Chinese symbol of royal power, and the king took the omen literally: He relocated his capital to the shores of the lake, the site of present-day Hanoi, and named his new city Thang Long, or "City of the Ascending Dragon." During the 11th century the old citadel was built, and 36 villages, each with its own specialized vocation, sprang up to service the royal court. This is the origin of the 36 streets that define the city's Old Quarter.

In 1428 King Le Loi is said to have driven Vietnam's Chinese overlords from the country with the help of a magic sword. Celebrating his success after the war with a boating excursion on Hoan Kiem Lake, Le Loi was confronted by a gigantic golden tortoise that retrieved the sword for its heavenly owner. Thus the lake became known as the Lake of the Restored Sword, or Ho Hoan Kiem. In 1789 the Chinese reconquered Hanoi but not for long. Nguyen Hue, leader of a rebellion in Tay Son (in the south), drove the Manchu invaders out of the country and crowned himself King Quang Trung. Officially, however, by then the country was led by the Nguyen dynasty, which moved the capital to Hue under the rule of Gia Long in 1802. This chapter in northern Vietnam's history was in part orchestrated by the French, who began to play a stronger role in the political and commercial fabric of the country.

The French usurped more and more control, setting up the protectorate of Annam in 1883–84, which meant the Hue royalty held the reins but only under the auspices of French rule. In the following years the French set up its administration and used Hanoi as the Eastern Capital, or Dong Kinh (the origin of Tonkin), of French Indochina. The Chinese character of the city was basically eliminated as the French filled in canals between Hanoi's many lakes and created a plain on which to remake the capital in its own mold. They constructed the large villas and administrative buildings that cluster in the streets around the present-day Presidential Palace and the Ho Chi Minh Mausoleum, as well as the grid of wide boulevards south of Hoan Kiem Lake. These streets and structures remain, and they continue to give the city a somewhat dilapidated but still striking colonial-era feel.

Once the French were defeated at Dien Bien Phu, Hanoi was again declared the capital of Vietnam. From 1954 until 1975 it was the seat of the Democratic Republic of Vietnam, or North Vietnam, from which Ho Chi Minh initiated his struggle to reunify the country. Despite American attempts to smash the Communist administration by bombing it from the air, the city survived the war with most of its grandeur remarkably intact. Given the country's experience with foreign rulers, it is not surprising that the post-1975 socialist order sought to seal off the city and, after the war with China in 1979, expel the ethnic Chinese, although many of these predominantly mercantile families had lived in Vietnam for generations.

In the decades after 1975 relations with the Soviet Union were strengthened. Tens of thousands of Russian advisers came to live in Hanoi and other parts of the country, leaving their mark in such buildings as the Viet Xo Cultural Palace and massive infrastructure projects like the Hoa Binh hydroelectric power station. But the '80s were tough times for Hanoians and everyone else. Natural disasters and international isolation led to near mass starvation. Come nightfall, city streets were deserted. Entrepreneurs were jailed for capitalist tactics they used to make ends meet.

Then in 1986, following the lead of Gorbachev's "perestroika" in the Soviet Union, the government suddenly took a bold "reform or perish" approach and proclaimed doi moi, the move to a market economy. The Soviet Union dissolved soon thereafter, taking with it billions of dollars of desperately needed foreign aid. But foreign investors had already

Hanoi

West Lake
(Ho Tay)

Truc Bach
Lake

Quan Thanh
Temple

Thanh Nien

Dang Dung

Quan Thanh

Thuy Khue

Phan Dinh Phung

Hoang Hoa Tham

Bach Thao
Botanical
Garden

Hung Vuong

The Citadel

BA DINH DISTRICT

Presidential
Palace

Nguyen
Lam

Ho Chi Minh
Mausoleum

Bac Son

Ngoc Ha

Ba Dinh
Square

Nguyen Tri Phuong

Ly Nam De

Cua Bong

Ho Chi Minh
Museum

One Pillar
Pagoda

Dien Bien Phu

Hoang Dieu

Ly Nam De

Doi Can

**SEE
AROUND THE HO CHI MINH
MAUSOLEUM AND
WEST LAKE DETAIL**

Army
Museum

Kim Ma

**GIANG
VO**

Museum
of Fine Arts

Nguyen Thai Hoc

Chi Lang
Park

Tran Phu

Tong
Duy Tan

Cai Linh

Trinh Hoai Duc

Yan Mieu

Nguyen Khuyen

**Hoa
(Han**

Temple of
Literature

Tran Quy Cap

Le Duan

**HAO
NAM**

Quoc Tu Giam

Phan

Bot Chau

Giang Vo

Ton Duc Thang

Hanoi Railway
Station

**V
Ce**

La Thanh

Kham Thien

Yet Kieu

Tran Binh Trong

**NAM
DONG**

Nam Dong

La Thanh

**THO
QUAN**

Cho Kham Thien

**TRUNG
PHUNG**

Tran Nt

Lenin
Park

DONG DA DISTRICT

Tu

Tay Son

Le Duan

**KIM
LIEN**

Bay Mau
Lake

0 ___ 400 yards

0 ___ 400 meters

Yen Phu

Long Bien Bridge

Hoe Nhai

Hang Dau

H. Giay   Gam Cau

Hang Khoai

Tran Nhat Duat

Phuc Tan

Hang Col

H. Luoc   D. Xuan Hang Duong

Hang Chieu

**SEE
THE OLD QUARTER
DETAIL**

Chuong Duong Bridge

Phung Hung

Hang Ga

Hang Ma   Cha Ca

H. Buom

H. Vai   P. Lan Ong

Luong Ngoc Quyen

Red River (Song Hong)

Bat Dan   H. Non

Hang Bo   Hang Dao   Hang Bac   Hang Mam

Tran Quang Khai

Luong V. Can

Hang V. Can   Cau Ga   Hang Thung

Hang Bong

Le Thai To

Hoang

Lo Su

Bach Dang

Hoan
Kiem
Lake

TRANG THI

Dinh Tien

Tran Nguyet Han

Chuong
Duong

**HOAN
KIEM
DISTRICT**

Indira
Gandhi
Park

Ioa Lo Prison
(Hanoi Hilton)

Quan Su

Trang Tien

Le Thai To

**Museum
of the
Revolution**

Ly

Hai Ba Trung

Ngo Quyen

**Opera
House**

**Museum
of History**

Bach Dang

Thuong Kiet

Ba Trieu

Phan Chu Trinh

**Viet Xo
Cultural Palace**

Tran Hung Dao

**SEE
THE FRENCH
QUARTER
DETAIL**

Le Thanh Tong

Tran Khanh Du

Hang Bai

Tran Quoc Toan

Hang Chai

Nguyen Du

Tran Thanh Tong

Thien
Quang
Lake

Ba Trieu

Nguyen Khoai

Nhan Tong

Tran Xuan Soan

Hue

Tue Tinh

Hoa Ma

Luong Yen

To Hien Thanh

Nguyen Cong Tru

Lo Duc   Yec Xanh

Nguyen Cao

Le Dai Hanh   Doan Tran Nghiep

Tho Lao

**VAN
HO**

Hue

**HAI BA TRUNG
DISTRICT**

Tran Khat Chan

Dai Co Viet

Lang Yen

started preliminary explorations of one of the world's largest untapped markets, and more and more foreign investment started coming, especially after the American embargo was lifted in early 1994.

More than a decade of economic reforms has changed the attitudes of the ruling party members considerably, and reformist city leaders are learning the ways of capitalism quickly—perhaps too quickly, according to some of the aging Communist Party cadres and conservative critics who pride themselves on their city's being the seat of Vietnam's socialist revolution. But few can argue that the last decade of change in Hanoi has been anything short of a godsend. In the past three years, as the economy has continued to open and the people have increasing amounts of disposable income, the city has modernized rapidly.

Nonetheless, Hanoi remains a city of academics, artists, diplomats—and contradictions. Although you will see people carrying their new TVs on the back of their Honda motorbikes, you will also see people carrying hundreds of pounds of rice on bicycles with no brakes. People may zoom around all day doing business, but they also take time out for long discussions over a cup of coffee in a café. Pete Peterson, once a prisoner in the Hanoi Hilton, is now the U.S. ambassador to Vietnam. On a Sunday you may see him cruising to a noodle shop on his motorbike with his new Vietnamese-Australian bride. (They married in Hanoi in May 1998, a wedding many observers touted as the ultimate symbol of reconciliation.) Octogenarian General Giap, who defeated the French at Dien Bien Phu, is involved in Vietnam's developing telecommunications industry. Like everyone else in Hanoi and all over Vietnam, General Giap is aware of his history but is moving on with the times.

Exploring Hanoi

Hanoi is divided into four main districts, or *quan*. The Hoan Kiem District, named after the lake at its center, is the hub of most local and tourist activity. Just north of the lake is the Old Quarter, a charming cluster of ancient streets. South of the lake is the modern city center, once the French Quarter, which houses grand colonial-style villas that have been turned into hotels and offices. The Ba Dinh District, west of the Old Quarter, contains the zoo, the Ho Chi Minh Mausoleum, the Presidential Palace, and areas around West Lake, a picturesque body of water north of the Ba Dinh and Hoan Kiem districts. The Hai Ba Trung District, in the southeast part of Hanoi, is a calm, elegant residential area, whose primary attraction is Lenin Park. The Dong Da District, to the southwest, is where the Temple of Literature can be found.

Getting around Hanoi on foot is not out of the question, but it can be tiring. So if you're intending to stick within the Old Quarter or elsewhere in Hoan Kiem District, break up your walks with a cyclo ride or two. Otherwise consider taking taxis, or if the weather is good and you're feeling a little more gung ho, rent a bicycle or hop on the back of a *xe om* (motorcycle taxi).

The Old Quarter

When Vietnam gained its independence from China in the 11th century, King Ly Thai To built his palace here, and the area developed as a crafts center. Artisans were attracted from all over the northern part of the country and formed guilds based on specialized trades and village affiliation. This area is referred to as the 36 Streets—actually now there are nearly 70. To this day the streets are still named after the crafts practiced by the original guilds. Note the slim buildings called tunnel or tube houses—with narrow frontage but deceiving depth—which combine workshops, storefronts, and living quarters. They were built this way because each business was taxed according to the width of its storefront. In addition to the specialty shops, each street has religious structures reflecting the beliefs of the village from which its guilds came.

A GOOD WALK

Begin your walk in the northern section of the Hoan Kiem District, at the **Dong Xuan Market** ① on Hang Chieu Street. From here you can dive right into the bustle of the ancient streets—but be careful in the traffic! From the intersection of Hang Chieu and Dong Xuan streets, head south on Dong Xuan, which immediately turns into Hang Duong (Sugar) Street and then into Hang Ngang Street. Spare a moment for 48 Hang Ngang, where President Ho Chi Minh wrote his country's Declaration of Independence. Continue south, to **Hang Dao Street** ②, which divides the Old Quarter and serves as a convenient corridor from which to venture down any of the appealing side streets. Once you come to busy **Hang Bac Street** ③, turn left.

Turning right down Hang Be Street brings you to the historic boat-building district. The bamboo rafts, called *cai mang,* that you may see here were designed especially for the shallow rivers, lakes, and swamps of Hanoi. From Hang Be Street take a right on Cau Go Street, the southeast border of the Old Quarter. This neighborhood was known for its flower market in colonial times, a vestige of which can be found at the intersection with Hang Dao Street. Just beyond this flower mart and to the left is the northern tip of **Hoan Kiem Lake** ④. On the left, or east, side is the distinctive red footbridge that leads to **Ngoc Son Temple** ⑤, the focal point for legends surrounding King Le Loi's encounter with the Ho Guom turtle.

Walk back to Cau Go Street and through the chaotic intersection here. Beyond this roundabout, Cau Go becomes **Hang Gai Street** ⑥, where you'll want to spend some time if you're shopping for embroidery, silk, or other souvenirs or if you want to wander through some art galleries. From here turn right (north) on Hang Hom Street, which leads to **Hang Quat Street** ⑦. This area is home to a few of the oldest musical instrument shops still standing in the Old Quarter. (Some shops here have turned to the more profitable business of selling paints and solvents.) A quick jog to the left on Hang Non Street brings you to Hang Thiec Street, where utilitarian tin chests and utensils dangle from every doorway. Farther north, this street becomes Thuoc Bac Street. The street has maintained quite a bit of its French-era Art Deco frontage. Eventually this street meets **Hang Ma Street** ⑧, which gets its name from the paper goods and fake money made for burning to appease ancestral spirits. East on Hang Ma leads you back to Hang Chieu Street and, to the left, the Dong Xuan Market.

TIMING

Since the Old Quarter is filled with shops, this 2.7-km (1.6-mi) route is the kind of walk that could take two hours or 10.

SIGHTS TO SEE

① **Dong Xuan Market.** Once conveniently accessible by riverboat, this market, the oldest (1947) and largest still standing in the city, has seen trading with the whole of Southeast Asia. "Still standing" may not be the appropriate term; the huge structure was destroyed by a massive fire in 1994—ironically enough on July 14, Bastille Day. The fire displaced 3,000 workers, caused millions of dollars in damage and losses, and took five human lives. (An untold number of exotic animals were burned alive.) The market reopened in December 1996; today it looks more like a concrete shopping mall but continues to offer all manner of local and Western goods. ✉ *Dong Xuan and Hang Chieu Sts.* ☉ *Daily 7–7.*

The Old Quarter

❸ Hang Bac Street. This street was originally dominated by silversmiths and money changers and still has a wide variety of jewelry shops. The Dong Cac jewelers' guild was established here in 1428, and it later erected a temple (now gone) in tribute to three 6th-century brothers whose jewelry skills, learned from the Chinese, made them the patron saints of Vietnamese jewelry. The Hanoi Cai Luong Theatre, at the corner of Ta Hien Street, is still in operation. Check inside for showtimes of the "*cai luong*" theater troupe.

❷ Hang Dao Street. Since the 15th century, when it was one of the original silk-trading centers, Hang Dao Street has been known for its textiles. When the French colonized Vietnam, Hang Dao Street became the center for all traffic in silk, with massive biweekly trade fairs. Indians who settled here at the turn of the century introduced textiles from the West, and today the street features ready-made clothing in addition to bolts of silk.

★ **❻ Hang Gai Street.** The Street of Hemp now offers a variety of goods, including ready-made silk, lovely embroidery, and silver products.

❽ Hang Ma Street. Here you can find *ma,* delicate paper replicas of material possessions made to be burned in tribute to one's ancestors. These faux luxury villas and Honda motorbikes can be found alongside more practical merchandise such as imported party decorations and kites.

★ **❼ Hang Quat Street.** The Street of Fans now features a stunning array of religious paraphernalia, including beautiful funeral and festival flags. It is one of the most atmospheric streets in Hanoi during holiday seasons.

★ **❹ Hoan Kiem Lake** (Ho Hoan Kiem or Ho Guom). The spiritual, legendary, and social heart of Hanoi, Hoan Kiem Lake, the Lake of the Restored Sword, is one of the most enchanting spots in the city. Taking a dip is not advised—not to mention illegal. Hanoi's sewer and plumbing systems are stressed to the limit, and the water is polluted. Unless drastic measures are taken, it may be only a matter of time before the lake's turtles—revered by locals as a link to Hanoi's legend-heavy past and proclaimed by scientists to be a species unto themselves—disappear forever.

⑤ Ngoc Son Temple (Den Ngoc Son). Enjoy a lazy game of Chinese checkers with the old gentlemen who frequent the courtyard of this quiet and well-manicured 18th-century shrine, whose name means "jade mountain." On an island in Hoan Kiem Lake, it is one of Hanoi's most picturesque temples. In the pagoda's anteroom is a 6-ft-long stuffed turtle that locals pulled from Hoan Kiem Lake in 1968. ⊠ *Dinh Tien Hoang St., Hoan Kiem District.* ☎ *12,000d.* ⊙ *Daily 8–5, later for festivals and 1st and 5th days of every lunar month.*

The French Quarter

Although much of the French Quarter's appeal lies in its grand but aging colonial architecture, the area is fast becoming a leading diplomatic and commercial section of the city. As you walk through this airy, surprisingly green district, note the considerable international presence here: More than a dozen embassies occupy renovated villas or compounds in the grid of avenues south of Hoan Kiem Lake, and 20-story office buildings have begun to shadow the streets of this lovely part of town.

A GOOD WALK

This 3.8-km (2.4-mi) walk, beginning southeast of Hoan Kiem Lake, ends not where it begins but on the west side of the lake, still in the heart of the city. If you've arranged for a driver to pick you up afterward, tell him to meet you in front of the Nha Tho Lon, the Grand Cathedral—also known as St. Joseph's.

Start on the steps of the downtown area's grandest building, the restored **Opera House** ⑨. From the Opera House steps turn sharply to the right and follow Trang Tien Street east to its end. Here, at No. 1, is the **Museum of History** ⑩, which houses some of Vietnam's dearest artifacts. Just up Trang Tien Street, at 25 Tong Dan Street, is the **Museum of the Revolution** ⑪.

Return to the huge intersection in front of the Opera House. From here head south on Phan Chu Trinh Street—that's the second road on the left if you're looking west from the Opera House steps. Turn right onto **Tran Hung Dao Street** ⑫. If you're pressed for time or want to rest your legs, hop into a cyclo here for a 1-km (½-mi) ride down Tran Hung Dao to Quan Su Street (it should cost a maximum of 10,000d, but you could try to bargain it down to 5,000d). If you choose to walk, you'll discover that this stretch of Tran Hung Dao Street is an embassy row of sorts.

At the intersection of Tran Hung Dao and Quan Su is the **Viet Xo Cultural Palace** ⑬, the Soviet Union's most striking architectural contribution to this district. At the end of Tran Hung Dao Street is the dreary Ga Hanoi, the main railway station whose name comes from the French: *gare.* Now travel north on Quan Su Street to the nearby **Ambassador's Pagoda** ⑭. At Ly Thuong Kiet Street, turn right, then left about 300 ft later at Hoa Lo Street. This is the site of the infamous **Hoa Lo Prison** ⑮, the turn-of-the-century "fiery furnace" that the French euphemistically called La Maison Centrale and that American prisoners of war sardonically nicknamed the Hanoi Hilton. Only about a third of the prison is intact, as a 22-story office tower and 14-story hotel complex was built in its place.

From Hoa Lo continue east on Ly Thuong Kiet for another block and a half. On the left is the entrance to a bustling market with CHO 19–12 (December 19th Market) written in red lettering on a flaking gray sign. (If you want to skip the market, continue down Ly Thuong Kiet Street—

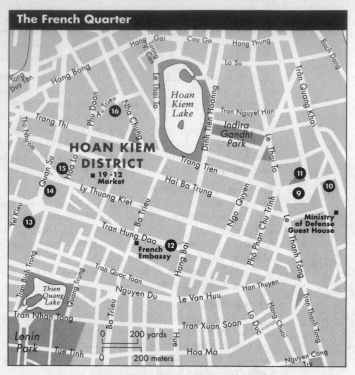

The French Quarter

where you'll find one of the ugliest new additions to the capital's chang-ing skyline, the Hanoi Central Office Building—and take a left on Quang Trung Street.) The north end of the market spills out onto Hai Ba Trung Street, named after the rebellious and heroic Trung sisters, who led a short-lived revolt against the Chinese in AD 40. Turn right on this street and then left on Quang Trung Street; at No. 1 is the main Vietnam Airlines ticketing office. Beyond Trang Thi Street, the road merges with Nha Chung Street. Continuing north on Nha Chung brings you to the Hoan Kiem District Culture Center (Nha Van Quan Hoan Kiem), a Soviet-style dance hall. Another 650 ft or so and you've reached **St. Joseph's Cathe-dral** ⑯, a proud but tired-looking stone-and-cement edifice that fronts a small square. From here it's just a two-block walk east to Hoan Kiem Lake or two blocks north to busy Hang Gai Street in the Old Quarter.

TIMING

This is a full-morning walk that could extend into the afternoon if you're keen on Vietnamese history. The museums, including the one at Hoa Lo Prison, are closed on Monday and at lunchtime. If you must see all three museums on this walk and you have other afternoon plans, start early. You can also save time by hopping in a cyclo or taxi.

SIGHTS TO SEE

⓮ **Ambassador's Pagoda** (Chua Quan Su). This stately prayer house once served the many ambassadors who called on the Le kings. As the pagoda is in part dedicated to a monk who is said to have saved King Ly Than Tong from his deathbed, many older women come here to pray for good health, especially on the first and 15th evenings of every month of the lunar calendar. ⊠ *73 Quan Su St., Hoan Kiem District,* ☏ *04/825–2427.* ☞ *Free.* ⊙ *Daily 7:30–11:30 and 1:30–5:30.*

⓯ **Hoa Lo Prison** (Hanoi Hilton). There's not much left of the infamous "Hanoi Hilton," the prison that once housed captured American servicemen during the Vietnam War, including U.S. Air Force pilot Douglas "Pete" Peterson, now the first American ambassador to Hanoi. These days it's the focal point of what the government plans as the central business district of the emerging metropolis of Hanoi. What does remain, however, is a small section of the old gaol, which is now the **Hoa Lo Prison Museum,** and the tree under which Do Muoi, the aging former General Secretary of the Communist Party, used to sit while writing epithets on the backs of leaves during his imprisonment by the French during the years of Viet Minh resistance. If you're looking for historical detail about the prison, bring your own well-informed guide; those available at the museum are far more inclined to talk about the size of the cells than reveal any nuggets about what once took place behind the musty yellow walls. Note, too, that at press time there was very little information in English at the museum. ⊠ *1 Hoa Lo St.* ☎ *Free.* ☉ *Tues.–Sun. 8:30–11 and 1:30–4.*

⑩ **Museum of History** (Bao Tang Lich Su). Opened in 1932 as the museum of the École Française d'Extrême Orient, this building has served in its present capacity since 1958, when the French finally handed it back to Hanoi authorities. It houses treasures from early history, particularly Vietnam's Bronze Age, and modern Vietnamese culture. Visiting the museum can be a frustrating experience: There is far too little explanatory text, and English-language translation is pitifully lacking. You would be best served accompanied by a translator and, if possible, a historian. ⊠ *1 Trang Tien St., Hoan Kiem District,* ☎ *04/825–3518.* ☎ *10,000d.* ☉ *Tues.–Sun. 8:45–11:45 and 1:15–4:30.*

⑪ **Museum of the Revolution** (Bao Tang Cach Mang). Built in 1926 to house the French tax office, this cavernous museum opened its doors in 1959. Exhibits focus on specific events or periods in Vietnam's arduous road to independence. Fortunately, just about all the exhibits have English and French commentary, so a few hours in here can actually be a learning experience. On the other hand it may be difficult to swallow some of the museum section titles. English-language guided tours must be arranged in advance. ⊠ *25 Tong Dan St., Hoan Kiem District,* ☎ *04/825–4151.* ☎ *10,000d.* ☉ *Sat. 8–11:30, Tues.–Fri. and Sun. 8–11:30 and 1–4.*

⑨ **Opera House** (Nha Hat Lon). The centerpiece of French architecture in Hanoi and one of the grandest buildings in the city, the Hanoi Opera House is a small-scale version of the Paris Opéra designed by Charles Garnier and completed in 1875. The Hanoi structure, finished in 1911, incorporates the same grand elements of Napoleonic architectural style. Despite (or because of) the theater's French history, its steps were the site of frequent denunciations against colonial rule. Today the Opera House is positively glowing after completion of the first stage of a three-year, $17 million restoration. Seeing a show as a VIP guest may be the only way to get into the Opera House, however, as its doors are usually closed; unfortunately, there aren't many performances yet. ⊠ *Trang Thien St.,* ☎ *04/824–8029.*

⑯ **St. Joseph's Cathedral** (Nha Tho Lon). French missionaries built the cathedral in the late 19th century and celebrated the first mass here on Christmas Day 1886. The small but beautiful panes of stained glass were created in Paris in 1906. Also of note is the ornate altar, with its high gilded side walls. The creaky wooden front doors open for Sunday Mass, but if you're visiting at midday, you'll have to walk through the iron gates to the left of the main entrance and enter through the side door. ⊠ *Nha Tho St., Hoan Kiem District,* ☎ *04/828–5967.* ☉ *Mass Sun. at 4:30 AM, 6:30 AM, 10 AM, and 6 PM; Mon.–Tues., Thurs., and Sun. at 5:30 AM; Wed. and Fri.–Sat. at 5:30 AM and 6 PM.*

Café Moca (✉ 14–16 Nha Tho St., ☎ 04/825–6334), opposite the
Cathedral, serves excellent coffees plus Vietnamese, Western, and Indian cuisine in an airy ambiance. Mr. Binh, Moca's charming young
maitre d', is a small-talk pro, but he's also a veteran of the Hanoi restaurant scene and will do what it takes to please. All he needs now is to
change the unwieldy chairs.

⑫ **Tran Hung Dao Street.** Once called Rue Gambetta, Tran Hung Dao Street
is now named after the revered 13th-century Vietnamese warrior who
repulsed Kublai Khan's Mongol hordes at a legendary battle on the
Bach Dang River, near present-day Haiphong. The boulevard is lined
with a number of diplomatic missions; among them, fittingly, is the
French embassy. Others are of the Philippines, Indonesia, India, Iraq,
and Cambodia.

⑬ **Viet Xo Cultural Palace** (Cung Van Hoa Viet-Xo). Never one to down-
play its influence, the Soviet Union assisted with the design and construction
of this "workers' cultural palace." Inaugurated September 1, 1985, the
rigid 120-room white colossus stretches from Yet Kieu Street to Tran Binh
Trong Road. The palace actually is three structures: the performance building houses a 1,200-seat concert hall, while the study and technology buildings contain a library, a conference hall, and an observatory. ✉ *91 Tran
Hung Dao St.,* ☎ *04/825–3787.* ✑ *Free.* ☉ *Daily 8–noon, 1–4:30.*

Around The Ho Chi Minh Mausoleum

Ask a cyclo or taxi driver to take you from Hoan Kiem Lake to the
Ho Chi Minh Mausoleum, in the Ba Dinh District. As you travel
northwest on Dien Bien Phu Street, you'll leave the tightly woven fabric of the Old Quarter behind and find yourself surrounding by sweeping French-era villas and massive ocher-color government buildings.
At the end of Dien Bien Phu Street is the minimally landscaped Ba Dinh
Square, in the center of which flutters Hanoi's largest Vietnam flag.
One can almost hear the echoes of Ho Chi Minh's voice ringing out
over loudspeakers to the half million northern Vietnamese who gathered to hear Uncle Ho's Declaration of Independence on September 2,
1945. On the west side of the square is the mausoleum itself.

A GOOD WALK

Start at the **Ho Chi Minh Mausoleum** ⑰. Once you have passed by the un-
flinching guards and through the mausoleum itself, you'll be directed
through large iron gates and toward **Ho Chi Minh's Residence** ⑱, which
is in the tranquil wooded compound of the **Presidential Palace** ⑲. Although
you are welcome to Uncle Ho's house, the palace itself is off-limits, as is
much of the surrounding parkland. Behind the Presidential Palace, however, is the large **Botanical Garden** ⑳, which is open to the public, although
the entrance is a bit far away, on Hoang Hoa Tham Street. A short path-
way leads from Ho Chi Minh's house to **One-Pillar Pagoda** ㉑, the reconstructed Buddhist tower in the center of a small square lake. To the
left is Dien Huu Pagoda; this charming but seldom-visited temple sits in
the shadow of the architecturally baffling **Ho Chi Minh Museum** ㉒.

Walk out the front doors of the museum and down the steps toward Ba
Dinh Square. Turn right on Hung Vuong Street, the road in front of the
mausoleum. Ahead and to the left is the six-story International Press Center. But turn left just before that building, on Le Hong Phong Street. At
No. 11 on this wide, tree-lined boulevard is the new International Conference Center, where the gathering of French-speaking nations, known
as the *Francophonie,* was held in November 1997. Le Hong Phong leads
back to Dien Bien Phu Street, where you should bear right. In about 200
yards you'll reach shady Chi Lang Park, where there's a statue of Vladimir
Ilyich Lenin, one of the last still standing. Lenin appears to be leaning

Around the Ho Chi Minh Mausoleum and West Lake

West Lake
(Ho Tay)

Truc Bach
Lake

THE CITADEL

Ministry of
Planning &
Investment

BA DINH DISTRICT

Ba Dinh
Meeting Hall

Ba Dinh
Square

Flag
Tower

Chi Lang
Park

GIANG
VO

Kim Ma
Bus Station

National
Stadium

HAO
NAM

Huu La Prison
(Hanoi Hilton)

Hanoi
Railway Station

Army Museum, **23**

Botanical
Garden, **20**

Fine Arts
Museum, **24**

Ho Chi Minh
Mausoleum, **17**

Ho Chi Minh
Museum, **22**

Ho Chi Minh's
Residence, **18**

One-Pillar Pagoda, **21**

Presidential Palace, **19**

Quan Thanh
Temple, **26**

Temple of
Literature, **25**

Tran Quoc
Pagoda, **28**

War Memorial, **27**

resolutely toward the **Army Museum** ㉓, just across the street. To the left is the 100-ft tower known as the Flag Pillar, the surviving remnant of the Nguyen dynasty citadel, which has become a historic symbol of the city.

From the Army Museum, retrace your steps to the intersection of Le Hong Phong, Dien Bien Phu, and Hoang Dieu streets. Turn left on Hoang Dieu and continue, past the Chinese embassy on your right, until you reach very busy Nguyen Thai Hoc Street. One block to the right is the **Fine Arts Museum** ㉔, set back in a courtyard. From here the **Temple of Literature** ㉕ is just across the street, secluded behind a low stone wall. To get to the entrance, proceed south down Van Mieu Street, opposite the art museum, and turn right on Quoc Tu Giam Street.

TIMING

Three hours should be enough to get from the Ho Chi Minh Mausoleum to the Fine Arts Museum, provided you don't venture over to the Botanical Gardens. Leave at least another 30–40 minutes for the Temple of Literature. Or conversely, you could start at the Temple of Literature—it opens in the summer at 7:30, in winter at 8—and make your way up to the Botanical Gardens or to West Lake, taking in the sights along the way. The only real delay is lining up to view Uncle Ho (keep in mind, too, that his mausoleum is closed in the afternoons).

SIGHTS TO SEE

❷❸ **Army Museum** (Bao Tang Quan Doi). The Army Museum is an intriguing example of Vietnam's continuing obsession with publicizing its past military exploits. The museum buildings were once used as French military barracks. Adjacent to the museum is the **Hanoi Flag Pillar.** Built in 1812, the pillar escaped destruction by the French when they leveled much of the citadel. ✉ *Dien Bien Phu St., Ba Dinh District,* ☎ *04/823–4264.* 🎟 *10,000d.* ☉ *Tues.–Sun. 8–11:30 and 1:30–4:30.*

☙ ❷⓿ **Botanical Garden** (Vuon Bach Thao). This 50-acre park behind the Presidential Palace was designed by French landscape engineers in 1890. Athletes in search of exercise congregate here. Between dusk and closing time—10 PM—the island retreat in the center of the park is definitely rated R. ✉ *Entrance on Hoang Hoa Tham Rd.* 🎟 *1,000d.* ☉ *Daily 7 AM–10 PM.*

★ ❷❹ **Fine Arts Museum** (Bao Tang My Thuat). The evolution of Vietnamese art is sparingly, if not lovingly, chronicled in this musty three-story museum, which opened in 1966 after serving as a boardinghouse for French girls living in Indochina. ✉ *66 Nguyen Thai Hoc St.,* ☎ *04/823–3084.* 🎟 *10,000d.* ☉ *Tues.–Sun. 8–noon and 1–4.*

★ ⓱ **Ho Chi Minh Mausoleum** (Lang Chu Tich Ho Chi Minh). It's hard to overstate Ho Chi Minh's heroic stature among the Vietnamese and the significance of his mausoleum. Although the number of citizens queuing up to see their late president has dropped significantly in the last few years, thousands of Vietnamese still visit the revered site each year to pay homage to "Uncle Ho." Had officials followed his wishes, this structure may never have been built, as Ho Chi Minh had expressed in his will his desire to be cremated. But the preservation of the Vietnamese leader and his memory has gone the way of such other Communist figureheads. Ho's embalmed body, touched up now and again in Russia, is virtually the only thing inside the mausoleum. The structure itself is a squat, cold, gray cubicle ringed by columns and topped by a flat square frieze adorned with the words "*Chu Tich* (President) Ho Chi Minh" in red plum marble.

When you enter the mausoleum, be aware of the strict propriety expected of visitors. Although you will see Vietnamese pilgrims moving in a solemn single-file procession, foreigners must sign in at an office on Chua Mot Cot Street, south of the mausoleum, then leave their possessions at another checkpoint closer to the actual tomb, where uninformative brochures are for sale. Your purchase of them amounts to your entrance donation. No cameras, hats, or bags of any kind may be brought in the building, and you are expected to behave respectfully. This means not wearing shorts or tank tops or putting your hands in your pockets while inside. Talking is also forbidden, and once inside the chilly room containing Ho's corpse you are discouraged from lingering for more than a few moments in front of the glass. ⊠ *Enter at corner of Hung Vuong and Le Hong Phong Sts.* ⊠ *Donation expected.* ⊙ *Sat.–Mon. and Wed.–Thurs.* 8 AM–11 AM. *Usually closed Oct. and/or Nov., when Ho's body is in Russia for maintenance.*

⑳ **Ho Chi Minh Museum** (Bao Tang Ho Chi Minh). Opened on May 19, 1990, on what would have been Ho's 100th birthday, this complex was established, in the language of the brochure that you can take on entering, "to satisfy the Vietnamese people's desire to express their deep gratitude to the President." This museum is a must-stop—if only for 15 minutes—on the Uncle Ho circuit. You must leave your cameras and bags at the reception area. There is an interesting gift shop. ⊠ *3 Ngoc Ha St. (also accessible from Chua Mot Cot St.), Ba Dinh District,* ☎ *04/846-3752.* ⊠ *5,000d.* ⊙ *Tues.–Sun.* 8–11:30 *and* 1:30–4.

⑱ **Ho Chi Minh's Residence** (Nha Bac Ho). After 1954 Ho Chi Minh had the run of the Presidential Palace, but the ostentation was too much for the austere president. Instead, he preferred the humble former home of the palace's electrician, where he lived for four years. Then, the story goes, in 1958 Ho Chi Minh moved to this simple but tastefully designed wooden house on stilts, which served as his living quarters and work space until his death in 1969. Regardless of Ho Chi Minh's faith in the accuracy of the city's antiaircraft gunners, some doubt must be thrown on the claim that Ho Chi Minh spent so much time in this open-air sanctum while American bombers targeted Hanoi during the Vietnam War. Indeed, Ho's Politburo ordered the construction of a nearby bomb shelter, later dubbed House No. 67. Legend holds that Uncle Ho refused to use the shelter as a home, preferring to confer with the Politburo in this fortified bunker but to sleep in his stilt house. You may want to purchase a 20,000d booklet entitled The Living Quarter and Working Place of President Ho Chi Minh, available at the entrance gate to the house. Though overwrought, it's actually quite informative. ⊠ *Hung Vuong Rd., Ba Dinh District.* ⊠ *3,000d.* ⊙ *Daily* 7:30–11 *and* 1:30–4.

㉑ **One-Pillar Pagoda** (Chua Mot Cot). The French destroyed this temple, once known as LienHoa Tower but now exclusively referred to as One-Pillar Pagoda, on their way out in 1954. It was reconstructed by the new government and still commemorates the legend of Emperor Ly Thai Tong. It is said that the childless emperor dreamed that Quan Am, the Buddhist goddess of mercy and compassion, seated on a lotus flower, handed him a baby boy. Sure enough, he soon met and married a peasant woman who bore him a male heir, and in 1049 he constructed this monument in appreciation. The distinctive single pillar is meant to represent the stalk of the lotus flower, a sacred Vietnamese symbol of purity. ⊠ *Ong Ich Kiem St., Ba Dinh District,* ☎ *no phone.* ⊠ *Free.* ⊙ *Daily* 7–5:30.

⑲ **Presidential Palace** (Cung Chu Tich). Constructed from 1900 to 1906, the bright, mustard-yellow building served as the living and working quarters of Indochina's general governors. When Ho Chi Minh returned to Hanoi after the defeat of the French in 1954, he refused to live in the palace itself but chose the more modest quarters of the palace electrician. Today the building is used for formal international receptions and other important government meetings. ⊠ *Hung Vuong Rd. and Hoang Van Thu St., Ba Dinh District. Not open to public.*

★ ㉕ **Temple of Literature** (Van Mieu). An unusually well-preserved example of Vietnamese architecture, this monument to Confucius was built in 1070 by Emperor Ly Thanh Tong. Soon after its construction, it became the site of Vietnam's first university, Quoc Tu Giam, which specialized in training students—many of them sons and daughters of emperors and other high-ranking dignitaries—to pass the rigorous examinations for government and civil-service posts. The achievements of several centuries of the university's doctoral recipients are recorded on 82 stelae (stone slabs), which rest on stone tortoises. The French later used the building as, appropriately, their school of civil administration. ⊠ *Quoc Tu Giam St., Dong Da District,* ☎ *04/845–2917 or 04/823–5601.* ☜ *12,000d; 20,000d for an English-speaking guide.* ☉ *Summer, daily 7:30–6; winter, daily 8–5.*

West Lake

About 3 km (2 mi)—10 minutes by taxi or motorbike—northwest of Hoan Kiem Lake lies West Lake (Ho Tay), another body of water that's steeped in legend. It is said a giant golden calf from China followed the peals of a monk's bronze bell to this spot. When the ringing stopped, the calf lost its direction and kept walking in circles, creating the basin of West Lake. Like Hoan Kiem's turtle, the calf is said to still dwell in the lake.

Development is changing the face of the shore, however, as luxury hotels and high-rent villas eat away at the traditional communities such as the flower village of Nghi Tam, near the Kim Lien Pagoda. The lake itself is a weekend boating spot for Vietnamese families. Afterward they stop in one of the floating restaurants for snails boiled in lemon leaves.

A GOOD WALK

Start your walk at the beginning of the wide causeway of Thanh Nien Street that divides West Lake from the smaller Truc Bach Lake. Thanh Nien means "youth"; the causeway was so named in honor of the young "volunteers" who helped build this roadway between the two lakes. Along the way note the floating seafood restaurants and the neon signs of the times—billboards for Carlsberg and Compaq. At the very beginning of Thanh Nien duck into ornate **Quan Thanh Temple** ㉖.

Staying on the same side of the street, walk for about five minutes to reach an unnamed **War Memorial** ㉗ to antiaircraft gunners stationed on the roof of a nearby factory who shot down 10 American planes in 1967. Walk about 650 ft, then cross the street to Hanoi's oldest pagoda, the delightful **Tran Quoc Pagoda** ㉘, on an islet jutting into West Lake. From there it's a 10- to 15-minute walk back to the beginning of Thanh Nien Street.

If you're up for walking at least part of the way back into the center of town from here, then go along Phan Dinh Phung Street. This beautiful shaded avenue leads past sprawling French villas and Chinese mandarin mansions, many occupied by long-serving party members, as well as the gracious but seldom-used Gothic North Door Cathedral (Cua Bac).

TIMING

The causeway can be traversed in about 20 minutes, but allow for an hour if you want to peek around the temples. Allow 90 minutes if you want to rent a dilapidated paddleboat from the quay on the Truc Bach side. The walk from the southeast corner of West Lake to the water tower at the edge of the Old Quarter is another 15–25 minutes.

SIGHTS TO SEE

㉖ **Quan Thanh Temple** (Chua Quan Thanh or Chan Vu Quan). Built by King Ly Thai To in the 11th century, this much-made-over temple was once known as the Temple of the Grand Buddha. Above the ornamented main gate is a 1677 replica of the bronze bell that supposedly lures the

West Lake's legendary golden calf from China. ✉ *Quan Thanh and Thanh Nien Sts.,* ☎ *04/823–4378.* 🎫 *5,000d donation.* ⊙ *Daily 8–4:30.*

28 **Tran Quoc Pagoda** (Chua Tran Quoc). Hanoi's oldest temple and an active monastery, dates from the 6th century, when King Ly Nam De had a pagoda, named Khai Quoc, built on the bank of the Red River. More than a thousand years later excessive erosion of the riverbank caused King Le Kinh Tong to move the pagoda to Goldfish (Ca Vang) Islet on West Lake, and a subsequent Le king renamed it Tran Quoc. ✉ *Thanh Nien St.* 🎫 *5,000d donation.* ⊙ *Daily 8–4:30.*

27 **War Memorial.** If you're interested in Vietnam War history, head for this small memorial between West Lake and Truc Bach Lake; it marks the capture of one of the war's most famous POWs. On October 26, 1967, Navy lieutenant commander John McCain's plane was shot down, sending him into Truc Bach Lake. Suffering from badly broken bones and severe beatings, he was imprisoned in the infamous "Hanoi Hilton" for over four years. He went on to become an Arizona senator and a vocal advocate of reconciliation between the United States and his former captors. ✉ *Thanh Nien St.*

Dining

The concept of an international cuisine industry is new to the capital despite the decades-long imposing presence of a culinary superpower: France. Fresh baguettes—and they're wonderful and cheap—are just about the only food link to that era. Virtually everything else at the international level has sprung up in the last half dozen years, leaving a Hanoi establishment's standing far more dependant on expatriate word of mouth and successful international management skills. Even the Vietnamese restaurants in Hanoi—and there are dozens of treats that await you—are confined to similar strictures; the hardscrabble north has understandably been preoccupied with more pressing issues than cuisine throughout most of this century. Keep such issues in perspective and you should be pleasantly surprised.

Though the establishments listed below have staying power, it is recommended you call before heading out to a particular restaurant, as Hanoi places close as suddenly as they open. In addition, it's not uncommon for owners and managers to change, transforming the whole restaurant—for better or worse. We have limited our list to restaurants only, though Hanoi's top hotels—particularly the Sofitel Metropole, the Guoman, the Daewoo, Horison, and Meritus Westlake—all have high-quality dining rooms.

Cafés

$ ✕ **Au Lac Café.** It's the perfect location for breakfast, an afternoon break, or an after-dinner espresso—at a table on the outdoor terrace of this café across from the new wing of the Sofitel Metropole. Don't confuse it with the copy next door, the Mai La Café, and pray it doesn't rain. ✉ *57 Ly Thai To St.,* ☎ *04/825–7807. No credit cards.*

¢ ✕ **Café 252.** This is the famous breakfast spot where Catherine Deneuve hung out while filming *Indochine*. Some say it's lost a dose of charm since remodeling in early 1998, but Mr. Chi and company still serve good pastries and the best fresh yogurt in town. ✉ *252 Hang Bong St.,* ☎ *04/825–0216. No credit cards.*

Chinese

$$$ ✕ **Quan Gio Moi.** The best part about this plain-looking restaurant is its perfect location overlooking a lake in Lenin Park. The food is good, though not superb. Try the hot-and-sour soup, the chili prawns, or the sweet-and-sour chicken. Eat here if you're in the area, but it's not worth

a special trip. ⊠ *63 Le Duan St., Lenin Park, Hai Ba Trung District,* ☏ *04/822–9839. No credit cards.*

French

$$$ ✕ **Le Splendide.** This French restaurant in the Hoa Binh Hotel is, as
★   the name claims, truly splendid for Hanoi. Sharp but unobtrusive service compliments the reserved sophistication, which is in stark contrast to the dilapidated, state-run hotel. The mussels in white wine sauce are excellent, as is the crème brûlée, and the $7 lunch special is a steal. ⊠ *Hoa Binh Hotel, 27 Ly Thuong Kiet St., Hoan Kiem District,* ☏ *04/ 826–6087. Jacket and tie. AE, MC, V.*

$$$ ✕ **President Garden.** Self-taught Belgian chef-turned-manager Daniel
★   Moreaux holds forth at this quiet, inoffensive villa a stone's throw from the U.S. Ambassador's residence. He has trained his local chefs to "respect culinary traditions," as he puts it, and prepare an array of pricey French delicacies with imported beef, lamb, and fish such as Norwegian salmon. Vietnamese cuisine on the patio. ⊠ *14 Tong Dan St., Hoan Kiem District,* ☏ *04/825–3606. MC, V.*

$$ ✕ **Hoa Sua.** Walk through a front courtyard off the street to find this
★   restaurant serving both French and Vietnamese food. It's a favorite of Francophiles and French expatriates. More than a restaurant, it's a humanitarian project: young people—particularly orphans—in need of assistance are trained as waiters and cooks. Outdoor seating is available on a terra-cotta patio surrounded by palms; indoors is equally charming, with wrought-iron furniture. Though the customer-server ratio often seems to be one-to-one, service is lax. Reservations are recommended for Sunday brunch. ⊠ *81 Tho Nhuom St., Hoan Kiem District,* ☏ *04/824–0448. No credit cards.*

Indian

$$ ✕ **Khazana.** Manager Shankar Dutta used to run this opulent tribute
★   to North Indian cuisine near the Temple of Literature. At press time, he was moving it downtown to cater to the international business community huddled in the vicinity of Hoan Kiem Lake. (It's also nearer his main Indian competition, the equally tasty and far cheaper Tandoor Restaurant on Hang Be St.) Curries, soups, and chutney, all created by his two Indian chefs and served with aplomb, have been worthy of the higher-than-average prices. Even so, Mr. Dutta promises the cost will drop by about 15% at the new location. ⊠ *41-B Ly Thai To St., Hoan Kiem District,* ☏ *04/851–7782. MC, V.*

International

$$$ ✕ **The Press Club.** Modern Mediterranean cuisine and fine wines are served at this elegant restaurant evoking the 1930s. Eat in the tasteful dining room or outside on the terrace surrounded by palms. Enjoy an aperitif or a sherry in the cigar bar. Private dining available. ⊠ *59A Ly Thai To St., Hoan Kiem District,* ☏ *04/934–0888. MC, V.*

$$–$$$ ✕ **Club Opera.** One of Hanoi's top all-around restaurants, Club Opera has been serving both Western fare (downstairs) and Vietnamese (upstairs) since 1993—an eternity in this town. But things change, and Clopera, as some call it, has just lost its lease on the second floor, bringing an end to the airy upstairs dining. The imported Australian beef tenderloin and such Vietnamese dishes as the shrimp compote served on stalks of sugarcane are excellent. ⊠ *59 Ly Thai To St., Hoan Kiem District,* ☏ *04/826–8802. AE, MC, V.*

$$ ✕ **Al Fresco.** This colorful south-of-the-border-cum-pizza restaurant a block south of Hoan Kiem Lake gets high marks from expats and travelers. Run by a friendly Aussie, the eclectic East-meets-West dining is coupled with a casual open-air ambience. Service, like the music, can be flighty. ⊠ *23L Hai Ba Trung St., Hoan Kiem District,* ☏ *04/826–7782. No credit cards.*

Italian

$$ ✕ **Il Grillo.** This popular Italian-run eatery serves authentic prosciutto and grappa. The rib-eye steak is highly recommended, as are the home-made pasta dishes. The restaurant has cheerful, cozy decor—like a cabin in the Dolomites. Dinner reservations are recommended. ✉ *116 Ba Trieu St., Hai Ba Trung District,* ☎ *04/822–7720. No credit cards.*

$$ ✕ **Mediterraneo.** Delicious, reasonably-priced Italian food is served in a California atmosphere at Mediterraneo. The pizzas, pasta specials, and spinach pie are surprisingly good, as is the interesting array of home-made high-octane grappa—try licorice or peach. ✉ *23 Nha Tho St., Hoan Kiem District,* ☎ *04/826–6288. MC, V.*

Japanese

$$ ✕ **Saigon Sakura.** The stamp of approval here is the number of ex-patriate Japanese regulars who frequent this take-off-your-shoes restau-rant. A clean Zen decor, good-value "lunch sets," and an attentive staff make this a Hanoi favorite. Private dining available upstairs. ✉ *17 Trang Thi St., Hoan Kiem District,* ☎ *04/825–7565. MC, V.*

Steak

$$$ ✕ **Galleon Steak House.** With beef imported from Australia and the United States and an American chef/manager—Richard Lee—who's man-aged to get it right, the meat here can satisfy most any carnivorous han-kerings. ✉ *50 Tran Quoc Toan St., Hoan Kiem District,* ☎ *04/ 822–8611. AE, DC, MC, V.*

Thai

$$ ✕ **Baan Thai Restaurant.** Saigon is Vietnam's preserve for Thai cuisine, but Baan Thai is one of a handful of restaurants that reminds us that good, cheap, and spicy Thai dishes are indeed available in the capital. ✉ *3-B Cha Ca St., Hoan Kiem District,* ☎ *04/828–1120. No credit cards.*

Vegetarian

$$ ✕ **Vegetarian Restaurant Com Chay Nang Tam.** An unusual array of vegetarian dishes, many prepared to resemble meat (careful: some ac-tually have meat!), are served in the back of a dimly lit villa. The warm corn squares are a pleasing starter, and the "ginger fish," made of tofu, is a good main course. Be aware that a few too many dishes are fried. ✉ *79A Tran Hung Dao St., Hoan Kiem District,* ☎ *04/826–6140. No credit cards.*

Vietnamese

$$$ ✕ **Indochine.** One of the older and better upscale Vietnamese dining establishments in town, Indochine is set back from a small street in a worn but elegant house. Live traditional music plays some nights, and the staff wears colorful traditional costumes. ✉ *16 Nam Ngu St., Hoan Kiem District,* ☎ *04/824–6097. Reservations essential. Jacket and tie. AE, MC, V.*

$$$ ✕ **Nam Phuong.** Upscale Vietnamese cuisine is served in an elegant French villa setting. Portions of the tasty and beautifully presented dishes (like the beef in coconut milk served in a coconut) are disappointingly scanty, however. Nouvelle cuisine Vietnamese style, perhaps? There's live traditional Vietnamese music in the evenings. ✉ *19 Phan Chu Trinh St., Hoan Kiem District,* ☎ *04/824–0926. AE, MC, V.*

$$ ✕ **Cha Ca La Vong.** Right in the thick of the Old Quarter is Hanoi's most famous purveyor of *cha ca* (boneless Red River fish cubes mar-inated in dill, grilled—with an alarming disregard for safety—at your table, and served with rice noodles and peanuts). The grease-covered walls add to the authentic, pungent experience. Don't wear your best threads; you'll likely be wearing some of that grease by evening's end. ✉ *14 Cha Ca St., Hoan Kiem District,* ☎ *no phone. No credit cards.*

$$ ✕ **Seasons of Hanoi.** English manager Justin Wheatcroft has done wonders with Seasons, where French elegance meets Vietnamese charm in a beautifully restored 1902 villa. The coconut and lemongrass chicken curry is a rich choice, and the fish baked in a clay pot is tasty but salty. Sunday brunch is popular. ⊠ *95B Quan Thanh St., Ba Dinh District,* ☎ *04/835–5444. AE, MC, V.*

$$ ✕ **Van Xuan.** Hue specialties are the order of the day in this expansive food hall that's half restaurant, half shopping mall. (The entire complex seems built by someone who didn't quite know what to do with the windfall of cash he stumbled into.) The menu is huge; try the prawns steamed in beer, or stir-fried frogs legs in coconut juice. Apparently Secretary of State Madeleine Albright appreciated the cuisine—photos of her digging in are everywhere. Although Van Xuan is open for lunch, the vast majority of its customers come for dinner, when there's live music. ⊠ *15 Hang Cot St., Hoan Kiem District,* ☎ *04/927–2888. MC, V.*

$ ✕ **Dac Kim Bun Cha.** After souvenir shopping on Hang Bac Street, con-
★ sider having lunch at this four-story Old Quarter institution. Ordering shouldn't be hard: The restaurant serves only two dishes, and locals say both are tops: Bun cha (grilled pork patties with rice noodles) is served with heaping plates of herbs and lettuce; as a side dish, try the huge pork- and crab-filled spring rolls. ⊠ *1 Hang Manh St., Hoan Kiem District,* ☎ *no phone. No credit cards. No dinner.*

$ ✕ **Hue Restaurant.** Come here for imperial Hue cuisine and other tra-
★ ditional Vietnamese fare in a rustic outdoor/indoor setting. Pork pie is a poor translation for culinary nirvana—a some-assembly-required platter of sugarcane-wrapped ground pork that you roll with greens and vegetables in rice paper and dip into a delicious peanut sauce. For those who wince at this carnivorous frenzy, vegetarian delights are plentiful. Warning: It's advised not to drink too much since the rest room here is essentially a sloping floor. ⊠ *6 Ly Thuong Kiet St., Hoan Kiem District,* ☎ *04/826–4062. No credit cards.*

Lodging

Hoan Kiem District

$$$$ 🏨 **Hotel Sofitel Metropole Hanoi.** The exquisitely renovated Metropole,
★ built by the French at the turn of the century, combines Old World European grandeur with modern convenience. And you can't beat the location, in the heart of Hanoi. The impeccably decorated rooms with French-style shuttered windows are luxurious if not incredibly spacious. ⊠ *15 Pho Ngo Quyen St., Hoan Kiem District,* ☎ *04/826–6919,* 𝔽𝔸𝕏 *04/826–6920. 244 rooms. 2 restaurants, 2 bars, air-conditioning, in-room safes, minibars, refrigerators, room service, pool, laundry service and dry cleaning, concierge, business services, meeting rooms, travel services, airport shuttle, car rental. AE, DC, MC, V.*

$$$–$$$$ 🏨 **Guoman Hotel.** Another property quick to win over business travel-
★ ers (with hefty discounts available for corporate guests) is the Malaysian joint-venture Guoman Hotel, a stately cream-color block of a building which sprouted up downtown in 1997. Function rules over elegance in the rooms, which often feel like, well, something's missing. Perhaps they lack character, the better to soothe the tired businessperson. The lobby and second-floor landing are a bit sparse as well. Better to relax in the plush bar, where half-priced drinks are served during the day and hotel GM John Simmons often wanders in to help guests improve their Guoman stay. Service is commendable, and the food in the 24-hour restaurant is first-rate. ⊠ *83-A Ly Thuong Kiet St., Hoan Kiem District,* ☎ *04/822–2800,* 𝔽𝔸𝕏 *04/822–2822. 152 rooms. Restaurant, lounge bar, in-room safes, minibars, fitness center, laundry service and dry cleaning, business services, meeting rooms, travel services, car rental. AE, DC, MC, V.*

$$$–$$$$ ☎ **Hanoi Opera Hilton.** Hilton International has defied the cynics and is going ahead with a major hotel in Vietnam's capital despite the various emotions attached to the term "Hanoi Hilton." The hotel was designed to complement the city's premier colonial-era edifice, the neighboring Opera House: it is the same height and will be painted the same color, and Hilton's interior decorators aim to reflect the opera's period elegance as well. It will have all the amenities that you would expect from this international hotel chain. Grand opening is slated for February 1999. ✉ *1 Le Thang Thong St., Hoan Kiem District,* ☎ *800/445–8667 in the U.S., no local phone at press time. 271 rooms. 3 restaurants, 2 bars, minibars, in-room safes, pool, fitness center, massage, shops, business services, meeting rooms. AE, DC, MC, V.*

$$$ ☎ **De Syloia Hotel.** Quietly tucked away on Tran Hung Dao Street, this
★ modest but exquisitely clean "boutique hotel" does a booming business, thanks to superior staff, elegant rooms, and the once-revolutionary concept that the customer always comes first. The De Syloia rises up from behind a red-tile colonial villa which serves as the entry way, lobby bar, and restaurant. Jean-Marie Bertron, the attentive general manager, says this Vietnamese-owned property is most popular with executive and business travelers, who appreciate the unswerving commitment to perfection. ✉ *17A Tran Hung Dao St., Hoan Kiem District,* ☎ *04/ 824–5346,* FAX *04/82–1083. 33 rooms. Restaurant, bar, in-room safes, minibars, refrigerators, room service, exercise room, laundry service and dry cleaning, business services, meeting rooms, travel services, car rental. AE, DC, MC, V.*

$$$ ☎ **Saigon Hotel.** A joint venture of Saigon Tourist and the Hanoi Rail-
★ way, this property offers superior-quality service and, despite the concrete '60s architecture, a pleasant ambience. Rooms are standard hotel-style, bordering on the dull. The rooftop garden is a terrific place for an evening drink, but you may feel like the only one in on the secret up there. ✉ *80 Ly Thuong Kiet St., Hoan Kiem District,* ☎ *04/ 826–8499,* FAX *04/826–6631. 44 rooms. Restaurant, 2 bars, in-room safes, minibars, refrigerators, room service, massage, sauna, laundry service and dry cleaning, business services, meeting rooms, travel services, car rental. AE, DC, MC, V.*

$$$ ☎ **Sunway Hotel.** Unassuming but modern, the Malaysian-invested Sun-
★ way, which opened in February 1998, is aiming its quiet charms and conveniences at the business traveler. It boasts triple-glazed windows, drinkable tap water, and fax-modem desk outlets in all rooms. Decor is unremarkable but ultimately acceptable—a feeling that translates to many of the hotel's qualities. ✉ *19 Pham Dinh Ho St., Hoan Kiem District,* ☎ *04/971–3888,* FAX *04/971–3555. 143 rooms. Restaurant, bar, in-room safes, minibars, refrigerators, room service, fitness center, laundry service and dry cleaning, business services, meeting rooms, travel services, car rental. AE, DC, MC, V.*

$$ ☎ **Chains First Eden Hotel.** In the Old Quarter, this establishment has all the makings of a first-class luxury hotel, except decent management. But it's an excellent departure point for walking through Hanoi. Rooms have all the amenities, but they also have bright orange curtains. ✉ *3A Phan Dinh Phung St., Hoan Kiem District,* ☎ *04/828–3897,* FAX *04/828–4066. 42 rooms. Restaurant, bar, air-conditioning, in-room safes, minibars, refrigerators, room service, health club, laundry service and dry cleaning, business services, travel services, car rental. AE, DC, MC, V.*

$$ ☎ **Galaxy Hotel.** Although built in 1918, this granite-faced hotel has
★ been fully renovated and seems wholly modern. The comfortable rooms have typical hotel decor and are quieter than you'd suspect given the hotel's proximity to the bustling Old Quarter; some have garden views. The attentive staff speaks English. ✉ *1 Phan Dinh Phung St., Hoan Kiem District,* ☎ *04/828–2888,* FAX *04/828–2466. 48 rooms. Restaurant, bar,*

air-conditioning, in-room safes, minibars, refrigerators, room service, laundry service and dry cleaning, concierge, business services, meeting rooms, travel services, car rental. AE, DC, MC, V.

$$ 🏨 **Government Guest House.** Welcome to 1975. This Soviet block a stone's throw from everything is a far cry from the elegant main guest house across the lawns of the quiet enclosed courtyard, where dignitaries and "friends" of Vietnam have been known to stay. A night in this nearly forgotten concrete hotel is a trip back to a simpler Hanoi. Despite modern conveniences like electricity (okay, the huge rooms do have IDD phones, satellite TV, hot water, air-conditioning, and some balconies), most furnishings here appear to be Late Cold War era. If it feels just a bit too spooky in these dark but clean hallways, it's because you're the only person in the place. ✉ *12 Ngo Quyen St., Hoan Kiem District, ☎ 04/825–5853, FAX 04/825–9227. 48 rooms. Restaurant, air-conditioning, minibars, meeting rooms, car rental. AE, MC, V.*

$$ 🏨 **Planet Hotel.** The Planet, in the Old Quarter overlooking West Lake, has plush rooms. Wooden touches offset the ultraslick modern edge and the profusion of granite. It's hard to imagine this place full of guests. Lovely views of West Lake from both the Penthouse Restaurant and the health club's hot tub. ✉ *120 Quan Thanh St., Hoan Kiem District, ☎ 04/843–5888, FAX 04/843–5088. 53 rooms. Restaurant, 2 bars, air-conditioning, in-room safes, minibars, refrigerators, room service, hot tub, sauna, health club, laundry service and dry cleaning, concierge, business services, travel services, car rental. AE, DC, MC, V.*

$–$$ 🏨 **Prince Hotel.** This smallish, comfortable minihotel has simple but elegant rooms, nice bathrooms, and an enthusiastic, English-speaking staff. The balconies block the noise from the street. It's near the train station and not too far from the city center. ✉ *96A Hai Ba Trung St., Hoan Kiem District, ☎ 04/824–8314, FAX 04/824–8323. 25 rooms. Restaurant, bar, air-conditioning, minibars, refrigerators, laundry and dry cleaning, business services, car rental. AE, DC, MC, V.*

$ 🏨 **Vinh Quang Hotel.** Aside from the cheap East-West fusion decor, the Vinh Quang has neat, efficient rooms and a great central location. Front rooms overlook the color and activity of Hang Quat Street, while back rooms have a more placid view of terra-cotta-tile roofs. ✉ *24 Hang Quat St., Hoan Kiem District, ☎ 04/824–3423, FAX 04/825–1519. 15 rooms. Restaurant, bar, air-conditioning, fans, minibars, refrigerators, laundry service, travel services. AE, MC, V.*

¢–$ 🏨 **Win Hotel.** At the top end of the budget accommodations, the Win
★   is immaculate and homey all at once. It's on a quiet street, a stone's throw from Hoan Kiem Lake. Carved hardwood furniture, tastefully arranged fake flowers, high ceilings, clean baths, satellite TV, and a fluffy dog in the lobby make you feel at home. ✉ *34 Hang Hanh St., Hoan Kiem District, ☎ 04/828–7371 or 04/828–7150, FAX 04/824–7448. 8 rooms. Air-conditioning, fans, minibars, refrigerators, laundry service, travel services, car rental. No credit cards.*

Around Lenin Park

$$$$ 🏨 **Hotel Nikko Hanoi.** Looming out of the tired neighborhood just above
★   Lenin Park is the imposing Japanese addition to Hanoi's hotel landscape. With it's grand opening set for October 1998, the Nikko had not proved itself by press time. But, with the Japan Airlines-owned Nikko Hotels International managing the property, one can rest assured the level of service will be high. ✉ *84 Tran Nhan Tong St., Hoan Kiem District, ☎ 04/822–3535, FAX 04/822–3555. 260 rooms. 3 restaurants, bar, pool, in-room safes, minibars, refrigerators, room service, TVs, massage, sauna, laundry service and dry cleaning, business services, meeting rooms, travel services, car rental. AE, DC, MC, V.*

$$–$$$ 🏨 **Eden Hotel.** The Eden—not to be confused with the other Eden Hotel on Tho Nhuom Street—offers minihotel luxury and service at its finest in a decent location near Thuyen Quang Lake. ✉ *94 Yet Kieu St., Hoan Kiem District,* ☎ *04/822–7465,* FAX *04/822–8235. 22 rooms. Restaurant, air-conditioning, minibars, refrigerators, laundry service and dry cleaning, concierge, travel services, car rental. AE, DC, MC, V.*

$$ 🏨 **Hawaii Hotel.** Ignore the name: this comfortable minihotel has spacious, tasteful rooms as well as a helpful, sweet staff that takes good care of guests from all over the globe. ✉ *77 Nguyen Du St., Hoan Kiem District,* ☎ *04/822–7517,* FAX *04/822–8698. 21 rooms. Restaurant, bar, air-conditioning, minibars, refrigerators, laundry service, business services, travel services, car rental. AE, DC, MC, V.*

Around the Ho Chi Minh Mausoleum/Ba Dinh District

$$$$ 🏨 **Hanoi Daewoo Hotel.** The pool here—the longest in Southeast
★ Asia—is just one example of the luxury of the Daewoo, whose Korean owners have awarded it five stars. Space is abundant—from the open marble lobby to the four restaurants. Rooms are big and tastefully decorated in better-than-average hotel-style furnishings. The main drawback is its distance from downtown; although there is a shuttle service, it doesn't run frequently enough. ✉ *360 Kim Ma St., Ba Dinh District,* ☎ *04/831–5000,* FAX *04/831–5010. 411 rooms. 4 restaurants, 2 bars, air-conditioning, in-room safes, minibars, refrigerators, room service, pool, hot tub, sauna, aerobics, health club, dance club, laundry service and dry cleaning, concierge, business services, meeting rooms, travel services, car rental. AE, DC, MC, V.*

$$$ 🏨 **Hanoi Horison Hotel.** Known as the "Emerald City" because of its green glass-fronted facade, the Horison is a joint Vietnamese-Indonesian project built on the site of a 100-year-old brick factory. (The remaining smokestack out front has become a hotel industry landmark.) The spacious marble lobby is a regular site for local gallery art exhibits. Rooms are luxurious if not overly large and are done in soothing pastels. At press time, the Horison had no plans to cancel the almost-50%-off special it has been running since opening in late 1997. ✉ *10 Cat Linh St., Ba Dinh District,* ☎ *04/733–0808,* FAX *04/733–0688. 324 rooms. 3 restaurants, bar, lobby lounge, air-conditioning, in-room safes, minibars, room service, pool, tennis court, exercise room, laundry service, business services, meeting rooms, travel services. AE, DC, MC, V.*

Around West Lake

$$$$ 🏨 **Meritus Westlake Hanoi.** This dapper new (1998) deluxe hotel overlooking West Lake and the Red River is hoping to take Hanoi's accommodation industry by storm. Its 20-story zig-zag facade rises monstrously above the surrounding minimalist rooftops. Rooms are luxuriously furnished, with classical lines and panoramic views. Meritus boasts Southeast Asia's only pool with a retractable roof, and with its grand ballroom, disco, swank karaoke rooms, and 1940s Manhattan-style rooftop lounge, it appears on its way to establishing itself as a hotel of note. ✉ *1 Thanh Nien Rd., Ba Dinh District,* ☎ *04/823–8888,* FAX *04/829–3888. 322 rooms (100 open at press time). 4 restaurants, 2 bars, fans, minibars, refrigerators, laundry service, pool, meeting rooms, travel services. AE, MC, V.*

Nightlife and the Arts

Bars and Clubs

Apocalypse Now (✉ 5C Hoa Ma St., Hai Ba Trung District, ☎ 04/971–2783), a tamer version of its Saigon sister, nevertheless trades on the mystique of the Francis Ford Coppola movie with Vietnam War and Hollywood props: revolving ceiling fans are painted as helicopter blades, and the DJ booth is the cockpit of a helicopter gunship. But the forty-something bald man at the bar isn't "Kurtz"—he's most likely the country manager for a stalled Vietnam project. It's very popular on weekends after midnight, when working girls rule the pool table, and it can get rowdy: watch your wallets.

K's Bar (⊠ 80 Hoa Ma St., Hoan Kiem District, ☎ 04/971–2138), at the top of a five-floor climb, is a friendly, no-fuss watering hole covered with supremely hip movie and concert posters and a bamboo rooftop. An eccentric Japanese expatriate set up this cramped bar in 1997 so he could bang on his drums and play his blues and jazz records. Regulars—K's faithful are religious about their allegiance—can choose from the extensive music collection and even strike up conversations with the introverted and oddly pretentious staff; newcomers will have to prove their loyalty to the place before enjoying such privileges, though they'll still be served a stiff bourbon.

Mai La Club (⊠ 23 Quang Trung St., Hoan Kiem District, ☎ 04/825–7799) is packed most nights with mobile-phone-wielding, Calvin Klein–clad local hipsters and their fashion-model girlfriends. Management has hoped to spice things up a bit by hiring scantily clad twins to gyrate on stage—an impossible scene only four years ago. Billiards upstairs. Cover charge.

Metal (⊠ 57 Cua Nam St., Hoan Kiem District, ☎ 04/824–1975), a theater-turned-club, is dark, pricey, and often void of style. That said, Vietnamese still enjoy coming here to schmooze with each other and stare at those getting down on the disco-ball-lit dance floor.

Met Pub (⊠ Sofitel Metropole, Ly Thai To St., Hoan Kiem District, ☎ 04/826–6919) is where businesspeople hang out, watch satellite TV, and drink martinis. There's a lively happy hour, and live jazz in the evenings.

Miró's Jungle Bar (⊠ 3 Nguyen Khac Can St., Hoam Kiem District, ☎ 04/826–9080) used to be Hanoi's most fashionable and stylish restaurant—until it's American management decided there's more of a future here in fine partying than in fine dining. "DJ Disco" Dan spins the city's most modern tunes up on the top floor, where the ambience is nouveau lounge. Friday and Saturday nights are popular with certain expatriates who settle in here for a few drinks and let the music pump them up before moving on to dance clubs after midnight.

The Pear Tree (⊠ 78 Tho Nhuom St., Hoan Kiem District, ☎ 04/825–7812) in the Eden Hotel was once the most popular expat bar in the city. Now it is dominated by wrought iron and two billiard tables. Satellite TV and good bar food draw a loyal clientele of French and Americans.

Polite Pub (⊠ 5 Ngo Bao Khanh St., Hoan Kiem District, ☎ 04/825–0959) is one of the nicer, quieter bars in town until Friday and Saturday nights, when it fills with unwinding expatriates and Vietnamese. Upstairs is a gargantuan snooker table, and next door is the rangy Gold Cock.

Queen Bee (⊠ 42 Lang Ha St., Ba Dinh District, ☎ 04/835–0938), the former preserve of cognac-sipping and karaoke-crooning Asian businessmen, has metamorphosed into Hanoi's hottest dance club. Weekend nights are steamy and loud, with a mix of live rock and disco music and a happy-go-lucky DJ's techno beats. A silly fog machine, a mike-wielding club manager ("Rock the house, Hanoi!"), and spontaneous R-rated stage antics may prove too much for the traditionalists who used to dance here with Hanoi women in *ao dai* (ubiquitous fitted one-piece dresses with slits). These days, exquisitely dressed and primped "Vinababes" hover around the bar and bust a move on the dance floor, sometimes making it hard to tell who's working and who's playing. Friday and Saturday nights, the party continues past 3 AM.

Vortex (⊠ 336 Ba Trieu St., Hai Ba Trung District, ☎ 04/978–0121) is a charming hole-in-the-wall club with an eclectic design and self-consciously groovy atmosphere. International student types have the run of the place weeknights (shouldn't they be hitting the books?), but the crowd diversifies on the weekends, when DJ Henry lays down the "phat" tracks that get people moving.

Opera, Theater, and Circus

Cheo Theater (⊠ 15 Nguyen Dinh Chieu St., Ba Dinh District, ☎ 04/826–7361), a tiny, simple drama house, seats 50 guests. Cheo is a form of "people's opera," incorporating both comic and tragic elements. The theater rarely has performances these days. Shows are usually on Monday, Wednesday, and Friday, but call or stop by to confirm. Ticket prices go up to 45,000d.

Chuong Vang Theater of Hanoi (⊠ 72 Hang Bac St., Hoan Kiem District, ☎ 04/825–7823) has performances of *cai luong*-style shows—the "renovated opera" that emerged in the early 20th century and is more similar to Western operas. Tickets are usually 20,000d for foreigners, and the curtain generally goes up at 8. Check for dates.

☾ **Municipal Water Puppet Theater** (⊠ 57 Dinh Tien Hoang St., on northeast shore of Hoan Kiem Lake, Hoan Kiem District, ☎ 04/825–5450) is the best place to see the thousand-year-old art of *roi nuoc*, or water puppetry. If you're in Hanoi on a package tour, it's likely you're already scheduled for a show. If not, get your tickets early (40,000d, including a tape of the music), as they sell out. The curtain goes up at 8 every night but Monday, and there's a 9:45 AM matinee on Sunday; occasionally there are 6 PM shows as well. There's a fee for taking pictures or videotaping.

☾ **Vietnam Circus** (Rap Xiec; ⊠ Tran Nhan Tong and Tran Binh Tong Sts., at north end of Lenin Park, Hoan Kiem District, ☎ 04/822–0268) offers an evening of guaranteed entertainment, as well as a significant bit of architecture: the distinctive 1,500-seat, round-topped building was constructed in 1985. In winter, bring a jacket. Shows last two hours and are held Tuesday–Sunday at 8 PM; ticket prices range from 15,000d to 30,000d.

Outdoor Activities and Sports

Biking

Vietnamese bikes and the ubiquitous Chinese Phoenix bicycles are for sale all over town for about $40 to $60. In Hanoi, cheap-o Chinese-made mountain bikes are for sale on Ba Trieu Street.

Memory Cafe (⊠ 33 bis Tran Hung Dao St., Hoan Kiem District) rents bicycles—as do many other backpacker-oriented cafés and minihotels.

Golf

King's Valley Golf Resort & Country Club (⊠ Dong Mo, Son Tay town, Ha Tay province, about 45 km/28 mi west of Hanoi, ☎ 034/846–373, 04/826–0342 Hanoi office) has an 18-hole course; greens fees are $50 for guests; clubs are extra. Other recreational possibilities here include tennis, horseback riding, boating on the reservoir, and trekking excursions. For information, ask at the Sofitel Metropole Hotel (☞ Lodging, *above*), which runs a weekly shuttle to the course.

Lang Ha Golf Driving Range (⊠ 16A Lang Ha St., Ba Dinh District, ☎ 04/835–0908) gives diehards a chance to practice their shots.

Health Clubs and Swimming Pools

A few major hotels in Hanoi allow you to purchase one-day memberships (about $10–$17) to their exercise facilities, even if you aren't staying at the hotel: **Clark Hatch Fitness Center** (⊠ Metropole Hotel Sofitel, 15 Ngo Quyen St., Hoan Kiem District, ☎ 04/826–6919, ext. 8881); **Daewoo Hotel Fitness Center** (⊠ Hanoi Daewoo Hotel, 360 Kim Ma St., Ba Dinh District, ☎ 04/831–5000, ext. 3309); **Meritus Lifestyle Club** (⊠ Meritus Westlake Hanoi, 1 Thanh Nien Rd., Ba Dinh District, ☎ 04/823–8888, ext. 5380).

Running

The best places to run in the city are around Lenin Park, the Botanic Gardens, or Hoan Kiem Lake. If you're an early riser, join the runners on the streets between 5 and 6:30 AM, but be aware that joggers are expected to be off the streets by 7 AM.

Soccer

No sport captures the attention and hearts of the Vietnamese quite like soccer. The religiously followed semi-professional national league packs them in at the new 20,000-capacity **National Stadium** (⊠ C orner of Nguyen Thai Hoc and Trinh Hoai Duc Sts., Ba Dinh District). The season runs roughly from October to May, but watch for news of international friendlies, which are occasionally played in Hanoi.

Shopping

Markets

Hom Market (Cho Hom; ⊠ Pho Hue St. and Tran Xuan Soan Sts., Hai Ba Trung District) is the biggest and most crowded market in town. **Dong Xuan Market** (Cho Dong Xuan; ⊠ Dong Xuan St., Hoan Kiem District) has been recently rebuilt after a disastrous fire in 1994. It's a textile center, but sells food and all sorts of items for the home. **19– 12 Market** (Cho 19–12; ⊠ Ly Thuong Kiet St. between Hoa Lo and Quang Trung Sts., Hoan Kiem District), the December 19th Market, has food and items for everyday use.

Shopping Districts

The area north of Hoan Kiem Lake is bustling with tiny shops carrying everything from shoes to clothes to antique timepieces. Hanoi is Vietnam's fine-arts capital, and running along the southern part of Hoan Kiem Lake, where Hang Khai Street turns into Trang Tien Street, are a number of arts-and-crafts galleries and antiques shops (note, however, that it is illegal to take antiques out of the country without permission from the government). You can find paintings and watercolors, as well as crafts such as lacquerware and puppets, on Trang Tien and F. ng Khai streets. Any number of shops along Hang Gai and Duc Loi streets, not far from Hoan Kiem Lake, can inexpensively produce custom-made clothes. Hang Gai is also good for souvenirs and antiques. Hand-embroidered linens are found on Hang Gai Street, which turns into Hang Bong Street. Most souvenir and silk shops in the tourist area of the Old Quarter are open to about 10 PM on weekends.

Specialty Shops

ART

When buying art in Vietnam, be careful of fakes. Paintings by Vietnam's most famous painters—Bui Xuan Phai, Nguyen Tu Nghiem and Le Thiet Cuong—are widely copied. **ATC Art Gallery** (⊠ 48 Lang Ha St., Dong Da District, ☏ 04/835–3179; ⊠ 22 Le Van Huu St., Hoan Kiem District, ☏ 04/825–0821). **Co Xanh** (Green Palm Gallery; ⊠ 51 Hang Gai St., Hoan Kiem District, ☏ 04/826–7116). **Galerie L'Atelier** (⊠ 6 Nha Tho St., Hoan Kiem District, ☏ 04/09121–6353 [mobile phone of curator]). **Hanart** (⊠ 43 Trang Tien St., Hoan Kiem District, ☏ 04/825–3045). **Hanoi Studio** (⊠ 33 Tran Quoc Tuan St., Hoan Kiem District, ☏ 04/943–1106). **Mai Gallery** (⊠ 3B Phan Huy Chu St., Hoan Kiem District, ☏ 04/825–1225). **Red River Gallery** (⊠ 71A Nguyen Du St., Hai Ba Trung District, ☏ 04/822–9064). **Salon Natasha** (⊠ 30 Hang Bong St., Hoan Kiem District, ☏ 04/826–1387). **Son Ha Art Gallery** (⊠ 35 Hang Than St., Hoan Kiem District, ☏ 04/826–9198). **Trang An Gallery** (⊠ 15 Hang Buom St., Hoan Kiem District, ☏ 04/ 826–9480).

CLOTHING AND ACCESSORIES

Some international fashion boutiques like Louis Vuitton have sprung up in Hanoi's top hotels. It's possible to have clothes made to order with enough time (one day to three weeks, depending on what you want made and how busy the tailor is). Keep in mind that you may need to return to have the clothes fitted. Good tailors include the following: **Huong Giang** (⊠ 58 Tue Tinh St., Hai Ba Trung District, ☎ 04/826−9372); **Tan My** (⊠ 66 Hang Gai St., Hoan Kiem District, ☎ 04/826−7081); **Tien Dat** (⊠ 75 Hang Gai St., Hoan Kiem District, ☎ 04/824−6244).

Ipa Nima (⊠ 30B Nguyen Huu Huan St., Hoan Kiem District, ☎ 04/934−0876) carries funky and fashionable handbags, as well as other accessories. **Kenly Silk** (⊠ 102 Hang Gai St., Hoan Kiem District, ☎ 04/826−7236) sells silk and linen clothes. **Khai Silk** (⊠ 121 Nguyen Thai Hoc St., Ba Dinh District and ⊠ 96 Hang Gai St., Hoan Kiem District, ☎ 04/823−3508) is where the Princess of Thailand shops for fine silk clothing and linens.

EMBROIDERY

Tan My (⊠ 66 Hang Gai St., Hoan Kiem District, ☎ 04/826−7081) is one of the most famous embroidery shops in Hanoi. **Tuyet Lan** (⊠ 65 Hang Gai St., Hoan Kiem District, ☎ 04/825−7967, FAX 04/826−5816) does beautiful embroidery and accepts credit cards.

HANDICRAFTS

Craft Link (⊠ 43 Van Mieu St., Ba Dinh District, ☎ 04/843−7710) is a terrific place to buy local handicrafts. A shop clumsily named **The Culture of Vietnam Ethnic Groups** (⊠ 44 Hang Ga St., Hoan Kiem District, ☎ 04/828−0509) offers a fine collection of handwoven baskets and other treasures. **Ngo Thu Huong's Souvenir Shop** (⊠ 62 Hang Ngang St., Hoan Kiem District, ☎ 04/828−1046) has real and imitation antiques. **Ngo Thu Huong** (⊠ 62 Hang Nhang St., Hoan Kiem District, ☎ 04/828−1046) is a reliable vendor of good-quality, 90%-silver and silver-plated items. **Pan Flute** (⊠ 42 Hang Bac St., Hoan Kiem District, ☎ 04/826−0493) is a small shop selling ethnic clothing and crafts.

Hanoi Essentials

Arriving and Departing

BY AIRPLANE

Many international airlines fly into Hanoi's **Noi Bai International Airport** (☎ 04/821−6660), about 35 km (22 mi) north of the city. **Vietnam Airlines** (⊠ 1 Quang Trung St., Hoan Kiem District, ☎ 04/826−9294) serves Danang, Dien Bien Phu, Ho Chi Minh City, Hue, Nha Trang, and Vinh. **Pacific Airlines** (⊠ 100 Le Duan St., Dong Da District, ☎ 04/851−5350) is Vietnam's smaller domestic carrier.

Vietnam Airlines runs a bus service from the airport into Hanoi; the trip takes about 40 minutes and tickets are 45,000d. A taxi into Hanoi should cost $20 or less. Buses to the airport depart from the Vietnam Airlines office (☞ *above*); book a seat in advance. If you're feeling bold, walk across the street from the Vietnam Airlines main office and haggle with the drivers there for an unofficial car out to the airport. If you're good you can get one for about $12.

BY BUS

Buses are uncomfortable and unreliable, but you can usually find minibuses parked near the terminals. For information, contact **Hanoi Bus Company** (⊠ 32 Nguyen Cong Tru St., ☎ 04/971−4590). **Gia Bat Bus Station** (Ben Xe Gia Bat; ☎ 04/864−1462) 7 km (4 mi) south of the Hanoi Railway Station, on Gia Phong Street, serves most southern routes. **Gia Lam Bus Station** (Ben Xe Gia Lam; ☎ 04/827−1529)

is across the Red River and just beyond the tollbooth, 100 yards off
Nguyen Van Cu Street on Ben Xe Street; it serves northern routes. **Kim
Ma Bus Station** (Ben Xe Kim Ma; ☎ 04/845–2846), at the intersection of Nguyen Thai Hoc and Giang Vo streets, in the Ba Dinh District, serves most routes to the northwest.

BY CAR OR MINIBUS

It's very unlikely that you'll arrive in or leave Hanoi by car, but if you
want to hire a car or minibus and driver, contact any hotel, large travel
agency such as **Vietnam Tourism,** or one of the tourist cafés.

BY TRAIN

The ticket office at the main Hanoi train station, Ga Hanoi (✉ Opposite 115 Le Duan St., at west end of Tran Hung Dao St., ☎ 04/825–
3549), is open 7:30–11:30 AM and 1:30–3:30 PM. There's a special
counter where foreigners buy tickets, and some of the schedules are
even in English. Another, smaller train station, up the tracks from the
main one, serves northern routes.

Trains leave four times daily for Ho Chi Minh City (soft berth $97–
$125, 40 hrs), but only one is an express. It stops at major cities, such
as Vinh, Hue (soft sleeper $57, including boxed breakfast and lunch;
daily, 12–14 hrs), Danang, and Nha Trang. Purchase a day in advance
to ensure a seat. Other destinations include Lang Son ($4, twice daily,
5 hrs); Lao Cai (hard berth $17, soft sleeper $22; daily, 11 hrs); and
Haiphong ($4, 4 times daily, 2 hrs).

Getting Around
BY BICYCLE
Bikes can be rented at hotels and cafés in the center of town for around
10,000d per day. Make sure the bike you get has a lock.

BY CYCLO

Cyclos (three-wheeled pedicabs) are a good way to get around Hanoi;
the fare is usually 5,000d to 10,000d, depending on the distance. Make
sure you're both on the same wavelength when you're talking money:
unsuspecting travelers have been known to agree to a fare of 10,000d,
only to have the cyclo driver later claim the agreed-upon figure was $10.

BY MOTORBIKE

Motorbike taxis, known as xe om, are another way to get around—if
you're brave. They'll find you. Many hotels and tourist cafés also rent
motorcycles (☞ Vietnam A to Z, *below*). Try the **Memory Café** (✉ 33
bis Tran Hung Dao St., ☎ 04/826–5854) and **Tourist Service Office**
(✉ 18C Ngo Quyen St., ☎ 04/824–7391).

BY TAXI

The moment you step into a cab, the meter (all cabs in Hanoi should be
metered) reads 14,000d; after that rates run about 5,600d per km (½ mi).
A trip across town will cost you about 25,000d. Hail a cab (a good place
is outside major hotels) or order a taxi by phone from the following: **Airport Taxi** (☎ 04/825–4250); **Hanoi Taxi** (☎ 04/853–5252); **Red Taxi** (☎
04/856–8686); **Taxi CP** (☎ 04/824–1999); and **Taxi PT** (☎ 04/856–5656).

Contacts and Resources
CURRENCY EXCHANGE
Most major international and large national banks in Hanoi have a
currency exchange. Hotels, too, can change money, as can some jewelry shops. But don't change money with the black-market money
changers who gather around the General Post Office (GPO). Many of
Hanoi's shops and upscale restaurants accept both dollars and dong.

Major banks in Hanoi include the following: **ANZ Bank** (Australia New
Zealand Bank; ✉ 14 Le Thai To St., ☎ 04/825–8190, FAX 04/825–

8189); **Bank of America** (✉ 27 Ly Thuong Kiet St., ☎ 04/824–9316, 𝔽𝔸𝕏 04/824–9322); **Citibank** (✉ 17 Ngo Quyen St., ☎ 04/825–1950, 𝔽𝔸𝕏 04/824–3960); and **Vietcom Bank** (Bank for Foreign Trade of Vietnam; ✉ 78 Nguyen Du St., ☎ 04/826–8035, 𝔽𝔸𝕏 04/822–8039).

EMBASSIES
Australia (✉ Van Phuc Quarter, Ba Dinh District, ☎ 04/831–7755, 𝔽𝔸𝕏 04/831–7711). **Canada** (✉ 31 Hung Vuong St., Ba Dinh District, ☎ 04/823–5500, 𝔽𝔸𝕏 04/823–5333). **New Zealand** (✉ 32 Hang Bai St., Hoan Kiem District, ☎ 04/824–2481, 𝔽𝔸𝕏 04/826–5760). **United Kingdom** (✉ 31 Hai Ba Trung St., Hoan Kiem District, ☎ 04/825–2510, 𝔽𝔸𝕏 04/826–5762). **United States** (✉ 7 Lang Ha St., Ba Dinh District, ☎ 04/843–1500, 𝔽𝔸𝕏 04/843–1510).

EMERGENCIES
Ambulance (☎ 15). **Fire** (☎ 14). **Police** (☎ 13).

Medical facilities in Hanoi are not up to international standards. A few foreign-run medical clinics offer basic treatment—at Western prices—and can arrange for emergency medical evacuation to Singapore or elsewhere in the region. **AEA International** (✉ 31 Hai Ba Trung St., Hoan Kiem District, ☎ 04/934–0555). **Emergency Viet Duc Hospital** (Benh Vien Viet Duc; ✉ 48 Tranh Thai St., Hoan Kiem District, ☎ 04/825–3531). **Hanoi Family Medical Practice** (✉ A-1 Bldg., Van Phuc Diplomatic Compound, Suite 109–112, Kim Ma Rd, ☎ 04/843–0748 or 09/040–1919 for emergency mobile phone). **Vietnam International Hospital** (Benh Vien Quoc Te Viet Nam; ✉ Phuong Mai Rd., next to Bach Mai Hospital, Hai Ba Trung District, ☎ 04/574–0740 or 04/574–1111 for emergencies).

ENGLISH-LANGUAGE BOOKSTORES
Look for books in English at the following: **The Gioi Publishers Bookshop** (✉ 46 Tran Hung Dao St., Hoan Kiem District, ☎ 04/825–4086); **Hien Sach Hanoi** (✉ 34 Trang Tien St., near the Metropole Hotel Sofitel, Hoan Kiem District, ☎ 04/824–1616); and the **State Bookshop** (✉ 40 Trang Tien St., Hoan Kiem District, ☎ 04/825–4282).

MAIL
The **General Post Office** (Buu Dien Trung Vong; ✉ 75 Dinh Tien Hoang St., Hoan Kiem District, ☎ 04/825–7036) has phone, fax, and express-mail services (open daily 6:30 AM–8 PM). Dozens of branch post offices dot the city.

TOUR OPERATORS AND TRAVEL AGENCIES
The following travel agencies offer visitor information, transportation and hotel bookings, car and bus rentals, guided tours, private tour guides, and visa extensions. Tourist cafés have many of the same services but usually at lower prices; it's mainly a walk-in business.

Ann's Tourist (✉ 26 Yet Kieu St., Hoan Kiem District, ☎ 𝔽𝔸𝕏 04/822–0018) is one of the best. **Exotissimo Travel** (✉ 26 Tran Nhat Duat St., Hoan Kiem District, ☎ 04/828–2150, 𝔽𝔸𝕏 04/828–2146). **Green Bamboo Café** (✉ 42 Nha Chung St., Hoan Kiem District, ☎ 04/826–8752, 𝔽𝔸𝕏 04/826–4949) is the best-organized tourist café in town. **Hanoi Tourism** (✉ 18 Ly Thuong Kiet St., Hoan Kiem District, ☎ 04/826–1627, 𝔽𝔸𝕏 04/824–1101; marketing office, ✉ 1 Ba Trieu St., Hoan Kiem District, ☎ 04/824–2330 or 04/826–5244, 𝔽𝔸𝕏 04/825–6418) is a big state-run agency. **Queen Cafe** (✉ 65 Hang Bac St. Hoan Kiem District, ☎ 04/826–0860, 𝔽𝔸𝕏 04/825–0000) is another good tourist café. **Saigon Tourist** (✉ 55 Phan Chu Trinh St., Hoan Kiem District, ☎ 04/825–0923, 𝔽𝔸𝕏 04/825–1174 for tours) is the largest agency in Vietnam. **Vietnam Tourism** (✉ 30A Ly Thuong Kiet St., Hoan Kiem District, ☎ 04/825–6916, 𝔽𝔸𝕏 04/825–7583) is another large state-run agency.

SIDE TRIPS FROM HANOI

Once you have seen the sights in Hanoi, it's time to jump off into the countryside—the "real" Vietnam—on day trips, using the city as your base. Less than an hour out of the capital in any direction brings you to stretches of rice paddies interrupted only by villages and jagged rocky outcrops. Trips organized by Hanoi's tourist cafés and travel agencies are usually the most time-efficient way to see this region.

Perfume Pagoda

60 km (37 mi) southwest of Hanoi.

Considered Vietnam's most important Buddhist site, the **Perfume Pagoda** (Chua Huong) is the largest of a cluster of shrines carved into the limestone of the Huong Tich Mountains. In the late spring the trails leading up to the shrines are clogged with thousands making their pilgrimage to pray to Quan Am, the goddess of mercy and compassion.

From the shores of the Yen River, you are ferried to the site, 4 km (2½ mi) away, on sampans that seem to be made of flimsy aluminum. After a spectacular ride past boats laden with fruit and farmers at work in their fields, you are let off at Chua Tien Chu. From there, follow a stone path uphill to the various pagodas and shrines. Three kilometers (2 miles) later you reach the Perfume Pagoda.

Hoa Lu

113 km (70 mi) south of Hanoi.

Hoa Lu, the first capital of independent Vietnam, is known as "Halong Bay without the water." The stunning natural beauty—limestone karsts rising from green rice paddies—and the historic interest of Hoa Lu's status as a 10th-century seat of power make for a worthwhile excursion. Much of the ancient capital of Hoa Lu has been destroyed or has succumbed to the forces of nature, but the two sanctuaries that do survive hint at the tastes of the emperor and his court.

Many travel agencies in Hanoi arrange tours to Hoa Lu—including entry tickets, lunch, and a boat ride on a lovely river, which winds between terraced rice paddies and passes through historic limestone grottoes. It takes less than two hours to get there. You can also rent a car or take the train. If you're en route to Hue, you can stop off at nearby Ninh Binh (stay at the Queen Minihotel), visit Hoa Lu, and reboard the next night for the rest of the trip.

Halong Bay and Cat Ba Island

★ *160 km (99 mi) east of Hanoi, 55 km (34 mi) northeast of Haiphong.*

Halong Bay's 3,000 islands of dolomite and limestone cover a 1,500-square-km (579-square-mi) area extending across the Gulf of Tonkin nearly to the Chinese border. According to Chinese legend this breathtaking land- and seascape (similar to the Guilin area of China) was formed by a giant dragon that came barreling out of the mountains toward the ocean. Geologists are more likely to attribute the formations to sedimentary limestone that formed here between 300 and 500 million years ago, in the Paleozoic Era. Boat trips through Halong Bay are the main attraction; they are often part of organized tours from the capital, and can be arranged by hotels or travel agencies in Hanoi or in the town of Halong Bay.

Onc of Halong Bay's most remarkable formations is **Cat Ba Island**, 354 square km (138 square mi) of wildly steep spines of mountains, narrow valleys and waterfalls, lush wetlands, golden beaches, and one of Vietnam's most beautiful national parks. In 1938 a French archaeologist found traces of an ancient fishing culture on the island dating from the end of the Neolithic Era. Today the population of more than 12,000 continues to subsist on fishing and rice and fruit cultivation, but tourism is quickly becoming Cat Ba's new cash crop. The park was established in 1986 to protect about half of the island. Included in these ecosystems are tropical evergreen forests, 15 kinds of mammals (including wild boars and hedgehogs), 200 species of fish, 21 species of birds, and 640 species of plants.

Hiring a car and driver in Hanoi or going with an organized tour (the fees are prepaid and a hike is mapped out) are the easiest ways to get to sites in the northeast, although many of the roads are in bad condition. Since the trip from Hanoi takes four to five hours you'll probably want to stay overnight in Halong City if your destination is Halong Bay; those going only to Cat Ba Island should go to Haiphong, the port city 100 km (60 mi) east of Hanoi, where daily ferries make the two- to four-hour ride.

Lodging

$$$ **Halong I Hotel.** The grande dame of Halong properties, this French
★ colonial restoration is evocative of a more sublime era—but with IDD phones. Don't expect fawning service here. Thankfully the whole place is quiet—except for the strains of karaoke wafting up from the roadside below. Try to book the Catherine Deneuve Room, where the French actress stayed while filming *Indochine.* ✉ *Halong Rd.,* ☎ *033/846320,* 𝖥𝖠𝖷 *033/846318. 23 rooms. Restaurant. AE, MC, V.*

$$$ **Halong Plaza Hotel.** This modern luxury hotel has a spacious front lobby with a glass-front entryway looking out onto the bay. Most of the rooms, too, have views of the bay, though some face the more industrial back side. ✉ *8 Halong Rd.,* ☎ *033/845810,* 𝖥𝖠𝖷 *033/846867. 200 rooms. 2 restaurants, bar, in-room safes, minibars, no-smoking rooms, pool, massage, exercise room, dance club, laundry service, business services, meeting rooms. AE, MC, V.*

$$$ **Heritage Halong.** This eight-floor, glitzy, international hotel soaks up much of the package-tour business in Halong Bay. Rooms are clean; those on the top floors in front have lovely views of the distant islands. ✉ *88 Halong Rd.,* ☎ *033/846888,* 𝖥𝖠𝖷 *033/846999. 101 rooms. Restaurant, café, pool. AE, MC, V.*

$ **Vuon Dao Hotel.** Ask for one of the top-floor rooms with a view of the sea at this three-story hotel run by Halong Tourist Company, the state-run travel agency. Breakfast is included in the room rate. ✉ *Halong Rd.,* ☎ *033/846427,* 𝖥𝖠𝖷 *033/846287. 77 rooms. Restaurant, air-conditioning. MC, V.*

Sapa

35 km (22 mi) south of Lao Cai, 170 km (105 mi) northeast of Dien Bien Phu, 350 km (217 mi) northwest of Hanoi.

Ringed by Vietnam's tallest peaks, Sapa is an enchanting hill-tribe village that has become the de facto tourist capital of the far northwest. It is part of the northwestern province of Lao Cai, which means "town of sand," and a 90-minute drive from the provincial capital—a dreary border town of 30,000 people. A pilgrimage to Sapa offers a glimpse of the country's most breathtaking mountain scenery as well as some of its ethnic minority cultures—the H'mong, the Dao, the Tay, the Giay, the Muong, the Thai, the Hoa (ethnic Chinese), and the Xa Pho. The hill tribes cultivate rice and ginger and hunt wild game by traditional methods; they continue as they always have to worship the soul of rice, their ancestors, and the spirits of earth, wind, fire, rivers, and mountains. To see them in their traditional style of dress—layers of indigo-dyed, brilliantly embroidered cotton, elaborate headdresses, and silver adornments—is to feel yourself caught in a time warp. Every Saturday there's a colorful market in Sapa; be sure to plan your trip so that it coincides.

The French dubbed the area around Sapa the "Tonkinese Alps." In 1922 colonial authorities displaced the minority residents and began building villas for themselves in the town, turning it into a kind of health resort and retreat from Hanoi's heat and the depot for a nearby mine. Between the end of French colonial rule in 1954 and national reunification 22 years later, the North Vietnamese government made weak attempts to grant the ethnic minorities political representation and the same constitutional rights as the majority Kinh population—provided they took up the struggle against the U.S.-backed Saigon regime. Since 1975 the government has pursued "integration" programs, providing free limited education and health care.

The protection of Sapa's cultural diversity and the environment seems to have little place on the state agenda, however. It appears that tourism may corrupt the integrity of the local populace and upset the area's fragile ecology. Some of the minority groups practice slash-and-burn agriculture, and along with the depredations of two centuries of outside interests, this has already reduced the virgin forest to a mere 12-square-km (4½-square-mi) area. Further destruction would be tragic, considering the area's remarkable natural gifts.

Sapa is part of the Nui Hoang Lien Nature Reserve, a mountainous 7,400-acre landscape covered by temperate and subtemperate forests. The reserve provides a habitat for 56 species of mammals—including tigers, leopards, monkeys, and bears—and an impressive 150 species of birds. (Don't expect a bird-watching bonanza, however. A tour leader researching Sapa in 1996 told Fodor's: "I saw two birds on my climb up Fansipan, and my guide shot them both for dinner.") Among the area's geological resources are marble; calcium carbonate; and kaolinite, or China clay, used in the making of porcelain. Guided walking tours of the nature reserve are recommended and are easily arranged through hotels in town.

Sapa is also the departure point for Mt. Fansipan, Southeast Asia's tallest peak at 10,372 ft. Hiking the mountain requires little technical expertise, but it does take three or four days, as you must depart from Sapa and hike down into the valley, then hike back up the other side. Bring your own tent and sleeping bag and warm clothes. You'll also want an experienced guide to help you navigate the wet, chilly mountainside and suggest the best route and places to camp. Hiking Fansipan is serious business and should not be taken lightly. Ask for details at the Auberge Hotel or the Green Bamboo Hotel.

One of the best ways to get to Sapa is with a tour organized by a travel agency or tourist café in Hanoi. By car, the trip takes 10 hours on Highway 1 to Lao Cai, then 90 minutes from Lao Cai on Highway 4. If you don't want to lose a whole day driving to Sapa, take the overnight train to Lao Cai. Most comfortable is the "luxury" train on Friday night (departs at 8:15 PM, takes 11 hrs), on which you get a soft sleeper in a four-person compartment ($10–$20). Currently tickets cannot be purchased more than two days in advance, so go to the Hanoi railway station Thursday morning. Minibuses can take you from the Lao Cai train station to Sapa (35 km/22 mi, 25,000d). You can buy your return ticket in Sapa (and check train and bus schedules) at the small post office next to Phan Xi Pan Hotel. Unfortunately, the night train from Lao Cai to Hanoi has only hard sleepers. Buses from Sapa to the Lao Cai train station depart at 6:30 AM and 2 PM, but you can also share a bus or Jeep with other travelers and leave at the time you want.

Dining and Lodging

$$ ⊡ **Hotel Victoria Sapa.** This international hotel was scheduled to open in late 1998. A French-designed pleasure palace on a hilltop overlooking town, it will have all the amenities, including a pricey restaurant and bar, room service, and plush rooms with bathtubs. Ask for information at one of Hanoi's many travel agencies. ⊠ *Overlooking town,* ☎ *no phone at press time. 81 rooms. Restaurant, bar, room service. AE, MC, V.*

¢ ✕⊡ **Auberge Hotel.** The best thing going in Sapa, this lovely, popular
★ hotel has exquisite views of the mountains. Rooms, particularly on the third floor, are cozy and clean and have functioning fireplaces. In the restaurant, feast on standard Vietnamese fare—and excellent spring rolls. The owner, Mr. Trung, and his son can help with all sorts of travel information. Reservations are a must. One major fault: Mr. Trung can't say "no," so overbooking is a serious problem. He rarely leaves anyone in the lurch, though you may find yourself with a room in the annex or in another minihotel altogether. ⊠ *On main road,* ☎ *020/871243,* FAX *020/871282. 12 rooms. Restaurant, laundry service, travel services, car rental. No credit cards.*

¢ ⊡ **The Green Bamboo.** Run by the Green Bamboo Café in Hanoi, this mountainside accommodation has small, sunny rooms decked out with satellite televisions, new but simple furniture, and private bathrooms. If you're looking for a quiet getaway, however, stay elsewhere on weekends. Reservations, which are recommended, can be made at the Green Bamboo Café in Hanoi (⊠ 42 Nha Chung St., ☎ 04/826–8752). ⊠ *On the main road,* ☎ *020/871214,* FAX *020/871411. 13 rooms. Bar, café, laundry service, travel services. No credit cards.*

HUE

Hue is 108 km (67 mi) north of Danang, 140 km (87 mi) north of Hoi An, 1,097 km (680 mi) north of Ho Chi Minh City, and 689 km (427 mi) south of Hanoi.

Bisected by the Perfume River and 13 km (8 mi) inland from the South China Sea in the foothills of the Annamite Mountains (Truong Son Mountains), Hue—pronounced "Hway"—stands as a reminder of Vietnam's imperial past. The seat of 13 Nguyen dynasty emperors between 1802 and 1945, Hue was once Vietnam's splendid Imperial City. Although it was devastated by the French in the 19th century and in the 1940s, and by the Americans in 1968, the monument-speckled former capital has a war-ravaged beauty. Imperial splendor may have long been gone, but a walk by the old citadel and into the emperor's palace can still conjure up images of eras past.

As early as the 2nd century BC, Hue was home to rulers: it was the seat of command for the Chinese Han army and was called Tay Quyen. By the 2nd century AD, Hue was captured by local chieftains, who renamed it K'ui Sou. Between the 10th and 14th centuries, the Cham and the Vietnamese fought for its control, and by the 15th century, the Vietnamese had succeeded and renamed it Phu Xuan. In 1558 Hue became the capital of a region ruled by Lord Nguyen Hoang, which established control of South Vietnam by the Nguyen lords. (During this time, the Nguyen lords, who controlled South Vietnam, and the Trinh lords, who controlled North Vietnam—fought for control of the whole country.)

Late in the 18th century, the Nguyen lords were temporarily defeated in the Tay Son rebellion, which arose from a general sentiment of discontent with both Nguyen and Trinh rule. The Tay Son emperor, Quang

Trung, ruled in Hue from 1786 to 1802, when the ousted Lord Nguyen Anh returned, with French backing. At the same time, Nguyen Anh captured Hanoi from the Tay Son rebels, who had defeated the Trinh and the Chinese-backed Ly Dynasty. In 1802, Nguyen Anh anointed himself Emperor Gia Long and made Hue the capital of a newly united Vietnam. Twelve Nguyen dynasty emperors followed him to the throne until the monarchy was abolished in the mid-20th century. Their impressive tombs and pagodas and the Imperial City are reminders of the important role Hue once played in the nation's affairs.

It was under Emperor Gia Long's rule that the city's architectural identity was established—and the prospect of French colonial rule in Vietnam initiated. With guidance, ironically from the French architect Olivier de Puymanel, Gia Long designed and built the city's surrounding fortress (the Citadel), in the style of the Forbidden City in Beijing. The result was a fairly modern structure that looked centuries old.

In the 1830s, voices of dissent arose against the French presence in Vietnam. The French responded by attacking Hue in 1833 (they had been looking for an excuse to assert their claims to the country in exchange for assisting Gia Long to the throne) and making the country—particularly, Tonkin and Annam—into a protectorate. During this time, a Western-style city was established across the river from the citadel to accommodate the French forces; some of these old French colonial buildings are still standing. In 1885, after repeated disagreements between the French and the emperors of Hue, the French pillaged the Royal Court, burned the Royal Library, and replaced Emperor Ham Nghi with the more docile Emperor Dong Khanh.

It was the Tet Offensive of 1968, however, that really destroyed large parts of the Imperial City. During one of the fiercest battles of the Vietnam War, the Viet Cong forces occupied the city for 25 days, flying their flag in defiance and massacring thousands of suspected Saigon Government sympathizers. The South Vietnamese and the Americans moved in to recapture the city with a massive land and air attack and in doing so further destroyed many of Hue's architectural landmarks. Overall, more than 10,000 people died in the fighting, many of them civilians.

Though much of the Imperial City was reduced to rubble, many sections still exist, and Hue's main draw continues to be the remnants of its glorious past. Today tourists keep the city thriving. There are many hotels and numerous cyclo drivers who can give you a tour of the Imperial City for only 50,000d. On top of it all, Hue is known for its outstanding cuisine.

Exploring Hue

Hue itself is quite small, and you can easily get around the Imperial City on foot. To visit the sprawling, majestic, imperial tombs, down the Perfume River—the Tomb of Tu Duc and the Tomb of Minh Mang—and the Thien Mu Pagoda on the outskirts of Hue, you need to go by boat or car—or by motorbike or bicycle, if you are more adventurous.

A Good Walk

You will probably be staying on the right (east) bank of the Perfume River, so you should begin your walk at the Phu Xuan Bridge and Le Loi Street. Cross the bridge to the west bank, turn left, and walk toward the entrance to the citadel, which is circled by a moat and ramparts. Along the way you'll see on your left the 122-ft Flag Tower. The citadel contains the Imperial City (where mandarins and the royal family conducted affairs of state), within which is the Forbidden Purple City, where the royal family lived. Cross the moat and pass through the Ngan Gate (Cua Ngan).

After entering, you will see four of the Nine Holy Cannons on your right. These bronze cannons commemorate the four seasons; the other five depict the Chinese elements—water, soil, wood, metal, and fire. Make your way along to the entrance of the Imperial City.

Enter this mostly ruined complex through the Noontime, or Royal, Gate (Cua Ngo Mon) and take an immediate left toward the Nine Dynastic Urns, symbols of the formidable Nguyen dynasty. Head back toward the entrance and turn left across the Golden Water Bridge (Trung Dao Bridge), once used only by the emperor. Straight ahead is one of the few intact structures in the Imperial City: the intricately decorated Palace of Supreme Harmony.

Exit the palace through the back of the gift shop. On either side of the path leading to the entrance of the Forbidden Purple City are the Halls of the Mandarins, where those court officials dressed in special attire before paying homage to the emperor. Through the courtyard in front of the halls, you can see the vast empty expanse that once was the Forbidden Purple City. To your right stands the Royal Theater or Festival Hall, largely intact, with behind it the partially restored Royal Library.

Heading east from the Royal Theater, exit the Imperial Enclosure through the beautiful and ornate Eastern Gate (Hung Khan Mon). Make a right on Doan Thi Diem Street and then take the first left on Le Truc Street to get to the Imperial Museum. Across the street are the unimpressive Military Museum and Hue's Archaeological Center, once a kind of prep school for male members of the royal court and now closed to the public.

Make a left out of the Imperial Museum and then another left onto Dinh Tien Hoang Street. Follow the street through what feels like a quiet suburban residential neighborhood for about 1 km (¾ mi). At the intersection with Tinh Tam Street is Tinh Tam Lake, overgrown with lotus flowers in spring and summer. Across Dinh Tien Hoang Street is another lake, Tang Tau, with a small island containing the Ngoc Huong Pagoda.

TIMING

This walk should take about four hours at a leisurely pace. Go in early morning or late afternoon, to avoid the midday heat.

Sights to See

The Citadel (Kinh Thanh). Seeking to secure his empire, Emperor Gia Long built this 1½-square-mi (3.88 square-km) citadel with a 65-ft-wide moat in the heart of Hue in 1804. Gia Long was assisted in the design by the French architect Olivier de Puymanel, and the result is a combination of French military architect Vauban's work and classical Chinese architecture. Enclosed in the citadel is the **Imperial City, or Imperial Enclosure** (Hoang Thanh), where official government activity took place. Within it is the **Forbidden Purple City** (Tu Cam Thanh; ☞ *below*), which was the private sanctuary of the emperors and their families. ⊠ *55,000d, which admits you also to the Imperial City and the Forbidden Purple City and their remaining buildings.* ⊙ *Daily 7–5.*

Flag Tower (Cot Co). This 112-ft structure is one of the symbols of Hue, and Vietnam's tallest flagpole. It was originally built in 1809 to serve as the Imperial Palace's central observation post. Like much of Hue, it has a history of being destroyed: it was toppled by a typhoon in 1904, rebuilt in 1915, destroyed again in 1947, and built anew in 1949. When the city was occupied by the Viet Cong during the Tet offensive of 1968, the National Liberation Front flag flew from the Flag Tower. The interior is closed to the public. ⊠ *In front of 23 Thang 8 St., facing Ngo Mon Gate.*

Forbidden Purple City (Tu Cam Thanh). This royal enclave was almost entirely destroyed during the Vietnam War and now is largely a wide-open field. In its day it housed members of the imperial family and the concubines and eunuchs who served them. Anyone else who entered was executed. After the 1968 Tet offensive, only the **Royal Theater** (Duyet Thi Duong) and the intimate and partially restored **Royal Library** (Thai Binh Lau) behind it remained intact. ⊠ *In Imperial City.* 🎫 *Included in admission to citadel.* ⊙ *Daily 8–5.*

Imperial City (Hoang Thanh). The Imperial City, or Imperial Enclosure, was once a complex of palaces and pavilions where civil and religious ceremonies took place and the region was governed. Now it betrays disappointingly few remnants of past glory beneath the sporadic vegetation that is taking over the ruins. There are four gateways into the Enclosure: the **Gate of Peace** (Cua Hoa Binh), **the Gate of Humanity** (Cua Hien Nhian), the **Gate of Virtue** (Cua Chuong Due), and the **South Gate** (Ngo Mon). ⊠ *Inside citadel.* 🎫 *Included in admission to citadel.* ⊙ *Daily 8–5.*

Imperial Museum. This beautiful wooden structure was constructed in 1845 and houses miscellaneous royal knickknacks such as wooden incense boxes, many inlaid with mother-of-pearl. ⊠ *On Dinh Cong Trang St., close to intersection of Doan Thi Diem St.* 🎫 *10,000d.* ⊙ *Daily 7–noon and 1:30–5.*

Nine Dynastic Urns (Cuu Dinh O The-Mieu). Cast in 1835 and weighing approximately 5,000 pounds each, these urns are dedicated to rulers of the Nguyen dynasty. Emperor Gia Long, the founder of this dynasty, is featured on the elaborately decorated, central urn. ⊠ *To left of the south gate into Imperial City.* ⊙ *Daily 8–5.*

Palace of Supreme Harmony (Thai Hoa Dien). In the 19th century, this palace, the site of special events, ceremonies, and festivals for the new moon, was where the emperor received dignitaries. Now it houses a gift shop. ⊠ *In the citadel.* ⊙ *Daily 8–5.*

Royal Library (Thai Binh Lau). The Royal Library, past the Palace of Supreme Harmony, on your right, is one of the few largely intact buildings in the citadel, although there are no books or other furnishings left. ⊙ *Daily 8–5.*

Thien Mu Pagoda. This Mahayana Buddhist temple contains one of Hue's most famous monuments, the seven-story, octagonal Phuoc Nguyen Tower, built in 1844 by Emperor Thieu Tri at a peaceful spot overlooking the Perfume River. Each of the tiers is dedicated to a different human incarnation of Buddha, and the main sanctuary houses a splendid, large Laughing Buddha. ⊠ *About 2½ km (1½ mi) southwest of Citadel on left bank of Perfume River.* ⊙ *Daily 7–5.*

Tomb of Minh Mang. Another Hue classic, this tomb is one of the most palatial, with numerous pavilions and courtyards in a beautiful pine forest. The route to the burial site is bordered with sculptures of mandarins, elephants, and lions. ⊠ *About 11 km (7 mi) south of Hue and 1 ½ km (1 mi) inland on left bank of Perfume River.* 🎫 *55,000d.* ⊙ *Daily 8–5.*

★ **Tomb of Tu Doc.** This tomb, one of Hue's most visited, has a lake and pine forest. Built in 1867 by thousands of laborers, it was once Tu Doc's second residence, to which he escaped to commune with nature and write poetry. You, too, may end up spending an hour here just wandering around the grounds. ⊠ *About 5 km (3 mi) south of Hue, on right bank of Perfume River.* 🎫 *55,000d.* ⊙ *Daily 8–5.*

OFF THE   **DMZ –** About 100 km (62 mi) north of Hue is the DMZ (Demilitarized
BEATEN PATH   Zone), site of some of the heaviest fighting of the Vietnam War. The

DMZ was established following the terms of the 1954 Geneva Accords, in which Vietnam was split in two along the 17th parallel at the Ben Hai River. Though it was supposed to have been temporary, enforced only until the elections in 1956, it existed until the country was reunified in 1975. The DMZ Tour Office (☞ Visitor Information and Travel Agencies *in* Hue Essentials, *below*) organizes trips to the area.

Dining and Lodging

Hue's cuisine, distinguished by the elegant radial symmetry of its presentation, is said to be the most sophisticated in Vietnam. Two specialties are *banh khoai,* a rice pancake filled with shrimp and pork, and *bun bo Hue,* a dish of rice noodles and broth topped with pork, beef, and pork rinds. Most of Hue's hotels are on the right (east) bank of the Perfume River. You have an excellent selection from which to choose in all price ranges, and you can often swim in a hotel's pool for a small fee, even if you're not staying there.

Dining

$$$ ✕ **Century Riverside Hotel Restaurant.** Perhaps the most upscale dining establishment in Hue, the Century serves two particularly tasty dishes: the grilled fish in banana leaves and the superb spring rolls. ⊠ *49 Le Loi St.,* ☎ *054/823390. AE, DC, MC, V.*

$$ ✕ **Club Garden.** A dimly lighted street leads to you the entrance of this small restaurant, where you can get a fabulous fixed-price five-course dinner for less than $10. The seafood and fish dishes are particularly good, as are the pork buns. ⊠ *12 Vo Thi Sau St.,* ☎ *054/826327. No credit cards.*

$$ ✕ **Huong Giang Hotel Restaurant.** From the windows of this spacious third-floor restaurant you get great views of the Perfume River. Large portions of very solid Vietnamese food and Western dishes, such as chicken and french fries, are served. Make a reservation if you want a seat by the window. ⊠ *51 Le Loi St.,* ☎ *054/822122. AE, DC, MC, V.*

$$ ✕ **Ngoc Anh.** This open-air restaurant, the Vietnamese version of a sidewalk café, serves high-quality Vietnamese and Chinese food in a relaxed atmosphere. The sizzling-hot clay-pot seafood special is exceptional. ⊠ *29 Nguyen Thai Hoc St.,* ☎ *054/822617. No credit cards.*

$$ ✕ **Ong Tao.** Ong Tao means "God of the Kitchen," and this restaurant exemplifies imperial cuisine. There are two locations. The citadel site serves lunch and dinner in an outdoor setting amid trees and ruins. Although swarming with tourists, it is still a pleasant place for lunch. The other location is less crowded. ⊠ *Inside Hien Nhou Gate, opposite College of Fine Arts,* ☎ *054/823031;* ⊠ *134 Ngo Duc Ke,* ☎ *054/ 822037. No credit cards.*

$ ✕ **Am Phu.** Excellent traditional Vietnamese cuisine is served at this restaurant. The nonglamorous atmosphere keeps this place relatively tourist-free. Although there are no prices listed on the menu, most dishes cost about 30,000d. ⊠ *35 Nguyen Thai Hoc St.,* ☎ *054/825259. No credit cards.*

$ ✕ **Lac Thanh Restaurant.** Packed with tourists and teeming with postcard and cigarette vendors, this dive (and its next-door copycat) serves the tastiest and cheapest meals in Hue. Some notable dishes include Asian basics like shrimp and vegetables over crispy noodles. ⊠ *6A Dien Tien Hoang St.,* ☎ *no phone. No credit cards.*

$ ✕ **Mai Huong.** Although it may not live up to your fantasy of a patisserie, this small "coffee shop" is a good place for a slice of coconut cake and a cup of tea. ⊠ *6 Nguyen Tri Phuong St.,* ☎ *no phone. No credit cards.*

$ ✕ **Tong Phuoc Nen.** Although soup—particularly different versions of eel soup—is the specialty of the house, you can also order a variety of fish dishes. Diners include somewhat adventurous tourists and lots of Vietnamese teenagers. ✉ *20 Ba Trieu St.,* ☎ *054/825264. No credit cards.*

¢   ✕ **Banh Khoai.** This two-table, family-run food stall serves some of the best banh khoai in town. The meat-filled rice pancake topped with bean sprouts comes to the table piping hot. Break it up with chopsticks into your small rice bowl, add the greens and sauce, and eat. ✉ *2 Nguyen Tri Phuong St., off Hanoi St.,* ☎ *no phone. No credit cards.*

¢   ✕ **Bun Bo Hue.** Close to the center of Hue, this very downscale sidewalk food stall serves wonderful bun bo Hue. This is the only dish served, and there is no menu. Order by pointing. ✉ *11b Ly Kiet St.,* ☎ *no phone. No credit cards.*

Lodging

$$$ 🏨 **Century Riverside Inn.** Although this large Western-style hotel on the river is the most luxurious in town, it's not opulent by Western standards. But it is very clean and comfortable. Ask for a room with a view of the river. ✉ *49 Le Loi St.,* ☎ *054/823390,* FAX *054/823399. 138 rooms. 2 restaurants, bar, minibars, refrigerators, room service, pool, massage, tennis courts, exercise room, shop, laundry service and dry cleaning. AE, DC, MC, V.*

$$$ 🏨 **Huong Giang Hotel.** Large rooms with traditional Vietnamese-style
★   decor and the most helpful staff in Hue make this hotel, on the north end of the east bank, the most pleasant in town. Request one of the renovated older rooms—they're better than the newer ones around the pool. The hotel also has a very good restaurant and rooftop bar-garden with panoramic views of the river. The travel office in the hotel is exceptional. ✉ *51 Le Loi St.,* ☎ *054/822122,* FAX *054/823102. 102 rooms. 2 restaurants, 2 bars, outdoor café, pool, tennis court, dry cleaning and laundry service, travel services. AE, DC, MC, V.*

$$ 🏨 **A Dong Hotel 1.** This pleasant, clean, and airy minihotel is a great budget alternative. Though there's nothing particularly charming about the place, it does have large, basic, immaculate rooms. It scores big, however, with fresh fruit and flowers delivered daily to your room. The staff speaks very little English but is eager to please. ✉ *1 Chu Van An St.,* ☎ *054/824148,* FAX *054/823858. 10 rooms. Restaurant, bar, air-conditioning, minibars, refrigerators, laundry service, travel services, car rental. AE, MC, V.*

$$ 🏨 **Dong Da Hotel.** This spacious hotel on a quiet street corner falls somewhere between a minihotel—one of the new, privately owned small places popping up all over Vietnam—and a Western-style accommodation. Rooms are clean and modern and have simple Japanese-style furnishings. All have TVs. ✉ *15 Ly Thuong Kiet St.,* ☎ *054/823071,* FAX *054/823204. 37 rooms. Restaurant, bar, air-conditioning, dance club, laundry service, travel services, car rental. No credit cards.*

$$ 🏨 **Hoa Hong Hotel II.** Almost as comfortable as its more expensive neighbors, the Century Riverside and the Huong Giang, this new hotel has similarly styled, semiluxurious, nondescript rooms. Though the hotel is not on the water, it is tall enough so that many rooms have excellent views of the river. In the restaurant are nightly shows of traditional music and dance. Credit cards are not accepted, but you can use traveler's checks. ✉ *1 Pham Ngu Lao St.,* ☎ *054/824377,* FAX *054/826949. 60 rooms. Restaurant, laundry service and dry cleaning, travel services. No credit cards.*

$$ 🏨 **Indochine.** It's run by the same management as the Huong Giang
★   (☞ *above*), but it has a more intimate environment and a new restaurant. The cozy, sunny rooms are arranged around a small garden.

Staying here, you sacrifice having access to recreational facilities, but you get the feel of a small inn and easy access to the center of town. ✉ *3 Hung Vuong St.,* ☎ *054/826070,* FAX *054/826074. 12 rooms. Restaurant, air-conditioning, fans, minibars, refrigerators, laundry service, travel services, car rental. AE, MC, V.*

$ ⬚ **Hoa Hong I.** The smaller and less luxurious of the Hoa Hong family of hotels, this place has comfortable rooms and bathrooms with tubs as well as IDD phones. Just ignore the fake-flower finishing touches and the overly cutesy pastel decor. ✉ *46C Le Loi St.,* ☎ *054/824377,* FAX *054/826949. 56 rooms. Restaurant, air-conditioning, minibars, refrigerators, TVs, laundry service, travel services. No credit cards.*

$ ⬚ **Saigon Hotel.** Don't be put off by the strangely decorated restaurant (with a neon backlit cow's head) in this new minihotel. Rooms are sunny and squeaky clean, and the bathrooms are in excellent condition and have tubs. ✉ *32 Hung Vuong St.,* ☎ *054/821007,* FAX *054/821009. 20 rooms. Restaurant, air-conditioning, fans, laundry service, travel services, car rental. No credit cards.*

¢–$$ ⬚ **Hung Vuong Hotel.** Both backpackers and nonbackpackers stay here, especially those taking the Sinh Café Bus (☞ Arriving and Departing *in* Hue A to Z, *below*), which drops off and picks up passengers here. There's a variety of clean rooms in a wide price range. The hotel adjoins the Thua Thien–Hue Tourism office and is near downtown Hue. ✉ *2 Hung Vuong St.,* ☎ *054/823866,* FAX *054/825910. 70 rooms, most with bath. Restaurant, air-conditioning, minibars, refrigerators, laundry service, travel services, car rental. No credit cards.*

Hue Essentials

Arriving and Departing
BY AIRPLANE
Vietnam Airlines (✉ 12 Hanoi St., ☎ 054/823249) flies to Hue's Phu Bai Airport, 15 km (9 mi) south of the city center, from Ho Chi Minh City (1 hr; $85 one way; 3 times a week); Hanoi (50 mins; $80 one way; 3 times a week); and Dalat (1 hr 20 mins; $105 one way; 2 times a week). The schedule changes frequently, so confirm departure times a day or two before your flight. Taxis will take you into town for about 90,000d (negotiable).

BY BUS
The **Sinh Café Bus** (✉ At Hung Vuong Hotel, 2 Hung Vuong St., Hue, ☎ 054/823866) stops in Hue on both its northbound and southbound routes (Hanoi to Hue takes about 12 hrs and costs $8; the trip from Ho Chi Minh City takes about 3 days and costs $14—you stop in Dalat and Nha Trang).

BY TRAIN
Trains from all over Vietnam come into the **Hue Railway Station** (Ga Hue; ✉ On right bank at southwest end of Le Loi St.). The ticket office is open daily 7:30–5. Four trains depart daily for Ho Chi Minh City (24 hrs, $60–$80 for a sleeping berth), and four depart daily for Hanoi (15 hrs, $40–$50 for a sleeping berth).

Getting Around
BY BICYCLE
An easy way to get around Hue is by bicycle, which you can rent from the Century Riverside Inn (☞ Lodging, *above*) and from a stand across the street from the Hung Vuong Hotel.

BY CAR OR MINIBUS
You can rent a minibus with a driver to take you to Hoi An, Danang, the imperial tombs, or other points near Hue; the cost is approximately

$25–$50 for the trip, depending on the kind of vehicle, its age, and whether it has air-conditioning. The additional cost of the services of a guide is $25–$50.

BY CYCLO

You can always find a cyclo outside hotels or cruising along the right bank. For 50,000d you should be able to get pretty much anywhere, although you will always have to negotiate. The Century Riverside Inn (☞ Lodging, *above*) posts suggested cyclo prices for those who hate to bargain.

BY TAXI

Taxis are metered. Expect to pay a few dollars for trips around town. Call **Hue Taxi ATC** (☎ 054/824500 or 054/833333) to arrange a ride, or just hail one on the street, though they are not always easy to find.

Contacts and Resources

CURRENCY EXCHANGE

The **Thua Thien–Hue branch of Vietcom Bank** (ICBV; ✉ 21 Le Duy Don St., ☎ 054/822281) changes money. It's open weekdays 7–11 and 1:30–3:30. You can also exchange money at most hotels.

EMERGENCIES

In case of emergency, contact **Benh Vien Trung Uong Hue** (Hue General Hospital; ✉ 16 Le Loi St., ☎ 054/822325). Some of the doctors speak English.

If you need to fill a prescription, the woman working at **Thuoc Tay** (✉ 5 Hung Vuong St.) speaks better French than English, but she is very helpful, especially if you write down what you need.

TOUR OPERATORS

A number of agencies organize boat trips on the Perfume River, which include stops at the tombs and the Thien Mu Pagoda. Most depart at 8 AM daily and cost 30,000d, excluding tomb and pagoda entry fees, which amount to about 50,000d each.

VISITOR INFORMATION AND TRAVEL AGENCIES

The following travel agencies arrange cars with drivers, tours of Hue, boat tours along the Perfume River, and excursions to the DMZ. **DMZ Tour Office** (✉ 26 Le Loi St., ☎ 054/825242). **Hue City Tourism** (✉ 18 Le Loi St., ☎ 054/823577). **Huong Giang Company** (✉ 17 Le Loi St., ☎ 054/820188, FAX 054/823102). **Thua Thien–Hue Tourism** (Cong Ty Du Lich Thua Thien–Hue; ✉ 30 Le Loi St. [and a branch at 2 Hung Vuong St.], ☎ 054/822369, 054/822288, or 054/822355).

THE CENTRAL COAST

Updated by
Andrew
Chilvers

The region south of Hue includes the port city of Danang, with an outstanding museum of Cham culture; the famous China Beach; the cave temples at the Marble Mountains; and the delightful town of Hoi An, a well-preserved 18th-century trading village on the sea, where families have lived in the same homes for more than 200 years.

Danang

108 km (67 mi) south of Hue, 30 km (17 mi) north of Hoi An, and 972 km (603 mi) north of Ho Chi Minh City.

Danang, an important port town at the end of the 19th century, may be familiar to you as a U.S. Air Force base during the Vietnam War. Today, it is a slightly run-down city that offers little in the way of sights except for the wonderful Cham museum. The city also has the region's largest airport for Hoi An and other points of interest in the region.

On display at the **Cham Museum** are artifacts from the ancient Kingdom of Champa, which existed from the 2nd to the 18th centuries around present-day Danang, Nha Trang, and Phan Rang. The Cham adopted many elements of Indian art and Sanksrit as their sacred language, and their religion combines native beliefs with elements of Indian culture and early Hindu thought (the god Shiva is often represented). Their kingdom stretched from the north of Hue to the Mekong Delta in the 10th and 11th centuries, between the Khmer to the south and the Viet to the north. In the 12th century, the Cham were under frequent attack by the Khmer. In the 13th century, backed by the Chinese, the Viet attacked in the north but were defeated in 1377 when the Cham reached an agreement with the Chinese. The Cham presence was substantial until the 1400s, when they were conquered by the Viet. After that, their influence receded until they were finally overthrown by the Viet in the 1700s. Remnants of the sandstone-and-brick towers built for Hindu worship by the Cham can still be found along the central coast, and descendants of the Cham continue to live in the highlands and along the coastal lowlands.

The Cham Museum was founded by the French in 1915 to exhibit Cham sculptures and fragments of temples and towers found by archaeologists. Exhibits are arranged chronologically, reflecting the changing seats of power in the kingdom, from Emperor Indrapura to Tra Kieu to My Son to Khuong My. The highly sensual, innovative, and expressive works from Tra Kieu's reign (7th century) and that of My Son (8th–9th centuries) and the abundant sandstone carvings of the god Shiva show the prosperity of the Kingdom of Champa.

As you walk through the museum, note that the Cham Buddha is displayed on a throne in an imperial pose, with his feet flat on the ground, not in the traditional lotus position. This subtle difference in Buddha styles reflects the Cham belief in the spiritual continuum between crown and divinity—the nobility were thought to be "higher up" because they were more directly connected to God. The symbol of fertility, Uroja (meaning female breast), which you will also see throughout the museum, reveals the esteem afforded women in Cham culture. ⊠ *Intersection of Tran Phu and Le Dinh Duong Sts.,* ☎ *no phone.* ▦ *20,000d.* ☉ *Daily 8–11 and 1–5.*

Lodging

$$$ ▦ **Marco Polo.** The only place that you would want to stay in town, the Marco Polo is a haven of Western-style efficiency (meaning: it has phones that work and an English-speaking staff). Rooms are large and tastefully decorated. ⊠ *11 Quang Trung St.,* ☎ *0511/823295,* FAX *0511/827279. 28 rooms. Restaurant, bar, minibars, refrigerators, room service, laundry service and dry cleaning, business services, travel services, car rental. AE, MC, V.*

Marble Mountains

11 km (7 mi) southwest of Danang, 19 km (12 mi) north of Hoi An.

Five beautiful limestone peaks, known as the Marble Mountains, rise above the beach south of Danang. A visit here can easily be combined with a trip to China Beach (☞ *below*). The Marble Mountains, named for the five basic elements of Chinese philosophy—earth, water, fire, wood, and metal—are riddled with caves, and over the centuries the **caves** (dong) in the Thuy Son Peak have been turned into temples and shrines. The first to exploit them were the Cham, who used them as Hindu shrines, but more recently, Buddhists have taken over, adorned, sanctified, and inhabited them.

The path leading to the various cave-pagodas is not particularly strenuous. It leads you into a cave filled with Buddhas, bathed in ethereal light from an opening high above, and then through the mountain into other shrines and out to spectacular views below. Polite children in traditional school uniforms may take you by the hand and lead you through the various caves, at the end offering you the "best price... for you only" for such marble souvenirs as miniature Marble Mountains and small mortar-and-pestle sets. ⊠ *About 11 km (7 mi) south of Danang; 9½ km (6 mi) north of Hoi An off Hwy. 1.* ▣ *40,000d.*

China Beach

12 km (7 mi) southwest of Danang, 45 km (28 mi) north of Hoi An.

Yes, the TV show *China Beach* was based on this place, but the China Beach that was an R&R resort for U.S. soldiers during the Vietnam War is actually 5 km (3 mi) north of what is now called China Beach (Bac My An). Activity here is limited to lazing on the sand and surfing. Surfboards can be rented from the Furama Resort, as can bicycles. It's best for nonsurfers between May and July, when the water is placid.

Dining and Lodging

$$$ 🏨 **Furama Resort.** This is one of Vietnam's premier resorts, a favorite
★   with the country's expatriates. Right on the beach, it comprises a group of French Vietnamese–style villas surrounding a man-made lagoon. The interior evokes the French colonial era, with a Vietnamese influence: shuttered windows, cane furniture, ceiling fans, and Vietnamese artifacts. The resort has a shuttle service from Danang's airport and can organize tours for you to Danang, Hoi An, and even Hue. ⊠ *68 Ho Xuan Huong St.,* ☎ *0511/847333 or 08/8211888 in Ho Chi Minh City,* ℻ *0511/847666. 200 rooms. 2 restaurants, 2 bars, in-room safes, minibars, room service, pool, sauna, driving range, 4 tennis courts, health club, surfing, bicycles, dry cleaning and laundry service, meeting rooms, travel services. AE, MC, V.*

Hoi An

138 km (67 mi) south of Hue, 30 km (17 mi) south of Danang, and 1,002 km (603 mi) north of Ho Chi Minh City.

Perhaps the most delightful of all Vietnamese towns, riverside Hoi An defies the insidious pace of modernization. The 18th-century houses, pagodas, and assembly halls built by the early Chinese communities remain in pristine condition; the bustling market makes you feel you've gone back in time. The crowded streets are lined with souvenir vendors and shops selling the rice-paper canvases of local artists. You'll also find great cuisine, tailors who can make you a nice suit in just one day, and a very pleasant sandy beach.

Hoi An, or Faifo as it was called, is a composite of many foreign influences. From the 2nd to 10th centuries, it was an important port town under the control of the Kingdom of Champa. During the 14th and 15th centuries, when the Cham and the Vietnamese fought for control, Hoi An ceased to be a trading center, but peace in the 16th century again saw the arrival of ships from all over Asia and Europe, bringing merchants in search of silk, porcelain, lacquer, and medicinal herbs.

During the Tay Son rebellion in the 1770s, Hoi An was severely damaged, but it was speedily rebuilt and once again became a major international port, where for two centuries Chinese, Japanese, Dutch, and Portuguese merchants came to trade. During the off-season, the merchants set up shop, and foreigners' colonies began to develop along the riverfront. To this day, ethnic Chinese make up a significant portion of the population. In the late 1800s, the French arrived and made

Hoi An an administrative post. Then, when the Thu ... to silt up, Danang gradually eclipsed Hoi An as the area ...

The old town, a combination of Vietnamese, Japanese, and C... architectural styles, is reserved for pedestrians, bicycles, and motor bikes—the perfect place for a walk. Get a map from your hotel or from the tourist office at the corner of Nguyen Hue Street and Phan Chu Trinh Street. Here you can also find an English- or French-speaking guide and buy the combined entrance ticket ($5) to the wonderful mix of Chinese assembly halls and temples, museums, and old teak houses. It admits you to three of the sites and the Japanese Bridge, which is actually a public thoroughfare.

A GOOD WALK

After purchasing your tickets, head to the small colonial-era **Museum of History and Culture,** approximately one block from the tourist office, at the corner of Tran Phu and Nguyen Hue streets. Walk across the courtyard filled with birdcages to get to **Quan Cong Temple,** dedicated to a deified Chinese general. Leave through the front entrance to find yourself directly opposite the **Central Market,** one of Vietnam's most pleasant.

Leave the market, and walk east on Tran Phu Street until you get to No. 178, the **Assembly Hall of the Hainan Chinese Congregation.** Continue east (Tran Phu Street turns into Nguyen Duy Hieu Street after it intersects with Hoang Dieu Street), and just past the intersection on the left, at No. 157, is the **Trieu Chau Assembly Hall,** with its fine wood carvings. Turn around and go back west on Tran Phu Street; cross Nguyen Hue, walk past charming small houses with teak columns and tile roofs, and on your right, at No. 46, is the colorful **Phuoc Kien Assembly Hall,** now a temple devoted to Thien Hau, the goddess of the sea. Just a few doors down is the **Assembly Hall of the Fujian Chinese Congregation,** also dedicated to Thien Hau. Continue along Tran Phu street until you come to No. 64, the **Chinese All-Community Assembly Hall** on your right; as its name implies, it was used as a meeting place for all the Chinese communities in Hoi An. Farther along on your left will be the ancient **Quang Thang House,** at No. 77.

At No. 80 is the Diep Dong Nguyen House, now the **Museum of Trade Ceramics,** and then, past Le Loi and Nhi Trung streets, on the north side, is the **Assembly Hall of the Cantonese Chinese Congregation.** Farther along Tran Phu Street, past a row of souvenir shops and the intersection with Nhi Trung Street, is the fascinating **Japanese Covered Bridge.** Keep going on Tran Phu Street, which becomes Nguyen Thi Minh Khai Street. At No. 4 is the **Old House of Phung Hung,** where eight generations of one family have lived for more than 200 years. Turn around and head back east; at the fork in the road after the Japanese Bridge, bear right onto Nguyen Thai Hoc Street and walk to No. 101, the **Old House of Tan Ky.** Continue east to Le Loi Street, and make a left. Cross Tran Phu Street, and on the corner of Phan Chu Trinh Street is the **Tran Family Chapel,** where a member of the family will show you around.

SIGHTS TO SEE

Assembly Hall of the Cantonese Chinese Congregation. The main altar of this hall, founded in 1786, is dedicated to Quan Cong, a revered General of the Chinese Han dynasty. ⊠ *176 Tran Phu St., at Nguyen Thai Hoc St.* 🎟 *In combination ticket.* ☉ *Daily 8–5.*

Assembly Hall of the Fujian Chinese Congregation. Built as a meeting place, this hall later became a temple dedicated to Thien Hau, the Fujian goddess of the sea and protector of fishermen. Thien Hau is represented in the mural near the entrance. Another mural depicts six Fujian families who fled from China to Hoi An in the 17th century. The gate is newer: it was built in 1975. ⊠ *Opposite 35 Tran Phu St.* 🔟 *In combination ticket.* ⊘ *Daily 8–5.*

Assembly Hall of the Hainan Chinese Congregation. This hall, founded by Chinese from Hainan, was constructed in 1883 in memory of more than 100 merchants who were mistakenly killed because they were thought to be pirates. ⊠ *178 Nguyen Duy Hieu St.* 🔟 *In combination ticket.* ⊘ *Daily 8–5.*

Central Market. Hoi An's wonderful market is one of the most enjoyable in Vietnam. The aisles are lined with silk shops that can fill custom clothing orders for little money in less than 24 hours (but beware of "cotton" that's part synthetic and "silk" that's really polyester). In the center are fresh and dried fruit and flowers; the daily catch is down by the river; and miscellaneous batteries, pajamas, and bicycle pumps pop up all over. ⊠ *Intersection of Tran Quy Cap and Tran Phu Sts.* ⊘ *Daily 6–dusk.*

Chaozhou Assembly Hall (Trieu Chau). Built by the Chaozhou Chinese community in 1776, this hall exemplifies Chinese wood carving of this period at its finest. ⊠ *157 Nguyen Duy Hieu St.* 🔟 *In combination ticket.* ⊘ *Daily 8–5.*

Chinese All-Community Assembly Hall (Chua Ba). This hall was built in 1773 as a meeting place for the Cantonese, Chaozhou, Fujian, Hainan, and Hakka families living in Hoi An. ⊠ *64 Tran Phu St.* 🔟 *In combination ticket.* ⊘ *Daily 8–5.*

Japanese Bridge (Cau Nhat, or Lai Vien Kieu). One of the city's landmarks, this red-painted, covered wooden bridge was originally built in 1593 by the Japanese to link their section of town to the Chinese quarter. Two small altars at one end are surmounted by charming statues of dogs and those at the other by statues of monkeys. A small temple on the north side, dedicated to Tran Vo Bac De (God of the North), is revered by sailors because he controls wind and rain. ⊠ *Tran Phu St.* 🔟 *In combination ticket.* ⊘ *Daily 8–5.*

Museum of History and Culture. This small museum—housed in just one large room—displays ancient bowls, cups, and other ceramics, many of them archaeological artifacts. ⊠ *7 Nguyen Hue St.,* ☎ *no phone.* 🔟 *In combination ticket.* ⊘ *Daily 8–5.*

★ **Museum of Trade Ceramics.** The ancient Diep Dong Nguyen House has been converted into a terrific small museum dedicated to the history of ceramics in Hoi An. ⊠ *80 Tran Phu St.* 🔟 *In combination ticket.* ⊘ *Daily 8–5.*

Old House of Phung Hung. Eight generations of the Phung Hung family have lived here since the house was built in 1780. Note the Japanese influences in the roof, the Chinese influences in the balcony, and the Vietnamese architectural style of the walls. ⊠ *4 Nguyen Thi Minh Khai St.* 🔟 *In combination ticket.* ⊘ *Daily 8–5.*

Old House of Tan Ky. One of the oldest in Hoi An, this private house has remained largely unchanged in the 200 years since it was built. Seven generations of the Tan Ky family have lived here. ⊠ *101 Nguyen Thai Hoc St.* 🔟 *In combination ticket.* ⊘ *Daily 8–5.*

Phuoc Kien Assembly Hall. This colorfully decorated building, built in 1690 and redone in 1900, is dedicated to Thien Hau, the goddess of the sea. It has a bright, airy garden. ⊠ *46 Tran Phu St.* 🔟 *In combination ticket.* ⊘ *Daily 8–5.*

Quan Cong Temple. Founded in 1653 by the Chinese c̶e̶... temple is dedicated to Quan Cong, a revered general of th̶... Han dynasty. The carp, symbolic of patience in Chinese mytho... displayed throughout. ⊠ *24 Tran Phu St.* 🎫 *In combination ticke̶...* ⊙ *Daily 8–5.*

Quang Thang House. Another of Hoi An's ancient family homes, built about 300 years ago, has beautiful wood carvings on the walls of the rooms surrounding the courtyard. ⊠ *77 Tran Phu St.* 🎫 *In combination ticket.* ⊙ *Daily 8–5.*

Tran Family Chapel. This house, built in 1802, is dedicated to the worship of the Tran family's deceased ancestors. ⊠ *21 Le Loi St.* 🎫 *In combination ticket.* ⊙ *Daily 8–5.*

Dining and Lodging

$$ ★ ✕ **Café des Amis.** There is no menu at the Café des Amis. Instead, your waiter will ask if you want seafood or a vegetarian meal, then start bringing you food. Expect five or six courses, sometimes excellent, sometimes ordinary; its popularity has made it unpredictable. The waterfront location makes for a great atmosphere. ⊠ *52 Bach Dang St.,* ☎ *0510/861616. No credit cards.*

$$ ✕ **Han Huyen Floating Restaurant.** It's a pleasure to sit on the breezy deck of this docked boat, whose menu serves Chinese and Vietnamese dishes, and specializes in game. ⊠ *Bach Dang St.,* ☎ *0510/61462. No credit cards.*

$$ ✕ **Vinh Hung Restaurant.** A peaceful oasis across the street from the Cantonese Assembly Hall, this restaurant serves superb seafood and such local specialties as White Roses, the delicious shrimp dumpling said to resemble a rose. Have a drink on the shady terrace, hung with bougainvillea and cages of singing birds, and watch the world go by. ⊠ *147b Tran Phu St.,* ☎ *0510/862203. No credit cards.*

$ ✕ **Bobo Cafe.** This neighborhood hangout has a pleasant shady terrace favored for breakfast by guests at the Thuy Duong Hotel across the street. It serves seafood and *cao lau* (a noodle dish topped with pork and bean sprouts) at reasonable prices. It's also a travel booking office. ⊠ *18 Le Loi St.,* ☎ *0510/861939. No credit cards.*

$ ✕ **Faifoo.** Come here for refreshing fruit shakes, as well as a great multicourse sampler menu of chicken and pork dishes, all for next to nothing. ⊠ *104 Tran Phu St.,* ☎ *0510/861548. No credit cards.*

$ ✕ **Ly Cafeteria 22.** Catering mostly to backpackers, this very friendly spot serves tasty local specialties such as cao lau and White Roses. This is a great place for a cheap lunch or dinner. ⊠ *22 Nguyen Hue St.,* ☎ *0510/861603. No credit cards.*

$ ✕ **Restaurant Thanh.** This open-air riverfront restaurant makes a splendid flounder (or whatever white fish happens to be fresh that day) cooked in banana leaves. The decor is shiny black and gold lacquered pillars, with pink walls, paper lanterns, and a voluptuous Thunbergia vine tumbling down. But the candlelight ambience is frequently disrupted by postcard vendors. ⊠ *76 Bach Dang St.,* ☎ *0510/861366. No credit cards.*

$$–$$$ 🏨 **Hoi An Hotel.** This hotel offers the best accommodation in town. It's also the only hotel that takes credit cards or traveler's checks. Rooms are comfortable, spotless, and spacious, with IDD phones and satellite TV. The outstanding Hoi An tourist office is in the lobby. ⊠ *6 Tran Hung Dao St.,* ☎ *0510/861445,* 📠 *0510/861636. 130 rooms. Restaurant, fans, pool, bicycles, laundry service, travel services, car rental. AE, MC, V.*

$$ 🏨 **Cua Dai Hoi An Hotel.** One of the nicest and newest accommodations in town, this plush minihotel has spotless, sunny rooms, many with

balconies. It's between the beach and the town center—both are just a bike ride away (you can rent bikes at the hotel). ⊠ *18A Cua Dai St.,* ☎ *0510/862231,* FAX *0510/862232. 17 rooms. Restaurant, air-conditioning, fans, bicycles, laundry service, travel services. No credit cards.*

$$ 🖭 **Thien Trung.** This hotel is very close to the bus station and only a short bike ride from the old town. Rooms are neat and bright. ⊠ *63 Phan Ding Phung St.,* ☎ *0510/861720 or 0510/861769. 16 rooms. Restaurant, air-conditioning, fans, laundry service, travel services, car rental. No credit cards.*

$$ 🖭 **Vinh Hung Hotel.** This Chinese-inspired hotel not far from the Japanese Bridge has dark wood paneling and carvings and a smiling Buddha in the lobby. Rooms are sunny and cheerfully decorated. The owners also run the popular Vinh Hung Restaurant on the corner. ⊠ *143 Tran Phu St.,* ☎ *0510/861621,* FAX *0510/861893. 12 rooms. Restaurant, bar, air-conditioning, fans, laundry service, travel services. No credit cards.*

$ 🖭 **Thanh Binh.** This centrally located hotel has clean rooms that get plenty of light. Get here early: the hotel often fills up by noon with budget travelers. ⊠ *1 Le Loi St.,* ☎ *0510/861740. 14 rooms. Air-conditioning, fans, laundry service, travel services, car rental, free parking. No credit cards.*

$ 🖭 **Thuy Duong Mini Hotel.** This nice budget hotel has two branches, and one of them is ideally located across from Bobo Cafe in the center of town. Rooms are large and are a great bargain at well under $20; the one on the second floor in the back has a sitting area and two exposures. ⊠ *11 Le Loi St.,* ☎ *0510/861574,* FAX *0510/861330. 11 rooms. Air-conditioning, fans. No credit cards.*

Central Coast Essentials

Arriving and Departing

BY AIRPLANE

Vietnam Airlines (⊠ 35 Tran Phu St., Danang, ☎ 0511/821130, FAX 0511/832759) flies to Danang's airport, 3 km (2 mi) southwest of the city, from Ho Chi Minh City (daily), Hanoi (daily), and Nha Trang (four times a week). A regular taxi to the airport should cost no more than 50,000d; to reserve one, call **Airport Taxis** (☎ 0511/825555), Danang's only taxi company.

BY BUS

Convenient tour buses that run between Hue and Hoi An ($3) stop en route at Danang's Cham Museum and at the Marble Mountains and China Beach.

BY CAR

Hue is about three hours north of Danang, and Hoi An is about one hour south. China Beach and the Marble Mountains are easily accessible by car from Danang, as is Hoi An. You can make arrangements at most hotels and from the **Danang Travel Information Center** (⊠ 3–5 Dong Da St., ☎ 0511/823431 or 0511/823298, FAX 0511/823431).

Getting Around

See Arriving and Departing, *above,* for information about renting cars with drivers; motorbikes can also be rented from many hotels and travel agencies. In Hoi An, **Mr. Loc** (⊠ 141 Tran Phu St., ☎ 0510/861447), can see to all your motorbike or taxi needs and even arrange a trip to My Son by boat. In Danang, taxi drivers hang out at the Cham Museum (count on about 50,000d a day), or you can take a taxi from the airport to Hoi An, stopping at Marble Mountains and China Beach.

NHA TRANG

Though it's a bustling city with a long stretch of developed beachfront, Nha Trang has its charms: swarms of high-school students bike to and from classes, and hordes of teenagers play soccer in the few waterfront lots that have not been turned into tourist sights. Recreational attractions include swimming, scuba diving, and snorkeling, and boat trips to neighboring islands—lush enclaves with isolated beaches and groves of palm trees. Recent dynamiting of coral reefs by fishermen has made scuba diving disappointing. For a good day trip you can travel by boat up the Cai River, which is wonderfully tropical, with lush palm forests lining the banks; it was reputedly the model for the journey upstream in *Apocalypse Now.*

Exploring Nha Trang

The beautiful **Long Son Pagoda,** built in the late 19th century and re-constructed a number of times since, is the town's most famous. A giant Buddha beckons you up a flight of stairs, at the top of which is a panoramic view of Nha Trang. The entrance to the pagoda itself is down below. The resident monks give tours of the main sanctuary. ⊠ *About 550 yards west of railroad station, opposite 15, 23 Thang 10.* ⊗ *Daily 8–noon and 2–4.*

One of the better preserved Cham ruins in Vietnam, the **Po Nagar Cham Towers** (Nha Trang Huu Duc), also called the Mother Goddess or Lady of the City Towers, was originally a 2nd-century site of Hindu worship. The present buildings were constructed between the 7th and 12th centuries, and it is still an active Buddhist shrine. Of the original eight towers, four remain, in various states of preservation. The North Tower (Thap Chinh), built during King Harivarman I's reign in AD 817, originally housed a lingam, a phallic stone, which was stolen and replaced by the statue of Uma that you see today. ⊠ *On north side of Cai River over Hai Ra and Xom Bong bridges.* ☎ 6,000d. ⊗ *Daily 8–5.*

On the same side of the river as the Po Nagar Cham Towers is the **Hon Chong Promontory,** where there are good views of the coastline and the surrounding islands. ⊠ *About ¼ km (⅛ mi) from intersection of Nguyen Dinh Chieu and 2 Thang 4 Sts.* ☎ 10,000d. ⊗ *Daily 8–4.*

A boat trip to the surrounding **islands**—Mieu Island (Tri Nguyen Island), Bamboo Island (Hon Tre), and Monkey Island (Dao Khi) can be arranged through any number of hotels and travel agencies (☞ Contacts and Resources *in* Nha Trang Essentials, *below*). **Mama Hahn's Boat Trips** are reputed to be the most fun; book through the Nha Trang Sailing Club (☞ Dining and Lodging, *below*).

North of town are two more isolated and less developed **beaches,** Doc Let (30 km/19 mi), and **Dai Lanh** (83 km/51 mi). To reach them it's best to hire a car and driver or simply catch a cab.

Dining and Lodging

$$ ✗ **Ngoc Suong.** This establishment a block from the beach serves the
★ best and the freshest seafood in town. Fish salad, made from marinated local seafood, is the specialty. ⊠ *16 Tran Quang Khai St., not far from Tran Phu St.,* ☎ 058/954516. *No credit cards.*

$$ ✗ **Nha Trang Sailing Club.** The liveliest of all the seaside cafés/restau-
★ rants in town, the Sailing Club is popular with expats, locals, and tourists. It's the place to go for food like burgers, fish-and-chips, and tomato soup. Boat trips can be arranged through the office just behind the restaurant. ⊠ *72–74 Tran Phu St.,* ☎ 058/826528, FAX 058/821906. *No credit cards.*

$ ✕ **Lac Canh.** Each table in this smoke-filled restaurant has a charcoal grill on which you make your own cheap and delicious marinated seafood and meat dishes. Just be prepared for one odd habit: diners pile empty beer bottles and other leftovers on the floor after they're done with them. ☒ *11 Hang Ca,* ☎ *058/821391. No credit cards.*

$ ✕ **Thanh Lich.** At this rustic family-run restaurant excellent seafood specials are prepared before your eyes. The sublime squid in ginger comes to your table as a raw marinade and is cooked on a portable charcoal burner at your table. ☒ *8 Phan Boi Chau St.,* ☎ *058/821955. No credit cards.*

¢ ✕ **Banana Split.** This small sidewalk café—open breakfast, lunch, and dinner—serves ice-cream sundaes, omelets, chicken, and burgers. It's a destination for Western travelers looking to meet other people. Boat trips and other travel arrangements can be made here. ☒ *58 Quang Trung St.,* ☎ *058/829115. No credit cards.*

¢ ✕ **Thanh The.** Locals and Vietnamese tourists pack this restaurant specializing in seafood and traditional Vietnamese fare. ☒ *3 Phan Chu Trinh St.,* ☎ *058/821931. No credit cards.*

$$$ ▦ **Ana Mandara Nha Trang Resort.** Completed in 1997, this beach-
★ front resort is the classiest and most comfortable place to stay in Nha Trang. Reminiscent of Balinese- and Thai-style resorts, it has private thatched cottages. ☒ *60 Tran Phu St.,* ☎ *058/829829,* ℻ *058/823629. 68 rooms. Restaurant, in-room safes, minibars, room service, pool, bicycles, motorbikes, library, laundry service and dry cleaning, meeting rooms, travel services. AE, MC, V.*

$$ ▦ **Bao Dai Villas.** Once the beach retreat of Emperor Bao Dai, this hotel has seen better days. As a state-run affair, it lacks overall quality and reminds you of sleeping in a museum, with its musty smells and the odd spiderweb and cockroach. The service, too, leaves a lot to be desired. Nevertheless, it's definitely worth a visit for its historic significance, and its peaceful hilltop location makes it a good place for a drink. ☒ *Cau Da-Vinh Nguyen,* ☎ *058/881471. 48 rooms, 45 with bath. Restaurant, air-conditioning, fans, room service, TV, tennis court, beach, snorkeling, boating, meeting rooms, travel services. No credit cards.*

$$ ▦ **Nha Trang Lodge Hotel.** Though this relatively new hotel (1996) is right across the street from the ocean, its tacky lobby and decor are reminiscent of roadside motels in the United States. But rooms are clean and comfortable, have satellite TV, IDD phones, and some have excellent views of the beach. The hotel can exchange money. ☒ *42 Tran Phu St.,* ☎ *058/810500,* ℻ *058/828800. 124 rooms. Restaurant, air-conditioning, room service, in-room safes, minibars, laundry service and dry cleaning, travel services. AE, MC, V.*

$$ ▦ **Seaside Hotel.** A plush, new minihotel just south of town on the coast, this place has some of the most tastefully decorated rooms in Nha Trang; a number even have ocean views. No services are offered, however, and the staff sleeps in the lobby at night. Nonetheless, it is one of Nha Trang's best. ☒ *96 Tran Phu St.,* ☎ *058/821178,* ℻ *058/ 828038. 15 rooms. Restaurant, air-conditioning, fans, laundry service. No credit cards.*

$–$$ ▦ **Thanh Thanh Hotel.** This efficient, brightly lit minihotel overlooks the water and is just south of town. ☒ *98A Tran Phu St.,* ☎ *058/824657,* ℻ *058/823031. 18 rooms. Restaurant, air-conditioning, minibars, refrigerators, room service, TVs, laundry service, travel services. No credit cards.*

$–$$ ▦ **Vien Dong Hotel.** One of the first large hotels in Nha Trang, the Vien Dong is a hub of tourist activity. Though popular with Westerners because it's close to the beach and has a pool, it's slightly run-down and overpriced—a charmless state-run affair with plastic furniture, polyester

curtains, and an abrupt and unhelpful staff. On the other
travel service is very good. ✉ *1 Tran Hung Dao St.*, ☎ *058*
FAX *058/821912. 86 rooms. Restaurant, bar, air-conditioning*
minibars, refrigerators, TV, pool, massage, laundry service, trav
vices, car rental. AE, MC, V.

Outdoor Activities and Sports

The Blue Diving Club (✉ 40 Tran Phu St., Coconut Grove, ☎ 058/
825390, FAX 058/824214), a very well-run Professionally Approved
Diving Institute (P.A.D.I.) center, offers beginning scuba instruction
in English and French and arranges guided excursions for all diving
levels.

Nha Trang Essentials

Arriving and Departing
BY AIRPLANE
The recommended way to get to Nha Trang is by plane. **Vietnam Air-
lines** (✉ 12B Hoang Hoa Tham St., Nha Trang, ☎ 058/823797) flies
daily between Nha Trang and Ho Chi Minh City (55 mins; $60) and
Hanoi (2½ hrs; $100), and three times a week to Danang.

BY BUS
The **Sinh Café** (☞ Getting Around by Bus *in* Vietnam A to Z, *below*)
bus links Ho Chi Minh City with Dalat and then Nha Trang.

BY CAR
Nha Trang is 448 km (278 mi) north of Ho Chi Minh City along Highway 1 (20 hrs by car) and 2,250 km (1,200 mi) south of Hanoi.
Danang is 541 km (225 mi) north of Nha Trang (10 hrs by car). A car
and driver can be hired from hotels and from private and state-run travel
agencies (☞ Contacts and Resources, *below*).

BY TRAIN
Nha Trang is served three times daily by both express and local trains
from Hanoi and Ho Chi Minh City. A soft sleeper to Ho Chi Minh
City costs $25–$35; to Hanoi it costs $80–$100, depending on whether
you take the express or the local train. The express train between Ho
Chi Minh City and Nha Trang takes 15 hours, the local 22 hours; between Hanoi and Nha Trang, the express takes 24 hours and the local
32. Note: the ticket office at **Nha Trang Railway Station** (✉ 26 Thai
Nguyen St., ☎ 058/822113) is open 7–2 only.

Getting Around
The easiest way to get around Nha Trang is by cyclo, which you can
find all over town. Be sure to bargain to get the best rate. Or you can
rent a bicycle at any travel agency and at most hotels for about
10,000d a day. Hiring a car with a driver is necessary only to go to
one of the beaches outside town. Renting a motorbike, with or without a driver, is another option—about 70,000d a day, from travel agencies and hotels.

Contacts and Resources
TRAVEL AGENCIES
Khanh Hoa Tourism (✉ 1 Tran Hung Dao St., ☎ 058/822753, FAX 058/
824206). **Nam-Viet** (✉ 2 Hung Vung St., ☎ 058/821428, FAX 058/
821428). **Nha Trang Tourism** (✉ 3 Tran Hung Dao St., Hung Dao Hotel,
☎ 058/821231).

THE CENTRAL
5 TO DALAT

...ending north and south from Dalat is the region known as the central highlands, an unspoiled landscape dotted with ethnic minority villages and religious complexes. Part of the southern end of the Truong Son range, this area of mountains, streams, lakes, and waterfalls covers the provinces of Lam Dong, Dac Lac (Dak Lak), Gia Lai, and Kon Tum. It is one of the few parts of the country where it is cool enough to wear a sweater, even in summer. The mountain resort of Dalat, the principal town, is somewhat shabby, but its lovely scenery continues to appeal.

The Central Highlands

The western part of the central highlands is home to a large population of ethnic minorities, called Montagnards, from the French for "mountain people." They are largely nomadic farmers who live an isolated existence in tribal villages. Some have been in Vietnam for thousands of years, others came from neighboring Thailand several centuries ago. The strategic Buon Ma Thuot, Pleiku, and Kontum provinces were major battlegrounds during the Vietnam War. Only now has the vegetation, including coffee trees, begun to recover from the napalm and defoliants.

At the **Dambri Falls** (about 233 km/149 mi northwest of Ho Chi Minh City and 75 km/47 mi southwest of Dalat), steep, slippery steps lead to excellent views of the 300-ft waterfalls. ☒ 10,000d. ☉ Daily 7–5.

Southeast of Dalat on Highway 20, just before you get to the semiarid twin cities of Phan Rang–Thap Cham, are the **Po Klong Garai Cham Towers,** four well-preserved Hindu temples that are remnants of a 13th-century Cham temple built during the reign of Cham King Jaya Simhavarman III, when the Kingdom of Champa ruled this part of Vietnam. ☒ Off Hwy. 20. ☒ 20,000d. ☉ Daily 8–5.

Dalat

308 km (191 mi) north of Ho Chi Minh City, 205 km (127 mi) southwest of Nha Trang.

Named for a river of the native Lat people, Dalat was "discovered" in the early part of this century by Alexandre Yersin, a protégé of the French scientist Louis Pasteur, and quickly became a vacation spot for Europeans escaping the infernal heat. During the Vietnam War the city was the favorite nonpartisan resting spot for high-ranking Vietcong and South Vietnamese officers.

Dalat today is a favorite of Vietnamese honeymooners, and attempts are being made to transform it into an international tourist destination. An 18-hole golf course is already in place, new hotels are planned, and old colonial villas are being converted into guest houses. The city vaguely resembles a small French town and is blessed with lovely weather, but it provides kitsch in unspoiled, unself-conscious abundance. The endless flora and fauna are mocked by plastic replicas decorating the white cars of the wedding processions that pass two or three times a day. Panoramic views of majestic mountains and placid lakes are often interrupted by incongruous Vietnamese dressed as American cowboys offering a ride and a photo opportunity.

Exploring Dalat

Dalat's prime sight is its market, which ranks among Vietnam's best. Several places outside downtown are also worth a visit, but since these are spread out across hilly Dalat, it is a good idea to hire a car with a driver and a guide. Decide what you want to see and leave the exact itinerary to your guide.

Dalat surrounds the dam-generated **Xuan Huong Lake** (Ho Xuan Huong), named for a 17th-century Vietnamese poet known for her daring attacks on the hypocrisy of social conventions. Circumscribed by a path and adjoining a beautiful 18-hole golf course, the lake is a hub of leisurely activity (including paddleboating). In April 1998 it was entirely dry, owing partly to drought and partly to ongoing repairs, and it was expected to be dry for at least another year.

Just west of the lake is the official center of Dalat, with its picturesque **Central Market** and its small collection of restaurants. Locals come here to buy and sell chickens, fruit, and vegetables, and specialties like dried strawberries. ⊠ *Nguyen Thi Minh Khai St.*

Bao Dai's Summer Palace (Biet Dien Quoc Truong), on the south side of the lake, is a wonderfully preserved example of modernist architecture—a yellow palace built in 1933 that still contains the original French furnishings of Emperor Bao Dai, the last emperor of the Nguyen dynasty, who ruled, with the support of the French, from 1926 to 1955. ⊠ *Le Hong Phong St.,* ☎ *063/822125.* ⊠ *10,000d.* ☉ *Daily 7 AM–8 PM.*

Visiting the **Hang Nga Guest House and Art Gallery,** west of Bo Dai's Palace, is an offbeat experience—Salvador Dali meets Swiss Family Robinson in the land of Disney. The designer/owner, daughter of the Vietnamese president, studied architecture in Russia and has created a fairy-tale landscape of huge convoluted trees and enormous fantastical animals, which contain the unique guest rooms, where your bed, your fireplace, and your bath are part of the fantastic sculptures.

The **Lam Ty Ni Pagoda** is the home of the multitalented, multilingual monk Vien Thuc, known as the Mad Monk of Dalat. An artist, poet, landscape architect, craftsman, and religious scholar, Vien Thuc is a living legend who will show you around and, if you're not careful, sell you one of his watercolors. ⊠ *2 Thien My St.* ☉ *Daily 9–5.*

One of Dalat's smaller waterfalls, lovely **Cam Ly Falls** is unfortunately crowded with Vietnamese and Western tourists and kids selling gum and dried meat, a Dalat treat.

If you love gardens, go to the European-style **Dalat Flower Garden (Vuon Hoa Dalat),** near the northeast end of the lake. ⊠ *2 Phu Dong Thien Vuong St.,* ☎ *063/822151.* ⊠ *8,000d.* ☉ *Daily 7–5.*

Dalat University (Truong Dai Hoc Tong Hop), on the north side of town, was established as a Catholic university in 1957 by Hue's archbishop, Ngo Dinh Thuc (President Ngo Ding Diem's brother). After 1975 it became a state school. ⊠ *1 Phu Dong Thien Vuong St.* ☉ *Daily 9–5.*

If you're a train buff or just want to see what Dalat was like in the 1920s, visit the **Crémaillère Railway (Ga Da Lat),** east of the lake. These days the train goes (8 AM departure) only to **Trai Mat,** an ethnic-minority village 8 km (5 mi) east of Dalat (you must hire a whole train car for $15 to take a ride). ⊠ *½ km (⅓ mi) east of Xuan Huong Lake.* ⊠ *10,000d to view station.* ☉ *Daily 8–5.*

The **Chinese Thien Voung Pagoda (Chua Tao Thien Voung),** southeast of town, is surrounded by gardens atop a steep mountain with great views. It was built in 1958 by the Chaozhou Chinese congregation. ⊠ *About 3 km (2 mi) southeast of center of town, following Khe Sanh St.* ☉ *Daily 9–4.*

A favorite of Vietnamese honeymooners is **Prenn Falls (Thac Prenn)**, where in the crowded park you can frolic over rope bridges and under the falls, or hike up the short path to a makeshift zoo. ⊠ *South of Dalat on Hwy. 20; look for Prenn Restaurant.* 🎫 *50,000d.* ⊙ *Daily 8–4:30.*

The Valley of Love (Thung Lung Tinh Yeu), north of the lake, is another pilgrimage site for Vietnamese honeymooners. On a walk around the lovely green valley you can see Vietnamese couples being photographed with locals on horseback dressed as cowboys. ⊠ *Approximately 3 km (2 mi) north of Xuan Huong Lake, following Phu Dong Thien Vuong St.* 🎫 *20,000d.* ⊙ *Daily 7:30–4.*

Dining and Lodging

$$ ✕ **Thanh Thanh.** This pleasant though unspectacular Vietnamese restaurant is one of the few formal establishments in Dalat. Because it's recommended by most of the local guides and hotel concierges, it's often filled with Western tourists. One of the better dishes on the menu is the tasty sugarcane shrimp. ⊠ *4 Tang Bat Ho St.,* ☎ *063/821836. No credit cards.*

$–$$ ✕ **Maison Hoa.** Billing itself as a "Restaurant de famille," this friendly place with its English-speaking owner is a welcome oasis. It's well located, close to the Central Market, and the Vietnamese-French food is good. ⊠ *6 Duong 3 Thang 2,* ☎ *063/822934. No credit cards.*

$ ✕ **Hoang Lan.** Come here for cheap and tasty traditional Vietnamese food served by a friendly staff. Don't expect atmosphere, though—the restaurant is nothing more than a group of large tables and plastic-covered menus. ⊠ *118 Phan Dinh Phung St.,* ☎ *063/822180. No credit cards.*

$$$$ ✕🏨 **Sofitel Dalat Palace.** Reminiscent of a French château, the Dalat
★ Sofitel is one of the best hotels in Vietnam. Overlooking Xuan Huong Lake, it has been renovated to recapture the grandeur and elegance of its original 1922 French design. Spacious rooms with tasteful antique reproductions, original moldings, and unobtrusive modern conveniences, combined with impeccable service under the new international management, make it a great place to stay. The French-influenced food in the beautiful Le Rabelais ($$) does not quite live up to its flawless service or impressive wine list. ⊠ *12 Tran Phu St.,* ☎ *063/825444,* FAX *063/825666. 43 rooms. Restaurant, café, lounge, piano bar, pub, in-room safes, minibars, no-smoking rooms, room service, 18-hole golf course, 2 tennis courts, mountain bikes, shops, baby-sitting, laundry service and dry cleaning, concierge, business services, meeting rooms, travel services, airport shuttle. AE, MC, V.*

$$$ 🏨 **Novotel.** The former DuParc, built in 1932, has been stylishly ren-
★ ovated to take its place as adjunct to the Sofitel, across the street, whose facilities are open to Novotel guests. The rooms are sleekly functional, though luxurious, with high ceilings, gleaming hardwoods and brass touches. The wonderful elevator cage reminds you that this place was built when no expense was spared. ⊠ *7 Tran Phu St.,* ☎ *063/825777,* FAX *063/825888. 144 rooms. Restaurant, café, bar, lobby lounge, in-room safes, minibars, 18-hole golf course, 2 tennis courts, laundry service, meeting rooms, business services, travel services. AE, D, MC, V.*

$$ 🏨 **Anh Dao Hotel.** This hotel is in a prime location overlooking the Central Market. Rooms are pleasant and modern, if a bit run-down. Some have Western conveniences such as in-room refrigerators, and the staff is eager to please. ⊠ *50–52 Hoa Binh Sq. (Nguyen Chi Thanh St.),* ☎ *063/822384. 27 rooms. Restaurant, bar, minibars, room service, laundry service and dry cleaning, travel services. MC, V.*

$$ 🏨 **Hang Nga Guesthouse.** Each of the unique rooms is an animal all its own—light your fire in an eagle's egg fireplace while momma eagle spreads her wings over the chimney. At this small guest house and art gallery close to the center of town, the wacky architecture makes for

a cheerful lodging alternative in an amusing ambience. ⊠ *3 Huynh Thu̇ Khang St.,* ☎ *063/822070. 10 rooms. Restaurant, travel services. No credit cards.*

The Central Highlands and Dalat Essentials

Arriving and Departing

BY AIRPLANE

Vietnam Airlines (San Bay Lien Khuong; ⊠ 5 Truong Cong Dinh St., Dalat, ☎ 063/822895) flies between Dalat's Lien Khuong Airport (30 km/19 mi south of town) and Hanoi, Ho Chi Minh City, and Hue several times a week; fares run $85–$115.

BY BUS

Dalat Tourist (⊠ 4 Tran Quoc Toan St., Dalat, ☎ 063/822125; ⊠ 21 Nguyen An Ninh St., District 1, Ho Chi Minh City, ☎ 08/8230227) runs daily minibus service between Dalat and Ho Chi Minh City. The trip costs 90,000d and takes 12 long hours; reserve one day in advance. **Sinh Café** (⊠ 179 Pham Ngu Lao St., District 1, Ho Chi Minh City, ☎ 08/835–5601) connects Dalat to Ho Chi Minh City (☞ Getting Around by Bus *in* Vietnam A to Z, *below,* for more information).

Getting Around

The best way to get around Dalat's narrow, hilly roads is by hired car and driver with a guide or on a rented motorbike. Try the **Dalat Tourist/ Lamdong Tourist Company** (⊠ 4 Tran Quoc Toan St., ☎ 063/822125, FAX 063/822661) who can also arrange a tour of the city.

HO CHI MINH CITY

Arriving in Ho Chi Minh City airport can be bewildering. The bustle of the crowds and the throngs of taxi drivers competing for business can be jarringly disorienting, especially if you're jet-lagged. But don't be put off—confusion and chaos are the very heart of the city.

Once romantically referred to by the French as the Pearl of the Orient, Ho Chi Minh City is still called Saigon by almost everyone who lives here (we use both names in this chapter). The city has a more cosmopolitan feel than Hanoi, although much of its French colonial quality is vanishing beneath the rapidly rising skyline. History, however, has bequeathed the city a kaleidoscopic melting pot of styles. For dinner you have your choice of not only Vietnamese food but also hamburgers; fine French cuisine; or black caviar at one of the Russian restaurants. Then you can head to one of the sleek, Western-style bars opening monthly.

At the teeming markets, tropical fruits, king cobras, barbecued dogs, and a hundred other such items are for sale; the sidewalks are crammed with noodle stands, cafés, and vendors selling fresh glasses of beer (*bia hoi*) for as little as 25¢. The roads are often gridlocked with motorbikes, scooters, bicycles, cyclos (pedicabs), buses, and a few cars (for now). All kinds of people travel around by bicycle or motorbike: women dressed in traditional ao dais, long gloves, and conical hats; and whole families—mother, father, and two children—all squeezed on one seat. Everyone seems to be going somewhere, no matter what time of day.

Ho Chi Minh City stretches northwest as far as Cu Chi, in Tay Ninh Province, and south to the upper reaches of the Mekong Delta. The part of the city known as Saigon comprises only districts 1 and 3 (there are 14). Bordered by the Thi Nghe Channel to the north, the Ben Nghe Channel to the south, and the Saigon River to the east, the city has served as a natural fortress and has been fought over by countless people during the past 2,000 years. The ancient empire of Funan made it a trading post, and the Khmer kingdom of Angkor transformed Prey Nokor, as it was called, into a flourishing trade center protected by a standing army. By the 14th century, while under Khmer rule, the city attracted Arab, Cham, Chinese, Malay, and Indian merchants. It was then known as the gateway to the Kingdom of Champa, the sister empire to Angkor.

In 1674 the Nguyen lords of Hue established a customs post at Prey Nokor to cash in on the region's growing commercial traffic, and Saigon (the Vietnamese name) became an increasingly important administrative post. The building in 1772 of a 6-km (4-mi) trench on the city's western edge (now District 5) marked the shift in the south from Angkor to Nguyen rule, and Vietnamese consolidation increased in 1778 with the development of Cholon, Saigon's Chinese city, as a second commercial hub. The Nguyen lords moved their power base from Hue to Saigon in 1789, after attacks by Tay Son rebels, who were unhappy with Nguyen rule. The rebels massacred most of the Nguyen clan and took control of the government—briefly. In 1802, Prince Nguyen Anh, the last of the Nguyen dynasty, defeated the Tay Son ruler—with French backing—regaining power and uniting Vietnam. He moved the capital back to Hue and declared himself Emperor Gia Long.

Gia Long's request for French help in quelling the Tay Son rebels came at a price. In exchange, he promised the French territorial concessions. Though the French Revolution and the Napoleonic Wars temporarily delayed any French claims, the concessions eventually cost Vietnam dearly. In 1859, tired of waiting for what they felt they deserved, the French seized Saigon and made it the capital of their new colony, Cochin China. This marked the beginning of an epoch of colonial-style feudalism and indentured servitude for many Vietnamese and ethnic minorities.

The catastrophe that was to overtake Saigon and the whole of Vietnam during the latter half of the 20th century was a direct result of French colonial interference. But despite France's role, the Vietnamese to this day, both north and south, maintain deep sentimental ties with French culture and art, as is apparent across the country. And perhaps even more surprising, they graciously welcome Americans with friendly interest, seemingly without rancor or blame.

Nowadays, without colonial or military occupation, the Saigonese are living life to the fullest—and trying to make money. This most Western of all Vietnamese cities has a broad range of international cuisine and Western-style high-rise buildings, although reminders of the past still poke through the headlong rush into capitalism. The Hotel Continental, immortalized in Graham Greene's *The Quiet American*, continues to stand on the corner of Rue Catinat (now Dong Khoi), the most famous thoroughfare of old Indochina; the city still has its central opera house and the old Hôtel de Ville, and it is still dotted with the bunkers and watchtowers of its more recent violent past.

Exploring Ho Chi Minh City

Ho Chi Minh City is not noted for tourist attractions. Although several of its sights should not be missed, its particular appeal is in its street life. From early morning to late at night, the sidewalks are home to hawkers and barbers, to noodle sellers and street artists, in a kaleidoscopic maze, with Western-style commerce right alongside traditional trades and practices.

Of the city's 14 districts, the three of most interest to visitors are Districts 1 and 3 (downtown Saigon) and District 5 (Cholon). The city's rather daunting layout and chaotic traffic tend to discourage leisurely walking, and the intermittent taxi, cyclo, or motorbike ride (6,000d–10,000d) is an enjoyable alternative. Any of the walks below could be done as a cyclo ride, an option particularly recommended on hot days.

Central Saigon (Districts 1 and 3)

A GOOD WALK

Although slightly away from the center, the provocative **War Remnants Museum** ① makes a good starting point. From here head northeast on Vo Van Tan Street toward tree-lined Nam Ky Khoi Nghia Street, and turn right. You will soon see the grounds of the modern **Reunification Palace** ②. Directly behind it is the old French sports club, the Cercle Sportif, now known as **Cong Vien Van Hoa Park** ③; to enter the park, turn right off Nguyen Du Street, along the side of the palace. Walk through the park into the grounds of the palace and on to Le Duan Boulevard. Walk northeast, and after passing Pasteur Street, you'll see the back of **Notre Dame Cathedral** ④, with its pink spires. Continue on Le Duan Boulevard, and a couple of blocks past Hai Ba Trung Boulevard is the now-dilapidated former **U.S. Embassy** ⑤; empty since 1975, and now being torn down to make way for the new American consulate. Continue on to the sprawling grounds of the **Zoo and Botanical Garden** ⑥ and the **History Museum** ⑦.

From the main entrance of the complex, walk southeast on Nguyen Binh Khiem Street to the intersection with Le Thanh Ton Street. Make a right, then take the first left at Ton Duc Thang Street, which turns and runs along the Saigon River. Walk south along the waterfront to the turn-of-the century **Hotel Majestic** ⑧, at the intersection of Ton Duc Thang and Dong Khoi streets. The hotel's rooftop bar provides magnificent views of the Saigon River and the Thu Thiem swamp district opposite. Turn right at Nguyen Hue Boulevard and make the first left onto Hai Trieu Street, also known as Whiskey Row. Take a right on Ham Nghi Street, where a bunch of international food stores (No. 64 is a good one) are jam-packed with Western specialties. Make a right onto Ton That Dang Street, where you can find everything from live eels to laundry detergent at the market that extends along intersecting Huynh Thuc Khang Street, a kind of electronics arcade. Continue a block past Huynh Thuc Khang Street, to Ton That Thiep Street, in the Indian quarter, and turn right.

Cross Nguyen Hue Boulevard, and turn left on Dong Khoi Street, which extends from the river to Notre Dame Cathedral. Along Dong Khoi Street is the **Delta Caravelle** ⑨, once a favorite haunt of war correspondents at cocktail hour. Opposite the Caravelle is the **Hotel Continental** ⑩. Although a shadow of its former self, it's still worth a visit. Sandwiched between the two at the end of Le Loi Boulevard is the **Municipal Theater** ⑪, recognizable by its inverted dome. Farther up Dong Khoi Street, past the Continental, is the main branch office of **Saigon Tourist** ⑫, on the corner of Le Thanh Ton Street. Next comes Notre Dame Cathedral—the front of the church this time. The beautiful French colonial **Central Post Office** ⑬ is on the right side of the square in front of the cathedral.

With your back to the cathedral, turn right on Nguyen Du Street, then take the first left onto Pasteur Street, and the first right onto Ly Tu Trong Street to get to the neoclassic **Museum of the Revolution** ⑭, or Army Museum. Return to Pasteur Street, and turn right to get to Le Thanh Ton Street and the **Old Hôtel de Ville** (City Hall) ⑮, now the People's Committee building. Follow Le Thanh Ton Street southwest, and make a right on Truong Dinh Street. In the middle of the block on your left is the **Mariamman Hindu Temple** ⑯, the last functioning one in the city.

Ho Chi Minh City

PHU AN DISTRICT

Nguyen Van Troi

Le Van Sy

Vo Thi Sau

Tran Quoc Thao

DISTRICT 3

Le Qui Don

Truong Dinh

Ly Chinh Thang

Vo Thi Sau

Tu Xuong

Dien Bien Phu

Nguyen Dinh Chieu

Truong Dinh

Ba Huyen Thanh Quan

Nguyen Thi Minh Khai

Cach Mang Thang Tam

3 Thang 2

Dien Bien Phu

DISTRICT 10

Nguyen Dinh Chieu

Cao Thang

Vo Van Tan

Cach Mang Thang Tam

Bui Thi Xuan

Le Thi Rieng

Ton That Tung

Nguyen Trai

Le Lai

Nguyen Thi Minh Khai

Cong Quynh

Pham Ngu Lao

Bui Vien

Ly Thai To

Hung Vuong

Trần Phu

Nguyen Van Cu

Tran Dinh Xu

Nguyen Trai

Nguyen Cu Trinh

Tran Hung Dao

Ho Hao Hon

SEE CHOLON DETAIL
← DISTRICT 5
(CHOLON)

Backtrack on Le Thanh Ton Street to where the busy **Ben Thanh Market** ⑰ spills out into the surrounding street.

TIMING

The walk could take a day or more, depending on how much time you spend at the sights.

SIGHTS TO SEE

★ ⑰ **Ben Thanh Market (Cho Ben Thanh).** Every imaginable item is sold here—look for a cheap meal, a hat, even live snakes. The market building was built in 1914 by the French. The best time to visit is first thing in the morning. ⊠ *At circular intersection of Le Loi Blvd., Pham Ngu Lao St., and Ham Nghi Blvd.* ⊙ *Daily 7–7.*

★ ⑬ **Central Post Office (Buu Dien Truing Tam).** This classic French colonial building was completed in 1891; inside is a huge map of old Indochina. To mail letters, enter the less romantic, Soviet-era expansion at 117 Hai Ba Trung Street. ⊠ *At the top of Dong Khoi St. opposite Notre Dame Cathedral.* ⊙ *Daily 7:30–7:30.*

🖑 ❸ **Cong Vien Van Hoa Park.** As the Cercle Sportif, the elite sporting club of the French bourgeoisie in colonial times, this park was barred to Vietnamese people. Today the sports club has tennis courts, a swimming pool, a gym and weight room, and a colonial clubhouse. To use the facilities will cost you no more than a dollar. ⊠ *Entrance on 115 Nguyen Du St.*

❾ **Delta Caravelle.** This recently renovated hotel is now the most popular in the city, with its ideal location and its modern cafés and bars. It was renowned in the 1960s as home to most of the foreign correspondents during the Vietnam War. During the 1968 Tet Offensive, several U.S. marines were killed here; journalists filmed the battle from the rooftop. The same rooftop is now the city's most popular bar, **Saigon, Saigon,** and the Hard Rock Cafe is set to move in soon. ⊠ *19 Lam Son Sq., District 1,* ☎ *08/823–4999,* 𝖥𝖠𝖷 *09/824–3999.*

Dong Khoi Street. Once named Rue Catinat, this was French colonial Saigon's Fifth Avenue or Rodeo Drive. During the Vietnam War it was Tu Do Street, the center of the infamous red-light district. These days the street remains the center of the old city, but most of the old-time bars have been replaced by restaurants and tourist-oriented shops.

NEED A BREAK?

The **Paris Deli** (⊠ 31 Dong Khoi St. District 1, ☎ 08/829–7533) is a European-style café serving excellent cappuccinos and pastries. **Java** (⊠ 65 Le Loi Boulevard—ground floor of the Saigon Centre, District 1), a hip, bar-style coffeehouse with TVs and magazines in the heart of downtown, also serves excellent food.

❼ **History Museum (Vien Bao Tang Lich Su).** Although the front door leads you right to a statue of ubiquitous "Uncle Ho," this museum is dedicated to Vietnamese history from the earliest inhabitants to 1930, when the Communist Party was established. Half the museum covers the history of the nation as a whole, while the other half focuses on the art and artifacts of southern Vietnam; the ethnography section is particularly interesting. The neo-Vietnamese structure was built by the French in 1929, and much of the current collection was compiled by the French Far Eastern Institute. ⊠ *2 Nguyen Binh Khiem, District 1,* ☎ *08/829–8146 or 08/829–0268.* 🎫 *10,000d.* ⊙ *Mon.–Sat. 8–11:30 and 1:30–4:30, Sun. 8:30–11:30.*

★ ❿ **Hotel Continental.** In French colonial days, the Hotel Continental's open terrace (now simply a sidewalk), shaded by broad tamarind trees, was the town's most sought-after lunch spot. During the Vietnam War, journalists and diplomats met on the terrace to discuss the latest events. Graham Greene's *The Quiet American* was set here. ✉ *132–134 Dong Khoi St., District 1,* ☎ *08/829–9201.*

★ ⑧ **Hotel Majestic.** Built in the late 19th century, the Majestic was one of the first French colonial hotels, and it still has the elegant decor of its origins. Go to the rooftop bar for an excellent view of the Saigon River. ✉ *1 Dong Khoi St., District 1,* ☎ *08/829–5512.*

⑯ **Mariamman Hindu Temple (Chua Ba Mariamman).** Vivid statues and colorful floral offerings at this temple create a microcosm of India in the streets of Saigon. Before its return in the early '90s to the Hindu community, the government used the temple as a factory for making incense and processing dried fish. ✉ *45 Truong Dinh St.* ☉ *Daily 7–7.*

⑪ **Municipal Theater (Nha Hat Thanh Pho).** This colonial-style theater was built as the opera house in 1899. Later it housed the National Assembly of South Vietnam, and after 1975 it became a theater again. ✉ *Intersection of Le Loi Blvd. and Dong Khoi St., District 1,* ☎ *08/825–1563.*

⑭ **Museum of the Revolution (Bao Tang Cach Mang).** Constructed in 1886 as the residence for the French governor of Cochin China, the building is now a museum dedicated to the Vietnamese struggle against the French and Americans. The displays are in Vietnamese, but you'll easily get the message. The neoclassic building is as interesting as the exhibits, with huge columns outside and ballrooms with high ceilings and frescoes inside. Beneath the building, in the concrete bunkers and tunnels connecting to the Reunification Palace, President Ngo Dinh Diem and Ngo Dinh Thuc hid before their capture and execution in 1963. ✉ *65 Ly Tu Trong St., District 1,* ☎ *08/829–9741.* 🎫 *Free.* ☉ *Tues.–Sun. 8–4:30.*

④ **Notre Dame Cathedral (Nha Tho Duc Ba).** This neo-Romanesque cathedral, prominent on the Saigon skyline, was built by the French in 1880 on the site of an old fort. Spanish, Portuguese, and French missionaries introduced Catholicism to Vietnam as early as the 16th century, and today Vietnam's 9 million Catholics are Asia's largest Christian population after the Philippines. The Mass celebrated at 9:30 AM on Sunday is quite a spectacle. ✉ *Top of Dong Khoi St.*

⑮ **Old Hôtel de Ville (City Hall).** Now called Ho Chi Minh City's People's Committee office, this yellow-and-white colonial-style structure built by the French between 1901 and 1908 now houses the city's main governing body. It is not open to the public. ✉ *Intersection of Le Thanh Ton and Nguyen Hue Sts., District 1.*

② **Reunification Palace (Hoi Truong Thong Nhat).** This modern palace—the symbolic center of the South Vietnamese government—was the scene of the dramatic seizure of Saigon by the National Liberation Front in 1975, when tanks smashed down the gates and an NLF flag was draped over the building's balcony. The president's mansion, designed by the European-influenced modernist architect Ngo Viet Thu in 1962, is classic '60s architecture. It was built after president Diem's own air force bombed him in the old French palace in an assassination attempt, and he decided he had an "image problem." It wasn't completed until after his death. Although tours are free to Vietnamese, foreigners must pay. ✉ *Visitors' entrance on 106 Nguyen Du St., District 1,* ☎ *08/829–4117.* 🎫 *10,000d.* ☉ *Daily 7:30–10:30 and 1–4.*

⑫ **Saigon Tourist.** This government-run travel service provides all kinds of visitor information and services (☞ Contacts and Resources, Travel Agencies *in* Ho Chi Minh City Essentials, *below*). ✉ *49 Le Thanh Ton St., District 1,* ☎ *08/823–0100.* ☉ *Daily 7:30–6:30.*

⑤ U.S. Embassy. At press time this historic building was being demolished to make way for the new U.S. consulate, scheduled to open in the summer of 1999. Nicknamed "the bunker" because it resembled just that, the embassy was built in 1967 with little thought for aesthetic appeal. A landmark of 20th-century history, this American symbolic stronghold was attacked during the 1968 Tet Offensive and finally seized at the capture of Saigon in April 1975. It was the site of a most memorable image: the U.S. ambassador, an American flag clutched to his chest, rushing into a helicopter waiting on the roof, while Marine guards pushed back mobs of South Vietnamese who had been assured of evacuation. ⊠ *Intersection of Le Duan Blvd. and Mac Din Chi St.*

① War Remnants Museum (Nha Trung Bay Toi Ac Chien Tranh Xam). You may instinctively shy away from this museum, which is dedicated to publicizing the horrors perpetrated by U.S. armed forces during the Vietnam War. You'll probably come away with mixed feelings about the one-sided propaganda—ashamed of the U.S. actions, angry about the Vietnamese inaccuracies in depicting them, or both. But it's a must-see if you're curious about the war. ⊠ *28 Vo Van Tan St., District 3,* ☎ *08/829–0325.* ⊠ *10,000d.* ☉ *Tues.–Sun. 7:30–11:45 and 1:30–4:45.*

☾ ⑥ Zoo and Botanical Garden (Thao Cam Vien). The fauna here does relatively well, and the flora thrives in its natural subtropical niche. After seeing the lackluster array of live animals, visit the eerie "taxidermy-go-round," where you can ride stuffed animals. ⊠ *Nguyen Binh Khiem St. at Le Duan Blvd.* ⊠ *2,000d.* ☉ *Daily 8–5:30.*

Circling Old Saigon

This tour covers the sights around the periphery of Old Saigon. South of District 1, on the broad waterfront along the Saigon River, is a less palatial section of the old city where the old docks and customs houses used to be. This was also the old banking district, and you can still see the colonial-era Hong Kong and Shanghai Banking Corporation, and Banque d'Indochine buildings. You might want to hire a cyclo to take you to some of the sights in this area.

SIGHTS TO SEE

⑲ Art Museum (Bao Tang My Thuat). Considering its grand colonial setting, this museum is a disappointment. The building is in classic French-Vietnamese architectural style (European-type stucco and Asian design). The first and second floors cover propaganda art of the Soviet socialist-realist variety. But the reason to visit the museum is on the third floor—the antique statues and other relics of the pre-Vietnamese south, objects from the ancient Funan and Chmer civilizations, and some good Cham art. ⊠ *97A Pho Duc Chinh St., District 1,* ☎ *08/822–2577.* ⊠ *Free.* ☉ *Tues.–Sun. 8:30–11:30 and 2–7.*

⑱ Ho Chi Minh Museum (Khu Luu Niem Bac Ho). This building, nicknamed the "Dragon House" (Nha Rong) for its architectural design, is far more interesting than most of the displays of Uncle Ho's personal belongings. It was constructed in 1863 as the original French customs house; Ho Chi Minh (1890–1969) passed through here in 1911 on the way to his 30-year sojourn around Europe and America. ⊠ *On Saigon Port at 1 Nguyen Tat Thanh St., by quayside on Ben Nghe Channel at far end of Ham Nghi Blvd.,* ☎ *08/839–1060.* ⊠ *Free.* ☉ *Tues.–Sun. 8:30–11:30 and 2–7.*

★ ㉑ Emperor Jade Pagoda (Chua Ngoc Hoang or Phuoc Hai Tu). Also known as the Tortoise Pagoda, this structure—the finest Chinese pagoda in Saigon—was built by the Cantonese community in 1909. A mixture of Taoist, Buddhist, and ethnic myths provide the sources for the pagoda's multitude of statues and carvings. Take a moment to note the main altar, the side panel's depiction of hell and, in the side room, the miniature female figures who represent the range of human qualities. ⊠ *73 Mai Thi Luu St., District 3.*

㉒ Ton Duc Thang Museum (Bao Tang Ton Duc Thang). Housed in a characterless Soviet-era building on the waterfront by the Vietnamese navy barracks, this unremarkable museum celebrates the life and times of president Ton Duc Thang (1888–1980), who succeeded Ho Chi Minh as head of North and later unified Vietnam. ⊠ *5 Ton Duc Thang St., District 1,* ☎ *08/829–4651.* ⌖ *Free.* ☉ *Tues.–Sun. 8:30–11:30 and 2–7.*

Cholon (District 5)

Southwest of central Saigon lies Cholon (District 5), a commercial mecca that's still the center of Chinese culture in Vietnam. Negotiate a price of about 55,000d with a cyclo driver to take you on a tour of the pagodas and mosques concentrated around Nguyen Trai Street and Tran Hung Dao Boulevard. There are no admission fees, but it is traditional to give a donation. When you've seen enough pagodas, tell your guide or cyclo driver, so you won't be taken to every single one. Spend the rest of the day exploring Cholon's streets, markets, shophouses (stores that double as the owners' homes), and restaurants, with their distinctive Chinese appeal.

A GOOD WALK

Begin at the bustling **Binh Tay Market** ㉒, and when you leave, turn left and walk along Phan Van Khoe Street until you get to Phung Hung Street; take a left and follow it until you reach the **Ong Bon Pagoda** ㉓, where you can pay your respects to the guardian of happiness and virtue. Leaving the pagoda, walk east on Hai Thuong Lan Ong Boulevard to the old colonial **Post Office** ㉔. Walk north up Chau Van Liem Boulevard to Tran Hung Dao Boulevard, the center of Cholon, with its street markets and old, small shophouses (and some newer, taller ones).

Continue north past Nguyen Trai Street (the heart of Cholon's pagoda district); turn right on small Lao Tu Street to reach the **Quan Am Pagoda** ㉕, known for its elaborately decorated scenes. Turn south on Luong Nhu Hoc Street to the **Ha Chuong Hoi Quan Pagoda** ㉖, at No. 802, one of the many temples devoted to the goddess of the sea. Take a left on Nguyen Trai Street and walk along until you come to the **Thien Hau Pagoda** ㉗, at No. 710, where sailors used to come before they went out to sea. Continue past the intersection of Trieu Quang Phuc Street, to No. 678, on the left, the **Nghia An Hoi Quan Pagoda** ㉘, famous for its detailed woodwork, and on the other side of the street, at No. 118, is the **Tam Son Hoi Quan Pagoda** ㉙, dedicated to the goddess of fertility. Keep on Nguyen Trai Street, past the intersection of Ly Thuong Kiet Street, until you reach the **Cholon Mosque** ㉚.

TIMING

Depending on how interested you are in pagodas, this walk could take three or four hours.

SIGHTS TO SEE

㉒ Binh Tay Market (Cho Binh Tay). Cholon's main market is in a colonial-era, Chinese-style building. The street outside is a frenzy of activity; inside you have to wend your way through very narrow aisles. ⊠ *On Hau Giang Blvd., District 6.*

㉚ Cholon Mosque. Built in 1932 by Tamil Muslims, the Cholon Mosque now serves Saigon's Indonesian and Malaysian Muslim community. ⊠ *641 Nguyen Trai St., at Ly Thuong Kiet Blvd.*

㉖ Ha Chuong Hoi Quan Pagoda. Like many pagodas built by Fujian congregations, this one is dedicated to Thien Hau, goddess of the sea and

Cholon

Tan Hu Channel

Ben Ham Tu

Ben Ba Dinh

Hung Phu

200 yards
200 meters
0
0

Nguyen Tri Phuong

Tran Phu

Nguyen Trai

Tran Hung Dao

Ngo Quyen

Tan Da

P. D. Vuong

30

28

Thien Quang Phuc

27

29

Luong Nhu Hoc

Lao Tu

25

26

Chau V. Liem

Ong

Van Kiep

Hai Thuong Lan

24

Tran Van Kieu

Ben Binh Dong

Tung Thien Vuong

Phung Hung

Tran Hung Dao

23

DISTRICT 5

Nguyen Trai

Thap Muoi

Tan Thanh

Pham Huu Chi

Hung Vuong

Xom Vo

Gia Phu

Nguyen Chi Thanh

Nguyen Thi Nho

22

Pham Dinh Ho

Phan Van Khoe

So 48

Lo Sieu

Le Quang Sung

Hung Vuong

Hau Giang

Ben Bai Say

Binh Tay Market, **22**
Cholon Mosque, **30**
Ha Chuong Hoi
Quan Pagoda, **26**
Nghia An Hoi Quan
Pagoda, **28**
Ong Bon Pagoda, **23**
Post Office, **24**

Quan Am Pagoda, **25**
Tam Son Hoi Quan
Pagoda, **29**
Thien Hau
Pagoda, **27**

protector of fishermen and sailors. Its four stone pillars encircled by painted dragons were brought from China when the pagoda was constructed in the 19th century. ⊠ *802 Nguyen Trai St.*

28 **Nghia An Hoi Quan Pagoda.** Built by the Chaozhou Chinese congregation in 1872, this pagoda is worth seeing for its elaborate woodwork. There is a large figure of the deified Chinese general Quan Cong's sacred red horse, as well as representations of Quan Cong himself with two guardians. ⊠ *678 Nguyen Trai St.*

★ **23** **Ong Bon Pagoda (Chua Ong Bon or Nhi Phu Hoi Quan).** Many deities are represented at this pagoda, but the main attraction is Ong Bon himself, the guardian of happiness and virtue. Ong Bong is also responsible for wealth, so people bring fake paper money to burn in the pagoda's furnace in his honor, hoping the year ahead will bring financial rewards. ⊠ *264 Hai Thuong Lai Ong Blvd. (parallel to Tran Hung Dao St.), at Phung Hung St.*

24 **Post Office.** This modernist building was constructed by the French in the 1920s. ⊠ *Intersection of Hai Thuong Lai Ong Blvd. and Chau Van Liem Blvd.* ☉ *Daily 7:30–7:30.*

25 **Quan Am Pagoda.** Dating from 1816, this pagoda was built by a congregation of Fujian refugees from China. It is notable for its busy array of scenes in lacquer, ceramic, gold, and wood illustrating traditional Chinese stories. ⊠ *12 Lao Tu St. (parallel to Huong Vuong Blvd. and Nguyen Trai St.).*

29 **Tam Son Hoi Quan Pagoda (Chua Ba Chua).** The Chinese Fujian congregation built this lavishly decorated pagoda dedicated to Me Sanh, the goddess of fertility, in the 19th century. Women—and some men—pray to the goddess to bring them children. ⊠ *118 Trieu Quang Phuc St.*

27 **Thien Hau Pagoda (Chua Ba).** Built by the Cantonese congregation at the beginning of the 19th century, this pagoda is dedicated to Thien Hau, the goddess of the sea and protector of fishermen and sailors. The turtles living on the grounds, symbols of longevity, are considered sacred. ⊠ *710 Nguyen Trai St.*

Dining

Central Saigon (Districts 1 and 3)

ECLECTIC

$$$ ✕ **Marine Club Restaurant.** Although more of a happening nightspot than a food mecca (☞ Nightlife, *below*), the Marine Club has the only wood-burning pizza oven in Saigon. ⊠ *17A4 Le Thanh Ton St., District 1,* ☎ *08/829–2249. AE, DC, MC, V.*

$$ ✕ **Café Mogambo.** A quirky restaurant-cum-burger bar with an African theme, Mogambo is run by an American expat and his Vietnamese wife. ⊠ *20 Bis Thi Sac St., District 1,* ☎ *08/825–1311. MC, V.*

$$ ✕ **Sapa.** This airy Swiss-run bar and restaurant is best known for its breakfasts, which include fine bacon, eggs, and hash browns. The Vietnamese-style chicken curry is also delicious. ⊠ *26 Thai Van Lung St., District 1,* ☎ *08/829–5754. No credit cards.*

FRENCH

\$\$\$\$ ✕ **Le Camargue.** Romantic and tastefully done, the French-influenced
★   Le Camargue is an exciting culinary forum. The cuisine is a mix of East
and West—with a good wine list to match. Dine on the elegant, plant-
filled terrace of the restored villa or in the warmly lighted dining
rooms. The restaurant also includes a tapas bar called Vasco's, which
is downstairs from the terrace. ⊠ *16 Cao Ba Quat St., District 1,* ☎
08/823–3148. Reservations essential. AE, DC, MC, V. No lunch.

\$\$\$\$ ✕ **Le Caprice.** Stodgy but run like a Swiss timepiece, this landmark pro-
vides Saigon's expat elite with unoriginal but fine French cuisine, passé
but well-maintained hotel decor, and a beautiful view of the Saigon River.
It's worth stopping by just to have a drink. ⊠ *Landmark Building, 5B
Ton Duc Thang St., 15th floor, District 1,* ☎ *08/822–8337. AE, DC,
MC, V.*

\$\$\$ ✕ **Augustin.** Small, intimate, and filled with comfortably solo expats
reading the newspaper at the bar, Augustin serves tasty French bistro
food to a predominantly international crowd. ⊠ *10 Nguyen Thiep St.,
District 1,* ☎ *08/829–2941. AE, DC, MC, V. No lunch Sun.*

JAPANESE

\$\$\$\$ ✕ **Sekitei Japanese Restaurant.** The fresh fish flown in daily from Japan
goes into the best sushi in Vietnam. Chefs Kori and Alex Ny also serve
well-executed regional Japanese dishes, like their wonderful shiitake-
and-chicken custard. ⊠ *188 Nam Ky Khoi Nghia, District 3,* ☎ *08/
825–1110. AE, DC, MC, V.*

MALAYSIAN

\$\$\$ ✕ **Spices.** One of the few Malaysian restaurants in Saigon, this is a good
spot to try spicier cuisine. Be sure to sample the excellent dry chicken curry
in banana leaves and the delicate wonton soup. ⊠ *Hai Van Nam Hotel,
132 Ham Nghi St. Blvd., District 1,* ☎ *08/821–1687. No credit cards.*

RUSSIAN

\$\$ ✕ **'A' The Russian Restaurant.** This is Saigon's premier Russian establishment, catering to the remaining members of that once-mighty
community. The restaurant has surprisingly good food—Siberian *pel-
meni* (dumplings), beef Stroganoff, and caviar with black bread—at
very reasonable prices. Endless amounts of vodka also flow. ⊠ *361/8
Nguyen Dinh Chieu St., District 3,* ☎ *08/835–9190. MC, V.*

THAI

\$\$–\$\$\$\$ ✕ **Chao Thai.** This sensational restaurant serves the finest Thai food
in the city. The cuisine is equal to the setting: a mock Thai longhouse
decorated with apsara dancers and wood carvings. ⊠ *16 Thai Van Lung
St., District 1,* ☎ *08/824–1457. AE, MC, V.*

VEGETARIAN

¢   ✕ **Bodhi Tree II.** Bodhi serves vegetarian delights in a quaint alley just
off Pham Ngu Lao Street. The eggplant sautéed with garlic, the vegetable curry, and the braised tofu in a clay pot are superb. The fresh-
fruit shakes are meals in themselves. ⊠ *175/6 Pham Ngu Lao St., District
1,* ☎ *08/839–1545. No credit cards.*

VIETNAMESE

\$\$\$ ✕ **Blue Ginger.** Dine on excellent Vietnamese cuisine in an elegant set-
★   ting with an international clientele. Traditional music shows are performed at 7:30. ⊠ *37 Nam Ky Khoi Nghia St., District 1,* ☎ *08/
829–8676. AE, DC, MC, V.*

$$$ ✕ **Lemongrass.** An expat and tourist favorite, Lemongrass serves ex-
★   cellent Vietnamese food in a French-bistro atmosphere. Almost every-
thing on the short menu is delicious, but the spicy mixed seafood soup
deserves special praise. ⊠ *4 Nguyen Thiep St., District 1,* ☎ *08/822–
0496. AE, DC, MC, V. No lunch.*

$$$ ✕ **Vietnam House.** Very popular with travelers and expats, Vietnam
House serves a wide selection of hearty noodle dishes and other Viet-
namese standards in a glossy Eurasian-style dining room. Live traditional music is performed every night upstairs. ⊠ *93 Dong Khoi St.,
District 1,* ☎ *08/829–1623. MC, V.*

$ ✕ **Restaurant 13.** This local and expat hangout, on a quiet road just
off Dong Khoi Street, serves delicious traditional local food in a no-
nonsense setting. (The nearby Restaurant 19 at No. 19, Hoang Yen at
Nos. 5–7, and La Fourchette at No. 9 are good bets, too.) ⊠ *11–17
Ngo Duc Ke St., District 1,* ☎ *08/829–1417. No credit cards.*

$ ✕ **Thi Sach Street Cafés.** Thi Sach Street is a must if you love seafood.
From 5 PM onward the top part of Thi Sach Street where it borders Le
Thanh Ton Street is literally impassable with street restaurants. Best
bets are the steamboat (boiling broth in which seafood and fish is cooked
at your table), freshwater crabs, and colossal tiger prawns. ⊠ *Thi Sach
St., District 1,* ☎ *no phone. No credit cards.*

¢ ✕ **Pho Hoa.** If you're not quite game for the sidewalk-food-stall eating experience, this open-air noodle kitchen is the next best thing. Just
say "chicken," "beef," or "pork," or point to whatever looks good at
the next table. ⊠ *260C Pasteur St., District 3,* ☎ *08/829–7943. No
credit cards.*

Lodging

Central Saigon (Districts 1 and 3)

$$$$ ▦ **Delta Caravelle.** This recently renovated hotel has quickly become
the most popular accommodation in the city. Ideally located opposite
the historic opera house, the new hotel is part of an international
chain catering to tourists and businesspeople. The rooftop bar, Saigon
Saigon, is an excellent venue in which to unwind and gives great views
across the downtown area. ⊠ *19 Lam Son Sq., District 1,* ☎ *08/823–
4999,* FAX *09/824–3999. 350 rooms. 3 cafés, 2 bars, lobby lounge, minibars, room service, pool, massage, sauna, exercise room, business
services, meeting rooms. AE, DC, MC, V.*

$$$$ ▦ **Hotel Continental.** If it's history you're after, stay here. But because
★   the Continental was renovated by the state-run Saigon Tourist agency,
it remains a shadow of its former self—the decor and finishing lack
the finesse and expert renovations of the hotel's international counterparts. Rooms facing the street are very noisy; ask for one overlooking
the inner courtyard. ⊠ *132–134 Dong Khoi St., District 1,* ☎ *08/829–
9201,* FAX *08/829–9252. 87 rooms. 2 restaurants, lobby lounge, in-room
safes, minibars, no-smoking rooms, refrigerators, room service, laundry service and dry cleaning, concierge, business services, meeting
rooms, travel services. AE, DC, MC, V.*

$$$$ ▦ **New World Hotel Saigon.** Along with the Omni Hotel, the New World
★   was one of Saigon's first international-chain hotels (1994). Its central
location—across the street from the Ben Thanh Market—makes it
very popular, particularly with tour groups and businesspeople. ⊠ *76
Le Lai St., District 1,* ☎ *08/822–8888,* FAX *08/823–0710. 541 rooms.
3 restaurants, bar, lobby lounge, in-room safes, minibars, no-smoking
floor, refrigerators, room service, pool, sauna, massage, driving range,
tennis court, exercise room, motorbikes, nightclub, piano, baby-sitting,
laundry service and dry cleaning, concierge, business services, meeting rooms, travel services, airport shuttle, car rental. AE, DC, MC, V.*

$$$$ 🏨 **Saigon Prince Hotel.** Rooms at the Saigon Prince are more spacious
★   and have higher ceilings and finer finishing touches than many of the
      other luxury hotels in the city. But the hotel has fewer facilities. The
      staff is competent and pleasant. The lobby bar is a nice spot for a calm
      midafternoon break, whether you are staying at the hotel or not. ⊠
      *63 Nguyen Hue Blvd., District 1, ☎ 08/822–2999, ℻ 08/824–1888.
      203 rooms. Dining room, sushi bar, lobby lounge, in-room safes, mini-
      bars, no-smoking rooms, refrigerators, room service, hot tub, massage,
      sauna, steam room, exercise room, nightclub, laundry service and dry
      cleaning, concierge, business services, meeting rooms, travel services.
      AE, DC, MC, V.*

$$$ 🏨 **Hotel Majestic.** The Majestic, on the waterfront overlooking the Saigon
★   River, is one of Vietnam's great colonial hotels. As with the Continental,
      the hotel was renovated by Saigon Tourist, so it still lacks the service
      expertise of the international chains. Nevertheless, the hotel's charm
      persists, and with its location, more than makes up for that. Be sure
      to have a drink at the rooftop bar overlooking the river. Rooms, with
      their high ceilings and the original woodwork, strike a delicate balance
      between airy and intimate. ⊠ *1 Dong Khoi St., District 1, ☎ 08/829–
      5512, ℻ 08/829–5510. 122 rooms. 2 restaurants, 2 bars, lobby
      lounge, outdoor café, in-room safes, minibars, no-smoking rooms, re-
      frigerators, room service, pool, massage, sauna, exercise room, piano,
      laundry service and dry cleaning, concierge, business services, meet-
      ing rooms, travel services. AE, DC, MC, V.*

$$$ 🏨 **Mercury Hotel.** This modern hotel combines warmth and elegance
      with modern conveniences. Rooms are reasonably sized and decorated
      in a luxurious yet utilitarian and unoriginal style. The hotel is closer to
      the budget traveler's haven—Pham Ngu Lao Street—than to the con-
      gregation of upscale hotels and restaurants around Le Loi and Nguyen
      Hue boulevards. ⊠ *79 Tran Hung Dao St., District 1, ☎ 08/824–2525,
      ℻ 08/824–2602. 104 rooms. 2 restaurants, bar, lobby lounge, in-room
      safes, minibars, no-smoking rooms, refrigerators, room service, mas-
      sage, health club, laundry service, dry cleaning, baby-sitting, business
      services, meeting rooms, travel services. AE, DC, MC, V.*

$$–$$$ 🏨 **Rex Hotel.** The Rex stands as a monument to Saigon's recent his-
      tory. Originally a French garage, it later became a hotel and then the
      base for American operations during the Vietnam War. Its conference
      room was the scene of the daily press briefings, or "five o'clock fol-
      lies," and in 1976 the unification of the country was announced in the
      same room. Today the hotel is filled with glorious kitsch (stuffed ani-
      mals, statues, crown-shape lamp shades), and the rooms are equipped
      with fax machines. Even if you don't stay here, it's worth a peek, and
      you should go up to the rooftop bar. The restaurants (breakfast is sat-
      isfactory), specialize in ordinary Vietnamese cuisine with a touch of
      French. ⊠ *141 Nguyen Hue Blvd., District 1, ☎ 08/829–2185, ℻
      08/829–1469. 207 rooms. 2 restaurants, lobby lounge, in-room safes,
      minibars, no-smoking rooms, refrigerators, room service, pool, beauty
      salon, massage, sauna, steam room, nightclub, laundry service and dry
      cleaning, concierge, business services, travel services. AE, DC, MC, V.*

$$ 🏨 **Mondial Hotel.** The renovated Mondial has small, tidy standard
      rooms. In the lobby are various large bas-relief wooden sculptures of drag-
      ons and mythical Vietnamese warriors. The hotel's Skyview restaurant

has traditional Vietnamese dancing and music nightly. ⊠ *109 Dong Khoi St., District 1,* ☎ *08/823–1359,* FAX *08/829–6273. 40 rooms, most with bath. Restaurant, lobby lounge, in-room safes, room service, nightclub, laundry service and dry cleaning, travel services. AE, DC, MC, V.*

$$ ⊡ **Norfolk Hotel.** This superslick establishment is between the Ben Thanh Market and the Hôtel de Ville in central Saigon. White and chrome dominate. Rooms are impeccable and comfortable if small and simple. Facilities are oriented primarily to businesspeople; there is even a resident interpreter. ⊠ *117 Le Thanh Ton St., District 1,* ☎ *08/829– 5368,* FAX *08/829–3415. 109 rooms. Restaurant, bar, lobby lounge, sports bar, in-room safes, minibars, massage, sauna, health club, baby-sitting, laundry service and dry cleaning, business services, meeting rooms, travel services. AE, DC, MC, V.*

$–$$ ⊡ **Bong Sen Hotel Annex.** This sparkling new minihotel in the heart of downtown has slick modern decor in its tidy but adequate rooms. Pale woods and plentiful light add to its appeal, as does the eighth-floor restaurant where breakfast is served (included in price) and the city views are splendid. ⊠ *61–63 Hai Ba Trung St., District 1,* ☎ *08/ 823–5818,* FAX *08/823–5816. 57 rooms. Restaurant, lobby bar, air-conditioning, minibars, laundry service and dry cleaning, airport shuttle, travel services. MC, V.*

$ ⊡ **Mogambo Guest House.** This minihotel above the restaurant of the same name (☞ Dining, *above*) is run by an American and is very popular with—guess who?—Americans. Like most of these small establishments, this one is unexceptional looking but has clean rooms that are suitable for a good night's sleep. Rooms have IDD phones and satellite TV. ⊠ *20bis Thi Sach St., District 1,* ☎ *08/825–1311. 10 rooms. Restaurant, air-conditioning. MC, V.*

$ ⊡ **Phuong Duong Hotel.** Another one of the city's minihotels, this one, too, is bare bones but comfortable and clean. Rooms have IDD phones and satellite TV. ⊠ *55B Nguyen Van Thu St., District 1,* ☎ *08/822– 2437,* FAX *08/822–1346. 10 rooms. Restaurant. MC, V.*

$ ⊡ **Spring Hotel.** In the hub of a major dining and nightlife area in District 1, this cozy, family-run minihotel has squeaky clean rooms with new moldings and fixtures made to look old. Some rooms have nice views of the street below, but the standard ones with no windows at all are a lot less expensive. ⊠ *44–46 Le Thanh Ton St., District 1,* ☎ *08/829–7362,* FAX *08/821–1383. 38 rooms. Bar, dining room, lobby lounge, air-conditioning, in-room safes, room service, travel services. AE, DC, MC, V.*

Cholon (District 5)

$$$$ ⊡ **Hotel Equatorial.** This luxury hotel is in an odd location—on the edge of Cholon, about 15 minutes from the downtown area. To date, bookings have been somewhat scarce because of this. Nonetheless, the hotel is one of the best in town. It also has Vietnam's nicest health club and a half-Olympic-size swimming pool. ⊠ *242 Tran Binh Trong St., District 5,* ☎ *08/839–0000,* FAX *08/839–0011. 333 rooms. Bar, café, lobby lounge, minibars, refrigerators, room service, pool, health club, nightclub, piano, laundry service and dry cleaning, business services, meeting rooms, travel services, car rental, free parking. AE, DC, MC, V.*

$$ ⊡ **Arc En Ciel Hotel.** This neon-clad hotel is done up in a mishmash of modern, '60s, and Chinese interior decor, with accommodations on the higher end of utilitarian. But overall it's a good deal—if you want to stay in Cholon. ⊠ *52–56 Tan Da St., District 5,* ☎ *08/855–2550,* FAX

08/855–0332. 91 rooms. Restaurant, bar, lobby lounge, outdoor café, in-room safes, room service, beauty salon, massage, sauna, exercise room, nightclub, laundry service and dry cleaning, concierge, business services, meeting rooms, travel services. AE, DC, MC, V.

$ 🏨 **Prince Hotel.** Not to be confused with the Saigon Prince in District 1, this small-time "royal" lodging in the middle of Chinatown provides charm and efficiency cheaply. Unlike many hotel restaurants, the Prince actually serves good food. ✉ *29 Chau Van Liem St., District 5,* ☎ *08/855–6765,* ℻ *08/856–1578. 25 rooms. Restaurant, bar, lobby lounge, outdoor café, air-conditioning, in-room safes, minibars, refrigerators, room service, travel services. AE, DC, MC, V.*

Phu Nuan District

$$$$ 🏨 **Garden Plaza Hotel.** Only about 10 minutes from the airport, this international establishment is one of the best (for now). It's a good 15–20 minutes from downtown, which could be a drawback, or a boon if you're eager to settle into town quickly. ✉ *309 Nguyen Van Troi St., Phu Nhuan District,* ☎ *08/842–1111,* ℻ *08/842–4370. 157 rooms. Restaurant, lobby lounge, pub, in-room safes, minibars, no-smoking rooms, refrigerators, room service, pool, sauna, massage, exercise room, motorbikes, shop, laundry service and dry cleaning, concierge, business services, meeting rooms, travel services, airport shuttle, car rental. AE, DC, MC, V.*

$$$$ 🏨 **Omni Saigon Hotel.** Built in the former CIA headquarters, with walls so thick mobile phones won't work, the Omni is one of the city's finest hotels. It has the essence of French elegance, with a hint of glitz and a touch of '60s bunker architecture. More important, it's one of the few international hotels to have sent its staff abroad for training, which shows in its excellent service. ✉ *251 Nguyen Van Troi St., Phu Nhuan District,* ☎ *08/844–9222,* ℻ *08/844–9200. 248 rooms. 3 restaurants, lobby lounge, pub, in-room safes, minibars, no-smoking rooms, refrigerators, room service, pool, beauty salon, sauna, massage, exercise room, motorbikes, nightclub, piano, baby-sitting, laundry service and dry cleaning, concierge, business services, meeting rooms, travel services, airport shuttle, car rental. AE, DC, MC, V.*

Nightlife and the Arts

Saigon's nightlife is thriving. But nightclubs here are subject to the erratic rules laid down by the authorities. One week they are open, and the next they are classified as social evils and are all shut down. Nightclub owners take this in stride. Check in "Time Out," the weekly English-language supplement in the Vietnam Investment Review, for up-to-date information.

Nightlife

BARS AND CLUBS

Apocalypse Now (✉ 2C Thi Sach St., District 1), one of the oldest clubs in Saigon, is loud, fun, and always packed with a cross section of expatriates, tourists, amiable pimps, and local prostitutes. Note: Take a taxi, not a cyclo, back to your hotel (cabs line up outside); cyclo drivers have been known to steal from drunken foreigners. Leave any jewelry, including watches, at your hotel.

Bar Rolling Stones (✉ 177 Pham Ngu Lao St., District 1), in the backpacker area of town, serves cheap beer and spills out onto the street with loud music. If you sit outside, hold your bag in your lap or wind the straps around your ankles.

Café Latin (✉ 25 Dong Du St., District 1) is a multilevel tapas bar with constructivist decor, and fine Australian and French wines.

Café Mogambo (⊠ 20 Bis Thi Sach St., District 1), run by an American expat and his Vietnamese wife, is a kind of self-parodying Reno-style roadside stop where you can get good draft beer in a kitschy environment all dressed up with African decor. (☞ Dining, *above*.)

Le Camargue (⊠ 16 Cao Ba Quat St., District 1), although really more a restaurant (☞ Dining, *above*), has an excellent terrace bar and also a pool table. A recent addition is a tapas bar, called Vasco's, on the ground floor.

Catwalk (⊠ 76 Le Lai St., District 1), in the New World Hotel, has private karaoke dens where you can sing to your heart's delight and a dance floor where dry ice creates a moody atmosphere.

Globo (⊠ 6 Nguyen Thipe St., District 1, ☎ 08/822–8855) looks like it could be in Paris and is very popular with the city's fashionable French set.

Gossip (⊠ 79 Tran Hung Dao St., District 1), in the Mercury Hotel, is one of the best discos in town. There is no admission charge for women, but men have to pay $8.

Hard Rock Cafe (⊠ 24 Mac Thi Buoi St., District 1), though not official, does a booming business. Plans are in the works for a real one, due to open in late 1998, in the renovated Delta Caravelle.

Long Phi (⊠ 163 Pham Ngu Lao St., District 1) is one of the few bars in town to attract expats, Vietnamese, and backpackers.

Marine Club (⊠ 17A4 Le Thanh Ton St., District 1), another expat favorite, is a very nice piano bar tastefully done with nautical paraphernalia.

O'Brien's (⊠ 72A2 Hai Ba Trung St., District 1), is a popular bar decked out with a trendy Parisian-style interior. It also has a garden terrace where you are served excellent pizzas straight out of the oven.

Q Bar (⊠ In the side of the Municipal Theater, off Dong Khoi St.)—a hip spot that looks like it could be in New York, London, or Paris—has become one of Saigon's not-to-be-missed. Bar food is served.

HOTEL BARS

A more civilized alternative to Saigon's bar scene is one of the many rooftop establishments at the city's hotels. Particularly noteworthy hotel bars include those in the **Caprice Hotel** (⊠ Landmark Building, 513 Le Ton Duc Thang St., District 1); the Saxophone Bar at the **New World Hotel** (⊠ 76 Le Lai St., District 1); the fifth-floor veranda at the **Rex Hotel** (⊠ Khach San Ben Thanh St., District 1); and the piano bar at the **Saigon Prince** (⊠ 63 Nguyen Hue Blvd., District 1). The newest, and without doubt best, is Saigon Saigon on the rooftop of the **Delta Caravelle** (⊠ 19 Lam Son Square, District 1).

The Arts
MUSIC AND THEATER

The only regular venue in town for classical music performances is the **Conservatory of Music** (Nhac Vien Thanh Pho Ho Chi Minh; ⊠ 112 Nguyen Du St., ☎ 08/839–6646); the seasons runs September–June. Built in 1899 by the French as an opera house and later used as the home of the National Assembly of South Vietnam, the **Municipal Theater** (Nha Hat Thanh Pho; ⊠ intersection of Le Loi and Dong Khoi Sts., District 1, ☎ 08/829–1249) became a theater again in 1975.

Outdoor Activities and Sports
Golf
There are two 18-hole golf courses outside Saigon. **Vietnam Golf and Country Club** (☎ 08/825–2951), in the outlying district of Thu Duc, 10 km (6 mi) north of Saigon, costs about $50 a day for a game. **Song Be Golf Resort** (⊠ 254B Nguyen Dinh Chieu St., ☎ 06/585–5802) is 20 km (12 mi) outside the city. Many of the club's facilities are still

under construction but will eventually include swimming pools, tennis courts, and restaurants. The cost for a day is $50.

Health Clubs and Swimming Pools

At the **Cercle Sportif** (⊠ In Cong Vien Hoa Park), once an elite French club, you can use the facilities for less than $1. **Hotel Equatorial** (⊠ 242 Tran Binh Trong St., District 5, ☎ 08/839–0000) has the best gym in town and a half-Olympic-size pool. The cost is $15 for the day. **Hotel Majestic** (⊠ 1 Dong Khoi St., District 1, ☎ 08/829–5514) has a small pool and gym that you can use as long as you order something from the bar. **New World Hotel Saigon** (⊠ 76 Le Lai St., District 1, ☎ 08/822–8888) charges $12 for use of its small pool and standard gym.

Running

Hot, crowded, polluted Saigon isn't really a good city for jogging, though some Vietnamese do go out around 5 AM, before the traffic begins. If you are set on running, contact the Hash House Harriers club, which meets every Sunday outside the **Century Hotel** (⊠ 68A Nguyen Hue Blvd., ☎ 08/845–3886).

Shopping

Ho Chi Minh City is a good place to have casual clothes made or to have designer apparel copied. The city is famous also for its lacquerware (boxes, trays, etc.) and its wood carvings of all kinds. As in the days when, as rue Catinat, it was French Saigon's main shopping thoroughfare, Dong Khoi Street between Le Loi Boulevard and the river is lined with art galleries and shops selling jewelry, antique watches (or lookalikes), lacquerware, wood carvings, and other souvenirs to mostly tourists (which doesn't mean there aren't good finds). No matter where you shop, if you are buying a large number of items, be sure to bargain. But be polite—the debate over prices is expected to be a very civil and friendly process. Also, most shops will take dollars or dong, though they often list prices in dollars only.

Department Stores

On the ground floor of the huge **Tax Department Store** (Cua Hang Back Hoa; ⊠ intersection of Nguyen Hue St. and Le Loi Blvd, ☎ no phone) you can change traveler's checks and find all kinds of souvenirs. But the best bargains in Vietnam are on the two upper floors: designer clothes and sneakers made in China but redirected to Vietnam; nice, inexpensive bags; and 24-hour tailors.

Markets

Clothing, shoes, bags, wood carvings, lacquerware, food, and more are available at the large **Ben Thanh Market** (Cho Ben Thanh). Keep careful watch of your belongings; pickpockets have been known to strike. **Cholon's Binh Tay Market** (Cho Binh Tay), on Hau Giang Boulevard in District 6 (near District 5), has all kinds of items—kitchenware, baskets, plastic goods (barrettes, magnets, toys), hats, shoes, and food. The charming **open-air market** on Ton That Dam Street, between Huynh Thuc Khang Street and Ham Nghi Boulevard in District 1, has everything from fish and produce to plastic toys and cleaning products. On the north side of Ham Nghi Boulevard, between Ho Tung Mau and Ton That Dam streets, you can find all kinds of international foods at the tiny, jam-packed European-style **specialty food shops.** For an assortment of **electronic equipment,** try Huynh Thuc Khang Street, Nguyen Hue Boulevard, and Pasteur Street.

Specialty Shops

ANTIQUES

It's against the law for foreigners to take antiques (anything older than 21 years plus a day) out of Vietnam, and it's also very difficult to distinguish between genuine and fake items, especially on Dong Khoi Street, where both sell at comparable prices. In particular, beware of restored antique timepieces, which often have a 1950s Rolex face, for example, covering the much cheaper works of a '70s Seiko. **Nguyen Freres** (✉ 2A Le Duan Blvd., District 1, ☎ 08/821–3716) sells antiques and replicas. The shop has French owners who guarantee that all products can be exported abroad and they now have outlets in both Paris and London, where their merchandise sells like hotcakes at much higher prices. Most popular items include beautiful French-Vietnamese antique and reproduction furniture and a range of prints of old colonial Saigon. Without doubt, it's the finest shopping of its kind in town.

ART

Taking fine art out of the country isn't as problematic as taking out antiques, but have a receipt for your purchase to show customs just in case. Many art galleries can be found on Dong Khoi Street and the surrounding area. Canvases fetch as much as $15,000 and as little as $30. Some good galleries: **Anh** (✉ 135 Nguyen Hue Blvd., District 1, ☎ 08/821–3716) sells ethnic folk art and fabrics. **ATC** (Art Tourist Services; ✉ 172 Nam Ky Khoi Nghia St., District 3, ☎ 08/829–6833, FAX 08/829–8947; ✉ 29B Dong Khoi St., District 1, ☎ 08/829–2695, FAX 08/829–8947; ✉ 2 Cong Truong Quoc St., District 3, ☎ 08/829–6833, FAX 08/829–8947) is a national art organization. **Fine Arts Museum** (✉ 97A Pho Duc Chinh St., District 1, ☎ 08/821–0001). **Galerie Lotus** (✉ 43 Dong Khoi St., District 1, ☎ 08/829–2695). **Hong Hac Art Gallery** (✉ 9A Vo Van Tan St., District 3, ☎ 08/824–3160). **Phuong Dong Gallery** (✉ 135 Nam Ky Khoi Nghia St., District 1, ☎ 08/822–1716). **Saigon Gallery** (✉ 5 Ton Duc Thang St., District 1, ☎ 08/829–7102).

CLOTHING

Linh Phuong Maison de Couture (✉ 38 Ly Tu Trong St., District 1, ☎ 08/824–2985) is very reliable for custom-made clothing for adults and children. **Tropic** (✉ 73A Le Thanh Ton St., District 1, ☎ 08/829–7452) carries contemporary and traditional clothing as well as some home furnishing items. **Zakka** (✉ 23 Dong Khoi St., District 1, ☎ 08/829–8086), next to the Hotel Majestic, sells fabric and beautifully designed clothing, shoes, and bags (with a Western influence).

HOUSEWARES

Home Zone (✉ 41 Dinh Tien Hoang St., District 1, ☎ 08/822–8022) sells stylish silverware, furnishings, and other housewares. **Mai Huong** (✉ 73 Le Thanh Ton St., District 1, ☎ 08/829–6233) is the place to go for beautifully embroidered tablecloths and bedspreads. **Q Home** (✉ 65 Le Loi St., 2nd floor, District 1, ☎ 08/821–4883) has colorful, contemporary-style ceramics.

LACQUERWARE

A number of galleries sell lacquerware on Dong Khoi Street (from No. 137 to No. 145) and in the Phu Nhuan District on Nguyen Van Troi Street (and on its continuation, Cong Hoa Street). **Heritage** (✉ 53 Dong Khoi St., District 1) has beautiful contemporary-looking lacquerware and outstanding replicas of antique Buddhas and statuary. **Tay Son** (✉ 198 Bo Thi Sau St., District 3, ☎ 08/820–2524, FAX 08/820–2526) is a large lacquerware distributor with a very wide selection and good prices.

SHOES

Tran Van My (⌧ 95 Le Thanh Ton St., District 1, ☎ 08/822–3041) is the place to go for ready-made, custom-made, embroidered, and leather shoes and sandals.

Ho Chi Minh City Essentials

Arriving and Departing

BY AIRPLANE

For major international airlines with flights to and from Ho Chi Minh City, *see* Vietnam A to Z, *below*. **Vietnam Airlines** (⌧ 116 Nguyen Hue St., District 1, ☎ 08/829–2118, FAX 08/823–0273), the Vietnamese national carrier, has international flights from Ho Chi Minh City as well as domestic flights to the following destinations: Buon Ma Thuot, Cantho, Dalat, Danang, Haiphong, Hanoi, Hue, Nha Trang, Phu Quoc, Pleiku, and Qui Nhon. Prices range from $60 to $150. It's best to book several days in advance and to reconfirm your flight; you can always change your reservation at branch offices all over the city.

Tan Son Nhat Airport (⌧ Hoang Van Thu Blvd., Tan Binh District, ☎ 08/844–3179), 7 km (4 mi) from central Saigon, is small and navigable. Depending on the officer behind the counter, getting through passport control is intermittently hassle-free.

Between the Airport and Downtown. Use the free hotel shuttle service if you're staying at one of the mid-range or high-end hotels. Or, choose an official-looking taxi from the throngs waiting outside. Though many now have meters, you should still try to negotiate a price before getting in: about $7–$10 (you can pay in dong or dollars), depending on the number of passengers and pieces of luggage. The ride takes about 20 minutes, depending on traffic.

BY BUS

Traveling by public bus around Vietnam is not recommended. You're better off taking one of the minibuses that leave from the bus stations (make reservations a day in advance through your concierge, a travel agent, or a travel café), or even better, a tour bus organized by one of the travel agencies or tourist cafés (☞ Travel Agencies, *below*).

BY CAR

One of the best ways to travel around Vietnam is with a car and driver, rented from one of the hotels or travel agencies (☞ Travel Agencies, *below*). You may want to be driven to sights around Saigon, though most people use a car only for excursions outside the city.

BY TRAIN

From Ho Chi Minh City there is local train service to Nha Trang, Qui Nhon, and Hue. The slightly faster **Reunification Express** goes to many of the larger coastal towns, from Phan Rang–Thap all the way north to Hanoi. Trains arrive and depart from the **Saigon Railway Station** (Ga Saigon; ⌧ 1 Nguyen Thong St., District 3, ☎ 08/823–0105), about 1 km (½ mi) from central Saigon. The ticket office (⌧ 275C Pham Ngu Lao St., District 1, ☎ 08/832–3537) is open daily 7:15–11 and 1–3, though it's best to ask a travel agent to call for ticketing and information. Note that Saigon Tourist does not provide any train service information.

Getting Around

BY BICYCLE

Bicycles can often be rented from your hotel; or ask there for a suggestion. Those available from shops on the street are generally unreliable.

BY BOAT

Boats touring the Saigon River start at 50,000d an hour and are available at the riverside on Ton Duc Thang Street, between Ham Nghi Boulevard and Me Linh Square. Negotiate an exact price with the owners before boarding. Ask at travel agencies for advice about which are the best trips.

BY BUS

Public buses are the cheapest way to get around town, though not the fastest, most convenient, nor most pleasant. Service is often erratic and painfully slow, and the buses generally have no air-conditioning and are often crammed full of people. You're better off taking a cyclo or a taxi. Nevertheless, it is important to know about the **Saigon–Cholon line,** which you are most likely to use; it starts in Me Linh Square at the Tran Hung Dao intersection and ends up at Cholon's Binh Tay Market. Tickets, available on board, cost 2,000d; look for signs reading *xe buyt* (bus stop).

BY CAR

See Arriving and Departing, *above.* To get around the city, use taxis or cyclos.

BY CYCLO

Although cyclos, or pedicabs, are only supposed to charge 2,000d per km (½ mi), 5,000d–10,000d is a decent rate (this includes the tip) for just about any destination within the same district. Going to districts in the outer suburbs obviously will cost you more. Cyclo drivers frequently speak English very well and can provide informative city tours for a small price (a generous half-day rate is about 30,000d–55,000d)—bargaining is advised. Drivers will wait for you when you visit sights; just don't leave any valuables in the cyclo. If you are happy with your driver, you can make arrangements to have him pick you up the next day.

BY MOTORBIKE

One of the quickest ways around the city is riding on the back of a motorbike taxi, known as a Honda *om* or *xe om.* This service usually costs about 10,000d. Motorbike drivers are everywhere—they'll just drive up alongside you and ask where you're going and if you're interested in a ride. You can also rent your own motorbike from any number of cafés, restaurants, and travel agencies, especially Sinh Café and Ann's Tourist.

BY TAXI

Taxis are available in front of all major hotels. Nowadays most taxis have meters, and most drivers speak a little English. An average journey across town starts at 20,000d–40,000d. The best taxi companies are: **Vina Taxi** (☎ 08/822–2990 or 08/842–2888) and **Saigon Taxi** (☎ 08/8226688). Other recommended companies include: **Airport Taxi** (☎ 08/844–6666); **Cholon Taxi** (☎ 08/842–6666); **Giadinh Taxi** (☎ 08/822–6699); and **Saigon Tourist** (☎ 08/822–2206).

Contacts and Resources

CONSULATES

Australia (✉ 5B Ton Duc Thang St., District 1, ☎ 08/829–6035). **Canada** (✉ 203 Dong Khoi St., District 1, ☎ 08/824–2000). **New Zealand** (✉ 41 Nguyen Thi Minh Khai St., District 1, ☎ 08/822–6907). **United Kingdom** (✉ 21 Le Duan Blvd., District 1, ☎ 08/829–8433). **United States** (✉ 51 Nguyen Dinh Chieu, District 1, ☎ 08/822–9433).

CURRENCY EXCHANGE

Although they don't always offer the best exchange rate, hotels are usually the easiest places to change money; they can also change traveler's checks. Banks and the small exchange shops offer the most competitive rates. Don't change your money on the black market. Many tourists lose out to sharks because the dong denominations are so confusingly high for the first-time visitor.

Major banks in Ho Chi Minh City include: **ANZ Bank** (Australia New Zealand Bank; ✉ 11 Me Linh Square, District 1, ☎ 08/829–9316); **Citibank** (✉ 8 Nguyen Hue St., District 1, ☎ 08/824–2118); **Hongkong Bank** (✉ 75 Pham Hong Thai St., District 1, ☎ 08/829–2288); **Standard Chartered Bank** (✉ 203 Dong Khoi St., District 1, ☎ 08/829–8383); and **Vietcom Bank** (✉ 29 Chuong Duong St., District 1, ☎ 08/823–0310). International ATMs can be found at ANZ Bank and Hong Kong Bank.

EMERGENCIES
Ambulance (☎ 15). **Hospitals:** Round-the-clock medical treatment is available at **Asia Emergency Assistance** (AEA; ✉ Han Ham Building, 65 Nguyen Du St., District 1, ☎ 08/829–8520), a clinic run by Western doctors. **Cho Ray Hospital** (✉ 201B Nguyen Chi Thanh St., District 5, ☎ 08/855–8074) has regular and 24-hour emergency treatment. **International SOS Assistance** (✉ 151 bis Vo Thi Sau St., District 3, ☎ 08/829–8520 for emergencies, 08/829–4386 for the clinic) can help with emergency care and evacuations. **Pharmacy:** My Chau Pharmacy (✉ 389 Hai Ba Trung St., District 1, ☎ 08/822–2266), recommended by the Travel Medical Consultancy, is open daily 7:30 AM–10 PM.

Police (☎ 13). For lost credit cards, contact **Vietcom Bank** (☎ 08/829–3068 or 08/822–5413), which is affiliated with Western banks.

ENGLISH-LANGUAGE BOOKSTORES
A few bookstores in Ho Chi Minh City sell English-language books. Many traveling street vendors have English–Vietnamese phrase books and dictionaries, travel guides, Graham Greene's *The Quiet American,* and other books on Vietnamese culture and history. **Xuan Thu** (✉ 185 Dong Khoi St., District 1, ☎ 08/822–4670) sells international newspapers and periodicals and Vietnamese–English phrase books. **Xunhasaba** (✉ 76E Le Thanh Ton St., District 1), the largest foreign magazine and newspaper distributor in town (which doubles as a tailor shop), sells nice, inexpensive art books and some novels (mostly classics) in English. Look carefully in Cholon (among other places) for shops buying and selling used paperbacks in English.

GUIDED TOURS
Guided tours of Ho Chi Minh City itself are virtually nonexistent; no one comes here for just the sights, but rather for the whole cultural experience. Furthermore, guides advertised as "English speaking" are often unintelligible in that language. You're better off exploring on your own or hiring an English-speaking cyclo driver (just make sure you can understand *his* English first).

On the other hand, do take advantage of the guided tours outside the city. For excellent tours to the Mekong Delta and the Cu Chi Tunnels and for various customized trips—some for as little as $5 per day with lunch included—check itineraries and schedules at the Saigon Tourist budget office or at any number of cafés and small travel agencies on Pham Ngu Lao Street (☞ Travel Agencies, *below*).

MAIL
The **Central Post Office** (✉ 2 Cong Xa Paris St., District 1), next to Notre Dame Cathedral, is open daily 7:30–5:30.

TRAVEL AGENCIES
Ann's Tourist (✉ 58 Ton That Tung St., District 1, ☎ 08/833–2564, FAX 08/832–3866), which also has an office in Hanoi, could very well

be your only tourist-information stop. The company arranges tours around Ho Chi Minh City and throughout the entire country, rents cars and books flights, does visa extensions, and provides all the historical, cultural, and orientation material you could possibly need. It's open Monday–Saturday 8–6, and Sunday 9–11.

Other privately run travel agencies include: **Exotissimo** (✉ 28 Dinh Tien Hoang St., District 1, ☎ 08/825–1723, FAX 08/825–1684), a more upscale tour operator headquartered in Hanoi but with an office in Saigon, and run by a helpful Frenchman. **Peregrine Tours** (✉ 24/9 Pham Ngoc Thach St., District 3, ☎ 08/829–6086 or 08/822–8464, FAX 08/829–6158), run by Australian John Powell, specializes in adventure tours as well as the more common package trip. **Vidotours** (✉ 41 Dinh Tien Hoang St., District 1, ☎ 08/829–1438, FAX 08/829–1435) specializes in upscale package and individual trips all over the country with excellent tour guides.

Saigon Tourist (✉ main office: 49 Le Thanh Ton St., District 1, ☎ 08/823–0100, FAX 08/822–4987; budget office [in Café Apricot]: ✉ 187 Pham Ngu Lao St., ☎ 08/835–4535) is the big government-run travel service. It can arrange just about everything you might need. Note that besides the price, the only difference between the luxury and budget excursions seems to be the size of the bus. It's open daily 7:30–6:30.

Other offices and agencies include: **Getra Tour Company** (✉ 86 Bui Vien St., District 1, ☎ 08/835–3021); **Thanh Thanh Travel Agency** (✉ 205 Pham Ngu Lao St., District 1, ☎ 08/836–0205); and **Vietnam Tourism** (✉ 234 Nam Ky Khoi Nghia St., District 3, ☎ 08/829–0776, FAX 08/829–0775).

Kim's Cafe (✉ 272 De Tham St., District 1) organizes inexpensive trips to regions such as the Mekong Delta. **Sinh Café Travel** (✉ 179 Pham Ngu Lao St., District 1, ☎ 08/835–5601) has Vietnam's greatest travel deal: a $35 open-ended ticket good for bus travel the length of the country. The café is open daily 7 AM–11 PM.

SIDE TRIPS FROM HO CHI MINH CITY

Cu Chi Tunnels

65 km (40 mi) northwest of Ho Chi Minh City via Hwy. 22.

The Cu Chi Tunnels—a 250-km (155-mi) underground network of field hospitals, command posts, living quarters, eating quarters, and trapdoors—stand as a symbol of the Vietcong's ingenuity in the face of overwhelming odds. (The term "Vietcong," used by the Americans and the Republic of South Vietnam, is used in this chapter because it is probably most familiar. It means, loosely, Vietnamese "Commies." The National Liberation Front [NLF] was the official name of the group fighting the southern government.)

These tunnels, first used in the late '40s against the French, made it possible for the Vietcong in the '60s to not only withstand massive bombings and to communicate with other distant Vietcong enclaves but to command a sizable rural area that was in dangerous proximity (a mere 35 km/22 mi) to Saigon. After the Diem regime's ill-fated "strategic hamlet program" of 1963, disenchanted peasants who refused to move fled to Cu Chi to avoid the aerial bombardments. In fact, the stunning Tet Offensive of 1968 was masterminded and launched from the Cu Chi Tunnels nerve center, with weapons crafted by an enthusiastic assembly line of Vietcong-controlled Cu Chi villagers.

Despite extensive ground operations and sophisticated chemical warfare—and even after declaring the area a free-fire zone—American troops were unable to control it. In the late '60s, though B-52 bombing reduced the area to a wasteland, the Vietnamese Communists and the NLF managed to hang on.

The guided tour includes a film that documents the handiwork of "American monsters" (with, of course, no mention of South Vietnamese involvement) and an array of booby traps demonstrated by former Vietcong soldiers. The claustrophobic might consider skipping the crawl through the hot, stuffy, and tight tunnels (though sections have been expanded to allow for tourists' bigger bodies). Amazingly, in these same tunnels many Vietnamese survived for months and even years.

The easiest and best way to visit is on a tour arranged through one of the travel agencies or tourist cafés (☞ Travel Agencies in Ho Chi Minh City Essentials, *above*), since every agency—state-run and private—does the identical trip. A day trip, which will run you about $40 per person, will generally combine the tunnels with a visit to the Cao Dai Holy See, in neighboring Tay Ninh.

Tay Ninh

95 km (59 mi) northwest of Ho Chi Minh City via Hwy. 22.

The town of Tay Ninh is home to Caodaism—an indigenous hybrid religion based on the major Eastern and Western religions—and to its

★   impressive, brightly colored temple, the **Caodai Holy See.** Founded in 1926 by a mystic named Ngo Minh Chieu, Caodaism is a fusion of a Mahayana Buddhist code of ethics with Taoist and Confucian components. Sprinkled into the mix are elements of Islam, Roman Catholicism, the cult of ancestors, Vietnamese superstition, and over-the-top interior decoration, encompassing a fantastic blend of architectural styles.

Caodai has grown from its original 26,000 members to a present-day membership of 3 million. Meditation and communicating with spiritual worlds via earthly mediums or seances are among its primary practices. Despite its no-holds-barred decorative tendencies, Caodaism emphasizes abstinence from luxury and sensuality as well as vegetarianism as means of escaping the reincarnation cycle. Although the priesthood is strictly nonprofessional, clergy are celibate.

Perhaps most important, the Caodaists believe the divine revelation has undergone three iterations: God's word presented itself first through Lao Tse and other Buddhist, Confucianist, and Taoist players; then through a second set of channelers such as Jesus, Muhammad, Moses, Confucius, and Buddha. Whether because of the fallibility of these human agents or because of the changing set of human needs, the Caodaists believe the divine transmission was botched. They see themselves as the third and final expression, the "third alliance between God and man." Since anyone can take part in this alliance, even Westerners like Joan of Arc, Victor Hugo, and William Shakespeare have been added to the Caodai roster.

The noon ceremony (others are held at 6 AM, 6 PM, and midnight) is one of the most fascinating and colorful religious vignettes to which you will ever be privy as a tourist. A finely tuned hierarchical procession of men and women of all ages parades through the temple's great hall, where great painted columns twined with carved dragons support sky-blue arched vaults; panels of stained glass with a cosmic-eye motif punctuate the walls. You are permitted to watch and take snapshots from the mezzanine. Ignore any feeling of complicity in what appears to be a collective voyeuristic sacrilege; the ceremony goes on as though you were not there.

Generally a visit to Tay Ninh is part of a day trip to the Cu Chi Tunnels (☞ *above*) arranged through one of the travel agencies in Saigon. A guide will accompany you, explain the history of the Caodai sect, and take you through the temple.

Mekong Delta

The northern delta, centered around My Tho and Can Tho, the region's capital, is accessible and can be managed in a day trip. Fruit grows here in abundance: orchards full of mangos, jackfruit, lemons, custard fruit, dragon fruit, pineapples, durians, and papayas. Lush green rice paddies stretch for miles. In the Mekong's remote southern section, steamy mangrove swamps and thick palm forests thrive on the flat, flooded delta, making the area difficult to navigate.

The heart of the delta is the Mekong River, also known as Song Cuu Long, or River of the Nine Dragons. The river carries with it and deposits every second 2,500 to 50,000 cubic yards of fertile soil, which created the delta and continues to make it grow. Descending from the Tibetan plateau, the Mekong River runs through China, separates Burma from Laos, skirts Thailand, passes through Cambodia, and flows through Vietnam into the South China Sea. As it enters Vietnam, the river divides into the Tien Giang (Upper River), which splinters at My Tho and Vinh Long into several seaward tributaries; and the Hau Giang (Lower River), which passes through Chau Doc, Long Xuyen, and Can Tho to the sea.

The Khmer once ruled this region but were slowly pushed out by the Vietnamese over the centuries. Uncertainty about who would have sovereignty over the Mekong Delta lasted until 1954, when the French bequeathed the area to the new country of South Vietnam. The Khmer have been disgruntled ever since. Under Pol Pot's rule in Cambodia, the Khmer again laid claim to the delta as their ancestral land, and there were frequent skirmishes between Khmer Rouge and Vietnamese soldiers along the border. During the Vietnam War defoliants like Agent Orange destroyed huge areas of natural wilderness. These were later resettled in the late '70s after the trees had regrown.

Most organized tours of the northern delta region include boat trips through the river tributaries to islands, such as Tan Long Island, crisscrossed with paths leading through orchards. Often you will stop to have a snack of exotic fruit and tea at someone's farm stand or home. You might visit a beekeeper or see rice noodles being made. Another popular stop on many tours is the Island of the Coconut Monk (Ong Dau Dua), about 2 km (1 mi) from My Tho, where you can have a full meal or a snack with rice wine and honey. Only ruins remain of a garish, eclectic religious complex built in the 1940s by a monk named Nguyen Thanh Nam, who was said to have once lived for years on nothing but coconuts.

There are only two ways to get to the Mekong Delta, both of which must be arranged from Ho Chi Minh City—hiring a private car with driver and guide through a travel agency or participating in an organized tour. The most scenic parts of the Mekong Delta are accessible only by boat. Boat trips are generally part of any prearranged tour or can be hired by your guide. Be sure to keep an eye on your bags and valuables during your boat trip.

VIETNAM A TO Z

Arriving and Departing

By Airplane

AIRPORTS

International flights from North America into Vietnam typically connect through hubs like Bangkok, Singapore, Manila, Hong Kong, Kuala Lumpur, and Taipei and fly into Ho Chi Minh City's Tan Son Nhat Airport and Hanoi's Noi Bai Airport. Ongoing negotiations to offer direct U.S.–Vietnam service may bear fruit by the end of the millennium.

For domestic air travel, major hubs are Ho Chi Minh City, Hanoi, and Danang, but there is also service to Ban Me Thuot, Dalat, Dien Bien Phu, Haiphong, Hue, Nha Trang, Phu Quoc Island, Pleiku, Quy Nhon, and Vinh.

AIRPORT TAXES

Every time you fly into or out of an airport in Vietnam, on a domestic or an international flight, you must pay an airport tax. For domestic flights it's either 15,000d or $2. For international flights it's either 130,000d or $10 if you depart from Hanoi or Ho Chi Minh City.

CARRIERS

Current international carriers with flights to Vietnam: **Asiana Airlines** (☎ 800/227–4262). **Cathay Pacific Airways** (☎ 800/233–2742 in the U.S., 800/268–6868 in Canada). **China Airlines** (☎ 800/227–5118). **Korean Air** (☎ 800/438–5000). **Malaysian Airlines** (☎ 800/552–9264). **Singapore Airlines**(☎ 800/742–3333). **Continental** (☎ 800/231–0856), **Northwest** (☎ 800/225–2525), and **United Airlines** (☎ 800/241–6522) have flights into Tokyo, Singapore, and Bangkok, which then connect with regional carriers.

There are no direct flights to Vietnam from the United Kingdom. Bangkok and Hong Kong are the easiest connection points. Contact **British Airways** (☎ 0345/222111), **Cathay Pacific** (☎ 0345/581581), or **Thai Airways International** (☎ 0171/491–7953).

Domestic routes in Vietnam are flown by **Vietnam Airlines** (✉ 1 Quang Trung St., Hanoi, ☎ 04/825–0888; ✉ 116 Nguyen Hue St., District 1, Ho Chi Minh City, ☎ 08/829–2118) and the smaller **Pacific Airlines** (✉ 100 Le Duan St., Hanoi, ☎ 04/851–5356; ✉ 177 Vo Thi Sau St., District 1, Ho Chi Minh City, ☎ 08/820–0978).

It is a good idea to confirm both domestic flights and flights out of Vietnam a day or two in advance. Also, be sure to arrive at the airport early. During rainy season avoid flying in late afternoon and early evening, when storms generally occur. Note that planes now include 10 Airbus A320s, 3 Boeing 767s, and a few German Fokker 70s and French ATR 72s. Vietnam's commercial fleet has retired its aging Soviet aircraft.

FLYING TIME

Flying time from Los Angeles to the Southeast Asian hub of Bangkok is approximately 18 hours, Chicago to Bangkok is 20 hours, and New York to Bangkok is 22 hours. Bangkok to Ho Chi Minh City takes 1 hour.

By Train

Trains leave Hanoi for Beijing twice weekly (55 hrs, $58–$88). The northeastern border crossing is at Dong Dang, just north of Lang Son. You need a standard tourist visa to enter China from Vietnam, as well as the appropriate exit permit attached to your Vietnam visa; inquire about this procedure when applying for your visa to Vietnam and at the Chinese embassy.

Getting Around

By Bus

Though an extensive and dirt-cheap public bus system serves every nook and cranny of the country, the buses are often overcrowded, cramped, unbearably hot, and notoriously loud. They also break down like clockwork and operate under arbitrary schedules. Air-conditioned minibuses, only slightly more expensive, are often available at or near most bus stations. An even better option is to take the more convenient, reliable, and infinitely more comfortable privately run tour buses organized by travel agencies, tourist offices, and travel cafés to most destinations. Even the most budget-conscious backpackers opt for the minivans or tourist buses.

Sinh Café Travel, in Ho Chi Minh City and Hanoi, runs the Sinh Café Bus. For $35 you get an open-ended ticket enabling you to break your journey for as long as you want at several points—Nha Trang, Dalat, Hoi An, Hue, and Ninh Binh—between Ho Chi Minh City and Hanoi.

By Car

At present, you, as a tourist, are not permitted to drive a car yourself. A rented car automatically comes with a driver who will, hopefully, speak some English. Cars and minivans with drivers are readily available from private and state-run travel agencies, tourist offices, and through most hotels in bigger cities. You are charged either by the kilometer or by the day, or both. A daily rate runs anywhere from $30 to $60, depending on the make of the car, the city in which you rent it, whether it has air-conditioning, and your bargaining skills. The agreed-on price should include gas and tolls (clarify all this before you set off).

The backbone of Vietnam's road system is Highway 1, extending from near the Chinese border, north of Hanoi, through Ho Chi Minh City and to the heart of the Mekong Delta. The major roads are for the most part paved, but they are still slow going (96 km/60 mi takes 90 mins–2 hrs). Those in the north are far worse than in the south, where the U.S. war effort built or paved many of them, but even the southern ones are suffering from neglect.

By Cyclo

Cyclos (pedicabs), the bicycle-powered buggies that are unfortunately on the verge of becoming outlawed, provide the most entertaining and cheapest means of transportation in Vietnam. Although cyclo drivers are supposed to charge 2,000d per km (½ mi), they definitely deserve more since many double as informed English-speaking tour guides. Plan to pay 10,000d–25,000d per hour. Bargaining is advised, but it's worth giving the guys a break (and a tip).

On Foot

The best way to get through traffic on foot is to walk at a steady pace across the street and, of course, watch out; the oncoming vehicles will have a better chance of avoiding you if the drivers can get a sense of where you will be going next. If you stop suddenly, it is harder for drivers to judge where you are in relation to them.

By Motorbike

One of the quickest ways to get around Vietnam's major cities is to ride on the back of a motorbike taxi. This service usually costs about 20,000d. They'll drive up alongside you and ask where you're going and whether you're interested in a ride.

You can also rent motorbikes and scooters in major cities at most travel agencies and some hotels for about 55,000d to 100,000d a day. A deposit is usually required along with a passport or a photocopy of one. But don't part with your deposit until you are convinced the place is legitimate (which usually means it has a line of motorbikes for rent and a standard ticket they give to all customers). Temporary insurance for tourists is almost nonexistent, and your own auto insurance generally does not apply. Make sure your medical insurance covers motorbike accidents, even if you are only a passenger. And ask for a helmet.

By Taxi
Metered taxis are common in Hanoi and Ho Chi Minh City and are becoming more common in smaller cities. Fares are quoted in dong, though you can always pay in U.S. dollars. Although tipping is not required, some cabbies have developed a habit of "not having change" in the hope you'll tell them to keep it. Though many cabbies act like reckless kings of the road, taxis are the safest way to get around the cities.

By Train
The 2,600-km (1,612-mi) rail system, built by the French, goes north–south, serving coastal towns between Hanoi and Ho Chi Minh City; another line goes both northwest and northeast (and on to China) from Hanoi. The main drawback is that the trains are slow. The quickest one, the Reunification Express, takes 36–44 hours, depending on how many stops it makes. Trains are good for overnight trips such as the hops between Hanoi and Hue, Hanoi and Lao Cai, and Ho Chi Minh City and Nha Trang (15–22 hrs, $25–$35).

You'll need separate tickets for each destination, and it's a good idea to book ahead, especially for overnight travel. When traveling long distances, reserving a soft-berth sleeper or soft seat is worth the small extra fare. You may want to take food and water with you, although they are available on some trains or from vendors in stations, and the fares on some routes include boxed meals.

Contacts and Resources

Customs & Duties
When you enter Vietnam, you will be given a yellow customs declaration slip and a green departure slip. You need these to get out of the country, so do not lose them. Do not bring weapons, pornographic materials, or anything that could be considered subversive into Vietnam, as you may receive a hefty fine, be detained, or in extreme cases, jailed. It's a good idea to declare cameras, camcorders, laptop computers, and any other expensive electronics that you want to take out of the country again, though it's not required. Keep receipts for all your purchases. Upon leaving Vietnam and reentering your country, be ready to show customs officials what you've bought. It is illegal to export antiques (anything older than 21 years and a day) and wooden furniture unless you get special permission to do so. If you buy an item that looks like an antique, be sure to get a note from the store owner stating that it is not.

Dining
MEALTIMES
Breakfast is served beginning at 6 at most sidewalk stalls and 7 at most restaurants; lunch is served anywhere between 11:30 and 2; and dinner any time after 5 and usually before 8. Restaurants are generally open daily (except major holidays), and although Vietnamese eat dinner fairly early, most restaurants remain open well into the night, even after they are supposed to close.

PRECAUTIONS

Be careful of what you eat and drink in Vietnam. Fresh, leafy vegetables are known to carry parasites, so avoid those of dubious origin or those likely to have been washed in tap water. Also, try to eat only fruit that has a peel. Drink only bottled water. Ice from Western-style restaurants is usually fine, but many visitors avoid it altogether. Note that monosodium glutamate (MSG) is used in many dishes in Vietnam, particularly in pho (noodle soup). That said, dining at street food stands can be as safe or safer than eating in restaurants, especially in cities. Be more careful away from urban areas. Most of all, use common sense and pick a food stand, restaurant, or café that looks clean, is crowded, and has fresh food.

Health and Safety

CRIME

Although it is widely accepted that Vietnam is safe for tourists, pickpocketing and bag snatching are becoming serious problems in Ho Chi Minh City, and even in Hanoi. Don't wear conspicuous jewelry. Walk with your bag on the shoulder away from the curb, and keep your hand or ankles through the straps when in a cyclo, as snatch-and-ride theft (on a motorbike or bicycle) is common. Put your wallet in your front pocket or in a zipped-up bag, and be alert in busy markets or crowds. Children or elderly people may act as decoys or pickpocket you themselves. When in a street café, keep your hands through the straps of your bag or put the strap around your neck, so no one can grab it. If someone does steal your bag, don't pursue the thief; bag snatchers often carry knives.

As for cyclos, don't go with a driver you don't feel comfortable with, and don't travel by cyclo after dark, especially in cities. Leave passports, cameras, laptop computers, and other valuables in your hotel room's safe, or in the hotel's safe, or with the front desk. It is wise to leave your passport in your hotel and carry a only photocopy with you. It's safe to walk around cities at night—even for women—but you should avoid dark, deserted streets. Minihotels in popular tourist areas such as Halong Bay seem to be thief magnets, so always keep your doors and windows locked.

MEDICAL CARE

Check with the Centers for Disease Control and your physician about current health risks in Vietnam and recommended vaccinations before you go.

Vietnam's medical infrastructure is not up to international standards. Hospitals and pharmacies are often undersupplied and out of date. Only a handful of Vietnamese doctors have top-quality Western training. Foreign insurance is very rarely accepted, so you should expect to pay immediately in cash. Foreign-run medical clinics offering basic treatment and 24-hour on-call services can guide you to local hospitals for more serious problems and can arrange for emergency evacuation. Embassies have duty officers on call who can assist with logistics. If you get sick outside Hanoi or Ho Chi Minh City, get yourself to those cities as soon as possible.

Language

Vietnamese, or *kinh*, is written in a Roman-based script called *quoc ngu*, devised by a French Jesuit scholar in the 17th century. Before that, the Vietnamese used a system called *nom*, which drew on the Chinese system of characters. Although the letters may look familiar and the words sometimes be recognizable, the tonal spoken language is quite foreign to Western ears. Barring a few exceptions in tones and words, written Vietnamese is homogenous throughout the country, though accents differ dramatically, particularly between north and south. It's best to use a phrase book as a point-and-show device, though a little Vietnamese goes a long way. English is by far the most widely used language in the tourist trade.

Mail

Packages mailed to and from Vietnam will probably be scrutinized at the post office. Videotapes, books, and compact discs are especially sensitive. Count on about two weeks, sometimes longer, for mail to arrive in the West from Vietnam. The main post offices in Hanoi and Ho Chi Minh City have Poste Restante, where you can have mail sent to you from abroad.

EXPRESS MAIL SERVICES

The **U.S. Postal Service, DHL** (✉ 150 Lang Rd. or 1 Le Thach St., Hanoi; ✉ 2 Cong Xa Paris St., District 1, Ho Chi Minh City); **FedEx** (✉ 6 Dinh Le St., Hanoi, ☎ 04/824–9054; ✉ 1 Nguyen Hau St., District 1, Ho Chi Minh City, ☎ 08/829–0747); and **UPS** (✉ 4C Dinh Le St., Hanoi, ☎ 04/824–6483; ✉ 80F Nguyen Du St., District 1, Ho Chi Minh City, ☎ 08/824–3597) all have express mail services to Vietnam, which, unfortunately, can take from four to seven days.

POSTAL RATES

On average, a postcard or letter to the United States costs about 13,000d; one to Europe costs about 11,000d. Stamps are sold at post office (*buu dien*) branches, which are generally open daily 6 AM–8 PM, and at many hotels and shops. Usually the postal clerk will cancel the stamps on your letter and give it back to you to put into the slot. This prevents the stamps being peeled off your letter for resale and your letter thrown away.

Money and Expenses

CURRENCY

The Vietnamese unit of currency is the dong (abbreviated as d throughout this guide), which comes in 100d, 200d, 500d, 1,000d, 2,000d, 5,000d, 10,000d, 20,000d and 50,000d notes. Since a 50,000d note is worth less than $5, you have to lug around quite a few notes. It's a good idea to keep plenty of 5,000d, 10,000d, and 20,000d notes handy for cyclos, cabs, and snacks.

EXCHANGING MONEY

The official exchange rate at press time was about 13,000d to the U.S. dollar, 9,100d to the Canadian dollar, and 20,830d to the British pound. Although traveler's checks are accepted at many places, cash—in the form of U.S. dollars or dong—is much more widely used. It's best to bring at least a few hundred dollars in cash or as much as you feel comfortable carrying. A money belt is good idea. The Bank for Foreign Trade of Vietnam, or Vietcom Bank, has branches all over the country and gives the official government rate. Although they don't often have the best exchange rates, hotels are convenient places to change money. You can usually get the highest exchange rates in gold or jewelry shops. The services of black-market money changers is a high-risk option. At many places you'll get a better exchange rate with higher-denomination bills.

FORMS OF PAYMENT

Credit cards have yet to catch on as a normal form of payment with ordinary merchants (ask first), but they are accepted at large hotels, upscale restaurants, better shops, large tour operators, and airline agencies. Hotels and shops sometimes insist on a service charge of up to 4% if you pay by credit card, however. MasterCard and Visa are the most widely accepted cards.

Technically it is illegal for many establishments to accept payment in anything but dong, but such rules are widely ignored. U.S. dollars are accepted almost everywhere, except at state enterprises—including train stations—which take only dong. You should carry both dong and dollars with you at all times; cash is definitely needed in rural areas and small towns.

WHAT IT WILL COST

Vietnam is still a relatively inexpensive destination. Though some upscale international hotels in Ho Chi Minh City and Hanoi charge more than $200 per night, most minihotels and guest houses there charge less than $35, and elsewhere they're even cheaper. Food can be a steal. If you eat at small local restaurants, street-side cafés, food stalls, or markets, you'll pay between $1 and $5. A meal at an upscale restaurant, including wine, costs an average of $15–$20. Be aware that Vietnam has an official dual-pricing system, so foreigners often are expected to pay more than double what locals do for trains, buses, flights, other goods and services, and admission fees.

Sample Costs: a cup of coffee in a street café will cost you 2,500d (20¢); a cyclo ride will generally cost from 5,000d to 10,000d (from 45¢ to 75¢) per km (½ mi); a liter of *bia hoi* (fresh draft beer) is 2,500d (20¢); bottled beer goes for between 12,000d and 25,000d (about $1–$2); and a bowl of noodles from a food stall is 5,000d (45¢).

National Holidays

The traditional lunar new year, known as Tet in Vietnam and celebrated throughout much of Southeast Asia, falls in January or February, depending on the lunar calendar. Other national holidays include: New Year's Day (January 1), the anniversary of the founding of the Vietnamese Communist Party (February 3); Liberation Day (April 30), commemorating the day the North Vietnamese army took Saigon; International Workers Day, or May Day (May 1, the date following Liberation Day, which means a two-day holiday); Ho Chi Minh's birthday (May 19); National Day (September 2); and Christmas Day (December 25).

Opening and Closing Hours

Small family-run shops seem to stay open indefinitely, primarily because living and working quarters are often one and the same. Many offices, museums, and government-run agencies are open weekdays and Saturday 7:30 or 8 to 11:30 and from 1 or 1:30 to 4 or 5. Banks are open weekdays and on Saturday morning until 11. Post offices are open seven days a week. Cafés and restaurants are open all day, almost every day. Most sidewalk stalls serving breakfast and lunch finish by 2 and reopen for dinner at 4. You can always find late-night noodle stands. Bars and nightclubs usually close at about 1 AM or whenever the last customer leaves.

Passports & Visas

To get into Vietnam, you need a passport and a visa. You are no longer required to carry your passport with you at all times, though most hotels will ask you for your passport when you check in.

Obtain a visa from the **Vietnamese Embassy** (⊠ 1233 20th St. NW, Suite 400, Washington, DC 20036, U.S., ☎ 202/861–0694, FAX 202/861–1297; ⊠ 12–14 Victoria Rd., London W8-5RD, U.K., ☎ 0171/937–1912, FAX 0171/937–6108; ⊠ 226 Maclaren St., Ottawa, Ontario, Canada, K2POL9, ☎ 613/236–0772, FAX 613/236–2704). The standard processing fee is $65 for a two-week turnaround and $80 for a four- or five-day rush turnaround. Although officially the embassy is only supposed to grant 30-day visas (that you may be able to extend once you're in Vietnam), persistent callers have been known to receive two-month visas.

Telephones

The country code for Vietnam is 84. Some city codes: Dalat, 063; Danang, 0511; Hoi An, 0510; Haiphong, 031; Halong Bay, 033; Hanoi, 04; Ho Chi Minh City, 08; Hue, 054; Nha Trang, 058; Phan Thiet, 062; Vung Tau, 064.

CALLING HOME

To call overseas from Vietnam, dial 00 + the country code (1 for the United States) + the area code + the number. Vietnam time is 12 hours ahead of Eastern Standard Time and 16 hours ahead of Pacific Standard Time.

International phone calls from Vietnam cost a small fortune. Many hotels have international direct dial (IDD) phones, but a better option is to buy phone cards at the telephone companies that are usually in or near post offices, and use them on special phones inside the phone company offices or in hotel lobbies. Card calls to the United States, Europe, and Canada cost about $4 for the first minute and about $3 for each additional minute. As of press time, access numbers for reaching U.S. long-distance operators do not work in Vietnam, though the phone companies claim otherwise. Collect calls are not allowed.

CALLING VIETNAM

To call Vietnam from overseas, dial the international access code (011 from the United States) + the country code 84 + the area code without the first 0 + the number.

Tipping

Tipping at restaurants is not common in Vietnam, although many upscale places are starting to add a service charge and/or gratuity to bills. If this hasn't been done and the service is good, you might consider leaving 5%–10%. Chambermaids and porters usually appreciate a small tip, though as you go farther north you may find that hotel employees will refuse tips, waving them off with a perplexed grin. Although it 's not necessarily expected, tour guides are more than happy to receive a tip. Many cyclo drivers will request in English a "souvenir" after you've paid the agreed amount.

Travel Agencies and Visitor Information

As of yet, there is no official source of tourist information abroad, but you might try calling the Vietnam embassy or consulate (☞ Passports & Visas, *above*) . The *Vietnam Business Journal* and *Vietnam Economic Times,* available internationally, provide some business information of interest to tourists. In Vietnam, travel agencies, tourist cafés, and hotels are your best sources of information.

Almost every city and province has a state-run tourist agency that does everything from book trains, planes, and automobiles to arrange guided tours and extend visas. The larger firms (**Vietnam Tourism, Saigon Tourist, Hanoi Tourism**) are huge agencies with fingers in many pies, but they are often pricey, slow, and not very helpful. In some smaller provinces, they're the only game in town. Hotels, big and small, are frequently affiliated with a travel agency, or they have their own travel services. In larger cities, there are also excellent, privately run travel agencies. Tourist cafés, though primarily oriented toward budget travelers, have many of the same services as large travel agencies and generally the best information, the widest selection of tours and day trips, and the lowest prices.

In Hanoi and Ho Chi Minh City travel agencies can provide English-speaking guides for about $15 a day. You may also be approached on the street by former U.S. Army interpreters or by cyclo drivers who will ask 50,000d for a day's work as a guide. This is a viable option, but make sure you understand their English by conducting an informal interview before you agree on a fee. Tourist agencies in cities like Hue, Danang, Halong Bay, and Haiphong all claim they can provide English-speaking guides. But outside the main cities, it's definitely hit or miss.

Vietnam Veterans

The **Vietnam Veterans of America Foundation** (VVAF)(⊠ 51 Ly Thai To St., Hanoi, ☎ 04/934–1607, FAX 04/934–1606) is involved in building long-lasting ties and increasing understanding between Vietnamese and Americans. Veterans returning to Vietnam are encouraged to contact the Hanoi or the Washington, D.C., office (⊠ 1224 M St. NW, Washington, DC 20005, ☎ 202/628–2700, FAX 202/628–5880). At least once a year VVAF organizes tours to Vietnam; contact the Washington office for information.

When To Go

During the festival of Tet, the lunar new year, accommodations are scarce; and museums, offices, and shops tend to close for days at a time.

Vietnam's climate varies widely from region to region; the best time of year in northern Vietnam is from October to December, when chilly, wet weather begins, which continues through March. Sweltering heat is common from May to early October, and flooding can be expected in summer. The Central Highlands are cool year-round and dry from December to March. Along the central coast, the rainy season runs from December to February; dry heat is the norm from June to October. In the south the best weather is from December to April. May to November generally brings the wet season and sporadic showers, usually during lunchtime. The rain shouldn't discourage you from visiting the south during this time (especially in late fall), though flooding in the Mekong Delta can make traveling there difficult. Overall, the best time of year to visit all of Vietnam is late September–December and March–April.

The following are average daily maximum and minimum temperatures for Hanoi and Ho Chi Minh City.

Climate in Vietnam

HANOI

Jan.	66F	19C	May	84F	29C	Sept.	82F	28C
	54	12		72	22		68	20
Feb.	66F	19C	June	88F	31C	Oct.	81F	27C
	55	13		73	23		68	20
Mar.	70F	21C	July	86F	30C	Nov.	75F	24C
	59	15		73	23		63	17
Apr.	77F	25C	Aug.	84F	29C	Dec.	70F	21C
	66	19		73	23		59	15

HO CHI MINH CITY

Jan.	84F	29C	May	88F	31C	Sept.	82F	28C
	68	20		75	24		73	23
Feb.	86F	30C	June	84F	29C	Oct.	82F	28C
	70	21		73	23		72	22
Mar.	88F	31C	July	82F	28C	Nov.	82F	28C
	72	22		73	23		70	21
Apr.	90F	32C	Aug.	82F	28C	Dec.	82F	28C
	75	24		73	23		68	20

8 Other Destinations

Pagodas in Burma, Khmer sanctuaries in Cambodia, and ancient Buddhist temples in Laos are begging to be rediscovered. Closed to visitors for decades, these countries are now opening their frontiers. Untainted, as yet, by mass tourism, their peoples greet outsiders with a natural warmth and hospitality.

T

HIS CHAPTER COVERS THREE COUNTRIES that are, as yet, secondary destinations on most Southeast Asian itineraries. Cambodia, Laos, and Burma (officially called Myanmar) are opening themselves up to international trade and tourism. Many tour companies offer trips covering these countries singly or in combination, but you can also travel independently. It's much easier than you would think. So long as you travel within secure areas, it's also reasonably safe (although banditry and guerrilla warfare make some towns and provinces dangerous). Locals—not yet inured to countless visiting foreigners—volunteer assistance and a friendly welcome. Moreover, because these countries are not yet commercialized and caught up in the techno-consumerism of the late 20th century, you can still experience the best of Southeast Asia's traditions and cultures. The easiest way into any of these countries is through Bangkok.

By Nigel Fisher

Dining

Price categories throughout the chapter are based on the following ranges (as a number of the countries covered have unstable currencies, prices are quoted in dollars):

CATEGORY	COST*
$$$$	over $20
$$$	$10–$20
$$	$4–$10
$	under $4

*per person for a three-course dinner, excluding tax, service, and drinks.

Lodging

Price categories throughout the chapter are based on the following ranges:

CATEGORY	COST*
$$$$	over $160
$$$	$100–$160
$$	$60–$100
$	$20–$60
¢	under $20

*for a standard double room in high season, excluding service charge and tax.

BURMA (MYANMAR)

The tale of modern Burma is a sad one. When it achieved independence from Great Britain in 1948, it was the rice bowl of Asia and potentially the richest country in the region. But the only person who had the strength of leadership and nobility of purpose to unite the independent-minded ethnic groups and establish a democracy was Aung San, and he was assassinated a few months before Burma was granted full sovereignty. Political squabbling, ethnic fighting, and communist terrorism became the rule, and in 1962 a military coup was engineered by General Ne Win, who for years presided over flagrant abuses of human rights and the disintegration of the country's economy. Although he resigned as president in 1982, his influence is still felt.

Popular resolve against the one-party rule of the Burmese Socialist Programme Party (BSPP), chaired by Ne Win, boiled over in 1988, and democratic demonstrations swept through the country. The government butchered the demonstrators—approximately 12,000 people disappeared or were killed—and the military seized absolute power on September 18, 1988. Since then the State Law and Order Restoration Council (SLORC), a 19-man military junta, has ruled by terror. Surprisingly,

SLORC permitted elections in 1990, expecting that their party would win. They totally miscalculated. Although the two leaders of the National League for Democracy (NLD), Aung San Suu Kyi and U Tin U, had been under detention since July 1989, the NLD won 82% of the 13 million votes cast. As expected, SLORC refused to hand over power and has tightened its grip, imprisoning any who speak out, many of whom "just disappear." Charles Humana, who produces a widely accepted index of human rights, has given Burma the lowest human-rights rating of any country in the world.

In 1997 SLORC renamed itself the State Peace and Development Council (SPDC), though SLORC is the acronym still commonly used. In an attempt to rescue the failing economy, it has embarked on a program to open the country to foreign investment and tourism. Visas are easier to obtain, travelers no longer have to exchange a minimum amount of money on arrival, and foreigners are no longer required to stay at government-run hotels. Better yet, independent travel is now possible, though most people arrange transport and accommodation through a tour operator. In 1996, 40,000 tourists are estimated to have entered the country. The government hopes to increase that figure to half a million in the next five years.

Herein lies your dilemma: by visiting Burma, are you contributing to the coffers of SLORC and its oppression of the people, or are you helping to bring about social and political change? Aung San Suu Kyi, who won the Nobel Peace Prize for her fight to win her people's freedom and is the most loved person in Burma, argues that foreign money (and that includes tourist dollars) should not be spent in Burma while SLORC denies freedom and human rights to the people. Others argue that so long as tourists purchase goods and services from the people and not from government-owned facilities, tourism may assist the Burmese in eventually overthrowing the SLORC dictatorship.

Pleasures and Pastimes

ARCHITECTURE

B rma is a land of pagodas—although "pagoda" is actually an English term and slightly misleading. The generic Burmese term for a Buddhist holy structure is *paya,* of which there are two types, the *zedi* and the *pahto.* Pahto is usually translated as "temple" or "shrine," but shrine is a better word. Monks are not necessarily in attendance, nor, more importantly, do Buddhist believers *worship* in the Western sense. Rather, they go to a shrine (which can be a building of almost any shape) for contemplation and meditation. The other pagoda form, the zedi (also known as a *chedi* or stupa), is a solid, bell-shape structure raised on a series of terraces and crowned by a golden finial called a *hti.* Zedis house important Buddhist relics, either objects taken from the Buddha or such holy materials as Buddha images and prayer tablets.

A paya can have both pahtos and zedis; Rangoon's Shwedagon Pagoda, for example, is a famous Mon zedi (the central one) that's surrounded by numerous pahtos where the devout go to pray. Most pagodas are open from dawn to dusk and are free, though at some, such as the Shwedagon, foreigners are required to make a donation.

DINING

Burmese food is disappointing. It has none of the intrigue and subtleties of Thai cuisine. Rice and rice noodles are the staples. Curries—of chicken, meat, or fish fried in peanut oil—are the usual substantive dishes. Unfortunately, these do not use all the herbs and spices found in Indian curries. At best, Burmese curries limit themselves to garlic, onions, tomatoes, turmeric, ginger, and chili peppers. Every meal comes with a bowl of clear soup, to offset the oiliness of the curries. If you don't like curries, seafood or simple fried chicken are your best, if not only, bets. In Rangoon and Mandalay, Western food is served in hotel dining rooms; in the smarter restaurants, Chinese recipes and perhaps a few Western dishes will be on the menu. In the larger provincial capitals and resorts, your only alternative to Burmese cooking is Chinese; in smaller towns, you won't have that choice.

LODGING

Burma has only just opened its doors to tourists, so hotels are few, far between, and often ugly. The Soviet-built Inya Lake in Rangoon and the Novotel in Mandalay were both early disasters—dreary inside and prisonlike outside. Both have revamped their interiors, but the outsides remain eyesores. The only first-class hotel in the entire country is the Strand in Rangoon—it costs a bundle—and the only hotel of old colonial charm is Candacraig (Thiri-myaing) in Maymyo, 67 km (41 mi) east of Mandalay.

In Rangoon, a few hotels have recently been built and more are under construction. Mandalay and Pagan are also slated to have new hotels by 2000. In other areas, you'll find places with little more than a bed, ceiling fan, and basic plumbing in the private bathrooms. Perhaps because they're limited in number, these basic hotels are surprisingly expensive—about $35 a night. Even the cheapest accommodation in Rangoon, where the bathroom is shared, runs $20 a night; in the country, a room with a cot, mosquito net, and washbasin costs $15.

THE PEOPLE

The greatest pleasure in Burma is meeting the people—excluding the military, of course. The Burmese are exceedingly congenial, polite, and generous in a way reminiscent of the Thai attitude toward visitors in the 1950s. They are eager to talk, to help, and to welcome you to their country. They give unstintingly of their warm sincerity—often all they have to give, considering the average per capita income of around $100 a year. Most are devout Buddhists who take their religion seriously by practicing good thoughts and deeds every day.

SHOPPING

Burma's range of goods is limited. While crafts are least expensive at the place where they are made, in Rangoon you can find lacquerware, tables, trays, and chests from Pagan; Shan shoulder bags, many from the Inle Lake region; and wooden chests made throughout Burma. Precious gems, for which Burma is known, are really no cheaper than in Thailand, and unless you are a gemologist, the risk of being taken is great.

Great Itinerary

Moving swiftly, you can cover the major sights in Rangoon, Mandalay, Pagan, and Inle Lake in little over a week. This certainly does not do justice to all the sights or give much of a chance to take in the depth of Burma's fascination, but it will be sufficient to whet your appetite. Our coverage of Burma includes only these most popular destinations, all of which have a tourist infrastructure sufficient to satisfy the demands of the international traveler. For those willing to rough it a bit, Burma has a lot more to offer, from beaches at Ngapali and Chaung Tha to the architectural wonders of Mrauk U.

IF YOU HAVE 10 DAYS

On day one, fly into **Rangoon** from Bangkok in the morning; in the afternoon, stroll around downtown, visit the National Museum, and shop at Bogyoke Aung San Market. Take dinner at a restaurant on Kandawgyi Lake and catch a "cultural show." Start the next day at the

Shwedagon Pagoda, and in the afternoon, take a tour of the outer townships to get a sense of the expanding city and to visit small pagodas.

On the morning of the third day, fly to **Pagan.** Spend that afternoon,
all of the next day, and the following morning visiting a few of the 2,000
monuments in the Pagan Architectural Zone. On the afternoon of the
fifth day, fly or go by road to **Mandalay.** For the sixth day, visit the
pagodas at the foot of Mandalay Hill and then tour the hills in **Sagaing,**
visiting the monasteries and taking in the breathtaking views. On the
way back, stop at U Bien Bridge in **Amarapura.** For the seventh day
take the ferry up the Ayeyarwady (Irrawaddy) to **Mingun** for its monuments and the world's largest uncracked bell. Return to Mandalay
for the afternoon; pay homage to the Buddha at the Mahamuni Pagoda,
and visit Shwe Kyaung palace. On day eight, fly out of Mandalay to
serene **Inle Lake.** Leave on the morning of the 10th day for Bangkok,
changing planes in Rangoon.

Rangoon (Yangon)

Only some 4 million people live in Rangoon, the capital, so named by
the British (the name Yangon, meaning "end of strife," was given to
the city in 1755 by King Alaungpaya after defeating enemy forces in
the south; both names are used here). Yet the city spreads over a wide
expanse, comprising teak forests, gardens, wide boulevards, lakes,
parks, and pagodas. The result is an open city. Turn a blind eye toward
the SLORC soldiers, the economic despair, and the crumbling buildings, and Rangoon could be an attractive place to live.

Rangoon is relatively new as a capital. The British chose it in 1885 for
its proximity to the sea, just 32 km (20 mi) away, and its natural de-
fensive position: the Rangoon River encases the city on its west and
south side, and the Pazundaung Canal, which flows south into the Rangoon River, flanks the east side. The city's heart is clustered close to
the riverbanks. Here colonial architecture is dwarfed by the buildings
put up in the boom created by foreign capital. Since 1992, when cap-
it. list-minded General Than Shwe became the head of SLORC, foreign investment and imports have been flooding into the city. People
still move slowly, but the traffic is building. One wonders if Rangoon
will go the way of Asian cities, bounding into the 21st century with
neon lights, traffic jams, and concrete high-rises.

Downtown is built on a grid system: minor north–south streets are
numbered, while the other streets often have both a pre- and post-in-
dependence name. Expect to be confused. The city is divided into
townships. Aside from the downtown area, the most important townships are Dagon (with the Shwedagon Pagoda, several embassies, and
a couple of hotels) and, slightly farther out, Bahan (with more hotels).

Your downtown landmark should be the **Golden Sule Pagoda** (Sule
Paya). Its octagonal shape rises 150 ft above the surrounding shops,
and the central stupa is said to contain a hair of the Buddha. The complex has been rebuilt so often that no one truly knows when it was
begun, but some suggest it may have been as long as 2,000 years ago.
🖼 *Free.* ☉ *Dawn–dusk.*

★ The country's best-known and most venerated pagoda is the **Shwedagon
Pagoda,** erected northwest of the city center 2,500 years ago, to house
eight sacred hairs of the Buddha. Its golden stupa, on Singuttara Hill,
rises to 320 ft, dominating the skyline, and its spiritual power reaches
out to all of Burma. Thousands come to pay homage each year.

At first, the pagoda was only 30 ft high, but successive monarchs have added to it, committing their empire's coffers to its restoration and elaboration. The dome is now covered with about 70 tons of gold, and the gilded hti on top is studded with rubies, sapphires, and topaz. The gold-and-silver weather vane is decorated with 1,100 diamonds; its orb is encrusted with 4,350 small diamonds and crowned with one of 76 carats.

Entrance to Shwedagon Pagoda is by four stairways, but foreigners may use only the southern one, from Pagoda Road (elevators are available). You enter the pagoda at the **Temple of the Konagama Buddha,** named for one of the four Buddhas that the Burmese believe preceded the Guatama Buddha (the Lord Buddha whose teachings form the basis of present-day Buddhism). From there, as you circle to the left around the golden stupa, you pass through a religious fairyland of pavilions and shrines, sculpted images, and small stupas. Plan on at least two hours here, which will allow you only to duck in and out of the two dozen or more small shrines. A guide is strongly recommended, as otherwise you will miss many of the fascinating details and intricacies of Burmese Buddhism. ⌨ *Admission.* ☉ *Daily 6 AM–10 PM.*

At the **Chauk Htat Gyi Pagoda** on Shwegondine Road, a short distance beyond the Shwedagon Pagoda, lies a reclining Buddha image, one of the largest in Myanmar. The original figure, built in 1907, suffered such damage from climate over the years that it was demolished in 1957 and rebuilt in 1966.

The **National Museum,** a five-minute walk from the historic Strand Hotel, contains the Mandalay regalia from Burma's last royal court and other artifacts. The showpiece is King Thibaw's 26-ft-high Lion Throne, which was originally in the Royal Palace at Mandalay. Once displayed in London's Victoria and Albert Museum, it was returned to Rangoon in 1964. ✉ *26 Pansodan St.* ⌨ *Admission.* ☉ *Weekdays 10–3.*

Bogyoke Aung San Market, Rangoon's largest and liveliest (still called by its old name, Scott's Market), throbs with activity, and it is here, more than anywhere else in Rangoon, that the depressed economy and oppressive rule of SLORC seem to be forgotten. In its maze of covered alleys, you'll find a huge collection of crafts from all over Burma, including the Shan states and Upper Burma. There are numerous jewelry stalls: search for **Su Yadana** (✉ *58 West D Hall*), whose owners are honest, fair, extremely helpful, and speak some English. Locals come to Bogyoke Market for dry goods, black-market items, gold, and clothes. Some stalls will change dollars at the black-market rate.

If you have time you may want to visit some of Rangoon's other sights. **Botahtaung Pagoda** (Bo means "leader" and tahtaung means "a thousand") commemorates the thousand military leaders who escorted relics of the Buddha brought from India more than 2,000 years ago. The present Botahtaung is hollow, and inside you can walk through a sort of mirrored maze with glass showcases containing many of the ancient relics and artifacts that were sealed inside the earlier pagoda. Above this interesting interior, the golden spire rises 132 ft.

The **Kaba Aye Pagoda,** dedicated to world peace (*Kaba Aye*), was built in 1952 for the Sixth Buddhist Synod, 1954–56. The 111-ft pagoda also measures 111 ft around its base. It stands about 11 km (7 mi) north of the city, a little beyond the Inya lake Hotel. **Mahana Guha,** an enormous artificial cave, 455 by 370 ft, was built close to the Kaba Aye Pagoda in the same compound. It was here that the Sixth Buddhist Synod was held, to coincide with the 2,500th anniversary of the Buddha's enlightenment, at which the participants recited, edited, and approved the entire Buddhist scripture, known as the Tipitaka. In **North Okkalapa,** a satellite town about 20 minutes' drive west from the city center, there is a whole cluster of spired pagodas and sculptured figures, of which the **Mai-Lamu Pagoda,** which has giant images depicting Buddha's earlier lives, is the most famous.

Dining and Lodging

$$ ✕ **Green Elephant.** This restaurant's popularity is based on its garden setting and its reasonably good menu, which has Chinese, Burmese, and Western dishes. Perhaps try the lime salad to whet your appetite, and continue with the river prawn curry. Arrive about 8 PM, when the air is cooler, and plan to spend a couple of hours relaxing over a dinner administered by friendly, attentive waiters. ⊠ *12 Inya Rd., ☎ 01/ 530263. No credit cards.*

$$ ✕ **Lone Ma Lay Restaurant.** One of several restaurants known more for its "cultural show" than its cuisine, Lone Ma Lay usually has a good repertoire of both traditional regional dances and contemporary acts. Food here is better than at most dinner-show establishments, perhaps because it has a number of Chinese dishes to supplement the Burmese. The restaurant also serves breakfast. It is just up the bank from Kandawgyi Lake, so the lights dance prettily on the water and a cool breeze wafts through the open-sided dining room. ⊠ *Natmauk Rd., Kandawgyi Lake, ☎ 01/50357. Reservations essential. No credit cards.* ⊙ *Dinner show starts about 8 PM.*

$ ✕ **Nan Yu.** Local businessmen come for lunch at this spot in the center of Rangoon. The hybrid Burmese-Chinese cooking is good; hot-and-sour fried prawns and fried chicken with green chili are good bets. A meal for two runs about $10, including a Mandalay beer. The decor is plain, but the tables have white cloths and a few photographs decorate the walls. ⊠ *81 Pansodan St., ☎ 01/577796. No credit cards.*

$ ✕ **Pole Star.** There are very few restaurants in the center of Rangoon that offer a good menu and are pleasant to sit in. Pole Star is not fancy by any stretch, but it does make the attempt to present itself smartly, with blue tablecloths on neatly lined-up tables and clean walls hung with pictures. The fare is Burmese and quite good, without excessive oil. Fish dishes, when available, are good choices, and the chicken curry is done with a mixture of spices that will excite your taste buds. The extensive menu will certainly have something to tempt you. ⊠ *No 81, Lanthit St., ☎ 01/222095. No credit cards.*

¢   ✕ **Schwe Ba.** This neighborhood spot on the north side of Shwedagon Pagoda is known throughout Rangoon for good local cooking. Sit at one of the long tables (where other diners may pull up a bench and join you), and an assortment of plates will be brought by—you pay only for those dishes that you accept. Try the *hingho* (clear soup), fried chicken, and *hin* (curries zesty with garlic, coriander, chili peppers, and onions, which have been fried in peanut oil). This homey spot is recommended for intrepid travelers; tables and plates may look a little grubby, but no stomach problems have been reported. ⊠ *U Wizara Rd., Dagon Township, ☎ no phone. No credit cards.*

$$$$ ▥ **Strand Hotel.** The cost of a room here for one night is exorbitant— ★   three times the nation's annual per-capita income—but if you do treat yourself, you'll find the experience well worth the tab. Founded in 1901 by the Sarkies brothers, the Strand reached its zenith in the 1920s, but after Burmese independence, it deteriorated into little more than a boardinghouse. It wasn't until the early '90s, when the property was purchased from the government and completely renovated, that the Strand returned to (or perhaps even surpassed) its former glory. You'll find all the conveniences of the late 20th century, done with impeccable Edwardian sensibilities. A tie and jacket at dinner are de rigueur, and sipping a pink gin in the wood-paneled bar seems entirely appropriate.

Throughout, 20-ft ceilings, potted palms, lazy overhead fans, and elegant wicker furnishings suggest colonial elegance. In the huge guest
rooms—on two floors, each with a valet on duty at all times—king-
size beds rest on highly polished teak floors; spacious tile baths have
separate shower and tub. The dining room is pleasantly formal, and
the food is the best that you will eat in Burma. Much of the produce
is imported, and there is a reasonable wine selection—choose an Australian, as that wine seems to travel better than the French ones do.
The attentive staff is eager to assist you in negotiating Burma, whether
you are a business traveler or a tourist. ⊠ *92 Strand Rd.,* ☎ *01/
220065; 800/447–7462 or 212/223–2848 in the U.S.; 0800/282684
in the U.K.;* FAX *01/22424. 32 suites. 2 restaurants, bar, room service,
laundry service, business services, travel services. AE, DC, MC, V.*

$$$ 🏨 **Inya Lake.** The Soviets built this hotel—that may account for its ugly
facade—but the interior has been revamped. A private management
team has taken over from the government, and service, rooms, and food
have greatly improved. The hotel's drawback is its location on 38 acres
near the airport and a good 9 km (6 mi) from downtown. Still book
ahead, as many tour groups stay here, and the government holds gem
auctions here each year, pocketing the revenue of Burma's rich min-
eral resources. ⊠ *37 Kaba Aye Pagado Rd.,* ☎ *01/662826,* FAX *01/
665537. 239 rooms. 4 restaurants, pool, 2 tennis courts, business ser-
vices, meeting rooms. AE, DC, MC, V.*

$$$ 🏨 **Summit Parkview.** For a strictly utilitarian hotel 3 km (2 mi) from
town, the Summit Parkview fills the bill. Its concrete curved building
is a bit of an eyesore, but all is new and it has been designed efficiently
for business travelers. The boxlike rooms are large and everything works.
Equally important, the staff is really friendly and speaks good English.
⊠ *350 Ahlone Rd., Dagon Township,* ☎ *01/227966,* FAX *01/227993.
152 rooms. Restaurant, business services. AE, MC, V.*

$$$ 🏨 **Traders Hotel.** The Traders hotels, a division of the Shangri-La
★ group, are geared toward providing top-quality accommodation with-
out the frills (and concomitant price tag) of a five-star hotel. This 22-
story property has all the modern facilities, including 24-hour medical
service, and in-house movies. Four restaurants provide Burmese, Jap-
anese, international, Cantonese, and Italian cuisines. Guest rooms are
of ample size and while not memorable are comfortable and functional.
⊠ *Bogyoke Aung San Rd.,* ☎ *01/248927,* FAX *01/248226. 500 rooms.
4 restaurants, pool, health club, business services, meeting rooms. AE,
MC, V.*

$$ 🏨 **Thamada.** The management of this 1998 hotel, part of the New World
Group, is efficient and geared to meet business travelers' needs. Rooms
are compact, especially singles, but the feeling is one of cleanliness. The
location is quite convenient, across the boulevard from the central Railway station and a five-minute walk from the Traders Hotel. Prices are
negotiable, so don't pay the printed rate. ⊠ *5 Signal Pagoda Rd.,* ☎
01/243639, FAX *01/245001. 58 rooms. Restaurant. AE, DC, MC, V.*

Inle Lake

*Nyaung Shwe, the main lake town, is 23 km (14 mi) southwest of Taung-
gyi, the capital of the Shan state. Taunggyi is 350 km (217 mi) northeast of Rangoon, a 14-hour bus trip, and 150 km (93 mi) southeast of
Mandalay, an eight-hour trip.*

Surrounded by mountains in the Shan state, which borders Thailand,
Laos, and China, Inle Lake is one of the most beautiful in Asia. It is
magical and serene, and is often spoken of in the same breath as the
lakes of Kashmir. If beauty isn't attraction enough, the fascinating and
friendly inhabitants add human interest. This narrow body of water—

30 km (18 mi) north to south and only 8 km (5 mi) wide—supports nearly 200 villages with a total population of 150,000.

Although the lake is in the Shan state, those that live on its shores are not Shan, but a Mon people known as the **Intha** (Sons of the Lake). The Intha have developed an ingenious way of farming the lake: they weave the rubbery tubes of hyacinths and rushes into gigantic mats, then dredge fertile mud from the lake's bottom and lay on a layer of humus. This floating garden is then staked in the water near a family's home. They also fish, with a unique style that involves rowing and using a large conical net simultaneously. With one leg wrapped around the oar, an Intha fisherman is able to move through the hyacinths cluttering the lake while leaving one hand free to control the net. When the fisherman spots a shoal of fish, down goes the net, allowing him to spear dinner at his leisure.

Boats depart at about 8 AM for a five-hour tour past floating gardens, one-leg rowers, and small lakeshore communities. Most tour boats head for the village of Ywama, where once every five days there is a colorful floating market. This is the ideal day to take the tour, but you'll have to be persistent to find out which day the market is being held—the guides often claim that there is a market every day. There will be places to stop for refreshment and lunch and you will need to be firm with your boatman on just how many shops and artist studios you want to see. Take a hat to wear under the merciless midday sun. You can hire a boat through your hotel for about 1,000 kyats or buy a ticket on a public boat (US$4 per person) at the tourist office at the pier in Nyaung Shwe, which puts the money into the junta's pockets.

Dining and Lodging

¢ ✕ **Bigdrum.** Shan food is served in this thatched restaurant with plain wood floors, a bar, and a jukebox. Posters and maps on the wall add some color, but otherwise it is very plain. The food is good, however, and usually you can try the best of the fish caught in Inle Lake. If you are less adventurous, you can choose from the Chinese dishes on the menu. The restaurant is next to the Golden Duck and the Queen Lodging House. ✉ *Nyaung Shwe, Inle Lake,* ☎ *no phone. No credit cards.*

$ ▥ **Golden Express Hotel.** This small two-story hotel on a shady street has a front courtyard where you can park your bike, and provides you breakfast with your room. The proprietor speaks some English, and the rooms are bright, with shiny satin bedspreads, print curtains and colorful layers of linoleum. If you you stay in room 105 you can watch the procession of monks at dawn with their begging bowls. ✉ *Road to Pier,* ☎ *no phone. 11 rooms. Breakfast room. No credit cards.*

¢ ▥ **Gypsy Inn.** This small, family-owned hotel is across from the canal that leads into the lake and only 20 yards from the pier where the tour boats come and go. The owner, who built the house himself in 1995, is extremely friendly—giving guests rides on the back of his motorbike and running them to the airport (for a fee) when his car is free. Rooms are basic, but clean, and they do have a private shower. They tend to be dark and gloomy, but the hotel's balcony looking out to the canal more than makes up for that. Free breakfast is served in the morning; coffee, tea, and beer are available all day. ✉ *82 Canal Rd., Win Quarter, Nyaung Shwe,* ☎ *no phone. 11 rooms. No credit cards.*

Pagan

450 km (279 mi) north of Rangoon. 193 km (120 mi) southwest of Mandalay, a four-hour drive by car or six-hour trip by local bus.

On the banks of the Ayeyarwady river stands astonishing, extensive Pagan (also called Bagan), once the seat of the mighty Myanmar kingdom, established by King Anawrahta (1044–77), the 42nd ruler of the Pagan dynasty. Pagan was probably founded around 849, but its Golden Age began when Anawrahta defeated his rivals, primarily the Mons from the south, and expanded his borders to include most of present-day Burma. Wealth poured in, and the building of pagodas began. At the same time, Anawrahta introduced Theravada Buddhism, and he was wise enough to incorporate into the cosmic whole of Buddhism the worship of *nats* (guardians of the spirit world that were part of the traditional animist Burmese religion).

After about two centuries of dominance, the Pagan dynasty began to be eaten away by corruption. The final blow came when Kublai Khan, the great Mongol lord, demanded that Pagan pay tribute. Pagan's ruler, the pompous King Narathihapati (1256–87), refused, and executed the Khan's messenger. Kublai Khan's army attacked, and the Pagan royal family fled.

★ Today more than 2,000 stupas, shrines, and monasteries remain from the 6,000 built during the Pagan dynasty, covering an immense area of 10,000 acres (or about 16 square mi) now known as the **Pagan Archeological Zone.** So as not to tire of seeing yet another stupa or shrine, limit yourself to a few of the most interesting and best preserved, three of which we detail below. Admission to the Pagan Archeological Zone is US$10. Transport is either by hired car, rented bicycle, or bullock cart. The latter is romantic, but even well-padded bones begin to crunch after four hours.

The most famous monument in Pagan is the **Ananda Temple.** Erected in 1091, it was reconstructed after the devastating earthquake in 1979. The shrine represents the endless wisdom of Buddha. The central square has 175-ft sides and rises in terraces to 168 ft. In the center of the cube are four vestibules, each with a standing Buddha that is 31 ft high. These statues represent the four Buddhas who attained Nirvana prior to Guatama Buddha. Only the images facing north and south are original; the east- and west-facing images are replacements for figures destroyed by fires. The base and the terraces are decorated with a great number of glazed tiles showing scenes from the Jataka, as tales of Guatama Buddha's prior lives are called. In the western sanctum, there are life-size statues of the shrine's founder, Kyannzittha.

Tradition has it that a holy tooth, collarbone, and frontlet relics of the Buddha are enshrined in the **Shwezigon Pagoda.** The chronicles relate that the tooth was presented by the King of Ceylon, and that King Anawrahta placed the bone relic on a jeweled white elephant and, making a solemn vow, said, "Let the white elephant kneel in the place where the holy relic is fated to rest!" It was at Shwezigon that the elephant knelt, and that is where Anawrahta built the pagoda. Anawrahta used this shrine to assimilate the old worship of nats into the new faith of Buddhism. Inside the building are murals of nats riding mythical animals. On the terraces are plaques with scenes from the Jataka.

The highest shrine in Pagan is the 200-ft-tall **Thatbyinnyut Temple,** built in the mid-12th century and repaired in 1979 after the earthquake. To give some idea of the enormous undertaking of building this temple, note the small shrine to the northeast. Known as the "tally pagoda," it was built with one brick for every 10,000 used in the main shrine and is, in theory, one ten-thousandth its big brother's size.

Dining and Lodging

Dining options in Pagan are limited; the River View is your best bet for dinner. Several hotels are under construction, including one under the auspices of Bangkok's Oriental Hotel, but currently the choice is limited. For now the Kumadara is the top spot.

$$ ✕ **River View.** The tables here are outside, along the Ayeyarwady, and candles provide the light (it's hard to see what you are eating—go with the mood and have faith). The Burmese curries and fish dishes are nicely prepared—not as oily as you often find—but service can be slow. ☎ *062/70099. Reservations essential. No credit cards.*

$$ 🏨 **Kumadara.** Scattered around the small garden behind the main building of this 1996 property are three long structures that house the guest rooms. These accommodations are quite basic, but each has cheerful draperies and bedcovers, and a small balcony. The bathroom has a good shower, which usually streams hot water. The restaurant— in the main house with the bar and reception—has quite good food. ✉ *Dawna St., Pyu Saw Hte Quarter, Pagan,* ☎ *062/70080,* 𝖥𝖠𝖷 *01/97486 in Rangoon. 42 rooms. Restaurant, bar. No credit cards.*

$ 🏨 **Queen Saw Guest House.** This small guest house in the village of New Pagan (the area where, in 1990, villagers were forcibly relocated from the Archaeological Zone) is owned by a very friendly, if rather shy, Burmese couple. The fan-cooled rooms are clean—choose one with a terrace—and the bathrooms have lukewarm showers. ✉ *Shwe Laung Kyan Sittya, New Pagan, Nyaung U,* ☎ *062/70032. 8 rooms. Breakfast room. No credit cards.*

Mandalay

193 km (120 mi) northeast of Pagan, 580 km (360 mi) north of Rangoon. Bus routes radiate out of Mandalay, including a long-distance bus to Rangoon that takes about 13 hours. The train between Mandalay and Rangoon takes approximately 14 hours.

In 1857 King Mindon decided to fulfil a sacred prophecy that a great city would be built at the foot of Mandalay Hill on the eastern bank of the Ayeyarwady River. All signs were auspicious for a great capital, and the time seemed right: it was the 2,400th anniversary of the founding of the Buddhist faith. King Mindon designed his new capital as a fortified city in a form of a square, each side of which was 10 furlongs (2,200 yards) in length. It is said that, following tradition, the king had 52 people buried alive beneath the four corners of the site to become guardians of the city. More prosaic protection was afforded by a moat, 225 ft wide and 11 ft deep. The battlements were made of brick and mud and rose to a height of 25 ft. Entrance was through 12 gates, three on each side and equidistant from one another. In the center was the king's palace. Four years after the foundations were laid, King Mindon moved his capital and his court, plus 15,000 of his subjects, from Amarapura to Mandalay.

The city's guardians, however, did not do their job: the British attacked the city 25 years later and annexed all of Upper Burma. Mindon's palace, renamed Fort Dufferin, became the British colonial barracks. Later, the Japanese made the palace their command headquarters, which prompted the British to drop bombs on it, and the ensuing fire destroyed a third of the city. For the next 40 years, the grounds and moat became not much more than a garbage dump. It wasn't until 1996 that the moat was cleaned out, largely in an effort to promote tourism and the "Visit Myanmar Year" campaign; the labor was provided by conscripted locals and chained convicts.

Part of the **Royal Palace,** in the center of the city, is also being partially reconstructed in cement at great expense and should offer an idea of what the original looked like. A sense of the beauty of the old palace can be gleamed from the scale model, made in 1952 and kept in an iron cage to the west of the old palace. The Lion Throne and several tons of regalia are in the National Museum in Rangoon.

The **Shwe Nandaw Kyaung** (Golden Palace Monastery) was the only palace of King Mindon that escaped bombing in World War II. It had been moved from the fortified city's grounds after King Mindon had inauspiciously died in it. This spectacular building is made of carved teak and mosaics. Inside it is held up by pillars, each a single trunk of teak. The original lacquering and gilding can still be seen on the pillars and walls. ⊠ *62nd St., south of Mandalay Hill and due west of Fort Mandalay.* ⌧ *Admission.* ⊙ *Daily 8–4.*

Near the foot of Mandalay Hill is the **Kyauktawgyi Pagoda,** famous for its huge Buddha statue carved from a single block of marble. Near the Kyauktawgyi Pagoda is the **Kuthadaw Pagoda,** built in 1857. King Mindon wanted to make Mandalay the world center of Buddhism, and he built the complex to house the entire Tripitaka, the Buddhist scriptures. These are inscribed on marble slabs and enshrined in 729 miniature pagodas. For this reason, the Kuthadaw is often referred to as the world's largest book.

The religious heart of Mandalay is the **Mahamuni Pagoda,** on the south side of town, which houses Mandalay's most venerated image of the Buddha. According to the Burmese, the image is one of only five that were molded to the actual likeness of Guatama Buddha. However, so much gold leaf has been affixed to the statue by the thousands of devotees who pay their respects each day that the shape of the body is now distorted. Only the gleaming, polished bronze face remains untouched. The approach to the shrine is lined with stalls and astrologers' booths. Follow the lines of pilgrims to the small room where the venerated Mahamuni image sits. Only men are permitted in this room; women must go off to the side and look upon the Buddha from a balcony. Pick up some gold leaf before you enter, and as you walk around the image, apply it to the surface. ⊠ *84th St., 5 km (3 mi) south of Fort Mandalay.* ⌧ *Admission.* ⊙ *Daily 8–5.*

Lodging

$$$ ⊞ **Novotel.** After renovations, this arc-shape building is now one of Burma's better modern hotels. Large, functional guest rooms have modern bathrooms and picture windows that face the hotel's gardens or Mandalay Hill (those at the back have the best view, with a pagoda or two in the distance). The "superior" rooms are even larger and worth the extra price. The hotel's best feature is a restaurant where the influence of the French management prevails. It's the only place in Mandalay to eat good European food; you may also want to try the Burmese buffet at lunch, where an array of dishes offers a crash course in the nation's cuisine. ⊠ *Oo Boke Taw Quarter, Aung Myea Township,* ☎ *02/35638,* 𝔽𝔸𝕏 *02/35671. 215 rooms. 2 restaurants, pool, health club, business services. AE, MC, V.*

Amarapura

19 km (12 mi) south of Mandalay.

Until King Mindon moved his court to Mandalay, Amarapura (the City of Immortals) was the capital of Upper Burma. Not much is left of the old town—a new township has taken its place. Most of the important buildings were dismantled and reassembled in Mandalay.

It's worth spending a couple of hours at the **U Bien Bridge.** The two-century-old footbridge, made from teak planks salvaged from yet another former capital, Ava, crosses the Taung Thaman lake. If you make the 1.2-km (¾-mi) hike, your reward will be the charming **Kyauk-tawgyi Pagoda,** with its immense jade Buddha inside. After you see the pagoda you can hang around the beginning of the bridge, where Burmese families come for afternoon picnics or eat at one of the several outdoor restaurants.

Ava

10 km (6 mi) southwest of Mandalay.

A few miles downriver from Mandalay stands what remains of Ava, one of the three cities around Mandalay that formerly served as capitals. In 1364, sometime after the fall of Pagan, Ava became the capital and remained the most important town in Upper Burma for the next four centuries. The city was largely demolished by an 1838 earthquake, and what did remain was dismantled and taken to Amarapura. Still discernible are the Namyin Watch Tower and some city walls. Only the **Maha Aungmye Bonzan monastery,** built of brick and stucco, remains intact, glaring white in the sun, but of little interest inside.

Sagaing

16 km (10 mi) west of Mandalay, across the Ayeyarwady River.

With a dozen monasteries and nunneries and 600 pagodas, Sagaing is regarded as the religious center of Burma. To reach the city, you'll travel across the 2,400-ft Ava Bridge, built by the British in 1934 and still the only bridge to cross the Ayeyarwady. (A new bridge is being built at Pyay, halfway between Rangoon and Mandalay.) Sagaing is a township, once the capital of an independent Shan state, and the area around it is known as the Sagaing Hills. On the tops and crests of these hills are the religious centers, some of which have tremendous views overlooking the Ayeyarwady. One of the best views is from **Soon U Ponya Pagoda** on Shin Bin Man Kai hill.

The largest of the pagodas is **Kaungmudaw,** built in 1636 by King Thalun and said to contain a tooth and strands of hair from the Buddha. Its perfectly hemispherical dome rises 150 ft; some government guides claim that it was modeled after the Mahaceti Stupa in Sri Lanka, although the more pragmatic of them suggest it represents the perfect and ample breast of King Thalun's favorite queen. Around the base of the stupa are 812 stone pillars, each of which has a small hollow for an oil lamp. At one time these lights illuminated the huge dome. Also around the base are 120 niches containing the images of nats. Over the last nine centuries, Buddhist kings and governments have tried to downplay the role of nats, but their worship is so embedded in Burmese culture that appeasing the nats is still part of everyday life.

The **Hsinmyashin Pagoda,** known as the Elephant Pagoda, is between the town of Sagaing and Kaungmudaw. Twenty-foot-high elephants stand guard at the gates of the temple, built in 1429 to house religious relics brought from Sri Lanka. They fell down on the job in 1985, when they failed to prevent the wrath of an earthquake. Much of the pagoda has since been restored, and it's one of the few where you can enter the relic chamber to see the display of votive tablets and images.

Mingun

13 km (8 mi) north of Mandalay by boat.

A popular day trip out of Mandalay is the hour-long boat ride up the Ayeyarwady to Mingun. Boats leave from Mandalay's Ma Yan Chan jetty from 8 AM on. You can either hire your own boat for about 1,000 kyats or take a public boat for 100 kyats. The hour on the river goes quickly as you pass by fishing communities on the riverbanks and bamboo rafts floating downriver to destinations as far off as Rangoon.

King Bodawpaya, the predecessor to King Mindon, was pleased with himself. He had expanded his kingdom by conquering Arakan. To celebrate, he had 20,000 Arakanese slaves build what was to be the biggest pagoda in the world, the **Mingun Pagoda.** He ran out of cash by 1819 and abandoned the project with a long way to go before reaching its projected 500-ft height. Nevertheless, with each of its four sides measuring 450 ft, it was and still is the largest brick-base structure in the world. You can climb the 150 ft to the unfinished top for the views, but it's really just the sheer mass of this vanity that's impressive.

As part of his grandiose aspirations, King Bodawpaya commissioned a **bell** for his pagoda. Finished in 1790 and hung on teak uprights, the bell weighed approximately 100 tons. It proved too much for the teak supports, and the 1838 earthquake brought it to the ground. Now, hung on chains and housed in a small shed, it remains the largest uncracked bell in the world. (One larger, flawed bell is in Moscow.) Give the bell a tap and hear its superb resonance.

The most charming structure in Mingun is the **Hsinbyame Pagoda,** built in 1816 by Bagyidaw, King Bodawpaya's grandson, in memory of his wife. He loved her beyond all else and was terribly upset by her death. It's a long way up the covered staircase to the shrine, an ascent you should think of as climbing Mount Meru, the center of the earth in Buddhist cosmology. Your earthly reward will be breathtaking views of the village below and of the timeless flow of the Ayeyarwady.

Burma A to Z

Arriving and Departing
BY AIRPLANE
The only way into Burma, other than by stepping off the occasional cruise ship or visiting a border town over the Thai frontier, is by plane. **Rangoon Airport** is on the northern edge of town, a 500 kyats ($4) taxi ride from downtown.

Carriers. Thai International Airways (☎ 02/234–3100 in Bangkok) has two daily flights from Bangkok to Rangoon; round-trip fare is around US$230. **Myanma Airways** (☎ 02/630–0338 in Bangkok) also flies between Bangkok and Rangoon for the same price. **Malaysia Airways,** in partnership with Myanma Airways, offers three flights a week from Kuala Lumpur to Rangoon; a round-trip ticket costs about US$180. A new route between Chiang Mai and Mandalay is operated by **Air Mandalay** (☎ 02/271–4375 in Bangkok), which makes the flight three times a week; round-trip fares cost around US$220.

At press time, there were no nonstop flights to Burma from North America or Britain, although several major airlines (among them British Airways, Lufthansa, and JAL) were in negotiations.

Getting Around
BY AIRPLANE
Government-owned **Myanma Airways** (✉ 77–91 Sule Pagoda Rd., Yangon, ☎ 01/283997), the privately owned **Air Mandalay** (✉ 146 Damazedi Rd., Bahan Township, Yangon, ☎ 01/525488), and **Yangon Airways** (✉ 22–24 Pamsodan St., Yangon, ☎ 01/250821) connect Burma's tourist destinations. There are direct flights from both Mandalay and Rangoon to Pagan and to Heho, the airport nearest Inle

Lake, 40 km (24 mi) from Taunggyi and 18 km (11 mi) from Nyaung Shwe. Air Mandalay has the best reputation of the three.

BY BUS OR CAR

Regularly scheduled buses run between Burma's towns and cities. Self-drive rental cars are not available, but you can hire cars with a driver. Travel agencies and tour operators can make the arrangements. The cost is about $40 to $50 a day; the driver will appreciate a gratuity of $5 a day. Roads are generally paved between the major destinations covered in this chapter. Off the main roads and in the Pagan Archaeological Area Area, expect gravel and potholes.

BY TRAIN

Tickets need to be purchased in advance. There is no first class on the train. Seats recline slightly in second class.

Contacts and Resources

CUSTOMS AND DUTIES

Tourists may bring into Burma 200 cigarettes, 50 cigars or ½ lb of tobacco, one quart of spirits, and one pint of perfume or eau de cologne. You are allowed to bring pets that are accompanied by health certificates. You may import unlimited amounts of foreign currency, but no local currency (kyats). The export of religious artifacts requires a permit, and you must show the bill of sale for any precious stones you are taking out of the country.

ELECTRICITY

The electrical current in Burma is 220 volts AC, 50Hz. You can expect occasional blackouts.

EMBASSIES AND CONSULATES

British Embassy (✉ Box 638, 80 Strand Rd., Yangon, ☎ 01/295300, FAX 01/289566). **Embassy of the United States of America** (✉ Box 521, 581 Merchant St., Yangon, ☎ 01/282055-9 or 01/282182, FAX 01/280409). Australia, Canada, and New Zealand are represented by the British Embassy.

EMERGENCIES

Ask your hotel or tour operator first for help in the case of medical and police emergencies. Provincial towns have clinics, but major medical emergencies are best attended to in Mandalay or Rangoon. Try the **Rangoon General Hospital,** an historic landmark (✉ Bogyoke Aung San St., ☎ 01/281722), or the **Diplomatic Hospital** (✉ Kyaikkasan Rd., ☎ 01/250149). Better yet, get back to Thailand for hospital treatment. If your passport is stolen or lost, notify your embassy immediately. The emergency telephone numbers in Rangoon are: ambulance, 192; fire, 101; police, 199.

HEALTH AND SAFETY

Don't drink tap water; bottled water is readily available. Stick to foods that are cooked. Crime is very rarely directed against foreigners, though the military police may shake you down for a bribe. Beware of people who want to talk politics. It is said that one out of eight Burmese is an informer for the military junta.

LANGUAGE, CULTURE, AND ETIQUETTE

The national language, Burmese, uses a non-Roman phonetic alphabet that is exceedingly difficult to comprehend, let alone read or write. Speaking Burmese is equally difficult, since it is tonal; in that regard it is similar to Thai. An amazing number of Burmese, particularly those in the travel industry, speak English. Burmese are very conservative in their dress: always smart and neat, never flaunting nakedness. Tourists should follow suit, especially in religious places—no short shorts or sleeveless shirts, for example. Shoes and socks should be removed before entering a temple. Feet are always seen as being a repository for bad things, so as in Thailand, it is insulting to point your feet at anyone and ill-mannered to put your feet on top of furniture. Never touch a person's head or the head of a Buddha image. So far, in Burma there's no discernible accommodation for or recognition of homosexuals. Discretion is evidently the rule, and public affection, hetero- or homo-, is frowned on.

MAIL

The easiest way to send mail in Burma is to hand it to your hotel reception clerk, who will often have postage stamps, too. In Yangon you can drop it in the pillar-boxes at the corners of all main roads and streets. The Central Post Office is at 39 Bo Aung Kyaw Street, at the corner of Strand Road. Mail is collected at 11 AM and 2 PM. Airmail letters (preprinted, prestamped forms, 3.50 kyats each) can be mailed anywhere. Basic overseas postage: Yangon to Australia/Canada/New Zealand/U.K./U.S. is 5 kyats. Yangon to Thailand/Hong Kong/Japan/Taiwan/Korea/Malaysia/Singapore is 4 kyats. All post offices are open weekdays 9:30–4:30. Addresses usually contain the block number of the office or housing unit, followed by the street, and then the township, which is often a subdistrict of the major city.

MONEY MATTERS

Costs. Burma can be surprisingly expensive. International-style hotels charge $150 and up for a double room, and even budget hotels with not much more than a cot and a shared bath charge as much as $30 in Rangoon. Air travel within Burma is expensive for foreigners; fares between Rangoon and Mandalay are approximately $100. However, bus and rail travel is very inexpensive—and uncomfortable. Taxis run about 100 kyats per kilometer. Local beer (Mandalay is the best) costs 180 kyats in a local café. At a hotel, an imported beer will cost about $4.

Currency. Burmese currency comes in kyats (pronounced chi-ats). Notes include the following denominations: 5, 10, 15, 20, 45, 50, 90, 10, and 500. (The 45 and 90 banknotes were the inspiration of Ne Win, who considered those numbers to be lucky.)

The official rate of exchange is 6 kyats to the U.S. dollar, the only western currency in common circulation. However, tourists may use cash or traveler's checks to purchase Foreign Trading Certificates (FTCs), on a one-dollar-to-one-FTC basis. These certificates may then be cashed at international hotels for about 175 kyats each. Most international hotels require guests to pay their bills in dollars or FTCs. Airline tickets also must be paid for in U.S. dollars or FTCs.

Independent travelers are required to change US$300 into FTCs immediately upon arrival. This is the minimum amount to be spent by a tourist during his or her stay in the country, and any unused FTCs out of this amount will not be reconverted. Any unused FTCs in excess of US$300 can be reconverted at the time of departure on presentation of the "Foreign Exchange Certificates Voucher" at the Foreign Exchange Counters. Those traveling on prepaid package tours are exempt from this requirement. (The type of Burmese visa in your passport informs immigration whether you are on a tour or not.)

Then there's the black market (really more of a gray market), where you can get an exchange rate of about 185 kyats to the U.S. dollar. (Other currencies and travelers checks are almost never accepted.) You cannot change kyats back into dollars. Most independent travelers change the minimum required amount into FTCs and use the black market to convert dollars into kyats for any remaining needs.

Credit cards are rarely accepted, except at international hotels. ATMs are *not* linked to such networks as Cirrus and Plus; it is possible to obtain cash from a bank with a MasterCard or Visa, but the rate of exchange is poor, the commission fees are high, and the paperwork is time-consuming.

Service Charges, Taxes, and Tipping. Government tax is 10% on hotels and restaurants. A service charge of 10% is added to the bill in tourist hotels. Tipping is not a widespread custom in Burma, but there are times when a gratuity is expected: a bellboy would like 100 kyats to take your luggage to your room, and the driver of your car may expect 500 kyats per day.

OPENING AND CLOSING TIMES

Offices tend to be open weekdays 9:30–4:30. Similar hours are kept by museums. Banks are open weekdays 10–2. Official holidays in 1999 are Independence Day (Jan. 4); Union Day (Feb. 12); Peasant's Day (Mar. 2); Armed Forces Day (Mar. 27); Thingyan (Apr. 13—Water Festival and Myanmar New Year); May Day (May 1—Workers Day); Martyrs' Day (July 19); National Day (Nov. 2); Christmas Day (Dec. 25).

PASSPORTS AND VISAS

All foreign nationals need a visa. Visitors from North America, Great Britain, Australia, and New Zealand can obtain a 30-day tourist visa within 48 hours from most embassies and consulates. The cost is approximately $10. Contact the **Union of Myanmar embassies** (✉ 2300 S St. NW, Washington, DC 20008, ☎ 202/332–9044; ✉ 10 E. 77th St., New York, NY 10021, ☎ 212/535–1310).

TELEPHONES

To call Burma from overseas, dial the country code, 95, and then the area code, omitting the first 0. Calling Burma is expensive—about $7 a minute from Pacific Rim countries, North America, and Europe. Phoning out of Burma is exceedingly expensive and time-consuming as there are not sufficient international lines available. Many of the international hotels have access to international lines, but, as they warn you, expect to pay through the nose. Burmese citizens must book overseas calls and are limited to five minutes per call. Public telephones, available at the airports, railway stations, and department stores, are only good for domestic calls. Coins are used. When calling long distance from inside Burma, dial the "O" of the area code.

TOUR OPERATORS AND TRAVEL AGENCIES

Abercrombie & Kent (✉ 4th floor, Silom Plaza, 491/29-30 Silom Rd., Bangkok 10500, ☎ 02/266–7660, FAX 02/266–7854; ✉ 1520 Kensington Rd., Suite 212, Oak Brook, IL 60521, ☎ 630/954–2944 or 800/323–7308, FAX 630/954–3324) arranges custom trips through Burma, including cruises up and down the Ayeyarwady.

Journeys International (✉ 4011 Jackson Rd., Ann Arbor, MI 48103, ☎ 313/255–8735 or 800/255–8735) has 8- and 15-day tours as well as group packages for five to 28 people. Unlike many U.S. tour operators, they do not use government guides, vehicles, and hotels—a plus in my book.

A very special, albeit expensive, way to visit the sights of Pagan and Mandalay is by taking the river cruise ship, *The Road to Mandalay*, operated and owned by the **Orient-Express Hotels, Trains, & Cruises** (☎ 800/5242420, U.S.; 0171/620–0003, U.K., FAX 0171/620–1210), the same company that operates the luxury train between Singapore and Bangkok. The ship, originally used on the Rhine, accommodates 138 passengers in 72 air-conditioned cabins, with en suite bathrooms and personal safes. On board there is a dining room (dress for dinner, please), swimming pool, and bar. The ship makes the day-and-a-half run on the Ayeyarwady between Mandalay and Pagan; you sleep on board for the two nights that it is berthed in Mandalay and two in Pagan. All sightseeing tours with guides are in the package.

VISITOR INFORMATION
If asked, the Union of Myanmar embassies (☞ Passports and Visas, *above*) will forward basic tourist information along with your visa application. The Burmese ministry of tourism is an arm of the SLORC and is not set up to assist travelers.

WHEN TO GO
The cool season is from late November through February, with temperatures in the 70°–85°F (22°–30°C) range. The hot season is March and April, when the mercury can peak at 110°F (46°C). May to October is the rainy season, which often makes the up-country roads impassable for a day or two.

The best festival is Thingyan, the Water Festival, which celebrates the Burmese New Year in April. The Burmese get carried away in dousing each other and being doused with water, and for three days the country comes practically to a standstill.

CAMBODIA

As the seat of the Khmer empire from the 9th to the 13th century, Cambodia developed a complex society based first on Hinduism and then on Buddhism. After the decline of the Khmers and the ascendancy of the Siamese, Cambodia was colonized by the French in the 19th century and became part of Indochina. Shortly after the end of World War II, during which the Japanese had occupied Cambodia, independence became the rallying cry for all of Indochina. Cambodia became a sovereign power with a monarchy and an elected government.

In the early '70s, the destabilizing consequences of the Vietnam War led Cambodia's political factions to take up arms. A very bloody civil war ensued, with the barbaric Khmer Rouge, under the French-educated Pol Pot, emerging as victors. A regime of terror followed. Under a program of Mao Tse Tsung–inspired re-education centered around forced agricultural collectives, hundreds of thousands of Cambodians died through torture and execution or from malnutrition and exhaustion in the camps.

Vietnam, unified under the Hanoi government, eventually intervened, partially defeated the Khmer Rouge, and brought back Prince Sihanouk as head of state. The United Nations was brought in as a peacekeeping force, and in 1996 a government was formed through democratic elections. In 1997, Hun Sen toppled the elected government, but political pressure forced new elections—monitored by the international community—in late summer 1998. Hun Sen won a plurality amid charges of election rigging and, through coercive tactics, formed a government. After the death of Pol Pot in mid-1998, the Khmer Rouge presence and its threat to the country's stability diminished. It remains to be seen whether foreign investment and the development of tourism will follow, whether domestic problems will be solved, and how the international community will accept Hun Sen's hard-line rule.

Great Itinerary
Though four days in **Siem Reap** would give the opportunity for a leisurely appreciation of the Khmer complexes at **Angkor,** most people limit their stay to two days and one night. The new Bangkok–Siem

Reap flight may change that. One day and night in **Phnom Penh** may be enough time to give a brief view of the city, but flight connections may require you to spend one night in Phnom Penh on the way to Siem Reap and one night on your return.

Phnom Penh

As the capital of the Kingdom of Cambodia, Phnom Penh is strategically positioned in the center of the country at the confluence of four branches of the Mekong River. Though it was founded in 1434, Phnom Penh is a small city with only a million inhabitants. There are only a few notable sights, which you can easily cover in a morning.

According to legend, a wealthy woman named Penh found four statues of the Buddha washed up on the banks of the Mekong, and in 1372 she commissioned a sanctuary to house them. **Wat Phnom,** Penh's temple, stands on a 90-ft knoll, visible from all parts of the city to which it gave its name—Phnom Penh means "Hill of Penh."

The **Royal Palace,** now the home of Prince Sihanouk, is a 1913 reconstruction of the one built in 1886. Though the royal palace itself is closed to the public, **Wat Phra Keo** (Temple of the Emerald Buddha), in the southern courtyard of the palace grounds, is open. The temple is often referred to as the Silver Pagoda because of the 5,000 silver blocks (6 tons of pure silver) that make up the floor. At the back of the temple is the venerated **Emerald Buddha**—some say it's carved from jade, while others hold that it's Baccarat crystal. Nearby is a 200-pound, solid-gold Buddha studded with 10,000 diamonds. Along the wall of the courtyard enclosing the temple complex are murals depicting scenes from the *Ramayana.* ⊙ *Tues.–Sun. 7–11 and 2–5.*

If the Silver Pagoda is a tribute to Cambodia and its civilization, the **Toul Sleng Holocaust Museum** is a horrific reminder of the cruelty humans are capable of. Once a neighborhood school, the building was seized in 1975 by Pol Pot's Khmer Rouge and turned into a prison; during its four years of operation as an interrogation center, some 20,000 Cambodians were tortured here. Fewer than 10 prisoners survived. The bodies of those that died under torture were tossed into the school's garden and playing fields; those that survived the torture went to the extermination camp outside of town called **Choeung Ek,** now known as the Killing Fields. A memorial stupa stands at Choeung Ek, 14 km (9 mi) southwest of Phnom Penh, filled with the skulls of Cambodians exhumed from the mass graves. ⊙ *Daily 8–11 and 2–5.*

The **National Museum,** a red building constructed in 1917 in the Khmer style, contains the nation's treasure of archaeological finds, from the pre-Angkor periods of Funan and Chenia (5th–9th centuries), the Indravarman period (9th–10th centuries), the classical Angkor period (10th–13th centuries), and the post-Angkor period up to the present. ⊙ *Tues.–Sun. 8–11 and 2–5.*

Lodging

Since most of the United Nations security forces have left Cambodia, accommodation at hotels in Phnom Penh has become easier to find. The Sofitel-managed **Cambodiana** (✉ 313 Sisowath Quay, ☎ 023/26288; U.S., 800/221–4542; ℻ 023/855–26290) is the best property. There is also the **Royal Phnom Penh,** close to the Mekong River, under the same management as the Raffles in Singapore. The rooms, at about $150, are completely refurbished, and the hotel has the good fortune to be set among beautifully tended gardens (✉ 26 August Site, Samdech Sothearoh Blvd. Sankat Tonle Bassac, ☎ 023/60026, ℻ 023/60036).

Shopping

While in Phnom Penh, find some time to visit a market or two. The largest is the **Central Market,** an art deco–style structure in the center of the city that sells foodstuffs, household goods, fake antiques, and some silver and gold jewelry; it's most active in the morning. **O Russel Market** has lots of food stalls and small shops selling jewelry. For serious shopping, go to **Tuol Tom Pong Market,** which has real and fake antiques, carved-wood furniture, and small Buddha statues.

Siem Reap

314 km (196 mi) north of Phnom Penh.

Siem Reap, meaning "Siam Defeated," is a small market town that has become a base for visits to the Khmer monuments at Angkor. During the Khmer Rouge era of the late 1970s, Siem Reap was largely destroyed and abandoned. With the Khmer Rouge's retreat into the jungles, hotels have reopened and the accommodation and feeding of visitors is becoming big business.

Angkor Temple Complex

★ *8 km (5 mi) north of Siem Reap.*

If Angkor had been discovered before the late 19th century, it certainly would have been classified as one of the Seven Wonders of the World. The Khmer Empire reached the zenith of its power, influence, and creativity from the 9th to 13th centuries, and Angkor, the seat of the Khmer kings, was one of the largest capitals in Southeast Asia. In all there are some 300 monuments scattered in all directions through the surrounding jungle. Only the largest and best preserved are mentioned here. Admission to the complex costs $20 per day.

If you are very energetic, only have one day, and want to cover as much as possible, then visit Angkor Thom and its two vast temple complexes, Bayon and Baphuon, in the early morning hours. Visit Ta Prohm, a wonderful 12th-century temple that has receded back into the jungle, by midday, and by midafternoon be at Angkor Wat, which faces west and is best seen and photographed as the sun sinks.

To get around, you need to hire transport and a guide. It's best to link up with a group traveling in a minivan, but you can hire a car and driver in Siem Reap for about $50 a day. Bicycles may be rented, but make sure that you know where you are going. *Never* stray off the beaten paths—live land mines still dot the area.

Angkor Thom

Angkor Thom was the last great Khmer City before the empire began to fall apart in the 13th century. The **Bayon** is the mystical and focal heart of the former capital, built by King Jayavarman VII (reigned 1181–1200). The central tower has 53 secondary towers, on each of which are four huge, strangely smiling faces of Bhodisattava Avalokitecvara in the likeness of Jayavarman. On the outer walls of the central sanctuary and on the inner walls of the laterite enclosure are marvelous bas-reliefs—1½ km (¾ mi) of them in all. On the outer walls, the depictions are of common man pursuing his mundane life; on the inner walls, the gods do legendary deeds.

The **Baphuon** was built in the 12th century, shortly before Bayon, by King Udayadityavarman II (reigned 1050–66). This is a fine example of poor planning: inferior architects erected the monument on a hill without the proper supports. When the earth shifted, collapse was inevitable. Much of what is there today is collapsed stone forming a chaotic ruin in the form of a pyramid with remarkable stone reliefs. Walk out past the moats and through the southeastern gate and you'll enter the Royal Enclosure. This vast rectangular yard was the epicenter of the Angkor empire. At the northeastern corner is what was perhaps a cremation tower, but is now known as the Terrace of Leper King. The 23-ft-high platform is carved with *apsaras* (dancing maidens) and mythological animals known to have inhabited the upper slopes of Mt. Meru, the Hindu and Buddhist center of the cosmos. To the north is the Terrace of the Elephants, which was used as a reviewing stand. The walls, measuring 1,150 ft long with a height of 10 ft, are sculpted with scenes showing hunting elephants, water buffalos, and lions.

Ta Prohm

Ta Prohm, between Baphuon and Angkor, has been kept more or less as it was when French explorers rediscovered Angkor at the end of the 19th century. Vines twist through pillars, and trees black out the sun. Here you can easily be transported back 800 years to the time when King Jayavarman VII had this structure built to honor his mother. Though you wouldn't know it today, this complex had 566 stone dwellings, 39 major sanctuaries, 18 chief abbots, 2,740 priests, 2,202 assistants, and 615 dancing girls to assist the priests. With all the sounds of the jungle around you and knotted trees contending for space, you can easily become lost and bewildered. Don't stray too far!

Angkor Wat

In the typical architectural art of the Khmers, the plan of Angkor Wat is simple and audacious. The five towers are the central element of the complex, forming a lotus bud (the emblem of the Cambodian flag). The reliefs of the lower gallery show scenes of daily life and war. The celebrated apsaras, or dancing ladies, surround the monument.

Angkor Wat was founded at the beginning of the 12th century and is the best preserved of the Khmer temples. It was erected by King Suryavarman II (reigned 1112–52) and dedicated to the Hindu god Vishnu. Like all the major monuments at Angkor, the buildings form a complex representing the Hindu (and Buddhist) universe. The central shrines symbolize Mt. Meru, while the gates and cloisters depict the successive outer reaches of cosmic reality. Moats represent the seven oceans that surround Mt. Meru.

Angkor Wat is reached by an impressive causeway, an avenue lined with balustrades in the form of serpents. The complex itself rises in three concentric enclosures and you must wander around the terraces marveling at the Hindu deities and Buddha images, many of which lost their heads to looters. The other amazing collection of images is sculpted on the 1-km- (½-mi-) long open colonnaded gallery. This collection tells the Hindu epics and Suryavarman's earthly deeds, both of which are celebrated by dancing apsaras.

Architecture and the fine reliefs symbolize the richness, power, and prosperity of the Khmer empire during this period, but such was the tremendous outlay required to build Angkor Wat that it nearly bankrupted the empire. It took 30 years to recover, and it was King Jayavarman VII who had the energy to revitalize the kingdom. Breaking with the established Hindu gods, he adopted Buddhism.

Banteay Srei

If you have the time, visit Banteay Srei (Citadel of Women), northeast of Angkor Wat, a magnificent 10th-century temple dedicated to Shiva. The fine sculptures of rosy sandstone are surprisingly realistic.

Dining and Lodging

Hotel builders always rush to fill a vacuum, even before need, and so there's a variety of new accommodations on the airport road and in Siem Reap proper, ranging from budget guest houses and stylish renovations to the luxurious palace we review.

$$$$ ✕⚏ **Grand Hotel d'Angkor.** This grande dame, built in 1930 and long fallen on hard times, was occupied by Khmer Rouge guerillas and then by the Vietnamese army. Now it has had a $30-million rejuvenation by Singapore-based Raffles International, and it's open for business, complete with gorgeous gardens, silken fabrics, and luxury throughout. ✉ *1 Vithel Charles de Gaulle,* ☎ *063/963888,* 𝔽𝔸𝕏 *063/963168. 150 rooms. Restaurant, travel services. MC, V.*

Cambodia A to Z

Arriving and Departing

BY AIRPLANE

Thai Airways International (☎ 023/855–232711 in Phnom Penh; 66/02/234–3100 in Bangkok) flies daily between Bangkok and Pochentong (PNH), Phnom Penh's International airport, 10 km (6 mi) from the city. Flights are quite heavily booked, so try to reserve in advance. **Bangkok Airways** (☎ 023/427429 in Phnom Penh; 02/229–3456 in Bangkok) and **Royal Air Cambodge** (☎ 023/428891 in Phnom Penh; 02/653–2261 in Bangkok), also fly this route. Royal Air Cambodge also operates internationally to Kuala Lumpur, Singapore, Ho Chi Minh City and Hong Kong. **Malaysia Airlines** flies from Kuala Lumpur; **Vietnam Airlines** from Hanoi and Ho Chi Minh City. **Lao Aviation** (☎ 021/212050 in Vientiane) flies from Vientiane. **Bangkok Airways** (☎ 063/380191 in Siem Reap) flies daily direct from Bangkok to Siem Reap. A tax of US$20 is levied on all international departures.

BY BUS OR CAR

Road travel between Phnom Penh and Ho Chi Minh City, Vietnam, either by hired car or by bus, poses no problem; it is only a matter of time and rough, bumpy travel. The bus trip is certainly cheap—approximately $10—and in four hours you're at the Vietnamese border. You walk across and get another bus on the other side for a five-hour ride to Ho Chi Minh City. You can hire a car and driver at most travel agencies or from the General Directorate of Tourism in Phnom Penh (☎ 023/426107) for about $50 for the trip to the border, but it is not always easy to find a car in Vietnam to take you to Ho Chi Minh City.

Getting Around

The road to Siem Reap from Phnom Penh is open, but most travelers find it more comfortable to fly. The truly intrepid can also go by riverboat up to Siem Reap. Government-run ferries depart from the Psar Cha Ministry of Transport Ferry Landing between 102 and 104 streets, and go to Kompong Cham, Kratie, Stung Treng, Kompong Chanang and Phnom Krom. Because of the present rise in crime, intercity boat travel should be restricted to the fast boats to Kompong Cham and Kratie. You can take buses (or a hired car) to the southern towns on the Gulf of Siam, and it is also possible, by way of bus and ferry, to enter Thailand's Trat province. Those planning such a trip should inquire in Phnom Penh about conditions, for they are continually changing.

Buses to Phnom Penh suburbs leave from the bus station at 182 Street (open 5:30 AM–7:30 PM). Cruising taxis are nonexistent, but service taxis can be hired at the Psar Chabam Pao Shared-Taxi Station between 367 Street and 369 Street. Few drivers speak English, but some remember their French, especially those found outside main hotels. Visitors can arrange to hire cars with a driver, with or without air-conditioning, from the General Directorate of Tourism for about US$40–US$50 per day.

Contacts and Resources

CUSTOMS AND DUTIES

Tourists are allowed to bring into Cambodia 200 cigarettes, 50 cigars or ½ pound of tobacco, and one quart of alcoholic liquor. You are not allowed to bring in or take out local currency. The export of antiques or religious objects requires a permit.

ELECTRICITY

Electrical current is 220 volts AC, 50Hz. Power cuts are frequent. Outside Phnom Penh, electrical power is provided only from around 6:30 PM to 9:30 PM.

EMBASSIES AND CONSULATES

Australian Embassy (✉ Villa II, Street 254, Chartaumuk, Daun Penh District, Phnom Penh, ☎ 023/426000/1). **British Embassy** (✉ 29 Street 75, Phnom Penh, ☎ 023/427124). Canadians should use the services of the Australian Embassy. New Zealanders should use the services of the British Embassy. **Embassy of the United States of America** (✉ 27 EO Street 240, Phnom Penh, ☎ 023/426436/8).

EMERGENCIES

For medical and police emergencies, use the services of your hotel. The best advice if you do get sick is to get back to Thailand as fast as possible, but if you wish to consult an English-speaking doctor, visit Dr. Gavin Scott at the Tropical & Travellers Medical Clinic (✉ 88 Street 108, Wat Phnom Quarter, Phnom Penh 3, ☎ 023/366802, mobile 015/912100). In the case of a lost passport, immediately notify your embassy.

HEALTH AND SAFETY

About a quarter of a million people enter Cambodia every year, either as tourists or on business. Although travel in parts of Cambodia is not advised—the killings and kidnappings of a number of Western tourists in recent years attest that remnants of the Khmer Rouge still roam the forests—neither Phnom Penh nor the Khmer ruins at Angkor are considered particularly dangerous. You are advised to drink bottled water and avoid uncooked food and vegetables. Cambodia's security is not especially efficient, and you're asking for trouble if you walk the streets alone at night or put your trust in the smiling hustler who knows all the right phrases to convey such interest in your well-being.

LANGUAGE, CULTURE, AND ETIQUETTE

The Cambodian language is based on the Khmer phonetic alphabet and is tonal. Within the tourist industry, English is spoken and, to a lesser degree, French. Many in Phnom Penh speak some English, from their dealings with the U.N. forces. Many of the older Cambodians know some French. As elsewhere in Southeast Asia, confrontational behavior and displays of anger are considered bad manners, as is nakedness and bare limbs at religious sites. Homosexuality is tolerated but not encouraged, and public displays of affection should be avoided.

MAIL

Airmail to Europe takes 4–5 days; to the U.S. 7–10 days. The Post & Telephone Office (PTT) in Phnom Penh is across from the Hotel Monorom at the corner of Achar Mean Boulevard and 126 Street; it's open 7–noon and 1–11. The main post office in Phnom Penh is on the west side of 13 Street between 98 Street and 102 Street and is open 6:30 AM–9 PM weekdays.

MONEY MATTERS

Costs. Hotel prices in Phnom Penh are quite high, around $180 a night, for very average accommodation. Western-style restaurants are also fairly expensive for very ordinary fare; expect to pay $20 a head. Local food is inexpensive. Air travel is expensive; buses are very inexpensive—and uncomfortable. Taxis run about $2 per kilometer. Local beer costs $1.50 in a local café. At a hotel, an imported beer will cost about $4.

Currency. The monetary unit in Cambodia is the rial, but U.S. dollars are in demand and it is best to take lots of low-denomination bills. Payment in dollars is required by hotels and airlines. At press time, the exchange rate was approximately 2,500 rials to the U.S. dollar.

Tipping. A bellboy would like a dollar for carrying your luggage. Guides may expect $5 for a day's sightseeing. At tourist hotels, gratuities are included in the cost of meals and accommodation.

OPENING AND CLOSING TIMES

Business hours are 7–11:30 and 2–5:30 weekdays. Generally, post office hours are weekdays 7:30–noon and 2:30–5 Public holidays for 1999 are: New Year's Day (Jan. 1); International Women's Day (Mar. 8); Cambodian New Year (Apr. 13); Labor Day (May 1); Visak Bochea (Buddha's Birthday; May 1); International Children's Day (Sep Bonn Phchum Ben; June 1); Constitution Promulgation Day (Oct. 12); Taing Tok Ceremony (Oct. 20–22); Paris Peace Agreement (Oct. 23); King's Birthday (Oct. 31); Independence Day (Nov. 9); Human Rights Day (Dec. 10).

PASSPORTS AND VISAS

All visitors are required to have a passport and a one-month visa, obtainable from the **Embassy of Cambodia** (⊠ 4500 16th St. NW, Washington, DC 20001, ☎ 202/726–7742).

Visas are also available for around $20 at travel agencies in Bangkok, who apply at the **Royal Cambodian Embassy** (⊠ 185 Rajdamri Rd., Lumpini, Patumwan, Bangkok, 10330 Thailand, ☎ 02/254–6630, FAX 02/253–9859). Allow five days. You can also collect a visa when you arrive at the airport in Phnom Penh, although this is not recommended. You could theoretically be denied entry, though nine times out of 10 there is no problem.

TELEPHONES

To call Cambodia from overseas, dial the country code, 855, and then the area code, omitting the first 0. The Phnom Penh code is 023. Calling overseas is very expensive, and you cannot do it from public telephones. If you have to make a call, either go to the main post office or, more conveniently, use your hotel's switchboard. Public phones take coins. For long-distance calls within the country, dial the zero as part of the area code.

TOUR OPERATORS

You can make tour arrangements (round-trip flight from Bangkok, Phnom Penh hotel, day trip to Angkor Wat, and visas) through a travel agency in Bangkok for approximately US$530. Strongly recommended is **Abercrombie & Kent** (⊠ 4th floor, Silom Plaza, 491/29-30 Silom Rd., Bangkok 10500, ☎ 02/266–7660, FAX 02/266–7854; ⊠ 1520 Kensington Rd., Ste. 212, Oak Brook, IL 60521, ☎ 630/954–2944 or 800/323–7308, FAX 630/954–3324).

VISITOR INFORMATION

A good travel agent is your best bet for assistance with travel in Cambodia. You may want to visit the knowledgeable, though expensive,

Diethelm Travel Ltd. (✉ House 65, Street 240, Box 99, Phnom Penh, ☎ 023/219151.).

WHEN TO GO

The dry season runs from November through March, with temperatures between 65°F (18°C) and 80°F (27°C). The monsoon season, with downpours for an hour or two on most days, lasts from April to October, and temperatures range from 80°F (27°C) to 95°F (35°C).

LAOS

Of all the peoples in Southeast Asia, Laotians seem the most gentle and peace loving, but this tiny landlocked nation, not much larger than Great Britain, has for centuries been a strategic battleground. Most recently, during the Vietnam War, the U.S. Air Force, in a vain attempt to disrupt the Ho Chi Minh Trail, dropped more tons of bombs on Laos than were dropped on Germany during World War II. Since the end of the Vietnam War, the People's Democratic Party has ruled the country, first on Marxist-Leninist lines and now on the basis of limited pro-market reforms. Overtures are being made to the outside, particularly to Thailand and China, to assist in developing the country—not an easy task.

Some changes are taking place. Blue jeans, motorcycles, and radios are creeping into Vientiane, the capital; a new airport is underway; and the road north to Luang Prabang, Laos's ancient capital, has just been paved. New hotels are opening, and the Friendship Bridge over the Mekong from Thailand's northern town of Nong Khai has made Vientiane accessible to trade from the south. The average annual income of $170 and a rugged landscape that makes transportation and communications extremely difficult have long made Laos a sleepy backwater, but "Visit Laos Year," 1999, is likely to wake the country up to lasting change.

Great Itinerary

If you limit your visit to the sights of Vientiane and Luang Prabang, a minimum of three days is required: one in Vientiane and two in Luang Prabang.

Vientiane

Vientiane is the quietest Southeast Asian capital. It's modern and small, with none of the imposing sights that you find in Bangkok. Notwithstanding the imports slipped in from Thailand and the occasional burst of pop music coming from newly acquired stereos, Vientiane's pace is as slow as the Mekong, which flows through town.

To immerse yourself in Vientiane, visit the morning **market** (Talat Sao) in the center of town, less than 1,000 yards northeast of the Presidential Palace and the bank of the Mekong.

The one temple worth finding is **Wat Phra Keo**, a name that has good reason for being similar to one in Bangkok's Royal Palace: the original Wat Phra Keo temple was built in 1565 to house the Emerald Buddha taken from the Thais by the Lao; the Buddha was recaptured by the Thai army in 1778 and taken to Bangkok. The present temple dates from 1936 and has become a national museum. On display are Lao wood sculptures and a vast array of Buddhas in different styles, including a Laotian interpretation of the walking Buddha first developed in Thailand's Sukhothai. There are also wonderful images of Khmer deities and a 16th-century door carved with Hindu images. ☉ *Tues.– Sun. 8–11:30 and 2–4:30.*

Dining and Lodging

$$ 🏨 **Novotel Vientiane.** This French-managed hotel between the airport and downtown is convenient and efficient, if not exactly charming. Rooms were refurbished in 1988, so everything is modern and spotless. It's not a place to linger, but for a stopover waiting for an outbound flight, you can't do better. ✉ *Unit 9, Samsenthai Rd.,* ☎ *021/ 213570,* ℻ *021/213572. 209 rooms. 2 restaurants, pool, dance club, business center, meeting rooms. AE, MC, V.*

$ 🏨 **Heuan Lao.** This new guest house built specially to accommodate the influx of travelers yet to come has large rooms that are both air-conditioned and fan-cooled. Bathrooms are modern and clean. Prices range from about $20 to $35; you can even splurge and have a suite, but that'll set you back about $80. ✉ *Friendship Hwy.,* ☎ *no phone. 15 rooms. Breakfast room. No credit cards.*

Luang Prabang

230 km (144 mi) north of Vientiane.

Most visitors to Laos don't go to see Vientiane, the present-day capital, but to see the ancient capital of Luang Prabang, a sleepy town of about 21,000 inhabitants that sits high on the banks of a peninsula where Nam Khan meets the Mekong. It is still, at least unofficially, the historic, religious, and artistic capital. Some 30 temples remain intact, making it a pleasant place to tour on a rented bicycle for a couple of days.

Start with a visit to the **Royal Palace Museum,** the former palace of the Savang family. (King Savang Vattana and his family were exiled to northern Laos in 1975 and have not been heard from since.) The most prized exhibit is the **Pha Bang,** a gold Buddha just inches under 3 ft tall and weighing more than 100 pounds. Its history goes back to the first century, when it was cast in Sri Lanka; it was brought to Luang Prabang in 1353 as a gift to King Fa Bang. This event is celebrated as the introduction of Buddhism to Laos, and Fa Bang is venerated as the protector of the faith. Also on display are excellent friezes removed from local temples, Khmer bong drums, elephant tusks with carved images of the Buddha, and a Luang Prabang–style standing Buddha. The eclectic assortment of items also includes, in the Queen's reception room, teacups presented by Mao Tse Tung and medals from Lyndon Johnson. In the king's reception room, the walls are covered with murals painted in the 1930s, depicting scenes of traditional Lao life.

Luang Prabang's most awesome temple is **Wat Xieng Thong.** Constructed in 1559, it is one of the few structures to have survived centuries of marauding Chinese and Thais. Low, sweeping roofs overlap to make complex patterns and create a feeling of harmony and peace. There are marvelous interior mosaics, and decorated wooden columns support the ceiling, which is covered with dharma wheels, suggesting the timelessness of life.

Several small **chapels** at the sides of the main hall contain images of the Buddha; the bronze 16th-century reclining Buddha was displayed in the 1931 Paris Exhibition. On the back wall of this chapel is a mosaic, an unusual creation that commemorates the 2,500th anniversary of Buddha's birth with a depiction of Lao village life. Another chapel, near the compound's east gate, contains the royal family's funeral statuary, including funeral urns and a 40-ft wooden chariot used as a hearse. The walls of the chapel are noteworthy for their gilt panels etched with erotic scenes from the *Ramayana*.

Lodging

$$ ⛏ **L'Auberge Calao.** This charming guest house was resurrected from a ruined mansion originally built by a Portuguese merchant in 1906. Four guest rooms upstairs open onto a colonnaded veranda, and all have air-conditioning. There is one small, fan-cooled room on the ground floor. Wholesome breakfasts are served; only snacks thereafter, but there are several restaurants down by the river, just 150 yards away. ✉ *River Rd.,* ☎ *no phone. 5 rooms. Bicycles. No credit cards.*

$$ ⛏ **Villa de la Princesse.** A former royal palace has been converted into a very commodious hotel. Although it may not offer modern five-star luxury, the rooms are simply furnished—with old-fashioned twin beds and table and chairs—in pleasing good taste. Hallways have bric-a-brac that, if not antique, certainly creates that atmosphere, and it's a treat to have drinks in the garden. The staff is wonderfully helpful, and the manager, Sant Inthavong, is anxious to please. The new annex around the corner is equally attractive; it looks as comfortably old-world as the main building. ✉ *Rue Sakkarine, BP 681,* ☎ ſ𝐀𝐗 *071/212267. 22 rooms. Restaurant, bicycles. No credit cards.*

Pak Ou Caves

25 km (15 mi) up the Mekong from Luang Prabang.

In high limestone cliffs above the river are two sacred caves stuffed with Buddha statues. The lower cave, **Tham Thing,** is accessible from the river by a stairway and has enough daylight to allow you to find your way around. The stairway continues to the upper cave, **Tham Phum,** for which you will need a flashlight.

It takes about two hours by boat to reach the caves. Along the way you pass small villages, and you'll probably stop at **Xang Hai** for refreshment. Be forewarned: The village makes *Lao Lao,* a potent, fermented rice drink. Try it, but don't try to dilute it with unfiltered water—better a temporarily swimming head than stomach troubles.

Laos A to Z

Arriving and Departing

BY AIRPLANE

You can fly from Bangkok to Vientiane's Wattai Airport, 4 km (2.5 mi) from the city, on **Thai International Airways** (☎ 021/225271 in Vientiane; 66/02/234–3100 in Bangkok). The national airline, **Lao Aviation** (☎ 021/212050 in Vientiane; 66/02/237–6982 in Bangkok), also connects Vientiane to Bangkok and to Hanoi, Phnom Penh, and Ho Chi Minh City. Departure tax is US$10.

BY BUS, CAR, OR TAXI

You can enter Laos from Northern Thailand by crossing the Friendship bridge at Nong Khai. Buses and taxis wait on the Laotian side to make the run into Vientiane, 19 km (12 mi) away.

Getting Around

Though you can go by road from Vientiane to Luang Prabang, it takes two days. Most people fly on Lao Aviation, which has daily flights that leave Vientiane early in the morning. The cost is approximately $50. River ferries also ply the waters between Vientiane and Luang Prabang. It takes three nights upstream and two nights coming down the Mekong. The fare is about $10 and you must bring your own food. You are also supposed to have a pass, but it is rarely requested.

Contacts and Resources

CUSTOMS AND DUTIES

Tourists are allowed to bring into Laos 200 cigarettes, 50 cigars or ½ lb of tobacco, and one quart of spirits. Bringing in or taking out local currency is prohibited, as is the export of antiques and religious artifacts without a permit.

ELECTRICITY

The electrical current is 220 volts AC, 50Hz. Outside of Vientiane and Luang Prabang, electricity is uncertain, and even in Luang Prabang there are frequent late-afternoon outages in hot weather.

EMBASSIES AND CONSULATES

Embassy of the United States of America (⊠ BP 114, rue Bartholomé, Vientiane, ☎ 021/212 581). Australian, British, Canadian, and New Zealand residents should contact their respective embassies in Bangkok for assistance in Laos.

EMERGENCIES

For medical and police emergencies, use the services of your hotel. In serious medical emergencies, get to Thailand as soon as possible. In the case of a lost passport, immediately notify your embassy.

HEALTH AND SAFETY

As in all of Southeast Asia it is advisable to drink bottled water and keep away from uncooked foods. Laos is fairly free of crime in the tourist areas, though traveling by road puts you at risk of highway thieves. Trekking is increasingly popular in Laos, but beware: there are still many unexploded mines and bombs left over from the Vietnam War. Do not photograph anything that may have military significance.

LANGUAGE, CULTURE, AND ETIQUETTE

In tourist hotels, the staff speaks some English. You will also find a smattering of English speakers in the shops and restaurants. A few old-timers know some French. The national language, Lao, is tonal; although a few words are similar to Thai, most are not, and the alphabet differs. Dress respectfully, and remove your shoes before entering a temple. Take your lead from these gentle, hospitable people and avoid displays of anger or confrontational behavior. Everyone should also avoid public displays of affection, which are considered offensive.

MONEY MATTERS

Costs. Anticipate spending $100 for a double room in a Western-style hotel that has private bathrooms. Dinner with Western food costs $18; in a local restaurant, a meal will cost less than $4. A local beer runs $1.50.

Currency. The local currency is the kip. It suffers inflationary pressure and continually drops against the dollar. Hence, dollars are preferred and are always used to pay hotel and airline bills. The Thai baht is accepted in Vientiane; it's better to use baht than kip, as any excess kip cannot be changed back into a hard currency. But because of the current instability of the baht, dollars are preferred. At press time the official exchange rate was 140 kip to the Thai baht, but the kip is likely to decline in value. Currently on the black market you can buy 3,000 kip for US$1. Credit cards are not used in Laos.

Tipping. Give bellboys a dollar. Guides expect $5 for a day's sightseeing. At tourist hotels, gratuities are included in the cost of meals and accommodation.

OPENING AND CLOSING TIMES

Business hours are 7–11:30 and 2–5:30 weekdays, and post offices keep the same schedule. Laotian public holidays are: New Year's Day

(Jan. 1); Army Day (Jan. 24); Lao New Year (Water Festival, Apr. 13–15); Labor Day (May 1); National Day (Dec. 2).

PASSPORTS AND VISAS

All visitors to Laos need a passport and visa. Most travelers obtain their visas in Bangkok, but for $50 you can get one in Vientiane, at the Friendship Bridge in Nong Khai, and also in Chiang Saen (near Chiang Rai). The process can be time-consuming, and sometimes the immigration officials want to see hard evidence that you have sufficient funds for your travels in Laos and an air ticket out of the country. Tourist visas are good for 15 days and can be extended for another 15. Because the rules are continually changing it is advisable to contact the **Embassy of the Lao People's Democratic Republic** (✉ Consular Section, 2222 S. St. NW, Washington, DC 20008, ☎ 202/667–0076) for the most recent entry requirements.

Visas (approximately $90) can also be applied for through a travel agency in Bangkok; allow a week for processing. In Rangoon, you can deal directly with the Laotian embassy and get a visa in about two days for about $20. Many travelers heading for Thailand from Hanoi prefer the cheaper five-day transit visa (which is, in any case, the only type issued from Hanoi), because with it they can fly cheaply from Hanoi to Vientiane and then take the Friendship Bridge across the Mekong to Nong Khai, Thailand—as opposed to paying US$180 for a flight from Hanoi to Bangkok.

TELEPHONES

To call Laos from overseas, dial the country code, 856, and then the area code, omitting the first 0. The outgoing international code is 00, but IDD phones are rare. If you have to make an international call from Laos, use your hotel's switchboard. This is a good idea even for local calls, since there are few pay phones.

TOUR OPERATORS

You can make tour arrangements (round-trip flight from Bangkok to Vientiane and Luang Prabang, hotels, guides, and visas) through a travel agency in Bangkok for approximately US$800. Strongly recommended is **Abercrombie & Kent** (✉ 4th floor, Silom Plaza, 491/29-30 Silom Rd., Bangkok 10500, ☎ 02/266–7660, FAX 02/266–7854; ✉ 1520 Kensington Rd., Suite 212, Oak Brook, IL 60521, ☎ 630/954–2944 or 800/323–7308, FAX 630/954–3324). **Journeys International** (✉ 4011 Jackson Rd., Ann Arbor, MI 48103, ☎ 313/255–8735 or 800/255–8735) also organizes tours to Laos.

VISITOR INFORMATION

A good travel agency in Bangkok is your best source of information on Laos (☞ Tour Operators, *above*). In Laos, you can get limited information from the **National Tourism Authority of the Lao People's Democratic Republic** (✉ BP 3556, Avenue Lang Xang, Vientiane, ☎ 021/212248). In Luang Prabang, try the **Luang Prabang Tourism Office** (✉ 72 Sisavangvong Rd., ☎ 071/212198). The office runs one- to six-day river tours that are worth checking out.

WHEN TO GO

The dry season is from December through May and is much cooler—even chilly at night—than the rainy season. Sudden downpours occur from June through November.

9 Portraits of Southeast Asia

Southeast Asia at a Glance:
A Chronology

Religion in Southeast Asia

Books and Videos

SOUTHEAST ASIA AT A GLANCE: A CHRONOLOGY

20,000 BC   First evidence of human settlement in the Philippines.

6000   Rice cultivation begins in Southeast Asia.

3000   Use of bronze begins in Thailand.

c. AD 150   Coastal Indonesians establish direct trade with South India. Early Malayan rulers adopt Indian Sanskrit.

c. 400   Chinese inscriptions from Province Wellesley (along the coast of Malay Peninsula) indicate presence of Mahayana Buddhism.

c. 638–700   Empire of Srivijaya emerges on Sumatra and power extends to Malay Peninsula and small archipelagoes to the south; West Java and southwest Borneo are influenced. Eighth-century inscriptions attest to "Old Malay," earliest-known use of national language in Southeast Asia.

c. 775–856   Under Sailendra dynasty Central Java prospers; great monuments are built in devotion to Mahayana Buddhism.

1000–1100   Suryavarman I of Angkor conquers area that is now Thailand and Laos. Old Javanese literature flourishes.

1100–1200   Singapore Island becomes prosperous trading center, while Kediri is chief political center in East Java. Khmer temples are built at Lopburi (the region now occupied by Thailand and Laos).

1230   Theravada Buddhist becomes ruler of Ligor (now Malaysia).

1291   Marco Polo arrives in Pasai, in northern Sumatra.

1292–93   Mongols attack Java. Northern Sumatran states adopt Islam.

1293   Majapahit, near present-day town of Modjokerto, is founded as capital of eastern Javanese kingdom.

1350–78   Siamese kingdom of Ayutthaya is founded and shortly thereafter conquers state of Sukhothai.

1364   Nagarajertagama (Old Javanese survey of Indonesian culture) is completed.

1402–1500   Melaka (Malacca), along southwestern coast of Malay Peninsula, becomes greatest international trading center in eastern world and is greatest diffusion center of Islam; Islam spreads throughout Sumatra and eastward to the Sulu Archipelago in the southern Philippines. Buddhist reforms begin in Burma region.

1431   Brahman political advisors are brought to Ayutthaya (capital of Siam), and king becomes divine monarch; Siamese sack Angkor.

1511   The Portuguese conquer Melaka.

1521   Ferdinand Magellan, on the first voyage to circumnavigate the globe, reaches what is now the Philippines; he is slain in battle by a local chieftain, Lapu-Lapu.

1525–36   Spanish expeditions, under Charles V, claim Philippines.

1596   The Dutch arrive in Indonesia.

1600–1700   Ayutthaya becomes principal port of Far East. The French, under Louis XIV, exchange embassies with Siam; European influence on Southeast Asia increases.

1633 The Dutch blockade Melaka, but don't gain control until 1641, when the Portuguese surrender the city.

1688 Siam enters a period of comparative isolation, not to be broken until the 19th century.

1767 The Burmese destroy Ayutthaya, and Sino-Siamese Phy Tak Sin becomes monarch; Siam's capital moves to Thonburi.

1781 The Philippines enter time of prosperity as the state holds monopoly on cultivation, manufacture, and sale of tobacco.

1782 The Chakri dynasty is established in Siam.

1795 Great Britain takes over Melaka.

1807 Organized by Herman Willem Daendels (governor general), Indonesian highway is constructed along northern coast of Java.

1811 British troops occupy Java.

1819 Under East India Company, Singapore becomes new British port south of Melaka.

1824 Britain returns Indonesia to the Dutch.

1826–32 Singapore joins with Penang and Melaka (both in present-day Malaysia) to form Straits Settlements; the territory then becomes seat of government.

1834 After years of clandestinely trading sugar and other tropical produce with Europe, Manila enters the world trade market.

1851 Siam's King Rama IV begins to reestablish previously severed diplomatic relations with Western powers.

1896–1901 The Philippines experience a countrywide revolt led by Katipunan Society; José Rizal, the Philippines national hero, is executed by the Spanish; General Emilio Aguinaldo declares the Philippines independent of Spain; instead of independence, sovereignty changes hands and United States takes control. Though Aguinaldo's troops refuse to recognize transfer, United States forces collapse of Filipino resistance.

1907–09 Siam cedes Laos and Cambodia to France, and recognizes British control over Kedan, Kelantan, Perlis, and Terengganu.

1916 The Philippines adopt bicameral legislature.

1922 Singapore chosen as principal base for defense of British interests in Far East.

1932 Western educated minority stages revolution in Siam, replacing absolute monarchy with a constitutional monarchy, though there's little change in policy.

1935 Primary education is made compulsory throughout Thailand.

1941–42 Japan occupies most of Southeast Asia (Malaya, the Philippines, Hong Kong, Singapore, Taiwan, Burma, Indochina).

1945–49 Indonesia stages resistance against Dutch and declares independence. Singapore liberated from Japanese by Great Britain.

1946 Straits Settlements are disbanded and Singapore becomes separate colony; Melaka and Penang are incorporated into Malaya. Republic of the Philippines becomes independent. U.S. economic assistance to Thailand begins. (More than $2 billion of aid sent between 1950 and 1975.)

1947–57 Thailand enters time of political unrest and flux of government policy until finally, in 1957, a state of national emergency is declared; Field Marshal Phibun is ousted and new elections are held.

1947–66 Indonesia's Communist Party becomes increasingly powerful, with several coup attempts; in 1965, political tension climaxes with coup that leads to more than 100,000 deaths. Sukarno replaced by Suharto, and Indonesia's Communist Party is banned.

1948–60 Federation of Malaya is proclaimed; Malaya enters 12-year state of emergency as Malayan Communist Party begins widespread terrorist campaign and attacks police stations, plantations, communication facilities; thousands murdered, including High Commissioner Sir Henry Gurney in 1951.

1953–57 Ramon Magsaysay elected President of Philippines; defeats Communist insurgents, the Huks.

1954 In hope of presenting a united front to forestall Communist aggression, Southeast Asia Treaty Organization (SEATO) is formed. Singapore's People's Action Party (PAP) is established under leadership of Lee Kuan Yew.

1958–63 Despite dissension among leading politicians, Thailand's economy grows under generals Sarit Thanarat and Thanom Kittikachorn.

1959 Lee Kuan Yew wins general elections (agreed upon by Great Britain in 1957) and becomes Singapore's first prime minister.

1963–65 Malaysia established, joining together the Federation of Malaya, Singapore, Sabah, and Sarawak; after two years Singapore secedes and becomes independent sovereign state.

1965 Ferdinand Marcos takes office as president of the Philippines. Singapore leaves the Federation of Malaysia.

1968 The Association of Southeast Asian Nations (ASEAN) is formed.

1972 Martial law, imposed by Philippine president Marcos, stifles dissent but increases armed insurgency. The country prospers for a while but by the 1980s falls into deep recession.

1973–76 Continual student demonstrations, strikes, and political assassinations occur in Thailand.

1974 Unrest erupts in Indonesia when students stage street demonstrations against the visit of Japan's premier.

1975 North Vietnam defeats the South; Vietnam is unified.

1977 SEATO is disbanded.

1978 Vietnam invades Cambodia, ousting Pol Pot and Khmer Rouge.

1979 Elections for lower house of legislature are held in Thailand.

1983 Benigno Aquino Jr., Philippines' opposition leader, is assassinated when he returns from exile; Marcos's downfall begins.

1984 Great Britain agrees that Hong Kong will revert to China in 1997.

1986 In a bloodless, four-day February Manila uprising known as "People Power," the Marcoses are forced into exile. The popular Corazon Aquino, widow of Benigno Aquino Jr., wins victory as president, and democratic rule is restored.

1989 Burma changes name to Myanmar; places Aung San Suu Kyi under house arrest.

1990 Powerful earthquake causes major destruction in Philippines.

1991 Military coup d'état in Thailand. Aung San Suu Kyi of Burma is awarded the Nobel Peace Prize. Mt. Pinatubo, dormant for 600 years, erupts in the Philippines, and this affects the global climate.

1992 Thais take to the streets in bloody demonstrations, forcing the military junta out of power and holding democratic elections. In the first freely held presidential elections since 1969, Fidel V. Ramos succeeds Corazon Aquino as president of the Philippines.

1993 U.N.-sponsored elections take place in Cambodia.

1994 United States lifts its embargo on Vietnam. The last U.S. military base in the Philippines is shut down, ending almost a century of U.S. military presence in the country.

1995 Burma's Aung San Suu Kyi is released from house arrest. Thailand holds general elections. The U.S. establishes full diplomatic relations with Vietnam.

1996 Two activists—Bishop Carlos Ximenes Belo and José Ramos-Horta—from the Indonesian island of Timor are awarded the Nobel Peace Prize.

1997 Regional financial crisis starts in July in Thailand and spreads through ASEAN.

1998 Pol Pot, notorious head of the Khmer Rouge, dies in his sleep in one of the jungles of Cambodia. Indonesia's President Suharto steps down after 32 years in power. His resignation followed rioting that left more than 1,000 dead in Jakarta, Medan, and Solo.

RELIGION IN SOUTHEAST ASIA

LIKE THE SHIFTING PATTERNS in a kaleidoscope, the rituals, ceremonies, prayers, and customs of all the world's major religions meet the eye of a visitor to Southeast Asia. Intrepid travelers will spend many hours "doing temples," and their weary feet will carry them up hundreds of steps and through miles of courtyards. Their cameras will click unceasingly, recording images of Buddha, of Jesus, of Rama, and of the pantheon of Hindu and Chinese gods. They will take pictures of mosques with golden domes and of minarets festooned with loudspeakers. At night, if they are in Malaysia or Indonesia, they may turn on the TV and listen to a Koran-reading competition.

A quick glance at the calendar in Singapore demonstrates the impact of multiple faiths on a modern society. The government of multiracial Singapore is basically Chinese. The only holiday when these hardworking people close up shop altogether is the Chinese new year. Nevertheless, the government recognizes holidays sacred to four religions. Important Buddhist, Islamic, and Hindu occasions are public holidays as well.

After all, the fact that it is nearly 2,000 years since the birth of Christ is not particularly meaningful for most Asians. Muslims date the era from the year of Muhammad's hegira in AD 622. The Buddhist year goes back to 563 BC. Christian dating, like the English language, is used for business, banking, and all international transactions. Many Asian calendars are bilingual, with Arabic numerals and Christian dates on one side and Chinese, Buddhist, or Islamic dates on the other. In Thailand, the cornerstones of important buildings usually carry two dates.

The calendar plays an important part in the lives of the people, because elements of astrology (both Hindu and Chinese) are taken into consideration when making important decisions. Statesmen, kings, and peasants refer to astrologers or *bomohs* or *dukuns* for help. The Chinese and Thais, for example, attach great importance to the year of a person's birth within a 12-year cycle, each year represented by an animal.

In most of Asia, time is regarded as cyclical, whereas for most Occidentals it is linear. For people in the Judeo-Christian tradition (and in Islam, which evolved from that tradition), each individual life is an entity—a unit—created at a specific moment in time. Death is considered the termination of the physical life of that individual, while the soul may continue to exist through eternity. The conditions of the afterlife, according to Christian and Muslim belief, depend in large part on the behavior of the individual during his or her earthly sojourn. Christians, according to most dogmas, believe in resurrection, but nowhere do you find any reference to the idea of reincarnation. And here is where the great schism between Eastern and Western thought begins. Hindus and Buddhists assume that life, as well as time, follows a cycle. The soul may endure over the course of many lives. Often the conditions of the new life depend on the behavior of the soul in its previous body. A Christian seeks eternal life through the teaching of Christ. A Buddhist seeks *nirvana*, or eternal nothingness, and follows the teachings of Buddha as set forth in his sermon "Setting in Motion the Wheel of Righteousness."

Buddhism

Buddhism, being a nontheistic religion, is tolerant of other faiths and beliefs. Thus elements of older religions turn up in the practices and customs of Buddhists. The cyclical notion of time and the idea of reincarnation were taken over by Buddhists from older Hindu and Vedic beliefs. Indeed, the Buddha was born a Hindu prince, and much of his teaching was aimed at a reform of the structure and complexities of Hinduism. For example, the Buddha, like another great Indian religious reformer, Gandhi, deplored the Hindu caste system.

The "historical Buddha" (the term "buddha" actually refers to an awakened or enlightened being) was born **Siddhartha Gautama** about 563 BC, near the border of Nepal. A wealthy prince, he lived in luxury, married happily, and had a son. Like many people of his class, he had been protected from viewing the harsher aspects of life. Legend has it that one day he went out from the palace and for the first time saw poverty, sickness, and death. Overwhelmed by these realities, he renounced his worldly position and became a wandering mendicant, seeking the meaning of life. After years of fasting, begging, and traveling, he sat down under a *bodhi* tree and sank into a deep meditation lasting 49 days. At last he achieved enlightenment, and Siddhartha became a buddha.

The answer he found after his contemplation was that to escape from suffering and misery, human beings must eliminate desire and attachment. In this world, he maintained, evil is caused by desire, which grows from ignorance caused by wrong thought and misdirected action. Thus, in order to achieve nirvana, an individual must extinguish desire by renouncing evil action and atoning for wrongs already done, either in this or in a previous life. Each life an individual passes through is another chance to escape the wheel. If he or she ignores opportunities for thinking and right action, in the next incarnation he or she will have to pay for past mistakes. The **Five Precepts** in Buddhist teaching resemble the Ten Commandments and prescribe guidelines for right living. They are: not to kill, steal, do sexual wrong, lie, or use any intoxicants. Thus, a devout Buddhist should be both a pacifist and a vegetarian.

Forms of Buddhism

As it spread from northern India throughout Asia, Buddhism branched into many schools and sects. The basic divisions are Theravada Buddhism (sometimes called Hinayana, or "Lesser Vehicle"), Mahayana ("Greater Vehicle"), and Tantric Buddhism. **Theraveda Buddhism** is closest to the original Buddhism of Gautama. It emphasizes that each person must seek salvation through enlightenment, attained by prayer, fasting, and the rigorous avoidance of temptation and evil. Theravada is a monastic religion, and people enter religious communities (the *sangha*) for mutual guidance and support.

Myanmar (Burma) and Thailand are both Buddhist countries where religion forms an integral part of life. In Thailand, for example, it is customary for every young man who can to spend at least three months of his youth as a monk, when he will eat only the food he has received as "merit" offerings by the people early in the morning. The remainder of the day is spent in study, prayer, and meditation. Buddhist monks appear at every official function, whether it be the opening of a village school or the inauguration of a military airfield.

Mahayana Buddhism originated in India but developed most fully in China, Korea, and Japan. The Greater Vehicle is so called because it acknowledges that most people do not have the fortitude to achieve enlightenment on their own. Believers in Mahayana sects such as the Pure Land School call upon the aid of saints to help them to salvation. These saints, called bodhisattvas, are fully enlightened beings who have voluntarily postponed their own entry into nirvana to help others along the way. In Southeast Asia, most Mahayana temples, such as the famous Ayer Hitam Temple in Penang (Malaysia), were founded by Chinese immigrants. These temples are filled with images of Kuan Yin, the Goddess of Mercy, and other bodhisattvas, which have become objects of devotion among the faithful.

Tantric Buddhism is a subsect of Mahayana Buddhism; it in turn has divided into various sects that are found most prominently in Tibet, but also in northern Burma as well as in China and Japan. Tantric Buddhism is also centered on monasteries, and emphasizes secret rituals designed to combat demons and overcome evil.

Hinduism

Hindu belief in reincarnation forms the basis of religious practice and faith. Unlike the Buddhist concept of nirvana, the Hindu notion is one of attained deliverance. Hindu dogma teaches that the soul can be released from the wheel of life only by the observance of dharma—doing one's duty according to one's position in life. The aim of each existence is to perform the dharma of that life so correctly that the soul will be rewarded with a higher station in the next life.

Hindu Deities

The Hindu godhead consists of a holy trinity: Brahma the Creator, Vishnu the Preserver, and Shiva the Destroyer. Each god appears in a number of different forms, or incarnations, and has a consort and many minor deities attached to his worship. Brahma is usually depicted with four heads to indicate his creativity and intellect. Vishnu is usually pictured with four arms, stressing his versatility and strength. His consort is the popular goddess of wealth and fortune, Lakshmi. Shiva is probably the most popular of the three, and the most widely worshiped. As he is the god of both destruction and regeneration, he is thought to be sympathetic to the human condition. In his incarnation as Shiva Nataraja, Lord of the Dance, he dances continuously to keep the world in existence. His consort, who is known by many names and is worshiped in several forms, is a source of comfort and inspiration. Her more familiar names are Kali, Parvati, or Dewi. Shiva has two sons: Ganesha, the elephant-headed god of knowledge and "remover of obstacles," and Subramaniam, god of war. Worship of the deities takes place daily in the home and in the temple on festival days. Thaipusam, which pays homage to Subramaniam, is celebrated widely in Singapore and Kuala Lumpur. The other major Hindu holiday is Deepavali, the autumn festival of lights.

Hinduism in Southeast Asia

Hindu-Brahmanic influence, which can be seen throughout Southeast Asia, is a relic of historical kingdoms that came under Indian influence in the 6th to 10th centuries. In Thailand some of these Hindu traditions came from the great Khmer kingdom that flourished in the 9th to 12th centuries. (The most spectacular example of the Khmer glories, of course, is the Angkor Wat complex of temples in Cambodia.) Thai royalty retains several court Brahman priests as a holdover from the times when they advised the king on heavenly omens so that he might rule more wisely. In modern times, these priest-astrologers advise only on special matters affecting the royal family and in connection with public ceremonies such as the annual opening of the plowing season, celebrated in Bangkok on the Pramane Ground.

The Hindu influence in Indonesia dates back to the powerful Srivijaya kingdom, which controlled much of Sumatra and the Malay Peninsula in the 10th century. In Java, a succession of empires combined several aspects of Hindu and Buddhist traditions so that in some instances Shiva, the Hindu god of destruction and regeneration, became merged with the Buddha—as can be seen in the temple at Prambanan near Yogyakarta.

The grounds of the Prambanan temple provide the setting for performances of a modern dance-drama based on the *Ramayana* and held during the summer months. One of two great Sanskrit epics (the other being the *Mahabharata*), the *Ramayana* narrates the life and adventures of Rama, an incarnation of Vishnu descended to earth in human form to subdue the demon Ravanna. The *Ramayana* story is narrated in dance, painting, and sculpture throughout Southeast Asia.

Hinduism on Bali

The advent of Islam in the 16th century, and its rapid spread thereafter, extinguished Hinduism in Indonesia except on the island of Bali. Balinese religion, which encompasses all aspects of life from work to play, from birth to death, is a rich mixture of Hindu mythology, animist beliefs, and an underlying awe of nature and God as manifest in the great volcano Gunung Agung. The Balinese, who accept the Hindu concept of Kali Yug—the last of the four great epochs before the end of the world—believe that in such times as these it is imperative to maintain a proper reverence for all the gods and spirits who dwell on the island, for their anger can be very destructive. Many Balinese believe that both the eruption of the volcano in 1963 and the wave of killings during the civil unrest in 1965 occurred because of religious improprieties.

Balinese Hinduism has absorbed so many local island deities that it has very little in common with Hinduism as observed by other communities in Southeast Asia. The two most famous local deities of Balinese Hinduism are the witch Rangda and her adversary, the lionlike beast called Barong. The Barong Kris dance performed daily at Batubulan is a modern, secular version of the very sacred *calonerang* exorcistic dance-drama that is used by the Balinese to protect their villages from evil; calonerang is rarely seen by outsiders, because it's performed at midnight at village crossroads and in graveyards. Both versions depict a struggle between Rangda, the personification of darkness and evil, and the protective Barong; the struggle always ends in a draw, because in the mortal world neither good nor evil can completely triumph.

Islam

Despite its long cultural and historical role, Hinduism is a minority religion in Southeast Asia today. The reason for this was the great Islamic expansion during the 15th and 16th centuries, when part of the Malay Peninsula (including the four southernmost provinces of Thailand), all of the Indonesian archipelago (with the exception of Bali), and the southern islands of what is today the Philippines became Muslim.

Islam, which is monotheistic (believing in one god), exclusive, and highly moralistic, came as quite a contrast to the pantheism of the Hindu and Buddhist religions it replaced. With the advent of Islam, the way of life in these areas changed. Some of the more obvious changes were in the calendar, the status of women, and the role of the state in regulating citizens' behavior.

The Islamic Calendar

The Islamic calendar is divided into 12 lunar months, as is the Chinese, so that all festivals move forward every year. Unlike the Chinese calendar, however, the Muslim lunar calendar does not attempt to make any accommodation to the solar year by adding "leap months" (7 months during the course of every 19 years). Muslim holidays, therefore, move forward 11 days each year, which explains why Muslims do not celebrate a fixed New Year's Day. Coincidentally, this system ensures that the month of fasting, Ramadan, rotates through the seasons and therefore is never confused with local planting or harvest festivities, which hark back to pagan customs and would be considered taboo for orthodox Muslims.

Islam and Women

Islam is often seen in the West as a religion that oppresses women. Muslims, however, contend that men and women are treated differently but equally. In Islam's Arabian homeland, the laws of the Koran regarding women were designed mainly to protect their personal dignity and legal rights. Women were expected to cover their hair (but *not* necessarily to wear a veil; that is a later development that varies widely in the Islamic world according to

local custom) and to be modest in their dealings with outsiders. They were also given the legal right to own property, and protection from arbitrary divorce. Muslim men may have up to four wives, if they can afford them and treat them all equally. A man may divorce his wife by saying "I divorce thee" three times, but both law and custom require a waiting period for the divorce to become final, and a woman who has borne a son may not be divorced except for grave, and legally specified, causes.

On the other hand, Islamic law clearly also makes women both separate and inferior. The Koran says: "Men have authority over women because God has made the one superior to the other . . . so good women are obedient." Among some orthodox groups in Southeast Asia, unmarried women are strictly segregated from men in schools and social organizations, and married women are expected to avoid any dealings with men outside their own families. But other groups have adapted Islamic law to local custom; among the Minangkabau of Sumatra and Malaysia, for example, women own most of the property and have a strong voice in community affairs. In other cases, women have received some protection from the strictness of Islamic law through parliamentary women's-rights legislation.

Islam and the State

In Southeast Asia, Malaysia and Brunei are avowedly Islamic nations; Indonesia has no official religion, but the population is overwhelmingly Muslim. Government departments include a bureau of religious affairs. Indonesia's constitution requires that every citizen must profess belief in a single deity. This law is inconvenient for the Chinese and Balinese, who have been forced rather artificially to add a "supreme deity" to their elaborate pantheons. In recent years many Chinese have become Christian to avoid harassment.

The Koran

Islam, like Christianity, is based on a specific holy scripture: the Koran, or Qu'ran, which is a collection of the words of God as revealed to his prophet, Muhammad. To a devout Muslim the book is the holy of holies, and much time is spent reading and studying it. The book must be treated with reverence, never handled carelessly, and should never be placed beneath any other books. One should never drink or smoke while the Koran is being read aloud, and it should be heard in respectful silence. In many villages children are taught to memorize great numbers of verses, and Koran competitions are annual events.

The Five Pillars of Islam

The Koran and Muslim tradition set forth the Five Pillars of Islam: the Profession of Faith, the Five Daily Prayers, the obligation to fast, the obligation to make the pilgrimage, and the obligation to give alms. The **Profession of Faith** is the familiar doctrine of the Unity of God, which is heard in every mosque and from every minaret: There is no God but God; Muhammad is the messenger of God.

The **Five Daily Prayers** are made at specific times of day: at dawn, at noon, in the afternoon, at sunset, and at night. The Muslim tradition gives specific instructions on how to say prayers: kneeling and bowing in the direction of Mecca (of course, in this part of the world to "face Mecca" means to turn west, not east). Because the Koran demands cleanliness before prayer (preferably a total bath, but if this is not possible then a ritual cleansing of face, hands, and feet), you will see tanks and basins of water outside all mosques.

The third Pillar of Islam is **fasting.** The ninth month of the year, Ramadan, is set aside for ritual fasting. For 30 days all adult Muslims are enjoined against taking any food, drink, or cigarettes from dawn to dusk. During this month, as one would expect, work efficiency tends to drop, because in addition to being hungry and thirsty, many Muslims are also sleepy because they have stayed up much of the night eating. Adherence to the tradition is quite strict, and in some villages special police prowl the streets looking for secret munchers. The Koran does, however, give dispensation to the sick and to those who must take a meal in the course of their work. The end of Ramadan is the great feast, Hari Raya Puasa. After a morning visit to the mosque, the family returns home for a memorable feast that more than makes up for the month of deprivation.

The fourth Pillar is the duty to make a **pilgrimage to Mecca.** Obviously for many Muslims in Southeast Asia this is an expensive and long journey, and therefore the pilgrimage is obligatory only for those who can afford it. Nevertheless, because of the honor and prestige accorded to those who have made the journey and because the pious regard it as a religious duty, every year thousands of men and women, many of them old, board pilgrim ships and planes for the long, arduous journey westward. Those who return are addressed as Haji (or Hajjah for women), indicating that they have fulfilled their obligation. The last Pillar is **almsgiving,** similar to the Christian custom of tithing. In Malaysia this money is collected by the Department of Religious Affairs and is used for welfare projects for the poor.

Christianity

Because of its claims to universal validity and the simplicity of its faith, Islam swept through the islands of Southeast Asia up to the Philippines, where it ran head-on into the Spanish Catholic Church. With the establishment of Spanish authority in Manila on June 3, 1571, Islam encountered a nearly impenetrable barrier to further expansion.

The Filipinos often pride themselves on having the only Catholic country in Asia, as well as the most westernized. Before the 16th century, the myriad islands that make up the Philippines had never reached the advanced stage of civilization of their western neighbors. The Filipinos accepted the Catholic teaching for a variety of reasons. In the first place, Catholicism did not have to contend with an organized, established religion because most of the indigenous beliefs involved ancestral spirits and nature gods; they offered neither a systematic theology nor a firm promise of salvation. So for the Filipino, acceptance of the new religion did not involve any deeply traumatic rejection of old ways. In fact, many of the older customs were absorbed into Catholic ritual. The second factor was the language problem. The islands were a hodgepodge of languages and dialects. Catholic schools, which taught Spanish as well as the catechism, gave the Spanish colonial authorities a means of unifying the country both religiously and linguistically. Furthermore, the church offered protection from marauding pirates and outlaw gangs—one of the terms for new Christians was "those who live under the bells." On the other hand, the Spanish friars were notorious for their abuses—one of the factors that contributed to the 1896 revolution.

As you travel through the Philippine countryside, you will come across some huge, stark, very un-Roman-looking cathedrals. These are the churches of an indigenous Christian faith, the Iglesia ni Kristo, which incorporates nationalistic feelings into a Protestant liturgy. It is estimated to have almost a million members.

Elsewhere in Southeast Asia, Christian missionaries, both Catholic and Protestant, followed the colonizing European powers. The lovely churches in Macau, Melaka (Malacca), and parts of Indonesia and along the coastal regions of Sri Lanka, where nearly all the fisherfolk are Catholic, are remnants of the Portuguese presence.

Missionary work in Southeast Asia did not disappear with the departure of the colonial powers. Indeed, in certain areas proselytizing church groups are now more active than ever. Much current missionary effort is directed toward the tribal peoples living in remote mountains and jungles, where pagan practices still prevail. Though Islam is Malaysia's national religion, the East Malaysian states are predominantly Christian.

Changing Times

Religion no longer plays the role in Southeast Asia that it once did, when personal identity was established by an individual's spiritual tenets. Educational, national, and professional ties have superseded the bonds that rituals in the home and ceremonies in the community once forged. Overcrowding in the cities has pushed people closer together, sometimes with unfortunate results, when vastly different customs clash with one another. The Call to Prayer, when amplified over a loudspeaker, becomes noise pollution to some ears; the clanging cymbals accompanying a Chinese funeral are equally unwelcome to the ears of others.

But just as people in the West have become aware of the value of tradition, so in the East old customs and rituals are undergoing a reassessment, both with regard to their importance for one's cultural identity and the spiritual sustenance they provide. During these transitional times a visitor to Southeast Asia has a unique opportunity to observe and participate in the customs, rituals, and ceremonies of many different religions. Nevertheless, sensitivity and good manners are essential. Do not persist in trying to enter a religious building if the people within ask you not to. Do not intrude on or photograph people at prayer. Remove your shoes when entering a mosque, and wear a waist sash when entering a Balinese temple. Dress modestly, as you would want strangers to dress if they visited your own church or synagogue.

Throughout Southeast Asia, religion has remained a more important feature of day-to-day social activity than it has in most of the West. Although the forms and nature of this religious feeling vary widely within the region, a large proportion of the population is actively involved in it. There is still a strong sense of traditional values, reflected in fundamental social attitudes.

BOOKS AND VIDEOS

Books

Southeast Asia

The Travelers' Guide to Asian Customs and Manners, by Kevin Chambers, advises on how to dine, tip, dress, make friends, do business, bargain, and do just about everything else in Asia, Australia, and New Zealand. *Shopping in Exotic Places,* by Ronald L. Krannich, Jo Reimer, and Carl Rae Krannich, discusses all major shopping districts and tells how to pick a tailor, how to bargain, and how to pack. For full reservation information with detailed descriptions of lodgings in 16 countries, read Jerome E. Klein's *Best Places to Stay in Asia.*

Video Night in Kathmandu, by Pico Iyer, is a delightful collection of essays on the *Time* correspondent's travels through Southeast Asia. Three highly recommended works on Southeast Asian history are *Southeast Asia,* 3rd edition, by M. Osborne; *Southeast Asia: A History* by Lea E. Williams; and *In Search of Southeast Asia: A Modern History,* edited by David J. Steinberg.

In *Beyond Belief* (Random House), a follow-up book to *Among the Believers,* V. S. Naipaul conveys the effects of Islam in Indonesia, Malaysia, Iran, and Pakistan. His account is rich and human—full of the people he encounters on his travels and their stories.

Southeast Asia was the inspiration for much of Joseph Conrad's work, including the novels *An Outcast of the Islands, Lord Jim, The Shadow-Line, Victory, Almayer's Folly,* and *The Rescue,* and the short stories "Karain," "The Lagoon," "Youth," "The End of the Tether," "Typhoon," "Flak," "The Secret Sharer," and "Freya of the Seven Isles."

SouthEast Asia Wildlife (APA Publications) is a collaborative effort by a number of the regions' top naturalists and explorers detailing the wildlife, national parks, and tourist facilities of Indonesia, Malaysia, Singapore, Thailand, and the Philippines. *Soul of the Tiger,* by Jeffrey McNeely and Paul Spencer-Wachtel, describes stories behind the region's customs and beliefs.

Cambodia

Cambodia: Report from a Stricken Land, by Henry Kamm, is a perceptive, angry account of the last 30 years—how the world betrayed Cambodia, and its leaders picked it clean.

Indonesia

Anthology of Modern Indonesian Poetry, edited by B. Raffle, provides insight into Indonesian society. Christopher Koch's *The Year of Living Dangerously* is a historical novel of the chaotic state of Indonesia in 1965. *The Religion of Java,* by Clifford Geertz, is a modern classic that describes the religious and social life of the Javanese.

Underwater Indonesia, by Kal Muller, is the best guide to diving in the archipelago—a must-read for anyone planning to scuba dive or snorkel here. Anne Richter's *The Arts & Crafts of Indonesia* is a beautifully photographed guide to handicrafts, costumes, and arts throughout the islands. *Adventuring in Indonesia,* by Holly S. Smith, is a guide to the nature and culture of the islands, including many national parks. Eliot Elosofan's *Java Diary,* Frances Yeager's *Jungle Woman,* and John MacKinnon's *In Search of the Red Ape* are classic accounts of explorers discovering wildlife and culture on Java, Sumatra, and Borneo, respectively.

Malaysia

Denis Walls and Stella Martin's *In Malaysia* is a dramatic novel set in Malaysia. Somerset Maugham's *Ah King and Other Stories* and *The Casuarina Tree* are two volumes of short stories that capture the essence of colonial life in Malaya. *Kalimantan* (Henry Holt), by C. S. Godshalk, is a fictional account of an Englishman who establishes a private raj on the north coast of Borneo in the 19th century.

Philippines

In Our Image, by S. Karnow, and *The Philippines,* by Onofre D. Corpuz, are good standard texts on the history of the nation. An excellent book dealing with the

1986 People Power revolution is *Endgame*, by Ninotchka Rosca, while José Sison's *The Philippine Revolution* places the People Power phenomenon in the context of earlier history. *Waltzing with a Dictator*, by R. Bonner, is an in-depth study of the relationship between the United States and the Philippines. Also try Bryan Johnson's *The Four Days of Courage: The Untold Story of the People Who Brought Marcos Down*. D. Schirmer's *Philippine Reader* is a good collection of left-wing essays. *Playing with Water: Love and Passion on a Philippine Island*, by James Hamilton Patterson, is a fascinating account of a year's stay on a small island.Singapore

Maurice Collis's *Raffles* is a rich biographical account of the founder of Singapore. *Singapore Malay Society*, by T. Li, is a solid historical reference. *Saint Jack* is a novel by Paul Theroux set in Singapore. JoAnn Meriwether Craig's *Culture Shock! Singapore* is a must for anyone spending more than a few days in the island nation.

Thailand

Monsoon Country is a contemporary novel by Pira Sudham, who portrays life in the northeast of Thailand. For insights into Thai culture and everyday life, read Denis Segaller's *Thai Ways* and *More Thai Ways*. For a humorous account of an expatriate's life in Thailand in the 1950s, read *Mai Pen Rai*, by Carol Hollinger. An excellent account of life in northern Thailand is provided by Gordon Young in *The Hill Tribes of Northern Thailand*.

Vietnam

Anthony Gray's *Saigon* takes the reader through all the major events from the 1920s to 1975. Neil Sheehan, a former New York Times reporter in Vietnam offers a very comprehensive look at America's involvement in Vietnam in *Bright Shining Lie*.

Videos

Cambodia's troubles and America's involvement in Southeast Asia are examined in *The Killing Fields* (1984). It is journalist Sydney Schanberg's (played by Sam Waterston) tale of the search for his Cambodian aide, Dith Prahn, who was left behind when Pnomh Penh fell to the Khmer Rouge in 1975. As a follow up to this movie, a must-see is Spaulding Gray's *Swimming to Cambodia* (1987). Gray weaves poetry, humor, political discussion, and personal confessions into an entertaining, insightful monologue linked to his small role in *The Killing Fields*, and to U.S. military aggression and the situation in Cambodia.

In *Indochine* (1991) Catherine Deneuve portrays a French colonial plantation owner who loses her way of life and her adopted Vietnamese daughter to the 1930s conflicts that begin to change the face of Southeast Asia. Linda Hunt won an Oscar for her performance as a male photographer covering strife-ridden Indonesia just before Sukarno's rule fell to Suharto in 1965 in *The Year of Living Dangerously* (1982). She plays alongside Mel Gibson and Sigourney Weaver. In *Beyond Rangoon* (1995), an American doctor (Patricia Arquette) finds herself caught up in the conflict between Burma's ruling facist regime and the dissident democratic movement.

There have been many films made about the military horrors of the Vietnam War, including the classic *Apocalypse Now* (1979), *Platoon* (1986), and *Full Metal Jacket* (1987). *Born on the Fourth of July* (1989) fully conveys the aftereffects of this war on the men who fought it.

VOCABULARY

To properly experience the culture of a foreign country, one must feast on its cuisine, learn the history of its monuments, and speak its native tongue. Southeast Asian languages, like its history, are as diverse as its people and customs.

To simplify communications, Fodor's has compiled a vocabulary chart of six languages you may encounter throughout your travels in the region. This easy-reference listing includes important words and significant phrases in English, Cantonese, Malay (which is usually similar to Indonesian), Mandarin, Tagalog, and Thai. Use the phonetical chart to assist you in getting around, asking directions, and dining out.

Note: In Bahasa Indonesia, the letter "c" is pronounced as "ch"; hence, *capcai*, a spicy vegetable dish, is pronounced "chap chai." Also the letter "y" is pronounced as "j"; thus, "Yogyakarta" is pronounced "Jogjakarta."

	English	Cantonese	Malay/Indonesian

Basics

	English	Cantonese	Malay/Indonesian
Yes/No	hai/mm'hai	ya/**tee'** -dak
Please	m'goy	**see**-la/**min**-ta
Thank you (very much).	doy-jeh/fehseng doh jeh	**tree**-ma **ka**-say (**ban**-yak)
You're welcome.	foon ying	**sa**-ma **sa**-ma
Excuse me.	dai'm jee	ma-fkan sa-ya
Hello	wa´	apa khabar or "hello"
Goodbye	joy geen	se-**la**-mat **ja**lan/ se-**la**-mat **ting**-gal

Numbers

One	yaht	sa-too
Two	eee	doo-a
Three	som	tee-ga
Four	say	em-pat
Five	m'	lee-ma
Six	look	e-nam
Seven	chut	tu-juh
Eight	baht	la-pan/**de**-lah-pan
Nine	gou	sem-bee-lan
Ten	sup	se-pu-luh

Days and Time

Today	gäm-yät	**ha**-ree ee-nee
Tomorrow	ting-yat	**ay**-sok (also **bay**-sok)
Yesterday	chum-yät	kel-**mar**-in/ke-**mar**-in
Morning	joo-joh	**pa**-gee
Afternoon	ahn-joh	**pe**-tang
Night	man-hak	**ma**-lam
Monday	lye bye **yaht**	**ha**-ree **iss**-nin/ **ha**-ree **se**-nin
Tuesday	lye bye **ee**	**ha**-ree se-**la**-sa
Wednesday	lye bye **som**	**ha**-ree **ra**-boo
Thursday	lye bye **say**	**ha**-ree **ka**-mees
Friday	lye bye m	**ha**-ree **ju**-ma-at
Saturday	lye bye **look**	**ha**-ree **sab**-too
Sunday	lye bye **yaht'**	**ha**-ree **a**-had (also **ha**-ree **ming**-gu)

Mandarin	Tagalog	Thai	English
shee/pu shee	oh-oh/hin-deé	khrap/mai khrap (M)/kha/mai kha(F)	Yes/No
ching	pah-keé	karoona	Please
sy-eh sy-eh nee	(mah-rah-ming) sah-lah-maht	khob (M)/kha (F) khun khrap	Thank you (very much).
boo sy-eh	wah-lahńg ah-noo-mahń	mai pen rai	You're welcome.
too-eh pu-shee	pah-oó-manh-hiń po	kaw-tōd	Excuse me.
way	kuh-moos-tah/ heh-ló	sa-wat dee khrap (M)/sa-wat dee kha (F)	Hello
tsay jen	pah-ah-lam nah pó	sa-wat dee khrap (M)/sa-wat dee kha (F)	Goodbye
ee	ee-sah	nung	One
err	dah-lah-wah	song	Two
san	taht-loh	sam	Three
soo	ah-paht	see	Four
woo	lee-mah	hah	Five
lee-oo	ah-neem	hōk	Six
chee	pee-toh	jet	Seven
bah	wah-ló	paat	Eight
joo	see-yahm´	kao	Nine
shur	sahm-poó	sip	Ten
chin tien	nga-yohń	wannee	Today
ming tien	boó-kahss	proong nee	Tomorrow
tso tien	kah-há-pon	moo-ah-wannee	Yesterday
shang wu	oo-mah-gah	torn-chao	Morning
shu wu	hußi pon	torn bai	Afternoon
wan shang	gah-beh	torn moot	Night
lee-pa-ee	loó-ness	wan-chan	Monday
lee-pa-ayr	mahr-tesś	wan-ung-khan	Tuesday
lee-pa-san	moo-yehŕ-koh-less	wan-poot	Wednesday
lee-pa-soo	hoo-whé-bess	wan-pru-roo-hud	Thursday
lee-pa-wu	bee-yehŕ-ness	wan-sook	Friday
lee-pa-ee-oo	sah-bah-doh	wan-sao	Saturday
lee-pa-tien	leeng-goh	wan-ar-teet	Sunday

English	Cantonese	Malay/Indonesian

Useful Phrases

English	Cantonese	Malay/Indonesian
Do you speak English?	nay gäng m' gäng ying män	**ta**-hoo-kah ber-ba-**ha**-sa **Ing**-gris?
I don't speak . . .	ah m' woiy gäng gäng doong wah.	**sa**-ya **tee**-dak ber-**cha**-kap ba-**ha**-sa
I don't understand.	äh m' sic	**sa**-ya **tee**-dak **fa**-ham/men-**ger**-ti
I don't know.	äh m' jee	**sa**-ya **tee**-dak **ta**-hoo
I am American/British.	ä hay may gäc yan/ying gäk yan	**sa**-ya **o**-rang Amerika/**Ing**-gris
I am sick.	ä beng **jah**	**sa**-ya **sa**-kit
Please call a doctor.	m goy nay gew yee sung	**see**-la ta-**lee**-pon **dok**-ter
Have you any rooms?	nay yaw mohfäng	**bi**-lik **a**-da
How much does it cost?	gay´ däh chien	**har**-ga-nya ber-**a**-pa
Too expensive	gai´ gway	ter-**la**-loo **ma**-hal
It's beautiful.	hoh leng	**chan**-tik
Help!	bong jô	**to**-long
Stop!	ting jee	ber-**hen**-ti

Getting Around

English	Cantonese	Malay/Indonesian
How do I get to . . .	deem yerng huy . . .	ba-gai-ma-na boh-lay per-gee-ke . . .
. . . the train station?	fäw ché jäm	**stay**-shen **kray**-ta a-pee dee **ma**-na
. . . the post office?	yaw jing gook	pe-**ja**-bat pos dee **ma**-na
. . . the tourist office?	le hang se´	ja-bat-ban pe-**lan**-chong/**kan**-tor **tor**-is dee **ma**-na
. . . the hospital?	yee´ yuen	**roo**-mah **sa**-kit dee **ma**-na
Does this bus go to . . . ?	ga ba se´ huy m huy . . .	a-da-kah bis ee-nee per-gee ke . . .
Where is the W.C.?	say soh gahn herng been doh	**tan**-das/way say a-da dee **ma**-na
Left	jäh	**kee**-ree
Right	yäw	**ka**-nan
Straight ahead	chiem mein	troos

Mandarin	Tagalog	Thai	English
nee fweh sho yung yoo má	mah-roo-nohng hoh kay-yohng mahg-Ing-glehs?	khun pood pas-sa ung-grid dai-mai	Do you speak English?
wo pu fweh sho (thai kway yoo)	hin-deé a-koh mah-roo-nohng mahg-tah-gaĥ-lohg	phom (M)/chan (F) mai pood pasa Thai mai dai	I don't speak . . .
wo pu lee-oo chee-ay	hin-deé koh nah-ee-een-tin-deé-hahn	phom (M)/chan (F) mai kao chai	I don't understand.
wo pu tung	hin-deé koh ah-lahm	phom/chan mai roo	I don't know.
wo sher may kwo jen/ing kwo jen	ah-ko ay Ah-meh-ree-kah-noh/Ing-glehs	phom/chan pen (American/ ung-grid)	I am American/British.
wo sheng ping ler	ah-ko ay may sah-kit	phom/chan mai sa-bai	I am sick.
ching chow ee sung lin	pah-kee-tah-wahg ang dook-tohr	dai-prod re-ak moa mai	Please call a doctor.
nee hay yoo fwang chien ma	may-roh-ohn kah-yong mang-ah kuh-wahr-toh	khun-mee hong-mai	Have you any rooms?
to shaw chien	mahg-kaĥ-noh?	tao rai	How much does it cost?
tao kwa la	mah-hal mah-shah-doh	pa-eng goo-pai	Too expensive
chen pee-ow lee-ang	mah-gahn-dah	soo-ay	It's beautiful.
choo-ming	sahk-loh-loh	choo-ay doo-ay	Help!
ting	hin-toĥ	yoot	Stop!
wo tsen yang tao . . .	pah-pah-no pah-poon-tah saĥ . . .	phom/chan ja pai . . . dai yangngai	How do I get to . . .
. . . fwa chu chan	ee-stah-syon nahng tren	sa-tai-nee rod-fai	. . . the train station?
. . . yu choo	post oh-pis/tahn-gah-pahn nahng koh-rco	pai-sa-nee	. . . the post office?
. . . kuan kuang choo	oh-pee-see-nah nahng too-ris-moh	sam-nak-ngan tóng-tee-oh	the tourist office?
. . . ee-yuen	oh-spee-tal	rohng-phayar baan	. . . the hospital?
chu pu pa shur tao . . . ma	poo-moo-poon-tah bah ee-tohngboos sah . . .	rod-mai-nee pai-nai . . . chai mai	Does this bus go to . . . ?
chaw soo tsai na lee	sah-ahn ahng bahn-nyoh	hong-nam tee-nai	Where is the W.C.?
tso	kah-lee-waĥ	sai	Left
yoo	kah-nahn	kwah	Right
ching sung chien tson	dee-reh-tsoh	trong-pai	Straight ahead

INDEX

NOTES

NOTES

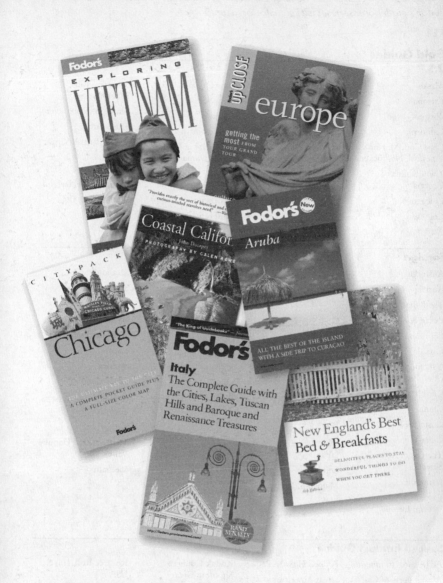

Fodor's Travel Publications

Available at bookstores everywhere. For descriptions of all our titles and a key to Fodor's guidebook series, visit www.fodors.com/books

Gold Guides

U.S.

Alaska
Arizona
Boston
California
Cape Cod, Martha's Vineyard, Nantucket
The Carolinas & Georgia
Chicago
Colorado

Florida
Hawai'i
Las Vegas, Reno, Tahoe
Los Angeles
Maine, Vermont, New Hampshire
Maui & Lāna'i
Miami & the Keys
New England

New Orleans
New York City
Oregon
Pacific North Coast
Philadelphia & the Pennsylvania Dutch Country
The Rockies
San Diego
San Francisco

Santa Fe, Taos, Albuquerque
Seattle & Vancouver
The South
U.S. & British Virgin Islands
USA
Virginia & Maryland
Washington, D.C.

Foreign

Australia
Austria
The Bahamas
Belize & Guatemala
Bermuda
Canada
Cancún, Cozumel, Yucatán Peninsula
Caribbean
China
Costa Rica
Cuba
The Czech Republic & Slovakia
Denmark
Eastern & Central Europe

Europe
Florence, Tuscany & Umbria
France
Germany
Great Britain
Greece
Hong Kong
India
Ireland
Israel
Italy
Japan
London
Madrid & Barcelona
Mexico

Montréal & Québec City
Moscow, St. Petersburg, Kiev
The Netherlands, Belgium & Luxembourg
New Zealand
Norway
Nova Scotia, New Brunswick, Prince Edward Island
Paris
Portugal
Provence & the Riviera
Scandinavia

Scotland
Singapore
South Africa
South America
Southeast Asia
Spain
Sweden
Switzerland
Thailand
Toronto
Turkey
Vienna & the Danube Valley
Vietnam

Special-Interest Guides

Adventures to Imagine
Alaska Ports of Call
Ballpark Vacations
The Best Cruises
Caribbean Ports of Call
The Complete Guide to America's National Parks
Europe Ports of Call
Family Adventures
Fodor's Gay Guide to the USA

Fodor's How to Pack
Great American Learning Vacations
Great American Sports & Adventure Vacations
Great American Vacations
Great American Vacations for Travelers with Disabilities
Halliday's New Orleans Food Explorer
Healthy Escapes

Kodak Guide to Shooting Great Travel Pictures
National Parks and Seashores of the East
National Parks of the West
Nights to Imagine
Orlando Like a Pro
Rock & Roll Traveler Great Britain and Ireland

Rock & Roll Traveler USA
Sunday in San Francisco
Walt Disney World for Adults
Weekends in New York
Wendy Perrin's Secrets Every Smart Traveler Should Know
Worlds to Imagine

Fodor's Special Series

Fodor's Best Bed & Breakfasts
America
California
The Mid-Atlantic
New England
The Pacific Northwest
The South
The Southwest
The Upper Great Lakes

Compass American Guides
Alaska
Arizona
Boston
Chicago
Coastal California
Colorado
Florida
Hawai'i
Hollywood
Idaho
Las Vegas
Maine
Manhattan
Minnesota
Montana
New Mexico
New Orleans
Oregon
Pacific Northwest
San Francisco
Santa Fe
South Carolina
South Dakota
Southwest
Texas
Underwater Wonders of the National Parks
Utah
Virginia
Washington
Wine Country
Wisconsin
Wyoming

Citypacks
Amsterdam
Atlanta
Berlin
Boston
Chicago
Florence
Hong Kong
London
Los Angeles
Miami
Montréal
New York City
Paris

Prague
Rome
San Francisco
Sydney
Tokyo
Toronto
Venice
Washington, D.C.

Exploring Guides
Australia
Boston & New England
Britain
California
Canada
Caribbean
China
Costa Rica
Cuba
Egypt
Florence & Tuscany
Florida
France
Germany
Greek Islands
Hawai'i
India
Ireland
Israel
Italy
Japan
London
Mexico
Moscow & St. Petersburg
New York City
Paris
Portugal
Prague
Provence
Rome
San Francisco
Scotland
Singapore & Malaysia
South Africa
Spain
Thailand
Turkey
Venice
Vietnam

Flashmaps
Boston
New York
San Francisco
Washington, D.C.

Fodor's Cityguides
Boston
New York
San Francisco

Fodor's Gay Guides
Amsterdam
Los Angeles & Southern California
New York City
Pacific Northwest
San Francisco and the Bay Area
South Florida
USA

Karen Brown Guides
Austria
California
England B&Bs
England, Wales & Scotland
France B&Bs
France Inns
Germany
Ireland
Italy B&Bs
Italy Inns
Portugal
Spain
Switzerland

Languages for Travelers (Cassette & Phrasebook)
French
German
Italian
Spanish

Mobil Travel Guides
America's Best Hotels & Restaurants
Arizona
California and the West
Florida
Great Lakes
Major Cities
Mid-Atlantic
Northeast
Northwest and Great Plains
Southeast
Southern California
Southwest and South Central

Pocket Guides
Acapulco
Aruba
Atlanta
Barbados
Beijing
Berlin
Budapest
Dublin
Honolulu
Jamaica
London

Mexico City
New York City
Paris
Prague
Puerto Rico
Rome
San Francisco
Savannah & Charleston
Shanghai
Sydney
Washington, D.C.

Rivages Guides
Bed and Breakfasts of Character and Charm in France
Hotels and Country Inns of Character and Charm in France
Hotels and Country Inns of Character and Charm in Italy
Hotels of Character and Charm in Paris
Hotels of Character and Charm in Portugal
Hotels of Character and Charm in Spain
Wines & Vineyards of Character and Charm in France

Short Escapes
Britain
France
Near New York City
New England

Fodor's Sports
Golf Digest's Places to Play (USA)
Golf Digest's Places to Play in the Southeast
Golf Digest's Places to Play in the Southwest
Skiing USA
USA Today The Complete Four Sport Stadium Guide

Fodor's upCLOSE Guides
California
Europe
France
Great Britain
Ireland
Italy
London
Los Angeles
Mexico
New York City
Paris
San Francisco

WHEREVER YOU TRAVEL, *H*ELP IS NEVER FAR AWAY.

From planning your trip to

providing travel assistance along

the way, American Express®

Travel Service Offices are

always there to help

you do more.